ROUTLEDGE COMPANION TO GLOBAL CYBER-SECURITY STRATEGY

This companion provides the most comprehensive and up-to-date comparative overview of the cyber-security strategies and doctrines of the major states and actors in Europe, North America, South America, Africa, and Asia.

The volume offers an introduction to each nation's cyber-security strategy and policy, along with a list of resources in English that may be consulted for those wishing to go into greater depth. Each chapter is written by a leading academic or policy specialist, and contains the following sections:

- overview of national cyber-security strategy;
- concepts and definitions;
- exploration of cyber-security issues as they relate to international law and governance;
- critical examinations of cyber partners at home and abroad;
- legislative developments and processes;
- dimensions of cybercrime and cyberterrorism;
- implications of cyber-security policies and strategies.

This book will be of much interest to students and practitioners in the fields of cyber-security, national security, strategic studies, foreign policy, and international relations.

Scott N. Romaniuk is a Postdoctoral Research Fellow in Security Studies at the China Institute, University of Alberta, Canada, and a Visiting Fellow at the International Centre for Policing and Security, University of South Wales, UK.

Mary Manjikian is Associate Dean of the Robertson School of Government at Regent University, USA.

ROUTLEDGE COMPANION TO GLOBAL CYBER-SECURITY STRATEGY

Edited by Scott N. Romaniuk and Mary Manjikian

Routledge
Taylor & Francis Group

LONDON AND NEW YORK

First published 2021
by Routledge
2 Park Square, Milton Park, Abingdon, Oxon OX14 4RN

and by Routledge
52 Vanderbilt Avenue, New York, NY 10017

Routledge is an imprint of the Taylor & Francis Group, an informa business

British Library Cataloguing-in-Publication Data
A catalogue record for this book is available from the British Library

Library of Congress Cataloging-in-Publication Data
Names: Romaniuk, Scott N, 1979- editor. | Manjikian, Mary, editor.
Title: Routledge companion to global cyber-security strategy / Scott N Romaniuk, Mary Manjikian.
Description: New York : Routledge, 2020. | Includes bibliographical references and index.
Identifiers: LCCN 2020024629 (print) | LCCN 2020024630 (ebook) | ISBN 9780367024239 (hardback) | ISBN 9780429399718 (ebook)
Subjects: LCSH: Cyberspace–Security measures–Government policy. | Cyberterrorism–Prevention–Government policy. | Computer crimes–Prevention–Government policy. | Computer security–Government policy. | Internet–Security measures–Government policy. | Computer networks–Security measures–Government policy.
Classification: LCC UA163 .R68 2020 (print) | LCC UA163 (ebook) | DDC 363.325–dc23
LC record available at https://lccn.loc.gov/2020024629
LC ebook record available at https://lccn.loc.gov/2020024630

ISBN: 978-0-367-02423-9 (hbk)
ISBN: 978-0-429-39971-8 (ebk)

Typeset in Bembo

CONTENTS

Contents

Contents

FIGURES

TABLES

CONTRIBUTORS

Kawser Ahmed was born in Bangladesh and immigrated to Canada where he earned his PhD in Peace and Conflict Studies from the University of Manitoba. He previously served in the Bangladesh Army and was an exchange officer to the Turkish Forces, an Observer to the UN Mission in Western Sahara (MINURSO), and attended the Near East South Asia Center for Strategic Studies (NESA) in Washington DC. His research interests include social conflict, peacebuilding, radicalism, violent extremism, and peacekeeping operations.

Joshua Oreoluwa Akintayo holds a Master's degree in Political Science from the University of Ibadan, Nigeria, where he is currently a PhD candidate. His research focuses on deradicalization, disengagement and re-integration programs of ex-terrorist groups, and state-society relations within the context of violence and conflict. His broad research interests are: terrorism, counter-terrorism, and development studies.

Nardine Alnemr is a PhD candidate at the Centre for Deliberative Democracy and Global Governance in the Institute for Governance and Policy Analysis at the University of Canberra. Previously worked as a teaching assistant in the political science department at the British University in Egypt and proposal writer for the Youth and Development Consultancy Institute.

Mostafa Amini's research interests lie at the intersection of computational analysis and social sciences, utilizing machine learning and information-extraction techniques to parse through various domains of knowledge, including religion, law, and healthcare. He currently works as a data scientist at Harvard Medical School.

Benjamin Ang is a Senior Fellow in the Centre of Excellence for National Security (CENS) at RSIS, and leads the Cyber and Homeland Defence Programme of CENS, exploring policy issues around the cyber domain, international cyber norms, cyber threats and conflict, strategic communications and disinformation, law enforcement technology and cybercrime, smart city cyber issues, and national security issues in disruptive technology. He is an Advocate and Solicitor of the Supreme Court of Singapore, and was a Certified

Novell Network Administrator. He serves on the Executive Committee of the Internet Society Singapore Chapter.

Rubén Arcos is lecturer and researcher of Communication Sciences at Rey Juan Carlos University in Madrid, and at the Centre for Intelligence Services and Democratic Systems. He is the coordinator of the master's program in Intelligence Analysis. He is a member of the research group Ciberimaginario and national member for NATO Task group SAS-114 on "Assessment and Communication of Uncertainty in Intelligence to Support Decision-Making." Arcos is deputy editor of *The International Journal of Intelligence, Security, and Public Affairs*.

Annamária Beláz, a PhD candidate at Óbuda University, Hungary, is a graduate of the National University of Public Service, Hungary, in Public Administration Studies.

Dániel Berzsenyi serves as a security policy analyst in Hungary's Ministry of Public Administration and Justice. A PhD candidate at the Military Science Doctoral School at the National University of Public Service, he focuses on Central European cybersecurity issues.

Kimeu W. Boynton received his JD from the University of Wisconsin (2000). He is currently an Assistant Professor of Sociology and Criminal Justice and Co-Director of the Law Studies Program at Delaware State University. His research interests include the sociology of law and criminal justice reform.

Oana-Elena Brânda is a Lecturer in International Relations at Titu Maiorescu University in Bucharest, Romania, with a focus on EU Studies, Geopolitics and Globalization, and Research Methodologies in International Relations. Her doctoral studies focused on the security dimension of the Anglo-American" special relationship" between 9/11 and the US' 2003 invasion of Iraq. Dr Brânda's main research interests include security and defense policies and their impact on world diplomacy.

Joost Bunk is a legal researcher and policymaker on Dutch cybersecurity. He holds a Public International Law LLM from Leiden University and is currently pursuing an IT-Law LLM degree from Groningen University.

Tobias Burgers is a project assistant professor at the Cyber Civilization Research Center, Keio University, Tokyo Japan, and a non-resident fellow at the Center for Security Studies, NCCU, Taipei. Taiwan. He holds a doctorate from the Otto Suhr Institute for Political Science, Free University Berlin.

Yu Cheng Chen is an Assistant Professor in the Graduate Institute of China Military Affairs Studies, National Defense University, and an active Lieutenant Colonel who served for more than fifteen years. His research interests include cyber security, Chinese propaganda and discourse, big data research, and security affairs in East Asia.

Mihai Chihaia, with the Bucharest-based think tank Strategikon, is a PhD candidate at University of Iasi, Romania. As an Erasmus+ Research Fellow at Tel Aviv University, he worked with the Secretariat General of the European Commission on political and security issues and has presented papers and policy briefs on regional EU/NATO security and hybrid warfare.

Michael Claus currently serves as a Legal Advisor at the NATO-affiliated think tank, The Center for Excellence for Confined and Shallow Waters, in Kiel, Germany. A US Navy Surface Warfare Officer who has deployed to the Arabian Gulf and Western Pacific, he received his Bachelor of Science degree in Economics from the US Naval Academy in Annapolis, MD, in 2011 and currently is a candidate for the Masters of Government degree in International Relations from Regent University in Virginia Beach, United States.

Fabio Cristiano is a postdoctoral fellow of The Hague Program for Cyber Norms and a lecturer at the Institute of Security and Global Affairs (ISGA) at Leiden University, The Netherlands. His research broadly lies at the intersection of critical security studies and cyber conflict, with a specific interest in automation, autonomy, and international norms.

Amber Darwish is an academic-practitioner who specializes in international security, particularly as it relates to weapons management and the prevention, identification, and criminal prosecution of smuggling and illicit trafficking of small, light and conventional arms. She is also interested in emerging issues of "weaponization" such as cyber security. In 2015, she was appointed to the UN "Panel of Experts" for Somalia and Eritrea, both investigating and providing capacity building as it related to these countries' compliance with international arms sanctions.

Tommaso De Zan is pursuing a DPhil in Cyber Security at the University of Oxford, where he analyzes policies aimed at reducing the cyber security skills shortage. In the context of his research, he conducted a six-month traineeship at the European Union Network and Information Security Agency (ENISA) in Athens and continues to collaborate with ENISA as a CEI Expert on topics related to skills development in the EU. Prior to his DPhil, he was an Associate Fellow at the European Union Institute for Security Studies and a Researcher at the International Affairs Institute (IAI). Before joining IAI, he interned at the International Peace Research Institute in Geneva. He holds a Master's degree in International Relations from the University of Bologna and he was an exchange student at the Hertie School, Josef Korbel School of International Studies and Université catholique de Louvain.

Dominika Dziwisz, PhD, is an assistant professor in the Institute of Political Science and International Relations of the Jagiellonian University in Krakow, Poland.

Ruben Elamiryan is an assistant professor and Chair of Political Governance and Public Policy at Public Administration Academy of Armenia, he also lectures at the Russian-Armenian (Slavonic) University on Ethno Politics, Political Globalization, Modern International Relations, and International Security Studies.

Tuba Eldem is as an assistant professor in the Department of International Relations at Istanbul Gedik University. She holds a Bachelor's degree in Political Science and International Relations from Boğaziçi University, Istanbul; a Master's degree in European Political Economy from the University of Birmingham, UK; and a PhD in Political Science from the University of Toronto, Canada. Widely published, she has also conducted post-doctoral research at the Research College of the Transformative Power of Europe, Free University of Berlin.

Ahmad El-Muhammady is a counter-terrorism analyst at the International Islamic University Malaysia. He also serves as the panel-member for the Special Rehabilitation Programme created by the Special Branch, Counter-Terrorism Division of the Royal Malaysia Police (RMP) to rehabilitate Malaysian detainees involved in militant activities.

Amparo Pamela H. Fabe is a Filipino economist/sociologist who trained at the University of the Philippines. She is the President of Bridges Unlimited, a group that offers psychosocial interventions to victims of conflict.

Adewunmi J. Falode a senior lecturer in International Relations and Strategic Studies at Lagos State University in Nigeria holds a PhD in History and Strategic Studies from the University of Lagos (2012). His areas of specialization include international relations, war studies, strategic studies, terrorism and counterterrorism studies, security studies, and contemporary Nigerian history.

James D. Fielder, USAF, serves as Assistant Professor of Political Science at the US Air Force Academy. With a PhD in Political Science from the University of Iowa, he has researched the effects of Internet access on protest movements in authoritarian states, cyber-mediated trust, social media politics, video game and virtual world interactions, and social mechanisms of cyber conflict. Having served as Electronic Warfare Squad Leader and Air Force Division Chief, he received a Bronze Star for meritorious achievement in Afghanistan in 2014.

Alexander Fotescu is a consultant for a political risk and international security firm. His research interests include identity and communication operations as well as institutional structural design, global governance, security, and competitive cultures.

Florent Frasson-Quenoz serves as a researcher at Externado de Colombia University and works on Colombia's cybersecurity policies. Co-founder of the first Colombian association for International Relations (IR), he wrote the first Spanish handbook of IR studies and a book on Brazilian military strategy. With interests in IR Theory and regional security (South America and Africa), he is a Professor at the Institute for Higher Studies for Development (IAED) in Bogotá, Colombia.

Laris Gaiser holds a PhD and MA from the Institute for International Political Studies (ISPI) of Milan, Italy, and serves as a manager, business and political adviser, and columnist. A Senior Fellow at the Centre for the Study of Global Issues (GLOBIS), he has lectured at University of Georgia (US), Diplomatic Academy of Vienna, University of Firenze, Catholic University of Sacred Heart, and Nova Univerza, Slovenia. Acting President at Euro Mediterranean University (EMUNI), he also serves on the Strategic Council in Slovenia's Ministry of Foreign Affairs.

Giampiero Giacomello is Associate Professor of Political Science at the University of Bologna, Italy, and at several American and European universities. Dr Giacomello reports on developments in Italy for the annual Freedom of the Net (Freedom House) and is a contributor on defense and security issues for Italian daily newspapers.

Lars Gjesvik is a Norwegian expert on cybersecurity in the European Energy Sector at the University of Oslo, and serves as a research assistant at the Norwegian Institute of

International Affairs (NUPI). He is also mapping cybersecurity in Myanmar as part of the Cybersecurity Capacity Building (CSCB) project in developing countries.

Miguel Alberto Gomez is a senior researcher at the Center for Security Studies and a PhD candidate at Cardiff University, holds a Master's in International Security from the Barcelona Institute of International Studies and has previously lectured at both the De La Salle University and the College of St Benilde, the Philippines. Serving in the Information Security field for the past eight years, his research is centered around cybersecurity with an interest in strategic use and emerging norms of cyberspace as an instrument of national power.

César Augusto Niño González is Associate Professor at the Sergio Arboleda University (Colombia) and Research Director of the Faculty of Political Science and International Relations. PhD in International Law (Spain) and Master of Arts in Seguridad Nacional y Defensa. Lecturer in International Relations. Advisor to the Colombian Escuela Superior de Guerra (2017-2018), author of *Terrorismo como régimen internacional subterráneo, más allá de una lógica convencional* (2017), various papers and commentaries, among which for *Foreign Affairs Latinoamérica*. He focuses on National and International Security in Colombia and the Americas.

Debarati Halder is Professor and Head at the Centre for Research on Law and Policy in United World School of Law, Gandhinagar, Gujarat. She is honorary managing director of the Centre for Cyber Victim Counselling (CCVC), India. She is the founder secretary of South Asian Society of Criminology and Victimology.

Alex Hardy is a Royal Leverhulme funded PhD candidate at Royal Holloway, University of London.

Bassant Hassib is a Lecturer in Political Science at the British University in Egypt. She earned her PhD in Euro-Mediterranean Studies in May 2017 from the Faculty of Economics and Political Science at Cairo University.

Suzette A. Haughton is a senior lecturer at the Department of Government, The University of the West Indies, Mona Campus where she lectures on International Security Issues. She specializes on security threats affecting people and the nation-state.

Moritz Hellmann is a doctoral law student in Germany, studied different aspects of Asian legal systems during an exchange year at Keio University, Tokyo Law School.

Louise Marie Hurel is a cybersecurity and Internet governance researcher. Researcher at the Brazilian Naval War College (NAC-EGN) and coordinator of the project "Cybersecurity and Digital Liberties" at Igarapé Institute. Her previous experience includes consultancy for UNESCO and research on Internet governance and privacy policies at the Center for Technology and Society at Getúlio Vargas Foundation (CTS-FGV).

Md. Shariful Islam is an Assistant Professor in the Department of International Relations at University of Rajshahi, Bangladesh. He specializes in international relations with research interests in critical security studies, Bangladesh foreign policy, and IR theories and pedagogies.

Karuppannan Jaishankar is Professor and Head of the Department of Criminology, Raksha Shakti University, Ahmedabad, Gujarat, India. He is the founding Editor-in-Chief *of International Journal of Cyber Criminology* and *International Journal of Criminal Justice Sciences.* He is the founder President of South Asian Society of Criminology and Victimology (SASCV) and founder Executive Director of Centre for Cyber Victim Counselling (CCVC).

Lucie Kadlecová is a PhD Candidate at Charles University in Prague, Czech Republic. A recent Fulbright scholar at the Massachusetts Institute of Technology, she previously served at the National Cybersecurity Centre of the Czech Republic and trained in the Cyber Defense Section of the NATO Headquarters and in the Cabinet of the Commissioner for Enlargement and European Neighborhood Policy at the European Commission in Brussels.

Filiz Katman received her PhD in International Security and Terrorism from the Defense Studies Institute of the Turkish Military Academy, and holds certificates from the Changing Character of War Programme at Pembroke College, Oxford University, and the War, Conflict and Order Program at Yale University. She is a lecturer in the Department of Political Science and International Relations (English) at Istanbul Aydin University, Turkey and Senior Fellow at the Centre for Syrian Studies at University of St Andrews, UK.

Yangmo Ku is Associate Professor of Political Science and Associate Director of the Peace and War Center at Norwich University, USA. He received his Ph.D. in Political Science from the George Washington University and previously taught at the School of International Service at American University. His research focuses on North/South Korean politics, East Asian security, U.S. foreign policy, and the politics of memory and reconciliation in East Asia and Europe. He also serves as founding Editor of an academic journal titled *Journal of Peace and War Studies.* He is often invited to teach intensive courses on the politics of the Korean Peninsula to U.S. federal government workers.

Phan Le is an Australian Awards scholar pursuing his PhD in Economics at the Australian National University. His areas of interests are international economics and the digital economy, particularly on the social and economic impacts of cybersecurity policies.

Luisa Cruz Lobato is a PhD candidate at the Pontifical Catholic University of Rio de Janeiro (PUC-Rio) and holds an MSc in International Relations from PUC-Rio. Researcher at the Igarapé Institute, where she also manages the "Cybersecurity and Digital Liberties" project. Visiting researcher at the Human Rights Law Clinic at Centro Universitário do Pará (CESUPA).

Mary Manjikian is Associate Dean of the Robertson School of Government at Regent University (US). She previously served as a US Foreign Service officer in The Netherlands, Russia, and Bulgaria and a Fulbright Scholar at Durham University's Institute of Advanced Study.

David Manley is an MA candidate in the Robertson School of Government at Regent University in Virginia Beach, Virginia, United States, serves as a Lieutenant and Surface Warfare Officer in the US Navy and is currently assigned in Yokosuka, Japan. He earned his BS in History from the US Naval Academy, where his studies focused on military strategy and the US civil war. His research interests include grand strategy, national security affairs, and naval warfare.

Luigi Martino is a PhD candidate in Human Rights and Global Politics and serves as Director of the Center for Cybersecurity and International Relations Studies at the University of Florence where he teaches Cybersecurity and International Relations. He also serves as project manager of the joint OSCE-University of Florence "Enhancing the Implementation of OSCE CBMs to Reduce the Risks of Conflict Stemming from the Use of ICTs" project.

Michael D. Miner teaches government at Harvard University focusing on strategy, intelligence, and cybersecurity. He is on the active roster of the Fulbright Specialist Program administered by the United States Department of State. Miner has written for or been quoted by the Wall Street Journal, Brookings, and the National Interest. He sits on the Board of Directors of the Massachusetts Fulbright Association and is a graduate of Dartmouth College.

David Andrew Omona, PhD, is a researcher and senior lecturer at Uganda Christian University, a transitional Justice fellow, trainer of trainees in peace-building and conflict management, and a national coordinator for a Justice and Peace Network in Uganda. He holds a PhD in Political Studies with a focus on International Relations and Diplomacy, MA in International Relations and Diplomacy, MA in Theology, BA with Education, and several specialized diplomas and certificates. He has authored several journal articles and book it in his areas of expertise. His research interests focus on international studies, security, ethics, and transitional justice.

Anwar Ouassini is at Delaware State University as an Assistant Professor of Sociology and Criminal Justice. His research interests include social movements, political sociology, and comparative criminal justice systems. He has worked on projects that explore the intersection of race and religious identities in the Arab World, the relationship between civil society, social movements, and democratic development in West Africa, and Criminal Justice Reform in the Maghreb.

Nabil Ouassini received his PhD in criminal justice from Indiana University at Bloomington. He is currently an assistant professor at Prairie View A&M University outside of Houston, Texas. Nabil's research interests include international criminology, comparative criminal justice systems, legitimation and legitimacy, and political violence.

Nick Robinson is an EPSRC funded PhD candidate in the Centre for Training in Cyber Security at Royal Holloway, University of London. His research is primarily grounded in Estonia, with a focus on the country's approach to cyber security, e-government, and the multitude of digital technologies the state has employed since the restoration of independence from the Soviet Union in 1991.

Saúl Mauricio Rodriguez-Hernandez is a historian from the National University of Colombia. He is a research-professor in conflict, peace, and post-conflict issues at Sergio Arboleda University (Colombia).

Scott N. Romaniuk is a Postdoctoral Research Fellow in Security Studies at the China Institute, University of Alberta, Canada, and a Visiting Fellow at the International Centre for Policing and Security, University of South Wales, UK. His teaching and research specializations include International Relations, Military and Strategic Studies, Critical Security Studies, Research Methods, and Terrorism and Political Violence. In addition to his research on terrorism and counter-terrorism, and violent extremism and de-radicalization, he examines China's global security and military roles, the rise of security architectures in Asia, robotic systems in international security, and technology and the future of warfare.

Niels Nagelhus Schia is a Senior Research Fellow at the Norwegian Institute of International Affairs (NUPI), heads NUPI's Cybersecurity Center. A former Fellow of NSSR (New School for Social Research), he earned his PhD in Social Anthropology from the University of Oslo. With a focus on the role of cybersecurity in International Relations, he tracks new developments in cybersecurity and provides expert analysis and strategic policy recommendations to governments and the UN.

Michaela Semecká, an analyst in the National Cyber & Information Security Agency of the Czech Republic, holds Masters degrees from the Department of War Studies at King's College London, and from Tel Aviv University. With prior experience serving at the United Nations, she worked in the Office on Genocide Prevention and the Responsibility to Protect.

Max Smeets is a cybersecurity fellow at ETH Zurich, Center for Security Studies, holds a DPhil (St John's College, Oxford) and MPhil (Brasenose College, Oxford) in International Relations. A Lecturer in Politics at Oxford's Keble College, he also served as Research Affiliate in the Oxford Cyber Studies Program, Carnegie Visiting Scholar at Columbia University SIPA, and as a Doctoral Visiting Scholar at Sciences Po CERI.

Brig. Gen. Steven J. Spano, USAF, Ret. is the President and COO of CIS (The Center for Internet Security). He is a graduate of Norwich University in Northfield, Vermont, and also served as General Manager of Defense and National Security for Amazon Web Service's Worldwide Public Sector as one the key leaders who launched the business in 2011. His service of over 28 years in the US Air Force, included Air Combat Command (ACC) Director of Communications at Langley Air Force Base in Virginia where was responsible for IT vision, policy guidance, and resource allocation supporting the warfighting mission. He was also responsible for IT policy, interoperability, and network operations for joint and coalition forces, and was the principal advisor to the Government of Iraq for ICT reconstruction.

Ilona Stadnik is a PhD candidate at Saint Petersburg State University whose focus is on global cybersecurity regimes and Russian cyber policy, is an Assistant Curator at the Digital Watch Observatory of the Geneva Internet Platform (GIP).

Raymond Steenkamp Fonseca is Senior Lecturer in the Department of Political Science (Military) at the University of Stellenbosch, South Africa. He also teaches International Relations and Political Economy at the South African Military Academy. Raymond's research publications focus on the role of security in Africa's socio-economic and democratic development.

Tim Stevens is a Senior Lecturer in Global Security at King's College London. His research looks critically at global security practices, with specific interests in cybersecurity and digital surveillance.

Ana Stuparu is a PhD Candidate at the National Security College, Australian National University. In her professional capacity, Ana is a Consultant in Cyber Risk with KPMG Australia.

Oleksiy Syvak served as a Senior Consultant at the National Security and Defense Council of Ukraine. He also has an experience of working for the Ministry of Foreign Affairs as a Specialist of the Department of European International Organizations. Dr Syvak is a graduate of the Naval Postgraduate School (United States), where he obtained his MA in International Security and Civil-Military Relations. He also holds MA and BA in International Relations from the Institute of International Relations of Taras Shevchenko Kyiv National University (Ukraine) and a PhD in Political Science from Taras Shevchenko Kyiv National University (2000). His current position is GR/Policy Director at CFC Big Ideas.

Tony Tai-Ting Liu is an Assistant Professor at the Graduate Institute of Future Studies, Tamkang University. He held previous visiting research positions at The University of Tokyo, Australian Catholic University and University of Tübingen. His research interests include international relations theory, international political economy, East Asia international relations, and China's foreign relations and foreign policy.

Jo-Ansie K. van Wyk lectures on International Politics in the Department of Political Sciences, University of South Africa, Pretoria, South Africa.

Nicolás G. Velásquez is a political and data scientist, Knight post-doctoral fellow at the Institute for Data, Democracy, and Politics at the School of Media and Public Affairs, George Washington University. He is a member and lead computational social science coder at the Online Dynamics Laboratory at George Washington's Department of Physics. Dr Velásquez also serves as Chief Data Scientist at Linterna Verde, a Colombian NGO focused on digital literacy and sociopolitical dimensions of the information revolution in civil society.

Aaron T. Walter serves as an assistant professor at the Faculty of Social Sciences of Sts Cyril and Methodius University in Trnava, Slovakia, and at the Faculty of Social Studies, Masaryk University in Brno, Czech Republic. With research interests in international relations with a focus on neoclassical realism and security studies, he also has interests in Israeli studies, and comparative European politics.

Christopher Whyte is an assistant professor in Homeland Security & Emergency Preparedness at the L Douglas Wilder School of Government & Public Affairs at Virginia Commonwealth University, teaching cybersecurity policy, conflict, and law, among other courses. His research interests include international security and IT related to war and peace, political communication, and cybersecurity doctrine/policy. He holds a PhD in Political Science from the Schar School of Policy & Government at George Mason University.

Cherry H. Y. Wong is the Research Coordinator at Cyber Civilization Research Center, Keio University, Tokyo, Japan.

Will Wrye holds an MA in Government with a focus in International Politics from Regent University in Virginia Beach, Virginia, United States. While interning at the College of International Security Affairs in Washington, DC, he researched numerous global issues and contributed to a newsletter on international trends, including cybersecurity. He led a student team in the Atlantic Council's 9/12 Cyber Challenge to present and defend a policy brief outlining three government response alternatives to a hypothetical attack on the US energy sector.

Olya Zaporozhets is Associate Professor of Mental Health Counseling and a Director of Ukrainian Institute for Education in Psychology & Counseling at Regent University. She is actively involved in building the field of counseling in Ukraine and mitigating the mental health effects of the Russian-Ukrainian hybrid war.

Ella Zarcilla-Genecela received her Bachelor of Arts in Mass Communication from San Sebastian College Recoletos de Manila, and her Master's degree in Foreign Service at Lyceum of the Philippines University, Manila. She is the Chief Operating Officer of Luciano Lingad Zarcilla Cybersecurity and Technologies Corporation and a Co-Owner of Navcomm Maritime Products in the Philippines.

FOREWORD: GLOBAL CYBERSECURITY IN THE 21ST CENTURY

In 2012, former FBI Director Robert Mueller famously said, "There are only two kinds of companies: Those that that have been hacked and those that will be." We might well say the same about nations within the international system. Though at present some nations – including the United States – are in the "top ten" of those states most targeted by cyber actors, no nation is immune to cyber-attacks. Indeed, we might argue that it is merely a matter of time before any nation becomes the target of a large-scale, devastating cyber-attack. For this reason, all nations would do well to develop an awareness of their vulnerabilities and to prepare for this eventuality.

In considering national vulnerabilities, we might, however, distinguish between those nations which have undergone major cyber-attacks or cyber breaches to either their military or civilian sectors with potentially devasting economic, social and political consequences; those which have undergone somewhat less significant breaches – with effects being felt regionally or locally, or within a limited sector – and those which have so far been spared a significant breach. Here, we might place Bangladesh in the major breach category as a result of the 2016 bank hack which resulted in the transfer of over one hundred million dollars from the nation's Central Bank into the accounts of hackers who were most likely state-sponsored. We might also place the United States in this category as the result of the 2016 data breaches of the US Democratic National Committee, as well attacks on the integrity of America's political system through the actions of state-sponsored Russian social media trolls. We might place Ukraine in that category as well as the result of Russia's use of social media and cyber warfare as part of a strategy of hybrid warfare more generally. We might place nations like India or France into a mid-range category, in which they have been the subject of significant and perhaps unrelenting cyberattacks on both their commercial/business and government sectors, but where so far we cannot point to one significant attack as devastating in its impact. Finally, we can point to nations in Latin America and the Caribbean which thus far have been least targeted by malicious cyber actors.

Romaniuk and Manjikian's *Routledge Companion to Global Cyber-Security Strategy* allows us to consider all three categories of nations, as it presents a variety of perspectives and lessons from nations throughout the international system. As the volume makes clear, not all nations are at the same stages when it comes to combatting and preparing for cyber events, either domestically or internationally. Some states have a unified program for implementing cybersecurity protocols within all sectors of society while others may still struggle to define the sectors where their nation is the most vulnerable, as well as to allocate the resources to address these threats. And as

Burt, Nicholas, Sullivan, and Scoles' *Cybersecurity Risk Paradox* report (2017) makes clear, nations may be at their greatest vulnerability to cyber risk when they are rapidly joining the online revolution – increasing connectivity and penetration rates, as well as increasing their reliance on connectivity in areas like the development of e-commerce and e-government. It seems typical for nations to undertake development projects in which their ability to innovate outpaces their ability to regulate and defend against outside threats. And states are most likely to be attacked during the window created by this paradox.

Despite this dire news, as this volume makes clear, there are a great many lessons which nations can learn from one another. In this volume, we can see how nations within the former Soviet Union and the former Eastern Bloc – from Armenia, to Ukraine, to Slovenia – have developed similar understandings regarding their nation's vulnerabilities to state-sponsored cyberthreats. In this way, being a late adopter rather than an early adopter can prove to be an advantage rather than a disadvantage. And in Whyte's essay on the Euroepan Union, we can see how nations which are preparing to face cybersecurity threats in a regional and a collective manner can benefit from economies of scale, and collective efforts.

This volume also makes clear how tightly interconnected nations are both regional and internationally – and how that often necessitates cooperation, even amongst nations which may differ from one another politically and ideologically. At the same time, as this volume makes clear, internet threats are no longer best understood as stand-alone threats. Throughout the volume, we see the ways in which internet threats have been part of hybrid war (as we see in Zaporozhet's essay on Ukrainian cybersecurity) as well as the ways in which international organizations like the North Atlantic Treaty Organization (NATO) have worked together to combat cyber threat. Finally, we see how cybersecurity is increasingly intertwined with all aspects of state security – from economic, to political to defense security, and the ways in which nations have thus worked to integrate cybersecurity into all aspects of national planning.

Finally, we are able to note the ways in which nations today are divided regarding whether the provision of a nation's cybersecurity is best approached as national or an international project. Throughout this volume, we see numerous references to "national cyberspace" (e.g., French cyberspace, German cyberspace, and Chinese cyberspace). At the same time, we see evidence of both ideological and monetary commitments to the creation and support of international agreements such as the Budapest Convention on Cybercrime. It may still be too early to say whether or not we will see the creation of broad and significant international norms governing cyberwarfare and cybersecurity in regard to critical infrastructure. However, the adoption of the United States Computer Emergency Response Team (CERT) model by many nations, as well as the creation of private-public partnerships suggests that there is reason to be hopeful about prospects for developing shared norms and agreements. This volume thus suggests that in the future, it is possible to look forward to the creation of a safer world where cyberconflict will continue to exist, but where it can be managed and regulated through international efforts.

Brig. Gen. Steven J. Spano (USAF, Ret.)
President and COO of The Center for Internet Security (CIS)

Reference

Burt, D., Nicholas, P., Sullivan, K., & Scoles, T. (2017). "The cybersecurity risk paradox: Impact of social, economic and technological factors on rates of malware." www.microsoft.com/en-us/cybersecurity/content-hub/cybersecurity-risk-paradox

INTRODUCTION

Cybersecurity strategy and policy in a comparative context

Mary Manjikian and Scott N. Romaniuk

In this volume, readers have the ability to familiarize themselves with cybersecurity policy developments and strategies across a wide variety of international settings. The chapters compiled here represent a broad cross-section of nations from all the world's regions, along with international actors like the North Atlantic Treaty Organization (NATO), the European Union (EU) and the African Union (AU). They can thus allow the reader to draw fruitful comparisons cross-nationally about the ways in which cybersecurity policy has evolved, been understood and been carried out.

Different understandings of cyber threat

Throughout this volume, there are several themes which can be identified. First, the volume makes clear that nations are universally concerned about emerging cybersecurity threats, and – it appears – all nations wish that they had more and better resources available to respond to these threats. Furthermore, as Brânda points out in her study of Romanian cybersecurity policy, state actors are always at a disadvantage in relation to threat actors who are often smaller, nimbler, nonstate entities. The crafting of legislation, the establishment of commissions and the creation of policies including regional and international coordination can be a slow and unwieldly process in comparison to how quickly such actors can organize. And in almost every national analysis presented here, the private sector has increasingly come to play a unique role in the provision of cyber hardware and software, as well as in the provision of cybersecurity. Thus, nations look alike in that they face similar challenges in terms of responding quickly to emerging cyberthreats, finding enough skilled personnel and enough resources to build a strong cybersecurity infrastructure, and articulating and implementing policies for working with private sector actors.

However, while nations may face similar challenges, this volume also makes clear that nations do not share a consensus regarding the particular ways in which cybersecurity threats are defined, nor in how they relate to a nation's overall national security. Thus, one overarching question which arises is: *Why have nations understood cyber threat so differently – within their own nations, within their own regions and internationally?* Here it is useful to consider Hurel and Lobato's argument (which they point out in their study of Brazil's cybersecurity policy) that risk may be understood differently depending on a nation's history and its political context. Thus, they argue, the understanding of risk and the variety of appropriate policy responses to that risk can be described as negotiated within a particular context. In their analysis, they illustrate how nations may choose to prioritize responding to one set of threats (such as managing the risks posed by foreign actors) over responding to another set of threats (such as managing risks posed by the rapid creation of infrastructure). As we see in this volume, policy actors from the legislature, to the Ministry of Defense, to a newly-created Ministry of Information, may all describe the universe of cyberthreat differently, and may also prioritize different strategies for addressing what they see as the most significant aspects of that threat.

Here Tuba Eldem's findings in regard to Turkish cybersecurity policy thus become salient. In her chapter, she describes how Turkey appears to have policies which are very much in line with European ideals in the areas of military cybersecurity and the combatting of cybercrime. However, she argues that in regard to considerations of whether Turkey owns "its cyberspace" and the amount of autonomy which Turkey's government has in terms of administering the sorts of debates and kinds of information which should be allowed into that cyberspace, these policies more closely resemble the policies implemented by actors such as Russia and China. Nations must thus balance competing concerns and influences in creating a cybersecurity policy which hopefully is coordinated between sectors.

But this need to agree upon which risks are most salient and to coordinate a national or regional policy response becomes even more complicated, as Whyte points out, when a multiplicity of actors is involved – as has occurred in the evolution of the European Union's cybersecurity strategy. Here he argues that all actors within the body have worked to ensure congruence of meaning on the nature of cybersecurity challenges. As a result, he notes, European Union policy has emerged only slowly.

As Manjikian suggests in her chapter on United States cybersecurity policy, a nation's ideology and political system can also affect how cyberthreat is understood and reacted to. She notes that democratic and autocratic nations can differ greatly in the threats which opening up one's nation to the outside through the Internet are seen as posing, and nations may also have markedly different types of resources at their disposal to manage these risks, depending on the legislative resources and cultural understandings which exist within their society. In some instances, the same event may be understood as an opportunity within one nation (such as the opportunity for academics to have increased international contacts with other academics worldwide) while it may be perceived as a threat within another.

As this volume makes clear, it is thus perhaps not useful to describe one nation as having a "better" cybersecurity policy than another – though international organizations have attempted to do exactly this, through issuing report cards and grades to nations based upon an analysis of their cyber-resiliency (Peter, 2017), or their cyber-capacity (Secure World News Team, 2019; Union, n.d.). However, as the case studies in this volume show, it is perhaps more important to consider how nations have mounted sector-specific problems to the unique cybersecurity challenges which have arisen in their own unique contexts. That is, one can identify specific issue-areas within cybersecurity – including in the areas of banking sector security, industrial systems security and transportation security. Nations may be more concerned with addressing threats in particular sectors and may have a more comprehensive and effective strategy in these areas. For example, maritime nations may experience specific threats related to cybersecurity attacks aimed at port or container security (Manjikian, 2020).

Here it is possible to identify nations which may have made great strides in one sector while at the same time continuing to struggle in other sectors. Here, we can consider how nations like Nigeria and South Africa still struggle with the threats posed by organized criminal activities which are being carried out via the Internet, despite making great strides to incorporate cybersecurity infrastructure into other areas of the economic, political and social systems of these nations. Thus, an in-depth analysis of each nation's challenges and opportunities may be more revealing than the creation of a single measure or score to convey that complexity.

And in considering the specific political, economic and social context in which cybersecurity policies are made today, Shariful Islam's insights into Bangladesh's speedy development as a cybersecurity player in the international system are also relevant. He argues that while the development of modern cyber capabilities, including the creation of a satellite for carrying data streams, has helped to increase the standard of living and development for the people of Bangladesh, at the same time it has presented new types of risks and challenges. Similarly, Fielder points to a dichotomy which he sees in the development of Kenya's cybersecurity policy − noting that while the development of the Internet has enabled such "good" aspects as continued economic growth and decreases in crime, at the same time, these same developments may be creating "bad" aspects such as the increased likelihood of human rights abuses being enabled by increasing surveillance capabilities, which the Internet has allowed.

Different policy responses

While states have differed in terms of how they understand cyber threat and cyber risk, they have also differed in terms of the resources they have brought to bear in response to these threats. Furthermore, states have mounted different organizational responses to these threats. As we see in this volume, in the past ten or so years, nations have come up with a variety of competing models for organizing the actors and activities which nations engage in related to cyberthreat. In some instances, a separate Ministry of Information or Ministry of Information Technology has been created, tasked with all responsibilities for administering cyber-related activities (from implementing defensive and offensive cybersecurity policies, to integrating cybersecurity activities within the private sector and the military, to overseeing the transition to a more highly technological structure for delivering education). In Kenya, China and Mauritius, for example, such activities are centralized within a Ministry of Information Communications and Technology, or a Ministry of Technology, Communications and Innovation.

In other instances, cyber activities have been placed in a subordinate status − placed under an existing ministry or program. Here, for example, we can consider the creation of a military cyber command as part of an integrated unit within the United States Department of Defense, as well as the creation of a unique cyber command within the North Atlantic Treaty Organization (NATO). In some instances, nations have created a cyber czar, tasked with overall responsibility for coordinating all things cyber, while others have doled out resources and responsibility between agencies and departments.

As van Wyk and Fonseca point out, South Africa's policy response has been the adoption of an inter-agency model. They write that "the cross-cutting nature of cybersecurity is that it cannot be addressed by one department only." And in Russia, as we have seen, offensive cyberwar capabilities carried out through social media have been coordinated by Russia's Ministry of Defense as well as its intelligence units (Meduza, 2017).

Both approaches come with inherent advantages and disadvantages as we see in these chapters. The free-standing, autonomous cyber ministry or cyber minister may have a preponderance of power to implement his or her objectives. This organization may also face fewer constraints on its behavior and fewer threats from competing actors – including those in the private sector or in other areas. However, this "all in one" approach may fall short when it comes to integrating these activities into the activities of other ministries and organizations.

Beláz and Berzsenyi's analysis of Hungary's cybersecurity policy also illustrates some of the dangers to democracy which might emerge in a system where a central organization plays a major coordinating role in the provision of cybersecurity. In their chapter, they describe the provisions of the Defense Act (Act CXIII of 2011) which describes the measures which Hungary's government can take – both online and offline – in response to a declared emergency, such as a terrorist attack. They write that:

> Although, there is no recent history of terrorism, in a terrorist emergency the government has the following powers to limit social and political freedoms:
>
> • The journalist, the correspondent and the producer of the press products can only use the information provided by authorized bodies, official spokesperson or the public service media.
> • Media product can be scrutinized and censored before their publication.
> • The government may order the suspension, limitation or control of postal and electronic communications services and IT networks.

In this way, they call the reader's attention to the social and political costs which sometimes result in prioritizing cybersecurity over other social values, such as freedom of assembly and freedom of information.

At the same time, when multiple organizations and actors must work together to address cyberthreats, the possibility of bureaucratic infighting is higher. In such instances a nation may struggle internally both in terms of clarifying and articulating a vision for cybersecurity (in a document like a National Cybersecurity Strategy) and may also struggle to implement these programs due to the need to pull resources from multiple places and agencies, as well as the need to work with multiple authors. In this scenario, the provision of cybersecurity measures may compete with other priorities within each division.

This picture is altered further when considering the environment in which autocratic rule is both present and thriving. In their chapter on Uganda, Romaniuk and Omona discuss the dangers of autocracy over the Internet and the management of information as a commodity that requires securing, amplified by the presence and threat of terrorism in and against the state and its people. In its efforts to ensure safety and security for the people within the country, the government sets in motion laws and measures that strictly govern how the Internet is used under the guise of protecting the people from those who wish to impose their values and practices on a sovereign state. The power of those laws and measures can be amplified when supported by supranational organizations encouraging states to become signatories of conventions aiming to extend the blanket of security though sometimes facilitating unintended consequences of misuse. Akintayo echoes this assessment in his chapter on the African Union, arguing that, "under the guise of enforcing AU cybersecurity policy, African governments are stifling civil liberties, thereby undermining democratic consolidation in the various nascent democracies in African countries."

The possibility of role confusion becomes even greater when, as we see in several chapters, the multiple actors whose efforts must be coordinated in the provision of cybersecurity include both state and private sector actors. Here, again we can consider the example of the United States, where it is sometimes unclear who is actually making policy – the state or the non-state commercial actors located within that state. As recent events involving actions taken by Facebook in particular in relation to the provision of United States election security and the sale of political advertising on its platform make clear, private actors in particular may not always have clearly articulated roles in reference to their responsibility to provide national level cybersecurity, nor do they share common understandings regarding their roles and responsibilities.

Catalyzing events for the provision of cybersecurity

For that reason, it may often be something like an outside public event that causes a nation to finally "get moving" in terms of implementing cybersecurity programs. We also see throughout this volume the ways in which states have and have not experienced their own Cyber Pearl Harbor or their own Cyber 9/11. Bangladesh, it can be argued, did experience a sort of defining moment as the result of the 2016 bank hack in which over one hundred million dollars were withdrawn from its Central Bank. Similarly, Ukraine became aware of its security vulnerabilities as the result of repeated cyber hostilities and cyber-attacks inflicted by Russia since 2014. In many instances the lessons drawn from these attacks have been promulgated throughout a region or internationally, with neighboring countries often beefing up their own cybersecurity measures in response, without having to bear the heavy costs of a cyber-attack upon their own citizens or infrastructure.

The issue of regional cooperation

Throughout this volume, the issue of regional and international cooperation also plays a central role. In the chapters about cybersecurity in Europe in particular, it becomes clear that states have been encouraged by both regional bodies and regional policies to pay more attention and devote greater resources to the issue of cybersecurity, as well as to create policies in key sectors such as military cybersecurity and the combatting of online crime which are in alignment with broader regional goals and requirements. At the same time, it also becomes clear that states have often been constrained in significant ways in creating their own cybersecurity policy. Here readers may wish to ask themselves whether the drive for regional alignment presents a positive good – leading all states to adopt more stringent requirements and procedures in the area of cyber security – or whether it represents a negative good – since the requirement that states adopt particular policies and technical standards in order to have interoperability within a region may lead to a fragmentation of the international Internet into regional blocs, characterized by shared technology standards as well as, perhaps, a particular ideological outlook.

The early adopter and today's cyber rankings

Finally, this volume, which provides both a historical tour d'horizon as well as a cross-cultural way of understanding cybersecurity policies, allows us to pose questions about how cybersecurity policies and capabilities have developed historically, and to ask whether the power rankings which held in the Internet's early days are salient now as Internet politics emerges from its infancy into its adolescence. Here, we can move beyond specific case studies to ask more broad-ranging questions including whether nations which have emerged as leading cyber powers always keep that edge.

That is, as you read this volume, you may wish to ask yourself: How much power do the early adopters or first movers in cyberspace have today – to define the terms of the debate, to define norms for the provision of cybersecurity, and to create the environment into which other nations will enter? That is, how well have nations like the United States, the United Kingdom and even Hungary been able to preserve the economic, political and technological advantages which they have accrued as first movers? Here, we can ask whether early adopters have an advantage in the configuring of cyberspace as a whole, and in the preservation of their own cybersecurity. Both Manjikian (United States) and Belaz and Berszenyi (Hungary) ask questions about early adopters which may fail to maintain that "leading edge" in cybersecurity relative to neighboring and rival states.

But as intriguing as the situation of the early adopter is, it is also important to note here that currently, according to the International Telecommunications Union, fifty percent of the world's nations do not yet have a formal cybersecurity strategy in place. This does not mean that they have not begun addressing issues related to cybersecurity – but rather that there is no one clear, coherent guiding strategy, nor is there an institutionalized set of responses to be deployed if the nation were to be the subject of a cyber-attack (Rayome, 2017).

An emerging academic consensus?

Finally, as you utilize this volume, you may find that it provides not only insights into individual nations' cybersecurity policies, but also insights into how academic and policy analysts in particular are beginning to think about and describe the making of cybersecurity policy. Here, we can identify an emerging trends within the academic study of cybersecurity. Increasingly, analysts from all regions (as illustrated by this volume) utilize the language of steering or building cybersecurity policy, rather than suggesting that such policies can or will somehow evolve organically. The older discourse of an evolving cybersecurity policy appears to have been pushed aside by a more activist narrative in which actors seek to create consensus, to articulate and build support for norms and to arrive at the achievement of specific objectives in creating cybersecurity policy. Here, this domestic discourse parallels the discourse taking place within the international cyber policy community – where the quest for Internet governance is similarly being described as a process which is being managed and coordinated, rather than merely evolving.

It is thus our hope that this volume, by providing resources for comparative analysis, can help to bring thinking about cybersecurity into the academic mainstream of both international relations and comparative politics. That is, cybersecurity policymaking should ideally be thought of not simply as a stand-alone subject. Rather, in considering how states have made policies in relation to cybersecurity in their nations, we can also draw broader insights into how states understand, measure and talk about threats, as well as how actors can work both cooperatively and competitively to mobilize resources to address specific threats. Here, readers are pointed to the chapter on Brazil in particular, which provides a case study of the politics of agenda-setting in the cyber arena. The insights generated by considering the "case of" cybersecurity may thus be adapted further to consider agenda setting in other areas, focusing on the ways in which cybersecurity policymaking both is and is not unique in relation to policymaking in general.

Finally, as scholars seek to extend their knowledge of cybersecurity policymaking, including the question of how norms emerge, are enforced and are institutionalized, this volume might be of use for dissertation writers and others to choose particular cases in order to engage in more broad-range theorizing, perhaps utilizing a most-different and a most-similar case approach (Lijphart, 1971).

References

Lijphart, A. (1971). "Comparative Politics and the Comparative Method," *American Political Science Review*, 65, 682–93.

Manjikian, M. (2020). *Introduction to Cyber Politics and Policy*. New York: SAGE.

Meduza. (2017, July 19). "Moscow Cyber-Defense: How the Russian Government Plans to Protect the Country from the Coming Cyberewar," https://meduza.io/en/feature/2017/07/19/moscow-s-cyber-defense

Peter, A. (2017). "Cyber Resilience Preparedness of Africa's Top-12 Emerging Economies," *International Journal of Critical Infrastructure Protection*, 17, 49–59.

Rayome, A. (2017, July 6). "UN Report: 50% of Countries Have No Cybersecurity Policy," *Tech Republic*. www.techrepublic.com/article/un-report-50-of-countries-have-no-cybersecurity-strategy-in-place/

Secure World News. (2019, July 15). "The List: Best and Worst Countries for Cybersecurity," www.secureworldexpo.com/industry-news/countries-dedicated-to-cybersecurity

Union, I. T. (n.d.). "Global Cybersecurity Index," www.itu.int/en/ITU-D/Cybersecurity/Pages/global-cybersecurity-index.aspx

PART I

Europe

1

SECURING THE KINGDOM'S CYBERSPACE

Cybersecurity and cyber intelligence in Spain

Rubén Arcos

Introduction

Cybersecurity is an important element in Spanish National Security; Spain adopted a specific National Cybersecurity Strategy in 2013. The Spanish Security Strategy of 2011 included – for the first time – cyber threats and attacks among the main threats to national security (Cendoya, 2016) and the National Defence Directive of 2012 also anticipated the development of a National Cybersecurity Strategy.

Spain's 2017 National Security Strategy, defined by the National Security Council, identifies cyberspace as a global common space (together with maritime, airspace, and outer space) as a particular area of vulnerability, either because of the use of the cyber environment for illicit purposes (terrorism, organized crime, and disinformation campaigns), or because of cyber threats such as information theft, hacking of devices, DDoS attacks, and attacks against infrastructures considered critical, among others.

The Kingdom of Spain has a high level of commitment to cybersecurity according to the International Telecommunications Union (ITU) and is a member country of the Freedom Online Coalition. Spain is ranked in 7th position globally (with a CGI score of 0.896) and 5th regionally in the ITU Global Cybersecurity Index which aims to "measure the commitment of countries to cybersecurity in order to raise cybersecurity awareness" (ITU, 2019). Analogously to the United Kingdom, the United States, France, and Lithuania, it scored highest in the legal ("existence of legal institutions and frameworks dealing with cybersecurity and cybercrime") and organizational ("existence of policy coordination institutions and strategies for cybersecurity development at the national level") pillars of the ITU framework (ITU, 2019: 8).

Spain's geographical setting and geostrategic position have implications in the domain of cyberspace. Its mainland national territory is located in Southwestern Europe, in the Iberian Peninsula; the Canary and Balearic Islands, as well other smaller islands and territories in North Africa, are also part of the Kingdom of Spain. As stated in the 2017 National Security Strategy:

> Spain's identity is at once European, Mediterranean and Atlantic. Its singular geo-
> strategic position and natural orientation towards different spaces requires it to have

its own strategic and dynamic vision. Its central position in key areas – between Europe and North Africa; between the Mediterranean and the Atlantic; and with peninsular territory, archipelagos, islands and the sovereign territories in North Africa – makes Spain a bridge between countries and cultures, conferring upon it a specific security profile.

(Presidency of the Government, 2017: 22)

The "physical segment of the cyberspace" is associated with the physical infrastructure of submarine and land cables as well as satellites providing connectivity across lands and seas (Sheldon, 2014: 287). As early as at the end of nineteenth century, during the Spanish-American War, Spain experienced the disruptive effects of telegraph cable-cutting operations carried out by the US Navy targeting the communications between Spain and its colonial territories.

Moreover, with over 95 percent of international communications and data transmission occurring via the global subsea network, routine activities like sending emails overseas, searching the Internet, downloading music or video, and the like are most likely to involve underwater fibre-optic cables (Carter & Burnett, 2015: 349).

Securing this physical segment in the strategic maritime domain is thus critical for a "maritime nation like Spain" (Departamento de Seguridad Nacional, 2013: 12). However, this physical infrastructure is mainly owned by private operators which has important implications for sovereignty and autonomy. For example, the transatlantic submarine cable MAREA[1] connects Sopelana (Spain) and Virginia (US) – its two landing points – and is owned by a partnership comprising Microsoft, Facebook, and Telefónica's Telxius. Also, in the Bay of Biscay, Tata Communications owns and operates VSNL Western Europe (formerly named TGN Western Europe), a submarine cable connecting Spain and Highbridge in the UK (Red Eléctrica de España, 2017; Telegeography, 2019). Figure 1.1

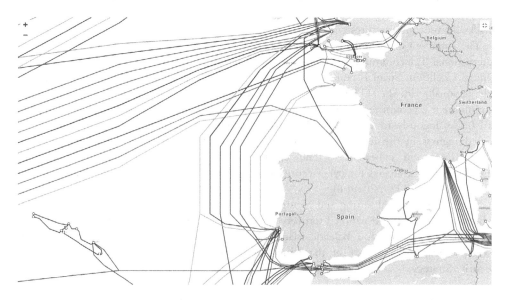

Figure 1.1 Submarine Communications Cable Map
Source: Telegeography (2019).

illustrates these submarine cable connections with Spain's mainland, as well as connections in and between the Canary and Balearic Islands, with North Africa.

As Sheldon (2014: 288–289) argues, "the ubiquity of cyberspace" should not obscure the role played by "geography and geopolitics in its use" since:

> the target itself is geographically located in that the computer network penetrated, the data pilfered or otherwise manipulated, and the political, economic, and military significance of the data are owned by and within the sovereign territory of some political entity.

The Spanish Maritime Security Strategy of 2013, highlights that "maritime connectivity between the mainland and the islands and the Autonomous Cities of Ceuta and Melilla is one of the pillars of Spain's geopolitical structure" and points out threats from cyberspace as one the potential risks and threats against the multiple national interests in the maritime security dimension (Gobierno de España, 2013).

National cybersecurity system

The National Cybersecurity Council (CNC) is the specialized committee and collegiate body for supporting the National Security Council (CNS) in the field of cybersecurity. The creation of the CNC was an initiative agreed at the CNS meeting of December 5, 2013. At that same meeting the first specific National Cybersecurity Strategy was adopted, this strategic document is the framework for reference regarding cybersecurity in Spain.[2] The National Cybersecurity Strategy was updated on April 12, 2019 after of the meeting of the CNS and was publicly released as the National Cybersecurity Strategy by the Order PCI/ 487/2019 of April 26. The National Cybersecurity Strategy 2019 specifies the components that make up the structure of the Spanish cybersecurity apparatus in the framework of the National Security System: (1) National Security Council (Government Delegate Commission for National Security); (2) Situation Committee for Crisis Situations; (3) National Cybersecurity Council; (4) Permanent Commission on Cybersecurity; (5) National Forum of Cybersecurity; and (6) competent public authorities and national Computer Security Incident Response Teams (CSIRTs) of reference (Orden PCI/487/2019).[3]

The CNS, in its capacity as the Government Delegate Commission for National Security, is the body responsible for assisting the Prime Minister in the direction of the Spanish National Security Policy. As stated in the strategy, the CNS acts through the Department of National Security (DSN) – which part of the Cabinet of the Presidency of the Government (Prime Minister) – as single point of contact for liaison and for ensuring cross-border cooperation with other member countries of the EU. The Situation Committee is also supported by the DSN and follows the direction of the CSN in crisis situations.

The National Cybersecurity Council met on April 9, 2019 with three main points on the agenda: (1) evaluation and monitoring of the work carried out in the preparation of the National Cybersecurity Strategy of 2019; (2) actions carried out to counter disinformation and protection of electoral processes – Spanish elections of April and European elections of May 2019; and (3) the security of 5G telecommunications networks (DSN, 2019b). On April 12, the National Security Council held its last meeting before the April 28 Elections and the Prime Minister, Pedro Sánchez, highlighted the key role of cybersecurity in "the preservation of the rights and liberties of citizens, the defence of Spain, as well as the transformation of our digital society necessary for progress, innovation and industrial development" (DSN, 2019c).

According to the ORDER PRA/33/2018 of January 22, the National Cybersecurity Council has, among others, the following functions: proposing guidelines on the planning and coordination of the National Security policy with regard to cybersecurity; supporting the CNS in its function of verifying the degree of compliance with the National Security Strategy in relation to cybersecurity; contributing to normative proposals for strengthening the National Security System in the field of cybersecurity; supporting CSN decision-making on cybersecurity matters, through analyses, studies and proposals; strengthening relationships with the relevant Public Administrations in the field of cybersecurity; the coordination, collaboration, and cooperation between public and private sectors; and assessing risk and threats as well as analysing likely crisis scenarios in support of the Situation Committee (ORDER PRA/33/2018). The presidency of the CNC is held by the Secretary of State Director of the National Intelligence Centre while the post of Vice-President is held by the Director of the DNS. The DNS is designated both as the permanent working body of the Cybersecurity Council as well as its technical secretariat (ORDER PRA/33/2018).

As stated above, the National Security Council, through the DSN, is the Spanish designated single point of contact for "coordinating issues related to the security of network and information systems and cross-border cooperation at union level"[4] – the NIS Cooperation Group – while the National Cryptologic Centre's CCN-CERT (public sector) and the National Cybersecurity Institute's INCIBE-CERT (private sector) are the designated national CSIRTs for the CSIRTs Network.[5] According to a press release by the French Agence nationale de la sécurité des systèmes d'information (ANSSI), on July 2019 the national cybersecurity authorities of 23 Member States, ENISA, and the European Commission gathered for the first time at high level in Paris to run the table-top exercise Blue OLEx – a joint proposal by France and Spain in which "on the basis of several short scenarios" the responsible authorities discussed on "the mechanisms that could be implemented to efficiently manage a cyber crisis affecting the EU Member States" (ANSSI, 2019).

The National Cybersecurity Strategy 2019 establishes both the Permanent Commission on Cybersecurity and the public–private National Cybersecurity Forum but these elements in the cybersecurity system require further development and implementation.

Relationships between relevant public cybersecurity organizations and private companies are solid as evidenced by different initiatives such as the establishment of the non-profit and independent association CSIRT.es, which integrates computer security incident response teams. According to official studies, the cybersecurity industry integrated over 530 active companies in Spain in 2014.[6] The CSIRT.es Forum's website includes some of the relevant membership CSIRT/CERT teams from private companies.[7]

The Royal Decree 12/2018, of September 7, of Security of Network and Information Systems, incorporates the European Network and Information Systems Directive, to the national legal framework. Articles 9 and 11 designate the competent authorities and the Computer Security Incident Response Teams of reference (CSIRTs) as illustrated in Table 1.1. Accordingly, the CSIRT/CERT of reference are:

1   For the operators of essential services:

    a   The CCN-CERT, of the National Cryptologic Center, which corresponds to the community of reference constituted by the public sector – as described in the Article 2, Chapter 1, of the Law 40/2015 of October 2.[8]

    b   The INCIBE-CERT, of the National Cybersecurity Institute of Spain, which corresponds to the reference community constituted by those entities not included in the subjective scope of application of Law 40/2015. The INCIBE-CERT is operated jointly by the INCIBE and the CNPIC (Ministry of Interior) in all that refers to the management of incidents that affect the critical operators.

c The ESPDEF-CERT, of the Ministry of Defense, which will cooperate with the CCN-CERT and INCIBE-CERT in those situations that they require in support of the operators of essential services and, necessarily, in those operators that have an impact on National Defense and that are determined by regulation.

2 For digital service providers that are not included in the CCN-CERT community of reference, the INCIBE-CERT is the CSIRT of reference. INCIBE-CERT is also the incident response team of reference for citizens, private law entities and other entities not included in the section 1 above (Royal Decree 12/2018).

Table 1.1 Royal Decree-Law 12/2018, of September 7, on Network Security and Information Systems

		Scope	*CSIRT of Reference*		*Authority of Reference*
Operator of Essential Services	Critical	Private Sector	ESPDEF-CERT (Joint Cyber Defence Command) Cooperation with the CCN-CERT and INCIBE-CERT in those situations that they require in support of the operators of essential services and, necessarily, in those operators that have an impact on National Defense and that are determined by regulation.	INCIBE-CERT	National Centre for Critical Infrastructure Protection and Cybersecurity (CNPIC) of the State Secretariat for Security (Ministry of Interior)
		Public Sector		CCN-CERT	
	Non-Critical	Private Sector		INCIBE-CERT	Sectorial Authority
		Public Sector		CCN-CERT	National Cryptologic Centre (CCN) (Ministry of Defence)
Provider of Digital Services	Critical	Private Sector		INCIBE-CERT	National Centre for Critical Infrastructure Protection and Cybersecurity (CNPIC) of the State Secretariat for Security (Ministry of Interior)
		Public Sector		CCN-CERT	
	Non-Critical	Private Sector		INCIBE-CERT	Secretariat of State for Digital Advancement (SEAD) of the Ministry of Economy and Business
		Public Sector		CCN-CERT	National Cryptologic Centre (CCN)

Source: CCN-CERT IA 13/19 and Royal Decree 12/2018.[9]

Regarding coordination between CSIRTS of reference, Spanish legislation determines that in exceptional cases requiring a high level of coordination, the CCN-CERT will exercise the national coordination of the technical response of the CSIRT (Royal Decree 12/2018). Additionally, when the activities may affect a critical operator, the legislation establishes that the CSIRTs of reference shall coordinate with the Ministry of Interior, through the Office for Cybernetic Coordination (OCC) of the CNPIC (Royal Decree 12/ 2018). The National Commission for Critical Infrastructures Protection (PIC Commission) has designated 132 essential operators, all of which are critical operators.[10]

Cyber intelligence

Clark and Oleson have pointed out the existence of three major categories of cyber operations: Computer Network Defence (CND), Computer Network Attack (CNA), and Computer Network Exploitation or Cyber Collection (Clark & Oleson, 2019: 14; see also, Clark, 2014). We agree with these authors in that cyber intelligence or Cyber INT cannot be separated easily from other INTs; there is some degree of overlapping with HUMINT, OSINT, and SIGINT (for example: the access to an isolated computer or network for cyber collection would likely be HUMINT-enabled or provided through social engineering; open source information can be very useful for producing cyber threat intelligence; and exploiting the material collected through cyber espionage may require cryptanalysis). And at the same time cyber intelligence

> has its own tradecraft; its practice requires unique technical expertise. Applying the tools and talents used in hacking; conducting forensics of the open, Dark, and Deep Webs; inserting malware into hardware and software – all depend on technical specialties that the five traditional INTs apply only peripherally. CYBERINT has its own specialized processing and analysis methods.
>
> *(Clark and Oleson 2019:16)*[11]

Similarly, Bonfanti (2018: 111–112) has argued that there two ways of looking at cyber intelligence: (1) intelligence *from* cyber to support decision-making in different domains, "not only to counter cyber threats" but beyond cybersecurity; and (2) intelligence *for* cybersecurity:

> that is, insight that is derived from an all-source intelligence activity occurring within and outside cyberspace. It is cyber intelligence *lato sensu* [...] It can draw from any intelligence discipline that supplies crucial knowledge, regardless of the source, method, or medium employed for crafting it. As such, cyber intelligence may therefore result from the combination of Open Source Intelligence (OSINT), Signal Intelligence (SIGINT), Geospatial Intelligence (GEOINT), Social Media Intelligence (SOCMINT), and Human Intelligence (HUMINT). From this point of view, cyber intelligence is less a discipline itself than an analytic practice relying on information/intelligence collected also through other disciplines and intended to inform decision makers on issues pertaining to activities in the cyber domain.

The Spanish National Cryptologic Centre (CCN), ascribed to the CNI – the all-source foreign and domestic intelligence service – in its 2015 Security Guide (CCN-STIC-401) understands cyber intelligence in this *lato sensu*, as "intelligence activities to support cybersecurity. Cyber threats are traced, the intentions and opportunities of cyber-adversaries are analyzed in order to identify, locate and attribute sources of cyber-attacks" (CCN-STIC-401). The National Intelligence Centre was created by Law 11/2002 of May 6, and its Secretary of State Director is also the National Authority for Intelligence and Counterintelligence, as well as the Director of the CCN. Established by the Royal Decree 421/2004 of March 12, the CCN shares with the CNI "means, procedures, regulations, and resources" (RD 421/2004, Art. 2). CCN-CERT, created in 2006, is thus accountable to CNI and its mission and objectives are:

> protection from cyber-attacks on classified systems and systems belonging to Public Administrations, and to companies and organizations of strategic interest (those essential for Spanish security and economy).
>
> Its mission is to strengthen cybersecurity in Spain. The CCN-CERT is the national alert and response centre, and helps provide quick and effective solutions to cyber-attacks and counter cyber threats in a proactive manner. It provides state coordination between the different Incident Response Teams and Cybersecurity Operation Centers.
>
> The ultimate goal of the CCN-CERT is to guarantee a safer and trustworthy cyberspace by protecting classified information (pursuant to article 4.F of Law 11/2002) and sensitive information, preserving the Spanish technological heritage, training experts, implementing security policies and procedures, and by using and developing the most adequate technology to this aim.
>
> *(see, CCN-CERT website)*[12]

The Joint Cyber Defense Command (MCCD) is

> responsible for the planning and execution of the actions related to cyber defense in the networks and information and telecommunications systems of the Ministry of Defense or others that may be entrusted, as well as contributing to the appropriate response in cyberspace against threats or attacks that may affect National Defense.
>
> *(Royal Decree 872/2014, of October 10, Art. 15)*

According to the Article 11 of the Order DEF/166/2015, the MCCD has the among others the responsibilities of directing and coordinating in the area of cyber defence, the incident response teams of the Armies and "exercising the timely, legitimate and proportionate response in cyberspace to threats and aggressions that my affect the National Defense" (Order DEF/166/2015). Within MCCD, the Operations Department is responsible for "executing cyber defense operations, through defense, exploitation and response activities" (ibid.).

The defense staff of the MCCD include a section of cyber intelligence and security, while the Operations Department includes, among other groups, the Response Group against threats or attacks (disruption, denial and other operations against information and systems of hostile actors) and the Exploitation Group that is "responsible for the execution of actions aimed at knowing capabilities for action in cyberspace of potential adversaries and hostile actors" (BOD, 2016: 1000). On January 29, 2019, the Spanish Ministry of Defense and the Royal Household of His Majesty the King, signed an agreement by which MCCD will: (1) perform system security audits and analysis of vulnerabilities; (2) act as a security operations center for the detection of cyber-attacks in the computer systems of the General Secretariat of the Royal Household; (3) act as an incident response team; (4) and provide other services that might be required.[13] According

Enrique Cubeiro, former Chief of MCCD's Defense Staff, the global Wannacry ransomware campaign helped to raise awareness of cybers attacks with businesses' top management (Cubeiro, 2018). On May 12, 2017, Spanish Telefónica and other companies were victims of a ransomware outbreak that received great media coverage.[14]

The Armed Forces Intelligence Centre (CIFAS) was created by a Ministerial Order in April 19, 2005 and is the military intelligence service responsible for disseminating military intelligence to the Minister of Defense, through the Spanish Chief of Defense Staff, and to other military authorities in order to provide the necessary support to military operations and warnings about potential crisis-risk situations of military interest coming from abroad (Order DEF/1076/2005). The tactical intelligence organizations of the Army, Navy, and Air Force are functionally dependent on CIFAS, which leads strategic and operational military information and intelligence (Arcos, 2014). CIFAS regulation specifies that its structure and functions are classified but a cyber section seems to be part of that structure, according to public presentations from CIFAS military officers.

Regarding Law Enforcement, the Central Unit of Cybercrime (UCC) of the General Commissariat of Judicial Police (Spanish National Police), has several branches and sections dealing with different kinds of criminal activities. The section on cyber threats is assigned to the Central Branch of IT Security. The UCC includes, among others, teams targeting the sexual exploitation of children on the Internet.[15] Regarding cyberspace, the General Commissariat of Information deals with its use by terrorist groups for different purposes.

The Group of Cyber Crimes (GDT) of the Guardia Civil's Operative Central Unit (UCO) and the EDITEs – the teams of the so-called peripheral organization assigned to the regions – are also an important part in the fight against cybercrime. The Department of Information of the Guardia Civil has structures for dealing with cyberterrorism as well.[16]

Besides the already mentioned National Centre for Critical Infrastructures and Cybersecurity of the State Secretariat for Security and its OCC, the Secretariat hosts the Intelligence Centre against Terrorism and Organized Crime (CITCO); it does not have an intelligence collection or operations remit, but produces analysis and assessments and co-ordinates when the National Police and the Civil Guard are working on the same investigations (Arcos, 2017). INCIBE has a model of intelligence for cybersecurity within INCIBE-CERT, that is fed by public and private sources of information.[17]

Private actors clearly have an important role to play as well, either by voluntary information sharing on cyber-attacks with the government authorities or by providing analyses and assessments for cyber security to other companies.

Cyber-incidents and targeted attacks

As stated in the 2018 Annual National Security Report, the 2017 Spanish National Security Strategy differentiates between cyber threats and the illegitimate use of cyberspace through illicit activities. Cyber threats are considered to be disruptions or malicious activities affecting technological elements, while the latter includes disinformation and propaganda activities as well as others such as the financing of terrorism and organized crime (DSN, 2019a: 61).

In January 2019, the National Cybersecurity Council approved the *National Guide of Notification and Management of Cyber-Incidents*, which includes the taxonomy of 38 potential types of incident (Gobierno de España, 2019a, 2019b). The March 2019 Annual Report of National Security, highlighted as a trend observed during the period 2013–2018 an increase in the number of cyber incidents affecting critical infrastructures, mainly malware and the exploitation of vulnerabilities. A total figure of 2,300 incidents involving critical operators were reported with the financial, energy, and transportation sectors being the most affected (DSN, 2019a: 62). On September 20, 2018, for example, the Port of Barcelona reported to have experienced a serious cyber-attack (see Figure 1.2).

In its May 2019 report on cyber threats and trends, the National Cryptologic Center's Information Security Incident Response Team, CCN-CERT,[18] reported to have managed 38,029 incidents in 2018 of which 2.7 percent were considered to be very dangerous or critical. This data represents an increase of 43.65 percent compared to the number of incidents experienced during the previous year (CCN, 2019: 108). The section of the report dedicated to the CNN's incident management activity during 2018 highlights APT campaigns from three threat actors: Carbanak/Cobalt (March 2018), Emissary Panda (April 2018), and APT29 (November 2018). According to the report (2019: 108):

> In the public sector, the main actor has continued to be APT29, which, in November 2018, launched a global campaign targeting an approximate total of 3,000 victims. The vector of attack was the use of a functionality of the operating system, which allowed the installation and execution of harmful code.

APT29 is considered to be a Russian cyber threat group targeting entities consistently with Russian State interest (Weedon, 2015: 69). Spain has been one of the countries in Europe most targeted by advanced targeted threats malware. Data from a 2015 FireEye's Regional Advanced Threat Report for EMEA, revealed that Spain was ranked 2nd in number (10 percent) of detected targeted attacks (FireEye, 2015: 6). Moreover, a CCN senior manager highlighted in a July 2017 interview that:

> Russia and China are the states that are most attacking Spain. We have that measured, but does that imply that we have the evidence? No. For the technical analysis we do and for the *modus operandi* we reach that conclusion [...] Russia for geopolitical interest and China for economic interest.[19]

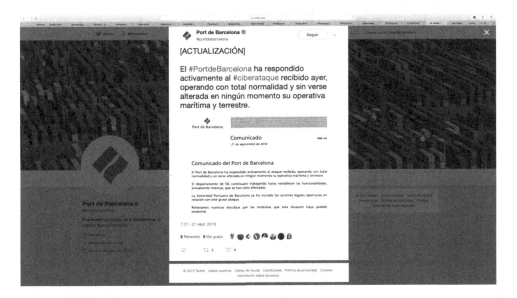

Figure 1.2 Tweet and Press Release Reporting on a Cyber-attack Affecting a Critical Infrastructure

Regarding the APT-style cyber-attacks campaign known as Carbanak/Cobalt, on March 26, 2018 the alleged leader of the cybercrime organization behind the targeted malware attacks on over 100 financial institutions worldwide was arrested in Alicante, Spain "after a complex investigation conducted by the Spanish National Police, with the support of Europol, the US FBI, the Romanian, Moldovan, Belarussian and Taiwanese authorities and private cyber security companies" (Europol, 2018a). The organization's activities started in 2013, attacking banks, e-payment systems, and financial institutions by means of malware of their own design (Anunak, Carbanak, and Cobalt) resulting in aggregate losses of over EUR 1 billion (Europol, 2018b). The attacks started with a priming phase of social engineering targeting bank employees that later were sent:

> spear phishing emails with a malicious attachment impersonating legitimate companies. Once downloaded, the malicious software allowed the criminals to remotely control the victims' infected machines, giving them access to the internal banking network and infecting the servers controlling the ATMs. This provided them with the knowledge they needed to cash out the money.
>
> *(Europol, 2018a)*[20]

This campaign provides an example of a non-state cyber threat group using sophisticated methods usually associated with cyberespionage operations of hostile foreign state actors.

On March 5, 2019, the Spanish Ministry of Defense detected an intrusion in its Wide Area Network for General Purpose (WAN PG) operated by the Centre of Systems and Information and Communication Technologies (CESTIC). According to a note released by the Ministry of Defense (2019):

> CESTIC provides the services of the Comprehensive Information Infrastructure for Defense (I3D): telephony, email, storage and information processing, access to databases, Internet browsing and Cybersecurity, among others. It provides services to all users of the Department: Central Organ of the Ministry, General Staff of Defense, Armies and Navy, UME and units deployed abroad in land and sea operations in more than 16 international missions, among other centers and agencies.[21]

The targeted network provides these services to over 50,000 authorized users[22] although does not host classified information.[23] The intrusion remained undetected during three months[24] and according to the information reported by Miguel González in El País the attack is attributed to an unnamed "foreign power" by those responsible for the forensic investigation (González, 2019).[25]

According to MCCD's Francisco Marín, "state players and professional criminals remain the most important threats, while cyberwar, cyberconflicts and hybrid warfare are becoming increasingly present throughout the world, always supported by actions in cyberspace" (author's interview, 2019).

#OpCatalunya

Hacktivist groups, as source of the cyber threat, have been involved in Spain's domestic politics, particularly in the Catalonian crisis.[26] On October 20, 2017 the Spanish Department of National Security (DSN) warned that "the hacktivist group Anonymous, through associated twitter accounts, is announcing a massive cyber-attack campaign for tomorrow day 21 under the name of '#OpCatalunya' and '#FreeCatalunya.' The last

Figure 1.3 Anonymous Operation Free Catalonia
Source: www.youtube.com/watch?v=f4cAkfTYDrA

weeks, state pages have received different cyber-attacks under these same slogans"[27] (DSN, 2017). As anticipated by this note, on October 21 the website of the Constitutional Court and other services experienced a DDoS attack.[28] The different DDoS attacks were preceded by the release of a video on September 24 by Anonymous (see Figure 1.3)

Intelligence-led strategic communication for public opinion influencing

Cyberspace has also emerged as a dimension for communication-led influence operations. Audience segmentation and profiling through open source collection, analytics, and social media listening is now at the hands of all kinds of actors – including governments, companies, and terrorist organizations. Research and analysis play a crucial role in strategic communication campaigns as a prior stage to planning and dissemination of key messages to target audiences, both in traditional channels and in the cyberspace. As pointed out by the Spanish National Cryptologic Centre:

> There are increasingly being more attacks against a country's interests through the cyberspace which do not consist of modifying the computer systems of companies and institutions but are aimed at altering the functioning of one of the main elements of the development of a liberal democracy and a modern nation-state: *the public opinion.*
>
> *(National Cryptologic Centre, 2019: 5)*

The above quotation is part of the CCN's guide *Disinformation in Cyberspace* and illustrates the increased attention of intelligence and cyber security institutions in Spain to hybrid influences and interference through information and communication activities by hostile actors, particularly after allegations of external meddling in the illegal Catalan referendum of October 1, 2017 (Arcos, 2018).

Spain is a member country of the Helsinki-based European Centre of Excellence for Countering Hybrid Threats – Hybrid CoE, which operates a Community of Interest on Influence, and of the Tallinn-based NATO Cooperative Cyber Defence Centre of Excellence – CCDCCOE.

Spain ranked 10th out of 28 EU member countries in the Digital Economy and Society Index (DESI), scoring 58.0. According to the European Commission:

> Overall, the use of internet services in Spain is broadly comparable with the EU average. People in Spain are keen to engage in a variety of online activities in line with the rest of the EU, the most popular online activity being downloading/ streaming music, videos and games with 83% of individuals engaged. 77% of Spanish internet users read news online (72% in the EU). The Spanish used social networks (68%), above the EU average, but the use of online banking and online shopping (55% and 59 %, respectively) is below the EU average.
>
> *(DESI country profile, 2018: 7)*

As reported by ONTSI, in 2017 the proportion of households with a computer was 86.7 percent, 56 percent also have at least one tablet, and almost the 98.5 percent of "Spanish households have at least one active mobile phone (used in the last month)" (ONTSI, 2018: 15).

The high penetration of Internet-connected devices such as computers, mobile phones, tablets and other connected devices, and the consumption of contents in social media networks provides opportunities to be exposed to computational propaganda (see, Woolley & Howard, 2019) from different actors, and particularly to covert influence actions that make use of the cyberspace which are difficult to attribute and to deter.

Hack-leak-publication patterns, disinformation, and amplification will continue to be likely tactics in the playbook employed by hybrid actors against democratic electoral processes, as well as cyber-attacks against election infrastructure (Arcos, 2019: 33). However, it should not be assumed that mere exposure to disinformation suffices to produce the intended cognitive, affective, or behavioral effects in targeted audiences in all cases.

The potential dissemination of AI-generated audio-visual forgeries in cyberspace could provide new opportunities for hostile actors to exploit societal vulnerabilities and influence public opinion in targeted countries or individuals for different aims.

Conclusion

Spain is well committed to cybersecurity and has developed a national system for countering cyber threats composed of different national structures to anticipate, prevent, and respond to cyber-attacks. Raising awareness on cyber threats, and developing the resilience capacity of the society will continue to be an important component of the response. Cyber intelligence is an important tool for supporting decision making in cybersecurity and the information flows between public institutions and practitioners in the private sector are particularly important. The establishment of forums of government CSIRT/CERT teams open to the private sector, and regional CERTs, is important for building trust and developing a sort of augmented Spanish cybersecurity community. Cohesion, coordination, and community-making at national and international levels between the cybersecurity/cyber defense, intelligence, and strategic communication communities and networks is important for dealing with hybrid actions from state and non-state actors.

Notes

1 "One of MAREA's main characteristics is its location, much farther south than other transatlantic cables, thus making it a very valuable asset for diversifying connectivity through the Atlantic. In addition, its landing stations in both Sopelana (Spain) and Virginia (US) are two key connectivity points with the United States, Africa, the Middle East and Asia. MAREA will greatly contribute to meet the growing data demand" Source: https://telxius.com/en/mareabrusa/

2 See, www.dsn.gob.es/es/sistema-seguridad-nacional/consejo-seguridad-nacional/reunión-del-con sejo-seguridad-nacional-5-diciembre-2013

3 The document can be accessed at: www.boe.es/diario_boe/txt.php?id=BOE-A-2019-6347

4 See, NIS Directive: https://eur-lex.europa.eu/legal-content/EN/TXT/PDF/? uri=CELEX:32016L1148&from=EN

5 For more information see: http://ec.europa.eu/newsroom/dae/document.cfm?doc_id=53682

6 See, www.red.es/redes/es/actualidad/magazin-en-red/infograf%C3%ADa-la-ciberseguridad-en-españa

7 Information about the membership can be accessed at: www.csirt.es/index.php/en/miembros-en-menu

8 See, www.boe.es/buscar/doc.php?id=BOE-A-2015-10566

9 See, www.boe.es/diario_boe/txt.php?id=BOE-A-2018-12257

10 For more information on the PIC Commission, essential services, and operators see: www.cnpic.es/Biblioteca/Noticias/listado_servicios_esenciales.pdf

11 For a constructive discussion on the concept, see also, Torres Soriano (2017).

12 See, www.ccn-cert.cni.es/en/about-us/mission-and-objectives.html

13 The agreement can be accessed at: www.boe.es/diario_boe/txt.php?id=BOE-A-2019-2759

14 For an illustration of the initial reactions to the campaign, see, https://elpais.com/tecnologia/2017/ 05/12/actualidad/1494585889_857386.html

15 For more information on UCC, see, www.congreso.es/public_oficiales/L12/CORT/DS/CM/ DSCG-12-CM-118.PDF

16 See, www.congreso.es/public_oficiales/L12/CORT/DS/CM/DSCG-12-CM-111.PDF

17 See, www.incibe-cert.es/servicios-operadores/information-gathering

18 "In compliance with this regulation, the CCN-CERT ensures protection from cyber-attacks on classified systems and systems belonging to Public Administrations, and to companies and organizations of strategic interest (those essential for Spanish security and economy)." See, www.ccn-cert. cni.es/en/about-us/mission-and-objectives.html

19 Pablo López, interviewed by Haridian Mederos, *La Provicia* – Diario de las Palmas, July 7, 2017. Translation by the author. Full interview available at: http://unedgrancanaria.es/docs/prensa/ LA_PROVINCIA_7_MAYO.pdf

20 See also, www.bitdefender.com/files/News/CaseStudies/study/262/Bitdefender-WhitePaper-An-APT-Blueprint-Gaining-New-Visibility-into-Financial-Threats-interactive.pdf

21 Translated by the author. See, www.defensa.gob.es/gabinete/notasPrensa/2019/03/DGC-190312-cestic.html

22 See, https://elpais.com/politica/2019/03/11/actualidad/1552308459_986467.html

23 See, https://elpais.com/politica/2019/03/11/actualidad/1552308459_986467.html. See also: www. defensa.gob.es/gabinete/notasPrensa/2019/03/DGC-190311-incidente-red-interna.html; https:// ssweb.seap.minhap.es/docconvenios/rest/descargaFicheros/v4/22071

24 See, https://cadenaser.com/ser/2019/03/14/politica/1552589479_582971.html

25 See, https://elpais.com/politica/2019/03/25/actualidad/1553543912_758690.html

26 According to Francisco Marín, "pro-independentism actors can be considered as a kind of hacktivist groups, which generally carry out cyber-attacks for ideological reasons. Such actions could grow in view of the increased availability of products, services and tools to develop attacks with a significant social impact," author's interview, July 25, 2019.

27 Translated by the author. The original note in Spanish can be accessed at: www.dsn.gob.es/es/ actualidad/seguridad-nacional-ultima-hora?page=144

28 See, https://elpais.com/politica/2017/10/21/actualidad/1508574710_898791.html

Suggested reading

Abellán, L. (2018, October 12). "Spanish security expert warns of 'critical risk' of a cyber-attack." *El País*. https://english.elpais.com/elpais/2018/10/10/inenglish/1539186888_353824.html

Cendoya, A. (2016). *National cyber security organization: SPAIN*. Tallinn, Estonia: CCDCOE. https://ccdcoe.org/uploads/2018/10/CS_organisation_SPAIN_092016.pdf

Centro Criptológico Nacional. (n.d.). "Spanish Approach to Cybersecurity." ccn.cni.es/index.php/en/menu-ccn-en/spanish-approach-to-cybersecurity

ENISA. (2019, January 4). "Spanish National Cyber Security Strategy." www.enisa.europa.eu/topics/national-cyber-security-strategies/ncss-map/national-cyber-security-strategies-interactive-map/strategies/the-national-security-strategy; www.mostrar/946824/theeconomyjournal.eu/texto-diario/cybersecurity-could-be-good-business-for-spanish-companies-in-latin-america

Rodríguez, M. (n.d.). "Cybersecurity could be good business for Spanish companies in Latin America," *The Economy Journal*.

References

ANSSI. (2019, July 1). "Blue OLEx 2019: member states' new initiative to develop the European cyber crisis management system," Press release. www.ssi.gouv.fr/uploads/2019/07/press-release-blue-olex-2019.pdf

Arcos, R. (2014). "Spain," in R. Dover, M. S. Goodman & C. Hillebrand (eds.), *The Routledge companion to intelligence studies* (pp. 235–242). London and New York: Routledge.

Arcos, R. (2017). "Co-ordinated strike: Spain acts to cut intelligence duplication," *Jane's Intelligence Review*, 29(2): 36–40.

Arcos, R. (2018, October). "Post-event analysis of the hybrid threat security environment: assessment of influence communication operations." Hybrid CoE Strategic Analysis Papers. www.hybridcoe.fi/wp-content/uploads/2018/11/Strategic-Analysis-2018-10-Arcos.pdf

Arcos, R. (2019). "EU and NATO confront hybrid threats in Centre of Excellence," *Jane's Intelligence Review*, 31(3): 28–33.

Boletín Oficial del Ministerio de Defensa. (2016, June 18). "Instrucción 65/2015, de 30 de diciembre, del Jefe de Estado Mayor de la Defensa, por la que se desarrolla la organización del Estado Mayor de la Defensa." www.emad.mde.es/Galerias/EMAD/files/ORGANIZACION_EMAD_ENE15.pdf

Bonfanti, M. E. (2018) "Cyber Intelligence: in pursuit of a better understanding for an emerging practice," *Cyber, Intelligence, and Security*, 2(1): 105–121. www.inss.org.il/wp-content/uploads/2018/05/Cyber-Intelligence-In-Pursuit-of-a-Better-Understanding-for-an-Emerging-Practice.pdf

Carter, L. & Burnett, D. R. (2015). "Subsea telecommunications," in H. D. Smith, J. L. S. de Vivero &T. S. Agardy (eds.), *Routledge handbook of ocean resources and management* (pp. 349–365). London and New York: Routledge.

Cendoya, A. (2016). *National cybersecurity organization: Spain*. Tallinn, Estonia: NATO Cooperative Cyber Defence Centre of Excellence. https://ccdcoe.org/uploads/2018/10/CS_organisation_SPAIN_092016.pdf

Centro Criptológico Nacional (CCN). (2015). "Guía de Seguridad (CCN-STIC-401) Glosario y abreviaturas." www.ccn-cert.cni.es/pdf/guias/glosario-de-terminos/22-401-descargar-glosario/file.html

Centro Criptológico Nacional (CCN). (2019, May). "CCN-CERT IA-13/19 Ciberamenazas y Tendencias. Edición." www.ccn-cert.cni.es/informes/informes-ccn-cert-publicos/3776-ccn-cert-ia-13-19-ciberamenazas-y-tendencias-edicion-2019-1/file.html

Clark, R. M. (2014). *Intelligence collection*. Thousand Oaks, CA: CQ Press.

Clark, R. M. & Oleson, P. (2019). "Cyber intelligence," *The Intelligencer: Journal of U.S. Intelligence Studies*, 24(3): 11–23. www.afio.com/publications/CLARK_OLESON_Pages_from_Vol24_No3_AFIO_INTEL_Winter_2018-19_FINAL.pdf

Cubeiro, E. (2018, October). "Interviewed by Virginia Lavín," *El País Retina*, 10: 42–49.

Department of National Security. (2013). "National cyber security strategy." www.dsn.gob.es/es/file/932/download?token=9-T_SSTE

Department of National Security. (2017, October 21). www.dsn.gob.es/es/actualidad/seguridad-nacional-ultima-hora?page=212

Department of National Security. (2019a). "Informe Anual Seguridad Nacional 2018. Ministerio de la Presidencia, relaciones con las Cortes e Igualdad." www.dsn.gob.es/es/file/2853/download?token=i8f5aG39

Department of National Security. (2019b). "Press Note: meeting of the National Cybersecurity Council 04.09.2019." www.dsn.gob.es/en/actualidad/sala-prensa/reunion-del-consejo-nacional-ciberseguridad-09042019

Department of National Security. (2019c, April 12). "Press note: meeting of the National Security Council." www.dsn.gob.es/es/actualidad/sala-prensa/reunión-del-consejo-seguridad-nacional-12042019 Last consulted: 4 August 2020.

European Commission. (2018). "Digital economy and society index 2018, country report Spain." http://ec.europa.eu/newsroom/dae/document.cfm?doc_id=52223

Europol. (2018a, March 26). "Mastermind behind EUR 1 billion cyber bank robbery arrested in Spain." www.europol.europa.eu/newsroom/news/mastermind-behind-eur-1-billion-cyber-bank-robbery-arrested-in-spain

Europol. (2018b). *Internet organised crime threat assessment.* www.europol.europa.eu/internet-organised-crime-threat-assessment-2018#:~:text=For%20the%20fifth%20year%20in,conducted%20and%2For%20facilitated%20online

FireEye. (2015). "Regional advanced threat report: Europe, Middle East, and Africa 2H2015." www.fireeye.com/current-threats/annual-threat-report.html

Gobierno de España. (2013). "National maritime security strategy." Department of National Security. www.dsn.gob.es/es/file/329/download?token=9Y92D968

Gobierno de España. (2019a). "Guía Nacional de Gestión y Notificación de Ciberincidentes." www.interior.gob.es/documents/10180/9814700/Gu%C3%ADa+Nacional+de+notificación+y+gestión+de+ciberincidentes/f01d9ed6-2e14-4fb0-b585-9b0df20f2906

Gobierno de España. (2019b). "Press note: España, primer país de la Unión Europea que desarrolla una Guía Nacional de Notificación y Gestión de Ciberincidentes." www.lamoncloa.gob.es/serviciosdeprensa/notasprensa/interior/Paginas/2019/230119ciberincidentes.aspx

González, M. (2019, March 27). "Una 'potencia extranjera' atacó los ordenadores de Defensa." *El País.* https://elpais.com/politica/2019/03/25/actualidad/1553543912_758690.html

ITU. (2019). *Global cybersecurity index (CGI) 2018.* Geneva, Switzerland: International Telecommunication Union. www.itu.int/dms_pub/itu-d/opb/str/D-STR-GCI.01-2018-PDF-E.pdf

Marín, F. (2019, July 25). "Interviewed by Rubén Arcos, Email exchange with LTC Francisco Marín Gutiérrez, Joint Cyber Defence Command (MCCD)."

National Cryptologic Centre. (2019). "Disinformation in Cyberspace, CCN-CERT BP/13, February 2019." Ministerio de Defensa. www.ccn-cert.cni.es/informes/informes-ccn-cert-publicos/3561-ccn-cert-bp-13-disinformation-in-cyberspace-1/file.html

ONTSI. (2018). *La sociedad en red. Informe anual 2017. Edición 2018.* Madrid, Spain: Ministerio de Industria, Turismo y Comercio. www.ontsi.red.es/ontsi/sites/ontsi/files/La%20sociedad%20en%20red.%20Informe%20anual%202017%20%28Edición%202018%29.pdf

Presidency of the Government. (2017). *National security strategy 2017.* DSN. www.dsn.gob.es/sites/dsn/files/2017_Spanish_National_Security_Strategy_0.pdf

Red Eléctrica de España. (2017, August). "Documento inicial del proyecto. Interconexión occidental España-Francia por el Golfo de Bizkaia-Gascogne." www.ree.es/sites/default/files/04_SOSTENIBILIDAD/Documentos/tramitacion_ambiental/DI/DI_GolfoBizkaia_v1.pdf

Sheldon, J. B. (2014). "Geopolitics and cyber power: why geography still matters," *American Foreign Policy Interests, 36*(5): 286–293.

Telegeography. (2019). *Submarine cable map.* www.submarinecablemap.com

Torres Soriano, M. R. (2017). "Concepto y niveles de la ciberinteligencia," *Revista de Aeronáutica y Astronáutica, 862*: 316–320.

Weedon, J. (2015). "Beyond 'cyber war:' Russia's use of strategic cyber espionage and information operations in Ukraine," in K. Geers (ed.), *Cyber war in perspective: Russian aggression against Ukraine* (pp. 67–77). Tallinn, Estonia: CCDCOE. https://ccdcoe.org/uploads/2018/10/CyberWarinPerspective_full_book.pdf

Woolley, S. C. & Howard, P. N. (eds.). (2019). *Computational propaganda: political parties, politicians, and political manipulation of social media.* New York: Oxford University Press.

2

ALBANIA'S CYBERSECURITY PIVOT

Between Western architectures and great power competition

Alexander Fotescu and Mihai Chihaia

Introduction

Albania, a small country with a population of nearly 3 million people, is an emerging parliamentary democracy. The country is ethnically diverse, with a population of 60 to 70 percent Muslim citizens, and is highly urbanized with approximately 60 percent of citizens living in cities. It also has one of the youngest populations in Europe. However, the country has a poverty rate of 35 percent, and is also significantly hampered in its development by problems related to brain drain. At present 30 percent of Albania's population lives outside of Albania and the World Bank forecasts that 280,000 people will emigrate from Albania by 2050. Indeed, demographers worry that Albania's population will continue to shrink in the future as a result of low birth rates and emigration.

In comparison to its neighbors, Albania also has a relatively low rate of internet connectivity – only 38 percent of households have fixed internet broadband. Rural areas hold 40 percent of the population but only 1 percent are connected to the internet. The International Telecommunications Union (ITU) 2017 Global Cybersecurity Index Report has labelled Albania as a "maturing" nation, signifying countries that have taken initiatives in this area and that developed on commitments, with the overall global rank of 88. The ITU score considers a nation's progress in five areas: legal (the development of cyber regulations), technical, organizational, capacity building (research, trainings), and cooperation (with other governments, private entities etc.). Albania's cybersecurity efforts were deemed noteworthy; advancements are highlighted in the areas of developing strong cybersecurity institutions, as well as for engaging in international participation and interagency cooperation. The ITU 2018 Report highlighted as important developments the Cyber Security Policy Paper 2015–2017 and the 2017 Law on Cyber Security. In addition, from 2017 to 2018, Albania climbed from 88 to 62 in the ranking of nations engaged in cybersecurity, indicating that considerable progress has been made from year to year.

That is, despite civil unrest, numerous transitions in Albania's government, and a slow rate of economic development, Albania has made great strides in recent years in the areas of cybersecurity policies. By 2018, the penetration rate for mobile phone use had reached 68 percent, and data usage increased by 30 percent from 2017 to 2018.

Much of the progress has occurred as a result of and alongside efforts at regional and international integration in other sectors. In particular, Albania's cybersecurity policy development has been strengthened as the result of relationships with the North Atlantic Treaty Organization (NATO), the European Union (EU), and Albania's neighbors, Turkey in particular.

Cyber security developments in Albania are almost 100% influenced by processes associated with NATO and the EU. NATO and EU requirements do not completely overlap, with NATO having a streamlined set of norms that apply to security and defense domains, while the EU approach is substantially more comprehensive, continuously evolving, applying to everything from infrastructure development to digital products and services standards, to international commerce and participation in collective scientific and technological frameworks. This peaceful partial overlap may change in the future, as it looks like NATO will be gaining an economic security dimension over the next 5–8 years, at which time the EU and the NATO frameworks may be partially contradictory, resulting in an even more constraining environment for the member states that wish to respect both frameworks.

While its NATO and EU memberships required the adoption of specific legal and institutional frameworks, Albania has not dragged its feet when it could have, instead being very proactive on cyber issues regarding fighting radicalization and the financing of terrorism. Albania prioritized making the most progress on security and external cooperation first, before it dealt with other EU requirements.

Cooperation with NATO in the provision of cybersecurity

Joining the Partnership for Peace (PfP) in 1994 was the first step towards joining NATO – a process finalized in 2009. Albania went through several essential steps in the integration process that focused on strengthening democratic processes, developing its economy and integrating it in the global system, developing its military and aligning to NATO standards. The country's orientation towards Euro-Atlantic integration was and is broadly supported by the population and the political class, making it a priority and advancing the process (Nichol, Morelli, Woehrel, & Belkin, 2009).

On the cyber side, Albania signed a Memorandum of Understanding with the NATO Cyber Incident Response Centre (NCIRC) on enhancing cyber defense in 2013, and adopted the Enhanced Cyber Defense Policy and committed to advance its national cyber defense capabilities in line with the Wales (2014) and Warsaw (2018) Summit conclusions. Furthermore, Albania also took part in the Cyber Coalition Exercise and is part of NATO cyber related projects such as the Multinational Cyber Defence Education and Training (MNCDE&T) (Minović, Abusara, Begaj, Erceg, Tasevski, Radunović, & Klopfer, 2016).

The Cyber Defence Strategy (2014), developed at MoD level, mandates the developing and enhancing of cyber capabilities, upgrading defense and information systems, the training of personnel, increasing cooperation at national and international levels, and engagement with other stakeholders such as the private sector. Regarding cooperation with NATO, it highlights the importance of participation in cyber defense operations and training.

Albania's National Security Strategy (NSS) (2014–2020) acknowledges the importance of cyber security in today's environment, describing it as part of an integrative process that constantly needs to be updated. Accession in the EU is described as the most important strategic objective of Albania (Albania, 2014).

The National Policy Paper on Cybersecurity (2015–2017) highlights the central role of cyber security in governance and society, the relevance of raising awareness, names the institutions that have competences in cyber security and cyber-crime, the need to enhance inter-institutional cooperation, the private sector, and universities, as well as with NATO and the EU. Highlighted weaknesses: lack of investments, of specialized human capital, of basic cyber awareness of the population.

Relevant institutions with responsibilities in the cyber area:

National Agency for Cyber Security (ALCIRT)
The Classified Information Security Directorate (CISD)
The National Authority for Electronic Certification (NAEC)
The National Agency on Information Society (NAIS)
The Albanian State Police and The General Prosecution Office
The State Intelligence Service (SIS/SHISH)
The Ministry of Defence and the General Staff of Armed Forces (with their subordinated departments and institutions with responsibilities in the cyber area)
The Electronic and Postal Communications Authority (EPCA)

Digital Agenda 2015–2020 Strategic priority: increasing safety of information networks through continuous update of norms, awareness raising, expertise development, identifying critical information infrastructures.

EU membership

In addition to the achievement of full NATO membership, Albania's most important strategic objective is EU integration. Although the process of achieving EU integration has been ongoing since the early 2000s, progress has been slow, and many do not expect to see Albania achieve full EU membership until 2030. Nonetheless, Albania has made significant progress in cooperation with the EU in the evolution of cybersecurity protocols and procedures, as well as the development of cybersecurity institutions. Albania is nominally up to date with EU norms regarding digital policies. However, an increase in pace of cyber developments on the EU side means that Albania will be in a continuous catch-up process over the next few years. Albania has been and is continuing to focus its efforts on the adoption of procedures, including legislation, in the areas of crime prevention, counterterrorism, and strengthening security in cyberspace.

The National Crosscutting Strategy on Information Security (NCSIS) (2008–2013) establishes the national Computer Incident Response Team for Albania (ALCIRT). Inaugurated in 2011, ALCIRT functions under the Office of the Prime Minister. In line with the EU framework, national CIRTs are the interlocutors of the EU Agency for Cybersecurity (formerly ENISA, the European Network and Information Security Agency). ALCIRT is the main institution in case of cyber incidents and response, advising and working with other institutions to increase cyber security, implement strategies and procedures, cooperate at international level, raise awareness and knowledge about cyber security issues at governmental, private sector, and citizens' level. The 2011–2013 USAID helped the Albanian government establish ALCIRT and runs a cyber training program for government officials.

The Crosscutting Strategy on the Information Society (CSIS) (2013–2017) was the first Albanian document that outlined future directions in the digital domain and the importance of cyber security. It mandated the establishment of a cyber-security authority and the development of cyber infrastructure, resulting in 2016 in the establishment of the National Authority for Electronic Certification and Cyber Security (AKCESK) (n.d.), which absorbed the former ALCIRT.

In the most recent 2019 European Commission report (EC, 2019) regarding Albania's evolution towards meeting EU criteria, Albania received rating of four out of a possible nine points in the area of fighting organized crime. The document suggested that Albania should in particular "adopt a cybercrime strategy and establish a more effective law-enforcement response focusing on the detection, traceability and prosecution of cyber criminals." In the same report, European Commission evaluators noted that "Albania's competitiveness is hindered by a lack of entrepreneurial and technological know-how and low education levels."

The Counter-Terrorism Directorate is the lead body on counter-terrorism, the others being the State Intelligence Service and the Defense Intelligence and Security Agency. In addition, the State Police's community policing personnel are involved in preventing radicalization and combating violent extremism. In 2018 former policing structures were upgraded to a National Coordination Centre for CVE.

On security measures, negotiations are continuing towards implementing the procedures for exchanging and protecting classified information, signed between the EU and Albania in 2016. Albania continued to actively participate in military crisis management missions under the Common Security and Defence Policy (CSDP), notably EUFOR Althea in Bosnia and Herzegovina and EUTM Mali. The country also offered to contribute to the EU battle groups in 2024.

The National Plan for European Integration 2018–2020 is the comprehensive outline of measures, institutions, and objectives, that need to happen for Albania to be in full compliance with EU norms (Albania, 2018).

The Law on Cyber Security 2017 is partly aligned with the EU Directive on security of network and information systems (NIS Directive). It outlines authorities, powers, and responsibilities, and defines measures to be followed in cases of crisis.

The EU's enhanced Agency for Cybersecurity's new mandate includes standardization of digital and ITC products and services across the EU, development of training, procedures, and doctrine for internal cyber security of member states, crisis response, and other aspects governing the EU cyber ecosystem, resulting in the establishment of a virtual EU cyber regime.

The EU's Joint Intelligence School was approved as a PESCO project in early 2019. Its cyber elements are likely to influence, in time, the benchmarking of the EU Agency for Cybersecurity. As a candidate country, Albania will have to adopt all EU developments prior to joining. Given its track record, it is likely that it will expedite their incorporation into its own frameworks. This will include the adoption of EU's (developing) concept of European Digital Sovereignty – the cyber segment of the wider concept of European Strategic Autonomy. Due to political and commercial factors, we are very likely to see a massive EU surge in cyber souveranist developments by 2021. In contrast to prior examples of EU strategic thought on cyber affairs, future developments will lean more towards the industrial, security and defense domains.

In 2018 the Council of Ministers approved the list of critical information infrastructures. The National Cyber Security Strategy is yet to be adopted (after August 2019).

Relations with neighboring states

As Albania–Turkey relations have improved, tighter regional cooperation in the area of cybersecurity has similarly evolved. In particular, Turkey has committed to the establishment of a High-Level Council of Cooperation, a cooperation mechanism similar to joint government meetings that Albania has with its neighbors in the region. Turkey remains the 5th largest trading partner and the sixth biggest foreign investor in Albania. Turkey has also continued to provide education and training for the Albanian Army and security forces including in the area of cybersecurity though primarily for defense.[1] After the coup attempt in July 2016, Turkey has been increasing pressure on Albania to deliver on dismantling the so-called Gulen/FETO structures in the country. The Marif Foundation, established by the Turkish government, is taking ownership of schools formerly owned by these structures.

Current cyber ecosystem, developments, and assessment

The National Authority on Cyber Security, AKCESK, is the foremost responsible institution in organizing awareness campaigns, trainings, and conferences on cyber and online security. The AKCESK also organizes training for government experts, implements regional and international capacity building projects, and the Albanian Cyber Academy for students, including promoting its activity in universities to attract students to join its ranks.

In the Albanian private sector larger companies take cyber security seriously, investing resources and developing their capabilities; small and medium sized enterprises (SMEs), however, have a limited understanding of the issues and afford to invest very little. InfoCom Albania is an important annual technology conference. It offers a platform for discussing cyber threats and digital regulations, enabling industry leaders and practitioners to share experiences and ideas.

In the area of civilian training and education, some efforts were made in universities to establish cyber security courses. The University of Tirana offers a Master's Degree in Information Security in the Economics Faculty; similarly, University College Luarasi offers a Masters in Cyber Security. While the programs show an early degree of positive outcomes, an issue that persists in both the academic and governmental environments is the lack of trained personnel – experts who could teach the curricula and train others.

In an interview for Euronews, (August 8, 2019) PM Edi Rama "warned against the EU dragging its feet on accession of Albania," raising concerns of other actors' meddling and stirring disentanglement and estrangement in Albania vis-a-vis Europe. The Albanians have proven very resilient, but conditions are changing, with increasing pressure from both the population and competitors of the EU, "at a time when the EU is starting to be perceived a hypocritical and betraying its own objectively set targets, due to internal political dynamics of some of the member states" (Euronews, 2019). In the fall of 2018, 23 percent of Albanians did not trust the EU. This figure grew to 27 percent within 6 months (Spring 2019 Eurobarometer).

In 2017, Edi Rama's Socialist Party won the parliamentary elections, with a majority and strong internal support, a clear Euro-Atlantic agenda, and with a set of high expectations. However, in 2019, after several years of continued reform, unexpectedly, the people decided to start mass protests, asking for the government's resignation. The mass protests paralyzing Albania since the beginning of 2019 are claimed to be due to pervasive corruption in the country. However, one might also suggest that the population has genuinely had enough of supporting a "security and international partners first" governmental policy. If this scenario were to constitute the more accurate description, then the natural implications are that the population will push back against any further tightening of the rule of law and cyber security efforts at the behest of the EU, resulting in implementations strictly on paper, most likely leaving the country particularly vulnerable. Considering the nature and character of asymmetric warfare, it is likely that foreign powers used the population's 24 years of reform fatigue and corruption annoyance to push the Albanian society into backtracking on transatlantic patience. While the overwhelming majority of the population supports NATO and EU membership, we are witnessing a social-, religious-, and identity-toughening stance.

The highest cyber security issues in Albania pertain to the category of "information operations," rather than the classical electronic attacks. The reason for this is the lack of any attack surface of consequence: IoT networks, businesses, and institutions online, etc., with high-speed internet still being an odd occurrence for the majority of the population. The second reason is that mobile internet is the main means by which the population has access to the internet – primarily smartphones. This creates the technical, societal, and behavioral conditions for the Albanian population to be particularly exposed to info-ops. We believe that it is a fair assessment that the Albanian society at large is highly vulnerable to disinformation and undermining campaigns that may be led against interfaith peace, NATO, the EU, or the rule of law, as well as any government, regardless of the electoral score, if it falls out of favor with the foreign governments operating in Albania and across the Western Balkans.

This situation is likely to persist, as fixed telco infrastructure development would depend more on the government, whereas mobile networks would rely primarily on private operators' investments. Much like other countries of Western Europe, Albania will likely adopt a strategy relying on mobile internet, as the more expedient and cheaper alternative to adequate fixed infrastructure development. Further trends to monitor are the purchase of local operators by companies east of Athens, which appeared to be turning into a trend during the second half of 2019.

Security and "souveranism"[2]

Albania has a very diverse cultural and historical heritage. With a moderate population and a tradition of fighting for independence and reunification, Albania was a good ground for developing a Euro-Atlantic understanding and perception of the cyber sector. Recently, with foreign actors' influence, increasing pressures from religious, sectarian, and propaganda movements, patience running low over EU's approach to Western Balkans integration, and unfiltered mass penetration of mobile internet, Albania is at very high risk of seeing its population influenced away from the ideals of a liberal, free, and open society. Albania will not renege on its NATO and security commitments, but if the current trend is allowed to continue, within a 3–5-year horizon it might start interpreting the EU Acquis more from a souveranist perspective.

Particular sensitive points have to do with surveillance, due to Albania's communist security services, oversight of religious activities and interference of foreign actors, and the fight against terrorism and Islamic radicalization. For now, the Albanian population is somewhat aware of such notions, but are generally open minded and have a neutral positioning. However, based on empirical evidence and precedent from other countries in the region, Albania is likely to have these three points used as triggers for developing adverse positions from those of the EU and NATO partners.

Albania sees itself primarily as a Mediterranean country, and with time, as more and more the country will be connected to European media, it will be pushed into taking sides on the narrative about Islam in Europe and migration from Africa and the Middle East. When accepted in the EU, Albania will also be the first majority-Muslim country of the Union.

An estimate of future developments

Due to weak administrative capabilities and an unstable political scene, Albania will not become a cyber security champion over the next 10–15 years; this is compounded by an undersized education and training capability and pressures from external state and non-state actors which are pushing the country, its people, and its politics in opposing directions. Foreign interference in Albania, the Western Balkans, and the wider Balkan region is intensifying, in a great power competition (GPC) manner, in which small Balkan states are under pressure from both regional middle powers as well as the global contenders. This will manifest only to a small extent as electronic warfare – and this will be mainly due to the fact that Albania is part of the EU integrated electricity grid, as well as being a NATO country. However, the prevalent means of cyber operations we will witness will come under the form of info ops. These will be about the weakening of the rule of law, central politics, eroding the stability of society and social and interfaith peace. Albanians, of whom a third live and work in the West, are convinced their country's future is about being part of the club. Since this entrenched cultural belief (for 30 years now) cannot be attacked directly, the main vectors will be undermining the image of Western actors, creating a perception that joining the EU will never happen, and providing alternatives that would answer the more immediate needs of the population still living in Albania. So far, the European Union has helped this undermining of faith and resilience by not acting upon the European Commission's recommendation to begin accession procedures with Albania and North Macedonia in summer 2019.

Albanians could play a relevant role in the EU, and an important one in the Balkans. With 1.5 million citizens already living in the EU, they would only start being seen, heard, and taken into account by the mainstream when they started making trouble. While the wide majority of Albanians have nothing to do with organized crime, those that are already on the precipice or are involved with organized crime, are likely to start joining paramilitary and organized networks whose purpose will shift from traditional sex slavery, credit card fraud, etc., to infiltrating operatives across borders, gaining access to corporate and international organizations networks, and organizing supra-national communities composed of first and prior generation migrants from the Balkans and CIS space, as well as from the Levant and Africa. Through mixed use of digital means, and digital–human communication networks, pockets of stirring of discontent may start happening.

It is important to emphasize that the Albanians' involvement in such operations would come about primarily due to external influences – due to the fact that Albanian crime rings are already in place and better organized than other groups, and they are more substantial in number compared to others from the Balkans. At the same time, the situation is not specific only to the Albanians. This combination of factors and pressures can be found acting upon all EU candidate or Eastern Neighborhood countries, most of which not only have visa requirements lifted for entering the EU, but are also part of at least one infrastructure and/ or cooperation network of the EU. For the Western Balkans candidates specifically, this means participation in the transport (TEN-T), energy (TEN-E), and digital (e-TEN) infrastructure networks, as well as borders, Europol, and other security cooperation frameworks which grant more or less access to shared EU data. For countries like Albania and Montenegro, which already are NATO members, the duty is even heavier, as the expectations from their side will be to positively influence developments with their neighbors, help provide extra security with regard to cyber security, disinformation, and timely flagging of emerging issues in the region (whether they be on the "human terrain operations" side, or in the cyber domain).

If all goes according to plan, Albania would be set to join the European Union anywhere between 2025–2030, this being a moderately positive scenario. At this point, this has less to do with Albania's technical preparedness level, but mostly with politics – internal instability in Tirana, as well as the political sentiment and calculations of a few EU capitals. While the most important factor regarding Albania's attitude as an ally and partner has to do with morale and the expectation of fully integrating into the Western club (NATO + EU), in terms of cyber security, this has to do with the length of candidate country status, as this keeps them one foot in, one foot out – with a target painted on their backs, but also not fully enjoying the umbrella of security membership and resources that the double membership would entail.

Strictly from a defense perspective, as NATO procedures and processes go, Albania will continuously work with alliance members to improve their technical skills and electronic capabilities to be on par with NATO requirements. This will spill over, to some extent, into capabilities of intelligence and security organisms, as they are tasked to handle counter terrorism duties. This, however, tells us little about the resilience and preparedness levels of both decision makers and society to confront an increasingly charged regional and global context. Best-in-class real-life examples have shown that it takes whole-of-society approaches and efforts to achieve the required resilience. This starts with building trust and cohesiveness, and as events in Albania since the beginning of the year have shown, neither of those seem to be at very high levels currently. It is important to point out that similar surges in public outcry, protests, and fragmentation have been attempted in the region since 2017, namely in Bulgaria, Greece, and North Macedonia. Albania seems to be the place where they also succeeded to an extent. This is the first red flag that the situation may be starting to slip and it concerns information operations and the penetration of human and digital networks with the objectives of undermining Albania's joining of the European Union and keeping the Balkans out of NATO.

Explicit geopolitical dynamics made a mark on Albania, with influences pulling it in different directions. Italy, France, and Germany have been positive influences and partners, but not to a sufficient extent to draw the Tirana government closer to them. In contrast, this is what Ankara succeeded in doing, exerting an oversized amount of influence on Albania while under the cover of NATO's membership umbrella. Due to the traditional NATO- and EU- accession succession, NATO has not engaged substantially with Albania as of late – at least not in a manner that would be evident from the public official documents. This tells a story of commitment and relevant contributions from Albania's part to both NATO and EU security frameworks and missions (defense, internal EU and national security, as well as law enforcement and fighting organized crime). The transition of the former communist Eastern European and Balkan countries to NATO and EU membership has always been driven by a narrative of increased engagement, partnership, and mutual benefits. This is currently absent in the country, resulting in what we suspect is an immeasurably demoralizing and demobilizing mindset for the population. Against this backdrop we see increasing pressures and influence from foreign Islamic state and non-state actors, and geopolitical and economic opportunity pressures from non-EU and non-NATO state actors.

Recommendations for the Albanian authorities and society include:

1   To start working on their own resilience strategy, one that involves both cyber coun-
    ter-measures, as well as societal preparedness and massive awareness and education cam-
    paigns through public media, schools, and institutions.
2   To develop a sustainability, social peace, and good governance strategy – a document
    that would provide the red wire to follow when crises and instability come, to keep
    everyone aligned and pursuing the higher interests of the country
3   To develop an integrated regional NATO action plan to support morale and higher
    national interests of the candidate countries of the Western Balkans. Lessons from previ-
    ous young member states showed that they tend to interact more with larger and/or
    early members. The Balkan region's specificities mean that intense cooperation with
    regional neighbors can be highly beneficial, particularly considering that Greece and
    Cyprus are the host countries to EU's Agency for Cyber Security and Joint Intelligence
    School, to name just two of immediate cyber interest.

Notes

1 With 5G and emerging technologies, frequency spectrum operations and normative frameworks
  tend to spill-over between civilian and military affairs.
2 "Souveranism" has become an EU-wide jargon term, from the French language, meant to denote
  a positioning/approach to both foreign policy and internal economic development policy that places
  national interests first, as opposed to what would be optimal in an open (and liberal) global system.
  Moreover, it embeds a security mode of thinking into all decision making under the aspect of "if
  we do this, will we still be able to keep control of the situation? Will we still have control of IP?
  Will we be able to shut things down as we need to?"

Suggested reading

Bahiti, R. & Josifi, J. (2015). "Towards a More Resilient Cyberspace: The Case of Albania," *Information
    and Security: An International Journal, 32*: 1–11.
Boga, G. (2018, December 27). "Albania: Cybersecurity 2019," *Mondaq*. www.mondaq.com/Technol
    ogy/766398/Cybersecurity-2019-Albania
Jica, H. (2013). "Cyber Security and National Security Awareness Initiatives in Albania: A Synergy
    Approach," *Mediterranean Journal of Social Sciences, 4*(10): 614–622.
National Authority for Electronic Certification and Cyber Security. (2018). "Report on Cybersecurity
    Maturity Level in Albania." https://cesk.gov.al/publicAnglisht_html/Publikime/2019/AlbaniaCMM
    Report.pdf
Global Cyber Security Capacity Centre, Oxford Martin School, Oxford University, commissioned for
    AKCESK. (2018). "Report on Cybersecurity Maturity Level in Albania." https://cesk.gov.al/Publi
    kime/2019/AlbaniaCMMReport.pdf
See-industry.com. (2018). "Cybersecurity Capacities of South-East Europe," *South-East European
    INDUSTRIAL Market, 2*. www.see-industry.com/en/cybersecurity-capacities-of-south-east-europe/
    2/1690/

References

Albania. Qendra e Botimeve Zyrtare [Official Publishing Center]. (2018). *The National Plan for European
    Integration 2018–2020*. www.qbz.gov.al/Botime/Akteindividuale/Janar%202018/Fletore%2069/
    VKM%20nr.%20246,%20date%209.5.2018.pdf
Albania. Strategjia e Sigurisë Kombëtare [National Security Strategy]. (2014). "Tirane." www.mod.gov.
    al/images/PDF/strategjia_sigurise_kombetare_republikes_se_shqiperise.pdf

Euronews. (2019, June 21). "EU Accused of Betraying Promises on Albanian Accession. Interview with Former Minister of Foreign Affairs." www.euronews.com/2019/06/20/eu-accused-of-betraying-promises-on-albanian-accession

European Commission. Commission Staff Working Document. (2019). "Albania 2019 Report." https://ec.europa.eu/neighbourhood-enlargement/sites/near/files/20190529-albania-report.pdf

International Telecommunications Union. (2018). "Global Cybersecurity Index Report." www.itu.int/en/ITU-D/Cybersecurity/Documents/draft-18-00706_Global-Cybersecurity-Index-EV5_print_2.pdf

"Law on Cybersecurity, 2017." https://cesk.gov.al/publicAnglisht_html/wpcontent/uploads/2016/04/Ligji%20_Per_Sigurine_Kibernetike_Nr_2_Date_26.1.2017.pdf

Minović, A., Abusara, A., Begaj, E., Erceg, V., Tasevski, P., Radunović, V., & Klopfer, F. (2016). *Cybersecurity in the Western Balkans: Policy Gaps and Cooperation Opportunities.* Geneva: Diplo Foundation. www.diplomacy.edu/sites/default/files/Cybersecurity%20in%20Western%20Balkans.pdf

National Authority for Electronic Certification and Cyber Security. (n.d.). https://cesk.gov.al/publicAnglisht_html/aktivitete/peereducator.html

Nichol, J., Ek, C., Morelli, V., Woehrel, S., & Belkin, P. (2009, April 14). "*NATO Enlargement: Albania, Croatia, and Possible Future Candidates,*" Congressional Research Service, Washington, DC.

3

ARMENIAN NATIONAL POLICY IN CYBER SPACE

Toward a global cyber security architecture

Ruben Elamiryan

Introduction

This chapter presents the cyber security of Armenia by considering its national security system, as well as integration into regional and global cyber security architectures. It demonstrates that currently Armenia is a less developed actor globally, however it is a factor of stability in the regional cyber security architecture. Nowadays Armenia is in the process of the establishment of a more comprehensive and sophisticated cyber security system to provide more active participation in the global cyber security. The major challenges which Armenia faces in cyber space are presented through three-level analysis: national, regional, and global. However, the more vital threats come from Azerbaijan and Turkey with regard to the Nagorno–Karabakh conflict and recognition of the Armenian Genocide of 1915.

At the same time, Armenia faces a transformation of the cyber security approaches caused by the rising challenges and threats in global and regional cyber space. Many of the concepts and norms in the field of cyber security expressed in Armenian documents in 2009 appeared to be influenced by Russian understandings (for instance, the use of term "information security," which integrates both information-psychological and information-technical components of cyber security); the draft version of the Cyber Security Strategy (HH kiberanvtangutyan nakhagits, 2017) provides more Western approaches to cyber security. However, having strategic relations with both the West and Russia, Armenia tries to integrate the best practices from all sides.

The above becomes clearer from the research of Armenia tightly cooperating, particularly in cyber security, with the North Atlantic Treaty Organization (NATO) while being a member of the Russia-led Collective Security Treaty Organization (CSTO) (NATO, 2016). The relations with other international organizations, such as the United Nations (UN), Organisation for Security and Co-operation in Europe (OSCE), International Atomic Energy Agency (IAEA), and Shanghai Cooperation Organization (SCO) witness rather "on hold" relations, at least publicly.

The concept of cyber security

The terms "cyber security" and "cyber defense" are multifaceted, leading to differing interpretations of each. Some perceptions concentrate solely on the military dimension of the issue, while others include a systems approach with both civil and military dimensions.

Based on the above, I will suggest the following definition of cyber security which will be the working one for this chapter:

> Cyber security is a set of technical and non-technical (policies, security arrangements, actions, guidelines, risk management) measures which provide for the social, ethnic and cultural evolutionary modernization of the critical cyber infrastructure, as well as protection of vital interests of human, society and state.
>
> *(Elamiryan & Bolgov, 2018)*

At the same time, a sophisticated cyber security system supposes forecasting and preventing cyber threats at early stages, as well as not only the ability to face challenges but also raise them when necessary.

Cyber security in the Republic of Armenia

The cyber security of Armenia is determined by a number of conceptual documents: The Military Doctrine of the Republic of Armenia, National Security Strategy of the Republic of Armenia, Strategic Defence Review, and the Public Information Concept of the Armenian Ministry of Defence. From 2009 the Concept of Information Security partially regulated cyber security issues in Armenia. However, it lost power in January 2018.

With regard to the cyber component of these documents, none of the above-mentioned strategic documents contains information strictly on cyber components. They do not bring clarity to the notion of critical cyber infrastructure, either. At the same time, for instance, the military doctrine of Armenia sets official views with regard to, specifically, the military-technical dimension of military security of the RA. Moreover, the technical and infrastructural components, as well as the information systems, are viewed separately as components of military security.

The research of the National Security Strategy of the Republic of Armenia concludes that cyber security is considered an instrument for effective functioning of information-psychological components of information warfare. For instance, it states: "Therefore, the Republic of Armenia aspires to … integrate into the international information area, to ensure professional promotion of Armenia and the Armenians, and to counter disinformation and propaganda" (National Security Strategy of the Republic of Armenia, 2007).

In this context, the Concept of Information Security (it is outdated, but we do not have a new one published yet) brings more clarity in the cyber field of Armenia. As in Russia and some other post-Soviet countries, it views cyber security in the broader context of information security, particularly, as the information-technical component under the umbrella term of information security. That is the reason why the Concept discusses cyber issues twice, but only in the context of cyber-crime issues.

However, the deeper comparison of the Armenian and Russian cyber security systems (Elamiryan & Bolgov, 2018) allows us to determine that, despite the tight military cooperation, the two countries do not share equivalent cyber security approaches. For instance, both countries do not have a centralized cyber command, however, Smirnov and Zhitnyuk believe that in Russia the technical aspects of cyber security are under the monopoly of the Federal Security Service (FSB in Russian), since all structures are obliged to use means of information protection, certified by the FSB (Smirnov & Zhitnyuk, 2010). In Armenia the provision of cyber security is rather de-centralized. Unlike Russia's troops of information operations, which were established in Russia in 2014 and whose functions include all aspects of information warfare: from psychological operations and propaganda (including the Internet) to the security of computer networks and cyberattacks on the enemy's information systems (Elamiryan & Bolgov, 2018), Armenia's cyber troops focus exclusively on the information-technological domain.

At the same time, while Russian analysts and policymakers tend to emphasize cyber sovereignty stating that "the main idea is that the government (in Russia) should have means of control over cyberspace and information traffic in order to ensure digital sovereignty but not to fence off the global network" (Elamiryan & Bolgov, 2018: 7), Armenian policymakers are more likely to provide rather liberal cyber space in Armenia, not really sharing Russia's understanding of cyber and digital sovereignty. The principle is "allow everything that is not prohibited," when prohibited are direct and clear criminal acts. For instance, the history of Internet in Armenia could hardly remember a single case when government blocked social media during anti-government demonstrations (Elamiryan & Bolgov, 2018).

It is also worth mentioning that the Russian analysts think that "the Russian approach focuses more on the security of information itself leaving the infrastructural level as a complementary component," when cyber space is considered to be a narrower notion as "a well-defined element of the information space" (Elamiryan & Bolgov, 2018: 1–2).

This demonstrates that nowadays (at least before the Armenian Velvet Revolution) Armenia is transforming its post-Soviet (Russian) view of information/cyber security to separation of the information-psychological and information-technological components of the general information security system. This is partially evident from the transformation of the names of documents: Information Security Concept (the Concept) in 2009 and Cyber Security Strategy (the Strategy) (HH kiberanvtangutyan nakhagits, 2017) in 2017–2018. Although the latter is not publicly available, its draft is available at the web site of the Ministry of Transport, Communication, and Information Technologies of the Republic of Armenia. The draft is a long-term cyber security development plan for Armenia and provides the relevant timeline for its implementation. It supports the above assumption on transformation of cyber security approaches from post-Soviet reality to more Western perceptions. Particularly, along with the clear-cut separation of the cyber security from information-psychological realm, the Strategy outlines a comprehensive development agenda, including establishment of a cyber security centre to coordinate the cyber security activities in Armenia (HH kiberanvtangutyan nakhagits, 2017). However, the implementation of this agenda is the matter of the upcoming future.

At the same time, despite the availability of a number of normative acts for cyber space in Armenia, it is hard to claim that they derive from the Concept. Rather, the transformation of cyber space in general, as well as the arising global, regional, and local threats and challenges provokes development of new regulations, for instance, the Law of the Republic of Armenia on Protection of Personal Data, which regulates the procedure and conditions for processing personal data, exercising state control over them by state administration or local self-government bodies, state or community institutions or organisations, legal or natural persons (Law of the Republic of Armenia, 2015).

Continuing the discussion about the normative part of cyber security in Armenia, an Armenian expert in cyber security, Samvel Martirosyan, put it the following way: "The normative part is rather underdeveloped, as most of the legal norms are rather old (except a recent law on personal data protection accepted in 2015)." He continues and explains that the Concept of 2009 was adopted based on the post-soviet experience of information security. In particular, it does not separate cyber security from propaganda/antipropaganda.

As a consequence, on one hand, it discusses the issue as a system, but on the other hand it brings uncertainty in the field. "Now we have the problem of clarification for ourselves the concepts of cyber security, cyber space, as well as critical cyber infrastructure." According to Martirosyan this situation causes very liberal cyber space in Armenia without filtering or blocking any cyber subject (except two short cases in 2008 and 2016). At the same time he mentions that the new cyber security strategy (accepted in 2017, but not yet publicly presented) "will allow us to develop the field more rapidly. And I think we will see it in the new concept of information security of Armenia."

Another Armenian expert, the CEO of the private cyber security company CYBER GATES, Samvel Gevorgyan, during the expert interview with me made for this chapter, clarified that the level of cyber security in Armenia is rather low, but it is experiencing a gradual rise. According to him, some parts of Armenian cyber space are protected by the National Security System of Armenia which led to the gradual decrease of successful cyber operations against the Armenian cyber space. At the same time the Ministry of Defence of Armenia, the Police, and the National Bureau at the National Academy of Sciences, as well as some private companies, work to provide security for specific fields in the cyber domain. "However the problem is that there is a low level of coordination among them," concluded Gevorgyan.

Rather problematically, the issue of the leading role in carrying out cyber security activities, as well as clear separation of responsibilities, are not addressed by the Concept or any other strategic document. This does not clarify if any ministry or organization is given this role, however it is not available publicly.

In this context Gevorgyan stresses the importance of public–private cooperation to provide cyber security for Armenia:

> Currently we face gradual rise of public–private cooperation in cyber security. For instance, as a private company we cooperate with the Police, National Security Service, and judicial system. Very often we start from one-time activity, which later transforms into long-term collaboration.

As a good example of private–public cooperation Gevorgyan mentions the functioning of the www.april2016.am website, which was established by private donors with the support of the Ministry of Defense of Armenia. The cyber protection of the website is provided by the private CYBER GATES. The website was established after the so called "April war" – a massive military escalation, initiated by Azerbaijan against the de-facto Nagorno-Karabakh Republic. As the website provides comprehensive information and the Armenian view of the "April war," it faces regular massive cyberattacks from Azerbaijan. "It is the number-one target, but the Azerbaijani hackers cannot eliminate it," states Gevorgyan. In addition, it is worth mentioning that this cooperation does not have strategic and/or normative basis and regulation, and is in the process of transforming its ad hoc nature into long-term reality.

Thus, we can see that the normative component of cyber security in Armenia currently experiences the process of strategic formation. As many other countries which recently came across the cyber issues, full scale cyber or hybrid warfare, Armenia first of all should clarify the general vision of its cyber security system. This will allow it to provide strategic and operational normative frameworks as the first step to formulate and implement practical policy-making in cyber domain.

In the meantime, this process should take place as soon as possible, because the cyber field is one of the most rapidly developing in the world and it will not wait for the actors of international relations to catch up with them. In this context the next section of this chapter draws out the main challenges and threats to the cyber security of Armenia which the country faces or could face in the near future.

Key challenges and threats to Armenian cyber security

The examination of the above presented strategic documents, as well as the necessity to provide multilayer security for critical cyber infrastructure of Armenia allows drawing out the most perilous symmetric and asymmetric threats and challenges to cyber security of Armenia. They could be grouped into the three-level system that follows.

The national level

This level includes threats to critical cyber infrastructure, lack of high-quality cyber security specialists, brain-drain, and limited digital literacy of the population, as well as too free internet space, and a low level of normative regulations. Particular threats come from social media and social networks. Another serious threat is the limited level of democratic development. In this regard Armenian scientist, Mamikon Margaryan (2013), believes that establishing the principles of "good governance," run by strategic leaders, can become an effective measure to modernize the cyber security system in the region of the South Caucasus, not only on an information-technology level, but also to increase the responsibility of political leaders and maximize improvement of cyber security in the RA.

In this context, Gevorgyan mentions the challenge of public awareness and Armenian mindset. According to him, on one hand the victims of cyberattacks in Armenia try to keep it secret when they are attacked and hacked. On the other hand, people and businesses do not want to pay for cyber security. As a result, these two factors together make the field more vulnerable. "It is very important to change this approach and as a private company we are working in this direction," states Gevorgyan. Interestingly, Gevorgyan finds the private sector in Armenia more secure then the public one. He explains: "Despite the private sector experiencing more deliberate attacks, but most of the private companies have their own rather professional cyber security teams (for instance banks). The public sector is protected only partially by, for instance, National Security Service."

The regional level

Being part of the South Caucasus and the Near East, Armenia faces a wide range of regional threats, particularly in cyber space. These issues deeply affect human security, which is a comprehensive set of threats directed against personal cyber security, as well as to control human feelings, emotions, psychological conditions, and the ability to objectively perceive physical and virtual realities (Elamiryan, 2015). A large volume of information appears daily in conventional and social media and is aimed at influencing human perceptions in different countries. The countries of both the South Caucasus and the Near East region strive to foster political stability and sustainable development. However, in our view, neither success nor failure in cyber operations can provide long-lasting sustainable development. At the same time the most vital threats to Armenian cyber security on a regional level come from its two neighbors Azerbaijan and Turkey. The reason is the ongoing Nagorno-Karabakh conflict between Azerbaijan and self-determined unrecognized Nagorno-Karabakh Republic. In this conflict Armenia (whom Azerbaijan claims to be the main side of the conflict) supports the

Armenian populated Nagorno-Karabakh Republic, while Turkey supports Azerbaijan. As a result, we now witness full-scale cyber warfare, to say the least, between Azerbaijan and Turkey, on one side, and Nagorno-Karabakh Republic and Armenia, on the other (Kotanjian, 2009; Elamiryan, 2015; Martirosyan, 2017).

There is no specific data on the quantity and quality of cyberattacks initiated by the two sides. However, frequently various local news agencies share information regarding successful or unsuccessful attacks on public and private resources committed by both sides (Jnews, 2011; Armenpress, 2012; The Register, 2016; Telecom Arka, 2018).

It is worth mentioning that full-scale cyber warfare accompanied the "April war." During the four days of war all the sides – Azerbaijan, Nagorno-Karabakh Republic, and Armenia – initiated and faced the whole spectrum of cyber operations, including DDoS attacks against news outlets and public institutions, operations in social medias (Facebook, Twitter), and so on (Tovmasyan, 2016).

Interestingly, in this context Gevorgyan thinks that Armenia gains much experience from Azerbaijani cyber operations. According to him, rather often these operations are successful, but they sophisticate the Armenian forces.

The global level

Globalization and development of networked society raises the issues of global cyber security due to the following:

- Vulnerability of the global cyber infrastructure, as a consequence of all the many actors involved in this process.
- The threat of communication manipulation.
- Underrepresentation in global cyber space.
- Crisis of multiculturalism.
- Dichotomy of traditional and modern values.
- Threats to sovereignty.
- Atomization of society, when a person only formally feels itself as a member of that society/state based on its current needs.
- International crime and terrorism, which are largely presented in cyber space.

Talking about regional and global threats towards the cyber security of Armenia, Martirosyan outlines the following:

- One of the main threats is Azerbaijan, which works against Armenia also in cyber domain. It takes place not only on state level, but also on behalf of formal-patriotic entities. "For instance the largest hacker group in Azerbaijan is called Anti-Armenia," Martirosyan clarifies.
- Another big issue for Armenia is the so-called state-sponsored attacks, which are directed deliberately against public figures and journalists in Armenia to receive information and frame public opinion. These attacks have different interested countries as subjects, not only Turkey and Azerbaijan.
- One more challenge is the attacks against the banking system, which gradually becomes a target. This is a relatively new challenge and banks have to work hard to be able to face the rising threats.

41

This section clearly demonstrates that nowadays Armenia faces a wide range of cyber challenges and threats, even cyber warfare, on national, regional, and global levels. At the same time, not a single small- or medium-size country is able to unilaterally provide effective solutions to the rising issue, let alone the development of early-prevention mechanisms. From this perspective Armenia does its best to integrate into regional and global security systems to provide more comprehensive and effective cyber security nationally, regionally, and globally.

Armenia within the context of regional and global cyber security architecture

Nowadays most of the international organizations (global and regional) have expanded their security agendas to reflect on rising challenges and threats of cyber security. The UN, OSCE, Shanghai Cooperation Organization (SCO), International Atomic Energy Agency (IAEA), NATO, Collective Security Treaty Organization (CSTO), and so on are developing strategies and operational capabilities to provide a more manageable and secure cyber environment.

Armenia, as an active member in the international community, is largely involved in the formation of global and regional cyber security architecture. In this regard Martirosyan thinks that Armenia is rather active in terms of international cooperation. However, the issue here is that the country has to work with and between both West and East, which very often have rather different approaches.

On the other hand, currently it is difficult to see any effective cyber security developments with the UN, IAEA, or OSCE, of which Armenia is a member. Moreover, the Memorandum on granting the Republic of Armenia the status of SCO dialogue partner was signed on April 16, 2016 at the SCO headquarters in Beijing. However, there is no publicly available information on the cooperation of Armenia with these organizations on cyber security issues. Due to the certain level of secrecy, the experts from government who are in charge of cyber security and work with these organizations also remain silent.

At the same time the following extract from the special address of the OSCE Secretary General Thomas Greminger on "The Future of European Security: Managing East-West Relations," chaired by Professor Wolfgang Danspeckgruber at the Liechtenstein Institute on Self-Determination at Princeton University on September 28, 2018, (with some reservations) could describe the situation with cyber security in institutions of collective security:

> Now in terms of thematic expertise, when it comes to relatively new security challenges, we still need to build our expertise on these issues. And this depends automatically on the will of participating states to give us the necessary resources. And here we clearly face challenge – we have [an] understanding of the relevance of these issues, and on the other side – strict budget policies, which makes it very difficult to develop this kind of issues. I am not going to tell you how many staff I have on cyber security, because you simply will not believe me. But this is a challenge. When it comes to more conventional security issues, we have fantastic capacity and institutions, but with new security issues, we face challenges to bring the necessary expertise into our discussions.
>
> *(Greminger, 2018)*

Based on the above, we should admit that at this point collective security organizations are less effective than collective defense ones. For this reason, this part will stop only on Armenia-NATO cooperation and Armenia's CSTO membership, where the results of collaboration are more or less tangible.

Armenia-NATO coperation: cyber security dimension

Armenia-NATO partnership started in 1992, when Armenia joined the North Atlantic Cooperation Council, later renamed the Euro-Atlantic Partnership Council. Later in 1994, Armenia joined the Partnership for Peace. Since 2006, Armenia-NATO cooperation has developed the framework of the Individual Partnership Action Plan (IPAP).

Key areas of cooperation include: security cooperation, defense and security sector reforms, civil emergency planning, science and environment, and public information. Currently, Armenia is implementing its fourth Individual Partnership Action Plan for 2014–2016, which was approved on May 23, 2014. At the same time, Armenia is an active contributor to NATO-led operations in Afghanistan and Kosovo. In 2007, a NATO information center officially opened in Yerevan (Relations with Armenia, 2016).

In this context, it is necessary to analyze the current state of Armenia-NATO relations in the cyber field, including the perspectives of each player regarding cyber security, as well as opportunities for further development in the cyber security field.

The 2014–2016 IPAP for Armenia lists five main actions to enhance Armenian capabilities for protecting critical communication and information systems against cyberattacks. They include conducting a study of international best practices in cyber security; establishing a network monitoring system in the National Security Strategy of Armenia; establishing response procedures for identified threats, providing methodologies, professional manuals, and other relevant materials to Armenia's cyber security state agencies, relevant departments, and professional training organizations; and harmonizing Armenia's national legislation with international legal norms addressing cyber space (IPAP, 2014).

A comparison of 2009 IPAP and 2014–2016 IPAP demonstrates the positive evolution of Armenia-NATO cyber cooperation in developing new approaches and addressing new elements of cyber security. However, interviews of experts lead to the conclusion that, in reality, Armenia-NATO cooperation in cyber security is limited to participation of the representatives of the Ministry of Defense and Armed Forces of the RA in NATO-organized seminars, conferences, and training. This development is partially reflected in Global Cybersecurity Index, as shown in Table 3.1.

Table 3.1 Global Cybersecurity Index – Armenia

Year	Country Index	Global Rank
2018	0.495	79
2017	0.196	111
2015	0.176	23
2014	0.176	23

Source: Global Cybersecurity Index (2014, 2015, 2017, 2018).

There was no change during 2014–2015. Interestingly there was a similar tendency of "stability" in the whole region of the South Caucasus for 2014 and 2015.

However, the International Telecommunication Union (ITU), which calculates Global Cybersecurity Index has changed the methodology for 2017. As a result, it completely changed the picture, as shown in Tables 3.2 and 3.3:

Table 3.2 Global Cybersecurity Index – Azerbaijan

Year	Country Index	Global Rank
2018	0.653	55
2017	0.559	48
2015	0.529	11
2014	0.529	48

Source: Global Cybersecurity Index (2014, 2015, 2017, 2018).

Table 3.3 Global Cybersecurity Index – Georgia

Year	Country Index	Global Rank
2018	0.857	18
2017	0.819	8
2015	0.500	12
2014	0.500	12

Source: Global Cybersecurity Index (2014, 2015, 2017, 2018).

Commenting on the low position of Armenia in Global CyberSecurity Index, Martirosyan and Gevorgyan agreed the calculation of the Index is rather technical and in practice Armenian cyber security capabilities are rather strong. "For instance, Georgia's position is high in the ranking as it is much more open to work with international agencies and follow their formal normative requirements, what we cannot say about Armenia", Martirosyan explains. This explanation could be true, as during this research I tried to implement expert interviews with government officials in cyber security, however I failed due to the certain restrictions and secrecy in work of the relevant agencies and their employees.

Continuing with the analysis of cyber security cooperation between the RA and NATO based on DOTMLPF II components – Doctrine, Organization, Training, Materiel, Leadership, Personnel, Facilities, Interoperability, and Information – there is a clear demonstration of rather well-developed cooperation in normative and education, but with greater potential for development in other fields.

From this perspective, DOTMLPF II could become the framework to modernize Armenia-NATO relations in cyber security (see Table 3.4).

Furthermore, Armenia-NATO cyber security cooperation must go beyond a purely technical and technological framework. Nowadays mankind, and specifically the nations of the South Caucasus, faces regional and global challenges and threats which undermine national, regional, and global stability. Consequently, humanization of cyber space and

Table 3.4 DOTMLPF II and Armenia-NATO Cooperation

DOTMLPF II Component	Possible Modernization
Doctrine	The IPAP for 2014–2016 covers the standard elements of Armenia-NATO relations. However, a separate joint strategy is needed and should be devoted specifically to cooperation in cyber security.
Organization	The actors can establish a joint center for coordination of cyber security in areas of mutual interest.
Training	Training in cyber security should be expanded for the Ministry of Defense and Armed Forces of the RA, and should include other ministries and civil institutions as deemed necessary.
Materiel and Logistics	A joint cyber infrastructure should be developed to predict and to eliminate threats in their early stages.
Leadership	Tighter cooperation and communication should be developed between the leaders of Armenia and NATO that are responsible for cyber security.
Information	Pertaining to the establishment of the joint center for cyber security coordination, a mechanism of information exchange on cyber issues of mutual interest should be developed.

Source: IPAP (2014).

development of a culture of cooperation in the South Caucasus will support sustainable development not only for that region, but also for wider areas of Eurasia and beyond. In this context, NATO can be one of the key actors in the humanization of cyber space, based on promoting a culture of peace and cooperation in the South Caucasus through, for instance, cyber security training, which NATO conducts for the countries of the South Caucasus.

The Collective Security Treaty Organization (CSTO)

Armenia became part of the then-Collective Security Treaty back in 1992 and from 2002 joined the then-newly formed CSTO (on the basis of Collective Security Treaty) as a full member.

The CSTO Charter's key Article 4 states that if one of the Member States undergoes aggression (armed attack menacing to safety, stability, territorial integrity and sovereignty), it will be considered by the Member States as aggression to all the Member States of this Treaty. Accordingly, all the other Member States at request of this Member State shall immediately provide the latter with the necessary help, including military assistance (Collective Security Treaty Organisation, 1992).

However, a question can be raised if this Article covers the issues of cyber security, too. Further clarification, particularly with regard to information field, is provided by Article 8 of the Charter, which states that, "… Member-states interact in fields of border protection, information exchange, information security, protection of population and territory from emergency situation of natural and technogenic character, as well as from dangers derived from military actions" (CSTO Charter, 2002).

More details in this regard are provided both in the "On the Strategy of CSTO collective security for the period till 2025", approved by the decision of the CSTO Council on October 14, 2016 (the Strategy 2025) and the Agreement on cooperation in provision of information security, accepted by the majority of the CSTO member states during the session of the CSTO Council on November 30, 2017. Particularly, the Strategy states that "one of the main modern threats and challenges to CSTO collective security is the aspiration to achieve strategic goals by use force, including information oppression, use of information-communication technologies to provide destructive impact on social-political and social-economic situation, manipulation of public consciousness in so called 'complex' or 'hybrid' technologies" (Strategy, 2016).

Generally speaking, the CTSO pays increasing attention to the provision of information security. However, neither the Charter nor various high-level declarations provide clue on whether Article 4 of the Charter also refers to information aggression, and how the CSTO member states would coordinate and combine their efforts to withstand information operations against any of them.

At the same time the Agreement (Republic of Kazakhstan, 2016) describes the CSTO perception of "threat to information security" as factors (integrity of factors), which create danger for people, society, and state in the information field. The document separates threats into three groups:

- Destructive impact on CSTO member states and the CTSO in general.
- Use of information-communication technologies by terrorist and extremist organizations and organized crime.
- Criminal acts with use of information-communication technologies.

What is interesting is that CSTO experts see cyber security (or the information-technological component of information security) as an integral component of broader information security. As a consequence, most of the CSTO strategic documents use the umbrella term "information security." The latter encompasses both information-technological (including cyber domain) and information-psychological components of the security architecture. We also see this approach in Armenia. At the same time neither the Strategy (2016), nor Agreement (Republic of Kazakhstan, 2016) and Charter (2002) use the term "cyber security" and "cyber warfare," in particular, in contrast to the NATO approach. Hypothetically, the terms differ from each other depending on the foreign policy of the country.

The Strategy (2016) emphasizes the formation of secure information space of CSTO member states as the main CSTO information security strategic goal, which undoubtedly also includes cyber domain. At the same time, according to the Strategy (2016), the CSTO should undertake the following set of actions to guarantee comprehensive information security for the member-states:

- Formation of CSTO member-states' information security system;
- Development of interstate and inter-institutional cooperation in information security;
- Modernization of mechanisms to counteract threats in information space;
- Implementation of joint events to counteract and neutralize threats in CSTO information-communication space;
- Interaction in international information security provision issues;
- Development of coordinated rules of behavior in information space and its promotion to international level;
- Development of conditions to establish basis for coordinated information policy.

Based on the Strategy (2016), the Agreement (Republic of Kazakhstan, 2016) presents more details and practical solutions to provide CSTO information security agenda on the ground. Article 4 of the Agreement defines the following directions of cooperation:

- Development of joint legal bases;
- Formation of practical mechanisms for joint reaction to threats to information security;
- Trust enforcement measures;
- Modernization of technological basis of information security;
- Establishment of the necessary conditions for the development of inter-institutional cooperation of the member states.

Articles 5 to 8 of the Agreement provide detailed clarifications and practical mechanisms on each above presented direction, which encompass a wide range of measures to coordinate and jointly secure CSTO information space from both information-psychological and cyber (not naming it) perspectives.

In this regard it is notable that back in 2014 information appeared that the CSTO member states were planning to establish a joint center for reaction to cyber incidents (CSTO will launch ..., 2014). However, we do not see any progress with regard to this suggestion either in Strategy 2025, or in the Agreement.

As effective implementation of any strategy demands well-organized structure, it is necessary to understand the relevant institutional framework, which is responsible for the functioning of the CSTO and, specifically, of its information security wing.

The CSTO organizational structure clearly demonstrates that there is only one division, which is directly responsible for the provision of information security (CSTO Structure, 2017). At the same time Bondurovskiy (2016) stresses the importance of the CSTO Parliamentary Assembly in information security as it coordinates the activities on harmonization of national legislatures.

Another two important organizations, which promote the CSTO information security, but are not direct divisions of the organization, are the Analytical Association of the CSTO and the CSTO University League. These two organizations provide academic partnership and university cooperation among the member states, organizing various academic-practical events (CSTO University League, 2014).

At the same time, one of the most successful proofs of the CSTO joint activities in information security could be the so-called PROKSI operations (from Russian, Counteraction to Crime in the Sphere of Information). The main goal of the operation is to reveal and suppress the functioning of such information resources in national segments of internet, the content of which damage or can damage national and collective security of the member states. PROKSI started in 2009. Since that time about 80,000 dangerous information resources were revealed (From Treaty to Organization, 2017).

Thus, we see that nowadays, in terms of information and cyber security on an institutional level, the Organization is in the process of development and operates mostly within the framework of the coordination of efforts. However, the problem is that the CSTO member states very often have, if not conflictual, at least different interests not only in terms of information security, but also with regard to the Organization's general activities. The latter largely impedes the effective functioning of the strategic goals for all member states, including Armenia.

Conclusion: the future of cyber security in Armenia

This chapter clearly demonstrates that nowadays Armenia is in the process of the development of a comprehensive and sophisticated cyber security system. In this process, Armenia conceptualizes cyber security as a combination of individual and collective good, which, as a consequence, should be pursued both unilaterally and through the development of regional and international regimes.

In this regard it is developing normative frames (cyber security strategy, laws, and so on), domestic institutions, and operational capabilities. On the other hand, Armenia integrates and develops in cooperation with regional and global international organizations. Particularly, we witness rather "on hold" relations (at least publicly) with the UN, OSCE, IAEA, and Shanghai Cooperation Organization and more active collaboration with institutions of collective defense such as NATO and CSTO.

With respect to the necessary developments in cyber security systems in Armenia, Martirosyan, during the expert interview, specified the following:

- Final clarification of the vision, ideology, and philosophy to provide security in cyber space.
- Modernization of the legal bases of cyber space.
- Establishment of an executive body or bodies to be responsible for cyber security.
- Development of public education in cyber security.

"This should be enough for the start, as it is dangerous to implement all the changes at once and all together. This can lead to enormous regulations and groundless restrictions to freedom in cyber space," stated Martirosyan in an expert interview arranged for the purpose of writing this chapter.

Agreeing with Martirosyan, however, it is necessary to emphasize that the main challenge to cyber space today is its internationally fragmented character. The problem is that the international community in general does not have a clear vision of tomorrow and, as a consequence, how to face the current and future challenges and threats in cyber space. This makes the countries deal with the threats alone – a task that is completely impossible for small and medium-sized entities. The rising regional and global uncertainties are also reflected in the cyber field, making it more essential to accelerate the modification of global and regional security institutions to bring more clarity, cooperation, and peace into the so called fifth geopolitical domain.

Suggested reading

Aliyeva, L. M. & Hwang, G. H. (2019). "The Model to Implement the Cyber Security Policy and Strategy for Azerbaijan Information System," *Journal of Digital Convergence, 17*(5): 23–31.
Garibov, A. (2018, November). "Azerbaijan, Georgia, Turkey: Advancing the Military Dimension of the Trilateral Relationship," Centre International de Formation Européenne, EUCACIS Online Paper, No. 3. www.cife.eu/Ressources/FCK/EUCACIS%20Online%20Paper%20No.%203%20-%20Azad%20Garibov_final.pdf
Gojayev, V. (2011). "The Struggle for Internet Freedom in Azerbaijan," Global Information Society Watch. www.giswatch.org/en/country-report/internet-rights/struggle-internet-freedom-azerbaijan
Panahov, H. (2016). "Cyber-Security Challenges in Azerbaijan," *Baku Dialogues, 3*(1): 1–6.
Runey, M. (2017, April 11). "Azerbaijan: State and Dissidents Acquire New Weapons for Cyber War," *Eurasianet.* https://eurasianet.org/azerbaijan-state-and-dissidents-acquire-new-weapons-cyber-war

References

Bondurovskiy, V. (2016). *Strategic Vector of International Information Security Provision*. SPIIRAN, Saint Petersburg, Russia.

"CSTO Charter." (2002). www.odkb.gov.ru/start/index_aengl.htm

"CSTO Structure." (2017). www.odkb-csto.org/structure/

"CSTO University League." (2014). www.odkbcsto.org/association/news/detail.php?ELEMENT_ID=4159&sphrase_id=25733

Collective Security Treaty Organisation. (1992). "Collective Security Treaty." https://en.odkb-csto.org/documents/documents/dogovor_o_kollektivnoy_bezopasnosti/

Elamiryan, R. (2015). "Human Security in Context of Globalization: Information Security Aspect," Materials of the International Scientific Conference on the Problems of National Security in Terms of Globalization (Interdisciplinary Aspects), RAU Publications, Yerevan, 173–179.

Elamiryan, R. & Bolgov, R. (2018). *Comparative Analysis of Cyber Security systems in Russia and Armenia: Legal and Political Frameworks*. Springer International Publishing, Cham. www.springerprofessional.de/en/comparative-analysis-of-cybersecurity-systems-in-russia-and-arme/16262586

"From Treaty to Organization. (1991-2017): 25 years of CSTO." (2017). www.odkbcsto.org/25years/index.php?sphrase_id=25732

"Global Cybersecurity Index." (2014). International Telecommunication Union. www.itu.int/en/ITU-D/Cybersecurity/Documents/WP-GCI-101.pdf

"Global Cybersecurity Index & Cyberwellness Profiles." (2015). www.itu.int/dms_pub/itu-d/opb/str/D-STR-SECU-2015-PDF-E.pdf

"Global Cybersecurity Index." (2017). www.itu.int/dms_pub/itu-d/opb/str/D-STR-GCI.01-2017-PDF-E.pdf

"Global Cybersecurity Index." (2018). www.itu.int/en/ITU-D/Cybersecurity/Documents/draft-18-00706_Global-Cybersecurity-Index-EV5_print_2.pdf

"Hay haqerneri hardzakumneri hetevanqov adrbejanakan mi sharq lratvakan kayqer ev nakhagahakani kayqy chen gortsum." (2012). https://armenpress.am/arm/news/691920/

"HH kiberanvtangutyan nakhagits." (2017). www.e-draft.am/projects/581/about

"Individual Partnership Action Plan 2014–2016." (2014). North Atlantic Council, NATO, Brussels, Belgium. http://mfa.am/u_files/file/NATO/INDIVIDUAL%20PARTNERSHIP%20ACTION%20PLAN%202014-2016.pdf

"Kiber hardzakum." (2011). "Hayastani teghekatvakan anvtangutyuny internetum," *Jnews*. www.jnews.am/Cyber_Attack

Kotanjian, H. (2009). "Complementarity in Developing the National Cybersecurity Strategy of the Republic of Armenia: Relevance of a Strategic Forum on Cooperation in Cyberspace." http://psaa.am/en/activities/publications/hayk-kotanjian/195-hayk-kotanjian-complementarity-in-developing-thenational-cybersecurity-strategy-of-the-republic-of-armenia-relevance-of-a-strategic-forum-oncooperation-in-cyberspace-arm

"Law of the Republic of Armenia on Protection of Personal Data." (2015). www.foi.am/u_files/file/Personaldataprotectionlaw_ENG.pdf

Leyden, J. (2016). "Azerbaijani Hacktivists Leak Armenian Security Service Docs," *The Register*. www.theregister.co.uk/2016/09/02/azerbaijani_hacktivists_ransack_armenia/

Liechtenstein Institute on Self-Determination at Princeton University. (2018, September 28). "Special Address by the OSCE Secretary General Thomas Greminger on 'The Future of European Security: Managing East-West Relations'." www.facebook.com/princeton.lisd/videos/249316699110227/

Margaryan, M. (2013). "'Good Governance' in the Context of Information Security of the Republic of Armenia," Proceedings of the International Conference on Innovation and Development, 58–63.

Martirosyan, S. (2017). "Hayastani tekhekatvakan anvtangutyuny ev kritikakan entakarutsvacqnery." http://noravank.am/upload/pdf/Samvel_Martirosyan_21_DAR_03_2017.pdf

NATO. (2016). "Relations with Armenia." www.nato.int/cps/en/natohq/topics_48893.htm?selectedLocale=en

"National Security Strategy of the Republic of Armenia." (2007). www.mfa.am/filemanager/Statics/Doctrineeng.pdf

"On the Strategy of CSTO Collective Security for the Period Till 2025." (2016). www.odkb-csto.org/documents/detail.php?ELEMENT_ID=8382&sphrase_id=25733

Republic of Kazakhstan. (2016). "Agreement on Cooperation in Provision of Information Security." mdai.gov.kz/sites/default/files/pages/soglashenie-1.doc

Smirnov, A. & Zhitnyuk, P. (2010). "Kiberugrozy realnyie i vydumannyie (Cyber Threats, Real and Imaginary)," *Global Affairs*, *2*: 186–196.

Telecom Arka. (2018, January 22). "Armenia Is at the Center of Cyber Attacks from Turkey and Azerbaijan." http://telecom.arka.am/en/news/internet/armenia_is_at_the_center_of_cyber_attacks_from_turkey_and_azerbaijan/

Tovmasyan, S. (2016). "Information Warfare: Armenia-Azerbaijan Cyber War Intensifies Amid Karabakh Clashes." www.armenianow.com/karabakh/71214/armenia_karabakh_azerbaijan_information_warfare

4

CZECH REPUBLIC

A new cyber security leader in Central Europe

Lucie Kadlecová[1] *and Michaela Semecká*

Introduction

The Czech Republic has a long history of industrial development and technological innovation. Since the nineteenth century, the nation has been famous for its prominent sectors of heavy industry and its technological prowess, which have provided its governments with a steady source of income. Not surprisingly, this historic heritage is reflected in present day Czech society, which has embraced a leading role in information technology (IT). Today, analysts recognize the international success of Czech IT companies such as Avast and AVG (both of which produce antivirus software) as well as the sterling reputation of the technical universities in Prague and Brno. The Czech Republic, and the city of Brno in particular, are sometimes referred to as the "Central European Silicon Valley." However, some critics allege that the Czech government initially underestimated the nation's great IT potential and the sector's importance to the development and security of Czech society, only beginning to take cyber security seriously after Czech cyber space suffered a major cyberattack in the spring of 2013.

Prior to the 2013 cyberattack that served as a wake-up call for Czech authorities, responsibility for cyber security was rather decentralized. Multiple ministries and government agencies exercised power over cyber space, resulting in various gaps and overlaps in their areas of responsibility. Only in late 2011 was the Czech National Security Authority (NSA) appointed as the main authority for cyber security. It was tasked with creating a National Cyber Security Centre (NCSC) in order to centralize and coordinate government action. Shortly afterward, a cyber security strategy for 2012–15, the first document of its kind in the Czech Republic, was adopted (National Cyber Security Centre, 2012). The strategy had two very basic but essential goals: to propose a legislative framework for addressing cyber security issues and to build the capabilities necessary to ensure a basic level of national cyber security. The latter task included the creation of a governmental Computer Emergency Response Team (CERT) in 2012. Although the 2012–15 strategy did not set out extremely ambitious goals, it laid a foundation for building the basic capacities and capabilities which guarantee a fundamental level of national cyber security and provide a solid basis for further development.

The impetus for the establishment of a more wide-ranging approach to cyber security came about in March 2013 when Czech cyber space was hit by a serious campaign of cyberattacks targeted at Czech media websites, the banking sector, and mobile telephone operators.[2] Although the disruption of services in those sectors lasted only couple of days, Czech authorities took it as a wake-up call requiring a series of complex actions, which followed not long after. First was the enactment by Parliament of an Act on Cyber Security and Change of Related Acts (Act No. 181/2014 Coll., 2014) which entered into force at the beginning of 2015. This comprehensive act replaced a hodgepodge of laws and regulations which had not fully addressed the entire spectrum of cyber activities. Before its enactment, the draft bill was scrutinized by various IT practitioners, companies, and experts, which allowed for broad debate on the topic and provided a valuable bottom-up perspective. This process initiated an ongoing program of cooperation between governmental institutions, the private sector and academia.

At the same time, a new National Cyber Security Strategy for the Period 2015–20 was adopted (National Cyber Security Centre, 2015). This strategy moved on from proposals for elementary capabilities envisioned in the first strategy to the ambitious goal of securing the highest possible level of cyber security in the Czech Republic. Most importantly for this chapter, the strategy outlined the Czech Republic's aspirations "to play a leading role in the cyber security field within its region and in Europe," which was highly ambitious but nevertheless reflected the swift progress of the country up to that point in improving cyber security (National Cyber Security Centre, 2015: 7). To fulfil this high aspiration and to adopt a truly comprehensive approach to cyber security, the Czech government agreed in winter 2016 to separate the NCSC from the NSA and form a National Cyber and Information Security Agency (NCISA), a civilian agency dedicated to cyber security. NCISA was authorized to undertake a wide spectrum of activities and provide a higher quality of service to the government and the IT sector. By 2025, NCISA will have grown ten-fold in budget and staff. It will acquire new premises around 2022. NCISA has been operational since August 2017, taking over and broadening the existing portfolio of the NSA's cyber activities.

Thus, despite a relatively late start, the Czech Republic has quickly adapted to the challenges inherent in the cyber space environment. With its government, the private sector, and academia working together, it has the potential to become a new leading regional player. Nevertheless, there still remain a number of unresolved cyber issues that first need to be addressed.

This chapter is divided into two main parts. First, the authors introduce two successes that highlight the Czech Republic's role as a regional cyber power. These are the development of highly advanced systems for identifying and protecting critical information infrastructure and for utilizing the great capacity of the Czech Republic's human resources in IT. Next, the chapter examines two issues that have slowed the otherwise rapid cyber development in the country and which need to be urgently addressed in the next few years in order to allow the country to become the region's cyber security leader. These are a low level of implementation of e-government, in which the Czech Republic has fallen behind the rest of developed Europe, as well as slow progress in building up cyber defense capabilities. The chapter's conclusion will wrap up the whole argument and point out a direction for future development.

Protection of critical information infrastructure:
a case of building trust

As in many European states, critical information infrastructure (CII)[3] protection has become the Czech Republic's top priority since it laid down the building blocks for better cyber security in 2011. CII includes the communication and information systems essential for the smooth functioning of a society and economy. CII is a valuable target for enemies that are both state and non-state actors in cyber space. Energy, finance, medical, transportation, and telecommunication assets located around the globe have been targeted for disruption by a wide array of actors. Given its importance and the increasing potential for exposure to cyberattacks, the need for protection of CII cannot be underestimated.

A strong foundation for CII protection begins with a comprehensive legal framework. In the Czech Republic, the cornerstone is the Act on Cyber Security (Act No. 181/2014 Coll., 2014) and its implementing regulations.[4] The Act, which preceded the 2016 EU Directive on Security of Network and Information Systems (NIS Directive) (European Union, 2016), entered into force on January 1, 2015 and was amended two years later based on the newly adopted EU legislation. It defines regulated entities and their obligations.[5]

The Act also gives the government authority to declare a state of cyber emergency.[6] In order to stop major incoming attacks, a declaration of a state of cyber emergency grants the NCISA authority to issue orders to internet service providers (ISPs), which are not regulated entities in normal situations. In practice, this measure is only likely to be used exceptionally. Cooperation between ISPs and the government CERT generally works well and orders could be issued after appropriate consultation and recommendation. No state of cyber emergency has yet been declared, but its use has been extensively tested both at the national and international level.[7] One of the hypothetical instances, when the cyber emergency could be used, would be a case of cyber terrorism as defined in the Czech Audit of the National Security (Ministry of Interior, 2018a).

A state of cyber emergency is something unique to the Czech Republic in the context of international cyber crisis management (Boeke, 2018). A declaration of a state of cyber emergency precedes a general state of emergency and gives NCISA an opportunity to handle a cyber incident by itself. Only if NCISA is unable to handle the situation within 30 days would the Prime Minister declare a state of emergency under the Crisis Act (Act No. 240/2000 Coll., 2000). No other European state has such a provision for declaring a state of cyber emergency, nor is there a similar EU policy. Most EU member states foresee declaring a full state of emergency immediately and handling the situation on the basis of their general crisis management acts, not their cyber-related legislation.

Although the Czech legislation creates a solid foundation for protection of CII, cyber security cannot be fully ensured unless the regulated entities are willing to maximize protection of their own systems. Therefore, the Czech legislation was drafted with trust and cooperation between the state and regulated entities in mind. All regulated entities were involved in the process of drafting the law. A map of institutions affected by the legislation was drawn up. Their representatives were invited to meetings in which they were given a chance to voice their doubts, provide feedback, and propose amendments to the wording of the legislation. Three years later, in 2017 when the Act on Cyber Security had to be amended to conform to the EU NIS Directive, the Czech Republic took the same approach again. Before the legislation was submitted to Parliament, a draft of the amended law was made public and was available for comment to anyone from the general public and the expert community.

By giving all the stakeholders a chance to influence the final wording of the cyber security law, the Act was perceived not as a purely authoritarian decree by the state but rather as the outcome of the cooperation of a number of subjects. Such an approach was promoted by several institutions and regulated entities on a number of occasions. It established a sound basis for further development of good relations with the private sector. NCISA is profiting from this approach, as it is still evident that regulated entities are more open to cooperation than they might otherwise be (Kadlecová, Bagge, Borovička & Semecká, 2017: 16).

One of the pillars upon which Czech cyber security legislation was built and which contributes to greater mutual trust is the minimal amount of state coercion that is applied. Operators of CII, like other regulated entities, have free choice in how they implement the security measures set forth in the Act on Cyber Security. Because the main responsibility for network protection lies with them and they are the ones most familiar with their own network infrastructure, they are best equipped to strengthen their own systems. Therefore, the legislation avoids setting rigid rules by indicating the desired end state of affairs and giving institutions free choice in how to reach it. Cyber security is a fast-developing field and national legislation should be flexible enough to accommodate new elements or tactics of protection. A similar approach may prove to be suitable, for instance, for the banking sector, which is well known for its emphasis on cyber security and the implementation of extra measures of security.

In the spirit of mutual trust, the state acts more as a partner than a sanctioning authority. NCISA, which controls implementation of the Act on Cyber Security, devotes considerable effort to explaining responsibilities to all regulated entities. The Agency keeps in close touch with CII operators, ready to assist them with implementing the legislation. Its goal is not to penalize but to help secure systems of critical infrastructure to the highest degree possible.

NCISA also strives to be a partner when it conducts cyber security audits of regulated entities. The primary aim of these controls is not to look for errors and impose penalties, but to help subjects to maximize the security of their systems and networks. Therefore, NCISA, which conducts the audits, highlights solutions and suggests remedies for shortcomings rather than simply identifying shortcomings, penalizing them, and leaving it at that. This "auditing to improve" is quite unique in the Czech state administration and has further increased mutual trust between the national cyber security authority and the operators of CII (Kadlecová, Bagge, Borovička & Semecká, 2017: 20).

As developments abroad have demonstrated, the Czech approach to protection of CII has been influential. Transposition of the EU NIS Directive into the national legislation of the Czech Republic has been relatively smooth and fast. Czech cyber security legislation is built around a right to undisturbed access to the Internet and information rather than on resolving conflict between security and personal data protection, as it is sometimes framed elsewhere. The EU NIS Directive is based on a similar logic. Czech experts are regularly being invited to visit partner states in the Balkans, Ukraine, and Morocco to help build local cyber security frameworks and draft legislation.

Trust between CII operators and the state is vital. Without trust, operators would be hesitant to share information about cyber incidents and the state would be left in the dark. It would not be able to help resolve cyberattacks and would not be able to perceive the bigger picture of cyber security in the country. Creating an environment in which all stakeholders are involved in formulating rules, in which the state is perceived as a partner rather than a sanctioning authority, and in which not errors but remedies for errors are highlighted, has proven to be one of the lasting building stones of national cyber security in the Czech Republic.

Investing in human capital: investing in the future of cyber security

People are the most important ingredient of cyber security. A state can possess all the latest technologies and have a comprehensive legal framework in place, but without a dedicated, skilled workforce not much success can be achieved. It is people who set forth visions and the steps to achieve them. It is people who build strong relationships with national and international partners. And it is people who come up with innovative ideas. The Czech Republic has proven that it has great capacity in terms of human resources, both in the state administration and in the private sector.

This strength has been confirmed during international cyber security exercises, in which the Czech team has constantly taken top positions. Locked Shields, organized by the NATO Cooperative Cyber Defense Centre of Excellence (CCDCOE), is the largest cyber security exercise and serves as an example. In its 2017 iteration, in which more than 900 experts from 25 countries took part, the Czech team won first place, followed by teams from Estonia and NATO's NCIRC. The Czech team was comprised of representatives of NCISA, the state administration, the intelligence services, the private sector, and academia. The exercise gave the Czech Republic's diverse team an opportunity to cooperate closely as they practiced handling a major cyberattack.

The potential of the Czech Republic's human capital has also been reflected in the successes of Czech IT companies, such as the antivirus companies Avast and AVG. Avast has more than 400 million users worldwide. Its success was put into the spotlight when its stock was listed on the London Stock Exchange in May 2018. The company was valued at £2.4 billion and was one of the UK's biggest technology listings ever (London Stock Exchange, n.d.).

The Czech Republic can be proud of its well-above-average programming talent too. Many countries face a lack of cyber security experts and it would be incorrect to say that the Czech Republic is in every way an exception. However, statistics indicate that the situation there is better than in most countries. Around 3% of the population are employed as software developers, whereas in the United States the number hovers around two to 2.5%. The number of programmers is enhanced by their quality. Statistics on GitHub (a web-based service for hosting open-source software projects) indicate that Czech software developers are creative and skillful. The Czech Republic ranks twenty-first among the countries of the world in the number of "pushes" on GitHub. In other words, it is the twenty-first-ranked country whose developers upload the most codes onto the platform (Štrosová, 2018). Combined with a stable economy, a favorable location, and a relatively low-cost workforce, it is not surprising that corporations such as Microsoft, IBM, and Red Hat have located their development divisions in the Czech Republic.

Thanks to Czech academia, the trend to a strong cyber security workforce is likely to continue in the foreseeable future. Strong cyber security teams can be found at the main universities – the Czech Technical University in Prague (ČVUT), the Technical University in Brno, Charles University, and Masaryk University are top European educational and research institutions in their fields. For example, the origin of the research cyber security team at Masaryk University in Brno, which is a member of the Forum of Incident Response and Security Teams (FIRST), dates back to the 1980s, when the university's computer network was being created. As the university team grew, more projects came in and more cooperation with other entities was established. In 2007, the university team reached an agreement with the U.S. Army. A few years later it commenced cooperation with NATO as well. Nowadays, it tests and improves the skills of its members in its own "cyber range" (Fojtů, 2018: 5). Another example of success is ČVUT, which is well-known for its Institute for Informatics, Robotics and Cybernetics, which strives to create synergies among different research projects and produce unique IT outcomes. Cyber security education programs at universities and high schools are constantly broadening and increasing in number, and with them the pool of future cyber security experts in the Czech Republic and beyond.

E-government: wasting an opportunity

E-government in the Czech context is understood as governance using modern electronic tools to make public administration more friendly, accessible, efficient, faster, and cheaper for its citizens (Ministry of Interior, 2018b). At least that is the perception of e-government as it is seen through the lens of the Ministry of Interior, the main national authority responsible for implementation of e-government in the Czech Republic. This definition is essentially correct, and if it is successfully implemented, it would help the Czech Republic to achieve its goal of becoming a regional leader in the cyber domain. However, the reality is far from the vision. The Czech authorities need to first overcome a series of shortcomings, such as the lack of stable leadership and a coherent framework for implementation of e-government.

At first glance, the Czech Republic appears to be a fairly well-interconnected and digitalized country with a high degree of dependency on information and communications technologies.[8] Based on the available data from Eurostat, the percentage of Czech households with internet access has gradually grown in recent years, reaching 83% in 2017, which is not that far off the European average of 87% (Eurostat, 2018a). A similar trend can be observed with regard to private enterprises in the Czech Republic, whose access to the internet even exceeded the European average of 97% in 2017 by one percentage point (Eurostat, 2018b). These seem to be promising indicators, which one would expect to be reflected in the development of e-government. However, the percentage of individuals using the internet for interaction with public authorities in the Czech Republic has shown a rather irregular trend of growth, which has caused the country to fall behind the European average in some respects. For instance, in 2010 the percentage of Czech individuals using the internet for communication with public authorities was 23%. That increased to 30% in 2012 and 32% in 2015, but it stagnated at 36% in 2016 when the EU average was already at 48% (Eurostat, 2018c). A similar picture from a different point of view is provided by the UN E-government Knowledge Database which positioned the Czech Republic in fiftieth place worldwide in 2016. That would not be a bad result if the country had not already placed at forty-sixth in 2012 and fifty-third in 2014, suggesting that there has not been much progress in Czech e-government in the past decade (UN, 2016).

The first e-government strategy was approved by the Czech government in 1999. Since then the most important phase in the development of e-government was the period 2007–13, when all activities in this regard were concentrated in the Ministry of Interior and the main pillars of e-government in the Czech Republic were built. The flagship project of this period was the creation of a network of one-stop access points to e-government services called Czech POINT in post offices and municipal buildings. Citizens can access all public records through the one-stop points and obtain transcripts from national registers, which reduces administrative burdens (Ministry of Interior, 2018c). Following the success of Czech POINT, the government initiated another scheme, a data-box project that has provided the general public with a secure repository for official electronic communications with the public authorities since 2009 (Ministry of Interior, 2018d). Finally, the third important and successful project of the era was the basic registers, a central information source aggregating the public authorities' information systems. The basic registers include, for instance, the register of inhabitants and the register of persons and companies. The basic registers also serve as a central hub for interchange of information held in information systems like those for vehicles and drivers (National Registers Authority, 2018). Since the implementation of these three projects, the Czech government has set further goals that do not seem to promise the relative success of Czech POINT, data boxes, and basic registers. An example of such projects is the introduction of new e-ID cards and the implementation of intelligent electronic forms that would facilitate citizens' interaction with the public authorities without the need for visiting offices in person.

With a closer look at recent developments in Czech e-government, three major shortcomings can be identified.[9] First of all is the low quality of the national strategies for e-government, which have rarely been re-evaluated or updated, resulting in a lack of detail about the effect of e-government implementation. Furthermore, most of the strategies can be criticized for their rather broad scope. Second, Czech e-government lacks stable political and executive leadership, which has resulted in a lack of a continuous vision and effort to implement goals for expanding e-government. Finally, the national government is often criticized for a strictly top-down approach to e-government, which fails to encourage participation by stakeholders during the preparatory phases of new legislature, strategic documents and e-government schemes (Špaček, 2015).

The Czech government tries hard not to be passive in the implementation of its e-government projects, as the examples of Czech POINT, the data boxes and the basic registers illustrate; nevertheless, it lags behind e-government role models such as Estonia and its highly developed digital society. The Czech projects currently are not evolving much further, and the Czech Republic is falling behind in the successful implementation of new schemes, as well as suffering from a number of other serious shortcomings. Although the Czech Republic might have the potential to take advantage of more advanced e-government services, it will not do so unless those deficiencies are addressed. The first step in this direction might be the Strategy for Coordinated and Complex Digitalization in Czech Republic 2018+ which promises to deliver a complex solution for digital agenda including e-government and which was approved by the government in October 2018 (Sedlák, 2018).

Active cyber defense: no legal framework – yet

To maximize national security in the country, there are still some issues that need to be resolved. Cyber defense is one of them and ensuring it is of fundamental importance to overall national security. A symbolic building block of cyber defense was laid with publication of the National Cyber Security Strategy for the Period 2015–20 and its Action Plan. In these strategy documents, the Czech government decided to create, under the aegis of military intelligence, a National Cyber Operations Center,[10] which is responsible for the cyber defense of the country. The center opened in 2016. Two years later it published its first cyber defense strategy, which was a necessary precondition for effective and complex cyber defense (National Cyber Operation Centre, 2018). In that strategy, the Center outlined its plans for developing active cyber defense capabilities. However, a law that would have framed its activities failed to pass through Parliament and as of mid-2018, the legal framework for cyber defense is still in limbo.

A mandate for cyber defense is essential to complete the spectrum of national security measures. Where cyber security[11] ends, cyber defense[12] begins. NCISA, the national authority in the field of cyber security, is responsible for handling cyber security incidents affecting its constituency. However, when cyberattacks are conducted on a massive scale and cannot be handled by traditional cyber security tools alone, military intelligence should step in and help to resolve the situation by active measures (Pačka, 2015). The exact situations that would trigger of use of active cyber defense are yet to be determined. Of course, cyber security and cyber defense are not two separate issues. In the event of a cyber security incident, military intelligence cannot suddenly take over responsibility from the civilian authorities. For cyber defense measures to be effective, military intelligence must be in contact with cyber security agencies on a daily basis. Therefore, a comprehensive cooperation framework between cyber security and cyber defense entities should be set up, applicable in both peacetime and conditions of war.

To create a stable environment for cyber defense activities, Czech military intelligence officials decided to anchor their cyber defense activities in legislation. In October 2016, they proposed an amendment to the Act on Military Intelligence, which was meant to clearly set forth their competencies in the area of cyber defense. In the amendment, it was proposed that Czech military intelligence have the right to introduce "technical means" onto "electronic communication providers' networks" (Military Intelligence, 2016). However, authority to conduct active cyber operations against a foreign adversary, which is the main element of cyber defense, was omitted.

The amendment was severely criticized by the community of experts in cyber security. Three major cyber security organizations – CZ.NIC, which operates the domain name registry for the ".CZ" domain and is the operator of the national Computer Security Incident Response Team (CSIRT); NIX.CZ, a trade association of Internet service providers in the Czech Republic; and the ICT Union, a professional association of companies active in the field of information technology – sent a letter to then Prime Minister Bohuslav Sobotka asking that the legislation be tabled and discussion with affected stakeholders reopened (CZ.NIC, 2017). They argued that the proposed new authority of military intelligence to place "technical means" onto the ISPs' networks would be problematic for several reasons. Their most serious concern was the issue of privacy. If devices were to be installed on the ISPs' networks, it would be technically possible to intercept and record most Internet traffic. Given that the purpose of military intelligence is to gather and assess information, it would be difficult to believe that they would refrain from reading the content of Internet traffic. In addition, such a measure would create a "single point of failure." If the military intelligence authorities lost control over its devices to a third party, its devices would be a place from which networks across the country could be attacked and possibly the Internet could be cut off altogether (CZ.NIC, 2017).

Military intelligence tried to dispel those doubts. Its representatives argued that they would be looking only for anomalies in network traffic, not content. If an anomaly appeared, intelligence officials would examine the content of a suspicious communication only after seeking and receiving permission from a court to do so. Despite those assurances, many critics still considered the "black boxes," as the media labelled the technical means of military intelligence, to be a threat to privacy (Ťopek, 2016).

The amendment to the Act on Military Intelligence did not pass. The Chamber of Deputies did not manage to enact the law before parliamentary elections in October 2017 and military intelligence still lacks legal authority to conduct active cyber defense operations.

In the summer of 2018, military intelligence issued its first Cyber Defense Strategy, which listed enactment of a legal framework as one of its priority goals (National Cyber Operation Centre, 2018). At the moment, however, it is still unclear when the amendment will be resubmitted to the Chamber of Deputies, how its wording will change, and to what extent those changes will be consulted with the expert community.

Conclusion

The Czech Republic is a latecomer to national cyber security in comparison to other countries which aspire to be or are considered to be leaders in the field. Nevertheless, the enormous progress in legislation, policy and leadership of the past few years shows the large cyber potential which the country possesses. The country's human resources and its advanced system for identifying CII and protecting it from attack are shining examples of that. This progress, together with the will of government authorities to continue it, can indeed ensure that the Czech Republic achieves its goal, outlined in the most recent cyber security strategy for the period 2015–20, of playing a leading role in the field of cyber security, not only in the region but in the whole of Europe. However, before that happens, the Czech authorities need to address several pressing issues which are holding the country back from fulfilling its ambition. E-government and cyber defense are examples of deficiencies that are closely linked to national cyber security. Ignoring them can have fatal impact on the reputation of the country abroad with regard to cyber issues. If those issues are addressed in the coming years, the Czech Republic will truly be the leader in cyber security that it hopes to become.

Notes

1 Lucie Kadlecová's work is supported by the Grant Agency of Charles University under grant number 250418.

2 For more details on the 2013 campaign of cyberattacks, see, Kadlecová, Bagge, Borovička and Semecká (2017).

3 CII is defined in the Act on Cyber Security as "an element or system of elements of the critical infrastructure in the sector of communication and information systems within the field of cyber security" (Act No. 181/2014 Coll., 2014: §2b).

4 Regulation No. 316/2014 Coll. on Security Measures, Cyber Security Incidents and Reactive Measures, Regulation No. 317/2014 Coll. on the Determination of Important Information Systems and their Determination Criteria, Decision of the Government No. 315/2014 Coll., which amends the Decision of the Government No. 432/2010 Coll. on the Criteria for the Determination of the Elements of the Critical Infrastructure, are available here: www.govcert.cz/en/legislation/legislation/.

5 Entities regulated by the Act are: (a) operators of critical information infrastructure systems, (b) operators of critical information infrastructure communication systems, (c) electronic communication service providers, (d) operators of important networks, and (e) operators of important information systems.

6 The Act on Cyber Security defines a state of cyber emergency as "a state in which there is a high measure of threat to the security of information of information systems or electronic communication network services or to the security and integrity of electronic communication networks, and this could lead to breaches or threats to the interests of the Czech Republic in line with the meaning of the Act on the Protection of Classified Information" (Act No. 181/2014 Coll., 2014: section 21(1)).

7 Crisis management is part of every national exercise the NCISA organizes. At the international level, it has been tested for example during NATO CMX in 2016 and 2017.

8 For detailed statistics, see, European Commission (2017).

9 David Špaček (2015) from Masaryk University in Brno has identified more shortcomings than the ones discussed here. Only the most significant ones were selected for the purpose of this chapter.
10 The National Cyber Operations Centre was originally called the National Cyber Forces Centre. It has changed its name with publication of the Czech Cyber Defense Strategy.
11 In the Czech Republic, cyber security is understood as a term encompassing a broad range of preventive and reactive measures intended to increase robustness and resilience of national information infrastructure. The exact wording of the Czech definition of cyber security can be found through the National Cyber Security Centre (2015).
12 There is no unified definition of cyber defense in the Czech Republic. For purposes of this article, cyber defense is understood as defense in cyber space and/or through cyber space.

Suggested reading

Act No. 181/2014 Coll. of July 23, 2014 on Cyber Security and Change of Related Acts. www.govcert.cz/download/kii-vis/preklady/Act_181_2014_EN_v1.0_final.pdf
National Cyber Operation Centre. (2018). "Strategie kybernetické obrany ČR 2018–2022." www.acr.army.cz/assets/informacni-servis/zpravodajstvi/strategie-kyberneticke-obrany.pdf
National Cyber Security Centre, National Security Authority. (2012). "Strategie pro oblast kybernetické bezpečnosti České republiky na období 2012–2015." www.govcert.cz/download/legislativa/container-nodeid-719/20120209strategieprooblastkbnbu.pdf
National Cyber Security Centre, National Security Authority. (2015). "National Cyber Security Strategy of the Czech Republic for the Period from 2015 to 2020." www.govcert.cz/download/gov-cert/container-nodeid-1067/ncss-15-20-150216-en.pdf

References

"Act No 181/2014 Coll. of July 23, 2014 on Cyber Security and Change of Related Acts." www.govcert.cz/download/kii-vis/preklady/Act_181_2014_EN_v1.0_final.pdf
"Act No 240/2000 Coll. on Crisis Management and on Amendments of Certain Acts." www.hzscr.cz/hasicien/file/crisis-management-act-n-240-2000-coll-pdf.aspx
Boeke, S. (2018, July). "National Cyber Crisis Management: Different European Approaches," *Governance: An International Journal of Policy, Administration, and Institutions*, 31(3): 449–464.
CZ.NIC. (2017, January 30). "Organizace CZ.NIC, ICT Unie a NIX.CZ se postavily proti novele zákona o Vojenském zpravodajství." www.nic.cz/page/3478/organizace-cznic-ict-unie-a-nixcz-se-postavily-proti-novele-zakona-o-vojenskem-zpravodajstvi/
European Commission. (2017). "Europe's Digital Progress Report 2017, Czech Republic." https://ec.europa.eu/digital-single-market/scoreboard/czech-republic
European Union. (2016). "Directive (EU) 2016/1148 of the European Parliament and of the Council of 6 July 2016 concerning measures for a high common level of security of network and information systems across the Union." https://eur-lex.europa.eu/legal-content/EN/TXT/?uri=uriserv:OJ.L_.2016.194.01.0001.01.ENG&toc=OJ:L:2016:194:TOC
Eurostat. (2018a). "Broadband and Connectivity – Households." http://appsso.eurostat.ec.europa.eu/nui/show.do?dataset=isoc_bde15b_h&lang=en
Eurostat. (2018b) "Internet Access." http://appsso.eurostat.ec.europa.eu/nui/show.do?dataset=isoc_ci_in_en2&lang=en
Eurostat. (2018c). "Individuals Using the Internet for Communication with Public Authorities." http://appsso.eurostat.ec.europa.eu/nui/submitViewTableAction.do
Fojtů, M. (2018). "Počítačová bezpečnost Česka se hlídá v Brně." *Absolvent*. http://absolventi.muni.cz/univerzita-absolventum/casopis-absolvent
Kadlecová, L., Bagge, D. P., Borovička, V. & Semecká, M. (2017). *The Czech Republic: A Case of a Comprehensive Approach toward Cyberspace*. NATO CCDCoE, Tallinn, Estonia.
London Stock Exchange. (n.d.) "AVAST PLC ORD 10P." www.londonstockexchange.com/exchange/prices-and-markets/stocks/summary/company-summary/GB00BDD85M81GBGBXSTMM.html?lang=en

Military Intelligence. (2016, October 5). "Návrh zákona, kterým se mění zákon č. 289/2005 Sb., o Vojenském zpravodajství, ve znění pozdějších předpisů, a některé další zákony." https://apps.odok. cz/en/veklep-detail?pid=ALBSA9LJNBUU

Ministry of Interior of the Czech Republic. (2018a). "Audit národní bezpečnosti." www.vlada.cz/assets/ media-centrum/aktualne/Audit-narodni-bezpecnosti-20161201.pdf

Ministry of Interior of the Czech Republic. (2018b). "Co je eGovernment?" www.mvcr.cz/clanek/co-je-egovernment.aspx

Ministry of Interior of the Czech Republic. (2018c). "Czech POINT." www.mvcr.cz/clanek/czech-point-czech-point.aspx

Ministry of Interior of the Czech Republic. (2018d). "Data Box – Another Step in Electronification of Public Administration." www.mvcr.cz/mvcren/article/data-box-another-step-in-electronification-of-public-administration.aspx

National Registers Authority. (2018). "Basic Registers." www.szrcr.cz/index.php?lang=2

National Cyber Security Centre, National Security Authority. (2015). "National Cyber Security Strategy of the Czech Republic for the Period from 2015 to 2020." www.govcert.cz/download/gov-cert/con tainer-nodeid-1067/ncss-15-20-150216-en.pdf

National Cyber Operation Centre. (2018). "Strategie kybernetické obrany ČR 2018–2022." www.acr. army.cz/assets/informacni-servis/zpravodajstvi/strategie-kyberneticke-obrany.pdf

Pačka, R. (2015). "Difference Between Cyber Security and Cyber Defence from a Czech Perspective," *Cyber Security Review*, 20–24.

Sedlák, J. (2018, October 3). "Digitální Česko: Tohle je státní plán, jak z ČR udělat digitální velmoc." www.lupa.cz/clanky/digitalni-cesko-tohle-je-statni-plan-jak-z-cr-udelat-digitalni-velmoc/?utm_sour ce=newsletter-html-d&utm_medium=text&utm_campaign=2018-10-04

Špaček, D. (2015). "E-Government Policy and Its Implementation in the Czech Republic: Selected Shortcomings," *Central European Journal of Public Policy*, *9*(1): 78–101.

Štrosová, S. (2018, September 8). "Technologie nejsou hokej. Česko je možná talent, ale rozhodně ne velmoc." www.forbes.cz/technologie-nejsou-hokej-cesko-je-mozna-talent-ale-rozhodne-ne-velmoc/

Ťopek, M. (2016, November 4). "Vojenská kontrarozvědka bude sledovat český internet, vláda jí chce svěřit kybernetickou ochranu." https://zpravy.aktualne.cz/domaci/vojenska-kontrarozvedka-bude-sledovat-cesky-internet-vlada-j/r~3f483e428a2611e682380025900fea04/?redirected=1521222256

UN E-Government Knowledgebase. (2016). "UN E-Government Survey 2016." https://publicadminis tration.un.org/egovkb/en-us/Reports/UN-E-Government-Survey-2016

5

CYBER SECURITY IN THE FRENCH REPUBLIC

Amber Darwish and Scott N. Romaniuk

Introduction: overview of national cyber security strategy

The French Republic (hereafter simply "France") has granted increasing national priority to responding to the growth in number, intensity and sophistication of information and communication technology (ICT or "cyber")-based threats, risks and vulnerabilities which can affect its security and stability. Although initially lagging behind its main strategic partners acting in this area, cybersecurity is now an integral part of the country's national defense and security posture, and the country has shown a consistent increase in its overall Internet penetration (92.3% as of 2019), which sits higher than the European Union (EU) average of 90.4% as of the same year (Internet World Stats, 2019). Its engagement on this issue broadly focuses on three pillars: governance, the economy and security.

With a highly connected population, France champions a vision of the cyberspace as a space of freedom, exchange and growth. It favors an open cyberspace that provides a sustainable source of prosperity and progress for French companies (including digital services, products and jobs) but which also asserts French democratic values and safeguards French citizens' digital lives and personal data. To this end, French cyber strategies place a heavy emphasis on maintaining the smooth running of everyday life in France, as well as the general competitiveness, trustworthiness and growth of French businesses and industry (Ministère de la Défense, 2013). French national cyber strategies are thus naturally tied to the country's national economic and industry policies, and a key component of the country's "road map for industrial renewal" (Ministère du Redressement Productif, 2013).

Nevertheless, France recognizes that the mass-digitization of societies presents serious governance challenges including unfair competition and espionage, disruption, disinformation and propaganda, terrorism and criminality. Moreover, the French administration has expressed concern that cyber technologies are transforming the relationships between states, non-state actors (NSAs) and the private sector, particularly by enabling the rise in power of new private actors which can challenge the traditional sovereign authority of states. It is the view of France that digital connectivity and technological innovation is now an integral part of the contemporary power strategies and power relations that govern international affairs. Strengthening stability and security in cyberspace is thus a priority objective for France, albeit one that must be carefully balanced with ensuring the maintenance of the autonomy of the country's actions and decisions.

Reflecting these considerations, France's approach to building its national cyber security centers on the mobilization of diverse resources, not only by government but also across civil society. Domestically, it is building its cyber security based upon collaboration between the state, the private sector and civil society to reinforce the resilience of essential services and systems in France (France Diplomatie, n.d.a). Internationally, it is working to establish a more secure cyberspace through a highly active program of international political diplomacy. Overall, this cyber security posture rests on seven key principles:

1 improving the protection of information systems within France;
2 repelling attacks through the building of France's defensive capabilities and resilience;
3 the affirmation and exercise of digital sovereignty in France;
4 a more effective criminal justice response to cybercrime;
5 the promotion of a shared culture of information security;
6 participation in the development of a secure and trusted digital Europe;
7 international action for collective governance and control of cyberspace.

Concepts and definitions

It is important to note that France does not tend to employ the term "cyber" as it relates to "information security," preferring instead the term "information systems security" (*sécurité des systèmes d'information*) or, more frequently, "cyber security" (*cybersécurité*). It is of the view that the term "cyber security" is more precise in that "it designates the resistance of a system to events from cyberspace that could compromise the availability, integrity or confidentiality of the data stored, processed or transmitted and of the related services that these systems offer or make accessible." The "cyberspace" is defined as "the communication space created by the worldwide interconnection of automated digital data processing equipment" (ANSSI, 2011).

France defines "cyber security" as:

> The desired state of an information system in which it can resist events from cyber-space likely to compromise the availability, integrity or confidentiality of the data stored, processed or transmitted and of the related services that these systems offer or make accessible.
>
> *(Republic of France, 2011)*

An "information system" is understood in a holistic sense to mean "an organised set of resources (hardware, software, personnel, data and procedures) used to process and circulate information" (ANSSI, 2011).

"Cyber defense" is defined as "the set of technical and non-technical measures allowing a state to defend in cyberspace information systems that it considers to be critical" (ANSSI, 2011). These include, but are not limited to, the networks of France's Ministry of Defense (discussed further in subsequent text).

National governance structures

Law No. 2013–1168 of December 18, 2013 stipulates that "the Prime Minister shall set policy and coordinate government action in the field of cybersecurity and cyberdefense." The Secretariat-General for National Defense and Security (*Secrétariat général de la défense et de la sécurité nationale*, SGDSN) is the principle government agency responsible for assisting the Prime Minister in exercising responsibilities in this area. The SGDSN is supported in this regard by the National Agency for the Security of Information Systems (*Agence nationale de la sécurité des systèmes d'information*, ANSSI), which is directly attached to the Head of the SGDSN, and operates under the authority of the Prime Minister. Currently under the direction of Guillaume Poupard, ANSSI was created in July 2009 pursuant to Decree No. 2009–834 of July 7, 2009, and is the national authority in the field of security and defense of French information systems, which monitors, detects and coordinates responses to cyberattacks, including through the protection of state information systems and critical infrastructures. This entity replaced France's central management of the security of information systems and operates with a substantial budget of €100 million – an increase of some €20 million over the past six years. In addition to its funding, ANSSI's staff complement has also seen an increase over that same period, rising from 350 personnel in 2014, to 500 by the end of 2015, and to 600 at the time of writing this chapter. While cyber security in general (including crisis management) is the responsibility of the Director General of ANSSI, the French Ministry of Defense (*ministère des Armées*) remains responsible for ensuring the protection of the networks underpinning its action and for integrating digital warfare into military operations. This represents a distinct separation between the country's defensive and offensive capabilities and missions with ANSSI playing an expanding role in the development of France's information systems security in direct and indirect ways (Gèry & Delerue, 2018).

Beyond these principal institutions, a large number of additional French institutions play a role in France's action and engagement on cyber issues. These include but are not limited to:

- The Ministry of Home Affairs (*ministère de l'Intérieur, de l'Outre-mer et des Collectivités territoriales*);
- Ministry of Foreign Affairs (*ministère de l'Europe et des Affaires étrangères*);
- The Defense Procurement Agency (*La direction générale de l'Armement*);
- The External Intelligence Directorate (*La Direction générale de la sécurité extérieure*);
- The Defense information and communication systems agency (*La direction des systèmes d'information et de communication*);
- The state agency responsible for information and communication systems (*Direction interministérielle des systèmes d'information et de communication de l'Etat*);
- The state agency responsible for the modernization of public policies (*Direction interministérielle pour la modernisation de l'action publique*);
- The Internal Intelligence Directorate (*La Direction générale de la sécurité intérieure*);
- The National Council on Economy, Industry, Energy and Technology (*le Conseil général de l'économie, de l'industrie, de l'énergie et des technologies*).

Key national strategies and initiatives

Cyber security initially emerged as a policy priority in the French government's third *White Paper on Defence and National Security*, released in June 2008 (Ministère de la Défense, 2013) and represented a climacteric in French cyber security and defense. The document mentions "cyber" no less than 40 times with specific reference to "cyber attack" and "cyber attacks" made 17 times, not including 13 references to "cyber-war" and "cyber-warfare." It further illustrates efforts towards the development of an offensive cyber capability and the need to develop the ability reach the safe spots of threats or points of origin in order to neutralize their destructive capacities during, after, or possibly before a cyberattack can be launched and distribute its destructive effects. Reflecting on the evolving global strategic context, the document set out a comprehensive 15-year strategic plan involving a significant overhaul of France's security and defense posture, taking France from a point of a

> passive defensive strategy to an active defensive strategy in depth, combining intrinsic systems protection with permanent surveillance, rapid response and offensive action, calls for a strong governmental impetus and a change in mentalities.
>
> *(Ministère de la Défense, 2013: 50)*

This included the introduction of a suite of targeted measures to enhance the country's capabilities to guard against the risks and threats of cyberattacks and cyberterrorism. An "in-depth" cyber defense posture would aim to strengthen the protection of critical information systems, enable the permanent monitoring of critical networks and ensure the capacity and capability for rapid response in the case of cyberattacks. The maintenance of France's strategic and political autonomy in the face of such events was a principle strategic objective.

With respect to the possibility of direct and indirect cyberattacks against France, the White Paper outline four key areas that require special attention and investment over the "long-term" to ensure national security:

- Definition, by the Joint Staff, of an overarching concept incorporating all actions involved in cyber-war;
- Development of specialized tools (networked digital weapons, technical and operations laboratory, etc.);
- Formulation of a body of doctrine for offensive cyber-war capabilities (planning, execution, evaluation of actions);
- Introduction of appropriate and regularly updated training for selected personnel, to be used flexibly in specialized units, overriding administrative considerations.

The establishment of ANSSI in 2009 was a crucial step in the implementation of this strategy. With continually expanding levels of technical and human resourcing, ANSSI has been instrumental to the design and enhancement of France's cyber security posture, policies and initiatives as well as the publication of numerous scientific publications and best practice guidelines for French industry and businesses. A key ANSSI publication was the *Cyberdefence and Cybersecurity Strategy* (ANSSI, 2011). This paper laid out four strategic objectives for France:

1 Be a global cyber defense power, taking its place in the inner circle of major nations in the field whilst preserving its autonomy;
2 Safeguard France's freedom of decision-making by protecting sovereign information;
3 Bolster the cyber security of national critical infrastructures;
4 Safeguard security in cyberspace.

The French position was gradually refined and detailed over a series of further papers and reviews that include:

- *The 2013 White Paper on Defense and National Security* (Ministère de la Défense, 2013);
- *The 2015 National Digital Security Strategy* (Premier ministre, 2015);
- The 2017 Defense and National Security Strategic Review (Ministre de l'Europe et des Affaires étrangères, 2017);
- The Strategic Review of Cyber Defense (Secrétariat général de la Défense et de la Sécurité Nationale, 2018).

In each, the national cyber security objectives remained largely unchanged, namely: (1) ensure national digital sovereignty; (2) provide a strong response against cyber-malicious acts; (3) inform and engage the general public, business and industry; (4) turn digital security into a competitive asset for French companies; and (5) strengthen France's voice internationally.

More recently, in February 2018, the *Strategic Review of Cyber Defense* (Secrétariat général de la Défense et de la Sécurité Nationale, 2018) presented a reappraisal of France's cyber strategy and associated military force structure. The paper recommended a restructure of France's cyber posture to focus on the following seven points:

1   Prioritize the protection of France's information systems;
2   Adopt an active stance of attack deterrence and coordinated response;
3   Fully exercise France's digital sovereignty;
4   Provide an effective penal response to cybercrime;
5   Promote a shared culture of information security;
6   Help bring about a digital Europe that is safe and reliable; and
7   Act internationally in favor of a collective and controlled governance of cyberspace.

The 2018 Review paved the way for a major shift, confirmed by French Minister of Defense Florence Parly in January 2019, from a defense doctrine of "active defense" to one of "offensive cyber capabilities." It reflects a view that has been gradually solidifying within French strategic circles that "[a]rmies must now, systematically, look at cybernetic combat as a mode of action in its own right, the effects of which combine with each other in a global maneuver" (French Republic, 2019, n.p.) – a concern most notably expressed by the announcement in October 2018 that the French Ministry of Defense and French National Assembly would no longer rely on foreign digital companies for their Internet usage. It also reflects and reinforces France's operational and organizational delineation between its defensive cyber operations (*lutte informatique défensive*) and its offensive cyber operations (*lutte informatique offensive*).

International law

As a key cyber power, France was designated by the UN Secretary-General to participate in work of the UN Group of Governmental Experts on Developments in the Field of Information and Telecommunications in the Context of International Security (UN GGE). In this capacity it was party to the GGE's reports (UNGA, 2013, 2015), adopted by consensus, that went some way in detailing a normative framework for responsible behavior of states in cyberspace. This included agreement with the view that the principles and rules of international law – not limited to the United Nations (UN) Charter, international humanitarian law and international human rights law – are applicable to the use of ICTs by States, including in the context of international and non-international armed conflict (UNGA, 2015).

France has encouraged more detailed specification of the behavioral norms, rules and principles for the use of cyberspace (French Republic, 2019). This is particularly the case given that the GGE reports have remained rather general in their discussion and recommendations (in large part reflecting the inability of the Group to reach a consensus on the question of the precise application of international law to cyberspace and cyber operations). Importantly, however, France does not support the creation to this end of any new legally-binding international instruments "specifically for cyber security issues" (French Republic, 2019); this suggests it favors instead the development of a "soft law" approach where existing international norms prove insufficient.

In developing its own cyber security strategies France has forged a strong vision of the rights and obligations of States in this domain. In particular, its 2018 *Strategic Review of Cyber Defense* reveals much about its stance on the specific application of international law as it applies to the use of ICTs (Gèry & Delerue, 2018). In some cases, its position on the interpretation and applicability of international law is not without controversy; it has, for example, expressed support for the legality of "pre-emptive self-defense" against cyberattacks (Gèry & Delerue, 2018; Secrétariat général de la Défense et de la Sécurité Nationale, 2018). The State's contributions to the follow-up Group of Governmental Experts on Advancing Responsible State Behavior in Cyberspace in the Context of International Security will be especially critical to future normative development in these areas.

International governance

In November 2018, France launched a major independent initiative entitled the "Paris Call for Trust and Security in Cyberspace" (*Appel de Paris* or "Paris Call"). The maneuver represented an attempt for France to "take charge" of the future global governance of cyberspace. The Paris Call proposes a series of common principles to guide the behavior of both state and non-state actors with a view to ensuring "an open, secure, stable, accessible and peaceful cyberspace." It points to the applicability of international law and human rights to the domain, and recalls a number of principles – such as responsible behavior of states, the state monopoly on legitimate violence and acknowledgement of the specific responsibilities of private stakeholders – that should inform the development of the governance framework, moving forward.

Importantly, the Paris Call promotes the achievement of trust and security in cyberspace as the shared responsibility of a wide range of actors. This incorporates the extension of international security responsibility in this domain to private actors, particularly as it relates to the design, integration, deployment and maintenance of their products, processes and digital services, throughout their life cycle and from one end of the supply chain to the other. The Paris Call proposes multi-stakeholder commitment and cooperative approach to cyber security, including measures to:

- increase prevention against and resilience to malicious online activity;
- protect the accessibility and integrity of the Internet;
- cooperate in order to prevent interference in electoral processes;
- work together to combat intellectual property violations via the Internet;

- prevent the proliferation of malicious online programs and techniques;
- improve the security of digital products and services as well as everybody's "cyber hygiene";
- curb online mercenary activities and offensive action by non-state actors;
- work together to strengthen the relevant international standards. The high-level political statement has since garnered the backing of a large number of states (including all European Union members) as well as a multitude of supporters spanning international and regional organizations, multinational companies (including Microsoft and Facebook), academic institutions, civil society organizations (CSOs) and private sector entities.

Partner institutions at home and abroad

France has developed a broad web of bilateral and multilateral cooperative partnerships to expand its impact and influence on cyber issues. Some of these partnerships and their initiatives are listed below.

European Union

France endorses the vision and concept of the EU Digital Single Market. The EU's Digital Single Market strategy aims to open up digital opportunities for people and business and enhance Europe's position as a world leader in the digital economy by providing for the free movement of persons, services and capital under conditions of a high level of consumer and personal data protection, irrespective of nationality or place of residence. France views this initiative as a key aspect of the EU's collective capacity for initiative and action, which will benefit France in terms of technology, regulation (including defense, security and privacy), and cyber capacity. To supplement this endeavor, France continues to encourage broad operational cooperation between EU member states, particularly as it relates to the prevention of and response to cyberattacks.

North Atlantic Treaty Organization

During the Warsaw Summit in June 2016, France spearheaded NATO's adoption of a Cyber Defense Pledge that treats cyberspace as an areas of operations where NATO will operate and engage in active defense as it does in other land, sea and air theaters of security and conflict (France Diplomatie, n.d.b). In May 2018, France hosted the first ever Cyber Defense Pledge Conference at which the NATO Allies agreed to set up a Cyberspace Operations Centre as part of NATO's strengthened Command Structure to facilitate the use of national cyber capabilities for its missions and operations.

Organisation for security and co-operation in Europe

France is playing an active role in the work of the OSCE to address the implications of cyber technologies both as an opportunity and a major vulnerability for states. This work focuses on the prevention of conflict arising from the use or misuse of cyber/ICT (preventative diplomacy). This includes through the adoption and implementation of 16 confidence-building measures (CBMs), which focus on enhancing interstate transparency and predictability of communication, preparedness and posturing in this area. France is facilitating the operationalization of these collective measures through its participation in capacity-building workshops, table-top exercises and the establishment of a crisis communication network.

United Nations

France has played a particularly active role in the UN in terms of debating and communicating the rules, standards and challenges in the cyber realm. France has been an active participant in the UN's past groups of government experts (GGEs) on cyber security, with France having participated in exchanges to contribute its view on international cyberspace regulation with a focus on the principles in the Paris Call (France Diplomatie, n.d.b). In May 2019, France presented its position to the UN on global cyberspace issues:

- The actions undertaken by France to strengthen its cyber defense apparatus and its policy of transparency regarding its international and national strategy;
- The ways it intends to prevent crises by strengthening cooperation, building international capabilities and developing norms regulating actors' behavior in cyberspace;
- The concepts and principles it advocates at the United Nations and the measures that would make it possible to bolster international security in cyberspace (France Diplomatie, n.d.b).

Group of seven (G7)

As a member of the G7, France endorsed the G7 *Declaration on Responsible States' Behavior in Cyberspace* (the Lucca Declaration) established in Lucca, Italy on April 11, 2017. This includes a commitment to contribute to international cooperative action and the protection against dangers resulting from the malicious use of ICTs, and to encourage similar commitments from other states. The Lucca Declaration also reaffirmed in this context the view of the G7 that international law and the UN Charter are vital for stability and for maintaining peace and security not only within the ICT context, but also offline, including as regards to the responses of states to wrongful or malicious acts conducted by other states. In this respect, the declaration reinforces and builds on the norms developed in the UN-GGE Reports. Another notable event occurred on April 6, 2019, when foreign ministers of the G7 countries gathered in Dinard, France, where they collectively launched a Cyber Norm Initiative that presented their "best practices" expectations regarding the cyber domain and state activity within it. The initiative drew from previous experiences, highlighting lessoned learned from past non-binding norms concerning state practices and behavior (France Diplomatie, n.d.b). Under its 2019 G7 Presidency, France has focused the G7's efforts on improving the resilience of the financial sector to cyber threats through crisis management exercises.

Wassenaar arrangement

In 2013, the French government was a principal negotiator for the addition of "intrusion software" and "[Internet Protocol] network communications surveillance systems" to the list of dual-use (civilian and military) technologies governed by the Wassenaar Arrangement. Intrusion software is defined as "software specially designed or modified to avoid detection by monitoring tools, or to defeat protective countermeasures" of a computer or network-capable device. The language of this amendment was subsequently modified in 2017 to address industry feedback in relation to potential unintended consequences of the trade control as initially worded for security vulnerability disclosure, collaborate malware analysis and cyber incident response that crosses national borders.

Other partnerships

France is a principal partner and financial sponsor of the Global Commission on the Stability of Cyberspace (GCSC). The GCSC is a global platform that aims to promote mutual awareness, normative understanding and policy development among the various cyberspace stakeholders to develop proposals for norms and policies to enhance international security and stability, and to guide responsible state and non-state behavior in cyberspace. France is also a founding member of the Global Forum on Cyber Expertise (GFCE), a global platform for countries, international organizations and private companies to exchange best practices and expertise on the use of the cyber domain for communication, innovation and sustainable social development and economic growth ("cyber capacity"). France is also a founding supporter of the SPARTA consortium, a network of actors which aims to develop and implement top-tier collaborative research, training and innovative actions on cyber issues. SPARTA is one of the four EU projects to prepare the European Cybersecurity Competence Network.

Acting on its 2015 national cyber security strategy, which promotes "cooperation between member states of the European Union (EU) in a manner favorable to the emergence of a European digital strategic autonomy, a long-term guarantor of a cyberspace that is more secure and respectful of our values," French activity in the cyber domain has benefited other countries. This is particularly the case as other look to France as a leader in this area, especially given the country's recognition as a "key cyber power" within the UN Group of Government Experts (UN GGE) on Advancing Responsible State Behavior in Cyberspace in the Context of International Security (formerly: Developments in the Field of Information and Telecommunications in the Context of International Security). This recognition has played a role in France's involvement in and contributions to other high-profile international organizations. For instance, France assisted in designing the cyber security policy of the Organisation for Economic Cooperation and Development's (OECD) Working Party on Information Security and Privacy (WPISP) and the Group of Eight (G8), as it was known until 2014 (Renard, 2014: 12).

Cybercrime and cyber-terrorism

France views terrorist use of the Internet as a global issue that needs innovative, international solutions. It has committed to work with state and non–state actors to prevent the dissemination of terrorist content online and the use of the Internet by terrorists and violent extremists to radicalize, recruit, inspire or incite. It encourages the leveraging of technology to identify and remove content of this nature, including the exploitation of artificial intelligence and machine learning to accelerate the identification of such content. It works in close partnership with the UN (including the Tech Against Terrorism initiative), the EU, the Global Internet Forum to Counter Terrorism and the Global Research Network on Terrorism and Technology.

France is a signatory of the 2001 Budapest Convention on Cybercrime. The French Ministry of Interior (*L'Office central de lutte contre la criminalité liée aux technologies de l'information et de la communication* or OCLCTIC, within the division of the national police responsible for work on organized crime) is the designated point of contact for this framework treaty.

Implications of cyber security policies and strategies

The development of France's capacity and capabilities in relation to both leveraging and defending against cyber technologies has important implications for France both domestically and internationally. Domestically, France's cyber security profits from a longstanding, highly centralized system of national governance, a system that has supported the rapid introduction of public and private measures for the protection of its critical information systems. These developments have enabled France to quickly secure its place as a leader in cyber security best practices. Internationally, however, its strong stance in this rapidly changing environment – particularly as it relates to the steadfast safeguarding and exercise of its "digital sovereignty" – has the potential to (or continue to) create divides at the international level. As it continues to pursue a controlled and collectively governed cyberspace, how France approaches such issues will thus have important ramifications not only for its domestic peace, prosperity and security, but also for international trade, development and stability.

Suggested reading

Baumard, P. (2017). *Cybersecurity in France.* Cham: Springer.

Grigsby, A. (2018, February 26). *Three Takeaways from the French Cyber Defense Review.* New York: CFR. cfr.org/blog/three-takeaways-french-cyber-defense-review; https://carnegieendowment.org/2020/02/26/cyberspace-and-geopolitics-assessing-global-cybersecurity-norm-processes-at-crossroads-pub-81110

Ruhl, C., Hollis, D., Hoffman, W. & Maurer, T. (2020, February 26). *Cyberspace and Geopolitics: Assessing Global Cybersecurity Norm Processes at a Crossroads.* Washington, DC: Carnegie Endowment for International Peace.

References

L'Agence nationale de la sécurité des systèmes d'information (ANSSI). (2011). "Information Systems Defence and Security: France's Strategy." www.ssi.gouv.fr/uploads/IMG/pdf/2011-02-15_Information_system_defence_and_security_-_France_s_strategy.pdf

France Diplomatie. (n.d.a). "Cybersecurity: Paris Call of 12 November 2018 for Trust and Security in Cyberspace." www.diplomatie.gouv.fr/en/french-foreign-policy/digital-diplomacy/france-and-cyber-security/article/cybersecurity-paris-call-of-12-november-2018-for-trust-and-security-in

France Diplomatie. (n.d.b). "France and Cyber Security." www.diplomatie.gouv.fr/en/french-foreign-policy/digital-diplomacy/france-and-cyber-security/

French Republic. (2019, May). "France's Response to Resolution 73/27 'Developments in the Field of Information and Telecommunications in the Context of International Security' and Resolution 73/266 'Advancing Responsible State Behaviour in Cyberspace in the Context of International Security'." www.un.org/disarmament/ict-security/

Géry, A. & Delerue, F. (2018). "The French Strategic Review of Cyber Defense." Commentary of 3 May 2018. Italian Institute for International Political Studies. www.ispionline.it/it/pubblicazione/french-strategic-review-cyber-defense-20376

Internet World Stats. (2019). "Internet Usage in the European Union." www.internetworldstats.com/stats9.htm

Ministère de la Défense. (2013). "White Paper on Defence and National Security." www.defense.gouv.fr/english/dgris/defence-policy/white-paper-2013/white-paper-2013

Ministre de l'Europe et des Affaires étrangères. (2017). "International Digital Strategy." (In French only). Ministre de l'Europe et des Affaires étrangères.

Ministère du Redressement Productif. (2013). "The New Face of Industry in France." www.economie. gouv.fr/files/nouvelle_france_industrielle_english.pdf

Premier minister. (2015). "National Digital Security Strategy: Meeting the Security Challenges of the Digital World." www.ssi.gouv.fr/en/actualite/the-french-national-digital-security-strategy-meeting-the-security-challenges-of-the-digital-world/

Renard, T. (2014, June). "The Rise of Cyber-Diplomacy: The EU, Its Strategic Partners and Cyber-Security." European Strategic Partnerships Observatory, Working Paper No. 7. files.ethz.ch /isn/181326/The%20rise%20of%20cyber-diplomacy_%20the%20EU,%20its%20strategic%20partners %20and%20cyber-security.pdf

Republic of France. (2011). "Information Systems Defence and Security: France's Security." www.ssi. gouv.fr/uploads/IMG/pdf/2011-02-15_Information_system_defence_and_security_-_France_s_strat egy.pdf

Secrétariat général de la Défense et de la Sécurité Nationale. (2018). "French Strategic Review of Cyber Defence." www.sgdsn.gouv.fr/uploads/2018/03/revue-cyber-resume-in-english.pdf

UNGA. (2013, June 24). "Report of the Group of Governmental Experts on Developments in the Field of Information and Telecommunications in the Context of International Security (A/68/98*)." https://undocs.org/A/68/98

UNGA. (2015, July 22). "Report of the Group of Governmental Experts on Developments in the Field of Information and Telecommunications in the Context of International Security (A/70/174)." https://undocs.org/A/70/174

6

GERMANY'S CYBERSECURITY STRATEGY

Confronting future challenges

Scott N. Romaniuk and Michael Claus

Introduction

Prior to 2005, cybersecurity had not been viewed as a national security issue. That changed in 2005, when Udo Helmbrecht, then president of Germany's Federal Office for Information Security (Bundesamt für Sicherheit in der Informationstechnik, BSI), penned a report in which he reasoned that Germany needed to seriously consider integrating cyber security into the state's national security calculus, thereby preparing for imminent threats in the cyber realm. The Bundestag heeded Helmbrecht's call for the state to assume a stronger position on the issue, incorporating cyber threats into its national security strategy (*Weißbuch*) with Chancellor Angela Merkel stating in 2006 that, "Germany's political and economic structures as well as its critical infrastructure have become more vulnerable as a result, not least where criminal activities, terrorist acts, or military attacks from or on cyberspace are concerned" (Bundesminister der Verteidigung, 2006: 17). Roughly a decade later, in 2016, Merkel emphasized the "spectrum of threats" inherent within the cyber and information domain in Germany's 2016 *Weißbuch*, describing cyberspace as "increasingly becoming a theatre of conflict; the internet is not only a force for good – ideologies of hatred and violence are also spread there" (Bundesminister der Verteidigung, 2016: 37 and 7).

Germany has endeavored to secure its information technology (IT) infrastructure since 2006 with the release of the 2011 Cybersecurity Strategy for Germany and the updated version published in 2016. After 2011, Germany became a frontrunner in cybersecurity efforts on an international scale and greatly enhanced its capabilities through the creation of new government agencies and strategic objectives. Agency creation was then followed by deepening of security roles and action on the part of cybersecurity agencies and institutions. The establishment of public–private partnerships illustrates an understanding on the part of the Bundestag concerning a comprehensive approach to securing IT-infrastructure. Its commitment, however, can be interpreted as a quasi-mobilization and deployment of Bundeswehr forces with its cyber defense activities an extension of the military armed forces of the country.

Germany, due to its history, has a particularly strongly developed set of cultural norms guiding its vision of the Internet, within the country, across the European Union (EU), and throughout Europe. These norms also permeate into how the German military approaches the cyber domain and give rise to associated legal dilemmas and public debate thus transforming the cyber and information domain as a subset of German society into a domain of tension in one sense, and a battlespace of federated cyber defense measures and ambiguously extensive cyber-offensive capabilities. At the same time, Germany has, in particular, evinced a strong discursive commitment to the protection of personal privacy, as well as its ongoing efforts to prevent and control the rise of hate speech discernable through initiatives to influence and pressure social media and tech firms in manner that curbs the effects of harmful expression online.

The evolution of Germany's cybersecurity strategy

Germany's cybersecurity strategy has slowly evolved over a period of approximately three decades, beginning in the early 1990s and following through to the present day. During this time, Germany's cybersecurity strategy has gone through three distinct transformation stages, with the concept of cybersecurity undergoing a maturation process that has taken it from a basic understanding entrenched in the security of the private individual to a state-level issues of security obliging the government to create enhanced defensive and offensive cyber and information competencies.

Stage one of Germany's cybersecurity evolution (1991–2011) – broadening the cybersecurity compass

The initial stage of Germany's cybersecurity strategy began in 1991, shortly after the reunification (Wiedervereinigung) of the two Germany's, and the end of the Cold War. In 1991, the German government moved to form a subsidiary agency within the Federal Ministry of the Interior (Bundesministerium des Innen, BMI) called the Federal Office for Information Security (Bundesamt für Sicherheit in der Informationstechnik, BSI) – Germany's primary national cybersecurity authority – with the general task of ensuring the security of "information technology" within Germany.[1] The emergence of technological means of communications, sharing information, and interacting via digital means, brought with it a range of risks that required government engagement to ensure that standards and responsibilities are met through the creation of sets of criteria, rules, and measures of use and abuse. The emergence of new and sophisticated technologies coincided with and upsurge of asymmetric threats such as transnational criminal organizations and terrorism. BSI was tasked with oversight of both systems and the use of such systems in everyday life. Over time, the BSI, in conjunction the federal government, set to define key terms and clarify their operationalization.

Roughly a decade after its creation, BSI was revamped vis-à-vis the Act on the Federal Office for Information Security (Gesetz zur Stärkung der Sicherheit in der Informationstechnik des Bundes, BSIG), which came into effect on August 20, 2009 (BSI Act of 2009). BSI thence became the central clearinghouse for IT security with expanded responsibilities based on renewed and updated definitions, and categorizing the domain of critical infrastructure to include nine distinctive sectors within the two broad categories: "technical basic infrastructures" and "socio-economic service infrastructures." Altogether, BSIG outlines 15 tasks for BSI to undertake. With the expansion of upgrading of definitions, outlining of new tasks and further responsibilities, the operational margins of BSI swelled to include broader and deeper work within and for the federal government as well as companies in the private sector. The federal government granted BSI increased responsibility but also defined its role and areas of operability, limiting its range to information infrastructure; however, as society has become increasingly digitized and nearly every aspect of society coming to depend on digital technology in one way or another, BSI's range of responsibility and protection has expanded.

Stage two of Germany's cybersecurity evolution (2011–2016) – from government to societal cybersecurity

The "Cyber Security Strategy for Germany," published in 2011 and updated in 2016 (representing the beginning of the third stage of Germany's cybersecurity evolution), is the primary document and foundation for the Federal Republic of Germany's cyber security strategy. The document, which was released in 2011 outlines potential threats, a framework for conditions, and outlines ten strategic objectives (BMI, 2011). Clear definitions are provided to standardize the use of critical vocabulary associated with the cyber domain as is the case with cyber security strategies of other countries. Within Germany, cybersecurity development comprised a stretching of digital and information security coverage resulting in a whole-of-society cybersecurity strategy. This strategic cybersecurity stretching saw all aspects (i.e., economics and many cultural elements) brought into the scope. The second stage of Germany's cybersecurity strategy thus extends the security blanket from the government and military to the civilian realm. Under the section, "Basic principles of the Cyber Security Strategy," the document states that:

> [t]he Cyber Security Strategy mainly focuses on civilian approaches and measures. They are complemented by measures taken by the Bundeswehr1 to protect its capabilities and measures based on mandates to make cyber security a part of Germany's preventive security strategy.
>
> *(BMI, 2011: 3)*

The document articulates the scope of the threat to include both the private and public sector, and includes organizations as well as the individual in Germany society. The introduction also expresses the complexities presented by an array of actors such as criminals, terrorists, spies, and militaries (BMI, 2011). When describing the "Framework Conditions" of the strategy, the cyber security strategy document stresses the need for the development of norms on an international scale to improve security and push it increasingly in a positive direction (BMI, 2011). Furthermore, the basic principles of the document highlights that the Strategy is primarily for the civilian sector and that a strategy from the military is supportive and serves as a compliment.

In total, 10 strategic objectives and measures serve as the epicenter of the Strategy:

1　Protection of critical information infrastructure;
2　Securitization of IT systems;
3　Strengthening of IT security in the public administration;
4　Creation of a National Cyber Response Centre;
5　Creation of a national Cyber Security Council (CSC);
6　Effective control of cybercrime;
7　Effective coordinated action to ensure cyber security in Europe and worldwide;
8　Use of reliable and trustworthy information technology;

9   Personnel development in federal authorities;
10 Tools to respond to cyberattacks.

Germany's updated National Cyber Security Strategy outlines 30 measures to improve cyber security. They can be categorized by the four following objectives: "[1] active position of GE in European and international Cyber Security policy discussion, [2] safe and self-determined action in a digitized environment, [3] powerful and sustainable Cyber Security architecture at the national level, and [4] joint effort of government and industries" (Rothenpieler, 2017). The Strategy gives special attention to Germany's commitment to encryption by expressing the government's desire to establish "security through encryption" and to enable "security despite encryption" (Schulze, 2017).

The original and updated version of Germany's Cyber Security Strategy includes a comprehensive approach to strengthen IT systems, aligns efforts and encourages collaboration on a domestic and international scale, and states the desire to create numerous public-private partnerships. The Strategy mentions periods of crises and the role of the National Response Centre, but does not articulate who, what organization, or what level (Federal or State) has decision-making powers for combating crises. While efforts from Germany's military (the Bundeswehr) will compliment this; however, there are no specifics mentioned to address information and intelligence sharing, any effort for offensive operations, or the inclusion of the Bundeswehr in the National Response Center or the National Council on Cyber Security. Overall, the Strategy focuses on the government and the private sector collaborating and takes a non-military approach. Lastly, the Strategy acknowledges Germany's willingness to assume a leadership role for the coordination of efforts and standards with multinational organizations.

Stage three of Germany's cybersecurity evolution (2016–2020) – Germany's "new powers" in a changing world

Germany's adoption of its second NCSS in November 2016 marks the beginning of a third stage of Germany's cybersecurity evolution and development. The German cabinet approved the most recent NCSS against a rise in attacks against German federal government institutions, Bundeswehr's websites and systems, and further harmful activity within the civilian realm, including attacks against critical infrastructures and private citizens' personal accounts and those of businesses. German authorities alongside its close partners and allies pointed to an escalation in attacks from Russia and China. Contributing to elevation of Germany's cybersecurity architecture is the creation of a mobile Quick Reaction Force (QRF) directly within the BSI. Similar units have been scattered throughout key government and law enforcement institutions and agencies such as the federal police (Bundespolizei, BPOL) and Germany's domestic intelligence service (Bundesamt für Verfassungsschutz, BfV). Initiatives in this area have sought to tighten the threats of Germanys cybersecurity network within the country by bringing all sectors into closer quarters with one another, thus augmenting aggregate capabilities accomplished through data and intelligence sharing, monitoring, communications, and assessment. The matter of critical infrastructure stands out in the government's strategy initiative given that, as mentioned previously, the digitization of society has resulted in a societal saturation technologically, leading nearly every societal function to have a relationship with digital technology in some form (e.g. processes, systems, facilities, networks, and services related to health, communications, travel, finances, food/water supplies and chains, and so on).

The 2016 NCSS has also set in motion efforts to have tech-knowledge and awareness trickle down from the upper echelons of the state (i.e., government, military) to ordinary Germans in communities across the republic through school training programs. The German government paid close attention to the surge in malware targeting Germany's IT systems. The Bundestag's IT system was shut down in August, 2015 after a cyberattack, allegedly by Russian hacker group Sofacy/APT 28. Thomas de Mazière highlighted China as a major source of cyberattacks against Germany. The attack against the Bundestag triggered a review of the government's systems and with called following for a complete overhaul – an enormous task to address the digital defenses of the Bundestag, which was referred to as an "open book" (Deutsche Welle, 2015). The attack sought to install a software on government computers systems that would enable the hackers to come and go as they please, and gain permanent access to the personal computers and files of politicians. In December 2019, the entire IT network in Frankfurt – home of the European Central Bank (ECB) and the Eurozone's financial capital – was shut down after an Emotet infection. The Frankfurt attack was the fourth of its kind in a two-week period with others having included the Justus-Liebig-University (JLU) Gießen, Bad Homburg, and the Katholische Hochschule Freiburg (Catholic University of Applied Sciences Freiburg) (Cimpanu, 2019).

The introduction of the 2016 NCSS coincided with the BMVg presenting its 2016 "military roadmap" as the 2016 White Paper, which stood as a major paradigm shift for Germany, just 20 years after Germany's Federal Court of Justice (Bundesgerichtshof, BGH) permitted the German state to participate in multinational peacekeeping operations and missions abroad. This shift was, in part, a response to significant changes that have taken place in the threat environment, including the digital and information domain. The White Paper mentions the term "cyber" 76 times, "cyber security" 13 times, and refers to the necessity of developing high-value "offensive capabilities" as part of Germany's comprehensive approach to addressing "the speed of innovation and the global nature of cyber threats" (BMVg, 2016: 93). Indeed, calls for Germany to play a stronger political and defense role in Europe and in and around the European periphery as well as further afield, in tandem with the country's new military strategy attracted major criticism. Stem (2016) called the "White Paper 2016 on German Security Policy and the Future of the Bundeswehr" as a "step in the revival of German militarism." Germany's previous White Paper (from 2006) was presented when Germany faced far fewer asymmetric threats, including cyber warriors of various stripe, multinational efforts to combat a rise in transnational crime and terrorism, Hamas' Gaza takeover, the Russo-Georgian war, Boko Haram, the Islamic State, Russia's hybrid warfare against and within Ukraine, the "Arab Spring," Libya, Syria, and other conflicts. Thus, the confluence of civil war, hybrid and asymmetric threats, and cyberattacks, necessitated the creation of a "whole-of-government /society" approach resembling that of the US (Chowdhry, 2016). US–Germany Cyber Bilateral Meetings in Washington, DC, rooted US–German cybersecurity collaboration and unified efforts in the cyber domain and as Germany deepened its aspects of its cyber defense handling at home, the Bundestag, with the support of an extensive range of constituents of German society, has sought to intensify the German states leadership in the context of multinationality and integrative cyber defensive and offensive capabilities.

International governance

The Cyber Security Strategy for Germany expresses that Germany's national efforts in regards to cyber security will be coordinated with international organizations and that they will ensure that their priorities are "pursued" in the organizations mentioned (Department IT, 2018: 13). While introducing new domestic legislation in 2015, the Federal Minister of the Interior, Thomas de Maizière, detailed Germany's desire to promote their proposals through similar legislation on an EU level, stating that the "German position is also understood at [the] European level. Germany has thus taken a leading role in an area that will become increasingly important at a time when digital vulnerability is growing" (Bundesministerium des Innern, für Bau und Heimat, BMI, 2015; BSI, 2015).

This would be indicative of the German government not only accepting and promoting efforts for international governance, but also assuming a leadership role in promoting cyber security within Europe foremost as well as beyond this immediate region and on the international level. Germany assumed the rotating, one-year chair position of the Organisation for Security and Co-operation in Europe (OSCE) in 2016. Frank Walter Steinmeier was designated as the Chair of the OSCE, who also, during the same time frame, served as Germany's Foreign Minister (Secretariat, OSCE, 2016). During his tenure, Germany's motto, according to Steinmeier was "renewing dialogue, rebuilding trust, restoring security" (Secretariat, OSCE, 2016).

In 2016, the OSCE passed a series of Confidence Building Measures (CBMs) that built upon "transparency measures" established in 2013. The CBMs in 2016 focused on attacks against critical infrastructure that affect multiple states and also incorporate considerations for Information and Communication Technologies (ICT) (Auswärtiges Amt, AA, 2016; Secretariat, OSCE, 2016). The CBMs developed in 2016 included efforts for improved regional collaboration, improved critical infrastructure protection, crisis communication channels, and public–private partnerships (Secretariat, OSCE, 2016). Additionally, in 2016, 90% of OSCE states enacted one of more cyber CBMs compared to just 61% in 2015 (Secretariat, OSCE, 2016). Furthermore, the establishment of additional CBMs in 2016 can be seen as a monumental success since the OSCE is the "only regional security organization with such a diverse constituency that has managed to reach agreement on CBMs focusing on the cyber domain" (Secretariat, OSCE, 2016).

Under the leadership of a German politician, Günther H. Oettinger, Commissioner for the Digital Economy and Society, the EU launched a European public–private partnership on cybersecurity. After the establishment of the partnership, Oettinger expressed his support by stating that, "[w]e call on Member States and all cybersecurity bodies to strengthen cooperation and pool their knowledge, information and expertise to increase Europe's cyber resilience" (Secretariat, OSCE, 2016).

In 2016, the EU passed the "first comprehensive EU-wide legislation" on cyber security, the Directive on Security of Network and Information Systems (NIS Directive) (Leisterer, 2016). This directive is aimed at creating common standards for risk mitigation and reporting for companies that conduct business throughout the EU, Germany views the NIS Directive as the starting point for cyber regulations for the EU and rejects further proposed legislation and regulations. During the Third European Cybersecurity Forum, CYBERSEC 2017, hosted by The Kosciuszko Institute in Krakow, Poland, Germany publicly pushed back on proposals to expand the EU's cyber efforts for expanded regulations and mandates. The head of international relations for BSI stated that,

> we [the EU] should not neglect that we first need to establish, I would like to call it basic reading and writing skills in Europe, as the NIS directive tells us to, before we get to the advanced mathematics level, as intended by the cybersecurity package.
>
> *(Leisterer, 2016)*

Germany's cultural understanding

Cultural understanding of the Internet in Germany is an extension and adaptation of existing laws and approaches associated to others sectors of society, particularly as Germany has "dialed-in" over the years and become highly-digitized. The overall German cultural understanding of the Internet is defined by positions concerning privacy, efforts for collaboration to collectively increase the security of IT infrastructure, the role and use of the military for offensive cyber operations, and the censorship of hate speech (Bundesminister der Verteidigung, 2016; Laub, 2019). These factors, among others, concern Germany's population of more than 80 million people (see Figure 6.1 for Internet users in Germany) as well as the diverse businesses and industries within Germany.

Both Germany and Brazil assumed the lead to reaffirm an individual's right to privacy at the UN, which led to the creation of UNGA Resolution 68/167. The Resolution is titled, "The Right to Privacy in the Digital Age" and was largely a reaction of the National Security Agency's (NSA) spying on Angela Merkel. Although the document is not legally binding, it represents Germany's attitude towards the human right of privacy by both governments and businesses (Minárik, 2014).

Understanding of protecting the privacy of individuals within Germany is also evident vis-à-vis monetary penalties integrated into laws for and the reporting of incidents by way of reports to the Bundestag. Fall-out from revelations from the Facebook scandal that erupted in April 2018 is building momentum for updating data-privacy laws in Germany primarily through the Bundesdatenschutzgesetz (BDSG) – Germany's Federal Data Protection Act. The young Coalition government (the Fourth Merkel Cabinet since 2018) called for an ethics committee to investigate the use of open information and will most likely lead to an updated data privacy and protection law in the near future. The same

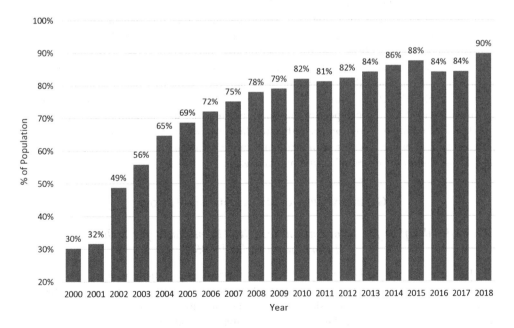

Figure 6.1 Percent of German Population Using the Internet
Source: The World Bank (2020).

document outlining the Coalition's common viewpoints and priorities, stressed the availability and access of end-to-end encryption for citizens.

The EU's General Data Protection Regulations (GDPR) has done little to adjust or change the legal landscape surrounding data protection in Germany, though the federal government has shown a rising concern over business practices those of tech firms. Without resorting to legal action, pressure has been applied to companies that are seen as engaging in questionable practices, and skirting the lines of illegality with Facebook having been restricted from data pooling as a result of activity and data availability through some of its popular online apps such as Instagram and WhatsApp. Earlier in 2020, Facebook was also criticized for failing to ask for users' consent prior to collecting users' personal data – a complaint brought forward to the German courts by the Federation of German Consumer Organizations (VZBV). In 2019, The German Federal Commissioner for Data Protection and Freedom of Information (BfDI) actioned a fine of €9.55 million against mobile services provider 1&1 Telecommunications for negligence with respect to the protection of customers' personal data and information in its call centers (Leprince-Ringuet, 2019). Greater degrees of scrutiny about how big tech firms gather, collect, and share the data of private citizens who are users of tech firms' apps in Germany are mirrored elsewhere in the EU and the world. Germany has presented itself as a leading actor in this regard, bringing stricter measures into play with respect to competition law and personal data protection with efforts on the part of the German state appearing to supported by the general population who want to enjoy using tech firms' apps but who also want to know that their privacy is not being compromised during the course of using them.

Germany has operated military cyber units since 2006 and initially revealed the capacity to conduct offensive cyber operations in 2012 (Shalal, 2017a). This issue in Germany recently gained momentum in the press since a new cyber command was established. In March 2017, German Defense Minister Ursula von der Leyen stated that the German military has the ability to respond to cyberattacks with cyberattacks. A *Rueters* article communicated the debate over offensive operations citing that the civilian officials warned that Germany may lack the legal framework to retaliate due to the Bundeswehr's status as a "parliamentary army" (Shalal, 2017b). This exchange between lawmakers, defense officials, and other civilian officials highlights Germany's reluctance to use military force other than when specifically sanctioned by international law and the extent to which the government is willing to apply self-defense principles to the cyber and information domain, and granted to the Bundeswehr. Still, the prospect of the Bundeswehr being unrestrained in such a way has found an uncomfortable position, or rather resulted in uncomfortable positions of many in German society who see this a militarizing move and one that departs sharply with Germany's "culture of restraint" in the military realm.[2]

Germany's key cybersecurity institutions

The Federal Office for Information Security (Bundesamt für Sicherheit in der Informationstechnik, BSI)

The BSI was founded on January 1, 1991 and is the lead government agency for the cyber domain and to promote the security of information technology (BSI, 2009). BSI is composed of eight primary divisions[3] under the direction of the president and vice-president. Each division (with the exception one division) leads its own cluster of branches, with their number varying from one division to another.

The spectrum of tasks for which BSI is responsible is enormous. Among its 15 tasks, the first and primary task is to "prevent threats to the security of federal information technology" (BSI, 2009: 2). However, the role and tasks of BSI extend well beyond the protection of federal IT systems and technology. Other tasks include supporting intelligence agencies, police, and state-level organization and offices (BSI, 2009). The four divisions of the BSI in simplified English are: Cyber Security and Critical Infrastructures; Consulting for Government, the Private Sector and Society; Cryptotechnology and IT Management for Increased Security Requirements, and; Digitalisation, Certification, and Standardisation (Federal Office for Information Security, 2017).

The Cyber Security Strategy highlights the importance of The National Cyber Security Council and The National Cyber Response Center. The National Cyber Security Council (NCSC), charter is to "advise businesses, government agencies, and policy makers on issues relating to cyber security and to strengthen the fight against cyber crime" (Cyber-Security Council Germany, n.d.). The organization is designed as a forum to collaborate and exchange ideas between industry, policy makers, academia, federal ministries, and international entities (Cyber-Security Council Germany, n.d.). It therefore brings together a large community of experts and knowledgeable personnel for the purpose of providing information and support. The NCSC was established in the original Cyber Security Strategy For Germany in 2011 and is led by three government agencies: the BSI, The Federal Office for the Protection of the Constitution, and the Federal Office of Civil Protection and Disaster Assistance. The role of the NCSC is to facilitate crisis response among government agencies to include the Germany military and Computer Emergency Response Teams (CERTs) (Hunton Privacy Blog, 2011).

National Cyberdefence Centre (Nationales Cyber-Abwehrzentrum, Cyber-AZ)

Germany's National Cyberdefence Centre in came into force as part of the state's broader cyber and security defense architecture in 2011 to "optimise operational cooperation between all state authorities and to improve the coordination of protection and response measures for IT incidents…" (ENISA, 2011: 5). This is done through a complete and sweeping integration of agencies and authorities (law enforcement, intelligence, and military organizations), as well state information infrastructure, and their skills. The overall objective is to bring into alignment the range of German cyber and security competencies and match them with the existing and emerging threats in the cyber and information domain – referring to any within the German state and well beyond that might and will eventually pose a threat to Germany, its citizens, business, industry, and armed forces, among other aspects of the German state. Rapid assessment of threats and fitting responsive and countermeasure capabilities with them is intended to facilitate equally rapid state response to them like an integrated meshwork and protection services, defenses, and action-based agencies and divisions.

The holistic approach to cybersecurity can amplify state response options and capacities by bringing into focus varying, whether competing or reinforcing, perspectives that enable efficacious reactions and possibly the expansion and fine-tuning of existing structures and forces. A "pooling" of knowledge can thus take place that yields exponential benefit across the agency and authority landscape. As BSI (n.d.: n.p.) describes the process, "[t]he BfV, the MAD and the BND rate it from an intelligence perspective. The BKA, the ZKA and the BPOL assess him from a police perspective. Finally, the BBK evaluates the aspects of disaster preparedness and critical infrastructure issues." This process has been established through a leadership cognizance that threats in the security environment are constantly changing and presenting authorities with new challenges. Cyber-AZ is therefore an embodiment of that threat-transmutation awareness, having evolved from a body that centered on a single function with broad purpose to what BSI (n.d.) characterizes as a "central cooperation platform of the IT security authorities."

Central Office for Information Technology in the Security Sphere (Zentrale Stelle für Informationstechnik im Sicherheitsbereich, ZITiS)

In April 2017, Germany's Interior Minister, Thomas de Maizière, founded its new cyber surveillance agency (receiving an initial €10 million financial infusion) with the purpose of establishing an independent resource from police and the secret service to conduct digital forensics to fight cybercrime and digital espionage, essentially the hacking agency for the German Government (Bundeskriminalamt, BKA, 2016; Bundesministerium der Verteidigung, n.d.). The agency also enables the promotion of Germany's dedication to encrypted services and communications. Within less than one year, the Agency experienced its first controversy when it was accused of identifying security flaws in commercial software and passing along this information to espionage agencies for exploitation (Heide, 2017). The establishment of ZITiS has also renewed the debate over the legal authority to conduct hack backs in Germany (*Reuters*, 2017). Independent of Germany's police and secret services, in principle ZITiS has the ability to conduct watch over virtually anyone in Germany via mass telecommunication surveillance, data encryption, and mass data collection practices. Implementation of ZITiS and allowing it to operate as a near-completely independent agency, serving the interest of the Germany state, fortifies the perspective that Germany has taken a step in the direction of centralizing state security practices.

Cyber and Information Space Command (Kommando Cyber- und Informationsraum, Kdo CIR)

The Bundeswehr launched a new Cyber Command in 2017 with its headquarters established in Bonn and headed by Lt. Gen. Ludwig Leinhos. Germany's Ministry of Defense (Bundesminister der Verteidigung, BMVg) reported that the Bundeswehr's IT systems were the subject of some 280,000 attacks in the first nine weeks of 2017 with Russian state-sponsored hackers suspected of contributing to a large portion of attacks (Delcker, 2017). Leinhos (quoted in Paganini, 2017) stated that German defense authorities "are in a constant race between the development of attack options and defensive capabilities." The Cyber and Information Space Command (Kommando Cyber- und Informationsraum, Kdo CIR) will reach full operational status in 2021 with a staff of over 13,500 and will include an innovation hub connecting the military to tech start-ups (Werkhäuser, 2017). Overall, Germany's primary institutions to conduct research, respond to threats, conduct research, and policy development fall under the responsibility of the BSI. The umbrella organizations are structured to integrate multiple government agencies and the private sector for both inputs and to exchange information (see Figure 6.2).

With the expansion of Germany's cybersecurity agencies and institutions, much debate has taken pace about the possible continued expansion and the instruments at the German government's disposal to operate in the cyber domain. In spite of palpable expansion that has taken place in over the past decade, German cybersecurity authorities, an extension of the German Armed Forces, remain restricted by firm legal rules and currently in place. The

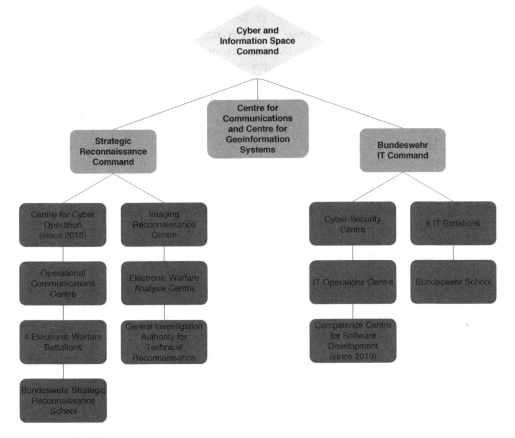

Figure 6.2 The Structure of the Cyber and Information Space Command (*Kommando Cyber- und Informationsraum, Kdo CIR*) of the Bundeswehr

Source: Authors' illustration based on data from Cyber-Peace.org (2016), Gotkowska (2017), Schallbruch and Skierka (2018), and the German government and Bundeswehr documents.

Bundeswehr is granted the powers to defend the German state and its people but has not been given a green light to operate freely and at its own discretion. The Bundeswehr's presence while having been expanded in the cyber and information domain, can still be seen as relatively limited in terms of its numbers. In the fullness of time, the parameters of the Bundeswehr's operationality will almost certainly be tested as its responsibilities are likely to cover new areas and threats. As mandates from the federal level and in the context of international partnerships and agreements, Germany's cybersecurity and cyber defense authorities will be tested and undergo further developmental and maturation processes. The Bundeswehr, however, has been unable to operate without the explicit approval of the Bundestag and beyond the confines of the German state and in defense of the German people.

The role of the private sector

Germany's private sector plays a critical role in ensuring the collective security of IT infrastructure in Germany. The Government works closely with industry through private–

public partnerships and initiatives such as "IT Security made in Germany" and "Industry 4.0." Both initiatives aim to increase the relevance of Germany's IT research and manufacturing capabilities ensuring that Germany remains competitive.

In the aftermath of the 2013 revelations that the NSA had conducted online surveillance against Germany's leaders and citizens – often with the collaboration of US-based private organizations like Google and Facebook – German private corporations led initiatives for so-called "data localization initiatives." In particular, Deutsche Telekom led an effort to create an internet network that would reside entirely in Germany (Dohmen, 2013). Deutsche Telekom lobbied the German Government to provide a legal framework that would prevent "lawsuits claiming discrimination or the curtailment of data traffic" (Dohmen & Traufetter, 2013). German internet providers perceived that American companies were not subject to the same privacy standards that German companies were subject to. Although efforts to create a national internet system in Germany did not come to fruition, Deutsche Telekom did create a European Cloud Service that they claim is "100% out of the reach of the US authorities" (*Financial Times*, 2015). The EU NIS Directive passed in 2016 which will be enforced in 2018 mandates that all companies that are considered operators of essential services or digital service provides, without a "physical presence" in the EU adhere to the data privacy laws in Europe and was seen as a way to limit competition from Silicon Valley firms (*Financial Times*, 2015; Katz & Larose, 2016). According to the Global Policy Institute, Germany "has become ground zero in the global regulatory battle on how to deal with hate speech on social media platforms" (Benner & Hohmann, 2017).

Private firms such as Google and Facebook are active in this debate and are vocal on policy positions. The most recent example is Facebook's vocal resistance to the Network Enforcement Act in Germany passed in 2017 and enacted in January 2018. The law was challenged in court months after going into force after Facebook deleted comments that were against its community standards for a somewhat inflammatory political post. The court ruled that Facebook was in the wrong for deleting the comments and blocking the user. The case is an early test for the law and evokes additional national debates on what is considered hate speech and the role of private companies to enforce such standards.

Legislation

In the past three years, Germany has passed three major pieces of legislation pertaining to IT and cyber systems as well as for the regulation of the internet. Data and privacy protection laws evolved and were amended with increasing technology and the widespread use of the internet. In April 2017, Germany passed a replacement for the Federal Data Protection Act that partially regulated data protection for the Internet (Hunton Privacy Blog, 2017). The new German Federal Protection Act (BDSG) incorporates changes and regulations contained in the EU General Data Protection Regulation (GDPR), which goes into effect in 2018 (Hunton Privacy Blog, 2017). Among many, the BDSG contains new provisions that dictate the appointment of a Data Protection Officer (DPO), establishes rights of data subjects, and establishes fines and jail times for the intentional misuse of personal data (Schonhofen & Hardinghaus, 2017). The new law was enacted in 2018 when the GDPR came into effect (Schonhofen & Hardinghaus, 2017). Germany also passed the Network Enforcement Law in April 2017 which forces social media platforms and search engines such as Facebook and Google to remove "fake news" and hate speech in a 24-hour time span or face steep fines up to €50 million (Tworek, 2017).

Primarily for the protection of critical infrastructure, Germany enacted the IT Security Act of 2015. The IT Security Act of 2015 also amended past laws such as the German Telemedia Act of 2003 and the now updated Federal Data Protection Act that both regulated online activates to a certain extent (Kuschewsky, 2015). The law passed in 2015 created certain minimum requirements for IT security, included a provision to mandate reporting requirements to the BSI, and required the designation of a single point of contact to the BSI (Heun, Niemann, Duisberg & Hinzen, 2015). The law is applicable to critical infrastructure and includes industries such as: energy, IT and telecommunications, transport and traffic, health, water, food, finance, and insurance (Heun, Niemann, Duisberg & Hinzen, 2015).

Conclusion

Germany's efforts and desire to combat cyber threats in the public and private sector continue to evolve as threats evolve. In addition, Germany is an active participant in efforts to clarify international law's application to the cyber domain and are deeply dedicated to following and perseverance of international law. Most importantly, the Bundestag from a very early stage understood that efforts to protect IT infrastructure, the basis of cyber security, is the collaboration between all private corporations, government agencies, and multinational organizations. Germany's current administration clearly realizes the essential role of the private sector and developed numerous private–public partnerships and established multiple strategic objectives to ensure German that manufacturing and technology sectors are capable to lead Europe. This again illustrates their comprehensive understanding of the required actions needed to properly ensure high levels of cyber security within Germany, the EU environment, in an interconnected global domain, and to limit the dominance of US Internet firms.

Legislation in Germany ensures that cultural priorities such as limiting hate speech, extremism, and, efforts divide society, and the protection of privacy is extended to the Internet. Their efforts to maintain high levels of privacy have not hampered or interfered with the private sector's development of encryption technologies impenetrable to hackers. This demonstrates the delicate balance of maintaining the capability of conducting investigations or to conduct anti-terrorism operations while respecting the privacy of German citizens and the free nature of the Internet. Germany, through its various efforts and continuous refinement of policies, regulations, and legislation, is currently poised to address challenges and threats inherent within the cyber domain. The forward-thinking nature of Germany's collective efforts presents the country a leader in the EU and on the global stage.

Notes

1 BSI is identified as the descendant of the Germany's Federal Intelligence Service (Bundesnachrichtendienst, BND) created in 1956 by the West German government. Responsible for foreign intelligence and reporting to the intelligence coordinator, the BND was once staffed by 7,500 personnel during the Cold War, though serious reductions in staff numbers followed with the end of the Cold War.

2 For an elucidating article on the topic, see Baumann and Hellmann's (2001) "Germany and the use of military force: 'total war,' the 'culture of restraint' and the quest for normality."

3 BSI's organization chart (BSI, 2016) can be accessed at: www.bsi.bund.de/SharedDocs/Downloads/EN/BSI/BSI/org_chart_IFG_pdf.pdf?__blob=publicationFile&v=8.

Suggested reading

Bundesministerium für Bildung und Forschung (BMBF) (Federal Ministry of Education and Research). (n.d.). "Cybersecurity research to boost Germany's competitiveness." www.bmbf.de/en/cybersecur ity-research-to-boost-germany-s-competitiveness-1418.html

CisoMag. (2019, October 7). "Negligent users are biggest cybersecurity threat to German Organizations: survey." www.cisomag.com/negligent-users-are-biggest-cybersecurity-threat-to-german-organiza tions-survey/

Deutsche Welle. (n.d.). "German cyber defense blends military and commerce." www.dw.com/en/ german-cyber-defense-blends-military-and-commerce/a-45636325

Gordon, J. (2019, February 24). "What 'God' taught us about Germany's cybersecurity." *Raconteur.* www.raconteur.net/technology/germany-cybersecurity

Guitton, C. (2013). "Cyber insecurity as a national threat: overreaction from Germany, France and the UK?" *European Security, 22*(1): 21–35.

Schallbruch, M. & Skierka, I. (2018). *Cybersecurity in Germany.* Cham: Springer.

Sprenger, S. (2020, February 4). "Germany moves to protect its military-cyber industry," *Fifth Domain.* www.fifthdomain.com/smr/munich-security-conference/2020/02/14/germany-moves-to-protect-its-military-cyber-industry/

References

AA. (2016, March 24). "Joint statement on U.S.-Germany cyber bilateral meeting." www.auswaertiges-amt.de/en/newsroom/news/160323-cyber-konsultationen-usa/279470

Benner, T. & Hohmann, M. (2017, April 20). *Internet Companies Cannot Be Judged of Free Speech.* Berlin, Germany: Global Public Policy Institute. www.gppi.net/publications/data-technology-politics/art icle/internet-companies-cant-be-judges-of-free-speech/

Bundeskriminalamt (BKA). (2016, July 1). *Cybercrime.* Berlin, Germany.

BMI. (2011, February). "Cyber security strategy for Germany." www.enisa.europa.eu/media/news-items/german-cyber-security-strategy-2011-1

BMI. (2015, March 16). "Improving IT security in Germany and the EU." www.bmi.bund.de/Share dDocs/Kurzmeldungen/EN/2015/03/exchange-with-eu-commissioner-oettinger-to-cyber-security. html

BMVg. (n.d.). "Entwicklung des Organisationsbereichs bei der Bundeswehr." bmvg.de/de/themen/ cybersicherheit/cyber-verteidigung/entwicklung-des-org-bereich-bei-der-bw

BMVg. (2006). "White Paper on Gemran Security Policy and the Future of the Bundeswehr." www. files.ethz.ch/isn/156941/Germany%202006%20white%20paper.pdf

BMVg. (2016). "White paper on security policy and the future of the Bundeswehr." www.gmfus.org/ file/8970/download

BSI. (2009, August 14). "Act to strengthen the security of federal information technology." www. bsi.bund.de/SharedDocs/Downloads/EN/BSI/BSI/BSI_Act_BSIG.pdf?__blob=publication File&v=1

BSI. (2015). "The state of IT security in Germany 2015." www.bsi.bund.de/SharedDocs/Downloads/ EN/BSI/Publications/Securitysituation/IT-Security-Situation-in-Germany-2015.pdf? __blob=publicationFile&v=2

BSI. (2016, November). "BSI organisation chart." www.bsi.bund.de/SharedDocs/Downloads/EN/BSI/ BSI/org_chart_IFG_pdf.pdf?__blob=publicationFile&v=5

Chowdhry, A. (2016, March 28). "U.S. and Germany expand cyber cooperation," *Federal Computer Week.* https://fcw.com/articles/2016/03/28/us-germany-cyber.aspx

Cimpanu, C. (2019, December 19). "Frankfurt shuts down IT network following Emotet infection," *ZDNet.* www.zdnet.com/article/frankfurt-shuts-down-it-network-following-emotet-infection/

Cyber-Security Council Germany. (n.d.). "About us." www.cybersicherheitsrat.de/english/about-us/

Cyber-Peace.org. (2016, April 27). "Details zum Abschlussbericht des Aufbaustab Cyber- und Informationsraum" ["Details on the final report of the Cyber and Information Space Command expansion team"]. https://cyber-peace.org/2016/04/27/auswertung_aufbaustab_cirk/

Delcker, J. (2017, March 20). "Germany fears Russia stole information to disrupt election." *POLITICO.* politico.eu/article/hacked-information-bomb-under-germanys-election/

Deutsche Welle. (2015, August 8). "Bundestag IT system shut down after hacker attack." dw.com/en/bundestag-it-system-shut-down-after-hacker-attack/a-18659654

Dohmen, F. & Traufetter, G. (2013, November 12). "Deutsche telekom pushes for all-German Internet," *Der Spiegel*. www.spiegel.de/international/germany/deutsche-telekom-pushes-all-german-internet-safe-from-spying-a-933013.html

European Commission. (2016, July). *Commission Signs Agreement with Industry on Cybersecurity and Steps Up Efforts to Tackle Cyber-Threats*. Brussles, Belgium. http://europa.eu/rapid/press-release_IP-16-2321_en.htm

European Union Agency for Cybersecurity (ENISA). (2011). "Cyber Security Strategy for Germany." www.enisa.europa.eu/media/news-items/german-cyber-security-strategy-2011-1

Federal Office for Information Security. (2017). "The German IT Security Certification Scheme." www.isccc.gov.cn/zlzx/kyxx/images/2017/09/10/AF5C39A704EA2F5CE84A2D0419EA383C.pdf

Financial Times. (2015, December). "Deutsche Telekom to offer 'secure' cloud storage." www.ft.com/content/2b5928dc-9cca-11e5-b45d-4812f209f861

Gebauer, M. & Gruber, A. (2016, Janurary 8). "eBundesregierung sucht Nerds," *Der Spiegel*.

Gotkowska, J. (2017). "*Obszar cybernetyczno-informacyjny: Nowa formacja w Bundeswehrze*" ["*The Cyber and Information Space: A New Formation in the Bundeswehr*"]. Warsaw, Poland: Ośrodek Studiów Wschodnich (Centre for Eastern Studies). www.osw.waw.pl/en/publikacje/analyses/2017-04-12/cyber-and-information-space-a-new-formation-bundeswehr

Heide, D. (2017, December 6). "Cybersecurity agency criticized as a double agent." https://global.handelsblatt.com/politics/cybersecurity-agency-criticized-as-a-double-agent-861980

Heun, S. E., Niemann, F., Duisberg, A., & Hinzen, S. (2015, July 29). *Germany Enacts IT-Security Act*. London, United Kingdom: Bird & Bird Lawfirm. www.twobirds.com/en/news/articles/2015/germany/july/germany-enacts-it-security-act

Hunton Privacy Blog. (2011, July 11). "Germany launches national cyber defense center." www.huntonprivacyblog.com/2011/07/07/germany-launches-national-cyber-defense-center/

Hunton Privacy Blog. (2017, April 28). "German federal parliament passes new German data protection act." www.huntonprivacyblog.com/2017/04/28/german-federal-parliament-passes-new-german-data-protection-act/

Katz, M. & Larose, C. (2016, July 11). "EU adopts cybersecurity directive: what US companies need to know," *Lexology*. www.lexology.com/library/detail.aspx?g=2d8054a8-a388-4b5e-a7fa-fc29d097c826

Kuschewsky, M. (2015, September 14). "What you need to know about Germany's cybersecurity law." www.insideprivacy.com/data-security/what-you-need-to-know-about-germanys-cybersecurity-law/

Laub, Z. (2019, June 7). *Hate Speech on Social Media: Global Comparisons*. New York: Council on Foreign Relations. cfr.org/backgrounder/hate-speech-social-media-global-comparisons

Leisterer, H. (2016, July 14). "New EU cyber security legislation: A Q & A with Andreas Schwab," *Policy Review*. https://policyreview.info/articles/news/new-eu-cyber-security-legislation-q-andreas-schwab/411

Leprince-Ringuet, D. (2019, December 12). "Data privacy: Germans dish out one of the biggest GDPR fines yet over lax call centers," *ZDNet*. zdnet.com/article/data-privacy-germans-dish-out-one-of-biggest-gdpr-fines-yet-over-lax-call-centers/

Minárik, T. (2014, December 18). "New UN resolution amplifies call for right to privacy in the light of mass surveillance." https://ccdcoe.org/new-un-resolution-amplifies-call-right-privacy-light-mass-surveillance.html

Paganini, P. (2017, April 1). "German military to launch the Bundeswehr's new cyber and information space command," *Security Affairs*. https://securityaffairs.co/wordpress/57607/cyber-warfare-2/cyber-and-information-space-command.html

Reuters. (2017, November 22). "German cyber agency calls for authority to hack back." www.reuters.com/article/us-germany-cyber/german-cyber-agency-calls-for-authority-to-hack-back-spiegel-idUSKBN1DM1XU

Rothenpieler, S. (2017, April 26). "National cyber security strategy 2016," *BSI*. www.enisa.europa.eu/about-enisa/structure-organization/national-liaison-office/meetings/april-2017/170426-bsi-enisa-nlo-presentation-v2.pdf

Schallbruch, M. & Skierka, I. (2018). *Cybersecurity in Germany*. Cham: Springer.

Schonhofen, S. & Hardinghaus, A. (2017, April 28). "German parliament voted 'yes' on new Data Protection Act to implement the GDPR." www.technologylawdispatch.com/2017/04/privacy-data-protection/german-parliament-voted-yes-on-new-data-protection-act-to-implement-the-gdpr/

Schulze, M. (2017, August). *Encryption under Threat.* Berlin, Germany: Stiftung Wissenschaft und Politik (German Institute for International and Security Affairs). www.swp-berlin.org/fileadmin/contents/products/comments/2017C31_she.pdf

Secretariat, OSCE. (2016, March 10). "OSCE participating states, in landmark decision, agree to expand list of measures to reduce risk of tensions arising from cyber activities." www.osce.org/cio/226656

Shalal, A. (2017a, April 5). "German military can use 'offensive measures' against cyber attacks: minister," *Reuters.* www.reuters.com/article/us-germany-cyber-idUSKBN1771MW

Shalal, A. (2017b, May 3). "Germany sees rise in cybercrime, but reporting rates still low," *Rueters.* www.reuters.com/article/us-germany-cybercrime-crime-idUSKBN17Z26S

Stem, J. (2016, July 15). "White Paper 2016: another step in the revival of German militarism," *World Socialist Web Site.* www.wsws.org/en/articles/2016/07/15/bund-j15.html

The World Bank. (2020). "Individuals using the Internet (% of population) – Germany." https://data.worldbank.org/indicator/IT.NET.USER.ZS?end=2018&locations=DE&start=1990&view=chart

Tworek, H. (2017, May 16). "How Germany is tackling hate speech," *Foreign Affairs.* www.foreignaffairs.com/articles/germany/2017-05-16/how-germany-tackling-hate-speech

Werkhäuser, N. (2017, April 1). "German army launches new cyber command," *Deustche Welle.* www.dw.com/en/german-army-launches-new-cyber-command/a-38246517

7

CYBERSECURITY OF POLAND

Legal and organizational framework

Dominika Dziwisz

Digital society in Poland

The history of the Internet in Poland is not very long compared to its history in Western European countries. The breakthrough date for establishing Internet in Poland was November 19, 1990, when the US Department of Defense gave the Institute of Nuclear Physics of the Polish Academy of Sciences the first Polish IP number, which made it possible to connect their 255 computers to the Internet (Instytut Fizyki Jądrowej PAN, 2019). Officially, Poland gained access to the Internet in December 1991. At that time, the Internet speed reached less than 10 KB/s and only a few companies and institutions used it (today Internet speed is up to 1 GB/s). It was not until 1996 that the main Polish telecommunications provider (Telekomunikacja Polska, TP) made it possible to connect to the network using a telephone modem and in 1999 SDI, i.e., Quick Internet Access, which did not block the telephone line, was launched. However, the service was still very expensive and only a few could afford it (Orange, 2019). Internet in Poland became more popular following a cheaper telecommunication provider offer for Internet access in 2004.

In 2018 in Poland, 84.2 per cent of households had access to the Internet and 79.3 per cent had a broadband Internet connection. This is still lower than the European Union average, but the number is growing (Information Society in Poland, 2018: 127). In comparison, the highest proportion (98 per cent) of households with Internet access among EU countries in 2018 was recorded in the Netherlands. In the United Kingdom, Germany, Finland, Denmark, Luxembourg and Sweden, more than 9 out of 10 households had access to the Internet (Eurostat, 2019). The lowest percentage of EU citizens using the Internet at home was reported in Bulgaria.

The share of enterprises with access to the Internet in Poland is slightly higher, exceeding 95 per cent. Among large enterprises this value fluctuates at around 100 per cent. Comparing results of the survey conducted in the EU Member States, the percentage of Polish enterprises with access to the Internet still is slightly lower than the EU average. It is interesting that in 2018 over two-thirds of enterprises equipped their employees with devices enabling mobile access to the Internet.

Polish citizens are increasingly using e-government services. In 2018, over 35 per cent of the population of people aged 16–74 had used public administration services in the last 12 months (Główny Urząd Statystyczny, 2018: 4). Compared to the previous year this showed a 4.7 per cent increase. Individuals use e-government services in order to obtain information from public authority websites (24.4 per cent), download official forms (22.1 per cent) and submit completed forms (24.6 per cent) (Statistics Poland, 2018: 165–166).

E-administration is an Internet service that entrepreneurs are more and more willing to use. Companies most often use e-administration to download and send back completed forms and obtain information. In 2017, 95.1 per cent of companies in Poland used e-administration services, representing almost all medium (98.9 per cent) and large companies (99.6 per cent). Today, Polish administration offers citizens the option of electronically utilizing a total of over 500 services (Ministerstwo Cyfryzacji, *Katalog cyfrowych usług*, 2017). Unfortunately, there is no centralized place where all electronic services offered by the administration are grouped. Currently, the Portal of the Republic of Poland (Portal RP) is being created, which will be the gateway to all public information and e-services.

The Ministry of Digital Affairs of Poland (Ministerstwo Cyfryzacji) is the main government department responsible for the development of e-administration. The ministry's mission is to "create a digital impulse for Poland's development. The main tasks include: development of broadband infrastructure, supporting the creation of Internet content and e-services, and promoting digital competences among citizens and officials" (Ministerstwo Cyfryzacji, *Jakie Instytucje*, 2017). In 2016, the Council of Ministers, the collective executive decision-making body of the Polish Government, adopted the National Integrated Informatization Program (Program Zintegrowanej Informatyzacji Państwa, PZIP), which is a strategic document describing how public services can be delivered to the public (an update of the program is under discussion now). In the program's annex the Minister of Digitization's plan of integrated activities was defined, aiming at improving the operation of public administration.

Poland is one of the fastest growing e-commerce markets in Europe (Statista, 2019). The number of registered e-commerce stores in 2019 reached almost 32,000 and this number rises regularly. Polish citizens increasingly shop online. In 2019, 62 per cent of Internet users made online purchases, which is 6 per cent more than one year ago (56 per cent in 2018). Shopping in foreign stores recorded a slightly slower increase. Currently, approximately 26 per cent of Internet users shop in foreign stores (23 per cent in 2018) (E-commerce w Polsce, 2019).

In 2017, the percentage of companies sending orders online was 33.6 per cent. The majority of enterprises used a website or mobile applications for this purpose (33.0 per cent), as well as, to a lesser extent, EDI messages (6.2 per cent). In 2017, 12.1 per cent of enterprises received electronic products, of which 9.4 per cent made sales via their own website or mobile application and 6.4 per cent via external online trading platforms. E-commerce in Poland is predicted to reach 11.64 billion USD in 2019 (Ecommerce News Europe, 2019).

Cybersecurity legal frameworks

The 2007 cyber-attacks against Estonia alerted European governments to the vulnerability of a computerized society. Among other things, one of the direct consequences of these attacks was the development of cybersecurity strategies by central European governments (Slovakia in 2009; Czech Republic, 2012; Hungary, 2013).

The first strategic document purely dedicated to the cybersecurity of Poland, the Cyberspace Protection Policy of the Republic of Poland, was published in June 2013 by the former Ministry of Administration and Digitalization (Ministerstwo Cyfryzacji i Administracji, MAC) and the Internal Security Agency (Agencja Bezpieczeństwa Wewnetrznego, ABW). The Cyberspace Protection Policy was replaced in May 2017 by a resolution on the National Cybersecurity Policy Framework of the Republic of Poland for

2017–2022. This document was developed by a group of experts composed of representatives of the departments of the Ministry of Digital Affairs (Ministerstwo Cyfryzacji), the Ministry of National Defense (Ministerstwo Obrony Narodowej), the Ministry of the Interior and Administration (Ministerstwo Spraw Wewnętrznych i Administracji) and officers and representatives of the Internal Security Agency, the Government Centre for Security (Rządowe Centrum Bezpieczeństwa), and NASK National Research Institute. As a result, the document was interdisciplinary and addressed a broad spectrum of needs in the field of cybersecurity. The main goal of the National Framework is to *ensure a high level of security for the public sector, the private sector and citizens in the provision or use of key services and digital services.* In addition, four specific objectives were identified, indicating the needs that arise from the development of a national cybersecurity system:

1. Achieving the ability to coordinate on a national scale in order to prevent, detect, combat and minimize the effects of incidents violating the security of ICT systems relevant to the functioning of the state.
2. Strengthening the ability to counter cyber threats.
3. Increasing national potential and competence in the field of security in cyberspace.
4. Building a strong international position for Poland in the field of cyber security. Because the National Framework takes the form of general objectives, guidelines and declarations, a group of experts developed a document that operationalized these objectives in January 2018 (NASK, 2018).

In January 2015, after more than a year of studies and drafting, the second strategic document, the Cyber Security Doctrine of the Republic of Poland (Doktryna Cyberbezpieczeństwa Rzeczypospolitej Polskiej), was published by the National Security Bureau (Biuro Bezpieczeństwa Narodowego, BBN). This doctrine is a conceptual and executive document linked to the National Security Strategy of the Republic of Poland 2014 (Strategia Bezpieczeństwa Narodowego Rzeczypospolitej Polskiej). It sets goals in the field of cybersecurity, describes the environment, indicating threats, risks and opportunities, and recommends the most important tasks that should be carried out as part of building the state cybersecurity system. The main operational objectives include:

- the assessment of both threats and opportunities that influence cyber security;
- cyber threat prevention (counteracting), reducing risks and taking advantage of opportunities;
- defense and protection of Poland's ICT system;
- combating sources of threats;
- restoring the efficiency and functionality of ICT systems after a possible attack.

Of particular importance is the fact that for the first time there was an official statement that not only defensive operations, but also offensive operations needed to be conducted at the national level. The doctrine is addressed to all entities whose involvement is necessary to ensure the cybersecurity of Poland: public administration, military, security services, the private sector and citizens.

The latest and most important strategic document, which replaces the National Framework of Cybersecurity Policy of the Republic of Poland for 2017–2022, is Poland's National Cyber Security Strategy for 2019–2024. This Strategy was first approved by the Council of Ministers and on October 29, 2019 was signed by the Polish Prime Minister

Mateusz Morawiecki (Ministerstwo Cyfryzacji, October 2019). The revision of the previous document was necessary due to the entry into force of the National Cybersecurity Act of July 5, 2018 (Ustawa z dnia 5 lipca 2018 r. o krajowym systemie cyberbezpieczeństwa), as well as the need to take into account new challenges related to cybersecurity, e.g., cloud computing security and 5G technology. The main goal of the strategy is "to increase the level of resistance to cyber threats and to increase the level of information protection in the public, military, and private sector and to promote knowledge and good practices, enabling citizens to better protect their information" (despite the strategy being adopted, its text has not yet been published; Uchwała Rady Ministrów w sprawie Strategii).

There are two overarching goals of the strategy:

- The first goal centers on the development of a National Cybersecurity System which will be subject to systematic assessment. In order to increase cyber security, among other steps, the system of exchanging information on cyber threats will be expanded, and cooperation and coordination of law enforcement agencies will be developed to increase the ability to combat cybercrime, including cyber espionage or hybrid incidents. The strategy also envisages closer cooperation with local government units.
- The second goal aims at increasing the resilience of public administration and private sector networks and ICT systems. The strategy also aims to achieve the ability to effectively combat the effects of cyber incidents, among others, by developing National Cybersecurity Standards to ensure that national entities meet the necessary organizational and technical requirements in this respect – relevant cloud computing standards or mobile application security.

The Minister of Digital Affairs is responsible for implementing the strategy. Within six months of adopting the Cybersecurity Strategy, he is obliged to develop, in cooperation with members of the Council of Ministers, heads of central offices and the Director of the Government Centre for Security, an action plan for implementing the Cybersecurity Strategy. This will specify specific tasks and activities for government administration bodies, along with a schedule for their implementation. The plan will also indicate sources of financing and measures to determine to what degree specific measures have been implemented.

Cybersecurity organizational structures

The responsibility of ensuring cybersecurity in Poland is divided mainly between two ministries. Protection of Poland's civil cyberspace is one of the main priorities and prerogatives of the Ministry of Digital Affairs. The Ministry of National Defense, on the other hand, is responsible for the development of cyber defense and attack capabilities. Specific cybersecurity competences have also been allocated to other ministries, agencies and public bodies.

Responsibilities of the Ministry of Digital Affairs

The Ministry of Digital Affairs was established by the ordinance of the Council of Ministers of December 7, 2015 (Rozporządzenie Rady Ministrów z dnia 7 grudnia 2015 r.), which transformed the former Ministry of Administration and Digitization. In accordance with the Cybersecurity Policy Framework of the Republic of Poland for 2017–2022, the Minister of Digital Affairs is a key figure responsible for the analysis and risk management system in Polish cyberspace. As part of the legislative work, the Minister of Digital Affairs, in cooperation with other ministries, is responsible for the review of sectoral and specific regulations that deal with the cyber issues. The Council for Digitization (Rada do Spraw Cyfryzacji) supports the minister in strategic decisions. This is a think-tank that gives opinions on strategic and other documents related to digitization, connectivity and the development of the information society. The minister cooperates with the council in areas such as digital integration, online privacy protection, elimination of barriers to the development of an electronic economy, and reform of intellectual property rights on the Internet (Ministerstwo Cyfryzacji, Rada do Spraw Cyfryzacji, 2019).

As part of the Ministry of Digital Affairs the Cyber Security Department was created in 2015 and is responsible for coordinating all cyber tasks. These include developing, implementing and reviewing strategic documents on cyber security issues; initiating research and development projects and disseminating knowledge on cyber security; organizing both national and international cooperation in the field of cyber security (especially with the European Union); developing training plans and exercises; keeping a register of cyber security plenipotentiaries; ensuring the execution of the minister's tasks in the field of state defense; handling matters pertaining to crisis management; acting as a national point of contact in order to collect information on cyber incidents on a national scale; and supervising the information and communication security of the ministry. The Cyber Security Department is also responsible for supervising the Research and Academic Computer Network (Naukowa Akademicka Sieć Komputerowa, NASK). NASK's mission is carrying out scientific and research and development activities in the field of security, organizing educational activities and popularizing the idea of an information society. NASK is also the Polish national registry of Internet names in the .pl domain (NASK, *About NASK*). CERT Poland, which operates within the structure of NASK, is responsible for responding to cyber security threats in the network.

On August 1, 2018, the President of the Republic of Poland signed the Act on the national cybersecurity system (Ustawa z dnia 5 lipca 2018 r. o krajowym systemie cyberbezpieczeństwa) prepared by the Ministry of Digital Affairs, which implements in Polish law a directive of the European Parliament and of the Council (EU) on the security of network and information systems (the Directive on security of network and information systems, NIS Directive; the first piece of EU-wide legislation on cybersecurity). The national cybersecurity system aims to provide cybersecurity at the national level, in particular: uninterrupted provision of key digital services, and to achieve a sufficiently high level of security of the ICT systems used to provide these services. The Act on the national cybersecurity system distinguishes several key sectors for the functioning of the state: energy, transport, banking and financial market infrastructure, health care, drinking water supply (including distribution) and digital infrastructure. The public authorities supervising these sectors are responsible *inter alia* for:

- Preparing recommendations for actions aimed at strengthening cybersecurity; in this respect they cooperate with CSIRT NASK, CSIRT GOV, CSIRT MON and sectoral cybersecurity teams;
- Conducting oversight of key service operators and digital service providers and calling on key service operators or digital service providers to remedy vulnerabilities that have or could have resulted in cyber incidents;
- Participating in cybersecurity exercises organized in Poland or the EU;
- If necessary, establishing a sectoral cybersecurity team for a given sector or sub-sector.

In addition to the Ministry of Digital Affairs and Ministries responsible for the security of key sectors, public authorities dealing with cybersecurity management also include (Świątkowska, Albrycht, & Skokowski, 2017):

- The Ministry of Justice (Ministerstwo Sprawiedliwości, MS), which sets the law on cybercrime and oversees its proper implementation.
- The Ministry of the Interior and Administration (Ministerstwo Spraw Wewnętrznych i Administracji, MSWiA), which supervises police forces in fighting cybercrime.
- The Internal Security Agency (Agencja Bezpieczeństwa Wewnętrznego, ABW) – a government institution responsible for protecting the internal security of Poland and its citizens, among others, by obtaining, analyzing and processing information about dangers.
- The CSIRT GOV Computer Security Incident Response Team, which is led by the Head of the Internal Security Agency, acts as the CSIRT National Level Team responsible for coordinating the computer incident response process.
- The Government Centre for Security (Rządowe Centrum Bezpieczeństwa, RCB) – an institution accountable to the prime minister that is responsible for conducting a comprehensive risk analysis, especially of the critical infrastructure in Poland including its cybersecurity dimension.
- The Office of Electronic Communications (Urząd Komunikacji Elektronicznej, UKE) – a regulatory authority which is responsible for the telecommunications market and frequency resources management. The Minister of Digital Affairs supervises the President of UKE in matters related to telecommunications.
- The Polish Financial Supervision Authority (Komisja Nadzoru Finansowego, KNF) – a public body whose mission is to ensure the stability and safe development of the financial market. The KNF provides recommendations on the Management of Information Technology and ICT Environment Security at Banks (Komisja Nadzoru Finansowego, 2013).
- The President of the Personal Data Protection Office (Prezes Urzędu Ochrony Danych Osobowych, PUODO) – a supervisory authority competent in the field of personal data protection. The president's tasks are strictly set out in the EU General Data Protection Regulation (GDPR). (NATO CCDCOE, 2017: 11–13)

Responsibilities of the Ministry of Defense

During the NATO summit in Warsaw in 2016, it was stated that defense of cyberspace was one of the basic tasks of NATO's collective defense. Consequently, cyberspace was recognized as an area of military operations. In the Polish government, the Minister of National Defense is the highest ranking official responsible for conducting a full spectrum of military operations in cyberspace. In the national cyber security system, the Minister of National Defense is, among other things, responsible for (Cyber.mil.pl, 2019):

- Cooperation of the Polish Armed Forces with NATO, the European Union and international organizations in the area of cybersecurity;
- Ensuring the ability of the Polish Armed Forces to conduct military cyber defense operations;
- Developing the skills of the Polish Armed Forces to ensure cybersecurity by organizing specialized trainings;
- Managing activities related to the handling of incidents during martial law and assessment of the impact of incidents on the state defense system;
- Coordinating the implementation of tasks of government administration and local government units during martial law regarding defense activities in the event of a cybersecurity threat.

In 2018 the Ministry of National Defense launched the cyber.mil.pl program to develop and strengthen the cybersecurity potential of Poland. This project focuses on the consolidation of already existing capabilities as well as building new ones and covers such broad topics as education, development of the research sector, and professional paths for specialists. The main goal of the program is to form Cyberspace Defense Forces. To this end, a representative of the Ministry of National Defense, who also assumed the position of director of the National Center for Cyberspace Security (Narodowe Centrum Bezpieczeństwa Cyberprzestrzeni, NCBC), was appointed for the creation of cyberspace defense forces. Thus, this figure will be responsible for the two key processes of consolidation and development of the capabilities of the Polish Armed Forces. Cyberspace defense forces will be created on the basis of the Cybernetic Operations Center (Centrum Operacji Cybernetycznych), i.e., a place that already brings together the most experienced Polish soldiers who specialize in IT security. A cyber component (Zespół Działań Cyberprzestrzennych, ZDC) of the Territorial Defense Forces is also planned, modeled on the United States National Guard and consisting of about 100 soldiers: 90 per cent of them will be volunteers performing territorial military service and 10 per cent will be professional soldiers (Wojsko Polskie, 2019).

On April 26, 2019, the Director of the National Center for Cyberspace Security signed a Polish–American Cyberspace Defense Cooperation Agreement (U.S. Embassy and Consulate in Poland, April 2019). The objectives of the agreement are the mutual exchange of information on cyber threats, training, education and cyber defense. The basic premise of this cooperation is to work together to develop capabilities concerning coordinated, defensive cyberspace operations. US–European Command's Joint Cyber Center director highlighted that "by establishing the framework for cyber information sharing, a successful attack against one should not equate to a successful attack against many" (U.S. Embassy, 2019).

Cyber incident management

The NIS Directive requires all EU Member States to guarantee a minimum level of national cybersecurity capabilities by establishing competent network and information security authorities as well as teams to respond to computer incidents. Technical cooperation between individual EU countries in the field of cyberspace protection is to take place through the European network of national CSIRTs (Computer Security Incident Response Team).

The National Cybersecurity Act of July 5, 2018 has established three national-level Computer Security Incident Response Teams: CSIRT GOV, CSIRT MON and CSIRT NASK. In accordance with the Act:

- CSIRT GOV (Internal Security Agency, ABW) coordinates the handling of incidents concerning government administration, the National Bank of Poland (Narodowy Bank Polski), the Polish National Development Bank (Bank Gospodarstwa Krajowego) and critical infrastructure operators.
- CSIRT MON (Ministry of Defense, MON) coordinates the handling of incidents concerning entities reporting to the Minister of National Defense, as well as enterprises of particular economic and defense importance. CSIRT MON is also responsible for all incidents related to national defense.

Both CSIRT MON and CSIRT GOV are competent in the event of terrorist incidents:

- CSIRT NASK (Scientific and Academic Computer Network, NASK) is responsible for coordinating incidents involving all other entities, such as the majority of key service operators, digital service providers and local government administration. Incidents can also be reported by ordinary citizens.

These three institutions are to cooperate with each other and the Ministry of Digital Affairs. The Government Plenipotentiary for Cyber Security was made responsible for coordinating the activities of these CSIRTs. The Plenipotentiary should also assess the state of security and develop new solutions based on aggregated data and indicators developed with the participation of these three CSIRTs.

The most important tasks of CSIRT MON, CSIRT NASK and CSIRT GOV include: monitoring cybersecurity threats and incidents at the national level; estimating the risk related to a disclosed cybersecurity threat and any occurring incidents, including dynamic risk analysis; providing information on incidents and risks to entities of the national cybersecurity system; and responding to reported incidents (Art. 26, Ustawa z dnia 5 lipca 2018 r. o krajowym systemie cyberbezpieczeństwa).

Law enforcement authorities and fighting cybercrime

According to the Report on the State of Security in Poland in 2016 (Raport o stanie bezpieczeństwa w Polsce w 2016 roku), cyberspace is an area of activity for individual criminals and organized crime groups as well as extremist and terrorist organizations. In most cases, however, cyberspace does not create a new type of crime, but merely provides new means or methods to conduct criminal activity or is a new space in which such activity is carried out. As has been emphasized, important types of threats in cyberspace include cyber-espionage campaigns. The aim of such campaigns is to obtain sensitive knowledge from ICT systems and networks of specific target groups, e.g., critical infrastructure, government agencies, representatives of powerful or decision-making groups. Information may be used in the context of a political or economic situation. The use of stolen information may additionally result in the unavailability or breach of data infrastructure integrity of the ICT.

To combat cybercrime more effectively, on December 1, 2016, by decision of the police general commandant and the Minister of the Interior and Administration, a specialized Counter Cybercrime Bureau was created at the General Police Headquarters of Poland (Biuro do Walki z Cyberprzestępczością, n.d.). The tasks of the Bureau include in particular:

- Supervising, coordinating and supporting activities aimed at fighting cybercrime carried out by the provincial police headquarters;
- Initiating and cooperating with government administration bodies, courts, prosecutors and state institutions as well as private entities;
- Conducting international cooperation, especially with European Union countries, and Europol;
- Recommending changes in the law in the area of cybersecurity.

The Bureau also carries out the tasks of the point of contact referred to in art. 35 of the Convention on Cybercrime of the Council of Europe.

The number of cases coordinated by the Bureau is growing every year. In 2017, the office coordinated 1,600 cases, while in 2018 there were already 2,183 cases. In 2017, 670 suspects were identified (749 in 2018), of which 82 were arrested (148 in 2018) (Policja, January 2019).

In April 2019 Poland joined the Joint Cybercrime Action Taskforce (J-CAT), which is an international initiative to combat cybercrime (Europol, April 2019). The Taskforce, launched in September 2014, is hosted within Europol's European Cybercrime Centre (EC3) headquarters in The Hague and comprises cyber liaison officers from 15 EU Member States as well as non-EU partners and 17 law enforcement agencies. Its main tasks include prosecuting cybercrime (such as malware, botnets and intrusion) or the people facilitating or mediating such activities (bulletproof hosting, counter-antivirus services, infrastructure leasing and rental, money laundering, including virtual currencies); fighting Internet fraud (online payment systems, carding, social engineering); and online child sexual exploitation (peer-to-peer networks and anonymized access like Darknet networks, live-streaming of child sexual abuse).

Suggested reading

Cerulus, L. (2019, August 29). "POLITICO Pro Cyber Insights: Ericsson in Poland – China's Business Surveillance – Banks and Data," *POLITICO Cyber Insights*. politico.eu/article/politico-pro-cyber-insights-ericsson-in-poland-chinas-business-surveillance-banks-and-data/ur

ENISA. (2017, November 30). "Polish National Cyber Security Strategy." www.enisa.europa.eu/topics/national-cyber-security-strategies/ncss-map/national-cyber-security-strategies-interactive-map/strategies/govermental-program-for-protection-of-cyberspace-for-the-years-2011-2016-2013

Świątkowska, J. (2012). "Cyberthreats as a Challenge to the Security of the Contemporary World," in J. Świątkowska (ed.), *V4 Cooperation in Ensuring Cyber Security – Analysis and Recommendations*. The Kosciuszko Institute, Kraków, Poland. http://pasos.org/wp-content/uploads/2012/08/kosciuszko_institute_v4_cybersec_062012.pdf

Świątkowska, J., Albrycht, I., & Skokowski, D. (2017). *National Cyber Security Organisation: POLAND*. NATO CCDCOE, Tallinn, Estonia. https://ccdcoe.org/uploads/2018/10/NCSO_Poland_2017.pdf

Tumkevič, A. (2016, December). "Cybersecurity in Central Eastern Europe: From Identifying Risks to Countering Threats," *Baltic Journal of Political Science*, *5*: 73–88.

References

Biuro do Walki z Cyberprzestępczością. (n.d.). http://policja.pl/pol/kgp/bwc/33358,Biuro-do-Walki-z-Cyberprzestepczoscia.html

Cyber.mil.pl. (2019, November 14). www.cyber.mil.pl/co-robimy/

Directive on security of network and information systems (NIS Directive). (n.d.). https://ec.europa.eu/digital-single-market/en/network-and-information-security-nis-directive

Doktryna Cyberbezpieczeństwa Rzeczypospolitej Polskiej, Biuro Bezpieczeństwa Narodowego. (2015). https://en.bbn.gov.pl/en/news/400,Cybersecurity-Doctrine-of-the-Republic-of-Poland.html

Ecommerce News Europe. (2019, September 2). https://ecommercenews.eu/ecommerce-in-poland-to-reach-e11-64-billion-in-2019/

E-commerce w Polsce, Gemius dla e-Commerce Polska. (2019). www.gemius.pl/wszystkie-artykuly-aktualnosci/raport-e-commerce.html,E-commerce_w_Polsce_2019.pdf

Europol. (2019, April 9). "Welcome on Board! Poland and Sweden Join the Joint Cybercrime Action Taskforce to Help Fight this Borderless Threat." www.europol.europa.eu/newsroom/news/welcome-board-poland-and-sweden-join-joint-cybercrime-action-taskforce-to-help-fight-borderless-threat

Eurostat. (2019, June). "Digital Economy and Society Statistics – Households and Individuals." https://ec.europa.eu/eurostat/statistics-explained/index.php/Digital_economy_and_society_statistics_-_households_and_individuals#Internet_access

Główny Urząd Statystyczny, Społeczeństwo Informacyjne w Polsce w 2018 r. (2018, October 22). https://stat.gov.pl/obszary-tematyczne/nauka-i-technika-spoleczenstwo-informacyjne/spoleczenstwo-informacyjne/spoleczenstwo-informacyjne-w-polsce-w-2018-roku,2,8.html

Instytut Fizyki Jądowej Polskiej Akademii Nauk. (n.d.). "Początki Internetu w Instytucie Fizyki Jądrowej i w Polsce." https://popul.ifj.edu.pl/historia/36/zobacz.html

Internal Security Agency, Ministry of Administration and Digitisation. (2013, June 25). *Cyberspace Protection Policy of the Republic of Poland.* www.enisa.europa.eu/topics/national-cyber-security-strat egies/ncss-map/copy_of_PO_NCSS.pdf

Komisja Nadzoru Finansowego. (2013, January). "Recommendation D on the Management of Information Technology and ICT Environment Security at Banks." Warsaw, Poland. www.knf.gov. pl/en/MARKET/Regulations_and_practice/Practice/banking_sector/Recommendations_of_th e_PFSA?articleId=44256&p_id=19

Ministerstwo Cyfryzacji. (2017, November 22). "Jakie instytucje odpowiadają za informatyzację?" www. gov.pl/web/cyfryzacja/jakie-instytucje-odpowiadaja-za-informatyzacje

Ministerstwo Cyfryzacji. (2017, November 22). "Katalog cyfrowych usług polskiej administracji." www. gov.pl/web/cyfryzacja/katalog-cyfrowych-uslug-polskiej-administracji

Ministerstwo Cyfryzacji, Rada do Spraw Cyfryzacji. (2019, April 30). www.gov.pl/web/cyfryzacja/rada-do-spraw-cyfryzacji

"National Cybersecurity Policy Framework of the Republic of Poland for 2017–2022." (2017). Ministry of Digital Affairs, Warsaw, Polska. www.enisa.europa.eu/topics/national-cyber-security-strategies/ncss-map/Cybersecuritystrategy_PL.pdf

NASK. (2018, January 18). "Plan Działań Na Rzecz Wdrożenia Krajowych Ram Polityki Cyberbezpieczeństwa Rzeczpospolitej Polskiej na lata 2017–2022." https://cyberpolicy.nask.pl/rb-dokumenty-krajowe-1-plan-dzialan-na-rzecz-wdrozenia-krajowych-ram-polityki-cyberbezpiec zenstwa-rzeczpospolitej-polskiej-na-lata-2017-2022/

NASK. (n.d.). "About NASK." https://eng.nask.pl/en/about-nask/about-nask/250,Research-and-Aca demic-Computer-Network.html

Orange. (2019, August 2). *Historia Internetu w Polsce.* www.orange.pl/poradnik/twoj-internet/historia-internetu-w-polsce/

Policja. (2019, September 1). *Mniej przestępstw kryminalnych, większa skuteczność i wykrywalność. Policja podsumowuje 2018 rok.* www.policja.pl/pol/aktualnosci/168195,Mniej-przestepstw-kryminalnych-wieksza-skutecznosc-i-wykrywalnosc-Policja-podsum.html

Projekt uchwały Rady Ministrów w sprawie Strategii Cyberbezpieczeństwa Rzeczypospolitej Polskiej na lata 2019–2024. (2019). https://mc.bip.gov.pl/projekty-aktow-prawnych-mc/projekt-uchwaly-rady-ministrow-w-sprawie-strategii-cyberbezpieczenstwa-rzeczypospolitej-polskiej-na-lata-2019-2024.html

Raport o stanie bezpieczeństwa w Polsce w 2016 roku, Ministerstwo Spraw Wewnętrznych i Administracji. (2018, August 6). https://archiwumbip.mswia.gov.pl/bip/raport-o-stanie-bezpie/18405,Raport-o-stanie-bezpieczenstwa.html

"Regulation (EU) 2016/679 of the European Parliament and of the Council of 27 April 2016 on the Protection of Natural Persons with Regard to the Processing of Personal Data and on the Free Movement of Such Data, and Repealing Directive 95/46/EC (General Data Protection Regulation)." (2016). https://gdpr-info.eu

Rozporządzenie Rady Ministrów z dnia 7 grudnia 2015 r. w sprawie utworzenia Ministerstwa Cyfryzacji. (2015, December 7). http://prawo.sejm.gov.pl/isap.nsf/DocDetails.xsp?id=WDU 20150002077

Statista. (2019). *E-Commerce in Poland.* www.statista.com/study/59880/e-commerce-in-poland/

Statistics Poland. (2018). *Information Society in Poland. Results of Statistical Surveys in the Years 2014–2018.* Statistical Office in Szczecin, Warsaw, Szczecin, Polska. https://stat.gov.pl/obszary-tematyczne/nauka-i-technika-spoleczenstwo-informacyjne/spoleczenstwo-informacyjne/spoleczenstwo-informa cyjne-w-polsce-wyniki-badan-statystycznych-z-lat-2014-2018,1,12.html

"Strategia Bezpieczeństwa Narodowego Rzeczypospolitej Polskiej." (2015). www.bbn.gov.pl/ftp/SBN per cent20RP.pdf

Świątkowska, J., Albrycht, I., & Skokowski, D. (2018). *National Cyber Security Organisation: POLAND.* NATO CCDCOE, Tallinn, Estonia. https://ccdcoe.org/uploads/2018/10/NCSO_Poland_2017.pdf

U.S. Embassy and Consulate in Poland. (2019, April 26). "U.S., Poland Sign Cyberspace Defense Cooperation Agreement." https://pl.usembassy.gov/cyberspace_agreement/

Ustawa z dnia 5 lipca 2018 r. o krajowym systemie cyberbezpieczeństwa. (2018, July 5). http://prawo. sejm.gov.pl/isap.nsf/DocDetails.xsp?id=WDU20180001560

Wojsko Polskie. (2019, June 10). "WOT zaczyna budowę komponentu 'CYBER'." www.wojsko-pols kie.pl/articles/tym-zyjemy-v/2019-06-102-wot-zaczyna-budowe-komponentu-cyber/

8

HUNGARY'S EVOLVING CYBER SECURITY STRATEGY

Annamária Beláz and Dániel Berzsenyi

Introduction

Hungary is committed to developing cyber space into a free, secure, and innovative environment as a key element of Hungary's drive for economic and social prosperity. The Budapest Convention (The Convention on Cyber Crime of the Council of Europe [CETS No. 185], known as the Budapest Convention) which was adopted in 2001 confirms that Hungary recognized the importance of cyber space in the early stages and acted as pioneer in this field. However, despite this key step, Hungary still took more than a decade to publish its first cyber security strategy.

Based on the ITU Global Cyber Security Index, Hungary, as one of the first adopters of cyber security strategies, ranked 6th on the global ranking and 3rd amongst European countries in 2013 (Boyd & Menting, 2015). Nevertheless, by 2017 (ITU, 2017) these numbers have changed dramatically. Now it ranks only 51st on the global and 24th on the European ranking; however, these numbers can be deceptive.

This chapter offers a review of the intensified Hungarian efforts in the field of cyber security from the beginnings to the present. It describes how the legal, technical, and organizational environment have been changed in the light of the evolving cyber security landscape during the recent years. Whether it be shaping international legislation or a nationwide attack against critical infrastructures, Hungary lost its initial advantage in cyber security as other nation-states and international entities caught up and overtook it.

Statement of national cyber security strategy

At the beginning of 2012, as part of a comprehensive program (called the Magyary Program), Hungary's entire system of strategic planning and control was reshaped. This change was induced by the recognition that the documents adopted earlier were inconsistent regarding their content and therefore difficult to implement. In 2012, Hungary introduced Government Degree 38, which called for the synchronization of strategic content.

The first national cyber security strategy (Government Decision No. 1139/2013 [March 21]; NCSS) was published in 2013. The Hungarian NCSS defines *cyber security* as follows:

> Cyber security is the continuous and planned taking of political, legal, economic, educational, awareness-raising and technical measures to manage risks in cyber space that transforms the cyber space into a reliable environment for the smooth functioning and operation of societal and economic processes by ensuring an acceptable level of risks in cyber space.
>
> *(NCSS, Art. 5.)*

However, it does not conform to the rules of the decree, and the NCSS is not listed as a strategic document. Despite its shortcomings, both from the professional and the public perspectives, NCSS reflects the importance of cyber security. At the same time, the government adopted the very first Hungarian Act on the Electronic Information Security of Central and Local Government Agencies (Act L. of 2013). These steps made Hungary one of the first adopters of cyber security strategies and legislation.

Hungary's cyber security strategy is connected to and coordinated with the national and international legal environment. It conforms to the Constitution (The Fundamental Law of Hungary (April 25, 2011)), the Budapest Convention, the EU Cyber security Strategy (EU Document 52013JC0001), and the NATO Strategic Concept (Strategic Concept for the Defense and Security of The Members of the North Atlantic Treaty Organization, November 19, 2010). In accordance with the Hungarian National Security Strategy (Government Decision No. 1035/2012 [February 21]) the NCSS elaborates the government efforts and responsibility laid down in Section 31 thereof.

The main objectives of the strategy are to build efficient response capabilities, create a secure environment for national data assets, meet the international requirements and standards, improve cyber security education, and provide a secure cyber space for future generations. The document highlights challenges emerging in cyber space, such as illegal acquisition of information and critical data, disruption of communication and information systems, information warfare, deficiencies in the operational security of information and telecommunication systems, and the new technologies like cloud computing and mobile internet are also identified as security risks. The NCSS mandates a comprehensive approach which includes stakeholders from governmental and non-governmental bodies, military, law-enforcement and civil sector, as well as national and international, economic, and political entities.

Although the original goal of the strategy planners was to provide clear and synchronized responsibilities in the field of national cyber security (Suba, 2014: 112), this goal was not reached. On the operational level the NCSS lacks the SMART elements (*Specific, Measurable, Achievable, Realistic, Timely*) which should create the criteria system and explicit guidance in the implementation process, for the relevant public and private stakeholders. Another weakness of the Hungarian NCSS is the lack of a thorough assessment of the cyber security environment. The strategy highlights a few challenges but fails to provide detailed description on the potential cyber threats affecting Hungary. The NCSS does not consider the implications of spying or terrorism in the cyber domain, nor does it recommend mitigation strategies. The details of educational and awareness raising programs and tools are also missing and the strategy does not explain the vision of the Hungarian government about international cooperation and information sharing, though these are critical details. The concept of cooperation between the government and private sector, including in the areas of research and development, is vague or unspecified.

In 2014 the draft version of the National Cyber Security Action Plan (NCSAP) was finalized by a dedicated working group and the document covered several important issues like the coordination of activities at the operational level, handling international cyber cooperation, management of research and development, and details on cyber education improvements (Kovács & Szentgáli, 2015: 6). The NCSAP has not yet been officially adopted by the government and its content is not publicly available.

By the end of 2016, the unclear vision of the NCSS, the missing action plan, and other shortcomings together with the new directive on network and information systems of the European Union (NIS Directive) led to the idea of a new cyber security strategy. At the beginning of 2017 a working group called the Information Security Strategic Committee was set up to create a new cyber security strategy. This effort focused on addressing the gaps in the previous strategy, as well as bringing it in line with international requirements, with the goal to lay down the basis of a new cyber security strategy. The main goal of the strategy planners was to correct the mistakes of the NCSS and bring the new strategy closer to the international requirements. The new strategy would have focused on the creation of a free, secure, and innovative cyber space; improvement of Hungary's cyber competitiveness; adoption of new technologies securely in the public and private sector; and raising awareness.

However, for unclear reasons, at the end of 2018 the legislators chose to keep the 2013 NCSS in force, and a new sectoral strategy has been adopted on network and infrastructure protection (Government Decree No. 838/2018. [XII. 28.]). This document details the strategic steps Hungary intends to take in order to implement the NIS Directive and the European Cyber Security Strategy. NIPS will be in force until 2022 and a detailed Action Plan will include the timespan of the actions, the necessary resources, and the stakeholders responsible for the different elements of the implementation.

The definitional landscape

The term of cyber security has been formed to determine the correlation between cyber space and security. This term is now widely used by consultants, analysts, lobbyists, and politicians. At this point, numerous questions could be raised regarding the meaning and usage of the term or even regarding the processes, tools, and users. The establishment of the conceptual framework of cyber security is also facing difficulties by the increasing popularity of the term in the media, where the term is used in a general, simplified form for every event concerning the malicious use of computers.

Regarding cyber security we can find other terms defined in different legal documents. These are the following:

- The formerly mentioned Act. L. explains the term of *cyber defense* as protection against the threats coming from the cyber space including the preservation of own cyber capabilities.
- *Cyber space* is also defined by the Act: Cyber space means the collective of societal and economic processes projected in the format of data and information through globally connected, decentralized, continuously growing electronic information systems and the systems themselves. The Ministry of Defense released the Professional Concept of Cyber Defense for the Military of Hungary (Ministry of Defense command No. 60/2013. [IX. 30.]; CoCD) which define the cyber space as a dynamically variable range that can be determined using electromagnetic spectrum and serves to handle data between interconnected networks, devices and additional physical infrastructures.
- A related specific term is the *Hungarian cyber space* that is defined in both the NCSS and the Act L. as:

The Hungarian cyber space includes the parts of the electronic information systems of the global cyber space which are located in Hungary, as well as the societal and economic processes appearing in and through the electronic systems of the global cyber space in the form of data and information that take place in, are directed to, or affect Hungary.

The CoCD includes several cyber related definitions and the terminology does not reflect a single military approach but rather makes the impression of a general policy mindset. Therefore, it is worth highlighting some definitions:

Cyber security: the state in which tools, policies, risk management approaches, operations, trainings, best practices, security procedures, and technologies for cyber space are applied.

Cyber threat: the unpredictable, constantly changing set of technologically, politically, personally, or by other means motivated malicious acts from cyber space.

Cyber attack: attack from the cyber space with the purpose to interrupt, disconnect, destroy, or acquire the right of custody of an information environment or infrastructure; destroy the integrity of the data being processed or obtain supervised data.

Cyber defense: the use of security measures designed to create cyber security of critical information infrastructure elements that may be targets of cyber-attacks to interrupt, terminate, or restrict their services or cause data breach. The most important tasks of protection are prevention, detection, analysis, evaluation, response, recovery, and service improvement.

Cyber terrorism cannot be found in the legal documents and there is no generally accepted definition in the professional literature. Although, the national Criminal Code states, that any person who commits a violent crime against the persons or commits a criminal offense that endangers the public or involves the use of arms in order to breach information system or data or compromise the integrity of the computer protection system/device is an act of terrorism. (Act. C of 2012 on the Criminal Code Art. 314 section i.)

International law

Hungary maintains the applicability of domestic law to the Hungarian cyber space. That is, Hungary claims sovereignty in cyber space, defining the term Hungarian cyber space in both the NCSS and the Act L. as mentioned above. The Fundamental Law of Hungary acknowledges the right to freedom of expression and defends freedom and diversity of the press, though Hungary regards the internet as part of its territory and holds the authority to control the flow of information and regulate speech on the internet if necessary. The Defense Act (Act CXIII. of 2011) regulates the measures which can be implemented in special legal order. Although there is no recent history of terrorism, in a terrorist emergency the government has the following powers to limit the social and political freedoms:

• The journalist, the correspondent, and the producer of press products can only use the information provided by authorized bodies, official spokesperson, or the public service media.
• Media products can be scrutinized and censored before their publication.
• The government may order the suspension, limitation, or control of postal and electronic communications services and IT networks.

At the same time, Hungary is looking forward and contributing to different initiatives in relation to international law and cyber issues.

The Budapest Convention on cyber-crime is the first international treaty on crimes committed through computer systems and networks. The treaty focuses on copyright infringements, computer related frauds, child pornography, and hate crimes while specific procedures and powers are defined for the search of computer networks and lawful interception. Hungary is a sponsoring nation of the NATO Cooperative Cyber Defense Centre of Excellence (NATO CCDCOE) that is dedicated to support its member nations and NATO in the field of international law of cyber operations among others. Hungary's memberships and roles in international organizations determine further compliance with international regulations such as the EU's NIS Directive and the GDPR, or the decisions adopted by the Permanent Council of the OSCE. This shows that Hungary has a supportive attitude towards the issues of international cyber law, but in the current stage, the rule of domestic law regarding cyber affairs is dominant.

International governance

NIS Cooperation Group and NLO Network

Given that Hungary has been a member state (MS) of the EU since 2004, international cooperation is crucial. Owing to the adoption of the NIS Directive, in 2016 an EU-level Cooperation Group was set up with the aim of improving cross-border exchange of information and trust building.

Hungary also participates in the National Liaison Officers Network, a statutory board of ENISA composed of representatives of all MSs. The Network facilitates the exchange of information between ENISA and the MSs, and supports ENISA in disseminating its activities, findings, and recommendations to the relevant stakeholders across the Union.

Central European Cyber Security Platform (CECSP)

The CECSP, established in 2013, is a regional-level strategic and operational cooperation of the four Visegrád countries and Austria. The platform's core purpose is to help collaborate, gather good practices, exchange experiences, and share know-how to ameliorate cyber security defense and resilience capabilities through regional cooperation. To achieve these goals, members of the Platform hold regular cyber security exercises as well as strategic and technical meetings.

The Meridian Process

Established in 2005, the Meridian Process aims to exchange ideas and initiate actions for the cooperation of governmental bodies on Critical Information Infrastructure Protection (CIIP) issues globally. It explores the benefits and opportunities of cooperation between governments and provides an opportunity to share best practices from around the world by creating a community of senior government policymakers in CIIP. Hungary represented by the Special Service for National Security has also participated in the Meridian Process initiative since 2005.

Global Forum on Cyber Expertise (GFCE)

The Global Forum on Cyber Expertise is a global platform for nations, international organizations, and private companies to exchange best practices and expertise on cyber capacity building. The aim is to identify successful policies, practices, and ideas and multiply these on a global level. The GFCE members and partners developed several practical initiatives to build cyber capacity; among these Hungary initiated, together with the Netherlands and Romania, the GFCE initiative for "Coordinated Vulnerability Disclosure" (Ethical Hacking) in 2016.

Hungary's cultural understandings

Regarding the cultural understanding of cyber space Hungary, as part of the EU, perceives privacy issues serious and applies the relevant national and international regulations accordingly. Hungary supported the suspension and termination of the Safe Harbor Act after the NSA surveillance scandals and fostered the EU's GDPR as well. The National Authority for Data Protection and Freedom of Information was among the first national level authorities that started to implement and enforce the GDPR rules with fines.

From this perspective, privacy protection in Hungary seems strong and healthy but "several privacy and digital rights organizations say the Hungarian authorities have purchased potentially invasive surveillance technologies over the past few years" (Freedom House, 2018). This is underpinned by the reports of the Canadian Citizenlab and the Wikileaks that uncovered a Finfisher command and control server in Hungary which is known as a governmental surveillance software package (Bodoky, 2013). Other resources reported that the Hungarian authorities have installed black boxes allowing them direct access to ISP networks and encrypted communication, however it is unclear how the access rights of the authorized intelligence agencies can be enforced in the case of end-to-end encryption.

In Hungary cyber space is considered as an innovative environment not just from the perspective of economic and social prosperity but from the aspect of intelligence and national security as well. Hungary has three classic security services and at least three additional special services that have various rights in cyber space to use surveillance technologies.

As the surveillance activities of the Hungarian National Security Services (NSS) fall under the scope of the Privacy Act, all remedies and redress mechanisms provided by the Act should be applicable to the surveillance activities of the NSS. In theory, every person concerned should have the right to access information on whether or not he/she was subject to surveillance, which body or organization conducted the surveillance operation, and for what purpose, though the general director of the national security services may deny the request to disclose information about the surveillance operation.

Hungary's institutions

Information systems and their management always required a level of central coordination. During the past decades, this task was dedicated to committees, individual organizations, and ministries showcasing the importance of the subject for the governing forces.

As computers appeared in personal use, the Ministry of the Interior and the Central Statistical Office were in charge of the regulation and management of information systems in Hungary. After the regime change, as the information security became a subject of interest the Statistical Office lost its regulating tasks. This led to the creation of the Information Society Interparliamentary Committee (ISIC) governed by the Prime Minister's Office between 1992 and 1998.

Around the millennium, ISIC became an institution called the Governmental Information and Social Relations Office and worked together with the Ministry of Informatics and Communications until 2006. In 2007 the Government appointed the Public Administration IT Committee with the mission to create organizational and technological recommendations to sustain a high level of information security.

Between 2010 and 2018 information technology and cyber security related issues were divided among the following institutions:

- Ministry of National Development Deputy State Secretary for Infocommunication;
- Ministry of Defence Deputy State Secretary for Defence Policy and Planning;
- Ministry of Foreign Affairs and Trade Minister of State for Security Policy and International Cooperation; and
- Ministry of Interior Deputy State Secretary for Informatics.

After the 2018 elections the overall management of cyber-related issues was transferred to the newly established Ministry for Innovation and Technology, though the Ministry of Defense and the Ministry of Interior still share an important role in questions connected to security.

The Ministry of Interior supervise the Special Service for National Security and its directorate the National Cyber Security Center (NCSC). The NCSC is responsible for the national incident management, security, and vulnerability assessment of public institutions and critical infrastructures. The organization also acts as the single point of contact on the security of network and information systems and is responsible for ensuring cross-border cooperation with the Member States and with the NIS Cooperation Group in the EU.

The strategic components of the organizational system are: (1) the National Cyber Coordination Council tasked with facilitating the coordination and monitoring of governmental implementation of the NCSS; (2) the Cyber Security Forum, established to channel private sector expertise into government decision-making; and (3) the cyber coordinator responsible for the professional coordination of the Forum. The Council's coordination activities and the implementation of its decisions are supported by sectoral and functional cyber security working groups, such as:

1 incident management;
2 internal security;
3 e-government;
4 energy;
5 child protection.

The role of the private sector

In Hungary, there are several multinational companies with which the State has signed a strategic cooperation agreement. The purpose of the partnership is the promotion of the investment of companies established in Hungary, an increase in employment, implementation of production of higher added value, integration of companies in vocational training, and the development of stronger ties with domestic suppliers.

Strategic partners from the ICT sector include: IBM, Microsoft, Huawei Technologies, Nokia Siemens Networks, IT Services Hungary, Samsung Electronics, Hewlett-Packard, Oracle, SAP, and General Electric. These partners are participating actively in the legislative process and in the working groups affecting Hungary's competitiveness in the ICT sector. SMEs are usually involved in the policy making by the means of different associations. ICT Association of Hungary is one of the main sectorial associations.

The Cyber Security Forum was established by the Government decree (Government Decree No. 484/2013 [XII.17.]) connected to Act L. with the aim to unite professional leaders from the private sector, civil organizations, cyber security scholars, and researchers to contribute to the work of the policy makers with suggestions and comments on cyber security legislation. One of the main areas of cooperation is 5G development. In the Hungarian context the best solution for deploying 5G is the mixed model, in which state and market players equally participate to create the best possible outcome. A 5G Coalition was established in 2017; the number of member organizations is currently 73, and 155 professionals participate in its working groups. The seven-member Presidency of the Coalition consists of senior leaders from the government, private sector, and academia.

The role of the legislature

In Hungary, until the mid-1990s, the average citizen seldom encountered the problem of information security. During the 1980s IT security was a trending issue internationally, however, in Hungary this topic slowly emerged into the political thinking only after the 1989 political transition. During this period, high-priority documents (such as Parliamentary resolution 94/1998 (XII. 29.) and Government Decision 2073/2004 (IV. 15.)), which established the country's security, identified no threats from cyber space. In the following 20 years, international recommendations and sectorial decrees were adopted and just a few laws were enacted on high priority areas (such as data protection, electronic signatures, electronic communication and media, electronic administration, and critical infrastructure protection).

With the constitutional reform in 2010 a new era started in Hungarian legislation with a clearly visible change on the viewpoint regarding cyber security. Cardinal laws on the protection of classified information (Act CLV. of 2009), privacy (Act CXII. of 2011), press and media (Act CIV. of 2010), general law on electronic administration (Act CCXXII. of 2015), information security (Act L. of 2013), and critical infrastructure protection (Act CXXVIII. of 2011) were adopted together with detailed sectorial decrees and the National Cyber Security Strategy. Nowadays, as the result of the new EU regulations the above-mentioned documents are subject to a complete revision.

Intellectual property (IP)

Intellectual property regulations date back to the early nineteenth century, when the famous scholar Ferenc Toldy (also known as Franz Karl Joseph Schedel) published two articles of outstanding importance (Schedel, 1838, 1840) to draw attention to the missing regulations related to copyright questions. In the following decades, due to the existence of the Austro-Hungarian Empire, the Hungarian regulation of IP continuously developed following the Austrian patterns. The Hungarian Intellectual Property Office was established more than 120 years ago on March 1, 1896 under the name of the Hungarian Royal Patent Office.

The extensive legislation of IP has taken place over the past 15 to 20 years, thanks to the World Trade Organization (WTO) where in the 1990s peripheral IP issues became a central question in international trade policy. New, more stringent requirements for the privatization and commercialization of IP have been expressed worldwide in the TRIPS Agreement (Act IX. of 1998, Annex 1/c). The current legal framework is in coherence with the EU regulation and international laws (Act LXIX. of 2015, Directive 2004/48/EC of the European Parliament and of the Council) and contains more than sixty laws and decrees on patent, plant variety protection, utility model protection, trademark, geographical indication, design, copyright, and related rights.

Cyber warfare

Cyber defense is dealt with in two paragraphs of the Warsaw Summit Communiqué (Issued by NATO, Warsaw, July 8–9, 2016), paragraphs 70 and 71. In these, the heads of state and government "reaffirm NATO's defensive mandate, and recognize cyber space as a domain of operations in which NATO must defend itself as effectively as it does in the air, on land, and at sea." Since cyber space was defined as a domain of operations, cyber defense and cyber operations are included in Hungary's National Security Strategy (Government Decree No. 1035/2012 (II. 21); HNSS) and Hungary's National Military Strategy (Government Decree No. 1656/2012 (XII. 20.); HNMS).

Although there is no explicit law on cyber warfare the HNMS states:

> The meaning of the concepts of war and attack have broadened, because the emerging asymmetrical challenges non-lethal in nature, and not linked to conventional weapons, are capable of inducing enormous material damage and chaos. Depending on the damage caused, a non-armed attack may be considered equal to an armed assault. Such threats are constituted primarily by cyber-warfare whose potential in its capability of creating material damages and obstructing public order is hardly less in significance than that of conventional weapons.

> Access to and use of cyber space constitute new challenges and potential sources of danger. The increasing number and potential damage caused by attacks against computer networks is especially threatening. The characteristics of cyber threats which are different from those of conventional threats necessitate a comprehensive review and possible amendment of our concepts of war.

To tackle the threats arising from cyber space in addition to strengthening the protection of the critical national information infrastructure, Hungary strives to enhance the security of information systems and to participate in the development of appropriate levels of cyber defense in cooperation with allies and fellow EU-members.

Cyber crime and cyber terrorism

The National Security Strategy of Hungary includes Section 31 which is dedicated to cybersecurity. The document states that there is an increased threat against the infrastructures of developed countries as other states, non-state actors (NSAs), or even terrorist groups can disrupt their proper functioning. The tasks are specified alongside the protection of the critical infrastructures and the international cooperation opportunities. The

Hungarian National Crime Prevention Strategy is in force until 2023. The document states that it is in alignment with the specific cybersecurity policies and focuses on the secure use of the Internet especially for youngsters. On the level of cybercrime counter activities and penalties, the Criminal Code of Hungary applies six different categories:

- Fraud using an information system;
- Prohibited data acquisition;
- Information system or data breach;
- Circumvention of the technical security measures of an information system;
- Copyright infringement;
- Circumvention of a protective measure.

Regarding law enforcement, there is an organization called the Intervention Police which is the superior body of the National Bureau of Investigation (NBI, established by the Ministry of Interior Decree No. 15/1994 (VII. 14.)). NBI has responsibilities in the field of cybercrimes with its High Technology Crime Unit and in the field of terrorist activities as well as its Unit for Combating Terrorism and Extremism. When a cybercrime or a terrorist activity violates the critical infrastructures or the national security, the Constitution Protection Office (counterintelligence) takes the responsibility to prevent, detect, and mitigate the homeland threat. Similar tasks are dedicated to the Information Office, which is another civilian intelligence agency responsible for non-military intelligence-gathering operations, primarily abroad. For all cases combating cyber terrorism Hungary has a dedicated Counter Terrorism Centre and a Counter-Terrorism Information and Crime Analysis Centre. In accordance with the applicable law the latter two authorities are in charge of counter-terrorism operations independently of their physical or cyber nature.

Societal implications

With respect to the definitions in the second subheading, Hungary as a state has never been a target of any cyberterrorist attack, though cyber-criminal incidents occur every day. During the last twelve months, in the course of the public sector organizations' auditing process, the National Cyber Security Center has uncovered a number of Cross-Site Scripting, SQL injection, Cross-Site Request Forgery, and input validation errors. According to the critical results, application developers face challenges in secure software development. Government websites were defaced or services were unavailable due to DOS attacks. These attacks usually generate high public interest and extensive media coverage.

In order to counter the threats and raise awareness several governmental programs are currently running under the ICT development umbrella project called "Digital Success Program" (more information is available at: https://digitalisjoletprogram.hu). These projects cover a wide range of society; all of the current programs share the same goal: secure digital development. The key programs are the following:

1 Digital Child Protection: Online safety and security of children is of significant import-ance. A peer-to-peer training system operates whereby the benefits and risks of using the Internet will be presented to children by their peers as part of more robust training program.
2 Digital Competence Building. The goal is the development of the national digital com-petence framework based on the current EU Citizens' Digital Competence Framework.

Named as DigKomp, the Hungarian system serves as a reference framework, but also as a unified system that will enable the definition, development, measurement, and evaluation of digital competence, as well as its validation and state recognition.

3   Digital Start-up Development: Aims to support the creation and development of innovative start-ups with high growth potential.

4   Smart Cities: The smart city concept and institutional system should be an integral part of the Hungarian public administration, primarily in the local and regional administrative procedures and regulation.

5   Digital Security: Capacity building for securing Hungarian cyberspace, and development of the information security/cyber security education and training concepts.

Conclusion

As an early adopter, Hungary has a long road behind it in the field of cyber legislation and strategy creation. The institutional structure responsible for cyber defense and security is well established and prospering. At the same time the competent organizations are fragmented, the extent of their authority is not always clearly defined, and the borders are sometimes blurred.

There is an ongoing process to close the gaps and make the organizational structure more unified. As most of the affected authorities are under the control of the Ministry of Interior, with clear political goals and ambitions the process can succeed, however from the perspective of administrative steps it can be a long-lasting transformation of the governmental cyber security institutions.

In the private sector Hungary is already hosting high-tech, world-leading cyber related solutions and services, but these are mostly connected to the presence of multinational companies with their shared service centers (SSC). As the cyber workforce is well trained and the salaries are among the lowest in the CEE region, during the next few years the biggest challenge for the nation will be to stop the brain drain in the field of cyber security. This challenge will be followed closely by the fast-growing demand for cyber security experts combined with the growing cyber security skills gap. To fight against these trends the only option for Hungary is to increase and improve the cyber security training and education at all levels as soon as it is possible.

Suggested reading

Cyber Threat Report, CEE. (2018). https://report.cybersechub.eu

Feledy, B. (2017, November 30). "Parallel Competences: The State of Cyber Security in V4." https://visegradinsight.eu/parallel-competences-the-state-of-cyber-security-in-the-v4/

Kovács, L., Nemeslaki, A., Orbók, K. & Szabó, A. (2017). "Structuration Theory and Strategic Alignment in Information Security Management: Introduction of a Comprehensive Research Approach and Program," *AARMS*, 16(1): 5–16.

Marek, G. (2018). "The Cybersecurity Strategy of the Visegrad Group Countries," *Politics in Central Europe*, 14(2): 75–98.

Parti, G., Kiss, T. & Koplányi, G. (2018). "Architecture of Aggression in Cyberspace: Testing Cyber Aggression in Young Adults in Hungary," *International Journal of Cybersecurity Intelligence & Cybercrime*, 1(1): 56–68.

Szádeczky, T. (2015). "Information Security Law and Strategy in Hungary," *AARMS*, 14(4): 281–289.

Török, S. (2012). "Hungarian Experiences in the Light of Cyber Attacks in 2011," *Hadmérnök*, 7(2): 342–350.

Tumkevič, A. (2016). "Cybersecurity in Central Eastern Europe: From Identifying Risks to Countering Threats," *Baltic Journal of Political Science, 5*: 73–88.

References

Act C. of 2012 on the Criminal Code §314 i.

Act CXIII. of 2011 on the Home Defense and on the Hungarian Defense Forces, and on the Measures to Implement in Special Legal Orders.

Act CLV. of 2009 on the Protection of Classified Information.

Act CXII. of 2011 on Informational Self- Determination and Freedom of Information.

Act CIV. of 2010 on the Freedom of the Press and the Fundamental Rules of Media Content.

Act CCXXII. of 2015 on the General Rules of Electronic Administration and Trust Services.

Act CXXVIII. of 2011 on Disaster Management.

Act IX. of 1998, Annex 1.c on "TRIPS = Agreement on Trade-Related Aspects of Intellectual Property Rights."

Act L. of 2013 on the Electronic Information Security of Central and Local Government Agencies.

Act LXIX. Of 2015 "Agreement on the Visegrad Patent Institute."

Active Engagement, Modern Defence: "Strategic Concept for the Defence and Security of The Members of the North Atlantic Treaty Organisation" Adopted by Heads of State and Government in Lisbon, November 19, 2010.

Bodoky, T. (2013). "Nem csak az USA szeme lát mindent." https://atlatszo.hu/2013/09/16/nem-csak-az-usa-szeme-lat-mindent-kormanyzati-kemprogram-magyarorszagon/

Boyd, A. & Menting, M. (2015). "Global Cyber Security Index & Cyberwellness Profiles 2015 Report," International Telecommunication Union. www.itu.int/pub/D-STR-SECU-2015

Directive 2004/48/EC of the European Parliament and of the Council of 29 April 2004 on the Enforcement of Intellectual Property Rights.

"Government Decision No. 1139/2013 (21 March) on the National Cyber Security Strategy of Hungary".

"Government Decree No. 38/2012 (12 March) on Strategic Management by the Government."

Government Decree No. 484/2013 (XII.17.) on the Rules of the Establishment and Management, as well as the Functions and Competence of the National Cyber Security Coordination Council, the Cyber security Forum and the Specialized Cyber Security Working Groups.

Government Decree 1035/2012. (II. 21) on Hungary's National Security Strategy.

Government Decree 1656/2012 (XII. 20.) on Hungary's National Military Strategy.

International Telecommunications Union, Global Cyber security Index. (2017). www.itu.int/dms_pub/itu-d/opb/str/D-STR-GCI.01-2017-PDF-E.pdf

Joint Communication to The European Parliament, The Council, The European Economic and Social Committee and The Committee of The Regions: Cyber security Strategy of the European Union: An Open, Safe and Secure Cyber Space – Document 52013JC0001.

Kovács, L. & Szentgáli, G. (2015). "*National Cyber Security Organization: Hungary*," NATO CCDCOE, Tallinn, Estonia. https://ccdcoe.org/uploads/2018/10/CS_organisation_HUNGARY_2015-10-12.pdf

"Magyar Honvédség Kibervédelmi Szakmai Koncepciója értelmében (60/2013). (IX. 30.) HM utasítás".

Schedel, F. (1838). "Néhány szó az írói tulajdonról, 's kérelem a' folyóiratok' kiadóihoz," *Athenaeum* 2. 1838/45. I., 705–717.

Schedel, F. (1840). "Az írói tulajdonról," *Budapesti Szemle* 1840/1, 157–237.

Suba, F. (2014). "Nemzeti Kiberbiztonsági Stratégia," in I. Dobák (ed.), *A nemzetbiztonság általános elmélete* (pp. 110–115). Nemzeti Közszolgálati Egyetem, Budapest, Hungary.

The Convention on Cyber Crime of the Council of Europe (CETS No.185).

The Fundamental Law of Hungary (25 April 2011), 838/2018. (XII. 28.) Government Decree on Hungary's Network and Infrastructure Protection Strategy.

Warsaw Summit Communiqué Issued by the Heads of State and Government participating in the meeting of the North Atlantic Council in Warsaw 8–9 July 2016.

9

ROMANIAN CYBERSECURITY EFFORTS

A work in progress

Oana-Elena Brânda

Introduction

One of the main challenges to states in the provision of cybersecurity is the speed at which new threats and risks materialize – often one step ahead of the legislation and institutional procedures meant to keep cyberthreats at bay. In a nation like Romania, where legislation needs to be coordinated through the EU process, states may find themselves working especially hard to keep up with new risks and challenges.

On an EU level, other than the General Data Protection Regulation (which deals with user privacy and the protection of personal data), the most significant piece of cybersecurity legislation is the NIS Directive on the security of network and information systems, which is a considerable part of the EU Cybersecurity Strategy. As an EU member since 2007, Romania is bound to transpose all EU legislation domestically and make the appropriate changes. Cybersecurity makes no exception in that regard, given the fact that unlike classical threats which require already established defense mechanisms, cyber-related threats demand constant adaptation of response mechanisms, as well as technological innovation, allocation of large sums of money, and clear-cut legislation that would tackle the threat at hand and possibly neutralize it at the source.

Although cyberthreats have been manifesting ever since processes like banking, transportation, water, healthcare, and industrial infrastructure came to be heavily internet dependent, Romania's cybersecurity capacity could be easily qualified as a long-term "work in progress." Thus, an investigation of Romanian cybersecurity efforts focusses on the following aspects: legislation and institutional framework, threats, and efforts made towards countering these threats.

Romanian legislation on cybersecurity

Romanian legislators have struggled to create definitions and frameworks of action that will be meaningful and accurate over the long term, despite the fast evolution of threats in this area. Such a rapid evolution turns the field into an unpredictable one; however, states (and in this case, Romania) need to be on their toes to immediately identify, react, and neutralize the threat.

Legislation has thus been two-fold: one part seeks to define terms related to cybersecurity and to establish appropriate infrastructure, while the other part is more responsive to specific cyberthreats as they have evolved. Overarching legislation thus comprises the following documents: Emergency Ordinance 98/2010 on the Identification, Designation and Protection of Critical Infrastructure and Law No. 182 on the Protection of Classified Information 2002, which requires specifically that any information pertaining to national defense and security, critical infrastructures, and foreign policy aspects be classified. The latter establishes levels of risk classification for each type of information received and classified (Parlamentul României, 2012).

The second set of applied legislative measures describes specific threats and establishes responses to them. There is a complex group of legislation providing the necessary means to combat. This group comprises the following: the Romanian National Defense Strategy for 2015–2019, the Romanian Cybersecurity Strategy, issued in 2013, in addition to Law No. 677/2001 on the Protection of Individuals with Regard to the Processing of Personal Data and the Free Movement of Such Data, and Law No. 506/2004 on the Processing of Personal Data and the Protection of Private Life within the electronic Communications Sector. Apart from these, there is the project of a Law on Cybersecurity, which has not yet been passed by Parliament.

Cyberthreats are viewed as major threats to national security, as defined by the National Defense Strategy 2015–2019 and the Romanian Cybersecurity Strategy of 2013. The National Defense Strategy 2015–2019, "A Strong Romania within Europe and the World" mentions cyber-attacks among the medium- and long-term evolutions affecting the security environment (Romania, The Presidential Administration, 2015: 11). Furthermore, cyberthreats are mentioned in Chapter III "Threats, risks, and vulnerabilities," subsection 3.1., as follows:

> The cyberthreats initiated by hostile entities, state or non-state, upon informational infrastructures posing strategic interest of the public institutions and companies, the cyber-attacks performed by cybercrime groups or the extremist cyber-attacks initiated by hackers alter directly Romania's national security.
> *(Romania, The Presidential Administration, 2015: 14–15)*

The same document provides the means to counteract such threats, which fall within the intelligence, counterintelligence, and security dimension, where lines of action are aimed at: "ensuring mechanisms to prevent and counteract cyberattacks targeting informational infrastructures of strategic interest, associated with promotion of national interests in the field of cybersecurity" (Romania, The Presidential Administration, 2015: 19–20). The presence of such elements within the Strategy highlights the degree of awareness existing among Romanian security and defense authorities, whose efforts are focused on counteracting and providing a legal framework of action against them.

A more proactive approach towards dealing with cyberthreats is made by the Romanian Cybersecurity Strategy, issued as a result of the Decision of the Supreme Council of National Defense No 16/2013 and Government Decision No.271/2013. This document establishes the conceptual, organizational, and action framework necessary for the provision of cybersecurity within Romania. The document also refers to the protection of cyber infrastructure in alignment with existing NATO and EU regulations. This document is critical due to the definitions it provides on "cybersecurity" and the emerging threats. Thus, cybersecurity is defined as:

normality resulting from the application of a set of proactive and reactive measures that ensure the confidentiality, integrity, availability, authenticity and non-repudiation in electronic information, resources and public or private services, in cyberspace. Proactive and reactive measures may include political, concepts, standards and guidelines for security, risk management, and training awareness activities, implement engineering solutions to protect cyber infrastructure, management identity and management consequence.

(Guvernul României, 2013: 3)

This document separates out cyberdefense from cybersecurity, noting that cyberdefense refers to "actions taken in cyberspace to protect, monitor, detect, counter aggression and ensure appropriate response against specific cyberthreats to national defense infrastructure" (Guvernul României, 2013: 3).

The Romanian Cybersecurity Strategy also differentiates between types of cyber aggression, placing them into categories such as: "cyber threat" (circumstance or event which constitutes a potential danger to cybersecurity) (Guvernul României, 2013: 3); "cyberattack" (hostile action in cyberspace held to affect cybernetics security) (Guvernul României, 2013: 3); "cyber incident" (event occurred in the cyberspace, whose consequences affect cybersecurity) (Guvernul României, 2013: 3); "cyber terrorism" (premeditated activities carried out in cyberspace by individuals, politically motivated groups or organizations, ideological or religious which may cause damage materials or victims, likely to cause panic or terror) (Guvernul României, 2013: 3); and "cybercrime" (all facts under criminal law or other special laws which constitute a social threat and are committed with guilt, through cyber infrastructure) (Guvernul României, 2013: 3). This differentiation is highly necessary as depending on the targeted infrastructure sector (energy, water, banking, healthcare, and national defense, to name a few) an act of cyber aggression could be easily transferred from one category to another. Here, moving on the incident–threat–terrorism axis is likely to impose different reaction mechanisms, made to render the respective aggression ineffective.

The main objective of the Strategy has been the creation of an integrated system – the National System of Cybersecurity (NSCS), which is the main body intended to supervise "the coherent implementation of all prevention and reaction measures to cyber-attacks against public institutions and private companies, and which reunites public authorities and institutions having responsibilities and capabilities in the field" (Ministerul Afacerilor Externe, 2019). Thus, NSCS is the platform for cooperation and harmonization of existing Romanian cyber capabilities. The NSCS has three main components: knowledge, prevention, and countering and it aims to combine different levels of interaction: military–civilian, public–private, and governmental–non-governmental. However, despite the multi-directionality and interdependence of the needed interaction, some of these levels have not yet been reached, as is the case of the public–private partnerships towards countering cyber aggressions.

Currently, Romania does not have a law on cybersecurity. Such an attempt was undertaken in 2014, with a project drafted and presented to Parliament. However, it was rejected due to the unconstitutionality objections raised towards it and accepted by the Romanian Constitutional Court Decision No. 17/21 January 2015, published in the Official Monitor No. 79 of 30th January 2015. The Romanian Constitutional Court claimed that the project infringed upon one's intimacy as well as one's private and family life and the confidentiality of correspondence (Badea, 2016). Although the project remained in limbo, and is currently off the agenda of the Ministry of Communication and Information Society, it was a noteworthy attempt to further enhance the existing framework of cybersecurity. Apart from the definitions it provided on the matter, the law enhanced in Art. 1 (2) the fact that "cybersecurity is a component of Romanian national security" (Camera Deputaților din România, 2014). Furthermore, it highlighted the fact that in order to provide effective means of control, the National System of Cybersecurity needs to establish cooperation between public institutions and authorities in the field, the private sector, academia, professional associations, and NGOs (Camera Deputaților din România, 2014).

Institutions and efforts towards countering cyberthreats

A plethora of public institutions have been engaged in the functioning of the National System of Cybersecurity (NSCS). Thus, the Supreme Council of National Defense is the authority coordinating on a strategic level the activity of the NSCS. The Romanian Government, through the Ministry of Communication and Information Society, focuses on the coordination of public authorities in order to achieve coherence among policies and the profound implementation of governmental strategies in the field (Ministerul Afacerilor Externe, 2019).

The NSCS comprises the following institutions: the Romanian Intelligence Service, Ministry of National Defense, Ministry of Internal Affairs, Ministry of Foreign Affairs, Ministry of Communication and Information Society, Special Communications Service, Foreign Intelligence Service, Protection and Guard Service, National Registry Office for Classified Information, as well as NGOs, professional associations, and companies.

Another institution dealing with cybersecurity is the Operative Council on Cybersecurity (OCCS) (Consiliul Operativ de Securitate Cibernetică – COSC), whose organization and functioning has been approved by the Supreme Council of National Defense Decision No. 17/2013 (Ministerul Afacerilor Externe, 2019). The council is composed of Secretary of State-level representatives from all national security-related institutions, and provides a unitary coordination of all NSCS activities. The technical coordination of the Council is provided by the Romanian Intelligence Service as a National Authority on Cybersecurity, through the National Cyberint Center, offering expertise on those cybersecurity incidents that can affect national security. On a technical level, the OCCS comprises the Technical Support Group (GST), composed of expert representatives from all national security institutions members of the OCCS. The OCCS delivers annual or upon-request reports on its activities, as well as on the trends within cyberspace that are likely to become vulnerabilities. These reports are classified and presented only to the habilitated authorities of the field.

As mentioned before, the Romanian Intelligence Service has played a significant role in cybersecurity protection since the National Cyberint Center became operational in June 2015, as a result of the Government Decision No. 241/2014 (Ministerul Afacerilor Externe, 2019). The main objective of the center was to contribute effectively to the securitization of cyber networks within national interest cyber infrastructures and to implement a cybersecurity management system on a national level, comprising four types of security techniques: prevention, detection, investigation, and correction (Dorobanțu, 2016).

As one of the institutions dealing with the implementation and coordination of Romanian cybersecurity efforts on a strategic level, the Romanian Intelligence Service issued a Guide of Good Practice on cybersecurity. The guide emphasized the need to carry out both proactive and reactive measures when dealing with cybersecurity threats, which comprise: "policies, concepts, security standards and guides, risk management, training and awareness activities, the implementation of technical solutions for the protection of cyber infrastructures, identity management, identity consequences" (Serviciul Român de Informaţii, n.d.). In addition, the guide focused on cyberhygiene measures to be enacted by users, including the use of a safe internet connection, and caution in the carrying out of internet payments and e-mail, in order not to fall prey to social engineering attacks and phishing, the protection of personal and bank data, through a careful choice of a strong password, the need to periodically update the operating system, performing back-up regularly, securing wi-fi access, safe use of smartphones and tablets, the protection of data during trips, and the safe usage of social media networks (Serviciul Român de Informaţii, n.d.). Such advice is easily accessible to the population, and can thus contribute to raising awareness on the matter and does not require additional training and supervision towards implementation.

Another result of the Cybersecurity Strategy is the National System of Cyber Alert (Guvernul României, 2013: 5), considered to be the main means of prevention and counteracting of those activities bound to affect cybersecurity. To make this system more efficient, Levels of Cyber Alert have been established through a thorough process of risk management such as: Level 1 – green – low; Level 2 – yellow – moderate; Level 3 – orange – high; Level 4 – red – critical. The change in levels of alert is decided upon by the Supreme Council of National Defense at the request of the Operative Council on Cybersecurity. Should the level of cyber alert be raised, all national authorities working in the field are compelled to upgrade their security mechanisms accordingly.

Finally, the Strategy provides for the creation of CERT-type entities that could become operational immediately and provide the interface between the Romanian end-user and the available regulations on an EU level and others. The Romanian CERT.ro (Computer Emergency Response Team) deals with threats both within public institutions as well as private ones.

Known as the National Response Center for Cybersecurity Incidents, CERT.ro (Guvernul României, 2015) is an independent structure, providing expertise and pursuing research and development activities in the field of cyber protection, in order to provide the end-user with data concerning the major threats in this field, as well as regulations and good practices that could be emulated in a simple, cost-effective manner by all users in order to ensure that the protection of cyber environment is performed not only by the state, through its provision of safety regulations and protocols, but also by the very user, through respect of minimal security standards. Its activity is regulated by Government Decision No. 494/2011 (Ministerul Comunicaţiilor şi Societăţii Informaţionale, 2011) and according to it, one of its many tasks is to issue alerts prior to cyber-attacks. CERT.ro is coordinated by the Ministry of Communication and the Information Society and is integrally financed by the state budget.

The most accurate document on cybersecurity protection in Romania remains the Cybersecurity Strategy of Romania, as it comprises the practices and tools to be put into place in order to guard against threats and vulnerabilities in this regard. However, the Romanian legislation in the field still needs considerable improvement, as there are no legal requirements in place on the establishment of a written information security plan, or of an annual cybersecurity audit plan. Furthermore, the government is not compelled in any legal manner to issue a governmental report on national cybersecurity capacity, nor are public institutions required to have a Chief Information/Chief Security Officer. Finally, public institutions are not bound in any legal capacity to report any cybersecurity incidents. Had it not been for the establishment of CERT-RO in 2011, the Romanian cybersecurity infrastructure would be feebler than at present.

Although the private sector comprises information technology-related industries, such as Bitdefender, there is no public–private sector partnership in store. This is a requirement to be fulfilled in the long term.

The NIS Directive 2016/1148 concerns measures to provide a high and unitary common level of security of network and information systems, all over the European Union. In Romania, the Directive was transposed by Law no. 362/2018. The aim of the Directive is to provide a common legal framework of response to all cybersecurity threats all over the EU, by imposing the creation of a Computer Security Incident Response Team (CSIRT), and the creation of the appropriate national response institution, which in the case of Romania is the CERT-RO authority, established within the Ministry of Communication and Information Society (EUR-Lex, 2016). The main feature of the NIS Directive is the identification of seven critical fields which need to receive extra measures of security: energy, transport, water, banking, financial market infrastructure, healthcare, and digital infrastructure.

Although the NIS Directive was supposed to be implemented by May 9, 2018, transposition is still a work in progress. Thus, Law No. 362/2018 was published in the Official Gazette only in January 9, 2019. Furthermore, the Ministry of Communication and Information Society took steps in issuing legislation in the field only recently, with Order no. 599/2019 (Ministerul Comunicațiilor și Societății Informaționale, 2019) approving the Methodological Norms on Identification of Operators of Essential Services and Providers of Digital Services (the "Methodological Norms"), issued on July 17, 2019. The next day, July 18, 2019, the Ministry published Order no. 601/2019 (Ministerul Comunicațiilor și Societății Informaționale, 2019) approving the Methodology for Establishing the Significant Perturbing Effect at the Level of Network and Information Systems of the Operators of Essential Services (the "Methodology"). This secondary legislation regulates the manner in which Operators of Essential Services (OSEs – they offer services related to energy, transport, banking, financial market infrastructure, health, drinking water supplies, and digital infrastructures) and Providers of Essential Services (PSEs – they offer services regarding the following areas: online market places, online search engines, and cloud computing) need to be identified for registration in specific registries, created especially for this purpose – the Registry for Operators of Essential Services (ROSE) and the Registry for Providers of Digital Services. The differentiation between the OSEs and PSEs is made on self-evaluation processes. Moreover, there are still gaps in the secondary legislation. For instance, there is no list of service providers that could be used by the government, as there is also no official approach towards measuring the impact of cyber-security incidents (Popescu & Ștefura, 2019).

Types of threats

In the past years, Romania fell prey to several cyber-attacks, some of them vicious ones, affecting critical infrastructures such as industry, healthcare, banking, and water supplies.

There are four major types of aggressors towards cybersecurity in Romania: state actors (which pose the greatest threat), organized crime actors, extremists, and terrorist organizations and terrorists (Vevera, 2016: 62). The first two are the strongest manifesting in Romania. As far as attacks perpetrated by state are concerned, they are of the Advanced Persistent Threat-type (APT), in which an unauthorized user gains access to a system or a network, not with the intention of de-stabilizing it, but rather to extra-filter sensitive data of the respective organization. The advantage of such attacks lays in the fact that the user can remain undetected for a long period of time (Olar, 2017).

In the past years Romania has responded to a number of cyberthreats, including APT28, Epic Turla/Snake/Uroburos Group, MiniDuke/TinyBaron/CosmicDuke, as well as Red October and Wanna Cry, the latter two being the most severe Romanian authorities had to confront.

The APT28 attack began in Europe in 2007, but was discovered in Romania in 2015. The main targets have been political and governmental entities, as well as communication and aerospace industries from Ukraine, Spain, Romania, the US, and Canada. The identification of vulnerable targets was an automatic one and was performed through the scanning of pre-determined IP addresses, from a specific area, with casualties being selected on an individual basis and later turned into priority targets (Olar, 2017). The Epic Turla/Snake/Uroburos Group attack targeted governmental institutions (Home Affairs and Foreign Affairs ministries, as well as intelligence services), as well as embassies, military companies, and educational and pharmaceutical entities. In Romania, there were 15 casualties: two ministries, two governmental institutions, private companies, as well as residential and mobile internet users. The aim of the attack was to obtain information regarding NATO and EU policies (Olar, 2017).

The MiniDuke/TinyBaron/CosmicDuke malware has been identified within Romanian systems since 2013. This threat mainly targeted governmental institutions. The number of casualties was 59, from 23 states, such as Romania, Belgium, Germany, Georgia, Hungary, Israel, Japan, Lebanon, Montenegro, Russia, Ukraine, and the US. The infection vector was corrupted PDF documents which were sent to the targets, ostensibly for a seminar concerning human rights, Ukraine's foreign policy, and plans on the country's future NATO membership (Olar, 2017).

Wanna Cry was a ransomware-type attack manifesting since May 2017. This type of threat develops through social engineering techniques which make the users prone to open emails containing malicious content. Unlike previous ransomware attacks, Wanna Cry has the capacity of lateral movement within the network, through the exploitation of the SMB protocol (CERT-RO, 2017). The root of the attack was the Eternalblue virus used by the American National Security Agency in its efforts to deal with espionage and hacking. According to reports issued by national authorities, Romania was the 9th most affected country by this attack, with the whole information system of the Mioveni factory collapsing, and the Renault Group reporting massive operational problems (Gândul, 2017).

By far the most vicious cyberattack Romania experienced in the past 20 years was Operation Red October or ROCRA. The origins of the attack date back to May 2007, but the Operation became of central interest only in October 2012, when Kaspersky Lab's Global Research & Analysis Team initiated research activities to document and counteract several attacks performed against international diplomatic service agencies. The investigation showed a specific pattern: the attack was aimed at governmental and diplomatic institutions of Eastern Europe and Central Asia, especially countries formerly a part of the USSR, with the intention of gathering intelligence from the computer systems, mobile connections, and network components of these organizations (Kaspersky, 2013). As far as Romania was concerned, according to the spokesperson of the Romanian Intelligence Service, the attack was intended to gain access to confidential, but not classified information, concerning Romanian foreign affairs, natural resources, Black Sea policy, and economy (Mihai, n.d.).

A guide issued by the Romanian CERT.RO in 2016 concerning generic threats of cybersecurity investigated the following most common threats: drive-by exploits, worms/

trojans, code injections against web apps, exploitation kits, based on drive-by downloads, botnet, denial of service, phishing, compromising confidential information, rogueware/scareware, spam, direct attacks, theft and loss of data, identity theft, information leakage, SEP of search engines, and fake digital certificates (CERT-RO, 2017).

Romania's CERT has multiple responsibilities. Along with serving as the designated Romanian authority charged with implementing the NIS Directive, the institution also needs to be notified after an entity has identified its status, either as an OSE, or as a PSE. In addition to this, the authority needs to be alerted in the event of a cybersecurity incident, as it is responsible for collecting the data and issuing annual reports on the state of cybersecurity threats in Romania and the level of response.

In the event of failure to notify CERT-RO, the respective entity can be charged with committing an administrative offence, and will have to pay a fine ranging between 3000 RON and 50,000 RON. Should the respective entity have a turnover of more than 2,000,000 RON in the previous year, the fine will take up to 0.5–2 per cent of the turnover, and may reach even 5 per cent of the turnover, should there be repeated offences (Parlamenttul Românie, 2019).

Furthermore, CERT-RO issues an annual report on the cybersecurity threats faced in the previous year. The report for 2018, entitled "Threat evolution in Romanian cyberspace 2018," was issued in June 2019 and contains an evaluation of both major and minor threats to cybersecurity. A hierarchy of threats showed that a large majority of them – 80.57 per cent – came upon vulnerable systems (Romanian National Computer Incident Response Team, 2019: 4), followed by botnet, compromised systems, attacks, malware, phishing, fast-flux, and spam (Romanian National Computer Incident Response Team, 2019: 4).

The dreaded Wanna Cry did not die away in 2018, but its impact was lesser – 1.18 per cent compared to other malware types, such as Andromeda (which was the most present and aggressive – 59.99 per cent); Confiker – 16.38 per cent; Sality – 7.41 per cent; and the new emerging ones – MoneroMiner malware, belonging to the crypto-hijacking attack phenomenon – 0.88 per cent; VPNFilter, affecting routers and storage devices and EITest – directing web traffic from the infected server to malicious and scam sites (Romanian National Computer Incident Response Team, 2019: 5).

As far as the geographical distribution of attacks is concerned, in 2018, attacks came from 193 states and territories, including Romania (0.28 per cent) (Romanian National Computer Incident Response Team, 2019: 7). The greatest number of assaults came from China (63.32 per cent), followed by Russia, USA, Ukraine, Germany, UK, Holland, France, Moldavia, and Brazil (Romanian National Computer Incident Response Team, 2019: 7).

Conclusion

Paradoxically, Romania has some of the fastest broadband internet speeds in Europe and the world. However, the institutional framework which regulates the use of the internet and the threats that might arise from excessive use are rather feeble. There is no real connection between the public sector and the private one, which would have the financial potential to create better tools for countering cyberthreats. The responsibility is unequally divided between the state and end-users who, should they undergo an attack, are left to protect themselves, as the existing legal framework is insufficient both for preventing and punishing cybersecurity events. Romania is adapting to the European Union framework in the field, finding its own particular way along the events it encounters. A national law on cybersecurity protection and defense is much needed as it would help create rights and responsibilities for all entities involved in this field, while the strategy, although helpful, has only a declaratory value, establishing a framework without a clear grid for punishments and indictments, should its provisions be violated. Until governmental authorities take steps towards regulating the legal framework, CERT-RO has assumed this role and performs prevention campaigns and creates weekly bulletins to inform the public on the status of cyberthreats in Romania. Nevertheless, its efforts need consistent support from the government authorities which should, sooner rather then later, address the need for coordinated actions with private entities as well.

Suggested reading

Gheorghe, G., Anghel, C. & Iulian, I. (2016). "Mechatronics and Cyber-Mechatronics in Intelligent Applications from Industry and Society," *Applied Mechanics and Materials, 841*: 152–159. https://doi.org/10.4028/www.scientific.net/amm.841.152

Nastasiu, C.-I. (2016). "Cyber Security Strategies in the Internet Era," Scientific Research and Education in the Air Force-AFASES 2016. http://ns.afahc.ro/ro/afases/2016/SOCIO/NASTASIU.pdf

Sabău-Popa, D., Bradea, I., Boloş, M. & Delcea, C. (2015). "The Information Confidentiality and Cyber Security in Medical Institutions," *Annals of the University of Oradea* (Economic Science Series), *24*(1): 855–860. http://steconomiceuoradea.ro/anale/volume/2015/n1/098.pdf

Turcu, D. (2016). "Considerations on Cyber Security Legislation and Regulations in Romania," International Scientific Conference "Strategies XXI," "Carol I" National Defence University, Bucharest, Romania. https://search.proquest.com/openview/6bd14a70aaa004a85e2b5404d0cbc07e/1?pq-origsite=gscholar&cbl=2026346

Vevera, V. A. (2016). "Cyber Space, Romania and the New Threats," *Studia Securitatis, 2*: 61–67.

References

Badea, D. (2016, April). "Consiliul Operativ de Securitate Cibernetică va coordona la nivel strategic activităţile destinate asigurării securităţii cibernetice a României," *Agerpres*. www.agerpres.ro/economie/2016/04/06/consiliul-operativ-de-securitate-cibernetica-va-coordona-la-nivel-strategic-activatile-destinate-asigurarii-securitatii-cibernetice-a-romaniei-18-38-04

Camera Deputaţilor din România. (2014). "Lege privind securitatea cibernetică a României (proiect de lege)." www.cdep.ro/proiecte/2014/200/60/3/pl263.pdf

CERT-RO. (2017, May 13). "WannaCry: o nouă ameninţare de tip ransomware cu victime la scară globală." https://cert.ro/citeste/wannacry-ransomware-alerta

Dorobanţu, I. (2016, June 30). "Logistica succesului. Reflecţii la proiectul Cyberint," *Intelligence Magazine*. http://intelligence.sri.ro/logistica-succesului-reflectii-la-proiectul-cyberint/

EUR-Lex. (2016, July 6). "Directive (EU) 2016/1148 of the European Parliament and of the Council of 6 July 2016 Concerning Measures for a High Common Level of Security of Network and Information Systems Across the Union." https://eur-lex.europa.eu/legal-content/EN/TXT/?uri=uriserv:OJ.L_.2016.194.01.0001.01.ENG&toc=OJ:L:2016:194:TOC

Gândul. (2017, May 13). "România, una din cele mai afectate ţări de atacul 'WannaCry'. Computerele, infectate şi fără accesarea e-mail-urilor sau link-urilor." www.gandul.info/stiri/romania-una-din-cele-mai-afectate-tari-de-atacul-wannacry-computerele-infectate-si-fara-accesarea-e-mail-urilor-sau-link-urilor-16299160

Guvernul României. (2013). "Hotărârea nr. 271/2013 pentru aprobarea Strategiei de securitate cibernetică a României şi a Planului de acţiune la nivel naţional privind implementarea Sistemului naţional de securitate cibernetică (Cybersecurity Strategy of Romania)." www.enisa.europa.eu/topics/national-cyber-security-strategies/ncss-map/StrategiaDeSecuritateCiberneticaARomaniei.pdf

Guvernul României. (2015, March 3). "Hotărâre privind Regulamentul de organizare şi funcţionare a Centrului Naţional de Răspuns la Incidente de Securitate Cibernetică." https://cert.ro/uploads/rof.pdf

Kaspersky. (2013, January 14). *"Red October" Diplomatic Cyberattacks Investigation.* https://securelist.com/red-october-diplomatic-cyber-attacks-investigation/36740/

Mihai, I.-C. (n.d.). "Octombrie Roşu – Cel mai puternic atac cibernetic la adresa României în ultimii 20 de ani," *Criminalitatea Informatică, Portalul de prevenire a criminalităţii informatice*. www.criminalitatea-informatica.ro/stiri-de-ultima-ora/octombrie-rosu-cel-mai-puternic-atac-cibernetic-la-adresa-romaniei-in-ultimii-20-de-ani/

Ministerul Afacerilor Externe. (2019). "Reglementarea domeniului securităţii cibernetice la nivel national." www.mae.ro/node/28367

Ministerul Comunicaţiilor şi Societăţii Informaţionale. (2011, June 2). "Hotărârea nr. 494/2011 privind înfiinţarea Centrului Naţional de Răspuns la Incidente de Securitate Cibernetică," CERT-RO, Guvernul României. https://lege5.ro/Gratuit/gi2tomzugu/hotararea-nr-494-2011-privind-infiintarea-centrului-national-de-raspuns-la-incidente-de-securitate-cibernetica-cert-ro

Ministerul Comunicaţiilor şi Societăţii Informaţionale. (2019, July 17). *Ordinul nr. 599/2019 privind aprobarea Normelor metodologice de identificare a operatorilor de servicii esenţiale şi furnizorilor de servicii digitale*, Ministerul Comunicaţiilor şi Societăţii Informaţionale. https://lege5.ro/Gratuit/gmztsnjvgeya/ordinul-nr-599-2019-privind-aprobarea-normelor-metodologice-de-identificare-a-operatorilor-de-servicii-esentiale-si-furnizorilor-de-servicii-digitale

Ministerul Comunicaţiilor şi Societăţii Informaţionale.. (2019, July 18). *Ordinul nr. 601/2019 pentru aprobarea Metodologiei de stabilire a efectului perturbator semnificativ al incidentelor la nivelul reţelelor şi sistemelor informatice ale operatorilor de servicii esenţiale*, Ministerul Comunicaţiilor şi Societăţii Informaţionale. https://lege5.ro/Gratuit/gmztsnrugm3q/ordinul-nr-601-2019-pentru-aprobarea-metodologiei-de-stabilire-a-efectului-perturbator-semnificativ-al-incidentelor-la-nivelul-retelelor-si-sistemelor-informatice-ale-operatorilor-de-servicii-esential

Olar, D. (2017, October 14). "România, în faţa inamicilor cibernetici," *Intelligence Magazine*. http://intelligence.sri.ro/romania-fata-inamicilor-cibernetici/

Parlamenttul României. (2019, January 9). "Lege nr. 362 din 28 decembrie 2018 privind asigurarea unui nivel comun ridicat de securitate a reţelelor şi sistemelor informatice." http://legislatie.just.ro/Public/DetaliiDocument/209670

Parlamentul României. (2012, April 12). *Legea Nr. 182 din 12 aprilie 2002 privind protecţia informaţiilor clasificate*. http://legislatie.just.ro/Public/DetaliiDocument/35209

Popescu, A. & Ştefura, F. (2019, July 24). "Romanian Legislation on Network and Information Systems Security: A Work in Progress," *Romanian Lawyers Week*. https://rlw.juridice.ro/15795/romanian-legislation-on-network-and-information-systems-security-a-work-in-progress.html

Romania, The Presidential Administration. (2015). "National Defense Strategy 2015-2019, A Strong Romania within Europe and the World." www.presidency.ro/files/userfiles/National_Defense_Strategy_2015_-_2019.pdf

Romanian National Computer Incident Response Team. (2019). "Threats Evolution in the Romanian Cyberspace 2018, Romanian National Computer Incident Response Team." https://cert.ro/vezi/document/cert-ro-cyberthreats-2018

Serviciul Român de Informaţii. (n.d.a) "Ghid de bune practici pentru securitate cibernetică, Serviciul Român de Informaţii." http://intelligence.sri.ro/logistica-succesului-reflectii-la-proiectul-cyberint/

Serviciul Român de Informaţii. (n.d.b) "Ghid – Ameninţări generice la adresa securităţii cibernetice." https://cert.ro/vezi/document/amenintari-generice-securitate-cibernetica

Vevera, A. V. (2016). "România în spaţiul cibernetic," *Revista Română de Informatică şi Automatică, 26*(1): 61–64. https://rria.ici.ro/wp-content/uploads/2016/03/08-art-6.-Adrian-1-2.pdf

10

ITALY'S CYBER SECURITY ARCHITECTURE AND CRITICAL INFRASTRUCTURE

Tommaso De Zan, Giampiero Giacomello, and Luigi Martino

Introduction

A long-standing member of the EU, NATO, OECD, and the group of G7 countries, Italy is by all measures a modern society with an advanced economy. Compared to other peers, however, such as France, Germany, Japan, or Canada, it is slower in adopting new technologies and integrating them into the economy. From the standpoint of cyber security, being a "sort of a latecomer" (Giacomello, 2005, 2018) allows the country to adopt policies and defenses already tested elsewhere. This lag, however, also means that Italy reacts to vulnerabilities slightly slower than other peers.

Italy's first computer network in 1980 was created by a group of nuclear physicists, with the intent of connecting all nuclear research institutes in the country (Siroli, Giacomelli, & Capiluppi, 1997) and it first connected to the internet (then ARPANET) on April 30, 1986, thus making Italy the *fourth* foreign country to do so (after the UK, Germany, and Norway). At the beginning, the internet was just one of several packet-switching networks that coexisted in Italy, while the dominant telecommunications firm at the time (SIP-Telecom) was trying to impose its privately owned system. Various cabinets at the time, aware of the importance of interconnectivity, supported integration among the networks. Ultimately, the adaptability and simplicity of the internet prevailed. Access to the internet was made available to private users after 1995, and the number of internet-service providers (ISPs) and users quickly soared. Since then, the Italian government has supported the internet as a catalyst for economic growth, increased tourism, reduced communication costs, and more efficient government operations. The most distinctive characteristic of Italy's information society, however, has been consumers' enthusiasm for mobile telephony and mobile internet, to the point that, already in 2009, Italy was in top position within the Organization for Economic Cooperation and Development (OECD) for mobile-phone penetration, with a rate of 151%.[1]

Broadly speaking, when it comes to cyber security Italy tries to stay within an "ideal" track represented by the EU on the one side and NATO on the other, incorporating directives and recommendations from both organizations, and trying to be a reliable partner (see, Dentons, 2018). This attitude is well illustrated, for example, by the events surrounding the visit of the Chinese president Xi Jinping in the spring of 2019. Worried that by signing a memorandum of understanding with China for the "One Belt, One Road Initiative," Italy was opening its 5G infrastructures to the Chinese, when the EU and the United States expressed serious concerns, the government had to rush and adopt a presidential decree that guaranteed greater oversight on telecom infrastructures.

Unsurprisingly, today's concept of cyber security is larger than the purely technical dimension of IT-security, as it involves actors, malicious or protective, policies, and their societal consequences (Martino, 2018a). While Italian authorities have engaged, now and then, in issuing formal requests for the removal of some particular content, or for whole websites, by and large, the public has unlimited access to the internet and social media. In fact, today, a most worrisome sign that cyber security should include policy for social media not only because of possible "perception management" activities (see Horowitz, 2018), but also for the increasing opposition of the public, expressed on the social media, to issues such as immigration.

The next three sections of this chapter examine (a) the current status of cyber security measures in Italy and (b) Italy's initiatives and commitment to international initiatives to foster security in cyberspace, and (c) the current status of public–private partnership in cyberspace.

Italy's cyber security governance and policy

Although an official registry for critical infrastructures (CI) is still missing in Italy, similar to other advanced societies, these sectors are considered part of the CI (Brunner & Suter, 2008: 211–212):

- Banking and finance
- Public safety and order
- Communications
- Emergency services
- Energy production, transportation, and distribution
- Public administration
- Health care systems
- Transportation (air, rail, maritime, roads) and logistics
- Water
- Information services and media
- Food supply

The CI along with the rest of cyberspace have recently become the focus of policy-makers and cabinets alike.

In Italy, cyber security governance and policy are outlined in two different documents, respectively the Quadro Strategico Nazionale (QSN), which defines the responsibilities and roles of the institutional actors involved in cyber security, and the Piano Nazionale (PN), which outlines national objectives and action plans to achieve them. Taken, together these two documents form the Italian cyber security strategy. In the context of regulatory developments in the European Union (EU) and internationally, the second Italian cyber security strategy was issued in 2017,[2] four years after the publication of the first strategy under the government of Mario Monti. The new strategy was formulated with the intent to streamline the institutional governance of cyber security and increase operational capacity in the wake of the entry into force of the Network and Information Security (NIS) Directive, which was nationally adopted in June 2018. This section argues that, whereas one can see clear developments in the institutional framework governing cyber security, Italian cyber security policy has not significantly changed since its inception in 2013.

With the new QSN, the main stakeholders within the Italian cyber security governance remain the President of the Council of Ministers (the Prime Minister) and the Interministerial Committee for the Security of the Republic (Comitato interministeriale per la sicurezza della Repubblica, CISR).[3] In terms of specific duties, while the President adopts the QSN/PN and gathers the CISR in the case of a cyber security crisis, the CISR proposes changes to the QSN/PN, monitors their implementation, smoothens collaboration among the various institutional actors, establishes national cyber security objectives, and proposes regulatory measures to strengthen cyber security, preventive, and mitigation measures. In terms of strategic policy making, the main difference from the cyber security governance set in 2013 is the role of the Director-General of the Security Intelligence Department (Dipartimento Informazioni per la Sicurezza, DIS), who has now gained a more direct and prominent role in defining the general policy aimed at improving the security of systems and networks.

At a lower level of the decision-making institutional layout, the two main bodies are the Technical CISR (CISR Tecnico, CISR-T), and the Cyber Security Unit (Nucleo Sicurezza Cibernetico, NSC). Chaired by the DIS's Director General, the CISR-T supports the CISR and implements the measures foreseen in the PN. Formally placed under the Office of the Military Advisor of the Prime Minister,[4] the NSC is now located within the DIS,

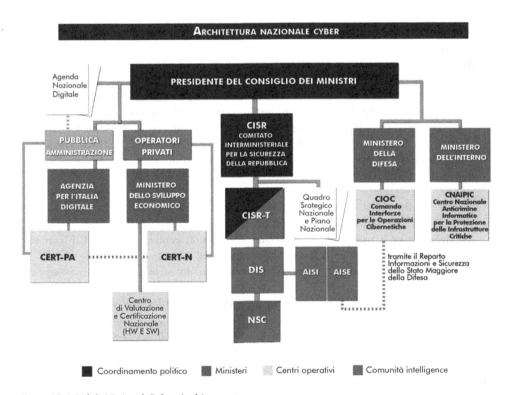

Figure 10.1 Italy's National Cyber Architecture

Source: Sistema di informazione per la sicurezza della Repubblica (2018).

and has the primary role to prevent and manage cyber crises, but also to promote cooperation among various ministries, coordinate information sharing activities, collect information regarding data breaches of ministries relevant to national security and, finally, be the main point of contact for international and regional organizations such as the EU, North Atlantic Treaty Organization, and United Nations. The NSC is chaired by the DIS's Deputy Director-General, who is the highest-ranking official of the Intelligence Department dealing almost exclusively with cyber security issues, including coordinating the various actors within the Italian cyber security governance and *de-facto* overseeing the implementation of the PN (Presidente del Consiglio dei Ministri, 2017).

The 2017 PN has the ultimate objective of developing the strategic objectives delineated in the QSN and, to achieve them, foresees 11 operational guidelines, which are the same guidelines of the 2013 PN. These are:

- strengthen intelligence, law enforcement, civil and military defense capability;
- strengthen coordination and interaction among private and public sector stakeholders;
- promote security culture, including education and training;
- international cooperation and exercises;
- increase operational power of national institutions dedicated to incident prevention, response, and remediation;
- international regulatory and compliance measures;
- compliance and security controls;
- support industrial and technological development;
- strategic communications;
- resources;
- implement a national cyber risk management system.

Compared to its predecessor, the new PN includes a separate Action Plan listing some priorities to ensure a rapid step change in the protection of the national cyber space in the years to come. After presenting the logic behind the establishment of the Joint Cybernetic Operations Command (Comando Interforze Operazioni Cibernetiche, CIOC), which is intended to achieve full operational capability by 2019 (Vestito, 2018), the Action Plan put forwards five new initiatives:

1 Merger of the CERT nazionale Italia and the CERT-Pubblica Amministrazione (CERT-PA) into a single operational structure called CERT-Italia;
2 Establishment of a national evaluation and certification center to verify ICT components embedded in strategic and critical infrastructures;
3 Creation of a foundation or venture capital fund to invest in innovative start-ups or relevant enterprises;
4 Establishment of a national research and development cyber security center in malware analysis, security governance, critical infrastructure protection, and threat analysis;
5 Creation of a national cryptography center involved in establishment of cyphers, development of a national algorithm and blockchain as well as security evaluations.

The NIS Directive came into force in Italian law in the form of legislative decree n.65 in June 2018 and spurred some relevant changes within the Italian cyber security institutional ecosystem. The DIS consolidated its position as the central Italian institution for cyber security policy, becoming the national contact point concerning information and systems security matters. As a national contact point, the DIS is the national representative to the EU Cooperation Group, formed by EU Member States, the Commission, and the European Union Network and Information Security Agency (ENISA), with the role to ensure strategic cooperation and the exchange of information among member states in cyber security.

The Decree also designated the competent authorities with the important role of monitoring the national application of the NIS Directives: 1) Ministry of Economic Development (Ministero dello Sviluppo Economico) for the energy and digital sectors (both services and infrastructures); 2) Ministry of Infrastructures and Transport (Ministero delle Infrastrutture e Trasporti) for the transport sector; 3) Ministry of Economy and Finance (Ministero dell'Economia e delle Finanze) for the banking and financial market infrastructures; 4) Ministry of Health (Ministero della Salute) for the health sector; 5) Ministry for Environment, Land and Sea Protection (Ministero dell'Ambiente e della Tutela del Territorio e del Mare) for drinking water supply and distribution. To smoothen national cooperation, the legislative decree makes all these be part of the Joint Technical Committee (Comitato tecnico di raccordo), within the Presidency of the Council of Ministers.

In line with the new 2017 PN, the legislative decree also established the Italian CSIRT (CSIRT Italiano) which has the role of a unified computer and emergency response team, merging the functions of the two previous CERTs (CERT-PA and CERT-N). The Italian CSIRT is placed under the authority of the Presidency of the Council of Ministers with a team of 30 professionals and a budget of €700,000 from 2019 onwards (with an initial investment of €2,000,000).[5] The NIS Directive also included the Italian CSIRT in the EU CSIRT's network, which comprises of representatives of Member States' CSIRTs and the CERT-EU.

Analysis of the 2017 national cyber security strategy and policy

Looking at the evolution of Italian cyber security, one can argue that between 2013 and 2018, most of the changes have regarded the institutional framework rather than the formulation of cyber security policy.

In the first strategy, some experts had underlined how the structure of Italian cyber security governance could be improved and streamlined (De Zan, 2016a). In particular, experts viewed the old structure as fragmented and suggested to further centralize it and/or reduce the number of actors whose tasks were overlapping. Since 2013, DIS has consolidated its role as central cyber security actor thanks to its operational role in the security of systems and networks in the period 2013–2016 and the implementation of the NIS directive in 2018. The Intelligence Department is now the key actor within the Italian cyber security governance, similar to what happens in the United Kingdom, where the NCSC-GCHQ is the cornerstone of various aspects of British cyber security. Moreover, the new QSN has assigned to the DIS's Director General a newer significant role in the definition of priorities on cyber security matters, possibly filling a gap in terms of strategic leadership able to link the strategic with the operational level which was missing in the previous institutional layout. Furthermore, the new placement of the NSC under the DIS rather than the Office of the Military Advisor of the Prime Minister is also another factor that could let us conclude that with the changes occurred in the new governance, some of the institutional asymmetries that had been previously considered as problematic have been removed.

Apart from these changes to the Italian institutional arrangement, little seems to have varied in Italian cyber security policy since 2013. In addition to a renewed emphasis on the enhancement of CERTs, intelligence, law enforcement, civil and military defense capabilities, the 2017 PN presents five initiatives (those contained in the separate Action Plan, seen above) that are innovative with the respect to the previous plan. Nevertheless, the 11 operational guidelines of the newer 2017 NP are almost identical to those already formulated in 2013, actually worded almost in the exact same way. This could lead some observers to ask whether any significative advancement has been made in the period 2013–2017 and to what extent the objectives of the previous PN have been achieved. Already in 2016, analysts were questioning what type of evaluation mechanisms were in place to inform advancements in Italian cyber security policy (De Zan, 2016b). Despite several official documents having reiterated that a formal evaluation and analysis of lessons learned had been set up to inform the new QSN and PN (Sistema di informazione per la sicurezza della Repubblica, 2017, 2018), possibly for national security reasons, there is no public account of this evaluation process and whether the objectives of the 2013 strategy have been fully, partially or not met. Regardless of how rigorous this evaluation process was, one can argue that the striking similarities between the 2013 and 2017 PNs suggest that the course of Italian cyber security policy has not significantly changed since the first Italian cyber security strategy in 2013.

The Italian contribution to secure cyberspace

Italy recognizes an important role for diplomacy in cyberspace, in particular the activities conducted in multilateral and regional forums, such as the activities promoted by the United Nations General Assembly, the Organization for Security and Cooperation in Europe (OSCE), and the G7. Italian cyber diplomacy was consolidated both under the presidency of the G7 in 2017 and during the Italian Presidency of the OSCE in 2018. There, a priority of the presidency was to improve collaboration and cooperation between participating states in the cyber domain (Martino, 2018b).

In Italy, according to the National Cyber Security Strategy, international initiatives in the cyber domain must be divided into two macro-activities: operational and institutional. The operational activities are the responsibility of the Cyber Security Unit – *Nucleo di Sicurezza Cibernetica* (NSC) in Italian. In fact, according to the provisions of Art. 9, letter f) the NSC

> constitutes a national reference point for relations with the UN, NATO, the EU, other international organizations and other states, without prejudice to the specific competences of the Ministry of Economic Development, of the Ministry of Foreign Affairs and International Cooperation, of the Ministry of the Interior, of the Ministry of Defence and of other administrations foreseen by the current legislation, ensuring any necessary connection in this matter.[6]

This activity is even more evident if we consider the legal framework produced by the NIS Directive which, at Member States level, establishes a national contact point in order to enhance the info-sharing mechanism at European Union level.

Meanwhile, the institutional and representative activities in international and regional forums are the responsibility of the Ministry of Foreign Affairs and Internal Cooperation (Ministero degli Affari Esteri e della Cooperazione Internazionale), which represents Italy in international forums and coordinates in close contact with the NCS.

Analysis of Italian cyber diplomacy

The Italian approach to cyber diplomacy relies firmly on international cooperation, favoring international and multilateral forums over bilateral ones. In particular, there are two initiatives that should be highlighted:

•   The activities promoted by Italy in the OSCE, especially the active role in the implementation of Confidence Building Measures in cyberspace (OSCE Permanent Council, 2013, 2016).
•   The proposals put forth during the Italian presidency of the G7 in 2017 – within the Ise-Shima Cyber Group of the G7 – regarding the declaration on the rules of responsible behavior of States in cyberspace, the so-called "Lucca Declaration," which highlighted, inter alia, the importance of applying existing international law in the cyber domain (Ministry of Foreign Affairs, 2017; Martino, 2018c).

In particular, the Italian international cooperation approach applied to the cyber diplomatic dimension is actively manifested both within the OSCE framework (OSCE, 2012),[7] whereas Italy, since 2012, has had a proactive approach within the Informal Working Group entirely dedicated to "cyber diplomacy," (c.d.) and within the G7 framework, where it is important to remember the work carried out under the Italian presidency of the IseShima Cyber Group.

As far as the G7 cyber activities are concerned, on the occasion of the Italian presidency of the ISCG, diplomatic initiatives were launched immediately to establish norms of responsible state behavior in cyberspace in alignment with the activities of UNGGE (Taormina Leader's Communiqué, 2017).

Although the negotiation process started from a proposal initially based on a "code of conduct" in cyberspace, with related appendices on verification and actions to be taken in case of attack and cyber incident, it evolved into a political declaration in the drafting phase. The declaration was then approved by the Ministers of Foreign Affairs as the *Declaration on Responsible States Behaviour in Cyberspace*, and finally endorsed in the *Leaders' Communiqué* of Taormina in May 2017. The "Lucca Declaration" recognizes the predominant role of states in the process of building a safer and more stable cyber environment; furthermore, it bases its legitimacy on the activities carried out by the UNGGE and the OSCE; finally, it recognizes the possibility of applying the existing international law to the cyber domain.

It is important to note that the work carried out by the ISCG, under the Italian presidency, has sought to intrinsically place the emphasis on the need to move from a predominantly technical approach (as it is currently the case at the UN where UNGGE has the power only to make recommendations and limits of "effectiveness" of this exercise are evident in the lack of consensus which caused the failure of the approval of the *report* 2017) to a purely political-diplomatic process that, ultimately, provides shared rules of conduct (with hope in the future also binding) valid for the specific case of cyberspace (Martino, 2018b).

The Italian public–private partnership approach in the context of cyber security

The existing national security policy framework refers to the public–private partnership as a more or less vague concept of protection of critical infrastructures from cyberattacks. In fact, although the Italian National Cyber Security Strategy recognizes the PPP as an appropriate instrument to enhance the critical infrastructures protection (CIP) from cyberattacks, this policy statement is addressed by generic political or administrative instruments such as *Protocolli d'Intesa* (i.e., Memorandums of Understanding), which, in general, are not legally binding.[8]

Moreover, in Italy – according to publicly available data – any kind of written or clearly formulated legally binding PPP contract, in terms of accountability, responsibilities, risk allocation, obligations, duration or budget constraints which should underline roles and commitments between the governmental or state authorities and private CI-enterprises in the context of protection of critical infrastructures from cyberattacks does not exist. The lack of any formal contracts (or national laws) defining participants, responsibilities, and risks allocation marks a specific difference between the current Italian PPP policy approach on CIP-framework from the conventional or "classic" concept of PPP, which instead foresees a long-term partnership based on a legal binding framework (such as a contract), which defines obligations among the partners and allows risks allocation properly in order to achieve the outcomes.

Conclusion

As recently noted by Catalano, Graziano, and Bassoli (2015: 749), the fact that the national administrative model is "characterized by a high formalism based on the primacy of law, and the administrative process must rigorously be pursued within the limits laid down by abstract rules and legal precepts" has not really helped Italy's path to modernity. Operating in cyberspace and managing cyber security are at the opposite ends of such attitudes. Indeed, they are incompatible.

In cyberspace and, consequently, cyber security, Italy presents innovative niches along with backward areas, both in the private sector and in the public administration. Membership of the EU has proved to be a mixed blessing, as funds and expertise are available but come with regulations and peer pressure for the country to conform its cyber defenses and policies to those of its European partners (Fritzon, Ljungkvist, Boin, & Rhinard, 2007). The net outcome for Italy has been that of an "elusive information society" (Giacomello, 2018). The vulnerabilities of critical infrastructures will not go away and societies' dependence on them can only increase. That cyber security should become everybody's concern is inevitable, in Italy, as elsewhere in advanced societies. Hence, the training/sensibilization for users and businesses to cope with disruption and malfunctioning and to adopt responsible behavior in cyberspace should be a priority for any future Italian government, no matter their political inclination.

Overall, it is evident that Italy too has greatly benefited from the growth of cyberspace, the diffusion of mobile phones, and online banking. Nonetheless, in case of critical infrastructures failure and cascading disasters, it would be the government that would have to "foot the bill" after the society suffered the consequences. To avoid such outcome, the government and the private sector, via the PPP and other solutions, try to prevent such ominous situation. Yet, organizational theories show that the risk of failure is embedded precisely in such solutions. As Charles Perrow (2011 [1984]) prominently noted, institutional fragmentation, that is, too many stake-holders, negatively affect the ability to reliably manage critical systems and that the consequences could be quite dear. This conclusion certainly applied to the Italian case, but also to several other countries examined in this volume.

Notes

1 Organization for Economic Cooperation and Development (OECD), "OECD Key ITC Indicators – Mobile subscribers in total/per 100 inhabitants for OECD, 2007" available at: www.oecd.org/sti/ICTindicators.

2 The QSN was approved as a decree of the President of the Council of Ministers ("Direttiva recante indirizzi per la protezione cibernetica e la sicurezza informatica nazionali") in February 2017. The related PN was made publicly available in March 2017.

3 The CISR is composed by: President of the Council of Ministers, Delegated Authority, Ministry of Foreign Affairs, Ministry of Interior, Ministry of Defence, Ministry of Justice, Ministry of Economy and Finance, and Ministry of Economic Development.

4 The NSC comprises all the ministries of the CISR-T in addition to representatives of the Italian intelligence services (AISE and AISI), Military Advisor (Consigliere Militare) of the President of the Council of Ministers, Department of Civil Protection, and the Agency for Digital Italy.

5 The total budget for the implementation of the NIS directive was €5,300,000 in 2018, and €3,300,000 from 2019 onwards (Art. 22).

6 See, www.sicurezzanazionale.gov.it/sisr.nsf/documentazione/normativa-di-riferimento/dpcm-17-febbraio-2017.html.

7 On April 26, 2012, the OSCE, with the decision of the Permanent Council n. 1039 (PC.DEC/1039), established the informal working group (IWG) aimed at developing CBMs to reduce the risk of conflicts in the cyber domain. The work of the IWG led to concrete results in 2013, when all 57 OSCE participating states, through the PC.DEC/1106, approved an initial set of 11 CBMs focusing mainly on transparency measures and communication channels and trust. In March 2016, the OSCE adopted additional CBMs contained in the Permanent Council decision n. 1202 (PC.DEC/1202). This second set focuses on measures based on cooperation between participating states in cyberspace, emphasizing, for example, the mitigation of cyberattacks against critical infrastructures and highlighting the risk of such attacks being able to have consequences, like a domino effect, on the entire organization. Finally, on December 9, 2016, the OSCE Ministerial Council, meeting in Hamburg, approved a specific decision on OSCE activities in cyberspace, marking the first document of this kind adopted by the highest political level of the Organization in the field of cyber security. It is useful to recall, for example, the direct involvement of Italy in the OSCE project "Enhancing the implementation of OSCE CBMs to reduce the risk of conflict stemming from the use of ICTs" carried out between 2016 and 2018 in collaboration with the University of Florence as an implementing partner and with other universities at an international level as project collaborators. The project, through a comparative analysis and a "cyber profiling" of the 57 participating states of the OSCE has allowed, among other things, to identify the obstacles that countries face in the application of Confidence Building Measures in cyberspace and to advance a Specific "Action Plan" for overcoming these obstacles through targeted capacity building programs.

8 As stated by the National Center for Counter Cyber Crime and Critical Infrastructures Protection (Centro Nazionale Anticrimine Informatico per la Protezione delle Infrastrutture Critiche, CNAIPIC), the national competent body to protect CI from cyberattacks: "The [CNAIPIC] operating model is based on the principle of 'public–private' partnerships: the CNAIPIC, in fact, assumes (through an operational room available 24/7) a central location within a network of critical infrastructural realities (institutional and business), and works in close connection with various organizations (national and international), engaged in the specific sector as well as on the issue of information security, with which it maintains constant relationships of information exchange and provides (through intelligence and analysis units) the collection and processing of data useful for the purpose of preventing and combating the threats. The aforementioned partnership relationship finds its moment of formalization in the stipulation of specific agreements [i.e., Protocolli d'Intesa]; since 2008, agreements have been stipulated, among others, with the following entities and companies: ENAV, Terna, Aci, Telecom, Vodafone, Ffss, Unicredit, Rai, Consob, Ansa, Atm – Milanese Transport Company, Abi, Banca D Italy, Sia Ssb, Intesa Sanpaolo, Enel, Finmeccanica, H3g, Atac, Expo 2015." See, Ministero dell'Interno, CNAIPIC "Comunicato Stampa," May 14, 2017, www.commissariatodips.it/uploads/media/comunicato.pdf; (Italian Original translated by Luigi Martino). As regards the Memorandum of Understanding see: Ministero dell'Interno, Accordo tra ministero dell'Interno e Terna per la sicurezza della rete elettrica nazionale, July 30, 2009, www1.interno.gov.it/

mininterno/export/sites/default/it/sezioni/sala_stampa/notizie/ministero/0519_2009_07_30_accordo_con_Terna_per_sicurezza_rete_elettrica.html_1840113086.html; Polizia di Stato "Intesa con Vodafone per la sicurezza informatica," January 20, 2010, www.poliziadistato.it/articolo/17950-Comunicazioni_intesa_con_Vodafone_per_la_sicurezza_informatica; Confederazione del Commercio Regione Lombardia, "Protocollo d'Intesa Cyber Security tra Polizia Postale e delle Comunicazioni Lombardia e Confcommercio Lombardia," August 2, 2017, www.confcommerciomantova.it/uploads/articles/1664/Protocollo%20d%27Intesa%20Cyber%20Security%20tra%20Polizia%20Postale%20e%20delle%20Comunicazioni%20Lombardia%20e%20Confcommercio%20Lombardia.pdf; Aska News, "Cyber crime, intesa Polizia-Mps" Cyber-Affairs, March 13, 2018, www.askanews.it/cronaca/2018/03/13/cyber-crime-intesa-polizia-mps-per-contrasto-a-reati-informatici-pn_20180313_00073/; Agenzia Regionale per la protezione dell'ambiente ligure ARPAL, "Firmato digitalmente protocollo di intesa Arpal – Polizia postale e delle comunicazioni" April 28, 2018, www.arpal.gov.it/articoli/58-temi-news/3521-firmato-protocollo-di-intesa-arpal-polizia-postale-e-delle-comunicazioni.html; Polizia di Stato, "Accordo tra Terna e Polizia di Stato contro i crimini informatici," May 10, 2018, www.polizia distato.it/articolo/135af4444513904707267764; Quotidiano Sanità, "Sicurezza informatica. Protocollo d'intesa tra l'Asp di Cosenza e la Polizia di Stato per contrasto a reati informatici," May 18, 2018, www.quotidianosanita.it/calabria/articolo.php?articolo_id=61921; (all documents consulted June 13, 2018). However, the specific aspects related to the Italian approach on CIP will be addressed in the section of this thesis entirely dedicated to the analysis of the Italian legal-political architecture in the context of critical infrastructure protection from cyberattacks, taking into account the legislative changes introduced by the aforementioned implementation of the European Directive "Network and Information Security."

References

Brunner, E. M. & Suter, M. (2008). *International CIIP Handbook 2008/2009*. ETH Zurich, Switzerland: Center for Security Studies.

Catalano, S., Graziano, P., & Bassoli, M. (2015). "Devolution and Local Cohesion Policy: Bureaucratic Obstacles to Policy Integration in Italy," *Journal of Social Policy, 44*(4): 747–768.

De Zan, T. (2016a). "Criticità nell'architettura istituzionale a protezione dello spazio cibernetico nazionale," n.117, Approfondimenti, Osservatorio di politica internazionale, www.parlamento.it/application/xmanager/projects/parlamento/file/repository/affariinternazionali/osservatorio/approfondimenti/PI0117App.pdf

De Zan, T. (2016b). "Nuova politica di sicurezza cibernetica per l'Italia," Affarinternazionali, www.affarinternazionali.it/2016/04/nuova-politica-di-sicurezza-cibernetica-per-litalia/

Dentons. (2018, November 21). "European cybersecurity Standards and Their Implementation within the Italian Legislative Framework." dentons.com/en/insights/articles/2018/november/21/european-cybersecurity-standards-and-their-implementation-within-the-italian-legislative-framework

Fritzon, A., Ljungkvist, K., Boin, A., & Rhinard, M. (2007). "Protecting Europe's Critical Infrastructures: Problems and Prospects," *Journal of Contingencies and Crisis Management, 15*(1): 30–41.

Giacomello, G. (2005). *National Governments and the Control of the Internet: A Digital Challenge*. London and New York: Routledge.

Giacomello, G. (2018). "Va Pensiero: The Evolution of Italy's Information Society," in M. Evangelista (ed.), *Italy From Crisis To Crisis: Political Economy, Security and Society in the 21st Century* (pp. 199–218). London and New York: Routledge.

Horowitz, J. (2018, March). "Will Russia Meddle in Italy's Election? It May Not Have To," *The New York Times*: A8. www.nytimes.com/2018/03/01/world/europe/italy-election-russia.html

Martino, L. (2018a). *Cyber Space and International Relations: Diplomatic Initiatives to Improve Cooperation and Mitigate the Risk of Military Escalation*. Toronto: Thomson Reuters.

Martino, L. (2018b). "National Regulatory Scenario: DPCM Gentiloni and the National Plan for Cyber Protection and IT Security," in R. Baldoni, R. De Nicola, & P. Prinetto (eds.), *The Future of cybersecurity in Italy: Strategic Design Areas* (pp. 18–24). Rome, Italy: Consorzio CINI.

Martino, L. (2018c). *Give Diplomacy a Chance: Give Diplomacy a Chance: OSCE's Red Lines in Cyberspace*. Milan, Italy: Istituto per gli Studi di Politica Internazionale. www.ispionline.it/it/pubblicazione/give-diplomacy-chance-osces-red-lines-cyberspace-20377

Ministry of Foreign Affairs. (2017, April 22). "G7 Declaration on Responsible States Behavior in Cyberspace." www.mofa.go.jp/files/000246367.pdf

OSCE Permanent Council. (2012, April 26). "Decision No. 1039: Development of Confidence-Building Measures to Reduce the Risks of Conflict Stemming from the Use of Information and Communication Technologies," OSCE document PC.DEC/1039. www.osce.org/pc/90169

OSCE Permanent Council. (2013, December 3). "Decision No. 1106: Initial set of OSCE Confidence-Building Measures to Reduce the Risks of Conflict Stemming from the Use of Information and Communication Technologies." www.osce.org/pc/109168?download=true

OSCE Permanent Council. (2016, March 10). "Decision No. 1202: OSCE Confidence-Building Measures to Reduce the Risks of Conflict Stemming from the Use of Information and Communication Technologies." www.osce.org/pc/227281?download=true

Perrow, C. (2011 [1984]). *Normal Accidents: Living with High Risk Technologies.* Princeton: Princeton University Press.

Presidency of the Council of Ministers. (2017). "National Plan for Cyber Protection and IT Security." www.sicurezzanazionale.gov.it/sisr.nsf/wp-content/uploads/2017/05/piano-nazionale-cyber-2017.pdf

Presidenza del Consiglio dei ministri. (2017). "Piano nazionale per la protezione cibernetica e la sicurezza informatica." www.sicurezzanazionale.gov.it/sisr.nsf/wp-content/uploads/2017/05/piano-nazionale-cyber-2017.pdf

Siroli, G., Giacomelli, R., & Capiluppi, P. (1997). "Internet e World Wide Web," in P. Capiluppi (ed.), *Reti Informatiche* (pp. 43–51). Le Scienze Quaderni No. 95. Milan: Le Scienze.

Sistema di informazione per la sicurezza della Repubblica. (2017). "Relazione sulla politica dell'informazione per la sicurezza 2016," Presidenza del Consiglio dei Ministri, Rome, Italy. www.sicurezzanazionale.gov.it/sisr.nsf/wp-content/uploads/2017/02/relazione-2016.pdf

Sistema di informazione per la sicurezza della Repubblica. (2018). *Relazione sulla politica dell'informazione per la sicurezza 2017.* Rome, Italy: Presidenza del Consiglio dei Ministri. www.sicurezzanazionale.gov.it/sisr.nsf/wp-content/uploads/2018/02/Relazione-2017.pdf

Taormina Leader's Communiqué. (2017, May 27). www.g7.utoronto.ca/summit/2017taormina/G7-Taormina-Leaders-Communique.pdf

Vestito, F. (2018). *The Italian Cyber Defence Build-Up.* Milan, Italy: Istituto per gli studi di politica internazionale. www.ispionline.it/sites/default/files/pubblicazioni/commentary_vestito_02.05.2018.pdf

11

DUTCH CYBER SECURITY STRATEGY

Joost Bunk and Max Smeets

Introduction

The Netherlands is one of the most connected countries in the world. This is largely due to three international hubs: the Port of Rotterdam, Schiphol Airport, and the Amsterdam Internet Exchange (AMS-IX). Spanning across all five continents, interconnecting more than 800 communication networks by offering professional peering services to Internet Service Providers (ISPs),[1] AMS-IX is one of the largest the internet exchanges in the world. The Netherlands is also a highly digitalized country. It has a large information communications technology sector, with innovative markets for services such as e-health and e-commerce. It has one of the strongest broadband connections in the world and a high internet penetration rate: about 95 percent of households have internet (The World Bank, 2019). The Dutch digital economy accounts for almost one quarter of the total Dutch economy (Organisation for Economic Co-operation and Development [OECD], 2015; The Hague Centre for Strategic Studies, 2016). This means the stakes are high when it comes to cyber security.[2] To capitalize on the social and economic opportunities offered by digitalization, over the past decade the Netherlands has started to recognize the importance of prioritizing cyber security though a series of policy initiatives and organizational reforms. The purpose of this chapter is to briefly review the Dutch government's efforts in establishing and implementing an active and coherent cyber policy.

Since 2010, the Netherlands has led a wide range of initiatives promoting cyber security and stability. The government currently engages with a variety of stakeholders – including the private sector, civil society, state actors, and intergovernmental organizations – across multiple fora and organizations. Rather than being a passive participant, the Netherlands has been a catalyst, driving change in the field of cyber security both domestically and internationally. Yet, the challenge which lies ahead for the Dutch government is to make sure their cyber efforts as a whole will become greater than the sum of its parts. It will require increased coordination and collaboration across initiatives to turn the current patchwork into a synergistic endeavor. Our argument is presented in four parts. The first part provides an overview of the national cyber security strategies published since 2011. It also addresses which key terms have been defined by the Dutch government. The second part discusses the Dutch government's views on sovereignty, international law and international cooperation. Part three analyzes the role of the private sector in the Netherlands. The final part concludes.

Statement of national cyber security strategy

General overview

The Dutch government has published several white papers and national strategies on cyber security. An overview of the most important government publications is provided in Table 11.1.[3] Issued by different government institutions with distinct organizational structure and mission, the publications listed in the table should *not* be seen as one continuous body of work by the Dutch government. Although some publications refer to and build on each other, there are inherent differences in where the focus of the publications lies.[4]

The first national cyber security strategy was published by the Dutch Ministry of Security and Justice in 2011. The document talks about the importance of secure and reliable ICT considering Dutch ambitions to become the "Digital Gateway to Europe" (Ministry of Security and Justice, 2011: 3). It addresses a range of issues that require consideration: improved coordination across initiatives, public–private cooperation, international cooperation in the EU and NATO context, the need for a balanced approach with respect to regulation, stimulating research and education, intensification of cybercrime forensics, enhancing the response capacity against cyberattacks, and building in resiliency of critical infrastructure. Yet, as the last sentence of the report indicates "[t]he activities listed above will be implemented within the existing budgets" (Ministry of Security and Justice, 2011: 15). In other words, there was a sense that much needed to be done within the government, but it lacked political consensus and urgency to spend significant resources on it. In more recent years, however, the Dutch budget for cyber security efforts has been steadily increasing. In the budget proposal for 2019, the Dutch

Table 11.1 Overview of Key Official Government Publications on Cyber Security

Title	Year	Published by
The National Cyber Security Strategy (NCCS)	2011	Ministry of Security and Justice
Defensie Cyber Strategie (*Defense Cyber Strategy*) 2012 (DCS 2012)	2012	Ministry of Defense
National Cyber Security Strategy 2 (NCCS 2)	2013	The National Coordinator for Security and Counterterrorism
Letter to Parliament Defensie Cyber Strategie 2015 (LPDCS)	2015	Ministry of Defense
The Cabinet's stance on Encryption (C-E)	2016	Minister of Security and Justice, & Minister of Economic Affairs
The Cabinet's response to AIV/WRR Reports (C-AIV/WRR)	2016	The Cabinet
The Digital Agenda 2016–2017 (DA)	2016	Ministry of Economic Affairs
International Cyber Strategy (ICS)	2017	Ministry of Foreign Affairs
National Cyber Security Agenda (NCSA)	2018	National Coordinator for Security and Counterterrorism
Defensie Cyber Strategie 2018 (DCS 2018)	2018	Ministry of Defense

government states it will invest 95 million euros in cyber security annually (Government of the Netherlands, 2019b: 16). The investment is dedicated to largely the same set of issues listed in the 2011 strategy.[5] Overall, whilst the priorities for cyber security have hardly changed, it can be argued that slowly but surely resources are becoming available to actually implement these measures.[6]

The Ministry of Defense published its first national cyber defense strategy in 2012. The Dutch Ministry of Defense recognizes cyberspace as the fifth domain for military operations, along with air, sea, land, and space (2012: 4). The strategy does not only focus on strengthening cyber defense but also on improving the Dutch intelligence position in cyberspace and developing the military capability to conduct cyber operations. More specifically, the Defense Cyber Strategy has six broad focal points: 1) a comprehensive approach, 2) defense, 3) offense, 4) intelligence, 5) adaptive and innovative, and 6) cooperation. The same six focal points are adopted in the updated defense strategy published in 2018, with the underlying strategic principles of deterrence and resilience remaining largely unchanged. This means that whereas the US DoD and Cyber Command transition to a new strategic approach in 2018 – moving away from deterrence towards a strategy of persistent engagement and defend forward – the Dutch largely maintained the same posture over the years.[7]

One notable inclusion in the 2018 defense strategy, however, concerns the discussion on the need for public attribution as part of the deterrence strategy. According to the strategy:

> [t]he increasing cyber threat requires a strong international response based on international agreements. That is still insufficient. The government wants to more frequently approach cyber attack perpetrators (publicly) about their behavior. [...] An active political attribution policy contributes to the deterrent ability and making the Netherlands less attractive as a target of cyber attacks. A state actor who (publicly) is held accountable for his actions will make a different assessment than an attacker who can operate in complete anonymity. The Netherlands thus contributes to combating impunity in the digital domain.
>
> *(Ministry of Defence, 2018: 7).*[8]

The discussion in the latest strategy of the Ministry of Defense follows two prominent public attribution cases by the Dutch government. In late 2018, it was announced that Dutch intelligence efforts in cooperation with UK counterparts helped to disrupt a cyber operation being carried out by a Russian military intelligence (GRU) team targeting the Organization for the Prohibition of Chemical Weapons (OPCW) in The Hague (Government of the Netherlands, 2018c). Equally, the revelation of Dutch reporters from *Nieuwsuur* and de *Volkskrant* that the Dutch Joint Sigint Cyber Unit (JSCU) gained access to computer systems of the Russian hacker group "Cozy Bear" in January 2018 reached international headlines – although there is no direct evidence which suggests this was a state-led effort to publicly disclose this information (Modderkolk, 2018; Smeets, 2018b). Both attacks were widely covered in the international media, praising Dutch cyber capabilities.[9]

Finally, Table 11.2 provides an overview of the cyber threat perception across all main government publications. As the table suggests, since 2011 almost every publication observes a growing cyber threat. However, the strategic documents avoid calling out specific threat actors – even when discussing the different categories of cyber threats. When it does discuss specific actors, it is usually in the context of attacks on *other* countries.[10] This is a significant

Table 11.2 Overview of the Perception of the Cyber Threat across Government Publications

	Cyber threat	*Key Threat Actors*	*Cyberterrorism*
NCCS	Moderately **higher**	**No**	**Yes,** briefly
DCS 2012	Considerably **higher**	**No**	**No**
NCCS 2	Considerably **higher**	**Yes,** briefly.	**No**
LPDCS	Moderately **higher**	**Yes,** briefly	**No**
C-E	**No mention**	**No**	**No**
C-AIV/WRR	**No mention**	**No**	**No**
DA	**Higher**	**No**	**No**
ICS	Considerably **higher**	**Yes (Russia)**	**No**
NCSA	Considerably **higher**	**Yes,** moderately	**No**
DCS 2018	**Higher**	**Yes,** briefly	**No**

difference compared to other countries. For example, the South Korean national strategy talks about the need to develop offensive cyber capabilities to counter North Korea, and the latest US DoD cyber strategy talks about the need to defend forward in cyberspace prioritizing four actors: China, Russia, Iran, and North Korea (US Department of Defence, 2018).

The Dutch talk about the threat environment in more detail in a separate annual publication series entitled the "Cyber Security Assessment Netherlands" by the National Cyber Security Centre. The publications however rarely mention against which specific actors the Dutch government should primarily seek to disrupt and deter.

Definitions

First, the NCSS 2011 defines cyber security as "freedom from danger or damage due to the disruption, breakdown, or misuse of ICT" (National Cyber Security Centre [NCSC], 2011: 4). ICT is subsequently considered to be a "an umbrella term referring to digital information, information infrastructures, computers, systems, applications, plus the interaction between information technology and the physical world that is the subject of communications and information exchange" (NCSC, 2011: 3). The paper goes on to discuss the consequences that the lack of cyber security could have, stating that "the danger or damage resulting from disruption, breakdown, or misuse may consist of limitations to the availability or reliability of ICT, breaches of the confidentiality of information stored on ICT media, or damage to the integrity of that information" (NCSC, 2011: 30). The latest National Cyber Security Agenda, published in 2018, provides an equally broad definition: "Cybersecurity is the entirety of measures to prevent damage caused by disruption, failure or misuse of ICT and to recover should damage occur" (Ministry of Justice and Security, 2018: 9; National Coordinator for Security and Counterterrorism, 2018a).

Second, cyberterrorism does not receive widespread attention in the strategy documents of the Dutch government. The national cyber security assessments, published annually, indicate that terrorists could have intentions to commit "terrorist attacks using digital tools" (National Coordinator for Security and Counterterrorism [NCSC], 2018a: 17). Yet, terrorism is not considered one of the most worrisome cyber threats. It argues that terrorists prioritize physical attacks over cyberattacks as it would be easier to wreak havoc. Instead, terrorists primarily use the digital domain for fundraising and propaganda.

Third, a white paper entitled "Resilient Critical Infrastructure – A Factsheet," published by The National Coordinator for Security and Counterterrorism (2018b), provides a detailed overview of what the Dutch government considers to be "critical infrastructure." Published in December of 2017, it describes a large number of processes that, in case of breakdown or disruption, could lead to serious societal disruption. The paper identifies the responsible parties and puts each process into category "A" or "B", depending on its importance to Dutch society and level of threat, i.e., "level of criticality" (NCSC, 2017: 1). The following processes are considered to be category A: 1) national transport and distribution of electricity, 2) oil supply, drinking water supply, 3) flood defenses and water management, and 4) storage, production and processing of nuclear materials. Over a dozen other processes are grouped into category B.

The Netherlands is an outlier in terms of how it defines critical infrastructure. Focusing on the processes themselves, like the distribution of electricity, rather than on broader sectors, like the electricity grid, its perspective on critical infrastructure is deliberately narrow. According to the Dutch government, this narrow understanding allows for more efficient allocation of sparse resources. The US government, in its 2001 Critical Infrastructures Protection, defined critical infrastructure more broadly as "systems and assets, whether physical or virtual" rather than processes (Cybersecurity & Infrastructure Security Agency [CISA], n.d.; Legal Information Institute, 2001). The British Centre for the Protection of National Infrastructure has a very broad definition, including not only systems, assets *and* processes, but also networks, facilities and even "essential workers that operate and facilitate them" (2019). Germany's Federal Office for Information Security (Bundesamt für Sicherheit in der Informationstechnik) defines critical infrastructure as consisting of physical structures and facilities; considerably different from the Dutch focus on less rigid and more specific aspects of the infrastructure, captured in the word "processes." However, the recent Directive on security of network and information systems (NIS Directive) has led to a convergence in EU-members' approach to critical infrastructure (European Commission, 2018).

International law and norms building

International law

The Dutch relation with international law and their position on the applicability is firmly rooted in Dutch history. This should be no surprise in the country of Hugo Grotius, a country with a strong tradition in international law, and in The Hague – city of peace and justice (Government of the Netherlands, 2018a). While the Dutch can pride themselves with centuries of engagement with international law, their official position on international law and cyberspace is fairly young. In 2012 the Dutch government explicitly acknowledged in the Adviesraad Internationale Vraagstukken, Commissie van Advies Inzake Volkenrechtelijke Vraagstukken (C-AIV/WRR: 4) the applicability of *jus ad bellum* in cyberspace: "the Government considers it important that the Committee stated that regarding digital attacks not a different regime applies then to violence in the physical domain." In the same letter the government acknowledges the applicability of *jus in bello* in cyberspace. In relation to *jus in bello* the government states that that digital acts of violence only fall under the law of armed conflict when they are committed in the context of an armed conflict, by the parties to that conflict. The government states that this is an important delimitation with respect to other actions of digital violence (C-AIV/WRR, 2011: 7).

In the NCSS 2 the Netherlands recalled its position in the wider debate of international law and formulated a goal with regard to cyber diplomacy: "Therefore, with its position in the area of international law, the Netherlands wants to contribute to the discussions about the application of legal rules in the digital domain" (NCSC, 2013: 21). In the 2013 Dutch response to Resolution 67/27, establishing the UN GGE of 2013, it is stated that the Netherlands supports the European Union's aims to ensure a secure Internet while promoting openness and freedom on the Internet, to encourage the development of confidence-building measures and norms of behavior and to apply existing international law in cyberspace (Secretary-General of the UN, 2013: 15). Furthermore, the Dutch government's belief is that the development of norms for state conduct does not require a reinvention of international law, but rather needs to ensure consistency in the application of existing international legal frameworks.

In 2015, during the hosting of the Global Conference on Cyberspace, through the Minister of Foreign Affairs, the government explicitly indicates that International Law as a whole – that is, all the conventional set of rules, agreements and treaties that are binding between countries – apply to cyberspace: "The rules and norms that apply offline, including the tenets of international law, most certainly apply online" (Government of the Netherlands, 2015: para. 20). In the Dutch response to Resolution 69/28, establishing the UN GGE of 2015, international human rights are emphasized, stating it is essential that fundamental rights are safeguarded. The Dutch response states that the same rights that people have offline must also be protected online. The submission furthermore commits the Netherlands to respect the following principles: the rule of law, legitimate purpose, non-arbitrariness, effective oversight, and transparency (Secretary-General of the UN, 2015: 8).

Equally, the Dutch response states in regard to the whole body of international law that the existing international frameworks of rules and restrictions equally apply to cyber operations. The submissions refer back to the "landmark achievement" of GGE 2013 and encourages further work to enhance States' understanding of how these existing rules apply. In particular the submissions points-out the examination of the international legal framework that applies to cyber operations that do not rise to the threshold of an armed attack. This includes the question of how the principle of state sovereignty applies and includes the question of the application of the principle of due diligence (UN, 2015: 89). From 2015 onward, the Dutch position is that existing international law, including international human rights law, is applicable in cyberspace. This position is reflected in various strategies such as the ICS and NCSA. Unlike other States the Netherlands has to this date not yet published publicly a specific position on sub questions on the application of international law in cyberspace. A letter to parliament detailing a more specific Dutch position is expected before the summer of 2019 (Government of the Netherlands, 2019a).

International governance

The international outlook of Dutch cyber security has been widely acknowledged (Luiijf, 2011: 14). Being one of the few states with an International Cyber Strategy suggests the Netherlands aims to play a substantial role in regional and international governance. As cyber security discussions cover a large number of overlapping topics, it is challenging to provide a comprehensive overview of Dutch engagement in the field of international governance.

The ICS details an overview of Dutch engagement regional and international governance. The ICS states that the government forms broad coalitions and partnerships to protect Dutch national and Internet interests. The Dutch do so at the UN-level by nominating an expert to the 2016–2017 GGE and national submissions in 2015 and 2017.[11]

The "Cyber Diplomacy Toolbox" was introduced during the Netherlands 2016 Presidency of the European Council. This initiative provides an inventory of possible diplomatic instruments that the EU institutions and Member States could use in response to adversarial cyberattacks (European Council, 2017). Following the public attribution of the cyberattack against the OPCW, the Dutch were part of a coalition of EU Member States pushing for the implementation of a "cybersanctions regime" as part of diplomacy toolbox (Drozdiak & Chrysoloras, 2018). The DCS 2018 states that NATO is the cornerstone of Dutch security policy. The Netherlands has, together with other allies, advocated recognition of cyberspace as a military domain (Ministry of Defence, 2018: 8). In further operationalizing this recognition, the Netherlands has offered cyber capacities to contribute to missions and operations of the alliance (Government of the Netherlands, 2018b: 3). According to the ICS, the Dutch government also closely cooperates with the Organisation for Economic Co-operation and the Development (OECD) and the Organization for Security and Co-operation in Europe (OSCE).

Norms development

The Dutch position on (the development of) norms has always been closely connected to its understanding of the application of international law. The Dutch response to Resolution 67/27, establishing the UN GGE of 2013, already indicated that the development of norms for State conduct does not require a reinvention of international law, but rather needs to ensure consistency in the application of existing international legal frameworks. The relation and potential tension between international law and the development of new norms, has been a topic of debate. The Dutch position is, however, that where there are gaps left by international law or questions unique to cyber security, additional non-binding, voluntary norms of responsible state behavior can be considered (Van Marissing, 2017: 30).

The Netherlands recognizes that the nature and dependence of the digital domain require restraint regarding activities that can touch the "public core" (Government of the Netherlands, 2017: 13). One particular norm the Netherlands has therefore sought to promote concerns the protection of *the public core* of the Internet. It was first publicly addressed by the Dutch Netherlands Scientific Council for Government Policy (Broeders, 2015). In the Dutch response to Resolution 69/28, establishing the UN GGE of 2015, further work is identified: to establish special normative protection for certain systems and networks, including critical infrastructure providing essential civilian services, civilian incident response structures, and certain critical components of the global Internet (UN, 2015: 8).

In the ICS the Netherlands acknowledged that it is working on developing norms and standards and has submitted an initiative proposal on the public core to the UN GGE of 2016–2017 (Government of the Netherlands, 2017: 11). However, the UN GGE 2016–2017 has not resulted in a consensus report. In addition, the Netherlands has launched the Global Commission on the Stability of Cyberspace, which will facilitate new voluntary norms of behavior in the cyber domain (Government of the Netherlands, 2017: 14). In 2017 the GCSC launched a "Call to Protect the Public Core of the Internet" and Norm Package Singapore featuring six new global norms for both state and non-state actors "to help promote the peaceful use of cyberspace" (Global Commission on the Stability of Cyberspace, 2018: para. 1). Through the Freedom Online Coalition (FOC), the Netherlands has also sought to add to the normative debate in the realm on human rights. A key priority of the FOC is "the shaping of global norms through joint action" (Global Commission on the Stability of Cyberspace, 2018: para. 1). Until early 2019, the FOC has published fifteen joint statements on a variety of freedom online related topics.

Role of the private sector

The Netherlands has a long tradition of public-private partnership. The almost mythical tale is that, with water as their shared enemy, the farmers and noblemen from the Middle Ages had to come together to decide on dikes and other measures against the water. The Treaty of Wassenaar from 1982 is seen as the modern starting point of this so-called "polder model": a consensus model in which employers, unions, and the government negotiate wages and labor conditions. The Treaty's agreement to hold down wages for the benefit of the Dutch economy's competitiveness was considered successful and is sometimes referred to as "the Dutch miracle." To this day, "polderen" (in its literal meaning "to create a polder", but often used as "to come to a solution through compromise") remains at the heart of Dutch culture and society. The question arises to what extent we see "cyber-polderen" in Dutch society.

According to Sergei Boeke, research fellow at the Institute of Security and Global Affairs, the institutional cyber security landscape resembles a participant-government connecting a variety of patterns on the basis of trust and equality (2017: 452). The scholar notes that cyber responsibilities and capabilities are decentralized in the country. In that sense, one can argue that there is a form of "cyber-poldering" in the Netherlands.

A textbook example of private-public partnership in the Netherlands is the Cyber Security Raad (Cyber Security Council) or CSR, a vehicle for public-private partnerships in the Netherlands for issues related to cyber security. The CSR is an independent advisory body that advises both public and private parties in the Netherlands on the issue of cyber security. The members of the CSR are leaders in business, government, and science. As such, a number of members in the board come from major Dutch companies. They are however, not supposed represent the specific companies' interests; rather, they act in the name of the entire sector their company is part of, and the organization that acts in that sector's interests.[12] The National Cyber Security Centre (NCSC), perhaps the country's main government institution for cyber security, considers public private partnerships particularly important for critical infrastructure protection. For the NCSC, this means that knowledge sharing and confidence building between the government and energy companies, telecommunication companies, and financial companies, among others, are considered especially important.

Conclusion

The purpose of this chapter was to provide a brief overview of Dutch cyber policy. As has become evident, over the past decade the Netherlands has led a number of new initiatives to promote cyber security. We can expect that for the coming years, the Netherlands will continue to invest in this field.

Our overview showed that the responsibilities of securing the Netherlands against cyber threats are spread across a range of government institutions, each establishing their own policy and initiatives on the basis of their own perspectives. The key challenge is to make sure that these policies and initiatives are synergistic rather than conflictual. This form of synergy can only come about if the Dutch government has a clear nation-wide vision of what it seeks to achieve, and continues to put the right levers in place to ensure coordination and collaboration.

Furthermore, the promotion of cyber stability has never been an endeavor a single government can take on. Early on, the Dutch government realized that cooperation with international partners – within the UN, EU, and NATO framework – is essential. This form of collaboration, especially amongst like-minded states, will only grow in importance in the years ahead. The future stability of cyberspace will rely on an ever-growing number of states, semi-state, and non-state actors working together.

Notes

1 For further information see, https://www.ams-ix.net/ams
2 Like the Dutch white papers and other official documents, this chapter uses the terms "digital security" and "cyber security" interchangeably.
3 The annual national cyber security assessments (CSAN), published since 2012, are not included in this table.
4 The CSAN, however, does provide an overview of this kind.
5 There is one exception: the government also seeks to invest money in their National Cyber Security Centre (not yet mentioned and established in 2011).
6 Also, the National Cyber Security Strategy 2 (NCCS 2) builds on, rather than deviates from, the NCCS 1.
7 It is said that the Dutch cyber command – and affiliated organizations – continue to struggle to operate effectively. For an overview see, Smeets, M. (2018a) and van Lonkhuyzen and Versteegh, 2018.
9 It remains unclear if the Dutch government has a framework for when and how to publicly attribute cyberattacks.
10 The annual reports of the Dutch intelligence services does pay specific attention to Russian threat.
11 The ICS further details that multilateral governance, such as before mentioned, should be complemented, where appropriate, through engagement with the technical community, non-governmental sector and academia through multi-stakeholder and public-private platforms such as the Internet Governance Forum (IGF) and the Internet Corporation for Assigned Names and Numbers (ICANN).
12 For example, Mr. Hans de Jong, President of a major Dutch technology company Philips, is co-chairman of the CSR. His task as a member is to represent the biggest Dutch employer organization, the VNO-NCW. Likewise, Mr. Farwerck is COO at the Netherlands' largest provider, KPN, but represents the organization of Dutch ICT companies, Netherlands ICT.

Suggested reading

Broeders, D. (2014, May 1). "Investigating the Place and Role of the Armed Forces in Dutch Cyber Security Governance," Ministerie van Defensie, The Hague, Netherlands. www.researchgate.net/profile/Dennis_Broeders/publication/280522039_Investigating_the_Place_and_Role_of_the_Armed_Forces_in_Dutch_Cyber_Security_Governance/links/55b74c8008aed621de045985/Investigating-the-Place-and-Role-of-the-Armed-Forces-in-Dutch-Cyber-Security-Governance.pdf
Cyber Wiser. (n.d.). "Netherlands (NL)." www.cyberwiser.eu/netherlands-nl
Hathaway, M. & Spidalieri, F. (2017, May). "The Netherlands Cyber Readiness at a Glance," Potomic Institute for Policy Studies, Arlington, United States. www.potomacinstitute.org/images/CRI/Final CRI20NetherlandsWeb.pdf
Huele, D. (2016, November). "SBIR Cyber Security Tender III." www.rvo.nl/sites/default/files/2016/11/Presentatie_SBIR_cyber_security_tender_III.pdf

Pieters, P. (2017, February 13). "Dutch Govt. Launches International Cyber Security Strategy," *NL Times*. http://nltimes.nl/2017/02/13/dutch-govt-launches-international-cyber-security-strategy

Van den Blink, E. A. (2018). "Public-Private Partnerships in Dutch Cyber Security Governance: An Analysis of Its Effectiveness" (Master's thesis), Universiteit Leiden, Netherlands. https://openaccess.leidenuniv.nl/bitstream/handle/1887/84042/Blink_van_den_CSM_2018.pdf?sequence=1

References

Adviesraad Internationale Vraagstukken, Commissie van Advies Inzake Volkenrechtelijke Vraagstukken. (2011). *Digitale Oorlogsvoering* (C-AIV/WRR). https://aiv-advies.nl/download/9fc55422-c96d-4563-9279-f434803c0afd.pdf

Boeke, S. (2017). "National Cyber Crisis Management: Different European Approaches," *Governance, 31* (3): 449–464.

Broeders, D. (2015). "The Public Core of the Internet. An International Agenda for Internet Governance," (WRR Report No. 94), The Netherlands Scientific Council for Government Policy, The Hague, Netherlands. https://english.wrr.nl/publications/reports/2015/10/01/the-public-core-of-the-internet

CISA. (n.d.). "Critical Infrastructure Sectors." www.cisa.gov/critical-infrastructure-sectors

Drozdiak, N. & Chrysoloras, N. (2018, October 11). "U.K., Netherlands Lead EU Push for New Cyber Sanctions," *Bloomberg*. www.bloomberg.com/news/articles/2018-10-11/u-k-netherlands-lead-eu-push-for-new-cyber-sanctions-document

European Commission. (2018). "The Directive on Security of Network and Information Systems (NIS Directive)." https://ec.europa.eu/digital-single-market/en/network-and-information-security-nis-directive

European Council. (2017). "Cyber Attacks: EU Ready to Respond with a Range Of Measures, Including Sanctions." www.consilium.europa.eu/en/press/press-releases/2017/06/19/cyber-diplomacy-toolbox/

Global Commission on the Stability of Cyberspace. (2018). "Global Commission Introduces Six Critical Norms Towards Cyber Stability." https://cyberstability.org/news/global-commission-introduces-six-critical-norms-towards-cyber-stability/

Government of the Netherlands. (2015, April 16). "Opening Speech GCCS Bert Koenders." www.government.nl/documents/speeches/2015/04/16/opening-speech-gccs-bert-koenders

Government of the Netherlands. (2017). "International Cyber Strategy." www.government.nl/binaries/government/documents/parliamentary-documents/2017/02/12/international-cyber-strategy/International+Cyber+Strategy.pdf

Government of the Netherlands. (2018a, June 20). "Speech by Minister Blok on First Anniversary Tallinn Manual 2.0." www.government.nl/documents/speeches/2018/06/20/speech-by-minister-blok-on-first-anniversary-tallinn-manual-2.0

Government of the Netherlands. (2018b). "Report of the NATO Summit 11–12 July." www.tweedekamer.nl/kamerstukken/brieven_regering/detail?id=2018Z14237&did=2018D40000

Government of the Netherlands. (2018c, October 4). "Netherlands Defence Intelligence and Security Service Disrupts Russian Cyber Operation Targeting OPCW." www.government.nl/latest/news/2018/10/04/netherlands-defence-intelligence-and-security-service-disrupts-russian-cyber-operation-targeting-opcw

Government of the Netherlands. (2019a, January 30). "Espionage by Russia." https://zoek.officielebekendmakingen.nl/h-tk-20182019-39-33.html

Government of the Netherlands. (2019b, September 18). "VI Justitie en Veiligheid Rijksbegroting 2019." www.rijksoverheid.nl/documenten/begrotingen/2018/09/18/vi-justitie-en-veiligheid-rijksbegroting-2019

Legal Information Institute. (2001). "Critical Infrastructures Protection Act of 2001 (42 U.S. Code §5195c)." www.law.cornell.edu/uscode/text/42/5195c

Luiijf, E. (2011). "Drie nationale cyber security strategieën vergeleken," *Magazine voor Nationale veiligheid en crisisbeheersing*, 14–15.

Ministry of Defense. (2012). *The Defense Cyber Strategy*. www.itu.int/en/ITU-D/Cybersecurity/Documents/National_Strategies_Repository/Netherlands_2012_NDL-Cyber_StrategyEng.pdf

Ministry of Defense. (2018). *The Defense Cyber Strategy.* www.defensie.nl/binaries/defensie/documen
ten/publicaties/2018/11/12/defensie-cyber-strategie-2018/web_Brochure+Defensie+Cyber+Strate
gie.pdf

Ministry of Justice and Security. (2011). *The National Cyber Security Strategy.* www.enisa.europa.eu/
topics/national-cyber-security-strategies/ncss-map/Netherlands_Cyber_Security_strategy.pdf/

Ministry of Justice and Security. (2018). *Nederlandse Cyber Security Agenda: Nederland digitaal veilig.* www.
rijksoverheid.nl/binaries/rijksoverheid/documenten/rapporten/2018/04/21/nederlandse-cybersecur
ity-agenda-nederland-digitaal-veilig/CSAgenda_def_web.pdf

Modderkolk, H. (2018, January 25). "Dutch Agencies Provide Crucial Intel about Russia's Interference
in US-Elections," *de Volkskrant.* www.volkskrant.nl/media/dutch-agencies-provide-crucial-intel-
about-russia-s-interference-in-us-elections~a4561913/

National Coordinator for Security and Counterterrorism. (2013). *"Cyber Security Assessment Netherlands
CSAN 2018."* https://english.nctv.nl/binaries/CSBN2018_EN_web_tcm32-346655.pdf

National Coordinator for Security and Counterterrorism. (2018a). "Cyber Security Assessment
Netherlands CSAN 2018." https://english.nctv.nl/binaries/CSBN2018_EN_web_tcm32-346655.pdf

National Coordinator for Security and Counterterrorism. (2018b). *Resilient Critical Infrastructure.* https://
english.nctv.nl/binaries/Factsheet%20Critical%20Infrastructure%20ENG%202018_tcm32-240750.
pdf

National Cyber Security Centre. (2011). *The National Cyber Security Strategy (NCSS): Strength through
Cooperation.* https://english.nctv.nl/binaries/cyber-security-strategy-uk_tcm32-83648.pdf

Organisation for Economic Co-operation and Development. (2015). "OECD Digital Economy Outlook
2015." www.oecd.org/internet/oecd-digital-economy-outlook-2015-9789264232440-en.htm

Secretary-General of the UN. (2013). "Addendum to the 2013 Report of the Secretary-General on
Developments in the field of information and telecommunications in the context of international
security," A/68/156/Add.1.

Secretary-General of the UN. (2015). "The 2015 Report of the Secretary-General on Developments in the
Field of Information and Telecommunications in the Context of International Security," A/70/172.

Smeets, M. (2018a). "Cyber: People, People, People: Vragen Over het DCC en Het Inzetten van
Cyberactiviteiten," *Atlantisch Perspectief,* 6: 30–34. www.atlcom.nl/upload/AP_6_2018_Smeets.pdf

Smeets, M. (2018b, February 8). "The Netherlands Just Revealed Its Cybercapacity: So What Does It
Mean?" *The Washington Post.* www.washingtonpost.com/news/monkey-cage/wp/2018/02/08/the-
netherlands-just-revealed-its-cybercapacity-so-what-does-that-mean/?utm_term=.c50daecc2e18

The British Centre for the Protection of National Infrastructure. (2019). "What We Do." www.cpni.
gov.uk

The Hague Center for Strategic Studies. (2016, December). "Dutch Investments in ICT and
Cybersecurity." https://hcss.nl/report/dutch-investments-ict-and-cybersecurity

The World Bank. (2019). *Indicators.* https://data.worldbank.org/indicator

US Department of Defense. (2018). *Summary Department of Defense Cyber Strategy 2018.* https://media.defense.
gov/2018/Sep/18/2002041658/-1/-1/1/CYBER_STRATEGY_SUMMARY_FINAL.PDF

van Lonkhuyzen, L. & Versteegh, K. (2018, December 18). "Het cyberleger kan en mag nog weinig,"
De NRC. www.nrc.nl/nieuws/2018/12/18/het-cyberleger-is-er-wel-maar-mag-weinig-a3099254

Van Marissing, R. (2017). "The Role of Cyber Diplomacy in Dutch Security Policy," *Atlantisch
Perspectief,* 3: 29–32.

12

NORWEGIAN CYBER SECURITY

A small-state approach to building international cyber cooperation

Lars Gjesvik

Introduction

As a small, open, and highly digitalized country, cyber security is an issue of growing policy importance in Norway. Yet, like highly technologically advanced states, Norway has faced difficulties in squaring national cyber security with private business interests and the multitude of actors. Recent years have seen efforts aimed at uniting disparate institutions and organizations into a coherent framework that works. This chapter will offer a brief summary of the relative criticality of cyber security for Norway as a state, examining the level of digitalization comparative to other states, before looking at the main tenets of Norwegian security policies since the Second World War. It will then examine the history, main documents, and publications delineating the Norwegian position, both nationally and internationally. Finally, remarks on the road ahead, and the challenges Norway faces when it comes to the issue of cyber security will conclude this chapter.

Background, digitalization, and security

Alongside the other Nordic countries Norway is among the most digitalized countries in the world, scoring above the EU average on all indicators on the DESI Index of 2018. The level of digitalization is especially comprehensive when it comes to the extent of services used, and the use of internet services and digital public services, such as banking, news, and eGovernment (European Commission, 2018). As a result, the Norwegian economy and society is highly dependent on digital services functioning properly. This high level of digitalization makes cyber security a concern of increasing importance, consistently ranking at the top of security agencies' lists of threats and risks in their yearly reports.

For years the defining aspect of Norwegian security policy has been its tiny population, extensive coastline, and land border with Russia (formerly the Soviet Union). As a small state, Norway has traditionally relied on foreign allies, and has also been dependent upon strong international norms and laws regulating state behavior (Riste, 2005). This has manifested in a support for rules-based approach to international affairs and institutions like the UN, minimizing the use of force and the risk of conflict (ibid.). In the event of hostilities and an international crisis, Norwegian security was to rely on its membership of the North Atlantic Treaty Organization (NATO). Generally, this approach has been consensus-driven and enjoyed widespread political support, with debates mainly centering on the extent of cooperation and integration (Tamnes & Eriksen, 1999).

But Norway's priorities and approach to cyber security differ for several reasons: first, the widespread private ownership of digital infrastructures requires closer cooperation between the public and the private sector in providing cyber security (see, Healey, 2013). Furthermore, most, if not all, cyber security incidents fall below the threshold of armed force, thus calling upon different mechanisms of international cooperation. Most cyber incidents are criminal in nature, and politically motivated cyber incidents frequently operate in a grey zone between criminal activity and clear-cut state use of force (see, Kello, 2017) that complicates the political responses, institutions, and organizations involved. Providing cyber security is a novel challenge for most societies, necessitating a variety of actors, practices, and concerns to meet a multifaceted challenge (Collier, 2018). As a result, cyber security is difficult to fit within traditional security frameworks such as NATO, as incidents do not necessarily fit into the high-politics framework of article 5 incidents (Fitton, 2016).

A brief history of Norwegian cyber security

Meeting this challenge has been an evolving practice, and one that has taken on different forms. As an early adopter of internet technologies, Norway has a fairly long history with attempts at securing digital networks. The early attempts, such as the 2001 White Paper from the Storting (Norwegian Parliament) on Security and Preparedness in the Communications Market (St. Meld. 47, 2000–2001) saw ICT-security as something primarily affecting the communications sector. This period is characterized by increasing acknowledgement of the importance of ICT infrastructures, yet an approach still seeing ICT security as a niche concern that did not necessitate coordinated action or a holistic national approach. Early years also saw the creation of a mechanism for surveilling data flows to critical private sectors (St. Meld. 17, 2001–2002), yet there were few coordinated efforts at addressing digital security issues. As digitalization picked up pace and encompassed ever more functions, the concern with the misuse of ICT technologies and its impacts on societies increased (see: St. Meld. 39, 2003–2004; St. Meld. 17, 2006–2007; St. Meld. 22, 2007–2008). This period also saw the creation of institutions like the National CERT in 2006, as well as expansion of existing infrastructures like the VDI and nationwide exercises like IKT 2008 (St. Meld. 22, 2007–2008).

A noted shift came with the increased prominence of societal security in the aftermath of the 2011 Utøya attacks. The perceived failure of the government response mechanisms became the starting point for a broad examination of how societal security could be enhanced (see St. Meld. 29, 2011–2012). This wider focus coincided with more cyber-specific examinations, most notably in 2015 with the publication of the report by the Committee of Digital Vulnerabilities in Society, headed by professor Olav Lysne (Norwegian Government, 2015). The committee had performed a broad-brush assessment of digital vulnerabilities in Norwegian society to be used as a basis for subsequent security work. The appointment of the committee came among growing awareness of the security risks digitalization entailed, in light of the rapid and accelerating digitalization (ibid.). The committee pointed out a long list of proposed suggestions to guide the work on ICT security, which to a large extent has been used as a framework for later publications and initiatives. Since then the work on strengthening Norwegian cyber security has grown significantly, also being influenced by the 2014 annexation of Crimea and a changing geopolitical climate, resulting in a long list of publications, documents, and strategies fleshing out the Norwegian approach to cyber security.

Cyber security: approach, main documents, and structure

The Norwegian approach to cyber security is firmly placed within a western understanding of multi-stakeholder cooperation between public and private actors. In this approach, stemming from the high degree of private ownership over critical infrastructures, cyber security is conceptualized as an "assemblage" of a variety of actors. These actors cooperate and contest the provision of societal security, making shifting arrangements as to who controls and secures what functions at what times (Collier, 2018). Taking this private–public cooperation as a vantage point has been the dominant framework for understanding the provision of cyber security in Norway, mirroring efforts in larger states like the US and the UK, traditionally the most important allies in Norwegian security policy. While the dominant strands in western thinking have been influential, the existing governmental and national structures have also been important, as shall be shown in greater detail later on, in determining the Norwegian approach. The combination of adopting "best practices" from similar countries, adapting them to Norwegian circumstances, as well as some efforts at innovation explain the majority of the Norwegian cyber security architecture and posture.

The Norwegian societal security architecture rests on four fundamental principles: responsibility, similarity, proximity, and cooperation. *Responsibility*: indicates that the organization in charge of day-to-day matters should also be responsible in the event of a crisis; *similarity*: that organizing for managing crises should resemble the normal organization; *proximity*: that any crises should be dealt with at the lowest possible level; and finally, *cooperation*: that every authority and actor involved in security has a responsibility to ensure the best possible cooperation between actors (St. Meld. 10, 2016–2017). In practice this has entailed a structure where each ministry has responsibility for providing security for their domains, with the Ministry of Justice and Public Security having a "coordinating" role in ensuring that the overall security work is sufficient (St. Meld. 10, 2016–2017). The main document outlining Norwegian policy is the 2012 Cyber Strategy for Norway. This strategy is, pending the ongoing work on a revised strategy, still the main document outlining the broad priorities for the country in the digital domain. The top priorities for the work going forward were laid out in four overarching goals consisting of: i) better coordination and common situational understanding, ii) robust and secure ICT infrastructure for everyone, iii) good ability to handle adverse ICT events, and iv) high level of competence and security awareness which was further operationalized into more measurable goals (Norwegian Ministries, 2012).

The cyber security approach mainly mirrors the overall approach to societal security with some additional components to cope with the national and cross-cutting nature of cyber security. A vital actor is the National Security Authority (NSM) co-owned by the Ministry of Justice and Public Security and the Ministry of Defense, which has the main responsibility for coordinating and monitoring protective security for critical systems and functions covered by the Security Act (National Security Authority, 2018b). In theory, NSM is only intended to serve critical infrastructures, as well as advise the various other organizations and institutions tasked with performing everyday cyber security, yet its ownership of the national response team and the newly established Cyber Security Centre implies that it is to have a larger role in managing incidents (National Security Authority,

2018a). It is also tasked with coordinating the emergency response team every ministry is supposed to maintain. These are to act as links of contact between NSM and NorCERT nationally and the various companies and organizations in the different sectors (Norwegian Ministries, 2012). One of the main rationales for these sectorial response teams is to combat the coordination problems stemming from the fragmented approach through enabling better information sharing between the public and the private sector, something that has been defined as problematic for some sectors (Muller, Gjesvik & Friis, 2017). In reality the extent of information exchange has been limited, with reports like "Mørketallsundersøkelsen"[1] claiming that the actual reporting by companies could be as low as 2 per cent of incidents (Næringslivets Sikkerhetsråd, 2018).

At the same time there are various other actors with responsibilities in the digital domain. The police have the main responsibility for investigating criminal actions and maintaining law and order online but have struggled to live up to this task. In 2018, a much sought after National Cyber Crime Center (NC3) was established, aimed at raising the competencies in investigating digital crimes by the Norwegian police. In addition to the police the various intelligence agencies also have responsibilities in identifying and responding to threats. The Norwegian Intelligence Service is tasked with foreign intelligence, and has certain offensive capacities, while the Police Security Service is tasked with protecting national security. The Cyber Coordination Center enables these various agencies to cooperate and coordinate their efforts (National Security Authority, 2017). The Norwegian Armed Forces Cyber Defense is tasked with the protection of the communication systems of the armed forces but has a limited role beyond this narrow mandate (Norwegian Government, 2012). The armed forces have admitted having some offensive capacities through its intelligence service, yet these are strictly used as tools for intelligence and do not have an important role in the broader cyber defense posture (Norwegian Ministries, 2012).

The large portion of private company ownership in critical services and infrastructures has been highlighted as a problem for modern societies, particularly when it comes to securing them from digital threats and risks (Dunn, Cavelty & Suter, 2009). Norway is no different in this sense, and the day-to-day security work is mostly done by private actors, of which Telenor, the main telecommunications provider, might be the most important. Security provision is also done by specialized private actors in digital security. For Norway the cooperation between these private actors and the government is crucial for maintaining sufficient levels of cyber security. Correspondingly there has been increased interest in various forums for fostering collaboration and mutual understanding, as well as formalizing the usage of these companies (National Security Authority, 2017). The establishment of the abovementioned Cyber Security Centre is intended to improve the cooperation between public and private in general, yet how it will do so remains to be seen. While cooperation exists, and is improving, there are differences in the levels of sophistication and approaches used from one sector to another. For cyber security, an issue spanning multiple sectors and demanding coordinated efforts, the tension between the need for actions at the national level and responsibility falling to individual ministries is particularly evident. The lack of a national entity tasked with ensuring across the board cyber security is noteworthy, as the lack of a coordinated effort could be seen as hampering developments. In 2017 the Ministry of Justice and Public Security decided to appoint a commission tasked with examining the regulations surrounding ICT security on a national level. The commission is yet to conclude at the time of writing (Norwegian Government, 2017).

Other vital publications delineating Norwegian division of responsibility and approaches for cyber security include the abovementioned mapping of digital vulnerabilities in Norwegian society (NOU, 2015: 13), the current state of addressing those vulnerabilities (St. Meld. 38, 2016–2017), new developments in societal security (St. Meld. 10, 2016–2017), the need for increased surveillance of digital information (Digitalt Grenseforsvar (DGF) 2016), new global security challenges (St. Meld. 37, 2014–15), as well as two outward-looking strategies in the form of an International Cyber Strategy (Norwegian Ministry of Foreign Affairs, 2017) and a Digital Strategy for Norwegian Development Policy (Norwegian Ministry of Foreign Affairs, 2018). In sum these various documents and publications aim to improve the competencies, strengthen the cooperation between the public and the private sector, and meet the twin goals of achieving increased efficiency through digitalization while maintaining secure and reliable services (St. Meld. 38).

A final document and development worth considering is the recently approved revised Security Act. One of the main impacts of the new regulations is a shift in conceptualization from the term "Critical Security Infrastructures" to "Critical Security Functions" (Lovdata, 2018). This more robust understanding of critical services was intended to reflect novel dependencies and give the Norwegian state the tools to secure these. The shift in understanding when it comes to critical functions could be partly seen as a response to the increasing concern with "hybrid warfare" aimed at unconventional targets. Beyond criminal acts the main concern for Norway when it comes to cyber security is its exposure to larger and more advanced nation states. Most notably Russia due to its proximity and worsening relations, but also China with which Norway had a strained relationship in the years after Liu Xiaobo was awarded the 2010 Nobel Peace Prize. Both China and Russia are regularly pointed to as actors in cyberspace in yearly reports by the intelligence services, mainly through cyber espionage. The close proximity to Russia is arguably guiding the work on cyber security, necessitating a shift away from deterrence and the signaling of offensive capacities and towards measures aimed at improving resilience. To avoid escalating tensions and creating enmity, prioritizing the defensive side of cyber security is a sensible choice for a small vulnerable state like Norway.

International outlook

The traditional Norwegian approach to issues of security has been outward-facing, frequently engaging international institutions and stressing the importance of norms regulating state behavior. NATO remains the dominant strategic pillar for national security, partially overlapping with cyber security issues. Beyond these two dominant foundations Norway also engages with a variety of partners and allies regionally, through for instance Nordic cooperation. European initiatives are widely implemented through the European Economic Area (EEA) agreement, yet the expansion of the EU into issues of societal security is a more difficult proposition as Norway in not a member of the Union.

The main document detailing this work is the 2017 "International Cyber Security Strategy." The strategy highlights the need for cooperation among states in order to promote peace and stability in the digital domain, in line with Norwegian support for international law. The document clearly states that international law in its current form is applicable to cyberspace as well, yet the way in which international law applies is described as "in need of international dialogue" (Norwegian Ministry of Foreign Affairs, 2017). As a small state with an interest in continuing a global order that is controlled by and is subject to international law, the adherence and call for deeper regulation of cyberspace on a global level is unsurprising. This makes the current gap in norms troubling, as Norway has neither the capacity nor desire for developing significant offensive capacities.

The above paragraph highlights the need for an international approach to issues of cyber security. As a small state with limited clout outside of international organizations the need for cyber security to be addressed globally through established and formalized institutions is recognized. The international strategy therefore highlights the need for Norway to participate and help further the work in international bodies like the EU, the UN, NATO, Organization for Economic Co-operation and Development (OECD), and Organization for Security and Co-operation in Europe (OSCE). The activities and engagements at an international level is further strengthened by a set of initiatives at a bilateral and regional level (International Cyber Security Strategy, 2017) exemplified by the call for greater collaboration on cyber and hybrid threats in the Nordic region (Republic of Estonia, 2017).

Furthermore, the strategy calls for a digital space that promotes innovation, trade, stability, and acts as a promoter of democratic governance and human rights. In particular the latter, highlighting the potential of digitalization to spread democratic forms of government, puts the Norwegian position at odds with the Russo-Chinese concept of "cyber sovereignty" and multilateral governance, instead favoring the western multi-stakeholder approach (Schia & Gjesvik, 2016). Overall, the Norwegian understanding of the applicability of international law in cyberspace is defined by a high adherence to international norms, and an understanding of those norms in line with a "western" interpretation of the issue. While firmly inside the western camp the official practice aims to acknowledge non-western concerns and viewpoints as well, believing in the need for international consensus on limiting the use of cyber weapons.

While this international approach on cyber security is in line with Norwegian foreign policy on most accounts, it is noteworthy for its exemptions. First of all, there is little engagement with international companies and multinational corporations, through for instance a cyber ambassador. Secondly, the potential for regional cooperation is uneven, with some sectors taking the lead in developing regional partnerships and others lagging behind. An example of a sector that is leading the way is the finance sector, where a Nordic cooperation on a financial CERT helps pool resources and competencies for greater security and resilience (FIRST, 2018). The differing international memberships of the Nordic countries is one explanation for this development (Norway being a member of NATO but not the EU, Sweden and Finland being the opposite and Denmark a member of both). Thus, the international and regional outlook of Norwegian cyber security has room for improvement, particularly considering Norwegian history and geopolitical context. The Nordic countries have a great deal in common, both when it comes to security context, culture, and societal structures, making any regional cooperation on security beneficial. For the issue of cyber security, where the highly limited resources available to all countries is putting strains on cyber security provision, pooling the existing competencies holds great potential.

A related, yet more complex, topic is the issue of the European Union. Norway's position as a member of the EEA, but not a member of the Union itself comes to a head on the topic of cyber security. As the issue covers both security topics and economic ones the inside-outside nature of the Norwegian approach gets challenged. So far Norway has implemented the GDPR regulations on data regulation and privacy, while the NIS directive on critical infrastructures had not been by the time of writing. In general, the Norwegian approach attempts to align itself with forthcoming EU regulations, yet Norway has a highly limited impact on how those regulations are created, resulting in concerns about a "democratic deficit" (Aale, 2012). Twice Norway has taken the question of membership to a popular vote, both time seeing membership rejected by the majority. Shifting geopolitical contexts and novel security threats like cyber attacks is making the issue of Norway's place in Europe more relevant.

Summary and way forward

While Norway was an early mover in digitalization the main body of work on cyber security has been done in recent years. This period has seen a concentrated effort in raising the level of cyber security provision among all parts of the government, and for large parts of the private sector as well. To some extent this has meant the establishment of new institutions and expanding the mandate of older ones, while it has also entailed increased investments in the competencies of traditional institutions like the police and intelligence services. The approach has been mainly defensive, through better security, incident handling, and cyber resilience, with a substantial part of the operationalized actual work on cyber security being supervised by the relevant ministries in a fragmented fashion. While the increased focus and resources has improved Norwegian cyber security there remains issues and structural challenges in the years to come.

A notable challenge is the changing international environment, which poses a series of difficult questions for the Norwegian state going forward. A more assertive Russia in conjunction with the insecurities stemming from the Trump presidency has introduced doubts into the foundations of Norwegian security policy. What is perceived to be a growing threat from Russia, manifesting itself in cyberspace with increased espionage efforts, challenges the ability of the Norwegian state to respond. The lacking international regulations over cyber operations is contributing to making responding to and deterring incidents increasingly difficult. With the publication of the International Cyber Strategy for Norway one could argue that this need for an international dimension has been realized, but it is too early to conclude on its impact. While the strategy puts forth some broad principles on how cyber security is to be achieved, it lacks in detail and omits important aspects like deterrence postures.

Beyond the international politics of cyber security, making the most out of limited resources will be crucial in the years to come. The need for skilled workers on cyber security has been recognized for some time, yet efforts at closing the gap are still wanting. As the talent pool remains limited, close cooperation between public and private actors, as well as allied countries, is needed to make the most out of the available competencies. An issue for improving public–private cooperation is building the right incentives so that private companies value the provision of security to a sufficient degree. Providing for a vibrant private cyber security sector, as well as incorporating it into the larger cyber security framework, will be crucial in making the most out of limited resources and capacities. The ability of Norway to keep cyber security issues at bay in the years to come is likely to hinge upon the ability to make the public–private cooperation work.

A related challenge is the trade-off between security and privacy. The existing system for gathering incidents through either the VDI or reporting by private companies is insufficient to deal with the cyber risks in the years to come. The proposed solution of digital surveillance at the border, under strict limitations and oversight, has been the source of fierce debates on the tradeoffs between security and privacy. The opponents of the proposed system mainly point to the ease with which these systems can be manipulated to surveil all citizens (Datatilsynet, 2017). Proponents argue, among other things, that the increasing digitalization leaves the government no choice, and that there is a lack of any viable alternatives (Løkke, 2017). In lieu of implementing the system, ensuring information sharing between the public and private companies will be even more crucial for maintaining an overall perspective of threats and developments.

The final point of emphasis centers on the necessity of making the security arrangements that are in place work, as well as filling the gaps that still exist. A persistent challenge is the gaps between various sectors and ministries when it comes to ensuring sufficient security practices. The lack of a centralized authority has resulted in varying security practices. While some are at the very front of security work, others are lagging behind and struggling. As long as the decentralized approach to security in collective terms remains, dealing with transnational risks like cyber security will be challenging. New initiatives to improve national coordination have been put into place, with long-awaited organizations like the national Cyber Security Centre and the NC3. Getting these new institutions to work within the current framework will be a main issue in the years ahead.

Note

1 A private-sector initiated publication on reported and unreported digital incidents.

Suggested reading

Norwegian Ministries. (2012). "Cyber Security Strategy for Norway." www.regjeringen.no/globalassets/upload/fad/vedlegg/ikt-politikk/cyber_security_strategy_norway.pdf
Norwegian Ministry of Foreign Affairs. (2017). "International cyber strategy for Norway." www.regjeringen.no/globalassets/departementene/ud/dokumenter/sikpol/cyberstrategy_2017.pdf
Norwegian Ministry of Foreign Affairs. (2018). "Digital Strategi for utviklingspolitikken." (Digital Strategy for Development). www.regjeringen.no/globalassets/departementene/ud/dokumenter/utv politikk/digital_strategi2018.pdf
NOU. (2015). 13 "Digital sårbarhet – Sikkert samfunn: Beskytte enkeltmennesker og samfunn i en digitalisert verden" (Lysne 1). www.regjeringen.no/contentassets/fe88e9ea8a354bd1b63bc0022 469f644/no/pdfs/nou201520150013000dddpdfs.pdf
St. Meld. 38. (2016–2017). "Cyber Security – A Joint Responsibility." www.regjeringen.no/en/doku menter/meld.-st.-38-20162017/id2555996/

References

Aale, P. K. (2012, January 16). "Rapport: EØS-avtalen er en demokratisk fiasko for Norge." *Aftenposten.* www.aftenposten.no/norge/politikk/i/8m8jQ/Rapport-EOS-avtalen-er-en-demokratisk-fiasko-for-Norge
Collier, J. (2018). "Cyber Security Assemblages: A Framework for Understanding the Dynamic and Contested Nature of Security Provision," *Politics and Governance*, 6(2): 13–21.
Datatilsynet. (2017). "Klart nei til digitalt grenseforsvar." www.datatilsynet.no/regelverk-og-verktoy/lover-og-regler/hoeringsuttalelser/20172/klart-nei-til-digitalt-grenseforsvar/
"Digitalt Grenseforsvar (DGF)." (2016, August 26). www.regjeringen.no/contentassets/ca1f705d bebd48cb9a61889d4cfee6bf/digitalt-grenseforsvar-lysne-ii-utvalget.pdf
Dunn Cavelty, M. & Suter, M. (2009). "Public–Private Partnerships are No Silver Bullet: An Expanded Governance Model for Critical Infrastructure Protection," *International Journal of Critical Infrastructure Protection*, 4(2): 179–187.
European Commission. (2018). "Digital Economy and Society Index (DESI) 2018." www.regjeringen.no/contentassets/5d2caddad8424250846b8dc93e259997/desi-indeksen_2018_norge.pdf
FIRST. (2018). "Nordic Financial CERT." www.first.org/members/teams/nordic_financial_cert
Fitton, O. (2016). "Cyber Operations and Gray Zones: Challenges for NATO," *Connections: The Quarterly Journal*, 15(2): 109–119.

Healey, J. (ed.). (2013). *A Fierce Domain, Conflict in Cyberspace 1986 to 2012*. Arlington, VA: Cyber Conflict Studies Association.

Kello, L. (2017): *The Virtual Weapon and International Order*. New Haven: Yale University Press.

Lovdata. (2018). "Lov om nasjonal sikkerhet (Sikkerhetsloven)." https://lovdata.no/dokument/NL/lov/2018-06-01-24

Løkke, E. (2017). "Trenger Norge et digitalt grenseforsvar?" *Minerva*. www.minervanett.no/trenger-norge-digitalt-grenseforsvar/

Muller, L. P., Gjesvik, L. & Friis, L. (2018): "Cyber-Weapons in International Politics – Possible sabotage against the Norwegian petroleum sector." NUPI report. www.nupi.no/en/Publications/CRIStin-Pub/Cyber-weapons-in-International-Politics-Possible-sabotage-against-the-Norwegian-petroleum-sector

National Security Authority. (2017): "Mnemonic AS tilfredsstiller kravene til NSMs kvalitetsordning for hendelseshåndtering." https://nsm.stat.no/aktuelt/nsm-mnemonic/

National Security Authority. (2018a, August 13). "NSM etablerer Nasjonal cybersikkerhetssenter." https://nsm.stat.no/aktuelt/nsm-etablerer-nasjonalt-cybersikkerhetssenter/

National Security Authority. (2018b). "About NSM." https://nsm.stat.no/english/

Norwegian Government. (2012, September 18). "Cyberforsvaret offisielt etablert i dag." www.regjeringen.no/no/aktuelt/cyber/id699271/

Norwegian Government. (2015). 13 "Digital sårbarhet – Sikkert samfunn: Beskytte enkeltmennesker og samfunn i en digitalisert verden" (Lysne 1). www.regjeringen.no/contentassets/fe88e9ea8a354bd1b63bc0022469f644/no/pdfs/nou201520150013000dddpdfs.pdf

Norwegian Government. (2017). "IKT-sikkerhetsutvalget." www.regjeringen.no/no/dep/jd/org/styre-rad-og-utval/tidsbegrensede-styrer-rad-og-utvalg/IKT-sikkerhetsutvalget/id2570775/

Norwegian Ministries. (2012). "Cyber Security Strategy for Norway." www.regjeringen.no/globalassets/upload/fad/vedlegg/ikt-politikk/cyber_security_strategy_norway.pdf

Norwegian Ministry of Defense. (2014). "Forsvarsdepartementets retningslinjer for informasjonssikkerhet og cyberoperasjoner i forsvarssektoren." www.regjeringen.no/globalassets/upload/fd/dokumenter/fdsretningslinjercyberoperasjoner.pdf

Norwegian Ministry of Foreign Affairs. (2017). "International Cyber Strategy for Norway." www.regjeringen.no/globalassets/departementene/ud/dokumenter/sikpol/cyberstrategy_2017.pdf

Norwegian Ministry of Foreign Affairs. (2018). "Digital Strategi for utviklingspolitikken." www.regjeringen.no/globalassets/departementene/ud/dokumenter/utvpolitikk/digital_strategi2018.pdf

NOU. (2015). 13 "Digital sårbarhet – Sikkert samfunn: Beskytte enkeltmennesker og samfunn i en digitalisert verden" (Lysne 1). www.regjeringen.no/contentassets/fe88e9ea8a354bd1b63bc0022469f644/no/pdfs/nou201520150013000dddpdfs.pdf

Næringslivets Sikkerhetsråd. (2018). "Mørketallsundersøkelsen 2018." www.nsr-org.no/getfile.php/1311303-1537281687/Bilder/M%C3%B8rketallsunders%C3%B8kelsen/M%C3%B8rketallsunders%C3%B8kelsen%202018%20low.pdf

Republic of Estonia. (2017, January 11). "Meeting of Nordic and Baltic heads of government focused on challenges of the modern era." www.valitsus.ee/en/news/meeting-nordic-and-baltic-heads-government-focused-challenges-modern-era

Rid, T. (2011). *Cyber War Will Not Take Place*. New York: Oxford University Press.

Riste, O. (2005). *Norway's Foreign Relations – A History*. Oslo: Universitetsforlaget.

Schia, N. N. & Gjesvik, L. (2016). "China's Cyber Sovereignty Concept." NUPI Policy Brief. https://brage.bibsys.no/xmlui/bitstream/handle/11250/2434904/NUPI_Policy_Brief_2_17_Schia_Gjesvik.pdf?sequence=4&isAllowed=y

St. Meld. 10. (2016–2017). "Risiko i et trygt samfunn – Samfunnssikkerhet." www.regjeringen.no/contentassets/00765f92310a433b8a7fc0d49187476f/no/pdfs/stm201620170010000dddpdfs.pdf

St. Meld. 17. (2001–2002). "Samfunnssikkerhet – Veien til et mindre sårbart samfunn." www.regjeringen.no/contentassets/ee63e1dd1a16409fa0bb737bfda9279a/no/pdfa/stm200120020017000dddpdfa.pdf

St. Meld. 17. (2006–2007). "Et informasjonssamfunn for alle." www.regjeringen.no/no/dokumenter/stmeld-nr-17-2006-2007-/id441497/

St. Meld. 22. (2007–2008). "Samfunnssikkerhet – Samvirke og samordning." www.regjeringen.no/no/dokumenter/stmeld-nr-22-2007-2008-/id510655/

St. Meld. 29. (2011–2012). "Samfunnssikkerhet." www.regjeringen.no/contentassets/bc5cbb3720b14709a6bda1a175dc0f12/no/pdfs/stm201120120029000dddpdfs.pdf

St. Meld. 37. (2014–15). "Globale sikkerhetsutfordringer i utenrikspolitikken." www.regjeringen.no/con tentassets/bdf4bd40d57d4dc79409de87419a2217/no/pdfs/stm201420150037000dddpdfs.pdf English version: www.regjeringen.no/en/dokumenter/meld.-st.-37-20142015/id2423339/

St. Meld. 38. (2016–2017). "IKT-sikkerhet – Et felles ansvar." www.regjeringen.no/contentassets/ 39c6a2fe89974d0dae95cd5af0808052/no/pdfs/stm201620170038000dddpdfs.pdf

St. Meld. 39. (2003–2004). "Samfunnssikkerhet og sivilt-militært samarbeid." www.regjeringen.no/no/ dokumenter/stmeld-nr-39-2003-2004-/id198241/sec8?q=digital#match_0

St. Meld. 47. (2000–2001). "Telesikkerhet og -beredskap i et telemarked med fri konkurranse." www. regjeringen.no/contentassets/c3b2c417894448b080313b190a540f28/no/pdfa/stm20002001 0047000dddpdfa.pdf

Tamnes, R. & Eriksen, K. E. (1999). "Norge og NATO under den kalde krigen." www.atlanterhavsko miteen.no/files/atlanterhavskomiteen.no/Tema/50aar/1a.htm

13

SEEKING A NEW ORDER FOR GLOBAL CYBERSECURITY

The Russian approach to cyber-sovereignty

Ilona Stadnik

Introduction

This chapter offers a complex analysis of the Russian key doctrines that shape infosecurity at home and define the policy for abroad. The Russian approach to cybersecurity and infosecurity is based on a strong commitment to national interests. As the time and practical policy decisions show, state interests are standing higher than individual ones. They aim not only to protect the information space, but also to control it in a preventive way. The same ideas are transmitted to the international community. The Russian concept of cyber-sovereignty exactly justifies such measures. Along with that, Russia has been actively engaged in international negotiations on cybersecurity since 1990s. The most prominent initiative was the creation of a special governmental group of experts on ICT use and the development under the auspices of the UN General Assembly. The group has made significant progress in elaborating a common understanding between states of security concerns and the applicability of international law in the recent decade. However, the last group convocation failed to build upon previous progress due to the deep political controversies between its main members. Despite this, Russia pushed for the continuation of efforts that led to the doubled track at the UN – OEWG and UN GGE. While the first was upheld mainly by states that sympathize with the idea of cyber-sovereignty, the second maintained its traditional format and values. Despite this, Russia participates in both initiatives. Another front to promote cyber-sovereignty is a new international convention to combat cybercrime, proposed by Russia. While the draft convention was not met with enthusiasm at the UN, Russia keeps pushing the need for a new treaty that will respect the sovereignty of states during cross-border investigation of cybercrimes.

Statement of the national cybersecurity strategy

Since cybersecurity is a buzzword for many policymakers today, this term has not been used in Russia at an official level. There is a wide range of definitions related to the ICT use and Russia prefers to talk about information security instead of cyber-derivatives. The reason for that is not just the language peculiarities; it indicates a conceptual difference in the security approaches.

The most common definition of cybersecurity refers to an operational and infrastructural level of information sharing, but not to its content per se. The common cybersecurity triad includes the principles of confidentiality, integrity, and availability. That means that information is available only for an intended circle of users, information is correct and complete without any breaches or unauthorized modifications, and that information can be accessed any time it is necessary. Parker (2002) added three more principles to the triad: possession or control, authenticity, and utility. The first principle indicates the necessity to maintain control over information because its loss threatens the security despite saving its confidentiality and integrity. The second principle is about the originality of authorship of the information. And finally, utility means that information is still usable after all other security precautions.

One can see these principles embedded in many western cybersecurity strategies. The majority of cyber threats listed relate to network infrastructures, objects of critical infrastructure dependent on electronic controls, importance of the free information flow for e-commerce, and the like. The Russian approach focuses more on the security of information itself leaving the infrastructural level as a default component. Further analysis of the official doctrines will describe the meaning of information security (infosecurity) and help to trace the crystallization of the term.

The first Doctrine on Information Security was established in Russia in 2000. It is a strategic document that formulates the notion of infosecurity from the national security angle where the national interest plays the key role. The infosecurity of Russia is a station of security of national interests in the sphere of ICT, defined by the aggregate of individual, societal, and national (state) interests. From there we can extract the basis for the triad important for infosecurity – an individual, the society, and the state. This triad is important for understanding the Russian perception of infosecurity threats as well as the Russian policy for ensuring infosecurity.

The doctrine of 2000 highlighted four components of national interest in infosecurity: 1) respect for freedom and the right to access and use of information; 2) information support (sensitization) to the Russian governmental policy towards its citizens and international community on its official stance on significant events and provision of access to open governmental info resources; 3) development of modern ICTs and the domestic information industry, ensuring the needs of the domestic market for its products and the entry of these products into the world market; and 4) protection of information resources from unauthorized access, ensuring the security of information and telecommunication systems, both already deployed and in the making in Russia ("Doctrine on Information Security," 2000: Part I, §1).

Threats and challenges were defined for those components and described in detail – the main objects under threat in each national interest priority, measures for ensuring security, and key sources of threats subdivided into internal and external ones.

Remarkably, international cooperation for infosecurity was highlighted too. The first area deals with prohibition of the development, proliferation, and use of "information weapons" ("Doctrine on Information Security," 2000: Part II, §7). Then, the ensuring of secure international information exchange and the safety of information during its transmission through national telecommunication channels. Another focus was the coordination of law enforcement agencies' activities worldwide to prevent computer crimes, as well as the prevention of unauthorized access to information from the international law enforcement organizations combating transnational organized crime, international terrorism, distribution of drugs and psychotropic substances, illegal trade of weapons and fissile materials, and also people trafficking. Safety of international banking telecommunication networks was also a priority for international cooperation. To fulfill these aims Russia started by establishing close cooperation with CIS countries and then focused on ensuring Russia's active participation in all international organizations active in the field of infosecurity, including standardization and certification of information security measures.

The last part of the doctrine contained a description of how infosecurity politics should be implemented: it differentiates powers between legislative, executive, and judicial branches on the federal and territorial levels. Thus, the state is the key stakeholder in infosecurity politics. It makes an analysis of infosecurity threats to Russia; organizes the work of state agencies to defend the country from the threats; supports the activity of public associations to protect society from distorted and inaccurate information; controls the development, use, export, and import of information security tools through their certification and licensing; protects domestic producers of infosecurity tools and takes measures to protect the national market against penetration by foreign poor-quality tools; promotes access to the world information resources, global information networks; and facilitates Russia's entry into the world information community on the basis of equal partnership ("Doctrine on Information Security," 2000: Part III, §8).

In a rapidly changing world and with the development of ICT, the strategy of infosecurity of 2000 has lost its relevance. In the interim, before the publication of the updated strategy in 2016, a draft *Concept of Cybersecurity Strategy* in Russia appeared in the public domain in 2013 (Council.gov.ru, 2013). It was an attempt to consolidate the two concepts: those of cybersecurity and infosecurity, and combine them in a new relevant strategy for Russia. The aim was to eliminate the existing gaps in the regulation of cybersecurity in Russia, and create a basis for the inclusion of civil society and business organizations in the process of ensuring cybersecurity on an equal basis with the state bodies in contrast to what had been fixed in the doctrine of 2000.

According to the Concept, cyberspace should be considered as a well-defined element of the information space, so it is a narrower notion. Thus,

> cyberspace is a sphere of activity in the information space, formed by a set of communication channels of the Internet and other telecommunication networks, technological infrastructure that ensures their functioning, and any forms of human activity carried out through their use (by individuals, organizations, and the state).
>
> *(Council.gov.ru, 2013)*

And cybersecurity is a "set of conditions under which all components of cyberspace are protected from the maximum possible number of threats and impacts with undesirable consequences." Interestingly, the Concept introduced the idea of multistakeholderism for the first time at such a high political level. The underlying principles of the prospective cybersecurity strategy included, among others, the principle of "constructive cooperation of all subjects of the information society – individuals, organizations and the state – in the field of cybersecurity." That meant the division of responsibilities between stakeholders: the state shall conduct legal regulation of cybersecurity and coordinate stakeholders' efforts; business shall ensure cybersecurity of critical information infrastructure in its ownership, implement and comply with cybersecurity standards; and society shall increase the level of digital literacy and provide feedback on efforts of the state and business.

Despite the Concept containing a range of progressive ideas for cybersecurity development, it was criticized by the industry for vagueness and the uncertainty of its provisions, as well as from state officials, as it "contradicts the state policy in this field"

(Коммерсáнтъ, 2013). After the parliamentary hearings on the Concept at the end of 2013, the Security Council had to consider it for further implementation. However, the fate of the project is not clear, and there is a reason to believe that it either got stuck at the approval stage or was rejected. At the 6th Russian Internet Governance Forum in 2015 the leader of the working group on the Concept said he was not going to push this project anymore as the main goal had been achieved – the public debate and legislative activity is spurred and ongoing.

By the end of 2016 the Russian president had signed the new "Doctrine on Information Security." There is a disclaimer in the introductory part that the Doctrine is the document of strategic planning in the field of national security in Russia, which develops the provisions of the national security strategy of Russia published in 2015.

The triad – an individual, the society, and the state – remained in the new doctrine. The infosecurity of Russia means:

> The station of security of an individual, the society and the state from internal and external information threats at which are provided: implementation of the constitutional rights and freedoms of an individual and the citizen; good quality of living for citizens; sovereignty, territorial integrity and sustainable social and economic development of the Russian Federation; defense and security of the state.
>
> *("Doctrine on Information Security," 2016: Part I)*

The Russian national interests in the information field are now "objectively significant *needs* of an individual, the society and the state *in ensuring their security* and sustainable development in the area of information."

More specifically, national interests include a number of responsibilities of the state and other actors, divided into five areas and consolidated around content security, cybersecurity of information infrastructure, advancement of technological potential, and international information security based on the principle of sovereignty ("Doctrine on Information Security," 2016: Part II, §8). First, to ensure the constitutional rights and freedoms of people to access and use information; protection of privacy in the use of ICT; information support to democratic institutions, with mechanisms of interaction between the state and civil society; and the use of ICT to preserve cultural, historical, and spiritual values of the multi-ethnic population of Russia. Second, to ensure stable and resilient functioning of the information infrastructure, primarily the critical information infrastructure of Russia and its unified telecommunication network in peacetime and wartime. Third, to develop the Russian ICT and electronic industry, and improve the development, production, and operation of information security tools, rendering services in the field of information security. Fourthly, to bring to the Russian and international public reliable information on state policy and its official position on socially significant events in the country and worldwide; to use ICTs to ensure national security in the field of culture. Fifthly, to assist in the formation of the international information security system aimed at counteracting the threats of the use of ICT for the purpose of violating strategic stability, and at strengthening the equal strategic partnership in the field of infosecurity, and also protecting the Russian sovereignty in information space.

Part III of the Doctrine describes the main concerns of the Russian government in infosecurity. The Doctrine distinguishes a set of threats and challenges:

1. The cross-border information flow is used in unlawful geopolitical purposes at the expense of strategic stability, as well as in terrorist and extremist purposes.

2. The enhancing capacity of foreign countries to influence the critical information infra-structure for military purposes as well as technical intelligence of Russian state agencies, scientific organizations, and military-industrial enterprises.
3. Foreign special services expand the use of information means of psychological influence aimed at destabilizing the internal political and social systems in various regions of the world that lead to undermining the sovereignty and territorial integrity of other states.
4. Increasing volume of information containing a biased assessment of the Russian state policy in foreign mass media together with blatant discrimination of Russian journalists abroad.
5. Increased number of computer crimes in the financial sector and violation of privacy in processing personal data.
6. Particular states use ICTs for military purposes that contradict international law, aiming to undermine the sovereignty, political and social stability, and territorial integrity of Russia and its allies and that pose a threat to international peace and global and regional security.

The Doctrine also marks the high level of import dependency on foreign ICT hardware and software that brings security risks in their use as well as the low rate of national R&D programs in infosecurity and their implementation. In addition, the current distribution of resources needed for secure and stable Internet functioning between countries doesn't allow equal and credibility-based Internet governance. Ultimately, the absence of international legal norms regulating interstate relations in infospace, as well as mechanisms and procedures for their application which will take into account the specifics of ICTs, makes it difficult to form an international information security system aimed at achieving strategic stability and equal strategic partnership ("Doctrine on Information Security," 2016: Part III).

The strategic steps to prevent the threats and meet the challenges listed above include a range of measures. For military politics it is prevention and containment of conflicts in infospace, advancement of armed forces capabilities to conduct information confrontation, and protection of Russian allies' interests in infospace. In the field of state and public security it is protection of sovereignty, political and social stability and territorial integrity, provision of basic human rights and freedoms, as well as protection of critical information infrastructure. For economic, science and technology development it is an increase in the share of the digital economy in the national GDP rate, import substitution for foreign ICT products, creation of a personnel reserve in infosecurity together with popularization of personal infosecurity culture.

The main aim for international cooperation is the formation of a stable system of non-conflict inter-state relations in the information space. To fulfill this aim Russia will protect its sovereignty in the information space through the implementation of an independent policy aimed at the realization of national interests. Firstly, Russia will actively participate in the formation of the system of international infosecurity providing effective counteraction to the use of ICT for military and political purposes contradicting international law. Secondly, Russia will seek the creation of international legal mechanisms to prevent and settle interstate conflicts in information space. Thirdly, Russia will promote its position to ensure equal and mutually beneficial cooperation of all interested parties in the information field at the key international organizations.

Remarkably, the last point on the list of strategic steps to be taken is the development of the national governance system of the Russian segment of the Internet. This provision gives a reference to the idea of information sovereignty and implies serious changes at an infrastructural level that is now underway in the form of a new legislation. The law on the stable operation of the Russian segment of the Internet was signed in May 2019. It aims to protect Runet from external threats through centralized Internet traffic routing and control together with the creation of the national domain system (Stadnik, 2019).

The Doctrine also designates the key role to the state agencies to provide infosecurity. However, among the "participants" there are owners of the objects of critical information infrastructure and organizations operating such objects, the media and mass communications, banking and other sectors of financial market operators, operators of information systems and service providers, organizations engaged in the development and operation of information systems and communication networks, the organizations performing educational activity in this field, public associations, other organizations and citizens who, according to the legislation of the Russian Federation, participate in the solution for tasks of ensuring information security. Thus, the Doctrine captures the multistakeholder principle, though remains blank in the scope of duties and abilities of each stakeholder in practice. In the meantime, the Doctrine sets principles for the government to hold constructive interaction between state bodies, organizations, and citizens in solving problems of information security and maintains a balance between the needs of citizens in the free exchange of information and restrictions related to the insurance of national security, including the information field.

To conclude the review of the doctrines, it should be said that despite the detailed description of threats to information security, none of them was actually named as being intrinsic to western cybersecurity strategies – neither has it named the opposing foreign countries, nor indicated particular terrorist groups, nor directly mentioned disapproval of the ICANN role in the distribution and governance of Internet resources.

International governance

Russia has been actively engaged in international infosecurity policy since 1998. That was the very first initiative – the letter to the UN Secretary-General about the emerging problem of international infosecurity, where Russia proposed the resolution on "Developments in the field of information and telecommunications in the context of international security." It formulated the necessity of preventing the information space from becoming a new domain for interstate confrontation and armed conflict. In addition, it suggested that UN member states inform the Secretary-General, on a yearly basis, about their views on the use of ICT for military purposes, the definition of "information weapons" and "information warfare", and the expediency of building international legal regimes to prohibit the development of particularly dangerous forms of information weapons. Since the resolution was adopted without a vote there have been annual reports by the Secretary-General to the General Assembly with the views of UN member states on these issues (UNGA, 1999).

The second part of the Russian initiative was the establishment of the Group of Governmental Experts (the UN GGE). Its aim was to examine the existing and potential threats coming from information space and to find possible cooperative measures to address them. The group assembled five times – in 2004, 2010, 2013, 2015, and 2017. The most prominent and fruitful were the consensus reports of 2013 and 2015. Participating states agreed on the key issue: international law is applicable to the cyber/information space as well as to the sovereignty concept. They also proposed norms, rules, and principles of responsible behavior of states in the ICT-sphere as well as confidence building measures, international cooperation, and capacity building (UNGA, 2015b). The Russian delegation was enthusiastic about the 2015 report because promotion of responsible state behavior is the key element of international infosecurity policy (Namib.online, 2013). Russia proposed documents for international discussion in different formats to the UN: the concept of the Convention on International Information Security of 2011 (Министерство иностранных дел Российской Федерации, 2011) and the International Code of Conduct for information security co-sponsored by SCO member states in 2011 and 2015 (UNGA, 2015a). These documents are based on sovereignty in the ICT environment together with the key role of states in Internet governance and provision of security in the information space.

Although the key feature of the SCO initiative is its peacemaking nature – and it is in contrast to the western initiatives to regulate cyber warfare – it did not get substantial enough support to be adopted even after the latest version included the human rights section, which establishes a duty-balanced approach to the issue and reaffirms that the rights that a person has in an offline environment must also be protected online. But the most unacceptable point is the internationalization of Internet governance promoted by Russia in connection with its skeptical attitude towards ICANN even after the IANA transition happened. The sole purpose of internationalizing the Internet is to prevent the political decision of the leadership of one country from limiting the functioning of the Internet in another country. Perhaps it is necessary to create an organization under the auspices of the UN Security Council that would make such decisions on the basis of international law instead of a private organization under the jurisdiction of a particular state.

Turning back to the rules of responsible state behavior, the work of the 5th UN GGE in 2017 ended without a consensus report. Despite the bitter taste of the failure to come to an agreement and suggestions from some group participants to wrap up this format (ECFR, 2017), Russia expressed its readiness to continue discussion of the responsible behavior of states in the UN. Definitely, the main fault line between two camps was the disagreement on the applicability of international humanitarian law as it "would legitimize a scenario of war and military actions in the context of ICT" (Cuba's Representative Office Abroad, 2017), the option that completely contradicts the Russian policy in international infosecurity. Mr Krutskikh, special representative of Russia on international cooperation in the field of infosecurity, confirmed the intention to introduce a new resolution. He mentioned that Russia seeks support for the document from the extended list of SCO members, including India and Pakistan, BRICS countries, Latin America, and the Middle East, in becoming co-sponsors (Международная Жизнь, 2017). By the end of 2018 a draft resolution calling the Secretary-General to convey a new Open-Ended Working Group (OEWG) was submitted to the General Assembly (UNGA, 2018a). Almost simultaneously, the United States submitted a similar document aimed at creating the 6th UN GGE in the traditional format. Finally, both resolutions were adopted. The mandate of OEWG is to discuss the implementation of the already agreed cyber norms from previous GGE reports, but there is an important addition to the list (UNGA, 2018b). The new added norm says that all charges against states regarding organizing and/or conducting illegal activities with the use of ICT need to be substantiated. The norm also touches on the problem of attribution, and the need to study all available information and the broader context of an incident. Some of the removed norms from the original draft resolution are borrowed from the SCO letters mentioned above. Instead they were partially included in the preamble of the resolution: new paragraphs indicate the growing concern of Russia and other countries with the issue of "dissemination of false or distorted news, which can be interpreted as interference in the internal affairs of other states." These provisions became the reason for 46 states, mainly western democracies, to vote against this resolution. The OEWG will provide its consensus report by 2020. The additional task is to study the possibility of institutionalizing the dialogue on the application of international law on a regular basis under the auspices of the UN. Russia will also participate in the 6th UN GGE as it did previously. The result will be a report in 2021 that does not require the consensus of all participants, but must contain an annex in which 25 UN GGE members will include their national positions on the application of international law in the ICT environment. Both groups agreed to keep their work complementary to each other (UNIDIR, 2019).

In the spring of 2017 there was more Russian input to the UN – the Draft UN Convention on Cooperation in Combating Cybercrime (UNGA, 2017). The document put the protection of state sovereignty at the top: "This Convention shall not authorize a State party to exercise in the territory of another State the jurisdiction and functions that are reserved exclusively for the authorities of that other State under its domestic law." Essentially, the Convention shall require the party-states to adopt necessary legislative and other measures to establish as an offence or other unlawful act under its domestic law the acts envisaged in the Convention, as well as procedures envisaged to prevent, suppress, and investigate crimes, and conduct judicial proceedings related to such crimes. Interestingly, Article 27 stipulates that states shall establish real-time collection of traffic data, thereby placing their citizens under surveillance. The document is full of other provisions unacceptable to democratic countries. At that date, the document did not gain any traction. However, Russia didn't give up this idea and submitted a new resolution to the 3rd Committee titled, "Countering the use of information and communication technologies for criminal purposes" – that was also adopted by a vote at the end of 2018. Importantly, it mandates a report by the Secretary-General with the views of member states on the challenges they face in countering the use of ICTs for criminal purposes, which is to be presented at the 74th UNGA session. Obviously, this resolution is aimed to push for a new treaty to replace the Budapest Convention on Cybercrime. While the text itself does not contain reference to the draft convention introduced by Russia in 2017, it creates a new specialized agenda item for the next UN session. At the opening of the 73rd UNGA session Russian Foreign Minister Sergey Lavrov reaffirmed the intent to start a process of negotiating a new convention on cybercrime (Министерство иностранных дел Российской Федерации, 2018a). Associations for progressive communications criticized the resolution for the vague term "use of ICTs for criminal purposes" since it may denote criminalization of online activity:

> specifically, cybercrime laws are being applied in ways that stifle dissent and gov-
> ernment criticism, outlaw peaceful protests, gain indiscriminate access to people's
> data, and crack down on tools that enable encryption and anonymity.
>
> *(APC, 2018)*

As such. the Russian national legislation on cyber and information security is developing in this direction.

National legislation on cybersecurity

The state policy towards the Internet and information space has been evolving in the last ten years. Before that time, the Russian segment of the Internet together with digital services could be characterized by a set of words: self-organization, self-regulation, and state non-interference. There is no definite answer to what had become a trigger for an active state interest in regulating the information space. Whether it was an explicable tendency to deal with the constantly growing potential and challenge of digitalization, or whether the ruling elite realized the force of ICTs to empower citizens to rise against the authorities, as happened during the Arab spring. The fact is that after post-election protests in Russia in the winter of 2011 the Parliament entered upon the regulation of dissemination of information on the Internet. It started with the out-of-court blocking of web pages and Internet resources which contained the prohibited information and creation of a "black list" of Internet resources.[1] Legislating activity followed with a federal law on "organizers of information dissemination on the Internet" (The Federal Law 97-FZ, 2014a) (all internet services that allow sending messages) that required them to keep within the territory of Russia the information on the facts of acceptance, transfer, delivery, and (or) processing of voice, text, images, sounds, or other electronic messages of users of the Internet and the information about these users within six months and provide it to the authorized state bodies performing operational and investigative activity.

Another federal law that caused trouble for Internet companies was the protection of personal data of the Russian citizens and its physical localization within the Russian borders (The Federal Law 242-FZ, 2014b). Though not all foreign Internet giants have yet fulfilled the requirements to organize the storage and processing of personal data in datacenters located in Russia, the professional network LinkedIn was blocked for incompliance. In 2016 the President signed a set of "anti-terrorist" amendments to the federal law on countering terrorism and to the Criminal Code, which got the name "the package of Yarovaya" (Meduza, 2016). With regards to infosecurity, it required telecom operators and providers to store any type of correspondence and user data for a particular period of time.[2] In addition, it obliges the organizers of dissemination of information on the Internet to decrypt the users' messages. At the request of the FSB, companies will be required to provide keys to encrypted traffic. Telegram messenger refused to provide encryption keys explaining that secret chats in Telegram use end-to-end encryption. However, it became a reason for the decision to block the messenger on Russian territory.

In terms of cybersecurity, in 2017 the Parliament passed the law FZ-187 on the security of Russia's critical information infrastructure (CII) (Consultant.ro, 2017). The law provided a definition of objects (i.e., physical objects that comprise critical infrastructure), and subjects (i.e., owners of objects) and their responsibilities in relation to the law. CII objects include information systems, information and telecommunication networks, and the automated control systems of CII owners. CII owners can include state institutions, Russian legal entities/individual entrepreneurs that interact with the above-mentioned systems, and networks in all sectors of the economy, energy, production, and defense. The law prescribes the subjects to categorize the CII objects in order to define their significance and prioritize their security, to ensure the integration of CII objects into GOSSOPKA, and finally, to take organizational and technical measures to ensure the security of CII. In addition, the law contains amendments (published in a separate FZ-194) to the Criminal Code that establishes criminal liability for wrongful/illegal acts against CII objects. Part of this law was the establishment the National Coordination Center for Computer Incidents (NCCCI) in July 2018. It is responsible for the exchange of information about computer incidents between CII objects, and also serves as a contact point for interaction with foreign CERTs (Официальный интернет-портал правовой информации, 2018b). All international incident response interactions must only go through NCCCI (except where there are special cooperation agreements, but even then NCCCI must be notified). It can refuse to share information about incidents with foreign counterparts if such information is deemed to threaten the national security of Russia. Additionally, the NCCCI is now adopting the functions and infrastructure of the GOV-CERT which was also established in 2012 by FSB for incident response in Russian government networks.

At last, the most prominent and ground-breaking law, which was mentioned in the first section, has been adopted just recently – on May 2019. This is the first law of its kind, aimed at regulation of the national segment of the Internet exclusively. The public named it "the Law on sovereign Runet" because of it highly restrictive and fragmenting nature (Официальный интернет-портал правовой информации, 2019). In brief, the law defines the main subjects responsible for stable operation of the Internet in Russia. They are telecom operators and owners and/or proprietors of: (1) technical communication networks (used for operations of transport/energy and other infrastructures not connected to the public communication network); (2) traffic exchange points; (3) communication lines crossing the state border; and (4) autonomous system numbers (ASN). All subjects must participate in the regular exercises to check the stability of the Runet operation. Roskomnadzor, a federal supervising body in the field of communication, IT, and mass communications, will execute the centralized management of communication networks in the event of threats to the stability and security of the Runet by defining routing policies for telecom operators and other subjects and coordinating their connections. Additionally, a new center for monitoring and control of public communication networks will appear under the Roskomnadzor supervision. Telecom operators are required to ensure in their networks the installation of state-sponsored technical means for countering threats to the stability, security, and integrity of Internet operations in Russian territory. These technical means will also serve the purpose of traffic filtering and blocking access to prohibited Internet resources. This practice is supposed to replace the existing system of "black list" where filtering and blocking is done by providers themselves. Finally, the law provides for the creation of the national domain name system that should ensure the accessibility of the Russian websites in the case of emergency. Though the law should have come into force on November 2019, it is still not ready for implementation due to the absence of the relevant orders and decrees regulating the technical nuances.

To conclude with the national regulation, we can see that most attention is paid to information security. The state's aim is to control the information flows and filter undesirable content at any expense. With regard to cyber security, it took several years to adopt the first law on critical information infrastructure, and now the government is striving to complete the work on the law that aims to control the Runet infrastructure and make it independent from any external shutdown in the case of emergency. For the government now it is vital not only to declare its sovereignty in cyberspace, but to ensure its technical implementation and align the Internet to its national borders (Mueller, 2017).

Notes

1 Prohibited information under the federal law 139-FZ includes child pornography, propaganda of drugs and suicide. Later, federal law 398-FZ added calls for mass riots, extremist activities, participation in mass (public) events conducted in violation of the established procedure as basis for blockage by the decision of the General Procuracy. Finally, 187-FZ, called antipiracy act, allows for blocking sites containing unlicensed content, at the request of the rights owner.
2 The law comes to the force in July 2018. In April 2018 the Russian government published a decree on the rules of data storage: 30 days for internet providers and 6 months for telecom operators. The metadata about facts of communication must be stored for 3 years. Yet nobody is implementing the law due to the absence of certified data-storage equipment of the necessary capacity.

Suggested reading

Compendium of Regulatory Legal Acts of the Russian Federation and the Strategy Planning Documents in the Sphere of Information Security, The Russian Federation contributions to the UN and other international organizations, Bilateral Agreements and Joint Declarations at the Highest Level and at Governmental Level with the Participation of the Russian Federation.

Demidov, O. (2012). "International regulation of information security and Russia's national interests." *Security Index: A Russian Journal on International Security*, 18(4). 10.1080/19934270.2012.714597

Krutskikh, A. & Streltsov, A. (2014). "International law and the problem of international information security." *International Affairs* 6, 64–76.

National Association of International Information Security (НАМИБ). "International information security legal acts and fundamental documents for Russia translated into English." http://namib. online/wp-content/uploads/2019/03/МИБ_английская-версия.pdf

Stadnik, I. (2019). White paper *Sovereign RUnet: What Does it Mean?* Internet governance project, Georgia Institute of Technology. www.internetgovernance.org/research/sovereign-runet-what-does-it-mean/

References

APC. (2018). "UN General Assembly adopts record number of resolutions on internet governance and policy: Mixed outcomes for human rights online." www.apc.org/en/news/un-general-assembly-adopts-record-number-resolutions-internet-governance-and-policy-mixed

Consultant.ro. (2017, 26, July). "Federal law dated, 26. 07.2017No187-FZ." www.consultant.ru/cons/cgi/online.cgi?req=doc&base=LAW&n=220885&fld=134&dst=1000000001,0&rnd=0.2477406265980837#07294351284912781 [in Russian].

Council.gov.ru. (2013). "Концепция стратегии кибербезопасности Российской Федерации" ["The Concept of the Russian Federation's Cyber Secuity Strategy]. http://council.gov.ru/media/files/41d4b3dfbdb25cea8a73.pdf [In Russian].

Cuba's Representative Office Abroad. (2017). "71 UNGA: Cuba at the final session of Group of Governmental Experts on developments in the field of information and telecommunications in the context of international security." http://misiones.minrex.gob.cu/en/un/statements/71-unga-cuba-final-session-group-governmental-experts-developments-field-information

"Doctrine on Information Security." (2000). Part I, §1.

"Doctrine on Information Security." (2000). Part II, §7.

"Doctrine on Information Security." (2000). Part III, §8.

"Doctrine on Information Security." (2016). Part I.

"Doctrine on Information Security." (2016). Part II, §8.

"Doctrine on Information Security." (2016). Part III.

ECFR. (2017). "The UN GGE is dead: Time to fall forward." www.ecfr.eu/article/commentary_time_to_fall_forward_on_cyber_governance

GOSSOPKA – the State system of detection, prevention and elimination of consequences of computer attacks on information resources, operated by FSB.

Коммерсáнтъ. (2013, November 29). "Koncepciya kiberbezopasnosti razoshlas's gosudarstvennoi strategiei Predlozheniya senatorov nravyatsya poka tol'ko obshchestvennikam i biznesu [Концепция кибербезопасности разошлась с государственной стратегией. Предложения сенаторов нравятся пока только общественникам и бизнесу]." Kommersant. www.kommersant.ru/doc/2355154

Международная Жизнь. (2017, December). "Cyber stability: Approaches, perspectives and challenges," International conference, Moscow, December 2017.

Meduza. (2016, June 22). "Irina Yarovaya's 'anti-terrorist' war on civil rights." https://meduza.io/en/feature/2016/06/22/irina-yarovaya-s-anti-terrorist-war-on-civil-rights

Министерство иностранных дел Российской Федерации. (2011, September 22). "Convention on international information security." www.mid.ru/en/web/guest/mezdunarodnaa-informacionnaa-bezopasnost/-/asset_publisher/UsCUTiw2pO53/content/id/191666

Министерство иностранных дел Российской Федерации. (2018a, September 28). "Foreign Minister Sergey Lavrov's remarks at the 73rd session of the UN General Assembly, New York, September 28, 2018." www.mid.ru/en/press_service/minister_speeches/-/asset_publisher/7OvQR5KJWVmR/content/id/3359296

Mueller, M. (2017). *Will the Internet Fragment? Sovereignty, Globalization and Cyberspace.* London: Polity.

Namib. online. (2013, July 24). "Основы государственной политики Российской Федерации в области международной информационной безопасности на период до 2020 года" ["Basic principles for State Policy of the Russian Federation in the field of International Information Security to 2020"]. Art. 11(б). http://namib.online/wp-content/uploads/2019/03/2013-07-24_Основы-гос политики-РФ-области-МИБ-на-период-до-2020-года.pdf [in Russian].

Официальный интернет-портал правовой информации. (2018b, September 6). "Приказ Федеральной службы безопасности Российской Федерации от 06.09.2018 No. 52107" ["Order of the Federal Security Service dated 09.06.2018 No. 52107"] http://publication.pravo.gov.ru/Document/View/0001201809100003?index=0 [in Russian].

Официальный интернет-портал правовой информации. (2019, May 1). "The Federal Law dated 01.05.2019No. 90-FZ." http://publication.pravo.gov.ru/Document/View/0001201905010025?fbclid=IwAR3POFABIeaD21PCGKdNDOMm-tDwZ-gU_uxyONSLw520E0cUT6x47m_sLjk [in Russian].

Parker, D. B. (2002). "Toward a New Framework for Information Security," In S. Bosworth, M. E. Kabay & E. Whyne (eds.), *The Computer Security Handbook* (4th ed.) (Chapter 3). New York: Wiley.

Stadnik, I. (2019). "A closer look at the 'Sovereign Runet' law," *CircleID.* www.circleid.com/posts/20190518_a_closer_look_at_the_sovereign_runet_law/

The Federal Law 97-FZ. (2014a).

The Federal Law 242-FZ. (2014b).

UNGA. (1999, January 4). "Developments in the field of information and telecommunications in the context of international security." UNGA A/RES/53/70 https://undocs.org/A/RES/53/70

UNGA. (2015a, January 15). "Letter dated 9 January 2015 from the Permanent Representatives of China, Kazakhstan, Kyrgyzstan, the Russian Federation, Tajikistan and Uzbekistan to the United Nations addressed to the Secretary-General." UNGA A/69/723. https://undocs.org/A/69/723

UNGA. (2015b, July 22). "Report of the group of governmental experts on developments in the field of information and telecommunications in the context of international security." UNGA A/70/174 https://undocs.org/A/70/174

UNGA. (2017, October 16). "Letter dated 11 October 2017 from the permanent representative of the Russian federation to the United Nations addressed to the Secretary-General." UNGA A/C.3/72/12. https://undocs.org/A/C.3/72/12

UNGA. (2018a. October 29). "Developments in the field of information and telecommunications in the context of international security." UNGA A/C.1/73/L.27/Rev.1 https://undocs.org/A/C.1/73/L.27/Rev.1

UNGA. (2018b). Developments in the field of information and telecommunications in the context of international security. UNGA A/RES/73/27. www.un.org/en/ga/search/view_doc.asp?symbol=A/RES/73/27

UNIDIR. (2019, June 6). "2019 cyber stability conference," United Nations HQ, New York.

14

SLOVAKIA

The Tatra Tiger without teeth

Aaron T. Walter

Introduction

In Slovakia, cybersecurity has recently been correctly placed in the independent area of national security from its obscure subsystem of information security. With the adoption of a new concept, the perspectives on a clearly defined terms of cyber related issues need to occur. Moreover, there is no distinguishing cyberattacks from cyber incidents in any draft legislation. This means that what one institution may regard as a cyberattack another one considers to be a cyber incident. This obviously causes confusion as different incident handling procedures are applied. Therefore, in Slovakia, unification of terminology is necessary to improve both intra-state and international cooperation. A cybersecurity committee of the Security Council of Slovakia has been established operating as a permanent working body to coordinate measures related to cyber-security. A priority is adopting planned legislation as well as increasing security consciousness. In addition, the government is committed to the provision of additional support. This is increasingly vital because of the threat of a DoS or DDoS (distributed denial-of-service) attack.

A cyberattack against a server occurs as a DoS or DDoS – when the bandwidth or specific system is not available due to multiple systems assaulting the server. An example of this massive overload is the attack upon Estonia in 2007 when a server's capacity with an excessive degree of false requests forces it to shut-down, restart, or unable to answer because the DDoS has come from dozens, often hundreds of thousands of computers or mobile phones interconnected. There are other terms to be aware of such as cyber threat, vulnerability, and exploit. A vulnerability is a "hole" in the system or the software that runs the system occurring unintentionally, creating shortcomings of the software. Exploit is the method by which such a vulnerability can be exploited by the attacker. Lastly, cyber threat is the term used by policy makers seeking to draw attention to the probable implications of exploiting the vulnerability to national security. How to determine what and if those risks are real is the task of agencies, programs, and personel. Within the individual Visegrád Four (V4) nations the essential fields of cybersecurity mentioned in the first section: data integrity, confidentiality, and availability, significant problems are present. Data integrity received or sent via the Internet is commonly altered and compromised via trolls or the planting of false stories.

While at present data confidentiality and authorization have not been compromised, interference with potential candidates and/or current politicians and groups is real. It is a cyber threat that no V4 nation is at present prepared to fight. Thus, when this occurs, a DOS or DDoS attack will happen. Slovakia, once described as the Tatra Tiger in reference to its economic performance in the early 2000s, is significantly behind in its cybersecurity. This chapter examines Slovakia's proposed and/or implemented strategy(ies) related to cybersecurity, while looking at the various domestic institutions responsible for cybercrime and cyberterrorism in the country. It also explores the role that the Slovak Parliament plays in the country's cybersecurity and cyber defense proposals and law-making, while looking at the influence of the private sector and NGOs in Slovakia on this topic.

National cybersecurity strategy of Slovakia[1]

There are two basic documents in Slovakia dedicated to cybersecurity. On June 17, 2015 the government of the Slovak Republic adopted resolution No. 328/2015 *Conception of Cyber Security of the Slovak Republic for Years 2015–2020* (Concept). The goal was to propose new institutional frameworks governing cybersecurity in the Slovak Republic. The government reacted as a priority to the proposal of the Directive of the European Parliament and the Council about measures to ensure a common high level of security of network and information systems in the European Union and specifying domestic competent bodies for security of the network and information systems.

Cybersecurity is a major competency that was assigned to the National Security Authority effective January 1, 2016. However, the Authority's activities in this area began long before the official handover date. In February 2009, the Authority was named the NATO contact point and began to shape itself as the national authority vis-a-vis the alliance in this specialized area. Within efforts to build out its competencies, the Authority regularly participated in international cyber training exercises (Cyber Coalition, Locked Shields, and Cyber Europe). Outside of NATO and EU activities, the Authority engaged in the informal Central European Platform for Cyber Security, which brings together security incident response centers in the countries of the V4 and Austria.

The Slovak government supported the Authority's ambitions in 2014 with the approval of the Preparations of the Slovak Republic to Fulfill Cyber Defense Tasks document and in particular a year later with the adoption of a key strategic document – the Cyber Security Strategy of the Slovak Republic for 2015–2020 – which lays out an institutional framework containing the Authority as the central body for cybersecurity. Specific proposals from the strategy have been transposed into amendments of the Act on Competencies, which resulted in the Authority becoming the central government body for cybersecurity.

Developments continued in 2016. A second-generation Memorandum of Understanding between NATO and Slovakia was signed in January and in March the Slovak government approved the Action Plan for Implementing the Strategy, which defines the methods and tools Slovakia will use to attempt to mitigate the risks and threats originating from cyberspace and adopt legislative, technical, and coordinating measures. Moreover, the action plan of the Concept fits within the time period beginning in 2015 and will conclude in 2020.

Proposal of the Action Plan was adopted by the Slovak government on March 2 in Resolution No. 93/2016. The Action Plan contains proposals of tasks which have the purpose to secure reasonable protection of cyberspace of the state against potential threats which could cause irrecoverable damage, and therefore the credibility of the state or organization could be threatened. The Plan provided for the Concept is one of the basic documents defining a list of tasks for the period 2016–2020 focused on creation of legislation, standards, methodical instructions, rules, security policies, international cooperation, increasing awareness of competences, as well as other activities required in order to ensure protection and defense of the national cyberspace. Per the NBUSR, individual tasks are grouped in eight priority areas with specification for a competent investigator and cooperating subjects, including time frame of its implementation. To better understand what the Concept of Cyber Security of the Slovak Republic is for the years 2015 to 2020, the material and Figure 14.1 summarize the current status of Slovak cyberspace security and how it is trying to establish some new rules and procedures, referring to the Action Plan.

Cooperation of the public sector with the private sector, the academic sphere, and civil society is not developed in vital range and also frameworks for systematic, coordinated, and effective cooperation, especially on strategic level, are missing. Cyber threats are not yet generally considered to be sufficiently urgent a problem. It is necessary to constantly warn of vulnerabilities to which current society is increasingly exposed. We also should increase the awareness of the general public and take action, which would lead to the elimination of threats and risks connected to the use of modern electronic, information, and communication technologies.

The most critical problem in the area of cybersecurity in the Slovak Republic is the fact that defense of the cyberspace, meaning cybersecurity of the Slovak Republic, are not yet complexly modified in legislation in force. Existing capacities and mechanisms in the area of network security and information technologies already do not suffice in order to keep up with the ever-changing environment of threats or secure a sufficiently high level of legally effective protection in all areas of the state governance and social life (NBUSR, 9). Figure 14.1 shows the draft framework for cybersecurity management.

As can be seen in Figure 14.1, a number of different agencies are involved in the provision of cybersecurity – including the government of the Slovak Republic, the Security Council of the Slovak Republic and the Committee for Cybersecurity, along with the National Security Office (NBU Authority) and the National Computer Emergency Repsonse Team/Computer Security Incident Response Team. This chart also illustrates the breakdown and assignment of responsibilities for responding to specific categories of cyber incidents and breaches. Here, one can note that incident response responsibilities are different depending on the target – information systems related to public administration; information systems related to critical infrastructure and other systems.[2] The draft document builds upon what Slovakia has had in place for institutional support in responsibility for cybercrime, now expanded to cyberterrorism.

As to the specific definitions and understanding of the terminology – cybersecurity, cyberterrorism, and critical infrastructure – these are defined within the draft framework. The framework follows the prescribed response from Brussels. Though, admittedly, prior to 2015 any institutional support within Slovakia was centered on the term cybercrime as understood in section two. As to the expansion of responsibility to cyberterrorism the Action Plan; creation of the Concept that contains the NBU is the logical next step and indicates that after several years of legislative indifference, Slovakia is getting serious about cybersecurity.

Responsibility for cybercrime and cyberterrorism

Establishment of a central body of public administration for cybersecurity: the National Security Authority (NBU) is already an existing institution, and is the central body for the

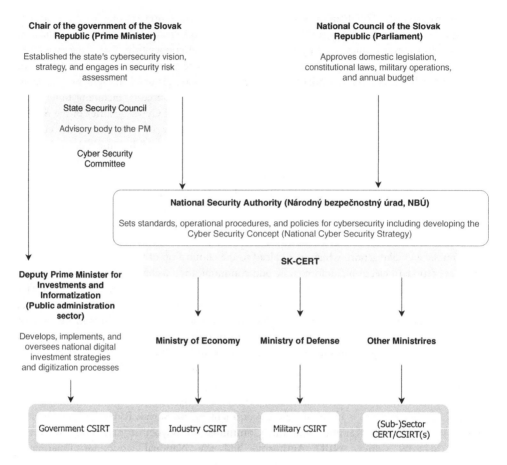

Figure 14.1 Slovakia Cybersecurity Organizational Chart

Source: Author's illustration as an adaptation of Hathaway, Spidalieri and Kaushik's (2019) organizational chart and information from government websites.

public administration for cybersecurity. The various roles of the NBU include the extended activity of the NBU as an existing independent central body in the public administration, supported by the text language of the Concept which recommends that the NBU is responsible for cybersecurity on the national level. In this activity the NBU protects network security and information systems within Slovakia. There are certain competences and responsibilities that the NBU undertake. These are as follows:

- Develops state policy in the area of cybersecurity and regulates its implementation in various branches of public administration;
- Prepares proposals of legislation and regulations, creates rules for incident solving procedures;
- Coordinates, follows, and controls fulfillment of tasks in the area of cybersecurity on the national level;

- Represents the central national contact point for the EU and NATO in the area of cyber security/defense;
- Within crisis management of the Slovak Republic, the NBU proposes and brings forward procedures in a case of a cyberattack;
- Performs incident solving.

The key recommendation from the Concept is that a new Law on Cybersecurity that coherently covers the area of cybersecurity be enacted (NBUSR, 20). While the proposed law is still in preparation, public input is being solicited through the Slovak parliament's website. The public may offer new proposals and amendments. The intention is not only coherence but to strengthen the weak record of legislation regarding cybercrime.

The role of the Slovak parliament in making laws

The Slovak parliament does have resolve in purpose, but there is fragmentation in practice on the topic of cybersecurity. Moreover, this question is even more relevant due to evidence of two additional problems. First, while attacks upon a country or people typically take the form of physical destruction, cyberpower does not necessary translate to this type of result from attack, making the assertion of such a "conventional" attack dubious. Second, international law operates on customary regimes and century-long traditions that may date as far back as the Westphalia peace of 1648, but in its current regime international security falls under the auspices of the Law of Armed Conflict based on Geneva Conventions, Hague Conventions, and UN Charter and the whole system that surrounds it (Kirsch, 630). Therefore, the relevance of international law and its application in cyberspace is a relevant question. Yet, determining if a nation has been "attacked" is harder to determine unlike in the Estonian and Georgian examples of 2007 and 2008 respectively. While the Slovak parliament has made efforts, as seen in the proposal for specific law on cybersecurity as discussed in the above paragraph, current Slovak law is lacking. In fact, there is no law on cybersecurity. What does exist is legislation pertaining to cybercrime. And here it can be said that it is very weak as well. Current legislation regarding cybercrime contains only a couple of paragraphs of the Criminal Code (Zákon 300/2005 Z.z.).

Generally speaking, while the Slovak Criminal Code contains a long list of criminal acts, information technology is only mentioned as one of the ways to carry out specific crime. In case of any criminal activity it is a role of bodies of the Ministry of Interior to provide evidence of the crime, to secure the perpetrator(s), to convict the guilty, and to arrest the perpetrator(s). The role of the Courts of Justice, which are under the Ministry of Justice, is to judge such perpetrator(s). However, only a few specific paragraphs of the Criminal Code mention criminal activities performed by information technologies. The following is the actual criminal code as written with translation from Slovak.

Slovak criminal codes

Abbreviated meaning

§122 ods. 2 písm. a:
(2) Trestný čin je spáchaný verejne, ak je spáchaný
a) obsahom tlačoviny alebo rozširovaním spisu, filmom, rozhlasom, televíziou, použitím počítačovej siete alebo iným obdobne účinným spôsobom
According to this paragraph, a crime is committed publicly if a computer network is used.

§194a ods. 1:
Kto úmyselne poruší právo iného na jeho súkromie v obydlí, právo na jeho súkromný a rodinný život vedený v obydlí tým, že bez jeho súhlasu zadovažuje pre seba alebo iné osoby neoprávneným sledovaním jeho obydlia poznatky o jeho živote a živote osôb, ktoré sa zdržiavajú v jeho obydlí, a s využitím informačno-technických prostriedkov a iných technických prostriedkov vyhotovuje z tohto pozorovania záznamy alebo inú dokumentáciu, potrestá sa odňatím slobody až na jeden rok.

It is forbidden to use information technologies and other technologies to make any records in order to knowingly violate someone's privacy of his/her own or his/her family without permission. Punishment is from one year, other paragraphs say from two to four years.

§132 ods. 5:
Detským pornografickým predstavením sa na účely tohto zákona rozumie živé predstavenie určené publiku, a to aj s využitím informačno-technických prostriedkov, v ktorom je dieťa zapojené do skutočného alebo predstieraného sexuálneho konania alebo v ktorom sú obnažované časti tela dieťaťa smerujúce k vyvolaniu sexuálneho uspokojenia inej osoby.

This paragraph specifies child pornographic performance and its unlawfulness to distribute it using information technologies.

The Slovak Criminal Code also adopted the legally binding regulation announced by the European Council. The Council decision, 2005/222/JHA, deals with cyberattacks against information systems (europa.eu). Both the proposed Slovak legislation on cybercrime the competencies are described in detail in Table 14.1.

Table 14.1 describes the creation of the institutional framework for the management of Slovakia's cybersecurity. It also defines responsible organizations involved in particular tasks. The specific abbreviations are seen in the table.

The NBU is considered to be an authority with the highest level of responsibilities in terms of cybersecurity. There have also been some competences held by the Ministry of Finance, but by establishing Prescription No. 171/2016, some competences were moved from Ministry of Finance to the UPVII (Úrad podpredsedu vlády pre investície a informatizáciu).

Deputy Prime Minister's Office for Investments and Informatization of the Slovak Republic

The full text and further description of Prescription No. 171/2016 can be found online at Slov-Lex, the Slovak legislation and information portal, as well as on the Deputy Prime Minister for Investment and Informatization homepage.

International governance

Slovakia does not, at this time, play a role in regional or international governance on the topic of cybersecurity. The government of the Slovak Republic is supportive of international governance institutions and has formally agreed with and implemented within domestic law, various codes, and language passed by the European Union, in accordance with being a member of such an international body. But, the bold vision and ideas laid out in the Koh speech and detailed within the Tallinn manual (Schmitt, 2012) simply do not exist within Slovakia.

Table 14.1 Creation of the Institutional Framework for the Management of Slovakia's Cyber Security

NBÚ	Národný bezpečnostný úrad *(National Security Office/Authority)*
ÚV SR	Úrad vlády Slovenskej republiky *(Government Office of the Slovak Republic)*
VPA	Vecne príslušná autorita pre kybernetickú bezpečnosť *(vecne príslušné autority definované v Akčnom pláne sú ÚOŠS SR (Competent Authority for Cyber Security [Competent authorities defined in Action Plan are Central bodies of the state administration])*
ÚOŠS	Ústredné orgány štátnej správy *(Central Bodies of the State Administration)*
MO SR	Ministerstvo obrany Slovenskej republiky *(Ministry of Defence)*
MF SR	Ministersvo financií Slovenskej republiky *(Ministry of Finance)*
AKOB	Akademická obec *(Academic community)*
ZaA	Združenia a asociácie *(Unions, associations, NGOs)*
MVSR	Ministerstvo vnútra Slovenskej republiky *(Ministry of the Interior)*
SIS	Slovenská informačná služba *(Slovak Information/Intelligence Service)*
NASES	Národná agentúra pre sieťové a elektronické služby *(National Agency for Network and Electronic Services)*
BR SR	Bezpečnostná rada SR *(Security Council)*
MDVaRR	Ministerstvo dopravy, výstavby a regionálneho rozvoja *(Ministry of Transport and Construction of the Slovak Republic)*

Source: Author.

Sovereignty

There is no legal understanding of Slovak cyberspace. Such an understanding may be found within other EU member states' legal codes or national legislation that defines sovereignty over cyberspace, as has been detailed within an Atlas of Cyberspace (Dodge & Kitchin, 2001), but this is not the case in Slovakia. No law or legal code exists at the moment that explicitly states such a thing and therefore the Slovak Republic does not claim sovereignty in cyberspace. As a liberal democracy which practices and allows free speech of its citizens and defends the rights of its citizens to free speech there has not been any effort to control the flow of information or to regulate speech on the Internet. In recent years this has begun to be an issue, arguably a negative one, as Russian propaganda, understood as an information-war, has worked increasingly well within Central Europe and Slovakia (Nimmo, 2015). How to balance citizens' rights while protecting citizens access to technology, as well as the national infrastructure and asserting sovereignty, are serious questions that are to be discussed, though within Slovakia it has so far been conducted in a haphazard fashion. As such, there is no Internet kill switch. While it is arguable as to the limits within a free and open and democratic society on speech, legislation and specific powers granted to Slovak authorities within law enforcement and the courts do not exist. It is possible that within the proposed legislation currently under review within the Slovak parliament clear definitions and regulations may be implemented, but speculation is not recommended at this time.

Cultural understanding

As a member of the European Union the concepts of free speech, privacy, surveillance, and intellectual property are known, accepted, and practiced. Moreover, the international scandals between governments date back to 2009 with Wikileaks and the "hacking" of nations, such as that which occurred in Estonia in 2007 and Iran with the Stuxnet virus that targeted Iran's nuclear program (Nicoll, 2011; Farwell & Rohozinski, 2013a; Collins & McCombie, 2012); the use of cyberwar towards Georgia in 2008 by Russia offers a warning to Slovaks. There is a cultural awareness of the positives and inherent disadvantages of technology. Furthermore, the advent and widespread use of social media in recent years has forced Slovaks and the government to take the appropriate steps both personally and legislatively to address cybercrime and cybersecurity to prevent worse events, such as the occasions of cyberterrorism. While the latter is currently not nearly as significant a threat to Slovakia as the threat of weaponizing cyberspace for information warfare by Russia (Darczewska, 2014: 9–10; Šnídl, 2015), it is necessary that Slovakia modernizes its response.

That is why the creation of the National Security Authority is important, as well as having the proposed legislation currently under review. The creation of a central body to handle cyber threats – whether crime or specifically terrorism – has increasingly become important and is widely accepted within Slovak culture. However, and this is crucial to understanding the critical situation within the country on cybersecurity, both salary differences and insufficient motivation exists. This is the critical situation in Slovakia where the nation faces resource difficulties, namely cybersecurity experts. The institutions that exist within Slovakia that hold decision making power are unilateral and important. Such importance can be observed in the National Security Authority. While there does not exist a Ministry of Information or Ministry of Information Technology in the Slovak Republic, the Action Plan as described in section one and the Authority in section two, offer explanations of its competencies.

Influence of the private sector and NGOs

Business leaders from the CEE region are most concerned about regulatory and operational risks. Risks related to cybersecurity are considered minor; only 5 per cent of the Slovak CEOs consider them as the major threat. It is a significant difference compared to the global level, where 30 per cent of executives link their major concerns with cybersecurity. These findings emerged from the latest KPMG Pulse of Economy Survey 2016. Within CEE, respondents are most concerned with regulatory (45 per cent), operational (37 per cent), talent and strategic risks (both 30 per cent). Cybersecurity was given little relevance as it at most concerns only 12 per cent of managers. In Slovakia it is even below the CEE average as it troubled only 5 per cent of respondents. However, our companies and consumers are exposed to such threats. Despite the fact that this type of attack does not usually go public, it is very possible that dangerous cyber threats – phishing and ransomware – have been recently observed in Slovakia and neighboring countries.[3]

There are multiple organizations involved in cybersecurity. Slovakia is a homeland of worldwide successful IT companies developing antivirus software and GPS navigating systems, but as far as I found out, they are not involved very much in the legislation process in terms of cybersecurity.

One of the most active civic associations consisting of professionals from the IT community is "slovensko.digital." Moreover, slovensko.digital is a respected organization where meaningful commentary is encouraged and accepted via an Internet platform which is used as an expert discussion forum with several threads still active. Most of the new law proposals are discussed personally in workgroups where representatives of various organizations are invited for advice and discussion.[4] The Slovak parliament has made no substantial effort directly through the legislative process to include the private sector and NGOs to manage the topics of cybercrime and cyberterrorism.

As for the role of the legislature, the key legislative developments that have occurred in policy making is offered in the third section. The intersection of private and public is at the present observed only within the context of the proposed cybersecurity law being open to the Slovak public for comment and suggestions.

Furthermore, as to the two topics under review in this chapter: cybercrime and cyberterrorism and how each are combatted in the Slovak Republic as well as what government ministry is responsible, the answers are provided in more detail in section two. However, while the NBU is responsible for combatting both cybercrime and cyberterrorism, the strength of the NBU is determined by legislative mandate and the existing authority is broad, while domestic law is small and not narrow or specific to the demands of twenty-first-century cyber defense at this time. Demands are complex and increasingly becoming interchangeable with day to day (Nye, 2010) threats to national as well as personal security.

Societal implications

The implications of cybercrime and cyberterrorism are grave. Both must be addressed in a clear, concise, and understood manner for Slovak society. While in the past there existed a lack of stable institutional coverage with the Ministry of Finance holding the role of information technology *and* cybersecurity, but with classified information placed under the supervision of the National Security Authority, the Ministry of Defense was responsible for the military aspects of cybersecurity, while the critical infrastructure was under the authority of the Ministry of Interior. Antagonism led to unwilling cooperation and information sharing between national institutions with international cooperation prioritized at the expense of national cooperation. This changed in a significant and positive way with Concept.

After the ConceptPlan15 took effect and NBU became a central authority, it serves as a central hub for all institutions on the matter of cybersecurity with responsibilities for the division of tasks and duties at the national level, instructing all sector oriented central state authorities. Moreover, with the international cooperation with fellow V4 countries and more broadly within the framework of the European Union laws, positive and protective steps are being taken for Slovak citizens, albeit slowly, and there remains a gap between implementation of legal mechanisms for protecting citizens. Both salary differences and insufficient motivation is the critical situation in Slovakia where the nation faces resource difficulties such as shortage of cybersecurity experts. This in turn has made Slovakia remain behind in comparison to other EU member states.

Conclusion

In Slovakia, the unification of terminology is necessary to improve both intra-state and international cooperation. Without such provisions, any statement of national cybersecurity strategy is necessarily defective or incomplete. The nickname, Tatra Tiger, is derived from the local Tatra mountain range in Slovakia and refers to the economy of Slovakia following liberal economic reforms from 2002–2007 and again after 2010. However, with reference to cybersecurity, Slovakia has lagged behind fellow Central European nations in addressing the significant digital threats. Slovakia as a member of both the European Union and NATO must implement serious measures to counter those threats.

While priority has been given to adopting planned legislation as well as increasing security consciousness, Slovakia is still behind other Central European nations, such as the Czech Republic. And though additional support for research and development in information and communication technologies and their security is known, little has been achieved. Such support is increasingly vital because of the threat of a DOS or DDoS attack as observed in fellow EU member nation Estonia or EU-aspirant nation, Georgia. Though Slovakia as an EU member state may have certain advantages that Georgia does not, at the domestic, institutional level, Slovakia's cybersecurity is insufficient in comparison to Estonia's efforts since 2007. In today's complex and dynamic Web 2.0 environment, Slovakia has made the necessary steps via public input on proposed legislation and engagement with the private sector. However, Slovakia remains the Tatra Tiger without teeth on the important, national security issue of cybersecurity preparedness.

Notes

1 The author wishes to acknowledge the research assistance in this section by Martin Rob, graduate student within the Department of Social Sciences, University of Ss. Cyril & Methodius in Trnava.
2 See, NBUSR Draft framework pages 12 and 13: www.nbusr.sk/wp-content/uploads/kyberneticka-bezpecnost/Koncepcia-kybernetickej-bezpecnosti-SR-na-roky-2015-2020-A4.pdf
3 The 2016 edition of KPMG's survey the Pulse of the Economy elaborates on current trends in economy and entrepreneurship, to measure the sentiment among the business leaders in Central & Eastern Europe (CEE).
4 Active forums include: https://platforma.slovensko.digital/t/zakon-o-kybernetickej-bezpecnosti/3201 and https://platforma.slovensko.digital/t/upvii-pracovna-skupina-k9-8-kyberneticka-bezpecnost/3307

Suggested reading

Goda, S. & Ušiak, J. (2016), "What Is the Threat Perception of the Slovak Republic?" *Central European Journal of International and Security Studies*, *10*(1): 61–87.
Górka, M. (2018). "The Cybersecurity Strategy of the Visegrad Group Countries," *Politics in Central Europe*, *14*(2): 75–98.
Tomic, D., Šaljić, E. & Cupic, D. (2018). "Cyber-Security Policies of East European Countries," in E. Carayannis, E. D. Campbell & M. Efthymiopoulos (eds.), *Handbook of Cyber-Development, Cyber-Democracy, and Cyber-Defense* (pp. 1039–1055). Cham: Springer.
Tumkevič, A. (2016). "Cybersecurity in Central and Eastern Europe: From Identifying Risks to Countering Threats," *Baltic Journal of Political Science*, *5*: 73–88.

References

Collins, S. & McCombie, S. (2012). "Stuxnet: The Emergence of a New Cyber Weapon and Its Implications," *Journal of Policing, Intelligence and Counter Terrorism*, 7: 80–91.
Darczewska, J. (2014). "The Anatomy of Russian Information Warfare," The Center for Eastern Studies, Warsaw, Poland. www.osw.waw.pl/sites/default/les/the_anatomy_of_russian_information_warfare.pdf
Dodge, M. & Kitchin, R. (2001). *Atlas of Cyberspace*. London: Pearson Education.
Farwell, J. & Rohozinski, R. (2011a). "Stuxnet and the Future of Cyber War," *Survival*, *53*: 23–40.
Hathaway, M., Spidalieri, F. & Kaushik, A. (2019, April). "Slovak Republic Cyber Readiness at a Glance," Potomic Institute for Global Studies, Arlington, United States. www.potomacinstitute.org/images/CRI/CRI_Slovakia_Profile-Digital.pdf
Nimmo, B. (2015). "Anatomy of an Info-War: How Russia's Propaganda Machine Works, and How to Counter It," Central European Policy Institute, Zurich, Switzerland. www.cepolicy.org/publications/anatomy-info-war-how-russias-propaganda-machine-works-and-how-counter-it

Nicoll, A. (2011). "Stuxnet: Targeting Iran's Nuclear Programme," *Strategic Comments*, *17*: 1–3. www.tandfonline.com/doi/abs/10.1080/13567888.2011.575612

Nye, J. (2010). *Cyber Power. In the Future of Power in the 21st Century.* New York: Public Affairs Press.

Rid, T. (2012). "Cyber War Will Not Take Place," *Journal of Strategic Studies*, *35*(1): 5–32.

Slov-Lex. Prescription No. 171/2016. www.slov-lex.sk/pravne-predpisy/SK/ZZ/2016/171/20160601

Šnídl, V. (2015). "Proruskú propagandu o zhýralom Západe u nás šíri 42 webov"/"The Prophet's Propaganda about the Spoiled West Spreads 42 Sites." https://dennikn.sk/57740/prorusku-propagandu-o- zhyralom-zapade-u-nas-siri-42-webov

15

SLOVENIA

A fragmented cyber security

Laris Gaiser

Introduction

The Slovenian Computer Emergencies Response Team (SI-CERT) was established as a public institute in 1995 to handle reports of security incidents. After that several proposals regarding the systemic regulation of cyber security were prepared; however, implementation never took place. Nevertheless, it became clear that the country needed a cyber security strategy that would join and direct the efforts of all stakeholders toward strengthening and systematically regulating this important area. Up until 2018, operational capacities regarding the response to cyber threats were distributed among SI-CERT as the national response center for network incidents; the Information Security Sector within the IT Directorate of the Ministry of Public Administration; the Ministry of Defense for the defense system and protection against natural and other disasters; the Slovenian Intelligence and Security Agency (SOVA) for counterintelligence activities; and the police, within its IT and Telecommunications Office and the Criminal Police Directorate mainly in the Centre for Computer Investigations, with capacities to combat cybercrime. The formal regulation of stakeholder cooperation in cyber security assurance did not happen until April 2018, when the National Assembly granted the country a clearly structured cyber security system by licensing the *Act on Information Security*.

The historical path

The general level of awareness regarding the dangers posed by cyber risks is relatively low in Slovenian society, and, according to the Institute of Corporate Security, the country's economic environment has always been unaware of the risk posed by cyber-related threats. Consequently, inadequate preparedness, staffing, and operational capabilities represented some of the main issues that national public authorities had to consider when preparing the most suitable cyber security system (Information Resources Management Association, 2019: 626).

As reported by SI-CERT, the 1990s, as well as the first decade of the new millennium, saw Slovenia become a place of ever-increasing IT tensions, exploited mostly by foreign operations as a place for botnet connections and by local hackers breaking into local systems or provoking denial of service attacks (SI-CERT, 2019). An advance in the quality of understanding of the risks posed by modern technological connections was achieved when

Slovenia took over the presidency of the European Union (EU) in 2008 for the first time. During that period authorities noted a rise in pressure on public administration networks and the fact that government employees became increasingly attractive targets for attacks. Several viruses were used against them. Tracks mainly pointed to China.

A turning point in understanding the serious threats that IT infrastructures pose to state security and stability was represented by the emergence of closed session recordings of the Republic of Slovenia government posted on YouTube and the discovery that one of Slovenia's electrical plants had a publicly accessible server embedded with a backdoor which could enable unauthorized entry or monitoring of the plant's control systems.

Despite both cases generating an impressive public debate, research continued to emphasize the existence of a certain distance between civil society and cyber security issues over the years. For example, Dernik and Preslan (2011) presented the results of their research carried out among small and medium enterprises from different sectors concerning their understanding of cyber terrorism and critical infrastructures security. The authors reported an alarming trend, the data showed that only 15 per cent of companies understood the phenomenon; moreover, an even lower percentage considered cybercrime to be an important issue, understanding it to be the same as other threats.

In order to tackle the major development gaps in the field of digital society, and to gradually shape the needed general legal framework, the Slovenian government have adopted several resolutions during the last decade.

The first was represented by the *Resolution on National Security Strategy* published in the Official Gazette of the Republic of Slovenia in April 2010. Despite Slovenia being a member of NATO since 2004 and leaders of the alliance already agreeing upon the establishment of a specific cyber defense program during the Prague Summit in November 2002, the resolution was the first document clearly connecting general cyber security with the country's national interest. Potential sources of threats are mentioned in Chapter 4.2 on Transnational Treats and Risks of National Security, such as cyber threats and the abuse of information technologies or systems. However, this chapter described Slovenia as strongly dependent on the continuity and reliability of information systems in both private and public sectors, with an emphasis on the key functions of state and society, but cyber space as a potential battlefield was only briefly mentioned. In section 5.3.5, responding to cyber threats and abuse of information technologies and systems, the Republic of Slovenia made a commitment to develop a national cyber defense program, including both public and private sectors as well as proposing the establishment of a new national coordinating body for cyber security in the near future. The Resolution on National Security Strategy had the great merit of giving, for the first time, visibility to cyber security connected issues while also proving that ICT security was still not a top national priority.

Nevertheless, since the publishing of the resolution, Slovenia has regularly participated in international cyber security exercises. In 2010, Slovenia took part in Cyber Europe exercises, organized by the European Network and Infrastructure Security Agency (ENISA), as an observer and by 2012 and 2014 was already an active participant. Furthermore, since 2013, it has actively participated in Cyber Coalition exercises within NATO. A national cyber security exercise has not yet been carried out, but participation in these exercises proved to be a good opportunity to check cyber security assurance capacities on a national level as well as to exchange, experience, and establish new connections between stakeholders.

As noted, Slovenia has, so far, been recording about a fifteen-year-long downward trend in its information society development level when compared with other EU member states, which has reflected negatively in other development areas (Ventre, 2012). This situation was the result of significantly low investment in the development of the information society, and insufficient general awareness of the importance of ICT and the internet for the development of the economy, state, and society in general. European competitors made higher and more systematic investments, which resulted in faster development progress than Slovenia was able to implement. By the inappropriate placement of ICT and the internet in its development efforts, Slovenia refused, as a society, to properly develop its potential. Consequently, the Slovenian government, understanding the general situation and attempting to reverse the country's cyclical decline, released the document *Digital Slovenia 2020* in March 2015, which can be viewed as the second main turning point toward the realization of a comprehensive national security environment.

Digital Slovenia wanted to represent a strategic commitment to the speedier development of digital society and the use of opportunities enabled by information and communication technologies as well as the internet for general economic and social benefits. Along with strategies from its scope, it envisages measures to tackle the major development gaps in the field of digital society: faster development of digital entrepreneurship, increased competitiveness in the ICT industry, overall digitization, digital infrastructure development, broadband infrastructure construction, strengthened cyber security, and the development of an inclusive information society. Among the objectives to be achieved by 2020 the document included an inclusive digital society and a safe cyber space (Republic of Slovenia, Digital Slovenia, 2015a: 3).

In order to foster the first, the government stressed the correlation between broadband penetration and economic growth, employment, and productivity, assessing the presence of high-capacity electronic communication infrastructure and accessible electronic communication services as a precondition of any future development. Therefore, Digital Slovenia proposed an economic and general development connecting society with the development of high-quality broadband infrastructure and proposed a strategic planning of an omnipresent high-capacity broadband infrastructure (fixed and mobile) that would be open and accessible to all end-users in order to avoid unequal possibilities of inclusion in the information society.

The second topic was addressed in paragraph 6.4, Cyber Security. In that paragraph, Slovenian authorities showed a full understanding of the complexity of cyber space-based threats, for the first time stressing that all interested parties should work together towards the safety and resilience of ICT infrastructures by focusing on prevention, readiness, and raising awareness, as well as developing efficient and coordinated mechanisms for reacting to new and increasingly complex forms of cyberattacks and cybercrime. Therefore, the main objective foreseen by the document was that of establishing a comprehensive cyber security system as an important integral factor of national security that could contribute to ensuring an open, safe, and secure cyber space. This would create a basis for a smooth functioning infrastructure, important for state entity operations as well as for the life of each individual. The establishment of an effective cyber security assurance system that would prevent and eliminate the consequences of security incidents was programmed to be attained by 2020.

The aforementioned document did contribute to change social attitudes towards ICT and the internet at the threshold of a new development period until creating a more stimulating environment for the faster and more harmonized development of an information society and ICT sector, especially considering the fact that the national government upgraded the strategy with its *Next Generation Broadband Network Development Plan* in March 2016, exactly one year later. Slovenia has one of the lowest population densities in

Europe, making infrastructure investments costlier. In February 2015, the European Commission approved Slovenia's *Rural Development Programme* 2014–2020, which was a joint program representing a basis for the absorption of the EAFRD funds. The measure under Focus Area 6C – enhancing the accessibility, use and quality of information, and communication technologies (ICT) in rural areas – was to improve rural access to broadband internet connections. Consequently, the aim of the proposed development plan – representing the basis for the allocation of EU cohesion policy funds in the period 2014–2020 (from ERDF and EAFRD) and other public funds in this area – was to support investments in broadband infrastructures in order to make them accessible throughout state territory, enabling a balanced development, reducing the digital divide, and increasing the involvement of individuals in contemporary social movements. In terms of directing development, the internet became a strategic tool for increasing productivity, creating innovative business models, products, and services, making communication more efficient and increasing the overall efficiency of society.

Symbolically, the approval of the above-described plan was contemporary with the release of the *Slovenian National Cyber Security Strategy* (2016). The strategy, based on three pillars – prevention, response, and awareness – became the milestone of all future choices in the field of IT-based infrastructure security, proposing the way a security assurance system should be organized together with the measures necessary for achieving set objectives. With more years of delay, if compared with all major European countries, Slovenia metabolized that strengthening the overall system was necessary because of the ever-growing importance of cyber security for the smooth functioning of systems the whole society depends upon.

Transposing strategies into law

The government wanted the *Cyber Security Strategy* to help Slovenia define its measures for establishing a national cyber security system that could facilitate a rapid response to the field's related threats and would serve to effectively protect ICT infrastructure and information systems, thus ensuring the continuous operation of both public and private sectors, and, in particular, the key functions of the state and society in all security situations. As the strategy stated, ensuring the security of cyber space and balancing it within the parameters of ensuring safety and economic viability as well as human rights and fundamental freedoms was a priority and the issue was addressed recalling the *Resolution on the National Security Strategy of the Republic of Slovenia* (2010), the *EU Cyber Security Strategy: Open, safe and secure cyberspace* (2013), and the then *Draft Directive on measures to ensure a common high level of network and information security across the Union*, which was adopted in June 2016 by the European Parliament as *The Directive on security of network and information systems* (NIS Directive).

Analysis of the ongoing situation showed that cooperation of stakeholders in cyber security assurance was not formally regulated and that society's overbearing dependence on ICT has increased the risks associated with general cybercrime, cyber warfare, and activities of foreign intelligence services given that various state or non-state stakeholders may exploit cyberspace to achieve their objectives, particularly by carrying out cyber-intelligence operations, which may, in certain segments, jeopardize the political, security, and economic interests of the Republic of Slovenia.

The strategy pointed out that successful high-level cyber security assurance requires the effective use of existing resources and appropriate multi-level organization, suggesting that Slovenia set up central coordination of the national cyber security assurance system and provide conditions for its stable operation. This coordination body shall synchronize cyber security assurance capabilities and policy planning at a strategic level to ensure the cyber security of the country's lower levels as well as representing a single point of contact for international cooperation (Republic of Slovenia, 2016: 9). The organization form of coordination functions shall be determined by the Government of the Republic of Slovenia. At the operational level of cyber security assurance, SI-CERT will operate within its capabilities on a national level, the Ministry of Defense in the field of defense and protection against natural and other disasters, the police in ensuring cyber security in the context of public safety and the fight against cybercrime, the Slovenian Intelligence and Security Agency (SOVA) in counterintelligence, and the emergent SIGOV-CERT in public administration. The cyber security assurance system shall also include other stakeholders as operators of critical infrastructure in both private and public sectors, particularly in the energy supply sector (electricity producers and distributors), and in the information and communication support sector (telecom operators, information society service providers). Given the above-reported analysis and vision, the implementation strategy suggested was to be based on the upgrade and update of existing cyber security system capabilities, monitored by the Government of the Republic of Slovenia, the central coordination of the national cyber security system and by relevant ministries in accordance with the grounds of jurisdiction set out in the Constitution and legislation.

Between 2008 and 2016 the number of cyber security incidents in Slovenia increased six-fold. SI-CERT reported 2,300 incidents in 2017 (STA, 2017). Starting to implement the strategy's provisions, and under pressure from a growing number of cyberattacks in January 2017, the Slovenian government officially determined that the institution suitable for assuming the competence of the National Cyber Security Authority should be the Government Office for the Protection of Classified Information. By April 2017, Slovenia adopted the resolution on the obligations and the organization of the established National Cyber Security Authority, thereby beginning to fulfill its commitment to NATO in order to prioritize strengthening of national capacities of cyber defense and applying the requirements, imposed by the NIS Directive on measures to ensure an overall high level of network and information security in the EU. The NIS Directive (European Commission, 2016) supports the establishment of country-based authorities that should manage all cyber and critical infrastructures' vulnerabilities at the local level, facilitating cooperation and exchange of information among states setting up a Critical Infrastructure Warning Information Network, a CSIRT Network, and favoring the necessary cross-border synergies.

Thus, central coordination of the national security system and conditions for stable operation have been established; though an official transposition of the NIS Directive into a national legal framework and clear legislation, defining the stakeholders' duties and responsibilities, on general national cyber-related as well as critical infrastructure security was still missing. For that reason, the government asked the Government Office for the Protection of Classified Information to prepare a legal proposal to be submitted to the National Assembly. The Act on Information Security was prepared in less than a year by the Government Office for the Protection of Classified Information in cooperation with the Ministry of Public Administration and unanimously approved by the National Assembly in April 2018.

The Slovenian cyber security system

By adopting the Act on Information Security, Slovenia concluded its long path of setting up a national framework for network and information security, which contained within it a national strategy, at least one response center, and a competent national authority to coordinate national-level activities. As requested by the NIS Directive, it established cooperation mechanisms at the EU-level and identified key service providers obliged to take on certain measures to increase the level of information security, including, inter alia, compulsory reporting of observed security incidents.

During parliamentarian procedures, some organizational responsibilities were redefined, not without a certain amount of surprise, and the Government Office for the Protection of Classified Information lost its leading role. Despite the initial governmental vision and Cyber Security Strategy suggestions (Republic of Slovenia, 2016: 8), it will not become the apical coordinating body for national cyber security. Within Parliament, a more fragmented idea of shared responsibilities among different governmental bodies prevailed instead of a broader concentration of duties under the direct control of the prime minister. Accordingly, the Government Office for the Protection of Classified Information must pass all competencies, no later than January 1, 2020, to the new national authority, the Information Security Agency (a body within the ministry responsible for information society, currently the Ministry of Public Administration), similar to the past decision for the Administration for Nuclear Safety Security. Until then, tasks are still performed by the government office that prepared the legislation. SI-CERT is confirmed as the body dealing with network and information security incidents in its role as National Response Center. The response center of state administration to deal with incidents in the area of network security is established as SIGOV-CERT at the ministry responsible for the management of information and communication systems, which is incorporated within the Ministry of Public Administration.

Article 5 of the Act states that three categories of service providers are subjected to it:

1   Providers of essential services (controlling critical infrastructures);
2   Digital service providers;
3   Public administration bodies.

The following sectors are listed as essential services:

1   Energy;
2   Digital infrastructure;
3   Drinking water supply;
4   Healthcare;
5   Transport;
6   Banking;
7   Financial market infrastructure;
8   Food supply;
9   Environmental protection.

Digital service providers are search engines, online marketplaces, cloud computing, and public administration bodies managing information systems and networks or providing information services necessary for the smooth functioning of the state or ensuring national security. They are obliged to provide minimum security requirements to information systems, notification of incidents and evaluation of incidents.

Digital service providers with less than 50 employees, or those having an annual turnover or annual balance sheet not exceeding €10 million, shall not be considered as providers of digital services while the identification of essential services providers is delegated to the government. It will define specific providers and critical infrastructure operators, basing the assessment on the type of services that are essential for the preservation of key social or economic activities, provided that the service depends on the networks and information systems and on the fact that a potential incident would have a significant negative impact on the provision of this service.

The Act demands that providers of any essential service must determine the contact person and their deputy for information security, forwarding their contact details to the competent national authority. Their duty is to report incidents to the Computer Emergency Response Team that will assess possible solutions. When in the presence of an event that negatively affects the confidentiality, integrity, and availability of a network, information system, or information service provider; an incident causing difficulties to the country's functioning, notably one affecting the defense information system, internal security, protection or rescue system; or the full disablement of an essential service or partially disabled operation of at least three essential service areas, CERT has to refer the incident immediately to the national competent authority. If the national competent authority assesses that the country is dealing with a cyberattack or a serious incident that could become critical, it must immediately inform the government and the National Security Council (the institution coordinating all the national security bodies, chaired by the prime minister). Additionally, the authority may determine the most appropriate and proportionate measures necessary to halt the incident or to eliminate its consequences. Instruction can be written or oral; the latter case must be confirmed in writing within 48 hours, maximum.

According to Article 24 of the Act on Information Security, Slovenia, instead of creating a specific agency with a broad range of powers, has decided to equip itself with a well-defined but fragmented system of cyber defense that becomes a domain implemented in coordination by the competent national authority, the national CERT, SIGOV-CERT, the Ministry of Defense, police, the Slovenian Intelligence and Security Agency, and other national authorities in accordance with their competencies in ensuring national security. The general public will be informed only if convenient with a communication that will be shaped by the Government Communication Office and which the media may only publish in an unchanged form. Taking this approach, the Slovenian decision makers have tried to respond urgently to the contemporary problems posed by the cyber world by avoiding potential conflicts with existing institutions defending their prerogatives.

Conclusion

Since 2010, Slovenia has carefully planned ways to reduce its delay in developing the necessary sensitivity to the digital world, its ability to guarantee the security of IT systems and its control of the vulnerability of critical infrastructures. A process of civil society modernization and updated legislation began in 2016 with the approval of the Cyber Security Strategy and was concluded in 2018 with the translation of the European NIS Directive into law. With the approval of the Act on Information Security, Slovenia has finally established a clear legal framework for managing risks arising from cyber space. During the legislative process, political factionalism, as well as a strategic unpreparedness of some institutions, prevented the country from establishing a new independent structure effective in the field of cyber security. Despite wishes expressed by many experts and it being an important part of the national security system, Slovenia lost the opportunity to become a point of reference in the sector. Only a fragmented cyber defense structure coordinated by the competent national authority – the Ministry of Public Administration – has been shaped.

Contrary to what was outlined in the Cyber Security Strategy, Slovenia did not give form to a body with both strategic and operational functions. It did not approve the transformation of the Government Office for Protection of Classified Information into a sort of National Security Agency dedicated entirely to data and infrastructure defense. By creating a competent national authority, the minimum requirements dictated by NATO and the NIS Directive have been met; however, an innovative and more dynamic environment has not emerged. A system that could guarantee a constant presence of national security in cyber space in order to meet the most updated requirements of deterrence, early warning, and improving international cooperation in case of cross-border incidents was not created (Gaiser, 2018). However, the progress that has been made within only eight years of Slovenia understanding its contemporary security needs is commendable.

Given that many of the ideas suggested by the Cyber Security Strategy have been implemented, the government urgently needs to update it as well as the Resolution on National Security Strategy in order to harmonize both with the current organizational reality. Finally, the most decisive step will be to implement an environment, based upon a shared security culture, able to better involve civil society and consequently make the country more resilient to any future stress.

Suggested reading

BSA. (n.d.). "COUNTRY: Slovenia." http://cybersecurity.bsa.org/assets/PDFs/country_reports/cs_slovenia.pdf

Cyber Wiser. (2017, July). "Slovenia (SI)." www.cyberwiser.eu/slovenia-si

Markelj, B. & Zgaga, S. (2016). "Comprehension of Cyber Threats and Their Consequences in Slovenia," *Computer Law and Security Review*, 32(3): 513–525.

Praprotnik, I., Podbregar, I., Bernik, I. & Tičar, B. (2013, March). "A Slovenian Perspective on Cyber Warfare." researchgate.net/publication/300463529_A_Slovenian_Perspective_on_Cyber_Warfare

Republic of Slovenia, Digital Slovenia. (2016, February). "Cyber Security Strategy: Establishing a System to Ensure a High Level of Cyber Security." gov.si/assets/ministrstva/MJU/DID/Cyber_Security_Strategy_Slovenia.pdf

References

"Act on Information Security 2018." www.pisrs.si/Pis.web/pregledPredpisa?id=ZAKO7707

Dernik, I. & Preslan, K. (2011, January). "Cyber Terrorism in Slovenia – Fact or Fiction," Paper presented to 2nd International Multi-Conference on Complexity, Informatics and Cybernetics, Orlando, United States. www.researchgate.net/publication/301626193_Cyber_terrorism_in_Slovenia_-_fact_or_fiction

European Commission. (2013). "Cybersecurity Strategy of the European Union: An Open, Safe and Secure Cyberspace." https://eeas.europa.eu/archives/docs/policies/eu-cyber-security/cybsec_comm_en.pdf

European Commission. (2016). "Directive on the Security of Network and Information Systems." https://eur-lex.europa.eu/legal-content/EN/TXT/PDF/?uri=CELEX:32016L1148&from=EN

Gaiser, L. (2018). "European Critical Infrastructure Protection: The Need for a Regional Approach and a Cyber Constant Contact Strategy," *National Security and the Future*, 19(1, 2): 6.

Government of the Republic of Slovenia. (2010). "Resolution on National Security Strategy of Republic of Slovenia." www.pisrs.si/Pis.web/pregledPredpisa?id=RESO61

Information Resources Management Association. (ed.). (2019). *National Security: Breakthroughs in Research and Practice: Breakthroughs in Research and Practice*. IGI Global: Hershey, PA.

Republic of Slovenia. (2015a). "Digital Slovenia 2020 – Development Strategy for the Information Society until 2020." www.mju.gov.si/fileadmin/mju.gov.si/pageuploads/DID/Informacijska_druzba/pdf/DSI_2020_3-2016_pic1.pdf

Republic of Slovenia. (2015b). "Next Generation Broadband Network Development Plan." www.mju. gov.si/fileadmin/mju.gov.si/pageuploads/DID/Informacijska_druzba/NGN_2020/NGN_2020_Slo venia_EN.pdf

Republic of Slovenia. (2016). "Cyber Security Strategy." www.uvtp.gov.si/fileadmin/uvtp.gov.si/ pageuploads/Cyber_Security_Strategy_Slovenia.pdf

SI-CERT. (2019). www.cert.si/en/

STA. (2017, June 16). "Debate Hears Slovenia Lagging behind in Cybersecurity." *Slovenian Times*. www. sloveniatimes.com/debate-hears-slovenia-lagging-behind-in-cybersecurity

Ventre, D. (ed.). (2012). *Cyber Conflict: Competing National Perspectives*. London: ISTE.

16

IN THE LINE OF RUSSIAN AGGRESSION

Ukraine, hybrid warfare, and cybersecurity defense

Olya Zaporozhets and Oleksiy Syvak

Introduction and background

Once a Soviet Union republic, Ukraine gained its independence after the Soviet Union collapsed in 1991. At that time 84 per cent of Ukrainians took a referendum vote in support of the Act of Declaration of Independence of Ukraine. This is an important fact to note for the future discussion of a hybrid war between Russia and Ukraine. The referendum of 1991 included Ukrainian citizens in Crimea and eastern Ukrainian territories whose decision to be a part of independent Ukraine was questioned by Russian President Putin in 2014. Putin justified his invasion of the Ukrainian territories by claiming that its purpose was to "protect Russian speaking population of Ukraine." That claim, like every other in informational wars, was only partially true as many villagers in eastern Ukraine spoke Ukrainian or a mix of the two languages and the majority of them supported the decision for Ukrainian independence with the National Referendum of 1991 and at the time of the Russian invasion in 2014.

The 1991 Declaration of Independence of Ukraine and the referendum provided a new historic beginning where this Eastern European nation of about 52 million people at the time started its path to democracy, breaking bounds with socialism and building democratic institutions, a free economic market, and new international relations. The initial years of Ukrainian independence were marked by a drastic economic crisis, formation of oligarchic elites, and the growth of corruption. Strategically located between Russia and the NATO countries of Slovakia, Hungary, Poland, and Romania, Ukraine was ambivalent in its foreign policy towards Europe, the US, and NATO, on the one hand, and towards Russia and the Customs Union that consisted of some former Soviet republics, on the other. Perhaps a bit naïvely, the Ukrainian government sought to cement its friendships with the West and

East by signing the Budapest Memorandum (1994), where it surrendered the world's third largest nuclear arsenal in exchange for guarantees of its territorial integrity and security from Russia, Great Britain, and the United States, initial signers of the memorandum, and later co-signed by France and China. For two decades after proclaiming its independence, many Ukrainians seemed to believe that there were no valid external threats to Ukrainian national security: the Russians were family and the West was friendly and civil.

However, the situation rapidly shifted as the Ukrainian government negotiated the European Association and Free Trade Agreement with the EU in 2014. Russia saw the threat of Ukraine joining the European community as it could mean NATO borders extending to the Russian backyard and Ukraine leaving the Russian sphere of influence. As Ukrainian President Yanukovich found himself caught in this East and West dilemma and refused to sign the European Association Agreement, the Ukrainian people started peaceful protests that lasted for three winter months and progressed to bloody street fights where over 100 protesters were shot. This protest was called the Revolution of Dignity, which only became possible with the utilization of real-time broadcasting, good communication between the protesters, and the ability to evaluate sources of information in initially government-controlled and Russia-influenced media communications. That experience was remarkable as we consider strategies for building national informational defense systems and bringing awareness about cybersecurity among the general public.

The Revolution of Dignity led to Yanukovich leaving office and fleeing to Russia. After that the Ukrainian Parliament (Verhovna Rada of Ukraine) appointed a transitional government and reelections. At this time of vulnerable transition, Russian President Putin invaded the Ukrainian Crimean Peninsula with a further illegal referendum and annexation that was not recognized by the international community. This was the first incident when Russia annexed occupied territories, as in the instances with Abkhazia, South Ossetia, Transnistria, and Nagorno-Karabakh, where Russia first would start with military aggression, then form the puppet governments of so-called people republics, but did not proceed to the official annexation of those territories. Apparently, the need for restoration of the Russian greatness in Russian society was so significant that it certainly outweighed the risks of international community reaction to this situation. Western leaders and international organizations were unable to enforce international law during previous Russian military occupational campaigns, so Putin, perhaps, decided to raise his electoral ratings with this Tsar conqueror invasion. In response, Ukraine proclaimed its territory as being occupied and appealed to the signers of the Budapest Memorandum to protect the integrity of its territory as one of the country-signers conducted the attack. That appeal was to no avail.

After the Crimean Peninsula occupation, Russia moved to gain control over Ukrainian eastern and southern territories, first by means of Russian inspired protests led by Russian special forces officers that soon turned into open military aggression by the Russian army with the use of hardware military equipment. It became known as the Russian Spring operation. The advancement of Russian military forces was stopped by the combination of revolution-inspired Ukrainian volunteer military groups and Ukrainian active duty military forces. NATO and Budapest Memorandum signers were unable to render any military support to Ukraine at that time. Russia gained control of 8 per cent of the Ukrainian territory that consisted of one third of two Ukrainian regions (oblasts) – Donetsk and Luhansk oblasts. This territory and Ukraine in general further became the field of a new hybrid war and a lab for Russian cyberattack training, which presented Ukrainians with unlimited opportunities to develop, update, and perfect informational defense and cybersecurity systems.

Hybrid war

To help illustrate Ukrainian–Russian hybrid warfare, there was one particular incident that deeply shocked and awakened the international community. It was the shooting down of the Malaysian commercial flight with the Russian Buk surface-to-air missile, a weapon of massive destruction, at an altitude of 33,000 feet in July of 2014. All 298 flight passengers and crew members were killed, out of which 80 passengers were children. Of course, the operation of surface-to-air missile equipment required several years of specialized military college training and, apparently, could not be done by anyone but Russian soldiers. The question remains, however, about the purpose of this attack in the context of Ukrainian–Russian hybrid war.

According to the head of the Security Service of Ukraine (SSU), Valentin Nalivaychenko (in office 2014–2015), the Buk crossed the Russian–Ukrainian border the night before the incident, and Russian soldiers simply confused two villages with the same name, Pervomayskiy. As a matter of fact, Donetsk area had as many as seven villages and towns with that same name. At the time of the incident there were two planes in the airspace flying at similar heights, one was Malaysian MH 17 and another one was Russian, Aeroflot flight SU2074. Nalivaychenko presented evidence that the Russian plane was the real target, not the Malaysian one, as its shooting down was supposed to create for Russians the "casus beli," the situation that would justify open Russian invasion of the Ukrainian territory (Espreso.TV, 2016).

This incident illustrates the essence of the informational war, how reality and facts can be distorted or confused to support conventional military operations. This also gives an insight into the kinds of challenges that Ukrainian military, Security Service, and Ukrainian people in general have to face daily in the area of informational defense in addition to typical challenges that are faced by any computer user, business, or government organization in every country of the world. According to the Head of Informational Security and Cyberdefense Council of Ukraine, Ellina Shnurko-Tabakova, the cybersecurity challenges of Ukraine are similar to other countries; Ukraine has "just as much [cyber] stealing as anywhere else in the world ... however, the rate of cyberaggression in Ukraine with no commercial interest is the highest in the world," she adds (personal communication, July 27, 2019). Shnurko-Tabakova further explained that the cyberattacks on business and government organizations are often done by Russian special forces as they are conducted in support of and in tandem with conventional Russian military actions. For example, the naval operations website was under cyberattack at the time of the Russians attacking and seizing Ukrainian military ships in Kerch Strait in November 2018. This cyberattack created barriers for the Ukrainian naval operations office to communicate about this incident for approximately five hours while the international community was struggling to learn the details about this situation and understand the facts in the news stream (Ellina Shnurko-Tabakova, personal communication, July 27, 2019).

The intent of Russian cyber- and informational attacks has also a purpose of psychological influence, such as discreditation of government or military leadership, especially during the time of critical military operations. As noted in Ukrainian scientific cyberliterature, informational attacks have a purpose of bringing chaos, challenging or breaking organizational structures, and causing emotional distress or turmoil to the point of self-destruction (Vorobyova, 2010). One example of informational attack in a hybrid war was evidenced during the Battle of Debaltseve. The Ukrainian military was surrounded by Russians in Debaltseve in Eastern Ukraine in January 2015, which resulted in 267 Ukrainian military deaths and over 100 military personnel taken captive. At the time of this operation, Russians spread messages through the news and social networks that Ukrainian generals were incompetent and unable to foresee a surrounding that apparently was obvious to all internet users. This, of course, presented a distorted picture of real facts which became exceptionally dangerous as sharing true facts by Ukrainian generals in that situation could lead to casualties in real time military operation. Again, this incident illustrated how the informational attack was synchronized with the military operation to magnify the offense impact. Such complex informational and cyberdefense situations require multilevel preparation and response, which we will discuss next.

Challenges of cybersecurity defense in the hybrid war

The first challenge that Ukraine faced in the Russian hybrid war was the inconsistency of Soviet and NATO cybersecurity standards. It is important to note that Ukraine inherited Soviet informational defense systems that, at the time of the Russian invasion, were dated and ineffective as they were based on the 1990s standards that were created before the internet became available to users, explains Ellina Shnurko-Tabakova (personal communication, July 27, 2019). The original Ukrainian Complex Informational Defense System is geared towards regulating physical requirements for data storage, coding, and location, while alternative EU and NATO security standards are concentrated on risk management, preparedness, and prevention that is described by the Informational Security Management System.

The hybrid war with Russia prompted the Ukrainian government to pass several informational defense laws and Presidential Mandates that set up a road map for reformation of the Ukrainian informational defense systems to adequately meet contemporary cybersecurity challenges. One such key Ukrainian document was the Strategic Defense Bulletin of Ukraine (2016) that focused on alignment of Ukrainian defense standards with the defense standards of NATO and the EU with the deadline of 2020 (see, Указ Президента України Про рішення Ради національної безпеки та оборони України від 20 травня 2016 року "Про Стратегічний оборонний бюлетень України" [The Mandate of the President of Ukraine about the Decision of the National Security and Defense Counsel of Ukraine "About Strategic Defense Bulletin"], 2016). The Ukrainian government also moved on identification of the cybersecurity problems and governmental structures responsible for cybersecurity defense and protection of people, outlining strategic goals and functions in the cybersecurity law "About Basic Principles of Cyber Security" of Ukraine, passed in 2017 (see Закон України Про основні засади забезпечення кібербезпеки України [About Basic Principles of Cyber Security of Ukraine], 2017).

While this law was criticized by the Ukrainian cybersecurity professional community for the lack of specificity and inefficiency, it allowed Ukrainian governmental and military agencies to start the process of incorporating western cybersecurity standards into their frequently outdated organizational systems and set up the course for their reformation. It also allowed business organizations to switch their focus from the obligation to fulfill certain static system defense requirements to more attuned and updated risk management systems. In addition, the Ukrainian president passed the decree where Ukrainian providers were not allowed to offer internet services that were operated on Russian servers and resources (e.g., mail.ru, yandex.ru etc.) (see, Указ Президента України Про рішення Ради національної безпеки та оборони України від 28 квітня 2017 року "Про застосування персональних спеціальних економічних та інших обмежувальних заходів (санкцій)" [The Mandate of the President of Ukraine about the Decision of the National Security and Defense Counsel of Ukraine "About Application of Special Personal Economic and other Restrictive Measures

(Sanctions)"], 2017). This mandate had an intent to limit the leaks of data and sensitive personal information to the Russian special cyber forces.

With all of this being said, it is also important to note the role of the volunteer civilians and organizations in reformation and cyber protection. Because the Revolution of Dignity had a strong democratic movement, the defense from Russian aggression that followed also inherited unprecedented support from the civil volunteer movement. Small and large civil volunteer groups and individuals actively responded to the needs of the military by the direct provision of equipment purchased from personal and donor funds, often imported from abroad. Perhaps, surprisingly for many, the update of military communication systems at that time also happened in a similar manner, where Ukrainian volunteers decided that purchasing IP telephony communication systems, which matched western standards, was more economical and presented a better communication solution for military needs than Ukrainian standard alternatives. Therefore, very early on in the hybrid war with Russia, Ukrainian military units were functioning with contemporary IP telephony communication equipment that was not in compliance with Ukrainian legislation and military regulations at that time. That, perhaps, gives a surprising insight, that like any other democratic change, cybersecurity informational defense preparedness in general could be initiated by the people and later legalized by the government.

This opens another important topic of discussion in cybersecurity and defense, an informational education of lay people that needs to start in elementary school. Ellina Shnurko-Tabakova shared that Ukrainian secondary schools and colleges started offering the Introduction to Cybersecurity class as the Ukrainian government recognized the need for each Ukrainian student to be able to critically evaluate the source of information, check the validity of facts, and protect devices from viruses (personal communication, July 27, 2019). At the end of the day, strong cybersecurity and informational defense are not defined by the response to the attack, but rather by the preparedness to prevent those attacks before they happen. "You should always overestimate your enemy and be ready," Shnurko-Tabakova adds (personal communication, July 27, 2019).

Conclusion

Ukraine's experience is unique as it has a direct hybrid war experience with Russia and was able to successfully mitigate the effects of purposeful Russian cyberattacks over the progression of the hybrid war, frequently unnoticed by the general Ukrainian public. Ukraine inherited Soviet systems of informational defense that were outdated at the beginning of the Russian–Ukrainian hybrid war. In such a situation Ukraine was able to make several impressive strides on multiple levels: legislative, people awareness, technological modernization of organizational equipment systems, and education. There is a lesson that Ukraine has to offer to the international community: not to be naïve about the enemy and be ready for the attack before it starts.

Suggested reading

CCDCOE. (2016, March 15). "Cyber Security Strategy of Ukraine." https://ccdcoe.org/uploads/2018/10/NationalCyberSecurityStrategy_Ukraine.pdf
Council on Foreign Relations. (2018, August 29). "How Ukraine's Government Has Struggled to Adapt to Russia's Digital Onslaught." www.cfr.org/blog/how-ukraines-government-has-struggled-adapt-russias-digital-onslaught#RejectSurvey

Greenberg, A. (2018, August 22). "The Untold Story of NotPetya, the Most Devastating Cyberattack in History," *WIRED*. www.wired.com/story/notpetya-cyberattack-ukraine-russia-code-crashed-the-world/

Miller, C. (2018, March 7). "What's Ukraine Doing to Combat Russian Cyberwarfare? 'Not Enough'," *Radio Free Europe*. www.rferl.org/a/ukraine-struggles-cyberdefense-russia-expands-testing-ground/29085277.html

OSCE. (n.d.). "Ukraine Information Security Concept." www.osce.org/fom/175051?download=true

Sanger, D. E. (2018). *The Perfect Weapon: War, Sabotage, and Fear in the Cyber Age*. New York: Crown.

Streltsov, L. (2017, November). "The System of Cybersecurity in Ukraine: Principles, Actors, Challenges, Accomplishments," *European Journal for Security Research*. DOI: 10.1007/s41125-017-0020-x

References

Espreso.TV. (2016, October 3). "Екс-глава СБУ Наливайченко – про доповідь слідчих щодо MH17" (Former Head of the National Security Service of Ukraine – About MH17 Investigation Report) [video interview]. http://flight-mh17.livejournal.com/184084.html

Vorobyova, I. V. (2010). "Information and Psychological Weapon as an Independent Means of Information-Psychological Warfare," *Системи озброєння і військова техніка* [*Journal of Military Weapons and Equipment*], *1*, 141–144.

"Закон України Про основні засади забезпечення кібербезпеки України" ["About Basic Principles of Cyber Security of Ukraine"], No. 45, §403 (2017, October 5). https://zakon.rada.gov.ua/laws/show/2163-19

Указ Президента України Про рішення Ради національної безпеки та оборони України "Про застосування персональних спеціальних економічних та інших обмежувальних заходів (санкцій)" ["The Mandate of the President of Ukraine about the Decision of the National Security and Defense Counsel of Ukraine 'About Application of Special Personal Economic and other Restrictive Measures (Sanctions)'"], No. 133/2017 (2017, April 28). www.president.gov.ua/documents/1332017-21850

Указ Президента України Про рішення Ради національної безпеки та оборони України від 20 травня 2016 року "Про Стратегічний оборонний бюлетень України" ["The Mandate of the President of Ukraine about the Decision of the National Security and Defense Counsel of Ukraine 'About Strategic Defense Bulletin'"], No. 240/2016 (2016, June 6). www.president.gov.ua/documents/2402016-20137

17

UNITED KINGDOM

Pragmatism and adaptability in the cyber realm

Tim Stevens

Introduction

The United Kingdom of Great Britain and Northern Ireland (UK) is one of the world's leading economies and has been able to marshal substantial national resources to address a range of cybersecurity issues. The UK's overt national cybersecurity program is a decade old and constitutes a sophisticated approach to cybersecurity involving multiple public and private actors. These operate in a robust planning framework that treats cyberspace as a strategic domain and cybersecurity as a means of pursuing the national interest at home and abroad. The UK recognizes that its prosperity and international visibility makes it an attractive target to cyber criminals and strategic adversaries and is developing ways of countering these threats. This chapter outlines the UK's cybersecurity strategy and its planning assumptions; sets out the main institutions and stakeholders; describes pertinent UK legislation; and discusses relevant aspects of UK foreign policy. It also looks ahead briefly to some of the societal implications of UK cybersecurity and concludes that while there are some strategic challenges to UK cybersecurity in the form of Brexit and Russian subversion, the UK is relatively well prepared to address the broad landscape of cybersecurity challenges.

National cybersecurity strategy

The UK's first national cybersecurity strategy (NCSS) was published in 2009, with subsequent iterations in 2011 and 2016 (Cabinet Office, 2011; HM Government, 2009a, 2016a). The current NCSS, issued in November 2016, is a mature statement of national cybersecurity aims, coupled with an ambitious auditing program for measuring progress towards its strategic goals. It is framed as a second five-year (2016–2021) National Cyber Security Programme (NCSP), following its 2011 predecessor, but looks beyond the 2021 time-frame to recognize evolving challenges from emerging technologies and adaptations in adversarial tools and capabilities. The NCSS prioritizes partnerships between government, industry, and society to deliver better national cybersecurity through multi-sectoral behavioral change but is driven by an important shift in government thinking. Government recognized that earlier reliance on the market to drive national cybersecurity innovation had engendered insufficient "scale and pace of change required to stay ahead of the fast moving threat" (HM Government, 2016a: 9). Accordingly, government has adopted a more interventionist stance to drive secure cyber behaviors across multiple sectors, supported by an enhanced financial investment of £1.9 billion over five years to "transform significantly" UK cybersecurity (HM Government, 2016a: 10). If successful, government will retreat from this central role, allowing the twin drivers of the market and technology to continue improving the cybersecurity of UK society and economy (HM Government, 2016a: 71).

The NCSS is organized around three mutually supporting themes – Defend, Deter, and Develop – undergirded by a renewed commitment to International Action to promote bilateral and multilateral cyber initiatives that advance UK national interests and promote collective security. "Defend" counters evolving cyber threats and promotes the protection and resilience of UK assets and society, including through public education and knowledge exchange with industry, particularly small-medium enterprises (SMEs). This includes an Active Cyber Defence (ACD) program, which claims to have "objectively" reduced through automated means the incidence and effects of common cyber threats across the public sector (gov.uk) domain (Stevens et al., 2019). "Deter" prioritizes actions to identify and pursue hostile actors in cyberspace and reserves the right to prosecute offensive actions against them if necessary. It emphasizes the development of sovereign capabilities, including cryptography, to reduce risk from cybercrime, cyberterrorism, and foreign cyber actors, both state and non-state. A core component of this effort is the establishment of a National Offensive Cyber Programme (NOCP) across the Ministry of Defence and GCHQ, the UK signals intelligence agency, which marks the present NCSS as more "offensive" in orientation than its defensively minded forerunners (Christou, 2016: 62–86; Lonsdale, 2016). The "Develop" strand promotes cybersecurity education, research, and training to reduce the cybersecurity skills gap, and support private-sector innovation and growth. Alongside a range of educational outreach and engagement programs, one highly visible component of "Develop" has been an increase to 19 in the number of accredited Academic Centres of Excellence in Cyber Security Research (ACE-CSRs) at UK universities.

Britain's perceived self-identity is an important driver in the framing of national cybersecurity and its strategic ambitions. Its historical contribution to digital innovation informs its status as "one of the world's leading digital nations" (HM Government, 2016a: 6). The UK is also, as attributed to Napoleon, "a nation of shopkeepers," by which is meant that England's wealth derived from commerce, rather than any innate material advantage. So too with cyberspace, which is seen as an opportunity to bolster and promote national economic productivity and prosperity. Indeed, as the NCSS makes clear, the "future of the UK's security and prosperity rests on digital foundations" (HM Government, 2016a: 9), an unsurprising conclusion for a country that generates upwards of 10 per cent of its gross domestic product from the digital economy, the highest proportion in the G-20 (Boston Consulting Group, 2015). Cybersecurity policy has always gone hand-in-hand with economic policy in the UK. The first national cybersecurity strategy, for instance, was launched together with the government's Digital Britain agenda, "a guide-path for how Britain can sustain its position as a leading digital economy and society" (HM Government, 2009b: 8). Subsequent strategies have reinforced the notion of the UK as a dynamic, outward-facing entrepôt nation and the potential of the cybersecurity industry itself to become a vibrant economic sector. Complementary ambitions are expressed in the Digital Economy Act (2017).

Institutions and stakeholders

No single government department or agency has sole responsibility for cybersecurity in the UK. Formally, the Cabinet Office, which sits at the heart of government and civil service, is responsible for developing cybersecurity policy and implementing the National Cyber Security Programme (NCSP) outlined therein. Many tasks are coordinated by the Cyber and Government Security Directorate (CGSD) in the Cabinet Office, which has its origins in the Office for Cyber Security (and, later, Information Assurance), founded in 2009. CGSD works with government partners, each of which has responsibility for various components of the UK cybersecurity architecture. The Department for Digital Culture, Media and Sport (DCMS) leads on the digital economy. The Home Office is the parent department for the Security Service (MI5) and National Crime Agency and guides cybercrime and counterterrorism operations. The Department for Business, Energy and Industrial Strategy (BEIS) oversees aspects of industrial cybersecurity outreach and engagement, including specific provisions for the civil nuclear industry. The Department for Education (DfE) delivers an extensive program for cybersecurity and online safety education in schools. The Cabinet Office itself controls the resilience agenda through the Civil Contingencies Secretariat.

The Foreign and Commonwealth Office (FCO) is responsible for the Secret Intelligence Service (MI6), GCHQ, and its offshoot the National Cyber Security Centre (NCSC) in London. It also handles diplomatic issues arising from foreign cyber actions, such as the 2018 attribution to Russian military intelligence of a series of hostile cyber operations (NCSC, 2018). The Ministry of Defence (MoD) harmonizes the activities of its service branches and executive agencies to develop sovereign capabilities and deliver operational advantage, including, in partnership with GCHQ, through the National Offensive Cyber Programme (NOCP). The UK was the first country in the world to admit to developing "a full spectrum military cyber capability" (Blitz, 2013), and joint cyber units at Cheltenham and Corsham deliver offensive and defensive capabilities respectively. These units and others, including the Joint Cyber Reserve, sit within the Joint Forces Cyber Group (JFCyG), created in May 2013 as a successor to the Defence Cyber Operations Group.

Previous investigations into UK cybersecurity suggest a rather haphazard, historical development of institutional capacity and responsibility (Harvey, 2013). This is broadly correct (although see, Pepper, 2010), but the present architecture represents a robust attempt since 2009 to establish cross-government cooperation, facilitated by a central coordinating body reporting upwards to the prime minister and cabinet and to the National Security Secretariat. Responsibilities are granted to departments with existing expertise and capabilities; where these need strengthening, additional funds have been allocated when possible from the £1.9 billion investment program announced in NCSS 2016. Cybersecurity is one of the few policy areas to receive additional funding when other budgets have been cut through spending reviews and financial austerity measures. Much of this is channeled into the intelligence agencies, an historical characteristic of all UK government cybersecurity (Stoddart, 2016). This raises questions about internal skewing of stated priorities and of bureaucratic land grabs, but the government would defend this on the basis that GCHQ, in particular, has the necessary technical heritage and resources to be a uniquely effective contributor to national cybersecurity.

As the government acknowledges fully, essential capabilities and knowledge exist outside the public sector too. The NCSS views the private sector as a key partner in achieving the stated ambitions of the NCSP, including the development of a robust cybersecurity export market (Department for International Trade, 2018). This is despite government's view that the market has not taken adequate account of cyber risk and has so far invested insufficiently in cybersecurity (HM Government, 2016b). Indeed, given private ownership of almost all critical national infrastructure, UK government has to look to public–private partnerships as a solution to a range of cybersecurity problems. These are well-established in the UK for purposes of threat intelligence sharing, knowledge exchange, capacity building, skills development, innovation partnerships, specialist outsourcing, supply of goods and services, and so on. Given the differing motives of the public and private sectors, the tensions inherent in such relationships can be ameliorated by embedding all actors early in the policy planning process (Carr, 2016). The UK therefore involves the private sector in a range of activities that feed into developing cybersecurity policy, in addition to the informal policy advice provided by commercial interest groups like the Information Assurance Advisory Council (IAAC), aerospace and defense industry organization ADS Group, and the Security and Resilience Industry Suppliers Community (RISC). Of particular note is the Defence Cyber Protection Partnership between MoD and industry which works to protect the defence supply chain from cyber threats. These initiatives ensure that government capitalizes upon private-sector skills and knowledge to understand the threat environment and available cybersecurity solutions. It also implicitly incentivizes commercial buy-in whilst staving off the twin perils of private-sector pushback on government policy and any immediate need for government regulation.

The NCSC is now a primary facilitator of public–private interaction, although by no means the only one. One of its key roles is to advise government departments and agencies on cybersecurity policy, including on how to "future-proof" policy in a dynamic technical environment. This is tied in to a broader horizon-scanning agenda across government and means that NCSC must seek expertise from outside government to inform its advice on cybersecurity science and technology (Cabinet Office, 2017). Industry representatives are integral to this process, through schemes like Industry 100, which embeds firms' employees in the NCSC to work on specific issues of technical and behavioral cybersecurity. This program acts as a knowledge exchange mechanism between industry and government to drive internal and external change but also assures the specialist advice that NCSC disseminates to other government partners and which forms the basis for policy development. Private companies are essential partners in establishing the NCSC as "the single authoritative voice for cyber security science and technology" policy advice (Cabinet Office, 2017: 17). Companies with national scope, like BT and Nominet UK, the official registry for .uk domain names, interface directly with various parts of government, including the NCSC. Nominet is also a key stakeholder, along with DCMS, in the UK Internet Governance Forum, which represents industry and third-sector views to policy-making organs of government. On occasion, companies are invited to present on specific policy issues to central government or parliamentary select committees, and extensive consultation with industry has occurred during the drafting of legislation (e.g., Investigatory Powers Act) and policy (e.g., DCMS, 2018).

Legislation

The UK Parliament has little direct involvement in cybersecurity policy and strategy, responsibility for which rests with government rather than the central or devolved legislatures. It has an important role, however, in shaping the legal environment in which cybersecurity operates and in exercising oversight over the activities of public and private cybersecurity actors. In the absence of a unified national legal framework for cybersecurity, Parliament has enacted a range of laws that impact upon cybersecurity and allied fields. The UK was one of the first countries to recognize the necessity of criminalizing certain computer-related crimes, leading to the Computer Misuse Act (1990). This has been amended over the years, most recently by the Serious Crime Act (2015). This legislation makes illegal a wide range of unauthorized access to and subversion of data and computer systems. Recent amendments have increased tariffs for some offences, whilst also criminalizing malicious cyber actions by British citizens outside UK territory.

Of particular interest to the intelligence community has been the sometimes awkward passage through Parliament of the Investigatory Powers Act (2016) (IPA). Nicknamed "the Snoopers' Charter" by critics, the IPA describes and expands the electronic surveillance powers of UK intelligence agencies but, in response to post-Snowden demands, also renders these more transparent and with greater safeguards on their use, including judicial review of warrants. It created an Investigatory Powers Commission and Investigatory Powers Tribunal to exercise oversight alongside the existing Intelligence and Security Committee (ISC) of Parliament. The IPA is in some respects an improvement on earlier legislation – and contrasts favorably, for example, with US surveillance law and intelligence community practice – but has been poorly received by privacy campaigners and civil liberties group, who continue to pursue legal actions against what they see as an authoritarian drift in UK government.

Another key area of legislative activity is data protection. Existing legislation includes the Data Protection Act (1998) and the Privacy and Electronic Communications Regulations (2003), which apply to all organizations handling personal information about living individuals, outlining their responsibilities and the penalties for non-compliance. Certain provisions have been strengthened by the incorporation into British law of the European Union General Data Protection Regulation (GDPR) in May 2018. A new Data Protection Act 2018 requires the Information Commissioner to be notified of all data breaches, with severe penalties – up to 4 per cent of annual turnover – for non-reporting and irresponsible data protection practices, and tightens up the data protection framework. This has elicited some concern from industry, not least from small-medium enterprises and charities struggling to understand, let alone comply with, the new regulation. NCSC has responded with a range of accessible resources to assist these organizations to do so. Government has also implemented the 2016 EU Directive on the security of network and information systems (NIS Directive), which identifies essential operators of UK information infrastructures and incentivizes better cybersecurity.

Foreign policy

The UK has repeatedly signaled its belief that international law applies to cyberspace, as it does in any other operational domain. The first national cybersecurity strategy hedged on the issue but, since the second strategy of 2011, national cybersecurity policy has expressed the existence of "a body of international agreed principles, behaviour and law which applies to cyberspace" (Cabinet Office, 2011: 18), even if it has side-stepped the issue of quite how these apply and the attendant implications. UK government also encourages the international community to act in accordance with international law and other norms of inter-state behavior (e.g., Wright, 2018). On those occasions when it has perceived other states to have challenged those frameworks, it has, consistent with articles of the NCSS (HM Government, 2016: 50), attributed cyber incidents to specific state actors. Notable in this respect are the public attribution of the WannaCry ransomware to North Korea and a range of aggressive cyber operations to the Russian Federation (Foreign and Commonwealth Office, 2017; NCSC, 2018). Its political legitimacy in this space has been challenged, including as a result of its involvement in transnational surveillance practices, as exposed by Edward Snowden in 2013. However, the UK is publicly committed to the rule of international law, both to constrain its actions and those of others, and to facilitate its own cyber operations within existing international legal frameworks.

A good example of this dynamic is provided by UK involvement in the Tallinn Manual process of the NATO Cooperative Cyber Defence Centre of Excellence (CCD COE) in Tallinn, Estonia. The two volumes of the Tallinn Manual (Schmitt, 2013, 2017) report on NATO's expert legal panel's explorations of the applicability of international humanitarian law to military cyber operations and other legal regimes' relevance to peacetime cyber operations, respectively. The first volume found that military cyberwarfare was regulated by the same international legal frameworks that shape and constrain other uses of military force. This is perhaps unsurprising, given the generally liberal-democratic character of the contributing NATO countries, but its rapid integration into national defense policy has been noteworthy. The UK quickly incorporated its findings into defense planning (Ministry of Defence, 2013) and, as a major player in NATO, also respects NATO's policy commitments to the Tallinn principles (e.g., NATO, 2014, 2016). UK military cyber doctrine is somewhat disconnected from national cybersecurity strategy (Ormrod & Turnbull, 2016), but the military and wider government both respect international law in the preparation and execution of cyber operations. In the military's case, as legal advice like the Tallinn principles trickles down into doctrine, this will constrain UK military cyber operations but also allow them to exploit the cyber environment fully by "playing to the edge" (Hayden, 2016) of the doctrinal box. Naturally, the UK's adoption – in common with NATO allies – of "modern deterrence" and cross-domain responses to cyber provocations (Donaldson, 2017; Lindsay & Gartzke, 2017) also means it must consider the applicability of other legal regimes to those response modes.

UK cybersecurity policy has insisted unwaveringly on the desirability of promoting international norms for responsible state behavior in and through cyberspace. These are expressed as "rules of the road" to be developed with international partners to "safeguard the long-term future of a free, open, peaceful and secure cyberspace" (HM Government, 2016a: 63). As a permanent member of the UN Security Council, the UK has been involved with the United Nations Group of Government Experts on Information Security (GGE) since its 2004 inauguration. The GGE has had some success in shaping the global cybersecurity agenda and in promoting the norm of the applicability of international law in cyberspace. However, the GGE is riven by a "Cold War" schism that prevented it reporting in 2016–2017. This is widely seen as a failure and an intractable obstacle to further global norms development. Despite this, the UK Foreign and Commonwealth Office remains committed to the spirit behind the GGE, even if it is unclear what may succeed it (Bowcott, 2017). It is also engaged fully with the new Sino-Russian Open-Ended Working Group on cyber issues, which started its UN General Assembly work in 2019.

The UK considers itself a "champion" of the multi-stakeholder approach to global internet governance (HM Government, 2016a, p. 63). It is proud of its heritage as a digital innovator – often invoking the likes of Alan Turing and Tim Berners-Lee – and has been a member of most organizations and institutions engaged in technical, regulatory, and policy aspects of internet governance since their inception. Whilst British influence is less than its closest ally the United States, the UK is an important actor in global internet governance and a net contributor to international cooperation and collaboration. In this, the UK considers government more a facilitator and guarantor of multi-stakeholder governance than a tool of control over the global internet (DCMS, 2013). This position does not disbar the UK from taking robust positions on global governance issues, including cybersecurity, but it does mark a conceptual boundary between it and those governments with more autocratic reflexes.

In the specific context of regional security governance, the UK is a key member of NATO, as previously mentioned, and of European institutions and organizations with critical roles to play in regional cybersecurity. It was an original signatory of the Council of Europe Convention on Cybercrime (2001), which seeks to harmonize international counter-cybercrime legislation and operations. Although it did not ratify the Convention until 2011, the UK is an active member of policing organizations that support the ambitions of the Convention, principally Europol, the law enforcement agency of the European Union, and its new European Cybercrime Centre (EC3). It also supports the work of the EU Agency for Network and Information Security (ENISA) and a range of other regional and supra-regional initiatives in critical infrastructure protection, cybersecurity, cybercrime, and counter-terrorism. The effects of the UK leaving the European Union in 2019 (Brexit) are unclear, particularly with respect to cybercrime policing, threat intelligence sharing, and its involvement with ENISA, although government officials have claimed Brexit will not impact UK–EU cybersecurity cooperation (Stevens & O'Brien, 2019). Parties to the exit negotiations have committed to maintaining close and strong links on security and intelligence matters, but the UK's interactions with regional cybersecurity arrangements will be subject to internal and external review (e.g., HM Government, 2017).

Like many former imperial powers, the UK maintains close ties with its erstwhile colonies, in this case through leadership of the Commonwealth of Nations. The UK acts as a source of advice and assistance to the 52 other countries in this intergovernmental organization and, by extension, to the population of 2.5 billion contained therein. This gives the UK unique reach into countries on every continent and allows it to shape cybersecurity to further its own national interest, particularly once it leaves the European Union. In addition to a host of bilateral capacity-building and advisory measures, the Commonwealth Telecommunications Organisation (CTO) has since 2010 organized annual forums to promote international cooperation on cybersecurity matters and to develop strategies for development and implementation, including its Commonwealth Cybergovernance Model (CTO, 2014). The Commonwealth Heads of Government 2018 meeting in London saw the launch by former Prime Minister Theresa May of the Commonwealth Cyber Declaration, a statement of principles and ambitions for improving cybersecurity across the community, although it remained focused principally on cybercrime (The Commonwealth, 2018).

Looking ahead

Like its immediate predecessors, the 2015 National Security Risk Assessment (NSRA) adjudged cyber threats a "Tier One" (high probability, high impact) risk to the UK over a five-year period, alongside terrorism, interstate war, pandemic disease, and natural disasters (HM Government, 2015). This explicitly referred to cyberattacks by hostile states and large-scale organized cybercrime but also interacts with other risk categories (Blagden, 2018). This assessment informs government cybersecurity policy and strategy and demands the cross-cutting, national response outlined above. From government's perspective, cybersecurity is key to national and economic security, without which national interests at home and abroad will be threatened. There are many positive outcomes to this way of thinking: greater public awareness of cyber issues; improved business cybersecurity; more sophisticated modes of cyber risk management; improved societal resilience, etc. However, internal government assessments have been critical of overall progress thus far (e.g., National Audit Office, 2019) and it is clear that planning for the next NCSS – due in 2021 – will have to address issues around resourcing, intra-governmental coordination, supply-chain cybersecurity, and critical infrastructure protection.

A key factor in the ongoing improvement of UK national cybersecurity has been the emergence of a more public-facing intelligence community, principally through the NCSC. This is the continuation of a longer process in which the secret agencies have "opened up" to public scrutiny since the 1990s. As the chief executive of NCSC observes, this is a necessity in the "team sport" of cybersecurity (Martin, 2016). There remain concerns that, despite this more open posture, the intelligence agencies at the heart of UK cybersecurity are unaccountable to the British public. The primary oversight mechanism of the parliamentary Intelligence and Security Committee, for instance, is thought to be less independent, and therefore less effective, than it might be (Defty, 2018). Coupled with weak parliamentary opposition to government security policy and a less than glorious track record on surveillance, it is unclear where meaningful resistance would emerge should the UK's whole-nation approach to cybersecurity overstep some as-yet unperceived line. The 2009 NCSS contained a short section observing that cybersecurity tools must meet criteria of necessity and proportionality and that a "clear ethical foundation and appropriate safeguards on use are essential to ensure that the power of these tools is not abused" (HM Government, 2009a: 10). This aspiration has yet to reappear in any formal national cybersecurity statements.

Conclusion

The UK can plausibly claim to have one of the most integrated approaches to national cybersecurity in the world. By its own admission, this can never be perfect, any more than any other form of security. Viewed as an exercise in risk management, therefore, the aim of UK cybersecurity is to minimize serious disruption and maximize economic prosperity, whilst maintaining its ability to project influence abroad and operate globally in the national interest. It is able to capitalize on extant sovereign capabilities whilst reaching out to partners across multiple sectors to assist in the national cybersecurity project. It views cybersecurity as an opportunity to promote itself in the world, both by example and as demonstration of its commitment to an open and secure global internet. Like most countries, it also faces challenges from a dynamic threat environment. It is a rich country that presents an attractive target for cybercriminals and a major, if waning, global power which must contend with other powerful states also seeking advantage in cyberspace. Its recent experiences with Russian cyber and informational subversion suggest a rocky road ahead and the very real prospect that deterrence simply is not working as well as it might. A new NCSS, scheduled for 2021, will have to take this into account. Its 2019 exit from the European Union also confounds predictions about future cybersecurity, but the UK is perhaps better placed than many to tackle the scale and scope of cybersecurity issues to which it is exposed.

Suggested reading

Harrop, W. & Matteson, A. (2015). "Cyber resilience: A review of critical national infrastructure and cyber-security protection measures applied in the UK and USA," in F. Lemieux (ed.), *Current and emerging trends in cyber operations* (pp. 149–166). London: Palgrave Macmillan.

HM Government. (2016). "National cyber security strategy, 2016–2021." https://assets.publishing.ser
vice.gov.uk/government/uploads/system/uploads/attachment_data/file/567242/national_cyber_se
curity_strategy_2016.pdf

Steed, D. (2019). *The politics and technology of cyberspace*. London, Routledge.

References

Blagden, D. (2018). "The flawed promise of National Security Risk Assessment: Nine lessons from the British approach," *Intelligence & National Security*, *33*(5), 716–736.

Blitz, J. (2013, September 29). "UK becomes first state to admit to offensive cyber attack capability," *Financial Times*. www.ft.com

Boston Consulting Group. (2015, May 1). "The internet now contributes 10 percent of GDP to the UK economy, surpassing the manufacturing and retail sectors." fromwww.bcg.com/d/press/1may2015-internet-contributes-10-percent-gdp-uk-economy-12111

Bowcott, O. (2017, August 23). "Dispute along cold war lines led to collapse of UN cyberwarfare talks," *The Guardian*. www.theguardian.com

Cabinet Office. (2011). "The UK cyber security strategy: Protecting and promoting the UK in a digital world." www.gov.uk/government/uploads/system/uploads/attachment_data/file/60961/uk-cyber-security-strategy-final.pdf

Cabinet Office. (2017). "Interim cyber security science and technology strategy: Future-proofing cyber security." www.gov.uk/government/uploads/system/uploads/attachment_data/file/663181/Embar goed_National_Cyber_Science_and_Technology_Strategy_FINALpdf.pdf

Carr, M. (2016). "Public-private partnerships in national cyber-security strategies," *International Affairs*, *92*(1): 43–62.

Christou, G. (2016). *Cybersecurity in the European Union: Resilience and adaptability in governance policy*. Basingstoke: Palgrave Macmillan.

Commonwealth Telecommunications Organisation. (2014, March 3-4). "Commonwealth cybergovernance model." www.cto.int/media/pr-re/Commonwealth per cent20Cybergovernance per cent20Model.pdf

The Commonwealth. (2018, April 20). "Commonwealth cyber declaration." www.chogm2018.org.uk/sites/default/files/Commonwealth per cent20Cyber per cent20Declaration per cent20pdf.pdf

Defty, A. (2018). "Coming in from the cold: Bringing the intelligence and security committee into parliament," *Intelligence and National Security*, *34*(1): 22–37.

Department for Digital, Culture, Media and Sport. (2013, October 28). "UK paper on the roles of governments in internet governance." www.gov.uk/government/uploads/system/uploads/attach ment_data/file/330740/UK_PAPER_ON_THE_ROLES_OF_GOVERNMENTS_IN_INTER NET_GOVERNANCE.docx

Department for Digital, Culture, Media and Sport. (2018). "Secure by design: Improving the cyber security of consumer internet of things." www.gov.uk/government/uploads/system/uploads/attach ment_data/file/686089/Secure_by_Design_Report_.pdf

Department for International Trade. (2018). "Cyber security export strategy." www.gov.uk//govern ment/publications/cyber-security-export-strategy

Donaldson, K. (2017, December 18). "UK would respond to a Russian cyberattack with the weapon of its choice," *Bloomberg*. www.bloomberg.com/news/articles/2017-12-18/u-k-would-respond-to-rus sian-cyberattack-with-weapon-of-choice

Foreign and Commonwealth Office. (2017, December 19). "Foreign Office Minister condemns North Korean actor for WannaCry attacks." www.gov.uk/government/news/foreign-office-minister-con demns-north-korean-actor-for-wannacry-attacks

Harvey, S. (2013). "Unglamorous awakenings: How the UK developed its approach to cyber," in J. Healey (ed.), *A fierce domain: Conflict in cyberspace, 1986-2012* (pp. 251–264). Arlington: Cyber Conflict Studies Association; Washington, DC: Atlantic Council.

Hayden, M. V. (2016). *Playing to the edge: American intelligence in the age of terror*. New York: Penguin Press.

HM Government. (2009a). "Cyber security strategy of the United Kingdom: Safety, security and resilience in cyber space." webarchive .nationalarchives.gov.uk/+/http:/www.cabinetoffice.gov.uk/media/216620/css0906.pdf

HM Government. (2009b). "Digital Britain: Final report." www.gov.uk/government/uploads/system/uploads/attachment_data/file/228844/7650.pdf

HM Government. (2015). "National security strategy and strategic defence and security review 2015: A secure and prosperous United Kingdom." www.gov.uk/government/uploads/system/uploads/attachment_data/file/478936/52309_Cm_9161_NSS_SD_Review_PRINT_only.pdf

HM Government. (2016a). "National Cyber Security Strategy 2016-2021." www.gov.uk/government/uploads/system/uploads/attachment_data/file/567242/national_cyber_security_strategy_2016.pdf

HM Government. (2016b). "Cyber security regulation and incentives review." www.gov.uk/government/uploads/system/uploads/attachment_data/file/579442/Cyber_Security_Regulation_and_Incentives_Review.pdf

HM Government. (2017). "Security, law enforcement and criminal justice: A future partnership paper." www.gov.uk/government/uploads/system/uploads/attachment_data/file/645416/Security__law_enforcement_and_criminal_justice_-_a_future_partnership_paper.PDF

Lindsay, J. & Gartzke, E. (2017). "Cybersecurity and cross-domain deterrence: The consequences of complexity," in D. van Puyvelde & A. F. Brantly (eds.), *US national cybersecurity: International politics, concepts and organization* (pp. 11–27). London and New York: Routledge.

Lonsdale, D. J. (2016). "Britain's emerging cyber-strategy," *The RUSI Journal, 161*(4): 52–62.

Martin, C. (2016, September 13). "A new approach for cyber security in the UK. Speech given at the Billington Cyber Security Summit." www.ncsc.gov.uk/news/new-approach-cyber-security-uk

Ministry of Defence. (2013). *Cyber primer.* Shrivenham: Development, Concepts and Doctrine Centre.

National Audit Office. (2019). "Progress of the 2016–2021 National Cyber Security Programme." www.nao.org.uk/report/progress-of-the-2016-2021-national-cyber-security-programme/

National Cyber Security Centre. (2018, October 3). "Reckless campaign of cyber attacks by Russian military intelligence service exposed." www.ncsc.gov.uk/news/reckless-campaign-cyber-attacks-russian-military-intelligence-service-exposed

NATO. (2014, September 5). "Wales summit declaration. www.nato.int/cps/en/natohq/of per centEF per centAC per cent81cial_texts_112964.htm

NATO. (2016, July 8). "Cyber defence pledge." www.nato.int/cps/en/natohq/of per centEF per centAC per cent81cial_texts_133177.htm

Ormrod, D. & Turnbull, B. (2016). "The cyber conceptual framework for developing military doctrine," *Defence Studies, 16*(3): 270–298.

Pepper, D. (2010). "The business of SIGINT: The role of modern management in the transformation of GCHQ," *Public Policy & Administration, 25*(1): 85–97.

Schmitt, M. N. (ed.). (2013). *Tallinn manual on the international law applicable to cyber warfare.* Cambridge: Cambridge University Press.

Schmitt, M. N. (ed.). (2017). *Tallinn manual 2.0 on the international law applicable to cyber operations.* Cambridge: Cambridge University Press.

Stevens, T. & O'Brien, K. (2019). "Brexit and cyber security," *The RUSI Journal, 164*(3): 22–30.

Stevens, T., O'Brien, K., Overill, R., Wilkinson, B., Pildegovičs, T. & Hill, S. (2019). "UK active cyber defence: A public good for the private sector." www.kcl.ac.uk/policy-institute/research-analysis/active-cyber-defence

Stoddart, K. (2016). "UK cyber security and critical national infrastructure protection. *International Affairs,*" *92*(5): 1079–1105.

Wright, J. (2018, 23 May). "Cyber and international law in the 21st century." www.gov.uk/government/speeches/cyber-and-international-law-in-the-21st-century

18

EUROPEAN UNION

Policy, cohesion, and supranational experiences with cybersecurity

Christopher Whyte

Introduction

Cybersecurity is one of the greatest areas of policy prioritization for the European Union (EU) (European Parliament and Council, 2016). Time and again, the statements of EU officials and the language of major policy documentation has emphasized the degree to which networks and network-enabled critical infrastructures constitute the foundation of the Union's economic and political processes. Today, the EU contains hundreds of millions of citizens using billions of Internet-connected devices to engage in commercial activity, to participate in politics and, perhaps most significantly, to communicate across the regional, national, and linguistic lines that so clearly define the European community.

In large part, it is the scope of the Union's supranational constitution that defines the nature of EU cybersecurity challenges and policy approach. Much as has been the case in other areas, the cohesiveness of policy intention and outcomes across all elements of the Union is the paramount concern of those institutions and individuals driving new formulations of approach to the various issues bound up underneath the "cyber" moniker. As Barrinha and Farrand-Carrapico (2018) note, however, the significance of coherence for the EU is not only the traditional need to square expectations and approaches across the naturally broad surface area of the continental bureaucracy (i.e., horizontal integration) and of the membership landscape (i.e., vertical integration) (Nuttall, 2005). Rather, the need for coherence stems from a deep-seated need to ensure congruence of meaning on the nature of cybersecurity challenges, the extent of EU responsibilities in the domain (both vis-à-vis member states and vis-à-vis private industry) and the potential for both to change (Cremona, 2008; Pomorska & Vanhoonacker, 2016). Here, the EU experience with cybersecurity is arguably unique by comparison with that of other major sovereign world powers. Even given that cybersecurity is itself an issue area perhaps best identified by its heterogeneous and changeable character, the pressures for EU policy that is comprehensively adaptive to changing circumstances are being felt exceedingly acutely, driven particularly by the need to protect (1) the single market and the euro, and (2) the political integrity of a membership body that has seen the rise of numerous threats to its credibility in recent years.

To many eyes, the European Union's effectiveness in responding to cyber imperatives has been slow to materialize. Ironically, this has likely been largely the fault of efforts to *ensure* cohesiveness in approach at early stages of the institutionalization process. Though the EU stands apart from other countries in that the impact of cybersecurity realization episodes (i.e., first-of-their-kind major cyber threat incidents prompting policy and political response) has naturally been less clearly felt due to the supranational setting of the broader community, its initial approaches have mirrored those seen in the United States, the United Kingdom, and elsewhere that saw too many engaged stakeholders and too little recognizable authority gimp the potential of new institutions (Healey, 2013). In Europe, early strategy emerged as a joint effort of multiple EU agencies and was framed broadly in its attempt to address crime, defensive issues, and the protection of critical infrastructures. Resultantly, this gave the EU only blunt tools with which to remedy the traditional tension bound up in determining who has responsibility (and, therefore, where capacity should be developed) for various cyber issues – the EU itself or member states?

The remainder of this chapter describes the state of cyber affairs within the European Union and contextualizes the nature of challenges to ensuring coherence in approach that, even given recent developments that streamline and centralize approaches to cybersecurity, appear likely to persist in years to come. After offering a brief perspective on the history of cyber threats to the supranational security and prosperity of the European experiment, the chapter details the development of strategy, institutions, and major cybersecurity initiatives over the past decade, culminating in the EU Cybersecurity Act in 2019 that overhauled Europe's cybersecurity agencies and granted a more concrete mandate for defense, development and standardization to the European Union Agency for Cybersecurity. Then, the chapter discusses the manifestation of enduring challenges in the drive to maintain coherence of approach amidst changing technological and political conditions.

Europe's experiences with cybersecurity

While a large number of Western countries can point to one or a few particularly pronounced early experiences with cyber threats to national security as the impetus for institution and strategy development on cybersecurity writ large, the pressure felt by the European Union to act on cyber issues has generally been brought to bear by threats more economic than geopolitical. In the spirit of the European experiment, the eyes of EU officials and other interested stakeholders have been drawn to cybersecurity threats wherein the eventual target appears to be prosperity and the integrity of those fundamentals that underlie economic potential. This focus, in many ways, makes the EU utterly unique as a cyber actor in international affairs. While many countries have allowed their institutions to be shaped by incipient cyber crises of varying flavor, the EU has been most clearly shaped by those cyber threats with the broadest implications for societal stability. In addition to the early experiences with seemingly unrestrained utilizations of malicious code like Conficker and ILoveYou, the European Union has taken point specifically from attacks on intellectual property and critical infrastructure. Some of these are discussed further below, but most recently the EU has been propelled to new heights of cyber institution development and coordination by worm-enabled ransomware attacks like WannaCry and NotPetya. These attacks took on an almost pandemic shape in their spread across sectors of European society, caused billions of dollars' worth of damage and spurred the EU on in what has been its most recent set of efforts to streamline and make coherent a strategic vision for a secure Europe online.

European Union cybersecurity policy: early efforts

Over the past two decades, the struggle within the European Union to better define the scope of cybersecurity issues relevant to the organization – and the responsibilities implied thereby – has reflected the challenges that countries like the United States have grappled with in attempting to determine what whole-of-government approaches to information technology issues should look like. Cybersecurity, to many, has consistently presented as either a somewhat esoteric area of concern or one characterized by such diverse prospective policy machinations as to not be particularly distinct from the generic focus on communications technologies as meaningful for economic function that came before. Resultantly, the 1990s saw initial focus on cybersecurity by the Union only as an adjunct element of core economic policy. A number of significant early documents – including the *White Paper on Growth, Competitiveness and Employment. The Challenges and Ways Forward into the 21st Century* (European Commission, 1993) and the *Report on Europe and the Global Information Society* (Bangemann Group, 1994) – identified information technologies as important to the growth of European markets, the development of the fundamentals of the single market, and the robust maintenance of Europe's innovation economy. In such documents, there was a clear implication that the role of information technologies in aiding democratic outcomes and ensuring stability in political engagement across the EU was a significant corollary of such objectives. Nevertheless, it is important to note even here that early EU focus on cyber issues reflected a focus on coherence of economic objectives and outcomes over and above salient social or political motivations.

As noted above, few major cybersecurity incidents had major impact on EU policy towards cyber issues until at least the late 2000s. Nevertheless, though security documents like the 2003 *European Security Strategy* remained mum on issues of information security,[1] the rise of cybercrime during the 1990s – typically unorganized, pedestrian criminal activity that nevertheless became remarkably common among the rapidly expanding community of Europeans with personal Internet access – did prompt a series of attempts to better square the development of the web with the governance responsibilities of the organization. Much as similar concerns led to the Computer Fraud and Abuse Act (CFAA) and subsequent legislation in the United States between the mid-1980s and the late-1990s, worry about harmful material and activity online produced a wave of initiative at the Union-level aimed at harnessing nascent member state capabilities and expanding awareness of potential cyber threats to consumers. During this period, which extended through at least the mid-2000s, much focus was placed upon coordination of knowledge initiatives for member state populations, building common definitions of what computerized crime looked like and standardizing language with a mind towards building consensus on what a secure web-enabled society in Europe should look like.[2]

The game-changer for EU cyber policy came in the mid-2000s, as the Western world grappled with the notion that global terrorism and "new" forms of interstate conflict characterized by the use of organized crime and other proxy actors were the most immediate threats to international security (European Union, 2016). The Global War on Terror, in particular, prompted many within the European Union to reassess the validity of approaches to organization policymaking that emphasized devolved governance over centralized management (Tickner, 1995; Bigo, 2000; Trauner & Carrapico, 2012). With the threat of international terrorism and organized crime (often linked to violent foreign political enterprise), it was envisioned that prospective member-level solutions would often be inadequate for a range of reasons. For one, such threats would likely be characterized by transnational targeting of European society. For another, the preponderance of new EU member states in Eastern and Southern Europe were dramatically less developed than the original members in Western Europe in terms of the resources available and institutions required to coordinate effective response, information sharing and more. Though motivation to effectively combat non-state and non-traditional threats to European security was equally enthusiastic across the organization, such differences presented as clear spoilers of the EU's capacity to defend European society.

By 2003–2004, these concerns and the implied shortcomings of member-level solutions were seen to apply directly to the security of information systems and digital communications as well. In particular, EU officials grew concerned about the manner in which different member states' laws diverged dramatically in their treatment of cybercrime and user protections (Cremona, 2008; Van Vooren, 2012). The result was a sea-change in the way that the EU approached cybersecurity, most notably in the shift from the use of non-binding instruments of supranational coordination to legally binding ones.

Cyber defense and the European Union

Since the mid-2000s shift in focus towards diminished reliance on member state solutions in favor of cohesive organization-determined ones, cyber policy under the EU has significantly focused on the protection of critical infrastructure and the mitigation of cyber-criminal threats (including the protection of the users of digital systems). A third area, cyber defense, has received somewhat less attention by the EU, despite growing transnational threats to Europe in cyberspace. As this area lies somewhat separate from other cyber policy efforts in the European context, the chapter discusses it separately here.

Through at least 2014, EU policy focus on cyber defense was largely driven by the threat of politically motivated industrial attacks from belligerent foreign powers. A substantial volume of malicious activity culminating in the theft of terabytes-worth of valuable industrial and government data through the early 2010s – particularly the "Gh0st RAT" series of intrusions – was seen by EU officials as a clear and present threat to the economic coherence of the continent. Likewise, the increasing use of malicious code to achieve very real disruptive outcomes presented European stakeholders with a form of cyber threat that for the first time seemed the direct relation of transnational terrorism. Stuxnet, the worm employed to actual destructive effect in Iran's uranium enrichment facility at Natanz, set Europe's cybersecurity community abuzz. Not only was the outcome of a cyberattack – for the first time under non-laboratory conditions – physical; the code itself was generic insofar as there was immense potential for tailoring the malware to be effective against any kind of industrial control system target (Langner, 2011; Lindsay, 2013). Two years later, the use of the Shamoon virus – ostensibly by the Iranian government – to "destroy" data on tens of thousands of Saudi Aramco's hard drives reinforced the emerging consensus position that the scope and nature of cybersecurity threats had evolved to such a form that it was no longer the stuff of "low" politics. Rather, cybersecurity was a cross-level issue that required coordinated response as much as it also necessitated diffuse efforts to better secure Europe's digital society.

The first major nods to cyber defense occurred in 2010, with the first enumerated focus on cyber capabilities as a critical national security development area appearing in the Capability Development Plan that year (and then endorsed in 2011) (Pupillo, Griffith, Blockmans & Renda, 2018). Early focus on cyber defense emphasized two main areas of activity – (1) the articulation of crisis response coordination mechanisms (and the role that the EU should play) and (2) the cultivation of national cyber capabilities. Over the next three years, EU organizations like the European Defense Agency (EDA) and the European Commission worked to stand up a range of programs designed to harden EU capabilities to coordinate member state defensive efforts. The EU Cyber Security Strategy (EUCSS) published in 2013 defined the relationship between these efforts as aimed at encouraging member states to adopt comprehensive roadmaps for the development of defensive capabilities, at filtering cyber response into crisis response infrastructures across member states, at generating and maintaining robust education opportunities and at creating synergistic initiatives that strengthen ties to private and non-EU cybersecurity stakeholders. On this last point, significant emphasis was placed – and has continued to be placed – on formal cooperation between the European Union and NATO, notably in the form of engagement between the EDA and NATO's Cooperative Cyber Defence Centre of Excellence (CCDCoE).

Since the publication of the EUCSS, the EU has increasingly recognized the need for better abilities to detect and recover from sophisticated digital threats alongside an obvious need to respond during crises (European Commission, 2017a). In many ways, the EUCSS stemmed from the formal recognition that cybersecurity was one of very few significant areas where the EU was pulling up short in terms of possessing necessary capabilities. Between 2016 and 2018, the organization took significant steps forward in developing such capabilities. In 2016, for instance, the European Union and NATO issued a Joint Declaration that announced cooperation on numerous cyber issues, including the need to combat hybrid threats to European sovereignty and the need to further harden continental digital defenses. In 2017, the Permanent Structured Cooperation (PESCO) framework was agreed by volunteer participants that included 25 of the 28 national armed forces of EU member states (PESCO, 2017). PESCO's aims revolve around the notion that community responses to cyber threats are likely to produce greater resiliency overall and greater response outcomes during crisis episodes. To these ends, PESCO signatories committed to the standard steps of creating Cyber Rapid Response Teams and better information sharing platforms.

Despite a range of promising developments focused on cyber defense, however, the European Union's response to cyber threats from a supranational security perspective remains somewhat fragmented. As Griffith notes, EU capabilities remain (as of 2018) relatively siloed within agencies and institutions whose missions and coordinative responsibilities are not always set out clearly in law and policy. One noteworthy issue that persists to this day is the response obligations of members under the Treaty on the European Union. The mutual assistance clause of the Treaty, Article 42(7), does not define "armed aggression" sufficiently to provide nuanced threshold criteria for determining the status of some cyber threats (say, large-scale denial of service attacks against a member state) vs. others (such as intrusions leading to theft of sensitive intellectual property) (Pupillo, Griffith, Blockmans & Renda, 2018). Secondarily, in cases where cyberattacks do not include an identifiable threat actor, it is unclear where the responsibility of fellow member states would lie (though this is somewhat controlled for via reference to the "solidarity clause" of the Treaty that allows for common security action against terroristic threats). Beyond response obligations, cyber defense also remains a fragmented affair in part because so much effort has been assigned to the construction of standard approaches to regulation of digital society across member states. In other words, cyber defense remains somewhat under-emphasized in no small part because of the top-down view that it should fit within a holistic framework for coherent action on the totality of cybersecurity issues facing the EU.

Integration, cohesion and conditions on the ground

Beyond the narrower scope of cyber defense issues, the European Union has been developing the institutional capacity to deal with cybersecurity in a comprehensive fashion – at least, ostensibly – since the mid-2000s. Over the past two decades, the EU has developed a robust and diverse ecosystem of agencies tasked with different elements of the cybersecurity mission, from the EDA and DG Migration and Home Affairs (tasked with a variety of cybercrime missions) to the DG for Communications, Content and Technology, the European Network and Information Security Agency (ENISA) and the full range of Computer Emergency Response Teams (CERTs).

In many ways, it is hard to avoid the picture of EU institutional development focused on cyber issues as one wherein coordination has been emphasized over the rapid construction of new capacities. From at least 2004, when ENISA came into existence (2004), emphasis has been placed on cohesion of the EU approach as an agreed set of mission objectives and institutional underpinnings as a necessary prerequisite to the broader protection of Europe's digital society. According to Carrapico and Barrinha (2017), this project of constructing cohesion has evolved along at least two lines and with both horizontal and vertical integration in mind. First, the EU (and the Council specifically) has attempted to build the institutional ecosystem necessary for securing European society online. In the context of member states themselves (i.e., horizontal relationships), this has meant efforts to reconcile policy instruments and national laws that pertain to cybercrime, user rights and more, as well as ensuring that approaches to coordination with the private sector are supported by EU institutions that offer frameworks and assurances to better chances for successful partnerships. Specifically, this has led the EU to develop numerous specialized agencies, from ENISA to elements of Interpol responsible for cyber-criminal investigation. Between member states and the EU (i.e., the vertical relationships) (Biscop & Andersson, 2008), this has involved ensuring that the EU itself has methods of assuring its own relevance and learns from its engagement with member state stakeholders. Second, the EU has attempted to ensure that there is common understanding of what the scope and objectives of the European cyber mission is. Horizontally, this has led to more than a decade of initiative aimed at aggregation and amalgamating understandings of the Internet's impact on European society. Likewise, this has meant significant investment in and negotiation around notions of responsibility on the part of member states, EU agencies and the private sector so as to ascertain what types of institutions will work most effectively to affect better cyber outcomes *supranationally*. Finally, the need to generate and maintain common meaning in cyber governance discourse has led to mechanisms for both accommodating and shaping national-level articulations of cyber priorities.

Overall, it should perhaps be unsurprising that this focus on cohesion preceding effectiveness has produced a cyber policy ecosystem within the EU characterized by gradualism. Many elements of the Union's approach to cyber issues are defined by international frictions that present obstacles to progress not found in other major polities around the world. While public–private partnerships are difficult to develop on cyber issues across the Western world, European Union agencies have faced particular issues in their development. After all, not only does the EU face the traditional issues of mismatch public–private interests (particularly vis-à-vis things like data sharing) and low historical involvement in loosely coupled infrastructural sectors (like the Internet technologies sector); it also finds itself forced to play a multi-level game with national governments that often, despite desiring progress on cybersecurity issues, are politically loathe to regulate private industry.

The NIS directive, ENISA and the EU cybersecurity act

EU gradualism on cybersecurity presents as a significant obstacle to effectiveness across a number of fronts. The multi-faceted nature of the EU's cyber ecosystem, in particular, has often meant a scarcity of resources (or, sometimes, simply a lack of access to the right resources) for agencies like ENISA, Interpol, and EDA. Likewise, there has rarely been an effective presentation of a strategic vision for EU interests and approaches to cybersecurity. While there have been numerous important strategies promulgated and vision statements published, it is hard to escape the fact that these have rarely implied a streamlined set of methods for rapid response to cyber crises at the organizational level. Moreover, barriers to cooperation – specifically, barriers to communication and transformation of *meaning* (Carrapico & Barrinha, 2017) – across EU stakeholders and counterparts in member states remain high to this day.

That said, recent years have seen several important steps taken towards mitigation of these challenges. In July 2016, for instance, Directive 2016/1148 (hereafter the "NIS Directive") (2016) was published to further streamline processes of cyber threat mitigation among member states. In many ways, the legislation, which was aimed horizontally at member states, is not unlike the voluntary National Institute of Standards and Technology (NIST) Cybersecurity Framework in the United States in that it offered for the first time definitions of the categories of operators, types of private industry stakeholders, and types of actions that should be addressed by state regulation (Markopoulou, Papakonstantinou & de Hert, 2019). It then mandated the adoption of these frameworks by national authorities via the publication of relevant strategies, the construction of rulemaking and enforcement agencies (where they did not already exist) and adherence to certain standards of national practice (regarding things like data breach notification).

The NIS Directive catapults ENISA, the EU's agency for cybersecurity, to a much more centralized, significant role in ensuring continental cybersecurity than has existed to this point. Under the Directive, ENISA is named as solely responsible for the provision of support by the EU to member countries and for the assurance of member state compliance with the Directive (Markopoulou, Papakonstantinou & de Hert, 2019). ENISA must provide relevant expertise to member state agencies and must help develop all guidelines for public–private cooperation to be utilized by the Cooperation Group (the EU sub-unit tasked with that support mission). Moreover, the Directive places ENISA in a mandatory consultative role wherein the EU Commission must be advised by the agency before taking formal action. These mandates, alongside the new role the agency is given under the Directive to help appoint representatives at various levels of coordination, situate ENISA as the nucleus of all decisions vis-à-vis the development of the EU's coordinative cyber workforce and the distribution of needed resources. By implication, they also put ENISA in a position to articulate more cohesive strategic visions going forward. The EU Cybersecurity Act (2019), adopted in mid-2019, augments this propulsion of ENISA to the fore of EU cyber policy enforcement by mandating that the agency be the sole and permanent authority for a range of operational-level initiatives to enhance cyber crisis response. Finally, these mandates also streamline the implications of cybersecurity activity in the EU in the context of the General Data Protection Regulation (GDPR). The GDPR, adopted alongside the NIS Directive, is a piece of broad-scoped regulation aimed at bettering data security for European citizens. Though there are numerous potential points of operational contradiction in instances where both pieces of legislation apply, such as when personal data is found during crisis response to a data breach, ENISA's placement at the heart of Europe's ecosystem for cyber policymaking and enforcement at least promises to help bring order where before there may have been confusion.

Conclusion

The architecture of EU cybersecurity policymaking and enforcement is complex, both in terms of the issues to be grappled with and along the traditional horizontal and vertical axes that have characterized integration on the continent for several decades. There remains a broad set of challenges facing the organization and the Single Market. More significantly, there remains a real need for greater cohesion of vision and subsequent action on the part of EU agencies, particularly when it comes to cyber defense. Recent developments have certainly made significant strides in streamlining the institutional landscape of cyber policy for the EU. In addition to the propulsion of ENISA to the fore of this ecosystem, new authority given to the European Council to sanction cyberattacks and the introduction of an EU-wide certification (among other developments) stand to make the continent more resilient than it has historically been. And yet, as President Jean-Claude Juncker stated in his 2017 State of the Union address, "Europe is still not well equipped when it comes to cyberattacks." To even the untrained eye, for instance, the absence of a true defense agency – an EU equivalent to the US Cyber Command, or at least to the Joint Task Forces that preceded it – should be glaring. It is also the absent development perhaps most indicative of an enduring problem stemming from the EU's unique status as a supranational body – much of what EU agencies do is advisory in nature. This is only not the case where years of horizontal and vertical negotiation has successfully allowed for concerted action among formally-committed stakeholders.

Moving forward, there is significant hope that the European Union can continue to capitalize on the momentum of progress over the past several years to become the effective international cyber authority it claims it can be. And yet, it would not do to end this brief recounting of Europe's experiences with cybersecurity and cyber policymaking on anything but a cautionary note. Cyber issues are heterogeneous and prone to transformation in a way that few issues are. What makes the European Union unique as a global cyber actor among other actors – that are, by-and-large, sovereign nations in their own rights – is its status as an advisory governance entity and the resultant gradualism that emerges from the need to ensure coherence in perspective among its members. The natural suggestion here, of course, is that the EU may suffer in a way that more organically coherent political entities might not when faced with radical transformation of the issue at hand (say, in the form of novel evolutions of artificial intelligence or unexpected manifestations of the Internet of Things). Indeed, even if gradualism comes to benefit Europe in this regard as caution leads to prudent policy evolutions, it seems not unreasonable to suggest that the EU approach will be vulnerable to the under-realization of new threat areas out into the future.

Notes

1 See, Toje (2005) for further details.
2 See, for instance, the *eEurope 2002 – Information Society for All – Action Plan* or the *Commission Communication on Improving the Security of Information Infrastructures and Combating Computer-related Crime.* See, Martin (2005) and Walden (2005) for further details.

Suggested reading

Calcara, A., Csernatoni, R. & Lavallée, C. (eds.). (2020). *Emerging Security Technologies and EU Governance: Actors, Practices and Processes.* Abingdon: Routledge.
Choucri, N. & Clark, D. D. (2018). *International Relations in the Cyber Age: The Co-Evolution Dilemma.* Cambridge, MA: MIT Press.

Christou, G. (2016). *Cybersecurity in the European Union: Resilience and Adaptability in Governance Policy (New Security Challenges)*. Basingstoke: Palgrave Macmillan.

Ilves, L. K., Evans, T. J., Cilluffo, F. J. & Nadeau, A. A. (2016). "European Union and NATO Global Cybersecurity Challenges: A Way Forward," *PRISM*, *6*(2): 126–141.

Wessel, R. A. (2019). "Cybersecurity in the European Union: Resilience through Regulation?" in E. Conde, Z. Yaneva & M. Scopelliti (eds.), *Routledge Handbook of EU Security Law and Policy* (pp. 283–300). Abingdon, Routledge.

Westby, J. (2019, October 31). "Why the EU Is about to Seize the Global Lead on Cybersecurity," *Forbes*, forbes.com/sites/jodywestby/2019/10/31/why-the-eu-is-about-to-seize-the-global-lead-on-cybersecurity/#38ffb62c2938

References

Barrinha, A. & Farrand-Carrapico, H. (2018). "How Coherent Is EU Cybersecurity Policy?" *LSE European Politics and Policy (EUROPP) Blog*. https://blogs.lse.ac.uk/europpblog/2018/01/16/how-coherent-is-eu-cybersecurity-policy/

Bangemann Group. (1994). "Report on Europe and the Global Information Society," *Bulletin of the European Union*, Supplement 2/94.

Bigo, D. (2000). "When Two Become One," in M. Kelstrup & M. C. Williams (eds.), *International Relation Theory and the politics of European Integration, Power, Security and Community* (pp. 171–205). London: Routledge.

Biscop, S. & Andersson, J. (2008). *The EU and the European Security Strategy: Forging a Global Europe*. Abingdon: Routledge.

Carrapico, H. & Barrinha, A. (2017). "The EU as a Coherent (Cyber) Security Actor?" *Journal of Common Market Studies*, *55*(6): 1254–1272.

Cremona, M. (2008). "Coherence through Law: What Difference Will the Treaty of Lisbon Make?" *Hamburg Review of Social Sciences*, *3*(1): 11–36.

Directive 2016/1148 of the European Parliament and the Council Concerning Measures for a High Common Level of Security of Network and Information Systems across the Union (the "NIS Directive").

European Commission. (1993, December 5). "Growth, Competitiveness, and Employment. The Challenges and Ways Forward into the 21st Century," COM (93) 700 final.

European Commission. (2017a, September 19). "State of the Union 2017 – Cybersecurity: Commission Scales up EU's Response to Cyber-Attacks," Press Release. http://europa.eu/rapid/press-release_IP-17-3193_en.htm

European Commission. (2017b, September 13). "Resilience, Deterrence and Defence: Building Strong Cybersecurity for the EU," Joint Communication to the European Parliament and the Council. https://eur-lex.europa.eu/legal-content/EN/TXT/?uri=JOIN:2017:0450:FIN

European Commission. (2019). "The EU Cybersecurity Act." https://eur-lex.europa.eu/eli/reg/2019/881/oj

European Parliament and Council of the European Union. (2016, September). "Directive (EU) 2016/1148 of the European Parliament and of the Council of 6 July 2016 Concerning Measures for a High Common Level of Security of Network and Information Systems across the Union," *Official Journal of the European Union*, L 194/119.

European Union. (2016, June). "Shared Vision, Common Action: A Stronger Europe – A Global Strategy for the European Union's Foreign and Security Policy." www.eeas.europa.eu/archives/docs/top_stories/pdf/eugs_review_web.pdf

Healey, J. (ed.). (2013). "A Fierce Domain: Conflict in Cyberspace, 1986 to 2012." Cyber Conflict Studies Association.

Langner, R. (2011). "Stuxnet: Dissecting a Cyberwarfare Weapon," *IEEE Security & Privacy*, *9*(3): 49–51.

Lindsay, J. R. (2013). "Stuxnet and the Limits of Cyber Warfare," *Security Studies*, *22*(3): 365–404.

Markopoulou, D., Papakonstantinou, V. & de Hert, P. (2019). "The New EU Cybersecurity Framework: The NIS Directive, ENISA's Role and the General Data Protection Regulation," *Computer Law & Security Review*, *35*(6): 105336.

Martin, B. (2005). "Information Society Revisited: From Vision to Reality," *Journal of Information Science*, *31*(1): 4–12.

Nuttall, S. (2005) "Coherence and Consistency," in C. Hill & M. Smith (eds.), *International Relations and the European Union* (pp. 91–112). Oxford: Oxford University Press.

"Permanent Structured Cooperation (PESCO) – Factsheet." https://eeas.europa.eu/headquarters/head quarters-Homepage/34226/permanent-structured-cooperation-pesco-factsheet_en

Pomorska, K. & Vanhoonacker, S. (2016). "Europe as a Global Actor: Searching for a New Strategic Approach," *Journal of Common Market Studies*, *53*(S1): 216–229.

Pupillo, L., Griffith, M., Blockmans, S. & Renda, A. (2018). "Strengthening the EU's Cyber Defence Capabilities," *CEPS Task Force Report*.

Regulation (EC) No 460/2004 of the European Parliament and of the Council of 10 March 2004 Establishing the European Network and Information Security Agency (Text with EEA Relevance), as Amended by Regulation (EC) No. 1007/2008 and Amended by Regulation (EC) No. 580/2011.

Tickner, A. (1995). "Re-Visioning Security," in K. Booth & S. Smith (eds.), *International Relations Today* (pp. 175–197). Cambridge: Polity Press.

Toje, A. (2005). "The 2003 European Union Security Strategy: A Critical Appraisal," *European Foreign Affairs Review*, *10*(1), 117–133.

Trauner, F. & Carrapico, H. (2012). "The External Dimension of Justice and Home Affairs after the Lisbon Treaty: Analyzing the Dynamics of Expansion and Diversification," *Foreign Affairs Review*, 17: 1–18.

Van Vooren, B. (2012). *EU External Relations Law and the European Neighbourhood Policy. A Paradigm for Coherence*. London: Routledge.

Walden, I. (2005). "Crime and Security in Cyberspace," *Cambridge Review of International Affairs*, *18*(1): 51–68.

19

ESTONIA

From the "Bronze Night" to cybersecurity pioneers

Nick Robinson and Alex Hardy

Introduction

Estonia is often lauded around the world for its leadership and expertise in cybersecurity and e-governance. Yet, for a relatively small country of just 1.3 million people, its role as a technological pioneer and "pathfinder" continues to surprise many. Such a position, however, can be evidenced by a number of developments to Estonia's "digital society" since it restored independence from the Soviet Union in 1991. In that time, Estonians have experienced what might be referred to as a "conveyor-belt period" of technological innovation and development, as the introduction of a mandatory national identity card (in 2002) arguably set about a long-line of digital "firsts" for the everyday Estonian. Today, the country arguably leads the way in digital service provision with 99 per cent of state services online, and with over 67 per cent of Estonians using their digital identity for e-services on a regular basis (e-Estonia, 2019). From health to banking and voting online, citizens rely on its state portal as a one-stop-shop for accessing an array of everyday digital services both securely and at ease.

Whilst Estonia's trajectory as an advanced digital society may herald many significant benefits (and plaudits), it is of no great surprise that its dependency on its digital ecosystem also brings with it a number of inherent risks. This was highlighted strikingly in 2007, when Estonia fell victim to what is widely believed to be the first instance of a state-sponsored cyberattack, targeting key state institutions and ICT infrastructure (see, case study below). Although damage and impact were fairly minimal, the attack not only served as a vital wakeup call for the Estonian government but equally brought the issue of cybersecurity and cyber defense into the mainstream and on to national security agendas around the world. At a local level, weaknesses were highlighted in government policy, legislation, and emergency response, whilst issues around national defense, international law, and capacity building on an international level were also brought to light.

In this chapter we focus exclusively on Estonia's contemporary cyber history from this point, and how the country's effective response to the attacks represent something of a distinct departure to its approach to national cyber defense (Hansen & Nissenbaum, 2009); we also reflect on how Estonia's subsequent expertise and maturity in this field has increased its international standing regarding such issues (see, Areng, 2014; Crandall, 2014). Two significant developments in 2008, in the immediate aftermath of the cyberattacks, point to such a trajectory. First was the prompt establishment of the NATO Cooperative Cyber Defence Centre of Excellence (NATO CCDCOE) in the country's capital Tallinn the following summer. Not only was its formation incredibly symbolic, recognizing the country's established expertise in cybersecurity in light of Estonia's response to the 2007 attacks, but was also a clear indication from within the NATO alliance that Estonia could lead on issues pertaining to cyber defense and international law. Second, and the focus of the remainder of this chapter, was the introduction of Estonia's first National Cyber Security Strategy (2008–2013). One of the first of its kind, the strategy introduced a flurry of newly formalized strategic targets, as well as developing a new legislative and organizational cybersecurity landscape.

Since that point, Estonia has produced a further two iterations of its National Cyber Security Strategy (2014–2017, 2019–2022). In this chapter we provide an overview of Estonia's approach to cybersecurity since 2007, charting the adoption of all three strategies and address the number of organizational, legislative, and diplomatic changes that have taken place since the introduction of the first strategy in 2008. In that time, we trace a shift in the government's approach from a deep concern over cyber defense to an understanding and wider recognition of the impact of cybersecurity upon wider society. For a country that has a growing dependency on its digital infrastructure, its more holistic approach today is a testament to Estonia's cyber maturity. As the government recognizes in its latest strategy, cybersecurity doesn't just revolve around the protection of technological solutions and critical infrastructure; but also means "protecting digital society and the way of life as a whole."

The "Bronze Night"

In this section, we will not attempt to provide anything other than a brief summary of the events surrounding the cyberattacks that affected Estonia in April and May 2007, often commonly referred to as the "Bronze Night" (for more detailed analyses see, Ehala, 2009; Kaiser, 2015; Ottis, 2008). The attacks were prompted by the removal of a Soviet World War II memorial in downtown Tallinn, in favor of relocation to a less centrally located military cemetery – an act which enraged Estonia's Russian speaking minority, as well as the Russian government. The decision to move the memorial was a highly contentious and politically motivated one; for many Estonian nationalists, it represented Soviet occupation, while for the Russian-speaking population, it represented the defeat of Nazi Germany and the sacrifices of the Red Army. Tensions soon escalated and culminated in violent clashes erupting on the streets of Tallinn between protesters and local authorities. Despite a sense of normality returning the following day, disruption continued online as Estonian authorities experienced what was seen as a deliberate, targeted distributed denial-of-service (DDoS) attack against the country, temporarily crippling state services and portals. Among those targeted were government websites, with a number of major banks, media organizations, and political parties also affected. Whilst most services were restored to normal within 24 hours, disruption continued for the next 22 days (April 27–May 18, 2007) as several waves of coordinated DDoS attacks continued to choke state information systems and government services. In the immediate aftermath, fingers began to point at Russia as political relations between both countries had all but collapsed in the weeks preceding the attack; however, such claims cannot be properly verified, with the involvement of the Russian government virtually impossible to prove (experts believe that politically motivated "hacktivists" were likely responsible).

In many ways, the "Bronze Night" can be seen as a pivotal moment in Estonia's recent history and the subsequent development of national cybersecurity defense and policy. There is a belief amongst some Estonians that the attacks were something of a blessing in disguise; for it was a vital wakeup call that spearheaded many changes in how the Estonian government approached cybersecurity. As highlighted above, it can be credited with the emergence of its first National Cyber Security Strategy (2008–2013), but also in spearheading many of the organizational, legislative, and technological changes witnessed since (as this chapter aims to elucidate below). Crucially, we must also recognize the impact of the attacks upon the wider global community. Not only did it serve as a wakeup call for not-yet-versed politicians and policymakers on the dangers of a cyberattack against the vital functions of the state, but it also provided an opportunity to learn from Estonia's experience, in order to drive developments in their own national cybersecurity policy and capabilities. Indeed, without the events of the "Bronze Night" in 2007, how long would it have been before we saw the emergence of many of the national cybersecurity strategies addressed in this edited collection?

First strategy (2008–2013): a new era for national security

Estonia is often credited with the world's first National Cyber Security Strategy (2008–2013). While this is a common misconception (the US actually released a "national strategy to secure cyberspace" back in 2003 under the George W. Bush administration), the Estonian National Cyber Security Strategy is often viewed as the forerunner for many contemporary cybersecurity strategies seen today. Approved by the Estonian government in May 2008, the document was the first formal cybersecurity strategy and framework released in the aftermath of the 2007 cyberattack and can be seen as a significant leap in terms of cybersecurity coordination, legislation, and the strategic goals of the country moving forward. Addressing a growing concern around asymmetrical threats and vulnerabilities faced in cyberspace (from cybercrime to cyber terrorism and cyberwarfare), the strategy identifies cyberattacks against critical national infrastructure and cybercrime as particularly pertinent. In light of events the previous year (and a growing number of incidents around the world), the strategy indicates the start of a "new era" regarding the security of cyberspace, stressing the importance of cybersecurity in terms of national security and putting it "on a par with traditional defence interests."

Following the 2007 cyberattack and prior to the adoption of the first strategy, the structure of Estonian cyber defense underwent significant organizational transformation, with the aim of improving cybersecurity coordination and collaboration efforts across government departments and institutions. The initial drafting and coordination of the strategy was undertaken by the Ministry of Defence (MoD), albeit with significant contributions from other government departments, including the Ministry of Education and Research, the Ministry of Justice, the Ministry of Economic Affairs and Communications (MoEAC), the Ministry of Internal Affairs, and the Ministry of Foreign Affairs. This inter-agency approach to develop the strategy would also see the inclusion of cybersecurity experts from the private sector. Many in Estonia point to the effective cooperation between the public and private sector as pivotal in coordinating a response to the 2007 DDoS attacks, with many large organizations such as Swedbank (Estonia's largest banking service) pooling resources and expertise to help cope after vital services were badly affected. In the strategy, the importance of the private sector is further underlined, particularly with regard to protecting critical national infrastructure (a relationship that still continues today). Prior to the attacks, in 2006, the Estonian government established CERT-EE (Computer Emergency Response Team of Estonia), a coordinating body that responds to cyber incidents. In 2007, CERT-EE became the coordinating body during the cyberattacks, and were largely praised for the handling of the crisis. CERT-EE's other duties include engaging local service providers and the provision of a network of IT professionals on a voluntary basis from both the governmental and commercial sectors who provide analysis of incidents (for further details see, Kaska, Talihärm & Tikk, 2010).

The strategy and wider principles were developed in conjunction with two national development plans: Information Security Interoperability Framework (2007) and Estonian Information Society Strategy 2013 (2007). The former developed a framework for smoother interoperable services across government, whilst the latter identified and prioritized the development of e-services across society (later becoming Estonia's Digital Agenda 2020 strategy – see below). The strategy itself has something of a disparate structure, with the document frequently discussing the need for individual departments to take responsibilities; however, following the creation of a more dedicated Information System Authority in 2011, a more coordinated chain of command began to form (see the next section).

The primary aim of the Estonian government's first National Cyber Security Strategy was to "reduce the inherent vulnerabilities of cyberspace in the nation as a whole." To accomplish this, the strategy identifies a number of specific goals. These included:

1   The establishment of a multilevel system of security measures;
2   Expanding Estonia's expertise in and awareness of information security;
3   Adopting an appropriate regulatory framework to support the secure and extensive use of information systems;
4   Consolidating Estonia's position as one of the leading countries in international cooperative efforts to ensure cybersecurity.

The development of security measures included conducting comprehensive risk assessments and establishing specific definitions of infrastructure. These definitions are laid out within the strategy's annex, identifying sectors of critical importance that depend on the security, operation, and availability of information infrastructure. These included:

*   Energy networks
*   Communications networks
*   Finance
*   Healthcare
*   Food safety
*   Water network
*   Transport network
*   State agencies and information systems

With reference to the 2007 cyberattacks, the strategy identifies further subgoals that aim to provide a comprehensive assessment of infrastructure interdependence, cross-dependencies, and the development of measures to protect it in the future. Other notable strategic goals include a commitment to cybersecurity education, research, and development, as well as strengthening Estonia's position as a leader in cybersecurity policy, defense, and the advancement of technological solutions.

Among the key goals of the first strategy was the introduction of appropriate regulatory frameworks and legislation to combat cybercrime and cybersecurity threats against the state. Notable contributions include the introduction of the Emergency Act (2009) – adopted to "improve national resilience to cyber threats" (Kaska, Talihärm & Tikk, 2010: 53) – as well as establishing legal definitions for cybersecurity and cybercrime. In order to improve overall cyber hygiene within the country, the strategy also introduced compulsory security measures and standards for critical infrastructure companies and minimum security-standards for all information systems. Furthermore, the penal code was updated to cases pertaining to cyber criminality such as attacks on information system and data.

Other priorities for the strategy included the development of EU Legal Framework and EU Law pertaining to the protection of personal data, electronic communications, the retention of data, the re-use of public sector information, and information society services. In what might be seen as a precursor to GDPR (see below), Estonia sought to be at the forefront in seeking international consensus and norm building in this area. The introduction of the Electronic Communications Act (2004) and the Personal Data Protection Act (2007) was highly influential in this regard. The first strategy makes significant note of the Council of Europe convention of Cyber Crime (2004) and frequently recognizes the Council of Europe as a platform for productive engagement, something lacking in later iterations, which place less value upon the institution.

In a brief summary, the main legislative achievements of the first strategy can be evidenced by the following:

- Adopting legislation which recognized that cyberattacks can constitute a national emergency;
- Re-definition of critical services and coordinating agencies in light of lessons learned from 2007 cyberattack;
- Implementation of compulsory baseline IT security standards for all organizations connected to the maintenance of critical infrastructure;
- Creation of the Estonian Cyber Defence League;[1]
- Significant alteration to Penal code to cover cybercrime (such as the distribution of spyware and malware – for detailed analysis of these updates see, Kaska, Talihärm & Tikk, 2010).

One crucial goal of the first strategy was to develop and further augment Estonia's position as a cybersecurity leader on the international stage. Recognizing the role it now plays post-2007, and the lessons that could be passed on to allies (namely in NATO and the EU), the strategy plans its approach through knowledge sharing, raising awareness, and supporting prevention and protection measures. The strategy identifies a number of platforms for engagement internationally, with both allies and enemies alike, including NATO, the EU, OSCE, the Council of Europe, and United Nations. As other chapters in this book show, platforms such as the EU and United Nations are vital for engaging with other states regarding capacity building, norms, and international law; whilst, for small states such as Estonia, providing a platform to showcase its expertise and cybersecurity capabilities on a global stage. Unlike its successors, the first strategy places a significant focus on the Council of Europe as a means to establish norms of cybercrime, with the target of utilizing the Council of Europe as a platform for consensus-building in Europe beyond the EU, and with the wider world.

A key security guarantor for Estonia, significant emphasis is also placed on the role of NATO within the strategy. Focusing on the role of cyber defense and the collaborative efforts of the recently opened NATO CCDCOE (mentioned above), the role of NATO with regards to Estonia's own cybersecurity capability (and vice versa) would continue to grow over the course of the first strategy. This can be first evidenced in the publication of the *Tallinn Manual* in 2013 which has sought to drive forward healthy debate and norms relating to cyberwarfare and international law (its successor, *Tallinn Manual 2.0*, was published in 2017); but also in the creation of the annual "Locked Shields" cyber defense exercise (first run in 2010) that has gone a considerable way in improving the cybersecurity awareness and training of NATO allies in the event of a potential crisis.

Second strategy (2014–2017): critical infrastructure, consolidation, and (digital) continuity

In September 2014, the Estonian government approved the second iteration of its National Cyber Security Strategy (2014–2017). The stated goal of the strategy was to "increase cybersecurity capabilities and raise the population's awareness of cyber threats, thereby ensuring continued confidence in cyberspace." As part of a much broader vision of ensuring Estonia's national security and the "functioning of an open, inclusive and safe society", the updated strategy aimed to build on the progress made by its predecessor whilst reflecting on lessons learned from its overall implementation, efficiency and impact (both domestically and internationally). In recognition of an evolving threat landscape, the document summarizes a number of current trends and challenges, from rises in cybercrime to threats posed to Estonia's highly sophisticated digital society. Pinpointing the state's dependency on its fundamental information systems and digital ecosystem, the strategy also places a greater emphasis on protecting Estonia's critical national infrastructure and the preservation of vital services in both the public and private sector.

With the first strategy taking great strides in setting the foundations from which the country's cybersecurity capabilities have since grown, the second strategy can be seen as a useful indicator of progress being made in terms of Estonia's cybersecurity capacity building and maturity across society. Its inception coincided with a number of key structural and policy changes in government (largely spearheaded by the previous strategy). The first key organizational adjustment was the decision to bring the direction and control of cybersecurity policy from under the auspices of the MoD to under the responsibility of the MoEAC. Such a decision reflected a wider understanding in government at the time that cybersecurity was more of an all-encompassing societal issue, whereas the previous strategy undoubtedly fitted within the remit of cyber defense in light of the 2007 cyberattack. Speaking to more of a horizontal approach that tackles cybersecurity across all areas of society, the MoEAC are believed to be better placed to address wider issues around economic growth, cybercrime, and ICTs.

The second major structural change was the creation of the Cyber Security Council – now forming a central component of the Estonian government's Security Committee. Established in 2009, just a year after the first strategy was adopted (and fulfilling one of its main goals), the council is tasked with the overall implementation of the cyber strategy's goals. Chaired by the Secretary-General of the MoEAC, the council also coordinates cybersecurity policy across other key ministerial departments and institutions.[2] The second strategy was also developed in concurrence with Estonia's Digital Agenda 2020 strategy. Building on the aforementioned Information Society Strategy 2013 (2007), the strategy's goals were to drive forward the country's ICT policies across society, including: citizen inclusion/participation in ICT and government services; the security and capability of eID and authentication services (including internet voting); and, the introduction of a "no-legacy" principle across the public sector.[3]

In a similar vein to its predecessor, the second strategy outlined the following five strategic objectives that went on to shape the Estonian government's cybersecurity policy for this period:

1   Ensuring the protection of information systems underlying important services;
2   Enhancing of the fight against cybercrime;
3   Development of national cyber defense capabilities;
4   Managing evolving cybersecurity threats;
5   Development of cross-sectoral activities.

Highlighted above, one major difference in the second strategy is the greater emphasis placed on the protection of the state's critical information systems. One of its main aims, addressed in its first strategic goal, is to ensure "the uninterrupted operation and resilience of vital services, and the protection of critical information infrastructures against cyber threats." Such a goal, in light of the 2007 cyberattack, is a reflection on the state's growing dependence on its information systems and digital ecosystem. A rapid process of digitization throughout the 1990s and 2000s (leading to developments such as a "paperless" governance policy in 2000 and nearly every government service becoming "digital first") meant that the vital, everyday functioning of the state was largely dependent on the security of its ICT infrastructure and e-services provided to its citizens. With critical databases such as the Land and Population Registry now only existing in digital form, and a realization that, in a time of crisis (e.g., cyberattack, natural hazard, or military occupation), vast quantities of Estonian records were at risk of being disrupted (or at worst, lost), many Estonian policymakers have reiterated to us how the notion of "returning to paper" in the event of a crisis was simply no longer feasible.

In an attempt to mitigate such risks, the strategy details a number of key specific actions on the protection of the state's vital information systems and services. First, in accordance with the government's own mandatory three-level baseline ICT security standard across the public sector (ISKE),[4] the strategy calls for the need to update, map, and manage dependencies that exist at the heart of national ICT infrastructure and the introduction of a comprehensive national "monitoring, analysis and reporting system." Progress in this area had already begun in 2010, after the Estonian government announced it would be upgrading the status of the Estonian Informatics Centre from a "ministry-administered state agency" into a "government agency with autonomous executive powers" (Kaska, Talihärm & Tikk, 2010: 63). Newly renamed as the Estonian Information System Authority (Riigi Infosüsteemi Amet – RIA), the more empowered agency is tasked with managing and protecting the state's critical information systems, as well as overseeing the wider architectural security of ICT infrastructure across government ministries.[5] Similar to the strategy, RIA was also brought under the general remit of the MoEAC (although still functioning as a separate agency – with its own director) and administers vital government services such as the State Portal (eesti.ee) that serve as a gateway to the state's digital ecosystem.

In addition, the Department of Critical Information Infrastructure Protection (CIIP) was established within RIA, tasked with orchestrating the protection of critical information infrastructure. As Kaska, Talihärm, and Tikk (2010) acknowledge, the CIIP's emergence was necessitated by the adoption of the aforementioned Emergency Act (2009), but functions at more of a strategic level than Estonia's CERT-EE (which sits at more of an operational level in terms of cyber defense).

In this strategy, we also denote a change in language and tone as, for the first time, the Estonian government proposes the use of "alternate" ICT infrastructure solutions, as well as the secure storage of data overseas, in the event of a large-scale disruption to state information systems (see, subgoal 1.1/1.3/1.6). The strategy highlights the necessity of ensuring the "digital continuity" of the state "regardless of Estonia's territorial integrity," and, with the benefit of hindsight, we now know that the use of such rhetoric by the Estonian government was a precursor to the establishment of the world's first "Data Embassy."[6] In order to manage evolving cyber threats and improve Estonia's cybersecurity capabilities, the strategy also expresses a desire to develop and adopt independent (or "in-house") security solutions. Building on the success of Estonian tech companies such as Cybernetica AS and Guardtime, such aspiration married the state's growing attention to R&D&I (Research and Design *and* Innovation – Kalvet, 2012) during this period. As well as supporting the development of national cybersecurity solutions and the next generation of cybersecurity professionals, the strategy also outlines its vision to become a key exporter in an increasingly competitive global market.

Such a vision complements a wider theme from the strategy, and one that builds on its predecessor, that aims to reach out beyond Estonia's borders, whether through international cooperation in areas of cybercrime and cyber defense (within institutions such as NATO and the EU), or through developing more robust foreign policy and "cyber diplomacy" on a global stage. The strategy reflects Estonia's intention to position itself as a "digital power" that has since allowed the country to gain a competitive advantage in niche areas such as cybersecurity and e-government (Areng, 2014).

One final key priority for the strategy was to enhance measures to tackle cybercrime across society more effectively, through both enhanced detections and by raising public awareness to its inherent dangers. Another vital structural development prior to the adoption of the strategy was made in 2012, consolidating the responsibility and investigative capabilities of cybercrime into a dedicated Cyber Crime Unit (part of the Police and Border Guard Board who are responsible for overseeing law enforcement and homeland security).

In 2018, the decision was taken to extend the strategy by a further year in order to fulfil its objectives to the highest standard. The decision may have also been made to ensure ample time to develop the strategy following the Estonian Presidency of the Council of the European Union in 2017 (September–December).

Third strategy (2019–2022): development, directives, and diplomacy

The Estonian government adopted its third and latest National Cyber Security Strategy (2019–2022) in October 2018. Introduced 10 years after its first iteration (and 11 years after the "Bronze Night"), the strategy is its most detailed and comprehensive to date, not only demonstrating the progress and lessons learned over the course of the last decade but also in positioning the country as a leader and pioneer in cybersecurity across areas of policy, defense, and technological solutions. Against an increasingly unpredictable security backdrop – from the ongoing conflict in Ukraine to the recent WannaCry/NotPetya cyberattacks in 2017 – its timely adoption is reflected in its overall vision and ambition to create "the most resilient digital society." Pointing to the inherent vulnerabilities Estonian society faces today, the strategy details the country's capacity to withstand cyber threats as a "secure and undisrupted digital society" whilst relying on the "indivisibility of national capabilities, a well-informed and engaged private sector, and an outstanding research and development competence." Recognizing the limitations of Estonia's small population, the strategy also highlights cybersecurity as a "shared responsibility" across society, and one that can be addressed through enhanced cooperation, the introduction of consolidation strategies and by reducing fragmentation – thus optimizing the country's limited resources.

At first glance, the strategy appears to be its most accessible and public-facing thus far, complete with its glossy, corporate design, and punchy goals (its previous iterations were somewhat faceless and uninspiring). This, as we show below, is important as it demonstrates the Estonian government's continuing desire to project its own cyber-power and diplomacy to a much wider audience. Unlike its two predecessors, the strategy does not propose any major organizational restructuring, thus adopting a similar framework to the previous strategy (see, Table 19.1); it does, however, propose the establishment of a national cybersecurity center during the current period of the strategy.

In order to ensure a "sustainable and secure digital society," the third strategy focuses on the following four strategic objectives:

1   A sustainable digital society;
2   Cybersecurity industry, research, and development;
3   A leading international contributor;
4   A cyber-literate society.[7]

Table 19.1 Timeline of Key Events

Date	Event
August 1991	Estonia restores independence from the Soviet Union
2002–2008	Estonia introduces a mandatory digital identity (eID), as well as introducing digital services such as e-health and i–Voting
2004	Estonia joins the European Union (EU) and North Atlantic Treaty Organization (NATO)
April-May 2007	**"Bronze Night" and subsequent DDoS attacks against Estonian institutions**
May 2008	**First Cyber Security Strategy (2008–2013) adopted**
May 2008	NATO CCDCOE established in Tallinn, Estonia
2009	Cyber Security Council established as part of Security Committee of central government
June 2011	Estonian Information System Authority (RIA) established – *formerly Estonian Informatics Centre*
September 2014	**Second Cyber Security Strategy (2014–2017) adopted**
July-December 2017	Estonia holds Presidency of the Council of the European Union
2018	*Domestic*: Cyber Security Act and Personal Data Protection Act come into effect *International*: GDPR and NIS Directive enter into force
October 2018	**Third Cyber Security Strategy (2019–2022) adopted**
June 2019	Estonia elected as non-permanent member of the UN Security Council (2020–2021)

In a similar guise to its predecessors, the primary purpose of the third strategy is to ensure the resilience of the state's vital functions – be it critical national infrastructure or wider components of Estonia's digital society. Recognizing that progress is still to be made in the management and protection of state information systems and e-services, the first goal is centered on measures that aim to future-proof the state, thus making it more technologically resilient and prepared in the event of a crisis. Developments proposed in the strategy include the continued use of its "no-legacy principle" (set as part of the aforementioned Digital Agenda 2020 strategy), further progress regarding a Data Embassy solution outside of Estonian territory, and addressing the use of next-generation technologies (e.g., AI, blockchain) across society.

For a country that relies so heavily upon the basic functioning and availability of its digital infrastructure, the Estonian government also acknowledges that its digital ecosystem is particularly sensitive to advances in cryptography. Emphasizing the potential risks around the advent of quantum computing and increasing cyberattack sophistication, the strategy highlights the risks posed towards the protection of state archives and the validity of digital signatures. This was put to the test in August 2017 after a vulnerability was discovered in the chip used by the Estonian ID card – putting approximately 800,000 ID cards at risk. The events that unfolded were unprecedented and subsequently led to the Estonian government revoking the digital certificates on all affected cards, whilst they were also praised for their overall transparency and handling of the crisis. In light of this, and in order to mitigate against such technological risks in the future, the strategy calls for the "long-term view" that ensures the adherence of key information security and data protection requirements and standards (e.g., security and privacy by design principles) across the state's information system architecture.

Such calls have since coincided with a number of legislative developments at both a domestic and supranational level, adopted concomitantly to the third strategy. Most notably, at an EU-level, the Network and Information Security (NIS) Directive and General Data Protection Regulation (GDPR) entered into force (both May 2018). For Estonia, its already joined-up approach to cybersecurity and existing robust data protection laws meant that their impact was fairly limited in comparison to other EU member states, but did lead to a number of domestic legislative changes. Central to these changes was the passing of Estonia's first Cyber Security Act (2018) and revised Personal Data Protection Act (2018)[8] in order to transpose upcoming requirements from the aforementioned NIS Directive and GDPR. Despite both regulations being fairly disparate in nature, the strategy is clear in asserting that, moving forward, the implementation of information security and data protection "must be treated as a whole."

Of the four strategic objectives in the third strategy, the advancement of cooperation and Estonia's international standing in cybersecurity is seen as a crucial goal and garners significant attention within wider government policy. Driven by certain geopolitical realities and recognition of the limitations of Estonia as a small state, such a position has been a strategic goal of Estonia for some time, highlighting the way in which small states often pursue specialized agendas and focus heavily upon alliance and consensus building in order to remain competitive within larger alliances and the international system (for a discussion on small European states see, Thorhallsson, 2017). Thus, Estonia actively seeks to advance close ties with allied states to elevate it's standing in international affairs, particularly in the realm of cybersecurity. The strategy notes that the Ministry of Foreign Affairs directs and coordinates international cooperation in this regard, as well as activities related to the strategy.

In the strategy, the Estonian government claims that it has retained its "international leading role" in the years since the previous strategy, and identifies maintaining credibility and capability to act as a leading actor in the international arena as a vital priority. This is to be achieved through increased cooperation and the promotion of sustainable capacity building. International leadership, the Estonian government claims, is to be achieved by strengthening the capacity to cooperate successfully with international partners in resolving cyber incidents and crises.

Illustrating Estonia's multifaceted and mature approach to cybersecurity and ICTs, the third strategy also places a notable focus upon development in the field of e-governance. A means for advancing development for humanitarian purposes, the document notes that ICT and e-state solutions in developing countries are crucial to the implementation of the Development Cooperation and Humanitarian Aid Development Plan 2016–2020, and these development goals are linked to wider Estonian foreign policy objectives. It is also Estonia's goal to raise awareness of the e-state internationally. This can be evidenced in the work of the e-Governance Academy, a leading Estonian consultancy and think tank, which provides research and practical expertise on how the e-state can be implemented to work alongside the EU's development policies. The strategy also stresses the importance of further developing platforms for outreach purposes, with the International Centre for Defence and Security (ICDS), a leading foreign policy think tank in Estonia, also mentioned. Furthermore, emphasis is placed on the development of cyber defense in education, noting the expertise of TalTech's (Tallinn University of Technology) Centre for Digital Forensics and Cybersecurity as a key contributor in this regard.

Similar to its predecessors, the strategy places a great deal of emphasis on its EU and NATO partners – through both their collaborative and deterrence stances. The importance of Estonia as the host country for the NATO Cooperative Cyber Defence Centre of Excellence (CCDCOE) is once again underlined, with a strategic interest in promoting the development of the center as an international organization of like-minded countries. In particular, Estonia's role in cyber exercises such as "Locked Shields" is again highlighted (now allowing non-NATO members to participate, including allies from Finland, New Zealand, and South Korea),[9] and points to its critical function in supporting national security and defense – whilst working alongside "trusted partners" and allies. As such, emphasis is also placed upon further cross-border cooperation, and streamlining information exchange and cooperation with other nations, as a pivotal pillar in Estonia's cybersecurity and information society strategies.

In June 2019, Estonia was elected for the first time as a non-permanent member of the UN Security Council (2020–2021). Delivering a clear message endorsing international cooperation on matters of security, trade, and more niche areas of cybersecurity and e-government, Estonia also believes they will give a voice and advocate the interests of other small states in the activities of the Security Council, as well as utilizing the platform for wider cybersecurity awareness building. Additionally, as of 2018, Estonia has appointed an "Ambassador at large" for Cyber Security, specifically to promote cyber norms and encourage stronger, bilateral ties with allies in the field of cyber security (RIA, 2018).

Also identified in the third strategy is the prospect of developing "cyber literacy." This is to be improved with a focus on building both the capability of citizens, and national capacity building. This approach is divided within the strategy as part of the following three pillars:

Protection

Based on the consolidation of state capabilities and maximizing output identified through continual audit, but also through maintaining an active cybersecurity community, developing comprehensive approaches to national defense (including areas such as the Cyber Defense League), and by ensuring the security and integrity of critical databases (such as the Data Embassy solution) and through the strengthening of cooperation with allies. The strategy also commits to the protection of internet freedoms.

Prevention

Based on the development of new services and databases (following the aforementioned security and privacy by design principles), the strategy promotes the adoption of risk-based approaches, an increase in state cooperation with private stakeholders, the security of essential services, and the fundamental acknowledgement of cybersecurity as a shared responsibility of both government and the individual.

Development

The development goals of a "cyber literate" society include ensuring a future supply of experts, organizing effective cooperation between state, academia and private sector partners. They also include support for cybersecurity within the economy, creating research and development plans for the cyber-sector, anticipating and responding to new risks, and promoting sustainable cyber capabilities in partner countries through international projects.

These goals are based within the wider targets of sustainability, internationalism, and support of private industry, research, and development identified by the strategy, as well as sufficient funding and administrative capabilities, and the minimization of "red tape" for both public and private sectors. In addition, the strategy also places an emphasis on retraining, based in an acknowledgement that Estonia's international reputation has caused the recent loss of talent overseas; and, as such, Estonia must continue to generate new talent from a relatively low base, or attract talent from overseas. In contrast to the second strategy, where a great deal of emphasis was placed on the exportable nature of Estonian cybersecurity solutions and expertise, a major consequence (and irony) has been that Estonian cybersecurity experts, policymakers, diplomats, and entrepreneurs have become increasingly desirable beyond Estonia's borders. The third strategy has thus prompted a reaction from the Estonian government to this brain drain by enacting lifelong learning strategies to maintain a digitally skilled workforce, with excellence in cybersecurity and digital technology a key priority. This, the strategy notes, is crucial given the growing digital dependency of both Estonia, and the wider modern world, brought about by the proliferation of internet connected devices and data-driven lifestyles for the everyday Estonian.

Conclusion

When the Estonian government adopted its first ever National Cyber Security Strategy in 2008, it was largely a step into the unknown. A little over a year had passed since the now infamous DDoS cyberattacks had targeted vital state information systems and services. The attacks were a significant trigger that set about a number of changes with regards to Estonia's approach to cybersecurity – from organizational changes at the heart of government to the drafting of new legislation that recognized cyberattacks can constitute a national emergency. The attacks were not only deemed a wakeup call for the Estonian government, but also sent shockwaves around the world regarding the threats posed by asymmetrical cyberwarfare or vulnerabilities in state infrastructure. The introduction of the first strategy, setting out Estonia's strategic goals and challenges for the years ahead, was a clear indication that Estonia could show strong leadership in cybersecurity whilst admitting lessons needed to be learned from its experience thus far. Now in its third iteration, there is a case to be made that Estonia's National Cyber Security Strategy is the most developed and comprehensive to date, offering a blueprint for many other states around the world regarding cybersecurity strategy and policy.

In this chapter, we have explored Estonia's journey and trajectory since 2007, providing an overview of its approach to cybersecurity through its National Cyber Security Strategy. Our aim was to illuminate the role the strategy has played not just in developing Estonia's cybersecurity capabilities (and its role as part of Estonia's wider national security), but also on its impact upon other states' approaches to cybersecurity around the world. We approached the strategies genealogically in order to compare and reconcile some of the key organizational, legislative and diplomatic changes that have taken place in that time.

The first strategy (2008–2013), in many respects, was ahead of its time, playing a vital role in establishing key institutions and principles that are still largely relevant today. Coordinated by the MoD in the aftermath of the 2007 cyberattack, there is a (expected) greater focus on national security, although the strategy should also be credited for the foundations it set for future strategies (and not just in Estonia) to build upon. The second strategy (2014–2017), whilst augmenting the progress made in the first, placed far greater emphasis on the protection of the country's critical infrastructure and digital ecosystem, with further progress made on tackling cybercrime and developing national cyber defense capabilities. Now under the coordination of the MoEAC, we note a clearer recognition of Estonia's digital dependency and the wider societal implications of cybersecurity. In its latest iteration (2019–2022), the strategy recognizes Estonia's growing importance as a cybersecurity leader and the role the country plays collaboratively within key global institutions such as the EU and NATO. Testament to the experience and expertise now formed within the country, the strategy sets out a blueprint for continuing Estonia's active engagement with the wider world through cyber exercises and new forms of diplomacy.

Taking all three strategies together, we note that Estonia's approach to cybersecurity hasn't taken any radical shifts since 2007, instead using each iteration as an opportunity to learn from its predecessor and add to its growing cyber capabilities. Its strategic goals have largely stayed the same during this time, with a clear focus throughout on protecting critical infrastructure, combatting cybercrime, and improving national security. Overall, Estonia's cybersecurity strategy has provided itself with the opportunity to project its capabilities, brand and power on a global stage. This, with the fourth strategy undoubtedly on the horizon in 2023, will continue to be a theme as the rest of the world looks towards this small Baltic Republic for leadership and direction on cybersecurity matters in the future.

Notes

1 The creation of the Cyber Defence League in 2011 received significant international attention, as a cyber defense force comprised entirely of volunteers, formed to defend vital infrastructure, and was a notable outcome of the first strategy, despite not being formally named as a strategic goal within the strategy.
2 The responsibility of implementing the agreed cybersecurity policy as part of the wider strategy lies with the government institution or agency identified by the Cyber Security Council. Similar to the

first strategy, the Estonian government calls for *all* government ministries and agencies to play their part in implementing the strategy, but largely falls under the remit of the Ministry of Economic Affairs and Communications, Ministry of Defence, the Information Systems Authority (RIA), Ministry of Justice, Police and Border Guard Board, the Government Office, Ministry of Foreign Affairs, Ministry of the Interior, and the Ministry of Education and Research. The government also calls for the coordination and cooperation of public/private sector bodies, NGOs and educational institutions in order to drive the implementation of the strategy forward.

3 The no-legacy principle mandates that ICT solutions in the public sector should not be any older than 13 years, meaning that outdated software and systems are replaced periodically and thus, in principle, improving the security of Estonia's wider information systems and architecture.

4 Adopted in 2003, ISKE is based on a German information security standard, IT Grundschutz. ISKE is a three-level baseline security system, meaning that every information system or database is measured and assigned on a three-tier security system (Low → Medium → High). In 2008, ISKE became obligatory for state and local government institutions that use databases.

5 RIA is composed of a number of units, most notably the Cyber Security Branch (which comprises of individual policy, standards and incident response departments) but also the State Information System Branch (which focuses on the preservation of the State Portal, electronic identity, data exchange and wider network/infrastructure security). Each branch is charged with formal duties, laid out in the statutes of the department established in 2011 (see www.ria.ee for more information on RIA and its structure).

6 Recently opened in Luxembourg, the Data Embassy allows the Estonian government to "backup" its most critical databases and information systems to a government-operated data center outside of its own borders, meaning the state can effectively operate in the event of an emergency (see Robinson, Kask & Krimmer, 2019).

7 Although each objective is rather vague, they each contain more specific subgoals or "activity areas" that define individual targets and set measures and performance indicators in order to reach such goals (for example, an activity area of creating "a cyber-literate society" is to "raise the cyber awareness of citizens, state and private sector").

8 The Personal Data Protection Act (2018) replaced existing legislation that was passed back in 2007. Interestingly, the Personal Data Protection Act is overseen by the Data Protection Inspectorate (DPI), a unique state agency body that acts as a supervisory body, defending individual rights to privacy and ensuring the state is transparent over its handling of data. The DPI also represents Estonia at an EU-level, and played a crucial role in the smooth transition of its latest Personal Data Protection Act (2018) and the introduction of GDPR.

9 Estonia has also benefitted from the running of national cyber exercises, conducting "live" Cyber Hedgehog and Cyber Fever exercises in 2010 and 2012.

Suggested reading

Adamson, L. (2019). "Let Them Roar: Small States as Cyber Norm Entrepreneurs," *European Foreign Affairs Review*, 24(2): 217–234.

Gold, J. (2019, May 27). *How Estonia Uses Cybersecurity to Strengthen its Position in NATO*. Tallinn, Estonia: International Centre for Defence and Security. https://icds.ee/how-estonia-uses-cybersecurity-to-strengthen-its-position-in-nato/

McGuinness, D. (2017, April 27). "How a Cyber Attack Transformed Estonia," *BBC News*. www.bbc.com/news/39655415

NATO Secretary General Praises Estonia's Commitment to Smart Defence. (2012, January 19). "NATO News." www.nato.int/cps/en/natolive/news_83519.htm

Ruus, K. (2008). "Cyber War I: Estonia Attacked from Russia," *European Affairs*, 9(1). www.europeaninstitute.org/index.php/component/content/article?id=67:cyber-war-i-estonia-attacked-from-russia

References

Areng, L. (2014). "Lilliputian States in Digital Affairs and Cyber Security," *Tallinn Paper No. 4*. CCDCOE, Tallinn, Estonia. https://ccdcoe.org/uploads/2018/10/TP_04.pdf

Crandall, M. (2014). "Soft Security Threats and Small States: The Case of Estonia," *Defence Studies, 14*: 30–55.

e-Estonia. (2019). "We Have Built a Digital Society and We Can Show You How." https://e-estonia.com/

Ehala, M. (2009). "The Bronze Soldier: Identity Threat and Maintenance in Estonia," *Journal of Baltic Studies, 40*(1): 139–158.

"First National Cyber Security Strategy." (2008–2013). www.enisa.europa.eu

Hansen, L. & Nissenbaum, H. (2009). "Digital Disaster, Cyber Security, and the Copenhagen School," *International Studies Quarterly, 53*: 1155–1175.

Kaiser, R. (2015). "The Birth of Cyberwar," *Political Geography, 46*: 11–20.

Kalvet, T. (2012). "Innovation: A Factor Explaining e-Government Success in Estonia," *Electronic Government: An International Journal, 9*(2): 142–157.

Kaska, K., Talihärm, A.-M. & Tikk, E. (2010). "Developments in the Legislative, Policy and Organisational Landscapes in Estonia since 2007," in E. Tikk & A. M. Talihärm (eds.), *International Cyber Security Legal and Policy Proceedings* (pp. 40–67. Tallinn: CCDCOE.

Ottis, R. (2008). "Analysis of the 2007 Cyber Attacks against Estonia from the Information Warfare Perspective," Cooperative Cyber Defence Centre of Excellence, Tallinn, Estonia. https://ccdcoe.org/uploads/2018/10/Ottis2008_AnalysisOf2007FromTheInformationWarfarePerspective.pdf

RIA. (2018). "Estonian Information System Authority Annual Cyber Security Assessment 2019." www.ria.ee/sites/default/files/content-editors/kuberturve/ktt_aastaraport_eng_web.pdf

Robinson, N., Kask, L. & Krimmer, R. (2019). "The Estonian Data Embassy and the Applicability of the Vienna Convention: An Exploratory Analysis," in Proceedings for the 12th International Conference on Theory and Practice of Electronic Governance (ICEGOV), Melbourne, Australia, April 3–5 2019, 391–396.

"Second National Cyber Security Strategy." (2014–2017). www.mkm.ee/sites/default/files/cyber_security_strategy_2014-2017_public_version.pdf

"Third National Cyber Security Strategy." (2019–2022). www.mkm.ee/sites/default/files/kyberturvalisuse_strateegia_2022_eng.pdf

Thorhallsson, B. (2017). *The Role of Small States in the European Union.* Abingdon: Routledge.

20

NATO'S EVOLVING CYBER SECURITY POLICY AND STRATEGY

Scott N. Romaniuk, Alexander Fotescu, and Mihai Chihaia

Introduction

The North Atlantic Treaty Organization (NATO) is adapting and adjusting its thinking, political, economic, technological, and innovative processes to new challenges. As before it used to look primarily at the Soviet Union and at the global "War on Terror" (WOT), now it begins to move toward a more forward-looking defense posture, with an emphasis on new geographies – Africa, the Middle East, and Central Asia – but also with domain-specific engagement like in the realm of the electromagnetic spectrum and cyber, space, quantum, and increasingly non-kinetic and non-hard power, those traditionally regarded as the purview of defense organizations.

While NATO is undergoing a transition and readjustment period internally, triggered by adjustments to globalization and anti-globalization, changes in the global relative positions of power of its members, and challenges both at its core and its periphery, the Alliance has, nonetheless, successfully orchestrated the inclusions of cyber security as a warfighting domain since 2016, and is accelerating towards a silo-reduced and more comprehensive understanding of cyber as a continuum between information operations (with subsets such as public diplomacy and NATO Strategic Communications Centre of Excellence, StratCom) and quantum capabilities at the very high-tech end.

It is important to acknowledge that NATO member's cyber capabilities, taken together, outweigh the NATO-available cyber capabilities aggregate, as cyber has become a significant contribution of the individual member countries, as well as the Alliance. European Union (EU) contributions to data security, privacy, and localization add a level of cyber security that, traditionally, is not counted towards defense structures, yet which does deliver a safer Alliance and cyber space for all its members.

This chapter looks at the cyber security policies, institutions, and initiatives of NATO, draws attention to cooperative efforts and partnerships with non-NATO countries, and sheds light on the current and future challenges facing NATO in the cyber realm. We highlight elements of NATO's cyber history, its pledge to be active in cyber defense, and the evolution of the Alliance's cyber security policy and strategy over the past two decades. Particular focus is placed on the NATO Cooperative Cyber Defence Centre of Excellence (CCDCOE) as an illustration of the Alliance's focus on interdisciplinary research and development, shared-learning and training, and cross-nation capabilities within a collective security arrangement.

The CCDCOE initiative, 12 years old as of 2020, has expanded to encompass key players extending beyond the state level, to include epistemic and knowledge communities, academics, and a wide variety of key actors in the private sector. Our emphasis of multifaceted partnerships, within and beyond the EU and NATO, is indicative of the Alliance's understanding and internalization of the importance of multinational collaboration and cooperation, leading to what we refer to as a "layered cyber defence shield."

Due to the rapidly changing cyber security environment and the continuous emergence of new challenges, NATO's policies and strategies and those of its members remain in a constant state of update and reviewing.

NATO's cyber history and key cyber structures

For nearly two decades, cyber defense has been a feature of NATO's strategic planning. As noted in the timeline illustrated in the following text, 2002 was a significant year for the Alliance, which witnessed the adoption of the Cyber Defence Program during the Prague Summit. This adoption, in part, was a reaction to what NATO saw as a changing cyber landscape, dappled with state and non-state actors (NSAs) with growing capabilities in the cyber realm and a clear indication that they were ready and willing to employ their abilities against the Alliance and its member states. Correspondingly, one should mention here the range of cyber strikes made against the Alliance predominantly during Operation Allied Force (OAF), NATO's air campaign against the Federal Republic of Yugoslavia launched on March 24, 1999 and lasting 78 days, perpetrated by Serbians objecting to NATO military activity as well as Russians and Chinese activists and cyber-militants. Their series of attacks raised awareness that NATO's cyber defenses were a possible weakness.

However, the 2007 cyberattacks on Estonia served as a wake-up call for NATO that despite being able to field sophisticated military forces, its cyber "under-belly" represented a potentially significant vulnerability of the Alliance. The implications of the attacks and the Alliance's vulnerabilities in the cyber domain received attention during the 2008 Bucharest Summit, where discussions presided over the Alliance's need to secure and safeguard its vital information systems, which by way of attacks against Estonia, proved to be at risk and subject to attackers that the Alliance could not necessarily track and engage. Since the high-level meetings in Bucharest, NATO's cyber security and defense trajectory crystalized with increasing speed. Both the Cyber Defense Management Authority (CDMA) and the CCDCOE soon emerged with the development of Rapid Reaction Teams (RRTs). NATO's cyber vision grew in the following years, and developed into a more comprehensive and sharpened program with attention given to the political and policy side of cyber security and cyber defense.

Since 2008 NATO has expanded its deterrent role and operational capabilities through the creation of new standards, clusters and networks of expertise, and experts from the military, civilian, and commercial worlds; has established relationships with allied organizations, including partnerships with the private sector, potential future allies, and partner countries (non-NATO and/or non-EU members); started engaging in awareness raising through public diplomacy, public events and conferences, and communication campaigns; and has adopted an active engagement posture, based on Article 5, with regards to cyber security risks as well as cyber enabled threats, such as hybrid and information operations, which are now considered under the expanded umbrella of cyber as the fourth operational domain of the Alliance. Cyber defense is core to the Alliance's collective defense, having affirmed that international law applies in cyberspace. NATO's main focus in cyber is to protect its own networks and enhance resilience across the Alliance.

NATO carried its cyber developments further in 2010 with its Strategic Concept 2010 "Active Engagement, Modern Defence" presenting the Alliance's strategic objectives and values for the decade that would follow. In its comprehensive coverage, Strategic Concept 2010 addresses the cyber element, both as attacks and pernicious threats, and as defense and deterrence imperatives. As part of NATO's wider security environment, cyberattacks were linked to the integrity of government, critical infrastructure on which societies depend, economies and vital supply chains/networks, thus equating a threat to "Euro-Atlantic prosperity, security and stability," identifying a fuller range of threat actors than previously identified or confronted by the Alliance. These threats necessitated increased focus on coordination of national cyber-defense capabilities, and tightening the cyber architecture of the Alliance, achieving centralized cyber protection. Under its "Defence and Deterrence" section, the Strategic Concept 2010 (NATO, 2019a) established NATO's aim to:

> develop further our ability to prevent, detect, defend against and recover from cyberattacks, including by using the NATO planning process to enhance and coordinate national cyber-defence capabilities, bringing all NATO bodies under centralized cyber protection, 17 and better integrating NATO cyber awareness, warning and response with member nations.

With its manifold changes, the NATO Strategy Concept 2010 took the Alliance to "NATO 3.0" and saw it "go global." It was a substantial upgrade from its previous strategic visions,[1] which thence took into account the rise of NSAs and asymmetric threats, the variations in the political landscape – within and outside of NATO and the EU – the dissolution of old states and emergence of new ones in the international system, and the development of new and innovative technologies and technological applications, and the Alliance's relationship with other countries, organizations, and supranational organizations, notably the United Nations (UN), including the UN Security Council (UNSC). Moreover, the Strategic Concept 2010 processed and facilitated the Alliance's operational adaptations to its geopolitical focus, specifically its expanding geographical treatment and turn to areas beyond the Balkans and elsewhere in European as well as Africa and Asia. Finally, revisions to the Strategic Concept accounted for the events of 9/11, and subsequent wars that have taken place in Iraq and Afghanistan.[2]

In April 2009, part of the lead up to the Lisbon Summit from November 19–20, 2010, NATO leaders approved the outline model for perhaps the most critical aspect of NATO's defense posturing, the NATO Defence Planning Process (NDPP). NATO Defence Ministers followed on this by approving its Implementation and Transition Plan in June that same year. The NDPP is a defense planning framework that "harmonizes" national and cross-NATO defense planning activities so as to streamline and enhance the efficiency of NATO operations and capabilities. As the Centre of Excellence for Operations in Confined and Shallow Waters (COE-CSW) (2013) describes, "[t]he NDPP provides a specific methodology and mechanism bringing the political and military strategic levels closer together and engaging them in a common, functionally integrated method towards Defence Planning."

With the implementation of the its Cyber Defense Policy in June 2011, the Alliance invested further in the growth of its cyber capabilities by pursuing cyber-force capabilities symbiosis across the entire Alliance. Responses to cyber events and incidents are prosecuted in accordance with the NATO governance structures pertaining to cyber defense and security, and as they related to other Alliance members through political channels. NATO's governance structures in the context of cyber defense and protection is illustrated in Figure 20.1.

NATO cyber structures and cooperative activities

The *NATO Cyber Committee* has the role of creating a bridge between NATO and the capitals and the relevant national authorities; it connects the technical and policy sides, ensuring that technical issues get translated at policy level and vice versa.

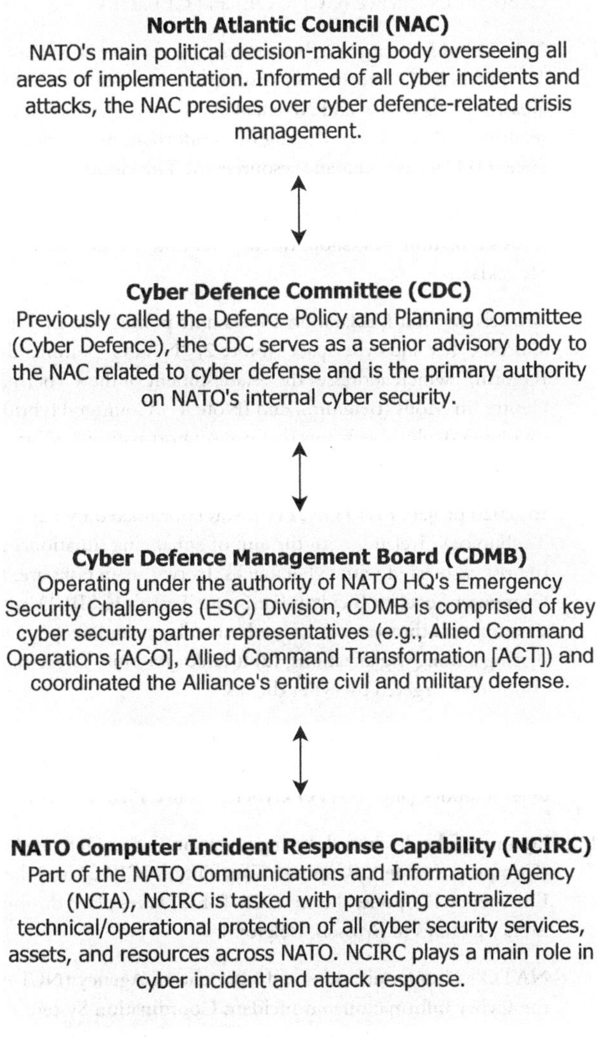

North Atlantic Council (NAC)
NATO's main political decision-making body overseeing all areas of implementation. Informed of all cyber incidents and attacks, the NAC presides over cyber defence-related crisis management.

Cyber Defence Committee (CDC)
Previously called the Defence Policy and Planning Committee (Cyber Defence), the CDC serves as a senior advisory body to the NAC related to cyber defense and is the primary authority on NATO's internal cyber security.

Cyber Defence Management Board (CDMB)
Operating under the authority of NATO HQ's Emergency Security Challenges (ESC) Division, CDMB is comprised of key cyber security partner representatives (e.g., Allied Command Operations [ACO], Allied Command Transformation [ACT]) and coordinated the Alliance's entire civil and military defense.

NATO Computer Incident Response Capability (NCIRC)
Part of the NATO Communications and Information Agency (NCIA), NCIRC is tasked with providing centralized technical/operational protection of all cyber security services, assets, and resources across NATO. NCIRC plays a main role in cyber incident and attack response.

Figure 20.1 NATO Cyber Defense Governance Relationship.
Source: Fidler et al. (2013), Shea (2013), Tsagourias and Buchan (2015), ATA (2018), Ablon et al. (2019).

Table 20.1 Timeline of Key NATO Cyber Events/Incidents

Date	Event(s)
2023	NATO's future Cyber Operations Centre (COC) in Mons, Belgium expected to be fully operational. The Centre will preside over, among other matters, military leadership and coordination, and situational awareness, and enhance NATO's collective cyber defense capacities overall.
2020, January 20–24	Exercise Crossed Swords 2020 in Riga, Latvia, achieves strides in the area of multinational and interdisciplinary cooperation with more than 120 technical experts, members of Cyber Command, and military personnel. The annual cyber exercise was organized by the NATO Cooperative Cyber Defence Centre of Excellence (CCDCOE) and CERT.LV.
2019, October 15–17	NATO holds its largest cyber security conference at Mons from October 15 to 17. The NATO Information Assurance Symposium (NIAS) address five key areas: (1) Traditional and AI-enabled information assurance; (2) Supply chain security challenges; (3) Moving from information assurance to mission assurance; (4) Data as a strategic resource; (5) The cloud.
2019, June 6	The GLOBSEC 2019 Forum serves as the forum for NATO's initial cyber crisis simulation workshop, titled, "Disruptive Dilemmas" in Bratislava, Slovakia.
2018, July 11–12	Brussels Summit Declaration covers nine points; two of which specifically address cyber and cyberspace: (Note 2) "NATO Command Structure Reform," which addresses the establishment of the Cyberspace Operations Centre, in Mons (Belgium), and (Note 4) "Counter-Hybrid Support Teams," involving deployable teams that can support national efforts in, among others, the cyber defense realm.
2016, September 1–August 31	EU2020 project PROTECTIVE was coordinated by Athlone Institute of Technology, Ireland, with the aim of enhancing situational awareness about the risk associated with cyberattacks. Its two main tasks are: (1) strengthen the Computer Security Incident Response Team's (CSIRT) awareness of potential or imminent threats via increased surveillance and deeper data/intelligence sharing among organizations; (2) it ranks potential threat damage to businesses/companies targeted by cyber threats.
2016, July 8–9	During the Warsaw Summit, NATO member states recognize cyberspace as a domain of military of operations and a core area of NATO's collective defense duties (also, NATO Cyber Defence Pledge, NATO-EU cooperation).
2016, February 10–11	Signing of the Technical Arrangement on Cyber Defence between NATO (Computer Incident Response Capability, NCIRC) and the EU (Computer Emergency Response Team, CERT-EU) takes place during the Defense Ministers Meetings in Brussels, Belgium.
2015, June	NATO's Communications and Information Agency (NCI Agency) develops the Cyber Information and Incident Coordination System (CIICS) to serves as the cyber division of the Alliance, maintaining 24/7 watch over cyber events. CIICS functions in conjunction with MNCD2.

(Continued)

Table 20.1 (Cont.)

Date	Event(s)
2014, September 17	NATO launches its Industry Cyber Partnership (NCIP) – endorsed at NATO's Wales Summit – to enhance the Alliance's cooperation with the private sector related to cyber threats and challenges.
2014, September 4–5	The Wales Summit serves as the venue where Allies pledge to make cyber defense a core part of their agenda. Allies state that a cyberattack would be an act of war and could trigger Article 5.
2014	MNCDE&T supports participant states (21 as of 2018) in identifying possible weaknesses in the areas of education and training. The project works with multiple EU groups/organizations: EU Military Training Group Cyber Defence Discipline, European Security and Defense College, EU Military Staff, European Defense Agency (EDA), and staff across NATO's various branches and divisions.
2013, June 4	NATO holds its first-ever meeting of ministers dedicated to cyber defense and aims to extend its cyber-shield to all networks operated by the Alliance.
2013	NATO begins its Computer Incident Response Capability (NCIRC) upgrade project, which entails the augmentation of NATO cyber defenses by the end of October, 2013. The project carries a budget of €58 million. Project aims to create better cyber defenses for the Alliance and address rising cyber incidents.
2013, March 14	The Multinational Cyber Defence Capability Development (MNCD2) is a "Smart Defence" addressing difficulties in NATO procurement of various materials/equipment due to irregularities in specialized technical knowledge. It assists states in optimizing their cyber defense capabilities by engaging in joint procurement addressing various constraints to procurement jointly.
2012, July 1	NATO Communications and Information Agency (NSI) is founded as the Alliance's cyber hub with four main campuses located in Brussels and Mons (Belgium), The Hague (The Netherlands), and Oeiras (Portugal), along with 30 other locations. NSI seeks to lead the enhancement of the Alliance's cyber capabilities.
2012, June	The Malware Information Sharing Platform (MISP) represents a knowledge community with expertise in cyber security threats and defense, including technical aspects of malware, for the detection of and protection against foreign intruders.
2011, June	NATO Defense Ministers adopt new Cyber Defense Policy on the guidance of the Strategic Concept. The primary aim is the prevention of cyber threats and building resilience across Allies. At the same time, the cyber defence Action Plan established to facilitate policy implementation.
2011, February 4	NATO Secretary General, Anders Fogh Rasmussen shares the idea of "Smart Defence" as a system of cooperation for the security and survival of states nearly a decade ago, which he described as, "ensuring greater security, for less money, by working together with more flexibility." The conception of

(Continued)

Table 20.1 (Cont.)

Date	Event(s)
	streamlining defense spending and measure incorporates Transatlantic Defence Technology and Industry Cooperation (TADIC).
2010, November 19–20	NATO holds major summit meetings of heads of state and government in Lisbon, Portugal, where a new "NATO 3.0" – adopted a new Strategic Concept, which outlined the Allies' ten-year plan. It was the first revised Strategic Concept since 1999. NATO's new agenda prioritized the "harmonization" of national defense plans with the Alliance's strategic objectives and priorities, notably the Alliance's view to "global engagement."
2008 August 9	Georgia's computer networks hacked by unknown foreign assailants in August. The cyber "hattack" appeared to be coordinated with Russian military activity during the Russo-Georgian conflict that took place between August 7 and 16, 2008.
2008, May	The Cooperative Cyber Defence Centre of Excellence (CCDCOE), based in Tallinn, Estonia, is a NATO advisory group on matters related to cyber defense but provides broader support in the areas concept development, education and training, exercises, political matters, legal issues, and military doctrine.
2008, April	The CDMA, based in Brussels, is the manifestation of efforts on the part of NATO to centralize the Alliance's cyber security and cyber defense capabilities across NATO member states.
2008, January	NATO adopts its first cyber defense policy.
2007, April (22-day attack)	Distributed denial-of-service (DDoS) attack perpetrated against the Estonian government by unknown assailants. "Attacks" described as cyber "protests," possibly in response to the Estonian government's decision to remove a Soviet war memorial (called the "Bronze Soldier") from the country's capital, Tallinn.
2002, November 21–22	At the Prague Summit, Allied leaders acknowledge the need to enhance NATO capabilities to defense against pernicious cyber threats. The summit marked the beginning of NATO's cyber focus.
2001, September 11	Terrorist attacks against the US on September 1 leads to NATO invoking Article 5 and deploys aircraft in the US.
1988-1990, November 2–May 5	The Morris Worm virus as the first major attack on the Internet launched from a computer at the Massachusetts Institute of Technology (MIT) and largely affected computers in the US.

Source: CORDIS (n.d.), Iasiello (n.d.), NCI Agency (n.d.a, n.d.b, n.d.c), Hughes (2009), NATO (2011a, 2011b, 2014a, 2014b, 2016d), Ringsmore and Rynning (2011), Czulda and Łoś (2013), Hallams et al. (2013), Healey and Jordan (2014), Academia Militar (2016), Butler (2017: 46), Lee (2017), Monteiro (2017), Rivas (2017), Besch (2018), FBI (2018), GLOBSEC (2018), NIAS19 (2018), Ottis (2018), Seffers (2018), CCDCOE (2019), De Carvalho (2019), Republic of Estonia, Defence Forces (2020)

The CCDCOE

The Tallinn-based *CCDCOE* is a NATO-accredited knowledge hub, think-tank, and training facility. With six branches under the Directorate (Technology, Strategy, Operations, Law, Education and Training, and Support), the Centre focuses on interdisciplinary applied research and development, as well as consultations, training, and exercises in the field of cyber security. The Centre's mission is to enhance capability, cooperation, and information-sharing between NATO, Allies, and partners in cyber defense. The Centre is staffed and financed by its member nations. The Centre is not part of NATO command or force structure, nor is it funded from the NATO budget (Republic of Estonia, Defence Forces, 2020). With cross-field specialties the Centre has benefitted from the incorporating of new members and integrating their specific knowledge and skill-sets. On June 13, 2019 the CCDCOE welcomed four new members – Bulgaria, Denmark, Norway, and Romania; the Centre now has 25 member-states, becoming the biggest among 25 NATO-accredited centers of excellence.

The three Pillars of CCDCOE are its *Tallinn Manual 2.0*, the most comprehensive guide for policy advisors and legal experts on how existing International Law applies to cyber operations; the *Exercise Locked Shields*, organized annually NATO, is the largest and most complex international live-fire cyber defense exercise in the world; the annual *International Conference on Cyber Conflict (CyCon)* bringing together decision-makers and experts from government, military, and industry to discuss legal, technological, and strategic perspectives of cyber defense. The Centre focuses mainly on research on cyber security as well as offering expertise and training and organizing cyber exercises where NATO member countries and partners take part.

NATO communications and information system services agency (NCIA)

NCIA plays a key role in delivering the technological aspects required for maintaining communications between the NATO member states. Created in 2012, "NCI Agency delivers advanced Command, Control, Communications, Computers, Intelligence, Surveillance and Reconnaissance (C4ISR) technology and communications capabilities in support of Alliance decision-makers and missions" (NATO, 2016a). This initiative allowed for the strengthening of national cyber defense capabilities by facilitating collaborative work and creating a framework through which mutual gains can be realized. Though disparate cyber doctrines and approaches between NATO members can create challenges to a unified command and coordination, different approaches and perspectives have been shown to strengthen the overall unified cyber defense capacities of the Alliance.

The NCIA contributes to enhancing cooperation and real time information exchange at the level of NATO members and in relations to the academia, think-tanks, and private sector. It develops industrial partnerships that boost cooperation in cyber defense, increase knowledge on cyber threats and how to deal with cyber-attacks, enhance situational awareness and security of networks as well as exchange best practices. NCIA also plays a key role being involved in the exercises organized at NATO level.

The *NATO Information Assurance Symposium (NIAS)* is the flagship NCIA yearly conference, intended to better connect industry with experts and governments, to address the latest developments in cyber innovation, and bring together new talent and new avenues of cooperation. It is also a platform to share best practices at national level that could be implemented by other actors or that could open new ways to work together at the

Alliance level. NATO is also present in the international debate held at the UN level regarding regulating international cyberspace, supporting the idea that international law is applicable in cyber space.

The *NATO Computer Incident Response Capability (NCIRC)*, part of the NCI Agency, is responsible for identifying and responding to cyber incidents against the networks of the Alliance. NCIRC also covers the cyber security protection and cyber defense at NATO sites across member states. Through the EU NATO Technical Agreement (2016), NCIRC shares best practices and participates in the enhancing of cooperation with CERT-EU.

The *NATO Cyber Operations Centre* (projected completion date set for 2023) in Mons, Belgium, will support military commanders with situational awareness, inform our operations and missions, and strengthen NATO's cyber defenses. The Centre will coordinate NATO's operational activity in cyberspace, "ensuring [NATO's] freedom to act in this domain and making operations more resilient to cyberattacks" (NATO, 2019a).

Through the *Cyber Defence Pledge* (2016 Warsaw Summit), the Allies committed to using part of the 2 per cent GDP target dedicated to defense towards cyber. The Pledge's seven key objectives:

1 Developing a wide range of capabilities to match requirements for cyber defense and treating cyber defense at the highest strategic levels
2 Dedicate the resources needed at national level to develop these capabilities
3 Strengthen cooperation between states
4 Sharing information and assessments to increase the knowledge on cyber threats
5 Raising awareness and develop skills across all actors involved in cyberdefense
6 Fostering training and education activities
7 Ensure quick implementation of agreed measures. (See reports on the implementation of the cyber defense pledge.) (NATO, 2016c)

The momentum of the cyber pledge was kept through an annual conference format which brings together officials from NATO, member states, and experts to look into developments around the key objectives and their implementation. NATO seeks to achieve mission assurance and to conduct cyberspace operations by 2021. Though it clearly stated it will not execute offensive cyberspace operations by NATO personnel under its own flag, it will, when deemed necessary, integrate sovereign cyberspace effects from allies who are capable and willing to provide them. Several nations have publicly declared their willingness and capability to do so, including the UK, the US, the Netherlands, Estonia, and Denmark (Lewis, 2019).

NATO's Cyberspace Operations Centre in Belgium, launched August 2018, is the central hub of cyberspace operations in the Alliance, with its primary role being to orchestrate the efforts of existing elements. As it stands, it is somewhat similar to EU envisioned cyber capabilities which are more about coordination than operations. The Centre's mission is three-fold: providing situational awareness of the domain, planning for the cyberspace aspects of allied operations, and managing the execution of operational direction to ensure freedom of maneuver in all domains affected by cyberspace activities. The Centre executes its mission at both the strategic and operational levels and has the central role of cyberspace defense.

CCDCOE's annual Cyber Conference (CyCon) serves as a platform to discuss the latest developments in cyber space as well as to gather together government representatives, policy makers, military, industry, and experts to analyze challenges and develop recommendations. It established itself as a high-level policy conference with a high academic focus.

Activities NATO undertakes in the cyber cooperation area focus on strengthening cyber defense in member states (supporting the creation of CERT centers in partner countries, training civil servants and members of armed forces, public events, awareness campaigns, exercises) and partners as well as expand cooperation with industry expert researchers. Further initiatives are directed at the inclusion of cyber threats into the NATO Crisis Management Exercise to educate NATO officials across the members states, at NATO Headquarters, Allied Command Operations, and Allied Command Transformation. Of particular importance for the enhancement and strengthening of NATO cyber capabilities is the NATO Cyber Range, in Tartu, Estonia, which provides the necessary infrastructure for cyber experts to build on existing knowledge and apply what they know through cyber exercises using computer simulated operational environments. During its twelfth iteration in 2019, exercises held in Estonia involved more than 900 participants coming from NATO and non-NATO states. Realistic scenario-based training and exercises are designed to crack NATO cyber defenses and reveal gaps in existence competencies.

Parallel to these initiatives, NATO organizes a variety of "Smart Defence" projects focused on pernicious software on its MISP, which allows for cross-nation sharing of private information and accommodates information and data sharing between NATO and EU member states. These are supported by the Smart Defence Multinational Cyber Defense Capability Development (MN CD2), and the Multinational Cyber Defence Education and Training Project (MN CD E&T) MN CD2 is synchronize with the Allied Command Transformation (ACT) Cyber Defence Programme of Work, drawing on the knowledge and experience of the NCI Agency as the main support structure for the Alliance's NCIRC Initial Operational Capability (IOC) and Full Operational Capability (FOC) projects. We turn our attention to these in the following sub-section.

Smart Defence

NATO's concept of "Smart Defence" in compatible with the idea of collaborative defense with flexibility, innovation, and greater efficiency as chief elements. The concept as policy innovation supports Allies in cooperative engagement for the development, acquisition, and maintenance of critical military capabilities in line with NATO's strategic concept. As an umbrella term, "Smart Defence" encompasses more than a hundred projects of various types, including: (1) Multinational Cyber Defence Capability Development Project (MNCD2), (2) MISP, and (3) Transatlantic Defence Technological and Industrial Cooperation (TADIC). These initiatives and projects have resulted in the development and implementation of critical defense systems, detection software/systems, coordination systems, information/data collection and sharing arrangements, and innovative planning with NATO members. Smart Defence capacity "pooling and sharing" (P&S)[3] – The "Ghent Initiative" recognized as the starting point (see Von Voss et al., 2013) – has led to a beneficial amalgamation of national resources and cyber competencies, enabling one NATO member state to benefit as a result of what another knows. This encompasses performance competencies and can be applied to long-term procurements.

Information and expertise sharing practices, as well as education, training, awareness raising, and communities of practice conferences are all part of an effort to consolidate NATO and partners' capabilities and interoperability in cyber defense (e.g., Cyber Defence Smart Defence Conference, CyCon, NIAS, and so on). Recognizing the importance of building relations with industry which drives the cyber security market innovation, NATO (through the NCIA) has taken active steps in this regard. One example is the NIAS annual conference. With the view that industry and industry leaders can be key deliverers of innovation that can benefit NATO cyber capabilities, the NIAS annual conference brings industry and military together. The annual conferences have provided NATO with immense support and has driven the Alliance's cyber security progress over previous years.

Partnerships struck with industry focus on sharing threat intelligence and early warning indicators. Taking into account that the cyber field is very much industry driven, these partnerships are essential for NATO to develop further its own tools. Cyber Conference CyCon is an annual conference organized by CCDCOE on cyber defense and related topics. It serves as a platform to discuss latest developments in cyber space as well as to gather together government representatives, policy makers, military, industry, and experts to analyze challenges and develop recommendations. It has established itself as a high-level policy conference that also focuses on the academic side of the aspects discussed. Papers submitted to the conference are published in its proceedings, outlining also focus on academic input of the Centre, contributing to expanding research in the academic world.

NATO–EU cooperation

Summit 2016 – the Joint Declaration on NATO–EU cooperation – established the basis for enhanced cooperation on multiple areas, which has been monitored through progress reports. Cooperation with the EU started to take shape with the Wales summit, and reached an important point in 2016 when the technical agreement was signed between the NCIRC Technical Centre and CERT-EU, its European counterpart. A major key decision was the mutual recognition of cyberspace as an operational domain, in which defense and offensive operations could and may be conducted. The newest frontier of operations was thus joined to existing land, sea, and air domains, bringing about new opportunities as well as deepening the challenges of defense and security. In spite of potential necessity to operate offensive, NATO has reiterated its strategy and posture in cyberspace remains strictly defensive. However, the linking of the newest domain with existing ones implies an expansive connectivity of defense across all sectors that can be interpreted as a pseudo-cyber build-up or mobilization of sorts.

The Brussels Summit 2018:

> Cyber defence is part of NATO's core task of collective defence. Strong cyber defence is an essential element of NATO's deterrence and defence posture. Allies work to implement fully the 2016 Warsaw Summit Cyber Defence Pledge on delivering strong national cyber defences. Moreover, cyberspace has become a domain of operations. Allies agreed to integrate sovereign cyber effects, 17 provided voluntarily, into Alliance operations and missions, under strong political oversight. Allies have also started to address the challenge of how to deter an adversary from launching cyber-attacks and how to combine "classic" deterrence, digital resilience and measures to be developed in order to be able to impose costs on those who would harm allied nations, with a view to discouraging them from launching significant, widespread cyber-attacks.
>
> *(Brauss, 2018)*

The second progress report (NATO, 2017b) on EU-NATO 2016 set proposals for the implementation of the Joint Declaration and takes stock of cooperation development in the cyber area, outlining the exchanges in concepts, education, and training practices. The third and fourth (NATO, 2018b, 2019b) progress reports illustrate the continued pursuit of an enhanced defensive posture and building on the previous 42 proposals for the implementation of NATO's Joint Declaration. This was followed by 32 further actions agreed upon by the two Councils on December 5, 2017. With the fourth progress report, NATO has implemented 74 common proposals. Cooperation in the cyber realm has accelerated after a sluggish beginning with heightened efforts focusing on information sharing, the coverage of tactical and strategic concepts pertaining to cyberspace, and revisiting strategic doctrines.

NATO emphasizes further cooperate on "cyber exercises" and attention to cyber threats and "cyber aspect of crisis management." Two workshops were held in September 2018 and April 2019, which enhanced existing exchanges between representatives of NATO states to understand and harvest the benefits of NATO-EU conceptual ideas. As such, mutual participation in NATO/EU exercises has built trust and strengthened cooperation at multiple levels. There are many opportunities to develop cooperation at the working level but agreement must start from the political level. Developing capabilities at national level must move forward first if NATO is to realize any appreciable degree of coordinated development.

The Cooperation Agreement includes a sanctions regime (economic, financial, and mobility) in response to attack on the EU and its member states. This brings political and economic bite to the NATO framework, as it, being a political-military alliance, could not by itself take such measures, which are the privilege of sovereign nation states.

The aspect of NATO-EU cooperation has become increasingly salient, as, due to political and policy developments within the EU, NATO has begun functioning like a two-pillar alliance. The EU's enlargement and deepening presents new horizons of opportunity and brings increased security to NATO and its members. The EU's shortcoming, however, is its slowness to (re)act, due to its architecture and the fact that some EU members are not also NATO members.

A significant doctrinal achievement has been persistent engagement. We are observing a gradual shift in NATO posture and operations in both Cyber and StratCom, brought about by the changing and evolving nature and volume of challenges by adversaries and/or third parties against the Alliance as well as against individual member states. This is happening in spite of decades of military doctrine and political preference of keeping the various elements of doctrine neatly separated as well as not adopting a posture that would be seen as threatening so as to warrant a negative response or from those feeling threatened by NATO or its members. However, with an increased tempo of attacks (whether cyber alone or in conjunction with other informational means), both attributable and non-attributable between 2010 and 2020, in a manner that is below the threshold of what would constitute an act of war – in other words deliberate planning, intensity, and in full awareness that they will become public – NATO members have been forced to adjust to a new and for some unfamiliar operational ecosystem. This is leading to an accelerated pace of adjustments.

Contrary to classical (kinetic) means of defense, the nature of cyber is pushing state and NSAs around the world to formulate new doctrine, processes, and operations – a threat landscape that the Alliance needs to adjust to as well. This will translate into a more agile environment and pace of change, and we will see cyber lead doctrine development, operations, and other allied joint actions spearheaded by cyber to a much greater extent than seen in previous defense cooperation domains and aspects. The gates of engagement opened by and the new perspectives stemming from the use of cyber by the NATO allies and third parties will almost certainly become a wellspring of norms, actions, and processes across domains and the geographies in which the Alliance has a presence. That is, due to the cyber element, the environment in which NATO exists and functions will become "hotter" than we have grown accustomed to over previous decades, and the operating margins will narrow down to incredibly thin margins. The level of complexity of decision making will increase significantly on the political side as well, while degrees of certainty and threat predictability and counter-action and adjustment will decrease in chorus, resulting in a much more challenging uptick for political decision making than the technical uptick seen on the operational side. This only comes to reinforce the call for specialized personnel and public managers who stand ready to deal with these hotter and more sensitive matters, going the full range from policy makers to crisis managers, security personnel, and politicians.

NATO – third country cooperation

NATO works with a number of partner countries to enhance international security based on shared values and common approaches to cyber defense, supporting a norms-based, predictable, and secure cyberspace, and protecting critical technology and infrastructure. We offer a snapshot a few of NATO's initiatives and programs with non-NATO members in and around Europe.

Azerbaijan

Through NATO Science for Peace and Security (SPS) Programme, training in the field of cyber defense is delivered to partner countries and civil servants who work in the area. The main aim is to increase cyber resilience and to share theoretical and practical knowledge and best practices and to develop talent in partners countries. Azerbaijan is a good example in this case, cooperation under the SPS program covering not only cyber but also energy security and natural disasters. In previous years, Azerbaijan hosted a number of key events that included leaders and delegates from the US and NATO divisions. These include a 2013 conference held in Baku focusing on the issues of energy security enhancement in the twenty-first century and was attended by members of the US State Department NATO's Emerging Security Challenges Division. Key agenda issues included cyber defense, terrorism and counter-terrorism, and infrastructure security (Mission of the Republic of Azerbaijan to NATO, n.d.). In 2019, Baku served as the venue for the "Advanced Cyber Defence Training Course for Azerbaijan" as part of the larger cooperative project between NATO and Azerbaijan called, the "NATO Science for Peace and Security (SPS) Programme" (AZERTAC, 2019). States can also apply for special NATO financial assistance pertaining to scientific projects.

Ukraine

NATO tailors its engagement with partner countries on a case-by-case basis, considering shared values, mutual interest, and common approaches to cyber defense. For example, in the NATO–Ukraine partnership, cyber plays an important role. Through the Trust Fund[4] (from 2014), the Ukrainian cyber security instruments are developed at the level of institutions that have responsibilities in this area, internal laws and policies. As part of the

Fund, assistance has been provided in opening a situational center for the security services, as well as equipment for ministries and trainings offered (Centre for Global Studies, 2019). NATO also provides support to Ukraine through the Defence Education Enhancement Programme (DEEP) under which different exercises have been developed, including an Advanced Training Course on "Cyber Defence in the Context of Energy Security," held in Kiev from May 22–26, 2017. Another initiative supported by NATO's SPS Programme, governments have expressed the value of such programs, especially as they are tailored to the specific requirements and contexts of the states that they target and with which NATO engages on the issues (NOAC, 2018). A great deal of interest has been shown in these programs and those of cyber defense broadly speaking, and quantum technology, advanced technologies such as sensors, nanoscience, unmanned aerial vehicles (UAVs), and soft policy specifically, have been especially sought after.

NATO Cyber Security Trust Fund for Ukraine is another instrument used by NATO to help Ukraine develop capabilities to investigate cyber security incidents in a purely defensive (e.g., CSIRT-type technical capacities) context (NATO, 2016b). Romania, the lead nation in the initiative and acting via the Romanian Intelligence Service (Serviciul Român de Informaţii, SRI) based in Bucharest, is supported by other national contributors (donors), including Albania, Estonia, Hungary, Italy, Portugal, Turkey, and the US. The direct beneficiaries are the State Communications Agency of Ukraine (SCA) as well as the Cyber Threat Response Centre (CRC) with a little more than €1.06 million (of some €3.26 million in international assistance to the field of cyber security) in support funds from December 2014–January 2017 (Steyne & Khudaverdyan, 2018: 85). Overall, the lead actor on the initiative is a Romanian state-owned and operated (and under the coordination of SRI) cyber-defense called "RASIROM R.A.," with a specific mandate to protect the critical infrastructure of Romania and elsewhere in Europe. While the company is officially mandated with securing the national strategic objectives of Romania, it clearly plays an important role as knowledge and experience contributor with its co-members states in NATO and NATO partner states.

Moldova

Under the SPS Programme, multiple projects in the cyber realm have been developed in the Republic of Moldova. Following the formulation of a cyber defense laboratory at the Technical University of Moldova in 2016, a multi-year project focused on developing cyber defense capabilities (and more specifically cyber incident response capabilities of the armed forces) was launched on February 13, 2018 (NATO, 2018a). The initiative marked the third project to be undertaken through the Defence and Related Security Capacity Building Initiative platform targeting and addressing Moldova and the country's developing cyber capacities. The Republic of Moldova has undertaken its cooperative efforts with NATO in augmenting its cyber security portfolio as part of its international commitments and in preparing the country for emerging security threats and challenges (MFA, Republic of Moldova, 2017).

Jordan

Through a similar project aimed at strengthening cyber capabilities, with a SPS project (started in 2014), the Jordanian CERT within the armed forces was established on July 19, 2017. The initiative has received support from several other NATO members to strengthen the cyber capabilities of states in the vicinity of the EU and Europe. Germany, with support from France and the US, played a key role with Jordanian experts in Jordan's Defence and Related Security Capacity Building (DCB) package (NATO, 2017a). An active player against security threats in the region, Jordan's small but well-trained armed forces is one of numerous countries seen by NATO as a key partner growing efforts to defend against Jihadist movements and other threats that lie just beyond NATO's borders (Ryan, 2018).

Through these instruments, NATO helps build expertise and shares its "best practices" with partner countries, contributing to enhancing cyber capabilities not only to member states but across its spectrum of partners.

Article 5 and cyberattacks

Since 1949, NATO has undergone a process of gradual enlargement with the exception of the 1960s and 1970s when NATO activity in the way of expanding stagnated. Enlargement was undertaken in tandem with NATO's cornerstone Article 5 within the Washington Treaty (codifying the idea of collective defense), which has been invoked on only a single occasion in the Alliance's history.[5] While 9/11 represented a milestone for NATO, showing the Alliance's adaptive capacity to a radically changing global security environment, the question of invoking Article 5 in the event of a cyberattack against one of NATO's member states has contributed to much lively discussion and debate. Whereas the impacts of international terrorism arguably represented an emerging frontier for NATO at the turn of the millennium, cyberspace has since been identified as yet another "new frontier" in both defense and collective defense terms.

Cyber defense falls primarily with Allied states, with NATO in a supporting role. Significant action is taken at the level of the NDPP. As of 2013, these had been introduced as part of the Cyber Defence Capability Targets that state the benchmarks Allied states commit to fulfil. Although NATO members collectively acknowledge that the cyber element will be an integral component of the way that future warfare is conducted, some member states have questioned the implications of Article 5 in the context of a cyberattack against a NATO member state and appropriate response (i.e., where does the threshold/red line exist over which the Alliance will respond?). Despite ongoing debate about the commitment of NATO members amid cyberattacks, the Wales Declaration clarifies that Article 5 is entirely applicable to cyberattacks with cases being determined by the NATO Atlantic Council. Beyond this determination, the subsequent efforts and responses by NATO remains as ambiguous politically for NATO members as it does a "grey zone" for military strategists. Presently, no universal standard exists by which to measure cyberattacks against NATO states, and could lead to enduring debate among members if a cyberattack were to take place.

In addition to the ambiguity of cyber event impact assessment and subsequent collective steps to be taken, a possible fault line is the existence of 29 different national security and defense strategies, almost all of which possess components of a cyber defense strategy. In theory, determining when collective defense is triggered is manageable, however, the added complexity of individual state capabilities alongside relative impacts and their polygonal effects reveals considerable deficiencies in existing guidelines and assessment instruments. For example, the impact of a cyber attack, especially within a multi-national alliance as NATO, means that the effects of a cyber event are never absolute. By virtue of NATO's diverse (small-, medium-, and large-) state membership, effects should be weighed against the resilience of a targeted state and the costs of damage against the impacts other members can withstand. Moreover, since attacks against a single state can vary, determining the exigency of collective response is contingent upon the impact of kinetic disruption versus disruption of critical infrastructure vital to state functions.

The lack of specific guidelines to assess an appropriate course of action and in the spirit of the Alliance's cornerstone article points to the existence of an equivocal cyber defense capacity on an alliance-level within limits, and a serious fault line within the Alliance that could invite costly and debilitating cyberattacks of opportunity, particularly amid the absence of norms of responsible cyber behavior. This point relates to the diverse range of members within NATO, all of which possess their own uniqueness, though similar and shared in many ways, and the stark contrast between the pursuit of soft forms of cyber power by some states and neorealist pursuit of cyber power-maximizing. The assertive posture of the US, as a pole in the international system and yet still a member of the NATO collective security arrangement, deeply clashes with the doves of NATO, Europe, and the EU that exercise soft power in cyberspace.

Future challenges

Increasing complexity of operating between the EU, US, and Alliance members

The Alliance is cooperating in cyber not only with its membership, but also with the Alliance's partners, as well as with the entirety of the EU, with countries like Ireland, Austria, and others as non-members of NATO. Cooperation structures such as the CCDCOE bridge the gap between the various jurisdictions and memberships. Aside from the CCDCOE, NATO cooperates with a number of states around the world either in capability development and/or in an operational capacity. A number of issues have recently plagued political concord within and around the Alliance, which are likely to perpetuate for the foreseeable future, and are already propagating into operations and the following technological aspects.

Great power competition

The mantra under which the Trump Administration has been operating for the past four years has determined the violent rejection of the presence of Chinese-manufactured equipment in the core networks (currently the most widespread use – by the EU – practice of limiting access to Chinese equipment) of NATO members and partners. Technical aspects aside, this has strained political and commercial relations, but also triggered what some are already calling a technological (not only a trading or economic) decoupling. Initially estimated to be just a decoupling between the US and China, the cascading effects of IP (intellectual property) governance and disagreements, banking and financial standards, technological standards and practices, privacy and human rights practices, as well as further considerations regarding the weaponization of information, international development crediting, and the outbreak of the New Corona Virus 2019, are leading to a decoupling between China and the rest of the world. Increasingly, countries around the world, beyond the traditional West, are faced with the decision of going the Western or the Chinese way on technology. Some chose not to go the Western way, and some of them are NATO partners and countries the various NATO members cooperate with. This will continue weighing and adding complexity to protecting the Alliance's infrastructure, data, and operations' integrity and ensuring continued operations regardless of technological decoupling, increased cyber competition, etc.

EU strategic autonomy

The emergent decoupling concept within the Alliance dictates that the EU needs to have its own capacity to act across all security and defense domains autonomously from the US. While there is no official doctrine concerning joint standards and practices, the acceleration of the political centrifugal tendencies of the two shores of the Atlantic community risks impacting technological and operational capabilities from a certain point onward. Strategic Autonomy is theorized to have its first deliverables by 2029; however, cyber being the most agile operational domain, it will be the most susceptible to political tugs of war and knee-jerk reactions when politicians will disagree again in the future. Due to the discipline and transatlantic cooperation tradition, so far, we have not publicly heard of troubles within the Alliance due to this (still) evolving mantra of the EU.

NATO's Middle East involvement

NATO's operations in the Middle East and North African (MENA) regions could turn into a contentious issue in the future. Threefold considerations: First, president Trump's request that NATO start being more actively involved in the Middle East at a time when US policy in the region has been erratic, leaving EU allies uncertain about the operating conditions at the EU periphery. Second, the EU reluctance, as a bloc, to get involved operationally outside its immediate vicinity – which so far only translates into the south shore of the Mediterranean. Third, Turkey's incursions and forays into adjacent territories and neighboring regions. These on the backdrop of a contested US presence in the region for, among others, the missile strike on Iranian military leader Qasem Soleimani, the fallout of which is yet to manifest.

Russian and Chinese expanded presence in the Middle East, Africa, and Central and South Asia

Due to accelerated security dynamics in Africa and the Indian Ocean, lines are becoming increasingly blurry between what is likely to constitute an encounter between NATO and Russia and/or China in Africa and the Indian Ocean, with all the countries composing the two continents and the region of the Indian Ocean being in some form of collaboration or partnership with either East, West, or both. Further complications may result from the presence of US and European multiple domain assets in places like the Persian Gulf, Djibouti, and various key and choke points across the Indo-Pacific. NATO had traditionally stayed away from being overwhelmingly and overbearingly present next to Russia or China. However, with an increasingly less dovish EU, and an ever-more assertive blue water Chinese presence, the opportunities to snoop around and naval- and aerial-assets close encounters are highly likely to increase.

Social engineering

While not an inter-allied issue, and not a hard-cyber security issue in itself, social engineering is, however, one of the main concerns of the entirety of the Alliance. However, the various blocks, states, and partners are dealing with these aspects in various ways. Though it emerged as an issue with the 2016 US elections, Brexit, and a number of other incidents (technical labelling as "incidents" may be missing from official public documents) since, it remains one of the main coagulating issues at a global scale. Social engineering, under hacking, disinformation,

242

propaganda, and other forms, is dealt with by the allies under both a cyber security and strategic communication heading. Gaps in privacy and data usage are gradually "patched" by legal and operational means. However, the weakening social cohesion and support for a previously commonly embraced vision and understanding of world order means that Allied societies are more vulnerable now than previously to social engineering.

Emerging technologies

Outer space

No longer a final frontier, outer space is already an operational domain and its militarization is an increasingly and overtly discussed (and observed) issue. Further complicating things, the cyber operational domain is the perfect storm of the conjunction between space, technological supremacy (see quantum supremacy), R&D, and upcoming semi- and autonomous platforms, with space being the "critical infrastructure" layer for all future kinetic and C4ISR capabilities.

Automation and Artificial Intelligence (AI)

Under their analytical, navigation, fire command, detection, battlefield integration, and other roles, AI is the most publicly discussed and contentious emerging technology. While countries on both sides of the Atlantic are pouring massive resources into developing AI (on their own), they have so far kept AI away from NATO (kinetic) capabilities. The challenge, however, is not any potential shortcoming in AI development, but the fielding of AI-enabled assets by Russia, China, and other actors. A few semi-autonomous and autonomous drones have already been deployed and used both in the Middle East and North Africa, with a perspective for strategic, global reach assets being fielded soon by a number of international actors. The proliferation of these platforms in the absence of any global conversation or process for the management associated with the risks entailed by automatic weaponry compounds the risks already associated with the use of such platforms.

Edge computing, 5G, and the frequency spectrum

Fifth-generation spectrum technologies known as 5G have attracted the attention of powerful states, including the US and China, due to opportunities they present in the areas of autonomous vehicles (AVs) or so-called "robo-cars" (e.g., robotic combat vehicles in the military realm at function alongside human assets, such as the Foster-Miller TALON tracked military robot made by US company, Qinetiq-NA), smart cities, and operation systems to dominate the conventional battlefields. Holding an advantage over another state mean significant benefits in the economic realm as much as the military realm. Applications of smart technology have attracted the attention of military organizations and alliances with NATO being no exception. Smart city technology (wireless radio-frequency identification [RFID] sensors for tagging) holds applications in the military dimension, notably the concept of the smart base with advanced networking technology/telecommunications capabilities and innovation alongside augmented and virtual reality with the aim of maintaining a military advantage over adversaries.

In line with US efforts to unfold military smart bases like Maxwell–Gunter Air Force Base, located at Montgomery, Alabama, NATO is endeavoring to transpose the benefits of civilian smart technology to the military domains – health systems, logistics applications, AVs, IoT capabilities that support tactical and operational situational awareness, targeting, and battle environment monitoring and surveillance. NATO has recognized the value of such applications to streamline and stealthize combat presence and movement. It has been working closely, under guidance by such bodies as the NATO Industrial Advisory Group (NIAG), with non-military personnel who are experts and industry leaders in their civilian fields to apply technological innovation to NATO's military and defense needs. Given the robustness of NATO's with its member states civilian sectors, there is room for significant development and application.

Place of origin, supply chain integration, and access vulnerabilities

Decoupling and parallel tech universes used to belong to the realm of geopolitics and trade conversations. With an increased siloing of the internet by Russia, China, and others, and the escalation of not only trade wars but also the "self-reliance" doctrine, present in the EU, China, Russia, North Korea, and possibly soon to emerge in other countries as well, the allies will be forced to address issues of origin, participants to the supply chain, and familiarity with the specs of the products used in a variety of networks, what crosses over between military equipment, dual-use, civilian, space-based assets, and land-based networks, whether they be critical infrastructure or networks in touch (capable of influencing, sensing, or controlling) with any of the above. This will increasingly include decentralized operating ecosystems, which currently are known primarily as "cloud" environments, but which will proliferate under various forms over the next decade, as concepts, technologies, and quantum capabilities are only in their infancy:

1   Strengthening of classical contenders (Russia, China, Iran, DPRK);
2   Emerging actors and/or capabilities (the proliferation and ease of access of anyone to cyber means);
3   AI, automated decision-making (not the operations themselves, but protecting the AI);
4   Quantum communications and satellites;
5   Increasing attack surface and vulnerabilities introduced by IoT, 5G, and a fully digital society.

Conclusion

In 2019, NATO celebrated its 70th anniversary. At the time of its founding, the world was undergoing strident technological change and advancement with the introduction of systems as wartime innovations that would determine the future of state conflict. The age of technology that began in the mid-1950s accelerated from the 1958 mark until the end of the 1970s, with achievements like the modem signaling the start of the computer age. At the time, the fifth domain of warfare had yet to emerge and conflict was still conducted on traditional and conventional battlefields. While technological development has taken place in leaps and bounds since the founding of NATO, the Alliance's need to continuously adapt to technological innovation and change has remained constant. The rapidly changing cyber security environment constantly brings new challenges and threats, many of which are markedly more complex and powerful than those previously faced, hence it requires states and international organizations to quickly adapt and tackle these issues in cross-field and cross-state fashion.

Against this backdrop, NATO needs, on one hand, to further develop its cyber capabilities and be regarded as a strong player in this field while, on the other hand, to enhance the capabilities of its member states and strengthen interoperability between them. NATO cyber security policy and strategy needs to strike a balance between innovative thinking at the political level, while observing the practical needs of the organization as a collective of societies and forces, each with distinct features and behaviors.

The bleed-through of security considerations across almost the full spectrum of civilian technologies due to digitalization, and the spill-over of anti-democratic behaviors into everyday communication, technology, economics, and primary resources, means that NATO will be faced with disruptive currents that will force it to reconsider well-established boundaries, and scope and breadth of its defense activities. Further, societies will be faced with the imposition to mainstream cyber defense and security into all aspects of their existence.

Notes

1 NATO's initial Strategic Concept, the Strategic Concept for the Defence of the North Atlantic Area, was followed by revisions to the agenda in 1957, 1968, 1991, and 1999.
2 See De Nevers (2007) for a critical engagement of NATO's role supporting the US-led WOT.
3 The Strategic Airlift Capability (SAC) is an example of pooled resources in NATO. Established in 2008 by NATO members, Bulgaria, Estonia, Hungary, Lithuania, and the Netherlands, and by Partnership for Peace (PfP) nations, Finland and Sweden, SAC facilitates optimal airlift capacity while diminishing national capabilities gaps. This applies to resources or capabilities sharing as well. Thus, NATO members benefit from strength accessibility and the mitigation of national weaknesses due to financial constraints, for example.
4 Many other trust funds are set-up by NATO to help non-NATO members (those facing particularly tough security challenges) with defense capacity building with institutional support in the areas of defense and security.
5 The decision about how each member state would contribute in the event of triggering Article 5 is left entirely up to the national authorities of each state.

Suggested reading

Burton, J. (2015). "NATO's Cyber Defence: Strategic Challenges and Institutional Adaptation," *Defence Studies*, 15(4): 297–319.
Efthymiopoulos, M. P. (2019). "A Cyber-Security Framework for Development, Defense and Innovation at NATO," *Journal of Innovation and Entrepreneurship*, 8(12). https://doi.org/10.1186/s13731-019-0105-z
Kovács, L. (2018). "Cyber Security Policy and Strategy in the European Union and NATO," *Land Forces Academy Review*, 23(1): 16–24.
Štitilis, D., Pakutinskas, P. & Malinauskaitė, I. (2017). "EU and NATO Cybersecurity Strategies and National Cyber Security Strategies: A Comparative Analysis," *Security Journal*, 30, 1151–1168.
Tikk, E. (2011). "Ten Rules for Cyber Security," *Global Politics and Strategy*, 53(3): 119–132.

References

Ablon, L., Binnendijk, A., Hogdson, Q. E., Lilly, B., Romanosky, S., Senty, D. & Thompson, J. A. (2019, June). *Operationalizing Cyberspace as a Military Domain*, Washington, DC: RAND. rand.org/content/dam/rand/pubs/perspectives/PE300/PE329/RAND_PE329.pdf
Academia Militar. (2016). "Multinational Cyber Defence Capability Development (MNCD2)." https://academiamilitar.pt/images/CDSDP2016/Apresentacoes/1.NATO-CD-Smart-Defence-Projects_MNCD2.pdf
ATA. (2018, March 9). "NATO's Cyber Defence Pledge: Developing the NATO Cyber Defence Capability and Capacity." www.atahq.org/2018/03/natos-cyber-defence-pledge-developing-nato-cyber-defence-capability-capacity/

AZERTAC. (2019, December 22). "Baku Hosts NATO Advance Cyber Defence Training Courses." https://azertag.az/en/xeber/Baku_hosts_NATO_Advance_Cyber_Defence_training_courses-1372909

Besch, S. (2018, October 31). *Protecting European Networks: What Can NATO Do?* London, United Kingdom: Centre for European Reform (CER). www.cer.eu/sites/default/files/insight_SB_31.10.18_2.pdf

Brauss, H. (2018, November). *NATO beyond 70: Renewing a Culture of Readiness.* Tallinn, Estonia: International Centre for Defence and Security. https://icds.ee/wp-content/uploads/2018/11/ICDS-Analysis_NATO-Beyond-70_Heinrich-Brauss_November-2018-1.pdf

Butler, L. R. A. (2017). *Transatlantic Defence Procurement: EU and US Defence Procurement Regulation in the Transatlantic Defence Market.* Cambridge: Cambridge University Press.

CCDCOE. (2019). "Exercise Crossed Swords 2019 Integrates Cyber into Full Scale of Operations." https://ccdcoe.org/news/2019/exercise-crossed-swords-2019-integrates-cyber-into-full-scale-of-operations/

Centre for Global Studies. (2019, October). "Ukraine – EU-NATO Cooperation for Countering Hybrid Threats in the Cyber Sphere." www.encouncil.org/wp-content/uploads/2019/10/ENG-Ukraine-EU-NATO-cooperation-to-counter-hybrid-threats-in-cyber-sphere.pdf

COE-CSW. (2013). "NATO Defence Planning Process." coecsw.org/our-work/activities/nato-defence-planning-process/

CORDIS. (n.d.). *Proactive Risk Management through Improved Cyber Situational Awareness.* Brussels, Belgium: European Commission. https://cordis.europa.eu/project/id/700071

Czulda, R. & Łoś, R. (2013). *NATO: Towards the Challenges of Contemporary World.* International Relations Research Institute in Warsaw, Poland.

De Carvalho, S. (2019). "Education and Training Towards Innovation and Capacity Building," in S. Gaycken (ed.), *Cyber Defense – Policies, Operations and Capacity Building* (pp. 107–112). NATO Science for Peace and Security Series. Amsterdam: IOS Press.

De Nevers, R. (2007). "NATO['s International Security Role in the Terrorist Era," *International Security*, *31*(4): 34–66.

FBI. (2018, November 2). "The Morris Worm." www.fbi.gov/news/stories/morris-worm-30-years-since-first-major-attack-on-internet-110218

Fidler, D. P., Pregent, R. & Vandurme, A. (2013). "NATO, Cyber Defense, and International Law," *Articles by Maurer Faculty*, Paper 1672. www.repository.law.indiana.edu/cgi/viewcontent.cgi?article=2673&context=facpub

GLOBSEC. (2018, December 17). "GLOBSEC European Security Initiative." www.globsec.org/

Hallams, E., Ratti, L. & Zyla, B. (eds.). (2013). *NATO beyond 9/11: The Transformation of the Atlantic Alliance.* Basingstoke: Palgrave Macmillan.

Healey, J. & Jordan, K. T. (2014, September). *NATO's Cyber Capabilities: Yesterday, Today, and Tomorrow.* Washington, DC: The Atlantic Council of the United States. www.atlanticcouncil.org/wp-content/uploads/2014/08/NATOs_Cyber_Capabilities.pdf

Hughes, R. B. (2009). *NATO and Cyber Defence: Mission Accomplished?* Carlisle, United States: Center for Strategic Leadership (CSL) Army War College. https://csl.armywarcollege.edu/SLET/mccd/Cyber SpacePubs/NATO%20and%20Cyber%20Defence%20-%20Mission%20Accomplished.pdf

Iasiello, E. (n.d.). "NATO's Cyber Operations Center – Will Russia Feel Threatened?" *The Cyber Research Databank.* www.cyberdb.co/natos-cyber-operations-center-will-russia-feel-threatened/

Lee, D. (2017, December). *How to Improve the ROK and U.S. Military Alliance against North Korea's Threats to Cyberspace: Lesson from NATO's Defense Cooperation.* Monterey, California: Defense Analysis Capstone, Naval Postgraduate School. https://apps.dtic.mil/dtic/tr/fulltext/u2/1053345.pdf

Lewis, D. (2019, February 4). "What Is NATO Really Doing in Cyberspace?" *War on the Rocks.* https://warontherocks.com/2019/02/what-is-nato-really-doing-in-cyberspace/

Mission of the Republic of Azerbaijan to NATO. (n.d.). "Science for Peace and Security." http://nato-pfp.mfa.gov.az/content/6

Monteiro, A. P. (2017, October 1). "Portugal at Forefront of Global Cyber Initiatives," *The Cyber Edge – Signal*, Armed Forces Communications and Electronics Association (AFCEA), Washington, DC. www.afcea.org/content/portugal-forefront-global-cyber-initiatives

NATO. (2011a, February 4). "NATO Secretary General Calls for "Smart Defence" at Munich Conference." nato.int/cps/en/natohq/news_70327.htm

NATO. (2011b, October 14). "'Smart Defence, Smart TADIC,'" Conference to address Trans-Atlantic Defence Technological and Industrial Cooperation (TADIC), Conference of Armaments Directors (CNAD). nato.int/nato_static/assets/pdf/pdf_topics/20120214_111014-smart_tadic_background.pdf

NATO. (2014a, October 20). "NATO Emerging Security Challenges Division Science for Peace and Security (SPS) Programme." www.nato.int/nato_static_fl2014/assets/pdf/pdf_2014_10/20141029_141020-8_Nunes.pdf

NATO. (2014b, November 18). "Largest Ever NATO Cyber Defence Exercise Gets Underway." www.nato.int/cps/en/natohq/news_114902.htm

NATO. (2016a, April 7). "NATO Communications and Information Agency (NCI Agency)." www.nato.int/cps/fr/natohq/topics_69332.htm?selectedLocale=en

NATO. (2016b, June). "Ukraine – Cyber Defence)." www.nato.int/nato_static_fl2014/assets/pdf/pdf_2016_07/20160712_1606-trust-fund-ukr-cyberdef.pdf

NATO. (2016c, July 8). "Cyber Defense Pledge." www.nato.int/cps/en/natohq/official_texts_133177.htm

NATO. (2016d, February 10). "NATO and the European Union Enhance Cyber Defence Cooperation." www.nato.int/cps/en/natohq/news_127836.htm

NATO. (2017a, July 19). "NATO Supports Jordan's National Cyber Defence Strategy." www.nato.int/cps/en/natohq/news_146287.htm

NATO. (2017b, November 29). "Second Progress Report on the Implementation of the Common Set of Proposals Endorsed by NATO and EU Councils on 6 December 2016." www.nato.int/nato_static_fl2014/assets/pdf/pdf_2017_11/171129-2nd-Joint-progress-report-EU-NATO-eng.pdf

NATO. (2018a, February 13). "NATO Launches Second Cyber Defence Project with Moldova." www.nato.int/cps/en/natohq/news_152364.htm?selectedLocale=en

NATO. (2018b, June 8). "Third Progress Report on the Implementation of the Common Set of Proposals Endorsed by EU and NATO Councils on 6 December 2016 and 5 December 2017." www.nato.int/nato_static_fl2014/assets/pdf/pdf_2018_06/20180608_180608-3rd-Joint-progress-report-EU-NATO-eng.pdf

NATO. (2019a, February). "NATO Cyber Defence." www.nato.int/nato_static_fl2014/assets/pdf/pdf_2019_02/20190208_1902-factsheet-cyber-defence-en.pdf

NATO. (2019b, June 17). "Fourth Progress Report on the Implementation of the Common Set of Proposals Endorsed by NATO and EU Councils on 6 December 2016 and 5 December 2017." www.nato.int/nato_static_fl2014/assets/pdf/pdf_2019_06/190617-4th-Joint-progress-report-EU-NATO-eng.pdf

NCI Agency. (n.d.a). "Cyber Security." www.ncia.nato.int/Our-Work/Pages/Cyber-Security.aspx

NCI Agency. (n.d.b). "Malware" Information Sharing Platform." www.ncia.nato.int/Documents/Agency%20publications/Malware%20Information%20Sharing%20Platform%20(MISP).pdf

NCI Agency. (n.d.c). "Multinational: MN CD2 – Cyber Defence Capability Development." www.ncia.nato.int/Documents/Agency%20publications/Multinational%20Cyber%20Defence%20(MN%20CD2).pdf

NIAS19. (2018). "NIAS19 – Digital Transformation." https://nias19.com/

NOAC. (2018, June 27). "Interview with Dr Deniz Beten, Senior SPS and Partnership Cooperation Advisor, NATO Emerging Security Challenges Division." http://natoassociation.ca/interview-with-dr-deniz-beten-senior-sps-and-partnership-cooperation-advisor-nato-emerging-security-challenges-division/

Ottis, R. (2018, October). *Analysis of the 2007 Cyber Attacks against Estonia from the Information Warfare Perspective*. Tallinn, Estonia: Cooperative Cyber Defence Centre of Excellence. https://ccdcoe.org/uploads/2018/10/Ottis2008_AnalysisOf2007FromTheInformationWarfarePerspective.pdf

Republic of Estonia, Defence Forces. (2020, February 12). "NATO Cooperative Cyber Defence Centre of Excellence." https://mil.ee/en/landforces/ccdcoe/

Rivas, J. A. Jr. (2017). "Cyber Defence Management Authority (CDMA)," in P. J. Springer (ed.), *Encyclopedia of Cyber Warfare* (pp. 46–47). Santa Barbara: ABC-CLIO.

Ringsmore, J. & Rynning, S. (eds.). (2011). "NATO's New Strategic Concept: A Comprehensive Assessment," Danish Institute for International Studies (DIIS) Report 2011: 02. www.econstor.eu/bitstream/10419/59845/1/656748095.pdf

Ryan, C. (2018, July 5). "What Jordan Means for NATO (And Vice Versa)," Istituto per gli studi di politica internazionale. www.ispionline.it/it/pubblicazione/what-jordan-means-nato-and-vice-versa-20934

Seffers, G. I. (2018, April 1). "The Cyber Ties That Bind," *The Cyber Edge – Signal*, Armed Forces Communications and Electronics Association (AFCEA), Washington, DC. www.afcea.org/content/cyber-ties-bind

Shea, J. (2013). "How Is NATO Dealing with Emerging Security Challenges?" *Georgetown Journal of International Affairs, 14*(2): 193–201.

Steyne, R. & Khudaverdyan, P. K. (2018). *Supporting Ukraine's Security Sector Reform: Mapping Security Sector Assistance Programmes*. Switzerland: The Geneva Centre for Democratic Control of Armed Forces (DCAF). www.dcaf.ch/sites/default/files/publications/documents/Ukraine_Mapping_2018_FINAL_web.pdf

Tsagourias, N. & Buchan, R. (2015). *Research Handbook on International Law and Cyberspace*. Cheltenham: Edward Elgar.

Von Voss, A., Major, C. & Mölling, C. (2013). *The State of Defence Cooperation in Europe*. Berlin, Germany: German Institute for International and Security Affairs. www.swp-berlin.org/fileadmin/contents/products/arbeitspapiere/WP_DefenceCooperationEurope_Voss_Major__Moelling_Dez_2013.pdf

PART II

Asia and Australia

21

JAPAN'S CHALLENGES, CAPABILITIES, AND PREPAREDNESS IN CYBERSPACE

Tobias Burgers, Scott N. Romaniuk, and Cherry H. Y. Wong

Introduction: statement of national cyber security strategy

Japan released its first significant document focused on cyber security in 2006, issued by its Information Security Policy Council (ISPC). Titled the "First National Strategy on Information Security,"[1] the document sought to establish a "Japan Model"[2] IT environment. It was followed by the second edition in 2009 and saw a subsequent number of strategy documents, discussing a range of topics concerning information security, in addition to human resource development, outreach, and awareness as well as research and development. In 2013, the term "information security" morphed to become "cyber security," and the first cyber security strategy was released. Two years later, in 2015, a second version was released, outlining the nation's cyber security strategy for the next three years. It was the first time the document was approved directly at the cabinet level, indicating how cyber security had grown in importance as a national security issue (Matsubara, 2015). The document differs from its predecessors in that it not only outlines risks, but also highlights the positive effect of the so-called cyber revolution. In 2018, the third edition of the document was released in which the tone of the second edition was carried forward, outlining the positive developments constantly emerging from cyberspace and information communication technologies (ICT) in general.

The optimistic tone can, to some extent, be explained by the government's desire to promote and revive the domestic ICT sector, and what appears to be the government's understanding that technology has the potential to positively address some of Japan's most pressing problems such as a declining population and aging society. Society 5.0., the government's flagship program formulated to address a multitude of Japan's problems via new technologies such as big data, deep learning, and artificial intelligence (AI), is not only foreseen as having a supposed positive impact on social issues of Japanese society, but also clearly has an economic angle. The government sees Society 5.0 as a vehicle to revive its economy and improve its (global) competitiveness. However, as Hathaway, Demchak, Kerben, McArdle and Spidalieri (2016) note, Japan is currently struggling economically with its domestic ICT sector – its importance in the total economy has declined and now accounts for only 9 per cent of GDP. Furthermore, its exports have been decreasing too. Keeping a positive tone in the nation's primary security document should be regarded as an incentive to revive this industry and serve as a key instrument in the country's overall readiness to defend against current and future cyberthreat.

A document that principally lists the risks of the cyber world and paints a bleak picture for the digital future of Japan would have a dampening effect on the possibilities of the digital world as a means to function as an economic revival monitor. That said, the strategy document does not ignore the risks that Japan faces in the cyber domain. As such, one dimension stands out among all others. The document acknowledges that, "the emergence of new products and services change peoples' awareness by changing their daily behavior and living environment, and this triggers the transformation of social systems and industrial infrastructures that include existing procedures, models, organizations, etc." (National Center of Incident Readiness and Strategy for Cybersecurity, 2018b: 1). It further addresses the potential risks to Japan's socio-economic stability. Among others, the socio-economic impacts discussed include data theft and attacks against critical infrastructure.

Preparing for the challenges of the cyber domain

Japan's Cabinet Office indicates that cyber threats pose a serious challenge for society, rather than a narrower technical threat isolated within the cyber domain. Indeed, one-third of the strategy is devoted to a pillar labeled, "Building a Safe and Secure Society for the People." This pillar outlines strategies undertaken by the government to develop a framework that would allow for active defense and combating cyberattacks across the board: from attacks with significant destructive impact, against such things as critical infrastructure, to smaller, disruptive attacks that would affect the security and well-being of the Japanese people.

The Tokyo 2020 Olympics and Paralympics,[3] in particular, are drivers of Japan's cyber security (among others, as discussed at a later point in this chapter), with an entire paragraph devoted to cyber security measurements concerning these major events (National Center of Incident Readiness and Strategy for Cybersecurity, 2018b: 3, 31). Moving beyond the Games, the document has a strong focus on the role of the private sector in cyber security. As opposed to other Western nations, Japan's private sector is lagging behind in addressing cyber security risks (IPA, 2017). A new strategy evidently seeks to improve corporate responsibility through several incentives, among them tax breaks and a so-called "best practices" that the private sector can follow in order to address the cyber security deficit in the private sector (Matsubara, 2018b).

The document presents a clear aim towards the private sector. This is noticeable in some of the other critical points of the document that focus either on the private sector, encouraging economic development in the cyber realm, or make a case for closer collaboration between the government and the private sector. Among these are a focus on the Internet of Things (IoT) systems, their added value to the economy, and possibly security risks. Furthermore, the concept of cyber security as a "Value Creating Driver" – changing the perception of cyber security from cost-based to investment-based to benefit the company and overall state of the national economy – in addition to addressing the many risks within supply chain management among small and medium enterprises (SMEs). Finally, the document illustrates Japan's position within the international global cyber debate. We discuss this in further detail later in the chapter.

The cyber strategy document wavers between a more traditional strategy policy document – akin to the priory released strategies in which governmental efforts to secure cyberspace are outlined – and a political call to improve cyber security beyond the direct governmental realm while outlining, albeit to a rather limited degree, the international efforts by the Japanese government to establish cyber defenses and security measures that are commensurate with the level of threats and challenges inherent in the contemporary cyber world.

Toward cyberspace – national security alignment

"The Basic Act on Cybersecurity (2014)" (サイバーセキュリティ基本法) defines "cyber security" as the necessary measures to be taken in order to manage information created by electronic or magnetic means within the telecommunications networks and information network in a safe, appropriate, and reliable manner (Ministry of Justice, 2014). The convergence of the cyber and physical space is highly recognized and underpins related policies emerging from the executive levels of government, though are oftentimes accompanied by a considerable measure of ambiguity. For example, inferences of appropriateness remain nothing more than inference and while the government clearly indicated that cyber security measures are to be formulated and implemented in a manner that serves the peoples' interests and rights, there have been a number of cases that suggest that: (a) the government of Japan lacks the requisite competencies to fulfil its own cyber security policies, and (b) its laws and regulations allow for maneuverability in non-transparent zones and grant agencies the authority to step beyond legal limits. This second point should be qualified by saying that the perceived legal over-step generally remains a matter of perception in that areas of operability and actions taken collectively constitute a legal grey zone and issues ethical management, as we discuss in greater detail in subsequent sections of the chapter.

In the "National Security Strategy (2013)," "cyberspace" is one of the main foci and recognized as the "global-domain of information network" and the increasing threats from cyberattacks at different levels are vital to secure national security (Cabinet Secretariat, 2013). To maximize the benefits streaming out of cyberspace and to recognize significant risks toward national security, Japan's cyber security strategy prioritizes "ensuring a free, fair and secure cyberspace for peace and stability of the international community and national security" (National Center of Incident Readiness and Strategy for Cybersecurity, 2015b). The balance between the free flow of information, application of rule of law, openness and autonomy of the system, and multi-stakeholder involvement creates a robust cyber security architecture in the Japanese strategy plan, and gradually a key to stabilizing the global market and innovation. A particular point of tension here rests in the relationship between the government's ability to ensure cyber security for private business, for example, and the role of private businesses as such to ensure that they are implementing necessary measures to prevent unauthorized access to sensitive data, especially as it may relate to government data and information such as defense materials, and so on.

International law

Japan adopts the policy of "Proactive Contribution to Peace" (平和への積極的な貢献 or "active contribution to peace") in recognition of a strategic approach based on international collaboration to facilitate national and international stability (Hornung, 2015; NISC, 2015b: 35). In particular, the free flow of information on a global scale is recognized and prioritized as the key to developing an internationally stable cyber environment. Japan has been taking a proactive role in developing the international rule of law in cyberspace. It is comprised of members of various working groups and committee members of international legal bodies related to rules and norm-settings in cyberspace: Group of Governmental Experts (GGE) at the First Committee of the UN General Assembly and Organization for Economic Co-operation and Development (OECD).

International governance

Given Japan's active role in the international arena in the areas of development, security, and international affairs, it should come as no surprise that within the debates on international cyber governance, Japan seeks, at least on a discursive level, to play an active and important role. The desire to fulfill such a role in this field is manifested in the recent cyber security strategy that was released in 2018. One of the three pillars refer to the Japanese government's position on international cyber governance. As part of Japan's emerging security legislation, its "Contribution to the Peace and Stability of the International Community and Japan's National Security," indicates the importance that the international debate holds for Japan's cyber security vision (see, Hosoya, 2016; MFA, 2017). Much of this vision centers on efforts to promote a free, fair, and secure cyberspace as well as promoting the rule of law in cyberspace. Given Japan's position as a liberally oriented international actor focused on multilateralism, these declarations harmonize with Japan's overall international profile. This has manifested itself in efforts to develop globally accepted norms and rules in cyberspace (MOFA, 2020). Accordingly, these efforts can be at least partially considered the second pillar of Japan's international cyber governance, which aims to develop confidence-building measurements. Establishing norms and rules, as well as internationally accepted red lines, are an essential part of confidence building efforts. The final "third leg" of its international cyber governance efforts focuses on capacity building cooperation.

Many of these efforts are promoted through bi- and multilateral dialogues, such as regional and global forums. Japan assumes a dual approach: participating in multilateral forums such as the Global Conference on Cyberspace (GCCS) – an annual Internet policy forum to discuss and establish internationally agreed rules and codes of conduct pertaining to cyberspace – and through existing forums that have thematic focuses on cyber issues, in particular, through the Asian Regional Forum (ARF).[4] Among these were the ARF Inter-Sessional Meeting on Security and the use of Information and Communication Technologies (ICTs), the ARF-ISM forum on ICTs Security, and the Association of East Asian Nations (ASEAN) Japan Cybercrime Dialogue. The regional focus of these forums indicates that Japan appears to be committed to establishing regional capacity building and establishing norms. In other words, it seeks to influence cyber governance primarily through efforts to develop cyber norms and rules in its immediate region – foremost with a focus on South East Asia.[5] Beyond multilateral forums, the Japanese government hosts a number of bilateral dialogues with nations beyond its direct orbit who are mostly its traditional conventional security allies. Among these are Australia, the European Union (EU), France, India, Israel, the United States (US), and the United Kingdom (UK).

Cyberspace and the question of Japanese sovereignty

In the nation's most recent cyber security strategy document or in the 2015 edition, one will not find a single mention of sovereignty. Only in the previous edition (2013 version) is sovereignty mentioned; yet, it only discussed how France has sought to exercise sovereignty over its cyberspace (Information Security Policy Council, 2013: 18). Beyond this single case, there is no mention of the notion of sovereignty in cyberspace or cyber-sovereignty in the key documents published by the Japanese government on the subject of cyber security. In a separate undated document by the Japanese Ministry of Foreign Affairs (MOFA) outlining their international cyber diplomacy, the concept of sovereignty within cyberspace is discussed. However, it is used here as an example of how nations might use the concept of sovereignty to prioritize internal *control* and limit the free flow of information. The concept is clearly used in a negative context and Japan, or at least MOFA, treats the concept as something that other, less-democratic or outright authoritarian or dictatorial states/regimes (e.g., China) would pursue to limit the development of open and free cyberspace. This mention, combined with the absence of a discussion on the notion of sovereignty in cyberspace, suggests two important points: (a) the minor relevance on this concept within the debate on cyber security in Japan (at least for the moment), and (b) as to the extent it is limitedly discussed – it is foremostly concerning how other nations (ab)use the concept to curtail Internet freedom.

As such, and unsurprisingly, one finds an absence of even moderate debate within Japan on the idea of an Internet "kill switch," or shutting down the Internet to any minor degree. Rather, Japan stands by and promotes the notion of an open and free Internet under any conditions and in any circumstances, in which information can flow freely. Through such a concept, the notion of sovereignty is contra to the ideals and vision of the Internet, as seen by the Japanese government and by extension, the Japanese people.

A cultural understanding of cyber security in Japan

Existing gaps in Japan persist between governmental efforts to ensure cyber security and those efforts in the private sector, which makes the private sector particularly vulnerable to cyber threats. This is a current issue, but also one that will increase in importance with the introduction of IoT systems and applications as part of the introduction of the aforementioned Society 5.0 when the degree of digitalization of Japanese society will increase. Much of the IoT revolution and Society 5.0 will be driven by private actors, with limited government oversight. As touched upon in the chapter's opening paragraphs, Japan's corporate sector sees cyber security as more of a corporate social responsibility as opposed to a security threat. This will be discussed in greater detail in the private sector section. However, there are some underlying cultural reasons for the deficit of qualified cyber experts in senior management positions across the country. Indeed, as Matsubara (2018b) notes in her discussion on the nation's most recent cyber security strategy, compared to other (Western) nations, Japan's private sector exhibits narrow understanding of cyber threats and concomitant cyber security matters. This is partially the result of the country's cultural focus and tendency to train CEOs and others in leadership positions for the sciences of economics, business, and law, rather than engineering or information and computer studies. This problem is further enhanced by the relationship between the government and the private sector. Rather than pursuing stronger and more responsible regulation via laws and regulations, the government pursues the collaboration of companies on a voluntary basis. Though chiming in harmony with the principles of liberal-democratic governance, to some extent, the offshoot of such an approach is a palpable cyber security deficit in the private sector being in part the result of the warm relationship between the government and the private sector: fostered by a culture in which consensus seems the norm and in which there exists longstanding warm and fuzzy relations between those who should propose and develop the law (the Parliament), those who execute the law (the Government), and those who find themselves on the receiving end of such laws (the business community).

Japan's turbulent history during the twentieth century, in particular, the pre-Second World War and Second World War periods of militaristic and imperialistic expansion, during which freedom of speech was suppressed and police surveillance and intimidation/coercion was prevalent, created a robust post-war desire among the Japanese for a near-complete departure from militaristic characteristics weaved into society, with emphasis on privacy and respect for human rights. This included a desire for the secrecy of communication, which was not the case during the prior era. As a result, in the constitution, the right to private communication was enshrined. This understanding has not changed over ensuing decades. Instead, it has been accepted within Japanese society on a broader scale and concretized. As such, even in the digital age, there exists an overt desire and demand by members of society, through non-governmental organizations (NGOs), to remind the government of the need to respect the secrecy of correspondence. This has resulted in a robust legal framework, that even as of today, protects digital communication within Japan.

Cyber security and Japanese institutions

The National Center of Incident Readiness and Strategy for Cybersecurity (NISC, 内閣サイバーセキュリティセンター) is the core coordination center responsible for the development and implementation of Japan's cyber security strategy. The Prime Minister had originally established the NISC a decade ago but the lack of legal authorization meant that it held little sway over other ministries and agencies. Thanks to the new law, NISC is responsible for developing national strategy and policy, ensuring the cyber security of ministries and agencies, and serving as a focal point for international cooperation. The law came into effect in 2014. With the emergence of Japan's Basic Act, Japan saw the prescription of the concept of cyber security and numerous roles and responsibilities of the government, local administrative bodies and agencies, and other relevant stakeholders defined. The Basic Act also designates the Cybersecurity Strategic Headquarters as the command and control body of national cyber security, and grants sharp authorities, such as making recommendations to national administrative organs, to the Cybersecurity Strategic Headquarters (see Figure 21.1). This mission document is to be formulated pursuant to the Basic Act that prescribes the government's responsibility to establish the Cybersecurity Strategy.

The role of the private sector

To improve cyber security capacities in Japan, several strategy papers highlight the critical responsibility and need by the private sector to improve its collective cyber security standing. In Japan, 90 per cent of information and communication assets belong to the private sector, illustrating the need for adequate cyber security operations and hygiene within this societal domain (Matsubara, 2018a). New business models and frameworks are suggested to adjust to and seize opportunities in this sophisticated business environment. It requires decision-makers or senior management executives to take appropriate account of risk management at all levels of business operations by utilizing advanced technologies. "Security by Design" (デザインによるセキュリティ) is one of the well-promoted approaches to consider cyber security measures at the point of product design stage, and establish a comprehensive and secure standard for IoT systems and implementations. However, the effectiveness of the development relies heavily on the literacy and mindset of business management, which as mentioned currently presents itself as a notable capacity deficit within the country. Thus, Japan is facing a cyber security talent gap problem caused by the low-income level and decreasing

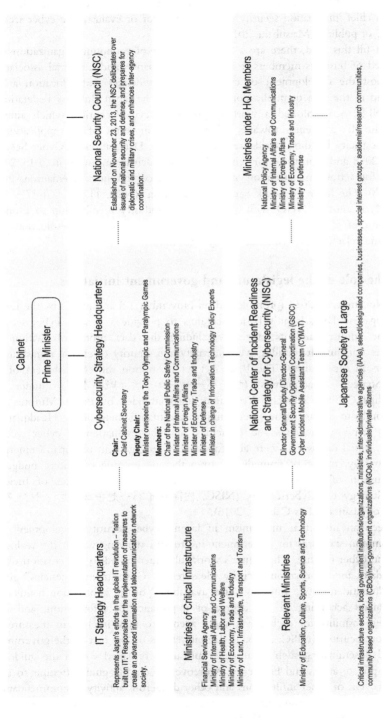

Cabinet

Prime Minister

National Security Council (NSC)

Established on November 23, 2013, the NSC deliberates over issues of national security and defense, and prepares for diplomatic and military crises, and enhances inter-agency coordination.

Ministries under HQ Members

National Policy Agency
Ministry of Internal Affairs and Communications
Ministry of Foreign Affairs
Ministry of Economy, Trade and Industry
Ministry of Defense

Cybersecurity Strategy Headquarters

Chair:
Chief Cabinet Secretary

Deputy Chair:
Minister overseeing the Tokyo Olympic and Paralympic Games

Members:
Chair of the National Public Safety Commission
Minister of Internal Affairs and Communications
Minister of Foreign Affairs
Minister of Economy, Trade and Industry
Minister of Defense
Minister in charge of Information Technology Policy Experts

National Center of Incident Readiness and Strategy for Cybersecurity (NISC)

Director General/Deputy Director-General
Government Security Operation Coordination (GSOC)
Cyber Incident Mobile Assistant Team (CYMAT)

Japanese Society at Large

IT Strategy Headquarters

Represents Japan's efforts in the global IT revolution – "nation built on IT." Responsible for the implementation of measures to create an advanced information and telecommunications network society.

Ministries of Critical Infrastructure

Financial Services Agency
Ministry of Internal Affairs and Communications
Ministry of Health, Labor and Welfare
Ministry of Economy, Trade and Industry
Ministry of Land, Infrastructure, Transport and Tourism

Relevant Ministries

Ministry of Education, Culture, Sports, Science and Technology

Critical infrastructure sectors, local government institutions/organizations, ministries, inter-administrative agencies (IAAs), select/designated companies, businesses, special interest groups, academic/research communities, community based organizations (CBOs)/non-government organizations (NGOs), individuals/private citizens

Figure 21.1 Japan's Cyber Security Policy Framework

Source: Illustration adapted from NISC with data from Kante (2000), Nitta (2014), Kawaguchi (2015), Yamauchi (2017), Fukushima and Samuels (2018), Liff (2018), NISC (2015a, 2018), Hashimoto (2019).

mobility as compared to other countries (Yatsu, 2019). It is also rare to have an in-house advocacy team within the Japanese business system – only 27 per cent of the Japanese companies hire a chief information security officer to monitor or evaluate the cyber security policies internally or publicly (Matsubara, 2018b).

To somewhat fill this void, there are a healthy number of economic organizations and NGOs, comprised of business members from leading companies and industrial associations in Japan, to boost the development of cyber security guidelines and education at the business level and in the area of public policy advocacy. The Japan Business Federation – "Keidanren"(経団連) – established a working group on cyber security, which aims to promote and raise the awareness towards cyber security in terms of the application of Society 5.0 and capacity building. Keidanren announced its Declaration of Cyber Security Management in 2018 and a proposal for reinforcing cyber security measures in 2015/2016/2017 with calls for action and attention among business communities (Keidanren, 2015, 2016, 2017, 2018). The Japan Network Security Association (JNSA, 日本ネットワークセキュリティ協会) is another NGO with a considerable industry membership to promote the standardization of a network system, a system of risk management evaluation, and education programs related to network security (JNAS, n.d.).

The role of the legislature and government initiatives

Introduced on November 6, 2014 (promulgated on November 12) and passed by the Lower House of the Japanese Diet, Japan's Basic Act aims to provide a general cyber security umbrella for the country and its citizens, including the data protection within the public and private domains. It presides over the safety and security of critical infrastructure business operators in the country. The Basic Act set in motion the establishment of the Cybersecurity Strategy Headquarters (サイバーセキュリティ戦略本部) (under the leadership of Chief Cabinet Secretary Yoshihide Suga) attended by Prime Minister Abe within a few months to discuss matters pertaining to the management of the Headquarters, serious incidents response measures and capacities, and the evaluation of cyber security policies in Japan. Initial discussions were also followed by engagement on Japan's emerging cyber security strategy, means of immediately strengthening existing capacities, budgetary issues, and discussion of cooperative efforts with Japan's National Center of Incident Readiness and Strategy for Cybersecurity (NISC, 内閣サイバーセキュリティセンター) (Prime Minister of Japan and His Cabinet, 2015).

NISC has been an important mechanism in Japan's cyber security development and works to set common standards for government institutions working within the realms of cyber security and cyber defense. The center's work subsequently led to the creation of the "Common Standards for Information Security Measures for Government Agencies" guide, which ensures, "'confidentiality', 'integrity', and 'availability' of the information handled by government agencies according to the degree of importance of information, and it is a fundamental responsibility for each government agency to duly implement measures to ensure information security" (NISC, 2016: 1). Despite efforts on the part of the government in preparing and disseminating such documents, measures contained within the guide are not imposed on private actors and businesses. Moreover, while the guide attempts to offer directions in the event of cyber infiltrations and other dangerous activity, recommendations for action are rooted in the assumption that individuals in positions to act possess the requisite knowledge and skill to do so effectively.

The Basic Act, as the name implies, is a foundational cyber security law that the government initially intended to expand upon. As the cyberthreat landscape within and surrounding Japan constantly evolves and morphs with emergent technologies and pernicious actors, the Basic Act allows for a variety of amendments and subsequent laws and regulations. The Act underwent further development following Cabinet's submission of a bill to amend the Act foremost for the purpose of preparing for the Tokyo 2020 Olympic and Paralympic Games. During one of the meetings, the political elites designed and subsequently introduced a five-stage index to be used to classify the impact of cyberattacks. These developments centered on enhanced cooperative capacities such as the sharing of cyber security information and data. Efforts to build on the existing Act can be interpreted as tightening maneuvers whereby a variety of actors and institutions in the cyber security realm are brought in closer quarters with one another and to see the creation of a Cyber Security Council, achieved on April 1, 2019. In addition to sundry other tasks, the Council's role includes representing "local administrative organs, principal infrastructure and cyber entities, educational or research institutions, experts and others" (Hirano & Shiraishi, 2019).

Deeper private–public cooperation and information sharing in the context of cyberthreats and possible attacks was also undertaken in preparation for the 2019 G20 Osaka summit, the Seventh Tokyo International Conference on African Development (TICAD 7), and the 2019 Rugby World Cup, hosted by venues across the country. Increased measures are constantly pursued to ensure greater protection of vital infrastructure, including the nation's energy grid and transportation hubs such as major airports, and key financial services. Thus, in light of previous mention of such key events as the Tokyo 2020 games, the Japanese government has used other major events as stimuli for the precipitous development of cyber security policy that casts a prism of security via proactivity.

The speed of development and attention that cyber security, both preemptive and responsive measures, has and continues to receive in Japan arguably speaks to the degree of a latent cyber security anxiety in the country, at least at the government level. One can assume that the general position of the state and its institutions is that cyberthreats are imminent and thus requiring state action to mitigate the impact, however possible. This idea is exemplified in the five-stage index of cyberattack severity. While major events have served as one of the primary impetuses for the creation and acceleration of cyber defensive warriors and postures in Japan, the Basic Law and subsequent laws, regulations, and institutions can and have been used to deploy a blanket of security across all aspects of the country. The assumption, however, that cyberattacks will take place is demonstrative of Japan's efforts needing to go further, and indeed it can be assumed that legislative efforts will continue to feed this trajectory.

Although Article 3 of the Basic Act emphasizes the government's responsibility to carry out its operations without infringing on the rights of citizens, under current legislation, Japan's cyber security activities indicate the potential for government agencies and institutions to operate beyond the public's understanding of responsible protection. Expansion of the nation's overall cyber security competencies and responsibilities has enabled institutions to conduct surveillance of citizens' communication and personal data under the guise of protecting national interests. Japan's National Institute of Information and Communications Technology (NCIT, 情報通信研究機構), for example, was granted legal permission to look at peoples' personal data on the justificatory basis that cyber security in the run-up to Tokyo 2020 needs to be augmented. NCIT hacking and surveillance of personal data is in effect a violation of the government's commitment to protecting the peoples' rights, as enshrined within the constitution, within the area of cyber security.

Although NCIT indicated that information will be securely stored and used only for the purpose of improving existing security measures, a mass hack of some 200 million users' private data put citizens' personal information as property at risk and their rights were violated in the name of national (cyber) security. Still, online concerns by security experts and members of the government are pushing to increase the pace of Japan's cyber security strides, particularly as cyber experts have routinely commented that Japan has fallen behind many other countries and non-state actors (NSAs), and therefore remains at risk of cyberattacks and cyberterrorism.

Cyberattacks, cybercrime, and cyberterrorism

An increase in cyber threats implicitly refers to threats from within and outside of Japan, and with the possibility of attacks being perpetrated by other states (e.g., being state-sanctioned) or by NSAs operating independently or in concert with agencies and organizations with ties to states. As such, Japan's increase in cyber security policies and measures can be considered a combination of two-interrelated verities: (a) tangible threats that pose a pragmatic threat to the Japanese nation, and (b) perceived or symbolic threats fueling measures as a result of both hypothetical scenarios and experiences of other states across the globe. Both have received significant attention by the Cabinet, ministries, and relevant agencies and institutions in Japan with the government publishing special action plans and procedures, including a public–private liaison and collaboration system, that are reviewed on a regular basis (NISC, 2000). In essence, every aspect of Japanese society is treated as a potential target and can be understood as being at risk at any given moment. This means that private citizens or individuals as well as companies in all sectors of the country, and even government institutions, are potential targets by cyber attackers.

Arguably no government is able to protect against every attack, as would-be assailants operate from the Internet depths and difficult-to-navigate and -trace virtual locales. NCIT observes cyberattacks on a daily basis and watches over some 300,000+ unused IP addresses. NCIT likewise monitors international cyber activity, noting that attacks on IoT devices (e.g., routers, antennas, microcontrollers, web cameras, sensors, etc.) have increased by a factor of 16 between 2013 and 2018, and nearly doubled between 2016 and 2018. Approximately half of all cyberattacks target IoT devices. These levels of attacks and their dramatic rise soberly attest to the vulnerability of private and public domains in Japan even in spite of promulgating of extensive cyber security documents and regulations.

In January 2020, Mitsubishi Electric, which works with institutions such as the Ministry of Defense, the Cabinet's office, the Nuclear Regulatory Commission, disclosed that it was subject to an attack in which as many as 8,000 personnel files were stolen (Naito, 2020). While the breach was significant, what stood out was that it took the company well over six months to make public that it had suffered a significant security breach in which personal information became subject to theft. In a series of attacks, Japan's information technology company, NEC Corporation, was targeted between 2016 and 2018, resulting in unauthorized access by cyber attackers to 27,445 files via unauthorized communications and file-sharing (Cimpanu, 2020). Stolen data included information related to work that NEC was doing with Japan's Defense Ministry. NEC reported a breach in January 2020, disclosing the extent of the attack only years after they were made. No explanation was given why the company decided to hide the fact it had been hacked for such a long time.

2019 was an active year for cybercriminals targeting Japan. On July 12, 2019, Japan's Remixpoint cryptocurrency exchange had ¥3.5 billion (US$32 million) in digital currencies stolen via "hot" wallets or Bitcoin wallets containing five currencies: Bitcoin, Bitcoin Cash, Litecoin, XRP, and Ether (Crypto World Journal, 2019; Paganini, 2019). Remixpoint was alerted by an error message related to the company's outgoing funds transfer system. Remixpoint temporarily suspend operations after learning of the incident. The perpetrator(s) of the act have never been identified and the methods of attacks remains unknown. Further incidents, such as the disastrous introduction of the 7/11 mobile payment app – 7py – as well as the Uniqlo hack on May 10, 2019, in which hackers stole at least 460,000 users' account information, are noteworthy (Du, 2019; Sim, 2019).[6] The Ursnif Malware cyberattack on Japanese banks took place on March 12, 2019. The Ursnif banking trojan, which also goes by the name Gozi ISFB, was first discovered in 2007. A popular malware, the Trojan steals data about Windows devices that have been infected (Bisson, 2019). The malware cyberattacks were supported by a distribution network of spam "robot networks" or botnets (malware- or virus-manipulated computers) and web servers that have been taken over in order to deliver the Trojan.

Other major companies holding sensitive information connected to the country's national defense agencies and critical infrastructure were attacked. In some cases, companies were unaware of attacks that had taken place until some time had passed (Nikkey Asian Review, 2020). The infamous WannaCry was effectively spread throughout domestic institutions in Japan in May 2017, causing system failures and other inconveniences and potentially dangerous situations. The attacks hit such areas as administrative agencies, private enterprises, and medical facilities like hospitals. JTB travel agency in Japan was the target of an attack on its servers on June 14, 2016 that resulted in a massive data leak of records for up to 7.93 million people who booked trips through the agency. As part of the attack, more than 4,300 valid passport numbers were disclosed. The source of the attack was a targeted email phishing campaign that exposed the company after a single employee opened the email attachment containing the stealthy PlugX trojan (The Japan Times, 2016; Jain, 2017). Tracing back to around 2012, PlugX is a multi-function remote access trojan (RAT). It can be easily overlooked as the trojan can be bundled with many legitimate applications and facilitates: keyboard capturing/ keystroke logging, screen captures, web operations, port listening/surveillance, disk information acquisition, and database theft.

Anonymous claimed responsibility for the January 13, 2016 cyberattack on Nissan (and a number of other major companies and organizations) that shut down two of the company's sites. The attack on Nissan was part of the group's "OpWhales" campaign, which staunchly opposed the killing of dolphins and whales (BBC, 2016; Reisinger, 2016). The attacks were allegedly to send a message to the Japanese government and punishment for supporting treatment of the marine life. Subsequent attacks in February 2016 targeted the websites of the Japan External Trade Organization (JETRO), Japan's National Tax Agency, and Japan Securities Finance Co., Ltd. (JSF).

Japan has seen a steady rise in both quantity and impact of distributed denial-of-service (DDoS) attacks over previous years. Attacks throughout 2015 targeted numerous government agencies, including the Japan Pension Service that saw some 1.25 million people's information compromised, (MOFA, 2019). A 2015 cyberattack on the Tokyo Olympic Games Organizing Committee website blocked access to the website by the Committee for 12 hours, raising concerns about further attacks and elevating a sinister specter for Japanese authorities given existing concern over the cyber security of the Tokyo 2020 games.

The prevalence of cyberattacks in Japan has raised sizable concerns about Japan's susceptibility to cyberterrorism and questions about the government's ability to adequately protect critical areas of the state. Japan sticks out among a surfeit of countries when it comes to cyberattacks and cyberterrorism. Building on the aforesaid attacks, the Japanese government and a wide range of public and private companies and organizations experienced nearly 12.8 billion cyberattacks in 2013. That number took off at jet speed over the following years with the total number of cyberattacks in Japan reaching over 128.1 billion in 2016. The pace of attacks represents a 999 per cent increase over a three-year period. Prior to this major surge in cyberattacks, in April 2009, Japan discovered that it was targeted through the well-known covert GhostNet attack, supposedly originating from mainland China. A massive cybermilitia-cyberterrorist network managed to penetrate Goo and Yahoo Internet portals with up to 100,000 accounts hacked and financial records accessed (Networkworld, 2013; Vaidya, 2015).

These attacks build a far more intricate portrait of Japan's susceptibility to cyberattacks than decades past, when on November 30, 1985, the 1,300-member-strong Japan Revolutionary Communist League (or Middle Core Faction, 中核派) attacked more than 30 major railway communications, signaling, and monitoring systems in outskirts of Tokyo and Osaka (Moosa, 1985). A second major event involved Chinese hacktivists who, in response to the Japanese government allowing a conference to be held by right wing Japanese historians who denied findings about the "Rape of Nanking," under the title, "The Verification of the Rape of Nanking: The Biggest Lie of the 20th Century," held on January 23, 2000. Although the conference attracted the indignation of some 100 Chinese and Japanese protestors outside the Osaka conference venue, Chinese nationals protested in their own way. The widespread cyberattacks targeted government emails, redirected visitors of government website to online pornography, and defaced sites with anti-Japanese hate and racist messages. The damage extended beyond this to encompass government statistical data being wiped and attempts to access numerous government agency sites, such as the Foreign Ministry, the Ministry of Finance, the Ministry of Agriculture, Forestry, and Fisheries, the Ministry of Defense, and Japan's Science and Technology Agency, among others (BBC, 2000; French, 2000). In the span of just seven minutes, around 1,600 attacks were made against the computer system of the Bank of Japan alone (Hughes, 2000, 2004: 84).

The two major incidents of 1985 and 2000 were a wake-up call for Japan in the area of cyber security, with the country learning through first-hand experience about the vulnerabilities of its institutions and IT environment. However, in spite of these cyber "9/11s," Japan has done more talk than walk despite the growing dangers embedded within ever-expanding cyber security climes. It is likely that such attacks will recur, even in spite of the proliferation of Japan's cyber security warriors and efforts to cover the island nation with a thick layer of discursive security. The most dramatic response to Japan's cyberthreats has been policy-oriented and instructive measures aimed at private citizens and companies to essentially do better when it comes to safeguarding sensitive data. While the government has made some progress since these two serious incidents, in addition to its skirt with a computer system that used software developed by the Japanese doomsday cult, Aum Shinrikyo, in 2000, cyber experts still level criticism against the Japanese government for taking an all-too-bureaucratic approach to combating serious threats rooted in areas that fall behind the competencies of the very institutions and agencies that are tasked with the peoples' protection.

Societal implications

In 2018, the Pew Research Center conducted a global survey on how societies viewed and ranked risks. Within Japanese public opinion, 81 per cent of respondents regarded cyberattacks as a significant threat to Japan's security (Poushter & Huang, 2019). They viewed cyberattacks and threats as a more urgent threat than climate change, the North Korean nuclear program as well as the rise of China (Poushter & Huang, 2019). Cyberthreats have only recently ranked among the top threats in Japan: Since a 71 per cent rate in 2016 its society has consistently ranked cyberthreats as the country's number one threat (Devlin, 2019; Poushter & Huang, 2019). These numbers illustrate that there is a keen awareness of cyberthreats, and as such, the assumption can be made that cyber security is a serious issue within broader Japanese society.

While the scope and seriousness of these incidents vary, they were widely reported by national news media sources. As such, the corporate sector's lukewarm efforts in taking cyber security seriously and the often clumsy post-cyber-breach response to attacks has created legitimate fears within Japanese society. At the same time, we contend that much of this fear is attached to the potential economic or financial impact of cybercrimes and cyberterrorism. Cyberterrorism remains a grey zone, with some attacks (and their potential effects) in Japan bearing characteristics of cyberterrorism, though this use of the Internet, notwithstanding the Middle Core Faction's attacks in 1985, has yet to transpire in Japan. Furthermore, cyber conflict, on a sophisticated state-to-state level, where opposing nations would have and deploy strategic cyber warfare capabilities, including the ability to destroy targets in the digital and physical domain, has yet to make an appearance. Nor does it seem likely that state actors, notably China and North Korea, would engage in such strategic cyber warfare behavior in the near future. As a probable worst-case scenario, Japan could become the victim of the incidental proliferation of cyberattacks, such as the virus that attacked Ukrainian targets, but then proliferated globally. However, most, if not all, nations in the world could be subject to such "incidental threats." Therefore, much of Japanese society's fear about cyberthreats could be focused on, adding to the economic and financial costs or fallout already mentioned, social issues, such loss of data, information, and related issues such as privacy. Concurrently, the absence of data on the kind of cyberattacks Japanese society views as the threats to the country, and what role and response measures the government would be expected to undertake, illustrate the need and necessity of further empirical research in this area.

Notes

1 The full strategy is available at: www.nisc.go.jp/eng/pdf/national_strategy_001_eng.pdf
2 The "Japan Model" IT environment refers to a "high quality, high reliability safety and security, or just simply to create 'a nation which should be revitalized by the value of trustworthiness'" (ISPC, 2006: 5).
3 This chapter was written prior to the outbreak of COVID-19 and its classification as a global pandemic. The chapter was subsequently revised in March 2020 to account for the International Olympic Committee's postponement of the 32nd Olympic Games ("Tokyo Games") and their rescheduling for 2021. See, www.olympic.org/news/joint-statement-from-the-international-olympic-committee-and-the-tokyo-2020-organising-committee.
4 The ARF is a regional forum promoted and organized by ASEAN in which other, mostly neighboring states who are not part of ASEAN also participate.
5 The focus on South East Asia as a regional focus can be geographically and politically explained. The remainder of its "close neighbors" have: (a) not always the best diplomatic relations with Japan, or (b) do not share Japan's stance towards a free, open, and secure Internet.

6 7pay was launched and had to be shut down within two days after it became apparent how easy it was to breach the security of users. Around 900 users' accounts were breached, with approximately 55 million JPY of losses. One of the factors contributing to the breach was the absence of a two-step factor authentication system: A common and widely accepted security tool that is found among most applications.

Suggested reading

National Center of Incident Readiness and Strategy for Cybersecurity. (2018, July 27). "Cybersecurity Strategy." www.nisc.go.jp/eng/pdf/cs-senryaku2018-en.pdf

Samuels, R. J. (2019). *Special Duty: A History of the Japanese Intelligence Community*. Ithaca: Cornell University Press.

Yanaga, M. (2017). *Cyber Law in Japan*. Alphen aan den Rijn: Kluwer Law International.

References

BBC. (2000, January 25). "Hackers Blast Japan Over Nanking Massacre." http://news.bbc.co.uk/2/hi/asia-pacific/618520.stm

BBC. (2016, January 13). "Anonymous Drives Nissan Offline in Dolphin Hunting Protest." www.bbc.com/news/technology-35306206

Bisson, D. (2019, March 13). "Threat Actor Targets Japanese Users with New Ursnif Variant," Security Intelligence. https://securityintelligence.com/news/threat-actor-targets-japanese-users-with-new-ursnif-variant/

Cabinet Secretariat. "National Security Strategy" (2013). www.cas.go.jp/jp/siryou/131217anzen hoshou/nss-e.pdf

Cimpanu, C. (2020, January 31). "Japanese Company NEC Confirms 2016 Security Breach." www.zdnet.com/article/japanese-company-nec-confirms-2016-security-breach/

Crypto World Journal. (2019, July 16). "Over US $32 Million in Cryptocurrencies Stolen from BITPoint." www.cryptoworldjournal.com/over-us-32-million-in-cryptocurrencies-stolen-from-bitpoint/

Du, L. (2019, May 14). "Uniqlo Says 460,000 Online Accounts Accessed in Japan Hack." www.bloomberg.com/news/articles/2019-05-14/uniqlo-owner-says-460-000-online-accounts-accessed-in-japan-hack

French, H. W. (2000, January 31). "Internet Raiders in Japan Denounce Rape of Nanking," *The New York Times*. www.nytimes.com/2000/01/31/world/internet-raiders-in-japan-denounce-rape-of-nanjing.html

Fukushima, M. & Samuels, R. J. (2018). "Japan's National Security Council: Filling the Whole of Government?," *International Affairs*, *94*(4): 773–790. https://dspace.mit.edu/bitstream/handle/1721.1/119205/Japan per cent27s per cent20National per cent20Security per cent20Council per cent20REVISED per cent20 per cent236 per cent20for per cent20Jen per cent20Greenleaf per cent20DSPACE.pdf?sequence=1&isAllowed=y

Hashimoto, Y. (2019, April). "Cyber Security Policy in Japan," The National Institute for Defense Studies, Tokyo. https://project.inria.fr/FranceJapanICST/files/2019/04/20190425-Cyber-Security-Policy-in-Japan.pdf

Hathaway, M., Demchak, C., Kerben, J., McArdle, J., & Spidalieri, F. (2016). *Japan Cyber Readiness at a Glance*. Potomac Institute for Policy Studies., Arlinton, TX. www.potomacinstitute.org/images/CRI/CRI_Japan_Profile_PIPS.pdf

Hirano, M. & Shiraishi, K. (2019, February). "Cybersecurity." https://gettingthedealthrough.com/area/72/jurisdiction/36/cybersecurity-japan/

Hornung, J. (2015, November 20). "Boosting Japan's 'Proactive Contributions to Peace'," *Nippon.com*. www.nippon.com/en/column/g00328/boosting-japan per centE2 per cent80 per cent99s-proactive-contributions-to-peace.html

Hosoya, Y. (2016). "Japan's New Security Legislation: What Does This Mean to East Asian Security?" *American Foreign Policy Interests*, *37*(5–6): 296–302.

Hughes, C. R. (2000). "Nationalism in Chinese Cyberspace," *Cambridge Review of International Affairs*, *13*(2): 195–209.

Hughes, C. R. (2004). "Controlling the Internet Architecture within Greater China," in F. Mengin (ed.), *Cyber China: Reshaping National Identities in the Age of Information* (pp. 71–90). New York: Palgrave Macmillan.

Information Security Policy Council. (2006). *The First National Strategy on Information Security - Toward the Creation of a Trustworthy Society*. Information Security Policy Council. www.nisc.go.jp/eng/pdf/natio nal_strategy_001_eng.pdf

Information Security Policy Council. (2013). *Cybersecurity Strategy – Toward a World-Leading, Resilient and Vigorous Cyberspace*. Information Security Policy Council. www.nisc.go.jp/eng/pdf/cybersecuritystrat egy-en.pdf

Information-Technology Promotion Agency. (2017). "企業の Ciso や Csirt に関する 実態調査 2017 －調査報告書－." www.ipa.go.jp/files/000058850.pdf

Jain, D. (2017, February 8). "JTB Breach Leaks 7.93 Million Customer Related Records," NSFocus. https://nsfocusglobal.com/jtb-breach-leaks-7-93-million-customer-related-records/

Japan Network Security Association. (n.d.). "What Is the JNSA?" www.jnsa.org/en/aboutus/index.html

Kantei.go.jp (2000, July 7). "Establishment of the IT Strategy Headquarters." https://japan.kantei.go.jp/it/council/establishment_it.html

Kawaguchi, H. (2015, January 21). "Cybersecurity Strategy in Japan," Japan Security Operation Center (JSOC). https://cs.kyushu-u.ac.jp/wp-content/uploads/17-kawaguchi.pdf

Keidanren. (2015, February 17). "Proposal for Reinforcing Cybersecurity Measures." www.keidanren. or.jp/en/policy/2015/017_proposal.pdf

Keidanren. (2016, January 19). "Second Proposal for Reinforcing Cybersecurity Measures." www.keidan ren.or.jp/en/policy/2016/006_proposal.pdf

Keidanren. (2017, December 12). "A Call for Reinforcement of Cybersecurity To Realize Society 5.0." www.keidanren.or.jp/en/policy/2017/103_summary.pdf

Keidanren. (2018, March). "Declaration of Cyber Security Management." www.keidanren.or.jp/en/policy/2018/018.pdf

Liff, A. P. (2018). "Japan's National Security Council: Policy Coordination and Political Power," *Japanese Studies*, 38(2): 253–279.

Matsubara, M. (2015, November 2). "Japan's New Cybersecurity Strategy: Security without Thwarting Economic Growth." www.cfr.org/blog/japans-new-cybersecurity-strategy-security-without-thwart ing-economic-growth

Matsubara, M. (2018a, June 26). "A Glimpse into Private Sector Cybersecurity in Japan," The Lawfare. https://assets.documentcloud.org/documents/4560424/A-Glimpse-Into-Private-Sector-Cybersecur ity-in.pdf

Matsubara, M. (2018b, June 4). "How Japan's New Cybersecurity Strategy Will Bring the Country Up to Par With the Rest of the World." www.cfr.org/blog/how-japans-new-cybersecurity-strategy-will-bring-country-par-rest-world

Ministry of Foreign Affairs. (2017). "Diplomatic Bluebook 2017 – Chapter 3: Japan's Foreign Policy to Promote National and Worldwide Interests." mofa.go.jp/policy/other/bluebook/2017/html/chap ter3/c030100.html

Ministry of Foreign Affairs. (2019). "Japan's Cyber Diplomacy." www.mofa.go.jp/files/000412327.pdf

Ministry of Foreign Affairs. (2020, February 7). "Japan's Security/Peace & Stability of the International Community-Cybersecurity." www.mofa.go.jp/policy/page18e_000015.html

Ministry of Justice. (2014). *The Basic Act on Cybersecurity, Tokyo*. Tokyo: Government of Japan. www.japaneselawtranslation.go.jp/law/detail/?id=2760&vm=04&re=02

Moosa, E. (1985, November 30). "Hundreds of Police Hunt for 300 Rail Saboteurs," *AP News*. https://apnews.com/eb2de145e6e22fb474d0500aa353cf28

Naito, T. (2020, January 20). "(独自) 三菱電機にサイバー攻撃　防衛などの情報流出か." www.asahi.com/articles/ASN1M6VDSN1MULFA009.html

Networkworld. (2013, April 4). "Japanese Web Portals Hacked, up to 100,000 Accounts Compromised." www.networkworld.com/article/2165028/japanese-web-portals-hacked–up-to-100-000-accounts-comprimsed.html

Nikkey Asian Review. (2020, January 31). "Japan Defense Data Feared Stolen in Cyberattacks on NEC." https://asia.nikkei.com/Business/Companies/Japan-defense-data-feared-stolen-in-cyberat tacks-on-NEC

NISC. (2000, December 15). "重要インフラのサイバーテロ," 対策に係る特別行動計画. www.nisc.go.jp/active/sisaku/2000_1215/pdf/txt3.pdf

NISC. (2015a). "サイバーセキュリティ戦略本部の運営について." www.nisc.go.jp/conference/cs/pdf/unei_kitei.pdf

NISC. (2015b). *Cybersecurity Strategy*. National Center of Incident Readiness and Strategy for Cybersecurity. www.nisc.go.jp/eng/pdf/cs-strategy-en.pdf

NISC. (2016, August 31). "Common Standards for Information Security Measures for Government Agencies (FY2016)." nisc.go.jp/eng/pdf/Common per cent20Standards(FY2016).pdf

NISC. (2018). *Cybersecurity Strategy*. National Center of Incident Readiness and Strategy for Cybersecurity. www.nisc.go.jp/eng/pdf/cs-senryaku2018-en.pdf

Nitta, Y. (2014, September). "Review of the Japan Cybersecurity Strategy," ISPSW Strategy Series: Focus on Defense and International Security, Issue No. 290. www.files.ethz.ch/isn/183668/290_Nitta.pdf

Paganini, P. (2019, July 12). "Hackers Stole $32 Million from Bitpoint Cryptocurrency Exchange," Securityaffairs.co. https://securityaffairs.co/wordpress/88293/data-breach/bitpoint-cryptocurrency-exchange-hacked.html

Poushter, J., & Huang, C. (2019). *Climate Change Still Seen as the Top Global Threat, but Cyberattacks a Rising Concern*. Pew Research Center. www.pewresearch.org/global/wp-content/uploads/sites/2/2019/02/Pew-Research-Center_Global-Threats-2018-Report_2019-02-10.pdf

Prime Minister of Japan and His Cabinet. (2015, February 10). "Cyber Security Strategy Headquarters." https://japan.kantei.go.jp/97_abe/actions/201502/10article4.html

Reisinger, D. (2016, January 14). "Anonymous Hacks Nissan Site to Support Whales," Fortune. https://fortune.com/2016/01/14/anonymous-nissan-whales-hack/

Sim, W. (2019, September 1). "Japanese Businesses, Consumers Vulnerable to Cyber Attacks." www.straitstimes.com/asia/east-asia/japanese-businesses-consumers-vulnerable-to-cyber-attacks

The Japan Times. (2016, June 15). "Japan Travel Agency Ordered to Probe Data Hack Affecting 7.93 Million People." www.japantimes.co.jp/news/2016/06/15/business/corporate-business/personal-info-7-93-million-people-may-leaked-japans-biggest-travel-agency/#.XlB5wZNKiqA

Vaidya, T. (2015). "2001–2013: Survey and Analysis of Major Cyberattacks," Georgetown University. https://security.cs.georgetown.edu/~tavish/cyberattacks_report.pdf

Yamauchi, T. (2017, April 24). "Cybersecurity Strategy in Japan," National Center of Incident Readiness and Strategy for Cybersecurity. https://project.inria.fr/FranceJapanICST/files/2017/05/TYamauchi_presentation_2017.pdf

Yatsu, M. (2019, August 27). "Why Japan Can't Fail Womenomics in Cybersecurity," *The Japan Times*. www.japantimes.co.jp/opinion/2019/08/27/commentary/japan-commentary/japan-cant-fail-womenomics-cybersecurity/#.XkOcwhMzZQI

22

AN EFFECTIVE SHIELD?

Analyzing South Korea's cybersecurity strategy

Yangmo Ku

Introduction

The Republic of Korea (ROK or South Korea) has earned fame as a "strong Internet nation," as the country contains cutting-edge digital technology, efficient computer networks, and the world's top high-speed Internet penetration rate. Behind these achievements, however, the nation has been vulnerable to cyber threats, particularly to those allegedly stemming from North Korea. Starting with multiple distributed denial-of-service (DDoS) attacks in July 2009, North Korea has frequently infiltrated and paralyzed South Korean government, finance, and critical infrastructure websites. These North Korean cyberattacks prompted South Korea to set safeguarding and securing cyber space as a priority for South Korean national security. To strengthen its cyber capabilities, South Korea has taken a series of measures, including developing firewalls, hiring cyber specialists, establishing a cyber warfare command, advancing educational organizations, and pushing forward legal frameworks advocating cyber protection.

With these facts in mind, this chapter addresses the following questions: What challenges has South Korea faced in the cybersecurity realm? How effective has the nation's cybersecurity strategy been? What measures are necessary for the strengthening of its cybersecurity strategy?

Answering these questions, the chapter highlights three primary cybersecurity challenges that South Korea confronts: the inherently vulnerable nature of cybersecurity, North Korean cyber threats, and the US–China cyber arms race. It then looks into the contents of South Korea's cybersecurity strategy ranging from the *National Cybersecurity Master Plan* forged in 2011 to the *National Cybersecurity Strategy and Basic Plan* adopted in 2019. The chapter then assesses South Korea's cybersecurity strategy in comparative perspective, emphasizing areas in need of further development in the nation's cybersecurity strategy, such as the strengthening of cybersecurity governance structure, the establishment of a comprehensive cybersecurity legal framework, more effective responses to North Korean cyberattacks.

South Korea's cybersecurity challenges

South Korea has faced three main challenges in its cybersecurity environment. First, like all nations, the ROK is not exempt from the inherently vulnerable nature of cybersecurity.

That is, it is almost implausible for a nation to completely protect its cyberspace, because state-sponsored and/or private hackers can penetrate any nation's cyber system by using well-developed cyber technology. Cyber hacking and espionage skills continue to develop in parallel with the unending advance of digital technology. As a result, according to Henry Nau (2019: 238), "it is estimated that 55,000 new pieces of malware are generated each day with some 200,000 computers becoming 'zombies' (computers controlled by outside actors) and millions of computers bundled into 'botnets' under the control of unauthorized personnel." There have been many other examples of such vulnerabilities all around the world, including North Korea's cyber strikes on Sony Pictures Entertainment in 2014 and Russia's hacks on the network of the US Democratic National Committee in 2015. In this regard, South Korean society, which is tightly connected through efficient computer networks, has been highly vulnerable to external cyberattacks and cyber espionage. For example, South Korea had more than 10,000 ransomware attacks over the three years from 2015–2017, thus suffering a financial loss of about one trillion Korean Won (Electronic News, 2018).

Second, in addition to nuclear and missile threats, North Korea has posed a serious cyber threat to South Korean government and private sectors. North Korea, which places a greater emphasis on cyber sovereignty, like China and Russia, than freedom in cyberspace as supported by western countries, has paid close attention to enhancing its regime's security by controlling information in the nation's limited cyberspace. Running counter to the increased sanctions imposed by the UN Security Council due to the nation's nuclear/missile provocations, North Korea has strived to develop its cyber capabilities in an attempt to conduct digital bank heists. North Korea's leader, Kim Jong-un, even regarded cyber capabilities as co-equal military importance with its nuclear and missile capabilities. Kim stated, "Cyberwarfare, along with nuclear weapons and missiles, is an all-purpose sword that guarantees our military's capability to strike relentlessly" (Sanger, Kirckpatrick & Perlroth, 2017).

Given these facts, North Korean hackers have frequently infiltrated and paralyzed South Korean government, finance, and critical infrastructure websites, although the North Korean government has vehemently denied any involvement (Hwang, 2017; Kong, Lim & Kim, 2019). Cyberattacks are very different from conventional attacks, particularly in two respects. First, precise attribution to specific actors is difficult in the case of cyberattacks. Second, it is very dangerous to respond to cyberattacks with a military response. For instance, if a country retaliates militarily based on erroneous forensics, such acts may unnecessarily and inadvertently spark a war (Chivvis & Dion-Schwarz, 2017). Using these unique features of cyberattacks, North Korea has performed a series of malicious cyber operations. North Korea's first recorded cyberattacks took place in July 2009. Pyongyang carried out multiple DDoS attacks on the websites of the ROK Presidential Office, the Ministry of National Defense, and the National Assembly. As a result, these websites were paralyzed by access requests generated by malicious software. In March 2011, North Korean hackers attacked South Korea's Nonghyup Bank, destroying 273 of the bank's 587 servers. They also executed the so-called "Dark Seoul Attack" in March 2013 that targeted South Korean public broadcasters KBS, MBC, and YTN, as well as financial institutions such as the Shinhan Bank, the Nonghyup Bank, and the Jeju Bank (Chanlett-Avery, Rosen, Rollins & Theohary, 2017). These attacks affected about 48,000 computers, and it took weeks for the systems to fully recover. Regarded as one of the most severe cyberattacks suffered by South Korea, North Korea's "Dark Seoul Attack" contributed to the international diffusion of the terms – Advanced Persistent Threat (APT) or cyber terrorism (Kim & Polito, 2019).

In addition to these DDoS attacks, North Korea has conducted numerous cyber espionage attacks and cyber thefts. For instance, in December 2014, North Korea targeted the Korea Hydro and Nuclear Power (KHNP), South Korea's nuclear power plant operator, resulting in "the leak of personal details of 10,000 KHNP workers, designs and manuals for at least two reactors, electricity flow charts and estimates of radiation exposure among local residents" (McCurry, 2014). This attack on KHNP increased concerns over North Korea's ability to cripple South Korea's infrastructure, thereby contributing to the diffusion of the "Cyber Pearl Harbor" narratives, which focuses on catastrophic physical impacts (Lawson & Middleton, 2019). A North Korean hacker group called Blunenoroff, a subgroup of Lazarus specializing in financial crime that began to operate in 2016, is believed to have performed financial gain attacks on South Korea's crypto-currency exchange institutions. Bitcoin exchange YouBit was attacked twice in April and December 2017 and went into bankruptcy after losing about US$20 million (BBC News, 2017). In June 2018, Conrail and Bithumb lost US$37 million and US$40 million respectively as a consequence of such North Korean cyberattacks (BBC News, 2018; Reuters, 2018).

Although it is difficult to clearly attribute all these attacks to North Korea, experts presume that North Korea was responsible for the cyber operations based on the composition of malicious codes used in those attacks and the way it worked (Hwang, 2017: 141). It is a well-known fact that many groups of North Korean hackers conduct such cyberattacks while residing in hotels in China, Southeast Asia, and East European nations (Reuters, 2017). North Korea has also committed numerous cybercrimes in the global community, including a series of cyberattacks on banks in Bangladesh and Southeast Asia in February 2016 and the 2017 ransomware attack called WannaCry. The former resulted in the theft of approximately US$81 million while about 300,000 computer users in at least 150 countries were reportedly affected by the latter ransomware (Chanlett-Avery, Rosen, Rollins & Theohary, 2017; Meyers, 2017; Potter, 2019; Sanger, Kirckpatrick & Perlroth, 2017; US Department of the Treasury, 2019).

Another challenge to South Korea is that the nation's cybersecurity environment resembles the geopolitical settings surrounding the Korean Peninsula. In the geopolitical environment, South Korea is sandwiched in between the two superpowers – the United States and China – whose strategic and economic rivalry began to intensify in the late 2000s. The deployment of the THAAD (Terminal High Altitude Area Denial) missile defense system in South Korea in 2015 demonstrates the agony of the relatively weak nation squeezed between the two great powers. In response to American persuasion and pressure, the South Korean government decided to deploy THAAD on its soil, but this decision brought sharp objections from China. Following the US' stated position, the ROK government argued that the THAAD system is mainly for protecting South Korea from North Korean missiles. However, China responded by claiming that THAAD's X-band radar could cover all of China, significantly weakening China's missile capabilities. The Chinese government then banned South Korean celebrities from holding performances in China and restricted Chinese tourists from visiting South Korea. Many South Korean products were also boycotted in Chinese markets, so that the South Korean economy, which is heavily dependent upon China, was seriously damaged (Ku, 2019: 125–132).

South Korea is affected by an intensifying cyber arms race between the United States and China. In response to China's increasing cyberattacks, the US has made every effort to strengthen its cyber capabilities by updating its cybersecurity strategy, restructuring cyber command, cultivating many cyber warriors, and promoting cybersecurity cooperation with anglophone intelligence allies, such as the UK, Canada, Australia, and New Zealand. After witnessing America's cutting-edge technology in the first and second Gulf Wars, China has also invested a huge amount of resources in advancing its cyber capabilities as part of its project to create a stronger military. To maximize its strategic and economic interests, the ROK needs to maintain its allied relationship with the US while simultaneously cultivating close cooperation with China. However, the intensification of US–China cyber power rivalry places South Korea in an ambivalent position. As mentioned above, many North Korean hackers reside in China to carry out cyberattacks. Given this fact, the US has pressured the Chinese government to resolve this issue, but China frames the issue of North Korean cyber threats as an excuse for the US to encircle China (Cha, 2019).

South Korea's cybersecurity strategy

Given these challenges, the South Korean government has sought to protect its national cyber space from cyberattacks. In August 2011, this effort culminated in the establishment of the *National Cyber Security Masterplan*, which was "a comprehensive response strategy at the national level in order to effectively deal with national cyber threats which are getting increasingly sophisticated and intelligent" (The National Cyber Security Council, 2011). The Masterplan had five major imperatives: (1) establishing a cyber threat early detection and response system comprised of private, public and military sectors working together; (2) strengthening the security of critical infrastructure and enhancing the protection of confidential information; (3) developing platforms to enable a stronger cybersecurity, such as the strengthening of legal frameworks dealing with cyber threats; (4) establishing deterrence against cyber provocation and strengthening international cooperation; and (5) elevating the security management of critical information and facilities, including the establishment of Information Protection Day (Wednesday of the second week of July) at the national level to raise public awareness.

In terms of the nation's cyber governance structure, the Masterplan included the establishment of differential but connected roles among relevant organizations. For instance, the National Intelligence Service (NIS) has overall control of cybersecurity in times of peace and crisis, while the Korea Communications Commission (KCC) supervises broadcasting and communications. The Ministry of Public Administration and Security (MOPAS) provides e-government services to the public. The National Computing and Information Agency (NCIA) that operates under MOPAS support cybersecurity activities of local governments. This Masterplan made important suggestions for South Korea's national cybersecurity, but it lacked implementation details. The rapid development of cyberspace and increased threats to cybersecurity demanded more proactive attention and action (The National Cyber Security Council, 2011).

To consolidate its cybersecurity strategy, the Moon Jae-in government's National Security Office unveiled the nation's first *National Cybersecurity Strategy* in April 2019. The South Korean government recognized the rapidly changing cyber environment and new challenges, including amplified vulnerability in cyberspace, the increasing severity of cyber threats, the intensified cybersecurity competition among states, and the enhanced harm to the public due to cybercrime. The *National Cybersecurity Strategy* set out South Korea's cybersecurity vision and goals and outlines the strategic tasks for individuals, companies, and the government. The Strategy's vision was to create a free and safe cyberspace to support national security, promote economic prosperity, and contribute to international peace. It presented three goals: (1) to strengthen the security and resilience of the nation's core infrastructure to enable continuous operation despite any cyber threats; (2) to enhance security capabilities to deter, detect, and block cyber threats quickly, and to respond to any incident promptly; and (3) to nurture a fair and autonomous ecosystem where cybersecurity technology, human resources, and industries are internationally competitive. The Strategy also had three basic principles: (1) to balance individual rights with cybersecurity; (2) to conduct security activities based on the rule of law; and (3) to build a participatory system with individuals, businesses, the government, and other nations (National Security Office, 2019).

In addition, the *National Cybersecurity Strategy* provided six strategic tasks: (1) to strengthen the security and resilience of the national core infrastructure against cyberattacks so as to ensure the continuous provision of critical services; (2) to expand the capacity to efficiently deter cyberattacks and respond to security incidents promptly; (3) to execute a future-oriented cybersecurity framework based on mutual trust and cooperation among individuals, businesses, and the government; (4) to create an innovative ecosystem for the cybersecurity industry in which to secure the competitiveness of technology, human resources, and industries that are critical to national cybersecurity; (5) to impress upon the public the importance of recognizing cybersecurity and persuade them to practice basic security rules, while the government concurrently respects citizens' fundamental rights when implementing policies and facilitates citizen participation; and (6) to become a leading country in cybersecurity by strengthening international partnerships and guiding the formation of international rules (National Security Office, 2019).

To implement this Strategy, in September 2019, South Korea's nine government ministries, including the Ministry of Science and ICT, the National Intelligence Service, and the Ministry of National Defense, crafted the *National Cybersecurity Basic Plan* with input from private companies and experts. By 2022, each government agency is supposed to establish its own guidelines to carry out the Strategy and the Basic Plan. The Basic Plan shares the same vision, goals, and strategic tasks as presented in the Strategy, but the Plan provided 100 detailed tasks, as shown in Table 22.1. The Basic Plan particularly highlights the importance of better coping with the emergence of the 5G hyper-connected world (Yonhap News, 2019).

Comparative assessment of South Korea's cybersecurity strategy

South Korea's *National Cybersecurity Strategy* and *Basic Plan* came out about ten years after the equivalent American strategy and five years later than Japan's version (Sohn, 2019). Despite this delayed publication, however, the establishment of the Strategy and Basic Plan was highly important as they were the first national-level comprehensive cybersecurity strategy produced by the nation's top leadership (Hong, 2019). The Strategy itself somewhat lacked details in implementation, but the subsequently published Basic Plan provided many concrete measures to enhance cybersecurity in South Korea. Despite this significance, however, the Strategy and Basic Plan have following weaknesses.

First, the two documents lack concrete, practical instructions for how to use the Blue House (Presidential Office) National Security Office as a control tower in the cases of a cybersecurity emergency. The South Korean government responds to cyber threats by categorizing them as private, public, and defense. The National Intelligence Service addresses cyber threats to governmental and public sectors, while the Ministry of Science and ICT and the Ministry of National Defense take charge of cyber threats to the private and defense sectors, respectively. However, this current system cannot be effective, because cyberattacks that occur in one sector can be easily transferred to other sectors. As a control tower in cyber

Table 22.1 South Korea's *National Cybersecurity Basic Plan*

Strategic Tasks	Primary Tasks	Detailed Tasks #
Increase the Safety of National Core Infrastructure	• Strengthen security of national information and communication networks • Improve cybersecurity environment for critical infrastructure • Develop next-generation cybersecurity infrastructure	24
Enhance Cyberattack Response Capabilities	• Ensure cyberattack deterrence • Strengthen readiness against massive cyberattacks • Devise comprehensive and active countermeasures for cyberattacks • Enhance cybercrime response capabilities	28
Establish Governance Based on Trust and Cooperation	• Facilitate the public–private–military cooperation system • Build and facilitate a nation-wide information sharing system • Strengthen the legal basis for cybersecurity	16
Build Foundations for Cybersecurity Industry Growth	• Expand cybersecurity investment • Strengthen the competitiveness of the cybersecurity workforce and technology • Foster a growth environment for cybersecurity companies • Establish a principle of fair competition in the cybersecurity marketplace	14
Foster a Cybersecurity Culture	• Raise cybersecurity awareness and strengthen cybersecurity practice • Balance fundamental rights with cybersecurity	9
Lead International Cooperation in Cybersecurity	• Enrich bilateral and multilateral cooperation systems • Secure leadership in international cooperation	9
Total	18	100

Source: The South Korean Government, 2019

emergencies, the National Security Office, which has significantly limited personnel and budget, would have difficulty establishing and implementing policy measures beyond coordinating various government agencies. Accordingly, it would be necessary for the ROK government to establish a separate organization, such as the National Cybersecurity Center under the chief of the National Security Office, which has adequate budget and personnel. The establishment of a National Cybersecurity Committee, in which private, public, and military personnel jointly monitor and respond cyber threats, would also yield considerable benefits (Boan News, 2019).

Second, there is little legal foundation for the South Korean government to consistently pursue the newly established *National Cybersecurity Strategy* and *Basic Plan*, regardless of the alternations of a ruling government. Japan enacted the Cybersecurity Basic Act in November 2014, which stipulated basic principles of its cybersecurity strategy and the responsibilities of central and local governments and other public agencies. This Act thus played a key role in laying out the groundwork for its cybersecurity strategy. A core part of the Act was the establishment of the National Center of Incident Readiness and Strategy for Cybersecurity (NISC) that works as a cybersecurity control tower. In December 2015, the US passed the Cybersecurity Act that directed private sectors to share their massive amount of personal information with US federal agencies when needed for cybersecurity. This Act resolved concerns over privacy rights raised by the sharing of cyber threat information (Kim, 2017). Therefore, it will be essential for South Korea to enact a comprehensive cybersecurity law for the successful implementation of the *National Cybersecurity Strategy* and *Basic Plan*.

Third, the Strategy and Basic Plan do not indicate the evident fact that North Korea has posed the primary cyber threat to South Korean society. The current Moon Jae-in government seems cautious in not wanting to irritate North Korea unnecessarily with cybersecurity issues, as the Moon administration desires to peacefully resolve the North Korean nuclear/missile challenge and improve inter-Korean relations. Considering the complicated, volatile security circumstances on the Korean Peninsula, this approach might be reasonable. Such a passive strategy, however, could inadvertently provide North Korea with the freedom to maintain its cyberattacks on South Korean society. To maximize the power of cyber deterrence, it will be necessary for the ROK government to clearly indicate the names of states and state-sponsored hacker groups that commit malicious cyberattacks on South Korean society in its official cybersecurity strategy (Park, 2019).

Also needed will be to set forth clear consequences for cyberattacks. The perils of redlines are a well-known fact: "too specific, and the adversary will press right up against the line; too vague, and the opponent will be left unsure about what conduct will trigger a response," as noted by Flournoy and Sulmeyer (2018). Nevertheless, it will be important for the South Korean government to give North Korea a clear warning about the costs of cyberattacks. The following American examples might provide reference points for the South Korean government. In the 2018 National Cyber Strategy, the Donald Trump administration distinctly pointed out that "Russia, China, Iran, and North Korea all use cyberspace as a means to challenge the United States, its allies, and partners, often with a recklessness they would never consider in other domains." The US National Cyber Strategy also aims to "preserve peace and security by strengthening the United States' ability – in concert with allies and partners – to deter and if necessary punish those who use cyber tools for malicious purposes" (The White House, 2018).

Concluding remarks with policy implications

South Korea faces significant challenges in the cyber domain, as the nation struggles with geopolitical complexities deriving from North Korea's nuclear/missile threats and the great power rivalry between the US and China. As noted already, North Korea has posed a serious cyber threat to South Korean society due to the inherently vulnerable nature of cybersecurity. On top of such North Korean cyber threats, South Korea is also sandwiched in between a cyber arms race by the US and China. Cyberspace has become an integral part of South Korea's financial, social, government, and political life. Thus, it is extremely important for the South Korean government to enhance its cybersecurity capabilities, just as geostrategic and economic capabilities are essential to its historical sense of national security.

As seen in the above analysis, South Korea places great emphasis on freedom, openness, and security in the cyber domain, similar to the US, Japan, and other western nations, rather than stressing cyber sovereignty. To enhance those values in cyberspace and better protect both governmental and private sectors from cyberattacks, South Korea first needs to establish a special agency that can effectively work as a cybersecurity control tower. As noted already, such an institution must have adequate personnel, a proportional budget, and strong authority to mastermind the nation's cybersecurity strategy. It should also have the role of coordinating other government and private agencies. It is also indispensable for the South Korean government to establish a solid legal framework to undergird the recently established cybersecurity strategy. Furthermore, the ROK should strive to elevate its deterrence against North Korea's cyber threats by incorporating North Korea's malicious cyber activities into the nation's cybersecurity strategy and sending North Korea clear warning signals about the consequences of its relentless cyberattacks. On top of these measures, since it is implausible for a nation to establish an effective cybersecurity shield on its own, the ROK government should make every effort to promote international cooperation with other like-minded nations, such as the Five Eyes plus three (the US, Canada, the UK, Australia, and New Zealand as well as Japan, Germany, and France).

Suggested reading

Butcher, L. (n.d.). "Defending Against Cyber Attacks in South Korea," Korea Economic Institute, Seoul, South Korea. http://keia.org/defending-against-cyber-attacks-south-korea
ENISA. (2013, December 30). "National Cyber Security Strategy of South Korea." www.enisa.europa.eu/topics/national-cyber-security-strategies/ncss-map/national-cyber-security-strategies-interactive-map/strategies/national-cyber-security-strategy-of-south-korea
Ikeda, S. (2019, January 27). "Lessons for Organizations from the South Korea Defense Agency Cyber Attack," *CPO Magazine*. www.cpomagazine.com/cyber-security/lessons-for-organizations-from-the-south-korea-defense-agency-cyber-attack/
Kang, T. J. (2019, March 8). "South Korea Cybersecurity," *The Diplomat*. https://thediplomat.com/tag/south-korea-cybersecurity/
National Security Office. (n.d.). "National Cyber Security Strategy." www.krcert.or.kr/filedownload.do?attach_file_seq=2162&attach_file_id=EpF2162.pdf

References

BBC News. (2017, December 19). "Bitcoin Exchange YouBit Shuts after Second Hack Attack." www.bbc.com/news/technology-42409815
BBC News. (2018, June 20). "Bithumb: Hackers Rob Crypto-exchange of $32m." www.bbc.com/news/technology-44547250
Boan News. (2019, October 24). "Intensification of Cyber Threats: Urgency of the Establishment of National Cybersecurity Control Tower." [in Korean] https://m.boannews.com/html/detail.html?idx=84004
Cha, J. (2019). "US-China Cyber Military Power Rivalry and the Rise of North Korean Threat: Implications for South Korean Cybersecurity," in S. Kim (ed.), *National Cybersecurity Strategy 2.0* (pp. 218–264). Seoul: Sahoepyungron Academy, Seoul. [in Korean].
Chanlett-Avery, E., Rosen, L. W., Rollins, J. W. & Theohary, C. A. (2017, August 3). "North Korean Cyber Capabilities: In Brief," Congressional Research Service, 7-5700. https://fas.org/sgp/crs/row/R44912.pdf
Chivvis, C. S. & Dion-Schwarz, C. (2017, March 30). "Why It's so Hard to Stop a Cyberattack—and Even Harder to Fight Back," RAND Commentary. www.rand.org/blog/2017/03/why-its-so-hard-to-stop-a-cyberattack-and-even-harder.html
Electronic News. (2018, February 6). "Ransomware Attacks Exceeded 10,000 Cases over the Last Three Years." http://m.etnews.com/20180206000358

Flournoy, M. & Sulmeyer, M. (2018, September/October). "Battlefield Internet: A Plan for Securing Cyberspace," *Foreign Affairs*. www.foreignaffairs.com/articles/world/2018-08-14/battlefield-internet

Hong, S. (2019, September 9). "What Should Be the Control Tower of National Cybersecurity? National Security Office or National Intelligence Service," *Popcorn News*. [in Korean] http://m.popcornnews.net/22550

Hwang, J. (2017). "North Korea's Cyber Security Strategy and the Korean Peninsula," *East West Studies*, *29*(1): 139–159. [in Korean].

Kim, C. W. & Polito, C. (2019). "The Evolution of North Korean Cyber Threats," Issue brief, The Asan Institute for Policy Studies, Seoul, South Korea.

Kim, S. (2017). "Cybersecurity Strategies of Major Powers in World Politics: From the Comparative Perspective of National Strategies," *International and Regional Studies*, *26*(3): 67–108. [in Korean].

Kong, J. Y., Lim, J. I. & Kim, K. G. (2019). "The All-Purpose Sword: North Korea's Cyber Operations and Strategies," 11th International Conference on Cyber Conflict: Silent Battle. https://ccdcoe.org/uploads/2019/06/Art_08_The-All-Purpose-Sword.pdf

Ku, Y. (2019). "Privatized Foreign Policy? Explaining the Park Geun-hye Administration's Decision-Making Process," *Korea Journal*, *59*(1): 106–134.

Lawson, S. & Middleton, M. K. (2019, March 4). "Cyber Pearl Harbor: Analogy, Fear, and the Framing of Cyber Security Threats in the United States, 1991–2016," *First Monday*, *24*(3). https://firstmonday.org/ojs/index.php/fm/article/view/9623/7736

McCurry, J. (2014, December 23). "South Korean Nuclear Operator Hacked amid Cyber-attack Fears," *The Guardian*. www.theguardian.com/world/2014/dec/22/south-korea-nuclear-power-cyber-attack-hack

Meyers, A. (2017, November 13). "North Korean Cyber Operations: Weapons of Mass Disruption," 38 North. www.38north.org/2017/11/ameyers111317/

National Security Office. (2019, April). "National Cybersecurity Strategy," https://www.itu.int/en/ITU-D/Cybersecurity/Documents/National_Strategies_Repository/National%20Cybersecurity%20Strategy_South%20Korea.pdf

Nau, H. (2019). *Perspectives on International Relations: Power, Institutions, and Ideas*. Washington, DC: CQ Press.

Park, C. (2019, April 21). "Superficial National Cybersecurity Strategy," *Digital Times*. [in Korean] www.dt.co.kr/contents.html?article_no=2019042202102369061001

Potter, R. (2019, August 5). "Toward a Better Understanding of North Korea's Cyber Operations," *38 North*. www.38north.org/2019/08/rpotter080519/

Reuters. (2017, May 20). "Exclusive: North Korea's Unit 180, the Cyber Warfare Cell that Worries the West." www.reuters.com/article/us-cyber-northkorea-exclusive/exclusive-north-koreas-unit-180-the-cyber-warfare-cell-that-worries-the-west-idUSKCN18H020

Reuters. (2018, June 10). "Bitcoin Tumbles as Hackers Hit South Korean Exchange Conrail." www.reuters.com/article/us-markets-bitcoin-korea/bitcoin-tumbles-as-hackers-hit-south-korean-exchange-coinrail-idUSKBN1J703I

Sanger, D. E., Kirckpatrick, D. D. & Perlroth, N. (2017, October 15). "The World once Laughed at North Korean Cyberpower. No More," *The New York Times*. www.nytimes.com/2017/10/15/world/asia/north-korea-hacking-cyber-sony.html

Sohn, Y. (2019, April 18). "The Blue House Security Office Published a Report 10 Years Later than the U.S. And 5 Years Later than Japan," *Joongang Ilbo*. [in Korean] https://news.joins.com/article/23444687

The National Cyber Security Council. (2011, August 2). "National Cyber Security Masterplan." www.sicurezzacibernetica.it/db/%5BSouth%20Korea%5D%20National%20Cyber%20Security%20Strategy%20-%202011%20-%20EN.pdf

The South Korean Government. (2019, September). "National Cybersecurity Basic Plan." [in Korean] msit.go.kr/cms/www/m_con/news/report/__icsFiles/afieldfile/2019/09/03/(%EC%B0%B8%EA%B3%A0)%20%EA%B5%AD%EA%B0%80%20%EC%82%AC%EC%9D%B4%EB%B2%84%EC%95%88%EB%B3%B4%20%EA%B8%B0%EB%B3%B8%EA%B3%84%ED%9A%8D.pdf

U.S. Department of the Treasury. (2019, September 13). "Treasury Sanctions North Korean State-Sponsored Malicious Cyber Groups." https://home.treasury.gov/index.php/news/press-releases/sm774

The White House. (2018, September). "National Cyber Strategy of the United States of America." www.whitehouse.gov/wp-content/uploads/2018/09/National-Cyber-Strategy.pdf

Yonhap News. (2019, September 3). "Seoul to Implement Comprehensive Cyber Security Strategy by 2022." https://en.yna.co.kr/view/AEN20190903002800320

23

IN THE LINE OF FIRE

Taiwan's legal, political, and technological cybersecurity posture

Tobias Burgers, Moritz Hellmann, and Scott N. Romaniuk

Taiwan's national cybersecurity strategy

Taiwan's national cybersecurity strategy is developed by the National Information and Communication Security Taskforce (NICST). This agency, part of the executive branch of the Taiwanese government – the Executive Yuan – formulated the first national cybersecurity strategy in 2009: The National Strategy for Cybersecurity Development Program (NCSP). In 2013 it was followed with a second edition of the nation's cyber strategy. Currently, the third version is in place, which will last until 2020. This document outlines in detail efforts to secure Taiwan cyberspace and targets and describes timelines, budget commitments, and implementation plans to enhance the security of Taiwan's cyberspace.

The current document starts with outlining the most pressing cyber issues and threats, globally, and for Taiwan (see National Information and Communication Security Taskforce, NICST, 2017). Among the threats it lists are data fraud, identity theft, large-scale cyber-attacks, and the breakdown of critical infrastructure via cyber means. In particular, the NCSP points to the latter issue as a significant problem that needs to be addressed urgently. The document notes that over 90 per cent of Industrial Control System (ICS) hosts – systems steering the machines that operate critical infrastructure – have vulnerabilities that can be exploited remotely, leaving them open to attack and subject tampering or destruction. This raises crucial cybersecurity issues in the eight critical infrastructure domains, essential for the well-functioning of Taiwan's society and the economy. These are defined in the report as government, energy, water, hi-tech industrial parks, information and telecommunication, transportation, banking and finance, emergency services, and public healthcare.

Furthermore, it argues that with the rise of the Internet of Things (IoT), Taiwan should seek to use the next generation of cyber technology to develop its economy further. At the same time, however, with the growing dependence on these new technologies, it requires government and private actors to enhance their cybersecurity efforts and decrease cyber vulnerabilities. This is a task for the NICST, in collaboration with private actors. Likewise, the rise of cloud computing, unmanned vehicles, and further use of mobile devices could spur economic development yet still poses significant cybersecurity risks. The second section of the current strategy discusses the organizational structure of Taiwan's government cyber security framework, promotes achievements made, and outlaws the (digital) environment in which it operates. The third and most extensive section outlines the blueprint for the future, building further on the points mentioned in the paragraph above. It outlines the vision for the next years, including objectives and strategies, and how progress can be achieved and measured.

International law and sovereignty

Questions of international law and sovereignty are tightly related in the case of Taiwan, whose statehood is subject to debate. Concerning the legal relations to mainland China (PRC), these questions are virtually inseparable. Coincidently, Taiwan's biggest cybersecurity concern is cyber-attacks from the PRC. Aside from the general problem of attribution of cyber-attacks to governments (cf. Geiß & Lahmann, 2013), respectively a duty of states to prevent such attacks on another state by private actors (cf. Pirker, 2013), we must ask ourselves: If Taiwan should not be a state, to what extent does international law prohibit PRC cyber operations against Taiwan?

The traditional view on both sides of the Taiwan Strait has been that there is only "one China" – with governments on each side claiming to be its legitimate representative. Taiwan has, perhaps consequently, not unequivocally declared its independence from the PRC. Together with a lack of recognition of Taiwan as a separate state (only a few states recognize Taiwan as a state and maintain formal relations with it, and no state maintains formal relations with both the Republic of China and the PRC), this has prompted Crawford (2006) to conclude that Taiwan is not a state. In light of the PRC's anti-secession law of 14 March 2015, it, however, appears somewhat paradox to rely on an unequivocal declaration of independence as the crucial factor: it is precisely such a declaration that the PRC has declared would prompt it to use force (cf. Roth, 2009).

Since the 1990s, the ROC has also increasingly been issuing statements and acted in a manner alluding to a drift towards "two Chinas" (Pei-Lun, 2015). Considering especially the involvement of the United States (Taiwan Relations Act of 1979, Section 2.b.4), any non-peaceful attempts at putting the matter to rest would likely "endanger the maintenance of international peace and security" under Art. 33 UN Charter (cf. Crawford, 2006). Thus Crawford (2006) finds, even if there is no "judicial boundary" between the parties, "the suppression by force of 23 million people cannot be consistent with the Charter. To that extent, there must be a cross-strait boundary for the use of force" (p. 220f). Others have argued that even if Taiwan is not a state, the result need not be that it belongs to the PRC (Chiang, 2004) or have argued that Taiwan constitutes a *de facto* entity that, like a state, is protected by the principles of international law regarding the non-use of force (Chiang, 2004).

Considering that international law prohibits cyber operations against states in two manners – as a use of force or as a violation of territorial sovereignty – there are thus in essence, three possible ways to look at PRC cyber operations against Taiwan. Firstly, Taiwan could be a sovereign state, and thus international law on the point would apply just like in the relations between any other two states. Secondly, it could be not a separate state, but form one state with the PRC. Then PRC cyber operations would be an internal affair, over which international law does not have much say. Or thirdly, Taiwan could be not a sovereign state, but – either as it does not belong to the PRC or for special status within it as a matter of international law – there would be a cross-strait boundary for the use of force. The latter option leads to the consequence that only cyber operations of a graver nature would be prohibited as a matter of international law, namely those that amount to a use of force, but not such that would only amount to a violation of sovereignty between states. A *Stuxnet*-like operation, damaging power plants in Taiwan would thus for example remain a prohibited cyber-attack amounting to a use of force (cf. Tallinn Manual, Rule 11), while e.g., coercive political interference in Taiwan, such as manipulation by cyber means of elections or public opinion, would not be prohibited under international law (cf. Tallinn Manual, Rule 10, para 10).

International governance

Taiwan's contested international position and its lack of official recognition have severely limited its ability to participate in international governance debates. It is a member of the ICANN; however, it is not a member of the ITU as China blocked Taiwan's efforts to join. To the extent that efforts have been undertaken to participate in international internet governance forums, such as the United Nations' Internet Governance Forum in Geneva in 2017, here, likewise, a strong reaction from China followed (Strong, 2017). Given the position of China, which has only intensified in the last two years, Taiwan has found it increasingly difficult to participate in international internet governance forums on a state level. Nevertheless, it is supportive of international governance efforts and can generally be considered as supporting the notion of free and democratic internet. As a result of its contested Taiwan international position, it has sought other opportunities and possibilities to influence the regional and global debate on internet governance and cybersecurity. Examples are the Taiwan International Governance Forum (TWIGF), which has been taking place since 2015. Furthermore, it has, through track two dialogues, sought to participate and contribute to regional and international internet and cyber governance efforts. Finally, given its unique position as the primary recipient of Chinese offensive cyber efforts and the expertise and knowledge it has gained through this, it is collaborating with other governments. However, much of this is conducted either through private enterprises or defense and intelligence agencies. As such is out of sight and hard to adequately guess or describe.

Taiwan's cybersecurity institutions

As mentioned throughout this chapter Taiwan has a rather unique cybersecurity culture that is fostered through a close collaboration between the government, private sector and white-hat hackers. This combined approach to cybersecurity is partly the result of the cultural understanding that has emerged as a result of the threat it faced from China. In this David versus Goliath scenario, Taiwan has limited means to defend and deter China – in the cyber realm and the physical military realm. As a result, it has fostered a culture of cooperation.

Policymaking was and is in the hands of the department of cybersecurity, which is part of the Executive Yuan branch. As Wu (2017) notes, it was this agency that was responsible for developing the Cybersecurity Management Act. The Cybersecurity Management Act, which will come in effect on a date set by the Executive Yuan, broadens the scope of cybersecurity efforts. The new Act includes not only governmental actors but also requires private actors, who are part of the critical infrastructure networks, to abide by the new cybersecurity policies and guidelines. Wu (2017) lists the following eight sectors which the new act considers part of the critical infrastructure: (1) energy, (2) water, (3) information and telecommunications, (4) transportation, (5) banking and finance, (6) emergency services and public healthcare, (7) central government, and (8) hi-tech industrial parks.

The recently established branch (2016), as Ferry (2018) describes, includes a "range of programs and taskforces, including the National Information and Communication Security Taskforce, the Cyberspace Protection System, and the Critical Infrastructure Protection System." It has set up a joint information-sharing center, in tandem with the National Communications Commission and Financial Supervisory Commission. This center aims to coordinate information about cybersecurity across the government, including possible, and actual breaches of civil government networks. In this, these agencies, foremost the Department of Cybersecurity, Executive Yuan, focus on the civil side of cybersecurity affairs. These legislative and policy efforts by the Department of Cybersecurity, Executive Yuan, are conducted in tandem with the Legislative Yuan – the Taiwanese parliament.

Responsibility for the military cyber realm rests with the Ministry of National Defense. A newly formed fourth branch of the military will focus on military cyber affairs (Wu, 2017). This Information, Communications, and Electronic Force, also known as the Electronic Warfare Command, is replacing the prior established MND's Information and Electronic Warfare Command, which had been in service since 2004. As Ferry (2018) notes, the new command aims at "consolidating cyber- and electronic-warfare components already existing within the armed forces." In these efforts, it will be supported by the Chungshan Institute of Science and Technology, as well as by civilian white-hat hackers groups (Ferry, 2018; Wu, 2018)

Role of the private sector

Taiwan has a lively and highly active white-hat hacker society, which has played an outsized role in the private sector. As Wu (2017) notes,

> Taiwan's ethical hackers are renowned in the global security community for vulnerability hunting and operational teamwork. [...] Interestingly, the Taiwan government has simultaneously worked to change the general public's perception of the hacker community. Now the government is aggressively supporting local cybersecurity communities, [...] with the Ministry of Economic Affairs' Industrial Development Bureau granting funds to such ethical hacker events.

These governmental efforts, as well as a strong entrepreneurial spirit among these groups, have fostered a private cybersecurity sector in which there is several highly sophisticated and capable startups and smaller companies – fewer than 50 employees – that tailor to specific cybersecurity needs within Taiwan and beyond (Huang & Li, 2018). These startups are collaborating with the government in developing tailored approaches to local cyberthreats and have fostered a large cybersecurity industry.

While smaller companies and startups have been leading the development of cybersecurity defenses, the larger enterprises involved in IT technology have illustrated a lesser ability to do so. As Wu (2017) notes, both the 2010 Stuxnet attack and the 2015 Duqu 2.0 attack used stolen digital certificates from leading Taiwanese ICT companies, Foxconn, JMicron, and RealTek Semiconductor, to gain access to the respective systems. Even more damaging was the news that the computer maker Asus was sending out "critical" updates that were infected with malware via Asus servers with an authentic security certificate for well over half a year (Kastrenakes, 2019). In this, there seems to be a discrepancy between smaller cybersecurity companies, who have an outsized role in the private sector, and larger ICT companies, the heavyweights of the Taiwanese economy.

While both are heavily involved in the nation's highly important ICT sector, the smaller cybersecurity-focused companies hold an outsized influence on the debate and direction of the debate within the country.

The role of the legislature

A critical legislative novelty is the Information and Communication Security Management Act, which passed the Legislative Yuan in May 2018 and came into effect 1 January 2019. It concerns the monitoring, detection, prevention, mitigation, and management of cybersecurity incidents and applies to government agencies, providers of critical infrastructure, state-controlled enterprises, and state-financed foundations. The Criminal Code of the Republic of China comprehensively penalizes cybercrime whose conduct or result takes place in Taiwan. Of further relevance is the Personal Information Protection Act, which governs the collection, storage, and use of personal data. Concerning intellectual property, it is noteworthy that Taiwan is not a party to the Berne Convention for the Protection of Literary and Artistic Works. Works by most foreign nationals do, however, enjoy copyright protection as Taiwan is a member of the World Trade Organization.

Combatting cybercrime and cyberterrorism

As Tsai et al. (2014) note, Taiwan has few to no significant international enemies besides the PRC. Partly the result of isolated geographical location, as well as its historical isolation, Taiwan has remained far away from the global terrorism focus. As a result of the limited terrorism threat, logically, the threat of cyberterrorism has been limited to non-existent. There are limited to no indications that Taiwan's absence of the global terrorism radar will change, and as such, it can be expected cyberterrorism will remain a topic of limited importance for Taiwan in the near future.

Cybercrime is widely present in Taiwan. However, before engaging in a more detailed study on cybercrime, a clarification on the concept of cybercrime is needed. Indeed, as Lin and Nomikos (2017) note in their study on cybercrime in Taiwan, the concept of cybercrime itself is contested. This chapter follows the definition of McGuire and Dowling (2013), who makes the distinction between two types of cybercrime. First, cyber-dependent crimes, also known as high-tech or advanced cybercrimes, and second cyber-enabled crimes. The first are crimes that solely can be committed through IT technology: hacking, DDoS attacks, spreading viruses, ransomware attacks. Second are "classical" crimes, such as fraud, theft, and spreading of illegal pornography.

Given Taiwan's high degree of digital penetration, as well as its widespread use of online communication, digital information sharing, and online and digital payments, it has become a target and hotspot for the cybercrime of the second tier. Lu et al. (2006, 11) suggest that the top five cybercrimes committed in the prior decades were all digital crimes in the second category: "trading sex on the Internet, Internet fraud, larceny, cyberpiracy, and cyber pornography." According to the number of the National Police Agency (NPA), a decade later, in 2015, these have largely remained unchanged. It is still cyber-enabled crimes that make up the bulk of cybercrimes committed within Taiwan. In particular, fraud is a core problem in Taiwan and beyond. Taiwan's criminal syndicates have become apt in fraud via digital means, with these syndicates now operating far beyond their borders – courtesy of the boundaryless nature of cyberspace. Nevertheless, in recent years, these types of crimes have seen the competition of the first type of crimes. Taiwan has become a leading recipient and distributor of spam. Much of this is the result of its high infection malware rates, turning legions of Taiwanese ICT systems into Botnet systems used for spam distribution and DDoS attacks (Lin and Nomikos, 2017). At the same time, it has become subject to several sophisticated heists by foreign actors. Most famously, the 2016 First Commercial Bank ATM hack, as well as the Far Eastern International Bank heist 2017, conducted by the North Korean linked Lazarus hacking collective (Boey, 2017; Hung, 2016, Wu, 2017). As a result of this persistent threat across multiple sectors, the government, in collaboration with the private sector, has, in recent years, undertaken several efforts to address the threats of cybercrime and to curb its negative impact.

Societal implications

Due to the impact of cybercrimes, as well as the persistent and advanced, sophisticated (cyber)threat from China, Taiwan long had a great need for a sophisticated cybersecurity ability to fend off criminal and nation-state cyber-attacks (Wu, 2017). The urgency for such has been further enhanced by the fact that Taiwan, as a highly digitalized society, with an economy dependent on the functioning of (new) IT technology, and of course, a large IT economic sector, has been highly vulnerable to attacks in the cyber domain (ibid.). The tandem of this has meant that Taiwan faced a unique, at least regionally, cyber threat scenario. Its ability to counter this threat has been hampered: The difference between the threats, who are legion, persistent, and ever-growing, and the ability of the government to counter these threats, which has been limited. Faced with this scenario, the government has engaged in structural effort to work with private sectors to increase the ability of the island to defend itself against cyber-attacks. In this, it has developed an influential collaborative culture in which government organs – civil and militarily – work in tandem with the private sector and (white-hat) hackers. Such efforts and the importance of achieving secure cyberspace can be witnessed in efforts undertaken by the Tsai government to develop an information security strategy 2.0.

This strategy, implemented from 2021 onwards, seeks not only to increase defenses – an ability the government can directly influence – but also foster further closer collaboration with the private sector and society. Among these are efforts to increase cybersecurity awareness, as well as cybersecurity training. With human errors still counting for the majority of the initial cyber breaches, such efforts to train society and raise cyber awareness are worthwhile, necessary and will improve the nation's security. Furthermore, and as emphasized in an earlier report by Tsai, prior to becoming president, in order to counter cyber threats, across the spectrum, there is a necessity, and utility in embracing small and medium enterprises, as well as individual hackers, to develop a collaborative effort in cybersecurity (Hsu, 2018; Tsai, 2014; Wu, 2017). In this, and the result of the unique threat situation it faces, Taiwan has developed a nation-tailored approach that encompasses and at the same time builds on the strength of the entire island.

Conclusion

As a result of its rather unique position within the international arena – in essence a country with sovereign borders and governance organs, but one that remains largely unrecognized – Taiwan has found itself in special cybersecurity situation. As result of Chinese pressure, it is not able to participate, at least openly, in global and regional cyber and cybersecurity forums. Furthermore, official cooperation in the international is neither possible. Instead, it has established a number of semi-official channels that are often fostered through non-governmental organizations. As such, Taiwan operates as state (too) in the cyber domain but remains an unrecognized entity within this domain on the international political level. At the same time, and owning to the persistent Chinese cyber threats, Taiwan has been forced early on to develop framework and policies to increase the nation's cybersecurity. Taiwan has developed an extensive cybersecurity framework. This framework encompasses legal efforts to ensure nationwide cybersecurity standards – in particular for what it deems organizations and enterprises that are part of the nation's critical infrastructure – as well as operational efforts to increase its cybersecurity defense.

In recent years, as the threat has intensified and as its society has further digitalized, the government has released a series of cybersecurity strategies and has actively sought to streamline and centralize its national cybersecurity efforts. Yet given the size of China, and its cyber abilities, and the limited capabilities – at least in regard to the Chinese threat – of the Taiwanese government, it has been forced to think beyond its traditional governmental domain. In this, it has sought the development of a cooperative framework in which private actors – large enterprises operating critical infrastructure as well SMEs and start-ups focused on niche cybersecurity focuses – play an important role in contributing to the nation's cybersecurity ability. Given the focus of the current Tsai government on cyber issues as well as active efforts by the government to sponsors private actors, it can be expected that governmental and private sector cooperation will only further increase in the near future. With the growing Chinese cyber threat – on a multitude of levels, ranging from APTs to digital election interference – it seems a necessary step. All in all, it seems Taiwan has been able to evaluate its cybersecurity policy in the recent years to a platform that seeks to establish a competent cybersecurity effort.

Suggested reading

BBC. (2019, November 4). "US and Taiwan Hold First Joint Cyber-war Exercise." bbc.com/news/technology–50289974

Finley, K. (2019, January 17). "Huawei's Many Troubles: Bans, Alleged Spies, and Backdoors," *WIRED*. www.wired.com/story/huaweis-many-troubles-bans-alleged-spies-backdoors/

Shay, A. (2020, February 14). "Cybersecurity Trends and Issues: Taiwan." www.internationallawoffice.com/OnDemand/Tech-Data-Telecoms-Media/Cybersecurity-trends-and-issues-/Taiwan/Shay-Partners

Yau, H. M. (2019). "A Critical Strategy for Taiwan's Cybersecurity: A Perspective from Critical Security Studies," *Journal of Cyber Security*, 4(1): 35–55.

References

Boey, D. (2017, October 17). "North Korean Hacker Group Linked to Taiwan Bank Cyberheist." Retrieved August 20, 2020, from: https://www.bloomberg.com/news/articles/2017-10-17/north-korean-hacker-group-linked-to-taiwanese-bank-cyberheist

Chiang, Y. F. (2004). "One-China Policy and Taiwan," *Fordham International Law Journal*, 28: 1–87.

Crawford, J. (2006). *The Creation of States in International Law* (2nd ed.). Oxford, U.K.: Clarendon.

Ferry, T. (2018, May 15). "Taiwan Gets Its Act Together on Cybersecurity." Retrieved August 20, 2020, from: https://international.thenewslens.com/article/95683

Geiß, R., & Lahmann, H., (2013). "Freedom and Security in Cyberspace: Shifting the Focus away from Military Responses Towards Non-forcible Countermeasures and Collective Threat-Prevention," in K., Ziolkowski (ed.), *Peacetime Regime for State Activities in Cyberspace. International Law, International Relations and Diplomacy* (pp. 621–657), Tallinn: NATO CCD COE Publication.

Hsiu-An Hsiao, A. (1998). "Is China's Policy to Use Force against Taiwan a Violation of the Principle of Non-Use of Force under International Law?" *New England Law Review, 32*: 715–742.

Hsu, P. (2018). *Taiwan's Emerging Push for "Cyber Autonomy"* (13th ed., Vol. 18, China Brief, Issue brief): Jamestown Foundation. Retrieved August 20, 2020, from: https://jamestown.org/program/taiwans-emerging-push-for-cyber-autonomy–2/.

Huang, H., Li, T. (2018). "A Centralized Cybersecurity Strategy for Taiwan." BASC Working Paper Series, Berkeley, CA: University of California.

Hung, F. (2016, July 13). "Taiwan Seeks Two Russian Suspects in $2 million ATM Malware Heist." Retrieved August 20, 2020, from: https://www.reuters.com/article/us-taiwan-banks-theft/taiwan-seeks-two-russian-suspects-in-2-million-atm-malware-heist-idUSKCN0ZT0Y6

Kastrenakes, J. (2019, March 25). "Asus software updates were used to spread malware, security group says." Retrieved August 20, 2020, from: https://www.theverge.com/2019/3/25/18280716/asus-update-tool-hacked-shadowhammer-malware

Lin, Lsf & Nomikos, J. (2018). "Cybercrime in East and Southeast Asia: The Case of Taiwan." DOI:10.1007/978-3-319-61729-9_4.

Lu, C., Jen, W., Chang, W., & Chou, S. (2006). "Cybercrime & Cybercriminals: An Overview of the Taiwan Experience," *Journal of Computers, 1*(6): 11–18. DOI:10.4304/jcp.1.6.11-18

McGuire, M., & Dowling, S. (2013, October). *Cyber Crime: A Review of the Evidence* (Home Office Research Report 75). Retrieved August 10, 2020, from: https://assets.publishing.service.gov.uk/government/uploads/system/uploads/attachment_data/file/246749/horr75-summary.pdf

National Information and Communication Security Taskforce (NICST). (2017, November). "National Cyber Security Program of Taiwan." Retrieved from: www.nicst.ey.gov.tw/en/DL.ashx?u=/Upload/RelFile/3172/760181/NationalCyberSecurityProgram.pdf

Pei-Lun, T. (2015). *The Application of International Human Rights Law to Unrecognised Entities: the Case of Taiwan.* PhD Thesis, Nottingham, UK: University of Nottingham.

Pirker, B., Territorial Sovereignty and Integrity and the Challenges of Cyberspace. In Ziolkowski, K. (2013), *Peacetime Regime for State Activities in Cyberspace. International Law, International Relations and Diplomacy* (pp. 189–216). Tallinn: NATO CCD COE Publication.

Roth, B. B. (2009). "The Entity that Dare Not Speak its Name: Unrecognized Taiwan as a Right Bearer in the International Legal Order," *East Asia Law Review, 4*: 91–124.

Strong, M. (2017, December 23). "China Protests against Taiwanese Minister Addressing UN Meet." Retrieved August 20, 2020, from: http://www.taiwannews.com.tw/en/news/3326879

Tsai, I. (2014, October). *Bolstering Taiwan's Core Defense Industries* (Defense Policy Blue Paper No.7). Retrieved August 20, 2020, from: New Frontier Foundation website: http://www.dppnff.tw/uploads/20141002201332_5490.pdf

Wu, B. (2017, August 24). "Taiwan Sees Its Cyber Capabilities as the Hard Reality of Soft Power." Retrieved August 20, 2020, from: https://www.nbr.org/publication/taiwan-sees-its-cyber-capabilities-as-the-hard-reality-of-soft-power/

24

SERVING THE PEOPLE

China's cybersecurity policy and its implications

Yu Cheng Chen, Tony Tai-Ting Liu, and Scott N. Romaniuk

Introduction

Since the end of the Cold War, the rise of China has reserved a spot in the study of international relations. As China's comprehensive power grew steadily after a period of economic reform, its influence in international society increased as well, particularly in the field of cyber and information technology. Currently, the revolution in information technology, including the internet, telecommunication networks, computer systems, and related virtual spaces, is changing human lifestyle and leaving deep imprints on the development of human society (Cyberspace Administration of China, 2016). For China today, the development of cutting-edge technology is at the heart of economic development and national security. The emergence of information and communication technology (ICT) companies is the key to the parallel rise of millions of Chinese citizens and consumers who actively participate in the age of information.

Nonetheless, while society is undergoing massive change, Beijing has come to realize that advancements in technology are outpacing improvements in the official capability to manage and control new technologies. Beijing has responded through the establishment of new institutions, laws, and policies to manage domestic software, hardware, and information. These developments are changing the characteristics of ICT companies and internet users both inside and outside of China (CSIS, n.d.). This chapter reviews the context that spurred the development of China's cybersecurity policy and observes the impact and meaning of such government policies, institutions, and legal norms. In addition, this chapter also discusses the implications of China's cybersecurity policy for international relations.

Domestic environment and the challenge of cybersecurity

While the internet brought about more conveniences and efficiency to daily life, the fact that China boasts the greatest number of internet users in the world and a corresponding high number of internet attacks is no trivial matter.

Development of the internet in China

To understand China's cybersecurity policy, it is important to first examine the history of internet usage in China. Interestingly, there exists no agreement on the first use of the internet in China. While records show that academic institutions sent out emails abroad in the 1990s, debate continues on when the first email was delivered in 1986 or 1987.

One claim, notes Wu Weimin, from the Chinese Academy of Sciences, was that the first email was sent to scientist Jack Steinberger of the European Organization for Nuclear Research (CERN) on August 25, 1986, from a work station in the Institute of High Energy Physics (IHEP). Another claim notes the first email as sent by a joint Chinese–German research team based at the Chinese Institute of Computer Applications (ICA) to the University of Karlsruhe on September 20, 1987 under the subject heading "Across the Great Wall, we can reach every corner in the world" (Goldkorn, 2012), which marked China's first step towards the internet age.

While the source of the first email remain debatable, China's official adoption of the internet is undisputed. On May 17 1994, IHEP and the Stanford Linear Accelerator Center (SLAC)'s TCP/IP connection marked China's entry into cyberspace. One week later, a 64K connection was established between the National Computing and Networking Facility of China and Sprint in the United States, realizing China's interconnection with the world (PC World, 2004).

ICT-led economic growth

Beijing views the development of the internet as a process in the evolution from an industrial society to an information society, or a process of "informatization" (PC World, 2004). In the past two decades, the Chinese government has clearly identified modernization policies in the digital age and adopted new information and communication technologies in departments spanning government, industry, business, education, and culture. Informatization is currently at the core of China's 13th Five Year Plan (2016–2020), which entails the application of advanced ICT in the political, economic, military, health, agriculture, and environmental sectors (Austin, 2016).

When the internet was first introduced in China, slow speed and limited infrastructure hampered its efficiency. Through land line connection, the speed of data transfer reached a mere 64 Kbps per second. On the other hand, in 1996, China hosted only 2000 computers that had internet connection ability. It was not until the subsequent appearance of corporations such as Sina, Sohu, and NetEase, that first generation internet users began to rapidly emerge in China. Despite being a cliché now, the internet is transforming the life and lifestyle of millions of average Chinese. In China today, people use personal computers (PC), tablets, and smartphones to check email and connect with others though social media applications. Thanks to the robust development of the information technology (IT) industry, millions of people began to launch private companies. Some Chinese companies have since became main participants in the global IT industry and are among the most successful firms in China today. E-commerce provides over 13 million employment opportunities in the country. Alibaba, one such Chinese company is currently the leader in online trade, with its annual trading numbers besting the combined sum of eBay and Amazon (FlorCruz & Sue, 2014).

In recent years, China has achieved eye-catching developments in the virtual world. Most notably, China boasts the greatest number of internet users; the number of Chinese netizens increased with explosive speed while internet technology grew rapidly. According to a report provided by the China Internet Network Information Center (CNNIC) in January 2018, China hosts a whopping 772 million internet users, which makes up 55.8 per cent of its total population (The Economic Times, 2018). Such a great number of netizens has translated into a driving force for economic growth. According to a whitepaper released by the Academy of Information and Communications Technology, a department under the Ministry of Industry and Information Technology (MIIT), digital or cyber economic activities including e-commerce, cloud computing, and online payment contributed to 3.35 trillion USD in 2016, leaping 18.9 per cent from the year before and making up 30.3 per cent of China's gross domestic product (GDP) (China Daily, 2017).

In short, the key to informatization is the internet. In China, infrastructure of the internet is either directly controlled by the government or owned by private corporations that work closely with the state. In such a sense, the internet seems more like an "intranet" within a company; the government is the service provider that is responsible for defending the internet. Such a characteristic stands in contrast with the US (Thomas, 2009: 455–456). In the eyes of China's political elites, the importance of cybersecurity is clear and the development of ICT is critical for the future of national security and development. As Chinese President Xi Jinping noted, cybersecurity and informatization are closely linked and related to national development, "there is no national security without cybersecurity, and no modernization without informatization" (Cyberspace Administration of China, 2014).

The increasing challenge of cybersecurity

As Joseph Nye points out, cybersecurity is mainly challenged by four types of threats: espionage, crime, cyber warfare, and cyber terrorism. Common explanations for the

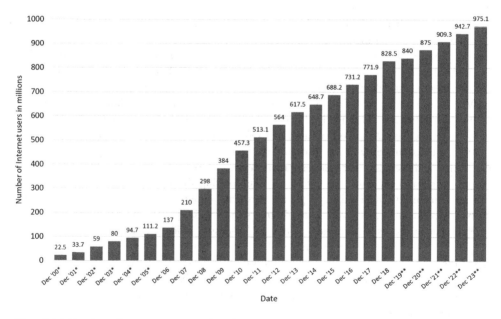

Figure 24.1 Number of Internet Users in China from December 2000 to December 2023 (in millions)
Source: Internet live States (2020) and Statista (2020).
*Data from Internet Live Stats.
**Projected.

challenges include defects in the design of the internet, defects in hardware and software, and the growing reliance on the internet as a storage space for important data systems (Clarke & Knake, 2010: 73; Nye, 2010: 16). On the other hand, official reports from the US also identify cyberattack and cyber espionage as the main challenges towards cybersecurity. Cyberattacks refer to offensive acts without an identifiable agent (Clapper, 2013: 1). The purpose of such attacks is to generate panic, or accomplish the goals of controlling, terminating, or deleting data.

While China boasts the greatest number of internet users in the world, it also faces an increasing number of cyberattacks. According to a 2016 report, the annual economic loss for China due to cybersecurity incidents amounted to as much as 915 million RMB (People's Daily, 2016). Trojan horse, botnet, mobile network, distributed denial of service (DDOS), software and hardware bugs, and security loopholes in websites were identified as the most common security issues (National Internet Emergency Center, 2017: 1). Correspondingly, in 2016, China released the National Cyberspace Security Strategy, which identified both domestic and external challenges to cybersecurity. For China, external challenges relate to the growing number of foreigners who exploit the internet to intervene in China's domestic politics. In addition, large scale web monitoring and espionage severely encroach on national security and user privacy, and may potentially damage critical information infrastructure or give rise to international conflicts. On the other hand, domestic challenges include online rumors, depressive and lewd culture, violence, and superstitious information that may erode culture security and the bodily health of young adults. Internet terrorism and criminal activities directly challenge social order and the life and property of Chinese citizens (Cyberspace Administration of China, 2016).

In technical terms, cybersecurity refers to the protection of software, hardware, and data from accidental or malicious damage, tampering, or disclosure. At the same time, internet service remains unterminated and in normal and successive functioning. From the perspective of social order, while Beijing recognizes the enormous economic benefit of internet technology, the circulation of uncontrolled information poses a serious threat to the regime – a phenomenon that is no doubt magnified by the Tiananmen Square Incident and the Jasmine Revolution. Therefore, for China, political stability remains the dominant priority for the establishment of policies and measures related to cybersecurity (Chang, 2014: 32).

In light of the Tiananmen Square Incident in 1989, it is not hard to understand China's emphasis on political stability. As social disruptions and upheaval in the aftermath of the incident brought the Chinese Communist Party (CCP) to the edge of collapse, Beijing came to keep a tight watch over all mass movements and unapproved political thought. The adoption of quick and determined suppression remains the justified response (Swartz, 2011: 1–5). On the other hand, noting how the Jasmine Revolution swept through the Arab world and how mass demonstrations disrupted peace in the region, for Beijing, the fear of the people turning against the CCP regime out shadows the concern for challenges such as corruption, wealth disparity, unemployment, and inflation (Swartz, 2011: 4).

Meanwhile, China remains vigilant of the fierce global competition in the development of ICT. Noting technological advancements by other states, as a main victim of cyberattacks and internet hacking, China recognizes the need to develop its internet capability and its ability to maneuver in the virtual world. Overall, China deems cybersecurity as a global issue that challenges national security, economic development, domestic politics, and society, and places emphasis on the defense of sovereignty, political order, and social stability (Raud, 2016: 6). In terms of cybersecurity, for China, security in the real world seems to matter more than security in the virtual world.

Development of China's cybersecurity policies

Over the years, Beijing has established laws, regulations, and institutions aimed at increasing the state's ability to monitor internet speech and prevent threats to the CCP. At the same time, institutions were established to realize the rule by law while cybersecurity laws were established to serve as non-tariff barriers against trade opponents. In this section, we survey the development of China's cybersecurity policies, including regulations, legal governance, and new cyber legislation.

Establishing regulations for cyber restraint

Not only does 1994 mark the official launch of China's internet age, it is also the starting point for cyber governance in the country. Since 1994, Beijing subsequently introduced a series of laws and regulations related to cybersecurity, including the National People's Congress Standing Committee's Decision on Safeguarding Internet Security, Telecommunications Regulations of the People's Republic of China (PRC), Regulation on Internet Information Service of the PRC, Computer Information System Security Protection Ordinance of the PRC, Regulations on the Administration of Foreign-Invested Telecommunications, International Networking of Computer Information Network Security Management Approach, and National People's Congress Standing Committee's Decision on Strengthening Network Information Protection (Yuxiao & Lu, 2015: 232).

Regarding internet censorship and control, it is hard to overlook the Golden Shield project headed by Chinese academician Fang Binxing, also known as the Great Firewall of China. China's "great firewall" contributes to censorship by blocking internet protocol (IP) and filtering domain name systems (DNS) and uniform resource locators (URLs) that are linked to sensitive terms or phrases or information that the central government does not want to be circulating online. Terms such as June 4 Tiananmen Square Incident, Taiwanese independence, Tibetan independence, Xinjiang independence, and Falungong are all tightly watched and often blocked by Beijing (Inkster, 2016: 32).

Besides the blockage of politically sensitive terms, Google, YouTube, and other media interfaces that exude free thought and free flow of information are all blocked by Beijing. Mainstream Western media that make serious accusations against China such as the *Wall Street Journal*, *Bloomberg News* and the *Washington Post*, and social media such as Facebook and Twitter, are all shut out by Beijing (Lindsay, 2014/2015: 18; Yuxiao & Lu, 2015: 232). It is clear that China's cybersecurity departments expend great efforts to control information and activities on the internet, in an effort to circumscribe all potential threats against the state.

Legal governance/rule by law

In recent years, Beijing has actively introduced and promoted cybersecurity policies of various types, in the hopes of bringing out the synergy between the party state and private business for technological advancements and expansion in the civil application of ICT. At the same time, however, Beijing has tightened its control over the use of the internet, which betrays the somewhat interesting phenomenon of co-evolution between development and restriction. For example, the Office of the Central Cyberspace Affairs Commission and the Cyberspace Administration of China (CAC) – formerly known as the Central Leading Group for Cybersecurity and Informatization – report directly to Xi Jinping.

The CAC was established by Xi Jinping in December 2013. Lu Wei, former head of the propaganda department of Beijing, served as the inaugural chair of the CAC (Perlez & Mozur, 2016). The purpose of the CAC is to redefine the digital information control system in China and confirm that the state has improved control over cybersecurity and internet services. Hence through censorship and surveillance, the CAC tightens its grip over online content. At the same time, the CAC also uses new technologies to carry out new forms of promotion and consolidate its hegemonic role over cyber governance (Raud, 2016: 18–19). As the chair of the CAC enjoys considerable power, observers have granted it the title of "internet Czar." In June 2016, Lu Wei resigned after being found guilty of violating government discipline.

On February 27, 2014, the Central Leading Group for Cybersecurity and Informatization was established. Led by Xi Jinping personally, the group aimed to readjust the institution for cyber management and improve on issues such as overlapping functions, accountability and efficiency (Cyberspace Administration of China, 2016; Inkster, 2016: 40–41). In addition to increasing the efficiency of cyber management, the leading group also contributed to Xi Jinping's anticorruption movement. Beijing's authority was severely damaged when online media and communities widely reported on the scandals of former Party Secretary of Chongqing Bo Xilai and Vice Mayor of Chongqing Wang Lijun in late 2012. Soon after, Beijing censored *New York Times* and other Western media that reported on the issue and adopted a hard hand against some foreign reporters by terminating the renewal of passports (PEN America, 2016: 31–32).

In an open statement in 2013, Xi Jinping emphasized the CCP's ambition "to establish a powerful team to occupy new grounds in the media" (Paulson, 2015: 370–372). Since then, the Chinese government employed a large number of cyber police to patrol and follow popular topics in online communities. As many as two million police or so called "public opinion analysts" reportedly patrol the virtual world (Xu & Albert, 2017). While anti-corruption was one of the main driving forces for establishing new institutions, Beijing also came to realize the popular influence of online media and note the need for a more effective system to control information (Lampton, 2014: 60–62). In other words, perhaps more than the protection of government authority, press freedom, and the freedom of speech are at the root of China's cybersecurity policies.

Besides official institutions, establishment of the Cyber Security Association of China (CSAC) in 2016 further buffers Beijing's attempt to strengthen cybersecurity. Established under the guidance of the CAC, the CSAC is a non-profit social organization approved by the State Council to reinforce China's cybersecurity through the organization and mobilization of different parties in society. The CSAC is an initiative aimed at cooperation among the government, business and academia for the goal of better cyber governance. In addition, the CSAC actively participates in policy discussions regarding China's cybersecurity and issues of global governance (O' Brien, 2016; *First Post*, 2016).

Finally, it is worth noting the contribution of the People's Liberation Army (PLA) towards legal governance. In *Strategic Studies* (*Zhanluexue*) published by the PLA Academy of Military Science in 2013, the existence of cyber troops in China was first described to the world. Besides emphasizing the troop's duty to safeguard cybersecurity, *Strategic Studies* also points out the importance of war and peace time cyber competition and tasks concerning offense and defense. In 2015, China's State Council released *China's Military Strategy* and emphasized the potential threat of penetration, subversion, and cultural erosion by Western countries through the exploitation of the internet (Kowalewski, 2017). Noting the strong impact such attacks may have on national security, the cyber division of the PLA is tasked with monitoring open information networks and preventing cyber espionage and attacks (The State Council of the People's Republic of China, 2014). In December 2015, Xi Jinping established the Strategic Support Force (SSF) as a part of his overall military reform. The SSF is a new operational force that will provide strategic support for the PLA on issues concerning outer space, cyber space, and electromagnetics, and plays a critical role in realizing integrated joint combat with other traditional forces (Costello, 2016).

Overall, the creation of cybersecurity policies and institutions not only demonstrates Beijing's desire to readjust the power structure on the leadership level and correct the problem of loose accountability, but also display the will of the political elites to push for more effective cyber policies through the efficient use of state resources.

New cyber legislation

It is easy to draw from the previous discussion that Chinese censorship on freedom of speech online has existed for quite some time. Since Xi Jinping's entry into office, besides the issue of free speech, one can also observe the issue of re-designation of power to state institutions to perform content review in the cyber world. As specific legislations remain unclear, some content is deemed to influence patent skills and intellectual property rights, and to encroach on individual privacy rights. Regardless, on December 27, 2016, Beijing released its Cybersecurity Strategy, which details China's determination to realize related laws and norms concerning cyber space and achieve effective governance. The following discusses some of the main developments in recent years.

On July 1, 2015, the Standing Committee of the Twelfth National People's Congress adopted the *National Security Law*, which in turn attracted considerable attention from observers concerned with the Chinese definition of cybersecurity. Clause 25 suggests the need for China to develop its capability to protect cyber space and information while emphasizing the importance of innovative research and application of ICT. Clause 59 further proposes that China should establish surveillance institutions and mechanisms for national security and carry out security reviews for foreign investment, specific resources, key technologies, and ICT products (National People's Congress, 2015). Through the *National Security Law*, for the first time, China clearly introduced the concept of "cyber sovereignty" or the extension of state sovereignty to the internet. Yet the question of how the state can execute jurisdiction in cyberspace remains unclear (Bennett, 2015; Panda, 2015).

On December 27, 2015, at the 18th meeting of the Twelfth National People's Congress, the *Counterterrorism Law* was adopted for implementation on January 1, 2016. The law bans the distribution of details related to terrorism and cruel or inhumane images, as Beijing thinks related reports may encourage imitation in the populace. Moreover, without official approval, individuals are outlawed from releasing information of terrorist victims and statements regarding state activities towards counterterrorism. While China is widely known for censorship, the *Counterterrorism Law* reinforces such control (BBC News, 2015; Xinhua Net, 2016).

On March 10, 2016, the State Administration of Press, Publication, Radio, Film and Television and the Ministry of Industry and Information Technology jointly issued the *Regulations on Online Publication Services* (Ministry of Industry and Information Technology of the PRC, 2016). For the first time in history, the regulations prohibit foreign investment and joint domestic and foreign investment companies from providing online publication services in China. In addition, cooperation between online publishers and foreign investment or joint domestic and foreign investment companies, foreign organizations, or foreign personnel are all subject to official review. Publishers are required to acquire the certificate for online publishing services before proceeding.

Finally, on November 7, 2016, China adopted the *Cybersecurity Law*, which came into full force in June 2017. The law reflects Beijing's emphasis on cyber sovereignty and information control. In terms of the former, making the analogy with borders in the real world, China makes the effort to draw out boundaries in cyber space. The concept of cyber sovereignty can be traced to the 2010 white paper on the internet in China, which noted the internet as an important state infrastructure, and the subordination of the internet to Chinese sovereignty within China (China Daily, 2010). China makes the distinction between domestic and foreign space. While businesses and civil society can develop through the internet, the state has the ultimate responsibility and authority to maintain peace and stability. In the face of cybersecurity, the market profit of business is secondary. In other words, in the eyes of Beijing, even though the internet may be global, when it comes to the issue of jurisdiction, state governments should still take the lead (Zhou, 2015: 4).

Overall, one can conclude that regarding cyber governance, China is stepping up its efforts towards management by taking punitive actions against both internal and external cyberattacks, cyber espionage, distribution of illegal and corrosive information, and criminal activities that disrupt social and state stability. Maintenance of cyber sovereignty and security and the development of basic interests remain the priorities for China. Meanwhile, laws and regulations that relate to censorship against foreign business remain a major concern for foreign companies both within and outside China.

Implications of China's cybersecurity policy for international relations

In terms of the international aspect of China's cybersecurity policy, the authors think that controversies center on the concept of cyber sovereignty. Noting the fundamental differences between China and Western democracies, in spite of the establishment of institutions and legal norms, China remains the target of attacks from observers who suspect China's continued encroachment on freedom of speech and individual privacy under the justification of national security. On the other hand, noting China's growing influence in international affairs, cyber sovereignty may be regarded as a new concept that may be used to reshape existing rules and principles that govern cyberspace. Finally, the concept of cyber sovereignty may also serve as an important way for Beijing to acquire foreign technologies and protect its trade against others.

First, upon a closer examination of the laws and regulations mentioned in the previous section, it is clear that cyber sovereignty is at the heart of the laws, which in turn produce influences on free speech and individual privacy. For example, in terms of the *Counterterrorism Law*, to a great extent, media is restricted from reporting on China's counterterrorist activities. Correspondingly, skeptics point out that the law serves the traditional goals of Beijing to maintain stability and authority by allowing the government to use various ways to prevent, suppress and deal with terrorist activities. The law allows Beijing strict control over private organizations and access to hitherto private information, which in turn challenges the freedoms to speech, peaceful assembly, and religion (Singh, 2016).

In terms of the *Regulations on Online Publication Services*, official consent is limited to "able Chinese citizens who reside in the country permanently" and "whose server and saving facility is located within China." If online publishers release material that touches on national security and social stability, the material must be filed with local authorities according to regulations stipulated by the State Administration of Press, Publication, Radio,

Film and Television, or is otherwise prohibited from pubic release (Chan, 2018: 8). On the other hand, the *Cybersecurity Law* demands foreign businesses store all personal information and data produced in China within the country, and that they cooperate and provide information to the government in the circumstance of investigations. Accordingly, individual users must register with their true identity when using China's telecommunication service (Mozur, 2016). In short, through large scale control, China's *Cybersecurity Law* directly and passively hurt the individual right to free speech and privacy (Creemers, 2017).

Second, concerning the incompatibility between China's conception of cyber sovereignty and existent concepts, in recent years, China is actively involved in global internet governance and makes great efforts to promote the concept of "cyber sovereignty," which emphasizes the extension of state sovereignty to virtual space and mutual respect among states concerning independent virtual space and jurisdiction over domestic internet activities. China's call received support from Russia, Algeria, United Arab Emirates, and some Central Asian states, which favor the tightening of restrictions on internet activities. The mentioned countries have all cooperated with China in raising proposals on important occasions including the General Assembly of the United Nations, to bring about the establishment of the concept of cyber sovereignty in international institutions. Such actions are clearly antithetical to the US emphasis on internet freedom and seek to produce certain legitimacy in international law (Nye, 2010: 18; Gechlik, 2017: 2–5).

A closer observation of the World Internet Conference (WIC) also reveals China's ambition to increase its global influence. In November 2014, at the first WIC held in Wuzhen, Xi Jinping re-emphasized that peaceful internet space undergirded by multilateral governance should be realized under the condition of mutual respect and trust (*The Economic Times*, 2014). In the second WIC in the following year, Xi further called on the international community to establish a virtual community of common destiny guided by the principle of cyber sovereignty (*China Daily*, 2015). Xi's calls expose the fact that China is dissatisfied with the current cyber governance regime and seeks a stronger leadership role in cyber space; China hopes the future development of the cyber world can be more aligned with its thoughts and desires (Rui, 2015).

Domestic law is an important tool used by Beijing to strengthen cybersecurity. Particularly in terms of the *Cybersecurity Law* and *Counterterrorism Law*, China's tightened grip on data storage worried foreign corporations that suspect that China has aims other than cybersecurity. The *Cybersecurity Law* stipulates that internet enterprises must provide technical support and accept examinations by security related departments out of consideration for national security. In addition, enterprises must conform to the limitation on outbound data transfer, or in other words, data from China must be stored within China. Such action is taken to be an example of Beijing placing restrictions on the products of foreign companies while promoting the development of the domestic ICT industry in the name of national and cybersecurity (The US Chamber of Commerce, 2016: 6–15). While China's new cybersecurity law is centered on the concept of cyber sovereignty and provides the state with jurisdiction to tackle cybercrime and safeguard cybersecurity, in certain aspects China falls suspect to protectionism for its domestic industry (Zhu, 2016).

In fact, the *Counterterrorism Law* stipulates that telecommunication operators and service providers should establish technological connection points within their product and service design and establishment and forward their encryption plan for review by related authorities. Backdoor investigation and conformance with regulations for decryption are also within the bound of the state demand for vigilance over terrorist activities (Blanchard, 2015).

Meanwhile, Western ICT companies fear that China may exploit the *Counterterrorism Law* and raise its trade barrier. In recent years, Beijing has made the claim that Cisco and certain software contain "backdoors," and demanded foreign software companies that deal with Chinese banks to submit the original code of their software for state examination. Needless to say, such demands add to the cost of development for companies and may trigger retaliatory measures against Chinese companies abroad, which in turn increases the risk of trade war (Livingston, 2015).

Conclusion: the future of cybersecurity in China

Based on the discussion of China's cybersecurity policies in this chapter, the authors conclude with some questions that remain to be explored in the near future.

First, while the Chinese government makes efforts towards maintaining control over the cyber world, it is also concerned with keeping up with economic growth in the real world. Deng Xiaoping's saying that "development is the absolute principle" continues to influence Beijing's policy decisions to this day. In response to China's slowing economy in recent years, Chinese President Xi Jinping proposed the Belt and Road Initiative (BRI), an initiative aimed at integrating the Eurasian continent and expanding the outlets and opportunities for China's excess production. Beyond the geopolitics and economics, a less discussed but nonetheless equally important development is the construction of the Digital Silk Road. The goal of the Digital Silk Road is to improve the internet infrastructure in Southeast Asia, Central Asia, the Middle East, and sub-Sahara Africa while promoting cooperation in electronic and satellite technology, e-commerce, and the development of smart cities. As such, a number of high-tech companies, including Baidu, Alibaba, Tencent, and Jing Dong, share the position of the government in expanding the influence of China through the promotion of China's telecommunication technology across the world.

A potential challenge of China's tech industry converging with the government position on the means of spreading Chinese influence is the effect of such phenomenon in other countries. For example, in Southeast Asia, where many Chinese high-tech companies have a footing, many governments in the region came to adopt or imitate the cybersecurity policies of China. In 2015, Thailand announced its desire to establish a censorship tool similar to China's Great Firewall, a wish that eventually fell short due to strong opposition from the population. In 2017, Indonesia adopted a law that demanded the localization of data collected by foreign companies. In 2019, Vietnam established a set of cybersecurity laws that boasts many similarities with its Chinese counterpart. Noting the developments, it is not difficult to make the connection between Chinese companies and Southeast Asian governments – how the former can influence and support the latter in cyber control and censorship – and how such challenge may be further strengthened with China's push for the Digital Silk Road.

Suggested reading

Austin, G. (2014). *Cyber Policy in China (China Today)*. Cambridge: Polity Press.

Austin, G. (2018). *Cybersecurity in China*. Cham: Springer. https://thediplomat.com/tag/china-cybersecurity/

Wagner, D. (2019, May 13). "What China's Cybersecurity Law Says about the Future," *International Policy Digest*. https://intpolicydigest.org/2019/05/13/what-china-s-cybersecurity-law-says-about-the-future/

Yang, Z. (2019, October 30). "China Cybersecurity," *The Diplomat*. https://thediplomat.com/tag/china-cybersecurity/

References

Austin, G. (2016, September 8). "Mapping and Evaluating China's Cyber Power," Lau China Institute, King's College London. www.unsw.adfa.edu.au/australian-centre-for-cyber -security/sites/accs/files/uploads/Greg_Austin_Chinapercent27s_Cyber_Power_Policy_Papers-Issue-2.pdf

BBC News. (2015, December 28). "China Passes Controversial New Anti-Terror Laws." www.bbc.com/news/world-asia-china-35188137

Bennett, C. (2015, May 8). "China Wants Cyber 'Sovereignty' in Latest National Security Law," *The Hill*. http://thehill.com/policy/cybersecurity/241420-china-wants-cyber-sovereignty-in-latest-national-security-law

Blanchard, B. (2015, December 28). "China Passes Controversial Counter-Terrorism Law," *Reuters*. www.reuters.com/article/us-china-security/china-passes-controversial-counter-terrorism-law-idUSKBN0UA07220151228

Chan, S. (2018, January 15). *Cybersecurity Under Xi Jinping*. Los Angeles, CA: Center for the Digital Future. www.digitalcenter.org/wp-content/uploads/2018/01/Cybersecurity-under-Xi-Jinping-analysis.pdf

Chang, A. (2014). *Warring State China's Cybersecurity Strategy*. Washington, DC: Center for a New American Security.

China Daily. (2010, June 9). "The Internet in China White Paper." www.chinadaily.com.cn/cndy/2010-06/09/content_9952206.htm

China Daily. (2015, December 21). "Infographic: Achievements of the 2nd WIC." www.chinadaily.com.cn/business/tech/2015-12/21/content_22761073.htm

China Daily. (2017, July 20). "China's Digital Economy Surges 18.9 per cent, Drives Growth." www.chinadaily.com.cn/business/2017-07/20/content_30179729.htm

Clapper, J. R. (2013, March 12). *Statement for the Record Worldwide Threat Assessment of the US Intelligence Community*. Washington, DC: US Office of the Director of National Intelligence. www.dni.gov/files/documents/Intelligence per cent20Reports/2013 per cent20ATA per cent20SFR per cent20for per cent20SSCI per cent2012 per cent20Mar per cent202013.pdf

Clarke, R. A. & Knake, R. K. (2010). *Cyber War: The Next Threat to National Security and What to Do About It*. New York: Harper Collins.

Costello, J. (2016, February 8). "The Strategic Support Force: China's Information Warfare Service," *Jamestown Foundation*. https://jamestown.org/program/the-strategic-support-force-chinas-information-warfare-service/

Creemers, R. (2017, January 10). "Is China's Cybersecurity Law Visionary?" *China-US Focus*. http://cn.chinausfocus.com/peace-security/20170110/11856.html#eng

CSIS. (n.d.). "China Cyber Outlook." www.csis.org/programs/technology-policy-program/technology-and-innovation/cybersecurity-and-governance/china

Cyberspace Administration of China. (2014a, February 25). "Xi Jinping tan guanyu jiakuai wanshan hulianwang guanli lingdao tizhi" ("Xi Jinping discussed the hastening of the improvement of the internet management and leadership system"). www.cac.gov.cn/2014-02/25/c_133142284.htm

Cyberspace Administration of China. (2016, December 27). "Guojia wangluo kongjian anquan zhanlue" ("National Cyberspace Security Strategy"). www.cac.gov.cn/2016-12/27/c_1120195926.htm

First Post. (2016, March 18). "China Launches First Cybersecurity Organisation." www.firstpost.com/tech/news-analysis/china-launches-first-cybersecurity-organisation-3679171.html

FlorCruz, J. A. & Sue, L. (2014, April 24). "From Snail Mail to 4G, China Celebrates 20 Years of Internet Connectivity," *CNN*. https://edition.cnn.com/2014/04/23/world/asia/china-internet-20th-anniversary/index.html

Gechlik, M. (2017). *Appropriate Norms of State Behavior in Cyberspace: Governance in China and Opportunities for US Businesses*. Washington, DC: Hoover Institution.

Goldkorn, J. (2012, August 2) "The Internet," *The China Story*. www.thechinastory.org/keyword/the-internet/; https://www.firstpost.com/tech/news-analysis/china-launches-first-cybersecurity-organisation-3679171.html

Inkster, N. (2016). *China's Cyber Power*. London: The International Institute for Strategic Studies.

Internet Live States. (2020). "China Internet Users." www.internetlivestats.com/internet-users/china/

Kowalewski, A. (2017, October 27). "China's Evolving Cybersecurity Strategy," *Georgetown Security Studies Review*. http://georgetownsecuritystudiesreview.org/2017/10/27/chinas-evolving-cybersecurity-strategy/

Lampton, D. M. (2014). *Following the Leader: Ruling China, from Deng Xiaoping to Xi Jinping*. Berkeley, CA: University of California Press.

Lindsay, J. R. (2014/2015). "The Impact of China on Cybersecurity," *International Security*, *39*(3): 7–40.

Livingston, S. D. (2015, April 22). "Will China's New Anti-Terrorism Law Mean the End of Privacy?" www.chinafile.com/reporting-opinion/viewpoint/will-chinas-new-anti-terrorism-law-mean-end-privacy

Ministry of Industry and Information Technology of the PRC. (2016, February 14). "Provisions on the Administration of Online Publishing Services." www.miit.gov.cn/n1146295/n1146557/n1146619/c4639081/content.html

Mozur, P. (2016, November 8). "China's Internet Controls Will Get Stricter, to Dismay of Foreign Business," *The New York Times*. www.nytimes.com/2016/11/08/business/international/china-cyber-security-regulations.html

National Internet Emergency Center. (2017). "2016 Nian Zhongguo Hulianwang Wanglu Anquan Taishi Zongshu."

National People's Congress. (2015, July 7). "National Security Law of the People's Republic of China." www.npc.gov.cn/npc/xinwen/2015-07/07/content_1941161.htm

Nye, J. (2010, May). "Cyber Power," *Harvard College*. http://belfercenter.ksg. harvard.edu/files/cyber-power.pdf

O' Brien, R. (2016, May 25). *What to Make of the Newly Established Cyber Security Association of China*. Washington, DC: Center for Strategic and International Studies. www.csis.org/analysis/what-make-newly-established-cybersecurity-association-china

Panda, A. (2015, July 1). "The Truth about China's New National Security Law," *The Diplomat*. https://thediplomat.com/2015/07/the-truth-about-chinas-new-national-security-law/

Paulson, H. M. (2015). *Dealing with China: An Insider Unmasks the New Economic Superpower*. New York: Hachette Book Group.

PC World. (2004, May 17). "China Celebrates 10 Years of Being Connected to the Internet." www.pcworld.idg.com.au/article/128099/china_celebrates_10_years_being_connected_internet/

PEN America. (2016), "Darkened Screen: Constraints on Foreign Journalists in China." https://pen.org/sites/default/files/PEN_foreign_journalists_report_FINAL_online per cent5B1 per cent5D.pdf

People's Daily. (2016, June 23). "Guoqu yinian woguo wangmin yin wanglu anquan shijian zaocheng jingji sunshi da 915 yi yuan" ("In the Past Year, Chinese Netizens Suffered an Economic Loss of 915 Million RMB Due to Cybersecurity Incidents"). http://sn.people.com.cn/n2/2016/0623/c190199-28556169.html

Perlez, J. & Mozur, P. (2016, June 29). "Lu Wei, China's Internet Czar, Will Step Down from Post," *The New York Times*. www.nytimes.com/2016/06/30/business/international/china-internet-lu-wei.html?_ga=2.36365474.346945526.1525389466-1633828418.1483632849

Raud, M. (2016, August). *China and Cyber: Attitudes, Strategies, Organisation*. Tallinn, Estonia: NATO CCDCOE. https://ccdcoe.org/sites/default/files/multimedia/pdf/CS_organisation_CHINA_092016_FINAL.pdf

Rui, Z. (2015, December 17). "China Headlines: Xi Slams' Double Standards, Advocates Shared Future in Cyberspace," *CCTV*. http://english.cntv.cn/2015/12/17/ARTI1450334752126739.shtml

Singh, A. P. (2016, March 29). *China's First Anti-Terrorism Law: An Analysis*. New Delhi, India: Institute for Defense Studies and Analyses. www.idsa.in/idsacomments/china-first-anti-terrorism-law_apsingh_290316

Statista. (2020). "Number of Internet Users in China from 2017 to 2023." www.statista.com/statistics/278417/number-of-internet-users-in-china/

Swartz, D. (2011, April 18). "Jasmine in the Middle Kingdom: Autopsy of China's (Failed) Revolution," *China Digital Times*. https://chinadigitaltimes.net/2011/04/jasmine-in-the-middle-kingdom-autopsy-of-chinas-failed-revolution/

The Economic Times. (2014, November 19). "Chinese President Xi Jinping Calls for International Cooperation on Cyberspace Security." http://economictimes.indiatimes.com/news/international/world-news/chinese-president-xi-jinping-calls-for-international-cooperation-on-cyberspace-security/articleshow/45205445.cms

The Economic Times. (2018, January 31). "China's Online Population Climbs to 772 Million." https://economictimes.indiatimes.com/news/international/world-news/chinas-online-population-climbs-to-772-million/articleshow/62726168.cms?from=mdr

The State Council of the People's Republic of China. (2014, August 25). "Ministry of Public Security." english.www.gov.cn/state_council/2014/09/09/content_281474986284154.htm

The US Chamber of Commerce. (2016, September 1). "Preventing Deglobalization: An Economic and Security Argument for Free Trade and Investment in ICT." www.uschamber.com/sites/default/files/documents/files/preventing_deglobalization_1.pdf

Thomas, T. L. (2009). "Nation-State Cyber Strategies: Examples from China and Russia," in F. D. Kramer, S. H. Starr & L. K. Wentz (eds.), *Cyberpower and National Security* (pp. 465–466). Lincoln: University of Nebraska Press.

Xinhua Net. (2016, August 6). "Xinjiang Issues China's First Local Counterterrorism Law." www.xinhuanet.com/english/2016-08/06/c_135567634.htm

Xu, B. & Albert, E. (2017, February 17). *Media Censorship in China*. Washington, DC: Council on Foreign Relations. www.cfr.org/backgrounder/media-censorship-china

Yuxiao, L. & Lu, X. (2015). "China's Cybersecurity Situation and the Potential for International Cooperation," in J. R. Lindsay, T. M. Chueng & D. S. Reveron (eds.), *China and Cybersecurity: Espionage, Strategy, and Politics in the Digital Domain* (pp. 225–241). New York: Oxford University Press.

Zhou, Z. (2015, December). "China's Draft Cybersecurity Law," *China Brief*, *15*(24). https://jamestown.org/program/chinas-draft-cybersecurity-law/.

Zhu, H. (2016, November 30). "China's New 'Cybersecurity' Rules Look Like Cyberprotectionism Instead," *The Diplomat*. http://thediplomat.com/2016/11/chinas-new-cybersecurity-rules-look-like-cyberprotectionism-instead/

25

CYBERSECURITY IN A ONE-PARTY STATE

Policies and implications for Vietnam's economy and online freedom

Phan Le

Introduction

In recent years Vietnam has emerged as one of the most promising and dynamic markets globally for information and communications technology (ICT) services. The number of Internet users grew 28 per cent in 2017 to reach 64 million, including 55 million users of social media (Kemp, 2018). Ninety-one per cent of the population use smartphones with an average Internet access of 25 hours per week (Export, 2018). There are currently 23 million people in the country who frequently use online shopping and this number will only continue to rise as more people are becoming familiar with e-commerce platforms such as Lazada, Tiki, or Shopee (Vietnamnet, 2018).

The rapid rate of Internet penetration has led to a boom of e-commerce activities. In 2017 alone, revenue from retail e-commerce rose 35 per cent – a rate that is expected to continue until at least 2020 (DTI News, 2018). In the same year, affiliate marketing[1] experienced an even more impressive growth of 200 per cent. The huge potential for e-commerce has attracted global investments into the country. In 2017, the Chinese e-commerce giant, Alibaba, invested over US$2 billion into the popular e-commerce site Lazada (Cheok, 2018). A year later, Amazon announced partnership with the Vietnam E-commerce Association (VECOM) in order to launch its first e-commerce services in the country (Nikkei, 2018). A recent forecast by VECOM sees a doubling of total e-commerce value within the next four years, from US$5 billion to US$10 billion by 2021 (Vietnamnet, 2018).

Further, the ICT sector is becoming a key driver of employment generation. During 2012–2017, the number of ICT jobs soared by 2.5 times and the sector has consistently led recruitment demand among all industries, according to the human-resource consulting firm Navigos. As of 2017 there were 600,000 people working in ICT, half of which were in the software and digital media industry; the figure will continue to grow as recruitment demand in the sector is forecasted to reach 1.2 million by 2020 (Navigos, 2017).

The rapid growth of the ICT sector, however, increases the country's exposure to cyberattacks and cybercrimes. In 2015, the Kaspersky Cyberthreat Real-time Map ranked Vietnam as the third most attacked country globally and fourth in terms of spam sending (Kaspersky, 2015). The domestic cybersecurity firm BKAV warned that 30 per cent of the country's banking websites had vulnerabilities, two thirds of which were in the dangerous and high level, and 85 per cent of computers in Vietnam suffered virus infection via USB (Duc, 2015). In July 2016, hackers attacked the computer system of the national flag-carrier Vietnam Airlines and leaked personal information of over 400,000 customers (Vietnamnews, 2016).

In light of these serious incidents, the Vietnamese government has quickly made cybersecurity its foremost priority. A series of strategies and policies has been enacted since 2010, such as Decision No. 63/QD-Ttg in 2010 approving the national planning on development of digital information security through 2020; the 2015 Law on cyberinformation security; Decision No. 05/2017/QD-Ttg on emergency response plans to ensure national cyberinformation security; or the most recent 2018 Cybersecurity Law. The government also encourages domestic firms to supply cybersecurity solutions to its digital economy development projects, such as the digital government development plan for 2018–2020, orientation towards 2025; or the recently approved sustainable smart city development plan for the period 2018–2025 with vision towards 2030.

Additionally, for the ruling Communist Party of Vietnam (CPV), the rise of online dissent through social media platforms is considered a challenge to its political legitimacy. As a consequence, the country's cybersecurity policies also include the regulation of informational content deemed harmful for the one-party regime. In other words, prioritizing cybersecurity is essential to ensure the security of the Party itself, whose power is affirmed in the 2013 Constitution as the sole "force leading the State and society."[2] The development of Vietnam's cybersecurity policies thus has important implications not only for its economy but also for online freedom of Vietnamese citizens.

The rest of the chapter is structured as follows. Section two reviews the evolution of Vietnam's cybersecurity framework through two periods, prior to 2010 and from 2010 to date. Section three assesses the implications of cybersecurity policies on Vietnam's economy and online freedom. The last section concludes.

Vietnam's cybersecurity framework

This section provides a comprehensive assessment of Vietnam's cybersecurity framework in two periods, prior to 2010 and from 2010 onwards. Notable cybersecurity-related strategies and policies are summarized and discussed. The section also analyzes the government's evolving view towards cybersecurity, and the comprehensiveness of objectives and proposed solutions in key cybersecurity documents.[3]

Prior to 2010

Before 2010, cybersecurity often took a back seat in national ICT strategies and policies (see, Table 25.1). There was yet to be a law[4] promulgated by the National Assembly, the country's legislative branch, that specifically targeted this topic. Many important ICT policies, such as the Prime Minister's Decision No. 246/2005 approving Vietnam's ICT development strategy to 2010 with orientation towards 2020, contain no section on cybersecurity.

Cybersecurity contents in this period, if present, lack both breadth and depth. Without clear and holistic objectives, various narrow aspects of cybersecurity are addressed in different policy documents, such as the Law No. 51/2005/QH11 containing a section on data security in e-transactions; the Law No. 67/2006/QH11 including provisions on protection of legitimate rights and interests of users of ICT products and services, the protection of the ".vn" domain name, protection of intellectual property rights in the ICT domain, prevention of spam and harmful software, and protection of children from accessing

Table 25.1 Notable Cybersecurity-Related Policies in Vietnam Prior to 2010

Document	Title	Issuing Authority	Key Cybersecurity Contents	Status
Decision No. 71/ 2004/QD-BCA (A11)	On ensuring safety and security in activities of managing, providing and using Internet services in Vietnam	Ministry of Public Security	**Chapter II** includes provisions on responsibilities of Internet service-providing enterprises, organizations and individuals participating in Internet activities, Ministries of Public Security and the General Department of Security. **Article 13** specifies sanctions for violations of regulations on information safety and security in activities of managing, providing and using Internet services, in accordance with *Decree No. 55/2001/ ND-CP* on the management, provision and use of Internet services, which was replaced in 2008 by Decree No. 97/2008/ND-CP.	Active
Law No. 51/ 2005/QH11	On e-transactions	National Assembly	**Chapter VI** includes provisions on security, safety, protection of data messages, confidentiality in e-transactions, and stipulates responsibility of online service-providing organizations (upon the request of competent state agencies). *Decree No. 26/2007/ND-CP* details the implementation of this Law.	Active
Law No. 67/ 2006/QH11	On information technology	National Assembly	**Section 4 (Chapter IV)** includes provisions on protection of legitimate rights and interests of users of ICT products and services; protection of ".vn" domain name; protection of intellectual property rights in the ICT domain; prevention of spam and harmful software; and protection of children from accessing harmful online information. **Chapter V** stipulates the settlement of disputes and handling of violations in the ICT domain.	Active
Decree No. 64/ 2007/ND-CP	On IT application in state agencies' operations	Government	**Section 3 (Chapter III)** includes provisions on assurance of state agencies' information safety in the network environment, such as procedures to assure data safety; process of managing technical	Active

(Continued)

Table 25.1 (Cont.)

Document	Title	Issuing Authority	Key Cybersecurity Contents	Status
			infrastructure safety; responsibility to settle and overcome information safety-related incidents; and coordination of activities of urgent rescue, fight against attacks and terrorism on the network. **Chapter IV** stipulates functions and tasks of different state units in the organization of IT application, i.e. heads of state agencies, specialized IT units, chief IT officers, Government Cipher Committee, and competent ministries.	
Decree No. 63/ 2007/ND-CP	On sanctioning of administrative violations in the IT domain	Government	**Chapter II** specifies various acts of violating regulations on IT application, IT development, measures to ensure IT application and development, procedures to report and submit to supervision and inspection of competent state agencies, and the corresponding legal penalties for each violation. **Chapter III** stipulates the competence and procedures for sanctioning administrative violations in the IT domain.	Expired in 2014
Decree No. 73/ 2007/ND-CP	On activities of studying, producing, trading, and using cryptography to protect information not classified as state secrets	Government	**Chapter II** stipulates the rights and obligations of organizations and individuals participating in activities of studying civil cryptography, producing, trading, and using civil cryptography products. **Chapter III** regulates state management on civil cryptography, including responsibilities of the Government Cipher Committee and of competent ministries, sectors and provincial/municipal People's Committees **Chapter IV** guides the inspection, examination, handling of violations and settlement of complaints and denunciations	Expired in 2016
Decree No. 90/ 2008/ND-CP	Against spam	Government	**Chapter III** stipulates the responsibilities of electronic mail service	Active,

(Continued)

Table 25.1 (Cont.)

Document	Title	Issuing Authority	Key Cybersecurity Contents	Status
			providers, Internet access service providers, organizations, and individuals sending text messages and/or using text message advertisement services in fighting electronic mail spam, including supplying information to state agencies upon request. **Chapter IV** specifies procedures for complaints, denunciations, and handling of violations, including penalties for different types of spam-related violations.	revised in 2012
Decree No. 97/ 2008/ND-CP	On the management, provision and use of Internet services and electronic information on the Internet	Government	**Chapter I** specifies prohibited acts in the provision and use of Internet services, such as opposing the State, undermining national security and social order and safety, or sowing hatred and conflict between nations, ethnic groups, and religions. **Chapter IV** regulates the distribution of electronic newspapers and publications on the Internet; licensing and revocation of licenses of general websites; and registration of the provision of online social services.	Expired in 2013
Law No. 41/ 2009/QH12	On telecommunications	National Assembly	**The Ministry of Information and Communications** assumes the leading responsibility for, and coordinates with the Ministry of National Defense, the Ministry of Public Security, and competent agencies in assuring the safety of telecommunications infrastructure and information security in telecommunications activities. **Article 12** specifies prohibited acts in telecommunications activities, such as opposing the State of the Socialist Republic of Vietnam, propagating and inciting violence, debauchery, depraved lifestyle, crimes, social evils, and superstitious practices. Detailed implementation of the Law is included in *Decree No. 25/ 2011/ND-CP*.	Active

Source: Author's compilation.

harmful online information; Decree No. 64/2007/ND-CP introducing provisions on assurance of state agencies' information safety in the network environment; Decree No. 63/2007/ND-CP sanctioning administrative violations in the IT domain; Decree No. 73/2007/ND-CP regulating the management, inspection, examination, handling of violations, and settlement of complaints in the domain of civil cryptography; Decree No. 90/2008/ND-CP containing provisions on fighting electronic mail spams; or Decree No. 97/2008/ND-CP regulating the distribution of electronic newspapers and publications on the Internet, licensing and revocation of licenses of general websites, and registration of the provision of online services.

However, there remained important aspects of cybersecurity that were not sufficiently addressed during this period. Cyberinformation was not classified by order of secrecy and as a consequence there was no clear procedure to protect different types of information. In addition, many cybercrimes were not mentioned in the laws. The 1999 Penal Code did not have a separate section on cybersecurity, and only three broad types of cybercrimes were listed: (1) Creating and spreading computer virus programs (Article 224); (2) Breaching regulations on operating and using computer networks (Article 225); and (3) Illegally using information in computer networks (Article 226). This left out common cybercrimes such as frauds in e-commerce or multi-level marketing, or spreading of malwares that are not computer viruses (i.e., adware, botnet, ransomware).[5] Sanctions for cybercrimes were disproportionate to the damage they could inflict and did not clearly distinguish different degrees of severity or between first-time offenders and recidivists. There was also no stipulation on the rights and responsibilities of firms providing cybersecurity products and services.

Further, policy measures to improve domestic cybersecurity capacity were scarce in this period. Only a few educational institutions offered formal qualification in cybersecurity. The government had yet to offer scholarships or set targets for cybersecurity training abroad. Programs to raise public awareness about cybersecurity remained lacking despite the rampant cybercrimes. IT infrastructures were undeveloped and dedicated cybersecurity bodies were few in number. Important ICT legislation did not specify coordination procedures among different governmental agencies in cyber emergency cases. International and regional cooperation efforts were still uncommon during this time.

From 2010

Since 2010, cybersecurity has become a foremost priority of the Vietnamese government. Policy documents in this period target cybersecurity more directly and holistically than before 2010 (see, Table 25.2). The first landmark legislation is the Prime Minister's Decision No. 63/QD-Ttg in 2010 approving the national planning on development of digital information security through 2020. Not only is this the first initiative that focuses directly on cybersecurity, but it also addresses the topic in a comprehensive manner. The Decision includes general objectives to 2020, short-term development objectives to 2015, proposed solutions to achieve the aforementioned objectives and specific tasks for competent ministries. The four general objectives to 2020 include safeguarding network and information infrastructure safety; ensuring safety for data and IT applications; developing human resources and raising awareness about information security; and ensuring an effective legal environment for information security. Six years later, in 2016 the new Prime Minister introduced Decision No. 898/QD-Ttg which adds more specific objectives to be achieved by 2020, such as reducing the rate of incidents of cyberinformation security loss due to poor awareness, subjectiveness, and carelessness to be below 50 per cent; removing Vietnam from the list of 20 countries with the highest rate of

Table 25.2 Notable Cybersecurity Policies in Vietnam Since 2010

Document	Title	Issuing Authority	Key Cybersecurity Contents	Status
Decision No. 63/ QD-Ttg in 2010	Approving the national planning on development of digital information security through 2020	Prime Minister	The Decision sets out the general objectives through 2020 in four areas: network and information infrastructure safety; safety for data and IT applications; human resources development and public awareness raising for cybersecurity; and legal environment for information security. It also establishes development objectives through 2015 and proposes solutions to achieve these objectives.	Active
Decree No. 72/ 2013/ND-CP	On the management, provision and use of Internet services and online information	Government	**Article 20** classifies websites in terms of electronic newspapers; news websites; internal websites; private websites; and specialized websites. Electronic newspapers must comply with the laws on press, publication, and advertising. News websites must specify authors or managing agencies of the official sources. The remaining three types are not allowed to post news. **Article 21** requires online service providers to reveal users' personal information at the request of competent authorities. *Decree No. 27/2018/ ND-CP* revises this Decree.	Active
Decision No. 99/ QD-Ttg in 2014	Approving the Project "Training and development of human resources for information security to 2020"	Prime Minister	Targets to be achieved by 2020: (a) Sending 300 lecturers and researchers for information security training abroad, 100 of whom are at the PhD level; (b) Training 2,000 information security graduates at the Bachelor's and higher levels; (c) Sending 1,500 information security personnel for short-term training abroad; and (d) Organizing short-term information security and IT training for 10,000 cybersecurity officers in governmental agencies.	Active
Law No. 86/ 2015/QH13	On cyberinformation security	National Assembly	**Chapter II** on assurance of cyberinformation security includes four sections on cyberinformation protection; protection of personal information; protection of information systems; and	Active

(*Continued*)

Table 25.2 (Cont.)

Document	Title	Issuing Authority	Key Cybersecurity Contents	Status
			prevention of online information conflicts. **Article 21** of this Chapter for the first time classifies security grades of information systems into five classes.	
Decision No.898/ 2016/ QD-Ttg	Approving the orientation, objectives and duties to ensure cyberinformation security for the period 2016–2020	Prime Minister	This Decision sets out four additional targets for the period 2016–2020: reduce the rate of incidents of cyberinformation security loss due to people's poor awareness and carelessness to be below 50 per cent; remove Vietnam from the list of 20 countries with the highest rate of malware and spam infection in the world; complete the technical regulation and standard system and the inspection and assessment system of information security; and develop at least five information security products with Vietnamese brand widely used in domestic market.	Active
Law No. 12/ 2017/QH14	On amendments to the Penal Code No. 100/2015/ QH13	National Assembly	This Law revises **Section 2, Chapter XXI** of the 2015 Penal Code, which specifies sanctions for offences against regulations on IT and telecommunications network. For example, it removes Article 292 of the 2015 Penal Code on illegal provision of services on computer network.	Active
Decision No. 05/ 2017/QD-Ttg	Providing for emergency response plans to ensure national cyberinformation security	Prime Minister	**Chapter II** assigns duties to implement emergency response plans to different units, including the National Steering Committee; the Ministry of Information and Communications; Steering Committees on IT of ministries, ministerial-level agencies, the Government's affiliates and People's Committees of provinces or central-affiliated cities; and specialized incident response units.	Active
Decision No. 1622/2017/QD-Ttg	Approving the project on strengthening the operations of incident response network, enhancing the capacity of	Prime Minister	The Decision sets out orientation towards 2025 and objectives to 2020, which includes strengthening the capacity of the Vietnam Computer Emergency Response Team (VNCERT); enhancing the operations of incident	Active

(Continued)

Table 25.2 (Cont.)

Document	Title	Issuing Authority	Key Cybersecurity Contents	Status
	public personnel and units specialized in incident response and national cyberinformation security through 2020		response network and specialized units; improving the capacity to monitor, collect, analyze, detect, and respond to cyber incidents; developing human resources for emergency response to ensure national cyberinformation security; raising public awareness and disseminating knowledge on cyber threats and plans to ensure national cyberinformation security; and promoting stronger international cooperation and better coordination among different computer emergency response teams from all over the world.	
Law No. 24/ 2018/QH14	On cybersecurity	National Assembly	**Article 26** requires domestic and foreign providers of telecommunications and Internet services to store data of users in Vietnam within the country for a specific period of time. Foreign enterprises must open branches or representative offices in Vietnam. Online service providers have the responsibility to provide users' information for professional security forces of the Ministry of Public Security upon request in writing to serve investigation into cybersecurity violations.	Active

Source: Author's compilation.

malware and spam infection in the world; and developing at least five Vietnamese information security products widely used in the domestic market.

In addition, many important aspects of cybersecurity that were inadequately addressed before 2010 are now covered in better details. The role of cybersecurity is recognized at the law-level – the second highest after the Constitution – with the introduction of the 2015 Law on Cyberinformation Security and the 2018 Cybersecurity Law. The 2015 Penal Code also adds a full new section on offences against regulations on information technology and telecommunications network. New cybercrimes are updated into the Code, with a wider range of sanctions based on degrees of severity and recidivism. Each cybersecurity law is accompanied with several government decrees and ministerial circulars guiding its implementation.

Further, cybersecurity concepts are better clarified in post-2010 policies. The 2018 Cybersecurity Law defines for the first time the concepts of "cyberattack," "cyberterrorism," and "cyberespionage" and specifies duties of competent authorities in the prevention and response to each cybercrime. Based on order of secrecy, the 2015 Law on Cyberinformation

Security classifies information into five security grades, each of which has a different protection mechanism: *Grade one* means that when an information system is sabotaged, it will harm lawful rights and interests of organizations or individuals but will not harm public interests, social order and safety, or national defense and security; *Grade two* means that when an information system is sabotaged, it will seriously harm lawful rights and interests of organizations or individuals or will harm public interests but will not harm social order and safety or national defense and security; *Grade three* indicates that when an information system is sabotaged, it will seriously harm production, public interests, and social order and safety, or will harm national defense and security; *Grade four* is when an information system is sabotaged, it will cause extremely serious harms to public interests and social order and safety or will seriously harm national defense and security; and *Grade five* means that when an information system is sabotaged, it will cause extremely serious harm to national defense and security.

In order to achieve the aforementioned objectives, Vietnamese policymakers have been implementing solutions in five areas: public awareness raising; international cooperation; cybersecurity assessment; human resources development; and organizational restructuring. Decision No. 893/QD-Ttg in 2015, for example, stresses the need to increase *cybersecurity awareness* in the general population, especially the youth, through incorporating cybersecurity materials into informatics courses and extracurricular activities for middle and high school. The Vietnam Information Security Day has been held annually by VNISA, the Authority of Information Security (AIS), the Vietnam Computer Emergency Response Team (VNCERT) and the Cyber Operations Command.[6] The annual event hosts various activities such as the national contest "Students with Information Security" for all universities and colleges, a series of workshops on the latest issues of cybersecurity, and a poll to select the highest quality domestic information security products and services.

Vietnam has also actively participated in *international and regional cooperation* efforts. The country is one of the founding members of the Global Forum on Cyber Expertise – a platform whereby countries can exchange experience and best practices on enhancing cybersecurity capacity (Global Forum on Cyber Expertise, 2018). Decision No. 1622/2017/QD-Ttg requires VNCERT to participate in at least three international cybersecurity drills annually. In addition, Vietnam has signed a memorandum of understanding on cybersecurity cooperation with Israel, Russia, India, and the Czech Republic.

In terms of *cybersecurity assessment*, on an annual basis VNISA reports the Vietnam's Information Security Index, which is adapted from the South Korea's model, while the Ministry of Information and Communications publishes its trademark Vietnam ICT White Book, including an important chapter on information security. Furthermore, in 2016 the Prime Minister issued Decision No. 898/QD-Ttg in 2016 approving the orientation, objectives, and duties to ensure cyberinformation security for the period 2016–2020. The Decision requires the Ministry of Information and Communications to coordinate with the Ministry of National Defense and the Ministry of Public Security to establish an interdisciplinary working group for annual inspection of cyberinformation security of ministries, sectors, and localities. The Ministry of Information and Communications is also in charge of coordinating with ministries, sectors, and enterprises to form a rapid response group to analyze and respond to malware incidents, and of coordinating with VNISA to classify and assess the quality of cybersecurity products and to annually evaluate cybersecurity practices in government agencies. Reports on such coordination must be submitted to the Prime Minister.

Regarding *human resources development*, in 2014 the Prime Minister introduced Decision No. 99/QD-Ttg approving the project "Training and development of human resources for information security to 2020," often referred to as "Project 99." This cornerstone project sets out clear targets to be achieved by 2020: (a) Sending 300 lecturers and researchers for information security training abroad, 100 of whom are at the PhD level; (b) Training 2,000 information security graduates at the Bachelor's and higher levels; (c) Sending 1,500 information security personnel for short-term training abroad; and (d) Organizing short-term information security and IT training for 10,000 cybersecurity officers in governmental agencies. To achieve these targets, the government has made cybersecurity a priority field to be considered for government scholarship schemes such as Project 911 on doctoral training for university and college lecturers or Project 599 on overseas training of public officials using state budgets. The government has also cooperated with eight domestic universities to open full degree courses on cybersecurity.

In terms of *organizational structure*, Vietnam has formed a number of professional units to handle different cybersecurity areas and stipulated coordination procedures among these units. Specifically, there are three major ministries in charge of cybersecurity, namely the Ministry of Information and Communications, the Ministry of Public Security, and the Ministry of National Defense.[7]

Under the Ministry of Information and Communications are four dedicated cybersecurity bodies: AIS; VNCERT; the Vietnam Internet Network Information Center (VNNIC); and the National Electronic Authentication Center (NEAC). Established in 2014, AIS serves as the key advising body to the Minister of Information and Communications. Some of its notable activities to date include the organization of seminars and training to improve capacity and disseminate knowledge on information security laws; tracking of attacks on domestic websites; organization of annual cybersecurity contests such as the White Hat Grand Prix; and participation in the oversight of Project 99 on developing human resources in cybersecurity domain. VNCERT, on the other hand, is responsible for the coordination of cyber incident responses nationwide; support for the establishment of CERTs in organizations and enterprises; and cooperation with foreign counterparts in annual events such as the Asia-Pacific Computer Emergency Rescue Teams (APCERT) drill, Japan-ASEAN drill, or the ASEAN CERTs Incident Drill (ACID). The longest-serving unit, VNNIC, manages the registration, suspension, revocation, and withdrawal of the national ".vn" domain names and collaborates with competent authorities in preventing the distribution of websites with international domain names that violate Vietnamese laws. Finally, NEAC manages the information security infrastructure for e-transaction activities, which includes digital signatures and electronic authentication.

Prior to August 2018, The Ministry of Public Security included three professional cybersecurity forces: under the General Department of Security were the Department of Network Security (A68) and the Department of Information Security and Communications (A87); and under the General Department of Police was the Police Department for Prevention and Fight against High-Tech Crime (C50). A68, established in 2014, was the lead ministerial unit overseeing the management and administration of network and cyberinformation security. A87 specialized in state management of culture, information, and communications security. Some of its notable activities include detecting VoIP frauds involving domestic and/or foreign subjects; preventing messages aimed to harass, defame, or threaten senior leaders of the Party and the State; exposing false personation crimes; handling cases of state secret leakages through the press and the Internet; and requesting news organizations to modify or remove contents that violate Vietnamese laws. C50 focused on the prevention and fight against high-tech crimes such as online gambling, malware distribution, or online investment scams. Since August 2018, C50 has been merged into A68, while A87 into the Department of Internal Political Security (A83) as the government carried out a major restructuring of the Ministry of Public Security.

Under the Ministry of National Defense are three key cybersecurity forces: The Government Cipher Committee; the Cyberspace Operations Command (Cyber Command 86); and Force 47. Under direct supervision of the Minister of National Defense, the Government Cipher Committee assists the Minister in the management of cipher and encryption products to protect state secret information. The Cyber Command 86 was founded in 2017 from the previous Information Technology Department under the Joint General Staff of the People's Army of Vietnam. Its main task is to research and predict online wars in order to protect Vietnam's sovereignty on the Internet. The last unit, Force 47, is a cyber-warfare task force of 10,000 military personnel aimed to counter what the CPV deem as "wrong" views on the Internet (Parameswaran, 2018).

The establishment of multiple cybersecurity units necessitates the stipulation of coordination procedures among them. In recent years, further policies have been introduced in this direction, such as the Prime Minister's Decision No. 05/2017/QĐ-Ttg providing for emergency response plans to ensure national cyberinformation security. According to the Decision, the Ministry of Information and Communications serves as the Standing Committee of the National Steering Committee on Emergency Response. It directs VNCERT to receive, collect and process information and reports on incidents that cause national cyberinformation insecurity and propose response plans; the Ministry then makes decision on which response plans to select and takes charge of instructing emergency response activities. VNCERT serves as the national coordination center for incident response and has the rights to mobilize and coordinate members of the National Cyberinformation Security Incident Response Network, containing key cybersecurity forces across ministries such as AIS, VNCERT, VNNIC and the Authority of Central Posts from the Ministry of Information and Communications; A68, C50 from the Ministry of Public Security; and Information Technology Department (nowadays Cyber Command 86) and Government Cipher Committee from the Ministry of National Defense.

Implications for Vietnam's economy and online freedom

The economy

There are multiple ways in which cyberattacks can inflict serious economic harms. Intellectual property and confidential information may get leaked to unwanted parties. Stolen credit card records and personally identifiable information are exploited to commit online frauds. Compromised e-commerce and financial services cause serious disruption to business operations and reduce confidence in online activities. Hacked companies suffer damages to their reputation and stock market valuation, while having to divert resources from productive use to pay for recovery from cyberattacks or purchase cyberinsurance (Lewis, 2018).

Vietnam has been a victim of cybercrimes for years. According to the Ministry of Public Security, from 2010 to 2014, the Police Department of Prevention and Fighting against High-Tech Crimes (C50) had detected 11,476 incidents of cybercrimes involving 3,220 subjects, with total damage of more than US$1 billion (Nguyen, 2014). Computer malware infection in 2015 alone cost Vietnamese users an approximate US$400 million (Luan, 2016). Since 2010, more than 18,000 websites of organizations and private enterprises were hacked, including 1,083 websites of governmental agencies and educational institutions (Van, 2017). The number of cyberattacks have only increased in recent years and more critical infrastructures are being targeted, notably the hacking of Vietnam Airlines in 2016 or of the Co-operative Bank of Vietnam in 2018 (Bao, 2018).

In this context, the government's efforts to increase penalties for cybercrimes while upgrading domestic cybersecurity capacity are a welcoming move for the economy. The 2015 Penal Code, for instance, incorporates a full new section on offences against regulations on information technology and telecommunications networks, compared to the 1999 version. New cybercrimes are added to the Code, such as the manufacturing, trading, exchanging, giving instruments, equipment, software serving illegal purposes (Article 285); the illegal collection, possession, exchanging, trading, publishing of information about bank accounts (Article 291); the illegal provision of services on computer network or telecommunications network (Article 292); the illegal use of radio frequencies dedicated to emergency services, safety services, search and rescue, or national defense and security (Article 293); or the deliberate harmful interference of radio frequencies (Article 294). The maximum fine for cybercrimes was raised to VND5 billion while the maximum term of imprisonment up to 20 years.

Further, the economy has benefitted from important government programs to upgrade domestic cybersecurity capacity. VNISA's annual awards for high-quality information security products and services encourage domestic innovation in the field, which now includes top-notch products from private firms such as BKAV Mobile Security (BKAV), CMC Internet Security Enterprise (CMC InfoSec), CyRadar Internet Shield (FPT), SecurityBox 4Network (MVS), or VNCS Web Monitoring (VNCS). After three years implementing Project 99, nearly five thousand students and professionals have received cybersecurity training, eight key institutions[8] have open graduate degrees in information security, and 81 university lecturers and researchers have been sent abroad for advanced cybersecurity training in 11 different countries: Russia, France, Australia, Ireland, Singapore, New Zealand, Belgium, Italy, Hungary, Austria and the Czech Republic (Trong, 2018a). Through preferential procurement policies, the government opens up market opportunities for domestic cybersecurity firms. SecurityBox, for example, has been providing comprehensive cybersecurity solutions to the Ministry of Public Security, Ministry of National Defense, provincial Departments of Information and Communications, and large state-owned banks since 2015 (Thu, 2018). At the end of 2018, the new Minister of Information and Communications affirms the government vision for Vietnam to become a cybersecurity powerhouse in the near future (Trong, 2018b).

However, one economic problem with Vietnam's cybersecurity framework is the corruption and abuse of power by cybersecurity units themselves. In 2018, for example, police arrested a Major General and also the former Head of the Police Department for Prevention and Fight against High-Tech Crime for his ironic protection of a transnational gambling ring, which he was supposed to take down. The former Director General of the Police General Department was sentenced to nine years in prison for "abusing position and power while performing duties" in the same case (Vu, 2018). This is just one example in the many documented cases of abusing position and power in the Ministry of Public Security and the Ministry of National Defense.

Further, Vietnamese policymakers need to pay more attention to the potentially negative impacts of some cybersecurity policies on the country's economic development trajectory. Since coming into power in 2016, the current Prime Minister, Nguyen Xuan Phuc, has emphasized the importance of creating a conducive business environment for start-ups. Within a year, the country climbed 14 places in the World Bank's Ease of Doing Business ranking, rated 68th among 190 economies in 2017 (The World Bank, 2018). Thus, there were significant concerns about Article 292 in the 2015 Penal Code on the illegal provision of services on computer networks or telecommunications networks. The Article specifies fines of up to VND5 billion and maximum prison sentence of five years for any person who provides the following online services without a license or against a license: trading gold on accounts; electronic commerce exchange; multi-level marketing; payment services; online video games; and other services on computer networks or telecommunication networks as prescribed by law. This Article imposed a burdensome barrier of entry to ICT start-ups, whose new products often begin with a small pilot before scaling up. Requiring start-ups to obtain a license even just for a pilot phase raises the cost of entering the ICT market. This policy, if passed, would have likely stifled domestic innovation in the ICT sector and made start-ups register in other countries with a better business environment such as Singapore. Fortunately, the 2017 Law on amendments to the Penal Code invalidated this Article.

More recently, the Prime Minister's Directive No. 16/CT-Ttg in 2017 on strengthening Vietnam's ability to access the Fourth Industrial Revolution[9] warns against failures to catch up with global or regional development, and stresses the importance of enabling people and businesses to easily and fairly grasp the opportunities for digital content development. If this Directive is to be taken seriously, Vietnamese authorities should realize that a critical aspect of business operations in the digital age is the free flow of data. Article 26 in the 2018 Cybersecurity Law, however, goes against this direction. The Article requires all foreign online service providers to open branches or representative offices in Vietnam, and to store data of users in Vietnam *locally* for a specific time period for the purpose of data security.[10] Policymakers however should be cautious with this line of reasoning. As Vietnam's ICT infrastructures and digital capabilities are still relatively less-developed, storing data locally may make them *less* secure than on multinationals' cloud systems. More importantly, the country's growth trajectory in the past three decades testifies the importance of economic opening and lowering the costs of doing business (Vanham, 2018). Article 26, while already a watered-down version of its earlier draft, still obstructs data flow and raises the cost of business operations in the ICT sector. While Vietnam is not the only country with data localization requirement, it wastes a valuable opportunity to gain an upper hand in attracting quality foreign investments through an open business environment that supports free data flow.

Online freedom

The non-governmental organization, Freedom House, has consistently ranked Vietnam as "not free" in its freedom status. In 2018, the country scored 6/7 in freedom rating, 5/7 in civil liberties, and 7/7 in political rights, on a scale of 1–7 in which 7 means the least free nation (Freedom House, 2018). This should come as no surprise for anyone living in the country. Leadership of the ruling CPV is not freely elected and operates without openness and transparency. Corruption is rampant, putting the country in the 107th place out of 180 countries in the Corruption Perceptions Index 2017 (Transparency International, 2019). Courts at all levels are controlled by the CPV, thus undermining Article 103 of the Constitution which requires judges and assessors to be independent and to obey only the law (DFAT, 2017). Defense lawyers have to bear criminal responsibility for failing to report certain crimes of their own clients. All print and broadcast media are under state control, with increasing number of "banned subjects" for journalists (Civius, 2016). The once promised Protest Law has now been postponed for years. Human-rights non-governmental organizations (NGOs) are mostly banned while dissident voices are heavily suppressed (Freedom House, 2018).

In light of this, online platforms have become an important venue for Vietnamese citizens to exercise their freedom of expression or organize peaceful protests. In 2015, for example, Hanoi's plan to chop down and replace 6,700 "dangerous" and "unsightly" trees had to be suspended due to several mass protests organized by three separate Facebook groups – "6,700 people for 6,700 trees"; "Green Trees"; and "6,700 green trees" (Brown, 2015). Online petitions to protect online freedom in Vietnam or to stop environmentally harmful industrial projects have been signed by thousands of people (Change, 2018). Independent candidates for the National Assembly such as the well-known singer and activist Mai Khoi or the reputed journalist Tran Dang Tuan have utilized social media to rally support. More recently, in June 2018 thousands of Vietnamese took to the streets to protest against the draft Law on Special Economic Zones, which many believe would grant China too much influence in Vietnam's economy, and the Cybersecurity Law, which is viewed as a further repression of the country's already limited online freedom.

For the CPV, online dissent presents a challenge to its legitimacy. Similar to the undemocratic one-party China, cybersecurity in Vietnam is inseparable from political stability. The 2006 Law on Information Technology prohibits the supplying, exchanging, transmitting, storing, or using digital information to oppose the State of the Socialist Republic of Vietnam. The 2009 Law on Telecommunications reiterates this doctrine and forbids the use of telecommunication activities to act against the ruling CPV, whose power is reaffirmed in the 2013 Constitution as the sole "force leading the State and society." Anyone who creates, possesses or spreads digital information that oppose the CPV can face maximum fines of VND1 billion and prison sentence of up to 20 years.

The repression of online dissent is aided with the enaction of Decree No. 72/2013/ND-CP on the management, provision and use of Internet services and online information ("Decree 72"), and the 2018 Cybersecurity Law. Decree 72 is arguably the worst blow to online freedom in Vietnam. Its Article 25 requires social networking sites to ensure that their users provide full and accurate personal information including real names and contact details, making it unsafe to blog or comment critically on sensitive subjects. Similar to other laws, "opposing the State" and "slandering reputation of organizations," which are vaguely defined, are strictly prohibited. All electronic newspapers and news websites have to obtain government approval while social networking sites have to provide private information of users who act against the State at the request of competent authorities. The Cybersecurity Law, in addition, requires all domestic and foreign online service providers to store data of users in Vietnam within the country for a specific period of time and provide users' information upon request in writing from the Ministry of Public Security. In the name of protecting Vietnamese data privacy, this mandate allows cybersecurity forces to better track anyone who is critical of the government.[11] As of 2018, these cybersecurity-related laws have led to the arrests and criminal convictions of more than two hundred bloggers, lawyers, journalists, human rights, and land rights activists (Vietnam Human Rights Defenders, 2018).

Conclusion

As an emerging one-party economy, Vietnam has to confront a multitude of cybersecurity challenges both for its *emerging* economy and for its *one-party* regime. On the economic side, the ICT sector has been a driver of growth and employment in recent years, making Vietnam one of the most promising markets globally for ICT products and services. The rapid growth of the ICT sector has nevertheless outpaced the development of cybersecurity capacity, leaving the country highly vulnerable to cyberattacks and cybercrimes. On the political side, the rise of social media platforms poses a challenge for the ruling Communist Party, who views cybersecurity as inseparable from its own political security.

Recognizing these challenges, the Vietnamese government has made cybersecurity its top policy priority. Since the first landmark legislation in 2010, the government has targeted the issue more directly and holistically than in the pre-2010 period. The role of cybersecurity is recognized at the law-level, with the enactment of the 2015 Law on Cyberinformation Security and the 2018 Cybersecurity Law. More cybercrimes are updated into the 2015 Penal Code with increasing sanctions for dangerous crimes. Cyberinformation is classified into five security grades, each having separate protection protocols based on level of secrecy. More importantly, the government has carried out comprehensive policy solutions in five areas: public awareness raising; international cooperation; cybersecurity assessment; human resources development; and organizational restructuring.

While the government's efforts are encouraging, massive challenges still lie ahead. Within the cybersecurity domain, in 2017 Vietnam fell 25 places to the 101st position out of 193 countries in the Global Cybersecurity Index (Vietnamnews, 2017). The VNISA's Information Security Index also downgraded Vietnam's score from 59.9 per cent in 2016 to 46.8 per cent in 2017, due to the cyberattack on Vietnam Airlines and the widespread Wannacry ransomware that affected 1,900 computers in the country, making it one of the twenty most affected nations in the world (Kaspersky, 2017). Turning Vietnam into a cybersecurity powerhouse as the government envisions remains an elusive dream in the near future.

Furthermore, a number of cybersecurity policies are a threat to the country's online freedom and economic development. Online dissent is heavily suppressed, with more than two hundred bloggers, lawyers, and activists being taken into custody for their critiques of the ruling party, whose political survival is of utmost importance in the existing cybersecurity laws. On the economic side, data localization requirements reduce the attractiveness of the Vietnamese market to foreign tech investments, while the benefits for domestic data security are seriously doubtful. If the CPV truly cares for its own security, it should know that squeezing online freedom and hampering economic development only serve to damage the one-party legitimacy. If anything, the 2018 mass protests against the Cybersecurity Law should be its wake-up call.

Notes

1 Affiliate marketing is a performance-based arrangement whereby external websites (affiliates) carry out marketing efforts to generate more sales/traffic for other online retailers, who pay them commissions in return.
2 See, Article 4 of the 2013 Constitution of the Socialist Republic of Vietnam.
3 The analysis framework is loosely based on Candice Tran Dai (2017).
4 Law has the second highest legal validity in Vietnam, only after the Constitution.
5 Adware is a type of malware that tracks people's online behavior without consent in order to serve them advertisements accordingly. Botnets are networks of computers connected together to perform some repetitive tasks, which can be exploited for illegal purposes. Ransomware locks victims' computers or networks and forces them to pay a ransom.
6 Previously the Information Technology Department of the Ministry of National Defense.
7 Some other important players in cybersecurity include VNISA, the first non-profit organization in cybersecurity recognized by the State, or the National Committee for e-Government which advises the Prime Minister on mechanisms and policies to promote the development of digital government, digital economy, and digital society.
8 These are the Post and Telecommunications Institute of Technology; Academy of Cryptography Techniques; Institute of Military Technology; People's Security Academy; Hanoi University of Science and Technology; Hochiminh University of Information Technology; Hanoi University of Engineering and Technology; and Danang University of Science and Technology.

9 The Fourth Industrial Revolution is characterized by "a range of new technologies that are fusing the physical, digital and biological worlds, impacting all disciplines, economies and industries." (Schwab, 2017: 1)

10 This final Law is already a watered-down version of the earlier draft, which requires all foreign online service providers to "store their Vietnamese users' data exclusively in Vietnamese data centres" (Le, 2018: 1).

11 Similar regulations have been enacted in China and Russia. Chinese law requires data of Chinese users and organizations to be stored within the country in data centers operated by Chinese enterprises. In a similar fashion, Russia requires "operators" to collect, store, and process data of users in Russia using databases located within the country.

Suggested reading

Dai, C. T. (2015). "Cybersecurity in Vietnam: Formulation and Implementation of a New Strategy," *Hérodote*, 2(157): 126–140.

Le, V. T., Nguyen, P. L. & Ngo, Q. D. (n.d.). "Cybersecurity Maintenance in Vietnam in 4.0 Era." www.interpa.org/Upload/editor/files/Quoc-Dung per cent20NGO.pdf

Nguyen, T. (2019, January 4). "Vietnam's Controversial Cybersecurity Law Spells Tough Times for Activists." *The Diplomat.* https://thediplomat.com/2019/01/vietnams-controversial-cybersecurity-law-spells-tough-times-for-activists/

Williams, S. (2019, September 4). "Vietnam Cybersecurity Market to Reach USD$215 million," *SecurityBrief.* https://securitybrief.asia/story/vietnam-cybersecurity-market-to-reach-usd-215-million

References

Bao, A. (2018, October 16). "Website of Vietnam's Co-Op Bank Hit by Hack, $100,000 Ransom," *Tuoitre News.* https://tuoitrenews.vn/news/business/20181016/website-of-vietnams-coopbank-hit-by-hack-100000-ransom/47238.html

Brown, M. (2015, March 22). "Hundreds of Hanoians Protest Tree-chopping Plan," *VOA News.* www.voanews.com/a/hundreds-of-hanoians-hug-trees-to-protest-chopping-spree/2690180.html

Change. (2018). "Protect Online Freedom in Vietnam." www.change.org/p/google-inc-protect-online-freedom-in-vietnam

Cheok, J. (2018, March 20). "Alibaba Pumps US$2b into Lazada to Wage War in SEA e-Commerce Market," *Business Times.* www.businesstimes.com.sg/technology/alibaba-pumps-us2b-into-lazada-to-wage-war-in-sea-e-commerce-market

Civius. (2016, April 20). "Intolerance of Civil Society in Vietnam: An Interview with Penelope Faulkner from the Vietnam Committee on Human Rights." www.civicus.org/index.php/media-resources/news/interviews/893-intolerance-of-civil-society-in- vietnam-an-interview-with-penelope-faulkner-from-the-vietnam-committee-on-human-rights

Dai, C. T. (2015). "Cybersecurity in Vietnam: Formulation and Implementation of a New Strategy," *Hérodote*, 2(157): 126–140.

DFAT. (2017, June 21). "DFAT Country Information Report: Vietnam," *Department of Foreign Affairs and Trade.* https://dfat.gov.au/about-us/publications/Documents/country- information-report-vietnam.pdf

DTI News. (2018, April 8). "Vietnam Has Huge e-Commerce Potential." http://dtinews.vn/en/news/018/55936/vietnam-has-huge-e-commerce-potential.html

Duc, T. (2015, August 6). "30 per cent Website Ngân Hàng Tại Việt Nam Tồn Tại Lỗ Hổng." *CafeF.* http://cafef.vn/tai-chinh-ngan-hang/30-website-ngan-hang-tai-viet-nam-ton-tai-lo- hong-2015080620454167.chn

Export. (2018, May 7). "Vietnam – Information and Communication Technologies." www.export.gov/article?id=Vietnam-Information-Technology

Freedom House. (2018). "Vietnam Profile." https://freedomhouse.org/report/freedom-world/2018/vietnam

Human Rights Defenders. (2018, October, 1). "Vietnam Holds 246 Prisoners of Conscience: Now! Campaign." www.vietnamhumanrightsdefenders.net/2018/10/03/vietnam-holds-246-prisoners-of-conscience-nowcampaign/

Kaspersky. (2015, July 30). "Kaspersky Lab Reporting: Mobile Malware Has Grown Almost 3-Fold in Q2, and Cyberespionage Attacks Target SMB Companies." www.kaspersky.com/about/press-releases/2015_kaspersky-lab-reporting-mobile-malware-has-grown-almost-3-fold-in-q2-and-cyberespionage-attacks-target-smb-companies

Kaspersky. (2017, May 13). "WannaCry: Are You Safe?" www.kaspersky.com/blog/wannacry-ransomware/16518/

Kemp, S. (2018). "Digital in 2018," *We Are Social*. https://digitalreport.wearesocial.com/

Le, P. (2018). "Vietnam's New Internet Law Will Make the Economy Lag," *East Asia Forum*. February 22, 2018. www.eastasiaforum.org/2018/02/22/vietnams-new-internet-law- will-make-the-economy-lag/

Lewis, J. (2018, February). "Economic Impact of Cybercrime – No Slowing Down," *McAfee*. www.mcafee.com/enterprise/en-us/assets/reports/restricted/rp-economic-

Luan, T. (2016, January 12). "Vietnam Computer Users Lose $387 Million to Viruses: Report," *Thanhnien News*. http://www.thanhniennews.com/tech/vietnam-computer-users-lose-387-million-to-viruses-report-58017.html

Navigos. (2017, November). "VietnamWorks Publishes Report on Recruitment Demand and Labor Supply in Vietnam Market for the First Half 2017." www.navigosgroup.com/vietnamworks-publishes-report-recruitment-demand-labor-supply-vietnam-market-first-half-2017/

Nguyen, D. M. (2014, November 17). "Đặc Điểm Tội Phạm Học Của Tội Phạm Sử Dụng Công Nghệ Cao Và Giải Pháp Nâng Cao Hiệu Quả Phòng Ngừa, Đấu Tranh," *The People's Police*. http://csnd.vn/Home/Nghien-cuu-Trao-doi/307/Dac-diem-toi-pham-hoc-cua-toi-pham- su-dung-cong-nghe-cao-va-giai-phap-nang-cao-hieu-qua-phong-ngua-dau-tranh

Nikkei. (2018, March 12). "Amazon to Enter Vietnam in Challenge to Alibaba." https://asia.nikkei.com/Asia300/Amazon-to-enter-Vietnam-to-take-on-Alibaba

Parameswaran, P. (2018, January 12). "What's Behind Vietnam's New Military Cyber Command?" *The Diplomat*. https://thediplomat.com/2018/01/whats-behind-vietnams- new-military-cyber-command/

Schwab, K. (2017). *The Fourth Industrial Revolution*. New York, NY: Penguin Random House.

The World Bank. (2018). "World Development Indicators." https://data.worldbank.org/indicator/

Thu, T. (2018, October 16). "SecurityBox Receives an Investment from VIISA Fund." http://www.antoanthongtin.vn/doanh-nghiep/securitybox-nhan-khoan-dau-tu-tu-quy-viisa-104890

Transparency International. (2018). "Corruption Perceptions Index 2018: Corruption in Vietnam's public sector is still perceived as highly serious." https://towardstransparency.vn/en/cpi_vietnam_2018_en/

Trong, D. (2018a, November 2). "Muốn Trở Thành Cường Quốc Kinh Tế, Việt Nam Phải Là Cường Quốc an Ninh Mạng," *Vietnamnet*. http://vietnamnet.vn/vn/cong-nghe/muon-tro- thanh-cuong-quoc-kinh-te-viet-nam-phai-la-cuong-quoc-an-ninh-mang-486561.html

Trong, D. (2018b, January 12). "Đề Án 99 Giúp Việt Nam Có Thêm Hàng Ngàn Chuyên Gia ATTT Cấp Quốc Tế," *Vietnamnet*. http://vietnamnet.vn/vn/cong-nghe/bao-mat/de-an-99- giup-vn-co-them-hang-ngan-chuyen-gia-attt-cap-quoc-te-423240.html

Van, A. (2017, June 28). "Hơn 6 Năm, Trên 1.000 Website Cơ Quan Nhà Nước Của Việt Nam Bị Hacker Tấn Công," *ICT News*. https://ictnews.vn/cntt/bao-mat/hon-6-nam-tren-1-000-website-co-quan-nha-nuoc-cua-viet-nam-bi-hacker-tan-cong-155491.ict

Vanham, P. (2018, September 11). "The Story of Viet Nam's Economic Miracle," *World Economic Forum*. www.weforum.org/agenda/2018/09/how-vietnam-became-an- economic-miracle/

Vietnamnews. (2016, July 29). "Chinese Hackers Attack VN's Airports and Vietnam Airlines' Website." https://vietnamnews.vn/society/300416/chinese-hackers-attack-vns-airports-and-vietnam-airlines-website.html#tyFVwEyMEKpekDmv.97

Vietnamnews. (2017, July 19). "VN Falls in World Cyber Security Index." https://vietnamnews.vn/economy/380338/vn-falls-in-world-cyber-security-index.html#MzW70b2JhCe2u0uk.97

Vietnamnet. (2018, July 16). "E-commerce Players Keep Burning Money." https://english.vietnamnet.vn/fms/business/204179/e-commerce-players-keep-burning-money.html

Vu, K. (2018, November 30). "Vietnam Jails Senior Police for Running Online Gambling Ring." *Reuters*. https://www.reuters.com/article/us-vietnam-security-trials/vietnam-jails-senior-police-for-running-online-gambling-ring-idUSKCN1NZ0ZS

26

THE PHILIPPINES' CYBERSECURITY STRATEGY

Strengthening partnerships to enhance cybersecurity capability

Amparo Pamela H. Fabe and Ella Zarcilla-Genecela

Introduction: the Philippines' cybersecurity strategy

Cybersecurity constitutes a new field of expertise in the Philippines. Faced with an increasing incidence of cyber-attacks on companies, individuals and corporate websites, the Philippine discourse reflected the idea that the country's reliance on technology also constituted a high security risk that needed to be properly addressed. The Philippine legislators passed Republic Act 10,844 which shall be known as the Department of Information and Communications Technology Act of 2015. In accordance with the law, the Department of Information and Communications Technology (DICT) shall be the primary policy, planning, coordinating, implementing, and administrative entity of the Executive Branch of the government that will plan, develop, and promote the national Information Communication Technology (ICT) development agenda. This law aims to provide a "strategic, reliable, cost-efficient and citizen-centric" ICT infrastructure as an instrument of good governance and global competitiveness (Department of Information and Communications Technology Act of 2015).

The Philippine Government is now cognizant of the strategic role of cybersecurity in all areas of business and commerce, and particularly in defense and security. In terms of the national cybersecurity strategy, Philippine Department of Information and Communications Technology (DICT) Secretary Gregorio Honasan, Jr. made three areas his priority: a) providing full internet access for all Filipinos; b) adopt a stronger Information Communications Technology infrastructure; and, c) reduce cybercrime and cyber terrorism activities (Speech of DICT Secretary Gregorio Honasan, January 2020).

Countries in Southeast Asia have revealed their respective masterplans to protect their countries' critical systems. According to a CSA Survey in 2017, almost half of Singaporeans suffered at least one cybersecurity lapse in the past year (CSA Annual Report, 2018). In 2017, the Philippines spent 0.04 per cent of its Gross Domestic Product on cybersecurity, compared to the other ASEAN countries which pegged an annual average of 0.07 per cent (AT Kearney, 2017). Risk awareness is growing, as evidenced by the increasing number of defensive measures initiated by both the public and private sectors. Philippine companies and Philippine websites have been the subject of regular cyber-attacks (*The Diplomat*, 2019).

Mars Buan, ADP Philippines Manager, stated that the greatest number of cyberattacks in the Philippines come from China and Russia (personal interview with Ms. Mars Buan). According to Frost and Sullivan (2017), the Philippines could sustain up to USD$3.5 billion of direct, indirect, and induced losses from breaches in cybersecurity.

The DICT is ably supported by the Philippine National Police (PNP)-Active Cybercrime Group Operations Center and the Armed Forces of the Philippines Cyber Crime Group to tackle cybercrime and cyber terrorism activities. In addition, DICT Secretary Honasan stressed the importance of good policy on innovation. Honasan stated that the culture of innovation is present in various private industries and there is a constant technological flux in the fields of block chain, e-money, logistics, data privacy, taxation, cybersecurity, and energy (Speech of DICT Secretary Honasan, 2019).

The vision of the DICT from 2020 to 2022 is to establish WiFi hotspots in the whole country. Secretary Honasan stated that the DICT's mission is to bridge access to millions of Filipinos by opening internet access points all over the country, setting up specific nodes in identified growth areas, installation of communication towers, and building 20 cable landing stations using submarine cables to bring in more connectivity. However, by knowing these goals such as establishing Wi-Fi hotspots within the country, a need to secure this field will require experts to deal with security matters in which the country has few (DICT Annual Report, 2019).

International law and cybersecurity

There are many international cybersecurity laws that have an impact on Philippine businesses. The European Union (EU) Cybersecurity Act entered into force on June 27, 2019. The act has these effects: a) the EU Cybersecurity Agency was established; b) the creation of a cybersecurity certification framework. This framework is meant to set the compliance standards for companies that are operating in EU countries (Carrapico & Barrinha, 2017).

Another EU Policy is the General Data Protection Regulation (GDPR) which requires organizations dealing with EU citizens to reassess their data-processing customs and set up safeguards that meet the standards set by the regulation. As the GDPR is applicable to all companies that do business in or with the EU, the Philippines is required to meet the new data protection standards. Failure to comply may result in a fiscal penalty and a potential ban from trading within the EU (Bendiek, Bossong & Schulze, 2017).

The sectors that could potentially be affected by the GDPR compliance requirements include retail, tourism, health care, and financial services (Stupp, 2015). Philippine companies that promote their compliance as a feature of their services, will make them more attractive to EU clients. Philippine firms need to invest in cybersecurity to boost their business credentials (Carrapico & Barrinha, 2017).

The local research agenda on cybersecurity has centered on the common practices and impact of the different forms of cybercrime, on how cyber criminals organize themselves and recruit others, and on whether existing legal frameworks and law enforcement responses can efficiently counter cybercrime (Bossler, 2017).

Directive 2016/1148 on security of network and information systems (the NIS Directive), is the first horizontal legislation which was passed at the EU level for the protection of network and information systems across the Union. The role of ENISA in implementing the Directive, as reinforced by the proposal for a new Regulation on ENISA (the EU Cybersecurity Act), is brought forward, before elaborating upon the – inevitable – relationship of the NIS Directive with the EU's General Data Protection Regulation (Markopoulou,

Papakonstantinou & de Hert, 2019). The NIS Directive derives its roots in the European Commission's Communication of 2009, which focuses on prevention and awareness and defines a plan of immediate action to strengthen the security and trust in the information society (Markopoulou, Papakonstantinou & de Hert, 2019).

ASEAN cybersecurity initiatives

The Association of Southeast Asian Nations (ASEAN) Blueprint for the Political-Security Community 2025 called for the strengthening of cooperation between member states in combating cybercrimes, and developing and improving relevant laws and capabilities to address cybercrime issues and enhance cybersecurity. An essential factor of this Blueprint is the establishment of a secure and connected information infrastructure to sustain regional economic growth and competitiveness (ASEAN Annual Report, 2018–2019).

A key goal of the ASEAN Economic Community (AEC), in particular, is to develop electronic transactions through e-ASEAN to further facilitate ICT trade and services between member states. Cybersecurity matters are embedded in various ASEAN institutional meetings. The Senior Officials Meeting on Transnational Crimes (SOMTC), for example, focuses on eight types of transnational crimes, including cybercrimes. At the 7th SOMTC in Vientiane, senior officials adopted a common framework for ASEAN cybercrime capacity-building to further enhance the cybersecurity capabilities of the Member States. In 2016, during the ASEAN Defense Ministers Meeting–Plus (ADMM-Plus), the defense ministers adopted the proposal of then-Philippine Defense Minister Voltaire Gazmin to create a cybersecurity working group that could facilitate the sharing of knowledge and expertise, and would also foster practical cooperation among all parties in addressing cybersecurity issues (ASEAN Annual Report, 2018–2019).

International governance

There is an ongoing US–ASEAN Cyber Dialogue which is meant to advance collaboration on this front. Cyber issues are significant for ASEAN countries. The United States wants to take the lead in areas such as 5G and advance capacity-building. The US–ASEAN Cyber Dialogue has a designated Digital Connectivity and Cybersecurity Partnership (DCCP). Cyber cooperation has also increasingly factored into US–Southeast Asia cooperation. The United States has been collaborating with Southeast Asian states be it through the US–Singapore Third Country Training Program or the establishment of new cyber centers. In 2019, the United States and ASEAN issued a separate ASEAN–US Leader's Statement on Cybersecurity Cooperation which laid out specific steps to advance collaboration, including advancing capacity-building, considering confidence-building measures, and promoting norms of responsible state behavior in cyberspace. During the dialogue, the countries exchanged views on national cyber priorities, issues impacting the cyber environment, joint cooperation on international venues, and cyber capacity-building in the region (ASEAN–US Leader's Statement on Cybersecurity Cooperation, 2019).

Partner institutions at home and abroad

The Philippine Department of Information and Communications Technology (DICT) has strong partners in the private and public sector, in the academe, and among industry practitioners. The other partners include Facebook, Microsoft, Voyager Innovations, Inc.,

State Grid Corporation of China (SGCC), the International Container Terminals Services, Inc. (ICTSI), Union Bank, SGV & Co., National Association of Data Protection Officers of the Philippines (NADPOP) and De la Salle University and the National Privacy Commission (NPC).

The DICT and the Department of National Defense (DND) launched the Cyber Bayanihan 2.0 which is aimed at securing and bolstering critical cybersecurity infrastructure across the country. This project is led by the Cyber Group of the Armed Forces of the Philippines (AFP) and a private company Synetcom Philippines Inc. The Cyber Bayanihan 2.0 involves information technology (IT) experts from Miscrosoft, Synetcom, Nexus, SES Networks, AhnLab, ePLDT, Genians, and Efficient IP. Cyber Bayanihan 2.0 was launched to address the current cybersecurity threats and attacks on cyberspace. Defense Undersecretary Cardozo Luna emphasized the need for military and civilian Information Technology experts to get involved in educating government agencies, communities, and vertical markets on the importance of new technologies in cyberspace to thwart cybersecurity threats. This project complements the government's public–private partnership programs to boost the country's cyber defense capabilities.

The DICT in partnership with the Department of Education (DepEd) launched the #BeCyberSafe project in a bid to teach Filipino school children to protect themselves from online child abuse. The DepEd launched the project in collaboration with Stairway Foundation and the Internet and Mobile Marketing Association of the Philippines (IMMAP). Education Secretary Leonor Briones explained that the project has three features, namely, Project for Keeps, Dalir-Eskwela, and Chatbot. Project for Keeps is a social media movement, created to empower children, with the help of their guardians, to take control of their online profiles and keep themselves safe from online predators. Dalir-Eskwela offers a range of educational materials including videos, brochures, and posters that discuss issues on cyber safety ranging from cyber bullying to pornography. This component of the #BeCyberSafe project emphasizes the power of the fingers in connecting a child to the online world, and the corresponding threats posed by online connectivity (Department of Education Annual Report, 2018).

The Chatbot is a social media page with a messaging feature which will be used as a helpline where child protection issues faced in cyberspace may be reported and addressed. According to Secretary Briones, this program is important because it protects children from threats that are posed through cyberspace. The Child Protection Policy of the Philippine Department of Education aims to nurture young learners in a safe environment not only in the physical sphere, but also in cyberspace. In this digital age when children socialize and spend considerable time online, the Department recognizes that their right to protection against violence and abuse should also be realized online (Personal Interview with Secretary Briones, February 2020).

Legislative developments and processes

The Philippine Government has recognized the importance of instituting mechanisms aimed at providing a conducive environment in ICT. The Philippines cannot take cyber-threats lightly as 37 per cent of Filipinos use the internet and more than 120 million have mobile cellular subscriptions. In 2012, the Philippines instituted Republic Act 10175, otherwise known as the Cybercrime Prevention Act, with the aim of preventing cybercrimes from being committed, protecting and safeguarding computers and other communication systems and networks from being exploited, abused, and illegally accessed.

According to the Philippine National Police Anti-Cybercrime Group (PNP-ACG), the Philippines experienced a total of 1,809 cybercrimes in 2015, around 800 more than 2014 (Philippine National Police Annual Report, 2014). The Philippine Government through the DICT works to ensure the full implementation of cybercrime laws and continues to mainstream the cybersecurity discussion in its National Security Agenda. It must also include cybersecurity management mechanisms in the discussions. Moreover, effective communication between concerned agencies is imperative. The Philippine Government launched GovCloud – an online portal for information, transactions, and services – by the Department of Information Communication Technology (DICT) in 2013. The National Cybersecurity Plan 2020 aims to reduce risks through the protection of critical information infrastructure, government networks, supply chains, and individuals (DICT National Cybersecurity Plan, 2020).

Dimensions of cybercrime and cyber terrorism

The Kaspersky Lab revealed that its users in the Philippines were still being attacked by cybercriminals through the popular attack method called drive-by download. The drive-by download attack works by accessing an infected website. The main reason for this is the lack of online security awareness among Filipino internet users (Kaspersky Security Bulletin, 2019). For example, the Philippines had moved up to fifth place from ninth a year earlier in Kaspersky Lab's global list of countries with most online threats detected in the second quarter of 2019. According to the Kaspersky Global Q2 2019 Security Bulletin, approximately seven million or 37.4 per cent of Kaspersky users in the Philippines were attacked by online threats during the period. The other most-attacked countries are Algeria (44.1 per cent), Nepal (43 per cent), Albania (40.1 per cent), and Djibouti (37.9 per cent). Another Philippine cybersecurity strategy has been the establishment of a cybersecurity management system to monitor cyberthreats. This is a joint venture between a local firm, the Integrated Computer Systems (ICS) and an Israeli company, Verint, over an initial licensing period till 2023.

The Philippine Government also launched an intelligence sharing platform under the Cybersecurity Management System Project (CMSP) in 2020. This centralized platform for intelligence sharing for the Philippines strengthens its ability to monitor cyberthreats as well as respond to attacks that occur. The DICT Assistant Secretary for Cybersecurity and Enabling Technology, Allan Cabanlong, said that 10 priority government agencies would be identified such as the Office of the President, the National Security Council, and the Department of National Defense. The platform constitutes one step toward the broader goal of achieving cyber resiliency for the Philippines. These public sector efforts made nonetheless constitute incremental progress in efforts to address the country's vulnerability to cyber threats (*The Diplomat*, 2019).

Implications of cybersecurity policies and strategies

The DICT Secretary Gregorio Honasan Jr. is co-chair of the National Cybersecurity Inter-Agency Committee as detailed in Executive Order No. 95. The Executive Order 95, signed by the President last November 15, 2019, had amended Executive Order 189 that created the government's cybersecurity group in 2015. The DICT Secretary takes the place of Secretary of the Department of Science and Technology as co-chair of the group. The DOST Secretary will instead serve as a member of the group (Office of the President, Executive Order 189). The order noted that Republic Act No. 10844 created the DICT in 2015. The Act transferred to it all powers and functions related to cybersecurity, such as the formation of a National Cybersecurity Plan. The cybersecurity inter-agency committee is currently chaired by the Executive Secretary with the Director General of the National Security Council as co-chair. The Executive Order 95 added four new members to the committee namely the Secretary of the Department of Transportation, Secretary of the Presidential Communications Operations Office, Executive Director of the Cybercrime Investigation and Coordinating Center, and the Governor of the Bangko Sentral ng Pilipinas. This committee is tasked to carefully assess the vulnerabilities and risks of the country's cybersecurity; generate updated security protocols to all government employees for the proper handling, distribution, and storage of all forms of documents and communication; and enhance public–private partnerships to deter cyberattacks, minimize cyber risks, and increase cyber resiliency (Office of the President, Executive Order 95).

In addition, the DICT officials regularly sought assistance from the representatives from the US Federal Bureau of Investigation and an American company, Booz Allen Hamilton, a private firm invited by the US Embassy to tackle cybersecurity issues that local government units (LGUs) may encounter as they implement their respective smart city projects. The DICT through the Cybercrime Investigation and Coordination Center (CICC), adapts to the new paradigm with the comprehensive National Cybersecurity Strategy Framework. The development of the Framework institutionalizes the adoption and implementation of Information Security Governance and Risk Management approaches. These globally recognized standards shall provide the government a systematic and methodical practice of ensuring the protection of our mission critical and non-critical assets. The government recently opened the National Computer Emergency Response Team (NCERT) (Parcon, 2017).

The DICT helps to

> ensure the rights of individuals to privacy and confidentiality of their personal information; ensure the security of critical ICT infrastructures including informa-tion assets of the government, individuals and businesses; and offer oversight over other government agencies regulating the ICT sector and ensure consumer protec-tion and welfare, data privacy and security, foster competition and the growth of the ICT sector.

The DICT has drawn up the National Cybersecurity Plan to address the urgent need to protect the nation's critical info structures, government networks, small and medium enterprises to large businesses, corporations and its supply chains. The primordial goals of the Philippine National Cybersecurity Plan are as follows: (1) guarantee the continuous operation of our nation's critical info-structures, public and military networks; (2) implement cyber resiliency measures to enhance our ability to respond to threats before, during, and after attacks; (3) effective coordination with law enforcement agencies; and (4) a cybersecurity educated society (Philippine National Cybersecurity Plan, 2017).

From 2003 to 2012, the PNP recorded a total of 2,778 cybercrime related offenses. From CY 2010 to CY 2012, the PNP has recorded a total of 1,184 incidents with the highest being the attacks targeting government websites where a total of 940 website defacements have been recorded. Another recent attack perpetrated by cyber criminals is the exfiltration of usernames and passwords from the DNS "Gov.Ph" registration site with an estimated 2,338 records and allegedly claimed by AnonTaiwan group (Philippine National Police Annual Report, 2012).

The timely police intervention against cybercrime in the country resulted in the arrest of 505 foreign nationals. The common cybercrimes that have been committed in the country were done either through the use of technology or the target of the crime is the technology itself, on the areas of national security matter, financially motivated offenses, crime directed against a person or the property, and those that involve crimes that violate public morals. Another aspect in the fight against cybercrime is the concern about online child victimization. In response to this international priority, the PNP is strengthening its children protection program by establishing a special taskforce known as the "Angel Net" which was established with the express purpose of addressing internet or technology-related child abuse and exploitation (Philippine National Police Annual Report, 2012).

Notable anti-cybercrime operations

These are some of the notable anti-cybercrime operations of the Philippine National Police (PNP). The DICT and the PNP continuously work closely together in order to craft a more coordinated response in case of cyber-attacks against Philippine targets consisting of company and government websites. The PNP conducted a search and seizure operation in 2011 against a group of alleged telecommunications hackers victimizing a US telecommunications company with the cooperation of the US Embassy in Manila. The US telecommunications company lost more than US$2M in revenues. The criminal group is allegedly connected to a foreign terrorist financing group responsible for financing the terrorist attack in Mumbai, India in 2008 (Philippine National Police Annual Report, 2011).

April 20, 2013 – The PNP officials arrested three Malaysian nationals in Iloilo City who were suspected of siphoning off money from ATM card holders. A small camera and a skimming device are placed in ATM booths. Credit card information stolen is cloned using sophisticated card tools to withdraw money from the victim's bank account. Suspects were charged for violation of R.A. 8484 "Access Device Regulation Act of 1998" (PNP Annual Report, 2013).

May 15, 2013 – The PNP-ACG officials together with local police officers had conducted search and seizure warrant at Interface Techno-Phil Cebu City. The call center was offering fraudulent waka gift vouchers to US nationals. The suspects were charged for violation of R.A. 8484 "Access Device Regulation Act of 1998" and Article 212 of the Revised Penal Code "Corruption of Public Officials" (PNP Annual Report, 2013).

July 11, 2012 – The PNP officers conducted a search and seizure warrant at "724 Care Call Center" employees in Mandaue City, Cebu for marketing and selling alleged counterfeit Pfizer medicines to US nationals online. They were suspected of violating of R. A. 8484 "Access Devices Regulation Act of 1998" (PNP Annual Report, 2013).

October 4, 2011 – The PNP officers arrested Shin Un-Sun in Batangas Province by virtue of an international warrant issued by Interpol and the Korea National Police for alleged hacking into the Hyundai customer database stealing around 420,000 customer records and he had extorted money from Hyundai. The suspect SUN was turned over to the Immigration Bureau for deportation to South Korea (PNP Annual Report, 2013).

Regulatory environment

The DICT offers a helpful and a positive regulatory environment for the highly engaged stakeholders of cybersecurity. This government agency is able to issue regularly some important guidelines and notifications to both the public and private companies and to the national government agencies to address the importance of fostering a digital governance through a strengthened cybersecurity framework. The DICT upholds the importance of international cooperation and partnership in strengthening cybersecurity.

The DICT is ably assisted by the PNP-ACG in its continuing fight against cybercrimes and cyber criminals. The PNP's main strategies encompass that of increasing the PNP's cybersecurity competence and capability, spreading a continuous public awareness of cybercrimes, fostering of an active cybersecurity private–public partnership, the enforcement of effective cybersecurity laws, and the fostering of international linkages in further strengthening cybersecurity and combating cybercrime and cyber-terrorism (Philippine National Police Annual Report, 2013).

Coherence has become a particularly crucial factor in the country's cybersecurity policy because, for some time now, its governance was uncoordinated and highly scattered, with relevant actors working independently from each other in areas. The serious pursuit of policy coherence, combined with the sustained increase in attacks on critical information infrastructures and on personal and commercial data, led the Philippines to further reinforce its new role by publishing its first cybersecurity strategy in 2019 (Philippine National Cybersecurity Plan, 2019).

This main strategy was primordially aimed at improving the private sector's resilience to cyber threats by encouraging a higher degree of cooperation among stakeholders, greater infusion of investment in national and private sector capacities to respond to cyber-attacks, the establishment and development of cyber defense capabilities, and a deep and a heightened engagement with identified international and local partners (Personal interview with DICT Secretary Honasan, January 15, 2020).

Moreover, the DICT has focused on the reinforcement of capabilities through the creation of several research and innovation funding streams for cybersecurity (Php 200 million for the period 2020–2030). The DICT also hopes to combine the further development of national infrastructures such as the establishment of cybersecurity centers for the public and the private sectors, i.e., the shipping sector, energy and power sector, the media sector, the police and military academies, as well as the resorts, hotel, and restaurant sectors (Philippine National Cybersecurity Plan of 2017).

Conclusion

The Philippine cybersecurity environment continues to grapple with these strategic issues: the lack of talent, and an obvious dearth of practical skills gap and education. The statistics behind crime rates connote that the government is still in the verge of creating a model for the majority to understand this era of Internet of Things (IoT). The government officials are not fully equipped to handle the fast-paced growth of this industry. The government agencies are aiming to be trained in their own way so as to view the bigger picture.

The Philippine Department of Information and Communications Technology through Secretary Gregorio B. Honasan Jr. has focused on three priority areas for the National Cybersecurity Strategy: a) providing full internet access for all Filipinos; b) adopting a stronger Information Communications Technology infrastructure; and, c) reducing cybercrime and cyber terrorism activities. The DICT has channeled substantial government investments to provide full internet access nationwide, provide added ICT infrastructure, and reduce cybercrime and cyber terrorism. This strong and renewed emphasis on focused priorities has made the DICT more poised to refine its cybersecurity strategy in the future. Continuous advocacies towards the cybersecurity agenda will help the Philippines to widen its views about the probability of future threats but will not guarantee to lessen cybercrimes due to continuous advancement of technologies.

Despite these great efforts which are carried out through the joint efforts of the DICT and the PNP, there remain a number of external and internal challenges that these two institutions need to contend with in the coming months: externally, there continues to be a lack of public awareness of cybersecurity risks among Filipinos, a reduced capacity on the side of the private sector to respond swiftly and capably to regular incidents such as cyber-attacks coupled with a reduced willingness to invest more seriously in the appropriate protection mechanisms, a massive expansion of the available tools to commit more cybercrime, and a continued difficulty in attribution. Internally, there is a dearth of progress in terms of countering the institutional fragmentation, defining the proper way of understanding resilience and how it should be achieved, and pushing for strong advancement towards binding legal norms, and obtaining the appropriate levels of funding for cybersecurity expansion and development.

Suggested reading

Lago, C. (2020, January 18). "The biggest data breaches in Southeast Asia," *CSO*. csoonline.com/article/3532816/the-biggest-data-breaches-in-southeast-asia.html

Republic of the Philippines. (2017). "National cybersecurity plan 2022." https://dict.gov.ph/national-cybersecurity-plan-2022/

Sosa, G. C. (n.d.). "Country report on cybercrime: The Philippines." www.unafei.or.jp/publications/pdf/RS_No79/No79_12PA_Sosa.pdf

References

"ASEAN Annual Report," 2018-2019. Jakarta, Indonesia, ASEAN Regional Headquarters.

"ASEAN-US Leader's Statement on Cybersecurity Cooperation," 2019. Jakarta, Indonesia, ASEAN Regional Headquarters.

AT Kearney. (2017). *AT Kearney Global Index*. Hong Kong: AT Kearney.

Bendiek, A., Bossong, R. & Schulze, M. (2017). "The EU's revised cybersecurity strategy: Half-Hearted progress on far-reaching challenges," *SWP Comments*.

Bossler, A. (2017). "Cybercrime research at the crossroads: Where the field currently stands and innovative strategies to move forward," in T. J. Holt (ed.), *Cybercrime through an interdisciplinary lens* (pp. 36–55). London and New York: Routledge.

Carrapico, H. & Barrinha, A. (2017). "The EU as coherent (cyber) security actor?" *Journal of Common Market Studies*, 55(6), 1254–1272.

"CSA Annual Report." (2018). US: Pricewaterhouse Cooper.

Department of Education Annual Report." (2018). Manila: Department of Education.

"DICT Annual Report." (2019). Manila: Department of Information and Communications Technology.

Frost & Sullivan. (2017). "Understanding the cybersecurity threat landscape in Asia Pacific: Securing the modern enterprise in a digital world," Washington, DC.

Honasan, G. B. Jr. "Speech entitled innovative Philippines: Transforming barriers to productivity, transparency and inclusive growth," ICT Summit, October 1, 2019, Manila, Philippines.

Kaspersky Annual Report. (2019). www.kaspersky.com

Markopoulou, D., Papakonstantinou, V. & de Hert, P. (2019). "The new EU cybersecurity framework: The NIS Directive, ENISA's role and the general data protection regulation," *Computer Law & Society Review*, 35(6), 1–11.

Parcon, R. J. M. L. C. (2017). "Addressing cyberspace vulnerability: The ASEAN and the Philippines," *CIRSS (Center for International Relations and Strategic Relations Commentaries) Commentaries*, IV(3). www.researchgate.net/publication/328496467_Addressing_Cyberspace_Vulnerability_The_ASEAN_and_the_Philippines

Pareswaran, P. (2019, January 23). "What's in the Philippines' new cyber platform?" *The Diplomat*. https://thediplomat.com/2019/01/whats-in-the-philippines-new-cyber-platform/

Personal Interview with ADP General Manager, Ms. Mars Buan, January 7, 2020.

Personal Interview with DICT Secretary, Gregorio B. Honasan Jr., January 15, 2020.

Personal Interview with Department of Education Secretary, Leonor Briones, February 1, 2020.

Philippine House of Representatives. "Department of Information and Communications Technology Act of 2015."

"Philippine National Police Annual Report 2011," Manila: Office of the Chief Philippine National Police.

"Philippine National Police Annual Report 2012," Manila: Office of the Chief Philippine National Police.

"Philippine National Police Annual Report 2013," Manila: Office of the Chief Philippine National Police.

"Philippine National Police Annual Report 2014," Manila: Office of the Chief Philippine National Police.

Stupp, C. (2015, July 31). "EU cybersecurity agency lacks funds for research on major tech issues," *EurActiv.* www.euractive.com/sections/infosociety/eu-cybersecurity-agency-lacks-funds-research-major-tech-issues-316729

27

MALAYSIA

Balancing national development, national security, and cybersecurity policy

Ahmad El-Muhammady

Introduction

The purpose of this chapter is threefold. First, to examine the Internet booms and the growth of the Information and Communication Technology (ICT) in Malaysia and how it impacts Malaysia's national security. Second, it also examines the nature and substance of Malaysia's cybersecurity frameworks. Third, it discusses Malaysia's strategy to manage the multitude of cybersecurity challenges within its border, including the emerging trend of security threats such as cyber warfare, cyberterrorism, and cybercrime.

Background

Since attaining independence in 1957, Malaysia has experienced a rapid development and economic growth manifested in the forms of infrastructure development, economic programs, and prudent policy formulation. With the current population of approximately 32 million people, comprising of multiethnic, religious, and cultural society, Malaysia continues to sustain its political stability under six prime ministers: Tunku Abdul Rahman (1957–1970), Tun Abdul Razak (1970–1976), Tun Hussain Onn (1976–1981), Mahathir Mohamad (1981–2003), Tun Abdullah Ahmad Badawi (2003–2009), and Najib Razak (2009–2018) (Kheng, 1999). Interestingly, after leaving politics for 15 years, Mahathir Mohamad made a comeback to the political arena and wrested the power from Najib Razak through a landslide victory during the General Election on May 2018. As the leader of Pakatan Harapan (Coalition of Hope), which consists of Parti Amanah, Parti Keadilan Rakyat (PKR), and Democratic Action Party (DAP), Mahathir Mohamad became the seventh prime minister of Malaysia. He is the first former prime minister returned to that position for a second time at the age of 93 (Teoh & Leong, 2018).

While previous prime ministers focused much on developing basic infrastructure and economic programs for a country that has newly attained independence, Mahathir (1981–2003) took a divergent approach to lay down a foundation to prepare Malaysia to become a self-sufficient industrialized nation by the year 2020. During his speech in the parliament in 1991, he announced Malaysia's Vision 2020 (Wawasan, 2020). Therein, he laid down the foundation for the development and growth of the Internet and ICT

(Hamid, 1993). The growth has been sustained in the subsequent two administrations during the era of Abdullah Ahmad Badawi (2003–2009) and Najib Razak (2009–2018).

The Internet boom in the 1990s

The Internet growth and diffusion in the United States in the 1990s produced strong "spillover effects" across the globe including in Malaysia. The advent of the Internet, according to some scholars, goes back to 1995, which was considered the beginning of the Internet age in Malaysia (Salman, Choy, Mahmud & Latif, 2013). This was indicated by the first Internet Users Survey (IUS) conducted from October to November 1995, which found that one out of every 1,000 Malaysians had access to the Internet, which means 20,000 Internet users out of a population of 20 million at that time (Salman, Choy, Mahmud & Latif, 2013). This number grew to 2.6 per cent of the population in 1998. A similar trend is observable in the sale of computer units which showed significant increase from 467,000 in 1998 to 701,000 in 2000 (Salman, Choy, Mahmud & Latif, 2013). On July 2012, the Internet users in Malaysia reached 25.3 million. Five million are broadband users, 2.5 million wireless broadband users, and 10 million 3G subscribers. According to the IUS report in 2018, the percentage of Internet users has continued to rise from 76.0 per cent in 2016 to 87.4 per cent in 2018. It should be noted however, that this kind of development is not sustainable without continuous support from the state (Salman, Choy, Mahmud & Latif, 2013).

Vision 2020, Multimedia Super Corridor (MSC) and Cyberjaya

Given the rapid growth of the ICT and the Internet capabilities globally in the 1990s, Malaysia decided to capitalize on this opportunity to become more economically competitive. To achieve this, in 1991, Mahathir announced his 29-year plan of how Malaysia is striving to become an industrialized nation by the year 2020 (Milne & Mauzy, 1999: 75–77). He also identified nine strategic challenges that Malaysia had to overcome in order to achieve the objectives. The challenges include:

1. Establishing a united Malaysian nation made up of one Bangsa Malaysia (Malaysian Race).
2. Creating a psychologically liberated, secure, and developed Malaysian society.
3. Fostering and developing a mature democratic society.
4. Establishing a fully moral and ethical society.
5. Establishing a matured liberal and tolerant society.
6. Establishing a scientific and progressive society.
7. Establishing a fully caring society.
8. Ensuring an economically just society, in which there is a fair and equitable distribution of the wealth of the nation.
9. Establishing a prosperous society with an economy that is fully competitive, dynamic, robust, and resilient.

In essence, Vision 2020 seeks to create and develop a fully developed nation state not only economically, but socially, politically, psychologically, morally, ethically, and of course technologically advanced. One of the key components in Vision 2020 is to establish scientific and competitive society that is able to play an active role in the global community. Definitely, given the new development of the time that is the rise of the Internet, focusing on developing the infrastructure, policy, and workable eco-system for encouraging the growth of the Internet and cyberspace become an important agenda.

As part of the 2020 strategy, Mahathir introduced the Multimedia Super Corridor (MSC) on February 12, 1996, a special economic zone and high technology business district covering a vast zone in the central-state of Selangor. MSC covers Petronas' Twin Tower at the heart of Kuala Lumpur, extended to Cyberjaya, Putrajaya, Sepang, Bandar Tun Razak, Puchong, Serdang, and ended at Nilai, the border of Negri Sembilan. However, to cater the specific needs of IT industries, Malaysia focuses on developing a very specific area known as Cyberjaya in May 1997 as the hub of ICT activities, much like Silicon Valley in California. Cyberjaya is an IT-themed city providing advanced telecommunication facilities for the domestic and international bodies to operate. The development of MSC and Cyberjaya especially provide conducive environment for the growth of ICT. However, it also exposes Malaysia to the cybersecurity threats.

Understanding cybersecurity context

The development of ICT and the Internet sectors have definitely brought about massive changes in Malaysian economy, industries, trades, social, and political life. Hyper-connectivity, open and borderless access to information highways, and users' ability to be anonymous exposed users, including in Malaysia to cybersecurity threats, domestically and externally.

Cybersecurity threats refers to any forms of premeditated attacks mounted by domestic and external parties with potentially catastrophic effects to information systems and critical information infrastructure in Malaysia. The open and borderless dimension of cyberspace, combined with easy and unlimited access to information, as well as the ability to maintain anonymity in cyberworld has also increased the potential risks of cyberattacks on Malaysia's critical information infrastructure, including abuse of the Internet, and cybercrime, cyberespionage, and cyberterrorism (National Security Policy, 2019). On April 2019, Deputy Prime Minister, Wan Azizah Wan Ismail informed Malaysian Parliament that "growing dependence on useful technology, at the same time, can pose threats and new challenges to national security management" (Ariff & Radhi, 2019).

Protecting critical information infrastructure is part of Malaysia's national security frameworks. Malaysia's National Security Policy (MNSP) defines national security as "a state of being free from any threats, whether internally or externally to its core values" (National Security Policy, 2019). The MNSP identifies nine Core Values that need to be "maintained, preserved and strengthened in order to guarantee its survival as an independent, peaceful and sovereign nation" (National Security Policy, 2019). The Core Values are as follows:

1. Territorial sovereignty and integrity;
2. Socio-political stability;
3. National integration;
4. Good governance;
5. Economic integrity;
6. Social justice;
7. Sustainable development;
8. People's security;
9. International recognition.

The MNSP also identified that 13 key imperatives existed in its national security environment such as fragility of national unity, challenges facing the national democratic system, illegal immigrants and "refugees," disputes over territorial claims, extremism and terrorism, cybersecurity, disasters, crises, transnational crime, pandemics and infectious diseases, energy security, food security, and proliferation of nuclear arms and arms development program (National Security Policy, 2019).

As stated, cybersecurity threats are one of the key components in MNSP that required serious attention. In describing the nature of cybersecurity threats, MNSP asserts that due to the rapid development of ICT and increased reliance of technology, it exposes Malaysia to "aggravating of cybersecurity threats." In 2018, the Security Intelligence Report (SIR) found that Malaysia has become extremely vulnerable to cyber-attacks based on data collected between January to December 2018 (Goud, n.d.). This view is validated by Dzahar Mansor, National Technology Officer, Microsoft Malaysia who was quoted saying that, "undoubtedly Malaysia has become a central hub for hackers to launch attacks on organizations operating in the region" (Goud, n.d.).

Microsoft identified three forms of cyber-attacks popularly launched against Malaysia:

1. **Cryptocurrency mining malware** such as cyber crooks who are reported to have increasingly used victims' personal computer to mine digital currency coins, enabling them to make smart profits. More attacks are observed as the rate of crypto currency fluctuates.
2. **Ransomware attacks**. According to the Microsoft research, on average "companies in western countries are observing a 73% rise in ransomware attacks, while in Malaysia it is encountering 100% more on average" (Goud, n.d.). The report also concluded that the volume of attacks may fluctuate but the severity of the attacks has not declined, especially in key areas such as transportation, traffic systems and hospitals (Goud, n.d.).
3. **Drive-by download pages** are another form of popular cyber-attacks in Malaysia, which shows a 544% increase on a global average as compared with only 22% rise in the world. Drive-by download pages are dangerous because they can affect a user's computer system simply by visiting the website planted with malware, even without downloading anything from it (Goud, n.d.).

Cybersecurity strategy

Realizing the potential risks posed by continuous cyber-attacks, the Malaysian government crafted the National Security Cybersecurity Frameworks (NSCF), which provides:

> a high-level perspective of all necessary components of cybersecurity to be considered by the respective Government ministries and agencies to protect their information (data) in cyberspace. Hence, with this framework and the Public Sector Cyber Security Policy, the Malaysian Public Sector ministries and agencies shall develop their individual organization cyber security policy to govern and ensure that all activities carried out in their organization adhere to the requirements stipulated in both documents. At the project level, all these documents shall be referred to and further guidance shall be sought from existing acts, regulations and guidelines related to cybersecurity that are in force to develop the information security plan for the ICT projects.
>
> *(The Malaysian Administrative Modernisation and Management Planning Unit, 2019)*

Malaysia's National Security Cybersecurity Frameworks consists of eight components:

1. To identify, which aims at identifying the business function environment, governance structure and policy as well as assets to be protected, the associated risks and risk management;
2. To protect requires the necessary security principles, technologies, processes, and people competencies to be determined in order to mitigate the risks identified;
3. To detect the objective of detecting malicious attacks through highlighting anomalies in usage and network traffic pattern;
4. To respond on the other hand is to ensure responses to these malicious attacks are being taken and to escalate communications to the stakeholders and the general public (if required);
5. To recover addresses the capability to be able to recover from the damages caused by malicious attacks and system failures to ensure availability of information;
6. To procure is to ensure that security measures and requirements are enforced throughout the entire lifecycle of the system regardless of the manner of acquisition, be it through external acquisition or through in-house development. This is a very important component that covers procurement specifications, vendor management, footprint of resources, system development life cycle, commissioning and decommissioning processes, and system disposal;
7. Security audit; and
8. To enforce cuts across all components to outline the scope of audit and enforcement carried out by the audit and enforcement agencies (The Malaysian Administrative Modernisation and Management Planning Unit, 2019).

This framework was used as point of reference and guideline in developing the National Cyber Security Policy (NCSP), basically to "facilitate Malaysia's move towards knowledge-based economy (K-economy)" (Ministry of Science, Technology and Innovation, n.d.). The NCSP was developed to address the potential risks to the Critical National Information Infrastructure (CNII) which comprises of the networked information systems of ten critical sectors:

1. National defense and security;
2. Banking and finance;
3. Information and communications;
4. Energy;
5. Transportation;
6. Water;
7. Health services;
8. Government;
9. Emergency services;
10. Food and agriculture.

The NCSP has stated its vision (National Cyber Security Agency, 2019):

> Malaysia's Critical National Information Infrastructure shall be secure, resilient and self-reliant. Infused with a culture of security, it will promote stability, social well-being and wealth creation, with its mission to: address the risks to the Critical

National Information Infrastructure (CNII); to ensure that critical infrastructure are protected to a level that commensurate with the risks; and to develop and establish a comprehensive program and a series of frameworks.

The policy also recognizes the "interdependent nature of the CNII" and thus, it seeks to "establish a comprehensive program and a series of frameworks that will ensure the effectiveness of cyber security controls over vital assets. It has been developed to ensure that the CNII are protected to a level that commensurate the risks faced" (National Cyber Security Agency, 2019). Similar strategy is echoed in Malaysia's National Security Policy Strategy No. 18 (see Table 27.1) asserting that the state has to "maintain cybersecurity and defense," with the objectives of "ensuring a secured cyber environment through comprehensive risk management involving the consolidation of the security and defense infrastructure, especially the Critical Information Infrastructure (CII) of the country" (National Security Policy, 2019).

Table 27.1 Eight Thrusts of Malaysia's National Cyber Security Policy (NCSP)

Thrust	Objectives
Effective Governance	• To centralize the coordination of national cybersecurity initiatives • To promote effective cooperation between public and private sectors • To establish formal and encourage informal information sharing exchanges
Legislative and Regulatory Framework	• To review and enhance Malaysia's cyber laws to address the dynamic nature of cybersecurity threats • To establish progressive capacity building programs for national law enforcement agencies • To ensure that all applicable local legislation is complementary to and in harmony with international laws, treaties, and conventions
Cyber Security Technology Framework	• To ensure that all applicable local legislation is complementary to and in harmony with international laws, treaties, and conventions • To implement an evaluation/certification program for cybersecurity products and systems
Culture of Security and Capacity Building	• To develop, foster, and maintain a national culture of security • To standardize and coordinate cybersecurity awareness and education programs across all elements of the CNII • To establish an effective mechanism for cybersecurity knowledge dissemination at the national level • To identify minimum requirements and qualifications for information security professionals
Research and Development Towards Self-Reliance	• To identify minimum requirements and qualifications for information security professionals • To enlarge and strengthen the cybersecurity research community

(Continued)

Table 27.1 (Cont.)

Thrust	Objectives
	• To promote the development and commercialization of intellectual properties, technologies, and innovations through focused research and development • To nurture the growth of cybersecurity industry
Compliance and Enforcement	• To standardize cybersecurity systems across all elements of the CNII • To strengthen the monitoring and enforcement of standards • To develop a standard of cybersecurity risk assessment framework
Cyber Security Emergency Readiness	• To strengthen the national computer emergency response teams (CERTs) • To develop effective cybersecurity incident reporting mechanisms • To encourage all elements of CNII to monitor cybersecurity events • To develop a standard business continuity management framework • To disseminate vulnerability advisories and threat warnings in a timely manner • To encourage all elements of the CNII to perform periodic vulnerability assessment program
International Cooperation	• To encourage active participation in all relevant international cybersecurity bodies, panels, and multi-national agencies • To promote active participation in all relevant international cybersecurity by hosting an annual international cyber security conference

Source: Author.

Based on the above, we can say that Malaysia's cybersecurity strategy was developed in order to achieve two major objectives. First, to encourage and sustain the growth of ICT and the Internet use. Second, to protect critical national assets as identified in the MNSP mentioned earlier. In order to achieve these objectives, various measures and initiatives are introduced as discussed in the following paragraphs.

Creating conducive eco-system for development and growth of ICT. As discussed earlier, Malaysia has taken various initiatives to create conducive eco-system to encourage the development and growth of the ICT and the use of the Internet. The development of Multimedia Super Corridor (MSC), Cyberjaya IT-themed park, supported by huge investment, government–private partnership, policy incentives, including offering of courses at the universities and college levels have produced positive outcome to accelerate the ICT growth in Malaysia.

Establishing institutions responsible to manage the ICT and Internet-related matters. In materializing the vision spelled out in the Vision 2020, Malaysia has created various institutions and agencies whose main responsibilities are to ensure the vision can be effectively translated into tangible forms. In the context of cybersecurity, besides creating institutions that promote the growth of ICT and the Internet, the government also institutionalized certain agencies to manage and govern the operation and activities in the cyberspace. This is evidenced with the creation of National Information Technology Council (NITC) in 1994, consisting of a group of national and international advisors responsible for advising the government on ICT matters.

Protecting cyberspace via legislative approach. Legislative approach constitutes an important component of Malaysia's cybersecurity strategy. Key legislation related to the cybersecurity is presented in Table 27.2.

Table 27.2 Key Cybersecurity Legislation

Type of Offence	Applicable Laws	Agencies/Jurisdiction
Sedition	Sedition Act 1948	Royal Malaysia Police
Threats to national security	Penal Code (Terrorism) 130	Royal Malaysia Police
Cheating/finance/trade/ commercial	Company Act 1965	Company Commission of Malaysia
	Financial Services Act 2013	Central Bank of Malaysia
	Direct Sales Act 1993 Consumer Protection Act 1999 (which includes online sale)	Ministry of Domestic Trade and Consumer Affairs
	Capital Markets and Services Act 2007	Central Bank of Malaysia
	Electronic Commerce Act 2006	Company Commission of Malaysia
	Penal Code (Section 420)	Royal Malaysia Police
Copyright	Copyright Act 1987	Ministry of Domestic Trade and Consumer Affairs
Defamation	Penal Code Defamation Act 1957	Royal Malaysia Police (civil)
Insulting religion	Syariah Criminal Offences Enactment	State Department of Religious Affairs
	Communication and Multimedia Act 1998	Malaysian Communication and Multimedia Commission (MCMC)
Pornography/ incest/prostitution	Communication and Multimedia Act 1998	Malaysian Communication and Multimedia Commission (MCMC)
Identity theft	Penal Code	Royal Malaysia Police
Sale/advertisement of medicine	Medicine (Advertisement and Sale) Act 1956	Ministry of Health
Distribution of weapons and explosive materials	Strategic Trade Act 2010	Ministry of International Trade and Industry Kementerian (MITI)

(Continued)

Table 27.2 (Cont.)

Type of Offence	Applicable Laws	Agencies/Jurisdiction
Gambling/betting	Common Gaming Houses Act 1953 Betting Act 1953 Pool Betting Act 1967	Royal Malaysia Police
Threats to life and property	Penal Code	Royal Malaysia Police
Hacking	Computer Crime Act 1997	Royal Malaysia Police
Abuse of personal data	Personal Data Protection Act 2010	Ministry of Communication and Multimedia
Terrorism	Penal Code (Offences relating to terrorism: 130B-130T) Security Offences (Special Measures) Act (SOSMA) 2012 Prevention of Terrorism Act (POTA) 2015 Prevention of Criminal Act (POCA) 1959. Anti-Money Laundering, Anti-Terrorism Financing and Proceeds of Unlawful Activities Act 2001	Royal Malaysia Police Malaysian Communication and Multimedia Commission (MCMC) Central Bank
Terrorism financing	Anti-Money Laundering Act	Royal Malaysia Police Central Bank

Source: Author.

The legal frameworks shown in Table 27.2 provide a solid basis of cyberspace governance, particularly to the law enforcement agencies. It also provides strong regulations, protection, and operation for users operating in the cyberspace.

Creating the culture of info-security to be well-informed users. Another key features of Malaysia's cybersecurity strategy aims at educating users on the culture of security in using the Internet services. CyberSecurity Malaysia, an agency established by Malaysian government to provide cybersecurity services states its aims as to "build a culture of security through awareness programs and best practices among children, teenagers, parents and organizations. We have organized and created many activities to improve the level of awareness in information security" (Ministry of Communications and Multimedia Malaysia, 2020).

Confronting a new security landscape

ICT and the Internet are double-edged swords. They can be used for good and bad purposes. While many users are benefitting immensely from the facilities provided by the advancement of technology and the Internet, some parties are capitalizing on this tool to achieve their selfish ends. In Malaysia, three emerging cybersecurity threats that become a cause for concern for the government and the public are the threats of cyberterrorism, cybercrimes, and cyberwarfare.

The use of social media platforms, banking facilities, and advanced technology in recruiting young people and performing illegal transactions to finance terrorism activities have increased in the past ten years. A study by the Institute of Youth Research (IYRES) Malaysia in 2017 found that 85 per cent of respondents, who were interviewed for terrorism charges, cited social media and the Internet as the main source of information and hub for recruitment (El-Muhammady, 2018: 103; Ringkasan Eksekutif Profail Belia Dalam Kegiatan Ekstrimisme, 2017: 26). Terrorist groups such as al-Qaeda and Islamic State of Syria and Iraq (ISIS) or Daesh also make use of ICT facilities to transfer funds, solicit money from followers, and distribute to its operatives for operation as evidenced in the Jakarta bombing in 2009 and 2016. Social media platforms and smartphone applications such as Telegram, WhatsApp, and Threema provide convenient methods of communication. That very convenience has been hijacked by certain parties to perform illegal activities. In Malaysian context, Royal Malaysia Police, Central Bank, and Malaysian Communication and Multimedia Commission (MCMC) work closely in tackling cyberterrorism threats especially in the last ten years.

In addition to cyberterrorism, criminals also incorporate the ICT and the Internet facilities as part of their modus operandi. On November 2019, the Malaysian Immigration Department arrested 680 Chinese nationals in IT-themed city of Cyberjaya for involvement in an illegal online gambling syndicate (Ross, 2019). It was hitherto the biggest arrest in one single operation conducted by the Immigration Department in Malaysia. Their choice of Cyberjaya city for illegal operations is quite telling, particularly because of superfast Internet speed and ICT facilities the city provided. The Macau Scam is another type of cybercrime in Malaysia, targeting especially pensioners and women. Their modus operandi is delicate and well crafted. According to the State Commercial Crime Investigation Department (CCID) chief, the scammers would impersonate personnel from Central Bank, the Malaysian Anti-Corruption Commission (MACC), police, post office, and Health Department among others. The scammer would instruct the panicked victim to follow their instructions in order to settle the problem, which definitely involved payment of large sum of money (Pei Pei, 2019). Despite continuous awareness campaign by the authorities, the report of Macau Scam activities continued to be featured in daily newspapers.

Cyberwarfare is another feature of a new security landscape in the region. Cyberwarfare "involves politically-motivated attacks by one nation on another nation, which involve the above groups to disrupt activities of an organization or nation-state. This is done especially for strategic or military purposes and cyber-espionage" (Satar, 2019). The "external threats, including espionage, sabotage and information warfare activities, come from criminal elements and also state-backed entities" (FMT Media, 2019). Given an increasingly challenging cybersecurity environment, it is suggested Malaysia develop "cyber force" to take charge of cyber defense operations (El-Muhammady, 2017). However, the most important constraint for Malaysia to confront the above challenges is the lack of professionals in the field, according to findings by Microsoft Malaysia in 2018 (Goud, 2019). This constraint may affect the efficiency and effectiveness of the cybersecurity activities in Malaysia.

Conclusion

While Malaysia envisages being a developed nation by 2020, through systematic economic program and developments, it also needs to deal with current realities posed by myriad challenges in its socio-political realities as well as in the cyberspace. Its ability to balance physical development, the need for preservation of "core values," and the Critical National Information Infrastructure (CNII), which also constitute key components of its national security, are vital to secure its cyberspace from domestic and foreign threats. Strong and effective cybersecurity laws, strategies, and operability are the cornerstones of its sustainable security in the future.

Suggested reading

Anbar, M., Adbullah, N. & Manickam, S. (eds.). (2020). *Advances in Cyber Security: First International Conference, ACeS 2019, Penang, Malaysia, July 30-August 1, 2019, Revised Selected Papers (Communications .. Computer and Information Science Book 1132)*. Singapore: Springer.

B Hashim, M. S. (2011). "Malaysia's National Cyber Security Policy: The Country's Cyber Defence Initiatives," Second Worldwide Cybersecurity Summit, London, United Kingdom.

Harris, A. R., Sarijan, S. & Hussin, N. (2017). "Information Security Challenges: A Malaysian Context," *International Journal of Academic Research in Business and Social Sciences*, 7(9): 397–403.

UNIDIR. (2019, January). "Malaysia – Cybersecurity Policy." https://cyberpolicyportal.org/en/state-pdf-export/eyJjb3VudHJ5X2dyb3VwX2lkIjoiNzUifQ

Yunos, Z. (2009). "Putting Cyber Terrorism into Context," *STAR In-Tech*. www.cybersecurity.my/data/content_files/13/526.pdf

References

Ariff, S. U. & Radhi, N. A. M. (2019, April). "National Cyber Security Strategy to Be Implemented Middle of This Year – DPM." www.nst.com.my/news/nation/2019/04/475821/national-cyber-security-strategy-be-implemented-middle-year-dpm

El-Muhammady, A. (2017). "External Threats and Malaysia's National Security: The Case of Daesh", *Journal of Defence and Security*, 8(1):42–56.

El-Muhammady, A. (2018, June 29). "The Role of Universities and Schools in Countering and Preventing Violent Extremism: Malaysian Experience." www.kas.de/documents/288143/288192/Terrorism_El-Muhammady.pdf/86c33d0c-53eb-4d6d-bf90-9aa528c95785

FMT Media. (2019, November 4). "Cyber Warfare to Be Part of Military 'Future Force'." www.freemalaysiatoday.com/category/nation/2019/11/04/cyber-warfare-to-be-part-of-military-future-force/

Goud, N. (2019). "Microsoft Says that Malaysia Has Become Extremely Vulnerable to Cyber Attacks." www.cybersecurity-insiders.com/microsoft-says-that-malaysia-has-become-extremely-vulnerable-to-cyber-attacks/

Hamid, A. S. A. (1993). *Vision 2020: Understanding the Concept, Implications, and Challenges*. Petaling Jaya: Pelanduk Publications. cnii.cybersecurity.my/main/ncsp/NCSP-Policy2.pdf www.straitstimes.com/asia/se-asia/mahathir-sworn-in-as-malaysias-7th-prime-minister

Kheng, C. B. (1999). "Politics: Malaysian Political Development from Colonial Rule to Mahathir," in A. Kaur & I. Metcalfe (eds.), *The Shaping of Malaysia* (pp. 105–116). New York: St. Martin's Press.

Milne, R. S. & Mauzy, D. K. (1999). *Malaysian Politics Under Mahathir*. London: Routledge.

Ministry of Communications and Multimedia Malaysia. (2020). "Frequently Asked Questions." www.cybersecurity.my/en/media_centre/media_faqs/media_faqs/main/detail/1691/index.html

Ministry of Science, Technology and Innovation. (n.d.). "National Cyber Security."

National Cyber Security Agency. (2019). "The National Cyber Security Policy." www.nacsa.gov.my/ncsp.php

National Security Policy. (2019). www.pmo.gov.my/2019/07/national-security-policy/

Pei Pei, G. (2019, December 11). "Macau Scam Targets Pensioners," *New Straits Times*. www.nst.com.my/news/crime-courts/2019/12/546843/macau-scam-targets-pensioners

Ringkasan Eksekutif Profail Belia Dalam Kegiatan Ekstrimisme. (2017). Institute for Youth Research, Kuala Lumpur, Malaysia.

Ross, C. (2019, November 23). "Malaysia: Police Arrests 680 Chinese Nationals Busting an Overseas Online Gambling Scam," *Casino Industry News*. https://casino.buzz/malaysia-police-arrests-680-chinese-nationals-busting-an-overseas-online-gambling-scam/

Salman, A., Choy, E. A., Mahmud, W. A. W. & Latif, R. A. (2013). "Tracing the Diffusion of Internet in Malaysia: Then and Now," *Asian Social Science, 9*(6): 9–10.

Satar, D. S. A. (2019, August 26). "Agencies Should Work Together to Protect Cyberspace," *New Straits Times*. www.nst.com.my/opinion/columnists/2019/08/516006/agencies-should-work-together-protect-cyberspace

Teoh, S. & Leong, T. (2018, May 11). "Mahathir Sworn in as Malaysia's 7th Prime Minister," *The Straight Times*.

The Malaysian Administrative Modernisation and Management Planning Unit. (2019). "Cyber Security Framework For Public Sector (RAKKSSA)." www.malaysia.gov.my/portal/content/30090

28

CYBER GOVERNANCE AND DATA PROTECTION IN INDIA

A critical legal analysis

Debarati Halder and K. Jaishankar

Introduction

With the introduction of United Nations Commission on International Trade Law (UNICITRAL) model law on e-commerce in 1996 (United Nations, 1996), several jurisdictions adopted focused law to regulate online commerce and related e-governance. The Indian parliament enacted its Information Technology Act, 2000 to incorporate essential provisions of UNICITRAL model law on e-commerce. This statute primarily catered to four basic needs, i.e., to recognize online transfer of data, to formulate a basic framework for e-governance, creation of framework for strengthening cyber security, and amending the existing laws including Indian Penal Code, Indian Evidence Act, Bankers Book Evidence law etc. for updating the traditional criminal laws in order to support the penology related to cyber security.[1] The 2000 version of the Information Technology Act was soon challenged by an enormous growth of information communication technology and criminalities in cyber space. The statute fell short of providing protection of data including sensitive personal data, addressing issues related to growth of e-commerce (Basu & Jones, 2003), crimes targeting women and children (Halder & Jaishankar, 2008), and cyber terrorism (Halder, 2011).

Countries including the United States of America, United Kingdom etc. had revamped their laws including cyber security policies post the 9/11 attacks (Collin, 1996; Trachtman, 2009; Wykes & Harcus, 2010). After the 26/11 Mumbai Taj Hotel attack, it was understood that the existing Information Technology Act, 2000 proved to be extremely weak for addressing cyber warfare and cyber terrorism (Halder, 2011). Even though Indian parliament had already framed a new Bill in 2006 to address data security including e-commerce, e-governance, and criminalities including cyber terrorism and cyber warfare, it could not provide much hope as cyber security experts assessed the inability of the Bill to address issues which it promised to address. The Bill therefore was revamped and in 2008 the new amended version of the Information Technology Act was implemented.

This amended Act emphasized economic fraud, e-service delivery, e-governance, and cyber terrorism: in short, it tried to holistically address cyber security aspects.[2] To execute the provisions of this law, several rules were introduced, including: (1) electronic service delivery; (2) reasonable security practices and procedures and sensitive personal data or information, intermediary guidelines; (3) procedures and safeguards for interception, monitoring, and decryption of information; (4) procedures and safeguards for monitoring and collecting traffic data or information; and (5) procedures and safeguards for blocking for access to information by the public. The Information Technology Act (IT Act) 2000 (amended in 2008) addressed electronic governance in chapter III, which included a discussion on legal recognition of electronic records and signatures, legal recognition of the use of the same by Government and its agencies, e-service delivery by service providers, retention of electronic records, auditing etc.

This chapter emphasizes the limitations of the Act insisting on accepting only e-documents.[3] The IT Act, 2000 also included detailed discussion on the role of body corporates in securing the data,[4] liability of individuals who may be empowered by the provisions of the IT Act, 2000 to deal with any data, information, policies etc., towards maintaining security and integrity of the data,[5] and liability of the service providers, intermediaries or any person who may be engaged in providing the services under this provision against disclosure of information in breach of lawful contract to any third party.[6]

While the amended version of the IT Act, 2000 promises to ensure cyber security and protection of data including sensitive personal data, this chapter argues that the provisions of this law still suffer from lacuna and three case examples are provided to defend the argument:

a) In 2009, the then Government of India rolled out the plan for 12-digit unique identification number for all residents of India (popularly known as Aadhaar), which would be linked to demographic and biometric data through the Unique Identification Authority of India (UIDAI). Later UIDAI became a statutory body under the provisions of the Aadhaar (Targeted Delivery of Financial and Other Subsidies, Benefits and Services) Act, 2016 ("Aadhaar Act 2016") 2016 (UIDAI, 2016). The objective of Aadhaar was to eliminate fake identities (UIDAI, 2016). This unique identity number or Aadhaar was also aimed at providing for targeted delivery of subsidies and services to individuals residing in India (UIDAI, 2016). Soon after, residents of India who were intended to be covered by the Aadhaar plan were informed by the banks that existing bank account verifications, opening of new accounts etc. may need Aadhaar details (Deepalakhshmi, 2017). This practice was soon followed by mobile telecom operators who insisted that Aadhaar number would be mandatory to get a new mobile phone connection and for verification of existing connections (TOI-Online, 2019). It was also understood that the Aadhaar number is necessary for registration of birth, marriage, death, getting any government subsidy especially in cases of public distribution system for food grains and cooking fuel (Business Today, 2017). However, Aadhaar and its database were soon questioned by privacy lawyers: K. S. Puttaswamy, a retired High Court judge, approached the Supreme Court with a plea to consider privacy as a core fundamental right and in the course of it, questioned the legality of Aadhaar which allegedly violated privacy norms as through this, the Government collected sensitive personal data including biometrics. Puttaswamy contended that India's privacy law including the data privacy law are ill equipped to handle private information including sensitive personal data of residents as the mechanism of collection of such data, processing of data, and retention of data is questionable (Justice K. S. Puttaswamy & Others v Union of India & Others, 2012). However, in the later part of 2016 when the Indian Government brought in plans for demonetization of bank currency notes to curb corruption, there was a sudden rise in the e-wallet market. While this case was finally settled in 2018, the court passed several interim orders in the period of 2012 to 2018 whereby it was made clear that Aadhaar is constitutional, but the Government cannot make it mandatory for any services other than public distribution services. The orders also relaxed the deadlines for connecting Aadhaar with bank accounts and mobile phone numbers (Justice K. S. Puttaswamy & others v Union of India & others). However, in the same year worldwide news media widely shared news of the hacking of UIDAI which however was denied by the UIDAI (Ganjoo, 2019). However, this allegation was feared to be true by several privacy rights activists especially because of third party involvement in collection, processing, and storing of information needed for UIDAI numbers.[7] This third party may actually be an agent of the Government or an individual, service provider etc. authorized by the Government in this regard under S.6A of the IT Act, 2000 (amended in 2008) and also The Information Technology (Electronic service delivery Rules) 2011. Information about the individual or intermediary or service provider may be available at the web portal of Common Service Centre (www.apnacscon line.in). This web portal was initiated by the Government of India as part of its national e-governance plan scheme (Apna CSC, 2017). Any individual above the age of 18 and a local resident may apply for Common Service Center through this e-platform provided he/she may have requirements and eligibility as may be indicated in the website. While such individuals may be commissioned by the Government to work for effective e-service delivery, proper auditing of their records and infrastructure needs to be done for secured e-service delivery. Several cyber security experts have expressed concern about such auditing.[8]

b) In 2013 the video image of an unidentified couple in a compromised position was captured inside a Delhi Metro station. This video was allegedly recorded from the live feed of the CCTV camera feed inside the Delhi Metro CCTV control room by a smart phone and it was uploaded on porn sites. The content became viral porn content. While Delhi Metro Railway Corporation (DMRC) lodged a complaint with the Delhi police against the unidentified couple for obscenity in a public place (CNN-IBN, 2013), this case also raised questions regarding privacy and cyber security loopholes in regard to audio-video clippings captured by CCTV cameras installed in public places by the Government agencies. Apparently, the Government department, or the authorized individual or the agency that has been authorized by the Government, that has installed CCTV cameras for security surveillance in a particular place that may come under its jurisdiction, is the sole authority responsible for confidentiality and integrity of the contents including electronic records that may have been created by way of capturing the audio video images. The Information Technology Act, 2000 (amended in 2008) confers the responsibility on such authority for protecting the confidentiality and integrity of the such records: breach of such responsibility has been held to attract penal liability on the said individual/authority under different provisions of Information Technology Act.

c) In 2019 October, several human right activists in India were targeted by WhatsApp snooping which had been allegedly carried out by an Israeli farm (Hopkins & Kirchgaessner, 2019). Interestingly a public interest litigation was filed by an activist in early November 2019 in the Supreme Court of India whereby the petitioner requested an investigation by the National Investigating Agency (NIA) for alleged surveillance by the Government using Pegasus software; the petitioner claimed that WhatsApp has mislead the Government by stating that the company uses end to end encryption, which will not allow any decryption at any point unless the sender and recipient themselves are revealing the information to any third party. The petitioner has also sought to restrain Government from using Pegasus software for the purpose of surveillance as it violates right to privacy (Nilashish, 2019). This case has pulled up huge debate over the use of S.69[9] and 69B[10] of the Information Technology Act, 2000 (amended in 2008).

While the first two examples may attract issues of privacy and security breach due to failure to protect the infrastructure in e-governance system, the third example attracts the issue related to breach of security and privacy from the perspective of an intermediary which is used by the general public for information and digital communication and Government agencies for e-governance (PTI, 2014). As stated above, after the Mumbai Taj Hotel attack, in view of cyber terrorism, Indian Information Technology Act, 2000 was made stronger by adding provisions to address cyber terrorism, attempts to commit cyber terrorism, and abetment to commit any offence including cyber terrorism in addition to prescribing stringent punishments for the said offences which extend to life imprisonment.[11] The Government also strengthened rules and policies for ensuring security for government infrastructure and data bases. However, this chapter claims that the law in this regard needs to be strengthened more; further, the execution of the existing laws, rules, and policies have remained extremely poor. This is mainly because several stakeholders including the government stakeholders may not be aware of cyber security measures that should be adopted to protect data.

This chapter carries on the discussion in three parts including the introduction. In the second part it discusses the existing laws and proposed Data Protection Bill that promises smooth conducting of e-governance. It will then discuss the possible lacunas in the laws including the bill that needs to be addressed for preventing the incidences of data privacy breach as shown in the three examples above. The third part is the conclusion and suggestions.

A critical review of laws meant for e-governance, service delivery for e-governance purposes, security surveillance by the government and data protection bill

In India, the primary law that regulates electronic governance, electronic commerce, and cyber security and cybercrime-related issues is the Information Technology Act, 2000 (amended in 2008) (IT Act).[12] With the implementation of the IT Act, India also recognized electronic records, electronic data, and electronic governance. The Information Technology Act, 2000 (amended in 2008) does not define the term "electronic governance." However, the other component parts of electronic governance, including electronic data, electronic records, and electronic signature have been defined by the IT Act.[13] Chapter III of the IT Act discusses electronic governance: the opening provision of this chapter, S.4 extends the scope of this law to accept electronic information submission for the purpose of e-governance. It states:

> Where any law provides that information or any other matter shall be in writing or in the typewritten or printed form, then, notwithstanding anything contained in such law, such requirement shall be deemed to have been satisfied if such information or matter is (a) rendered or made available in an electronic form; and (b) accessible so as to be usable for a subsequent reference.

S.5 further emphasizes that need of signature for any authentication of any information submitted by anyone, may be satisfied by affixing digital signature. S.6 contains the heart of the third chapter of the IT Act by stating that filing of any form, issuing of any license etc. by the Government or by Government authorized agencies and receipt of any payment etc. may be accepted by the Government if done by electronic form.[14] This provision also indicates that such filing, issuance of such certificates etc. and receipt of payments etc. must be made as per proper format prescribed by the Government. S.6A of the IT Act speaks about service delivery including e-service delivery for the purpose of electronic governance. It states:

1   The appropriate Government may, for the purposes of this Chapter and for efficient delivery of services to the public through electronic means authorise, by order, any service provider to set up, maintain and upgrade the computerised facilities and perform such other services as it may specify, by notification in the Official Gazette. Service provider so authorized includes any individual, private agency, private company, partnership firm, sole proprietor form or any such other body or agency which has been granted permission by the appropriate Government to offer services through electronic means in accordance with the policy governing such service sector.
2   The appropriate Government may also authorize any service provider authorized under subsection (1) to collect, retain and appropriate service charges, as may be prescribed by the appropriate Government for the purpose of providing such services, from the person availing such service.
3   Subject to the provisions of sub-section (2), the appropriate Government may authorize the service providers to collect, retain and appropriate service charges under this section notwithstanding the fact that there is no express provision under the Act, rule, regulation or notification under which the service is provided to collect, retain and appropriate e-service charges by the service providers.
4   The appropriate Government shall, by notification in the Official Gazette, specify the scale of service charges which may be charged and collected by the service providers under this section: Provided that the appropriate Government may specify different scale of service charges for different types of services.

A clear reading of the above-mentioned provision may indicate that the Government may not only appoint authorized service providers to collect, retain, and process data[15] for the purpose of proper e-service delivery and e governance, such service providers may also decide upon service charges for their services independently. However, the IT Act, 2000 (amended in 2008) also provides and check and balance provision in S.7A which speaks about auditing of the documents in electronic form. It states:

> Where in any law for the time being in force, there is a provision for audit of documents, records or information, that provision shall also be applicable for audit of documents, records or information processed and maintained in electronic form.

The above provision may imply that auditing of the documents, data, and databases is an inherent responsibility of the data collectors, retainers, and processors. It may be interesting to note that India has come across incidences of data and information security breaches for critical information infrastructures including the Central Bureau of Investigation (CBI) and the security experts have expressed their concerns about lacuna in cyber security and auditing of the documents and databases by the Government as well as Government authorized stakeholders (PTI, 2010). The Government of India has however taken several precautionary measures to improve the situation such as introducing more rules for stronger protection of data. However, it is also noteworthy that while India is the biggest market for social media websites and messaging services like WhatsApp, the majority of the Indian population, including the senior citizens, may not be comfortable in using e-governance mechanisms including e-service mechanisms. This was noted by some researchers during the demonetization drive in India in 2016–2017 (Pavan, 2016). The IT Act, 2000 (amended in 2008) has offered alternative solution for such incidences in S.9., which states that:

> Nothing contained in sections 6, 7 and 8 shall confer a right upon any person to insist that any Ministry or Department of the Central Government or the State Government or any authority or body established by or under any law or controlled or funded by the Central or State Government should accept, issue, create, retain and preserve any document in the form of electronic records or effect any monetary transaction in the electronic form.

This implies that electronic governance and e-service delivery system for the purpose of e-governance and e-commerce may not be forcefully imposed on anyone.

As such, several beneficiaries of e-governance may be provided services for e-filing, e-receipts etc. without properly sensitizing them. The Information Technology Act 2000 (amended in 2008) has accommodated the authorized individuals or companies etc. who may collect, retain, and process data for e-governance and e-commerce purposes as "body corporates" and has provided special responsibilities to such body corporates. The lead author in her earlier research observed as follows:

> In India data privacy has been recognised as an important factor from the very beginning of the initiation of Information Technology Act (IT Act) way back in 2000 when the first version of this law was created. The 2000 version of the IT Act had provisions to criminalise infringement of privacy by recognising it as a case for civil penalty (S.43), as well as criminal penalties (S.66). But it did not recognise the liabilities of the Body Corporates for data security of their customers/subscribers. This was modified by the 2008 amendments which added S.43A after S.43 to the IT Act to ensure Body Corporates' liability for data safety and also compensation for breach of data safety to the victim. S.43A titled "Compensation for failure to protect data" is a liability of civil nature on the Body Corporates for failure to protect data. It needs to be remembered that in the IT Act, along with S.43A, there exist two more provisions to penalise infringement of privacy; these include S.72, which prescribe punishment for breaching of confidentiality and privacy and S.72A, which prescribes punishment for disclosure of information in breach of lawful contract. These provisions were created in support of computer related offences including breaching of privacy, which were criminalised under Chapter IX (civil in nature) and XI (criminal in nature). But these two later provisions differ from S.43A in their scope and nature. S.43A is essentially for Body Corporates, whereas Ss.72 and 72A cover "any individual" who may come under the purview of these two provisions.
>
> It has been seen that due to the special scope of S.43A, the provision has been used to restore justice for victims who may have suffered due to negligence of the

Body Corporates. But such Body Corporates are mostly the financial institutions ... . S.43A ... prescribes punishment for a Body Corporate by stating that "Where a Body Corporate, possessing, dealing or handling any sensitive personal data or information in a computer resource which it owns, controls or operates, is negligent in implementing and maintaining reasonable security practices and procedures and thereby causes wrongful loss or wrongful gain to any person, such Body Corporate shall be liable to pay damages by way of compensation, not exceeding five crore rupees, to the person so affected." The term Body Corporate is further defined by explanation (i) of this provision as "any company and includes a firm, sole proprietorship or other association of individuals engaged in commercial or professional activities."

The concept of Sensitive personal data or information that forms the core subject to be protected by the Body Corporates, is defined by Rule 3 of the Information Technology (Reasonable security practices and procedures and sensitive personal data or information) Rules, 2011 as "such personal information which consists of information relating to; − (i) password; (ii) financial information such as Bank account or credit card or debit card or other payment instrument details; (iii) physical, physiological and mental health condition; (iv) sexual orientation; (v) medical records and history; (vi) Biometric information; (vii) any detail relating to the above clauses as provided to Body Corporate for providing service; and (viii) any of the information received under above clauses by Body Corporate for processing, stored or processed under lawful contract or otherwise." This provision exempts those information which are already available in the public domain or may have been accessed by way of Right to information Act or any other law that may make it compulsory to furnish some personal information for public knowledge. ... Taking help of S.43A of the IT Act read with Rule 3 of the Information Technology (Reasonable security practices and procedures and sensitive personal data or information) Rules, 2011, some victims of identity theft and phishing have successfully made the banks to compensate the loss.

(Halder, 2017)

However, it can be noted that the authorized agencies at the grassroots level who may be data collectors working on behalf of the body corporates who may be the authorized agents of the Government to collect and retain data might not be sensitized enough for taking basic security measures to protect the confidentiality of any data collected from the beneficiaries. This has resulted in data and information security and privacy breaches affecting private individuals, financial sectors like banks, and government sectors. Consider the cases of CCTV footage leaking, alleged Aadhaar data breaches, bank phishing cases etc. discussed in the introductory part of this chapter: each of them supports the above-mentioned opinion of the authors. Ironically, India's cyber security laws have been strengthened enough to prohibit and penalize attacks on critical information infrastructure[16] systems and critical sectors[17] concerning confidential Government data, certain types offences targeting individuals including unauthorized access to computers and computer system (Halder, 2016), impersonation, voyeurism, and stalking (Halder & Jaishankar, 2016).

However, we argue that the creation of such laws could not fully cure the problems of cyber security issues. After the 26/11 Mumbai Taj Hotel attack by terrorists, the Government brought in several amendments in the IT Act and this included provisions to include punishment for cyber terrorism under S.66F (Halder, 2011), the Government's power to issue directions for interception or monitoring or decryption of information through any computer resource under S.69, power to issue directions for blocking for public access of any information through any computer resource under S.69A and power to authorize to monitor and collect traffic data or information through any computer resource for cyber security under S.69B. The parliament however had taken enough caution to ensure proper implementation and execution of these laws through Rules including the Information Technology (Procedure and safeguards for interception, monitoring and decryption of information) Rules 2009 and Information Technology (Procedure and Safeguards for Blocking for Access of Information by Public) Rules, 2009. These Rules suggest that interception, monitoring, collecting of traffic data, and blocking of contents may be done only under certain conditions, by authorized officers, and the data collected must be destroyed after the purpose of the collection and monitoring of data traffic is over.

However, at various times the provisions meant for interception, monitoring, and decryption of data have been challenged by privacy advocates in India.[18] The Supreme Court however offered for more cautious use of such provisions rather than scrapping the provisions *in toto*. A clear reading of the Information Technology (Procedure and safeguards for interception, monitoring and decryption of information) Rules 2009 may suggest that both the Government and intermediaries who may be collaborating with each other for the purpose of interception, decryption, monitoring of traffic data etc., must follow stringent security procedures and the rules to ensure protection of privacy of data and data owners (Information Technology (Procedure and safeguards for interception, monitoring and decryption of information) Rules 2009). However, the recent report of WhatsApp snooping (CNN-IBN, 2013) may suggest that such provisions have raised wider risks related to cyber security in India.

Further, S.69A of the IT Act (which empowers the Government to block for access of information) and the Information Technology (Procedure and Safeguards for Blocking for Access of Information by Public) Rules, 2009 have also attracted severe criticism from the free speech advocates especially after the Government decided to ban and block access to 857 websites which allegedly provided porn contents (PTI, 2018). It has been seen that such blockage has not provided any fruitful suggestions especially when there are glaring examples of defying the rules for cases like sharing of rape videos through social media and porn sites (Tripathi, 2019), circulation of confidential video clippings which are supposed to be protected by body corporates who may be authorized by the Government to protect the same.

In the aforementioned context, it becomes necessary to critically analyze the Personal Data Protection Act, 2018 which is still in the form of a Bill named the Data Protection Bill, 2018 when this chapter was being written. There are four main purposes for the enactment of the Data Protection Act, these are (1) to ensure privacy for information; (2) to guarantee privacy of communication for e-commerce purposes; (3) to ensure autonomy for the data owners; and (4) to lay stronger rules for data processing. This proposed Act provides guidelines for secure processing of personal data which may be used for e-governance and e-commerce purposes. It also lays down guidelines for consensual data processing and right to confirmation and access of data, right to be forgotten and right to data portability. Further, the proposed Act also lays down guidelines for proper categorization of data such as health data, financial data, personal data etc., which, if accessed unauthorizedly or if processed non consensually, may attract legal sanctions (Data Protection Bill, 2018). Notably, the Data Protection Act is made on the basis of EU General Data Protection Regulation.

As may be understood from the above discussions, India is equipped with cyber security laws to provide protection for critical infrastructure information, critical sectors, and personal data to a certain extent. However, the three case studies discussed above may show that, in spite of the existing laws, the Government is not able to provide full satisfactory protection for the data.

Conclusion

As discussed above, e-governance may necessarily impose the responsibility of data protection on the data collectors, data retainers, and data fiduciaries. After witnessing several misuses of the Internet to target the government, corporations, and individuals by terror organizations, scammers, hackers, and private stakeholders who would be using the data illegally collected for unethical gain, the Indian Government proposed more stringent laws to prohibit and penalize criminal activities. However, this has given rise to confusion and abuse of laws. In Shreya Singhal's case, it was observed by the courts that draconian drafting of laws has created more trouble for civil citizens rather than solving the problems (Halder, 2017). Further, the recent WhatsApp snooping case (Hopkins & Kirchgaessner, 2019), may show that the procedure for monitoring, decryption, and collection of traffic data has not been followed as per the existing rules which say that such surveillance activities may not be permitted unless and until there is urgent need for doing so and other alternative mechanisms for surveillance may not be applicable.[19] Further, it has been universally accepted that personal data collected by authorized government agencies and private stakeholders for e-governance purposes and e-commerce purposes may not be properly protected and may be misused. The situation may improve if the Government emphasizes proper auditing of the documents and data retained and stored by stakeholders including child care institutions, education sectors, financial sectors, health care sectors, and criminal justice machinery including the courts who may generate data for victims and accused and crime location data. The Government must consider training and sensitizing data handlers and it is expected that if such suggestions are considered, the existing laws may be properly implemented and executed.

Notes

1 For a deeper understanding, see the objectives of the Information Technology Act, 2000.
2 Chapters IX and XI of the IT Act are specifically mentionable here.
3 S.9 of the IT Act) says "Nothing contained in sections 6, 7 and 8 shall confer a right upon any person to insist that any Ministry or Department of the Central Government or the State Government or any authority or body established by or under any law or controlled or funded by the Central or State Government should accept, issue, create, retain, and preserve any document in the form of electronic records or effect any monetary transaction in the electronic form."
4 S.43A of the IT Act covers the same.
5 S.72 of the IT Act discusses this. These provisions would be discussed in later parts.
6 S.72A of the IT Act) discusses this. These provisions would be discussed in later parts.
7 Even though UIDIA has clearly stated that it is responsible for Aadhar enrolment, authentication, and governance by virtue of S.6A of the IT Act, the Information Technology (Electronic service delivery Rules), 2011 provides that government may consider appointing any agent for e-service delivery.
8 S.72 of the IT Act discusses this. These provisions would be discussed below.
9 S.69 of the IT Act discusses power to issue directions for interception or monitoring or decryption of any information through any computer resource. Discussions on this provision would be carried out in the later parts of this chapter.

10 S.69B of the IT Act discusses power to authorize to monitor and collect traffic data or information through any computer resource for cyber security.

11 S.66F of the IT Act addresses cyber terrorism and related issues.

12 IT Act, Act no 21 of 2000.

13 For example, S.2(o) defines data, which means a representation of information, knowledge, facts, concepts or instructions which are being prepared or have been prepared in a formalized manner, and is intended to be processed, is being processed or has been processed in a computer system or computer network, and may be in any form (including computer printouts magnetic or optical storage media, punched cards, punched tapes) or stored internally in the memory of the computer.

S.2(t) says electronic record means data, record or data generated, image or sound stored, received or sent in an electronic form or micro film or computer generated micro fiche; 2(p) addresses digital signature and explains it as authentication of any electronic record by a subscriber by means of an electronic method or procedure in accordance with the provisions of section 3;

2(ta) discusses electronic signatures and explains them as authentication of any electronic record by a subscriber by means of the electronic technique specified in the Second Schedule and includes digital signature.

2(r) says electronic forms with reference to information, means any information generated, sent, received, or stored in media, magnetic, optical, computer memory, micro film, computer generated micro fiche, or similar device.

14 S. 6 of the IT Act states "(1) Where any law provides for (a) the filing of any form, application or any other document with any office, authority, body or agency owned or controlled by the appropriate Government in a particular manner;

(b) the issue or grant of any license, permit, sanction or approval by whatever name called in a particular manner;

(c) the receipt or payment of money in a particular manner such requirement shall be deemed to have been satisfied if such filing, issue, grant, receipt or payment, as the case may be, is effected by means of such electronic form as may be prescribed by the appropriate Government."

15 S.7 of the IT Act, 2000 (amended in 2008) speaks about retention of electronic data and states that:

"(1) Where any law provides that documents, records or information shall be retained for any specific period, then, that requirement shall be deemed to have been satisfied if such documents, records or information are retained in the electronic form, – (a) the information contained therein remains accessible so as to be usable for a subsequent reference; (b) the electronic record is retained in the format in which it was originally generated, sent or received or in a format which can be demonstrated to represent accurately the information originally generated, sent or received; (c) the details which will facilitate the identification of the origin, destination, date and time of dispatch or receipt of such electronic record are available in the electronic record: Exception to this provision states that this clause does not apply to any information which is automatically generated solely for the purpose of enabling an electronic record to be dispatched or received.

Subclause (2) further says Nothing in this section shall apply to any law that expressly provides for the retention of documents, records or information in the form of electronic records."

16 Rule 2(d) of Information Technology National Critical Information Infrastructure protection center and manner of performing functions and duties Rules, 2013 defines the term "Critical Information Infrastructure" as the "computer resource, the incapacitation or destruction of which, shall have debilitating impact on national security, economy, public health or safety." (explanation to S.70 (1) IT Act, 2000 (amended in 2008).

17 Rule 2e of Information Technology National Critical Information Infrastructure protection center and manner of performing functions and duties Rules, 2013 defines the term "Critical Sectors" as "those sectors which are critical to the nation and whose incapacitation or destruction will have a debilitating impact on national security, economy, public health or safety: these will include Defense, Transport, Public, banking/health/education system, Telecom Biometric data base/ Unique Identification Authority of India."

18 This can be seen in the case of Shreya Singhal vs Union of India & others. WRIT PETITION (CRIMINAL) NO.167 OF 2012.

19 See, Ministry of Electronics and Information Technology (2009), Rules 4–12 of the Information Technology (Procedure and safeguards for interception, monitoring and decryption of information) Rules 2009.

Suggested reading

Dua, S. (2017). "Digital India: Opportunities & Challenges," *International Journal of Science Technology and Management, 6*(3): 61–67. https://thediplomat.com/2019/12/indias-national-cybersecurity-policy-must-acknowledge-modern-realities/

Mishra, S., Dir, S. & Hooda, M. (2016). "A Study on Cyber Security, Its Issues and Cyber Crime Rates in India," in H. Saini, R. Sayal & S. Rawat (eds.), *Innovations in Computer Science and Engineering: Advances in Intelligent Systems and Computing*, Vol. 413, (pp.249–253). Singapore: Springer.

Roy-Chaudhury, R. (2019, November 22). "India–UK Cybersecurity Cooperation: The Way Forward," The International Institute for Strategic Studies. iiss.org/blogs/analysis/2019/11/sasia-india-uk-cyber-security-cooperation

Shukla, S. & Agrawal, M. (eds.). (2020). *Cyber Security in India: Education, Research and Training (IITK Directions)*. Cham: Springer.

Waghre, P. & Mehta, S. (2019, December 20). "India's National Cybersecurity Policy Must Acknowledge Modern Realities," *The Diplomat*. https://thediplomat.com/2019/12/indias-national-cybersecurity-policy-must-acknowledge-modern-realities/

References

Apna CSC. (2017). "Common Service Center." www.apnacsconline.in

Basu, S. & Jones, R. (2003) "E-Commerce and the Law: A Review of India's Information Technology Act, 2000," *Contemporary South Asia, 12*(1): 7–24.

Business Today. (2017, December 15). "Supreme Court Extends Aadhaar Linking Deadline: Here's a Five-Year Timeline." www.businesstoday.in/current/economy-politics/aadhaar-linking-deadline-supreme-court-timeline-pan-card-bank-account/story/266066.html

CNN-IBN. (2013). "CCTV Footage of Couples in Delhi Metro Leaked on Porn Sites." www.news18.com/news/india/delhi-metro-cctv-622454.html

Collin, B. (1996). "The Future of Cyber Terrorism," Proceedings of the 11th Annual International Symposium on Criminal Justice Issues, The University of Illinois at Chicago, United States.

Data Protection Bill. (2018). "The Personal Data Protection Bill." https://meity.gov.in/writereaddata/files/Personal_Data_Protection_Bill,2018.pdf

Deepalakhshmi, K. (2017, March 24). "The Long List of Aadhaar-Linked Schemes," *The Hindu*. www.thehindu.com/news/national/the-long-list-of-aadhaar-linked-schemes/article17641068.ece

Ganjoo, S. (2019, September, 12). "UIDAI Refutes Aadhaar Software Hacking Reports, Says Aadhaar Can't Be Hacked." www.indiatoday.in/technology/news/story/uidai-refutes-aadhaar-software-hacking-reports-says-aadhaar-can-t-be-hacked-1338357-2018-09-12

Halder, D. & Jaishankar, K. (2008, June). "Cyber Crimes against Women in India Problems, Perspectives and Solutions," *TMC Academy Journal, 3*(1): 48–62.

Halder, D. (2011). "Information Technology Act and Cyber Terrorism: A Critical Review," in P. M. S. Sundaram & S. Umarhathab (eds.), *Cyber Crime and Digital Disorder* (pp. 75–90). Tirunelveli: Publication Division, Manonmaniam Sundaranar University.

Halder, D. & Jaishankar, K. (2016). *Cyber Crimes against Women in India*. New Delhi: SAGE Publications.

Halder, D. (2017). "Corporate Liability for Data Protection in India: A Critical Analysis of S.43A of the Information Technology Act, 2000 (Amended in 2008)," in N. Saxena (ed.). *Cyber Crimes in 21st Century* (pp.328–337). New Delhi: Manakin Press.

Hopkins, N. & Kirchgaessner, S. (2019). "WhatsApp Sues Israeli Firm, Accusing It of Hacking Activists' Phones." www.theguardian.com/technology/2019/oct/29/whatsapp-sues-israeli-firm-accusing-it-of-hacking-activists-phones

Justice, K. S. "Puttaswamy & Others v Union of India & Others," Writ Petition no. 494 of 2012.

Nilashish, C. (2019, November 4). "'Pegasus Surveillance': RSS Ideologue KN Govindacharya Moves SC Seeking NIA Investigation against WhatsApp, Facebook, NSO Group." www.livelaw.in/top-stories/kn-govindacharya-nia-investigation-whatsapp-facebook-nso-group–149476

Pavan, K. (2016). "An Empirical Study of the Effects of Demonetization in India in the Year 2016 and Analyzing Shifting Trends in Marketing/Purchasing to the Alternative Options," *Journal of Management Engineering and Information Technology, 3*(6): 2394–8124.

PTI. (2014). "Delhi Police Launches WhatsApp Helpline to Curb Corruption." https://indianexpress.com/article/cities/delhi/delhi-police-launch-whatsapp-helpline-to-curb-corruption

PTI. (2018). "Telecom Department Asks Internet Providers to Block 827 Porn Websites." www.economic times.indiatimes.com/articleshow/66351252.cms?from=mdr&utm_source=contento finterest&utm_medium=text&utm_campaign=cppst

PTI. (2010). "CBI Website Hacked by 'Pakistani Cyber Army'." http://timesofindia.indiatimes.com/arti cleshow/7038524.cms?utm_source=contentofinterest&utm_medium=text&utm_campaign=cppst

Ministry of Electronics and Information Technology. (2009, October 27). "The Information Technology (Procedure and Safeguards for Interception, Monitoring and Decryption of Information) Rules 2009." https://meity.gov.in/writereaddata/files/Information%20Technology%20%28Proced ure%20and%20Safeguards%20for%20Interception%2C%20Monitoring%20and%20Decryption%20of %20Information%29%20Rules%2C%202009.pdf

TOI-Online. (2019, October, 15). "Why Linking Your Mobile Number with Aadhaar Is Important?" http://timesofindia.indiatimes.com/articleshow/62752460.cms?utm_source=contentofinterest&utm_medium=text&utm_campaign=cppst

Trachtman, J. P. (2009). "Global Cyberterrorism, Jurisdiction, and International Organization," in M. F. Grady & F. Parisi (eds.), *The Law and Economics of Cybersecurity* (pp. 259–296). New York: Cambridge University Press.

Tripathi, K. (2019, December 3). "Rape Victim Anonymity: Delhi HC Issues Notice on Plea for Action against Media for Revealing Identity of Rape Victim." www.livelaw.in/news-updates/delhi-hc-issues-notice-in-a-plea-seeking-action-against-media-for-revealing-the-identity-of-rape-victim-150438

UIDAI. (2016). "About UIDAI." https://uidai.gov.in/about-uidai/unique-identification-authority-of-india/about.html

UN. (1996). "UNCITRAL Model Law on Electronic Commerce Guide to Enactment with 1996 with Additional Article 5 as Adopted in 1998." www.uncitral.org/pdf/english/texts/electcom/05-89450_Ebook.pdf

Wykes, M. & Harcus, D. (2010). "Cyber-terror: Construction, Criminalisation and Control," in Y. Jewkes & M. Yar (eds.), *Handbook of Internet Crimes* (pp. 214–229). Cullompton: Willan Publishing.

29

CYBERSECURITY

A national priority for Bangladesh

Md. Shariful Islam

Introduction

Bangladesh's cybersecurity policies became well-known internationally in 2016 when the country's central bank was the subject of one of the largest digital bank heists to date. Notably, on February 2016, US$101 million was stolen from the Bangladesh Bank's account with the New York Federal Reserve Bank by hackers (*The Daily Star*, 2016). This is a major loss for Bangladesh. In fact, in this age of growing cyber insecurities, no nation, whether powerful or weak, big or small, developed or developing is immune to cyber-attack. Though Bangladesh is a very small country, covering an area of 1,47,570 square km, the country has already been affected by several cyber-attacks ranging from its foreign ministry website to security infrastructure (Islam, 2013). In addition, cyber-attacks in critical financial infrastructures in Bangladesh in 2016, as mentioned earlier, have proven the importance of cybersecurity in the country. Bangladesh becomes vulnerable to cyber-attacks considering its poor resources and lack of skilled manpower to defend or protect its cyberspace. This chapter contends that there is no alternative to promoting cooperation at both the regional and international level to ensure cybersecurity for Bangladesh. It is also worthy to note that there is no scholarly work on cybersecurity in Bangladesh. And therefore, the chapter fills the existing knowledge gap.

Bangladesh's National Cyber Security Strategy

Bangladesh adopted its *National Cyber Security Strategy* in 2014 to face cyber threats, risks, and challenges to its national security. According to the *National Strategy*, three dimensions will be prioritized, i.e., legal measures; technical and procedural measures; and organizational structures (Ministry of Post, Telecommunications, and Information Technology, 2014). The first priority will focus on the development of cybercrime legislation to deter cybercrime in the country. Cybercrime laws will be based on the global conventions, i.e., ITU Toolkit for Cybercrime legislation. According to the *National Strategy*, "[t]he alignment of our [Bangladesh's] cybercrime legislation with the ITU Toolkit for Cybercrime helps international cooperation and addresses jurisdictional and evidentiary issues" (Ministry of Post, Telecommunications, and Information Technology, 2014: 9706). Also, the Convention on Cybercrime (2001) will be consulted to draft the cybercrime laws in Bangladesh. It is worthy to note that Bangladesh's cybercrime policy is in line with international and global norms. This also applies to all aspects of Bangladesh's cybersecurity policies.

Technical and procedural measures include creating organizational structure at national and regional levels to facilitate communication and information exchange. The structures will be imperative to recognize digital credentials through a national cybersecurity framework, securing government infrastructure and protecting critical information infrastructure. The third priority, organizational structure, focuses on the role of government, the National Cybersecurity Council, and public–private partnership to ensure cybersecurity in Bangladesh. It also highlights the national management capacity, cybersecurity skills and training, and national culture on cybersecurity.

The *Strategy* asks for the collaboration of resources of the government, organizations across all sectors, individuals, and international partners in mitigating threats to its cyberspace. It prioritizes the development of national cybercrime legislation, raising awareness among different stakeholders, promoting dialogues, cooperation, and coordination in dealing with cyber threats (Ministry of Posts, Telecommunication and Information Technology, 2014: 9705). Additionally, Bangladesh has drafted the *Digital Security Act 2016* to address "the need for cybercrime legislation" (Jamal, Mahtab & Sajen, 2016). The draft was approved in August 2016 by the cabinet, the Government of Bangladesh. Bangladesh is trying to pass the *Digital Security Bill* consulting with the relevant stakeholders.

Definitions

Cybersecurity can be defined as the securing of one's cyber space from internal or external cyber-attacks. Bangladesh has defined several key terms about its cybersecurity. In the draft of *Digital Security Act, 2016*, cyber terrorism has been defined as:

> Any person, entity, company or foreign national with a view to restrain the government or any company or any person to do any work through creating panic among people for endangering the integrity, solidarity, public security or sovereignty of Bangladesh.
>
> *(Ministry of Posts, Telecommunication and Information Technology, n.d.)*

International law, cooperation and governance

Bangladesh accepts the generally accepted understanding regarding the applicability of international law to cyberspace. Bangladesh believes that cyber threat is a global issue which requires international cooperation. According to the *National Cybersecurity Strategy*, Bangladesh commits itself to "join regional and international partnerships creating solutions for addressing the cyber security challenges regardless of threat" (Ministry of Posts, Telecommunication and Information Technology, 2014: 9703). Bangladesh has prepared its *National Cyber Security Strategy* following the Pillars of the International Telecommunication Union's Global Cybersecurity Agenda (GCA).

Bangladesh has sought cooperation from the major powers including Russia and India to face growing cyber insecurities. Notably, Bangladesh and Russia have agreed to form a joint working group to combat cybersecurity risks. They have agreed to establish a "Centre of Excellence in Cyber Security" (Dhaka Tribune, 2018). Bangladesh has also signed a Memorandum of Understanding (MoU) with India with regard to cybersecurity cooperation in April 2017. The agreement was signed between the Indian Computer Emergency Response Team (CERT-In) and Bangladesh Government Computer Incident Response Team (BGD e-Gov CIRT) (India Today, 2017). The Agreement would be implemented through a duly set up joint committee on cybersecurity. It is expected that the implementation of the agreement will be highly imperative to secure the cyber space of Bangladesh.

Bangladesh's cultural understandings

Though the number of smartphone and internet subscribers is increasing rapidly in Bangladesh, the level of awareness of cybersecurity among the users is at the lowest level. Also, the level of responsibility among the users is not satisfactory. Due to lack of knowledge and awareness, people are becoming involved in different cybercrimes like cyberbullying, hate speech, defamation and radicalization. And even Buddhist and Hindu temples were destroyed based on a Facebook post (Islam, 2016). Therefore, the *National Cybersecurity Strategy* identifies some steps to promote cybersecurity culture in Bangladesh, i.e. increasing cybersecurity awareness among the users and institutions, introducing cybersecurity education at the national education curriculum, engaging the civil society organizations (Ministry of Posts, Telecommunication and Information Technology, 2014: 9715).

Institutions dealing with cybersecurity

What are the key institutions involved in addressing cybercrime in Bangladesh? The Ministry of Science and Information & Technology is mainly responsible for addressing cyber insecurities in Bangladesh. The Ministry has already adopted some policies to tackle cyber threats. The *National ICT Policy*, *Cyber Law*, and *Electronic Transaction Act* are a few examples. Moreover, the Post and Telecommunications Ministry and Bangladesh Telecommunication Regulatory Commission are also involved in dealing with cybersecurity in Bangladesh. For instance, in association with the Asia-Pacific Telecommunity, the Post and Telecommunications Ministry and Bangladesh Telecommunication Regulatory Commission arranged the 8th APT Cyber Security Forum, titled "Cyber Security in Data-Driven Society" in Dhaka in October 2017. Such developments in the cybersecurity domain of Bangladesh occurred as a reaction to the 2016 Bangladesh Bank heist. Bangladesh also plans to establish "Cyber Security Agency" to curb cyber insecurities in the country. State Minister for Post and Telecommunications, Tarana Halim, points out that the "cyber security issue is being prioriti[z]ed and [the] formulation of the 'Cyber Security Law' is on the cards. After the law, [a] cyber security agency will be established and it will act under the Prime Minister's Office" (BSS, 2017).

Role of private sector

Alongside the state, non-state actors are also involved in ensuring cybersecurity in Bangladesh. For instance, Cyber Security Forum, an NGO, focuses on the awareness-building programs, i.e., organizing workshops, seminars, and conferences regarding cybercrime and cyber threats. The role of media is also critically important as it works as a medium of debate, discussion, and critical analysis of cybersecurity issues. Media also educates people about cyber threats. Against the context of *Digital Cyber Security Act*, "the civil society and public interest groups have already engaged in debate in respect of whether cybersecurity is something for systems, rather than people" (Siddiqui, 2018).

Financial institutions are mostly vulnerable to cyber-attacks. In a study conducted by the Bangladesh Institute of Bank Management (BIBM), it is revealed that bank officials in Bangladesh are largely ignorant to the issue of cybersecurity. The study also found that among the respondents of the study, some 28 per cent were found to be "totally ignorant" and another 20 per cent "ignorant." Only 20 per cent of respondents showed "some knowledge" on the issue (bdnews24.com., 2017). This issue requires serious attention to ensure cybersecurity in Bangladesh as all the actors involved need to play their part.

Cybercrime and cyberterrorism in Bangladesh

What is the nature of cybercrime and cyberterrorism in Bangladesh, and what might be its societal and security implications for the country? According to the *National Cybersecurity Strategy*, the cyberspace of Bangladesh:

> faces a range of threats. Cyber threats range from espionage directed towards obtaining political intelligence to phishing to facilitate credit card fraud. In addition to Government information, espionage now targets the intellectual property of commercial enterprises in areas such as communication technologies, optics, electronics and genetics.
>
> *(Ministry of Posts, Telecommunication and Information Technology, 2014: 9703)*

The number of internet users is increasing rapidly in Bangladesh. For instance, according to the Bangladesh Telecommunication Regulatory Commission, as of February 2018, the number of internet users in Bangladesh was estimated at 83 million, which was estimated at only 31 million in February 2012. Due to the increased number of users, the volume of cybercrime is also on the increase. In this context, Post and Telecommunications Ministry's Secretary Shyam Shunder Sikder admits that "although a number of initiatives were taken to increase internet penetration, we are lagging behind in terms of ensuring cyber security" (New Age, 2017). Religious fanaticism has also increased in Bangladesh due to easy cyber access. Also, on August 21, 2004, Bangladesh experienced an unprecedented terrorist incident in a series of grenade attacks at a high profile Awami League rally, leaving 23 people dead and 200 injured. In the following year on August 17, 2005, another incident occurred with the explosion of over 450 bombs in 63 out of 64 districts of Bangladesh, all within 40 minutes of each other. The Gulshan attack in July 2016 resulted in 22 deaths, including nine Italians, seven Japanese, a US citizen and an Indian, and demonstrates the magnitude of terrorist incidents in Bangladesh. One can also link the terrorist incidents and easy cyber access.

Earlier, crimes happened through traditional means in the physical world. But in the twenty-first century the nature of the crime, as well as warfare, has been changed radically. In this age of internet revolution, there is no need for the physical presence of the terrorists to attack a country or an organization or an individual. The term "cyber army" has gained momentum in this age. It can be argued that no country or organization or individual is safe in cyber space. Among other notable examples, the Bangladesh Foreign Ministry website was hacked twice in 2012. Furthermore, in 2008, the website of law enforcement agency Rapid Action Battalion (RAB), Bangladesh was also hacked. Tapan Kanti Sarkar writes that "of late, in Bangladesh, the financial services industry, which is a vital component of a nation's critical infrastructure, is under persistent threat" (Sarkar, 2016).

The institutions in Bangladesh are vulnerable to cyberattacks because of their apathy towards cybersecurity. In this regard, IT specialist, Tapan Kanti Sarkar writes that "out of my 35 years of experience in IT, I have developed an impression that the organizations are never willing to invest in IT security until and unless they are targeted and fallen as victims" (Sarkar, 2016). According to Kaspersky Lab Malware Report, Bangladesh ranked the second position after Iran about the top 10 countries attacked by mobile malware in 2017 (ranked by percentage of users attacked) (Unuchek, Sinitsyn, Parinov & Liskin, 2017). Furthermore, *Kaspersky Security Bulletin: Overall Statistics for 2017* notes that among the top 20 countries "where users face the greatest risk of online infection" Bangladesh ranked 19th position where 30.37 per cent of users were attacked (Kaspersky, 2017: 22). Bangladesh is not only vulnerable to external threats but also local threats. The *Kaspersky Security Bulletin* also notes that Bangladesh positioned 10th regarding local infection where 58.09 per cent of unique users were affected in 2017 (Kaspersky, 2017: 27). Thus, it can be claimed that on the one hand, Bangladesh is vulnerable to growing cyber threats. On the other hand, private sectors are not interested much in investing in cybersecurity though it is different in the case of the Bangladesh government.

Societal implications

Due to the easy accessibility of smartphones and the internet to the general public in the country, there is an increasing level of cybercrime in Bangladesh. Cybercrime has wider societal implications for Bangladesh. Considering the level of education, many people in the country do not have any idea about cybersecurity. In this regard, MS Siddiqui writes that "[c]yber security is still a subject to understand" (Siddiqui, 2018).

In an editorial, the *Daily Star*, the leading English daily in Bangladesh urges for the strong cyber safety and notes that the teenagers in Bangladesh are more vulnerable than others to cyber threats. In a study done by Unicef, it is revealed that 13 per cent of teens in Bangladesh face harassment on social media, and this is happening because of the ignorance of people about cybersecurity (*The Daily Star*, 2018). Additionally, there are also reports about online sexual harassment in Bangladesh (Rob, 2019). The editorial also claims that "[i]t is not just online bullying. We have faced the horror of terrorist attacks perpetrated by young adults barely out of their teens, and they were radicalized through the internet" (*The Daily Star*, 2018). State Minister for Post and Telecommunications, Tarana Halim, admits that cyberbullying took place on social media like Facebook, which sometimes results in the suicide of girls for disclosure of indecency (*New Age*, 2017). In addition, moral decay among the young generation is manifested, which will have long-term negative societal implications. For instance, increased cyber violence has become a common phenomenon among the young generation in Bangladesh, which merits serious attention.

Conclusion

This chapter concentrated on the adoption of *National Cyber Security Strategy* in Bangladesh and its role in facing growing cyber insecurities. It has also focused on the nature and scope of cyber insecurities and the actions taken by the state to address those insecurities. The chapter has also concentrated on the role of non-state actors to address cyber risks in the country. There is hardly any country that has not experienced cyber-attack. In this age of cyber insecurity and since no country is in isolation in cyber space, there is no alternative to building up capacity at the national level. Therefore, it discusses the role of international governance and cooperation at a regional and global level to ensure cybersecurity for the countries. Bangladesh needs to be prepared to face any future nuclear catastrophe. Rooppur Nuclear power plant needs to be given the utmost importance to secure it from any cyber-attack. It is expected that after five or ten years, Bangladesh will be cited as one of the cyber secured countries in the world since the country is highly committed to secure its cyber space, which is manifested through the steps taken by the country.

Suggested reading

Ahmed, N., Kulsum, U., Bin Azad, I., Momtaz, A. S. Z., Haque, M. E. & Rahman, M. S. (2017). "Cybersecurity awareness survey: An analysis from Bangladesh perspective," 2017 IEEE Region 10 Humanitarian Technology Conference (R10-HTC), Dhaka, Bangladesh. https://ieeexplore.ieee.org/abstract/document/#

Global Cyber Security Capacity Centre. (2019). "Bangladesh: Cybersecurity Capacity Review 2019." www.sbs.ox.ac.uk/cybersecurity-capacity/content/bangladesh-cybersecurity-capacity-review–2018

Hossin, A. Md., Sarker, N. I. Md., Xiaohua, Y. & Frimpong, A. N. K. (2018). "Development dimensions of e-commerce in Bangladesh: Scope, challenges and threats," Proceedings of the 2018 International Conference on Information Management & Management Science. https://dl.acm.org/doi/pdf/10.1145/3277139.3277152?download=true

Joveda, N., Khan, T. Md. & Pathak, A. (2019). "Cyber Laundering: A Threat to Banking Industries in Bangladesh: In Quest of Effective Legal Framework and Cyber Security of Financial Information," *International Journal of Economics and Finance, 11*(10): 54–65.

Sarker, K., Rahman, H., Rahman, K. F., Arman, S. Md., Biswas, S. & Bhuiyan, T. (2019). "A Comparative Analysis of the Cyber Security Strategy of Bangladesh," *International Journal on Cybernetics & Informatics, 8*(2): 1–12.

References

bdnews24.com. (2017, May 17). "Banks in Bangladesh 'Ignorant' about Cyber Security: Research." https://bdnews24.com/business/2017/05/17/banks-in-bangladesh-ignorant-about-cyber-security-research

BSS. (2017, May 17). "Govt to Form Cyber Security Agency: Tarana."

Dhaka Tribune. (2018, March 15). "Dhaka, Moscow Agree to Form Joint Working Group to Ensure Cyber Security." www.dhakatribune.com/technology/2018/03/15/dhaka-moscow-agree-form-joint-working-group-ensure-cyber-security

India Today. (2017, July 12). "Cabinet Informed about India, Bangladesh Cyber Security Pact." www.indiatoday.in/pti-feed/story/cabinet-informed-about-india-bangladesh-cyber-security-pact-996683-2017-07-12

Islam, A. (2016, October 31). "Islamists Vandalize Hindu Temples in Bangladesh Over Facebook Post," *DW.* www.dw.com/en/islamists-vandalize-hindu-temples-in-bangladesh-over-facebook-post/a-36211956

Islam, M. S. (2013, June 2). "Cyber Security: It Merits Serious Attention," *The Financial Express.* www.thefinancialexpress-bd.com/old/index.php?ref=MjBfMDZfMDJfMTNfMV8yN18xNzEzNjg

Jamal, E. M., Mahtab, M. & Sajen, S. (2016, October 29). "Digital Security Act, 2016," *The Daily Star.* www.thedailystar.net/opinion/interviews/how-does-it-affect-freedom-expression-and-the-right-dissent-1305826

Kaspersky. (2017). "Kaspersky Security Bulletin: Overall Statistics for 2017." https://kasperskycontenthub.com/securelist/files/2017/12/KSB_statistics_2017_EN_final.pdf

Ministry of Posts, Telecommunication and Information Technology. (n.d.). "Digital Security Act 2016 Draft."

Ministry of Posts, Telecommunication and Information Technology. (2014). *National Cyber Security Strategy.* Dhaka: Government of Bangladesh. www.dpp.gov.bd/upload_file/gazettes/10041_41196.pdf

New Age. (2017, October 24). "Bangladesh Lags Behind in Cyber Security." www.newagebd.net/article/26874/bangladesh-lags-behind-in-cyber-security

Rob, R. (2019, May 31). "Online Sexual Harassment: Exposing Dark Secrets in the Digital Corners of Bangladesh," *The Daily Star.* www.thedailystar.net/crime/news/online-sexual-harassment-exposing-dark-secrets-the-digital-corners-bangladesh-1751242

Sarkar, T. K. (2016, May 3). "Cyber Threat and Security," *The Daily Star.* www.thedailystar.net/business/banking/cyber-threat-and-security-1217542

Siddiqui, M. S. (2018, May 27). "Digital Security Law: Security of Individual or Government," *Daily Asian Age.* https://dailyasianage.com/news/123154/digital-security-law-security-of-individual-or-government

The Daily Star. (2016, March 15). "$101m Heist: Atiur Quits as Governor of Bangladesh Bank." www.thedailystar.net/business/101m-heist-bb-governor-ready-quit-791542

The Daily Star. (2018, April 1). "Editorial: Ensuring Cyber Safety Crucial." www.thedailystar.net/editorial/ensuring-cyber-safety-crucial-1556152

Unuchek, R., Sinitsyn, F., Parinov, D. & Liskin, A. (2017, November 10). "IT Threat Evolution Q3 2017 Statistics, Kasperisky Lab," *Kaspersky.* https://securelist.com/it-threat-evolution-q3-2017-statistics/83131/

30

MANAGING A DIGITAL REVOLUTION

Cyber security capacity building in Myanmar[1]

Niels Nagelhus Schia and Lars Gjesvik

Introduction

Digitalization is exposing developing countries to a growing number of risks as well as opportunities associated with connecting to the Internet. Myanmar stands out as a critical case of both the pitfalls and the benefits Internet connection can bring. Amidst a political transition from military rule to a functioning democracy Myanmar is adding ICT to key areas like banking and e-government. Having been one of the least connected countries in the world only five years ago the country is now connecting to the Internet at an unprecedented pace, with few institutions in place to ensure the transition goes smoothly. The rapid expansion of Internet connectivity is connecting ever more people to an international world of business, discourse, and entertainment, but also crime, subterfuge, and discord. A crucial aspect for development in the years to come will be the harnessing of the benefits, as well as mitigating the downsides that inherently follow in the wake of Internet access (Schia, 2018). In this chapter, we examine the risks and potential benefits of Myanmar's embracement of digital technologies.

History and digital revolution

In 2010 Myanmar held its first general election in over 20 years. This was the fifth step in a seven-step transition roadmap to democracy. In 2011 the military junta was dissolved and replaced by a civilian government. In 2015 Aung San Suu Kyi won both houses and the freely elected Myanmar Parliament convened for the first time, after being under the thumb of military rule for over half a century. As the country has recently emerged from oppressive rule at the hands of the military junta, the military continues to hold a strong position in Myanmar politics, but the country has taken important steps towards a democratization of the society (Chan, 2016). In coexistence with this move towards a more open society the country has also tried to develop its economy and its capabilities on several issues, among these connecting to the Internet. Myanmar has moved rapidly from one of the countries with the least ICT coverage in the world to one where connectivity is growing at an unprecedented pace (Vota, 2015).

In 2011 the country was rated as the second-least connected country in the world, beating only North Korea, with an Internet penetration of under 1 per cent. The rapid connectivity is part of a government-initiated effort at modernizing the country that started in parallel with the democratization in 2011 (Calderaro, 2014). By the end of 2015 the number of subscribers in the country had ballooned to almost 50 per cent, indicating an increase in Internet subscribers of around 300 per cent yearly. The growth has been mostly related to smartphones, which make up around 80 per cent percent of all mobile phones in the country, a share that is higher than in most developed countries (Vota, 2015). While the fixed broadband Internet penetration is low, the mobile market has grown significantly since 2013, when the two foreign telephone operators Telenor (Norway) and Ooredo (Qatar) began investing in the Internet infrastructure in the country. In 2018, Myanmar is among the countries with the most substantial progress in the world concerning internet users.[2]

Cyber security challenges in Myanmar

Being new to digital technologies the country still has significant unresolved issues relating to the securing and managing of this transition. A further complicating element is that Myanmar is undergoing this rapid transformation into the digital age at the same time as the country is undergoing a profound political transition. The precariousness of political institutions combined with the known security threats emanating from digital technologies are both undermining the cyber security of Myanmar society. Adding internet connectivity as the same time as the country transitions away from a suppressive regime is heightening the risk that the technology can be used to exert government control and a return to old sins in acting as a tool for repression of minorities in the country (Calderaro, 2014).

As Myanmar struggles with an unstable political situation, the country is seeing new kinds of societal vulnerabilities emerging from digitalization, among them hate speech, cybercrime, and cyberattacks. The transition from military rule to a more democratic form of government, along with the recurring theme of ethnic conflict, creates an environment that is favorable to criminals and *bulletproof hosting*.[3] Already cybercrime is an existing, and growing, concern in Myanmar. As the growth in cybercrime rapidly outpaces the growth in digital transactions globally and the issue of criminal activities is set to grow in importance over the coming years. Due to the fluid nature of these criminal activities, states lacking legal frameworks and enforcements like Myanmar are likely to see a disproportional part of this growth (Threat Metrix, 2016).

As the country has connected to the Internet citizens have been allowed access to a wealth of information, resulting in a renaissance of sorts for independent media outlets and civil society groups. People have embraced social media and messaging applications such as Facebook and Viber, using these as their main, and often only, access point to the Internet. Facebook is in fact widely perceived as "the Internet" and is being used as a replacement for missing company websites, channels for file sharing, and communication between employees in public and private sector. This tendency has also been propelled by the collaboration between some social media companies and telephone operators. Telenor has for instance offered free Facebook through Telenor subscriptions. Despite this apparent positive development there are huge concerns relating to the security of these websites, as many of these applications are also pre-installed when purchased.

In 2010 Myanmar was on the receiving end of what was at the time one of the largest Distributed Denial of Service-attacks (DDoS) to date. The attacks, which consists of flooding connection points with massive amounts of online traffic until they collapse, came in the run-up to the 2010 general election (Labovitz, 2010). As the infrastructure at the time was dependent on a single submarine fiber-optic cable, the attack succeeded in disconnecting the entire country from the Internet. Airline companies, public sector institutions, and citizens were cut off from online services for one month. The connection at the time was so limited that the attack was several hundred times larger than needed to shut down the connection. The government did not have the expertise or any established strategies to deal with the situation. China remedied the situations by providing Internet services for the important ministries through their border. While the source of the attacks has not been made public to this date, suspicion has been directed towards the military junta that governed the country, as dissident websites hosted outside of Myanmar had been targeted earlier in the year (Reporters Without Borders, 2010). There were also similar accusations raised at the Burmese military and government following restrictions of access and information in 2007 (Nizza, 2007).

This underlines the risks that digital technologies will erode the turn towards democratic governance, and whether controlling the political discourse has merely taken on another form. The most concerning development has been the rise of vigilante groups pushing a nationalistic agenda by attacking websites and news outlets that are critical of the government, or in some way positive to the country's Muslim minority (Hindstrom, 2016a). The most active of these group has been identified as the "Blink Hacker Group" which has targeted numerous media websites over the last few years. This group has been linked to the Myanmar military by the Swedish-based cyber security firm *Unleashed Research Lab* (Hindstrom, 2016b). Their report on the attacks tied the hacker-collective to military servers and training facilities, while the group itself has admitted on Facebook that it consists in part of "Pro-government" members (Unleashed, 2015). This is coupled with a general rise in Islamophobia, and the use of social media as an instigator of violence between differing ethnic groups, and mainly aimed towards the ethnic Rohingya-minority.

The combination of ethnicity, suppression, and digital technologies has come under increased focus lately. Myanmar is one of the most ethnically and culturally diverse countries in the region, with a persistent tension between the Burman central government and the various minorities. The most well-known tension runs between the Buddhist majority, and the ethnic Rohingya Muslim minority. A tension that has been transferred into the cyber realm with a growing number of incidents of hate-speech, as identified by a survey on digital security by the Myanmar Center for Responsible Business (Myanmar Centre for Responsible Business, 2015). A glaring problem in Myanmar's online world is in this sense the addition of social media to an already combustible ethnic situation. This mixture has already led to violent riots with two casualties as the result of rumors spread online (Calderaro, 2015). Since then hate speech has continued to spread and is becoming an increasingly pressing problem. Most of the hate speech is directed towards the Muslim majority, with a significant part of the hate speech including calls for violence and even killing of Muslims (Ibid.). In 2018 investigations by Reuters journalist Steve Stecklow exposed how the dependence on Facebook for digital communication acted as a driver for the genocide aimed at the Rohingya minority, highlighting the damaging potential digitalization and social media has in tense ethnic conflicts (Stecklow, 2018).

Cyber security in Myanmar

Contextual factors

While leapfrogging into the digital age creates new opportunities and greater connectedness, it also creates challenges and pitfalls. Technological development and progress move fast, while norms and policy production move slowly and create a lag between policy and practice; this has become symptomatic for the digital age. The lag creates a huge gap between political regulation on the one hand and practice on the other, both internationally and nationally. This gap is also pertinent in Myanmar. Interviewees from fieldwork in 2016 and 2017 pointed at the need for cyber security capacity building within the state institutions; for improving legal regulations and mechanisms; and for awareness campaigns, better knowledge, and education. The new and distinct societal challenges and vulnerabilities stemming from digitalization vary from nation to nation and are shaped by the interface between digitalization, local and national policies, and large-scale global forces, elsewhere also described as the "cyber frontier" (Schia, 2018). Cyber security and digital pitfalls must be understood and contextualized to local circumstances. Even though the digital age is relatively new, there are already several examples showing how this technology can be utilized either for democratization trends or by authoritarian regimes to suppress public interests, democratic processes, and freedom of speech. Any outcome will depend on an interplay between the new technology and pre-existing political and economic circumstances. Digital technology may help authoritarian regimes regain control during democratic transition. Some scholars have found that authoritarian regimes or states wanting to repress an independent public sphere were more likely to adopt and expand the Internet than were other autocracies (Rød & Weidmann, 2015).

Myanmar's current political transition in tandem with the digital revolution is perhaps the country's most distinct feature in this context. Certainly, one of the main factors determining the limited ability to provide digital security in Myanmar is the glaring lack of resources, both human and financial. The lack of qualified personnel with sufficient training and skills in IT security is obvious, and not just restricted to the public sector but private companies as well. This limitation puts severe strain on all aspects of cyber security provision, from the development of regulations and policies to the day-to-day management of digital events. Raising the competencies and resources available will be critical to enhance cyber security and cyber resiliency in the years going forward. One initiative that has already been taken is *The Digital Myanmar Study* (2018). This is a self-assessment of the country's cyber security capacities that was hosted by the Ministry of Transport and Communication and facilitated by the World Bank, the Global Cyber Security Capacity Centre at the University of Oxford (the GCSCC), and the Norwegian Institute of International Affairs (NUPI).[4] This evaluation identified challenges and produced useful recommendations to the Myanmar government in five societal dimensions; cyber security strategy and policy, cyber security culture and society, cyber security education, training and skills, as well as on standards, organizations, and technologies. However, it is not clear to what extent the Myanmar government has had the capacity to follow up on the recommendations identified in this study.

The outreach to Oxford also highlights an important issue for Myanmar going forward, namely which approach and understanding of cyber security will be implemented. States approach cyber security from two main vantage points: one being championed by western states and forming the basis for initiatives like the Oxford review takes a multi-stakeholder approach to cyber security where this security is conceptualized as a public good. The other camp, most prominently championed by Russia and China, has a more state-centric approach to cyber security. This "cyber sovereign" approach does not separate state authority in cyberspace from state authority over the physical domain, and as such implies larger acceptance for surveillance and control. The majority of states, however, do not fall into one of these categories but are understood as either uncommitted or "digital deciders"; states who are undecided but who have significant regional influence. For the ASEAN region Singapore is one such critical case that could have large regional influence, and a relationship that is worth paying attention to.

However, the most crucial relationship for Myanmar has historically been China. As long as Myanmar was a pariah state globally its relationship with its giant northern neighbor resembled that of a client state. China has also been tentatively identified as the culprit in several espionage campaigns where Myanmar was one of the victims. A 2015 FireEye investigation into the APT 30 group found that the group had been active in targeting ASEAN member-states (like Myanmar) for several years. While the group's targets pointed towards the Chinese government, the group has not as of yet been definitely linked to any actor (FireEye, 2015). A similar pattern vas evident in the 2015 Arbor Networks investigation into the "Trochilus" campaign (Metzger, 2016). While both reports are hesitant at attributing China directly, other experts have hinted toward China being the likely culprit. The recent democratization has changed the relationship between the two countries as Myanmar looks for other international engagements, and until very recently enjoyed improved relationships with western states (Maini & Sachdeva, 2017). This makes the choices and trajectory of the Myanmar cyber security approach in the years to come an interesting case in how developing states will place themselves within the increasingly contested battle on how to define cyber security. Stating which direction Myanmar will take is so far rather premature, as the approach and strategies are too underdeveloped to be accurately defined, a point we will turn to next.

Official policies and legal framework

In general, the approach to cyber security in Myanmar is at a start-up stage, with an ad-hoc approach to capacity and blind spots in both official policies, regulation and competencies to deal with the challenges posed by digitalization. Some initial discussions and needs-assessment exercises have been run, but there is currently no official national cyber security strategy, few cyber security units in the public departments, and weak coherence in sets of policies across the ministries.[5] This can partly be traced back to the newness of digital technologies in Myanmar, the revolutionary uptake of mobile connectivity in later years has necessarily led to a lag in political activity. Partly the general political upheaval of post-junta Myanmar has meant a flurry of political activity wherein digital regulations has not been given prominence. Finally, the issues of Myanmar in managing digital technologies politically could be seen as a symptom of a larger trend wherein developing nations are struggling to provide digital security in a rapidly shifting technological environment.

The most clear-cut example of the inability to provide sufficient security is the lack of a cyber security strategy or any overarching coherent framework for guiding the work on cyber security. While a draft strategy has been under development for a long time, being the work of the Ministry of Transport and Communications in cooperation with the Asian Development Bank, no finalized version exists as of yet. Beyond the non-existence of an actual framework, the process with which the strategy was developed involved a small number of ministries of agencies and taking in very little input from private companies or critical infrastructure owners. As a consequence, questions can be raised regarding the applicability of the strategy when it comes into force. The non-inclusion of the very companies that will be tasked with providing cyber security in developing the strategy can be seen as troubling.

The lack of an overarching strategy in turn fragments the approach by various ministries and agencies, as a cross-sectorial issue is met by isolated initiatives. As ministries and agencies operate within their respective silos when it comes to detecting and responding to various risks and threats. As Myanmar has rapidly digitalized, the frequency of cyber incidents is growing rapidly and the fragmented approach is hampering the ability to manage it sufficiently. This is further complicated by the byzantine bureaucratic processes and structures that define much of the governmental work. For the issue of cyber security providing meaningful legislation and regulations is for instance dependent on the cooperation between the Ministry of Transport and Communication and the Ministry of Planning and Finance, a cooperation which so far has been limited and strained. Providing a clear overarching direction for these various approaches and conflicts of interests necessitates a cyber strategy tailored to the situation in Myanmar, providing clear incentives, benchmarks, and divisions of responsibility.

The lack of top-down political leadership is further reflected in the absence of awareness about critical infrastructures and their importance for modern societies. The very concept of critical infrastructures is not widely established, and subsequently neither is the cyber security of said infrastructures. The lacking mapping, categorization, and understanding of different infrastructures and the role they play in society limits the ability to secure them in a sufficient manner. As there does not exist any legal definition of what a critical infrastructure is, the framework for mapping and categorizing them is non-existent. As a first step creating a legal framework for what is considered critical infrastructure, as well as giving the responsibility of protecting said infrastructures to an institution, would be a starting point to improve critical infrastructure protection in Myanmar. The increasing number of cyber incidents targeting institutions and infrastructures that are widely categorized as "critical" in other states, such as the central bank, highlights the importance of improving on this issue.

Moving towards the regulatory regime, the state of Myanmar cyber security legislation is also at an early stage, with large gaps and insufficient existing frameworks. Some laws are in place that cover some aspects of cyber security, notable examples being the *Electronic Transactions Law (State Peace and Development Council Law No 5/2004)* covering some aspects of electronic data and cybercrime. This law defines the distribution of information that causes harms to minors (see, section 34(d)) via digital technology and networks as illegal, and it also allows electronic evidence to be brought before the court. The *Telecommunications Law* regulates access to and the use of telecommunication services (Electronic Transactions Law, 2004). Legislation covering issues like human rights, data protection, and child pornography is however not in place, making the overall legislative framework highly insufficient for responding to rapidly evolving digital threats. Beyond the actual legal framework, the implementation of existing laws is also lacking, as there are limited resources, competencies, and abilities to investigate and prosecute cybercrime both in the police and the judiciary. Some initiatives have been taken, such as the Cybercrime Division at the National Police Criminal Investigation Department, but also here, the unit suffer from limited capacity. Very few cybercrime cases have been brought to court. Prosecutors and judges need training on cybercrime and how to make use of digital evidence.

One of the institutions that has been established is a national Computer Emergency Response Team (CERT), with mmCERT (Myanmar Computer Emergency Response Team) being established as early as 2004 by e-National Task Force. The CERT's mission is to do incident handling, public awareness in security, to provide cyber security advice to Myanmar Internet users, and to prevent cyberattacks. It is also mmCERT's responsibility to function as a coordinator of incident responses with other teams, organizations, security experts, and law enforcement agencies nationally and internationally. In 2010 mmCERT came under the responsibility of Myanmar's Ministry of Transport and Communications. This ministry also has its own cyber security unit aiming to enhance the cyber security capacity in the country. The CERT is also an operational member of the Asia Pacific Computer Emergency Response Team (APCERT) and the International Multilateral Partnership Against Cyber Threats (IMPACT). While it's ostensibly providing technical assistance, cataloguing incidents, collaborating with international partners, and assisting police and other agencies its limited resources significantly hamper its ability to deliver on its mandate. The lack of financial resources available for mmCERT results in insufficient technical equipment, lack of human resources, and limited ability to operate as intended. And outside of its international affiliations, private companies and stakeholders in Myanmar hold that mmCERT is not adequately capable of addressing cyber security threats in Myanmar (Myanmar Centre for Responsible Business, 2015). In addition, there is little awareness of the role and functions of mmCERT, resulting in a lack of information being shared with the organization. While the leading companies, particularly the international ones, have capacities to manage incidents, the cooperation between government and private actors are minimal, further limiting the ability of mmCERT to work as intended.[6]

When it comes to regional collaborations these are limited. Among the more effective collaborations described by interviewees during fieldwork in 2016 and 2017, was the engagement with Interpol. This was pointed at as an important channel for cross-border collaboration and information sharing. Interpol, ITU, and ASEAN deliver capacity building programs to the cybercrime unit at the national police, although not on a regular basis. Regional initiatives through ASEAN intend to develop better, more accessible, and more affordable IT infrastructure. These goals have been established and endorsed in an ASEAN broadband corridor study that also identified key drivers for broadband rollout and recommendations for government initiatives (ASEAN, 2016) as well as improved capacities, knowledge and awareness (ASEAN, 2015). Some regional measures have also been taken to mitigate possible bullet-proof hosting, weak links, and havens of vulnerable ICT architectures in the CLMV countries – Cambodia, Laos, Myanmar, and Vietnam (Heinl, 2014). The collaboration with other ASEAN member states on mutual legal assistance treaty in criminal matters has not been ratified to include cases concerning cybercrime, and Myanmar has not signed the Budapest Convention or any other multilateral or regional cybercrime agreement.

Cultural and societal factors

Cyber security is provisioned by a multitude of actors frequently described as an "assemblage" of private, public, and private citizens (Collier, 2018). To fully comprehend the work on maintaining a safe and reliable cyberspace for citizens one needs to broaden the view to include not only the government initiatives but also the leading private companies and individual citizens. For Myanmar there is a widespread lack of attention being afforded to the security implications of rapid digitalization. This holds true for both public and private sector employees as well as the general public at large. It can be seen through widespread usage of pirated software and unsecured mail accounts for employees, as well as a limited level of awareness on the security issues modern societies face. The most problematic account however related to the understanding of cyber security dangers in the public at large. Taking a broad understanding of cyber security, including such concerns as the dissemination of fake news, there was a noted lack of skepticism surrounding claims made online. Furthermore, there is little to no awareness about the dangers of handing out private data or sensitive information online among the general public, providing an ample breeding ground for cybercrime.[7] Seen in correlation with the incitement towards ethnic violence mentioned above, the lack of awareness and competencies when it comes to navigating digital media is troubling.

The main exceptions to the rule of low awareness about cyber security is an issue in the private sector, and most notably among the two leading telecommunication operators in the country. After a 2012 licensing-round, licenses were awarded to Qatari telecoms operator Ooredoo and Norwegian operator Telenor (Calderaro, 2014). In Myanmar, there has been a shared responsibility for the development of the telecommunications sector: while the government is focused on developing laws and regulations extending connectivity has fallen into the hands of foreign companies. A large part of the task is thus dependent on the companies doing so in a manner that highlights their corporate social responsibility. A 2013 Human Rights Watch report underlined the potential positive impacts of the Internet and digitalization in societies such as Myanmar. However, the report also stressed the risk that this technology would be used by the regime to crack down on dissent, used for illegal surveillance, and as a way to enforce censorship. The call was for companies involved in improving the ICT-infrastructure in Myanmar to refrain from cooperating with the government on matters that would undermine the rights of its citizens (HRW, 2013).

Whether the companies do so is up for debate. The smaller of the companies is Ooredoo, which has no clear published guidelines and a spotty record on protecting the rights of its users. The company in fact has a history of accepting censorship by the Qatari government and installing filters in accordance with the wishes of autocratic regimes (Calderaro, 2014). Telenor on the other hand is widely regarded as having one of the more advanced policies on social responsibility, however there are some concerns raised over its shutting down of its services at the behest of the Thai military junta in 2014. There are also some uncertainties over the extent to which telephone operators are willing to pass information over to the government and whether these policies are clearly enough formulated to withstand potential pressures (Calderaro, 2014).

The way forward

When addressing the question of Myanmar's preparedness and development on the issue of cyber security, a starting point is mapping the landscape of digital infrastructure and its trajectory. The infrastructure in Myanmar is disproportionately based on mobile broadband access and not fixed broadband, which translates into lower speeds and worse service. Myanmar is thus a typical case of early stage Internet development, while there has been an immense growth in spreading internet coverage nationally, the underlying structure and backbone of the Internet remains weak. This is important as most websites, both foreign and domestic, are based on servers outside the borders of Myanmar. A stable connection to the outside world is thus important to gain access to most of the websites that residents want to access. Up until very recently Myanmar was served by a single submarine cable, creating both large vulnerabilities in the infrastructure and a slow connection (Telegeography, 2020).

In general Myanmar's cyber security "maturity" is at the start-up level, very few actions, other than some initial discussions on this topic, have been taken. There are however some indications on clear progress towards a more formative level in the education sector, the legal and regulatory framework, and on establishing better standards. Nevertheless, Myanmar remains among the countries in the Asia-Pacific region with the least attention to cyber security. Reports have pointed to large issues and gaps in the approach to the issue. Beyond the military aspect of cyber security Myanmar is among the lowest scoring countries in all categories in a comparison between Asian countries, highlighting a long list of issues that needs to be addressed (ASPI, 2017). A shortage in skilled labor is one of the main issues, as the ICT sector is regulated and run by a small group of public employees tasked with managing the rapid transition. The digital transformation, coupled with the democratic transition, is dependent on the development of a long list of technical standards and regulation, as well as reinventing the educational system to meet new demands. On top of this, the interconnected nature of the ICT sector, and the fact that Myanmar has already become entangled with foreign actors after years of isolation, points to the scope of the challenge Myanmar is facing to make the transition run smoothly (Myanmar Centre for Responsible Business, 2015). Moreover, while the government drafted a master plan for telecommunications in 2015 its implementation has been severely postponed and uneven, undermining the efforts at creating a sound political environment. This is mirrored in the regulatory sector wherein the existing rules and regulations are aimed at control and censorship, and not on cybercrime and related issues (ASPI, 2017).

A subdivision of the political and regulatory capacity is a country's participation in international foras and programs. This is an area of particular importance in cyberspace, where the government challenges are often global in nature. One of the main ways for countries with less-developed cyber security maturity is to engage in cooperation between Computer Emergency Response Teams (CERTs). There are some regional initiatives enabling this, such as the APCERT which covers the Asia-Pacific Region and where Myanmar is a member. This is a positive, both for the development of capabilities within countries and to foster cooperation and information-sharing between countries and national CERTs. While Myanmar participates in APCERT, as well as some bilateral capacity building programs with India and Singapore, among others, the country has not so far engaged other countries beyond capacity-building programs (ASPI, 2017).

In the midst of a democratic transition, Myanmar is trying to utilize ICT and digital technologies to jump-start its development. The potential for ICT to do so is great, but so are the risks inherent in connecting to the Internet. Due to its fragile political state, turbulent regional politics, and fraught social cohesion, Myanmar faces a set of unique challenges. Building cyber security is paramount to avoid a scenario wherein digital technologies act as a catalyst of destructive forces, and not as a vehicle for development. Expanding and developing cyber security capabilities should therefore be a priority as key financial and governmental functions are moved online, otherwise the digitalization of Myanmar risks being a curse disguised as a blessing.

Notes

1 This chapter builds on fieldwork in Myanmar in 2016 and 2017 and further develops findings from a NUPI-policy brief and working paper: Managing a digital revolution – Cyber Security Capacity Building in Myanmar (2018).
2 In wireless and household Internet penetration.
3 Rogue states and countries in the Global South become hosts to outlaw servers, so-called "bullet-proof hosting." The hosts of these servers operate beyond the reach of most law enforcers, and make cybercrime possible elsewhere (Schia, 2018: 826).
4 For more about this see, www.sbs.ox.ac.uk/cybersecurity-capacity/content/cmm-assessments-around-world, and www.nupi.no/en/About-NUPI/Projects-centres-and-programmes/Cybersecurity-Capacity-Building-2.0-Bridging-the-digital-divide-and-strengthening-sustainable-development

5 This was confirmed by several officials from various ministries in Myanmar during fieldwork and interviews in 2016 and 2017.
6 This was confirmed by several officials from various ministries in Myanmar during fieldwork and interviews in Nay Pyi Taw and Yangon in 2016 and 2017.
7 Field assessment findings, fieldwork in Myanmar 2016 and 2017.

Suggested reading

Chang, L. Y. C. (2017). "Cybercrime and Cyber Security in ASEAN," in J. Liu, M. Travers & L. Chang (eds.), *Comparative Criminology in Asia* (pp. 135–148). Cham: Springer.

Clark, D. B. (2017, September 28). "Myanmar's Internet Disrupted Society – And Fueled Extremists," *WIRED*. www.wired.com/story/myanmar-internet-disrupted-society-extremism/

Myanmar Centre for Responsible Business. (2019). "Policy Brief: Cyber Security and Cyber Crime: Issues or Myanmar." www.myanmar-responsiblebusiness.org/pdf/2019-Policy-Brief-Cyber-Security-and-Cyber-Crime_en.pdf

Singh, R. (2019, July 5). "Myanmar's March Towards a Digital Future," *Internet Society*. www.internetsociety.org/blog/2019/07/myanmars-march-towards-a-digital-future/

Unleash Research Labs. (2016). "Unleashed: Unveiling Cyberwar in Myanmar." http://unleashed.blinkhackergroup.org/op-its-time/3/

References

ASEAN. (2015). "ASEAN ICT Masterplan 2015." www.asean.org/storage/images/2015/December/telmin/ASEAN per cent20ICT per cent20Completion per cent20Report.pdf

ASEAN. (2016). "Masterplan on ASEAN Connectivity 2025," https://asean.org/wp-content/uploads/2016/09/Master-Plan-on-ASEAN-Connectivity-20251.pdf

Calderaro, A. (2014). "Digitalizing Myanmar – Connectivity Developments in Political Transitition," *Center for Global Communication Studies*. https://global.asc.upenn.edu/publications/digitalizing-myanmar-connectivity-developments-in-political-transitions/

Calderaro, A. (2015). "Internet Governance Capacity Building in Post-Authoritarian Contexts," *Internet Policy Observatory*. https://papers.ssrn.com/sol3/papers.cfm?abstract_id=2686095

Chan, S. (2016, February 2). "First Freely Eleceted Parliament after Decades of Military Rule Opens in Myanmar," *The New York Times*. www.nytimes.com/2016/02/02/world/asia/first-freely-elected-parliament-after-decades-of-military-rule-opens-in-myanmar.html?_r=0

Collier, J. (2018). "Cyber Security Assemblages: A Framework for Understanding the Dynamic and Contested Nature of Security Provision," *Politics and Governance*, 6(2): 13–21.

Electronic Transactions Law. (State Peace and Development Council Law No 5/.2004, http://unpan1.un.org/intradoc/groups/public/documents/un-dpadm/unpan041197.pdf (accessed 31 October 2018)

FireEye. (2015). "APT30 and the Mechanics of a Long-Running Cyber Espionage Operation." www2.fireeye.com/rs/fireye/images/rpt-apt30.pdf

Heinl, C. H. (2014)."Regional Cybersecurity: Moving Towards a Resilient ASEAN Cybersecurity Regime," *Asia Policy*, 18: 131–159.

Hindstrom, H. A. (2016a). "The Perils of Burma's Internet Craze," for *Foreign Policy*. 01. 04.2016, http://foreignpolicy.com/2016/04/01/the-perils-of-burmas-internet-craze/

Hindstrom, H. B. (2016b): "Is Myanmar's Military Behind Shadowy Cyber Attacks?" for *The Diplomat*, 27. 02.2016 https://thediplomat.com/2016/02/was-myanmars-military-behind-shadowy-cyber-attacks/

HRW. (2013, May 19). "Reforming Telecommunications in Burma." www.hrw.org/report/2013/05/19/reforming-telecommunications-burma/human-rights-and-responsible-investment-mobile

Labovitz, C. (2010, November 3): "Attack Severs Burma Internet," *ASERT*. https://asert.arbornetworks.com/attac-severs-myanmar-internet/

Maini, T. S. & Sachdeva, S. (2017, November 14). "China Faces Increasing Competition in Myanmar," *The Diplomat*. https://thediplomat.com/2017/11/china-faces-increasing-competition-in-myanmar/

Metzger, M. (2016, January 13). "'Trochilus' RAT Targets Government of Myanmar," *SC Media*. www.scmagazineuk.com/trochilus-rat-targets-government-myanmar/article/1477758

Myanmar Centre for Responsible Business. (2015, September 24). "Sector-Wide Impact Assesment of Myanmar's ICT Sector." www.myanmar-responsiblebusiness.org/swia/ict.html

Nizza, M. (2007, September 28). "Burmese Government Clamps down on Internet," *The New York Times.* https://thelede.blogs.nytimes.com/2007/09/28/burmese-government-clamps-down-on-internet/

Reporters Without Borders. (2010, May 10). "Stop Cyber Attacks on Independent Burmese Media." https://rsf.org/en/news/stop-cyber-attacks-against-independent-burmese-media

Rød, E. G. & Weidmann, N. B. (2015). "Empowering Activists or Autocrats? The Internet in Authoritarian Regimes," *Journal of Peace Research, 52*(3): 338–351.

Schia, N. N. (2018). "The Cyber Frontier and Digital Pitfalls in the Global South," *Third World Quarterly, 39*(5): 821–837.

Stecklow, W. (2018, August 15). "Why Facebook Is Losing the War on Hate Speech in Myanmar. www.reuters.com/investigates/special-report/myanmar-facebook-hate/

Telegeography. (2020, August 14). "Submarine Cable Map." https://www.submarinecablemap.com/#/

Threat Metrix. (2016). "Q1 Cybercrime Report." www.threatmetrix.com/wp-content/uploads/2017/04/cybercrime-2016-q1-1492588964.pdf?_ga=2.203348887.767081945.1493862414-973637201.1493760913

Unleashed. (2015). "Unleashed – Unveiling Cyberwar in Myanmar." http://unleashed.blinkhackergroup.org/

Vota, W. (2015, September 30). "Wow! Myanmar Is Going Straight to Smartphones," *ICT Works.* www.ictworks.org/2015/09/30/wow-myanmar-is-going-straight-to-smartphones/

31

AUSTRALIA'S CYBER SECURITY

A unique opportunity

Ana Stuparu

Introduction: statement of national security strategy

Australia's national Cyber Security Strategy ("the Strategy") was released in April 2016 by the Department of Prime Minister and Cabinet, under Prime Minister Malcolm Turnbull's government. The Strategy is the second of its kind for Australia, being preceded only by the 2009 Cyber Security Strategy (CSS), and has been perceived as being more "in touch" with Australia's cyber needs (Stuparu, 2016), also providing broader strategic direction and deliverables,[1] though some still found it to be vague, especially around lack of funding (Austin & Slay, 2016).

The Strategy covers five key areas:

1   A national cyber partnership;
2   Strong cyber defenses;
3   Global responsibility and influence;
4   Growth and innovation; and
5   A cyber smart nation (PMC, 2016: 5).

Since 2016, substantial progress has been made in the first and fourth areas, especially through the work of the Australian Cyber Security Growth Network (AustCyber). The second area also saw the Australian Signals Directorate update the Information Security Manual (ISM) and Essential Eight,[2] as well as complete a network of Joint Cyber Security Centres across Australia, among other successful initiatives. The third area was addressed through the creation of Australia's International Cyber Engagement Strategy (DFAT, 2017), a document which will be discussed in further detail in the International Governance section below. The fifth and final key area has seen some more modest progress through enterprises such as the ACSC Threat Report release (ACSC, 2017) and those on the education front; for example, vocational education agreed to a national curriculum for a Certificate IV in Cyber Security (Sadler, 2018).

A point which has, however, been heavily criticized is that of the Strategy's promised annual updates (Bashfield, 2019), of which only the first was delivered in 2017 (PMC, 2017), while Australia was still under the Turnbull government.

Though not officially announced as yet, a new Cyber Security Strategy is expected in 2020, as the current Strategy refers to its themes of action "over the next four years to 2020" (PMC, 2016) and the present government has arguably demonstrated a lack of action on progressing the existing Strategy (Bashfield, 2019).

A few months prior to the Strategy's release, namely in February, Australia also put out the 2016 Defence White Paper ("the White Paper"). Unlike the Strategy, the White Paper focused purely on defense capacity and capability plans over the coming years, along with some broad budgetary allocations. It is a very different document in style and purpose, representing "how Defence meshes with national efforts" to achieve long-term cyber resilience in Australia (Scully, 2016: 115).

It is important to recognize, however, that the White Paper "gives us no hint as to whether Australia recognises cyber space as a discrete domain of warfare" in the way the United States of America "formally recognised cyber space as a fifth domain" in 2010 (Scully, 2016: 116).

Its main cyber-related outputs are articulated in a broad section entitled "Intelligence Surveillance and Reconnaissance, Space, Electronic Warfare, and Cyber Security." The focus is on intelligence gathering and electronic warfare support to the existing services, and one notable point is that of the Information Warfare Division's creation, a "unit of keyboard soldiers," initially 100 personnel-strong but set to grow to 900 within 10 years (McGhee, 2017).

It is worth mentioning that other areas of government have also published their own cyber strategies, applicable to their own department, such as the Department of Human Services' Cyber Security Strategy 2018–22 (DHS, 2018).

Definitions

Australia has defined a number of key terms which are relevant to the basis of the national cyber conversation. Examples include cybersecurity, cybercrime, cyberterrorism, and critical infrastructure, for which definitions are provided below. Though not word-for-word, and though not all defined in the one place in Australia's case, these broadly align with the views that Five Eyes partners seem to have on the matters.[3]

First, and "[i]n simple terms, *cybersecurity* involves the protection of computer systems connected to the Internet" (APH, n.d.b). Otherwise put, it is "an ongoing journey (…) about protecting your technology and information from accidental or illicit access, corruption, theft or damage" (Australian Government, n.d.b).

In terms of *cybercrime*, the Australian Government equates it to "computer crime," and states that it "involves using computers and the internet to break the law. Common kinds of cybercrime include: identity theft and fraud; online scams; [and] attacks on your computer systems or websites" (Australian Government, n.d.b). Moreover, the Australian Federal Police (AFP) thinks of cybercrime as "[c]rimes such as fraud, scams, and harassment [which] can be facilitated by using technology [and] which bring unique challenges to old crimes" (AFP, n.d.a).

Though "[t]here is no universally agreed upon definition of *cyberterrorism*, […] the term generally refers to an attack which uses electronic means (such as a computer worm, virus or malware) to penetrate and seriously interfere with critical infrastructure" (Hardy, 2017). This general definition is a relevant working one in Australia, however, under the Australian Criminal Code Act 1995, one can only find a formal definition of a terrorist act, which can then be applied to cyberspace:

an action or threat of action where: (a) the action falls within subsection (2) and does not fall within subsection (3); and (b) the action is done or the threat is made with the intention of advancing a political, religious or ideological cause; and (c) the action is done or the threat is made with the intention of: (i) coercing, or influencing by intimidation, the government of the Commonwealth or a State, Territory or foreign country, or of part of a State, Territory or foreign country; or (ii) intimidating the public or a section of the public.

(Australian Government, 1995: 83)

According to the Department of Home Affairs, "[c]ritical infrastructure provides services that are essential for everyday life such as energy, food, water, transport, communications, health and banking and finance" (Australian Government n.d.a). More complexly, the Trusted Information for Sharing Network (TISN), another government agency, defines critical infrastructure as

[t]hose physical facilities, supply chains, information technologies and communication networks, which if destroyed, degraded or rendered unavailable for an extend period, would significantly impact on the social or economic wellbeing of the nation, or affect Australia's ability to conduct national defence and ensure national security.

These "[e]ssential services we all rely on in our daily lives (…) [include] power, water, health, communication systems, and banking" (Australian Government, 1995: 83).

International law

Australia is at the forefront of international law in general, and is "a country that has actively encouraged the development and spread of international law and has integrated it into its national law to an extent unimaginable when the first edition of *International Law in Australia* was published in 1965" (Rothwell & Crawford, 2017). Indeed, Australia has a permanent Office of International Law (OIL) within the Attorney-General's Department, providing relevant advice to the Government (AG, n.d.).

In terms of international cyber law, much of Australia's viewpoint is tightly interlinked with that on international governance, and is articulated in its International Cyber Engagement Strategy (DFAT, 2017), which will be discussed in the following section.

A summary of Australia's commitment to cyber international law is perfectly captured by the current Minister for Foreign Affairs, Senator the Hon Marise Payne, as she states that Australia is "very proud to [have] chair[ed] the UN GGE[4] in 2013 when it agreed that existing international law applied in cyberspace," and is "urging like-minded nations to throw their support and resources behind these international efforts that will build trust and transparency" (Payne, 2019).

Among the most recent actual examples of Australia's understanding of the applicability of international law in cyberspace was the 4th Japan–Australia Cyber Policy Dialogue Joint Statement, whereby "Japan and Australia reaffirmed their commitment to continue to enhance cooperation and information sharing on responses to malicious cyber activities, including deterring and responding to significant cyber incidents, consistent with relevant domestic and international law" (MOFA, 2019). This illustrates Australia's commitment to international law and cooperation on cyber issues with a number of international geopolitically strategic partners, including outside of the Five Eyes alliance.

International governance

In terms of regional governance, Australia holds the "leading role in the region's largest cyber security community with the Australian Cyber Security Centre re-elected as Chair of the Asia-Pacific Computer Emergency Response Team (APCERT) Steering Committee in Shanghai on 23 October 2018" (ACSC, 2018a). This is an interesting point, as Australia unmistakably aims to balance out China's power in the region (Huang, 2017).

Indeed, regional cyber governance initiatives abound for Australia;[5] for example, "[t]he Pacific Cyber Security Operational Network (PaCSON), [was] launched in Brisbane [Australia] on 30 April 2018 with 14 foundation member countries from the Pacific"[6] (Australian Government, 2018). Moreover, Australia and New Zealand jointly recently reaffirmed their commitment to enhance collective regional cyber resilience, notably "bringing Australia's total investment in cyber cooperation to $38.4 million to 2022" (Australian Government, 2018).

The regional cyber governance involvement is part of a broader international cyber governance plan, detailed in the International Cyber Engagement Strategy ("the International Strategy") (DFAT, 2017). The document makes a number of international commitments, and dedicates an entire section to "Internet Governance & Cooperation" (DFAT, 2017: 56–64). International cooperation is central to the document, through "multi-stakeholder Internet governance," all with an aim to reduce the risk of cybercrime, promoting peace and stability in cyberspace, "particularly in our [Australia's] region" (DFAT, 2017: 10). DFAT has also released a 2019 Progress Report for the International Strategy (DFAT, 2019).

As previously mentioned, Australia chaired the 2013 UN GGE whereby nations agreed that international law applied in cyberspace, thus avoiding the UN having to create a new global legal framework. Australia also supported the 2015 UN GGW, whereby "nations agreed to a set of 11 international norms in cyberspace" (Stilgherrian, 2019b). It continues to back the UN's international cyber governance efforts, openly supporting both its present progress initiatives, namely a GGE proposed by the United States of America, and an Open Ended Working Group (OEWG) put forth by Russia, viewing the two as "complementary" (Stilgherrian, 2019b), and sending the Director of Cyber Policy at DFAT to represent Australia in those conversations (Stilgherrian, 2019b).

Two final things are noteworthy as relating to the Cyber Security Strategy here; first, the creation of an Australian Ambassador for Cyber Affairs ("Cyber Ambassador") position as part of the Department of Foreign Affairs and Trade (DFAT), allowing Australia to pursue its interests and project its principles (as articulated in the International Strategy, such as advocating an "open and free internet among the international community" [Holding, 2018]) on a more interpersonal level. Second, stability in the region and a strong international system can arguably not be approached without the "carrot and stick" concept, and, as such, Australia has openly confirmed its possession and further development of offensive cyber capability (Holding, 2018).

Sovereignty

Australia, a sovereign nation state with a stable democracy of nearly 120 years (Lohman, 2011), has not formally claimed sovereignty over "its" cyberspace. Whilst it does not regard the Internet as its territory, it certainly seeks to protect Australia's "sovereignty, (...) economy and (...) national security" (Turnbull, 2019) from cyberthreats though, and, to this effect, has both defensive and offensive military cyber capabilities,[6] and a set of relevant internal legislations.

Australia has never in its history shut down the Internet; though the government has the actual legal ability to do so, "with emergency powers," this is highly unlikely to occur (Lohman, 2011). It does, nevertheless, maintain a degree of control over the flow of information and regulating of speech on the Internet; this is done within specific legal frameworks and addresses primarily censorship around child pornography, sexual violence, and terrorism (Crozier, 2019), as well as piracy (Copyright Amendment [Online Infringement] Bill, 2015), practical aspects of suicide (2006 Suicide Related Materials Offences Act), and "abhorrent violent material" (Criminal Code Amendment [Sharing of Abhorrent Violent Material] Bill, 2019).

Restrictions must normally be ordered by the Australian Communications and Media Authority, however, as demonstrated in the aftermath of the 2019 Christchurch mosque shootings, Australian Internet Security Providers (ISPs) have the ability to act independently in blocking the content ahead of any governmental directive (Barnett, 2019). It is worth noting that, as is to be expected in a federal system like Australia's, state and territory laws also have additional provisions, particularly in relation to banning the transmission of material deemed unsuitable for minors.[7]

Australia does not, otherwise, censor free speech around political opinions or any other societal aspects that may be controlled under various other regimes. An interesting, tangent point worth mentioning, however, is that of the new, contentious anti-encryption law (Telecommunications and Other Legislation Amendment [Assistance and Access] Act, 2018) that was recently passed. A first in the world, this law aimed at enhancing national security – but arguably posing great risks to privacy – requires "technology companies to provide law enforcement and security agencies with access to encrypted communications."[8] The law is undergoing review but is currently being enforced. In the same vein, the Australian government has the legal right to request access to metadata from various organizations (telecommunication companies, and others that might be of interest, such as transport) in the interest of national security, and has done so "nearly 60 times" over the course of the past year (Shields, 2019).

Another rather fascinating debate took place in 2018; should Chinese planes, for example, flying in Australian airspace, abide by Australian law in terms of Internet censorship (or lack thereof?) (Xiao, 2018). Which country's laws ought to come into effect when a plane is Chinese territory, but the airspace is Australian? This made for an interesting food-for-thought point, and, to date, Chinese flights offering Wi-Fi and flying in/out of Australia apply Chinese laws to their available Internet content.

Australia's cultural understandings

Australia has been labelled a "cultural, ethnic and political melting pot" (Vosloo, 2014) and is one of the most stable democracies in the world, as previously mentioned (Lohman, 2011). In stark antithesis to China, the regional pole of power, Australia aims for this open democracy and its respective founding values and principles to be exported in the Asia Pacific region, and indeed, to the world (DFAT, 2017: 5). Overall, Australians favor "an open, free and secure Internet, achieved through a multi-stakeholder approach to Internet government and cooperation" (DFAT, 2017: 9).

A number of understandings around privacy vs. national security in particular have changed in the past decade, granting more surveillance rights to the government (such as those discussed in the previous section around the anti-encryption laws) – which is indeed presently seeking additional "spying powers" (Karp, 2019).

This was heavily influenced by the rise in terrorism and specifically ISIS radicals leaving to fight, then seeking to return to Australia. In parallel, for example, the broader community debate extended to sometimes depict Muslims in an unfavorable light, and whilst this may not necessarily affect cyberspace issues directly, much of this proliferation of information and opinions around Islamophobia has been achieved digitally (Chamas, 2019).

As a nation, Australians have been known to enjoy sharing – and, in fact, oversharing – a substantial amount of information from their daily lives online; it is fair to say it has become a cultural Australian trait (Golbeck, 2014). There is an interesting paradox to be noted here around the value still placed on privacy (hence the general discontent with the current administration's surveillance intents) and the yet the expectation that the government ought to protect its citizens from cyber threats in spite of this voluntary information dissemination. Indeed, in private as much as in business circles, Australia has an overall degree of naivety when it comes to cyber security (Calic, Pattinson, Parsons, Butavicius & McCormac, 2016: 17–18). This characteristic could be said to be a cultural trait, as traditionally Australia's population has been quite fortunate and sheltered from cyber threats in comparison to the United States and certain European states, for example. This is also underlined by the fact that it is one of the Strategy's main aims to make Australia a "cyber smart nation" (PMC, 2016: 51), though it has a way to go yet.

Australia's institutions

Australia does not currently have a Ministry of Information or Information Technology – but perhaps it should. This would not only demonstrate its commitment to the "cyber future," but would also enhance and streamline Australia's cyber policies and capabilities in the present, which could be perceived as rather fragmented.

Cyber security is currently under the umbrella of the newly (2017) formed Department of Home Affairs, an organization responsible for national security, law enforcement, emergency management, border control, immigration, refugees, citizenship, and multicultural affairs (Commonwealth of Australia, 2017: 4–5).

Other parts of government that have a say in cyber security policy and decision-making are, primarily, the Department of Prime Minister and Cabinet, the Attorney-General's Department, the Department of Foreign Affairs and Trade, the Department of Defence, and the statutory Australian Signals Directorate (with the Australian Cyber Security Centre under it).

The position of Cyber Ambassador driving DFAT's International Strategy has been mentioned previously, and was established as part of the national Cyber Security Strategy in 2016. Other roles which were created at the same time as part of the Strategy were that of Special Adviser to the Prime Minister on Cyber Security and Minister Assisting the Prime Minister on Cyber Security (APH, n.d.a). Following a resignation without succession (Stilgherrian, 2019a) and as part of a cabinet reshuffling respectively (Stilgherrian, 2018), both of these positions have quietly vanished from Australia's present cyber landscape, as of mid-2019.

There are a number of digital agencies and divisions across the Australian government which have strong cyber interests and are worth noting, including the Digital Transformation Agency, the Australian Digital Health Agency, the Office of the eSafety Commissioner, and the Office of the Australian Information Commissioner. Overall, Australia is driving digital transformation across the board in government, even if some agencies may be taking the lead over others.

Interestingly, the inaugural 2009 Cyber Security Strategy was released by the Attorney General's Department, while the 2016 one was put out by the Department of Prime Minister and Cabinet. This shift illustrated the then-Prime Minister's priorities; however, it is safe to assume that the next one is likely to be published by the Department of Home Affairs, which now has cyber under its umbrella.

Role of the private sector

Australia's Cyber Security Strategy prides itself on having been written following extensive private sector consultation (also including academia), and has, as its first goal, to achieve an increasing degree of synergy and partnerships between government decision-makers and industry (PMC, 2016: 21).

AustCyber (the Australian Cyber Security Growth Network) was established in this scope, "growing Australia's cyber security ecosystem" (AustCyber, n.d.). The organization also ensures the continuing communication link between government and industry insofar as national cyber policy, and is also involved in multiple educational initiatives connected to industry.

The private sector has the democratic right to lobby the government on a number of issues, having the potential to influence cyber policy making. In particular, large telecommunication companies (telcos) such as Telstra or Optus are consulted and heavily involved in legislative changes, and often the four largest banks are too (due to their central importance in funding and critical role in the economy), among other industry stakeholders. That being said, protest though they might some proposed legislation, it can be passed without their full agreement or support; for example, the top three Australian telcos objected to this, but did not sway the government:

> The parliament of Australia passed a metadata retention bill back in October 2015; according to this law, all the Telcos and ISPs in the country will be legally responsible for storing the user's metadata for a time period of 2 years. The data will be stored for the purpose of investigations and proceedings by law enforcement agencies in Australia.
>
> *(Ali, 2018)*

Indeed, the metadata retention laws are a continuing sore point between government and telcos, with "back door to access data 'deliberately left open'" and 21 agencies authorized access without a warrant (Schliebs, 2019).

Another group worth mentioning in terms of private sector involvement in the making of Internet policy in Australia is that of consulting firms. The Big Four (KPMG, Deloitte, EY and PwC), alongside other smaller firms, have a very substantial amount of advisory (among other) work in government organizations (Belot, 2018).

Finally, an example of a private corporation that has had much contentious publicity of late is Huawei. As of 2019, allegations were circulated that the company, a large player in the Australian tech market, shared information with Chinese intelligence agencies. As such, it was banned from being a supplier to Australia's 5G mobile phone network, which sparked continued controversy, and indeed strained Sino–Australian relations. It is therefore worth mentioning Huawei in the context of a private sector entity that directly (albeit unwillingly) affected a specific Australian policy (Ryan, 2019).

Role of the legislature

Though some were discussed in the "Sovereignty" section of this chapter, a few key pieces of Australian federal legislation relating to cyberspace are mentioned below, in chronological order of passing, or latest relevant amendment:

- *Broadcasting Services Act 1992* deals with issues to do with ownership of media and content regulation;
- *Telecommunications (Consumer Protection and Service Standards) Act 1999* is very broad legislation covering public interest and telecommunications services;
- *Suicide Related Material Offences Act 2006* forbids the sharing of practical aspects of suicide online;
- *Telecommunications (Interception and Access) Amendment (Data Retention) Act 2015* introduced a statutory obligation for telcos to retain for two years users' metadata, and makes provisions for law enforcement agencies' access to this under certain circumstances;
- *Copyright Amendment (Online Infringement) Bill 2015* deals with piracy over the Internet;
- *IP Laws Amendment Act 2015* is applicable to cyber Intellectual Property or IP stored online;
- *Enhancing Online Safety Act* 2015 (amended in 2017) is a comprehensive mandate from the eSafety Commissioner around ensuring Australians are and feel safe digitally;
- *Privacy Amendment (Notifiable Data Breaches) Act 2017* mandates organizations to disclose online breaches by notifying/reporting them to the Office of the Australian Information Commissioner;
- *Telecommunications and Other Legislation Amendment (Assistance and Access) Act 2018* requires technology companies to grant access to encrypted communications to specific law enforcement, intelligence and security agencies;
- *Criminal Code Amendment (Sharing of Abhorrent Violent Material) Bill 2019* for virtual content deemed abhorrently unacceptable.

As previously mentioned, state and territories also have additional legal provisions, notably around banning the transmission of material deemed unsuitable for minors.[9]

As yet, there is no specific law relating to cyberwarfare, and the Australian legal community is still working on "anticipating potential legal issues that might arise" from it (ANU, 2019).

The current Minister for Home Affairs has recently put forward a proposal which, if approved, would give the Australian Signals Directorate the power to be involved in domestic work, something that has been mediatized as an effort to spy on the Australian people (Karp, 2019). This is still under consideration, but, if approved, would represent a significant development in the area of surveillance in Australian policy.

Cybercrime and cyberterrorism

In Australia, responsibility is shared between internal- and external-facing federal and state/territory security and intelligence agencies, depending on the type of cyber issue, its scale, where it originates, whom it affects and how.

Broadly, whole-of-nation level cyberattack and potential acts of cyberwar would be dealt with by the Department of Defence. Under certain circumstances, the latter may be able to assist on a national level also (e.g., in case of a large-scale act of cyberterrorism, including on critical infrastructure) via the Information Warfare Division; though this assistance has not been required as of yet, discussion is taking place around provisions to facilitate such a maneuver (Borys, 2019).

Cybercrime and identity security, in terms of final responsibility, falls under the Department of Home Affairs as part of criminal justice; this is, however, only the umbrella organization for the frontline entities mentioned below (DHA, n.d.).

The Australian Federal Police deals with high tech crime (defined as including computer intrusions, unauthorized modification or destruction of data, and Distributed Denial-of-Service attacks among other elements), and provides overarching support and assistance when/as required to state/territory police, as it is often otherwise deemed not to have jurisdiction to intervene, and moreover noting they all have their "own legislated computer-related offences which are similar to the Commonwealth legislation" (AFP, n.d.b).

The Australian Security Intelligence Organisation (ASIO) – under the Department of Home Affairs (ASIO, n.d.) – alongside the Office of National Intelligence (ONI) – under the Department of Prime Minister and Cabinet (ONI, n.d.) – gather and analyze relevant intelligence and data that underpins the work of law enforcement agencies in the terms of countering national cybercrime, cyberterrorism and cyberespionage.

The Australian Signals Directorate is a statutory entity that provides intelligence for, and supports primarily, the Department of Defence and Australia's international partners in cyber endeavors (ASD, n.d.).

Though the ASD is an external facing entity, under it falls the Australian Cyber Security Centre (ACSC), a multi-stakeholder initiative for national cyber resilience, indeed a "hub for private and public sector collaboration and information-sharing, [which exists] to prevent and combat cyber security threats and to minimize harm to all Australians" (ASD, n.d.). The ACSC in turn oversees the Computer Emergency Response Team (CERT), which responds to cyber threats and incidents within Australia (ASD, n.d.).

The ACSC published the Threat Report 2017, detailing who was affected by cybercrime and divulging some alarming national statistics. It also provided guidelines for reporting and assistance that could be provided to affected stakeholders, as well as outlined and recommended pre-emptive cyber security measures (ACSC, 2017). Another such report has not come out since.

It is worth mentioning that thus far, Australia has not suffered major cyberattacks, be they deemed cyberterrorist ones or other. Although instances like the hacking of the Australian Parliament (Remeikis, 2019) or the Australian National University (McGowan, 2019) are becoming more frequent, instances such as WannaCry malware attacks have been avoided.[10]

Societal implications

Cyberspace has become a shaping means to society's evolution – that is certainly Australia's case, just like most other nations. Malicious cyber activity is also an avenue to strike at society, and especially civilians on a large scale (e.g., social engineering in instances like federal elections), using methods that may not even initially appear malign.

As previously mentioned, Australia has not suffered a critical attack as yet, but has seen a staggering number of individuals and organizations breached, hacked or infected, to which most people did not know how to respond or did not have the means to, and, as such, Australia suffered considerable financial damage to its economy (ACSC, 2017).

The Australian Cyber Security Centre states it exists to provide "information, advice and assistance to all Australians" (ASD, n.d.), but building nation-wide cyber resilience is not an easy goal to reach, which is why it comes into focus in the Cyber Security Strategy (PMC, 2016: 4).

The ongoing societal debate around whether Australians value privacy or security more is illustrated in the previously mentioned recent outrage at the Minister for Home Affairs' proposed more "invasive" legislation (Karp, 2019). Nevertheless, admittedly, the government can only go so far in protecting those who may not want that protection or disregard the risks, as shown by the enthusiastic uptake of Australian citizens in the controversial FaceApp, in spite of possible implications (Blau, 2019).

Nationally, people are becoming more interested in hearing about issues relating to cyber security, whether media-sensationalized or rationally analyzed. The Australian Strategic Policy Institute's International Cyber Policy Centre, one of Australia's leading think tanks, has an ever-growing following (as shown, for example, by their constantly increasing number of Twitter followers and commentators) (ASPI, 2019).

Similarly, in the private sector, lawyers and insurance firms, for example, are beginning to offer more, and diversified, services in this space.[11] Technology, IT and cyber education is being developed at all levels, as well as in terms of research,[12] and employers are (as is the case in most countries around the world) asking for more professionals to deal with the workforce shortage and skills gap (Pearce, 2018).

It could overall be said that although a threat will likely always have a negative impact, a positive implication for the likes of cybercrime and cyberterrorism is the fact that Australians are embracing the challenge, and growing increasingly aware and savvy, albeit slowly, and are taking the opportunity to play in the innovation space which these threats create.

Conclusion

In conclusion, Australia is making progress in terms of cyber security policy and legislation, as well as in its international involvement. Much change has occurred at structural level nationally in terms of government responsibility for cyber policy, legislation and security in the past five years. Some strategic movement in the cyber sphere can also be seen from a private industry perspective, as well as an educational and cultural one. The nation still has a way to go in comparison to some allies and contenders, however, given its resources, population, and typical federal government mechanism, it is "holding its own" as a middle power.

Importantly, Australia is presently at a unique East-West confluence; "for the first time in its history, Australia's major trading partner, China, is an authoritarian state while Australia's major security partner, the United States, is China's strategic rival" (Spry, 2019). There is a prospect for Australia to redefine its cyber self with the 2020 upcoming cyber strategy, and focus in further on what can make a difference immediately, but also consider and address longer term implications – will the current government take this opportunity?

Notes

1 Eighty-three outcomes have been mentioned specifically, though some are not quantifiable (Hawkins & Nevill, 2017: 3).
2 The Australian Signals Directorate's (ASD) baseline cyber mitigation strategies, which are not mandatory for government departments (Sadler, 2019).

3 Definitions and terminology around cyber in the other Five Eyes nations can be found here: United States of America (NICCS, n.d.), Canada (CCCS, n.d.), United Kingdom (UKGov, n.d.), New Zealand (NZGov, 2019).
4 United Nations Group of Governmental Experts.
5 For an overview of Australia's involvement with individual Pacific nations' cyber capacity, see Spry, 2019.
6 See, the Strategy and the White Paper for further detail.
7 See, for example: (1) In Victoria, Classification (Publications, Films and Computer Games) (Enforcement) Act 1995 – Section 58; (2) In New South Wales, NSW Internet Censorship Bill 2001; (3) In South Australia, Classification (Publications, Films and Computer Games) Act 1995 – Section 75D.
8 Such as the Australian Parliament (2019), among others.
9 See, for example: (1) In Victoria, Classification (Publications, Films and Computer Games) (Enforcement) Act 1995 – Section 58; (2) In New South Wales, NSW Internet Censorship Bill 2001; (3) In South Australia, Classification (Publications, Films and Computer Games) Act 1995 – Section 75D.
10 Some have argued that insofar as WannaCry is concerned, Australia simply got lucky because of its time zone, and the fact that the devastating effects in the rest of the world were broadcasted mainstream by the time Australia woke up (Smith & Han, 2017). It is unclear how the situation would have been dealt with exactly and by whom, should Australia have been affected to the extent other nations were.
11 Such as Sladen Law's cyber practice offerings (SladenLegal, n.d.) and AIG cyber insurance (AIG, n.d.) among many others that did not exist a few years ago.
12 For example: (1) At primary and secondary level, the Technologies Curriculum was recently rolled out; (2) At professional training level, a national curriculum was developed for a Certificate IV in Cyber Security (AustCyber, 2019); (3) At university level, most universities now offer a program in tangent with technology or cyberspace (Austin & Slay, 2018); (4) Cyber Security Cooperative Research Centre (CSCRC) has been created with branches across Australia (CSCRC, n.d.).

Suggested reading

Australian Government. (2020). "Australia's 2020 Cyber Security Strategy." www.homeaffairs.gov.au/reports-and-publications/submissions-and-discussion-papers/cyber-security-strategy-2020
Hanson, F. (2019, September 10). "Australia's Cyber Strategy, Version 2.0," *The Strategist*, Australian Strategic Policy Institute, Barton, Australia. www.aspistrategist.org.au/australias-cyber-strategy-version-2-0/
Joiner, K. F. (2017). "How Australia Can Catch up to U.S. Cyber Resilience by Understanding that Cyber Survivability Test and Evaluation Drives Defense Investment," *Information Security Journal: A Global Perspective*, 26(2): 74–84.
Leuprecht, C. & MacLellan, S. (ed.). (2018). "Governing Cyber Security in Canada, Australia and the United States," Special Report, Centre for International Governance Innovation, Waterloo, Canada. www.cigionline.org/sites/default/files/documents/SERENE-RISCweb.pdf
Mikolic-Torreira, I., Snyder, D., Price, M., Shlapak, D., Beaghley, S., Bishop, M., Harting, S., Oberholtzer, J., Pettyjohn, S., Weinbaum, C., & Westerman, E. (2017, August). "Exploring Cyber Security Policy Options in Australia." RAND, Santa Monaca, CA. https://nsc.crawford.anu.edu.au/sites/default/files/publication/nsc_crawford_anu_edu_au/2017-08/issues_and_options_paper-3_2_0.pdf

References

ACSC. (2017). "ASCS Threat Report 2017."
ACSC. (2018a). "Australia Maintains a Key Role in International Cyber Security Community."
ACSC. (2018b). "Strengthening Cyber Security across the Pacific."
AFP. (n.d.a). "Cyber Crime."
AFP. (n.d.b). "High Tech Crime." www.afp.gov.au/what-we-do/crime-types/cybercrime/high-tech-crime
AG. (n.d.). "International Law."

AIG. (n.d.). "CyberEdge," AIG Cyber Insurance. www.aig.com.au/business/products/financial-lines/cyberedge

Ali, Z. (2018). "Mandatory Data Retention in Australia," *PrivacyEnd*, www.privacyend.com/mandatory-data-retention-australia/

ANU. (2019). "Cyber Warfare Law," Australian National University, ANU School of Law https://programsandcourses.anu.edu.au/2019/course/LAWS8035

APH. (n.d.a). "Cybersecurity, Cybercrime and Cybersafety: A Quick Guide to Key Internet Links."

APH. (n.d.b). "National Security – Cybersecurity."

ASD. (n.d.). "Cyber Security," Australian Signals Directorate. www.homeaffairs.gov.au/about-us/our-portfolios/criminal-justice/cybercrime-identity-security

ASIO. (n.d.). "What We Do," Australian Security Intelligence Organisation. www.asio.gov.au/what-we-do.html

ASPI. (2019). "ASPI Cyber Policy," *Twitter*. https://twitter.com/aspi_icpc?lang=en

AustCyber. (2019). "TAFECyber Initiative – A Year in Review," AustCyber. www.austcyber.com/news-events/tafecyber-initiative

AustCyber. (n.d.). "Home," AustCyber. www.austcyber.com/

Austin, G. & Slay, J. (2016, May 31). "The Australian Government Must Take Cyber Security More Seriously," *The Conversation*. https://theconversation.com/the-australian-government-must-take-cyber-security-more-seriously-60231

Austin, G. & Slay, J. (2018). "Development in Training and Education for Australian Cyber Security: Filling the Gaps," *Journal of the Colloquium for Information System Security Education*, 5(2): 1–27.

Australian Government. (1995). "Criminal Code Act 1995."

Australian Government. (2018). "Australia and New Zealand: Pacific Cyber Cooperation," Minister for Foreign Affairs, Minister for Women.

Australian Government. (n.d.a). "Critical Infrastructure Resilience."

Australian Government. (n.d.b). "What Is Cyber Security?"

Australian Parliament. (2019). "Review of the Telecommunications and Other Legislation Amendment (Assistance and Access) Act 2018, Parliamentary Joint Committee on Intelligence and Security," Parliament of the Commonwealth of Australia.

Barnett, K. (2019, April 8). "Censorship Is the Wrong Response to Christchurch," *Spiked-Online*. www.spiked-online.com/2019/04/08/censorship-is-the-wrong-response-to-christchurch/

Bashfield, S. (2019). "Australia Needs a New National Security Strategy," *The Diplomat*. https://thediplomat.com/2019/02/australia-needs-a-new-national-security-strategy/

Belot, H. (2018, August 17). "Big Consultancy Firms Call the Federal Government 'The Dairy' because They Milk It for All It's Worth, Inquiry Hears," *ABC News*. www.abc.net.au/news/2018-08-17/consultancy-bosses-quizzed-on-government-nickname-the-dairy/10132264

Blau, A. (2019, July 18). "Tried the Viral FaceApp Transformation? Here's What Might Happen to Your Photo Now," *ABC News*. www.abc.net.au/news/2019-07-18/faceapp-privacy-concerns-dampen-viral-challenge/11321728

Borys, S. (2019). "Senior Defence Figure Raises Concerns about Future Cyber Attacks – And the Scenario Costing Him Sleep," *ABC News*.

Calic, D., Pattinson, M., Parsons, K., Butavicius, M., & McCormac, A. (2016). "Naïve and Accidental Behaviours that Compromise Information Security: What the Experts Think," Proceedings of the Tenth International Symposium on Human Aspects of Information Security & Assurance, HAISA. https://pdfs.semanticscholar.org/b553/7b5368c9e0955b82d3dd93fd3fe4d2bb8f11.pdf

CCCS. (n.d.). "Cyber Threat and Cyber Threat Actors."

Chamas, Z. (2019, May 17). "Australia Vote: Concern about Islamophobia among Smaller Parties," *Al Jazeera*. www.aljazeera.com/news/2019/05/australia-vote-concern-islamophobia-smaller-parties-190517074521443.html

Commonwealth of Australia. (2017). "The Consititution – Amendments to the Administrative Arrangements Order."

Crozier, R. (2019). "Govt Expands Socmed Crackdown Laws, Including Jail Time, to Internet, Content and Hosting Providers," *ITNews*. www.itnews.com.au/news/govt-expands-socmed-crackdown-laws-including-jail-time-to-internet-content-and-hosting-providers-523352

CSCRC. (n.d.). "About," Australian Cyber Security Cooperative Research Centre. www.cybersecuritycrc.org.au/

DFAT. (2017). "Australia's International Cyber Engagement Strategy."

DFAT. (2019). "2019 Progress Report."

DHA. (n.d.). "Cybercrime and Identity Security," Department of Home Affairs, www.homeaffairs.gov.au/about-us/our-portfolios/criminal-justice/cybercrime-identity-security

DHS. (2018). "Cyber Security Strategy 2018–22."

Golbeck, J. (2014). "Why We Overshare Online," *Psychology Today*. www.psychologytoday.com/au/blog/your-online-secrets/201410/why-we-overshare-online?amp

Hardy, K. (2017). "Is Cyberterrorism a Threat?" *Australian Institute of International Affairs*. www.internationalaffairs.org.au/australianoutlook/is-cyberterrorism-a-threat/

Hawkins, Z. & Nevill, L. (2017). "Australia's Cyber Security Strategy: Execution & Evolution," Australian Strategic Policy Institute, Barton, Australia. https://i.nextmedia.com.au/Assets/ASPI_cyber_security_strategy_review.pdf

Holding, M. (2018). "Australia Is Set to Future-Proof Its Cyber Foreign Policy," Australian Institute of International Affairs, Deakin, Australia. www.internationalaffairs.org.au/australianoutlook/white-paper-cyber/

Huang, K. (2017, November 23). "Australia Looks for Balance to China's Rising Power in Indo-Pacific Region," *South China Morning Post*. www.scmp.com/news/china/diplomacy-defence/article/2121245/australia-looks-balance-chinas-rising-power-indo

Karp, P. (2019, June 16). "Peter Dutton Confirms Plan to Create New Spying Powers Still Being Considered," *The Guardian*. www.theguardian.com/australia-news/2019/jun/16/peter-dutton-confirms-plan-to-create-new-spying-powers-still-being-considered

Lohman, T. (2011, January 31), "Can Australia's Internet Be Switched Off, Too?," *ComputerWorld*, www.computerworld.com.au/article/374883/can_australia_internet_switched_off_too_/

McGhee, A. (2017, June 29). "Cyber Warfare Unit Set to Be Launched by Australian Defence Forces," *ABC News*. www.abc.net.au/news/2017-06-30/cyber-warfare-unit-to-be-launched-by-australian-defence-forces/8665230

McGowan, M. (2019, June 6). "China behind Massive Australian National University Hack, Intelligence Officials Say," *The Guardian*. www.theguardian.com/australia-news/2019/jun/06/china-behind-massive-australian-national-university-hack-intelligence-officials-say

MOFA. (2019) "The 4th Japan-Australia Cyber Policy Dialogue Joint Statement."

NICCS. (n.d.). "Explore Terms: A Glossary of Common Cybersecurity Terminology."

NZGov. (2019). "New Zealand's Cyber Security Strategy 2019."

ONI. (n.d.). "What We Do," www.oni.gov.au/what-we-do

Payne, M. (2019, March 12). "Marise Payne on Australia's International Cyber Strategy," Lowy Institute, Australia. www.lowyinstitute.org/publications/marise-payne-australia-s-international-cyber-strategy

Pearce, R. (2018). "$400 Million: The Cost of Australia's Cyber Security Skills Shortage," *ComputerWorld*. www.computerworld.com.au/article/650122/400-million-cost-australia-cyber-security-skills-shortage/

PMC. (2016). "Australia's Cyber Security Strategy."

PMC. (2017). "Australia's Cyber Security Strategy – First Annual Update."

Remeikis, A. (2019, February 8). "Australian Security Services Investigate Attempted Cyber Attack on Parliament," *The Guardian*. theguardian.com/australia-news/2019/feb/08/asio-australian-security-services-hack-data-breach-investigate-attempted-cyber-attack-parliament

Rothwell, D. & Crawford, E. (2017). "International Law: Is Australia a Good International Citizen?" Australian Institute of International Affairs, Deakin, Australia. www.internationalaffairs.org.au/australianoutlook/international-law-australia-good-citizen/

Ryan, P. (2019, July 17). "Huawei Protests 5G Mobile Phone Network Ban, Saying 'Australia Can Trust Huawei,'" *ABC News*. www.abc.net.au/news/2019-07-18/huawei-protests-5g-mobile-phone-network-ban/11320426

Sadler, D. (2018). "National Plan for Cyber Studies," InnovationAus. www.innovationaus.com/2018/01/National-plan-for-cyber-studies

Sadler, D. (2019). "Govt Won't Mandate Essential Eight, InnivationAus." www.innovationaus.com/2019/04/Govt-wont-mandate-Essential-Eight

Schliebs, M. (2019). "Back Door to Access Data 'Deliberately Left Open'," *The Australian*. www.theaustralian.com.au/nation/back-door-to-access-data-deliberately-left-open/news-story/9416da34adac9d6dcf24e14c836d1b15

Scully, T. (2016). "Cyber Security and the 2016 Defence White Paper," *Security Challenges Journal, 12*(1): 115–126.

Shields, B. (2019, July 8). "Federal Police Accessed the Metadata of Journalists Nearly 60 Times," *The Sydney Morning Herald*. www.smh.com.au/politics/federal/federal-police-accessed-the-metadata-of-journalists-nearly-60-times-20190708-p52598.html

SladenLegal. (n.d.). "Cyberlaw." https://sladen.com.au/cyberlaw

Smith, P. & Han, M. (2017, May 14). "Wake up Call for Aussie Business after 'Lucky Escape' from WannaCry Ransomware Attacks," *Financial Review*. www.afr.com/technology/wake-up-call-for-aussie-business-after-lucky-escape-from-wannacry-ransomware-attacks-20170514-gw4kbb

Spry, D. (2019, March 24). "What Australia's Cyber Strategy Means for Asia Pacific," *GovInsider*. https://govinsider.asia/innovation/what-australias-cyber-strategy-means-for-asia-pacific/

Stilgherrian. (2018, August 26). "Cyber Defence Goes Missing in Australian Cabinet Reshuffle," *ZSNet*. www.zdnet.com/article/cyber-defence-goes-missing-in-australian-cabinet-reshuffle/

Stilgherrian. (2019a, May 6). "Australia's Cybersecurity Chief Alastair MacGibbon Resigns," *ZDNet*. www.zdnet.com/article/australias-cybersecurity-chief-alastair-macgibbon-resigns/

Stilgherrian. (2019b, April 16). "Australia to Keep Playing the UN Cyberspace Norms Game," *ZDNet*. www.zdnet.com/article/australia-to-keep-playing-the-un-cyberspace-norms-game/

Stuparu, A. (2016). "Australia's New Cyber Security Strategy: A Critical Outlook," *The Interpreter*. www.lowyinstitute.org/the-interpreter/australias-new-cyber-security-strategy-critical-outlook

Turnbull, M. (2019). "Statement to the House of Representatives on Cyber Security," Prime Minister of Australia.

UKGov. (n.d.). "What Is Cyber Security?"

Vosloo, E. (2014, August 28). "Australia: A Cultural, Ethnic and Political Melting Pot," *Australian Times*.

Xiao, B. (2018, September 7). "The Complexities of Cyber Sovereignty in Chinese Airlines over Australian Skies," *ABC News*. www.abc.net.au/news/2018-09-08/i-confronted-the-great-firewall-of-china-in-australian-airspace/10159900

32

SINGAPORE

A leading actor in ASEAN cybersecurity

Benjamin Ang

Introduction and overview of national cybersecurity strategy

Singapore set up a Cyber Security Agency (CSA) in 2015, as the national agency overseeing cybersecurity strategy, operation, education, outreach, and ecosystem development. The CSA reports directly to the Prime Minister's Office and is managed by the Ministry of Communications and Information. While the CSA oversees civilian cybersecurity issues, the C4 (Command, Control, Communications, Computer) Command in the Singapore Armed Forces' (SAF) and Defence Cyber Organisation in the Ministry of Defence oversees military cyber issues. One year after its formation, the CSA published Singapore's Cybersecurity Strategy in October 2016. The Strategy sets out Singapore's vision, goals, and priorities in the area of cybersecurity and outlines the country's plans to build a resilient and trusted cyber environment for Singapore and Singaporeans.

The Cybersecurity Strategy has Four Pillars:

1   **Building a resilient infrastructure to strengthen the critical infrastructures by working closely with private sectors and cybersecurity community**. Singapore's Government works closely with private sector operators and regulators responsible for Critical Information Infrastructure (CII) that supports essential services. Singapore has identified 11 Critical Information Infrastructure (CII) sectors: Government, telecommunications, energy, aviation, maritime, land transport, healthcare, banking and finance, water, security and emergency, and media. The Strategy seeks to establish "robust and systematic cyber risk management processes, as well as response and recovery plans, across all critical sectors." The Cybersecurity Act was introduced in 2017, to provide a legal framework for implementing this pillar of the Strategy.

2   **Creating a safer cyberspace by promoting involvement from not only government but also industry and the public**. For the rest of the nation, who are not part of Critical Information Infrastructure, the Strategy outlines efforts by various agencies to combat cybercrime and protect data, including the National Cybercrime Action Plan. The plan also addresses cyberhygiene, and presents everyone in society as having a responsibility to understand cybersecurity issues and adopt good practices.

3 **Developing a vibrant security ecosystem by working with industry and academia to grow the cybersecurity workforce**. The Strategy next calls on Government to collaborate with industry and Institutes of Higher Learning (universities and polytechnics) to grow the cybersecurity workforce. The private sector and academia will also receive incentives to develop technologically advanced companies and nurture local start-ups.

4 **Strengthening international partnerships, especially among the ASEAN members, to address transnational cybersecurity issues**. Last but not least, Singapore commits to actively cooperating with the international community, particularly ASEAN, to address transnational cybersecurity and cybercrime issues, champion initiatives for cyber capacity building, and facilitate global exchanges on cyber norms, policy and legislation.

International law

Consistent with the fourth pillar of the Cybersecurity Strategy, Singapore views a rules-based cyberspace as essential to protect nations in the ASEAN region, and recognizes the application of international law and the adoption of voluntary operational norms as a vital part of this. As Singapore's Commissioner for Cybersecurity (who is also Chief Executive of CSA), David Koh said in his speech to the Atlantic Council in 2018 (Ghosh, 2019):

> Cyberspace should not be any different from the physical domain … For example, in the maritime domain, there are rules that govern how a nation-state should behave, such as through the United Nations Convention on the Law of the Sea. And similarly in the aviation domain, we abide by the rules set by the International Civil Aviation Organization. These rules underpin our modern economies and our security … Otherwise, the alternative is a world order where might makes right, where rules and norms are routinely flouted, and where there is considerable uncertainty about the sanctity of international agreements and norms … A small state like Singapore is like an ant in a jungle full of elephants, and we must do what we can to better secure ourselves, especially when the elephants fight.

ASEAN had embraced the concept of the rule of international law ever since its formation. International law continues to be a cornerstone of ASEAN policy, and is enshrined in the ASEAN Charter. The Secretary-General's words in 2018 illustrate this (ASEAN, 2018):

> The ASEAN Way has brought us to where we are now. War among the ASEAN Member States is unthinkable. And we are one of the fastest growing regions in the world today.

At the same meeting, it was noted that the ASEAN Ministerial Conference on Cybersecurity (AMCC) of September 2018:

> reaffirmed the importance of a rules-based cyberspace as an enabler of economic progress and betterment of living standards, and agreed in-principle that international law, voluntary and non-binding norms of State behaviour, and practical confidence building measures are essential for stability and predictability in cyberspace and in which ASEAN Member States agreed to subscribe in-principle to the 11 voluntary,

nonbinding norms recommended in the UNGGE 2015 Report, as well as to focus on regional capacity-building in implementing these norms.

(CSA, 2018)

Here the "11 voluntary, non-binding norms" refer to those recommended in the 2015 Report of the *United Nations Group of Governmental Experts on Developments in the Field of Information and Telecommunications in the Context of International Security*.

The 11 UNGGE 2015 norms include norms against knowingly allowing one's territory to be used for internationally wrongful acts using ICTs; against conducting or knowingly supporting ICT activity contrary to international law that damages critical infrastructure; responding to appropriate requests for assistance by another state whose critical infrastructure is subject to malicious ICT acts; taking reasonable steps to ensure the integrity of the supply chain; and responsible reporting of ICT vulnerabilities.

Unfortunately, the UNGGE process was unable to reach consensus in 2017 on how to implement the norms. The process resumes again in 2019, and Singapore has been selected, for the first time, to be a member of the Group.

The UNGGE process is now one of two separate working groups approved by the United Nations General Assembly First Committee for developing rules for states and responsible behaviour in cyberspace; the other is the Open Ended Working Group (OEWG) that was proposed by Russia and which also started in late 2019. The difference is described by Colatin of NATO CCDCOE as:

from one side, some states are advocating for the protection of fundamental freedoms in the use of ICTs and promoting the use of legal instruments in response to cyber threats; on the other side, states are more concerned about their capacity to control ICT infrastructures and regulate activities within their domestic online environment.

(Colatin, 2019)

Singapore is an active participant in both processes, and seeks to promote the rules-based world order in whichever forum it can. At the first substantial meeting of the OEWG in September 2019, Singapore presented its support for the application of international law to cyber operations, and set out the cyber threats which it considers most significant.

The GGE will also hold its first meeting in 2019 and is to submit its final report to the General Assembly in 2021. The group will be comprised of 25 members and its Chair will hold two informal consultations with all UN Member States in between its sessions.

The mandate also includes consultations on the subject to be held with regional organizations, such as the African Union, the European Union, the Organization of American States, the Organization for Security and Cooperation in Europe, and the Regional Forum of the Association of Southeast Asian Nations (also known as the ASEAN Regional Forum or ARF) (UNODA, 2019). The last of these regional consultations (for the ARF) is being hosted by Singapore, most likely during Singapore International Cyber Week 2019.

International governance

Singapore has taken steps towards cooperation with other states on cyber-issues. In the Cybersecurity Strategy, Singapore has committed to strong international collaboration in cybersecurity; active cooperation with the international community, particularly ASEAN, to address transnational cybersecurity and cyber-crime; champion cyber-capacity building initiatives;

and facilitate exchanges on cyber-norms and legislation. This includes setting aside US$7.3 million (S$10 million) over 10 years for the ASEAN Cyber Capacity Programme (ACCP).

Singapore carried these efforts into its chairmanship of ASEAN in 2018, playing a leading role in the region's cybersecurity agenda; investing resources in building operational, policy, and legal capacity in other member states (through a multi-million dollar ASEAN Cyber Capacity Building Program), and building partnerships with the UN and international, multi-stakeholder initiatives like the Global Commission on Stability in Cyberspace. The annual Singapore International Cyber Week has been a useful event in convening important meetings as well as announcing initiatives, such as setting up a Singapore-funded multi-disciplinary physical facility called the ASEAN-Singapore Cybersecurity Centre of Excellence (ASCCE), which will function as a Cyber Think-Tank and Training Centre, a Computer Emergency Response Team (CERT) Centre and a Cyber Range Training Centre.

The ASEAN Member States participate in various activities to build cooperation in cyber issues:

*   The ASEAN Regional Forum (ARF) was established to foster constructive dialogue and consultation on political and security issues of common interest and concern, and to make significant contributions towards confidence building and preventive diplomacy in the Asia-Pacific region.
*   The ASEAN Network Security Action Council (ANSAC) was set up as a multi-stakeholder organization to promote CERT cooperation and sharing of expertise.
*   The ASEAN CERT Incident Drill (ACID) is an annual exercise aimed at strengthening cooperation among CERTs in ASEAN and its Dialogue Partners. The exercise tests the coordination amongst the incident response teams and their incident handling procedures. Singapore has convened ACID since 2006.

Bilateral cooperation

Singapore's concern for international partnership is driven by the recognition that cyber threats do not respect sovereign boundaries, cyber-attackers can come from almost anywhere in the world, attackers can exploit jurisdictional gaps between countries, and cyber-attacks disrupting one country can have serious spill-over effects on others, because of increasing global connectivity in trade, logistics, and financial markets.

Singapore has signed bilateral memoranda of understanding with eight countries to date. The common features of these agreements are mutual assistance and information sharing to "strengthen the cybersecurity landscape of both countries" and "working together to promote voluntary norms of responsible state behaviour to support the security and stability of cyberspace" (Cyber Security Agency, 2016). The agreements as of early 2019 are as follows:

1   **France (May 2015)**: Singapore and France agreed to strengthen national cybersecurity capabilities through more regular bilateral exchanges, sharing of best practices and efforts to develop cyber security expertise.
2   **United Kingdom (July 2015)**: Singapore and the United Kingdom agreed to cooperate in four key areas, including cybersecurity incident response and cybersecurity talent development; and also on joint cyber-research and development collaboration between the UK and Singapore, with funding being doubled over three years, from S$2.5 million to S$5.1 million.

3   **India (November 2015)**: Singapore and India agreed to establish formal cooperation in cybersecurity between the Singapore Computer Emergency Response Team (SingCERT) and the Indian Computer Emergency Response Team (CERT-In). The MOU focused on five key areas of cooperation. They are (i) the establishment of a formal framework for professional dialogue; (ii) CERT-CERT related cooperation for operational readiness and response; (iii) collaboration on cybersecurity technology and research related to smart technologies; (iv) exchange of best practices; and (v) professional exchanges of human resource development.

4   **The Netherlands (July 2016)**: Singapore and The Netherlands committed to regular bilateral exchanges, sharing of cybersecurity best practices and strategies aimed at protecting critical information infrastructures as well as access to training and workshops.

5   **United States (July 2016)**: Singapore and the United States agreed to cooperate through regular CERT-CERT information exchanges and sharing of best practices, coordination in cyber-incident response and sharing of best practices on Critical Information Infrastructure protection, cybersecurity trends and practices. They also committed to conducting joint cybersecurity exercises and collaborate on regional cyber-capacity building and cybersecurity awareness building activities.

6   **Australia (June 2017)**: Singapore and Australia agreed to cooperate in key areas similar to the other MOUs, such as sharing of information and best practices, cybersecurity training, joint cybersecurity exercises with a focus on the protection of Critical Information Infrastructure and a commitment to promote voluntary norms of responsible state behaviour in cyberspace. As a first step, the two countries will organise an ASEAN cyber-risk reduction workshop at the end of 2017.

7   **Germany (July 2017)**: Singapore and Germany agreed to cooperate in regular information exchanges, joint training and research; and sharing of best practices to promote innovation in cybersecurity. Both parties also committed to promote voluntary norms of responsible state behaviour in cyberspace.

8   **Japan (September 2017)**: Singapore and Japan agreed to cooperate in regular policy dialogues information exchanges, collaborations to enhance cybersecurity awareness, joint regional capacity building efforts, and sharing of best practices.

Legislative developments and processes

The key legislation that Singapore has passed so far in respect of cybersecurity are the Computer Misuse Act, the Personal Data Protection Act and the Cybersecurity Act.

Singapore's Computer Misuse and Cybersecurity Act (Chapter 50A of the 2007 Revised Edition) was originally enacted in 1993, pre-dating the Cybersecurity Strategy by decades, and updated most recently in 2017. The Act makes provision for securing computer material against unauthorised access or modification and other related matters, including:

* Section 3 – Unauthorised access to computer material
* Section 4 – Access with intent to commit or facilitate commission of offence
* Section 5 – Unauthorised modification of computer material
* Section 6 – Unauthorised use or interception of computer service
* Section 7 – Unauthorised obstruction of use of computer
* Section 8 – Unauthorised disclosure of access code

- Section 8A – Supplying, personal information obtained in contravention of certain provisions
- Section 8B – Obtaining, items for use in certain offences
- Section 9 – Enhanced punishment for offences involving protected computers

The Singapore Police Force has successfully prosecuted numerous cases under the Computer Misuse Act, putting many credit card skimmers and hackers behind bars.

Personal Data Protection Act

The next Act to be enacted was the Personal Data Protection Act 2012 (PDPA) which came into effect, after a transition period, in 2016. Personal data refers to "data, whether true or not, about an individual who can be identified from that data; or from that data and other information to which the organisation has or is likely to have access" (PDPC, 2019).

The PDPA establishes a data protection law that comprises various rules governing the collection, use, disclosure and care of personal data. It recognises both the rights of individuals to protect their personal data, including rights of access and correction, and the needs of organisations to collect, use or disclose personal data for legitimate and reasonable purposes.

If the Personal Data Protection Commission (PDPC), which is the government agency enforcing the PDPA, finds that an organisation is in breach of any of the data protection provisions in the PDPA, it may direct the organisation to stop collecting, using or disclosing personal data in contravention of the Act; destroy personal data collected in contravention of the Act; provide access to or correct the personal data; and/or pay a financial penalty of an amount not exceeding $1 million.

A 2019 study showed that 26 companies in Singapore were fined a total of S$1.28 million for breaching the PDPA in 2019, a record high since the PDPA came into effect in 2016, with the finance, retail, and non-profit sectors leading the way.

Cybersecurity Act 2018

The most important legislation in implementing the Cybersecurity Strategy is the Cybersecurity Act which was passed in 2018. The Act's four key objectives are to:

1 **Strengthen the protection of Critical Information Infrastructure (CII) against cyber-attacks**. The Act provides a framework for the CSA to designate a computer system as CII and its owners as "CII owners," then and sets out specific obligations on these CII owners to proactively protect the CII from cyber-attacks.

2 **Authorise CSA to prevent and respond to cybersecurity threats and incidents**. The Act empowers the Commissioner of Cybersecurity to investigate cybersecurity threats and incidents, even for computer systems that are not CII, to determine their impact and prevent further harm or cybersecurity incidents from arising. Three levels of severity of cybersecurity threat or incident are provided, with equivalent powers given to respond accordingly.

(Section 2, Personal Data Protection Act 2012)

The second level or "serious" cybersecurity threat or incident is one that (a) creates a risk of significant harm being caused to a critical information infrastructure; (b) creates a risk of disruption to the provision of an essential service; (c) creates a threat to the national security, defence, foreign relations, economy, public health, public safety or public order of Singapore; or (d) is of a severe nature, in terms of the severity of the harm that may be caused to persons in Singapore or the number of computers or value of the information put at risk, whether or not the computers or computer systems put at risk are themselves critical information infrastructure (Section 20, Cybersecurity Act 2018).

In such a scenario, the Commissioner can direct any person to carry out remedial measures, or to cease carrying on such activities, such as (a) the removal of malicious software from the computer; (b) the installation of software updates to address cybersecurity vulnerabilities; (c) temporarily disconnecting infected computers from a computer network until paragraph (a) or (b) is carried out; and (d) the redirection of malicious data traffic towards a designated computer or computer system (Section 20, Cybersecurity Act).

The Commissioner can also require the owner of a computer or computer system to take any action to assist with the investigation, including (i) preserving the state of the computer or computer system by not using it; (ii) monitoring the computer or computer system for a specified period of time; (iii) performing a scan of the computer or computer system to detect cybersecurity vulnerabilities and to assess the manner and extent that the computer or computer system is affected by the cybersecurity incident; and (iv) allowing the incident response officer to connect any equipment to the computer or computer system, or install on the computer or computer system any computer program, as is necessary for the purpose of the investigation.

Other extensive powers include the ability to enter premises if the incident response officer reasonably suspects that there is within the premises a computer or computer system that is or was affected by the cybersecurity incident; to access, inspect, and check the operation of a computer or computer system that the incident response officer has reasonable cause to suspect is or was affected by the cybersecurity incident, or use or cause to be used any such computer or computer system to search any data contained in or available to such computer or computer system; perform a scan of a computer or computer system to detect cybersecurity vulnerabilities in the computer or computer system; take a copy of, or extracts from, any electronic record or computer program contained in a computer that the incident response officer has reasonable cause to suspect is or was affected by the cybersecurity incident; and to take possession of any computer or other equipment (with the consent of the owner) for the purpose of carrying out further examination or analysis.

These extensive powers caused some concern in the private sector during the public consultation. Responding in Parliament, the Minister for Communication and Information that the measures and requirements under the Bill are mainly technical, operational, or procedural in nature and are "non-intrusive with respect to personal privacy," and any information required to deal with threats would also be "primarily technical and not personal."

This limitation would presumably not apply to the most severe "emergency" situation envisaged by Section 23, which would arise if the Minister is satisfied that action is necessary for the purposes of preventing, detecting, or countering any serious and imminent threat to (a) the provision of any essential service; or (b) the national security, defence, foreign relations, economy, public health, public safety or public order of Singapore. In this emergency scenario, the Minister has sweeping powers to authorise or direct any person or organisation to "take such measures or comply with such requirements as may be necessary to prevent, detect or counter any threat to a computer or computer system or any class of computers or computer systems."

1   **Establish a framework for sharing cybersecurity information**. The Act allows for information sharing between government and owners of computer systems to identify vulnerabilities and prevent cyber incidents. The Act also provides a framework for CSA to request information, and for the protection and sharing of such information.
2   **Establish a light-touch licensing framework for cybersecurity service providers**. After a lengthy public consultation, in which the private sector gave extensive feedback, CSA adopted a light-touch approach to license only two types of service providers: penetration testing and managed security operations centre (SOC) monitoring. These two services were prioritised because of their access to sensitive information.

Other Acts

Singapore has defined cybersecurity in its statutes as:

the state in which a computer or computer system is protected from unauthorised access or attack, and because of that state –

(a)   the computer or computer system continues to be available and operational;
(b)   the integrity of the computer or computer system is maintained; and
(c)   the integrity and confidentiality of information stored in, processed by or transmitted through the computer or computer system is maintained.

(Section 2, Cybersecurity Act 2018)

This clearly does not cover the information or content passing through the said computer systems, unlike many other countries in the region which have enacted cybersecurity legislation that also serves to regulate content. In this respect, Singapore's approach to cybersecurity legislation to date is more similar to the nations proposing the UNGGE process for developing international law, than to the nations proposing the OEWG process. This is not to say that Singapore does not have an interest in regulating online falsehoods, hate speech, or other online content which could disrupt its society.

The Sedition Act (Chapter 290, [Revised Edition] 2013) has remained on the books since 1948 and prohibits speech which would (a) bring into hatred or contempt or to excite disaffection against the Government; (b) excite the citizens of Singapore or the residents in Singapore to attempt to procure in Singapore, the alteration, otherwise than by lawful means, of any matter as by law established; (c) to bring into hatred or contempt or to excite disaffection against the administration of justice in Singapore; (d) raise discontent or disaffection amongst the citizens of Singapore or the residents in Singapore; (e) promote feelings of ill-will and hostility between different races or classes of the population of Singapore.

The Protection from Online Falsehoods and Manipulation Act 2019 was passed in early 2019 to

prevent the electronic communication in Singapore of false statements of fact, to suppress support for and counteract the effects of such communication, to safeguard against the use of online accounts for such communication and for information manipulation, to enable measures to be taken to enhance transparency of online political advertisements, and for related matters.

Finally, the Minister for Law and Home Affairs has announced that Singapore will enact a law to counter attempts by foreign elements to influence domestic politics and opinion, as part of the country's sovereign right to protect its national security. This will give the government powers to tackle foreign interference attempts through targeted, surgical interventions, and to investigate and respond quickly to "hostile information campaigns" which can be carried out both offline (in real life) and online (through automated and inauthentic accounts, which Singapore does not believe the social media platforms will do enough to stop unless they are forced to by legislation).

Dimensions of cybercrime and cyber terrorism

CSA's annual "Singapore Cyber Landscape" publications identify cyber threats and trends that Singapore faced in the previous year. The 2018 report noted that the number of common cyber threats detected in Singapore decreased, but that cybercrime continued to rise. Online crime now accounts for almost a fifth of all crime in Singapore (CSA, 2019). Recognizing the transnational nature of the problem, Singapore has been working closely with regional and international partners.

Singapore is ASEAN's Voluntary Lead Shepherd on Cyber-Crime. It leads ASEAN Member States (AMS) in coordinating the regional approach to cyber-crime, and working together on capacity building, training, and the sharing of information.

Singapore hosts the INTERPOL Global Complex for Innovation (IGCI), which is INTERPOL's global hub on cyber-crime, and has led the IGCI Working Group and INTERPOL Operational Expert Group on Cybercrime, working with other INTERPOL member countries to define INTERPOL's cyber-crime programme. This is part of partnership efforts with INTERPOL and other countries in capacity building, and in bringing global experts and thought leaders together to discuss the latest threats, trends, and solutions in the cyber-domain, and share best practices and solutions.

Singapore, INTERPOL, and Japan completed a two-year (2016–2018) ASEAN Cyber Capacity Development Project, which hosted workshops for Decision Makers and Heads of Cybercrime Units of ASEAN Member States, to raise the level of awareness and knowledge in the region.

Other capacity building programmes include the Singapore-United States Third Country Training Programme, and the ASEAN Plus Three Cybercrime Workshop (Plus Three refers to the People's Republic of China, Japan and the Republic of Korea).

During the annual Singapore International Cyber Week conference, Singapore hosts the ASEAN Cybercrime Prosecutors' Roundtable Meeting for cyber-crime prosecutors and law-enforcement experts from across ASEAN, to take stock of the legal capacities of ASEAN, and to raise the overall capabilities in the region.

In 2013, Malaysian police, acting on information provided by their Singapore counterparts, illustrated the close cooperation between states with the arrest of the "Messiah" hacker James Raj Ariokasamy (who had breached numerous high profile Singapore sites) in Kuala Lumpur (Lim, 2019). Subsequently in 2018, Singapore Police Force's Technology Crime Investigation Branch (TCIB), in cooperation with US Law Enforcement officials, arrested a Singaporean computer hacker who had infiltrated the US National Football League's official Twitter account in 2016 (Blake, 2018).

Implications of cybersecurity policies and strategies

Singapore's Cybersecurity Strategy can surely take some credit for the nation's top 10 ranking in last year's Global Cybersecurity Index (GCI), prepared by the United Nation's International Telecommunication Union (ITU) – above countries such as the United States and the United Kingdom (Singapore Business Review, 2019).

However, the nation is not to rest on its laurels, especially when cyber threats still loom large. In 2018, a total of 1.5 million SingHealth patients' non-medical personal data were stolen, as well as 160,000 patients' dispensed medicines records. One of the victims was Prime Minister Lee Hsien Loong, with the attackers "specifically and repeatedly targeting" his personal particulars and information of his outpatient dispensed medicines. CSA confirmed that the attack was a "deliberate, targeted and well-planned cyberattack" and was not the work of casual hackers or criminal gangs, but did not name any nation state suspected of this attack "because of operational security reasons." None of the stolen data has surfaced in the public domain, including that of the prime minister (Kwang, 2018).

Following this incident, the Smart Nation and Digital Government Group (SNDGG) completed its review of cybersecurity policies and will implement additional measures for critical government systems, to strengthen the ability to detect and respond quickly to cybersecurity threats. The Cyber Security Agency of Singapore also instructed the 11 Critical Information Infrastructure (CII) sectors to raise their respective level of network security including (a) removing all connections to unsecured external networks; (b) if there are strong business or operational reasons to keep open connections, these should be mediated through uni-directional gateways (e.g., data diodes) to prevent data leakage; and (c) if two-way communication between the secured network and unsecured external network is required, a secured informational gateway has to be implemented (SNDGG, 2019).

The Government, which is one of the 11 CII sectors, has implemented significant measures in the last three years to comply with these cybersecurity guidelines, such as "Internet Surfing Separation" to remove unnecessary external connections with unsecured networks (SNDGG, 2019).

Suggested reading

Baharudin, H. (2019, October 1). "New Cyber-security Masterplan Launched to Protect Critical Sectors," *The Straits Times*. straitstimes.com/tech/new-cyber-security-masterplan-for-operational-technologies-launched-to-protect-critical-sectors

Henderson, J. (2020, March 10). "The State of Cyber Security in Singapore," *CSO*. www.csoonline.com/article/3531459/the-state-of-cyber-security-in-singapore.html

Majulah Singapura. (2016). "Singapore's Cybersecurity Strategy." www.csa.gov.sg/news/publications/singapore-cybersecurity-strategy/~/media/0ecd8f671af2447890ec046409a62bc7.ashx

Parameswaran, P. (2019, October 4). "What's behind the New US-ASEAN Cyber Dialogue?" *The Diplomat*. https://thediplomat.com/2019/10/whats-behind-the-new-us-asean-cyber-dialogue/

Vu, C. (2016, November). "Cyber Security in Singapore," Policy Report, S. Rajaratnam School of International Studies, Singapore. https://css.ethz.ch/content/dam/ethz/special-interest/gess/cis/center-for-securities-studies/resources/docs/RSIS-Cybersecurity%20in%20Singapore.pdf

References

ASEAN. (2018). "East Asia Summit Leaders Statement on Deepening Cooperation in the Security of Information and Communications Technologies and of the Digital Economy." www.asean2018.sg/Newsroom/Press-Releases/Press-Release-Details/EAS_InformationCommunication

Blake, A. (2018, April 6). "Singapore Sentences Twitter Hacker Over NFL Breach: Report," *The Washington Times*. www.washingtontimes.com/news/2018/apr/6/singapore-sentences-hacker-over-nfl-twitter-breach/

Colatin, S. D. (2019). "A Surprising Turn of Events: UN Creates Two Working Groups on Cyberspace," *CCDCOE*. https://ccdcoe.org/incyder-articles/a-surprising-turn-of-events-un-creates-two-working-groups-on-cyberspace/

CSA. (2016, October 10). "Singapore's Cybersecurity Strategy." www.csa.gov.sg/news/publications/singapore-cybersecurity-strategy

CSA (2018 19 Sep). "ASEAN Member States Agree to Strengthen Cyber Coordination and Capacity-Building Efforts" https://www.csa.gov.sg/news/press-releases/amcc-2018

CSA. (2019, June 18). "Singapore Cyber Landscape 2018." www.csa.gov.sg/news/publications/singapore-cyber-landscape-2018

Ghosh, N. (2019, April 23). "Singapore's Cyber Security Chief Says International Norms, Partnerships Are Key Issues," *The Straits Times*. www.straitstimes.com/singapore/singapores-cyber-security-chief-says-international-norms-partnerships-are-key-issues

Kwang, K. (2018, October 18). "Singapore Health System Hit by 'Most Serious Breach of Personal Data' in Cyberattack; PM Lee's Data Targeted," *Channel New Asia*. www.channelnewsasia.com/news/singapore/singhealth-health-system-hit-serious-cyberattack-pm-lee-target-10548318

Lim, A. (2019, September 26). "Singapore Needs Laws to Tackle Foreign Meddling in Its Affairs: Shanmugam," *The Straits Times*. www.straitstimes.com/singapore/spore-needs-laws-to-tackle-foreign-meddling-in-its-affairs-shanmugam

Singapore Business Review. (2019). "Singapore Ranks 10th in Global Cybersecurity: Study." sbr.com.sg/information-technology/news/singapore-ranks-10th-in-global-cybersecurity-study

Smart Nation and Digital Government Office (SNDGG). (2018, August 3). "The Government Is Lifting the Pause on New ICT Systems Which It Announced on 20 July, following the Attacks on SingHealth's System." www.smartnation.sg/whats-new/press-releases/the-government-is-lifting-the-pause-on-new-ict-systems-which-it-announced-on-20-july–following-the-attacks-on-singhealths-system

UNODA. (2019). "Informal Intersessional Consultative Meeting of the OEWG with Industry, Non-Governmental Organizations and Academia (2-4 December 2019)." www.un.org/disarmament/oewg-informal-multi-stakeholder-meeting-2-4-december-2019/

PART III

The Middle East

33

BETWEEN MULTI-STAKEHOLDERISM AND CYBER SOVEREIGNTY

Understanding Turkey's cybersecurity strategy

Tuba Eldem

Introduction

The mysterious explosions at the Baku-Tbilisi-Ceyhan oil pipeline attack near the eastern Turkish city of Erzincan in August 2008 may be considered as a "cyber wake-up call for Turkey" (Kasapoğlu, 2015: 13–14). The fire caused by an explosion without triggering any sensors or alarms happened on August 5, 2008 two days before the conflict between Russia and Georgia began over the South Ossetia region. Although it was ruled at the time to be an accident resulting from a mechanical failure, the subsequent investigations linked it to a cyber attack, which according to some sources "rewrites the history of cyber war" (Robertson & Riley, 2014).

Turkey has experienced several other cyber attacks over the last decade; some were openly disclosed as such, and others swept under the rug due to either poor post-attack investigation or governmental choices (Basaran, 2017). One of the openly disclosed attacks occurred between December 14 and 21, 2015, when Turkish internet servers suffered one of the most intense cyber attacks ever seen in the country. Massive distributed denial of service (DDoS) attacks claimed by the hacker group "Anonymous" took nearly 400,000 websites with the extension ".tr," including almost all of the websites of public institutions, offline. Another attack in April 2016 resulted in the leaking of nearly fifty million Turkish citizens' personal data.

Indeed, Turkey has been one of the top ten countries experiencing cyber attacks in the last few years. It is in fifth place among nations experiencing botnets, malicious software and exploit kits attacks (Fortinet, 2017), and DDoS attacks (Akamai, 2016). In terms of targeted malware detections, Turkey received 77 per cent of all incidents occurring in Europe in 2016 (Fireye, 2017: 7) and ranks among the top three countries preceded by China and Taiwan in 2017 (Comparitech, 2018). Turkey is also ranked as the most affected country in Europe for online banking system attacks and the eighth in the world (Trendmicro, 2016).

How Turkey responds to such threats constitutes the central theme in this chapter. Despite its prominence in global discourse, Turkish cybersecurity policy has been somewhat neglected in the academic literature. This chapter addresses this gap, discussing Turkey's national cybersecurity strategy, setting out the main institutions and stakeholders and describing pertinent legislation. The chapter considers Turkey's cooperation with international organizations and understanding of the norm of national sovereignty. The main argument of the chapter is that while Turkey generally conforms to the emerging cybersecurity norms in the Euro-Atlantic alliance around the protection of critical infrastructures, cybercrime, cyberwarfare, and ICT security, it converges towards the Sino-Russian model when it comes to information controls in national cyberspace.

National cybersecurity strategy

Turkey took its first step related to cybersecurity at the executive level in October 2012 with the Council of Ministers' Decision (2012) on the "Execution, Management and Coordination of National Cyber Security Activities," which authorized the Ministry of Transport and Infrastructure (MTI)[1] to prepare policies, strategies, and action plans on ensuring cybersecurity at the national level. The cabinet decision established the National Cyber Security Board (NSCB) "to determine the precautions to be taken for cyber-security, to approve – and to ensure implementation and coordination of – the plans, schedules, reports, procedures, principles and standards that have been prepared." The following year, the MTI released the country's first National Cyber Security Strategy (NCSS) and 2013–2014 Action Plan. The action plan aimed to create the national cybersecurity infrastructure that will protect information systems of critical infrastructures and of public organizations and agencies, and that minimize the effects of cybersecurity incidents (MTI, 2013: 10). In order to create such a cybersecurity infrastructure, the action plan listed seven action items and 29 sub-action items scheduled to take place in 2013–2014. From MTI (2013), they included:

1 Carrying out legislative activities such as updating the current laws in the area of cyber security, defining the duties, powers, and responsibilities of the public organizations and agencies, and adopting regulatory measures to remove the existing problems in the management of cybersecurity (23–24).
2 Procuring reliable and high-tech recording mechanisms to strengthen evidence-based judicial processes (25).
3 Creating the national cyber incidents response organization (26–27).
4 Strengthening the national cyber security infrastructure through carrying various activities such as information security management programs in critical infrastructures and in public sectors, determining the critical infrastructures that could be the direct target of cyber threats, providing trainings in public organizations and agencies, organizing cyber security exercises, determining the secure communication rules for the public sector, and establishing a cyber threat detention center (28–37).
5 Carrying our human resources education and awareness-raising activities on cyber security such as educating academics, promoting cyber security curricula in universities, creating scholarship programs, implementing cyber security expertise programs for university students, and promoting cyber security trainings across primary, secondary, high school, and non-formal education platforms (38–42).
6 Developing national technologies in cyber security through stimulating R&D activities, establishing R&D laboratories, and promoting the development of national products (43–45).

7   Extending the scope of the national security mechanisms through integrating national cyber security concepts into the national security context, determining the responsibilities of public organizations and ensuring their coordination, determining high priority potential attack scenarios and their effects, and determining priority actions to be used in case of potential cyber security incidents (46).

The MTI released the revised National Cyber Security Strategy and 2016–2019 National Cyber Security Action Plan in March 2016 with a mission to determine, coordinate, and implement efficient and sustainable national cybersecurity policies. Reflecting a continuing commitment to multi-stakeholder*ism*, the revised NCSS was prepared after having a series of assessment meetings with relevant public institutions, critical infrastructure operators, the IT sector, non-governmental organizations, and universities.

The primary aim of the revised NCSS is to integrate cybersecurity into national security strategy and to acquire the administrative and technological competency for maintaining the absolute security of all systems and stakeholders in national cyber space (MTI, 2016: 11). To reach these two objectives, it identifies three strategic sub-targets:

1   Safeguarding the security, confidentiality and privacy of all services, transactions and information/data provided through information technologies as well as systems used for their provision.
2   Determining cybersecurity actions to minimize the effects of cybersecurity incidents, recovering systems quickly, and ensuring higher efficiency in the judicial investigation of cyber-crimes.
3   The national development of critical technologies and products or otherwise, taking measures to ensure that technology and products procured from abroad shall be solely and safely used for ensuring cyber security, confidentiality, and privacy (11–12).

To reach these strategic targets, the action plan identifies five strategic actions to be taken for the 2016–2019 period: Strengthening the cyber defense and protection of critical infrastructures; combating cybercrime; improvement of awareness and human resources; developing a cybersecurity ecosystem; and integration of cybersecurity to the national security policy (20–23).

Overall, Turkish strategy and action papers consider cybersecurity as a matter of national security and economic prosperity and favor a multi-stakeholder governance model to secure cyberspace (MTI, 2013: 15, 2016: 4). The revised NCSS expresses this idea in its vision statement as to create

an eco-system that has international competitive power in the field of cyber security, in which all stakeholders related to cyber security manage risks at cyber space in a competent manner in cooperation with each other in order to benefit from information and communication technologies in the most efficient way for the purpose of contributing to wealth and security of society, as well as national economic growth and efficiency.

(MTI, 2016: 10–11)

The NCSS views state cooperation with the public and private sectors, universities and non-governmental organizations as essential for the governance of cybersecurity. It also underlines "full cooperation with the private sector, including the participation into decision-making mechanisms" as vital for ensuring the security of critical infrastructures. The NSCC identifies energy, water management, electronic communication, transportation, critical public services, and banking and finance as critical infrastructure sectors.

Turkey's understanding of cybersecurity includes five distinct dimensions including "protection of information systems forming cyber space from attacks, assuring confidentiality, integrity and availability of information/data processed in this environment, detection of attacks and cyber security incidents, activation of counter-response mechanisms and recovering systems to conditions prior the cyber security incident" (MTI, 2016: 10). Using a holistic top-down risk management strategy, it identifies the following threats: Denial of service (DoS) attacks and similar targeted attacks on information systems used by public and critical infrastructures, targeted attacks focused on acquiring trade secrets and know-how of institutions and organizations engaging in research, development, and production; hacktivism for political propaganda purposes; the DoS and similar attacks on e-commerce companies, e-mail and social media service providers; and bulk mail, malware, and similar attacks directed against the citizens (17–18).

Turkey's strategy paper, however, fails to explain how or why these threats have emerged, why they are growing so fast, and how such risks can most effectively be minimized. The NSCC also does not offer a specific roadmap as to how to renovate Turkey's outdated operating systems and generally improve poor IT management compared to other European countries, both of which contributes significantly to the prominence of targeted, complex cyber-attacks in Turkey. The International Telecommunications Union (ITU) ranked Turkey 67th among countries worldwide based on 11 different indicators, including fixed telephone line subscriptions, mobile subscriptions, internet bandwidth, internet access, and mobile broadband. Turkey's rather weak ICT infrastructure has become even under more risk due to the malicious software that it hosts more than any other European country (Fireeye, 2017: 7).

Another important omission in Turkish strategy concerns the lack of a sophisticated understanding of the inherently international dimensions of cyberspace security. Although there is acknowledgement in the document that cyberspace is global, there is a lack of depth about the full scope of the issues involved including a role for foreign policy in Turkey's cyber-security strategy. There is also under-appreciation of the extent to which the cyber threats Turkey faces domestically cannot be solved in isolation, or in a traditional statist manner. After all, in addition to infrastructural and technical deficiencies, the geopolitical tensions surrounding Turkey, including ISIS, the civil war in Syria and the ensuing refugee influx, as well as Turkey's contentious relationship with two of its most powerful neighbors, Iran and Russia, increase Turkey's risk of being a target of complex cyber-attacks.

Institutional framework of cybersecurity governance in Turkey

Policymaking, regulation, and operation functions in the area of cybersecurity are also addressed under the basic laws of the telecommunications sector. At the political and strategic level management, the Ministry of Transport and Infrastructure (MTI) is the main institution responsible for policymaking in the areas of information and communication technologies and the national cybersecurity. It is responsible for preparing cybersecurity strategy and actions plans, ensuring the security and privacy of information; safeguarding information and communication technologies infrastructures, systems, and databases; determining critical infrastructures and strengthening these systems against cyber threats and attacks. The MTI is also responsible for promoting the development and production of national cyber-attack intervention tools; planning and coordinating the development and training of specialized personnel for critical institutions and positions; cooperating with other countries and international organizations; and increasing awareness and training about cyber-security. The MTI has been overseeing and conducting cybersecurity activities at the strategic level with the NCSB and at the operational level with the Turkish National CERT directed by the Information and Communication Technologies Authority (Bilgi Teknolojileri ve İletişim Kurumu, BTK).

The NCSB, founded in 2012, is the top governmental organization regarding national cybersecurity governance. It is responsible for developing a national policy to counter the cyber threats and to protect key strategic assets. The NSCB approves the plans, programs, reports, procedures, principles, and standards prepared by governmental bodies, ensures their implementation and coordination, and determines the measures to be taken in relation to national cybersecurity. It also submits proposals for the identification of critical infrastructures and determines the institutions and organizations to be exempted from all or some of the provisions related to cybersecurity. The NSCB is headed by the Minister of Transport and Infrastructure and composed of the undersecretaries of the Ministries of Foreign Affairs, Interior, National Defense, as well as of the Transport and Infrastructure. The undersecretaries of the Public Order and Security, and National Intelligence Organization (MIT) and the heads of Turkish General Staff Communication, Electronic and Information Systems (TGS CES), the Information and Communication Technologies Authority (BTK), the Scientific and Technological Research Council (TÜBİTAK), Financial Crimes Investigation Council, and Telecommunications Communication Presidency (TIB) are also members of the board.

While cybersecurity policymaking is the responsibility of the MTI and the NCSB, the regulatory function is assigned to the Information and Communication Technologies Authority (Bilgi Teknolojileri ve Iletisim Kurumu, BTK), a department under the MTI. The BTK was founded with the Electronic Communication Law No. 5809 adopted on November 10, 2008 replacing the Telecommunications Authority established under Telegram and Telephone Law in January 2000. The BTK has regulatory and supervision duties in the electronic communication sector. It is tasked with authorization, inspection, dispute resolution, protection of consumer rights, regulation of sectoral competition, issuing of technical regulations, and spectrum management and inspection. Since mid-2016, it has also become the main authority for surveillance of communication assuming the responsibilities and duties of the Presidency of Telecommunication and Communication (TİB), which was closed after the failed coup in July 2016, due to suspicions that it was used by – the once an ally now an enemy – Gülenist community led by Preacher Fetullah Gülen as a "headquarters for illegal wiretapping."

At the operational level, the BTK has been overseeing and conducting cybersecurity activities with the Turkish National Computer Emergency Response Center (TR-CERT, Ulusal Siber Olaylara Müdahale Merkezi, USOM). USOM has established under BTK in November 2013 in order to specify threats against national cybersecurity, take measures for reducing or eradicating the impact of cyberattacks, and coordinate cybersecurity activities in public and private sectors. In addition to these tasks, USOM monitors cybersecurity incidents, issues warnings and announcements, and assists the associated organizations to found their own computer emergency response centers (CERTs). USOM is divided into two subgroups including institutional CERTs responsible for the main governmental institutions and sectoral CERTs responsible for private sector providing critical infrastructure services such as transportation, energy, electronic communications, finance, and water management. Institutional CERTs are also responsible for coordinating critical infrastructure operators in both public and private sectors on a sectoral basis when it is needed.

The main national research and development center in the field of cyberspace is the Informatics and Information Security Research Centre (BİLGEM) of the Scientific and Technological Research Council of Turkey (TÜBİTAK). TÜBİTAK had been the main authority for cybersecurity until October 2012 when it transferred this responsibility to the MTI (Cabinet Decision No. 2012/3842). TÜBİTAK BİLGEM was founded in 2010 as an umbrella institution comprising the existing Information Technologies Institute (BTE) and National Research Institute of Electronics and Cryptology (UEKAE). In 2012, three more institutes – the Software Technologies Research Institute (YTE), Cyber Security Institute (SGE), and Advanced Technologies Research Institute (İLTAREN) – were included under the roof of TÜBİTAK BİLGEM (see Figure 33.1). The Center with its five institutes and more than 1600 staff, carries out research and develops products in the fields of information security, communications, information technologies, cybersecurity, software technologies, microelectronics, optoelectronics, and advanced electronics. Since 2007, TÜBİTAK BİLGEM has participated in NATO exercises with its products, coordinated joint CERT exercises among institutional CERTs, held "cyber-security maneuvers" similar to war games carried out by conventional militaries. In 2013, BİLGEM designed and produced Turkey's first Real-Time Operating System. In the forthcoming years, TÜBİTAK BİLGEM aims to

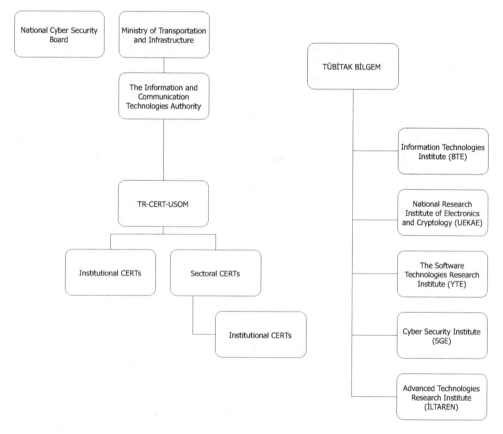

Figure 33.1 The Institutional Actors in Turkey's Cybersecurity Governance
Source: Author's conception.

strengthen Turkey's technological independence in the fields of information security and informatics by more closely collaborating with national industry players.

The role of private cybersecurity organizations

Both the number and capacity of private cybersecurity companies in Turkey have increased rapidly over the last decade. Today, more than 100 companies carry on business in the field of cybersecurity, often as part of a public–private partnership. While initially most were distributors for global companies offering information security counseling and penetration testing, in the last couple of years, they have begun developing products and technologies, cybersecurity solutions and operational services. For example, top national defense industry companies, including Aselsan and Havelsan, provide services to fight cyberattacks on institutions and critical infrastructure. While Aselsan offers national solutions in the areas of cybersecurity, information security and cryptology, Havelsan provides defense services with its three products – watch, barrier, and shield – to various institutions (HDN, 2019). In 2013, BİLGEM signed an R&D agreement with NATO and a Memorandum of Cooperation with HAVELSAN.

Another defense industry company STM founded Turkey's first Cyber Fusion Center in May 2016 to proactively detect cyber threats and take preventive actions to protect critical technology and data asset. The STM also took part in Europe's New Strategic Cyber Security Initiative undertaken by the European Commission and the European Cyber Security Organisation (ECSO), of which Turkey's STM is a founding member. This new Public–Private Partnership Initiative, seeking to improve the cybersecurity industry of Europe through strategic research and innovation, is expected to invest €1.8 billion into information security by 2020. It will set a joint strategy against the cyber-attacks for both public and private sectors and offer hi-tech solutions against any cyber-attack in energy, healthcare, transportation, and finance industries. The Commission will assess the progress and related results under the European Network and Information Security Agency (ENISA).

The Turkish government's efforts to strengthen public–private partnerships in the field of cybersecurity have increased in the last few years. The Presidency of Defense Industries invited the major cybersecurity companies in the private sector in October 2017 to strengthen mutual trust and public–private cooperation opportunities. These meetings commenced in the Turkish Cyber Security Cluster project, which aims to expand the number of cybersecurity companies in Turkey and to encourage national and domestic technologies in the field of cybersecurity. The project brings together public agencies, organizations, and representatives of the private sector and academia.[2]

Legislation

The Turkish Parliament has little direct involvement in cybersecurity policy-making and not enacted a unified law on cybersecurity. There are, however, a range of laws that impact on different dimensions of cybersecurity. The first relevant legislation concerning cybersecurity goes back to the Law No. 3756, which introduced Information Technology (IT) Crimes in Turkish Criminal Code in 1991. The law defined IT crimes as illegally obtaining software and other electronic data from a computer or the use, transmission or copying of such with the aim of harming any party (Article 20). The scope of cybercrime was broadened with the new Turkish Penal Code No. 5237, adopted in September 2004. The following were included: illegal access to a computer network system (Article 243); preventing the functioning of a system and deletion, alteration or corrupting of data (Article 244); misuse of bank or credit cards (Article 245); prohibited devices and programs (Article (245/a); implementation of security measures on legal entities (Article 246); obscenity (child pornography) (Article 226); gambling (Article 228); computer and communications fraud (Article 158/1-f); theft committed by use of data processing systems (Article 142/2.e); and counterfeiting (Article 245/3).

Turkey signed the Council of Europe's Cybercrime Convention in 2010 in Strasbourg. The Convention, adopted in 2001 in Budapest, came into force in 2004 and is the first international treaty on crimes committed via the Internet and other computer networks. It deals particularly with copyright infringements, computer-related fraud, child pornography, and violations of network security. Considering the Budapest Convention as a guideline, Turkey's Ministry of Foreign Affairs has prepared a Draft Law on the Approval of the Convention on Cybercrime in December 2012. The Convention was approved by the Turkish parliament in May 2014 and a working group under the Directorate General of Laws of the Ministry of Justice was accordingly formed to harmonize the domestic legislation with the Convention (Law No. 6533, 2014). In compliance with Article 35 of the Budapest Convention, a 24/7 point of contact based in the National Police Cybercrime Department was established, which is also used for the G8 and INTERPOL networks.

The EU has put considerable effort into strengthening Turkey's capacity against cybercrime through funding capacity-building and twinning projects since 2009. Turkey has also signed the Council of Europe's "Additional Protocol to the Convention on Cybercrime" concerning the criminalization of acts of a racist and xenophobic nature committed through computer systems on April 19, 2016, but ratification is still pending. Specific provisions related to cybercrime were also included in Criminal Procedure Code No. 5271, Law No. 6706 regarding International Legal Cooperation in Criminal Matters and Law No. 5651 on Regulating Broadcasting in the Internet and Fighting Against Crimes Committed through Internet Broadcasting and the Law No. 3713, the Anti-Terror Law.

Turkey adopted its first online content-regulation legislation in May 2007 with an aim to the protect minors and families (Akgul & Kirlidog, 2015). The Law No: 5651 on "Regulation of Publications on the Internet and Suppression of Crimes Committed by means of Such Publications" put forward the criteria for blocking websites and the responsibilities of content providers, hosting companies, mass-use providers, and Internet Service Providers (ISPs). The law set out seven categorical crimes (incitement to suicide, facilitation of the use of narcotics, child pornography, obscenity, prostitution, facilitation of gambling, and slandering of the legacy of Ataturk – the founder of modern Turkey) and authorized the Presidency of Telecommunications and Communication (TIB) to combat with such crimes. As a result, between 2007 and 2009 approximately 3,700 websites were blocked (Akdeniz, 2010: 4). The restrictions on Internet access has accelerated to such an extent that on March 11, 2010, Turkey was added to the list of "countries under surveillance" by Reporters Without Borders. The European Court of Human Rights (2013) has ruled that Turkish Internet law violates freedom of expression guaranteed under the European Convention on Human Rights (Akgul & Kirlidog, 2015). Despite the ECHR ruling, the amendments of the Internet Law in February 2014 (Law No. 6518), September 2014 (Law No. 6518/89), and March 2015 (Law no: 6639/29) broadened the power of the TIB to block content and required ISPs to retain user data and make it available to authorities upon request both without a court order (Akgul & Kirlidog, 2015; Biçakci, Ergun & Çelikpala, 2015; Yesil, Sozeri & Khazraee, 2017).

State capacity for cyber-surveillance has been expanded by the amendments made on Law no: 6532 on State Intelligence Services and MIT in April 2014. The amended law empowered the MIT by allowing the organization to access personal data without a court order and by granting MIT agents immunity from prosecution for violations of law they might commit in the course of their work. Under the amended law, the MIT is authorized to monitor and collect private data on "external intelligence, national defense, terrorism, international crimes, and cybersecurity" passing through telecommunication channels without a court order (HRW, 2014a, 2014b). The amendments also provided for an up to nine years of prison sentence for publishing information leaked from intelligence sources (HRW, 2014a).

The package Law No. 6638 dated March 27, 2015 amending the Law on the Powers and Duties of Police further expanded the state surveillance over cyberspace by extending permissible warrantless wiretapping period for police from 24 hours to 48 hours (Article 5). The coup attempt organized by the Gülenist community on July 15, 2016 prompted a new wave of surveillance and gave additional powers to the police. Under a state of emergency lasting from July 20, 2016 to July 20, 2018, the executive adopted a total of 32 decrees in the force of law, with the declared objective of taking the necessary measures with respect to the attempted coup and the fight against the "Fethullahist Terror Organization/Parallel State Structures" ("FETÖ/PDY"). The Decree-Law no. 670 dated August 17, 2016 allowed for the interception of digital communications of those users who are under a coup-related or FETO-related investigation and the collection of their private data from all public authorities and private companies during the state of emergency period (Article 3).

The Emergency Decree No. 671 authorized the BTK to fulfill the TIB's duties including taking "any necessary measure" to "uphold national security and public order; prevent crime; protect public health and public morals; or protect the rights and freedoms" and inform operators, access providers, data centers, hosting providers, and content providers of the said measure, who then need to enforce government orders within two hours (Article 25). Emergency Decree-Law 680 amended the Law No: 2559 on Police Duties and Responsibilities to grant police the authority to access information on the identity of Internet users and to conduct cyber inquiries for purposes of investigating cybercrimes. Access providers, host providers, and content providers are required to share the requested information to the relevant police unit (Article 27). The authority of the Turkish National Police is expanded to monitor data traffic between the Internet connection addresses and the Internet resources; evaluate signal information; and detect, monitor, and record the data transmitted through cyberspace (Article 28).

In terms of online privacy and data protection, Turkey has adopted the long-awaited Data Protection Law No: 6698 on April 7, 2016 prepared in line with the EU acquis. The issue of data protection was, first, appeared on the national agenda in 2003, when the EU emphasized data protection as a prerequisite for membership. Yet, no step was taken until the Syria refugee crisis. The refugee influx necessitating Turkey's cooperation with EU legal and police institutions EUROJUST and EUROPOL facilitated the adoption of the data protection law (Unver, 2018). Turkey has also ratified the CoE Convention on the Protection of Individuals with regard to Automatic Processing of Personal Data and its additional protocol on May 2, 2016. Data protection legislation was accordingly adopted in March but the legislation is not yet in line with European standards. The data protection legislation contains only general requirements with regard to the security of personal data and there is a long list of exceptions on particular issues for processing personal data by judicial and law enforcement authorities (European Commission, 2016: 83). There are also concerns over the effective independence of the Personal Data Protection Agency. The European Commission (2018: 41) in its progress report requests Turkey "to align [her] legislation on personal data protection with European standards and implement the necessary requirements for the negotiations of an international agreement allowing for the exchange of personal data with Europol."

International law and governance

Turkey conforms with the generally accepted understandings regarding the applicability of international law to cyberspace. The NCSS recognizes the importance of international cooperation and information sharing for achieving and maintaining cyber space security (MTI, 2013: 15–16) and calls for the harmonization of domestic cybersecurity legislation with international agreements and regulations. Turkey participates in several regional and international cooperation initiatives. Turkey joined as sponsoring nation to the NATO Cooperative Cyber Defense Center of Excellence (CCDCOE) in 2015. In line with NATO's understanding, Turkey recognizes cyberspace as a distinct military domain. Turkey regularly participates in international exercises including NATO's Cyber Coalition, Locked Shields, and Crisis Management Exercises. Annual national cyber defense exercises are conducted to assess the capability of the public institutions against cyber threats and to strengthen Turkey's cyber resilience.

In terms of the ICT standards, Turkey also conforms to the emerging global practice. Turkey is a member of the International Telecommunication Union (ITU) – the International Multilateral Partnership Against Cyber Threats (IMPACT) initiative and it has access to relevant cybersecurity services and actively involved in the standardization work on cybersecurity within ITU-T. USOM is also candidate for FIRST and Trusted Introducer Membership. Turkey participated in Applied Learning for Emergency Response Team (ALERT) 2012 held in Bulgaria during the ITU Regional Forum on Cybersecurity for Europe and CIS in 2012. The International Cyber Shield Exercise 2014, which was co-organized with ITU-IMPACT, was held in Istanbul on May 14–15, 2014 with the participation of 17 countries: Albania, Angola, Azerbaijan, Bosnia and Herzegovina, Bulgaria, Georgia, Italy, Jordan, Lithuania, Malaysia, Romania, Sri Lanka, Senegal, Spain, Sudan, Turkey, and Ukraine (ITU, 2014a). The event, linked to the ITU Global Cybersecurity Agenda and Hyderabad Action Plan Program 2, aimed to enhance security and build confidence in the use of ICTs and to share information on the effective handling of incidents by CERTs. Participating national CERTs engaged in a series of real-life cyber threat simulations to assess their incident handling capability. In addition to CERT practitioners, the exercise brought together senior government officials, cybersecurity experts, related industry players, and other stakeholder groups from ICT and security sectors.

Turkey also hosted the G20 Summit in November 15–16, 2015, which released the G20 Leaders' Communiqué on cybersecurity. The Communiqué emphasized the UN Group of Governmental Experts' consensus report on cybersecurity concerning norms, rules or principles of the responsible behavior of states in the cyber-sphere as well as confidence-building measures, international cooperation, and capacity building. It also included provisions relating to ICT-enabled theft of intellectual property, commercial cyber-espionage, privacy, and the application of international law, in particular the UN charter in cyberspace (Para. 26). In addition to holding dialogues and co-operation with international organizations, Turkey also contributes to regional efforts such as the European Cyber

Security Protection Alliance (CYSPA), which was founded in 2015 as an outcome of a European project run by 17 partners and four supporting organizations from 10 countries working in industry and research. The aim of the Alliance is to increase the capacity of industry to protect itself from cyber disruptions by bringing together EU stakeholders working together to articulate, embody and deliver the concrete actions needed to reduce cyber disruption in Europe and beyond.[3]

Since 2004, Turkey has also been a member of the RACVIAC – Centre for Security Cooperation, which is a regional international organization aiming to foster dialogue and cooperation on security matters in Southeastern Europe including cybersecurity. Turkey's MTI and Ministry Foreign Affairs in partnership with RACVIAC organized a Cyber Security Advanced Training Course in Antalya, Turkey in 2017. The aim of the event was to promote and increase cooperation by using dialogue and exchange of information and transfer of knowledge and ideas, as well as to disseminate international standards by bringing together the representatives of the relevant national institutions dealing with cybersecurity issues from the SEE region.

To facilitate sharing of cybersecurity assets across borders or with other nation states, Turkey has also officially recognized partnerships with several countries including Albania, Azerbaijan, Bosnia and Herzegovina, Bulgaria, Kosovo, Kyrgyzstan, Macedonia, Montenegro, Morocco, Niger, Republic of Sudan, Senegal, Serbia, Tunisia, Iran, Thailand, Egypt, and Ukraine (ITU, 2014b: 2).

Sovereignty in cyberspace

Despite the prevalent discourse on multilateralism, Turkey's policy toward Internet freedoms converges towards the Sino-Russian model characterized by increasing efforts to establish its digital sovereignty in its cyberspace. The Turkish strategy and action plan, for instance, defines "the environment that is composed of public information systems and information systems operated/used by natural and public persons" as its *national cyber-space* (MTI, 2016: 8) and considers "cyber security provided at a national scale for any hardware and software systems associated with all services, transactions, information/data provided through the information and communication technologies" as constituting its *national cyber security* (MTI, 2016: 10).

Turkish authorities have, particularly since 2013, extended their power to control the flow of information and regulate speech online. Five political developments have been instrumental in this process: Gezi protests in Summer of 2013, the leakage of wiretapped conversations of government members allegedly involved in corruption in December 2013, the Syrian Civil War and the consequent refugee influx since 2011, successive terrorist attacks in major cities in 2015–16, and the failed coup attempt in July 2016. The total number of blocked websites has accordingly raised from about 40,000 in 2013 to more than 245,000 in 2018 (Akdeniz & Guven, 2019). Popular social media platform, such as YouTube (2008–2010), Twitter (March 21–April 2, 2014), Imgur (since 2015) were blocked. More than 10 VPN services, as well as the circumvention tool Tor have been banned since November 2016. Wikipedia remains inaccessible since May 2017.

In addition to extensive blocking, Turkish authorities are active in requesting removal of content both on international social media platforms, and on popular Turkish websites. Twitter declared on March 26, 2014 that it had started to use its Country Withheld Content tool for the first time in Turkey. Since then, Turkey has been the country with the highest volume of removal requests submitted to Twitter. Turkey requested more than

52 per cent of removal requests worldwide between 2014 and 2017. Bandwidth throttling as well as the Internet kill switch have also been employed (Yesil, Sozeri & Khazraee, 2017). These new tools were employed during major political events such as detention of representatives of Pro-Kurdish party (HDP) in 2016 or during security crises such as military coup attempt in 2016 and terror attacks in Istanbul, Ankara, and Suruc between 2015 and 2016.

Conclusion

Turkey has devoted substantial efforts to develop its cybersecurity infrastructure with a vision to form a cybersecurity eco-system that has international competitive power in the field of cybersecurity. With this aim in mind, it has published strategy and action papers, created several new institutions, and re-tasked existing ones with the mandate oversee cybersecurity. Several important steps have also been taken to combat against cybercrime, to improve R&D, and human resources and to develop a national cybersecurity governance model based on public–private partnership. Turkey has also actively participated in several regional and international cooperation initiatives and complied with the international norms and regulation concerning cybercrime, cyberwarfare, and ICT security. Turkey has also strong diplomatic and security relationships with Western liberal democracies that champion the multi-stakeholder model.

On the other hand, Turkey's increasingly "security-first" outlook in cyberspace, particularly after the failed coup of July 2016, detaches Turkey from Western alliance and brings it closer to the Russia-China Axis, which prioritizes claim "information security" and "digital sovereignty" in cyberspace. The harmonization of Turkey's legislation in accordance with the recommendations of the Council of Europe, the rulings of the ECHR, and the principles of the European Convention on Human Rights to which Turkey is a party of could be instrumental for the construction of a delicate balance between security and human rights. The establishment of independent and effective oversight mechanisms to monitor the surveillance and censorship, notably over implementers such as the BTK, ideally through the equal representation of all political parties in the parliament, and with the ad hoc participation of other stakeholders, including academia, civil society and industry could also help to find a balance between what John Stuart Mill called "liberties and authorities."

Notes

1 The decree in the force law no. 703 dated July 9, 2018, changed the name of the "Ministry of Transport, Maritime Affairs and Communications" to the "Ministry of Transport and Infrastructure."
2 Further information can be accessed at: https://siberkume.org.tr/en/homepage/.
3 For further information please see: https://cordis.europa.eu/project/rcn/106313/factsheet/en.

Suggested reading

Çakır, S. (2017, April 24). "Cyber (In)security in Turkey," *Medium.* https://medium.com/wonk-bridge/cyber-in-security-in-turkey-cb65b74aaba
Şeker, E. & Tolga, İ. B. (2018). "National Cyber Security Organisation: TURKEY." CCDCOE, Tallinn, Estonia. https://ccdcoe.org/uploads/2018/10/CS_organisation_TUR_112018_FINAL.pdf
Şentürk, H., Çil, C. Z., & Sağıroğlu, Ş. (2012). "Cyber Security Analysis of Turkey," *International Journal of Information and Security Science,* 1(4): 112–125.

References

Akamai. (2016). "State of the Internet Security," Report Q4 2016. www.akamai.com/us/en/multimedia/documents/state-of-the-internet/q4-2016-state-of-the-internet-security-report.pdf

Akdeniz, Y. (2010). "Report of the OSCE Representative on Freedom of the Media on Turkey and Internet Censorship," Organization of Security and Cooperation in Europe. www.osce.org/fom/41091?download=trueinternet_censorship.pdf

Akdeniz, Y. and Guven, O. (2019). Engelli Web 2018, Ifade Ozgurlugu Dernegi, Istanbul, https://privacy.cyber-rights.org.tr/wp-content/uploads/2019/06/EngelliWeb_2018.pdf

Akgul, M. & Kirlidog, M. (2015). "Internet Censorship in Turkey," *Internet Policy Review*, *4*(2). http://policyreview.info/articles/analysis/internet-censorship-turkeyu

Basaran, A. (2017). "Turkey Under Cyber Fire," *Turkish Policy Quarterly*, *16*(1): 95–102. http://turkishpolicy.com/files/articlepdf/turkey-under-cyber-fire_en_4590.pdf

Bıçakcı, S., Ergun, F. D., & Çelikpala, M. (n.d.). "The Cyber Security Scene in Turkey," EDAM: The Centre for Economics and Foreign Policy Studies, Istanbul, Turkey. http://edam.org.tr/document/CyberNuclear/edam_cyber_security_ch2.pdf

Comparitech. (2018). "Cybercrime and Cybersecurity Statistics & Trends." www.comparitech.com/vpn/cybersecurity-cyber-crime-statistics-facts-trends/

"Emergency Decree Law No. 670, Official Gazette No: 29804." (2016, August 17). www.resmigazete.gov.tr/eskiler/2016/08/20160817-17.htm

"Emergency Decree No. 671, Official Gazette No: 29804." (2016, August 17). www.resmigazete.gov.tr/eskiler/2016/08/20160817-18.htm

"Emergency Decree No: 680, Official Gazette No:29940." (2017, January 6). www.resmigazete.gov.tr/eskiler/2017/01/20170106M1-2.htm

European Commission. (2016). "Commission Staff Working Document: Turkey 2016 Report, SWD (2016) 153," Strasbourg, France. https://ec.europa.eu/neighbourhood-enlargement/sites/near/files/pdf/key_documents/2016/20161109_report_turkey.pdf

European Commission. (2018). "Commission Staff Working Document: Turkey 2018 Report, SWD (2018) 153," Strasbourg, France. https://ec.europa.eu/neighbourhood-enlargement/sites/near/files/20180417-turkey-report.pdf

European Court of Human Rights (ECHR). (2013). Case of Ahmet Yildirim v. Turkey. Strasbourg, https://hudoc.echr.coe.int/fre#{"itemid":["001-115705"]}

Fireeye. (2017). "Marsh & Mclennan Cyber Risk Report A Perfect Storm about to Hit Europe?" www.fireeye.com/content/dam/fireeye-www/global/en/current-threats/pdfs/rpt-world-eco-forum.pdf

Fortinet. (2017). "Threat Report, FortiGuard Eye of the Storm." www.fortinet.com/content/dam/fortinet/assets/threat-reports/Threat-Report-FortiGuard-Eye-of-Storm.pdf

"G20 Leaders' Communiqué," Antalya Summit 2015, November 15–16. www.mofa.go.jp/files/000111117.pdf

HDN. (2019, March 8). "Turkey Fights Cyber-Crimes with Own Capabilities." www.hurriyetdailynews.com/turkey-fights-cyber-crimes-with-own-capabilities-141742

HRW. (2014a, April 29). "Turkey: Spy Agency Law Opens Door to Abuse." www.hrw.org/news/2014/04/29/turkey-spy-agency-law-opens-door-abuse

HRW. (2014b, September 2). "Turkey: Internet Freedom, Rights in Sharp Decline." http://bit.ly/1r1kJ0F

ITU. (2014a). "Cyberwellness Profile Turkey." www.itu.int/en/ITU-D/Cybersecurity/Documents/Country_Profiles/Turkey.pdf

ITU. (2014b). "International Cyber Shield Exercise 2014, 15–16 May 2014, Istanbul, Turkey." www.itu.int/en/ITU-D/Cybersecurity/Pages/Turkey_cyberdrill_2014.aspx

Kasapoğlu, C. (2015). "Turkey's Future Cyber Defense Landscape," in S. Bicakci, D. Ergun, A. K. Han & M. Celikpala (eds.), *A Primer on Cyber Security in Turkey and the Case of Nuclear Power* (pp. 2–21). EDAM: The Centre for Economics and Foreign Policy Studies, Istanbul, Turkey.

Law No. 6518. (2014, February 6), "Official Gazette No.28918 Dated 19 February 2014." www.mevzuat.gov.tr/MevzuatMetin/1.5.5651.pdf

Law No: 6532. (2014, April 17). "Law Amending the Law on the State Intelligence Services and the National Intelligence Organization, Official Gazette No. 28983 Dated June 26, 2014." www.resmigazete.gov.tr/eskiler/2014/04/20140426-1.htm

Law No. 6533. (2014, May 2). "On the Approval of the Convention on Cybercrime, the Official Gazette No. 28988."

Law No. 6638. (2015, March 27). "Law on Amending the Police Powers and Duties Law, Law on the Gendarmerie's Organization, Duties and Authorities, and Some [Other] Laws." www.tbmm.gov.tr/kanunlar/k6638.html

Law No. 6639. (2015, March 15). www.mevzuat.gov.tr/MevzuatMetin/1.5.5651.pdf

Robertson, J. & Riley, M. (2014, December 10). "Mysterious '08 Turkey Pipeline Blast Opened New Cyberwar," *Bloomberg*. www.bloomberg.com/news/articles/2014-12-10/mysterious-08-turkey-pipe line-blast-opened-new-cyberwar

The Council of Ministers. (2012, October 20). "Decision on the Execution, Management and Coordination of National Cyber Security Activities, the Official Gazette No: 28447."

The Ministry of Transportation, Maritime and Communication. (2013, June 20). "The National Cyber Security Strategy and 2013–2014 Action Plan, the Official Gazette No. 28683." www.udhb.gov.tr/doc/siberg/ActionPlan2013-2014.pdf

The Ministry of Transportation, Maritime and Communication. (2016). "2016-2019 National Cyber Security Strategy." www.udhb.gov.tr/doc/siberg/UlusalSibereng.pdf

Trendmicro. (2016). "TrendLabs 2016 Security Roundup: A Record Year for Enterprise Threats." https://documents.trendmicro.com/assets/rpt/rpt-2016-annual-security-roundup-a-record-year-for-enterprise-threats.pdf

Unver, H. A. (2018). "The Logic of Secrecy: Digital Surveillance in Turkey and Russia," *Turkish Policy Quarterly*, *17*(2): 93–103.

Yesil, B., Sozeri, E. K., & Khazraee, E. (2017). "Turkey's Internet Policy after the Coup Attempt: The Emergence of a Distributed Network of Online Suppression and Surveillance," An Internet Policy Observatory Publication. http://globalnetpolicy.org/wp-content/uploads/2017/02/Turkey1_v6-1.pdf

34

ISRAEL

Cyber defense and security as national trademarks of international legitimacy

Fabio Cristiano

Introduction

In the last two decades, Israel established itself as a leading actor in the global arena of cyber security governance, strategy, and industry. Transferring knowledge from the military to the civilian sphere, the country can today be considered as a normative power for its cyber security policies, research, and innovative market ventures. Thanks to its notorious – yet contentious – operations, the Israel Defense Forces (IDF) are internationally recognized as pioneers in the field of offensive cyber defense. Different elements contribute to Israel's national success in cyber security, and this chapter maps them through a critical perspective on the country's conflation of military strategies with cyber security governance and market initiatives. This problematic merging of different domains in fact creates the conditions for a distinctive – and growlingly exported abroad – profitable approach to the securitization and militarization of cyberspace.

Between defense and security: a governance model-in-the-making

In a cyber context characterized by rapid changes and continuously renewed security needs, Israeli authorities have – through the years – adopted diverse institutional arrangements to govern national cyber security (Tabansky & Ben Israel, 2015; Housen-Couriel, 2017). The governance of national cyber security commonly separates the military domain, and the protection of critical infrastructures, from civilian cyber security and crime. Whereas the governance of cyber defense involves the cooperation between the army and national security agencies, national cyber security traditionally rests in the hands of law enforcement and local system administrators (Galinec et al., 2017; Carr, 2016; Mueller, 2017). This common setup reflects an understanding of cyberspace as a network constituted of nodes that can be governed and protected independently (on this debate, see Broeders & van der Berg, 2020). Different levels of fragmentation in fact attribute calibrated protection and assign the responsibility to respond to each nodal unit, this way oscillating between different degrees of trust and control (van den Berg & Keymolen, 2017). The breakup of national cyber security governance into smaller units tends to be praised for enhancing organizational networking and effectiveness (see Shackelford, 2013 on "polycentric" cyber security governance). Governance fragmentation, however, poses the risk of prioritizing particular cyber security concerns, and areas, over others while delegating national security to private "trustees."

Applying a centralized – but incomplete in its scope – governance approach, the Israeli government initially assigned responsibility for cyber security to the Shabak/Shin Bet (the Israel Internal Security Service), through a specific sub-unit: the National Information Security Authority (NISA). Besides administering national internet infrastructures as an element of information security, one of NISA's tasks included the safeguarding of cyber security for those public organizations that, by their very nature, were considered to be mostly at risk: the Israel Electric Corporation and the national water supplier Mekorot. Similarly, on the trail of a traditional defense-based approach, major national service providers were included in the compass of critical infrastructures to be protected (Tabansky, 2013). At this stage, in 2002, the majority of Israeli networks had to henceforth arrange their cyber security independently, making the entire national network more vulnerable, as the country lacked a central unit of control for cyber security, and part of a unified national strategy (Cohen et al., 2016).

Once authorities recognized the limitations and potential risks connected to such an approach, in 2011 an ad-hoc team of experts was given a prime minister's mandate to assess existing national cyber security shortcomings and to produce relevant recommendations. The so-called "National Cyber Initiative" (NCI) concluded that the country needed a substantial restructuring of its cyber security governance (Adamsky, 2017). Besides insisting on the crucial need of investments to bridge automated activities with manned ones, the team emphasized the necessity to strengthen cyber security for those nodes of the national network that were, at that point, not part of a nationally-integrated system of protection and control. In other words, the NCI argued in line with a national strategy that would regard cyberspace as "one and unified" national milieu, with no substantial distinction between its critical/military infrastructures and civilian nodes. Acting on these suggestions, the Israeli government established the Israeli National Cyber Bureau (NCB) that, reporting directly to the prime minister, produced a new and comprehensive national strategy for cyber security (Benoliel, 2014). In particular, the NCB highlighted the country's need to institute an operational body to oversee, expressly, at affairs related to civilian cyber security (Tabansky & Ben-Israel, 2015).

In 2017, the government aligned to this mission goal by giving the newly founded National Cyber Security Authority (NCSA) the specific mandate of governing security for Israeli civilian cyberspace (NCB, 2017). At the operational level, the NCSA relied on the CERT (Computer Emergency Response Team) that, together with its subordinated units, monitored and protected civilian organizations from minor and major cyberattacks (such as the infamous Wannacry, NotPetya, and more), regardless of their political or criminal nature. For its globally acclaimed expertise and renowned preventive abilities, NCSA also partnered with analogous international units to cooperate on matters related to the prevention of cyber threats.

Later in 2017, the NCSA received the additional task of putting in place cyber security measures to protect the Israel Electric Company and Israel Railway, as well as to develop pedagogical activities to engage the Israeli society at large (such as specific trainings targeting the ultra-orthodox communities).[1] During the same year, the NCSA published the "Cyber Defense Methodology for an Organization," a thorough guide that outlines foundational elements of organizational cyber security as well as practical measures to be taken for securing networks and infrastructures (NCSA, 2017). Introducing local network administrators to practical security solutions, as well as to a broader systemic perspective, the methodology guide aimed at fostering cohesiveness and ownership towards the establishment of a unified national vision for cyber security. At the same time, this methodology extended the military language of 'cyber defense' to national cyber security.

As soon as the mission of the NCSA – i.e., progressing civilian cyber security at the same level of excellence of military cyber defense – appeared to be accomplished, the government decided to merge, in December 2017, both cyber security tracks (military and civilian) into the National Cyber Directorate (NCD). Part of the prime minister's office, the NCD aims at erecting a unified "cyber-shield" to protect the entire national internet network and its ramifications. With the NCD guiding national cyber security as an *unicum*, military and national security personnel ultimately took on a directing role within the directorate, thus supervising both military/public and civilian cyber security.

Encouraging the continuous exchange of military/civilian and public/private know-how, the NCD unceasingly consolidates the Israeli cyber security ecosystem as a focused and unified national enterprise. Going back to its origins – i.e., assigning major responsibilities to a single unit – Israeli authorities organized national cyber security in light of the understanding of cyberspace as an integrated national space. If on one hand this governance model benefits the country by assisting authorities to control network nodes in unison, on the other it raises a set of ethical and political questions regarding the risks associated to the merging of military/public governance and technologies with civilian ones, as well as to the militarization of cyberspace.

The role of the military

Long-since targeted by cyberattacks,[2] the Israeli military developed unique expertise and responsiveness in the context of cyber-defense, at a time when many major global powers had not yet taken significant steps in securing their national networks (Tabansky 2013; Grauman, 2012). IDF's cyber-operations – both defensive and offensive – are in fact internationally recognized for their sophistication and innovativeness (Baram, 2017). On one hand, this level of military expertise can be explained as a natural consequence of the contested political role played by the country, and its defining security concerns and defensive needs. On the other, looking at its development over time, this expertise rather emerges as the result of a long-term governance strategy that, fruitfully combining military and civilian approaches, created strategic advantages for the country in the field of cyber security as a whole.

At the center of a highly cooperative organizational structure, the Computer and IT Directorate – which comprises four subunits – monitors the security of information, networks, and communication within the army. Existing military intelligence capabilities, and infrastructures, also contributed to shape Israel's preparedness once, particularly in the last decade, cyber-warfare emerged as a significant strategic domain. Founded in 1952, four years after the creation of the state of Israel, IDF's Unit 8200 holds major responsibility for gathering signal intelligence and writing code decryption (Cordey, 2019). Upholding a primary role in defining security priorities and strategies, in fact the unit constitutes the largest division within the army. In particular, one of its operational sub-units – the Urim SIGINT Base (unknown to the public until 2010,[3] and located in the Negev desert) – intercepts communication of interest and reports to the main unit, or pertinent agencies, for analysis and investigation.

IDF units also hold major responsibilities for information security, a domain traditionally overseen by other national security agencies. Through predictive policing techniques – such as algorithmic scanning and data analytics – these technologies are used to identify presumed early warnings of violence midst Palestinians' online contents. Primarily targeting social media, these controversial practices have led to the arrest of hundreds of Palestinians, both in Israel and in the West Bank (Cristiano, 2019a; 7amleh, 2019). The army has been criticized for its aggressive methods and for conducting intrusive operations to control and blackmail Palestinians, both in Israel and in the occupied territory (Cristiano, 2019b; Zureik, 2020). While the history of espionage and monitoring of Palestinians dates back, and even precedes, the foundation of the Jewish state (see, Friedman, 2019), digital communications and the internet constitute a new source of private data for the Israeli army and security agenciesIn 2014, forty-three agents of Unit 8200 undisclosed a report describing that private data and communication of Palestinian users are constantly subjected to the Unit's hacking and data manipulation (Derfner, 2014; Levy 2014). These violations of privacy and digital rights intentionally target vulnerable subjects – such as women and homosexuals[4] – forcing them into sharing security-relevant information with Israeli security agencies.

IDF's strategy to foster national cyber-defense also contemplates the recurrence to offensive methods, often justified through logics of prevention, deterrence, and pre-emptive self-defense (Tabansky, 2020; Garwood-Gowers, 2011). In September 2007, the Israeli air forces conducted a nighttime strike on Deir-al-Zor (also referred to as Al Kibar) in Syria on a nuclear facility under construction. Prior to the airstrike, an Israeli cyberattack decisively compromised the Syrian government's monitoring systems, to the point they altogether failed to detect Israeli airplanes. Thank to this expedient, the airstrike efficaciously destroyed the facility, killing seven North Korean technicians who were working on its development (IAEA, 2008). Exemplifying a perfect mixture of cyber-espionage techniques with conventional cyber-attacks, the so-called "Operation Orchard" succeeded thanks to the cooperation between the IDF and the Mossad (see Harel & Benn, 2018).

Moreover, the operational mechanics suggest two relevant considerations. First, its backstory would strikingly point at the importance of imagining, and protecting, national cyberspace as "one." Installing a trojan malware on a Syrian officer's laptop, during a 2006 short visit to London for a conference, Mossad agents accessed confidential data and kept track of the Syrian officer's communication. At a first glance, none of the intercepted information appeared to be of security relevance. However, once they came across the picture of an Eastern Asian-looking man posing in the desert with a local, they commenced an investigation on the issue. Additional evidence ultimately pointed at a Syrian-North Korean partnership for the construction of a nuclear facility in Eastern Syria.[5] As a result, an individual's negligence – in securing a single computer – lead to the disclosure of a secret nuclear plan, and eventually to the bombardment of its facilities.

The Unit 8200 also holds allegedly responsibility for developing and deploying the multi-model computer worm Stuxnet through a partnership with the United States (Zetter, 2014; Langer, 2013). In 2010, this worm seriously compromised the programmable logic controllers of vital Iranian nuclear machines. As these are responsible for the automatic activation and control of mechanic operations as well as crucial industrial processes, for the first time, cyber-attacks appeared to raise to the level of cyberwar. A typical distinctive trait of these circumstances, neither country claimed responsibility for the attack, but strong evidence points at an Israeli-American partnership in designing and launching the offensive, with analysts attributing Stuxnet to Israeli Unit 8200 (Sanger, 2012; Cordey, 2019).

Whereas Stuxnet appeared as an unprecedented – and still today unmatched – moment of cyber-warfare for its destructive outcome, Israeli cyberattacks have also manifested in more hybrid forms, in fact uniquely questioning the distinction between information and cyber warfare. Defined by Symantec (2011) to be "nearly identical to Stuxnet," 2011's malware Duqu is also believed to be a Unit 8200's creation. Gathering information, rather than compromising mechanic operations, its activities consisted in data theft and espionage. With an identical genesis and goal, 2014's Duqu 2.0 damaged Kaspersky Lab's systems, and was detected on the computers of the hotel hosting the negotiations for the Iranian Nuclear Deal (Bencsáth, Pék, Buttyán & Félegyházi, 2012; Kaspersky Lab, 2015).

Beside enforcing defensive and offensive cyber-strategies, the Unit 8200 also contributes to the mainstreaming of cyber security in Israeli society at large, establishing this field as a recognizable national trait, which unfolds through the conflation of military and civilian activities. Most of Unit 8200's officers are teenage-conscripted soldiers, who are selected for their tech abilities and innovative thinking. In line with the substantial efforts made by the national education system to include cyber security as an independent topic of school programs,[6] the military functions as the primary *locus* where cyber security thinking and entrepreneurial spirit are matched and activated.

Conclusion: from the cyber-battlefield to the market, and back

Benefiting from a highly interconnected military-industrial complex, Israel has been often considered an exception when analyzing the negative impact that military expenditures can have on national economic growth (see Swed & Butler, 2013). The overall consensus in macroeconomic studies asserts, in fact, that high military spending has a negative impact on a country's aggregated economic performance (Lifshitz, 2003). Disproving this assumption, Israel successfully combines growing investments for the military with national economic growth (Broude, Deger & Sen, 2013). The cross-fertilization of military expertise with a favorable environment for hi-tech entrepreneurship constitutes one of the driving forces behind this positive, yet exceptional, correlation. Acquiring know-how and extensive training in various IDF units, veterans often develop their hi-tech careers outside the military (Senor & Singer, 2009) – with cyber security becoming a privileged market sector.

Assisting these entrepreneurial ventures to disclose their full potential – i.e., creating innovative cyber security solutions and marketable products – the Israeli government also directs extensive financial support[7] to dozens of promising enterprises. To guide the transition from the army to the market, the Israel Innovation authority (IIA) – previously known as the Office of the Chief Scientist – manages public and private financial support, thus arising as an additional piece of the complex governance puzzle that governs Israeli cyber security. Established in 1974 to support innovative economic initiatives, the IIA functions today as an important node of a network connecting military, businesses, investors, governmental units, research institutes, and the global market. Besides encouraging large and comprehensive partnerships with other countries, the IIA targets international investors in order to boost cooperation across the international public/private divide. The authority also supports R&D activities and – thank to its renowned incubators[8] – provides crucial support for newly formed cyber security startups. Moreover, the IIA regularly produces research reports focusing on market trends, intelligence analysis, and commercial opportunities. These reports are meant to advise governmental and security entities, thus making the multi-stakeholder Israeli governance model of cyber security to come full circle.

Fabio Cristiano

Operationalizing considerable public/private financial investments, Israeli integrated governance model has escorted Israeli companies to the acquisition of a stable leadership in the global market of cyber security products. With extensive resources available for R&D, Israeli companies are encouraged to envision future security scenarios and to produce timely solutions. Besides a consolidated dominant position in the market of traditional cyber security products – such as email security, firewalls, antiviruses, and more – Israeli companies are placing themselves at the forefront of emerging market areas (such as IoT and cognitive cyber security). Similarly, Israeli enterprises also specialize in developing security solutions for cryptocurrencies, blockchain, SDP technologies, and cloud-native security. In this scenario, a recent INCB's report (2018) estimates that Israeli cyber security exports – presently constituting ten per cent of the entire global market – are expected to rise substantially in the upcoming years.

Israeli headship in the market of cyber security contributes to foster transnational collaborations with international allies and their markets (such as the United States and its market). Profiting on a long-sighted governance strategy, the country has made its cyber security technologies (and knowledge) attractive, and at times indispensable, to other countries. For this reason, a growing number of countries (such as India, Singapore, and Romania) relies on partnerships with the Israeli government, army, and private companies to secure their national networks. Widening the spectrum of military and security related exports, cyber security products bring much more to the country than ever-growing market revenues: other countries' reliance on Israeli tech exports ensures renewed legitimacy and political support for the country.

From this perspective, it can be argued the extensive governmental support for cyber security pays back in multiple ways: economic development, up-to-date knowledges available for national cyber-defense, and strengthening the political/diplomatic role of the country in the international arena. The growing involvement of Israeli prime minister's office[9] in the coordination of multiple actors – such as authorities, military, businesses, and universities/research centers – indicates the strategic relevance that cyber security holds for the country. At the same time, as elucidated by the recent restructuring of cyber security governance through the NCD, integrating military and civilian cyber security appears, once again, to have consigned an important sector of Israeli society to its security and defense elites.

Notes

1 Through the years, religious authorities have attempted to discourage internet diffusion amongst the ultra-orthodox community. Targeting in particular the young generations, these internet-ban campaigns seem to have failed in isolating the community from the online world. In 2016, the Israel Democracy Institute published the "Statistical Report on Ultra-Orthodox Society in Israel" that outlines major social changes occurring within the ultra-orthodox society in Israel. Amongst these, the report indicates a substantial increase in internet use among ultra-orthodox Israelis, from 28 per cent in 2009 to 43 per cent in 2016. In particular, women access the internet more than men – 47 per cent versus 39 per cent. The full report is available at: https://en.idi.org.il/articles/20439

2 Already in 2000, Hizbollah's hackers attacked Israeli government, IDF and major e-commerce websites (Kuntsman & Stein, 2015).

3 In September 2010, for the first time, an article authored by Nicky Hager on *Le Monde Diplomatique* provided detailed evidence regarding the existence of Urim SIGINT Base and its location. The article can be accessed here: https://mondediplo.com/2010/09/04israelbase

4 With homophobia increasing in Palestinian society (Whitaker, 2006), Israeli security agencies have recurred to the blackmailing of Palestinian homosexuals into sharing information of interest in exchange for secrecy regarding their sexual orientation.

414

5 Israeli authorities officially admitted responsibility about the attack only in March 2018. The IDF also undisclosed classified footage, photographs, and intelligence documents about the airstrike.
6 In Israel, cyber security is part of school programs already in middle school. Through high school, the topic can be chosen as an undergraduate specialization. As the country was the first to host a specific PhD program in Cybersecurity, there are today six different university research centers dedicated to the topic.
7 In 2018, the IIA, the Ministry of Economy and Industry, and the NCD announced a three-year plan to further boost the cyber security industry. The plan, particularly encouraging Israeli ventures abroad, included a public investment of ca USD$24 million.
8 Offering long-term technological, business, and administrative supports, IIA's incubators program supports Israeli startups in turning innovative ideas into commercial ventures through generous funding for R&D. A 2018 report published by data firm CB Insights indicates that Israel accounted for the second-highest number of global deals in cyber security – with the country's share of 7 per cent only surpassed by the United States' share of 69 per cent.
9 A recently proposed bill, advanced by the prime minister to the Knesset, aims at expanding NCD powers in such a way that would further make its decisional process independent from the Parliament. As the NCD falls under prime minister's supervision, critics have argued this might lead to an imbalance amongst institutional and decisional powers.

Suggested Reading

Baram, G. (2017). "Israeli Defense in the Age of Cyber War." *Middle East Quarterly*, *24*(1):1–10. Available at: www.meforum.org/middle-east-quarterly/pdfs/6399.pdf
Council on Foreign Relations. (2018, July 2). "A Look at Israel's New Draft Cybersecurity Law." cfr. org/blog/look-israels-new-draft-cybersecurity-law
Housen-Couriel, D. (2017). *National Cyber Security Organisation: ISRAEL.* NATO CCDCOE. Tallinn, Estonia: NATO CCDCOE. Available at: https://ccdcoe.org/uploads/2018/10/IL_NCSO_final.pdf
Press, G. (2017, July 18). "6 Reasons Israel Became A Cybersecurity Powerhouse Leading The $82 Billion Industry." *Forbes*. Available at: forbes.com/sites/gilpress/2017/07/18/6-reasons-israel-became-a-cybersecurity-powerhouse-leading-the-82-billion-industry/#2d2c4ee6420a

References

Adamsky, D. (2017). "The Israeli Odyssey Toward Its National Cyber Security Strategy." *The Washington Quarterly*, *40*(2): 113–127.
Argaman, S., & Siboni, G. (2014). "Commercial and industrial cyber espionage in Israel." *Military and Strategic Affairs*, *6*(1).
Benoliel, D. (2014). "Towards a Cybersecurity Policy Model: Israel National Cyber Bureau Case Study." *The North Carolina Journal of Law and Technology*, *16*: 435.
Bencsáth, B., Pék, G., Buttyán, L. & Félegyházi, M. (2012). "The Cousins of Stuxnet: Duqu, Flame, and Gauss." *Future Internet*, *4*(1): 971–1003.
Broeders, D., & van den Berg, B. (2020). Governing Cyberspace. *Governing Cyberspace: Behavior, Power and Diplomacy*, Lanham: Rowman & Littlefield.
Broude, M., Deger, S. & Sen, S. (2013). "Defence, Innovation and Development: The Case of Israel". *Journal of Innovation Economics & Management*, *12*(2): 37–57. doi:10.3917/jie.012.0037.
Carr, M. (2016). "Public–private partnerships in national cyber-security strategies." *International Affairs*, *92*(1): 43–62.
Cohen, M. S., Freilich, C. D., & Siboni, G. (2016). "Israel and cyberspace: Unique threat and response." *International Studies Perspectives*, *17*(3): 307–321.
Cordey, S. (2019). *The Israeli Unit 8200–An OSINT-based study: Trend Analysis.* ETH Zurich.
Cristiano, F. (2019a). "Internet Access as Human Right: A Dystopian Critique from the Occupied Palestinian Territory," in G. Blouin-Genest, M. C. Doran & S. Paquerot (eds.), *Human Rights as Battlefields* (pp. 178–201). Basingstoke: Palgrave Macmillan.
Cristiano, F. (2019b). "Deterritorializing cyber security and warfare in Palestine: Hackers, sovereignty, and the National Cyberspace as normative." *CyberOrient*, *13*(1): 28–42.

Derfner, L. (2014, September 16). "Against Spy Revelations, Israel Doth Protest Too Much," *+972mag.* Available at: https://972mag.com/against-spy-revelations-israeldoth-protest-too-much/96781

Friedman, M. (2019). *Spies of No Country.* Chapel Hill: Algonquin Books.

Galinec, D., Možnik, D. & Guberina, B. (2017). "Cybersecurity and Cyber Defence: National Level Strategic Approach." *Automatika, 58*(3): 273–286.

Garwood-Gowers, A. (2011). "Israel's Airstrike on Syria's Al-Kibar Facility: A Test Case for the Doctrine of Pre-emptive Self-Defence?" *Journal of Conflict and Security Law, 16*(2): 263–291.

Grauman, B. (2012). *Cyber-Security: The Vexed Question of Global Rules. An Independent Report on Cyber-Preparedness around the World.* Brussels: Security & Defence Agenda (SDA) and McAfee Inc. (Security & Defence Agenda).

Harel, A. & Benn, A. (2018, March 23). "No Longer a Secret: How Israel Destroyed Syria's Nuclear Reactor." *Haaretz.* Available at: www.haaretz.com/world-news/MAGAZINE-no-longer-a-secret-how-israel-destroyed-syria-s-nuclear-reactor-1.5914407

Housen-Couriel, D. (2017). *National Cyber Security Organisation, Israel.* Washington, DC: NATO Cooperative Cyber Defence Centre of Excellence.

IAEA. (2008). "Implementation of the NPT Safeguards Agreement in the Syrian Arab Republic." Report by the Director General. Available at: https://isis-online.org/uploads/isis-reports/documents/IAEA_Report_Syria_19Nov2008.pdf

Kaspersky Lab. (2015). "The Duqu 2.0: Technical Details." Available at: https://media.kasperskycontenthub.com/wpcontent/uploads/sites/43/2018/03/07205202/The_Mystery_of_Duqu_2_0_a_sophisticated_cyberespionage_actor_returns.pdf

Kuntsman, A., & Stein, R. L. (2015). *Digital militarism: Israel's occupation in the social media age.* Stanford, CT: Stanford University Press.

Langner, R. (2013). *To Kill a Centrifuge: A Technical Analysis of What Stuxnet's Creators Tried to Achieve.* Hamburgh/Munich: The Langner Group.

Levi, E. (2014, December 9). "IDF Intelligence Soldiers Refuse to Serve: We Won't Work against Innocent Palestinians." *Ynet.* Available at:www.ynetnews.com/articles/0,7340,L-4570256,00.html

Lifshitz, Y. (2003). *The Economics of Producing Defense: Illustrated by the Israeli Case.* Amsterdam: Kluwer Academic Publishers.

Lindsay, J. (2012). "Stuxnet and the Limits of Cyber Warfare." *Security Studies, 22*(3): 365–404.

Mueller, M. (2017). "Is cybersecurity eating internet governance? Causes and consequences of alternative framings." Digital Policy, Regulation and Governance.

NCB. (2017). *Israel National Cyber Security Strategy.* Tel Aviv: Israel Prime Minister's Office – National Cyber Bureau.

NCSA. (2017). *Cyber Defense Methodology for Organizations.* Tel Aviv: Israel Prime Minister's Office – National Cyber Security Authority.

Rid, T. & Buchanan, B. (2015). "Attributing Cyber Attacks." *Journal of Strategic Studies, 38*(1): 4–37.

Sanger, D. E. (2012). *Confront and Conceal: Obama's Secret Wars and Surprising Use of American Power.* New York: Crown.

Senor, D. & Singer, S. (2009). *Start-Up Nation: The Story of Israel's Economic Miracle.* New York: Hachette Book Group.

Shackelford, S. J. (2013). "Toward Cyberpeace: Managing Cyberattacks through Polycentric Governance." *American University Law Review, 62*(5): 1273–1364.

Siboni, G. & Assaf, O. (2016). *Guidelines for a National Cyber Strategy.* Tel Aviv: Institute for National Security Studies.

Swed, O. & Butler, J. S. (2013). "Military Capital in the Israeli Hi-tech Industry." *Armed Forces & Society, 41*(1): 123–141.

Symantec. (2011). "W32.Duqu: The Precursor to the Next Stuxnet." Available at: www.symantec.com/connect/w32_duqu_precursor_next_stuxnet.

Tabansky, L. (2013). Cyberdefense Policy of Israel: Evolving Threats and Responses. *Chair de Cyberdefense et Cybersecurite.*

Tabansky, L. & Ben-Israel, I. (2015). *Cyber Security in Israel.* New York: Springer.

Tabansky, L. (2020). "Israel Defense Forces and National Cyber Defense. Connections." *The Quarterly Journal,* 19(1), 45–62.

Tan, T. C. C., Ruighaver, A. B. & Ahmad, A. (2010) "Information Security Governance: When Compliance Becomes More Important than Security," in K. Rannenberg, V. Varadharajan & C. Weber, (eds.), *Security and Privacy – Silver Linings in the Cloud* (pp. 55–67). Berlin: Springer.

van den Berg, B., & Keymolen, E. (2017). "Regulating security on the Internet: control versus trust." *International Review of Law, Computers & Technology*, 31(2), 188–205.

Whitaker, B. (2006). *Unspeakable Love – Gay and Lesbian Life in the Middle East.* Berkeley: University of California Press

Zetter, K. (2014). Countdown to Zero Day: Stuxnet and the launch of the world's first digital weapon. Broadway books.

Zureik, E. (2020). "Settler Colonialism, Neoliberalism and Cyber Surveillance: The Case of Israel." *Middle East Critique*, 1–17.

35

PALESTINE[1]

Whose cyber security without cyber sovereignty?

Fabio Cristiano

Introduction

A number of elements contributes to the absence of a centralized internet governance and coherent strategy for national cyber security across the Palestinian territory. With Israel in full control of network infrastructures, the Palestinian Authority (PA) and the Hamas administration retain limited sovereign functions with regards to cyberspace. Furthermore, the Palestinian governance of cyber security unavoidably echoes those territorial and political fractures that set apart the Palestinian Authority (PA) in the West Bank from Israeli-annexed East Jerusalem as well as from the Hamas administration in Gaza. These divergences are strikingly revealed in their dissimilar ways to engage with Israel: whereas the PA's approach takes the connotations of a cyber security cooperation, Hamas extensively recurs to its cyber-wings to launch attacks aimed at breaking the Israeli cyber-blockade. As a peculiar case of fragmented governance and limited sovereignty, Palestine provides an unique perspective to situate the concept of cyber sovereignty outside its traditional authoritarian narratives and to reveal its emancipatory potential.

Palestinian Authority: the paradox of security without cooperation

National control over the infrastructural elements of cyberspace constitutes the primary condition for a country's ability to exercise its sovereignty online (Wu, 1997; Mueller, 2010; Jensen, 2015; Broeders, 2017). As an element of territorial sovereignty, countries ordinarily include 'their' national cyberspace in the compass of national security. Whereas cyber and digital sovereignty have been primarily engrained in those national narratives envisioning a tight control on cyberspace (Zeng et al., 2017; Budnitsky and Jia, 2018), these concepts assume an emancipatory connotation when applied to the context of Palestine.

In 1995, the Oslo II framework explicitly set forth the Palestinian Authority's (PA) right to nurture an independent ICT sector and autonomous national infrastructures: "the right to build and operate separate and independent communication systems and infrastructures including telecommunication networks, a television network and a radio network." (Annex III – Art. 36). In full violation of the peace agreement, however, Israel has until today precluded the possibility for Palestinians to fulfil their right to infrastructural autonomy (Abduaka, 2016). A 2016 World Bank report indicates that, besides retaining full control on the infrastructure, Israeli authorities regularly block the import of ICT equipment and technologies from abroad as well as their transit across the Palestinian territory (Rossotto, Decoster, Lewin, & Jebari, 2016). This tight control on infrastructural development also affects Palestinian mobile networks, a sector of rising significance for cyber security. With Oslo I (1993) granting Israel jurisdiction over Area C – presently ca. 60 per cent of the West Bank[2] – Palestinian operators require multiple authorizations for importing and installing technologies in the area (AbuShanab, 2018). Indicating security concerns, the Israeli Civil Administration (ICA) regularly turns down Palestinian requests. Since 1967, Israeli authorities implement a building permit regime that hinders Palestinian construction and development in the West Bank and East Jerusalem. From 1993, and the institution of Area C, the bureaucratic procedures for Palestinians became even harder. Figures for 2016 (OCHA) indicate that the ICA rejected ca. 91 per cent of Palestinian building applications in Area C.

At the same time, and contrary to other network-based services – such as water and electricity – the architecture of cyberspace assigns control functions to the different nodes of the network, in a way that detaches sovereignty from infrastructural control (Mueller, 2019). Instead of a central unit governing the entire infrastructure, the national internet backbone comprises a conglomerate of main data routes that, connecting principal computer networks, sustains internet traffic and data mobility (van den Berg & Keymolen, 2017). This suggests that important sovereign functions are exercised through service provision: ISPs hold in fact a critical responsibility in securing the national cyberspace (also because they often own important data routes of the backbone), thus becoming crucial allies for national authorities (Yarden, 2005). In the current situation, however, Palestinian ISPs continue to be dependent to their Israeli homologues to provide internet connectivity across the PA-controlled areas of the West Bank. Part of the PALTEL Group – a public sharing company founded in 1995 – the ISP Hadara controls the Palestinian market in its entirety, also thank to its controlled virtual operators.[3] Furthering the consequences of the Israeli occupation (cfr. UNCTAD, 2018), this *de facto* monopoly forces Palestinians to purchase an obsolete connection services at non-market prices. With these conditions, many prefer to purchase, illegally, internet services from Israeli operators. At the same time, Oslo I (1993) allows Israeli operators to supply internet connections and mobile services to illegal Jewish settlements in Area C. In East Jerusalem, Palestinian residents forcedly rely on Israeli internet service providers: putting "facts on the ground", Israeli annexation also bans Palestinian carriers and ISPs in their designated capital.

Lacking control over the infrastructure, and with very limited powers over service delivery, the PA holds a certain degree of regulatory prerogatives on information security, the primary element of interest for the most prominent narratives on cyber sovereignty (China and Russia). Operating through two focal aspects – content management/censorship and data traffic/access – the 2018 PA's cybercrime law[4] proposes to protect "national unity" and "social harmony" (Article 51) in its national cyberspace. Regarding the first aspect, it urges Palestinian ISPs – and hosting services – to take down those websites, blogs, and online contents that PA and its security agencies consider to be a threat to national security and values (cfr. Abdeen, 2018). With Palestinian contents already subjected to Israeli predictive policing and algorithmic scanning (Cristiano, 2019a), PA's surveillance further restricts freedoms for Palestinians. As second focal point, the PA's legislation regulates access and data traffic for endpoints. Referring to security needs, the PA devoted various norms – as Article 31 – to outlaw connection via alternative routes, such as VPNs and the like (mesh networking, I2P, and more).[5] At the cost of violating liberties for users, banning these methods purports to constrain traffic along the national backbone. In the specific case, as this falls under Israeli control, the PA's ban on alternative connection methods ultimately forces Palestinian traffic on Israeli infrastructural networks. Peculiarly, the PA potentially punishes – with forced labor or jailtime – those users who recur to alternative connection methods to elude Israeli blocks and surveillance.

Concluding, despite its peculiarities, the PA case corroborates the argument of an accurate correspondence between national cyberspace and territorial sovereignty. The Israeli ban for Palestinian ISPs in East Jerusalem in fact extends the city's annexation to cyberspace. In the West Bank, Oslo's governance fragmentation and the Israeli occupation – with their complex regimes of access/mobility and regime of permits – are mirrored in PA's reduced sovereignty on its fragmented cyberspace. At the same time, the Palestinian case also suggests how sovereignty in cyberspace does not manifest solely as a function of infrastructural control, or service provision. Rather, PA's cyber security legislations reveal how implementing restrictive measures with regards to information security does not only violate digital rights, but ultimately gives away sovereignty functions and political authority on the altar of cyber security.

Hamas and the Gaza Strip: breaking the cyber-blockade

Palestinian internal fragmentation – both political and territorial – directly manifests in its divided national cyberspace. Following Hamas' 2006 victory in the Palestinian elections,

Israel has imposed an illegal blockade on the Gaza Strip (Erakat, 2012). Severely limiting the mobility of goods and people, this measure further isolates the area from the rest of the Palestinian territory and results in the Strip's full reliance on Israeli infrastructures for the provision of basic services – such as electricity, water, and sewage treatment (The World Bank, 2018). Likewise, Israeli authorities and operators control Gaza's entire communication system, including wired and wireless internet services. With the extension of the blockade to bandwidth, spectrum, and frequencies allocation, Israeli authorities force the area into a state of technological obsoleteness (Fatafta, 2018).

In the Gaza Strip, internet governance shadows the one in place for the West Bank: relying on Israeli infrastructures, Palestinian ISPs deliver the service across the Hamas-controlled region (Tawil-Souri, 2012). Beyond this face-value equivalence, however, the overall service quality in the Strip endures the consequences of recent years' Israeli raids[6] on ICT infrastructures and of regular electric power cuts (Weinthal & Sowers, 2019). These, together with Israeli restrictions on Palestinian ISPs regarding infrastructural maintenance, often result in the area being disconnected from the internet (see Jalal, 2017).

In absence of regionally controlled infrastructural networks, and with extensive obstacles to regulate service delivery, the Hamas-led government ultimately retains marginal powers with regards to its national cyber security. In 2012, the party introduced a ban on the use of Israeli communication services (Ghraieb, 2012): with unavailable valid alternatives, this ban produced few results in gaining back control on traffic and market shares. Concerning information security, Hamas security agencies – through extensive monitoring – largely rely on policing users' data and contents to motivate arrests of political opponents and dissidents (AbuShanab, 2018). These same techniques are used for policing compliance to Islamic precepts: besides having enforced a ban on immoral websites[7] through ISPs, Hamas security forces regularly raid internet cafes to police users' online navigation. With little or no authority on infrastructures and service delivery, Hamas political strategy unfolds by tightening control on information security.

Besides implementing invasive security measures on its domestic information, Hamas' affiliated[8] cyber-wings routinely recur to disruptive operations to break the cyber blockade by targeting Israeli cyberspace, on both its military and civilian nodes. Hamas' offensive tactics include intrusive operations for gathering intelligence as well as disruptive ones. Whereas these intensify during Israeli raids on the Strip, they constitute an constant feature of regional warfare for the last ten years. Despite vastly asymmetric potentials in offensive and defensive cyber capabilities, these campaigns proved to constitute a great asset for Hamas' political strategy. They commonly rely on somewhat unsophisticated coding but advanced social hacking techniques, crediting their success to highly designed baits. Targeting specifically military and governmental personnel, hackers recur to gaming, dating, and sport apps, or false links to leaked pictures and videos of IDF soldiers, to target users through highly tailored contents (IDF, 2017; ClearSky, 2018). In 2018, for instance, Hamas hackers implanted a spyware into an app mimicking the Red Alert, a service that alerts

Israeli users in the event of imminent rocket attacks from Gaza (ClearSky, 2019; Cristiano 2019b).

On other occasions, Hamas hackers combine complex operations with well-developed social hacking techniques. One of Israel's basic cyber defense provision consists of blocking data coming from the Strip in order to prevent them reaching its network endpoints (AbuShanab, 2019). At these conditions, the success of Hamas' cyberattacks primarily depend on the ability of circumventing the Iron Dome-like barrier that extends the Israeli blockade to cyberspace. In 2015, Hamas hackers launched a massive spear-phishing attack on Israeli cyberspace: bypassing the blockade, the operation compromised and accessed databases belonging to public offices, military departments, private companies, and individual users (TrendMicro, 2015). On one hand, the hackers leveraged these attacks – referred to as Operation Arid Viper – on servers based in Germany: through this expedient, the Israeli cyber-Dome failed to detect them as originating from Gaza and thus approved their passage. On the other, the attack employed diverse bait contents for different targets, in line with social hacking's precept that envisions network vulnerability as the effect of users' behavior rather than of an ineffective strategy of cyber security or defense (Bullée et al., 2018). In 2019, Hamas' offensive cyber warfare also lead to the first example of a real-time physical attack in response to a cyber-attack (cfr. Newman, 2019). With a tweet, the IDF in fact publicly announced that: "We thwarted an attempted Hamas cyber offensive against Israeli targets. Following our successful cyber defensive operation, we targeted a building where the Hamas cyber operatives work. HamasCyberHQ.exe has been removed."

Conclusion

Palestinian cyber security (and the lack thereof) reveals the complex relationship between territorial sovereignty and cyberspace. Limits to Palestinian autonomy in cyberspace do not only depend on lacking control over infrastructures, but also on the ways service delivery and the security of information are (not) governed by the Palestinian Authority in the West Bank and East Jerusalem, and Hamas in the Gaza Strip. In other words, claiming sovereignty over a national cyberspace requires more than controlling principal network routes and the infrastructure. As argued throughout this chapter, the complex territorial realities across the Palestinian territory put into question this equation. That is to say that cyber sovereignty decisively plays out as a function of information security, regardless of national control over the infrastructure.

The imposed restrictions to Palestine by the Israeli occupation appear to indeed create a continuity between national territory and cyberspace. The exceptionality of the Palestinian case, however, illustrates how a country's sovereignty and its security in cyberspace appear to shape not only in terms of infrastructural control, but also as a result of dynamical political deeds. Above all, the PA cooperation on cyber security with Israeli security agencies – with the emblematic outsourcing of its organizational cyber security to the Israeli tech firm Check Point, Ltd. – accentuate the limits to its sovereignty in cyberspace. Pivotal in this cooperation, the 2018 PA cybercrime law hinders digital rights for its citizens while furthering Israeli control on Palestinian cyberspace. Adding on these, Palestinian users are subjected to two complementary regulatory regimes regarding the ways they can access the internet, protect their data, as well as sharing and managing their own contents.

Similarly, Israeli blockade on Gaza also manifests in the imposed siege on the Strip's cyberspace. In lieu of control on infrastructures and service delivery, Hamas authorities enforce their sovereignty and security through restrictive policies of information security. Along the same lines, the Islamic party's cyber-operations – through social hacking and expedients for bypassing territorial blocks – somewhat disown the argument that the national boundaries of cyberspace can be identified through its physical infrastructures or territorial identifiers (e.g., IPs, domain names). In other words, sovereignty is configured as a dynamic and political feature of cyberspace.

In terms of cyber security, accounting for this dynamicity requires envisioning cyberspace as more than a nationally controlled infrastructural system. In this light, the Palestinian case evokes the importance of including service provision and information security into the compass of a long-sighted national strategy.

Notes

1 In accordance with resolutions of various bodies of the United Nations, its General Assembly, and Security Council, this chapter employs the nomenclature "Occupied Palestinian Territory" or "territories" to refer to the Gaza Strip and the West Bank, including East Jerusalem.
2 Estimations regarding the extension of Area C vary. This variation depends on whether percentage includes East Jerusalem, the so-called "no man's land," and the Palestinian share of the Dead Sea. The extension of Area C underwent different changes throughout recent history. During the first phase (1993–1995), Area C constituted a total of 72–74 per cent of the West Bank. In accordance with the Wye River Memorandum, an additional 13 per cent should have been incorporated in Area B through Israeli withdrawal from Area C – thus reducing its area to a total of 61 per cent. In contravention of the memorandum, Israel only withdrew from a total of 2 per cent, which eventually re-occupied in 2012. As a result, as of 2013 the common figure estimates Area C to constitute the 63 per cent of the West Bank.
3 Virtual mobile operators (VMOs) resell internet services without having ownership of the infrastructures. Their activities and degree of independence are contingent on contracts and partnerships they stipulate with ISPs. VMOs commonly develop their own branding, marketing, sales and invoicing systems, as well as customer support.
4 The full English translation of the Presidential Decree No. 16 is available at: https://goo.gl/Dj1t1Q
5 Besides VPNs, other methods exist to re-route one's connection outside main national data routes. Commonly used by large companies and institutions, proxy servers allow to encrypt data through connecting one's device, a single endpoint, with a remote small network (or a single endpoint) that obtains content on device's behalf. Using end-to-end encryption, the invisible internet protocol (I2P) enables anonymous connection through a global network of over 55k volunteer computers. Based on a similar cooperative structure, a particular type of local network topology – referred to as meshnetworking – allocates to each network node the possibility to connect directly and dynamically.
6 Since 2008, Israeli military conducted three major assaults on Gaza that inflicted enormous damages to ICT infrastructures.

7 Part of a broader strategy to forcefully "re-establish morality and protect Gaza's social fabric," in 2008 Hamas had already signed an agreement with PALTEL for applying access filters on websites displaying explicit contents. In 2012, the Islamic group extended this measure to all ten ISPs operating in the Strip.
8 Because of the illicit nature of their activities, unless self-claimed, the relationship between Gaza hacker groups and Hamas remains unclear. The ties between cyber-armies, proxies, hacker groups with states often tend to be ambiguous. Whereas some national armies officially set up cyber-units (as, for instance, in the case of the cyber-wing of the IDF), others do so without officially disclosing the existing connection between the state and the cyber-army. Intuitively, this allows countries to elude state attribution with regards to illegal cyber-operations.

Suggested reading

Al Jazeera. (2018, August 25). "Censored and Surveilled: The Digital Occupation of Palestinians." Available at: www.aljazeera.com/programmes/listeningpost/2018/08/censored-surveilled-digital-occupation-palestinians-180825122608591.html
Belal, M. (2018, September). "Cybercrime as a Matter of the Art in Palestine and Its Effect on Individuals." *International Journal of Wireless and Microwave Technologies*, 5: 19–26.
HRW. (2017, December 20). "Palestine: Reform Restrictive Cybercrime Law." Available at: www.hrw.org/news/2017/12/20/palestine-reform-restrictive-cybercrime-law
Tawil-Souri, H. & Aouragh, M. (2014). "Intifada 3.0? Cyber Colonialism and Palestinian Resistance." *The Arab Studies Journal*, 22(1): 102–133.

References

Abdeen, I. (2018). "Measures Taken by Al-Haq to Counter the Law by Decree on Cybercrimes." *Ramallah: Al-Haq Law for Human Rights*. Available at: www.alhaq.org/publications/Measures_Taken_by_AlHaq_to_Counter_the_Law_by_Decree_on_Cypercrimes.pdf
Abduaka, M. (2016). "The Telecommunication and IT Sector in Palestine." *TWIP*, 223(1): 17–23.
AbuShanab, A. (2018) "Connection Interrupted: Israel's Control of the Palestinian ICT Infrastructure and Its Impact on Digital Rights." *7amleh – The Arab Center for the Advancement of Social Media*. Available at: https://7amleh.org/wp-content/uploads/2019/01/Report_7amleh_English_final.pdf
AbuShanab, A. (2019). "Hashtag Palestine 2018: An Overview of Digital Rights Abuses of Palestinians." *7amleh – The Arab Center for the Advancement of Social Media*. Available at: https://7amleh.org/wp-content/uploads/2019/03/Hashtag_Palestine_English_digital_pages.pdf
Broeders, D. (2017). "Aligning the international protection of 'the public core of the internet' with state sovereignty and national security." *Journal of Cyber Policy*, 2(3): 366–376.
Budnitsky, S., & Jia, L. (2018). "Branding Internet Sovereignty: Digital Media and the Chinese–Russian Cyberalliance." *European Journal of Cultural Studies*, 21(5), 594–613.
Bullée, J., Montoya, L., Pieters, W., Junger, M. & Hartel, P. (2018). "On the Anatomy of Social Engineering attacks: A Literature-based Dissection of Successful Attacks." *Journal of Investigative Psychology and Offender Profiling*, 15(1): 20–45.
ClearSky. (2018, July 3). "Infrastructure and Samples of Hamas' Android Malware Targeting Israeli Soldiers." Available at: www.clearskysec.com/glancelove/
ClearSky. (2019). *Year of the Dragon: 2018 Cyber Events Summary Report*. Cambridge: Clearsky Security, Ltd.

Cristiano, F. (2019a). "Internet Access as Human Right: A Dystopian Critique from the Occupied Palestinian Territory," in G. Blouin-Genest, M.-C. Doran & S. Paquerot (eds.), *Human Rights as Battlefields* (pp. 178–201). Basingstoke: Palgrave Macmillan.

Cristiano, F. (2019b). "Deterritorializing Cyber Security and Warfare in Palestine: Hackers, Sovereignty, and the National Cyberspace as Normative." *CyberOrient* 13(1): 28–42.

Erakat, N. (2012). "It's Not Wrong, It's Illegal: Situating the Gaza Blockade between International Law and the UN Response." *UCLA Journal of Islamic and Near Eastern Law*, 11(37): 40–83.

Fatafta, M. (2018). "Mapping of Digital Rights Violations and Threats". Published by 7amleh – The Arab Centre for Social Media Advancement and The Association for Progressive Communications (APC).

Ghraieb, O. (2012, September 3). "New Internet Censorship Rules Take Effect in Gaza." *The Jerusalem Post*. Available at: www.jpost.com/Middle-East/New-Internet-censorship-rules-take-effect-in-Gaza

IDF. (2019, May 5). "CLEARED FOR RELEASE: We thwarted an attempted Hamas cyber offensive against Israeli targets. Following our successful cyber defensive operation, we targeted a building where the Hamas cyber operatives work. HamasCyberHQ.exe has been removed." Available at: https://twitter.com/IDF/status/1125066395010699264

IDF. (2017, April 5). "Hamas Uses Fake Facebook Profiles to Target Israeli Soldiers." Available at: www.idf.il/en/articles/hamas/hamas-uses-fake-facebook-profiles-to-target-israeli-soldiers/

Jalal, A. (2017, July 9). "How Gazans are Dealing with Internet Crisis," *Al Monitor*. Available at: www.al-monitor.com/pulse/originals/2017/07/gaza-power-cuts-electricity-crisis-internet-israel.html

Jensen, E. T. (2015). "Cyber Sovereignty: The Way Ahead." *Texas International Law Journal*, 50: 275.

Mueller, M. L. (2010). *Networks and States: The Global Ppolitics of Internet Governance*. Cambridge, MA: MIT Press.

Mueller, M. L. (2019). "Against Sovereignty in Cyberspace." *International Studies Review*.

Newman, L. H. (2019). "What Israel's Strike on Hamas Hackers Means for Cyberwar." *Wired*, June 5. Available at: https://www.wired.com/story/israel-hamas-cyberattack-air-strike-cyberwar/

OCHA. (2017). *oPt Fragmented Lives: Humanitarian Overview 2016*. East Jerusalem: United Nations Office for the Coordination of Humanitarian Affairs Occupied Palestinian Territory.

Rossotto, C., Decoster, X. S., Lewin, A. & Jebari, I. (2016). *The Telecommunication Sector in the Palestinian Territories: A Missed Opportunity for Economic Development*. Washington, DC: The World Bank Group.

Tawil-Souri, H. (2012). "Digital Occupation: Gaza's High-Tech Enclosure." *Journal of Palestine Studies*, 41(2): 27–43.

TrendMicro. (2015). "Operation Arid Viper: Bypassing the Iron Dome." TrendMicro Research Team.

United Nations Conference on Trade and Development. (2018). "Report on UNCTAD's Assistance to the Palestinian People: Developments in the Economy of the Occupied Palestinian Territory." Geneva, Switzerland: United Nations.

van den Berg, B. & Keymolen, E. (2017). "Regulating Security on the Internet: Control versus Trust." *International Review of Law, Computers & Technology*, 31(2): 188–205.

Weinthal, E. & Sowers, J. (2019). "Targeting Infrastructure and Livelihoods in the West Bank and Gaza." *International Affairs*, 95(2): 319–340.

The World Bank. (2018). *Economic Monitoring Report to the Ad Hoc Liaison Committee*. Washington, DC: The World Bank Group.

Wu, T. S. (1997). "Cyberspace Sovereignty: The Internet and the International System." *Harvard Journal of Law & Technology*, 10(3): 647–666.

Yarden, J. (2005, December 16). "Should ISPs Be Accountable for Overall Internet Security?" *TechRepublic*. Available at: www.techrepublic.com/article/should-isps-be-accountable-for-overall-internet-security/

Zeng, J., Stevens, T., & Chen, Y. (2017). "China's Solution to Global Cyber Governance: Unpacking the Domestic Discourse of 'Internet Sovereignty'." *Politics & Policy*, 45(3): 432–464.

36

THE "SILICON VALLEY OF THE MIDDLE EAST"

Cybersecurity, Saudi Arabia, and the path to Vision 2030

Anwar Ouassini and Kimeu W. Boynton

Introduction

In 2017, after a series of crippling cyber-attacks, King Salman of Saudi Arabia issued a royal decree to establish the National Cybersecurity Authority (NCA). This institution would serve under the jurisdiction of Crown Prince Muhammed Bin Salman (MBS) to combat the successive cyber-attacks on critical infrastructure, reinforce national security, and pursue the long-touted Vision 2030 to diversify the Saudi economy and establish it as the "Silicon Valley of the Middle East." To address these challenges, the NCA under MBS has restructured existing information and communications technology organizations, integrated legal and Islamic-criminological frameworks on cyber-criminality, secured regional and international partnerships with leading tech firms, and created a burgeoning cybersecurity economic sector. While the Saudis have made tremendous strides, they are still contending with daily cyber-attacks from foreign actors, international criticism and distrust of the regime and its use of this technology in curtailing individual freedoms, and the lack of infrastructure and technological know-how to accomplish its Vision 2030 goals. This chapter explores these issues by examining the history of the Saudi information and communications technology infrastructure through to the development of the National Cybersecurity Authority in 2017. The chapter will then discuss the Saudi cybersecurity paradigm shift by contextualizing it in the political and economic reforms pursued by MBS, the reform of legal and Islamic criminological frameworks, and finally discuss the implications of Saudi cybersecurity policies at home and abroad.

The internet in the Kingdom of Saudi Arabia

The development of the internet began in the academic laboratories of American and European universities in the 1960s and 1970s. At the outset, there was sponsorship and influence from the United States Department of Defense, as its ARPANET system had been in development since 1969 (Salus, 1995). It is not uncommon for academic institutions to assist, host and/or cosponsor governmental and defense-related research projects. The internet, in its contemporary form, was an outgrowth of the ARPANET system and other digital networking systems that allowed the connectivity and internetworking of computers between cities in the early 1990s. The early protocols that governed digital networking systems began to show commercial value and by 1995, the internet as we now know it became a common tool for information retrieval and data sharing (Salus, 1995).

Given the above, it is fitting that the first internet connection in the Kingdom of Saudi Arabia, like many other countries at the time, started at the tertiary academic level. In 1993, King Fahd University of Petroleum and Minerals (KFUPM) in Dharan hosted the first connection through its College of Computer Sciences and Engineering (Al-Tawil, 2001). This early connection was made via satellite link to Bethesda, Maryland. Initially, two domain names were designated to KFUPM: kfupm.edu.sa and kfupm.edu. Due to slow connection speeds and limited bandwidth, internet functionality was limited to email between university faculty and staff. As systems improved, the use of the internet grew to include academic, medical, and governmental institutions in the Kingdom (Hathaway, Spidalieri & Alsowailm, 2017). However, throughout most of the 1990s, access to and use of the internet was not fully available for commercial and/or private use.

Many of the institutions accessing the internet in the 1990s were headquartered in Riyadh. Their connection protocols came under the authority of the King Abdulaziz City for Science and Technology (KACST), then the nation's central hub for administration of the internet and digital connections. In 1994, the domain suffix ".sa" became the Kingdom's official internet domain designation (Hathaway, Spidalieri & Alsowailm, 2017). Incidentally, in 1995, the Kingdom's oil company, Saudi ARAMCO, also acquired internet access for its staff. The following year, a commission that included religious clerics was set up by the government to debate whether access to the internet provides any societal benefits (*maslaha*) for Saudi citizens. Ultimately, in 1997, the Council of Ministers decided to allow public access to the internet, via a proxy server, so that Saudi authorities could ensure that the Kingdom's residents would not be subjected to inappropriate content. KACST's Internet Service Unit began working with the private sector and governmental units to roll out internet service to Saudi citizens in 1997 and by 1999, internet services were available to all Saudi citizens (Hathaway, Spidalieri & Alsowailm, 2017).

As the internet became widely available to Saudi citizens, the ISU and the Saudi Telecommunications Commission (STC) began to draft rules and regulations related to governance and censorship of anti-Islamic, inappropriate, and illegal online materials. They instituted filtering measures that required ISPs to run all their traffic through the main proxy server at ISU. Though ISPs were not given a mandate to block any internet information, they were required to keep monthly logs on user activity. As the commercial potential and appeal of online services grew around the world, it also began to be realized in the Kingdom. Internet usage in the Kingdom grew from 100,000 in 1999 to more than 21 million in 2017. Increasingly, since the early 1990s, the internet has been embraced by governmental and academic institutions and commercial industries (Hathaway, Spidalieri & Alsowailm, 2017).

Cybersecurity in the Kingdom of Saudi Arabia

In order to diversify the economy and mitigate the country's reliance on oil production and refinement revenue, the Kingdom's Vision 2030 sets out a series of ambitious goals for economic growth and expansion. Though not a central or primary goal of Vision 2030, strategies surrounding the development of information technology sectors have been crucial to providing a path for international investment in Kingdom's new ventures (Hathaway,

Spidalieri & Alsowailm, 2017). These strategies have focused primarily on streamlining the roles of governmental bodies by concentrating on project management and process improvement programs. This would, in turn, assist the private sector with new job creation opportunities for Saudi citizens and offer greater services to the public.

In 2007, the Kingdom passed two major laws dealing with cybersecurity. The Electronic Transaction Law and the Anti-Cyber Crime Law (ETL, 2007) were aimed at addressing emerging cybercrime and cybersecurity issues. Specifically, the Electronic Transaction Law sought to bring regulatory legitimacy to electronic transactions in the areas of e-commerce, education, e-government, and e-payment systems. In addition, it sought to protect digital information and records from fraud abuse and theft, while also bringing parity to electronic transactions, as if they were traditional in-person transactions. Lastly, it gave legal validity to electronic signatures. It must also be noted that the Electronic Transaction Law created the Communications and Information Technology Commission (CTIC), chiefly responsible for implementing the regulatory rules under the act and issuing licenses to authentication services providers (Hathaway, Spidalieri & Alsowailm, 2017). Under the regulatory auspices of the newly enacted law, the Minister of Interior and the Ministry of Communication and Information issue policies and develop plans for electronic transactions and signatures. (Hathaway, Spidalieri & Alsowailm, 2017).

The Anti-Cyber Crime Law (ACCL), at its core, sought to protect internet users from cybercrimes, including fraud and theft of assets. However, its main purposes, according to Article two of the law are: 1) Enhancement of information security; 2) Protection of rights pertaining to the legitimate use of computers and information networks; 3) Protection of public Interest, morals, and common values; and 4) Protection of the national economy (ACCL, 2007). The law provides a legal framework for the prosecution of cybercrimes but also criminalizes and creates a set of penalties for those convicted of said crimes. The law authorizes the CITC to provide technical support and assistance to security agencies tasked with investigating cybercrimes. The Kingdom's Bureau of Investigation and Public Prosecution is authorized to carry out investigations and prosecutions under the law. One central criticism of ACCL is that it also criminalizes acts that create threats to public order, religious morals, and public morals. Violations of this part of the law are punishable by up to five years in prison and fines up to five million riyals. As a result, there have been prosecutions, convictions, and prison sentences imposed against Saudi citizens who have used social media networking applications like Twitter and WhatsApp to criticize Saudi officials and their respective policies (Bruton, 2018).

Furthermore, due to the unstable regional-political environment including Islamic extremism, terrorism, the civil war in Syria, the war in Yemen, ongoing violence in Iraq, and the proxy war with Iran have increased the private sector's concerns about investment in the Kingdom's ventures. Threats, like the ones previously mentioned, are not limited to violent physical action. They also took the form of cyber-attacks on vital infrastructure. This is evident in the 2012 cyber-attack on the state-run oil company, Saudi ARAMCO. Malicious malware, Shamoon, infiltrated ARAMCO's IT system and corrupted the company's IT infrastructure. This malware attack created a wave of global concern, as it was a sophisticated attack that potentially could have undermined stability in Saudi Arabia and the global economy. The attack itself was a wakeup call to the Kingdom. They, like other countries at the time, realized that cyber warfare, like its conventional counterpart, could have devastating effects on infrastructure and economic output (Quadri & Khan, 2019).

The Kingdom realized the necessity to bolster information security as a result of the ARAMCO attack. It provided the Ministry of Communications and Information

Technology the incentive to implement the National Information Security Strategy (NISS) that was developed the year prior in 2011. The NISS provided a well-researched framework for the Kingdom to address the areas of risk mitigation, information security, and resilience its abilities to protect information assets and became the basis for future cybersecurity development (Hathaway, Spidalieri & Alsowailm, 2017). In 2017, King Salman organized, via a series of royal decrees, the Kingdom's cybersecurity assets under the National Cybersecurity Authority (NCA) which would be directly controlled by the Presidency of State Security (PSS). This newly formed agency would be responsible for counter-terrorism and intelligence, but it would also encompass many other domestic agencies that had long been a part of the emergency response and security apparatuses of the Kingdom (Taher, 2019). Most importantly, the NCA and the newly established National Cyber Security Center (NCSC) would facilitate government agencies and vital political and economic institutions to cooperate in building the capabilities to strengthen and defend the nation from all cyber-threats (Taher, 2019). This new consolidated group of agencies came under the authority of King Salman and principally, the Crown Prince Mohammad bin Salman.

Cyberattacks in Saudi Arabia

The digital revolution that the Kingdom has undertaken to accomplish the Vision 2030 goals has exposed private and public sector institutions to searing attacks from state and non-state actors. The necessity to engage and create a robust cybersecurity apparatus has emerged as a result of the lessons learned from previous cyber-attacks. The defining attack that reinforced this paradigm shift in Saudi cybersecurity policy was the infamous Shamoon Virus. On August 15, 2012, a virus was dispatched overriding files on nearly 30,000 workstations in the largest state-owned company in Saudi Arabia, ARAMCO and replaced them with an image of a burning US flag. This virus not only corrupts the files that it infects but also destroys the computer hardware that holds them. The impact of this virus on operational and intellectual property was devastating as it caused tremendous disruption to the everyday activities of ARAMCO, even raising the prospect of disrupting oil production (Alelyani & Kumar, 2018; Quadri & Khan, 2019).

This event would have had tremendous regional and international consequences for the global economy if not contained. Ultimately, ARAMCO was able to address the in-house threats and restore network services with the aid of international cybersecurity firms. The Shamoon cyberattack received a lot of press from the US government including former US Secretary of State, Leon Panetta who said, "the scale and speed with which it happened was unprecedented" (Stewart, 2012) and assured that new strategies would be composed to protect Saudi and US companies in the region. While several hacktivist organizations claimed responsibility there was a lot of speculation from the US and Saudi intelligence that this attack was orchestrated by Iranian affiliated actors. Through the convening years, Saudi authorities have made tremendous strides in developing their cybersecurity apparatus but still didn't have the adequate infrastructure or the local know-how to combat the successive threats.

In 2014 and 2015, a Saudi-based hacking outfit called Cyber-Emotion hacked Saudi government websites after warning the authorities that they were vulnerable and unsecure stating the "government websites ignored our warnings about a possible attack, the group announces today that it has targeted poorly-protected government websites" (The New Arab, 2015). The intended goal was to challenge the claims by the government that the cybersecurity infrastructure had adequately responded to the Shamoon attack and that "had it been hacked by enemies, your personal information, emails, and registration data would have been compromised" (The New Arab, 2015). Moreover, they alerted the public on Twitter that it took no more than a couple of riyals to conduct this attack while inferring that the government has claimed to spend millions on cyber-defense (The New Arab, 2015).

Their predictions came to fruition in November 2016 as a second Shamoon attack was employed on Saudi organizations and political institutions. The attack followed the same structure as the first Shamoon attack by posting a photo on infected computers of Alan Kurdi, a Syrian child who made international headlines when he was found drowned on the beach in the Mediterranean. The second Shamoon attack didn't focus on one target as the first Shamoon cyber-attack, but was intentionally transmitted to several organizations to gather information and gain access to critical servers. The attack was immediately headed off and controlled by several agencies (Saudi and foreign) to ensure there was minimal damage to the internet and the communications technology network. The second Shamoon attack compelled the national authorities to increase investments in the Kingdom's cybersecurity apparatus and the national information infrastructure. Especially as Saudi Arabia is increasingly finding itself: 1) In direct conflict with Iran, a cyber-technological powerhouse in the region; 2) Shifting towards a knowledge-based economy that necessitates a highly developed digital infrastructure.

Islamic law and cybersecurity

Another unique development in the institutionalization of cybersecurity structures in Saudi Arabia has been the way the state has integrated Islamic *shariah* law to legitimize the institutions but also develop a succinct Islamic perspective on addressing cybersecurity in the criminological and civil context. The legislation on cybersecurity laws builds on the fundamental Islamic legal principle that individual privacy is a God-given right that should be safeguarded at the personal and institutional level (Maghaireh, 2009). The Saudi Basic Law of Governance which is a constitution of sorts lays out a broad framework of how Islamic law is to be conceptualized and implemented in Saudi Arabia. It states that "property, capital, and labor are basic constituents of the economic and social structure of the kingdom. They are private rights which fulfill a social function in accordance with Islamic *Sharia*" (Basic Law of Governance, 1992). The shift towards the digital economy in Saudi Arabia has simultaneously produced new discussions on the religious necessity (*darura*) to protect individual privacy online and to ensure that the national cybersecurity policies conform to Islamic Shariah Law.

The Kingdom's efforts to construct a cybersecurity agenda reflecting their Islamic tradition allows Saudi interpretations of Shariah Law to play an active role in both criminalizing cybercriminal activities, but also producing a robust cybersecurity strategy. The 2007 Anti-Cyber Crime Law (ACCL) does this by integrating the five foundational categories that Islamic Shariah is intended to protect including the sanctity of human life, intellect, lineage, wealth, and religion (Maghaireh, 2009). The characterization of cybercrime as a violation of these sacred values legitimizes the role of Islamic judges (*Qadis*) in enforcing these laws in Saudi courts.

Islamic criminal law is framed around three legal categories to protect these values including *Hudud* (crime against God; prescribed punishments set in *Shariah*), *Qisas* (crimes against a person; prescribed punishment set in *Shariah*), and *Taazir* (general crimes; no prescribed punishments in *Shariah*) (Algami, 2010). Since *Hudud* and *Qisas* punishments are for criminal acts directly mentioned in the Quran and Hadith they have not been used to address the new subset of questions surrounding cybercrime. Consequently, Islamic scholars have employed the *Taazir* category to construct criminal labels and punishments set out in the ACCL. While the ACCL has codified punishments for violating the cybercriminal laws, Islamic judges have ultimate discretion in the punishment, which is often shaped by the cultural and political context (*urf*) and the perceived benefit to the community (*maslaha*).

The expansive Islamic legal framework allowed Saudi legislators to formulate policies to adapt to the digital shift that occurred post-Shamoon. The government approached the problem of cybercrimes from the perspective of the victims including individuals, property, and the State (Algami, 2010). The process of Islamicizing cybersecurity both in infrastructure and the criminal code promotes acceptance in society while limiting resistance to its introduction in the Kingdom. Moreover, Article two and six of the ACCL are clear that the purpose of the law is the "protection of public Interest, morals, and common values" (ACCL Article 2, 2007) and to prosecute individuals participating in the "production, preparation, transmission, or storage of material impinging on public order, religious values, public morals, and privacy, through the information network or computers" (ACCL Article 6, 2007). This allows for the ACCL to be viewed in line with the Islamic legal and cultural norms but also provides the Saudi judiciary discretion to impose their own religious jurisprudential opinions on cybercriminal cases. The ACCL law and its accompanying punishments are not exhaustive, but they did set the basis for the Saudi state to begin anchoring their cybersecurity strategies for the years to come (ACCL, 2007).

Saudi Arabia, GCC, and social media

The expansion of the Saudi cybersecurity sector is framed in the context of both economic growth (Vision 2030) for the increasingly diversified Saudi economy and to expand its influence in the Arab and Muslim world. This was realized as a result of the post-Arab Spring context and in the aftermath of the Shamoon attack in which the American and Saudi intelligence communities concluded that the Iranian regime was responsible. The Saudi strategic response was focused on using internet technologies to consolidate power and dissent internally while ensuring their regional rivals, Iran does not undermine their interests in the Arab Gulf and the Muslim world. The Kingdom lobbied the United States to not only support the development of its cybersecurity program but also composed a $110 billion deal with the US to modernize its defense sector including it cybersecurity apparatus (Phelps & Stuyk, 2017). The Saudi goal is to implement the National Strategy and create new institutional structures under the control of MBS that would enforce the top-down change throughout Saudi Arabia. This includes digitizing all government services, protecting the Royal Family and its regional allies from cyberattacks and political dissent, enforce the ACCL laws, and advance the capabilities of Saudi intelligence agencies to counter Iranian cyber-attacks and Islamic extremists' organizations in the region (Al Sharif, 2018).

Another component of the cybersecurity strategy that Saudi Arabia has sought to control is the role and power of social media. Especially, as Saudi citizens are one of the biggest consumers of social media platforms in the region. Social media has caused Saudi authorities tremendous problems in the domestic front as thousands of Saudis have been recruited online to terrorist organizations in the region. This has undermined the Kingdom's domestic security, international relations, and global standing. Moreover, the relationship between social media and regional forces has become central to the Saudi state and its cybersecurity agenda as they have learned from the Arab Spring experience that protests and conflicts that originate in the GCC or the broader Arab world can "travel" to the borders of Saudi Arabia and have a devastating impact on domestic stability.

While the cybersecurity apparatuses' control of social media has been crucial in capturing intelligence and building the necessary capacity to curtail potential terrorist attacks in and outside of Saudi Arabia; it has also undermined political dissent locally and globally. In 2019, the Saudi government used Article 6 of the ACCL law which states that "production, preparation, transmission or storage of material impinging on public order, religious values, public morals, and privacy" (ACCL, 2007) to force Netflix to pull one of the episodes on the comedy show, The Patriot Act. The show was critical of the Saudi government's involvement in the murder of journalist Jamal Khashoggi in the Saudi Arabian embassy in Turkey in 2018 (Petkar, 2019).

Conclusion

The growth of the Saudi cybersecurity sector is expected to increase to $5 billion by 2022, establishing Saudi Arabia as a major player in the region in cybersecurity technology and policy (Mehio, 2019). With Vision 2030 in mind, the cybersecurity strategy under the tutelage of the National Cyber Security Authority (NSAC) and MBS has announced the construction of smart cities beginning in 2020, the full implementation of E-Government and E-Commerce services, and national investments in emerging technologies and the defense industries (Khwaja, 2017). The Saudi government and MBS, in particular, view cybersecurity as central to shifting away from their economic reliance on oil, but also as a way to head off cyberattacks and threats that can have devastating consequences on the Kingdom's economy and society. Moreover, the emerging cybersecurity apparatus reflects the all-embracing need by the Saudi government to control cyber technologies to enforce political stability, economic growth, and ultimately gain unprecedented authority in Saudi Arabia, the GCC, and the Arab world.

Suggested reading

Anti-Cyber Crime Law (ACCL). (2007). "Royal Decree No. M/17 8 Rabi' 1 1428/26 March 2007 Kingdom of Saudi Arabia Bureau of Experts at the Council of Ministers Official Translation Department Translation of Saudi Laws." www.citc.gov.sa/en/RulesandSystems/CITCSystem/Docu ments/LA_004_%20E_%20Anti-Cyber%20Crime%20Law.pdf

Hathaway, M. & Spidalieri, F. & Alsowailm. (2017). "*Kingdom of Saudi Arabia Cyber Readiness at a Glance*," Potomac Institute for Policy Studies, Arlington, United States. https://potomacinstitute. org/images/CRI/CRI2_0_SaudiArabiaPofile.pdf

Quadri, A. & Khan, M. (2019). "Cybersecurity Challenges of the Kingdom of Saudi Arabia." www.gfcy ber.org/cybersecurity-challenges-of-the-ksa-past-present-and-future/

References

Alelyani, S. & Kumar, H., (2018). "Overview of Cyberattack on Saudi Organizations," *Journal of Information Security and Cybercrimes Research*, 1(1): 42–50.

Algami, A. F. (2010). "Is a Shari'ah-based Law Compatible with Cybercrime? an Inquiry in the Saudi Regulations on Internet Fraud," *In-Spire Journal of Law, Politics and Societies*, 5(2): 1–17.

Al Sharif, D. T. (2018). "How Saudis are Protected against Cybercrime," *Arab News*. www.arabnews. com/node/1282571

Al-Tawil, K. M. (2001). "The Internet in Saudi Arabia, Telecommunications Policy," *Elsevier*, 25(8–9), 625–632.

Anti-Cyber Crime Law. (2007). Royal Decree No. M/17 8 Rabi' 1 1428/26 March 2007." Kingdom of Saudi Arabia Bureau of Experts at the Council of Ministers Official Translation Department Translation of Saudi Laws. www.citc.gov.sa/en/RulesandSystems/CITCSystem/Documents/ LA_004_%20E_%20Anti-Cyber%20Crime%20Law.pdf

Basic Law of Governance. (1992). "Basic Law of Governance. Royal Order No. (A/91) 27 Sha'ban 1412H/1 March 1992." www.wipo.int/edocs/lexdocs/laws/en/sa/sa016en.pdf

Bruton, F. B. (2018). "Saudi Cleric Salman al-Awda Called for Reform. Now He's in Solitary Confinement," *NBC News*. www.nbcnews.com/news/mideast/saudi-cleric-salman-Al-awda-called-reform-now-he-s-n840916

ETL. (2007) "Electronic Transactions Law Royal Decree No. M/18, 8 Rabi' 1-1428H – 26 March 2007." Kingdom of Saudi Arabia Bureau of Experts at the Council of Ministers Official. Translation Department Translation of Saudi Laws. http://www.iracm.com/wp-content/uploads/2013/01/electronic-transactions-act-2007-1462.pdf

Elnaim, B. M. (2013). "Cyber Crime in Kingdom of Saudi Arabia: The Threat Today and the Expected Future," *Information and Knowledge Management*, 3(12), 14–18.

Hathaway, M. & Spidalieri, F. & Alsowailm. (2017). "*Kingdom of Saudi Arabia Cyber Readiness at a Glance*," Potomac Institute for Policy Studies, Arlington, United States. https://potomacinstitute.org/images/CRI/CRI2_0_SaudiArabiaPofile.pdf

Khwaja, H. (2017). "What Vision 2030 Means for the Information and Communication Technology Sector in Saudi Arabia," *Tamimi*. www.tamimi.com/law-update-articles/what-vision-2030-means-for-the-information-and-communication-technology-sector-in-saudi-arabia/

Maghaireh, A. (2009). "Shariah Law and Cyber-sectarian Conflict: How Can Islamic Criminal Law Respond to Cybercrime?" *International Journal of Cyber Criminology*, 2(2), 337–445.

Mehio, R. (2019). "Fighting Hackers: The Development of Cybersecurity in Saudi Arabia," *Step Feed*. https://stepfeed.com/fighting-hackers-the-development-of-cybersecurity-in-saudi-arabia-8579

Petkar, S. (2019). "What Is Saudi Arabia's Anti-cybercrime Law and Why Was an Episode of Patriot Act Removed by Netflix?" *The Sun*. www.thesun.co.uk/news/8104632/saudi-arabia-cybercrime-law-netflix/

Phelps, J. & Stuyk, R. (2017). "Trump Signs $110 Billion Arms Deal with Saudi Arabia on 'A Tremendous Day,'" *ABC News*. https://abcnews.go.com/Politics/trump-signs-110-billion-arms-deal-saudi-arabia/story?id=47531180

Quadri, A. & Khan, M. (2019). "Cybersecurity Challenges of the Kingdom of Saudi Arabia." www.gfcyber.org/cybersecurity-challenges-of-the-ksa-past-present-and-future/

Salus, P. H. (1995). *Casting the Net: From ARPANET to Internet and beyond* …. Boston, MA: Addison-Wesley Longman.

Stewart, P. (2012). "Shamoon Virus Most Destructive yet for Private Sector, Panetta Says," *Reuters*. www.reuters.com/article/us-usa-cyber-pentagon-shimoon/shamoon-virus-most-destructive-yet-for-private-sector-panetta-says-idUSBRE89B04Y20121012

Taher, A. (2019). "Saudi Arabia's Efforts to Ensure Cyber Security," *Almajalla*. https://eng.majalla.com/node/65466/saudi-arabia%E2%80%99s-efforts-to-ensure-cyber-security%C2%A0

The New Arab. (2015). "Saudi Group Hacks Government Websites 'As a Cyber-security Warning.'" www.alaraby.co.uk/english/news/2015/8/17/saudi-group-hacks-government-websites-as-a-cyber-security-warning

37

THE ISLAMIC REPUBLIC OF IRAN'S CYBER SECURITY STRATEGY

Challenges in an era of cyber uncertainty

Filiz Katman

Introduction

Cyber security is one of the main areas of comprehensive security approaches that attract global attention. In the cyber era, cyber security has been increasingly located on top in national security agendas. Cyber-attacks on critical institutions have been challenging national security; thus, a comprehensive mechanism is required for countering such technology-based threats. The Islamic Republic of Iran, as a key actor in the Middle East with nuclear capacity, is also targeted in cyber-espionage attacks.

In this chapter the cyber wellness profile of the Islamic Republic of Iran will be evaluated in terms of a comprehensive cyber security strategy, responsible agencies, cyber security awareness, and international cooperation. Diverse perspectives will be elaborated with a multidisciplinary approach including both defensive and offensive considerations. It will reveal types of cyber threats, cyber-attacks, cybercrime, cyber warfare, policy mechanisms, regulatory and preparedness schemes, cyber security, and nuclear security relations. Cyber programs, cyber defense, cyber force building, and cyber espionage in Iran will be evaluated. Iran is targeted at not only national level, but also its universities and private industries. Thus, a broad analysis of cyber security in Iran will be discussed in all dimensions.

This study first analyzes the comprehensive cyber security strategy of Iran. In order to frame the strategy the national security strategy, which is based on deterrence (Tabatabai, 2019: 7), will be evaluated. Iran, allegedly dreaming of a reborn Persian Empire (*New York Post*, 2015), has always been one of the most significant actors in the Middle East. In order to achieve such a vision, Iran should tackle contemporary challenges and opportunities. Thus, national security of Iran includes the elements of change and continuity. Cyber security is a vital and significant element of change in the strategy, and it is referred to as a comprehensive cyber security strategy. It is reported that Iran perceives cyber-attacks as a greater threat than actual war and is prepared to defend itself against them (Reuters, 2012).

In order to realize such a comprehensive strategy legal measures, technical measures, organization measures, capacity building, and cooperation will be discussed as main components of the strategy. In terms of legal measures, legislation and regulations will be explained. Then, in terms of technical measures, the content of the Cyber Incident Response Team (CIRT), standards, and certification will be analyzed.

Organizations should also be organized and assigned to certain tasks of cyber security. Considering the characteristics of the state, the Supreme Leader and the Ayatollahs have major control (Rattray, 2018: 7). Organizational structure of cyber security structures will be analyzed within the comprehensive cyber security strategy. In terms of organizational measures policy, roadmaps, responsible agency, and national benchmarking will be analyzed.

In terms of capacity building, standardization development, manpower development, professional certification, and agency certification will be discussed. A vital component of security in general, cooperation will be discussed in intra-state cooperation, intra-agency cooperation, public sector partnership, and international cooperation.

The Islamic Republic of Iran has ambitious goals in the region, allegedly extended to a reborn Persian Empire. In order to achieve such ambitions, national security strategy has a military doctrine in largely defensive and asymmetric terms with a strong military and the capabilities to deter enemies and raise the costs of conflict (Tabatabai, 2019: 7). In this framework, it has elements of continuity and change. Cyber security composes the element of change and cyber threats are referred to as greater threats than actual war. Thus, a comprehensive framework of cyber security strategy is designed in terms of legal, technical and organizational measures, capacity building, and cooperation. Such a comprehensive cyber security strategy mainly aims to deter cyber threats, create awareness, provide preparedness schemes, and connect cyber security with nuclear security.

National security strategy of the Islamic Republic of Iran

In framing and modelling the national security strategy of the Islamic Republic of Iran, a bargaining process based on infighting (division) and consensus building (consensus) is followed in an anarchic structure (Tabatabai, 2019: 3). Bargaining takes place in areas other than redlines drawn by the Supreme Leader. In this process, the Supreme National Security Council (SNSC) facilitates the process through presenting the outcomes of bargaining and highlighting the consensus to the Supreme Leader. National security policy is debated at the SNSC, composed of the representatives of the following state organs: the final arbitration of disputes by the Supreme Leader, the legislation by the Majles, execution held by the President, judiciary, and the Iranian armed forces composed of the conventional military by the Artesh, and Islamic Revolutionary Guard Corps (IRGC) (see Figure 37.1).

Aside from the aforesaid, within the office of the Supreme Leader (*beyt-e rahbari*), various advisory bodies including political, military, intelligence, security, and international affairs oversee internal and external affairs. In terms of division of labor in national security issues, relations with international powers are under the authority of the executive branch while relations with regional powers are dominantly held by the IRGC. Considering their relatively small role in national security, the Artesh and the Majles can be listed but their role is primarily in shaping public opinion and bringing the public opinion to the decision-making and embedding policies into the system through law making.

Within the national security framework of the Islamic Republic of Iran, main factors can be listed such as religion, nationalism, ethnicity, economics, and geopolitics (Byman, Chubin, Ehteshami, & Green, 2001: 1). It is also inseparable from domestic and foreign policies. While it is a mix of Islamic and nationalist objectives and while geopolitics

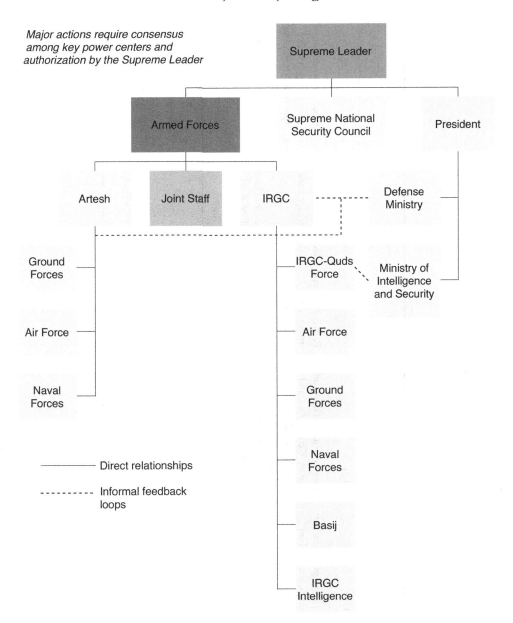

Major actions require consensus among key power centers and authorization by the Supreme Leader

Figure 37.1 Key Power Centers in National Security Decision-Making
Source: Tabatabai, A. M. (2019).

contribute and economics, ethnicity, and communal divisions play roles in terms of regional stability, so it results in favoring more cautious policies. Thus, it can be argued that Iranian policy is based on the combination of factors with varying degrees of importance in different periods with ethnicity and economics dominating in numerous key areas (Byman, Chubin, Ehteshami, & Green, 2001: 19).

Table 37.1 Comparative Drivers of Iranian Foreign Policy

Select Issues	Revolutionary Islam	Geopolitics	Nationalism	Ethnicity	Economics	Actual Policy
Defense spending level	–	Low	High	–	Low	Low
Ties to revolutionary movements	Strong ties to Muslim groups, particularly Shi'a	Ties to groups in key states, such as Iraq	Ties to groups in the Gulf region, Central Asia, and other historical areas of interest	Reject most ties; strong ties to governments	Reject most ties that might hinder trade or stability	Cautious ties to various religious groups; decline in support in recent years
Relations with the Gulf States	Competition and rejection of legitimacy	Attempt to decrease US influence	Seek recognition of Iran's leadership	Avoid policies that might anger Arab Iranians	Seek close ties to gain goodwill of West, improve oil cooperation	Steady rapprochement
Relations with Central Asia and the Caucasus	Competition and rejection of legitimacy	Balance Azerbaijan (and Turkey) with Armenia	Seek influence in Tajikistan and other Persian areas	Strong ties to governments to prevent irredentism	Pursue close economic ties	Pursue economic ties; good relations with regional governments
Relations with the United States	Reject ties	Recognize US power; avoid confrontation; minimize US influence	Reject ties, particularly if perceived as subordinate	–	Seek good relations with Washington	Continued resistance to normalization

Source: Tabatabai (2019: 3).

The strategic culture of Iran is composed of the powerful national cultural identity with regional hegemonic ambitions and theocratic ruling necessitating a strong military culture leading to confrontation and rivalries with regional foes and it dictates Iran's foreign policy and military activities in general, and its cyber warfare activities in particular (Rattray, 2018: 7) (see Table 37.1).

Comprehensive cyber security strategy of the Islamic Republic of Iran

Cyber security has been considered as a vital element of national security since its uranium enrichment centrifuges were hit in 2010 by the Stuxnet computer worm, allegedly emanating from Israel or the United States (Reuters, 2012). As reflected in the words of Abdallah Araqi, Deputy Commander of Ground Forces, Iranian Revolutionary Guard (Rattray, 2018: 98), "we have armed ourselves with new tools, because a cyber war is more dangerous than a physical war." Cyber security is considered more important, moreover, cyber is used as a weapon not only to preserve and protect the regime but also for the offensive purposes against the adversaries (Rattray, 2018: 7).

Since the first connection to the internet in the early 1990s, the Supreme Council of the Cultural Revolution controlled cyber activity in the country. IRGC supervises cyber activities in Iran. With the popular dissent relying more on new information and communication technologies (ICT) in 2009, the Green Revolution led the Iranian authorities to rely on cyber surveillance as an effective counter-strategy tool. In order to avoid a more widespread popular uprising in Iran like those which, through the power of networks, toppled regimes in Tunisia and Egypt in 2011, Iranian security forces expanded their ability to monitor and disrupt online dissent as part of a broader crackdown on opposition activities after the Green Revolution in 2009 (Lewis, 2014: 2).

As the success appears, government-sponsored cyber and hacking capabilities developed such as offensive strategies to use these capabilities against external targets, such as the Saudi oil company Aramco and the banking sector in the United States (Rattray, 2018: 99).

Cyber policies are aimed at leveraging its influence in the region and cyberwarfare is added to its arsenal "as a deterrence weapon against foreign threats to the regime, as well as a way to spy on foreign nations" (Rattray, 2018: 105). In 2011, the hack of the Netherlands internet company DigiNotar allowed Iran to read Iranian dissidents' emails secretly (BBC, 2011).

Legal measures

In the cyber security strategy of the Islamic Republic of Iran, criminal legislation and regulations compose legal measures leading to cyber justice such as the 2009 Computer Crimes Law (criminal legislation, regulation). In this process, numerous arrangements were made including the Protection of Software Copy Right Act in 2000, Electronic Commerce Act (ECA) in 2003, Military Criminal Act in 2003, Free Access to Information Act 2007, Audio-video Crimes Act in 2008, and Cyber Crimes Act (CCA) in 2009.

In the evolution of the cyber area in the Islamic Republic of Iran, the very first institution that used internet through satellite was the Theoretical Physics Research Center in 1992; then, universities received services in 1993, meaning joining the World Wide Web. Thus, it necessitated preparation for a law on cybercrime which was initiated with a committee composed of legal and information technology (IT) experts for drafting the laws regarding cybercrimes in 2002 and the draft of the Cyber Crime Act (CCA) in 2004 which was approved by the Majles in 2009 with some modifications (Pakzad & Ghassemi, 2012: 140).

Cyber security strategy has been through an evolutionary process. First, in 2007, the Fourth Development program introduced strengthening and improvement in computer information systems (both qualitative and quantitative) and development of information society and e-commerce. In order to do this, necessary legislations for securing cyber space and confronting cyber organized crimes (such as guidelines for cyber space security) were also instructed.

In 2009, the Comprehensive Statute of Security in Production and Exchanging Data (AFTA) passed in order to establish an information transfer system. In terms of criminal legislation, a specific legislation on cybercrime has been enacted: the Computer Crimes Law No. 71063 in 2009. It was mainly inspired by the European Convention on Cyber Crimes, for the prosecution and repression of cyber activities with 56 articles on internet usage and online content with two main parts (crimes and punishments and prosecution of cybercrimes) and one miscellaneous part. In an attempt to make it understandable, simplifications led to some ambiguities. It has articles on the punishments for spying, hacking, piracy, and publishing materials deemed to damage "public morality" or to be a "dissemination of lies." Article 18, inter alia, provides for imprisonment up to two years and a fine up to 5,000,000 Iranian Rial for anyone found guilty of "disseminating false information likely to agitate public opinion." The main categories of criminal content can be listed as immoral content, anti-Islamic content, anti-security and disturbing the public peace, criminal content regarding intellectual property and audio and visual issues, content which encourages, invites, or provokes others to commit criminal acts, content against state and public institutions and their responsibilities, and content used to facilitate other computer crimes (GlobalVoices, 2010).

In 2010, development of national information network, electronic state, economy, commerce, justice, national defense etc. with the aim of providing internet access for 60 per cent of Iranians by 2016 was included in the Fifth Development Program.

Technical measures

The National CIRT of the Islamic Republic of Iran, namely the Computer Emergency Response Team (CERT) also known as MAHER, was established with the goal of coordinating cyber space incident handling activities in the country for developing secure communication mechanisms for safe and secure communication among all teams (Radkani, 2013). It is composed of an incident response and response coordination team, an assessing and analyzing team, a monitoring, data gathering and updating team, a maintenance and supporting team, a malware and vulnerability analysis team, and a training team.

The CERT works on reporting and handling the incident, analyzing and reporting vulnerability, consultation on security advisory of security articles and reports, malware analysis at a malware analysis lab and reporting and comparing antivirus, guiding malware removal, developing malware toolkit – HoneyNET – and organizing seminars and conferences. Iran does not have any officially approved national- or sector-specific cyber security framework for implementing internationally recognized cyber security standards. Iran also does not have any cyber security framework for the certification and accreditation of national agencies and public sector professionals.

Organizational measures

In the comprehensive cyber security strategy of the Islamic Republic of Iran, the National Information Network has the capacity to disconnect Iran from the global internet. There is no national governance roadmap for cyber security in Iran. The laws and regulations on the cyber area also necessitate professional law enforcement agencies. Iranian lawmakers recognizing this reality have established professional divisions within the justice system for the investigation and prosecution of cyber criminality. BASIJ, IRGC, the Ministry of ICT, Iran's Passive Defense Organization, and the Information Technology Organization of Iran are such enforcement agencies responsible for cyber security oversight in the Islamic Republic of Iran.

In 2011, the Cyber Police – FATA (*Polis-e Faza-ye Towlid va Tabadol-e Ettela'at*; Iran Cyber Police) – was formed belonging to NAJA (*Niru-ye Entezami-ye Jomhuri-ye Eslami*; Law Enforcement Force). It has provincial branches in order to fight against phishing, forgery, internet theft, hacking, organized internet crime, pornography, violation of privacy, to secure and preserve order, defend religious and national identity, protect private sphere and legal liberties, protect national interests, secrets, and authority, secure the fundamental infrastructures against electronic attacks, and maintain public peace.

In order to determine which content is criminal, the Iranian Judicial Administration established the Committee for Determining the Instances of Criminal Content within the Office of the State Prosecutor General. It is composed of Ministers of Education, ICT, Intelligence, Justice, Science, Research and Technology, Culture and Islamic Guidance; the President of the Islamic Propagation Organization; the head of the Islamic Republic of Iran Broadcasting; the Commander-in-Chief of the Police; an expert of ICT chosen by the Commission of Industries and Mines of the Majles; and a member of the Legal and Judicial Commission of the Islamic Consultative Assembly chosen by the Legal and Judicial Commission and confirmed by the Majles.

The Prosecutorial Office holds the judiciary process in the prosecution of cybercrimes. It is necessary for prosecutors and judges to have capacity in cyber space, thus, since 2005, there have been training courses and workshops for judicial staff to add current special prosecutorial office for cybercrimes in Tehran (Pakzad & Ghassemi, 2012: 143). Iran does not have any officially recognized national benchmarking or referential for measuring cyber security development.

Capacity building

There is no information on any program or project for research and development of cyber security standards, best practices, and guidelines in Iran. In order to create cyber security awareness in the Islamic Republic of Iran, ASIS Cyber Security Contest has been organized since 2015. Iran does not have the exact number of public sector professionals certified under internationally recognized certification programs in cyber security. Iran does not have any certified government and public sector agencies certified under internationally recognized standards in cyber security.

Cooperation

The Fourth Development program introduced in 2007 encourages cooperation with regional and international institutions and unions of information and communication technology. There is no information on any framework for sharing cyber security assets across borders with other nation states. Iran does not have an officially recognized national- or sector-specific program for sharing cyber security assets within the public sector. There is no officially recognized national- or sector-specific program for sharing cyber security assets within the public and private sector in Iran.

MAHER is involved in the international arena through membership in the Organization of Islamic Conference OIC-CERT and ITU-IMPACT, and cooperation with other CERT in cyber-attacks like phishing, waterhole attacks, botnet etc. It has achievements on disabling some reported phishing sites, identification, analysis and disinfection of several malware attacks (such as flame, narilam, batch wiper), and developing a widespread honeypot network over the country.

Categories of cybercrime

According to the CCA and ECA cybercrimes may be categorized into the following types: offences against the confidentiality of data and systems, offences against the authenticity of data and system, offences against the integrity of data and system, and offences related to the availability of data and systems, computer related crimes, accessory crimes, and e-commerce crimes.

Offences against the confidentiality of data and systems refer to illegal accesses to a computer or communication systems, interception without right, made by technical means, of nonpublic transmissions of computer data to, from, or within a computer system including electromagnetic emissions from a computer system carrying such computer data, and espionage. Illegal access is punished with 91 days to 1 year of imprisonment or fines of 5–20 million Rials or both (Article 1), if there is an intention to gain access to secret date, Article 3 is applied. Illegal interception is punished with 6 months to 2 years of imprisonment or 10–40 million Rials of fine or both (Article 2).

Espionage refers to violation of security measures of computer transmitting or storing secret data. One to 3 years of imprisonment or 20–60 million Rials of fine or both is the punishment for gaining access to, obtaining, or intercepting secret data (Article 3a) while 2 to 10 years of imprisonment is the punishment for providing access to secrets for incompetent people (Article 3b), and 5 to 15 years of imprisonment is the punishment for disclosure of access to secret data for foreign states, organizations, companies or groups, or their agencies (Article 3c). Six months to 2 years of imprisonment or 10–40 million Rials of fine or both is the punishment for violating security measures of computer information systems with secret data (Article 4). Ninety-one days to 2 years of imprisonment or 5–40 million Rials of fine or both in addition to 6 months to 2 years of imprisonment during the dismissal of offender from the governmental duties is the punishment for disclosure of secret data to incompetent people out of carelessness, negligence, or infringement of the security measures by officials (Article 5).

Offences against the authenticity of data and system refer to computer-related forgery and the use of false data. In computer-related forgery (Article 6), input or alteration of reliable data or fraudulent creations or input of such data and alteration of data or signals of memory or processable cards in computer or telecommunication systems or chipsets, or deceitful creation or import of data or their signals to them are considered as criminal activities. The punishment for such crimes is 1 to 5 years of imprisonment or 20–50 million Rials of fine. Use of false data (Article 7) is also punishable with punishment of forgery.

Offences against the integrity of data and systems refers to data interference, system interference, and cyber terrorism. In data interference (Article 8), deletion, destruction, disturbance of others' data or making them non-processable without permission is punished with 6 months to 2 years of imprisonment or 10–40 million Rials of fine or both. In system interference (Article 9), damaging or disturbing the functioning of computers or telecommunication systems by inputting, transmitting, distributing, deleting, interrupting, manipulating, and deteriorating data or electromagnetic or optical emissions is punishable with 6 months to 2 years of imprisonment, or a fine of 10–40 million Rials, or by both (Article 9). Using internet in terrorist activities is referred to as cyber terrorism against network, data, information, and computers for a political cause, specifically Article 11 defines it as deletion, destruction, disturbance of others' data or making them non-processable and damaging or disturbing the functioning of or denial of access to data or system with punishment of 3 to 10 years of imprisonment (Article 11).

Offences related to the availability of data and systems refers to the violation of the principle of accessibility of data and system, and the accessibility of prohibited data and system out of omission of an internet service provider. In case of a denial of access to both data and systems, the punishment is 91 days to 1 year of imprisonment or 5–20 million Rials of fine or both (Article 10). In case of failing to prevent access to criminal content, the punishment is being banned from service, in case of repetition of the same crime, it is punished with the closure of business for 1 to 3 years (Articles 21 and 23). Illegal use of bandwidth is punished with 1 to 3 years of imprisonment or 100 million–1,000 million Rials of fine or both (Article 24).

Computer-related crimes refer to theft, fraud, and offences against public decency and morals. In theft, the punishment is harsher in case of complete removal of data. In case of the first act, the punishment is 1–20 million Rials of fine, in case of the second act, it becomes 91 days to 1 year of imprisonment or 5–20 million Rials of fine or both (Article 12). In fraud, gaining property or financial means is punished with 1 to 5 years of imprisonment or 20–100 million Rials of fine or both (Article 13). In offences against public decency and morals, obscene pornographic content is punished with 91 days to 2 years of imprisonment or 5–40 million Rials of fine while indecent pornographic content is punished with the minimum amount of the aforementioned term.

In the case of encouragement, provocation, or threatening or convincing people to access, the gravely obscene content is punished with 91 days to 1 year of imprisonment or 5–20 million Rials of fine while indecent content is punished with 2–5 million Rials of fine (Article 15a). In the case of the act of encouragement, provocation, threatening, facilitating, convincing, or training, the punishment is 91 days to 1 year of imprisonment or 5–20 million Rials of fine or both (Article 15b). Offences against dignity include following acts: fabricating, distorting, or altering the video, voice, or picture of a person and its distribution, by means of computer or telecommunication systems (Article 16), distributing or making available voice, picture, private, or family video, or others' secrets concerning another person without their permission (Article 17), disseminating of false news through computer and telecommunication systems, with the intention to harm others or disturb public peace (Article 18). In such cases, the punishment is 91 days to 2 years of imprisonment or 5–40 million Rials of fine or both. If the content is pornographic, the maximum amount is applied.

Accessory crimes refer to following acts: production, distribution, making accessible, or trading data, software, malware or any other electronic devices to commit computer crimes; distribution or making accessible of the training materials and contents on how to commit cybercrimes, sale and distribution of passwords or providing access to them or any data to unauthorized people. Article 25 refers to 91 days to 1 year of imprisonment or 5–20 million Rials of fine or both.

The Electronic Commerce Act (ECA) 2003 regulates e-commerce crimes (WIPO, 2020). E-crimes cover crimes violating the declared rights of the author related to data messaging and crimes violating individual rights. Crimes violating the declared rights of the author related to data messaging include violation of intellectual property rights, crimes against commercial secrets and signs. Article 74 of ECA refers to 3 months to 1 year of imprisonment and 50 million Rials of fine in case of violation of intellectual property rights. Article 75 of ECA refers to 6 months to 2 and half years of imprisonment and 50 million Rials of fine in the crime against commercial secrets. Article 76 of ECA refers to 1 to 3 years of imprisonment and 20–100 million Rials of fine in case of crimes against commercial signs. Crimes violating individual rights include violation of consumer rights and false commercial advertisement. Articles 33 to 43 of ECA refer to 10–50 million Rials of fine for the violation of consumer rights (to deliver effective information, giving information, right to canceling the deal, to return the money to consumer). Article 70 of ECA refers to 20–100 million Rials of fine for fraudulent, unhealthy, ambiguous, anonymous advertisement, hiding the identity or brand. Article 71 of ECA refers to 1 to 3 years of imprisonment for the violation of personal data.

Cyber operations as a weapon of deterrence

Protection of the regime from internal and external sources is the primary impetus in the national security strategy of the Islamic Republic of Iran. Thus, cyber is used not only in a defensive but also in an offensive manner against adversaries. Such offensive strategy includes internal espionage, sabotage against neighboring Arab countries, using proxies for the inclusion of Iraqi groups (including Hezbollah, the Syrian Electronic Army, and Kata'ib Hezbollah in Iraq, in an attempt to create a "Cyber Shi'ite Crescent" [Rattray, 2018: 113]), cyber-attacks against Israel and Gulf countries, data mining and cyber operations targeting infrastructure, military operations and businesses in the region (for e.g. the attack on Saudi Arabia's oil company Aramco and the attack on Qatar's Ras Gas company as a response to the Stuxnet attack) and Western countries (Rattray, 2018: 7–8). Specifically, the energy sector has been critical.

Among the cyber offensive cases of the Islamic Republic of Iran, the following cases raise serious considerations of the cyber capacity of the Islamic Republic of Iran as a so-called "second-tier" cyber power (Rattray, 2018: 110). These were the indictment on hacking American banks and the indictment on the attempt to hack the computerized controls of upstate New York's Bowman Avenue Dam. It was argued that allegedly water level and temperature information to operate the floodgate remotely was obtained. Interestingly, it was considered as part of a plot to breach or paralyze 46 of the largest American financial institutions and to block access to the bank accounts online. Considering the cyber capacity, the strategy of the Islamic Republic of Iran focuses on maximizing the damage with significant political and economic outcomes through some of the most sophisticated, costly, and, consequentially, invasive and destructive cyber operations in the history of the internet (Rattray, 2018: 111).

In terms of disrupting military operations, bases are targeted via the National Passive Defensive Organization (NPDO), an elite cyber force of the Islamic Republic of Iran. Formed in October 2003 after Operation Iraqi Freedom, NPDO can be termed as quasi-military body responsible for the protection of national infrastructure of the Islamic Republic of Iran in countering "power to coerce" (P2C) (RAND Corporation, 2016) focusing on "the use of nonlethal means in order to enforce adversaries into compliance" (Nadimi, 2018). It was given authority to use "all national cyber and non-cyber resources to deter, prevent, deny, identify, and effectively counter any cyberattack against … Iran's national infrastructure by either hostile foreign states or (domestic) groups supported by them" (Nadimi, 2018). In line with that, Telegram, an application for sending messages, was blamed for popular protests.

According to law, it was formed in order to deal with cyber, chemical, biological, radioactive, and economic threats through "policymaking, planning, directing, organizing, coordinating, monitoring, and operating the passive defense and civil defense … activities of enforcement agencies" (Nadimi, 2018). In line with the hybrid characteristics of the warfare in the twenty-first century, NPDO is given the multitask character of containing hard and soft threats such as internal and external security for nuclear sites and the financial, construction, industrial, telecommunications, media, energy, food security, transportation, and defense sectors. In such a complex structure of duties requiring coordination with other institutions, it has authority to make agreements with other institutions of civilian, military, and security sectors for effective cooperation and coordination. Its structure is composed of staff from IRGC and BASIJ since it was formed under the Armed Forces of the Islamic Republic of Iran (AFGS), thus it was financed by the AFGS until 2015 reaching USD$34 million budget just a few years ago (Nadimi, 2018).

In using cyber strategy not only for defensive but also for offensive purposes, the NPDO handles "services to other countries within the limits of (Iran's) national defense diplomacy" in order to accomplish "regional resistance doctrine" and in this manner, it is argued that the NPDO has been working closely with Syria, Iraq, and Lebanese Hezbollah, as mentioned by the chairman of the NPDO in October 2017 (Nadimi, 2018). It was argued that the regime in Syria received training and technology for the interception of communications and monitoring of the internet in order to track down and oppress political opponents (Rattray, 2018: 109). Moreover, it was argued that the Islamic Republic of Iran has hosted Hezbollah officials for "Cyber Hezbollah" conferences since September 2010 (Rattray, 2018: 113).

In combatting a diverse set of threats posed to the regime (i.e. military and non-military tools including economy, popular protests and the Velvet Revolution), the aim is to gain popular support and legitimate grounds for the prosecution of domestic opposition. The AFGS used such attacks on the Iranian nuclear and energy facilities such as those in 2009, 2011, 2012, 2017, and 2018, popular protests facilitated by social media, the 2010 Stuxnet attack on nuclear facilities, and the 2012 Flame attack on oil facility as a grounds to form a Cyber Defense Headquarters in October 2011 (Nadimi, 2018). By February 2012 it had reached a point of calling for the formation of an Iranian Cyber Army (ICA) in the coordination of surveillance of citizens' online activities and, allegedly, conducting offensive cyber-attacks in cooperation with the IRGC-BASIJ cyber command. The cyber-attack aimed to sabotage the operations and trigger an explosion in a petrochemical company in Saudi Arabia in August 2017 (Rattray, 2018: 109).

In the sanctions list of the European Union, namely the Decision of the Council of the European Union 2010/413/CFSP concerning restrictive measures against Iran, Brigadier General Gholam-Reza Jalali, former IRGC, PDO chairman, was named in the list of persons with the duty of "selection and construction of strategic facilities, including – according to Iranian statements – the uranium enrichment site at Fordow (Qom) built without being declared to the IAEA contrary to Iran's obligations (affirmed in a resolution by the IAEA Board of Governors)" (The National Archives, 2010).

It is also argued that the Islamic Republic of Iran aims at developing its cyber capability as the fourth leg of deterrence aiming at gaining "ability to disrupt maritime traffic in the Strait of Hormuz; conduct unilateral and proxy terrorism on several continents; and launch long-range missile and rocket strikes against targets throughout the region" (Rattray, 2018: 107).

The tools used by the Islamic Republic of Iran are numerous. Installation of malicious code in counterfeit computer software, blocking of computer communications networks, and development of viruses took place in the 2012 attack on Saudi Aramco resulting in destroying 35,000 computers. Tools for penetrating computers to gather intelligence occurred in the attack on the Sands Las Vegas Corporation-LVS in 2014. The development of tools with delayed action mechanisms or mechanisms connected to control servers was observed in the attack of malicious domains emulating the ones used by the American Israel Public Affairs Committee – AIPAC (Rattray, 2018: 111).

In considering the cyber capacity and the national security strategy, the attacks aim "to disable critical infrastructure, create confusion, distrust, deception, disruption, support or to drive psychological operations that deter hostile activity or otherwise achieve strategic or tactical objectives" (Rattray, 2018: 111). The ultimate form of such goals led to the creation of the Iran Cyber Army by the Intelligence Unit of the IRGC, arguably the second-biggest cyber army in the world (Rattray, 2018: 114).

In countering the cyber capacity of the Islamic Republic of Iran, the vital element is the Joint Comprehensive Plan of Action (JCPOA), also called the Iran nuclear deal, an agreement reached between Iran and the P5+1 together with the European Union in Vienna on July 14, 2015. Recent developments on the JCPOA after the withdrawal of the United States of America challenge the argument that cyber threats emanating from Iran decreased after the JCPOA (Rattray, 2018: 115). Such consideration is made due to the fact that the Islamic Republic of Iran aims to deter threats to the regime and become a reborn Persian Empire.

Conclusion

The Islamic Republic of Iran is forced to have a contemporary national security strategy in order to counter contemporary challenges like cyber threats. Considering the unique characteristics of the Islamic Republic of Iran, the main factor of the cyber strategy is "as a deterrence weapon against foreign threats to the regime, as well as a way to spy on foreign nations."

In achieving such a goal, a comprehensive cyber security framework is highly critical. In order to achieve that, the Islamic Republic of Iran focuses on legal, technical, and organizational measures together with capacity building and cooperation. In terms of legal measures, legislation and regulations provide measures to deter such threats via framing such acts as crimes. In terms of technical measures, a response team named MAHER has a reputation with its capacity, activity, and cooperation with international organizations. In terms of organizational measures, since the main factor is to deter the foreign threats against the regime, a main body of national security, namely the IRGC, plays a vital role but it also has other units in order to work in coordination with each other.

Th ECA and CCA are the main elements of cyber security legislation and the acts classified as crime are defined in detail in the cyber area. The uniqueness of the cyber security legislation of the Islamic Republic of Iran lies in its moral values, which are highly strengthened in the cyber security legislation. Since the cyber threats are highly contemporary, it necessitates the Islamic Republic of Iran to counter such contemporary challenges with continuous updates in the legislation, technical capacity, organization, capacity building, and cooperation.

In deterring internal and external threats to the regime and challenging the region as a hegemonic power, both defensive and offensive strategies are considered in the comprehensive cyber security strategy framework of the Islamic Republic of Iran in order "to disable critical infrastructure, create confusion, distrust, deception, disruption, support or to drive psychological operations that deter hostile activity or otherwise achieve strategic or tactical objectives" through developing cyber capability as the fourth leg of deterrence.

Recent attempts to develop the cyber capacity of the Islamic Republic of Iran, namely NPDO, ICA, and Cyber Hezbollah, aim at transforming from a "second-tier" cyber power position to the second-biggest cyber army in the world. Adversaries observe such ambition and they weigh options available in the post-JCPOA including cyber warfare as well.

Suggested reading

Article 19. (2012). "Islamic Republic of Iran: Computer Crimes Law." www.article19.org/data/files/medialibrary/2921/12-01-30-FINAL-iran-WEB per cent5B4 per cent5D.pdf

Baldino, D. & Goold, J. (2014). "Iran and the Emergence of Information and Communications Technology: The Evolution of Revolution?" *Australian Journal of International Affairs*, 68(1): 17–35.

Carnegie Endowment for International Peace. (2018, January 4). "Iran's Cyber Threat: Conclusion and Prescriptions." https://carnegieendowment.org/2018/01/04/iran-s-cyber-threat-conclusion-and-prescriptions-pub-75143

Doffman, Z. (2020, January 11). "Iran's 'Critical' Cyberattack Threat: This Is What Is Really Happening Right Now." www.forbes.com/sites/zakdoffman/2020/01/11/irans-critical-cyberattack-threat-this-is-what-is-really-happening-right-now/#79e6a7184f78

O'Flaherty, K. (2020, January 6). "The Iran Cyber Warfare Threat: Everything You Need To Know," *Forbes*. www.forbes.com/sites/kateoflahertyuk/2020/01/06/the-iran-cyber-warfare-threat-everything-you-need-to-know/#35d56ac215aa

Vicens, A. J. (2020, January 3). "Here's What a Cyber Attack by Iran Might Look Like," *Mother Jones*. www.motherjones.com/politics/2020/01/heres-what-a-cyber-attack-by-iran-might-look-like/

References

BBC. (2011, September 5). "Fake DigiNotar Web Certificate Risk to Iranians." www.bbc.co.uk/news/technology-14789763

Byman, D., Chubin, S., Ehteshami, A. & Green, J. D. (2001). "*Iran's Security Policy in the Post-Revolutionary Era,*" RAND Corportation, Santa Monica, United States. www.rand.org/pubs/monograph_reports/MR1320.html

GlobalVoices. (2010). "Iran: We Are All Computer Criminals." https://globalvoices.org/2010/11/23/iran-we-are-all-computer-criminals/

Lewis, J. A. (2014). "*Cybersecurity and Stability in the Gulf, Gulf Analysis Paper,*" Center for Strategic and International Studies, Washington, DC. https://csis-prod.s3.amazonaws.com/s3fs-public/legacy_files/files/publication/140106_Lewis_GulfCybersecurity_Web_0.pdf

Nadimi, F. (2018). "Iran's Passive Defense Organization: Another Target for Sanctions," Washington, DC. www.washingtoninstitute.org/policy-analysis/view/irans-passive-defense-organization-another-target-for-sanctions

The National Archives. (2010). "Council Decision 2010/413/CFSP." www.legislation.gov.uk/eudn/2010/413/2020-01-31

The New York Post. (2015). "The Iranian Dream of a Reborn Persian Empire." https://nypost.com/2015/02/01/the-iranian-dream-of-a-reborn-persian-empire/

Pakzad, B. & Ghassemi, G. (2012). "Cybercrimes in Iran: Perspectives, Policies and Legislations," in S. Manacorda (ed.), *Cybercriminality: Finding a Balance between Freedom and Security* (pp. 139–163). Milano: ISPAC.

Radkani, E. (2013). "MAHER (Iran National CERT." www.itu.int/net/WSIS/implementation/2013/forum/agenda/session_docs/Day4/113/Panelist3-Radkani.pdf

RAND Corporation. (2016). "The Power to Coerce: Countering Adversaries without Going to War." www.rand.org/pubs/research_reports/RR1000.html

Rattray, G. (2018). "Strategic Culture and Cyberwarfare Strategies: Four Case Studies," SIPA Capstone Workshop. https://sipa.columbia.edu/file/7168/download?token=qLvPL-J8

Reuters. (2012). "Iran Sees Cyber Attacks as Greater Threat than Actual War." www.reuters.com/article/net-us-iran-military/iran-sees-cyber-attacks-as-greater-threat-than-actual-war-idusbre88o0my20120925

Tabatabai, A. M. (2019). "*Iran's National Security Debate, Implications for Future U.S.-Iran Negotiations,*" RAND Corporation, Santa Monica, United States. www.rand.org/content/dam/rand/pubs/perspectives/PE300/PE344/RAND_PE344.pdf

World Intellectual Property Organization-WIPO. (2020). "Electronic Commerce Law of the Islamic Republic of Iran." www.wipo.int/edocs/lexdocs/laws/en/ir/ir008en.pdf

PART IV

The Americas

38

CANADA'S CYBER SECURITY IN A GLOBALIZED ENVIRONMENT

Challenges and opportunities

Kawser Ahmed

Introduction

A couple of events dominate 24-hour news cycles nowadays. Among them, an alleged Russian hacking into the 2017 Democratic National Convention (DNC), UK-based Cambridge Analytica's data manipulation of 80 million Facebook users, a Russian global hacking effort to gain access to the UK and the US infrastructure as well as home Wi-Fi users, and last but not least, the use of social media platforms to wage "troll wars."[1] Although Facebook data manipulation or trolling might not fit into typical cyberattack profiles, these instances drew wider attention because they were carried out with malicious intent. Obviously, these nefarious cyber activities simply exposed the vulnerability of our Information Technology (IT) platforms; however, the above-mentioned incidences are unique in terms of the magnitude of data breach and the subsequent social-political fallouts. Nevertheless, there are two types of cyberattacks, one that is directed against states and their apparatuses and the other that is carried out against both the public and private sectors such as financial, service, and Internet service providing institutions.[2] The vast number of cyberattacks actually fall in the latter category.

This chapter is organized into two main parts. The first part deals with the global cyber security and cyber threat environment where the concept of sovereignty in cyber space including the current state of international governance is illustrated. The second part opens up with the statement of Canada's cyber security strategy including Canadian context on cyber security where Canada's cultural understanding, institutions, the role of the legislature, and the societal implications of cyber security are discussed. Data is gathered from various Internet sources as well as government and non-government policy papers.

Global cyber security and cyber threat environment

In general, cyber attackers target either *data* (most common form causing service disruption) or *control systems* (a rare form intended to manipulate physical infrastructures). Considering these two forms of attack, experts contend that physical damage due to cyber terrorism has not taken place on a large scale in the past although technology and motivation of numerous actors are growing in leaps and bounds. Despite the fact that non-state actors, for example, terrorists and hackers, would continue to vie for their share to access resources to attack, "sophisticated espionage and sabotage in the cyber-domain still needs the capabilities, determination, and cost-benefit-rationale of a nation-state [and] the most dangerous actors in the cyber-domain are still nation-states" (Theiler, 2015). Additionally, an American law enforcement agency noted a new kind of "hybrid cyber threat … in which nation-states work with criminal hackers to carry out malicious activities" (The US Department of Justice, 2017). In this regard, it might be worthwhile to review important cyber threat terminology. Depending on actors' goals and motivations, although experts and practitioners differ widely in defining various forms of cyber threats, generally agreed upon common definitions of *cybercrime*,[3] *cyber terrorism*,[4] *cyberattacks*,[5] *cyber espionage*,[6] and *cyber warfare*[7] are appended here (Alexander, 2014a, 2014b). Nevertheless, one of the ways to understand different forms of the cyber threats is to judge the intention of an attacker (i.e., the motive).

The concept of sovereignty in cyber space

Merriam-Webster defines sovereignty in three ways: 1) supreme power especially over a body politic; 2) freedom from external control or autonomy; and 3) controlling influence (Merriam-Webster, 2018). According to the "Westphalian" notion of a nation-state where clear-cut boundaries delineate one state from the other, modern nation states also assert their inalienable rights over their cyber space. But now the concept of sovereignty also includes virtual space where non-state actors not only outnumber state actors but are also free to engage in a wide variety of actions. Nevertheless, there are no agreed upon terminologies such as *Russian* or *Japanese* or *US cyber spaces* as everyone perceives to have the rights to be in the virtual space. Here three contradictions, which capture the essential debate on *state sovereignty* and *cyber space* are worth mentioning.

> First, the contradiction between cyber sovereignty and the spirit of the internet; the exclusivity of classical state sovereignty runs contrary to the spirit of the internet, which rests on the concept of unrestricted inter-connectivity. Second, the contradiction between cyber sovereignty and human rights. The third is the contradiction between cyber sovereignty and involvement of multiple stakeholders in governance.
>
> *(Yeli, 2017: 109)*

In order to strengthen the security of global information and telecommunications systems, the UN established a Group of Governmental Experts (GGE) in 2004. One of its reports suggests that

> state sovereignty and the international norms and principles that flow from it apply to States' conduct of [Information Communication Technology] ICT related activities and to their jurisdiction over ICT infrastructure within their territory; States must meet their international obligations regarding internationally wrongful acts attributable to them.
>
> *(United Nations, 2015: 2)*

However, after witnessing the futile attempts by the GGE to formulate a standard norm to address the issues pertaining to state sovereignty, experts, as well as policymakers in the US, have put forward two sets of arguments. One suggests building norms with the US adversaries who traditionally challenge US hegemony on cyber matters. This approach would enable the setting of ground rules that would allow the US to assess threats to its sovereignty and allocate resources to defend it. While the other suggests they "… build a coalition of norm adherents or good guys" so that collaborative defensive actions can be taken against the violators; this approach would also act as a deterrent to potential aggressors (Segal, 2017).[8]

GGE consists of 25 members comprised of legal and government experts who have held five sessions on international governance. It postulates a "coherent system of rules based on the premises that international law governs everything virtual just as it does everything tangible" (CCDCOE, 2017). GGE's principles of governance are also published in 2013 and 2015 GGE reports. Similarly, the Tallinn Manual 2.0 prepared by an international group of experts also suggested a "rules-based system" for the member nations of the OSCE and ASEAN. Such an expression was further reflected in the G7 Lucca Declaration.

Although fraught with challenges, Microsoft propagates the idea of a "digital Geneva Convention" where state and non-state actors can collaborate and agree upon certain norms and using such a platform the companies can become a "neutral digital Switzerland" (Smith, 2017). This initiative was pitched at the 2017 RSA Cybersecurity Conference (RSA Conference, 2017) that contained three elements: "the substance of a Digital Geneva Convention for peacetime; a Tech Accord to protect people in cyber space, and the possibility of creating an 'International Cyber Attack Attribution Organization'" (Mueller, 2017). In this initiative, experts who gathered at the conference strongly supported the proposal to establish a "Tech Accord" which would act as a collective platform containing "a common set of principles and behaviors in cyber space," such as "no assistance for offensive cyber operations," and a refusal to "traffic in cyber vulnerabilities" (ibid.).

Canada's cyber security strategy

Canada defines cyber space as "… the electronic world created by interconnected networks of information technology and the information on those networks. It is a global commons where more than 1.7 billion people are linked together to exchange ideas, services, and friendship" (Public Safety Canada, 2010: 2). This was mentioned in Canada's first Cyber Security Strategy (CCSS) which was released in October 2010. This strategy assumes four key characteristics of a cyber threat including three types of cyber threats depending upon the nature of targets, methods of attack, motivations, and intent of the attacker.[9] Additionally Canada's vision of cyber security is explained in the following way, "strong cyber security is an essential element of Canadian innovation and prosperity" where it is mentioned that the government and its partners would continue to work on three core themes: security and resilience, cyber innovation, and leadership and collaboration (Government of Canada, 2018b).

In CCSS, partnerships between provincial, territorial, and private sectors are mentioned as a crucial element. However, the importance of such a partnership is also mentioned in the *National Strategy and Action Plan for Critical Infrastructure* (Public Safety Canada, 2018b) through which Canadian law enforcement community is able "to work with partners and international allies" in curbing illegal activities committed in cyber space (for more details see Government of Canada, 2018b). The strategy has three pillars and five essential elements.[10] The CCSS also emphasizes the complementary nature of the US, UK, and Australia's strategies so that all of these countries can share information on threats and resources to deter cyberattacks together. More so, Canada being the only non-European country which is a signatory of the Council of Europe's *Convention on Cyber Crime* (also known as the Budapest convention, which was ratified by Canada on July 8, 2015) collaborates with European nations on cyber matters as well (Government of Canada, 2015). Additionally, in 2014 Canada launched its Digital Canada 150 Strategy where 39 initiatives were announced. As a follow-up, version 2.0 of the strategy tracked the progress of the earlier initiatives and added 31 new initiatives to secure Canada (Innovation Science and Economic Development Canada, 2017). "Get Cyber Safe" is another tool that provides news and guidance for individual Canadians and Canadian corporations on cyber security (Government of Canada, 2018c).

Canadian cyber security context

Canada is not immune to cyber threats according to the Canadian Internet Registration Authority's (CIRA) latest Internet Factbook (Coop, 2017) and Scalar survey.[11] In the Internet Factbook, 75 per cent of Canadians expressed their concerns about cyberattacks, a 13 per cent increase from the previous year. However, its cyber security is intertwined with the national security similar to most of the Western nations. It relies heavily "on the uninterrupted functioning of its critical infrastructure [CI], disruptions of which can have a serious impact on lives, the safety of communities and the economy" (Public Safety Canada, 2016b).[12]

The government has also established the Canadian Cyber Incident Response Centre (CCIRC) to monitor and provide mitigation advice on cyber threats, and coordinate the national response to any cyber security incident (Public Safety Canada, 2016a). Nine Government of Canada organizations are responsible for implementing the CCSS.[13] The CCIRC is situated at the junction of private and public sector collaboration in Canada where partnerships with Canadian owners and operators of CI are of particular importance.

Canada is one of the G7 nations and along with its counterparts in October 2017 it endorsed the G7 Fundamental Elements of Cyber Security for the Financial Sector guidelines to implement its cyber security and outline a strategy to deal with cyber risks.[14] The guideline describes "eight basic building blocks" for crafting cyber security strategy that include: 1) Cyber security strategy and framework, 2) Governance, 3) Risk and control assessment, 4) Monitoring, 5) Response, 6) Recovery, 7) Information sharing, and 8) Continuous learning (Freedman, 2017). Among these "building blocks" mentioned, monitoring, response, information sharing, and continuous learning are important to take into account while evaluating Canada's cultural understanding of cyber security. Moreover, G7 foreign ministers met on April 23, 2018, in Ottawa to discuss cyber security threats making it an important topic of nations' ongoing efforts on this matter. Additionally, Canada has a number of institutions to deal with cyber security threats.[15]

Canada's cultural understandings, role of private sectors, and legislature

In Canada, in 2017, 59 publicly reported data breach incidents took place of which 17 incidents were categorized as critical and severe (Gemalto, 2017). A cursory look into different types of cyberattacks, data breaches, and the state of cyberattack preparedness reveals certain patterns of organizations and individuals in Canada. In this backdrop, several cultural understandings related to cyber security are discussed in the following paragraphs.

First, at the organizational level, a general understanding of a cyberattack and its consequences vary between government and non-government organizations (NGOs). For example, at the three levels of federal, provincial, and municipal governments, resource allocation in cyber security varies widely, which is rooted in individual organization's work culture. Typically, most government organizations other than those that deal with national security have some guideline in place outlining the nature of cyber security that includes a periodic review of employees' roles and noting precautionary measures. Although an IT department monitors data breaches and conducts such awareness programs, individual branches at the division or sub-division level lack resources to train employees and enforce rules. On the other hand, non-governmental agencies, especially the commercial ones, invest heftily in cyber defense infrastructure, monitor their employees effectively for potential data breaches, and share information with others in a collaborative way. As transpired, these NGOs are agile and can adapt to changes as they enjoy more organizational flexibility than government agencies. Nonetheless, the necessity of changing the mindsets of government agencies to deal with evolving cyber threats is a need of our time. Most importantly, a shift of mindset from data *breach prevention* towards the notion of institutionalizing data *breach acceptance* is important. Regardless of all the sorts of cyber defensive capabilities in place, a cyber attacker might find a way inside a system because the threat of attack comes from within (i.e. a rogue or a careless employee, for example, Canadian Forces Sub-Lt. Jeffrey Paul Delisle who worked for the Russian embassy at Ottawa) (KERA News, 2012).

Second, at the individual level, culturally, cyber security is often perceived in terms of a *fear* resulting from the likelihood of loss of personal data either through government security agencies using mass surveillance tools or by anonymous hackers, known corporations, and business firms. Nonetheless, according to a new survey conducted by the Canadian federal privacy commissioner, "Canadians deeply value privacy, but fear they are losing the control they have over their personal information" (Office of the Privacy Commissioner of Canada, 2018b). Canadians also feel that they need to be in control of their private data. This is why in another survey, 78 per cent of Canadians broadly supported the requirement of government agencies to properly safeguard the personal information and 71 per cent opined to modernize the existing Privacy Act so that it could be applicable to the Prime Minister's Office (PMO) and the offices of cabinet ministers (CISION, 2017).

Third, organizational resilience against a cyber threat is an important aspect of cyber defense that is gaining traction now. Thus, a Public Safety document entitled Fundamentals of Cyber Security for Canada's CI Community asserts, "building true resiliency usually requires active engagement from a number of different players" (Public Safety Canada, 2016b). Resilience is predicated upon the fact that cyberattacks in today's context are not about the question of where but when the attack will happen; therefore, people as well as systems must remain ready to absorb an attack and return to normal operation. Here the concept of resiliency should be envisioned as both a bottom-up and a top-down process. The bottom-up process involves organizational rules in terms of security awareness including procedures in place, which employees must follow diligently (Solomon, 2017). The top-down approach involves an organization's hardware capabilities to defend itself, repulse an attack and get back to a normal operation with a minimum loss (both material and downtime). In an ideal situation, both these approaches should converge and create a resilience system.

Fourth, the government of Canada enacted legislation that ensures mandatory reporting of data breaches given the fact that most organizations feel reluctant to report data breaches due to the fear of losing organizational reputations. Such a mindset needs to be changed in order to safeguard the personal data of clients for business as well as government organizations. In this regard, in 2015, the Bill S-4 (i.e., the *Digital Privacy Act*) amended Canada's private sector privacy law (i.e. the *Personal Information Protection and Electronic Documents Act* – PIPEDA) in a number of areas including the establishment of mandatory data breach reporting requirements (Government of Canada, 2017). Although the responsibility for overseeing compliance with PIPEDA rests with the Privacy Commissioner, various service providers are expected to come onboard to implement the law.

Fifth, the role of the private sector in cyber security in Canada is important for two reasons: it contains millions of Canadians' personal information and at the same time many of them work for government organizations and deal with sensitive data. In this regard, the Global State of Information Security Survey of 2018 provided four valuable lessons for private sectors worldwide. One, the growth in digital devices is driving risk management (hinting at the explosion of handheld mobile devices). Two, business leaders see new risks tied to emerging technologies (for example, GPS, monitoring technologies, profiling through the use of social media data. Three, cyber threats to the integrity of data (data sharing across many digital platforms as well as data encryption). And four, current employees remain the top source of security incidents (lack of control over employees at work) (PWC, 2018).

Sixth, legislature plays a key role in assessing a situation and enacting appropriate laws in conjunction with regional and global partners. In terms of legislation, Canada has enacted the following: 1) Anti-Spam Legislation (CASL – July 1, 2014) (Government of Canada, 2018a), 2) the *Digital Privacy Act* (also known as Bill S-4), and 3) the PIPEDA. A key change in PIPEDA was the establishment of mandatory data breach reporting requirements (Government of Canada, 2017). The CRTC has the primary enforcement responsibility for the anti-spam law. On March 10, 2015, Protecting Canadians from Online Crime Act came into force. This legislation provides law enforcement agencies with new, specialized investigative powers to help them take action against Internet child sexual exploitation, and disrupt online organized crime activity (Global Affairs Canada, 2018).

In the above paragraphs, variation of monitoring aspects in government and non-government agencies are highlighted based on organizational culture. Response is mentioned in terms of gaining resilience against any cyberattack as well as information sharing among and between government agencies and private businesses were two important aspects in understanding cyber security environment of Canada.

Canadian uniqueness and societal implications of cyber law

In general, Canadians are aware of their cyber vulnerabilities (CIRA, 2018) yet they believe that cyber security laws[16] offer a collective good in securing their safety by providing them suggestions and guidelines for cyber preparedness according to a report published in 2016 (CGI, 2016). In view of this, the government of Canada published the Cyber Incident Management Framework – a comprehensive document that shows nature of cyber threats, various steps, and roles of agencies and stakeholders in dealing with such situations (Public Safety Canada, 2018a). Nonetheless, on the eve of the 2018 G7 summit that was hosted in Canada, the CCIRC emphasized physical aspects of cyber defense.[17] In this context, Canada has two unique conditions in the defense of its cyberspace as a member of the

5-Eyes group (Hanna, 2017) as well as through one of its institutions (i.e., Office of the Privacy Commissioner of Canada – OPC) that safeguards individual rights to privacy.

Global cooperation and understanding between the government and the private sector providing IT services are crucial in safeguarding individual cyber space. In line with this concept, the 5-Eyes group was created following the UK–USA agreement of 1946 (Farrell, 2013). Primarily, in this agreement, the member states – Australia, New Zealand, Canada, the United Kingdom, and the USA – agreed upon data sharing to protect their national security. In its recent communique, the danger from the "new vectors for harm" was highlighted and IT companies (i.e. the Global Internet Forum to Counter Terrorism, where Google, Facebook, Microsoft, and Twitter are members) were urged to support their intelligence communities in tackling terrorist fundraising and child exploitation (Harris, 2018). Thus Canada, being a member of this group, truly enjoys some unique advantages regarding data sharing among the most developed nations on earth whose citizens use technology the most. Additionally, the Communication Security Establishment (CSE) is Canada's largest and most prolific organization that is tasked with safeguarding national interest related to cyber security. CSE's mandate and jurisdiction are defined in National Defence Act, and its mission is "to provide and protect information of national interest through leading-edge technology, in synergy with [its] partners" (Communications Security Establishment, 2014). However, CSE is also part of the 5-Eyes group of countries with whom it has shared intelligence for decades.

Canada has a unique establishment, the OPC, which provides "advice and information for individuals about protecting personal information" as well as "enforce[s] two federal privacy laws"[18] that regulate federal government institutions and guide private businesses in handling personal information. This office carries out investigations on privacy breaches and advises lawmakers on issues that affect the privacy rights of Canadians. Additionally, the OPC plays a crucial role in monitoring and advising policymakers about maintaining a balance between individual rights to privacy versus security. As a matter of fact, the need for protecting the safety and security of Canadians unquestionably rests on the government's shoulders, however this must not come at the expense of Canadians' privacy. In the age of violent extremism where the Internet remains the primary domain to spread hate and recruit extremists, OPC oversees law enforcers so their work is consistent with the rule of law while protecting individuals from terrorism. OPC also carries out research on matters related to privacy protection in cyber security activities (Office of the Privacy Commissioner of Canada, 2018a). With regards to mapping societal implications of cyber laws, OPC's 2016 survey helps us to identify key trends in this field (Office of the Privacy Commissioner of Canada, 2016). Two main perspectives that are derived from the survey are appended below.

First, 74 per cent of Canadians felt that they have less protection of their personal information than they did ten years ago. However, they prioritize privacy over other matters and strongly believe in non-interference of government agencies in their private lives. In this regard, one can observe several trends in the 2016 Survey of Canadians on Privacy. For example, between the years of 2014 and 2016, Canadians' *very good knowledge* on privacy rights increased from 5 per cent to 16 per cent and *good knowledge* increased from 27 per cent to 49 per cent. Similarly, within the same period, Canadians' concerns about the protection of personal privacy increased from 34 per cent to 37 per cent. This trend shows that Canadians are increasingly becoming aware of the predicament of digital privacy matters and they are learning how to protect personal data. That is why they are more cognizant of cyber security laws and their ramifications.

Second, despite living in the age of ever-diminishing privacy, the survey asked participating Canadians how they felt about "Government monitoring of citizens activities for national security or public safety purposes." In response, 26 per cent expressed that they were extremely concerned and 40 per cent suggested that they were somewhat concerned, making it 66 per cent of Canadians that were generally concerned. This finding tells us that government agencies spying on its citizens without justified cause is not accepted and it stems from the fact that Canadians prefer privacy over safety. In the same vein, 70 per cent of Canadians expressed that law enforcement agencies should disclose at what frequency they collect citizens' personal information within a scheme of general *intelligence gathering* without court authorization. Although 50 per cent said that law enforcement agencies currently do not have enough jurisdiction or legal power to collect citizens' private information for national security or public safety, conversely, 33 per cent do not agree that these agencies need more power to collect information. This data illustrates that while the majority of Canadians value the need to monitor citizens who might be a national security threat, they do not support a blanket approval of intelligence gathering.

Conclusion

The more our private and public lives are becoming digitized, the more we are prone to interference either by state or non-state actors. In this regard, the only way we can improve our vulnerabilities is by being aware of our vulnerabilities in the cyber world and knowing the appropriate tools that we have at our disposal for reducing vulnerabilities. In a similar vein, like other governments Canada also enacted laws, passed legislation, and founded institutions yet the onus remains on Canadians to defend themselves against cyber threats.

In this chapter, global cyber security and cyber threat environments were discussed first, followed by the concept of sovereignty in the cyber world and international governance in cyber domain. One thing that contributes to not being able to formulate an agreed upon international law/norm governing state behaviors is that powerful cyber capable nations do not want to become hostage to cyber laws as they seem to remain flexible to attack others. Afterward, this chapter examined Canada's cyber security environment that includes cultural understanding, its institutions, the role of the legislature, and societal implications. Two things stand out clearly: Canadians are more aware of cyber laws and they do not want interference in their private lives in the name of collecting data for national security. Canada also has unique characteristics being a member of 5-Eyes in defense of its cyber environment and an organization such as OPC that oversees implementation of cyber laws in the country.

Research on cyber security needs to go on due to the fact that cyber threats evolve and according to the analyses made in the cultural understanding of Canadian cyber security environment above, it is reasonable to understand that stakeholders' awareness and cooperation are the two most important elements for Canadian cyber defense in the future. However, to bolster its cyber defense, Canadian private business sectors and government agencies should work together in bringing changes to its culture of data protection and sharing while maintaining a balance between privacy and national security.

Notes

1 "The art of deliberately, cleverly, and secretly pissing people off, usually via Internet, using dialogue. Trolling stands for an attempt to feed mis- and disinformation to manipulate public perceptions." www.urbandictionary.com/define.php?term=Trolling

2 For example, the case of the disruption of Estonia's government sites in April 2007 by hackers through Distributed Denial of Service (DDoS) attacks, which ultimately triggered article 5 of NATO's collective defense; the Russian DDoS attack in response to Georgia's South Ossetia incursion in 2008; and the computer worm Stuxnet, which infected Siemens computers at Iranian nuclear facilities in 2009–2010 to name a few. In the latter category, the examples are attacks on Sony, JP Morgan, Saudi Aramco, and the US Office of Personnel Management.

3 A "cybercrime" is "enabled by or […] targets computers [and] can involve the theft and damage to property as well as fraudulent and espionage-related activities." Source: Alexander, Dean, Cyber Threats Against the North Atlantic Treaty Organization (NATO) and Selected Responses (2014) Turkey. http://dergipark.gov.tr/download/article-file/89251

4 "Cyber terrorism" is defined as unlawful attacks and threats of attack against computers, networks, and information stored therein – carried out through the computers, Internet, or the use of flash drive storage devices – when done to intimidate or coerce a government or its people in furtherance of political or social objectives (ibid.).

5 A "cyberattack" (or computer network attack) can disrupt computer equipment and hardware reliability, change computer-processing logic, steal or corrupt data; "… cyber attacks include the loss of integrity, availability, confidentiality, and physical destruction. Cyber attacks most frequently target critical infrastructure (financial services, manufacturing, telecommunications, electricity, water). However, they increasingly inflict damage on government targets, including the military, intelligence, and law enforcement" (ibid.).

6 "Cyber espionage is the use of computer systems or information technology to illegally obtain confidential/secret information from the government, private sector, or some other entity" (ibid.).

7 Cyber is the fifth domain of the battlefield after air, land, sea, and space. Cyber warfare is utilizing computers and other instruments to target an enemy's information systems rather than attacking an enemy's armies or factories. War in the Information Age: A Primer for Cyberspace Operations in 21st Century Warfare. www.dtic.mil/dtic/tr/fulltext/u2/a514490.pdf

8 Some experts believe that sovereignty should not be viewed as a state's prerogative in controlling its resources; it also should make a state responsible for its conduct and behavior in cyber-space. Concerning states becoming self-responsible, one can refer to June 2017 China and Canada's agreement not to conduct cyber espionage for a commercial gain against each other (Reuters Staff, 2017). China also followed it through and signed similar agreements with the US, UK, Australia, the G-7 and G-20 nations.

9 Characteristics are: "1) inexpensive (tools to carry out attack can be purchased from open sources); 2) easy (only basic essential computer skills are needed to carry out attack); 3) effective (in terms of damage that an attack can cause); and 4) low risk (attackers' capability to evade detection and prosecution). Threats are: 1) state-sponsored cyber espionage and military activities; 2) terrorist use of the Internet; and 3) cybercrime. Public Safety Canada (2010). From, Canada's Cyber Security Strategy: For a stronger and more prosperous Canada (Vol. 2018). Ottawa.

10 These are: 1) securing Government of Canada systems; 2) partnering to secure vital cyber systems outside the Government of Canada, and 3) helping Canadians to be secure online. The elements are: 1) reflects Canadian values such as the rule of law, accountability and privacy; 2) allows continual improvements to be made to meet emerging threats; 3) integrates activity across the Government of Canada; 4) emphasizes partnerships with Canadians, provinces, territories, business, and academe; and 5) builds upon our close working relationships with Canadian allies" Public Safety Canada (2018b). Get Cyber Safe Guide for Small and Medium Businesses. www.getcybersafe.gc.ca/cnt/rsrcs/pblctns/smll-bsnss-gd/index-eng.aspx

11 Scalar – the cyber security advocacy firm – surveyed the Canadian landscape and reported that on average, Canadian organizations are attacked 455 times per year; 9 breaches resulted from these attacks, and 20 per cent of the attacks were considered high impact. In terms of damage assessment, Scalar also indicates that it cost Canadians $3,679,090, caused 90 hours of downtime, resulted in 16 days of recovery time, and files containing personal private data due to the breach was 47 per cent. For details, see Scalar survey infographics. www.scalar.ca/wp-content/uploads/2018/03/Scalar_Survey graphic v6.pdf

12 Critical infrastructure (CI) refers to processes, systems, facilities, technologies, networks, assets and services essential to the health, safety, security, or economic well-being of Canadians and the effective functioning of government. Critical infrastructure can be stand-alone or interconnected and interdependent within and across provinces, territories, and national borders. Disruptions of

critical infrastructure could result in catastrophic loss of life, adverse economic effects, and significant harm to public confidence. www.publicsafety.gc.ca/cnt/ntnl-scrt/crtcl-nfrstrctr/index-en.aspx

13 Public Safety (PS), Communications Security Establishment (CSE), Shared Services Canada (SSC), Department of National Defence/Defence Research and Development Canada (DND/DRDC), Treasury Board of Canada Secretariat (TBS), Global Affairs Canada (GAC), Justice Canada (JUS), the Royal Canadian Mounted Police (RCMP), and Canadian Security Intelligence Services (CSIS). www.publicsafety.gc.ca/cnt/rsrcs/pblctns/vltn-cnd-scrt-strtg/vltn-cnd-scrt-strtg-en.pdf

14 Cyber risks are the risks of loss and liability (e.g. business disruption, financial loss, loss to stakeholder value, reputational harm, trade secret disclosure and other competitive harm, legal noncompliance liability and civil liability to customers, business partners and other persons) to an organization resulting from a failure or breach of the information technology systems used by or on behalf of the organization, including incidents resulting in unauthorized access, use or disclosure of regulated, protected or sensitive data. http://blg.com/en/News-And-Publications/Publication_4694

15 For example, the Canadian Anti-Fraud Centre and several training resources offered by the CCIRC (i.e. Advanced Persistent Threat Guide (APTG), Cyber Security Technical Advice/Guidance/Training, DDOS Mitigation guide, Cyber Safe Guide for Small and Medium Businesses, Malware Removal Guide, and Industrial Control System (ICS) Guide. Additionally, the Canadian Radio-television and Telecommunications Commission (CRTC) scam reporting system has an elaborate guide explaining how to protect Canadians from scams.

16 "In 2015, the Government of Canada introduced a number of legislative amendments and programs in an effort to keep pace with the digital economy and growing cyberthreats to Canadian businesses and citizens. These initiatives, meant to strengthen our collective cyber resiliency, require Canadian businesses of all sizes, and any Canadian organizations that store personal data, to update their cyber road maps to bring them into compliance". Source: CGI (2016). Will Canada's Cybersecurity Legislation Impact Your Business? Be aware of your obligations. Canada. www.cgi.com/sites/default/files/white-papers/canada-cybersecurity-legislation-white-paper.pdf

17 "Achieving 'perfect' cyber security is a wasted effort if the cyber components of critical cyber systems are physically accessible by unauthorized personnel. Securing critical systems inside fortress-like facilities will not achieve the desired effect if personnel who have access to these facilities have not been properly vetted. Information Security measures can only go so far if procedural security measures – such as not having several levels of approval in place within an organization prior to authorizing the transfer of funds based on an online or telephone request – are not in and of themselves rigorous" (p. 5). Public Safety Canada. "Cyber Security Guideline for the G7 Summit." Ottawa: Canadian Cyber Incident Response Centre, 2018.

18 The Privacy Act, and the Personal Information Protection and Electronic Documents Act (PIPEDA).

Suggested reading

Fundamentals of Cyber Security for Canada's Critical Infrastructure Community. *Building a Safe and Resilient Canada*. www.publicsafety.gc.ca/cnt/rsrcs/pblctns/2016-fndmntls-cybr-scrty-cmmnty/2016-fndmntls-cybr-Scrty-cmmnty-en.pdf

Public Safety Canada. "Cyber Incident Management Framework for Canada." www.publicsafety.gc.ca/cnt/rsrcs/pblctns/cbr-ncdnt-frmwrk/index-en.aspx

Public Safety Canada. "National Strategy for Critical Infrastructure." www.publicsafety.gc.ca/cnt/rsrcs/pblctns/srtg-crtcl-nfrstrctr/index-en.aspx

Public Safety Canada. "Canada's Cyber Security Strategy: For a Stronger and More Prosperous Canada." http://publications.gc.ca/collections/collection_2010/sp-ps/PS4-102-2010-eng.pdf

Public Safety Canada. "Canadian Cyber Incident Response Centre (CCIRC)." www.publicsafety.gc.ca/cnt/ntnl-scrt/cbr-scrt/ccirc-ccric-en.aspx

References

Alexander, D. C. (2014a). Cyber threats against the North Atlantic Treaty Organization (NATO) and selected responses. *İstanbul Gelişim Üniversitesi Sosyal Bilimler Dergisi (Istanbul Gelisim University Social Sciences Journal)*, 1(2), 1–36.

Alexander, D. C. (2014b). "Kuzey Atlantik Antlaşması Örgütü'ne (NATO) Karşı Siber Tehditler Ve Seçilmiş Yanıtlar," *İstanbul Gelişim Üniversitesi Sosyal Bilimler Dergisi, 1*(2): 1–36.

CCDCOE. (2017). "Back to Square One? the Fifth UN GGE Fails to Submit a Conclusive Report at the UN General Assembly Estonia: NATO Coopeative Cyber Defence Center of Excellence."

CGI. (2016). "Will Canada's Cybersecurity Legislation Impact Your Business? Be Aware of Your Obligations." www.cgi.com/sites/default/files/white-papers/canada-cybersecurity-legislation-white-paper.pdf

CIRA. (2018). "2018 CIRA Canadian Internet Security Survey."

CISION. (2017). "Majority of Canadians Support Privacy Act Reform, Greater Transparency by Government, Businesses: Poll." www.newswire.ca/news-releases/majority-of-canadians-support-priv acy-act-reform-greater-transparency-by-government-businesses-poll-611876805.html

Communications Security Establishment. (2014). "Mission, Vision and Values." www.cse-cst.gc.ca/en/ about-apropos/vision-mission

Coop, A. (2017). "Cyber Security a Growing Concern for Canadians." www.itworldcanada.com/art icle/cyber-security-a-growing-concern-to-canadians/399641

Farrell, P. (2013). "History of 5-Eyes – Explainer." www.theguardian.com/world/2013/dec/02/history-of-5-eyes-explainer

Freedman, B. J. (2017). "Cyber Risk Management – G7 Cybersecurity Guidelines For The Financial Sector." http://blg.com/en/News-And-Publications/Publication_4694

Gemalto. (2017). "Data Breach Database." https://breachlevelindex.com/data-breach-database

Global Affairs Canada. (2018). "Cybercrime." www.international.gc.ca/crime/cyber_crime-criminalite. aspx?lang=eng&_ga=2.127330884.892494619.1525240450-492751339.1521087974

Government of Canada. (2015). "Canada Completes Ratification of Convention on Cybercrime." www. canada.ca/en/news/archive/2015/07/canada-completes-ratification-convention-cybercrime.html

Government of Canada. (2017). "Breach of Security Safeguards Regulations." www.gazette.gc.ca/rp-pr/ p1/2017/2017-09-02/html/reg1-eng.html

Government of Canada. (2018a). "Canada's Anti-Spam Legislation." www.fightspam.gc.ca/eic/site/030. nsf/eng/h_00241.html

Government of Canada. (2018b). "Canada's Cyber Security Strategy: For a Stronger and More Prosperous Canada." http://publications.gc.ca/site/eng/9.693830/publication.html

Government of Canada. (2018c). "Getcybersafe." www.getcybersafe.gc.ca/index-en.aspx

Hanna, J. (2017). "What Is the Five Eyes Intelligence Pact?" www.cnn.com/2017/05/25/world/uk-us-five-eyes-intelligence-explainer/index.html

Harris, K. (2018). "'Five Eyes' Allies Urge Digital Industry to Stop Child Pornographers, Terrorists." www.cbc.ca/news/politics/digital-security-online-five-eyes-pornography-terrorism-1.4803122

Innovation Science and Economic Development Canada. (2017). "Version 2.0 – Digital Canada 150 2.0." www.ic.gc.ca/eic/site/028.nsf/vwapj/DC150-2.0-EN.pdf/$FILE/DC150-2.0-EN.pdf

KERA News. (2012). "A Rare Case: Canadian Navy Officer Pleads Guilty To Selling Secrets To Russians." http://keranews.org/post/rare-case-canadian-navy-officer-pleads-guilty-selling-secrets-russians

Merriam-Webster. (2018). "Sovereignty." www.merriam-webster.com/dictionary/sovereignty

Mueller, M. (2017). "Debates on Global Governance and Cybersecurity." www.internetgovernance. org/2017/04/03/debates-on-global-governance-and-cybersecurity/

Office of the Privacy Commissioner of Canada. (2016). "Public Opinion Survey." www.priv.gc.ca/en/ opc-actions-and-decisions/research/explore-privacy-research/2016/por_2016_12/#fig1

Office of the Privacy Commissioner of Canada. (2018a). "Privacy and Cyber Security: Emphasizingprivacy Protection in Cyber Security Activities." www.priv.gc.ca/en/opc-actions-and-decisions/research/ explore-privacy-research/2014/cs_201412/

Office of the Privacy Commissioner of Canada. (2018b). "Privacy Breaches." www.priv.gc.ca/en/priv acy-topics/privacy-breaches/

Public Safety Canada. (2010). "Canada's Cyber Security Strategy: For a Stronger and More Prosperous Canada." http://publications.gc.ca/collections/collection_2010/sp-ps/PS4-102-2010-eng.pdf

Public Safety Canada. (2016a). "Canadian Cyber Incident Response Centre (CCIRC)." www.publicsaf ety.gc.ca/cnt/ntnl-scrt/cbr-scrt/ccirc-ccric-en.aspx

Public Safety Canada. (2016b). "Fundamentals of Cyber Security for Canada's Critical Infrastructure Community," *Building a Safe and Resilient Canada.* www.publicsafety.gc.ca/cnt/rsrcs/pblctns/2016-fndmntls-cybr-scrty-cmmnty/2016-fndmntls-cybr-Scrty-cmmnty-en.pdf

Public Safety Canada. (2018a). "Cyber Incident Management Framework for Canada." www.publicsaf ety.gc.ca/cnt/rsrcs/pblctns/cbr-ncdnt-frmwrk/index-en.aspx

Public Safety Canada. (2018b). "National Strategy for Critical Infrastructure." www.publicsafety.gc.ca/ cnt/rsrcs/pblctns/srtg-crtcl-nfrstrctr/index-en.aspx

PWC. (2018). "The Global State of Information Security® Survey 2018." www.pwc.com/us/en/ser vices/consulting/cybersecurity/library/information-security-survey.html

Reuters Staff. (2017). "China, Canada Vow Not to Conduct Cyber Attacks on Private Sector." www. reuters.com/article/us-canada-china-cyber/china-canada-vow-not-to-conduct-cyber-attacks-on-pri vate-sector-idUSKBN19H06A

RSA Conference. (2017). "Power of Opportunity." www.rsaconference.com/events/us17

Segal, A. (2017). "The Development of Cyber Norms at the United Nations Ends in Deadlock. Now What?" www.cfr.org/blog/development-cyber-norms-united-nations-ends-deadlock-now-what

Smith, B. (2017). "The Need for Digital Geneva Convention." https://blogs.microsoft.com/on-the- issues/2017/02/14/need-digital-geneva-convention/

Solomon, H. (2017). "Focus on Security Basics and Be Good at Them, Says Risk Consultant." www. itworldcanada.com/article/focus-on-security-basics-and-be-good-at-them-says-risk-consultant/ 398876

The US Department of Justice. (2017). "Canadian Hacker Who Conspired with and Aided Russian FSB Officers Pleads Guilty." www.justice.gov/opa/pr/canadian-hacker-who-conspired-and-aided-rus sian-fsb-officers-pleads-guilty

Theiler, O. (2015). "New Threats: The Cyber-dimension." www.nato.int/docu/review/2011/11-sep tember/Cyber-Threads/EN/index.htm

United Nations. (2015). "*Group of Governmental Experts on Developments in the Field of Information and Telecommunications in the Context of International Security Seventeeth Session, Developments in the Field of Information and Telecommunications in the Context of International Security.*" New York: UN General Assembly.

Yeli, H. (2017). *A Three-Perspective Theory of Cyber Sovereignty* (Vol. 2). China: China International Institute for Strategic Society.

39

THE UNITED STATES

A declining hegemon in cyberspace?

Mary Manjikian

Introduction

In considering the cybersecurity policy and position of the United States, in particular, it is necessary to begin with the unique circumstances surrounding the creation of the internet itself. Beginning in the 1960s, the United States led the effort to create what became today's internet. That is, the bulk of the research and funding for the initial creation of the internet was provided by the United States government, while the bulk of early technology development took place in California's Silicon Valley. As a result, it would not be a stretch to say that the internet itself was born in the United States. US government efforts to create an interconnected system for carrying data began in 1966, with the allocation of resources for this project taken from the US Defense Department's Ballistic Missile Program. The original ARPAnet, begun in 1969, connected four research facilities in the United States. New civilian, military, and academic nodes were added throughout the 1970s and 1980s, with the technology gradually spreading to include overseas addresses. In 1990, the US military withdrew from its controlling position within the internet, although the US government continued to offer financial support to international groups like the International Commission for the Assignment of Network Names (ICANN) and the Internet Society with funds administered by the United States' National Science Foundation.[1] The construction of physical hardware (the internet's "backbone") to carry the data internally within the United States and eventually to overseas locations as well was administered by the National Science Foundation and constructed by American-based international corporations including IBM and MCI (Tyson, n.d.).

America's historic leading role in cybersecurity development

Owing to the fact that the internet was born in America, the United States arguably has historically enjoyed certain built-in advantages in regards to developing its cybersecurity posture. US planners and technology developers have made decisions which have established procedures and rules for how the internet has been structured and how it behaves. Such acts include investing in the creation and placement of vital hardware including data cables to setting precedents in regard to issues like data storage and data transmission protocols. As a first mover in this new environment, US protocols and procedures have often proven to be the blueprint which other nations have followed as they move into this technological sphere. That is, the United States has historically acted as a norm giver in establishing behavioral expectations in the online environment.

In its initial phases of development, the internet itself might have been described as having a uniquely "American flavor" since many software and hardware designers believed in and advanced principles such as minimal regulation and state interference (aligning with the political philosophy of libertarianism) (Manjikian, 2020). At the same time, US foreign policy initiatives aimed at extending the internet's reach globally were often intertwined or linked with foreign policy goals such as overcoming global poverty including information poverty and advancing causes such as freedom of information and freedom of the press (Manjikian, 2020).

The United States has also played a key role in setting the terms and standards of the debate regarding how best to defend "national cyberspace." The US was the first nation to draw up a National Strategy to Secure Cyberspace in 2003. This document, issued by America's then new Department of Homeland Security, described the threat posed to American cyberspace, including the possibility that terrorists could use this space to mobilize support for their message and draw adherents. The United States was also the first nation to establish a national military Cyber Command in 2009 and took an early lead in drawing up strategic doctrines governing what it has dubbed the Fifth Domain (Manjikian, 2020) (the other strategic domains are land, sea, air, and space). Indeed, the notion of utilizing cyberspace technology for offensive purposes (as a WME or Weapon of Mass Effect) can be traced back to the US Strategic Deterrence Joint Operating Concept of 2004.

The United States is also credited with having jointly developed one of the first cyberweapons, along with Israel, in 2005. The Stuxnet worm, which targeted Iran, caused substantial damage to Iran's nuclear program.

Today, US planners are key framers of strategic cyberspace doctrines in areas such as active cyber defense, as well as in the increasing use of artificial intelligence to identify and respond to emerging cyber threats. The United States also developed what has come to serve as the model for cyberthreat intelligence sharing and cyber emergency response between the commercial and government sectors, through the creation of Cyber Emergency Response Teams (CERTs). Indeed, the first CERT was developed in 1988 at Carnegie Mellon University. This model has been widely adopted throughout the world, based on the US example.

US military and civilian government officials were also among the first analysts to identify the ways in which cyber threats were not freestanding but were instead intimately intertwined with all sectors of a nation's economic, political, and social infrastructure. Beginning in 2005, the United States Department of Homeland Security defined the notion of critical infrastructure, pointing to sixteen sectors of America's infrastructure (from water purification to transportation) which were uniquely vulnerable to cyber-attacks, and which required specific measures to harden the targets and put in place measures to assure their resilience (Brown et al., 2006). At the same time, the United States government worked to defend American economic assets in cyberspace, through, for example, lobbying for the extension of intellectual property protections to work which existed and was stored in cyberspace.

An early awareness of the deadly potential of cyberconflict and the possibility that conflicts which began in cyberspace could escape cyberspaces' "leaky borders" with real world consequences also caused the United States government to take a leading role in the development of rules and procedures aimed at stemming and preventing cyber conflict on a global scale. For this reason, the United States has played a key role in the development of international legal frameworks for governing cyberspace. The lead analyst involved in the development of NATO's Tallinn Manual 1.0 and Tallinn Manual 2.0, both of which deal with the applicability of international law, including the Laws of Armed Conflict to cyberspace, is an American academic, Michael Schmitt.

The United States US Cyber Command has taken a key role in crafting cyber deterrence strategies, as well as in the area of creating confidence-building measures in cyberspace, seeking to prevent the escalation of conflicts between states through the creation of information sharing mechanisms and joint cyber exercises (Manjikian, 2015). At the same time, the United States Department of Commerce has been involved in efforts to prevent the export of cyberweapons to American adversaries, and to prevent the deployment of cyber code in ways which would violate citizens' rights to privacy and freedom of expression. Such efforts have included the extension of export regimes now in use for other types of weapons – such as biological and chemical weapons – to the export of cyberweapons and surveillance software through the international Wassenaar Arrangement agreement (Manjikian, 2020).

From an American perspective, such developments might appear to be largely positive, and indeed, US politicians have argued historically that the United States has a unique responsibility, as the internet's founder, to act as a guard of international system space and as a guarantor of peace and stability within that environment.

Is America still the hegemon in cyberspace?

At the same time, however, despite its leading position as a developer of cyberspace doctrines and capabilities, the United States has certainly not been immune from being the subject of cyber-attacks itself. Indeed, the 2018 US National Cyber Strategy notes that the United States has in recent years been the target of cyber-attacks by Iran, North Korea, and Russia, as well as the target of large-scale Chinese industrial espionage (DeVore & Lee, 2017). In addition, the United States was the subject of significant and large-scale attempts at hacking during the 2016 American president election. Therefore, we might ask if the seeming inability of the United States to defend against Russian attacks upon its electoral system beginning in 2016 suggest that it is perhaps poorly equipped or even failing in its attempts to defend its cyberspace and its population (Deval, 2019). Has the US begun to lose its leading position?

In recent years, analysts have begun to suggest that any unique advantages which the United States might have enjoyed in cyberspace as a result of its initial leading position in this environment have been waning, with new competitors in cyberspace increasing in number and power (Gilli & Gilli, 2019). The 2018 United States Department of Defense Cyber Strategy notes that the US is engaged in a "long-term strategic competition with China and Russia" (United States Department of Defense, 2018). Here, US analysts have identified three types of advantages which China may have, in comparison to the United States, in increasing its power position in cyberspace. First, China has been engaged in long-term, coordinated efforts to carry out cyber espionage, stealing US trade secrets and deploying the resulting technologies for commercial advantage. Next, China has engaged in a long-term, coordinated effort to build influence within the region of Asia through investment in the so-called One Belt, One Road initiatives, including the creation of a so-called Digital Silk Road which would stretch throughout Southeast Asia to Pakistan. Finally,

China perhaps enjoys advantages as an autocratic, one-party state, since it has the ability to compel both public and private actors to carry out defense measures that would be questionable in a democratic regime.

In contrast to the United States, China's government is able to filter and control internet content going into and out of China, as well as seeking to roll-back the anonymous nature of the internet (as traditionally understood) in favor of building a more restrictive domestic internet in which citizens are not anonymous but rather registered, with their digital and real identities closely linked (Segal, 2018). Indeed, as Klimburg has noted, in today's environment authoritarian regimes – including Russia – may have an advantage in defending their cyberspace, since they are in a better position to compel private internet service providers to implement specific policies in the areas of surveillance and cybersecurity (Klimburg, 2011). In recent years, nations like India, Russia, and China, as well as a number of nations in Africa, have been successful in utilizing a so-called "internet kill switch" to shut down regional and national internet communications during periods of social, economic or political disruption. In contrast, the notion that the United States should have an internet kill switch available to the president – in order to respond to, for example, the quick spread of an internet virus, was widely opposed by citizens and government officials when President Obama broached it during his tenure in office (Stoddart, 2016).

That is, American culture has historically been libertarian and distrustful of "big government" solutions to economic, political, and social problems. Americans often express distrust of what they view as government overreach into their private lives. Not surprisingly, a majority of Americans (57 percent) feel that it is unacceptable for the government to monitor their private internet communications, or to view their private data – unless a citizen is suspected of having committed a crime, including terrorism (Geiger, 2018). In the American climate, then, legislators like New York State Representative Alexandra Ocasio-Cortez have voiced their opposition to new forms of biometric surveillance, arguing that adopting such technologies is inappropriate in a democratic regime (Darnell, 2019).

At the same time, recent events in the United States, such as the large-scale Russian attack on America's electoral system carried out through the vectors of social media beginning in 2016, suggest that American planners may have seriously underestimated America's vulnerability to new and novel forms of information warfare and cyberwarfare – including those associated with age-old Russian strengths in the areas of psychological operations and disinformation. Here it is possible that the significant advantages which America enjoyed for so long as the "internet's creator" may have led American military and intelligence analysts to become complacent. Believing that the United States enjoyed a commanding lead in both cyberspace defensive and offensive capabilities, America's defense community failed to recognize the fact that social media represented an undefended flank which was ripe for attack by America's adversaries (Riotta, 2019).

In addition, many of the specifically "American" facets of the internet – such as the capacity for anonymous communication and an absence of filtering – are being rethought in other nations, as governments strive to articulate and implement their own visions for "their" cyberspace. While previously such capacities were regarded as innate facets of the internet itself, in point of fact new nations are creating their own versions of the internet which do not include such abilities. Indeed, analysts now suggest that an open, free internet may be uniquely positioned as a threat vector in ways that a more authoritarian internet might not be. The threat, for example, of widespread societal disruption created through forms of online psychological warfare and social media engineering, is much greater in a society characterized by freedom of expression and lacking a filtering mechanism like China's "great firewall." As a result, technological and political characteristics of the American internet which previously appeared as strengths now increasingly appear to be weaknesses.

A waning capabilities gap between the US and its competitors

Analysts like Joseph Nye have warned, quite presciently, that the United States should not expect to maintain its significant leading position as *primus inter pares* (or first among many) in the international rankings of cybersecurity powers. In comparison to the resources required (including money, education, and manpower) to achieve a leading position in the development of conventional or nuclear weapons, a nation can relatively cheaply and quickly increase its rankings among cyber powers (Nye, 2016). For that reason, cyberweapons are viewed as an asymmetric threat which could as easily be wielded by a small nation as by a powerful nation.

Global rankings of cyber capability are thus extremely dynamic. Today, Sanger suggests that there are actually seven significant cyber powers (which he refers to as the "seven sisters of cyber conflict"), namely the United States, Russia, China, Britain, Iran, Israel, and North Korea. These are nations with established cyber capabilities which have carried out significant events in the cyber arena. However, he notes that there are other nations – from Vietnam to Mexico – who are closing in as players in this arena (Sanger, 2018). Indeed, China in particular has articulated its desire to "catch up and overtake" the United States in cyber power rankings, describing its wish to "leapfrog" over existing powers to take the lead (Brenner & Lindsay, 2015).

As other nations are achieving significant cyber capabilities, they are also making claims to have the ability to articulate cyber doctrines in keeping with their own national norms and forming new alliances and power groupings. Here, we can point to the creation of new players in cyberspace like the Shanghai Cooperation Organization (SCO), formed in 2001 (India Today, 2018).

At the same time, American efforts to guide and steer the development of the internet – politically, economically, and culturally – have been met with suspicion by many other nations, including America's historic adversaries. The understanding that America has a unique role to play in the internet's development has been interrogated, particularly in the wake of developments such as the 2013 revelations by Edward Snowden regarding the extent of internet surveillance occurring by the United States National Security Agency. Today, the United States lags behind other actors – like the European Union – in the articulation of doctrines related to information and data privacy, for example. The EU has taken the leading role in articulating norms and policies related to protecting user privacy and combatting cybercrime. At the same time, other nations – like China – have sought to change their own identities – moving from a position of being "norm takers" to instead being "norm setters" in the international environment. – through the advancement of initiatives like China's Digital Silk Road (Zeng, 2017).

Today, we have good reason to ask if the United States is still, and will remain as primus inter pares, serving as a global hegemon within the internet – or if instead the global internet is already in the process of fragmenting into regional blocs or along national lines. Particularly within the last ten years, we can identify national responses by other nations aimed at advancing and defending claims to administer and steer the development of their own national cyberspace. Nations like China and Russia in particular have questioned the notion that the United States should play a leading role in the development and administration of international cyberspace and have furthermore raised questions regarding whether today's internet even requires a global hegemon.

Roadblocks to the development of US cybersecurity policy

In recent years, information security professionals have begun to speak of "information security culture" which can be defined as the package of both attitudes and procedures which members of an organization maintain and follow in reference to the preservation of a company's information security. Information security culture includes such factors as how employees understand their roles and responsibilities in maintaining information security, the ways in which information security breaches are addressed by a company's leadership and how people understand the risks associated with information security breaches (Beaver, 2015).

One might argue that nations also have information security cultures. The citizens of a nation may have different attitudes regarding how they view their rights and responsibilities in the online environment, how they view the role of government in policing and securing that environment, and what they regard as acceptable and unacceptable uses of the online environment. Nations may also have different policies and procedures for addressing information security breaches – and may differ in terms of which actors are involved and how those actors interact with the national government.

In thinking about the challenges which the United States in particular has encountered in developing cybersecurity policies, it can be argued that US information security culture is unique in three aspects: First, the United States is unique in that many of the major non-state actors who have been key figures in shaping and creating the online environment (such as Twitter, Google, and Microsoft) were created within and are located within the United States. Such corporations thus work closely with the United States government. However, at the same time, these corporations do not conceptualize themselves as uniquely American corporations, nor do they necessarily regard their position of adherence to American rules, procedures, and norms as primary to their identities. Thus, in the years since the advent of these actors, the United States has struggled to manage these actors, and to articulate the exact nature of its relationship to these actors.

Here, Segal suggests that in recent years, a sort of "divorce" has taken place between Silicon Valley and Washington, DC. In many aspects, private actors still do cooperate with government actors, namely through the creation of public–private partnerships (PPPs), particularly in areas like combatting online crime. Today, public–private partnerships include the Online Trust Alliance (OTA) and the Industry Botnet Group (IBG). In addition, groups like the National Cyber-Forensics and Training Alliance (NCFTA) – with more than 80 businesses – provide cyber threat intelligence to national and international CERTS (U.S. Senate, 2014). Microsoft maintains a Cyber Threat Intelligence Program (C-TIP) which makes information about botnets available to both internet service providers and US-government sponsored Computer Emergency Response Teams (CERTs). Microsoft is also working with states internationally, including making an agreement with Spain's Computer Emergency Response Team, INTECO. Today, Microsoft also maintains a Digital Crimes Unit (DCU) with more than 100 technical and legal experts, who work to fight cybercrime and improve cybersecurity.

However, American-based technology corporations have also articulated policy positions which have been at odds with stated American cybersecurity aims. For example, in the aftermath of the 2015 San Bernardino terrorist attack, the United States Federal Bureau of Investigation sued the Apple Corporation for access to the cellphone records belonging to one of the terrorists. An ongoing legal dispute centered around whether US cellphone manufacturers should be required to build a "back door" into their devices which would allow US law enforcement to access user information. Secondary issues centered around the territorial jurisdictions in which US requests might prevail (for example, if data produced by an American user was stored outside the United States at an Apple facility in Europe, was Apple still legally obligated to turn over this information to US law enforcement?). And in 2016, Facebook founder Mark Zuckerberg testified before the US Congress regarding the fact that Facebook had sold advertising of a political nature on its platform in the months leading up to the US presidential election. US legislators argued that Zuckerberg and his team should have exercised due diligence in verifying who the purchasers of these advertisements were in order to safeguard against undue foreign interference in an American election. Zuckerberg famously responded that Facebook is merely a "platform which hosts content," and that its ethical and legal responsibility for policing that content was therefore limited (Chander, 2012). Furthermore, he seemed to suggest that Facebook did not have a greater responsibility towards the American government in this regard than it had towards any other government.

America is thus in a unique position. As the territorial host of many of these international technology corporations, the US is obliged to work closely with them, particularly in regard to combatting issues like the growth of hate speech or terrorist organizing online. However, due to the fact that these actors are private corporations, the final responsibility for deciding, for example, which actors are too dangerous to be allowed to have a social media presence (and should therefore be "deplatformed") will ultimately be not the state's but rather the corporations' (Chander, 2012). At the same time, there is not strong legislation mandating that such corporations prioritize US security interests over their other corporate policies and priorities, nor are there corporate norms regarding this issue (in contrast, private corporations headquartered in China and Russia may encounter much stricter legal regulations regarding their policy priorities and responsibilities).

Today, American legislators have proposed breaking up monopoly corporations like Facebook in order to stem the power which nonstate actors have for deciding such issues, in comparison to the limited powers of the states. Other initiatives have focused on creating new types of public–private partnerships in which states and corporations will work together to combat such threats. As corporations create new technologies in fields like artificial intelligence and data analytics, the need to more clearly articulate and regulate how states will work together with these actors becomes clear.

A second unique aspect of America's cybersecurity culture today is the fact that throughout the Trump Administration's tenure in particular, American foreign policy has tended towards a position of isolationism and an "America First" agenda, which has been perceived by many as a relinquishing of America's leading role in the world. As Wickett, Smith, and Smart (2017) note:

> Trump's outlook is more nationalist than isolationist. He is not proposing US withdrawal from the world *per se*, but he has a narrower interpretation of vital American interests than his predecessors did and will likely assess international engagements in more transactional terms. His "America first" campaign posture implies limited recognition of the global common good, or appetite for intervention to uphold it.

A weaker commitment to a "global public good," might easily translate into a weaker US commitment towards supporting the continued resilience and security of the internet itself as a global public good. Particularly if President Trump achieves a second term in the 2020 election, we might expect to see a weaker American financial and organizational commitment to supporting initiatives such as the sharing of cyberthreat intelligence and cybersecurity training opportunities with allies, including those within the European Union and NATO. Such an outcome could create a markedly differently cyber landscape not only in the United States but globally. At present, one cannot identify a significant American response to China's Digital Silkroad initiative, for example, and despite the American announcement that steps are being taken towards the development of a Space Command to provide for the security of digital satellites and data streams, few concrete steps have been taken towards the securing of this objective.

In addition, we might expect that private corporations will step into a void left by a decreased US presence internationally, particularly in the area of cybersecurity. Thus, it is not surprising that, for example, private corporations have cooperated to issue the 2017 International Asilomar Declaration on the ethical development of artificial intelligence, laying out principles for the ethical development of artificial intelligence from an industry perspective. Here, private corporations have been quicker to articulate principles, form a consensus, and issue statements than any official bodies, like the United States Department of Defense, have (Alexander, 2017).

A final aspect of United States cybersecurity culture which can be described as unique is the way in which American cybersecurity actors have sought to balance the twin requirements of articulating pragmatic procedures for reacting to specific actual and proposed cybersecurity breaches, while simultaneously seeking to articulate a more broad set of principles at a higher level of abstraction. Under President Obama's leadership, the United States was faulted for framing responses to specific incidents, but without laying out a global theory regarding what sorts of cyber-attacks would lead to what specific consequences. However, more recently analysts have argued in discussing a security breach which targeted the United States Office of Management and Budget, that the United States has perhaps proven to be better at the articulation of large-scale strategic doctrines and blueprints than it has been in implementing specific cybersecurity practices (Dourado & O'Sullivan, n.d.).

That is, while the US Cyber Command has articulated key doctrines in the areas of cyber deterrence, cyber arms control and active cyber defense, it is still unclear what, if anything, the United States will do if attacks occur on the 2020 national election. (Here, as Dora Devin points out, it may be that the exact response which are taken in cyberspace are by definition less public than a conventional response might be, and a result there is a coherent policy which is classified and of which observers are unaware. However, if this is the case, it has perhaps not been effective up until now.)

The American experience is thus unique – while other countries may have begun from a position of weakness to build a strong cybersecurity culture, legislation, and policies, the United States may be in the position of watching its innate advantages as an early adopter decay over time. And just as early internet analysts suggested that only a devasting event like a "cyber Pearl Harbor" would be sufficient to make policymakers and citizens alike aware of the dangers created by an insufficiently strong cyber policy, one might again ask what sorts of events could potentially lead to a rethinking of America's current cybersecurity postures in the areas of public–private cooperation and the commitment of strategic resources.

Note

1 This is not to say, of course, that the United States was solely responsible for the internet's creation – or indeed that the United States could have created the internet independently as its own product. Indeed, the technology known as packet switching which enabled the transfer of information across networks was developed by British computer scientist Donald Davies and developed in the United

Kingdom. And many of the key developers of anti-virus and computer security software worked for companies outside the United States, including in Russia and India. However, the bulk of the organizing and funding for the original project was American and thus the development of the internet could be described as American-led.

Suggested reading

CSIS. (2020). "Significant Cyber Incidents." https://csis-prod.s3.amazonaws.com/s3fs-public/200306_Significant_Cyber_Events_List.pdf?qRZXF65CUUOKTOl9rLVBMJhXfXtmJZMj

Taylor, R. W., Fritsch, E. J., Saylor, M. R. & Tafoya, W. L. (2018). *Cyber Crime and Cyber Terrorism*. London: Pearson.

Valeriano, B. & Jensen, B. (2019, January 15). *The Myth of the Cyber Offense: The Case for Restraint*. Washington, DC: CATO Institute. cato.org/publications/policy-analysis/myth-cyber-offense-case-restraint

Van Puyvelde, D. & Brantly, A. (2017). *US National Cybersecurity: International Politics, Concepts and Organization*. Abingdon, Routledge.

The White House. (2018, September). "National Cyber Strategy of the United States of America." www.whitehouse.gov/wp-content/uploads/2018/09/National-Cyber-Strategy.pdf

References

Alexander, S. (2017, February 6). "Notes from the Asilomar Conference on Beneficial AI." https://slatestarcodex.com/2017/02/06/notes-from-the-asilomar-conference-on-beneficial-ai/

Beaver, K. (2015, September 28). "The Importance of a Security Culture across the Organization," Securityintelligence.com. https://securityintelligence.com/the-importance-of-a-security-culture-across-the-organization/

Brenner, J. & Lindsay, J. R. (2015). "Correspondence: Debating the Chinese Cyber Threat," *International Security*, 40(1): 191–195.

Brown, G., Carlye, M., Salmeron, J. & Wood, K. (2006). "Defending Critical Infrastructure," *Interfaces*, 36(6): 530–544.

Chander, A. (2012). "Facebookistan," *North Carolina Law Review*, 1807(90). https://scholarship.law.unc.edu/nclr/vol90/iss5/15Facebookistan

Darnell, C. (2019, May 22). "Concern over Facial Recognition Technology Unites Progressive and Conservatives in Congress," Yahoo News. https://news.yahoo.com/concern-over-facial-recognition-technology-unites-progressives-and-conservatives-in-congress-234327186.html

Deval, D. (2019). "The U.S. Response to the 2016 Russian Election Meddling and the Evolving National Strategic Thought in Cyberspace: (Part 2)," *Academic and Applied Research in Military and Public Management Science*, 18(1): 59–77.

DeVore, M. R. & Lee, S. (2017). "APT (Advanced Persistent Threat)s and Influence: Cyber Weapons and the Changing Calculus of Conflict," *The Journal of East Asian Affairs*, 31(1): 39–64. Retrieved from www.jstor.org/stable/pdf/44321272.pdf

Dourado, E. & O'Sullivan, A. (n.d.). "Poor Federal Cybersecurity Reveals Weakness of Technocratic Approach." www.mercatus.org/publications/technology-and-innovation/poor-federal-cybersecurity-reveals-weakness-technocratic

Geiger, A. W. (2018, June 4). "How Americans Have Viewed Government Surveillance and Privacy since the Snowden Leaks," *Pew Research*. www.pewresearch.org/fact-tank/2018/06/04/how-americans-have-viewed-government-surveillance-and-privacy-since-snowden-leaks/

Gilli, A. & Gilli, M. (2019). "Why China Has Not Caught up Yet: Military-Technological Superiority and the Limits of Imitation, Reverse Engineering and Cyber Espionage," *International Security*, 43(3): 141–189.

IndiaToday.in. (2018, June 10). "What Is the Shanghai Cooperation Organization and Why Is Its Membership Crucial for India?" *India Today*. www.indiatoday.in/education-today/gk-current-affairs/story/what-is-shanghai-cooperation-organisation-and-why-does-its-membership-matter-for-india-1256624-2018-06-10

Klimburg, A. (2011). "The Whole of Nation in Cyber Power," *Georgetown Journal of International Affairs*: 171–179. www.jstor.org/stable/pdf/43133826.pdf?refreqid=excelsior%3A76a84e45ce1ae5ce3507a0e ea771e4c6

Manjikian, M. (2020). *Cyber Politics and Policies*. Washington, DC: CQ Press.

Manjikian, M. (2015). "Confidence-building in Cyberspace: A Comparison of Territorial and Weapons-based Regimes," Strategic Studies Institute, US Army War College, Carlisle, United States.

Nye, J. (2016). "Deterrence and Dissuasion in Cyberspace," *International Security*, *41*(3): 44–71.

Riotta, C. (2019, October 9). "Russia Used Social Media to Support Trump in 2016 at Direction at Kremlin, Senate Intelligence Report Says," *Independent*. www.independent.co.uk/news/world/americas/ us-politics/trump-russia-2016-intelligence-report-read-kremlin-facebook-a9148036.html

Sanger, D. E. (2018). *The Perfect Weapon: War, Sabotage, and Fear in the Cyber Age*. New York: Crown.

Segal, A. (2018). "When China Rules the Web: Technology in Service of the State," *Foreign Affairs*, *97* (5): 10–18.

Stoddart, K. (2016). "Live Free or Die Hard: US-UK Cyber Policies," *Political Science Quarterly*, *131*(4): 803–842.

Tyson, J. (n.d.). "How Internet Infrastructure Works." https://computer.howstuffworks.com/internet/ basics/internet-infrastructure4.htm

United States Department of Defense. (2018). "Summary: Department of Defense Cyber Strategy." https://media.defense.gov/2018/Sep/18/2002041658/-1/-1/1/CYBER_STRATEGY_SUMMARY_ FINAL.PDF

U.S. Senate, Committee on the Judiciary, Subcommittee on Crime and Terrorism. (2014, July 15). "Taking Down Botnets: Public and Private Efforts to Disrupt and Dismantle Cybercriminal Networks." www.judiciary.senate.gov/meetings/taking-down-botnets_public-and-private-efforts- to-disrupt-and-dismantle-cybercriminal-networks

Wickett, X., Smith, J., & Smart, C. "America's International Role under Donald Trump." Chatham House Reports. January 18, 2017. https://www.chathamhouse.org/publication/americas-international- role-under-donald-trump

Zeng, J. (2017). "Does Europe Matter? the Role of Europe in Chinese Narratives of 'One Belt, One Road' and 'New Type of Great Power Relations,'" *Journal of Common Market Studies*, *55*(5): 1162–1176.

40

JAMAICA'S CYBERCRIME AND CYBER-SECURITY

Policies, laws, and strategies

Suzette A. Haughton

Introduction

Cybercrime is a global problem and trends have indicated that the financial sector is a highly targeted area for cyber criminals. In 2015, the global estimate of the cost of cybercrime stood at USD $500 billion and projections are that by December 2019 cybercrime cost will increase to USD $2 trillion. However, these estimates are modest as the Global Risk Report (2016) noted that significant incidents of cybercrimes go undetected (The Global Risk Report, 2016). The threats posed to states are glaring as their internet interconnectivity and computer usage increases. Hence, rising cyber dependency is ranked among the 13 risks identified on the *Risk Trend Interconnections Map* produced by the 2018 Global Risk Report. Cyber-attacks and data frauds or theft were also listed as critical risk-imperatives for 2018 (The Global Risk Report, 2018).

Brenner (2012) argues that policing cybercrime is challenging for law enforcers. She noted that this difficulty is further complicated as the commission of cybercrimes involve the perpetrators and victims residing in separate countries. Therefore, the authority of police officers is restricted to the state's territorial borders and unlike cybercriminals they must operate within their respective nation-states. Additionally, globalization is fueling cybercrimes into what Castells (1998) refers to as the global criminal economy, including cybercrime, terrorism, drugs, and people trafficking.

The globalization of markets and interconnectedness of states coupled with the reliance on information and communication technologies require that developed and developing states must institute measures to address cybercrime. As a developing country, Jamaica is particularly vulnerable to cybercrime attacks. In the past decade, it has exponentially increased its internet usage among businesses, the state, and citizens. Additionally, cybercriminals may view Jamaica as a soft target to launch cyber-attacks due to calculations that the state's weak financial status could impact on its acquisition of sophisticated cyber detection and prevention tools. Given this reality, cyber-security is a policy priority identified by the Government of Jamaica as it is important to protect personal, businesses', and the state's data, networks, and systems in cyberspace.

This chapter addresses the challenging problem of curtailing cybercrime for the Jamaican state. First, it explores the definition of cybercrime and cyber-security within the context of the agreed definitions used by the international community of states. It notes the integrated relationship existing between both terms while also discussing their differences. Second, the chapter assesses Jamaica's cyber-security strategies used in curbing cybercrimes. In this regard, it discusses Jamaica's Cybercrimes Act, its Cyber Security Strategy and two tangential Acts which support the Cybercrimes Law. Third, it assesses the role of the hemispheric group, the Organization of American States (OAS), in shaping Jamaica's cyber-security strategy. It also discusses cooperative mechanisms used in strengthening Jamaica's cyber-security policies and laws in order to confront cybercrimes.

Defining cybercrime and cyber-security

There is no consensus on the precise definition of cybercrime (Yar, 2013). Global norm-creating agencies have advanced different definitions of this concept. One such agency, the International Telecommunications Union (ITU) defines cybercrime as activities in which computers or networks are employed as tools, targets, or places for the execution of criminal acts. This definition broadly explains cybercrime although it places emphasis on the activity and not the actor who executes these criminal acts. Hence, it is difficult for researchers to operationalize it to specifically address cybercriminals in the penal system.

Wall (2007) defines cybercrimes as crimes occurring within cyberspace and involves online insecurity and risks (Wall, 2007: 10). A more precise definition of cybercrime is provided by the Council of Europe's Convention on cybercrime. It stipulates four categories of cybercrime. The first category covers offences contrary to confidentiality, integrity, and availability of data and computer systems. Matters such as hacking, phishing, interception, and interference are included under this category. The second category refers to content offences inclusive of child pornography, hate message, libel, and spam. The third category covers computer-related offences such a fraud, forgery, identity theft, and money laundering. The final component covers copyright and trade-mark related offences such as music downloads and file sharing (Convention on Cybercrime, 2001).

Some scholars, such as Wall (2001) and Yar (2013), have categorized cybercrimes into four categories. These are cyber-trespass, cyber-deceptions and theft, cyber-pornography, and cyber-violence. Cyber-trespass involves the entry into others' property and this normally results in damage. Examples of cyber-trespass include hacking, defacement, and viruses. Cyber-deception and theft normally include the stealing of money or identity through credit card frauds, identity theft, or intellectual property violations. Cyber-pornography violates laws on sexual vulgarity. Finally, cyber-violence involves the imposition of psychological or physical harm by violating the rights pertaining to the protection of persons, such as inciting violence through hate speeches or by stalking (Wall, 2001; Yar, 2013).

The Council of Europe and the classifications advanced by scholars have provided a comprehensive guide on the categories of cybercrime. However, the definitions do not capture the transnational complexities of cybercrime since these crimes transcend national geographic borders and are often complex, multifaceted acts which span multiple categories. Nevertheless, these two definitions from international sources form the authority on cybercrime in the absence of a global consensus-based definitional framework on this concept.

On the other hand, ITU (2018: 13) provides a comprehensive definition of cyber-security.

the collection of tools, policies, guidelines, risk management, approaches, actions, trainings, best practices, assurances and technologies that can be used to protect the availability, integrity and confidentiality of assets in the connected infrastructures pertaining to government, private organisations and citizens, these assets include connected computing devices, personnel, infrastructure, applications, services, tele-communications systems and data in a cyber-environment.

In other words, cyber-security is the strategies employed to reduce the threats of damage, theft, or misuse posed to electronic devices and information. Cyber-security therefore aims to protect data but also computer systems and networks used by citizens, the public, and the private sector. Cyber-security is important because computer systems and networks are often connected to the internet and hence are vulnerable to cyber-attacks. Hence, securing computer systems and networks is central to protect data integrity and cyber-physical systems from threats posed by cyber-attackers.

Cybercrimes occur when criminals violate cyberspace to defame others, for ideological reasons and to obtain monies through fraudulent means. The adoption of cyber-security measures is therefore important to stem the flow of cybercrimes. The subsequent section assesses the intricate connections between both concepts.

The relationship between cybercrime and cyber-security

There is a profound connection between cyber-security and cybercrime. Cyber-security broadly provides the state's guidelines and policies designed to curtail cybercrime. In this regard, Tropina and Callanan (2015) have argued that given the nature of cybercrimes and the governmental necessity to provide regulation in cyber-security to protect critical information infrastructure, cyber-security has now emerged at the top of states' policy agendas.

However, there are four main differences emerging in the literature between cyber-security and cybercrime. First, there are different targets in the criminal acts committed under the umbrella of cyber-security and cybercrime. The crimes affecting cyber-security normally target computer networks, their hardware, and their software. These crimes popularly include viruses, worms, ransom-ware, and the denial of services as a result of the attack. Governmental agencies, their networks, and websites are particularly the target of such attacks. For instance, in 2015, the Jamaican State Minister of Science, Technology, Energy and Mining reported that the state-owned Jamaica Information Service (JIS) and five other entities were attacked by hackers who hit the JIS website and shut it down. The JIS website was replaced with a black screen with the caption "hacked by Team System DZ: I am Muslim & I love jihad. I love Islamic State." In the body of the message were these words:

> Message to all the peoples of the world and especially to governments, Islamic State List to restore the rights of Muslims who have been killed by your governments savage and unjust, Islamic State will restore dignity for Muslims. Will purge the land of the Muslims from hypocrite infidels. It intervenes you will equip you to dwell in cemeteries. Op USA & Israel. Hackers Islamic State/.2015 "Facebook."
>
> *(The Jamaica Observer, 2015)*

Though the language is not eloquently written, the message was nonetheless conveyed by the hackers in terms of the words expressed and the ability to deface the government's website. Given this situation, the State Minister noted that the Jamaican Constabulary Force (JCF), the national police, was investigating with the aim to find the source of the attack. Further, Jamaica's Cyber Incidents Response Team (CIRT), which comprises computer technical experts and cross-governmental agency representation, worked to plug loopholes so as to minimize similar future attacks. Unlike attacks targeted at cyber-security, cybercrime attacks target individuals and their data. The popular cybercrimes affecting people are cyberbullying, child pornography, sexting, and hate speech. Similarly, cyber deception and theft affect individuals through credit card fraud and identity theft.

Another major difference between cyber-security and cybercrime but which is related to the previous point concerns the profile of victims of the attack. In this regard, cyber-security attacks tend to target large corporations and state-run agencies while cybercrime victims are normally ordinary citizens or individuals. Waller, Bailey, and Johnson (2015) conducted a comprehensive study on the fear of cybercrime in Jamaica and Barbados. They found that risk perception was higher among non-users as compared to users of online banking. This is possibly the case because non-users lacked confidence in the internet banking system due to financial and credit card fraud perpetuated against individuals. However, the knowledge users have about the protection mechanisms in place made them less fearful as this knowledge was balanced with the risks involved in using online platforms.

The third distinction between cyber-security and cybercrime concerns the fact that much of the literature on cybersecurity is written within the broad field of computer science while much of the works on cybercrime are confined to the disciplines of security studies, criminology, and psychology. Hence, the works on cyber-security surround issues of computer semantics, coding, and secure network strategies to minimize unauthorized access to computer hardware, software, and systems. However, the research on cybercrime provides an explanation of the fear of cybercrime and understanding of theories shaping crime and criminal behavior.

Jamaica's cyber-security strategies in curbing cybercrimes

A legal and regulatory framework shapes Jamaica's strategy to combat cybercrimes. These are instituted to prevent, combat, and mitigate criminals' actions to filtrate computer systems, infrastructure and data. Jamaica has no Cyber-Security Act instead it has a Cyber Security Strategy which feeds into its Cybercrimes Act. The Cybercrimes Act attached punitive measures to cyber and cyber-related acts committed by individuals as a means to punish as well as to deter future acts.

The following section discusses Jamaica's Cyber Security Strategy as the national policy framework to protect critical infrastructure from cyber-attacks.

Jamaica's National Cyber-Security Strategy

The seriousness with which Jamaica views cybercrime has been evidenced in its policy imperatives. In 2015, Jamaica developed its National Cyber-Security Strategy. The Organization of American States (OAS) provided technical assistance to state officials in the development of this Strategy. Further, the National Cyber-security Strategy resulted from a coordinated collaboration involving not only technical support from the OAS but financial assistance from Canada, the United Kingdom, and the USA as well as organizational support from the Commonwealth Cybercrimes Initiative, the Commonwealth Telecommunication Organisation, and the University of Oxford's Global Cyber Security Capacity Centre. The

Strategy aims to provide security in protecting individuals, businesses and the government against cyber-security attacks.

Four main pillars form the National Cyber-Security Strategy. These are *technical measures, human resources and capacity building, legal and regulatory framework,* and *public education and awareness. Technical measures* provided a platform which combined physical infrastructure with human capacity in combating cybercrime. The rationale underlying this pillar is that countering cybercrime requires robust critical infrastructure systems primarily because all entities, institutions, and businesses depend on information technology systems to execute their daily activities. Cybercrimes warrant inter-agency cooperation and cross-national collaboration; hence, the Strategy supports law enforcement information sharing in an attempt to reduce cybercrime breaches.

The pillar of *human resources and capacity building* aims to build capacity to combat cybercrimes by working with Jamaican universities to maintain a highly trained and skilled pool of professionals in information systems and network security. Therefore, the academic community is integral in supporting the development and growth in this area, and the government plans to develop a national cyber-security professional register, with details of such persons having the accredited skills and competencies in cyber-security.

The *legal and regulatory framework* aims to provide protection for the public and private sectors through periodic reviews of existing laws to ensure parity with the dynamic nature of cybercrimes. To this end, the Strategy intends to cover online and offline transactions and data protection. An effective local and regulatory framework remains essential in the investigation and prosecution of cybercrimes. Currently, the JCF has the capability to investigate cybercrimes, primarily, through the use of computer and mobile forensics. Likewise, the Office of the Director of Public Prosecutions (DPP) has established a specific unit, the Digital Evidence and Cybercrimes Unit. This Unit is charged with the responsibility to prosecute cybercrimes.

The final pillar in the Strategy is *public education and awareness.* This pillar educates and informs citizens about the types of cybercrimes as well as their vulnerabilities to such problems based on their online and internet usage. It also proposes mechanisms which may be adopted to minimize cyber-attacks. Accordingly, public education and awareness programs sensitized the Jamaican public on appropriate online behavior that reduces the risks of cyber-induced crimes (The National Cyber-Security Strategy, 2015). One important public education campaign undertaken through this Strategy was called "Everyone is at risk to Cybercrimes." As part of this Strategy, the Government of Jamaica supports the international designation of October being cyber-security month. Every year during this month, it organizes a number of media-related and other activities targeting its populous and through which it disseminates information on cybercrimes to the nation.

In accordance with the third pillar of Jamaica's Cyber-Security Strategy, a discussion on the legal and regulatory framework in the form of the Cybercrimes Act and other institutional responses are explicated below.

Jamaica's Cybercrimes Act

In 2010, the Cybercrimes Act was announced in the Jamaican Parliament. However, the passage of the Cybercrimes Act and its subsequent amendments meant that a legal structure was in place to charge cybercriminals in the Jamaican courts. The 2015 Cybercrimes Act is a comprehensive Act aimed to legally protect Jamaican citizens from cybercriminals. This Act makes cybercrime a criminal act in Jamaica and by so doing, provides greater enforcement authority by which law enforcers can police this crime. Section 4(1) of this Act makes it an offence for any person to "access any programme or data held in a computer with the intent to commit or facilitate any offence" (The Cybercrimes Act, 2015). For purposes of this Act, a "computer means any device or group of interconnected or related devices, one or more of which, pursuant to a programme, performs automatic processing of data" (Section 2, Cybercrimes Act, 2015).

Jamaica's Cybercrimes Act is divided into four parts. Part I addresses the preliminary definitional interpretation of the terms used. Part II is captioned "offences" and covers nine penalties stipulated under this Act. It also specifies that compensation may be accorded to victims who suffered damage or loss through the commission of offences outlined under this Act. Part III is titled "investigations" and includes four critical investigative aspects of cybercrimes namely, matters concerning preservation of data, issues of searches and seizure warrants, production orders, and the recording of the seized material. Finally, Part IV broadly encompasses the matters of jurisdiction, regulations, power to modify monetary penalties, and mechanisms to review the Act two years after its passage.

Part II, Section 1 of the Cybercrimes Act makes it a punishable offence for a person to obtain unauthorized access to a computer's program or data. Section 3 (a) of the Act, upon conviction in a Resident Magistrate Court, punishes this offence through a fine of no more than two million dollars or to imprisonment not longer than two years or to both a fine and imprisonment. The fines are increased to three million dollars and imprisonment time of no more than three years if damage results from the commission of this offence. However, the punishment is harsher upon conviction in a Circuit Court where the imprisonment should not exceed five years and if damage is caused the imprisonment term should not exceed seven years.

Another offence stipulated under Jamaica's Cybercrimes Act is that of accessing computer programs or data with the intention to facilitate or commit a crime. Section 5 makes it an offence for a person to cause an unauthorized modification to a program, data, or computer system. Section 6 makes it an offence for a person to obtain unauthorized access to a computer system and for the direct or indirect interception of the functioning of a computer. Section 8 makes it an offence for a person to possess, receive, manufacture, sell, import, distribute, or disclose an unlawfully obtained device or data communication. Section 9 stipulates that the violation or unauthorized access to a protected computer is punishable before a Circuit Court and a person who is guilty of this offence is subjected to a fine or prison term not exceeding ten years. Further, individuals convicted through the Cybercrimes Act may be required to pay compensation in addition to penalties in the form of fines and prison time, to the victims who suffered because of the commission of the cybercrime offences.

Section 16 allows for the documentation of records that have been seized in executing a warrant. Further, a copy of the list of seized items should be given to the occupier of the residence or to the person to whom the warrant targets. Section 18 stipulates the jurisdiction applicable to the Act. It is applicable to conduct that has happened in Jamaica, on Jamaican aircraft and on Jamaican vessel and committed by a Jamaican citizen. Finally, Section 20 empowers the Minister to modify monetary fines imposed by the Act but only after an affirmative resolution and subsequent to its publication in the Gazette.

The Larceny Act and the Interception of Communications Act

Two previous laws have also strengthened the ability of the Jamaican state in its efforts to stem cybercrimes. These are the Larceny Act and the Interception of Communications Act. Lloyd (2017) noted that governments have a well-established interest in maintaining the ability to intercept communications, especially to safeguard citizens against abuse. Section 4(1) of Jamaica's Interception of Communications Act allows for an authorized officer to apply to a judge for a warrant to intercept public or private communications network. Section 4(1A)(a) makes it possible for the disclosure of the intercepted communication to be given to a foreign government where there is a mutual exchange agreement between Jamaica and the foreign government and the Jamaican Minister deems the disclosure necessary in the public interest. Further, Section 14(1) of the Interception of Communications Act also provides for admissibility of evidence from "sensitive information" and for witnesses not to be questioned in a manner to disclose the source of such information. Provisions within the Interception of Communications Act may therefore support the Cybercrimes Act in the investigation and successful prosecutions of cybercrimes.

Section 11 of Jamaica's Larceny Act makes it an offence for a person to fraudulently destroy, damage, or carry away any record relating to a civil or criminal matter. A person who is found to be guilty of this offence is liable to imprisonment not exceeding three years. Further, Sections 33 and 35 of the Larceny Act make it a felony with imprisonment not exceeding five years upon conviction for a person who falsely or deceitfully impersonates another person with the intent to fraudulently obtain money or property. Section 46(1) of the Larceny Act stipulates that anyone who receives stolen property is guilty of an offence. Section 66 of the Larceny Act mandates a person found guilty under this Act to pay restitution to the victim or the property owner.

The Larceny Act supports the Cybercrimes Act by creating part of a legal framework which may be used to charge people who engage in fraudulent acts. It also ensures that restitution is made to the victims who suffer from the actions of those who impersonate others either through credit card scams or other online computer-related acts, which deprive them of their monies.

Jamaica's Cyber Incident Response Team

In 2014, Jamaica established a Cyber Incident Response Team. The main role of the Cyber Incident Response Team is to provide information on existing and new cybersecurity threats. It is also responsible to provide warnings to businesses, citizens, and the government on cybercrimes that are projected to affect the integrity of their computer systems.

This Team formed a part of Jamaica's Strategy in strengthening its cyber-security apparatus. By establishing the Cyber Incident Response Team, Jamaica received technical assistance in the form of finances to purchase equipment critical to the reduction of cybercrimes. Training was also extended to key personnel. This assisted in building the technical capacity to detect and respond to instances of cyber-attacks. Further, the Cyber Incident Response Team facilitated greater collaboration with two important agencies, the International Telecommunications Union (ITU) and the OAS's Inter-America Committee against Terrorism (CICTE). Both of these agencies also provided training and financial support to Jamaica's anti-cybercrime efforts.

Other collaborations

Additionally, Jamaica benefited from a wider pool of technical assistance provided to Latin American and Caribbean countries by the Inter-American Development Bank (IDB). This assistance fed into the country's cyber-security policy and supported Jamaica's technologically driven society through specialized training to create a more secure environment.

Training

In 2012, Jamaica's Communications, Forensics and Cybercrimes Unit noted a number of cyber-related incidents that were reported to the JCF. Among the reports given to the police were 299 instances of website defacement, 108 instances of electronic fraud, 1509 mobile phone-related cyber instances, and 564 other digital media-related incidents (National Cyber-Security Strategy, 2015). From 2014 to 2017, 149 persons were arrested on cybercrime charges in Jamaica (The Jamaica Observer, 2017). The individuals arrested were charged with electronic fraud, namely, credit card scamming, and online bank robbery. Others were charged for obscene publication, possession of child pornography, and using computer technology to transmit malicious communication.

To improve the robustness of computer systems and state officials' cyber-detection capacity, the Jamaican government utilized technical assistances from external sources. In this regard, training to combat cybercrimes included programs on digital investigations, the utilization of electronic devices and legal interception of communication technology.

The Government of Jamaica also conducted training, which was coordinated at the Ministerial levels of government. In 2017, Jamaica's Ministry of National Security facilitated the training of ten cybercrime experts at the cost of JMD12 million. The training equipped the experts to analyze electronic equipment, namely, computers and cellular phones, to ascertain their use in the commission of acts defined as criminal offences under Jamaica's Cybercrimes Act. This training provided cybercrime experts with the technical knowledge required to collect evidence that could support criminal convictions of perpetrators of illegal acts. Additionally, in 2017, 22 police officers developed and launched a computer application called the "JCF docs." This app provides easy retrieval of relevant JCF documents such as the Acts needed by the JCF police officers in the daily execution of their tasks. Hence, the app uses technology to readily provide the cybercrimes law to law enforcers in order to better police matters concerning cybercrimes and to increase arrests in these areas.

In 2018, the Department of Legal Cooperation of the OAS has provided three days of training to judges. This training covered cybercrimes investigation techniques and the consideration of electronic evidence. Jamaican judges participated in this training session as well as judges from Antigua and Barbuda, the Bahamas, Belize, Dominica, Grenada, Guyana, St. Vincent and the Grenadines, St. Kitts, Nevis, St. Lucia, Suriname, and Trinidad and Tobago (OAS, 2018). Prior to this, in 2012, the OAS extended to Caribbean leaders a workshop on cyber-security and cybercrime. The workshop covered matters on global and regional cyber conventions, the Caribbean cybercrimes landscape, cybercrimes and cyber-security agenda setting, and cybercrimes legislation as a legal and procedural tool for policing and investigations. The Jamaican authorities benefited from this workshop as it assisted in shaping Jamaica's Cyber-Security Strategy three years later.

The OAS plays an integral role in working with states to address the challenges that they confront. The subsequent section addresses the role of this institution in strengthening member states to respond to cyber-security challenges.

The Organization of American States

The OAS plays an important role in assisting member states to strengthen their cyber-security capabilities in protecting their critical infrastructure from attacks. There are a number of commitment instruments spearheaded by the OAS to which member states governments signed up. In 2004, the Comprehensive Inter-American Cyber-Security Strategy was passed by the OAS General Assembly. Thereafter there was the 2012 Declaration on Strengthening Cyber-Security in the Americas. By 2015, the OAS adopted the Declaration on Protection of Critical Infrastructure from Emerging Threats. These OAS regional instruments laid the foundation for the promotion of cyber-security policies across the Americas. They also formed the framework upon which member states cyber-security policies aimed at improving their critical infrastructure rests.

Increasingly, governments have relied on critical infrastructure of internet networks to provide essential products and services to their citizens. Hence, cyber-attacks on these infrastructures may compromise the state's ability to provide essential services to its populous. For instance, disruptions in the transportation, energy, and financial sectors, which utilize both basic and sophisticated technologies will inevitably result in disruptions in the functioning of the state and disturb people's daily activities. The disruption may even be more widespread as it may filter to other sectors which may ultimately result in massive disruptions for the public and private sectors alike.

The OAS has strengthened cyber-security capabilities of its member states by providing policy frameworks and training. It engages in the training of senior management officials, policy makers and security technicians to detect and bolster their systems against cyber-attacks and infiltration. As an OAS member state, Jamaica has benefited from the OAS's training and capacity building initiatives.

The OAS encourages public–private sector cooperation. It views cyber-security as a shared responsibility hence, governments, the private sector, civil society, and academia must work in unison to provide a more secure cyberspace. In this regard, the OAS Cyber-Security Program aims to sensitize stakeholders about best practices in strengthening their cyber-security and critical infrastructure against cyber threats. This is a seven point program. First, it engages civil society and the private sector. Civil society is important in lobbying for citizen's protection and the private sector owns more than 80 per cent of the internet infrastructure (OAS, 2015).

Second, the OAS raises awareness by encouraging states to develop cyber-security policies as well as embarking on programs designed to raise the awareness of individuals by explaining the cyber-security risks and measures to take in order to improve their own cyber-security. Third, the OAS assists countries in developing broad-based strategies on cyber-security. This assistance is utilized in the establishment of state's national cyber security strategy. The national cyber-security strategy provides clear responsibility among state agencies in attempting to address cybercrime matters. It allows for the coordination of state agencies with relevant stakeholders in efforts to curtail cybercrimes. In this regard, the OAS has promoted the development of Jamaica's Cyber-Security Strategy and framework, which was documented in 2015.

Fourth, the OAS supports states by assisting them with the establishment of a national Computer Security Incident Response Team (CSIRT). The establishment of Jamaica's Cyber Incident Response Team flows directly from the role the OAS plays in strengthen states cyber-security capability. The OAS also facilitated the delivery of technical training on a number of relevant areas of cyber-security to public sector officials. As indicated earlier, Jamaican public sector employees have been the recipient of some of these training to build their technical knowledge to combat cybercrimes.

Fifth, the OAS executes crisis management exercises so that states may engage in simulations to develop responses to cyber-attacks and to strengthen their partnerships with other states in responding to this threat. Sixth, the OAS makes recommendations to states based on their needs, which the OAS determines following technical assistance endeavors involving site visits, policy reviews, and local authority presentations. Finally, the OAS is establishing a Regional CSIRT, comprising national CSIRTs and other cyber-security agencies. The Regional CSIRT will facilitate timely communication and information sharing among states in their efforts at curtailing cybercrimes (OAS, 2015). This Regional CSIRT will be very beneficial, especially for Caribbean states to share their experiences and better coordinate their efforts in the fight against cybercrimes.

Conclusion

Cybercrimes threaten the stability of states by compromising their critical high value sectors and through disrupting peoples' lives. Jamaica has taken steps in the development of a legal and regulatory framework to protect citizens against cybercrimes and to promote confidence in a safe and secure cyber-environment. As discussed above, such framework includes the adoption of the Cybercrimes Act, which makes cybercrime activities punishable offences through fines or imprisonment or by both fines and prison time. Further, this framework incorporates compliance with Jamaica's regional commitments adopted through its membership in the OAS.

Jamaica is among the states which have established a National Cyber-Security Strategy. This Strategy was developed with technical experts from the OAS's Cyber-Security Program. Additionally, Jamaica has built its capacity to enforce this framework by strengthening its national capabilities and through international collaboration with other entities in its efforts at combating cybercrimes.

Nevertheless, despite the government's efforts, it is well established globally and in Jamaica that cybercrimes prevention is a utopian goal, which is difficult to achieve. Hence, Jamaica has opted to use its technical assistances obtained from external partners to focus its efforts on cybercrime detection and response. Ideally, once breaches have been detected, the mechanisms in place should allow for swift response in order to minimize disruptions.

Continuous cybercrime detection and response training must be given to Jamaican technical experts so that they can be kept abreast of the fast changing and dynamic nature of the cybercrime environment. Further, there is the need for greater cross-border collaborative efforts among states to determine best practices in addressing cybercrime matters. Finally, the strengthening of private–public cooperative forums and joint task force initiatives are important platforms to confront cybercrime challenges faced by businesses and the public sector. This is important as shared responsibility at the national, regional, and international levels remain the best way to conquer the threat posed by cybercrime.

Suggested reading

Coble, S. (2019, December 4). "Jamaica to Create a National Cybersecurity Policy in 2020," *Info Security*. www.infosecurity-magazine.com/news/jamaica-to-create-cybersecurity/
Government of Jamaica. (n.d.). "National Cyber Security Strategy." www.oxfordmartin.ox.ac.uk/down loads/cybersecurity/Jamaica%20National%20Cyber%20Security%20Strategy.pdf
Lewis, C. B. (2015). "Social Media: Cyber Trap Door to Defamation – Jamaica's Defamation Act 2013 Examined," *Masaryk University Journal of Law & Technology*, 9(1): 65–84.
RJR News. (2020, January 8). "Heightened Risk of Cyber-attacks - Says JN Cybersecurity Unit." http://rjrnewsonline.com/business/heightened-risk-of-cyber-attacks-says-jn-cybersecurity-unit
Schatz, D., Bashroush, R. & Wall, J. (2017). "Towards a More Representative Definition of Cyber Security," *Journal of Digital Forensics, Security and Law*, 12(2): 53–74.

References

Brenner, S. (2012). *Cybercrime and the Law: Challenges, Issues and Outcomes*. Lebanon: Northeastern University Press.

Castells, M. (1998). *The Information Age: Economy, Society and Culture*. Oxford: Blackwell Publishers.

"Convention on Cybercrime." (2001). Council of Europe, European Treaty Series, No. 185, Budapest, Hungary.

"The Cybercrimes Act." (2015). Ministry of Justice, L.N. 92c/2012, Kingston, Jamaica.

The Global Risk Report. (2016). World Economic Forum, Geneva, Switzerland. www3.weforum.org/docs/GRR/WEF_GRR16.pdf

The Global Risk Report. (2018). World Economic Forum, Geneva, Switzerland. www3.weforum.org/docs/WEF_GRR18_Report.pdf

International Telecommunication Union. (2018). "Guide to Developing A National Cybersecurity Strategy: Strategic Engagement in Cybersecurity." www.itu.int/dms_pub/itu-d/opb/str/D-STR-CYB_GUIDE.01-2018-PDF-E.pdf

The Jamaica Observer. (2017, September 7). "$12m to Be Invested in Training 10 Cybercrime Experts – Montague." www.jamaicaobserver.com/latestnews/$12m_to_be_invested_in_training_10_cybercrime_experts_Montague?profile=1228

The Jamaica Observer. (2015, June 22). "Update: JIS Website Hacked." www.jamaicaobserver.com/news/UPDATE–JIS-website-hacked-, 26 December 2018.

"The Larceny Act." (1942). Ministry of Justice, Kingston, Jamaica.

Lloyd, I. (2017). *Information Technology Law* (8th ed.). Oxford: Oxford University Press.

"The National Cybersecurity Strategy." (2015). www.mset.gov.jm/sites/default/files/Jamaica%20National%20Cyber%20Security%20Strategy.pdf

OAS. (2018). "Three Days of Training for Judges on Cybercrime Investigation Techniques and the Consideration of Electronic Evidence, Department of Legal Cooperation." www.oas.org/juridico/english/cyber_events.htm

OAS. (2015). "Report on Cybersecurity and Critical Infrastructure in the Americas, OAS, the Trend Mico Incorporated." www.sites.oas.org/cyber/Certs_Web/OAS-Trend%20Micro%20Report%20on%20Cybersecurity%20and%20CIP%20in%20the%20Americas.pdf

Tropina, T. & Callanan, C. (2015). *Self and Co-regulation in Cybercrime, Cybersecurity and National Security*. Cham: Springer.

Wall, D. (2007). *Cybercrime: The Transformation of Crime in the Information Age*. Cambridge: Polity Press.

Wall, D. (2001). *Crime and the Internet*. New York: Routledge.

Waller, L., Bailey, C. & Johnson, S. (2015). *Fear of Cybercrime: Lessons for the Global e-Banking Sector*. Kingston: Ian Randle Publishers.

Yar, M. (2013). *Cybercrime and Society* (2nd ed.). Santa Monica: SAGE.

41

MEXICO AND CYBERSECURITY

Policies, challenges, and concerns

Saúl Mauricio Rodriguez-Hernandez and Nicolás Velásquez

> The risks and threats in cyberspace may become a possible attack on human dignity, on the integrity of people, on the credibility, reputation and assets of companies and public institutions, and have effects on public safety or even national security.
>
> (*Mexican National Cybersecurity Strategy*, 2017)

Introduction

In late 2011, an unusual security event evolved in cyberspace. The Mexican drug cartel "Los Zetas" and the hacktivist collective Anonymous were involved in a major cyber-battle. Los Zetas – a criminal structure due to the elite Mexican military origin of its founding members – kidnapped one member of Anonymous in retaliations for the hacktivist campaign against political corruption in Mexico. The cybergroup countered with a threat to release secret information about the illegal connivance between prominent elected officials, civil servants, and members of the social elites with the drug cartel. Unabated, Los Zetas threatened an indiscriminate campaign against innocent people if any kind of information was posted online. The crisis was resolved through a sort of stalemate, with the Zetas freeing the hacktivist and Anonymous announcing it would stop monitoring this particular Cartel (Clark, 2011).

According to Paul R. Kan this *sui generis* episode proved that the Mexican government had no jurisdiction in cyberspace, and the possibilities to "prevent, intervene, or respond" in this or another similar situation was almost impossible to deal with for any government but particularly for Mexican civilian and military authorities (Kan, 2013: 48). In this respect, as it is pointed out by Yeo, Birch, and Jörgen, in cyberspace there is no state monopoly of violence in the Westphalian way and anarchy seems to be one of the main traits within this realm (Yeo, Birch, & Bengtsson, 2016). At the same time, the cyber-realm is a space where state, economic, social, and political actors interact in ways that both expand the capacity of any of them to penetrate society and institutions, for instance, enabling making visible activities of both state and non-state social actors. Thus, as authors like Mann and van Haaster have stressed, a less Weberian interpretation of social power that does not conflate military and political capacities, nor power sharing (i.e. regime) with public policy implementation (i.e. infrastructural power) capacities might help us understand the evolution of challenges, capacities, and policies (Mann, 2013; Van Haaster, 2016).

This chapter offers an overview of Mexico's cybersecurity landscape from the perspective of the trends and evolutions of its policies and challenges but will also address them critically stressing the concerns on security, human and digital rights, and inclusiveness. We offer a general technopolitical context and then follow that with a recapitulation of relevant cyber threats and attacks, the evolution of domestic norms and capacities, and a review of Mexico's multilateral role in cybersecurity and internet governance. A small reference section with further resources is attached.

Social, technical, and political context

Mexico presents many of the contradictions of the developing world. On the one hand, this country has mid-level economic development with a well-developed industrial complex deeply inserted into the North American and Trans-Pacific trade networks. In fact, market analysis firms consider that with internet access and e-commerce this country will be one of the top ten economies in the world in the coming years (Stratiss-LookingGlass, 2018). Likewise, democracy is rooted in the national essence and freedom has become an important value across society including the use of internet as a way of communication, social interaction, and economic empowerment.

On the other hand, intra- and cross-society economic inequality continues to be high, corruption is widespread, and criminality and violence are a common feature in this country. In this respect, the intersection between mid-level economic development, widespread use of the internet, and presence of criminality makes the country so fragile regarding any kind of illegal action in cyberspace ranging from cybercrime in the form of stealth information, financial frauds, and attacks to governmental platforms, to cyberterrorism.

In this respect, Leuprecht and Tupler (2018: 1) pointed out accurately "Now that cyber vulnerabilities pose serious risks to prosperity, democracy and social harmony, cyber security has become a complex and all-encompassing political, social, economic and technological phenomenon." Latin America and Mexico are not exemptions, if we consider not just the case shown above but also the vulnerability of Mexico to similar kinds of situations in both public and private sectors due to its fast connection to the cyber world. According to the Federal Institute of Telecommunications, in 2018 of the countries in Latin America, Mexico suffered the second highest number of cyberattacks and approximately half of the private companies have asserted that they were victims of cyber delinquency (2018: 4).

In this anarchical scenario, multiple actors are involved including international institutions, the Mexican state, financial actors, non-state organizations like hacktivists and criminals, and even ordinary citizens as passive actors, who often suffer as victims unaware of the crimes themselves until after these situations happen. In this line, legal actors are concerned about the actions to regulate, repel, and organize the cyberspace in order to minimize the risk and vulnerabilities related to the interaction between these actors. Therefore, international and local strategies are the forefront of these actions, however with a different kind of scope and effectiveness.

As a new topic and concern, cybersecurity has been a challenge for many actors involved in the prevention and action to avoid criminal activities in the cyberspace, this is understood as the technological space where different actors interact and share data and information. In this respect, the steps to enhance the awareness and action regarding this topic were slow just a few years ago but have become faster recently due to international and domestic pressures both from legal and illegal actors. According to the Mexican National Cybersecurity Strategy released in 2017, cybersecurity is understood to be "[a] set of policies, controls, procedures, risk management methods and standards associated with the protection of society, government, economy and national security in cyberspace and public telecommunications networks" (Presidencia de la República, 2017: 27). The main goal is to protect the public and private good with the critical role of the state; however, multiple actors are part of this complex architecture to avoid harmful activities.

Recent threats and cyberattacks

In general terms, the trends of cyberattacks and vulnerabilities faced by Mexico reflect both the country's rapid increase in connectivity and reliance on information systems, and its national economic and political conditions. Among the latter, we can identify the following as factors that define Mexico's cybersecurity challenge landscape: Its condition as a mid-level economy deeply inserted in North American and trans-Pacific trade dynamics; its role as a Latin American regional power; the particular security risks posed by the ongoing war on drugs with a substantial presence of organized crime; and finally, the pervasive corruption that permeates the public sector.

During the first decade of the twenty-first century, literature on Mexico's cybersecurity focused on the threat posed by viruses, malware, ransomware, and poorly secured IT infrastructure. A dual culture of lax IT security and an appetite for pirated software made Mexico, with its considerable domestic market, a prime target for digital fraudsters, hackers, and "herders" of "zombie" PCs infected by remote-access enabling malware (Kshetri, 2013: 140–141; Espinosa, 2015; Saucedo & Retama, 2010: 7 and 9–10). By the early 2010s, Mexico faced a dramatic increase in cases of digital identity theft and production and distribution of child pornography distributed through the internet. Some legislators considered that between 2011 and 2013 Mexico was the world leader in cybercrime cases (Stone, 2011; Cawley, 2013; Southwick, 2013). While the exactitude of such a claim can be questioned, there was no doubt that Mexican society faced a difficult cybersecurity scenario, and that the general security crisis brought about by organized crime was spilling into the digital realm.

Statistics on cyberattacks to critical infrastructure are not readily available. Nonetheless, Luis Parraguez from the Wilson Center's Mexico Program compared the official list of key infrastructure facilities compiled by the government of Mexico against a report by the United States CERT (US-CERT) to identify that by 2013 almost one third of known cyberattacks targeted energy companies (Parraguez, 2017: 14). Adolfo Arreola, on a working paper by the Mexican Navy's Institute of Strategic Research, identified significant cyber-attacks to Pemex – the national petroleum company; the CFE – the national electric utility; and the Presidency itself (Arreola, 2018: 3).

Two highly publicized cases of state-sponsored cyberattacks against Mexico's interests include the United States and North Korea. The 2013 "NSA files" released by Edward Snowden made clear that the US's NSA had intercepted private communications of Mexican presidents Felipe Calderón, Peña Nieto, ministries and other public institutions, including the Public Security Ministry (Louv, 2014). Later in the decade, the United States Department of Justice and Federal Bureau of Investigation would present evidence against North Korean agents of the "Lazarus Group" that had targeted with malware the IT systems of institutions in Mexico, the US, and a number of other countries during 2014 the "WannaCry 2.0" ransomware attacks (Department of Justice, 2018).

Confidential and sensitive documents from the Mexican embassy in Guatemala were dumped by what appeared to be a single hacker in April 2019. The documents included visas, confidential diplomatic communications, and documents related to defendants in criminal cases (Proceso, 2019; Whittaker, 2019). In November 2019 a new ransomware attack targeted PEMEX, knocking down its email servers and other information systems. The attackers demanded 565 bitcoins (around 5 million USD), although former PEMEX security engineers did not discard that the goal of the attack would be to delete compromising information involving past administrations (Cruz, 2019; Barrera & Satter, 2019). However, perhaps the most perplexing cybersecurity threat in the Mexican contest is posed by the State itself. There is ample evidence that state-owned surveillance and penetration tools have been illegitimately employed to target, harass, and even locate in order to assassinate a number of activists, journalists, and members of congress (Centeno, 2018; Rivas & Mantovani, 2018; Velasco, 2019: chap. 5).

One of the best documented cases is the abusive use of the penetration Pegasus of the Israeli firm NSO. Pegasus can infect Android and iOS phones, even compromising communication platforms with basic encryption like Facebook's WhatsApp or VKontakte's Telegram. This software, which nominally should be useful to combat the intricate drug cartels and organized crime structures, has nonetheless been used against journalists that cover extrajudicial massacres within the war on drugs (Scott-Railton, Marczak, Anstis, Abdul, Crete-Nishihata, & Deibert, 2018), public health activists demanding more controls over edulcorated beverages (Scott-Railton, Marczak, Guarnieri, & Crete-Nishihata, 2017), and members of congress that objected to certain public policies of the Peña Nieto administration (Scott-Railton, Marczak, Razzak, Crete-Nishihata, & Deibert, 2017). While a judicial inquiry by the former Procuraduría (Federal Attorney Office) on those abuses has been publicized, to this date it has not yielded results. Invoking technical difficulties, the Mexican executive requested the assistance of the United States' authorities. Yet, according to the *New York Times*, "American officials decided not to get involved, leery that the Mexican government had little interest in actually solving the case because a serious investigation might implicate some of its most powerful figures" (Azam, 2018).

As shown in the opening paragraphs of this chapter, social networking and Internet 2.0 platforms like Twitter, WhatsApp, and YouTube are one integral battleground in the ongoing war with the drug cartels. As these organized criminal enterprises have deployed de-facto power to violently repress free press and journalism in several Mexican regions, journalists, activists, and citizens turned to these digital platforms to broadcast content and critical opinions that traditional media outlets did not dare or were unable to publish. As social media researcher Nilda García has pointed out, the cartels themselves have answered by strategies to coopt social media channels and to swarm comments and referral sections with their own narratives (García, 2017: chaps. 3–5).

Legislative development and public policies

There is a wide consensus amid scholars and analysts that Mexico has an adequate and updated normativity regarding telecommunications and e-commerce, an adequate set of pre-information revolution legacy norms that have been interpreted to cover basic cybersecurity scenarios, and a mixed record in terms of public policies and legislative efforts to update cybersecurity normativity (Espinosa, 2015: 115; Isla, 2015: 44–45; Parraguez, 2017: 2–3; Cancino, 2019: 160; Velasco, 2019: paras. 713 and 796).

The 2013 Constitutional Reform updated the communications and telecommunications concepts at the higher level, and – at least on paper – sets a mandate on the State to guarantee access into the "information and knowledge society." The 2014 Federal Law on Telecommunications and Broadcasting (FLTB) consolidated into a single body disperse codes for different forms of broadcasting, including digital and internet channels. Both the Constitution and the FLTB define telecommunication infrastructure and communication as a social service that are central not only to social cultural and economic development, but also to the capacity of the Mexican State to implement its policies and project its power domestically. The FLTB is much more concerned with trade, intellectual rights, and customer rights than with security. Nonetheless, along with the Federal Civil and Criminal Codes, the Constitution and the FLTB provide a framework where cybersecurity and information/privacy rights are – at least in theory – guaranteed under a democratic rule of law. Yet, beyond the written law, the Mexican cybersecurity landscape is characterized by critical challenges, voids, and contradictions.

As mentioned in previous pages, both cybercrimes against citizens and companies as well as cyberattacks by either state or organized non-state actors against key infrastructural assets are very common. Furthermore, the updated legislation did not address the building of cybersecurity safety culture, resiliency, and response capacities, thus relegating such key items to the purvey of the Executive Branch. Alas, different presidential administrations have not granted cybersecurity the level of priority it deserves in the age of the information revolution. For instance, CERT and digital forensic teams have been attached to preventive and judicial police institutions at the federal level. Alas, Mexican police and security services have been characterized by both corruption and institutional instability. At the federal level, preventive police and judiciary police services have undergone six rounds of structural reforms during the past 20 years, with cybercrime and CERT units constantly having to migrate from one dissolved police institution into the newer one (Espinosa, 2015: 131; Riquelme, 2018, 2019). Finally, there is ample evidence that state-controlled surveillance resources have been illegitimately deployed against peaceful activists, government critics, and even members of Congress in order to illegally monitor their activities (Scott-Railton, Marczak, Razzak, Crete-Nishihata, & Deibert, 2017). In several cases such monitoring was instrumental in the assassination or extrajudicial killings of the victims (Scott-Railton, Marczak, Anstis, Abdul, Crete-Nishihata, & Deibert, 2018).

In that regard, analysts are more concerned with the lack of a robust and long-term cybersecurity public policy than with the need to update the current civil, criminal, and telecommunications federal codes to cope with emerging technologies and definitions. The sustained growth in internet coverage across Mexico has been accompanied – and often supported – by public policies related to connectivity and access rights. Yet, only in 2017 did the administration of President Peña Nieto release the first white-book type "National Cybersecurity Strategy (NCS)" (Presidencia de la República, 2017).

According to the NCS document, that Strategy had its roots in the Peña Nieto administration's National Development Plan. Nonetheless, in said document the concept of cybersecurity was only mentioned once, within the chapter about Mexico's international role, in a paragraph that identified the need for research projects to identify the needs of the civil and military intelligence communities to properly defend against threats to National Security (Presidencia de la República, 2013: 107).

Nonetheless, both a civilian (as opposed to a military) focus and an international cooperation approach have characterized the exploration and administrative processes that led to the NCS. The discussions that led to the drafting of the NCS involved the input of different stakeholders, including the industrial and financial sectors, scholars, information technology specialists, and civil society actors. It was supported by the active advice of the Organization of American States (Treppel, 2017; Velasco, 2019).

The NCS claims three guiding principles: A human rights-based perspective, a risk management-based approach, and a cooperative and multidisciplinary implementation. It also sets five strategic goals: To ensure that civil society can enjoy and profit from a safe cyberspace; to protect the economic sector from cyberthreats as well as to promote the domestic cybersecurity industry; to protect the State's IT infrastructure; to strengthen preventive and reactive cyber capacities by domestic law enforcement agencies; and to develop capacities related to cyber-defense and to guarantee national security interests in cyberspace. While – on paper – these seem appropriate guiding principles, legal scholars and social scientist have warned that it is by no means clear that the 2017 NCS will enjoy the political backing or administrative consensus required for it to be effectively implemented across Mexico's bureaucracy (Rodríguez, 2019; Velasco, 2019: para. 809).

During the current and past two legislatures a number of legislative bills have tried unsuccessfully to pass a cybersecurity law (Barrera, 2019; Velasco, 2019: para. 761). In March 2019 Senator Lucía Trasviña presented a bill to modify the Federal Criminal Code and to enact a novel Information Security Law (Trasviña, 2019). At the time of this writing (December 2019) the bill had not yet gained additional endorsements and was not scheduled for initial debate in the committees. On the other hand, several reforms to the Criminal and Telecommunications codes have successfully updated legislation related to child pornography.

The current administration of President Andres M. López has neither offered an alternative to his predecessor's cybersecurity policies nor has reneged on it. Rather, cybersecurity as a subject has been almost absent from López's public policies and narratives. Some critics interpret this as a negligence (Rodríguez, 2019), but other see it as a deliberate – albeit politically counterproductive – effort to conduct a reform in silence, away from social stakeholders (Chávez, 2019).

This silence is in stark contrast with other dimensions of security, which are a central part of López's proposed reforms. For instance, the National Development Plan describes an ambitious plan to rethink security policies in order to move away from the interdiction model employed in the "war on drugs," the remnants of the Cold War era's National Security Doctrine, and institutionalized corruption in Mexico's security services towards a much more citizen- and community-oriented paradigm aligned with democratic practices (Presidencia de la República, 2019: chap. 1). Yet, within this ambitious plan, there is not a single mention of cybersecurity or technological rights.

Agreements, international governance, and domestic ambivalence

Mexico has a long tradition of multilateralism and international cooperation which extends into recent international cybersecurity and information technologies governance mechanisms. Driven mostly by its traditional multilateral stance and by the other requirements of trade deals, Mexico has been an active part at the United Nations, Hemispheric, South-South, North American, and trans-Pacific levels of cybersecurity, fight against cybercrime, financial technologies (Fintech), and intellectual rights international pacts. Yet, as critics of Mexican domestic policies remind us, Mexico has also a tradition of being very supportive of a liberal and prodemocratic regime at the international level that does not lives up to its own domestic standards (Centeno, 2018: 5).

Mexico supported the ICANN's 2004 Working Group on Internet Governance that included state, industry, academic, and civil society representatives (Bhuiyan, 2014: 55–58). Furthermore, Mexico has also been an active member of the United Nations' Group of Governmental Experts (GEG, 2004–2018) and the Open-Ended Working Group on Cybersecurity (OEWG, 2019–present). Both initiatives held a multi-stakeholder approach, including civil society and industry presence and inputs. While scholars like Parraguez consider that the GEG failed at consolidating an international agreement (2018: 3), Mexico sees the OEWG – under the auspices of the UN's Office of Disarmament Affairs – as representing a renewed effort at an international compact (Permanent Mission of Mexico to the United Nations, 2019: 5).

Mexico's central bank is a founding member of the Center for Latin American Monetary Policy (CEMLA – the regional central banks' think tank and multilateral forum) and is an active member of its Fintech initiatives, like the Fintech Regulatory forum. In 2019 CEMLA praised Mexico's new Fintech Law as "channel and activity" focused rather than "provider" focused normativity that could serve a regional framework to regulate financial technologies (Fintech Regulatory Aspects Working Group, 2019: 7). The OAS, and specially its Inter-American Committee against Terrorism (CICTE) have been key strategic development partners for several Latin American and Caribbean countries' cybersecurity capacities and resilience policies (Treppel, 2017; CICTE, 2019). The Mexican National Cyber Security Strategy recognizes CICTE's contribution (Presidencia de la República, 2017: 11–12). Furthermore, compliance with two strategic international trade agreements have pushed Mexico to harmonize – or at least commit to harmonize – its regulations and policies on IT security, Fintech, and intellectual property rights: The Trans Pacific Partnership and the North America's USMCA (the successor to NAFTA) agreements (Mishra, 2017; Keitner & Clark, 2019: 2). A regional Latin American trade pact, the "Pacific Alliance" is mentioned in the 2017's Cybersecurity Strategy as another harmonizing initiative where Mexico has a leading role (Subgrupo de Agenda Digital, 2017).

Considering Mexico's traditional multilateral stance and support for international cooperation, it is somewhat striking that it has yet not yet become a full ratifying member of the 2001 Budapest Treaty that creates a common framework to deal with cybercrimes and digital rights. Some researchers consider that this is due to the lack of political will by Mexican authorities to update their criminal legislation up to international standards, due at least in part to the widespread violations of due processes by the security services and judicial police (Centeno, 2018: 10). This treaty – drafted by the Council of Europe – has nonetheless been ratified by several American nations including the US, Brazil, and Colombia. Therefore, the main concern about some international and domestic regulations are related to the thin line between cybersecurity and freedom of expression as asserted by Bhuiyan (2014: 136).

Conclusion

The Mexican society and economy are deepening their reliance on the tools and networks of the Information Economy, the fourth industrial revolution. Mexico is in fact an important member of both North American and trans-Pacific trade and production networks. Its government, historically weak and politically unaccountable for industrial and democratic nation standards, has nonetheless been one of the Global South's staunchest supporters of the international liberal regime, and multilateralism as a tool to face global issues. Both these characteristics are indeed reflected in the policy and governance dimensions of the Mexican cybersecurity scenario. Furthermore, the de-facto power wielded by organized criminals like the drug cartels and the pervasive corruption networks that coopt not only the civil service but also the security and police services represent the most urgent current challenge to the Mexican citizens' capacity to employ the tools of the information revolution to further their social, economic, and political rights.

Suggested reading

CICTE. (2019). "The Organization of American State's Committee against Terrorism Prepared a Comprehensive Report on Mexico's Financial Cybersecurity Landscape." www.oas.org/en/media_center/press_release.asp?sCodigo=E-052/19

Instituto Federal de Telecomunicaciones. (2018, November). "Plan de Aciones en Materia de Ciberseguridad: Unidad de Política Regulatoria Dirección General de Regulación Técnica." www.ift.org.mx/sites/default/files/contenidogeneral/transparencia/upr-planaccionesciberseguridad.pdf

Magrana, E. (2018). *Digital Rights in Latin America and the Caribbean*. Rio de Janeiro: FGV Direito Rio. https://itsrio.org/wp-content/uploads/2018/01/digital-rights.pdf

Pérez, F. M. (2019a). *Riesgo cibernético y ciberseguridad*. Documento de Trabajo No. 181. Ciudad de México, México: Search Results Web Result with Site Links Secretaría de Hacienda y Crédito Público. www.gob.mx/cms/uploads/attachment/file/478193/181.-_Riesgo_Cibern_tico_y_Ciberseguridad_2019.pdf

R3D. https://r3d.mx/

Velasco, C. (2019). *Cyber Law in Mexico* (4th ed.). Alphen aan den Rijn: Wolters Kluwer.

References

Arreola, A. (2018). "Ciberseguridad Nacional En México y Sus Desafíos," *Documentos de Trabajo IIE Armada de México*.

Azam, A. (2018, February 20). "Mexico Spyware Inquiry Bogs Down. Skeptics Aren't Surprised," *The New York Times*. www.nytimes.com/2018/02/20/world/americas/mexico-spyware-investigation.html?

Barrera, A. & Satter, R. (2019, November 12). "Hackers Demand $ 5 Million from Mexico' s Pemex in Cyberattack," *Reuters*. www.reuters.com/article/us-mexico-pemex/hackers-demand-5-million-from-mexicos-pemex-in-cyberattack-idUSKBN1XN03A

Barrera, R. (2019). "Necesario Construir Marco Jurídico Enfocado a Garantizar La Ciberseguridad," *Boletín de La Cámara de Diputados*. www5.diputados.gob.mx/index.php/esl/Comunicacion/Boletines/2019/Noviembre/05/2692-Necesario-construir-marco-juridico-enfocado-a-garantizar-la-ciberseguridad-Barrera-Badillo

Bhuiyan, A. (2014). *Internet Governance and the Global South: Demand for a New Framework*. New York: Palgrave Macmillan. www.palgrave.com/gp/book/9781137344335

Cancino, B. (2019). "Mexico," in N. Parker & A. Rendell (eds.), *Cybersecurity 2020* (3rd ed.). London: Global Legal Group. https://iclg.com/practice-areas/cybersecurity-laws-and-regulations

Cawley, M. (2013). "Mexico Is World Leader in Child Pornography: Officials," *Insight Crime*. September 27, 2013. www.insightcrime.org/news/brief/mexico-is-world-leader-in-child-pornography/

Centeno, D. (2018, August 21). *México y El Convenio de Budapes: Posibles Incompatibilidades*. Ciudad de México, México: Red en Defensa de los Derechos Digitales. www.derechosdigitales.org/publicaciones/mexico-y-el-convenio-de-budapest-posibles-incompatibilidades/

Chávez, G. (2019, September 30). "El Gobierno de AMLO Avanza En Ciberseguridad, Pero a Puerta Cerrada," *CNN Expansión*. https://expansion.mx/tecnologia/2019/09/30/el-gobierno-de-amlo-avanza-en-ciberseguridad-pero-a-puerta-cerrada

CICTE. (2019). *The State of Cybersecurity in the Mexican Financial System*. Washington, DC: Organization of American States. www.oas.org/en/sms/cicte/Documents/reports/The-State-of-Cybersecurity-in-the-Mexican-Financial-system.pdf

Clark, A. (2011, November 4). "Anonymous and the Zetas Cartel Declare a Truce," *The Atlantic*. www.theatlantic.com/technology/archive/2011/11/anonymous-barrett-brown-armed-mexican-drug-cartels/335861/

Cruz, N. (2019, November 19). "Ciberataque Vulneró 60 Áreas de Pemex; Temen Pérdida de Datos," *El Universal*. www.eluniversal.com.mx/cartera/ciberataque-vulnero-60-areas-de-pemex-temen-perdida-de-datos

Department of Justice. (2018). "United States vs Park Jin Hyok." www.justice.gov/opa/press-release/file/1092091/download

Espinosa, E. (2015). "Hacia Una Estrategia Nacional de Ciberseguridad En México," *Revista de Administración Pública, 50*(1): 115–146.

Fintech Regulatory Aspects Working Group. (2019). *Key Aspects around Financial Technologies and Regulation Policy*. Ciudad de México, México: Center for Latin American Monetary Policy. www.cemla.org/fintech/docs/2019-06-KeyAspectsAroundFinancialTechandRegulation.pdf

García, N. (2017). *The Dark Side of Social Media*. United States: University of Miami. https://scholarlyrepository.miami.edu/oa_dissertations/2009/

Isla, J. N. (2015). *Examen de La Armonización de La Ciberlegislación En América Latina*. Geneva, Switzerland: UNCTAD. https://unctad.org/es/paginas/PublicationWebflyer.aspx?publicationid=1630

Kan, P. R. (2013). "Cyberwar in the Underworld: Anonymous versus Los Zetas in Mexico," *Yale Journal of International Affairs*. http://yalejournal.org/article_post/cyberwar-in-the-underworld-anonymous-versus-los-zetas-in-mexico/

Keitner, C. & Clark, H. (2019). "Cybersecurity Provisions in Trade Agreements: The State of the Art," *Harvard Business Law Review, 10*(1). www.hblr.org/volume-10-2019-2020/

Kshetri, N. (2013). *Cybercrime and Cybersecurity in the Global South*. London: Palgrave Macmillan.

Lara, J. (ed.). (2016). *Internet En México: Derechos Humanos En El Entorno Digital*. Santiago: Derechos Digitales. www.derechosdigitales.org/wp-content/uploads/Internet-en-Mx-2016.pdf

Leuprecht, C. & Tupler, J. (2018). "Introduction," in C. Leuprecht & S. MacLellan (eds.), *Governing Cyber Security in Canada, Australia, and the United States* (pp. 1–3). Waterloo: Centre for International Governance Innovation.

Louv, J. (2014, February 24). "The NSA Has Set Up Shop at the US Embassy in Mexico," *Vice*. www.vice.com/en_us/article/vdpvza/the-nsa-has-set-up-shop-at-the-us-embassy-in-mexico

Mann, M. (2013). *The Sources of Social Power. Globalizations, 1945-2011* (Vol. 4). Cambridge: Cambridge University Press.

Mishra, N. (2017). "The Role of the Trans-Pacific Partnership Agreement in the Internet Ecosystem: Uneasy Liaison or Synergistic Alliance?" *Journal of International Economic Law, 20*(1): 31–60.

Parraguez, L. (2017). *The State of Cybersecurity in Mexico: An Overview*. Washington, DC: Wilson Center. www.wilsoncenter.org/publication/the-state-cybersecurity-mexico-overview

Parraguez, L. (2018). *Quo Vadis? Mexico's National Cybersecurity Strategy*. Washington, DC: Wilson Center. www.wilsoncenter.org/person/luisa-parraguez-kobek

Permanent Mission of Mexico to the United Nations. (2019). *Position Paper, 74th Ordinary Session of the UN General Assembly*. New York: Secretaría de Relaciones Exteriores. www.gob.mx/sre/prensa/mexico-takes-part-in-the-74th-un-general-assembly?idiom=en

Presidencia de la República. (2013). *Plan Nacional de Desarrollo 2013–2018. Gobierno de La República*. Ciudad de México, México: Presidencia de la República. www.gob.mx/epn/acciones-y-programas/plan-nacional-de-desarrollo-2013-2018-78557

Presidencia de la República. (2017). *National Cybersecurity Strategy*. Ciudad de México, México: Presidencia de la República. www.gob.mx/cms/uploads/attachment/file/271884/Estrategia_Nacional_Ciberseguridad.pdf

Presidencia de la República. (2019). *Plan Nacional de Desarrollo 2019–2024*. Ciudad de México, México: Presidencia de la República. https://lopezobrador.org.mx/wp-content/uploads/2019/05/PLAN-NACIONAL-DE-DESARROLLO-2019-2024.pdf

Proceso. (2019, April 2019). "Hackean y Hacen Públicos Pasaportes, Visas y Papeles de La Embajada de México En Guatemala." www.proceso.com.mx/580466/hackean-y-hacen-publicos-pasaportes-visas-y-papeles-de-la-embajada-de-mexico-en-guatemala

Riquelme, R. (2018, February 5). "¿Cómo Es Un CERT Desde El Interior?" *El Economista*. www.eleco nomista.com.mx/tecnologia/Como-es-un-CERT-desde-el-interior-20180205-0042.html

Riquelme, R. (2019, July 31). "División Científica de La Policía Federal, En Proceso de Transición Hacia Guardia Nacional," *El Economistata*. www.eleconomista.com.mx/tecnologia/Division-cienti fica-de-la-Policia-Federal-en-proceso-de-transicion-hacia-Guardia-Nacional-20190731-0063.html

Rivas, D. A. P. & Mantovani, C. (2018). "Lawful and Unlawful Surveillance in Mexican Democracy/ Vigilancia Legal e Ilegal En La Democracia Mexicana," *Revista Internacional de Comunicación y Desarrollo*, 2(7): 111–129.

Rodríguez, G. (2019, March 14). "Preocupante Ausencia de La Ciberseguridad En La Agenda Oficial: Entrevista Con El Maestro Arturo García Hernández," *América Latina En Movimiento*. www.alainet. org/es/articulo/198730%0AEntrevista

Saucedo, G. & Retama, C. (2010). "Informe de Seguridad Informática En México," *Sistemas*, 115: 1–16. http://acistente.acis.org.co/typo43/index.php?id=1490

Scott-Railton, J., Marczak, B., Anstis, S., Abdul, B., Crete-Nishihata, C. & Deibert, R. (2018, November). "Reckless VI. Mexican Journalists Investigating Cartels Targeted with NSO Spyware Following Assassination of Colleague," *Citizen Lab Research Report*. https://citizenlab.ca/2018/11/ mexican-journalists-investigating-cartels-targeted-nso-spyware-following-assassination-colleague/

Scott-Railton, J., Marczak, B., Guarnieri, C. & Crete-Nishihata, C. (2017, February). "Bitter Sweet: Supporters of Mexico's Soda Tax Targeted with NSO Exploit Links." *Citizen Lab Research Report*. https://citizenlab.ca/2017/02/bittersweet-nso-mexico-spyware/

Scott-Railton, J., Marczak, B., Razzak, B. A., Crete-Nishihata, M. & Deibert, R. (2017). "Reckless Redux. Senior Mexican Legislators and Politicians Targeted with NSO Spyware," *Citizen Lab Research Report*. https://citizenlab.ca/category/research/targeted-threats/

Southwick, N. (2013, October 10). "Norton Says Cyber Crime Costs Mexico $3B per Year," *Insight Crime*. www.insightcrime.org/news/brief/cyber-crime-cost-mexico-2b-in-2012-report/

Stone, H. (2011, March 3). "Mexico Moves into Cyber Crime." www.insightcrime.org/news/analysis/ mexico-moves-into-cyber-crime/

Stratiss-LookingGlass. (2018). *Mexico: Cyber Threat Landscape*. Reston (VA): LookingGlass Cyber Solutions. Available at https://www.lookingglasscyber.com/wp-content/uploads/2019/03/STRA TISS-Cyber_Landscape_Mexico.pdf

Subgrupo de Agenda Digital. (2017). *Hoja de Ruta Agenda Digital*. Cali: Alianza del Pacífico.

Trasviña, L. (2019). *Proyecto de Decreto Que Reforma y Deroga Diversas Disposiciones Del Título Noveno, Libro Segundo Del Código Penal Federal y Se Expide La Ley de Seguridad Informática*. Ciudad de México, México: Senado de la República. www.senado.gob.mx/64/emergente/fichaTecnica/index.php? tipo=iniciativa&idFicha=8426

Treppel, A. (2017). *Inauguración Tercera Semana Nacional De La Ciberseguridad*. Washington, DC: Organization of American States. www.oas.org/es/centro_noticias/discurso.asp?sCodigo=17-0168

Van Haaster, J. (2016). "Assessing Cyber Power," in NATO CCDCOE (ed.), *International Conference on Cyber Conflict, CYCON* (pp. 7–21). Tallin, Estonia. https://ccdcoe.org/uploads/2018/10/ CyCon_2016_book.pdf

Velasco, C. (2019). *Cyber Law in Mexico* (4th ed.). Alpen aan den Rijn: Kluwer Law International.

Whittaker, Z. (2019). "Hacker Dumps Thousands of Sensitive Mexican Embassy Documents Online," *TechCrunch*. https://techcrunch.com/2019/04/19/mexican-embassy-hack/%0AHacker

Yeo, S., Birch, A. S. & Bengtsson, H. I. J. (2016). "The Role of State Actors in Cybersecurity," in E. de Silva (ed.), *National Security and Counterintelligence in the Era of Cyber Espionage* (pp. 217–246). Hershey: IGI Global.

42

COLOMBIA'S CYBERSECURITY PREDICAMENT

State making, strategic challenges, and cyberspace

Florent Frasson-Quenoz and César Augusto Niño González

Introduction

Since the late 1990s, Colombia has been growing its economy, has been an active protagonist of the 2015 Paris summit on climate change, has been able to sign an historic peace agreement with the FARC-EP (Revolutionary Armed Forces of Colombia-Popular Army) in 2016, and has been successful in its commitment to join the OECD (May 30, 2018). But, Colombia is still fueling its economy through extractive activities, more than a quarter of its people still live under the poverty line (26.7 per cent in 2017) (World Bank, 2019), it still has the largest number of internally displaced people in the Americas (7,671,624, according to the UNHCR, 2019), it still is the world's hub for cocaine trafficking (UN, 2020), and it still has to wrestle with internal political conflicts and criminal groups (ELN, National Liberation Army, and "*las BACRIM*," *las bandas criminales*, Criminal Gangs).

On cybersecurity issues, the Colombian landscape is dominated by: (a) the country's long-term struggle to achieve internal stability and sustainable economic growth; (b) its positioning on the international stage; and (c) its relationship with International Organizations. Three characteristics that Mohammed Ayoob (1995) or Carlos Escudé (2012) would surely understand as typical of "third world" states.

If we do point to those different readings of IR, it is because cyberspace can be understood in many ways. In fact, as Manjikian (2010) points out, we apply to this new dimension of our social life the same narratives we normally use to understand spaces occupied, and consequently theorized, long before. Therefore, cybersecurity can be understood in terms of capacities (realist theories), in terms of legal framework, sensitivities and vulnerabilities between actors (liberal theories), or in terms of cyber-insecurities, either related to state's autonomy (Ayoob's and Escudé's theories) or to individual freedom (Welsh School of Security Studies). Following the Copenhagen School, it could be said that

Colombian governments never really promoted their own discourse on cybersecurity. But this does not mean that cyberspace has not been securitized.

As elsewhere in the world, cyberspace has been presented as one of many dangers for its people, for the government, and for the state. But in the last couple of years, as President Iván Duque's statements reveal, the securitization process is following the lines of a material-rationalist narrative: "As it stands today, due to cybersecurity breaches, the country is losing a fortune in dollars! This same money could be invested elsewhere" (Iván Duque; MINTIC, 2018).

Since 2000, the administration made a push to "modernize" itself using the e-government. In the last decade, Colombia has been able to limit cybercriminal activities because of the capacities acquired during the counter-insurgency fight. But today the country seems to have reached its limits. What are Colombia's cybersecurity challenges?

Both in the physical and the cyberspace, Colombia is a "land" of contrasts that generates specific challenges in terms of global governance (I.) and presence in the cyberspace (II.).

Governance of cyberspace

Colombian strategy

Colombia faces circumstances of internal armed conflict at least since 1964, a situation that has inspired a national security doctrine coded in the counter-insurgency fight. On the other hand, for more than a century now, Colombia's security agenda has been defined by its relations with the United States. From the US meddling in Panama, the Cold War, and 9/11, US security dynamics have always dominated Colombian politics in international security matters. Since the 1920s this phenomenon has been known in Colombia as "*la política réspice polum*" (the looking north policy), coined by former Colombian president Marco Fidel Suárez. This combination makes for a realist reading of security. Furthermore, and until recently, classic theaters of war dominated in high levels of government. Therefore, the Colombian state has been building its policies and strategies primarily to shield itself from those types of threats.

If we were to consider the historic bases for this construction, we should mention the National Economic and Social Policy Council – CONPES, in Spanish – created in 1958. This institution is the highest planning authority and an advisory board to the government regarding the national economic and social development (Departamento Nacional de Planeación, 2015). The CONPES operates under the direction of the President. Its permanent members, the Vice President, Ministers, the Director of the Administrative Department of the Presidency, the Director of the National Planning Department, and the Director of the Administrative Department of Science, Technology and Innovation, are all entitled to speak and vote, being traditional or non-traditional actors of the security sector.

The most relevant cybersecurity document, CONPES 3854 on National Digital Security Policy, was published in 2016 and included the Ministry of Information and Communication Technologies, the Ministry of National Defense, the National Intelligence Direction, and the National Department of Planning. Through this document the government aimed at updating its public institutions in terms of digital security. CONPES 3854 establishes that cybersecurity and cyber defense policies must focus on neutralizing the increase in cyber threats, aim at defending the country, and fight against cybercrimes

(Consejo Nacional de Política Económica y Social, 2016). But the first policy guidelines enforced by the Colombian state for cybersecurity and cyber defense to fortify its digital security were underlined in 2011 (CONPES, 2011). The main achievement was the strengthening of the institutional framework and the creation of relevant bodies to deal with this important issue.

When Colombia turned its attention to the cyberspace, the decision-making process was unusually quick. In a few years, six entities were created to respond to the perceived threats, increasing the capacity to act, at the expense of coordination (see Table 42.1).

International law

As Egan (2017) reasons, one could argue that, even though the international legal framework is always adapting to the ever-evolving cyberspace, the basic principles of international law should apply to it. But, as it is often the case with technological innovations, there is no international consensus on the matter yet. Most countries are asking

Table 42.1 Institutional Organs

Institution	Acronym	Objective
Grupo de respuesta a emergencias cibernéticas de Colombia (Colombian Cybernetic Emergency Response Group)	colCERT	To coordinate the necessary actions for the protection of the critical infrastructure of the Colombian State, when facing cybersecurity emergencies that threaten or compromise national security and defense (colCERT, 2017).
Comando Conjunto Cibernético del Comando General de las Fuerzas Militares de Colombia (Colombian Military Forces' Cybernetic Joint Command)	CCOC	To coordinate the decision making of the three cybernetic units of the Military Forces. Capacities, joint operations, research, and cyber defense of critical cybernetic infrastructure (CCOC, 2015).
Centro Cibernético Policial de la Policía Nacional de Colombia (Colombian National Police's Cybernetic Center)	CCP	To prevent, recommend, and respond to civilian cyber threats (CCP, 2017). It operates in sync with INTERPOL and other police bodies of the world.
Equipo de respuesta a incidentes de seguridad informática de la Policía Nacional (National Police's Digital Response Team)	CSIRT PONAL	To address the needs of prevention, attention and investigation of digital security situations (CSIRT, 2017).
Delegatura de protección de datos en la Superintendencia de Industria y Comercio (Data Protection Office of the Commerce and Industry Superintendence)		To pronounce the declarations of conformity on the international transfers of data (Delegatura para la Protección de Datos Personales, 2016).
Subdirección técnica de seguridad y privacidad de tecnologías de información (Subdirection of Information Technologies Security and Privacy)		To promote the research, development, and innovation in the field of cybersecurity, to provide information technology solutions required by the State (Subdirección de seguridad y Privacidad de TI, 2017).

Source: Authors' elaboration (2018).

for more and better international regulation but, on the other hand, some have contested the very applicability of international law to cyberspace. In the same fashion that the nineteenth century international legal framework was thought as a shield for second and third tear states from invasion by the more powerful, we could consider that the same phenomenon occurs for cyberspace: most states conceive international law as the basic tool in their search for security against state aggression.

If we were to accept the existence of an international order founded on liberal principles and lead by the United States – the "Liberal Leviathan" as Ikenberry coined it (2011) – we should underline the relevance of the legal considerations in the case of Colombia.

From the second half of 2000 onward, Colombia has been actively looking for international partners to fight against cyberthreats. In this context, the Colombian predicament could be described as such: To increase the general efficiency of the Colombian economy and reassure foreign investors, the state decided to modernize its administration privileging the use of the e-administration. For instance, as soon as 2014 65 per cent of Colombians had already had an interaction with the state through internet (it was the case for 81 per cent of private businesses) (Medina, 2015). This growing reliance on the internet has created challenges that were, until very recently, problems of more developed countries. For a mid-range income country like Colombia, it is a nearly impossible task to guarantee by itself the security of its data (being public or private). At the same time, because Colombia was looking to integrate into the OECD, the government felt the need to accelerate its modernization process and, consequently, did not – and still doesn't – have much room to act independently. In this matter, cooperation with the US explains a lot, from the fact that Colombia has fully embraced a narrative that combines military and economic considerations, to its cyber military command structure (there are four in the US, one central and one for each military branch).

International governance

As noted, Colombia has been relying heavily on international cooperation, specifically the US and Israel.[1] If this is the case, it is not only because of the traditional and strategic relation that the US and Colombia have had since the beginning of the twentieth century, but also because of the American interest in consolidating the idea that the principles of international law should/do apply to the cyberspace. Even if the US does not directly drive Colombia in matters of cybersecurity, the very fact that Colombia is looking to consolidate international legislation through international cooperation does serve American interests.

If we consider international law as a regulatory tool, then, this tool appears to be in the hands of those who have the capacity to create and enforce the law. As such, Colombian efforts to create regulation are overshadowed by its relative incapacity to enforce it. Transferring Mohammed Ayoob's theoretical framework – subaltern realism – to the cyberspace it could be said that Colombia, as a "third world" state, has no choice but to follow the guidelines that more powerful states promote on the international stage. By doing so, Colombia can try to position itself as a representative of the interests of the region in the construction process of the international legal framework. In relation to cybersecurity, the two main alarms, as far the United States and OECD's members are concerned, are set on data integrity and economic growth and, as we said, those two are the guidelines that Colombia follows.

In order to understand the way Colombia participates in the global cyberspace governance process we would like to make an analogy with the way Colombia participates in the UN security council. Since the creation of the United Nations, Colombia has been one of the most called upon Latin American states to participate in the UN security council activities (7 times; 10 for Brazil and 8 for Argentina). One of the main explanations for this is the fact that Colombia manifested, on the one hand, its willingness to follow to the letter the guiding principles of the organization and, on the other, its eagerness to be perceived as the legitimate representative of the region despite its internal difficulties. As such, Colombia showed its more powerful partners that it can be relied on.

Since the 2008 successful military operation in Ecuadorian territory against "Raúl Reyes," second in command and spokesperson of the FARC-EP, Colombia has been gaining in international credibility. Using its decryption capabilities, Colombia was able to establish its conviction that the FARC-EP were linked to the Venezuelan government. In a few years, Colombia was able to strengthen its ability to survey and draw attention to cyberthreats, internally and internationally. But Colombia does not stand as the most well-organized of Latin American states. Uruguay, Brazil, and Argentina are perceived as more prepared. Nonetheless, the fact that Colombia has a good and long-standing relationship with the US and that it has been able to respond to its internal cybersecurity threats will help the country follow through with its strategy of compliance and Latin American leadership.

It is important to point out the fact that international organizations do play a role in this debate on the Latin American stage. When mentioning "standards and standardization" the Inter-American Development Bank (IDB) and Organization of American States' (OAS) 2016 report focus on the necessity to use cybersecurity as another tool for maximization of trust between states. This move corresponds to the behavior liberals predict for international institutions. In this case, the IDB and the OAS act as predicted and can barely hide their eagerness to promote their own standards as the "good standard" (2016: 15).

The "Colombian" cyberspace

Definitions

Nonetheless, the Colombian State has adopted its own conceptual definitions regarding the strategic cybersecurity vocabulary. Some of those are shared with international institutions and organizations, while others are not. It is important to mention that in terms of cybersecurity, not only is the Ministry of Defense involved, but also other specialized bodies that do not belong to the traditional security sector. That said, here are some of those definitions aiming at creating a lexicon.

Cyberattacks are understood as organized and/or premeditated actions by one or more people in order to cause damage or problems to a computer system through the cyberspace (Ministerio de Defensa, traditional/US definition).

Cybersecurity is understood as the capacity of the state to minimize the level of risk to which citizens are exposed, in the face of threats or incidents of a cybernetic nature (Consejo Nacional de Política Económica y Social, non-traditional/international).

Cyber defense is the use of military capabilities when facing cybernetic threats or hostile acts that affect society, national sovereignty, independence, territorial integrity, constitutional order, and national interests (Ministerio de Defensa, traditional).

Within the State, **Cyberspace** has been understood as the physical and virtual environment formed by computers, computer systems, computer programs (software), telecommunications networks, data, and information that is used for the interaction between users (Resolución CRC 2258/2009 of the Comisión De Regulación De Comunicaciones, non-traditional/international).

A **Cyber Threat** is understood by the Colombian State as the appearance of a potential or current situation where an agent has the capacity to produce a cybernetic aggression against the population, the territory, and the political organization of the State (Ministerio de Defensa, traditional/own).

But the main challenge, the process of internalization of those definitions, still stands.

Specificities

The IDB's 2016 Cybersecurity Report is the best method at our disposal to draw the map of the cyberspace-related culture in Colombia. In this report, one can observe that it is amongst the most established in South America: only Uruguay seems to have acquired a better grasp of the risks that exist in the cyberspace.

The Observatory of Cybersecurity in Latin America and the Caribbean assesses the culture of cybersecurity using ten criterions. We shall focus our attention on three of them: cybersecurity mind-set in the society, confidence and trust in e-government, and online privacy standards. We shall compare Colombia to the other top four countries in South America, ranked by efficiency: Uruguay, Brazil, Chile, and Argentina.

In Colombia as well as in Uruguay, "societal consciousness of the secure use of online systems has been developed; a growing proportion of users have the skills to manage their privacy online, and protect themselves from intrusion, interference or unwanted access of information by others" (IDB & OAS, 2016). This established cybersecurity mind-set is unmatched in South America. The other top countries (Brazil, Chile, and Argentina) are less consistent on this front.

As far as confidence and trust in e-government are concerned, Colombia ranks second in South America just a step behind Uruguay. In Colombia, breaches have been identified, acknowledged, and disclosed in an ad-hoc manner by the government. The public sector coordinates actions to avoid attacks on personal information. High level internet crimes are prioritized and compliance to internet and web standards to protect the anonymity of users is promoted (IDB & OAS, 2016).

Finally, regarding online privacy standards, Colombia ranks fifth amongst the five first South American countries. Whereas in Uruguay actors, policies, and practices shaping freedom of expression and privacy are clearly identified and are central to informing decisions, in Colombia as well as in Brazil, actors from civil society are the ones actively driving change in practices, laws, and regulations that impinge on freedom of expression or privacy issues. Concerning the most relevant feature, that of the compliance to the universal declaration of human rights, Uruguay is the most efficient of South American countries. In Colombia, the government is only considering the adoption of human rights legislation with a focus on privacy, especially data of private enterprises.

Clearly Colombia sees the cyberspace as a space to be protected for it to generate aggregate value to the economy. But the fact remains, the criterions used to assess the situation are the same as those used by Occidental countries. The vision defended by experts is militarily and economically oriented.

Cyberspace and its challenges for Colombia

Colombia is a country that has more territory than state; that is, a country where state institutions do not reach every territory and community. Despite its significant institutional advances – cyberspace has been added to the national security strategy – institutions and capacities still needs to be strengthened.

In traditional terms, cyberspace combines sensitivities and potential vulnerabilities capable of rearranging political doctrines and the crucial elements of prevention, intelligence, and offensive actions. This dimension, unexplored or relegated within the strategic priorities of a "Third World" country, clusters two major problems for Colombia: cybercrime and cyberterrorism. Thirty years ago, the state understood that the involvement of both public and private sectors in a coherent strategy to minimize vulnerabilities and increase response capacities to face adverse phenomena, would build a security culture, increasing institutional resilience.

In 2014, the Global Cybersecurity Index (GCI) of the International Telecommunications Union (ITU) assessed the degree of cybersecurity development in each country, aiming to foster a cybersecurity culture and its integration in the core of information and communication technologies. This index ranked Colombia fifth within the Americas, and ninth in the world, sharing the position with France, Denmark, Spain, and Egypt as the countries with the best cybersecurity indicators. The United States was ranked first, and Timor-Leste last. In its 2015 report, the GCI showed the same results, ranking Colombia in fifth and ninth respectively (Global Cybersecurity Index, 2015). The above rating reflects a certain degree of effectiveness; that is, a process of institutionalization of international norms and internalization of the "northern" narrative on cyberspace and cybersecurity. However, the fact that in 2017 Colombia was ranked 46th on the GCI (2017) is indicative of its relative incapacity to deal with the threats this narrative does identify. For all states, threats go much faster. But for some the task to overcome them, only underlines their structural fragility.

Illustrative of this paradox, in 2009 Colombia became one of the first countries in the world to enact a law specifically targeting cyberspace (Superintendencia de Industria y Comercio, 2009): Law 1273, by means of which the Penal Code was amended, and a new legal right was created: "the right to the protection of personal information and data." Since then, the state's capacity to safeguard that right has not grown significantly, unveiling its "cyber"-security predicament (Ayoob, 1995).

The fact remains that, in traditional terms, cybercrime is not a simple security preoccupation anymore, it is a risk. This transformation is due to structural events related to the vulnerabilities of different sectors of the society. In 2017, this type of crime increased around 28 per cent according to figures from the Bureau of Judicial Investigation – DIJIN – and INTERPOL (Revista Semana, 2017).

That same year, figures of the National Police estimated that around 6,372 citizens reported internet fraud, for up to 5 billion US dollars. Colombia has been reported as the first victim of ransomware in Latin America in 2018. The authorities have related the use of virtual currencies with illegal activities and, in 2017, have warned of "cyber pyramids" in 11 cities of the country, considerable in a country where more than 50 per cent of the population lives in only four cities (Bogotá, Medellín, Cali, and Barranquilla). This urban/ rural divide is of importance when we consider that segregation between communities repeats itself, from the physical to the virtual space, along the lines of social and economic constructs (intersectional narrative).

In addition, Colombia is still vulnerable to risks from outside its digital borders. In 2017, WannaCry reached the country, the police attended 52 victims of global attacks and alerted on 59 possible international threats (Revista Semana, 2017).

One last consideration must be pondered: due to their definitions, the limit between cybercrime and cyberterrorism is quite thin, one could say fuzzy. In Colombia, cyberterrorism is "the use of cyberspace as an end or as a means, with the purpose of generating terror or generalized fear in the population, nation or state, resulting in a violation of the people's will" (Ministerio de Tecnologías de la Información y las Comunicaciones, 2016). As stated, cyberterrorism seeks to alter critical infrastructure and moves away from cybercrime. The first concept aims at generating instability and threatens the existence of the state, while the other aims at benefitting from illegal activities. But, because terrorism is illegal and generates profits through drug trafficking and organized crime (unlicensed copying, credit card fraud, and phishing attacks against the retail industry) separating one from the other opens the way for abuses and discriminatory measures and, ultimately, for the decline of the Rule of Law. In very recent history, it has been easy for the state to use the terrorist semantic in order to undermine human rights.

Colombia's current cybersecurity challenges can be summarized accordingly:

- Defend state integrity;
- Increase its cyber reach;
- Apply and promote international norms in order to gain recognition on the international stage;
- Protect data privacy and promote economic growth;
- Guarantee a stable and business friendly environment for foreign investors;
- Strengthen internal institutions and their accessibility;
- Reclaim and order the cyberspace against non-traditional and non-state actors;
- Respect and promote human rights.

Some final considerations

As a mid-range income country, Colombia has identified itself with the norms of cybersecurity promoted by Occidental countries within the international society. Nonetheless, Colombia faces specific social challenges related to its situation of extractive and agriculturally based economy on the one hand, and its situation regarding its long-lasting internal conflict heritage – internal displacement and a much-needed land reform – on the other.

In Colombia, there are few debates on the construction and access to databases regarding the historical memory of the conflict and few debates about the limit between private and public data. This point is relevant when we consider the fact that private actors like multinational corporations possess information that could be important for the reconciliation process but are strictly covered by the law on data privacy.

By the same token, the Colombian State does not seem to be concerned with protecting some basic and free access to vital information for its communities, being either native, black, afro, or rural. For instance, the state has not been concerned with providing free meteorological data to those rural and native communities in need whose living conditions could decide the success or failure of the peace process. Sometimes, preoccupations about the Orange/creative economy have had the tendency to occupy public debates, revealing the profound and persisting divide between urban and rural populations.

Notwithstanding, cybersecurity has been one of the central axes of Colombian policies in the last decade. Its commitment has been significant and particularly visible in the region. In this sense, Colombia's cybersecurity policy has constituted an opportunity for the state to make its presence felt on the international stage. One could argue that, apart from the signing of the peace treaty in November 2016 and in pair with environmental ones, cybersecurity issues have been the most fruitful in terms of international insertion, specifically within the OECD.

Note

1 Interview with Colonel Jaime Ariza Girón who was director of Intelligence and Counterintelligence of the Colombian National Army. Interview conducted on November 30, 2017.

Suggested reading

Kshetri, N. (2013). *Cybercrime and Cybersecurity in the Global South.* Basingstoke: Palgrave Macmillan.
Patiño, A. M. S. & Ramírez, D. P. G. (2019, May 15). "A technological analysis of Colombia's cybersecurity capacity: a systemic perspective from an organizational point of view," *Ingeniería Solidaria, 15*(2): 1–30. https://revistas.ucc.edu.co/index.php/in/article/view/2750/2702
Subrahmanian, V. S., Ovelgonne, M., Dumitras, T. & Prakash, B. A. (2015). *The Global Cyber-Vulnerability Report.* Cham: Springer.

References

Ayoob, M. (1995). *The Third World Security Predicament. State making, Regional Conflict, and International System.* Boulder, CO: Lynne Reinner.
CCOC. (2015). "Comando Conjunto Cibernético." www.cno.org.co/sites/default/files/documentos/actas/150304 per cent20Presentaci per centC3 per centB3n per cent20CNO-2015.pdf
CCP. (2017, December 12). "Centro Cibernético Policial." https://caivirtual.policia.gov.co/
colCERT. (2017, July 12). "Grupo de Respuesta a Emergencias Cibernéticas de Colombia." www.col cert.gov.co/?q=acerca-de
Consejo Nacional de Política Económica y Social. (2011). "*Lineamientos de política para la Ciberseguridad y Ciberdefensa,*" Bogotá: Ministerio de Tecnologías de la Información y las Comunicaciones.
Consejo Nacional de Política Económica y Social. (2016). "*Política Nacional de Seguridad Digital.*" Bogotá: Departamento Nacional de Planeación.
CSIRT. (2017, December 12). *Equipo de Respuesta a Incidentes de Seguridad Informática de la Policía Nacional.* https://cc-csirt.policia.gov.co/Publicaciones/quienes_somos
Delegatura para la Protección de Datos Personales. (2016, August 16). "Superintendencia de Industria y Comercio." www.sic.gov.co/sites/default/files/files/Superintendente_Proteccion_Datos_Personales.pdf
Departamento Nacional de Planeación. (2015, April 12). "El Consejo Nacional de Política Económica y Social, CONPES." www.dnp.gov.co/CONPES/Paginas/conpes.aspx
Egan, B. J. (2017). "International law and stability in cyberspace," *Berkeley Journal of International Law, 35* (1): 169–180.
Escudé, C. (2012). *Principios de realismo periférico. Una teoría y su vigencia ante el ascenso de China.* Buenos Aires: Ediciones Lumiere.
Global Cybersecurity Index. (2015). "Global Cybersecurity Index & Cyberwellness Profiles." *The International Telecommunication Union.*
Global Cybersecurity Index. (2017). "Global Cybersecurity Index & Cyberwellness Profiles." *The International Telecommunication Union.*
IDB & OAS. (2016). "Cybersecurity: are We Ready in Latin America and the Caribbean. 2016 Cybersecurity Report." https://publications.iadb.org/bitstream/handle/11319/7449/Cybersecurity-Are-We-Prepared-in-Latin-America-and-Caribbean.pdf?sequence=1&isAllowed=y

Ikenberry, G. J. (2011). *Liberal Leviathan: the Origins, Crisis, and Transformation of the American World Order*. Princeton, NJ: Princetown University Press.

Manjikian, M. M. (2010). "From global village to virtual battlespace: the colonizing of the internet and the extension of realpolitik," *International Studies Quarterly*, *54*(2), 381–401.

Medina, C. M. A. (2015, August 3). "La hoja de ruta para la ciberseguridad," *El Espectador*. www.elespectador.com/noticias/economia/hoja-de-ruta-ciberseguridad-articulo-576914

Ministerio de Tecnologías de la Información y las Comunicaciones. (2016, September 30). www.mintic.gov.co/portal/604/w3-article-18728.html

Ministerio de Tecnologías de la Información y las Comunicaciones. (2018). "Ivan Duque habla de factura electrónica, ciberseguridad y acceso a las tecnologías," C34 N3. www.youtube.com/watch?v=X2BwuNZz9pY

Resolución CRC 2258 de 2009. (2011, December 23). "Comisión de Regulación de Comunicaciones." www.alcaldiabogota.gov.co/sisjur/normas/Norma1.jsp?i=38498

Revista Semana. (2017, December 28). "El cibercrimen en 2017: la amenaza crece sobre Colombia." www.semana.com/nacion/articulo/cibercrimen-en-colombia-balance-de-2017/551979

Subdirección de seguridad y Privacidad de TI. (2017, August 29). "Ministerio de Tecnologías de la Información y las Comunicaciones." www.mintic.gov.co/portal/604/w3-propertyvalue-6198.html

Superintendencia de Industria y Comercio. (2009, June 12). "Protección de datos personales: aspectos prácticos sobre el derecho de Habeas Data." www.sic.gov.co/sobre-la-proteccion-de-datos-personales

UN. (2020). *UN Wolrd Drug Report 2020*. https://wdr.unodc.org/wdr2020/index.html

UNHCR (2019) *Global Trends: Forced Displacement in 2018*. Geneva, Switzerland: UNHCR, p.68

World Bank. (2019). https://data.worldbank.org/indicator/SI.POV.NAHC?locations=CO

43

CYBER SECURITY GOVERNANCE IN BRAZIL

Keeping silos or building bridges?

Louise Marie Hurel and Luisa Cruz Lobato

Introduction

The year is 2008. This was the very first time that the Brazilian national defense strategy recognized cyberspace as one of the strategic domains for the country's defense and national security. At that time, cyber attacks were becoming notorious and ever more reflective of geopolitical tensions. One year earlier, Estonia had suffered a major cyber attack from Russia, followed later on by further Russian attacks in Georgia. Not that differently from the growing global concern with cyber security, Brazil had then started to witness what would become a decade of fundamental institutional developments aimed at consolidating an architecture for cyber security governance within the federal government and a national cyber security agenda informed by concerns with external threats, "cyber wars," and the country's existent problem of terrorism. These initial concerns would later be replaced by an emphasis on combating cybercrime and digital propaganda – but not before bequeathing a set of institutional arrangements and organizations that have become part of the government's cyber infrastructure. At the same time, the institutional legacy from this period came to coexist and interact with existing non-governmental organizations involved in technical response to cyber incidents and with developing Internet policy (Hurel, 2019).

How has this change taken place? How did the Brazilian cyber security ecosystem come into existence and how can we make sense of the *shifts* in the cyber threat landscape in the past decade? Additionally, how can we make sense of these shifts institutionally, within the federal government? In posing these questions, this chapter provides an overview of the state-of-art of cyber security governance in Brazil, presenting a complex landscape of actors and institutions responsible for the country's cyber incident response, cyber policy, information security, and cyber defense strategies. It points to the current challenges that institutions and actors working with cyber security in Brazil face, including a persisting misalignment between threat perception and response, and a lack of concerted action among the variety of governmental and non-governmental bodies. The governance of cyber security in Brazil is characterized by a continuous tension between isolated responses to threats and attempts of concerted action, which substantially affects the effectiveness and coherence of existing strategies vis-à-vis actual threats, in addition to making it hard for extensive collaboration outside of already established niches sharing a similar understanding of threats.

The chapter is structured in four sections. The first section will draw a map of the cyber threat landscape in Brazil, which includes dimensions of defense policy, concerns with cyber terrorism, and cybercrime. It traces the shifting threat concerns since the initial build-up of the government's cyber infrastructure and points to how it slowly adjusted to respond to high impact/low probability threats – instead of focusing on high probability ones. Second, the chapter presents an overview of the cyber security institutional landscape and the main concepts from the country's national cyber security documents that have contributed to structuring the contemporary governance landscape. It then traces the challenges and opportunities for political action, concluding with the diagnosis that one of the main challenges faced by those engaged in cyber security policy making is the poor alignment between strategy and actual threats.

Cyber security in Brazil

Risk landscape

Cyber security emerged as a national concern in Brazil following profound transformations deriving from the digitalization of infrastructures, society, economy, and politics. Between 2008 and 2017, the country's digital penetration rate jumped from 18 to 61 per cent (TIC Domicílios, 2018), financial institutions have gone fully digital with more than 604 financial start-ups across the country (FintechLab, 2019), and social media has achieved a central role in the creation and mediation of public opinion – with more than 120 million users in Brazil. On the other hand, reports from the Brazilian National Computer Emergency Response Team (CERT.br) highlight that the number of registered incidents increased from 3,107 in 1999 to 833,775 in 2017 – reaching its peak in 2014, with more than a million incidents reported. These incidents include Distributed Denial of Service Attacks (DDoS), computer invasion, scans, worms, fraud, and web attacks.

Understanding which cyber risks are established, prioritized and how they feed into institutional responses to perceived threats is fundamental to the task of tracing the architecture of cyber security governance in Brazil, not least because they tell us what kind of institutional setting is prioritized as the most suitable to responding to upcoming threats. Thus, for example, a focus on cyber war might likely lead to a protagonism of military doctrines and rationales as adequate responses and, thus, to an allocation of resources to military or defense-oriented actors. Likewise, a focus on "domestic threats," i.e., local hacktivism and online political activism, or on "cybercrime," might foster a greater investment on intelligence, surveillance, or investigative capacities within the current institutional landscape or even lead to the establishing of new organizations and institutions.

Risks are significantly distinct from threats, despite the fact that both are profoundly entangled when it comes to security (National Research Council, 1991). Whereas *threats* suggest the existence, present or *in potentia*, of *something* that can explore a vulnerability, cause damage, or destroy an asset; *risk* refers to the possibility of a threat to effectively cause destruction or damage (Dunn Cavelty, 2009). That is to say, risks are associated to threats in their *potential*, always pointing towards a future (immediate or not). Defining risks is a normative action that relies on the mobilization of a "risk grammar" that seeks to trigger actions to *prevent* the occurrence of or *mitigate* the impacts related to a particular risk. Risk is a call for action (both material and discursive) in face of uncertainty (Lobato, 2016).

Risks and threats are culturally and historically constructed. Not only they are mutable across time and space, but they are most intimately dependent on and responsive to shifts in the political context (Giddens, 1990; Beck, 1992). This is important as it provides us with at least two considerations that inform the analysis of the competing notions of risks in Brazil. First, it allows us to consider *who* can "call to action" – identify risks or define priorities. Second, it places the notion of risks and threats in a wider horizon of political, social, and economic dynamics. Thus, the exercise of understanding cyber risks in Brazil should not be limited to actions and/or mitigation strategies (such as the repair, maintenance, and management of infrastructures). Rather, we should also consider how these priorities are negotiated and resources mobilized within this cultural and political context.

In this section we (i) identify the dominating understandings of cyber threats at the national level and (ii) trace the emergence and change in the perception of risks and threats in light of the shifts in the socio-political context. We contend that the institutional development of cyber security in Brazil was marked by specific concerns related to external threats such as espionage and foreign interference. However, the growing political instability in late 2015 onwards combined with the fast digitization of society created new conditions for a shift in threat perception. That does not necessarily mean that new threats emerged, rather that already-existing perceptions of risk/threats linked to cybercrime could emerge within this particular context. What is more, it sheds light to the competing and, at times, complementary perceptions of threat.

Brazil hosted five "mega-events" in a period of four years, starting with the Rio+20 Conference for Sustainable Development in 2012 and closing with the Olympic Games in 2016. The imminence of the so-called "mega-events" in the country, that is, large-scale international events that are characterized by the large-scale attraction of visitors, significant media outreach, high costs, and big transformations in the urban infrastructure, environment, and population (Müller, 2015), raised substantial concerns as to which would be the main sources of threats to the country's Internet infrastructure. Scholarly literature (Gaffney, 2010; Cardoso, 2013) has noted that these events act as key moments for the transformation of public security governance (see Figure 43.1).

Consecutive events, such as the Confederations Cup, World Cup, and the Olympic Games, prompted preparatory responses by the federal government, which culminated in the creation of organizations and institutions that would add to the burgeoning Internet infrastructure (De Carvalho & Cukierman, 2015). Here we explore two dimensions of the threat landscape in the years that followed 2012.

The first dimension of the governance of national cyber security threat landscape in Brazil was one of combatting and identifying *external threats*. Between the years of 2012 and 2014

Figure 43.1 Timeline of "Mega Events" Hosted by Brazil Since 2012
Source: Authors' illustration.

the main national concern revolved around low probability and high impact threats, such as cyber war and cyber terrorism. The early perception of cyber risks was substantially influenced by the – then – "newfound" threats to state security in cyberspace. Realization of these threats was intensified by media coverage and scholarly debates focusing on international events such as the cyber attacks against Georgia (2008) and Estonia (2007) and the discovery of the Stuxnet worm in the Iranian nuclear plant in Natanz (2010) (Dunn Cavelty, 2007). Alarmism regarding the imminence of a cyber war and the cyber terrorist threat raised substantially in this period. Not only did it overshadow the public debate to actual high-risk cyber security threats – such as fraud (Nery, 2017), cybercrime, data breaches, and theft – but also raised ambiguous notions of cyber war and terrorism to the political agenda with little conceptual clarity to follow (Diniz, Muggah & Glenny, 2014).

This ambiguity provides a fertile ground for the redefinition and contestation of red lines. Some policymakers, for example, have highlighted that the unauthorized access to government sensitive information should be configured as an act of war (Senado Federal, 2012). According to the National Cyber Defense Policy, cyber war is defined as the use of a set of offensive and defensive measures to deny, explore, corrupt, and destroy opponent's values through information, information systems, and computers (Defesa, 2012). At that time, mainly 2012, the concern – at least, discursively – was with capabilities, that is, how ready the government was to address cyber terrorism and cyber war – despite the fact that both were not concrete nor imminent threats to the country.[1]

Distinctly from Western countries, cyber terrorism lags behind as a national security concern in Brazil and the country has not faced substantive terrorist threats in its history. Many scholars have argued that the misalignment between the perceived terrorist threat or the expectation of potential cyber war are indicators of the securitization of cyberspace by the state (Diniz, Muggah & Glenny, 2014; Cepik, Canabarro & Borne, 2014; De Souza & De Almeida, 2017; Hurel, 2019). Despite this, more recently, debates on cyber terrorism have been gradually returning to the political agenda as the Senate discusses a new anti-terrorist law that seeks to incorporate the Internet as one dimension of the means and expressions of terrorism (Senado Federal, 2017).

According to the government, both information security and cyber security are becoming a priority for the strategic functions of the State. This includes the protection of critical infrastructures, information, individual rights such as privacy, and national sovereignty. Based on media articles and computer security companies' reports (Kaspersky, 2017; Symantec, 2019), Figure 43.2 illustrates the likelihood and impact of the cyber events that were most highlighted during the mega-events period in the country, having as reference the national defense framework that guided most of debates in this period. As shown, it considers as high impact attacks those actions that could likely result in loss of human life, sensitive government information, or political instability.

However, if we change the reference point to the market sector and consider the main impacts in terms of financial costs, the figure substantially changes (see Figure 43.3).

This shift suggests that prioritization of a group of risks associated to threats to national defense has substantially shaped efforts to create and/or establish adequate responses to them. At first, Brazil's cyber security governance architecture adjusted to respond to high impact, low probability threats partly as a strategy to address the international attention received during the Olympic Games and the World Cup, and partly as the continuation of a trend to focus on military and national defense issues on cyberspace (i.e., cyber war and cyber terrorism).

Whilst external threats such as cyber war and terrorism characterize the predominant government perspective in the early years of the "mega-events," in particular 2012 and

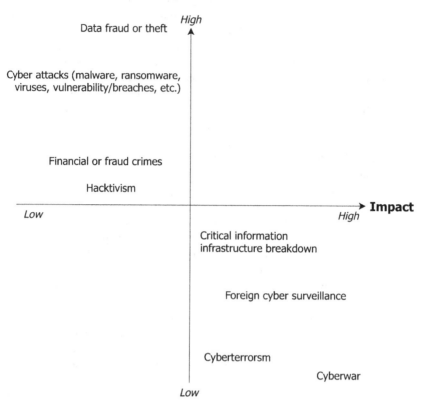

Probability of occurrence

Figure 43.2 The Cyber Threat Landscape in Brazil, 2012–2016 – (National Defense-Oriented)

Source: Authors' illustration.

*The figure portrays the 2012–2015 Brazil cyber threat landscape from the perspective of the national defense sector. It replicates the "perspective" of national defense institutions, including their threat characterizations and prioritizations. The figure splits the risk of a cyber threat to occur along two axes: the horizontal axis comprises the expected impact of such risk, ranging from "low" to "high," whereas the vertical comprises the probability of a risk to take place and also ranges from "low" to "high." Defining whether a risk is of low/high probability/impact depends on the estimated frequency of the event, on the one hand, and its expected financial, economic, information, or human loss, on the other. Our risk matrix adapts Bostrom's and Ćirković's (2008) three variables of risk severity into two variables: *impact* and *probability*. In terms of impact, the severity of a risk depends on how many people it would affect (and how badly) and, in terms of probability, it depends on how likely it is to occur, provided the best evidence available at the time in which this judgment took place. High impact events would have to affect entire populations and cause great damage (thousands of fatalities, compromise of critical health and supply/transport infrastructures or pose great danger to national security), in contrast to low impact events which damage may include limited financial losses, minor nuisances and temporary suspension of non-essential services. Whether an event probability is high or low depends on the frequency with which it occurs.

2013, it is far from portraying the risk landscape in its entirety. In addition to the late 2000s cyber war debates, an important risk-driver during 2014 was precisely the impact of the revelations of US mass surveillance and how it targeted Brazilian institutions. The Snowden

Probability of occurrence

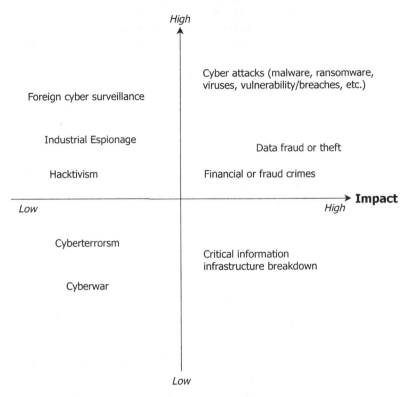

Figure 43.3 Cyber Threat Landscape in Brazil, 2012–2016
Source: Authors' illustration.
*This figure illustrates the cyber threat matrix using a market-oriented approach.

Revelations surfaced major concerns with foreign interference and espionage as well as resulted in direct political leadership engagement from former president Dilma Rousseff after having been targeted by the US government. It was also followed by key political and strategic responses, such as: (i) the approval of the Brazilian Internet Bill of Rights, (ii) the organization of NetMundial[2] in São Paulo; and (iii) the elevation of privacy and security as allies in the national political agenda (Hurel & Santoro, 2018).

However, shortly after, political instability crept in as the country approached its presidential elections at the end of 2014, opening up space for a major political and economic crisis which later led to the impeachment of president Dilma, in 2016. During this period, waves of protest across the country preannounced a shift in the risk landscape from *external* to predominantly *internal* threats. Increasing polarization and use of social media created new conditions for the emergence of fake news, crimes, whistleblowing, and hacking as synonyms to risks associated with cyber security.

While political and economic instability contributed to a greater focus on domestic politics and threats, parallel events such as the 2016 Olympics also reflected similar internally focused concerns. In preparation for the international mega-event, the Brazilian intelligence agency publicly called attention to the role of hacktivism as one of the key drivers of potential attacks. The intelligence sector concerns with hacktivism prior to the Olympics was rooted on the experience with the cases reported during the Confederations Cup, in 2013, the massive street protests in the same year, and the 2014 World Cup, when government webpages were defaced with politically motivated messages (Abin, 2016).

An ever-present and yet rather forgotten dimension of cyber security debates during this period was cybercrime – mainly characterized by economically motivated and computer-mediated breaches, data theft, fraud, and financial crimes (Diniz, Muggah & Glenny, 2014; Kaspersky, 2017). The costs of cybercrime in Brazil are particularly alarming – McAfee estimate losses reach approximately US$10 billion (Machado, 2018) – and the country has been at the epicenter of a global cybercrime wave (Muggah & Thompson, 2015). It ranks second in consumers losses by cybercrime (Statista, 2019a) and is the most targeted country in Latin America (Statista, 2019b). This scenario should also be read in the context of Brazil's banking sector's innovations and rising e-commerce infrastructure. Not only is the country an early adopter of secure Internet banking (Rosenthal, 2012; Fernandez, 2016), but also of emerging technologies such as biometric ones (Schmidt, 2013). According to Brazilian Federation of Banks (FEBRABAN), 40 per cent of all transactions in 2018, that is, 31.3 billion, were solely through mobile banking (Febraban, 2019). Being the "avant garde" of transformation of digital economy, however, also comes with a greater attack surface for crimes – such as online fraud schemes which include, but are not restricted to, the creation of fake banking web pages to lure customers into giving sensitive information.

A recent dimension of cyber risks that was left out of both Figures 43.2 and 43.3 is the impact of misinformation campaigns in Brazilian democratic institutions. Whereas formerly comprised in national defense concerns, impacts of digital technologies in regime stability was not a source of concern during the "mega-events" period and the institutional build-up of Brazil's cyber security governance architecture. Attention was directed to this phenomenon after the election of US president Donald Trump and the Cambridge Analytica scandal and promptly fostered research on the impact of computational propaganda in Brazil (Arnaudo, 2017). As in the US case, the dynamics of misinformation in Brazil are closely related to the protection – or lack of thereof – of databases containing users' personal information. The emergence of social media platforms and business models focused on collecting as much data as possible about users' behavior in order to improve services and allow for targeted advertising potentialized propaganda in a rather unforeseen fashion. Not only does it serve as a means for manipulation, influence campaigns, and other mechanisms for disputing and changing public opinion, but it provides new grounds for charismatic leadership to communicate with and identify their particular audience. In light of how such means are associated to the election of Brazil's president Jair Bolsonaro and his communication, the following years will likely see in-depth assessments regarding the actual impact and reach of these efforts.

Furthermore, the politicization of the image of the hacker and its constitution as a politically invested agent has characterized the recent scandals involving the leaking of online correspondence between public prosecutors from the Operation Car Wash ("Lava Jato") (Fishman, Martins, Demori, De Santi & Greenwald, 2019), which investigated a high-profile corruption scandal involving government and business representatives. In reaction to accusations of partiality, illegality, and judicial misconduct during the investigations which culminated in the conviction of Brazil's former president Luiz Inácio Lula da Silva, prosecutors, the minister of justice, and president Jair Bolsonaro have questioned the authenticity of the messages, suggesting that they were hacked and were therefore illegal.[3]

These developments suggest a continuation and possible deepening of actions and responses oriented towards an "internal" threat. That is to say, the prioritization of threats and consequent allocation of resources will likely keep following concerns with the possibility of disruption (technical and political) caused by the actions of the much-fantasized threat of the hacker and an anxiety with tracing and monitoring "disruptive" subjects online. In practice, this would align with a build-up of investigative and monitoring capabilities of the Federal Police, ABIN and, possibly, CDCiber. The immediate imprisonment of four people by the federal police (headed by Sergio Moro) for allegedly hacking into public authorities' phones could be indicative of how investment in investigative and monitoring capabilities strengthens the role of this particular institution.

Institutional and political landscape

Cyber threat awareness was significantly pushed forward by (i) the military sector's perceptions of international cyber security incidents and framing of the issue in terms of cyber war; (ii) rising cybercrime costs; and (iii) concerns with cyber attacks and cyber terrorism during the mega-events years. These three phenomena influenced different aspects of what should be called the "Brazilian cyber security strategy." Officially, there is not a single document unifying this strategy, as in the case of the US or many EU countries; instead, there are three core documents that summarize the country's national strategy to address cyber threats: The National Defense Strategy of 2008, its revision of 2012, the National Information Security Strategy of 2015, and the National Information Security Policy of 2019. This section analyses the same timeline of events however, it departs from the understanding of the institutional and normative developments that both underpinned and emerged from the shifts in the risks landscape.

Concerns about cyber war, surveillance, and other foreign threats resulted in the inclusion of cyberspace as one of the key strategic sectors in the 2008 National Defense Strategy. This was a significant step, and perhaps the foundational moment for a national cyber security architecture to emerge under the auspices of the Ministry of Defense. The emphasis in this document paved the way for the government to create a new portfolio of activities and projects that would fall under the coordination of the Ministry of Defense and the Brazilian Army.

Cyber security's ascent within the national agenda was not merely discursive, it also led to a significant resource mobilization. That does not come as a surprise as some companies and governments have a political and economic interest (and expectation of profitability) in echoing narratives of imminent cyber threat (Lindsay, 2017). The 2012 White Book of National Defense estimated 900 million Brazilian reais (approximately 220 million US dollars) in investments between 2011 and 2035 (Brasil, 2012a) for the army to establish a protection system for national cyberspace protection. This budget further included a list of six subprojects, three of which focused on the implementation of the: (i) National Cyber Defense Center (CDCiber), (ii) the Armed Forces' Cyber Defense Command (ComDCiber), and (iii) the National School for Cyber Defense. That was the same year that the army had just established CDCiber and received a multi-year budget of 370 million to develop a national system for cyber defense (Brasil, 2012b). Moreover, 20 million reais were allocated solely for an integrated center for cyber security for that particular "mega-event" (Andrade, 2012).

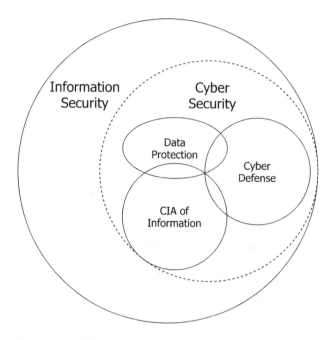

Figure 43.4 Thematic Institutional Competencies

Source: Authors' illustration, based on the Strategy for Information, Communications, and Cyber Security (see Brasil, 2015).

The Brazilian institutional architecture distinguishes cyber security competencies from information security and cyber defense (see Figure 43.4). This division follows competencies among different branches in the federal government, particularly as it incorporates military-civilian distinctions (cyber security vs. cyber defense) and – institutionally – differentiates security of the communications infrastructure (information security) from the security of machines and systems. In practice, this means attributing the competency for cyber defense to the armed forces (CDCiber and ComDCiber) while leaving information security within the institutional responsibility of the federal government through the Institutional Security Cabinet (GSI) and the Brazilian Intelligence Agency (ABIN).

The GSI is responsible for coordinating the information security activities and maintaining the Centre for Incident Response of the Governmental networks (CTIRgov) (CTIR, 2018). It is the main organisational body in charge of developing guidelines, strategies, and policies for information security at the national level. The CDciber, on the other hand, integrated the Cyber Defense Command (ComDCiber). Its key activities are risk analysis, automatic incident detection, incident analysis, alert diffusion, and statistic recommendations.

To map and delve deeply into the different institutions that emerged in the past two decades would be a paper in itself. Figure 43.4 (Hurel & Lobato, 2018) is a representation of the key sectors and competencies that currently compose the wider national cyber security governance landscape. What is important within this panorama is to understand that though securitizing trends and predominant external threat perceptions have made the steep institutional inflation of governmental bodies and armed forces, operationally and strategically, cyber security is much broader in the sense that it entails coordination efforts.

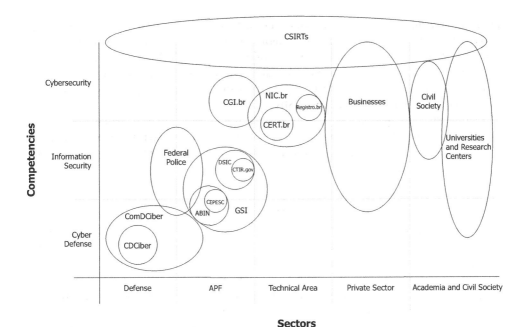

Figure 43.5 Domestic Cyber Security Governance (Post/Olympics and Marco Civil Law)
Source: Hurel and Lobato (2018).

This was evident during the "mega-events" where different technical bodies came together to establish coordination and integration efforts to respond to cyber attacks and vulnerabilities (Figure 43.5). During the 2014 World Cup, CDCiber established a center for operations with a central cyber defense body in charge of coordinating 13 teams scattered in key cities all across Brazil (CDCiber, Diniz, Muggah & Glenny, 2014). In 2015, collaborative efforts continued to take place whilst preparing for the Olympics in the following year. However, paradoxically, these exercises and actions were considerably restricted to the government bodies such as the Federal Police, National Telecommunications Agency, National Intelligence Agency, and specific representatives from academia (Agência, 2015).

Conclusion: a strategic approach to national cyber security in-the-making

To better understand the progression of cyber security governance in Brazil, we separate the institutional development into three stages. These should be understood as a framework of reference rather than an attempt to portray the totality of factors that play in the temporal development of national cyber security.[4]

Early stage

The years of 2008 to 2012 were key for the normative and strategic consolidation of cyber security in the national security landscape. It was during these years that the concepts of information security, cyber security, and cyber defense began to take shape in the strategic agenda. Even though, historically, these terms appeared in 2000 in the Green Book on Information Society issued by the Ministry of Science and Technology, it was only after 2008 that a strategic pool of resources were allocated to support the construction of a cyber security organizational complex that would join both GSI (presidency), Armed Forces, and Computer Incident Response Teams (CSIRTs).

During the same period Internet governance was slowly maturing within the country. Thus, new technical organizations, such as the national Computer Emergency Response Team (CERT.br), were created, in order to act as a designated focal point for reporting threats, incidents, and attacks.

Mid stage

These were the years of the "mega-events." In Brazil, such events acted as important "contextual triggers" to the institutional and operational development of national cyber security. These years served as testing grounds for the newly established CDCiber and ComDCiber, mobilized financial resources, and began to consolidate specific networks of cooperation within the government and with some strategic sectors (critical infrastructure, federal police) through integrated centers of command and control.

The exercise of tracing threat perception in Brazil is a particularly relevant one as it enables us to unpack the factors which have substantively shaped the construction of the country's national cyber security governance. As illustrated in the first section of this chapter, Brazil's cyber risk landscape has been significantly affected by a series of internal and external events. The years preceding the World Cup (Diniz, Muggah & Glenny, 2014) and the Olympic Games (2016) in Brazil saw the progressive consolidation of an architecture of governance composed of actors from both the civilian and the military branches of the government, the private and financial sectors, and groups in the technical community. This architecture was however deeply shaped by militarized responses to a very specific set of projected cyber risks and included the build-up of a cyber defense system within the army which kicked off in 2008, with the publication of the National Defense Strategy. As of the moment of the writing of this chapter there were, at least, three branches of the army addressing some aspect of cyber defense: The Army Electronic Communications and Warfare Command, established in 2009, the Cyber Defense Center (CDCiber), created in 2010, and the Cyber Defense Command (ComDCiber), established in 2016 to integrate joint responses to cyber threats from the army, the navy, and the air force.

Current stage

With (i) institutions set in place within the government's organizational structure, (ii) operational experience from an exceptional period of "mega-events," and (iii) a consolidated repository of doctrines, strategies, and white papers to guide the actions of government bodies approach to information security and cyber security, Brazil has been shifting its efforts to refining information sharing, cooperation, and coordination practices. At the technical and operational level, some best practices include the establishment of cross-sector exercises to enhance information sharing in identifying and mitigating incidents. One example is the Guardião Cibernético, an exercise developed by CDCiber and universities to explore alternative threat scenarios whilst integrating more sectors to the coordination of incident handling and response (Grossmann, 2019).

In contrast, policymaking processes still struggle to transcend the centrality of bodies such as GSI and the Armed Forces, leaving civil society and academia side-tracked. One example is that the National Policy for Information Security (published in 2019) mentioned that different parts of society and private sector would be included in the development of the National Cyber Security Strategy. In practice, that was not the case. The draft Strategy will only gather public comments during the already foreseen period of consultations. Cases such as this shed light on the existing gaps in communication, collaboration, and governance. An important part of building a culture of cyber security depends on the inclusion of these sectors in the actual "making" of policies. This also results in a poor alignment between threats and the strategies designed to counter them and can further enhance a dichotomous view of privacy and security – all of which are central to the development of policies and efficient mechanisms for cooperation among stakeholders. A more balanced policy development approach would likely benefit from increasing cross-sector dialogues.

Furthermore, with a shift in the nation's focus from combating *externally generated threats* to combating predominantly *internal* threats, the initial turn to militarized solutions has been gradually obfuscated by a concern with cyber crime and digital malfeasance (such as fake news and misinformation). In the case of cyber security threats, the fluidity of action and the transnational nature of actors, practices, and attacks repositions the notion of security as the state where "a set of dangers is counteracted or minimised" (Giddens, 1990: 36; see also, Beck, 1992). Whereas managing, repairing, and maintaining surely add to the prevention of risks, this reposition also implies responses that include regulating, prosecuting, tracing and taking down illegal flows, malicious activities, misinformation, and other identified threats.

Politically, the development of laws, regulations, and policies shape the understanding of threats, security, and risks. Two examples are worth mentioning. First, the approval of Brazil's National Data Protection Law. Information security and cyber security are associated with the integrity, reliability, and confidentiality of data (see Figure 43.4). However, with the approval of the Data Protection Law, the understanding of security is less contrasting with data protection, rather it is complementary in the sense that both governments and companies are required to have minimum security standards to safeguard data. Second, the emergence of sectoral regulations that seek to establish minimum security standards. That is the case of the Central Bank's 2018 regulation that sets specific security and cloud requirements for all financial organizations operating within the country.

Whereas cyber security has always been transversal to the operation and governance of companies and governments, there remains a large gap between recognition of this fact and cyber threat response in Brazil. In fact, the recognition of the transversality of cyberspace (across borders, domains, and competencies) vis-à-vis the framing of threats as either internal and external has been a constitutive tension during the institutional build-up of cyber security in the country and likely contributed to shape (either coordinated or misaligned) institutional responses to these threats. The contrasting of responses that sought, on the one hand, the build-up of a militarized architecture, and responses that have, on the other hand, recurrently focused on "domestic" events – such as hacktivist campaigns, "politically invested hackers," and even electoral misinformation propaganda – have very much contributed to a misleading stabilization of notions of internal vs. external threats as the basis of action. Not surprisingly, responses have either come within "silos" of organizations and institutions with similar competencies and threat grammar, with limited space for (truly) concerted multi-stakeholder action in this field.

Notes

1 This was also a time when cyber terrorism reached main international media headlines, with the early accounts of the Islamic State and their use of social media tools for global terrorist recruitment (see Weimann, 2005; Awan, 2017).
2 International event for advancing a rights-respecting and multi-stakeholder Internet governance that was held in April 2014 following the Snowden Revelations.
3 There was no contestation to the content of the chats.
4 Scholars such as Souza and Almeida have suggested a different approach in the analysis of the institutionalization of cyber security in Brazil. Adopting a securitization theory lens, they contend that the first stage (until 2000) was one of non-politicization, from there on, politicized, and after 2008, securitized.

Suggested reading

Arnaudo, D. (2017a). "Computational Propaganda in Brazil: Social Bots during Elections," *Oxford Internet Institute Working Paper 2017*. 8. http://blogs.oii.ox.ac.uk/politicalbots/wp-content/uploads/sites/89/2017/06/Comprop-Brazil-1.pdf

Diniz, G., Muggah, R. & Glenny, M. (2014). Deconstructing cyber security in Brazil: Threats and responses," *Instituto Igarapé*, 3–32. https://igarape.org.br/en/desconstruindo-a-seguranca-cibernetica-no-brasil-ameacas-e-respostas/

Hurel, L. M. & Lobato, L. C. (2018). A Strategy for Cybersecurity Governance in Brazil," *Igarapé Institute* Strategic Paper no. 30. https://igarape.org.br/wp-content/uploads/2019/01/A-Strategy-for-Cybersecurity-Governance-in-Brazil.pdf

Hurel, L. M. & Santoro, M. (2018). "Brazil, China and Internet Governance: Mapping Divergence and Convergence," *Journal of China and International Relations*, 6(1): 98–115. https://journals.aau.dk/index.php/jcir/issue/view/218

References

Abin. (2016, April 04). "Agência expõe ameaças cibernéticas contra os Jogos Olímpicos em CPI da Câmara." www.abin.gov.br/agencia-expoe-ameacas-ciberneticas-contra-os-jogos-olimpicos-em-cpi-da-camara/

Agência. (2015, September 21). "Forças Armadas e órgãos públicos e privados trabalharão para segurança do ciberespaço." www.fab.mil.br/noticias/mostra/22963/olimpíadas--forças-armadas-e-órgãos-públicos-e-privados-trabalharão-para-segurança-do-ciberespaço/destaquese054.html?ajax_load=1

Andrade, H. D. (2012, May 28). "Rio+20 terá 15 mil homens na segurança e centro contra ataques cibernéticos, diz ministro." https://noticias.uol.com.br/cotidiano/ultimas-noticias/2012/05/28/rio20-tera-15-mil-homens-na-seguranca-e-centro-contra-ataques-ciberneticos-diz-ministro.htm

Arnaudo, D. (2017). "Computational Propaganda in Brazil: Social Bots during Elections," Oxford Internet Institute Working Paper 2017. 8. http://blogs.oii.ox.ac.uk/politicalbots/wp-content/uploads/sites/89/2017/06/Comprop-Brazil-1.pdf

Awan, I. (2017). "Cyber Extremism: Isis and the Power of Social Media," *Social Science and Public Policy*, 52(2): 138–149.

Beck, U. (1992). *Risk Society: Towards a New Modernity*. London: SAGE.

Bostrom, Nick & Cirkovic, Milan M. (eds). *Global Catastrophic Risks*. Oxford: Oxford University Press, 2008.

Brasil. (2012a). "*Livro Branco de Defesa Nacional.*" Brasília: Ministério da Defesa.

Brasil. (2012b). *Ações Orçamentárias Integrantes da Lei Orçamentária para 2012.* Brasília: Ministério do Planejamento e Gestão.

Brasil. (2015). *Estratégia de Segurança da Informação e Comunicações e de Segurança Cibernética da Administração Pública Federal 2015-2018.* Brasília: Gabinete de Segurança Institucional.

Cardoso, B. D. V. (2013). "Megaeventos esportivos e modernização tecnológica," *Horizontes Antropológicos*, 40, 119–148.

CTIR. (2018). "Oficina Equipes de Tratamento e Resposta a Incidentes em Redes Computacionais – ETIR [PowerPoint slides]." www.ctir.gov.br/arquivos/eventos/1_Oficina_2018/Oficina2018_Palestra01_CTIR_Democlydes.pdf

De Carvalho, M. S. R. M. & Cukierman, H. L. (2015). "The Dawn of the Internet in Brazil," *IEEE Annals of the History of Computing, 37*(4): 54–63. https://ieeexplore.ieee.org/document/7343726

Diniz, G., Muggah, R. & Glenny, M. (2014). "Deconstructing cyber security in Brazil: Threats and responses," *Instituto Igarapé*: 3–32. https://igarape.org.br/en/desconstruindo-a-seguranca-cibernetica-no-brasil-ameacas-e-respostas/

Dunn Cavelty, M. (2009). Securing the digital age: The challenges of complexity for critical infrastructure protection and IR theory," in J. Eriksson & G. E. Giacomello (eds.), *International Relations and Security in the Digital Age* (pp. 85–105). New York: Routledge.

Dunn Cavelty, M. (2007) *Cyber-Security and Threat Politics: US Efforts to Secure the Information Age.* CSS Studies in Security and International Relations. London: Routledge.

Febraban. (2019). "Pesquisa FEBRABAN de Tecnologia Bancária de 2019." https://cmsportal.febraban.org.br/Arquivos/documentos/PDF/Pesquisa-FEBRABAN-Tecnologia-Bancaria-2019.pdf

Federal, S. (2012). "Inimigos invisíveis: A guerra cibernética," *Em Debate – Revista de Audiências Públicas do Senado Federal, 3*(10). www.senado.gov.br/noticias/Jornal/emdiscussao/defesa-nacional/razoes-para-a-implementaao-da-estrategia-nacional-de-defesa/inimigos-invisiveis-a-guerra-cibernetica.aspx

Fernandez, A. N. (2016, November 1). "Americans are finally about to get online banking features that Brazil has enjoyed for years." https://qz.com/823178/the-zelle-app-will-change-online-banking-and-money-transfers-in-america-but-brazil-has-been-enjoying-that-for-years/

FintechLab. (2019, June 12). "8a Edição do Radar FintechLab Registra mais de 600 iniciativas." https://fintechlab.com.br/index.php/2019/06/12/8a-edicao-do-radar-fintechlab-registra-mais-de-600-iniciativas/

Fishman, A., Martins, R. M., Demori, L., De Santi, A. & Greenwald, G. (2019, June 9). "Breach of ethics: Leaked Chats Between Brazilian Judge and Prosecutor Who Imprisoned Lula Reveal Prohibited Collaboration and Doubts Over Evidence." https://theintercept.com/2019/06/09/brazil-lula-operation-car-wash-sergio-moro/

Gaffney, C. (2010). "Mega-events and socio-spatial dynamics in Rio de Janeiro, 1919-2016," *Journal of Latin American Geography, 9*(1): 7–29. www.jstor.org/stable/25765282

Giddens, A. (1990). *The Consequences of Modernity.* Cambridge: Polity Press.

Grossmann, L. O. (2019, July 4). "Guardião Cibernético testa reação a ataques contra redes de telecom." www.convergenciadigital.com.br/cgi/cgilua.exe/sys/start.htm?UserActiveTemplate=site&UserActiveTemplate=mobile per cent252Csite&infoid=51121&sid=18

Hurel, L. M. & Santoro, M. (2018). "Brazil, China and Internet Governance: Mapping Divergence and Convergence," *Journal of China and International Relations, 6*(1): 98–115. https://journals.aau.dk/index.php/jcir/issue/view/218

Hurel, L. M. (2019). "Securitização e a Governança da Segurança Cibernética no Brasil," in J. Reia, P. A. P. Francisco, M. Barros & E. Magrani (eds.), *Horizonte Presente: Tecnologia e Sociedade em Debate* (pp. 320–342). Belo Horizonte: Editora Letramento.

Hurel, L. M. & Lobato, L. C. (2018). "A Strategy for Cybersecurity Governance in Brazil. *Igarapé Institute*," Strategic paper no. 30. https://igarape.org.br/wp-content/uploads/2019/01/A-Strategy-for-Cybersecurity-Governance-in-Brazil.pdf

Kaspersky. (2017, March 27). "Cybersecurity in financial institutions 2016 — And what 2017 holds." www.kaspersky.com/blog/from-the-perils-to-strategies/6682/

Lindsay, J. (2017), "Restrained by design: The political economy of cybersecurity," *Digital Policy, Regulation and Governance, 19*(6): 493–514.

Lobato, L. (2016). "Unraveling the cyber security market: The struggles among cyber security companies and the production of cyber (in)security," [Master thesis]. www.maxwell.vrac.puc-rio.br/colecao.php?strSecao=resultado&nrSeq=27784@2

Machado, F. (2018, February 21). "Brasil perde US$ 10 bilhões por ano com cibercrime, diz McAfee." https://veja.abril.com.br/economia/brasil-perde-us-10-bilhoes-por-ano-com-cibercrime-diz-mcafee/

Muggah, R. & Thompson, N. (2015, September 17). "Brazil's Cybercrime Problem," *Foreign Affairs*. www.foreignaffairs.com/articles/south-america/2015-09-17/brazils-cybercrime-problem

Müller, M. (2015) "What makes an event a mega-event? Definitions and sizes," *Leisure Studies, 34*(6): 627–642.

National Research Council. (1991). *Computers at Risk: Safe Computing in the Information Age.* Washington, DC: National Academy Press.

Nery, C. (2017, March 14). "Prioridade é Combater Fraudes." www.valor.com.br/empresas/4898002/prioridade-e-combater-fraudes

Rosenthal, J. (2012). *The Economist: International Banking: Retail Renaissance*. London: Penguin.

Schmidt, A. (2013, August 6). "Brazilian banks lead way on biometrics." www.marketplace.org/2013/08/06/brazilian-banks-lead-way-biometrics/

Senado Federal. (2017, October 16). "Audiência aponta que terrorismo usa tecnologia para crescer." www12.senado.leg.br/noticias/materias/2017/10/16/audiencia-aponta-que-terrorismo-usa-tecnologia-para-crescer

Statista. (2019a). "Consumer loss through cyber crime worldwide in 2017, by victim country (in billion U.S. dollars)." www.statista.com/statistics/799875/countries-with-the-largest-losses-through-cybercrime/

Statista. (2019b). "Countries in Latin America most targeted by cyber attacks in 2017." www.statista.com/statistics/818412/latin-american-countries-highest-share-cyber-attacks/

Symantec. (2019). "Relatório de Ameaças à Segurança na Internet de 2019." www.symantec.com/pt/br/security-center/threat-report

TIC Domicílios. (2018). "TIC Domicílios 2017." https://cetic.br/media/analises/tic_domicilios_2017_coletiva_de_imprensa.pdf

Weimann, G. (2005). "Cyberterrorism: Sum of All Fears?" *Studies in Conflict & Terrorism, 28*(2): 129–149.

PART V

Africa

44

SECURITIZING CYBERSPACE IN EGYPT

The dilemma of cybersecurity and democracy

Bassant Hassib and Nardine Alnemr

Introduction

States are developing technologies to combat cyberthreats but the dilemma remains in balancing human rights and national security. Whereas Egypt ranks 14th globally and 2nd in the Arab region on the Global Cybersecurity Index (GCI) in terms of legal, technical, capacity building, and cooperation initiatives, these initiatives do not balance national security and netizens' rights. Instead, it diverts cybersecurity from promoting digital citizenship and Information Communication Technologies (ICT) for development to another tool of state sovereignty in cyberspace.

After the Arab Spring, the democratization potential of the Internet was highlighted. In reaction, Egypt implemented measures to circumvent users' online freedom of assembly, expression, and access, in the name of preserving "national security" and "religious identity." Society is socialized into thinking "security" and "democratization" are dichotomies.

In reference to the Copenhagen school's securitization theory, Buzan, Wæver, and de Wilde (1998) categorize issues in state politics into three main categories: non-politicized, politicized, and securitized. Issues that are not publicly debated or a matter of state concern are in the non-politicized category. Once they are brought into public debate they become politicized. Securitization occurs when politicized issues are framed as security concerns; "securitization can thus be seen as an extreme version of politicization" (Buzan, Wæver, & de Wilde, 1998: 23), thereby, necessitating above-politics arrangements. Underlying securitization is a military-political understanding that security is countering a direct threat to *survival* but it depends on how it is defined (Buzan et al., 1998). Moreover, effective securitization is audience-centered where rhetoric resonates with the audience based on a consensus of what symbolizes a security/survival threat (Balzacq, 2005).

Public consensus was based on how the securitizing agent propagated cyberspace as a threat to "national security and identity" in media and policy. To combat this threat state sovereignty is extended to cyberspace (cybercontrol) whereby the 2018 Anti-Cybercrime Law (ACL), equates vaguely defined cyber-"crimes" to "state security" threats (Arab Republic of Egypt, 2018).

This chapter analyses Egypt's cyberpolicy and the ACL, and examines the different online surveillance tools and policing measures. In light of the flawed governance apparent in drafting the ACL, the main question is what are the implications of excessive cyberspace securitization on digital rights and democracy?

Developing norms and concepts: Egypt's role in regional and international Internet Governance

Egypt's leading status on the GCI reflects its involvement in Internet Governance (IG) since 2003. It is a member of the UN Government Group of Experts (GGE) on cybersecurity, chaired the ITU Working Group for Child Online Protection, and was a founding member of the African Computer Emergency Response Team (CERT) as well as having its own EG-CERT to combat cybersecurity threats (International Telecommunications Union, 2017). Nevertheless, Egypt is only leading in technical capacity and lags on human rights.

Pre-2011 cybersecurity: from a development tool to a state surveillance tool

The two World Summits on Information Society (WSIS) inspired Egypt's international and regional IG efforts. Internationally, it contributed to the 2005 report of the Working Group on Internet Governance (WGIG) (Kamel, 2005). Nationally, Egypt established the National Telecommunication Regulatory Authority (NTRA) by Telecommunications Law. The NTRA is an arbiter between three stakeholders: government, businesses, and users. It is entrusted with the protection of national security and hence more than 30 per cent of its Board of Directors are from the state security apparatus.

Regionally, Egypt hosted and led the Arab Working Group to create an Arab development-based IG framework. These efforts resulted in two documents: the "Cairo Declaration" and "Towards an Arab Information Society: A Framework for Collaborative Action" (Arab Council of Ministers of Communications and Information, 2003a, 2003b). The Declaration and Framework mirror the WSIS conclusions on increasing netizens' connectivity and resolving the "digital divide." Given the context of developing this Framework (pre-2011 events), information society (IS), ICT, and cyberspace have been conceptualized as socioeconomic development tools. It emphasizes enabling citizens' access to local information, and financial, educational, governmental, and health services. It stresses the roles of national governments, the private sector, civil society, donor agencies, and international community in building the IS (Arab Council of Ministers of Communications and Information, 2003b: 4ff.). Thus, cyberspace is viewed as a development tool rather than a tool for democratization.

The Framework did not view cyberspace as an extension of territorial sovereignty. Instead, cybersecurity is defined as the technical capacity of Arab countries to combat privacy violations, cyberthreats, cybertheft, cybercrimes, cyberterrorism, and cyberwar. The definition of each is absent (Arab Council of Ministers of Communications and Information, 2003b: 17).

Egypt hosted and organized the second Pan-Arab Conference on WSIS and avidly updated the *Geneva Plan of Actions* on the Arab and African levels (Ministry of Communications and Information Technology, 2018; ESCWA, 2015: 2). The former Minister of Communication and Information Technology (MCIT), Tarek Kamel, defined the Internet as a development tool to enhance citizens' use of ICTs. He stressed the importance of multi-stakeholder governance yet admitting that Egypt fell short of strengthening civil society's role in consumer protection and technological awareness. Moreover, Egypt was among 174 countries adopting the *Tunis Commitment* and *Tunis Agenda for the Information Society*, which emphasize enhancing "cybersecurity" (Kamel, 2005; ESCWA, 2015: 2). Similarly, the 2007 EU–Egypt Action Plan specifies mutual cooperation and capacity building of the NTRA in IG, Internet for socioeconomic development, and combating cybercrimes and cyberterrorism (European Commission, 2007). Hence, the transfer of knowledge and resources is to develop Internet infrastructure and not cybercontrol. Consequently, the Cairo Declaration against Cybercrime 2007 was adopted at the first regional conference on cybercrime, hosted by the Council of Europe. The Declaration emphasized the need for national cybercrime legislations reflecting the 2001 Budapest Convention, which balances human rights and prosecution of cybercrimes (Council of Europe, 2001; 2007).

The Mahalha protests in 2008 shifted the state's approach to cybersecurity. Opposition groups blogged, tweeted, and assembled on Facebook to mobilize and organize their protests. This highlighted the importance of cyberspace as a tool for political change, hence increasing Mubarak regime's interest in online surveillance. Surveillance technologies were imported to target the opposition, such as: 1) FinSpy software from the Germany-based Gamma International, a "high-level security system hacking into personal Skype accounts, email accounts, and completely controls targeted computers" (Raoof, 2011); and 2) the Remote Control System (RCS) from the Italy-based Hacking Team – for targeted surveillance (Kimball, 2015; Ramy Raoof, digital security research fellow at Citizen Lab, February 25, 2018, personal communication). This was revealed in documents retrieved by protestors after raiding the Egyptian State Security Investigation (SSI) in 2011. Cyberpolicy before the ACL is found in the 2003 Telecommunication Law where surveillance is permitted under Articles 65 and 67 that give state security institutions the authority to control all telecommunication services, resources, and administration in the case of general mobilization (Arab Republic of Egypt, 2003).

Given this new context, conceptualizing cybersecurity as state security came with the 2011 "Arab Roadmap for Internet Governance" (ARMIG) by the Economic and Social Commission for Western Asia (ESCWA). ARMIG proposed defining cybersecurity in terms of network assets e.g. hardware, software, connectivity, and individual assets i.e. user data and devices. ARMIG highlights the importance of "internet openness" where security from social harm is in the lack of freedom of expression. Hence, privacy and anonymity are important for these rights. In contrast, "protect[ing] Arab Internet users against harmful content and cybercrimes" by "establishing policy and legal frameworks for content filtering and censorship" (ESCWA, 2011: 16f.). These contradictory objectives place Arab governments as online watchdogs, extending their sovereignty over cyberspace.

It is argued that cultural experiences shape policy developments and attitudes, which explains the gap between the Arab and "developed" countries. ESCWA acknowledges that openness is a "grey-zone" where there is no clear regulation established for Internet freedoms. ARMIG proposed to "decrease restriction on access to knowledge" but this cannot be reconciled with censorship (ESCWA, 2017: 17f.).

The Arab convention: extending state sovereignty to cyberspace

Sovereignty as a cybersecurity concern was introduced in the "Arab Convention on Information Technology Offences." Adopted in December 21, 2010, the Convention consists of 43 articles, 21 of which are about crimes, and 8 are procedural concerning authorizing agencies to collect information, track users, and control materials stored on computers and devices of individuals and organizations, defining *"organized cybercrime"* as: money laundering, drug dealing, human and organ trafficking, and illicit arms trade. The provisions of this Convention legitimate the 2006 UAE, 2007 Saudi and 2010 Jordanian cybercrime laws. Its preamble and phrasing underscore *"sovereignty."*

The Convention's provisions are loosely defined but also violate international norms. Regarding criminalization, collection of data and information, and the general principles on which it was based, it disregarded the principles of precision and clarity (United Nations Human Rights Committee, 2011: 6). Moreover, most of the public in Arab countries are not aware of it. This is another violation of international law, as people should "know in advance what the law demands of them, what the law grants to them, and what sorts of behaviour they can expect from officials" (Majambere, 2011). It affirms commitment to human rights conventions yet does not cite any of these rights or the Budapest Convention. Also, the governance process was exclusive to Ministries of Interior and Justice without considering other stakeholders. Thus, it adversely affects online rights and a wide range of electronic and technical activities.

First, the Convention defines cybercrimes based on religious ethics, Islamic Sharia, and Arab heritage governing society. This is problematic as the interpretation of Sharia and ethics is subjective and depends on religious institutions, which are mostly mobilized by governments. Second, it overlooks technical digital security developments; Article 9 criminalizes the acquisition of any software that can crack passwords or access unauthorized sites, thereby penalizing network security professionals. Article 12 expands *"cybercrime"* to include the display or dissemination of "indecent" content. This includes the "storage/ possession" of child pornographic material, sexual exploitation, or gambling. While important, it does not outline "indecent" material. This allows governments to criminalize any online content, and has been used before to criminalize offline freedom of expression. In 2008 the comic novel *Metro* was banned for "offending public morals" for discussing corruption and oppression under Mubarak (Arabic Network for Human Rights Information, 2009). Similarly, Article 15 defines *"cyberterrorism"* as propagating extremism, financing terrorism, facilitating communication between terrorist organizations, circulating bomb-making how-to, and speech that encourages discrimination or "defamation" of religion. Since no precise definition of "defamation" is specified, opinions may be considered blasphemy and be penalized.

Third, Article 14 limits privacy to "private life" overlooking violations committed by states. No obligation of confidential data collection is guaranteed thereby disregarding Articles 57 of the Egyptian Constitution and 17 of the ICCPR.

Fourth, in Article 21, traditional crimes committed using ICTs are more harshly penalized; states' offline repression of political activism, civil society, freedom of thought and expression, privacy, and assembly, is intensified when "crimes" are committed online. Article 25 gives "respective authorities" the competence to issue orders to combat cybercrimes, with no reference to the requirement of a court ruling. In Articles 35, 36 and 38, the "supreme interests of the state" and "political crimes" are justifications allowing states to cooperate by sharing citizens' data with one another. Such vague terms allow governments to prosecute and penalize content or activities that challenge their hegemony. In effect, the Convention legitimates the violation of privacy, arbitrary arrest, and imprisonment of online activists who challenge the political order.

Arab Spring revelations: cyberspace as a new national security threat, and the tools and targets of state surveillance

Protesters who raided the SSI building in March 2011 were able to disclose meeting minutes on tenders for Internet circumvention tools and spyware. The leaks reveal that private telecommunication companies released user data without judicial orders based on government demands. SSI convened periodical meetings with the three private telecommunications companies in Egypt (Vodafone, Mobinil, and Etisalat), Ministry of Interior (MoI), General Intelligence, Ministry of Defense (MoD), and MCIT. Companies allowed call and text message interception, installation of spyware, blocked websites, and agreed to Internet shutdowns (Raoof, 2011).

The relationship between the state security apparatus and the private telecommunication sector is defined in Articles 64, 65, 67, and 68 of the Telecommunication Law. Internet service providers (ISPs) are obliged to cooperate with security institutions in case of general mobilization. Article 68 incentivizes private companies to comply with the law trading users' data and information to the state in exchange for operation permits and business expansion (Kimball, 2015). Additionally, Article 69 gives the NTRA, the Armed Forces, and any National Security body the right to prosecute any cybercrimes under this law, upon a resolution by the Minister of Justice. As Table 44.1 illustrates, private telecommunication companies, in compliance with the law, blacked out communication for the 18 days of the 2011 protests.

This aligns with the Arab Convention's vision of a heavily restricted cyberspace. As a security researcher for the "The Onion Router project" (TOR) attested: Arab officials meet annually to discuss TOR circumvention tools and blocking websites (Kimball, 2015).

After 2011, surveillance turned from targeted to mass. In August 2012, Egypt purchased security software and devices from the US company BlueCoat to censor and intercept online content, which was installed on the private ISP "Etisalat" and to be used for mass surveillance, especially on social media (Marquis-Boire, Dalek, McKune, et al., 2013). This follows the mandates of the Telecommunication Law yet violates rights to privacy and open

Table 44.1 Timeline of Communication Shutdown in Egypt during the January 25, 2011 Revolution

Timeline	Online Communication Shutdown
January 25	Twitter.com and Bamuser.com are blocked
	Activists' mobile lines are shutdown
	Network coverage in Tahrir square is shutdown
January 26	Facebook.com is blocked
January 27	Internet is shutdown
January 28	Short messages services and mobile phone calls are shutdown
	Landlines are shutdown in some areas
January 31	ISPs are shutdown
February 2	Internet service is restored
February 5	Short messages services are restored

Source: A modified version of a visual timeline developed by cybersecurity expert, Ramy Raoof. https://c2.staticflickr.com/4/3198/5814392791_1a39ac54c0_b.jpg

access. Further documents were leaked in 2014 on cybersecurity technology tenders for the MoI. This defies the constitutional right to privacy, international law's principle of "proportionality and necessity" and the requirement of obtaining judicial orders to justify surveillance (Amnesty International, 2014). Before 2011, judicial orders were politicized and used to overrule NTRA data protection regulations (Ezzat, 2014). Now, mass surveillance technologies allow MoI to surpass the judiciary and NTRA.

In parallel, Egypt signed the 2014 *African Union Convention on Cybersecurity and Personal Data Protection (AUCC)*. It emphasizes that cybersecurity legislation and mechanisms shall respect individual freedoms and rights, based on the United Nations Human Rights Council (UNHRC) (2012) resolution, which extends protection of rights online. The gap between Egypt's regional and international commitments and its national practices is centered on the "security-human rights" dilemma where security always prevails.

In November 2014, the Arab Convention came into force as President Al-Sisi approved Egypt's accession to the Convention; which Egypt's ACL came to reflect (League of Arab States, 2010; MENA, 2014). In parallel, some Arab cybercrime laws were enacted while others were amended. Oman issued its cybercrime law in 2011, sanctioning prosecution of content curators at home and in exile (Gulf Center for Human Rights, 2017). The UAE has issued new cybercrime legislation in 2012 to cover a wider scope of cyberoffenses. Content critical of national and regional leaders and policies is to be penalized (Amnesty International, 2017). Jordan amended clause 11 of its cybercrime law in 2015, which was considered a violation of freedom of electronic journalism, prosecuting written and non-written content (Freedom House, 2017; Ma'ayeh, 2017). Saudi Arabia proposed amendments to its cybercrime law to limit Twitter and Facebook, targeting accounts that promote adultery, homosexuality, and atheism (Saudi Gazette, 2014).

The permanent representative of the League of Arab States (LAS) in Geneva, Dr. Sameh Aboul-Enein (2015), justifies viewing the cyberspace as a "security concern" following the Arab Spring as it was prominently used as an alternative space for mobilization. Furthermore, cybersecurity threats are equated to offline national security threats, thus, requiring new legislation; extending state sovereignty. Similarly, President Al-Sisi's opening speech at the 26th LAS Summit in 2015 raised concerns regarding the implications of the Internet on national and regional security. The speech viewed the Internet as an "unconventional threat for Arab nation-states," for encouraging terrorist rhetoric, ideas, and mobilization. Arab Internet users are viewed as complicit either by being a passive audience of terrorist rhetoric or by being potential recruits for these groups (CNN, 2015).

In contrast, ESCWA released a draft for public comments on the Second ARMIG in December 2017, in which it stresses the importance of ICT for development, paving the way to re-steer the vision for 2017–2018 IG from a territorial and securitized point of view to a developmental application. Unlike the state-centric security approach of the first ARMIG, this draft positions cybersecurity as a question of users' security that promotes their trust in using the Internet; it does not recommend censorship as a measure of cybersecurity, yet acknowledges that users are liable to online obligations and ethics such as combating hate speech. Legislation should address: 1) Internet misuse, e.g., cybercrimes; 2) netizens' rights, like protecting users' privacy against applications that rely on user data, e.g., AI; 3) cyberwarfare, e.g., WannaCry. However, it is underdeveloped in the sense that it does not specify the degree to which state sovereignty is extended or how regional cooperation should proceed, and fails to name the government institutions expected to develop cybersecurity measures.

Egypt's national legislation on cybersecurity: securitization of cyberspace and the question of online rights

Egyptian authorities were concerned with the creation of executive institutions entrusted with direct IG without a respective law. Egypt's international commitment to adopt a multistakeholder IG model was not upheld. Instead, IG institutions created were the General Agency for Combating Cybercrimes (Cyberpolice) and the Supreme Council for Cybersecurity Council (SCC), in 2002 by the MoI and in 2014 by the then-Prime Minister Ibrahim Mahlab, respectively. The Minister of CIT heads the SCC and it includes officials from the MoI, as well as the MoD. The SCC intensifies state surveillance on civil society, activists, and "deviant" public opinion (Kimball, 2015). Mahlab issued another decree to establish a committee tasked with filtering "terrorist" online content, which is headed by the Minister of Justice and consists of representatives from the Ministries of Interior, Defense, Military Production, Foreign Affairs, and Communications. The definition of "terrorist content" is vague, but the Committee felt justified as support for military missions in Sinai under the umbrella of counterterrorism (Ahram Online, 2015). In May 2015, the cabinet tasked Military Intelligence, General Intelligence, the National Security Agency, and the Cyberpolice to install a nationwide camera surveillance system (Raoof, February 25, 2018, personal communication).

The Constitution, Anti-Terrorism Law, and Media Regulation Law extend sovereignty to cyberspace. In the Constitution, cybersecurity equals national security as specified by Article 31. Articles 70, 71, and 72 ensure freedom and independence of the press, online and offline, and prohibit censorship, confiscation, suspension, or shutdown of newspapers and media outlets. However, under Article 71, "limited censorship" is allowed in times of war or general mobilization. Article 73 protects citizens' rights to privacy and public and private assembly, without state authorities monitoring such meetings. Article 65 guarantees the freedom of thought and opinion. As such, mass surveillance by state authorities is unconstitutional.

The Anti-Terrorism Law controls digital media to the extent of shutting down websites and monitoring online communication to combat terrorism. Cyberterrorism is not explicitly defined in the text of the law, yet online activities, broadly and imprecisely defined in Article 29, and communication to carry out an attack are criminalized. Article 15 further criminalizes using the Internet to learn any technology that could be used to commit terrorist crimes. Under the Media Regulation Law, Article 3 tasks the Supreme Council for the Regulation of Media to ensure the compliance of audio-visual, print, and digital press with public ethics and national security (Supreme Council for Media Regulation, 2018). Subsequently, Article 26 (based on Article 211 of the Constitution) allows the Council to block media content, which may harm national security (Supreme Council for Media Regulation, 2018).

Anti-cybercrime law: pitfalls and implications

The 2012–2017 National ICT Strategy recommended changes in the Telecommunications Law. It proposed amendments to Article 65 to limit the state's ICT control to the cases of "international tension, threat of war, actual war, natural or environmental disaster, or crises threatening national security," while retaining the initial vagueness of the original article. Article 67 to be amended so that a written Presidential decree, approved within 15 days by the parliament, is required for Internet shut down. National security remains as a strategic pillar in the strategy; however, the development of cybersecurity for digital citizenship, and information security of private sector and civil society for the use of ICT, is articulated. The strategy puts a blueprint for a national cybercrime law, taking into consideration national security dimension and stiffens the penalty for material distributed, created, or duplicated in violation of "public decency" (MCIT, 2013).

Building on this, MPs whose seats are controlled by the pro-government "Support Egypt Coalition" (Ahram Online, 2016), prepared new legislation that further threatens digital rights. The press coverage of the law insinuates its relevance as a necessary intervention for counterterrorism (Rabie, 2018; Sobhy, 2018).

There were two preceding drafts to this law. The first draft was submitted by the MoD to the Legislative Reform Committee (LRC) in February 2015, and approved a year later. Hisham Hilmi, the Secretary General of the Committee, asserts that the definition of cybercrime in the draft is that of the MCIT: "An electronic crime is any unlawful act committed using a computer or a network whether the computer or the network were subjects of the crime or the tool to commit it" (Al-Ahram, 2016). Regarding governance, a full draft of the bill was not provided, despite constant pressures from civil society. According to Al-Ahram (2016), the LRC consulted the Ministries of Interior, Communications, General Intelligence, and Administrative Control. Independent ICT experts, relevant civil society organizations (CSOs), and the National Council for Human Rights were not invited to attend the discussions nor to submit proposals (Moghazi, 2017).

The Ministry of Justice (MoJ) submitted to the cabinet the second draft on March 24, 2015. This draft was widely criticized by CSOs and ICT experts for violating a number of fundamental rights, as it holds the victims of cybercrimes accountable under the claim of negligence. The draft did not regulate the role of Cyberpolice (Almasry-Alyoum, 2015).

Both drafts mirror the Arab Convention in its imprecision. For example, blocking websites that threaten national security or sites containing pornographic content, without defining them.

MP Tamer El Shahawi – a retired Military Intelligence Officer, introduced the draft of the current law in 2016. The articles of the 2018 "Anti-Cyber and Information Technology Crimes" Law are similar to the draft submitted by the MoI. The law has multidimensional shortcomings: the legal phrasing and definitions, penalties, respect of civil and political rights and freedoms, and the impact on the ICT industry and R&D. It is designed to legitimate cybercontrol by the authorities.

First, the law uses imprecise legal phrasing for its terms and definitions. Article 1 defines a "website" as any medium identifiable by a hyperlink accessible on the World Wide Web, hosting data and information. The definition is intentionally broadly defined so as to include public pages and personal accounts on Facebook, Twitter, and other platforms. Similarly, the Egyptian Initiative for Personal Rights, Support for Information Technology Center, and Association of Freedom of Thought and Expression (2016) highlight that the imprecision of the language and the unnecessary definitions of tools such as "website" and "email," instead of identifying private communication and public content regardless of the technology used, is an indicator of the legislator's lack of expertise, which impact the proper prosecution of crimes. This is due to the lack of good governance, excluding the input of cybersecurity legal and tech experts, and representatives from CSOs. Instead the articles are skewed towards limiting cybercrimes to ICT tools and not the actual crime committed.

Also, Article 27 criminalizes any user who runs or uses a "website" that propagates committing any of the crimes in the law and by other body of laws. Article 34 imposes imprisonment without parole for any of these crimes, which disrupt society's security, national unity, social cohesion, or state's economy. To reiterate, without clear definition for such crimes, mirroring the Arab Convention in broadly defining cybercrimes of financial fraud, copyrights infringement, and terrorism.

Second, it legalizes mass surveillance and violation of privacy. Article 2 requires ISPs to store and provide to authorities with data on users' identification, the content of the information system, and the equipment used.

Second, it penalizes the acquisition and/or usage of ICT, not the crime. Thus, it aborts a number of cyberactivities and research on IS security and programming, as Article 22 criminalizes purchasing, selling, acquiring, exchanging, exporting, importing, manufacturing, producing devices, tools, programs, access codes, passwords with the aim of using them to commit, facilitate, or conceal a crime, thereby blanketing a lot of network security professionals, students, researchers, and investors; crippling R&D, investment in digital economy, and the ICT industry.

Third, the law imposes heavy penalties, from three-years imprisonment to imprisonment without parole. Similarly, fines range from 5,000 EGP to 2 million EGP. Article 29 further penalizes victims of cybercrime, on grounds of negligence and not taking the necessary precautionary measures to prevent these crimes, without specifying a threshold for such precautionary measures. Article 35 penalizes administrators of "websites" that are subject to fraud, phishing, or similar cybercrimes with a minimum of three-months prison sentence and 100,000 EGP fine, for failing to report to the authorities any cyberattack. Article 7 permits state authorities to censor content or completely block access to websites that operate from Egypt or overseas, if the material in question threatens national security. This is cemented by Article 30, which penalizes ISPs with a minimum of one-years prison sentence and a fine of 2 million EGP for not abiding by censorship or blocking rulings. In case of failure to comply with the court ruling, resulting in someone's death, they are subject to imprisonment without parole.

Fourth, the law stiffens penalties for crimes already penalized in other laws, just because they are committed over the cyberspace. For example, Articles 27 and 34 could be used to penalize a person for online calls to protests, for a minimum of two-years imprisonment and a maximum of imprisonment without parole and a fine of no less than 100,000 EGP; while Article 21 of the 2013 Protest Law penalizes protesting without notice, for just a fine not exceeding 30,000 EGP (Ahram Online, 2013).

Fifth, the law is discriminatory in terms of "whose security." It sidelines holding-state officials accountable in case of a cyberattack by their side or by using any of their resources. As for the same crime, according to Articles 18 and 21, penalties are harsher if the offence is against public institutions. The Egyptian Initiative for Personal Rights et al. (2016) argue that the law protects the cybersecurity of the powerful – state institutions; i.e., the private communication of a state employee, using a government account, which does not hold any value to public interest should not be guaranteed more online security than that of an academic or a journalist, who are researching public concerns.

Sixth, for compatibility with international laws and agreements, it disregards the *Budapest Convention*. While the 2015 draft referred to Article 3 of the convention (which calls on party states to establish legislative measures to validate their concerns about an offence, or else illegal interception is a violation of security of computer data and systems), it was not included in the current law. The excessive criminalization of netizens demonstrates why the legislators dropped this article. Furthermore, the UNHRC 2016 Resolution (A/HRC/32/L.20) urges the extension of offline human rights to the cyberspace. Although Egypt is party to the UNHRC, the law, governance structure, and statements by public figures articulate that human rights are not central to Egypt's agenda.

Conclusion: the future of democracy under a securitized cyberspace

Egypt exhibits a strong cybersecurity profile, which places it as a leading country in the GCI. However, this cybersecurity is not society-centric, contrary to its supposed objectives. First, legislation does not offer precise definitions of cybercrime, cybersecurity, and cyberterrorism. Instead, definitions are vague, giving leeway to penalize cyberactivity or target individuals posing "threats" to the regime, penalizing the use of ICT, not the crime. Second, they sideline holding state officials accountable for infringing on netizens' privacy and the use of surveillance; cybersecurity in Egypt is the security of the state, not that of netizens. Third, beyond the question of a democratic cyberspace, current cybersecurity measures cripple the potential of investment in the digital economy, R&D, and the ICT industry.

As in the Russian and Chinese models, by extending state sovereignty to cyberspace, excluding CSOs and technical experts from the governance process, this enables government/security agencies to violate netizens' privacy, monitor their activity and impose censorship. The implication will be a government crackdown on political activists and human rights defenders for: destabilizing social morals, defaming religion, and thus, threatening national security. As such, despite its international commitments to strengthen and promote IS, and utilize e-economy, Egypt's actions will have a two-fold effect. A portion of Egyptian society will become "technophobic"; they will not be able to recognize the importance of digital rights for human development and democratization, to the extent that they surveil and report their fellow citizens. In stark contrast, other factions of society will develop increasingly creative methods in circumventing government authority, such as resorting to the use of VPNs and TOR.

Egypt's excessive securitization of cyberspace will diminish international trust in its human rights record, risking future cybersecurity cooperation. As a regional leader in the domain of cybersecurity, the implications are national and regional, impacting the status of democracy and human rights in the Arab region.

Suggested reading

Aboul-Enein, S. (2017). "Cybersecurity Challenges in the Middle East," GCSP Geneva Paper No. 22/17, Geneva Centre for Security Policy, Geneva, Switzerland. www.gcsp.ch/News-Knowledge/Publications/Cybersecurity-Challenges-in-the-Middle-East

Kshetri, N. (2013). "Cybercrime and Cybersecurity in the Middle East and North African Economies," in N. Kshetri (ed.), *Cybercrime and Cybersecurity in the Global South* (pp. 119–134). New York: Palgrave Macmillan.

Radsch, C. (2016). *Cyberactivism and Citizen Journalism in Egypt: Digital Dissidence and Political Change.* New York: Palgrave Macmillan.

Salhi, H. (2007). "Assessing Theories of Information Technology and Security for the Middle East," in J. Eriksson & G. Giacomello (eds.), *International Relations and Security in the Digital Age* (pp. 106–131). New York: Routledge.

Thompson, K. (2011). "Not like an Egyptian: Cybersecurity and the Internet Kill Switch Debate," *Texas Law Review, 90*, 465–495.

References

Aboul-Enein, S. (2015). *Themes and Concepts for Cyber Security Development* (Group of Governmental Experts (GGE). Geneva Centre for Security Policy, Geneva, Switzerland. www.gcsp.ch/download/4216/102453

African Union. (2014). *"African Union Convention on Cyber Security and Personal Data Protection."* https://au.int/sites/default/files/treaties/29560-treaty-0048_-_african_union_convention_on_cyber_security_and_personal_data_protection_e.pdf

Ahram Online. (2013, November 25). "Full English Translation of Egypt's New Protest Law." http://english.ahram.org.eg/News/87375.aspx

Ahram Online. (2015, February 17). "Egypt to Block Websites Linked to 'Terrorism.'" http://english.ahram.org.eg/NewsContent/1/64/123290/Egypt/Politics-/Egypt-to-block-websites-linked-to-terrorism.aspx

Ahram Online. (2016, May 9). "'Support Egypt' First Coalition to Receive Recognition in Parliament." http://english.ahram.org.eg/NewsContent/1/64/211447/Egypt/Politics-/Support-Egypt-first-coalition-to-receive-recogniti.aspx

Al-Ahram. (2016, February 3). الإصلاح التشريعي» توافق على مشروع قانون مكافحة الجرائم» الإلكترونية ("Legislative Reform Approves the Cybercrime Law Draft"). www.goo.gl/h7wcM8

Almasry-Alyoum. (2015, May 27). النص الكامل لقانون الجرائم الإلكترونية ("Full-text of the Cybercrime law"). www.almasryalyoum.com/news/details/742625

Amnesty International. (2014, June 4). "Egypt's Plan for Mass Surveillance of Social Media an Attack on Internet Privacy and Freedom of Expression." www.amnesty.org/en/latest/news/2014/06/egypts-attack-internet-privacy-tightens-noose-freedom-expression/

Amnesty International. (2017, March 29). "UAE: Prominent Academic Jailed for 10 Years over Tweets in Outrageous Blow to Freedom of Expression." www.amnesty.org/en/latest/news/2017/03/uae-prominent-academic-jailed-for-10-years-over-tweets-in-outrageous-blow-to-freedom-of-expression/

Arab Council of Ministers of Communications and Information. (2003a). "Cairo Declaration." www.itu.int/net/wsis/docs/cairo/declaration.pdf

Arab Council of Ministers of Communications and Information. (2003b). "Towards an Arab Information Society: A Framework for Collaborative Action." League of Arab States, Cairo, Egypt. www.itu.int/net/wsis/docs/cairo/towards_is.pdf

Arab Republic of Egypt. (2003). "Egypt Telecommunication Regulation Law: Law No. 10 of 2003." www.goo.gl/cR8gSc

Arab Republic of Egypt. (2018). "Law No. 175 of 2018 on Anti-Cyber and Information Technology Crimes." https://drive.google.com/file/d/1ra7NlKn7Uh_YU5fL7NBKt18JE2mKAKm8/view

Arabic Network for Human Rights Information. (2009, March 31). "Author and Publisher of 'Metro,' Egypt's First Graphic Novel, Face up to Two Years in Prison for Material Deemed 'Contrary to Public Morals'." www.ifex.org/egypt/2009/03/31/author_and_publisher_of_metro_egypt/

Balzacq, T. (2005). "The Three Faces of Securitization: Political Agency, Audience and Context," *European Journal of International Relations*, 11(2), 171–201.

Buzan, B., Wæver, O. & de Wilde, J. (1998). *Security: A New Framework for Analysis*. Boulder: Lynne Rienner.

CNN. (2015, March 28). السيسي يؤيد القوة العربية المشتركة ويحذر من خطر غير تقليدي لاستخدامات الانترنت ("al-sisi Supports the Joint Arab Force and Warns against the Unconventional Uses of the Internet"). https://arabic.cnn.com/middleeast/2015/03/28/egypp-al-sisi-speech-arab-summit

"Constitution of the Arab Republic of Egypt." (2014). www.sis.gov.eg/Newvr/consttpercent202014.pdf

Council of Europe. (2001). "Convention on Cybercrime" (European Treaty Series No. 185), Budapest. www.europarl.europa.eu/meetdocs/2014_2019/documents/libe/dv/7_conv_budapest_/7_conv_budapest_en.pdf

Council of Europe. (2007). "Cairo Declaration against Cybercrime." www.coe.int/t/dg1/legalcooperation/economiccrime/cybercrime/cy per cent20activity per cent20Cairo/CairoDeclarationAgainstCC2007_EN.pdf

Economic and Social Commission for Western Asia. (2017). "Arab Roadmap for Internet Governance: Provisional Second Edition," United Nations, Beirut, Lebanon. www.unescwa.org/sites/www.unescwa.org/files/events/files/171220-arab-roadmap-internet-governance-en.pdf

Economic and Social Commission for Western Asia. (2011). "Arab Regional Roadmap for Internet Governance: Framework, Principles and Objectives" (Technical Paper No. 5), United Nations, New York, United States. www.unescwa.org/sites/www.unescwa.org/files/publications/files/ictd-10-tp-5.pdf

Economic and Social Commission for Western Asia. (2015). *Policy Recommendations on Cybersafety and Combating Cybercrime in the Arab Region*. United Nations, New York, United States. www.unescwa.

org/sites/www.unescwa.org/files/uploads/policy-recommendations-cybersafety-arab-region-summary-english.pdf

Egyptian Initiative for Personal Rights, Support for Information Technology Center & Association of Freedom of Thought and Expression. (2016). معاداة التقنية ("Anti-Technology"). https://eipr.org/sites/default/files/reports/pdf/cybercrime.pdf

European Commission. (2007). "EU/Egypt Action Plan," Brussels, Belgium. https://eeas.europa.eu/sites/eeas/files/egypt_enp_ap_final_en.pdf.

Ezzat, A. (2014, September 29). "'You Are Being Watched!' Egypt's Mass Internet Surveillance," *Mada Masr*. www.madamasr.com/en/2014/09/29/opinion/u/you-are-being-watched-egypts-mass-internet-surveillance/

Freedom House. (2017). "Jordan: Country Profile" (Freedom on the Net). https://freedomhouse.org/report/freedom-net/2017/jordan

Gulf Center for Human Rights. (2017, October 8). "Oman: Supreme Court Ruling Closes 'Azamn' Newspaper Forever." www.gc4hr.org/news/view/1703

International Telecommunications Union. (2017). "Global Cybersecurity Index (GCI) 2017." www.itu.int/dms_pub/itu-d/opb/str/D-STR-GCI.01-2017-R1-PDF-E.pdf

Kamel, T. (2005, November 15). "Statement by HE Dr. Tarek Kamel, Minister of Communications and Information Technology, Arabic Republic of Egypt," International Telecommunication Union. www.itu.int/net/wsis/tunis/statements/docs/g-egypt/1.html

Kimball, S. (2015, March 9). "After Arab Spring, Surveillance in Egypt Intensifies," *The Intercept*. https://theintercept.com/2015/03/09/arab-spring-surveillance-egypt-intensifies/

League of Arab States. (2010). "Arab Convention on Combating Cybercrime" (Convention). Cairo, Egypt. https://cms.unov.org/DocumentRepositoryIndexer/GetDocInOriginalFormat.drsx?DocID=3dbe778b-7b3a-4af0-95ce-a8bbd1ecd6dd

Ma'ayeh, S. (2017, November 1). "Jordan's Top Cartoonist Faces Charges of Insulting Religion," *The National*. www.thenational.ae/world/mena/jordan-s-top-cartoonist-faces-charges-of-insulting-religion-1.672024

Majambere, E. (2011). "Clarity, Precision and Unambiguity: Aspects for Effective Legislative Drafting," *Commonwealth Law Bulletin*, *37*(3): 417–426.

Marquis-Boire, M., Dalek, J., McKune, S., Carrieri, M., Crete-Nishihata, M., Deibert, R., Khan, S. O., Noman, H., Scott-Railton, J. & Wiseman, G. (2013). *Planet Blue Coat Mapping Global Censorship and Surveillance Tools* (Free Expression Online). The Citizen Lab, Toronto, Canada. https://citizenlab.ca/2013/01/planet-blue-coat-mapping-global-censorship-and-surveillance-tools/#26

MENA. (2014, November 14). "Sisi Approves Egypt's Accession to Arab Convention to Combat Cyber Crimes," *Egypt Independent*. www.egyptindependent.com/sisi-approves-egypt-s-accession-arab-convention-combat-cyber-crimes/

Ministry of Communications and Information Technology. (2013). "Egypt's ICT Strategy 2014–2017." www.mcit.gov.eg/Publication/Publication_Summary/660

Ministry of Communications and Information Technology. (2018). "WSIS." www.mcit.gov.eg/International_Relations/Cooperation_with_International_Organizations/wsis

Moghazi, A. (2016, February 4). قانون الجريمة الإلكترونية: التورنت يحملك إلى طرة ("Cybercrime Law: Torrent Takes You to Torah"), *Almanassa*. https://almanassa.com/ar/story/1019/collaboration

Rabie, A. (2018, March 12). القاضي يكشف ملامح قانون مكافحة الجريمة المعلوماتية وعقوباته ("al-qady Reveals Features of the Cybercrime Law and Its Punishments"), *Al Watan News*. www.elwatannews.com/news/details/3157598

Raoof, R. (2011, April 7). "Egypt: How Companies Help the Government Spy on Activists," *Global Voices*. https://advox.globalvoices.org/2011/05/07/egypt-how-companies-help-the-government-spy-on-activists/

Saudi Gazette. (2014, June 2). "Saudi Arabia Amending Laws to Monitor Social Media," *Al Arabiya*. http://english.alarabiya.net/en/media/digital/2014/06/02/Saudi-Arabia-amending-laws-to-monitor-social-media.html

Sobhy, M. (2018, February 23). النائب تادرس قلدس: قانون الجريمة الإلكترونية مشاركة للدولة في حربها ضد الإرهاب ("representative Tadris Kaldis: Cybercrime Law Is the State's Contribution in Its War against Terrorism"), *Youm 7*. www.goo.gl/scUwJW

Supreme Council for Media Regulation. (2018). "Law No. 180 of 2018 on Regulating the Press, Media, and the Supreme Council for Media Regulation". goo.gl/cQ6tuw

United Nations Human Rights Committee. (2011). "General Comment No. 34, Article 19: Freedoms of Opinion and Expression" (General Comment No. 34). United Nations, Geneva, Switzerland. www2.ohchr.org/english/bodies/hrc/docs/gc34.pdf

United Nations Human Rights Council. (2012). "Promotion and Protection of All Human Rights, Civil, Political, Economic, Social and Cultural Rights, Including the Right to Development" (Resolution No. A/HRC/20/L.13). www.ohchr.org/Documents/HRBodies/HRCouncil/.../A. HRC.20.L.13_en.doc.

United Nations Human Rights Council. (2016). "Promotion and Protection of All Human Rights, Civil, Political, Economic, Social and Cultural Rights, Including the Right to Development" (Resolution No. A/HRC/32/L.20). http://digitallibrary.un.org/record/845728/files/A_HRC_32_L.20-EN.pdf.

45

SECURITY THROUGH THE ARAB WINTER

Cyber strategies in post-revolutionary Tunisia

Nabil Ouassini

Introduction

In the past decade, governments have become more cognizant of how cybersecurity threats can impact domestic and national security within political, economic, and military institutions. Although internet access in Africa is lacking when compared to other regions in the world, many governments in the continent are starting to pay more attention to their cybersecurity capabilities (Kshetri, 2019). Global connectivity, social media and networking, the expansion of e-commerce, international investment, and economic growth in Africa are attracting more cybercriminals as internet access expands to a billion people across the continent by 2022 ("Africa will break through," 2017). In 2019 cybercrime cost the African economy an estimated $3.5 billion (Mathe, 2019). In the African fight against cybercrime, Tunisia is an example of a nation that has a mixed record in confronting cyber threats. Tunisia's lengthy history with cybersecurity emerges with its first connection to the internet in 1991 (El Gody, 2007). In the years that followed, the former president Zine El Abidine Ben Ali's (1987–2011) regime became the authoritarian standard for severe censorship and absolute control of the Tunisian cybersphere. By 2011, the Arab Spring protests and eventual ending of Ben Ali's 23-year dictatorship would have been unfeasible without the sophisticated use of Twitter, Facebook, blogs, and e-mails to maneuver around the Tunisian government's lagging censors. A near decade after the Jasmine Revolution, the lessons learned from the Arab Spring and other incidents show the preservation of a safe, secure, and robust cyberspace as one of the top priorities in Tunisia's national security. The following provides an overview of post-revolutionary Tunisia's cyber strategies. First, the chapter discusses Tunisia's cyber history, infrastructure, and legislation. The chapter then outlines current trends in Tunisian cybersecurity and concludes with implications and future policies.

Background

Since the advent of the internet in Tunisia, the government has deliberately restricted the political content Tunisians can access (Saidin, 2018). When proclaiming independence from the French, Habib Bourguiba's (1957–1987) one party state ruled Tunisia with a paternalistic authoritarian approach that ensured his role as president for life (Hopwood, 1992). Ben Ali's medical coup d'état during Bourguiba's ill health in 1987 offered new optimism in Tunisia but this ultimately regressed by the 1990s. During the early years of the Tunisian public's access to the internet, Ben Ali recognized the potential threats of the new medium and calculatedly passed laws that censored internet activities (Honwana, 2011). The regime filtered web content and dissident web sites experienced a barrage of cyberattacks and shutdowns. The 404 Page Not Found screen was the standard with illegal web pages. "Ammar 404" became the term for the error message that was displayed on computer screens as Ammar became the personified name of Tunisia's version of Big Brother (Abrougi, 2014). In social media sites, the regime conducted mass surveillance on users and even resorted to blocking Facebook a couple times. Academics, activists, and journalists were deliberately targeted and regularly appeared in court for violating laws, codes, and regulations that focused on protecting the regime from online criticisms. One human rights lawyer was sentenced to three and a half years during this time period for simply publishing a report accusing the government of torture on a banned web site. At times the situation became so dire that one journalist, Ziad El Heni along with the Tunisian Union of Free Radio Stations and the Unionist Freedoms and Rights Observatory filed an audacious lawsuit against the government that was dismissed without explanation (Deibert, Palfrey, Rohozinski, & Zittrain, 2010). Throughout these official policies of cyber repression, the Ben Ali regime further developed its cybersecurity capabilities and even went as far as to host the 2005 World Summit on the Information Society (WSIS) in Tunis. The United Nations-sponsored summit was focused on bridging the digital divide between Northern and Southern countries through the spread of internet access. For Ben Ali, cybersecurity policies were essentially concentrated on the preservation of the regime as much as protecting Tunisia's internet infrastructure against cyber threats.

By 2010, an economic crisis, a growing disenfranchised young population, and stronger opposition to repression started to boldly question the regime's legitimacy. It was the tragic death of a street vendor, Mohamed Bouazizi (1984–2011) that sparked the 2011 revolution. Posts, pictures, and articles about Bouazizi's experiences of abuse, harassment, injustice, and humiliation at the hands of government officials and his subsequent self-immolation fueled widespread protests throughout Tunisia. The unique role of the internet and social media became obvious at the onset of the revolution. The policies of banning web sites and blogs that worked in the past were insignificant in the era of social media sites, blogs, satellite channels, and foreign news agencies. According to Marzouki, Skandrani-Marzouki, Béjaoui, Hammoudi, and Bellaj (2012) web sites like Facebook and Twitter accelerated the Jasmine Revolution; named after Tunisia's national flower. Honwana (2011) contends that cyber-activism was at the center of the revolution as protestors communicated through cyberspace about the regime's crackdown and counter actions against protestors. The government attempted to ban a number of web sites that include Twitter, Facebook, YouTube, and the French video sharing platform DailyMotion but protestors simply switched to SMS networks as a means of communicating (Howard & Hussain, 2013). It was during this time that the international hacktivist group, Anonymous, launched denial of service cyberattacks against Tunisian government web sites. In what became known as Operation Tunisia, Anonymous also revealed damaging documents pertaining to corruption of the Ben Ali regime and incriminatory information on repression to the world (Norton, 2011). By January 14, 2011, Ben Ali went into exile as his regime collapsed.

The events in Tunisia were replicated in a few other Arab countries in the forerunning of what became known as the Arab Spring. Ben Ali went into exile in Jeddah, Saudi Arabia where he remained until his death in 2019. However, the role of cyberspace in overthrowing the North African dictatorship captivated the world and showed the potential political power of the internet. The communication of information through Twitter and Facebook was essential to the mobilization of the Tunisian masses against Ben Ali's regime (Marzouki, Skandrani-Marzouki, Béjaoui, Hammoudi, & Bellaj, 2012). Unlike the Arab coups in previous decades, this revolution was the first popular uprising that forced a leader out of power in the modern Arab world (Gelvin, 2012). In the aftermath, Tunisia became the only democratic government to emerge from the protests, demonstrations, and revolutions of the Arab Spring and has become the litmus test for democracy in the Middle East and North Africa (MENA) region (Arieff, 2012).

During the Ben Ali regime, Tunisia developed an international reputation for censorship that included the suppression of information on cyberspace. One of the encouraging outcomes of the Jasmine Revolution is the new Constitution that was adopted in 2014. Progressive articles in the Constitution include that the "freedom of opinion, thought, expression, information and publication shall be guaranteed," and that "these freedoms shall not be subject to prior censorship" (Tunisian Constitution, Article 31, Chapter II). Nevertheless, there are still many issues and concerns regarding Tunisia's current cyber strategies. The next section will discuss these predicaments through the various components of Tunisia's contemporary cyber institutions, laws, and trends.

Tunisian cyberspace

National agency for computer security

With internet penetration hitting a little over 50 per cent of Tunisia's population of 11.5 million people, the government has tasked the Ministry of Communication Technology and Digital Economy with the responsibility of cybersecurity (International Telecommunication Union, 2016). In 1999, a micro-Computer Emergency Response Team (CERT) unit was formed to handle any problems generated from the Y2K bug (ANSI, n. d.). The unit was a task force that brought together Tunisian experts that met regularly to design strategies and plans for cybersecurity. It was in the early 2000s that these experts established the National Agency for Computer Security (ANSI) as the official government agency to maintain and execute national plans, strategies, and policies in cybersecurity. ANSI is the government's principal agency responsible for securing Tunisian cyberspace, benchmarking and measuring cybersecurity development, providing educational and professional training, and promoting cybersecurity courses to the private and public sectors. The government agency protects citizens against cyber threats by investing in experts and writing legislation and regulations that are favorable to protecting the nation's cybersecurity. Furthermore, the ANSI web site mentions additional missions of the agency that include coordinating between Defense, law enforcement, and National Security; the development of technical guides for publication; and the incessant inspections of Tunisia's computer systems and networks (ANSI, n.d.).

As the core agency overseeing the nation's cybersecurity, ANSI has delegated the response to emergencies to its CERT teams. The Tunisian Computer Emergency Response Team or TunCERT plans and executes national strategies and guidelines, develops warning systems, periodically tests these systems, coordinates between different private and public groups, and spreads public awareness on cyberattacks (ANSI, n.d.). The web site (www.ansi. tn/) provides contact information for Tunisians to report cybersecurity incidents with an email, telephone number, and physical address of the agency. Currently, TunCERT is developing a national child online protection strategy to keep children from cyber threats (Ghajati, 2018). In the political realm, TunCERT helps shape the legal aspects of cybersecurity along with policies for national information systems and is the face of Tunisian cybersecurity in the assistance of and cooperation with national, regional, and international communities. An example of its national effort is in the interaction between TunCERT, NGOs, and civil society organizations to raise awareness on cyber risks (African Union Commission, 2016). Through the years, TunCERT has created NGOs that include the Tunisian Association for Numerical Security and the Tunisian Association of the Experts in Computer Security (Cole, Chetty, LaRosa, Rietta, Schmitt, Goodman & Atlanta, 2008). Along with TunCERT, Tunisia has become one of the few African and Arab countries to have two CERTs certified by the Forum of Incident Response and Security Teams (FIRST, 2019). The second CERT is CSIRT.tn (http://csirt.tn/), a private team within the international cybersecurity company Keystone Group. Future Tunisian CERTs will focus on banking and financial institutions to thwart cyberattacks targeting the Tunisian economy (Tunis Afrique Press, 2019).

Technical telecommunications agency

In November of 2013, the Tunisian government founded a new surveillance agency called the Technical Telecommunications Agency (ATT) to "exploit national monitoring systems of telecommunication traffic" and to offer "technical support to the judicial investigations into the information systems of crimes and communications" (Ben Hassine, 2016: 23) The agency is controversial as some have called it Tunisia's own "law abusing agency" or the "Tunisian NSA" (Abrougi, 2013) which many human rights organizations and privacy advocacy groups have criticized for its lack of transparency (Freedom House, 2018) and vague definitions of its tasks in investigating crimes. Despite the criticism, the agency is still conducting surveillance for the state with powers that allow its activities to remain closed to public scrutiny (Freedom House, 2018).

Cybersecurity and the law

The laws during Ben Ali's presidency permitted government officials to spy and repress voices of dissent. In the overthrow of the regime, citizens assumed that these laws would be largely reversed. However, these same laws endure and are used in Tunisia's war against terrorism. Tunisia has experienced numerous terrorist attacks carried out by members of Al Qaeda in the Islamic Maghreb (AQIM) and the Islamic State of Iraq and the Levant (ISIL) in the last five years. The deadliest attacks intentionally targeted Tunisia's tourism industry and occurred in the Bardo National Museum and hotel resorts in Sousse; they tragically left 60 dead and close to 100 injured. The challenge for legislators is striking a balance between combatting serious cybercrimes involving terrorism and the safeguarding of Tunisian civil and human rights. The next few paragraphs will highlight the key cybersecurity laws in Tunisia.

The first major cybersecurity law is the *Tunisian Electronic Exchange and Electronic Commerce Law* enacted in August of 2000. The law was passed to create a legal framework that was designed to develop Tunisia's e-business. This law established the rules on electronic signatures, cybercrimes, privacy and personal data, as well as e-commerce and business (Ben Ayed, 2017). In 2004, Tunisia passed numerous laws in the realm of cybersecurity.

That year, the government created the National Institute for Personal Data Protection to monitor and protect data amongst its citizens. That same year, legislation established ANSI with regulations pertaining to its administration, financial/legal rules, measures, and procedures (ANSI, n.d.). Tunisia also passed the National e-Commerce Law of 2009 in an effort to build the legal groundwork for e-commerce (Ben Ayed, 2017). Other laws were proposed to the Tunisian parliament but never passed due to their perceived controversy. One example is the Tunisian National Cyber Criminal Law that gave the government flexibility to inhibit voices with vague legal language that criminalized criticism. Another law in 2018 proposed the criminalization of online defamation (Freedom House, 2018). The brief review of Tunisia's cyber laws reveals the government's deficient legal framework and legislation in cybercrime (Oleksiewicz, 2019).

Current trends in cybersecurity

Thus far, most indicators suggest that Tunisia's cybersecurity is advanced when compared to countries within its vicinity, but still nevertheless lags behind internationally. According to Freedom House (2018) international report, Tunisia is categorized as "partly free" and had a freedom score of 38/100 (the higher the score the less free). Deficiency of cybersecurity is a concern since Tunisia was listed as one of the top 25 countries in the world that is vulnerable to cyberattacks (Pandalabs, 2017). The Global Cybersecurity Index (2018) ranked Tunisia's cybersecurity as 9th amongst the 28 members of the Arab world and 76th in the world. The ranking measures each country's commitment to cooperation along with other legal, technical, and organizational measures. Present-day cybersecurity concerns for Tunisia include DDoS attacks, viruses, sniffing attacks, software piracy and copyrights, and cyberterrorism (Ben Ayed, 2017). Hybrid cyberterrorism or the use of the internet to disseminate propaganda, recruit and radicalize potential terrorists, fundraise, train and plan terrorism online is Tunisia's biggest national security concern (Zerzri, 2017). The description of ISIL as Al Qaeda 2.0, comes from the terrorist organization's innovative cyber approaches to propaganda, recruitment, training, and psychological warfare using social media networking sites. This is especially troublesome because of the more than 5,500 Tunisians that left for ISIL in Iraq, Syria, and Libya in the last six years (Raghavan, 2018). In fact, one of the most committed groups within the ISIL organization are the Tunisian hacking team called the Fallaga. The group has been successful in hacking numerous government, news, and personal websites of individuals and organizations in the United States, United Kingdom, and France. In an interview with VICE, one member of the Fallaga hackers describes the concept of "*Al Jihad Électronique*" as a modern form of holy war against those perceived to be against Islam (Moore & Saltzstein, 2013). Cyber defense and the deterrence of cyberterrorism is one of the top priorities for the Tunisian government.

In Africa, Tunisia is one of the most proactive countries in its cybersecurity efforts. As mentioned, the Tunisian government is actively cooperating with other nations and the international community. Tunisia is a member of AfricaCERT ever since it was launched in 2010. Tunisia continues to cooperate with other African countries in developing CERTs for those nations where they do not exist. Tunisia is also a member of the International Communication Union and its United Nations backed International Multilateral Partnership against Cyber Threats (IMPACT) with access to its cybersecurity services. Tunisia has also been a member of the Global Forum on Cyber Expertise (GFCE) that exists as "a global platform for countries, international organizations and private companies to exchange best practices and expertise on cyber capacity building" (GFCE, 2019). The Tunisian government is actively involved with Project Cybersouth in cooperation with the European Union and the Council of Europe. Project Cybersouth has conducted numerous events with the Tunisian government to improve cybersecurity legislation, specialized services, judicial training, institutional capacities, international cooperation, and strategies in cybercrime and electronic evidence (Council of Europe, 2019). In 2018, Tunisia was invited to strengthen its legal framework on cybersecurity by acceding to the Budapest Convention on Cybercrime (Freedom House, 2018). This trend will align Tunisia's cybersecurity laws with those held by the international community. Draft laws will be designed for submission to parliament that protect personal data that is in line with universal human rights standards (Freedom House, 2018).

The future of Tunisian cyberspace

The aftermath of the Jasmine Revolution in Tunisia continues to reverberate in the Arab world until this day. Unfortunately, the revolutions in Egypt, Libya, Syria, Yemen, and other parts of the Arab world have turned the Arab Spring into the Arab Winter. The reemergence of repression, religious extremism, and autocratic rule is partly the result of Gulf monarchies leading a counter-revolution. Even in Tunisia, the UAE intelligence services plotted a coup d'état in 2018 against the democratically elected government that was thwarted with the help of Algerian, French, and German intelligence (Beau, 2018). As this is the only democratic government in the MENA region, the Jasmine Revolution has for the most part been auspicious.

In the cybersecurity arena, there is a great deal of work yet to be completed by the government. Despite its standing as one of the first African and Arab countries with internet access, two CERTs, and a cybercrime legislative framework, the government still trails behind the majority of the world's nations. The government is trying to progress with initiatives to transform Tunisia into a Smart country with the Smart Gov 2020 and Digital Tunisia 2020 plans that would simplify international investment through e-business and an e-Government (Taamallah, Khemaja, & Faiz, 2019). Cooperation with international organizations, the African Union, the European Union, the Council of Europe, and the United Nations will ensure that Tunisia's cybersecurity practices also proceed in the right direction.

The greatest concern for Tunisia's cyber strategies rests in countering all the threats to Tunisian society without compromising citizens' civil and human rights. Since the revolution, Tunisians have experienced unprecedented access to online content that was unconceivable during Ben Ali's regime. The legal framework from the Ben Ali regime and the limited legislation in the cyber realm threatens Tunisia's democratic progress. The need for protecting Tunisia from cybercrimes and terrorism is a foreseeable risk to the nation's ongoing experiment with democracy. The terrorism incidents in Tunisia are alarming but like so many other countries, the issue of terrorism can be used as a pretext to limit liberties, control the flow of information, and silence criticism made against the government. These concerns are not without warrant when considering recent events in Tunisia. One proposed law on the agenda called the "Repression of attacks against armed forces," would criminalize criticism of security forces while granting them immunity from prosecution in cases of unnecessary use of lethal force (Amnesty International, 2017). In 2018, the Interior Minister openly admitted to spying on and wiretapping a journalist's phone (Amnesty International, 2018). Several Tunisians have also been arrested for their online activities. One Tunisian blogger by the name of Nabil Rabhi was sentenced to six months in prison and ordered to pay 1,200 dinars for posting defamatory statements about Tunisia's president on his Facebook page (Ben Hassine, 2017). In another example, Yassine Ayari, a member of parliament was sentenced to three months in prison for a Facebook post that mocked the appointment of a military commander (Human Rights Watch, 2019).

In the context of the Arab Winter, Tunisia should depart from the political trends in the region and avoid shortsighted cybercrime legislation that dishonors its citizens by reverting back to the surveillance, censorship and crackdown on dissent that reflected the Bourguiba and Ben Ali regimes. Tunisia is a country that has the capability to balance the nation's cybersecurity concerns with policies that are harmonious with international standards of human rights. This will be in the spirit of those who sacrificed their lives in the Jasmine Revolution and utilized the Tunisian cyberspace for attaining freedom and dignity.

Suggested reading

Loghmari, N. (2016). "Tunisian Experience in the National Cyberspace Security," Agence nationale de la sécurité informatique, Tunis, Tunisia. www.itu.int/en/ITU-T/Workshops-and-Seminars/cyberse curity/Documents/PPT/S7P2_Nadhir_L.pdf

Mehrez, H. B. (2017). "Tunisia," Global Information Society Watch. https://giswatch.org/sites/default/files/gw2017_tunisia.pdf

Privacy International. (2019, March 14). "State of Surveillance Tunisia." https://privacyinternational.org/state-privacy/1012/state-surveillance-tunisia

Yakinthou, C. & Croeser, S. (2016). "Transforming Tunisia: Transitional Justice and Internet Governance in a Post-Revolutionary Society," *International Journal of Transitional Justice, 10*(2): 230–249.

References

Abrougi, A. (2013, November 26). "Will Tunisia's ATT Ring in a New Era of Mass Surveillance?" *Advox Global Voices*. https://advox.globalvoices.org/2013/11/26/will-tunisias-att-ring-in-a-new-era-of-mass-surveillance/

Abrougi, A. (2014, May 6). "Ammar 404 Is Dead. Long Live Ammar 404!" *PEN/Opp*. www.penopp.org/articles/ammar-404-dead-long-live-ammar-404

Africa will break through 1 billion mobile internet connections by 2022. (2017, November 15). "Ovum." www.consultancy.africa/news/30/africa-will-breakthrough-1-billion-mobile-internet-con nections-by-2022

African Union Commission. (2016). "Cyber Crime & Cyber Security Trends in Africa." www.thehaguese curitydelta.com/media/com_hsd/report/135/document/Cyber-security-trends-report-Africa-en.pdf

Arieff, A., (2012, June 18). "Political Transition in Tunisia." Congressional Research Service, Washington, DC. www.everycrsreport.com/files/20120618_RS21666_781751299464fd009bddbb543f66539 fde30f699.pdf

Amnesty International. (2017, July 13). "Tunisia: Proposed Bill Could Give Security Forces Carte Blanche to Use Unnecessary Lethal Force." www.amnesty.org/en/latest/news/2017/07/tunisia-pro posed-bill-could-give-security-forces-carte-blanche-to-use-unnecessary-lethal-force/

Amnesty International. (2018, February 12). "Tunisia: Attack on Freedom of Expression Must End." www.amnesty.org/en/latest/news/2018/02/tunisia-attack-on-freedom-of-expression-must-end/

ANSI. (n.d.). www.ansi.tn/en/pages/historique.html

Beau, N. (2018). "Tunisie, les ambitions déçues de Lotfi Brahem," *Le Monde Afrique*. https://mondafri que.com/tunisie-lalliance-ratee-des-emiratis-avec-lotfi-brahem/

Ben Ayed, A. (2017). "Nature of Cyber Crimes and Legislation in the Republic of Tunisia," *International Journal of Advanced Research in Computer Engineering & Technology*, 6(3): 241–244.

Ben Hassine, W. (2016). "The Crime of Speech: How Arab Governments Use the Law to Silence Expression Online," *Electronic Frontier Foundation*. www.eff.org/files/2016/04/28/crime-of-speech. pdf

Ben Hassine, W. (2017, August 15). "In Tunisia, a Blogger Is Jailed for Criticizing the President on Facebook," *Access Now*. www.accessnow.org/tunisia-blogger-jailed-criticizing-president-facebook/

Cole, K., Chetty, M., LaRosa, C., Rietta, F., Schmitt, D. K., Goodman, S. E. & Atlanta, G. A. (2008). "Cybersecurity in Africa: An Assessment," Sam Nunn School of International Affairs, Georgia Institute of Technology, Atlanta, United States.

Council of Europe. (2019). "*Cybersouth Objectives*." www.coe.int/en/web/cybercrime/cybersouth

Deibert, R., Palfrey, J. G., Rohozinski, R. & Zittrain, J. (2010). *Access Controlled: The Shaping of Power, Rights, and Rule in Cyberspace*. Cambridge: MIT Press.

El Gody, A. (2007). "New Media, new audience, new topics, and new forms of censorship in the Middle East," in P. Seib (ed.), *New Media and the New Middle East* (pp. 213–234). New York: Palgrave Macmillan.

Freedom House. (2018). "Freedom on the Net 2018: Tunisia." https://freedomhouse.org/report/freedom-net/2018/tunisia

Forum of Incident Response and Security Teams. (2019). "Membership." www.first.org/

Gelvin, J. L. (2012). *The Arab Uprisings: What Everyone Needs to Know*. Oxford: Oxford University Press.

Global Forum on Cyber Expertise. (2019). "GFCE Cyber Monitor." www.thegfce.com/

Index, G. C. (2018). "Global Cybersecurity Index 2018," ITU Publications. www.itu.int/dms_pub/itu-d/opb/str/D-STR-GCI.01-2018-PDF-E.pdf

Ghajati, F. (2018, December 4). "The Tunisian Computer Emergency Response Team: The Tunisian Cyberwall Face to Cyberthreats," *Medium*. https://medium.com/@alghajati/the-tunisian-computer-emergency-response-team-the-tunisian-cyberwall-face-to-cyberthreats-6e38161410a5

Honwana, A. (2011). "Youth and the Tunisian Revolution." *Conflict Prevention and Peace Forum Policy Paper*, Social Science Research Council. http://webarchive.ssrc.org/pdfs/Alcinda_Honwana%2C_Youth_and_the_Tunisian_Revolution%2C_September_2011-CPPF_policy%20paper.pdf

Hopwood, D. (1992). *Habib Bourguiba of Tunisia: The Tragedy of Longevity*. New York: St. Martin's Press.

Howard, P. N. & Hussain, M. M. (2013). *Democracy's Fourth Wave? Digital Media and the Arab Spring*. Oxford: Oxford University Press.

HRW. (2019). "Tunisia: Prosecutions for Online Commentary Repressive Laws Sap Free Expression." www.hrw.org/news/2019/10/15/tunisia-prosecutions-online-commentary

International Telecommunication Union. (2016). "Percentage of Individuals Using the Internet, Fixed (Wired) Internet Subscriptions, Fixed Broadband Subscriptions." www.itu.int/en/ITU-D/Statistics/Pages/stat/default.aspx

Kshetri, N. (2019). "Cybercrime and Cybersecurity in Africa," *Journal of Global Information Technology Management*, 22(2): 77–81.

Mathe, A. (2019, July 10). "The Misunderstood World of Cybersecurity in Africa," *Policy Center for the New South*. www.policycenter.ma/opinion/misunderstood-world-cybersecurity-africa#.XfcjpuZtfpU

Marzouki, Y., Skandrani-Marzouki, I., Béjaoui, M., Hammoudi, H. & Bellaj, T. (2012). "The Contribution of Facebook to the 2011 Tunisian Revolution: A Psychological Insight," *Cyberpsychology, Behaviour and Social Networking*, 15(5): 237–244.

Moore, I. & Saltzstein, H. (2013, June 25). "We Skyped with a 19-Year-Old Islamist Hacker from Tunisia," *VICE*. www.vice.com/sv/article/xdpeyq/we-skyped-with-a-19-year-old-islamist-hacker-from-tunisia

Norton, Q. (2011, January 11). "2011: The Year Anonymous Took on Cops, Dictators and Existential Dread," *WIRED*. www.wired.com/2012/01/anonymous-dicators-existential-dread/

Oleksiewicz, I. (2019). "Policy to Prevent and Combat Cyber-crime in Africa," *Humanities and Social Sciences*, 7(4), 138–146.

Pandalabs. (2017). "Panda Security Annual Report 2017." www.pandasecurity.com/mediacenter/src/uploads/2017/11/PandaLabs_Annual_Report_2017.pdf

Raghavan, S. (2018, September 8). "Tunisia Feared the Return of Militants from Abroad the Threat Now Is Those Who Never Left," *The Washington Post*. www.washingtonpost.com/world/tunisia-feared-the-return-of-militants-from-abroad-the-threat-now-is-those-who-never-left/2018/09/07/aafa6c84-aacf-11e8-9a7d-cd30504ff902_story.html

Saidin, M. I. S. (2018). "Rethinking the 'Arab Spring:' the Root Causes of the Tunisian Jasmine Revolution and Egyptian January 25 Revolution," *International Journal of Islamic Thought*, 13, 69–79.

Taamallah, A., Khemaja, M. & Faiz, S. (2019). "The smart city of Tunisia," in L. Anthopoulos (ed.), *Smart City Emergence* (pp. 421–433). Amsterdam: Elsevier.

Tunis Afrique Press. (2019, April 29). "Second Tunisian Cyber Attack Alert and Response Centre Joins FIRST." www.tap.info.tn/en/Portal-Economy/11398178-second-tunisian

Tunisian Constitution. (2019). "Tunisia's Constitution of 2014. Constitute Project." www.constitutepro ject.org/constitution/Tunisia_2014.pdf

Zerzri, M. (2017). "The Threat of Cyber Terrorism and Recommendations for Countermeasures," *Policy Advice and Strategy Development, 4*, 1–6.

46

CYBER SECURITY IN KENYA

Balancing economic security and internet freedom

James D. Fielder

Introduction

The year 2010 was a momentous one for Kenya's human rights and global connectivity, ushering in both a new constitution and linking to the Eastern African Submarine Cable System undersea fiber optic cable. The latter event marked Kenya's third of three undersea connections, which dramatically increased Kenya's internet bandwidth. Online in various forms since 1995, Kenya has long strived to lead East Africa's information and communication technology (ICT) development and in many ways has achieved the distinction: Kenya was one of the first countries in Africa – if not the world – to establish national cyber governance and associated institutions. Kenya further recognized the importance of ICT to economic development and has thus weaved ICT-focused economic policies into its cyber strategy, and has done so surprisingly (but not perfectly) free of corruption and ethnic tensions. Cyber crime and information distortion, however, have stymied Kenya's cyber ambitions, further aggravated by the Government of Kenya's (GoK) top-down chilling effects on online freedom of expression and ongoing difficulties in backing strategy with actionable plans or resources.

This chapter examines Kenya's national cyber security policy evolution from Kenya's first Internet connection in 1995 through the 2017 Kenyan elections, with particular focus on the dichotomy between Kenya's internet-mediated economic growth, cyber crime efforts, and digital human rights abuses since the release of Kenya's 2014 National Cyber Security Strategy. Kenya's historically permissive Internet governance has fostered remarkable economic advances while at the same time scoring high marks in independent security assessments. However, Kenya's security efforts have yet to find pace with policy recommendations, resulting in the Kenyan economy losing KSh 21 billion ($210 million) to cyber crime in 2017. Moreover, Kenya's anti-terrorism efforts have resulted in legal abuses against online civil liberties couched under the umbrella of national security, sparking concerns that Nairobi is casting wider surveillance scrutiny on previously open and vibrant internet discourse.

A brief history of Kenya's internet growth and governance

Kenya first dialed in to the internet in 1995 and soon after liberalized the country's communications market through the Kenya Communications Act 1998 (Souter &

Kerretts-Makau, 2012). This was followed in 1999 with the Government of Kenya (GoK) establishing the Communications Authority of Kenya (CA or CAK) as the country's regulatory authority for the communications sector, responsible for "facilitating the development of the information and communications sectors including; broadcasting, cyber security, multimedia, telecommunications, electronic commerce, postal and courier services" (CAK, 2018: para 2). From 1995 to 2009 Kenya depended on slow and expensive satellite internet at the national backbone level, further brought to a crawl through wired dial-up modem speeds and burgeoning cellular connectivity. Between 2009 and 2010, however, Kenya connected to the SEACOM, East Africa Maritime System (TEAMS), and Eastern African Submarine Cable System (EASSy) undersea fiber optic cables, which dramatically increased Kenya's nation-wide bandwidth and cellular capacity (Bright, 2016; Okuku, Renaud, & Valeriano, 2015; Souter & Kerretts-Makau, 2012). Kenya now has the highest estimated Internet penetration in Africa, with internet penetration increasing from 1 per cent in 2002 to 85 per cent by the end of 2017 (Barnes, 2015; IWS, 2018; Mutisya, 2018; Turianskyi, 2018). Kenyans also fully embraced Web 2.0 social media applications, with 12 million Kenyans using the WhatsApp messaging program by the end of 2017, followed by 8 million on YouTube, 7 million on Facebook, 4 million on Instagram, and 1 million on Twitter (BAKE, 2018; Crabtree, 2018; IWS, 2018).

In addition to social use, numerous literatures also find that ICTs boost economic growth and improve government efficiencies, and Kenya's ICT governance has certainly made good faith attempts to bottle both (Aker & Mbiti, 2010; Deloitte, 2012; Hjort & Poulsen, 2017). For example, ICT sector grew approximately 20 per cent annually between 1999 and 2009 and added an additional 1 per cent to Kenya's GDP over the same period (Sunday & Makau, 2017). Moreover, in 2007 GoK unveiled *Kenya Vision 2030*, a long-term development plan designed to transform Kenya into a modern, globally competitive, middle income country based on three developmental pillars (Kenya Vision 2030, 2018):

- Economic Pillar: This pillar aims to achieve an average economic growth rate of 10 per cent per annum and sustain the same until 2030.
- Social Pillar: This pillar seeks to engender just, cohesive, and equitable social development in a clean and secure environment.
- Political Pillar: This pillar aims to realize an issue-based, people-centered, result-oriented, and accountable democratic system.

The GoK followed up in 2014 with a National ICT Masterplan, which rests on three foundations of human capital development, effective ICT cost and delivery through integrated architecture, and improved e-government services via integrated information architecture; and additionally, three pillars of efficient e-government services, ICT driving industry, and globalized ICT businesses (GoK, 2014a; ICTA, 2018). The ICT Masterplan suggested a bold way forward, forecasting ICT contributing at least 8 per cent to the GDP annually, the creation of 180,000 ICT-related jobs, and 50 per cent of adults accessing at least one e-government service. Reports on the plan's success are mixed, with some data depicting a slowdown of Kenyan ICT-related economic growth since 2014 (Sunday & Makau, 2017) and opposing data suggesting ICT successes and growth over 10 per cent annually since 2014, albeit the latter comes from government reporting (Kazeem, 2018; KNA, 2018). Even so, multi-source analysis suggests that the GoK can readily claim positive ICT-related economic growth.

Kenya's greatest economic success story is the M-Pesa mobile money service (Barnes, 2015; Corkin, 2016; Souter & Kerretts-Makau, 2012). In brief, M-Pesa allows users to deposit and withdraw money, transfer money to other M-Pesa users and non-users, pay bills and purchase mobile phone minutes (Corkin, 2016). Further, by eliminating the time, cost, and risk involved in real currency remittances, estimates suggest that by 2016 Kenyan household income had increased between 5 per cent and 30 per cent solely due to mobile money's conveniences (Corkin, 2016; The Economist, 2015). Prior to M-Pesa's 2007 launch (let alone prior to Kenya's access to broadband) only 25 percent of Kenyans had access to banking; but, by 2015 over 17 million Kenyans were using M-Pesa, with roughly 25 per cent of Kenya's GDP crossing through cellular towers (The Economist, 2015). Given Kenya's mobile penetration rate, Kenyans have almost universal access to M-Pesa and other mobile money platforms.

Kenya's recent ICT governance efforts also dovetail with the country's relatively new (2010) Constitution, which established stronger commitments to privacy of communications, freedom of expression, and free media, which are derived from the Universal Declaration of Human Rights (Branch, 2011; Souter & Kerretts-Makau, 2012). In turn, Kenya's Access to Information Act 2016 dramatically opened citizen access to online government services, such as access to marriage certificates, driver's licenses, visas, and other civil services and databases (Turianskyi, 2018: 9). Article 33 guarantees freedom of expression and Article 31 the right to privacy, but both also disavow propaganda, hate speech, and incitement to violence. Hate speech is penalized under the 2008 National Cohesion and Integration Act, passed in response to widespread ethnic violence during the 2007 elections. Indeed, the Government of Kenya threatened an Internet shutdown during the August 2017 presidential and parliamentary elections in order to prevent electoral violence (Turianskyi, 2018).

Kenya's cyber governance efforts have resulted in successes in terms of reasonably free self-expression and measurable economic growth. For example, in 2017 Freedom House ranked Kenya as a free state with internet connections surpassing the global average and the ITU ranked Kenya as a "highly committed" cyber security state in their 2017 Global Cyber Security Index. The same report further notes that there are no economic constraints on Kenyan online media and online political content is rarely censored in Kenya, although content deemed to violate social mores is occasionally restricted. Indeed, Kenya boasts a lively information environment, with multiple issues and viewpoints shared freely across numerous traditional broadcast and Web 2.0 social media platforms (see also, Barnes, 2015; Branch, 2011; Freedom House, 2017; Souter & Kerretts-Makau, 2012). Unfortunately, Kenya's launch into the broadband era coincided with the continent's skyrocketing growth as a cyber crime hub, and the GoK's focus on economic growth largely overlooked security until fairly recently.

Putting the internet access cart before the cyber security horse

In 2010 Rowe, Reeves, Wood, & Brown (Kritzinger & von Solms, 2012) reported that roughly 80 per cent of all personal computers in Africa were infected by malicious software, or malware, which has since metastasized thanks to the continent's explosive bandwidth and wireless infrastructure growth – and more specifically, Kenya's (Kaimba, 2017; Mutisya, 2018). Such woes have also been further aggravated by poor technical security measures, user security training and awareness, and ill-defined official public and private security policies (Akuta, Ong'oa, & Jones, 2011; Kritzinger & von Solms, 2012; Mutisya, 2018).

Kenya ranks third in Africa and 45th globally in the ITU's 2017 World Cyber Security Index, with common security threats including identity and data theft, phishing, online fraud scams, and ransomware (Mutisya, 2018; Okuku, Renaud, & Valeriano, 2015). Kenya lost almost KSh 18 billion ($175 million) to cyber crime in 2016 and over KSh 21 billion in 2017, the second highest in Africa behind Nigeria, despite also having the second highest number (1,600) of trained cyber security professionals (Kaimba, 2017). 72 per cent of Kenyans also reported being cyber crime victims in 2017 and 41 per cent of mobile money users lose between KSh 1,000 and KSh 5,000 a month to cyber crime (Amadala, 2018; Kaimba, 2017; Mutisya, 2018). A notable example was the 2017 Public Likes scam that cost Kenyans KSh 2 trillion. The scam was a pyramid scheme in which users purportedly earned money by clicking advertisements, but could earn more by "upgrading" to higher payout levels (Kaimba, 2017; Kassujja, 2017; Omondi, 2017). Moreover, the M-Pesa mobile money service stands out as a particularly lucrative target (Sutherland, 2018). Mobile money's speed, convenience, and simplicity loses allure when lax security grants similar benefits to criminals if they gain access. This requires informed cyber security hygiene along all points of the transfer chain.

Alas, a joint 2017 survey by the by the Kenya National Bureau of Statistics and the Communications Authority of Kenya revealed that over 48 per cent of government agencies and over 6 per cent of business reported data loss due to malware, yet only 15 per cent of reporting organizations had intrusion detection capabilities (Macharia, 2017). Another report by Deloitte revealed that Kenyan banks lost KSh 17.1 billion in 2016 and KSh 21 billion in 2017, with dozens of firms hit by the 2017 WannaCry ransomware infection. Yet, only 96 per cent of banking intrusions were reported, as firms fears that reporting attacks will shake public trust and confidence and due loss of customers (Amadala, 2017; Kamau, 2018). Threats posed by malicious software, though, pale in comparison to the human element, ranging from outright insider threats to simple user error associated with poor security education (Mutisya, 2018; Okuku, Renaud, & Valeriano, 2015). Insider threats occur when organizations fail to administer layered security accesses – or any access limits for that matter. Thus, a terminated employee with data access and a grudge could wreak havoc on organizational files. Or, lower-level employees with full user permissions could potentially access higher-level confidential information. As for simple user error, personal threat defense requires users to understand technical threat basics, such as how phishing scams function on a social level, how malware spreads via removable media such as USB memory sticks, and the importance of strong passwords. Speaking to the latter, a recent Kenya CA report noted how brute force attacks against weak passwords – admin, password, and 123456, among others – are still surprisingly effective methods. Yet, the same Deloitte report mentioned previously found that most Kenyan firms spent less than $5,000 annually on security measures and nothing on staff training (Amadala, 2017; Kamau, 2018; Rogito, 2017).

Cyber crime is not limited to Kenyan shillings lost, however, as information has also been targeted. In January 2012 an Indonesian hacker defaced over one hundred Kenyan government websites, and in May 2016 the hacking collective Anonymous launched a sophisticated hack on the Kenyan ministry of foreign affairs, stealing data and confidential files, including email conversations and security-related communications (Souter & Kerretts-Makau, 2012; West, 2017). There has also being ongoing concern towards terrorist use of the internet, notably al-Shabab and al-Qaeda affiliates (Mwangi, 2018; Souter & Kerretts-Makau, 2012). However, there is little evidence to suggest that al-Shabaab has acquired the technology to deploy a cyber or electronic attack, although the group has targeted telecommunication installations (West, 2017). The GoK, however, expends considerable effort tracking online discourse and money flows as part of its overall anti-terrorism program, which has resulted in abuses of civil liberties (Mwangi, 2018). Public and private organizations' fears of shaken public confidence are not misplaced, as the above-mentioned cyber breaches have fostered doubt towards the Government of Kenya's cyber security capabilities. Cyber security incidents have occurred from the highest GoK levels down to the pocketbooks of the average Kenyan. Thankfully, this is not to say that the GoK has sat entirely idle as criminals, hackers, and uneducated users respectively looted electronic coffers, pilfered online data, or unintentionally installed viruses at the local internet café.

19 years after dialing in: Kenya's 2014 Cyber Security Strategy

Despite Kenya's years of internet access and concurrent growth of cyber security threats, the Government of Kenya did not release a unified cyber security strategy until 2014. Kenya's strategy was actually predated two years by establishment of the Kenya National Computer Incident Response Team Coordination Centre, or KE-CIRT/CC. The KE-CIRT/CC was chartered to provide national-level cyber security expertise and 24/7 operational response, to include national cyber security policy implementation, cyber security awareness socialization, national threat coordination, and international cyber security partner engagement (Gagliardone & Sambuli, 2015; ITU, 2017; The National KE-CIRT/CC, 2012). There were almost immediate concerns that the KE-CIRT/CC sorely lacked resourcing for both technical capacity and sufficient adequately trained staff; however, the KE-CIRT/CC has demonstrated the capability to identify and resolve threats. Just between January and March 2018 for example, the KE-CIRT/CC tracked over almost 8 million cyber attacks against Kenyan ICT systems and responded to over 4,000 critical events (Matinde, 2018).

The Government of Kenya followed with release of its first National Cyber Security Strategy in 2014, which prioritized securing national cyber space so as to inspire public confidence, facilitate economic growth, and embed cyber security within Kenya's *Vision 2030* plan (GoK, 2014b). Interestingly, *Vision 2030* (GoK, 2014b: 8) boldly accepts Kenya's, "relatively immature [cyber security posture] in the face of the growing complexity and sophistication of cyber threats" noting that Kenya's long-term economic and social growth depends on ICTs. Moreover, the Strategy proposed four strategic goals: enhancing the nation's cyber security posture in a manner that facilitates the country's growth, safety, and prosperity; building national capability by raising cyber security awareness and developing Kenya's workforce to address cyber security needs; fostering information sharing and collaboration among relevant stakeholders to facilitate an information sharing environment focused on achieving the Strategy's goals and objectives; and providing national leadership by defining the national cyber security vision, goals, and objectives and coordinating cyber security initiatives at the national level (GoK, 2014b: 11). The strategy also touches on specific actions and responses such as business impact analysis, continuity of operations, disaster recovery, and security awareness and training; however, the strategy provides no specifics for task implementation or capacity building (Gagliardone & Sambuli, 2015; GoK, 2014b: 5; Okuku, Renaud, & Valeriano, 2015).

Kenya's cyber security strategy is also notionally backed by a robust legal framework. In 2017 Kenya approved a computer and cyber crime bill that targets intentional unauthorized infiltration of a computer system and unauthorized data interception and transmission over a telecommunications system. The bill further states any ICT-based interference or tampering that threatens national security, causes injury or death, or threatens public health and safety carries a ten-year prison sentence or a fine of up to $20,000 (Wabuke, 2017). Moreover, individuals found guilty of spreading hate speech, broadly defined, can be fined up to KSh 1 million, sentenced to up to three years in prison, or both (Freedom House, 2017). Additionally, the Kenya Information and Communications Act (KICA) further prohibits unlawful monitoring and interception of communications, but the Prevention of Terrorism Act 2012 permits limits to constitutional freedoms during terrorist investigations. Amendments to the Prevention of Terrorism Act in 2014 also explicitly allow national authorities to intercept communications during antiterrorism operations (Freedom House, 2017; Wabuke, 2017). While the GoK clearly recognizes the relationship between cyber security, public trust, and economic growth, the latter amendments have lamentably either resulted in false positive arrests at best, or at worst have been misapplied to stifle anti-government dissent.

Cyber governance versus cyber mobilization

2007 marked the first Kenyan elections where Kenyans unleashed grievances over keyboards and cellphones, in this case to protest incumbent presidential candidate Mwai Kibaki's reported electoral rigging. Although the Kenyan Ministry of Security ordered suspension of television and radio broadcasts to limit growing public ire, blocking older mediums did little to stop the spread of ethnically charged calls for violence. 2007 was the first election in which a majority of Kenyans owned mobile phones, and unfortunately the first in which mass messages such as "fellow Kenyans, the Kikuyu's have stolen our children's future… we must deal with them in a way they understand … violence," and, "We will slaughter [Luo] right here in the capital city," spread via short messaging (Branch, 2011; Goldstein & Rotich, 2008: 4; Kagwanja & Southall, 2009; Mäkinen & Kuira, 2008). The ensuing violence resulted in 1,000 people killed and over 500,000 displaced.

Social media tools like wikis, blogs, Facebook, Flickr, YouTube, and Twitter, were used to share information and mobilize, and Kenyan developers further created the Ushahidi crowdsourcing app, which allowed users to geotag text, photos, and videos onto Google Maps (Bright, 2016; Goldstein & Rotich, 2008; Mäkinen & Kuira, 2008; Turianskyi, 2018). Individual Kenyans, civil groups, and political parties continued using social media during the 2013 and 2017 elections, and in between elections senior government officials have been fired over corruption charges thanks to reporting via social media and online journalism (Bright, 2016; Turianskyi, 2018). Further, during the 2017 elections opposition party members argued that the election commission system had been hacked and its servers compromised in favor of the incumbent. In conflicting responses, the electoral commission first denied any hacking attempts and later said the hacking attempts had been thwarted (Campbell, 2017; Kaimba, 2017; Wabuke, 2017).

Section 29 of Kenya's Information and Communications Act of 1998 criminalizes improper use of a licensed telecommunications gadget, which grants officials broad authority to illegalize online content and arrest users accused of criticizing government officials (Turianskyi, 2018). Human Rights Watch documented 17 separate incidents between 2013 and 2017 in which 23 journalists and bloggers were physically assaulted by government officials or suspected affiliates, and at least 60 bloggers were arrested in 2016 (Freedom House, 2017; Human Rights Watch, 2018a; Kakah, 2018). Human Rights Watch (2018b) has also reported on Kenyan authorities withholding payments to media companies in attempts to prevent government criticism.

The Kenyan High Court, however, has generally sided with constitutional freedoms. In 2018 Kenyan bloggers filed a lawsuit arguing that portions of the new cyber crime law contained wording that, "deny, infringe and otherwise threatened freedom of expression, media and persons besides the right to privacy, property and a fair hearing" (Kakah, 2018, sec 2, para 3). The challengers further argued that Section 29 of the Kenya Information and Communication Act and Section 194 of the penal code were applied to enforce the new law. The Kenyan High Court ultimately declared portions of the new law unconstitutional, stating that the wording was too broad and violated constitutional freedoms (Kakah, 2018; Turianskyi, 2018). The High Court previously declared Section 132 of the penal code unconstitutional in April 2017 for similar reasons, and also suspended use of a communications monitoring system designed to track "illegal" mobile network traffic on the basis that it could erode personal privacy (Freedom House, 2017; Human Rights Watch, 2018a; Matinde, 2017).

What is particularly interesting here is that, despite Kenya's record of corruption, nepotism, and ethnic tensions (see Branch, 2011), Kenya's 2010 Constitution and post-2014 cyber security governance efforts have reasonably functioned as advertised. From a purely legal perspective, Kenyan courts have displayed considerably more power compared to years prior to the new constitution and certainly far more since the Arap Moi administration (Mutua, 2001; Wesangula, 2017). When weaved within cyber governance initiatives, security has tipped in favor of user rights while recognizing the need to prevent ICT-mediated violence. This is not to say efforts are perfect, however. Preventing a Kikuyu from slitting a Luo's throat is on par with guaranteeing M-Pesa data integrity, but shaping political narrative through government-level gatekeeping risks undermining what is Kenya's otherwise forward-thinking network protection initiative.

Conclusion: matching cyber security strategy to action and freedom

The Central Bank of Kenya went on the security offensive in both 2017 and 2018, issuing guidance notes in both years requiring finance institutions to implement local policies, procedures, standards, and training, with all efforts demonstrably led by top management and available to external audit (CBK, 2017; Olingo, 2018). Even more remarkable though is requiring institutions to report all major cyber security incidents and associated recovery efforts within 24 hours so as to improve transparency and technological responses. The long-term effort here is to remove the trust stigma associated with reporting and inspire public confidence via documented action rather than hiding heads in the sand. This recent development illustrates that the Government of Kenya is attempting to supply its cyber security strategy with actual teeth.

Kenya has sought regional ICT leadership since connecting its first collective modem in 1995 and by many measures has succeeded. Kenya's internet story has been one of economic growth and largely free of the antagonists that have historically plagued Kenya's offline governance. Moreover, Kenya's cyber security strategy lays out a reasonable understanding of the threats and required social, technical, and legal solutions. However, thieves still freely raid online shilling chests and citizens face the new specter of violence via text message, although 2007's electoral violence has yet to be eclipsed; that, and cyber security must target the threat rather than become a tool for stifling civic discourse. Kenya's cyber security strategy still lacks necessary funding, technical capacity, and sufficient training efforts – and for the latter, not just professional training, but also necessary security awareness socialized to the average user. Kenya's cyber security strategy succeeds at the policy guidance and legal levels, but requires greater translation into technical tools, risk management, and information assurance. While the KE-CIRT/CC was a move in the right direction both in terms of internal sovereignty and international collaboration, Kenya cannot wait another 19 years to put cyber security policies into action while remembering civic engagement is not the target.

Suggested reading

Kaimba, B., Kimani, K., Mwangi, M., Munyendo, B., Mueni, F., Ndegwa, D., Wanjuki, S., Rishad, N., Keige, S., Karanja, J., Soita, J., Musuva-Kigen, P., Onyibe, S., Mugure, P., Mbae, K., Karumba, N., Ngari, A., Owino, E. & Paladion Team. (2016). "Kenya Cyber Security Report 2016," Serianu Cyber-Threat Command Centre, Nairobi, Kenya. www.serianu.com/downloads/KenyaCyberSecuri tyReport2016.pdf

Kigen, P. M., Kisutsa, C., Muchai, C., Kimani, K., Mwangi, M. & Shiyayo, B. (2014). "Kenya Cyber Security Report 2014: Rethinking Cyber Security – 'An Integrated Approach: Processes, Intelligence and Monitoring'," Serianu Cyber-Threat Command Centre, Nairobi, Kenya. www.researchgate.net/ publication/306918414_Kenya_Cyber_Security_Report_2014_Rethinking_Cyber_Security_- _An_Integrated_Approach_Processes_Intelligence_and_Monitoring

Muendo, M. (2019, December 2). "What's Been Done to Fight Cybercrime in East Africa," *The Conversation*. http://theconversation.com/whats-been-done-to-fight-cybercrime-in-east-africa-127240

Njanja, A. (2019, July 3). "Kenya Cyber Attacks Rise to 11.2 Million in First Quarter," *Daily Nation*. www.nation.co.ke/business/Kenya-cyber-attacks-rise-to-11-2m/996-5182266-el3o65/index.html

Serianu. (2015). "Africa Cyber Security Report – Kenya: Achieving Enterprise Cyber Resilience through Situational Awareness." www.serianu.com/downloads/KenyaCyberSecurityReport2015.pdf

Serianu. (2017). "Africa Cyber Security Report – Kenya: Demystifying Africa's Cyber Security Poverty Line." www.serianu.com/downloads/KenyaCyberSecurityReport2017.pdf

Serianu. (2018). "Africa Cyber Security Report – Kenya." www.serianu.com/downloads/KenyaCyberSe curityReport2018.pdf

Tubei, G. (2019, May 27). "Kenya Is a Sitting Duck in Cybersecurity as the Country Boasts Too Few Cybercrimes Professionals Despite Having a Big Name in African ICT Circles," *Business Insider*. www.pulselive.co.ke/bi/strategy/kenya-is-a-sitting-duck-in-cybersecurity-despite-boasting-big- name-in-ict/nvcd12h

References

Aker, J. C. & Mbiti, I. M. (2010). "Mobile Phones and Economic Development in Africa," *Journal of Economic Perspectives*, 24(3): 207–232.

Akuta, E., Ong'oa, I. & Jones, C. (2011). "Combating Cyber Crime in Sub-Sahara Africa: A Discourse on Law, Policy and Practice," *Journal of Peace, Gender and Development Studies*, 1(3): 129–137.

Amadala, V. (2017, August 23). "Banks Given up to Nov 30 to Present Cybersecurity Plans," *The Star*. www.the-star.co.ke/news/2017/08/23/banks-given-up-to-nov-30-to-present-cybersecurity- plans_c1621157

Amadala, V. (2018, August 20). "CBK in New Cybersecurity Rules to Stem Mobile Money Deceit," *The Star*. www.the-star.co.ke/news/2018/08/20/cbk-in-new-cybersecurity-rules-to-stem-mobile- money-deceit_c1805190

Barnes, S. (2015). "How Better Connectivity Can Transform Africa's Economies," *World Economic Forum*. www.weforum.org/agenda/2015/06/how-better-connectivity-can-transform-africas- economies/

Bloggers Association of Kenya. (2018). "State of the Internet in Kenya 2017." www.ifree.co.ke/wp-con tent/uploads/2018/02/State-of-the-Internet-in-Kenya-report-2017.pdf

Branch, D. (2011). *Kenya: Between Hope and Despair, 1963–2011*. New Haven, CT: Yale University Press.

Bright, J. (2016, May 5). "A Brief Overview of Africa's Tech Industry – And 7 Predictions for Its Future," *World Economic Forum*. www.weforum.org/agenda/2016/05/a-brief-history-of-africa- s-tech-industry-and-7-predictions-for-its-future/

Campbell, J. (2017, November 3). "What Went Wrong with Kenya's Elections?" *Council on Foreign Relations*. www.cfr.org/expert-brief/what-went-wrong-kenyas-elections

Central Bank of Kenya. (2017). "Guidance Note on Cybersecurity for the Banking Sector." www.central bank.go.ke/wp-content/uploads/2017/09/GUIDANCE-NOTE-ON-CYBERSECURITY-FOR-THE-BANKING-SECTOR.pdf

Communications Authority of Kenya. (2018). https://ca.go.ke/

Corkin, L. (2016). "Kenya's Mobile Money Story and the Runaway Success of M-Pesa," *Observer Research Foundation*. www.orfonline.org/expert-speaks/kenyas-mobile-money-story-and-the-run away-success-of-m-pesa/

Crabtree, J. (2018). "Cambridge Analytica and Its Role in Kenya 2017 Elections," *CNBC*. www.cnbc.com/2018/03/23/cambridge-analytica-and-its-role-in-kenya-2017-elections.html

Deloitte. (2012). "What Is the Impact of Mobile Telephony on Economic Growth?" GSM Association, London, United Kingdom. Retrieved from www.gsma.com/publicpolicy/wp-content/uploads/2012/11/gsma-deloitte-impact-mobile-telephony-economic-growth.pdf

Freedom House. (2017). "Freedom on the Net 2017." https://freedomhouse.org/report/freedom-net/freedom-net-2017

Gagliardone, I. & Sambuli, N. (2015). "Cyber Security and Cyber Resilience in East Africa (No. 15)," Chatham House, London, United Kindom. www.cigionline.org/sites/default/files/no15_web_0.pdf

Government of Kenya. (2010). "The Constitution of Kenya." www.icla.up.ac.za/images/constitutions/kenya_constitution.pdf

Government of Kenya. (2014a). "The Kenya National ICT Masterplan." www.kenyagreece.com/sites/default/files/ict-master-plan.pdf

Government of Kenya. (2014b). "Government of Kenya Cybersecurity Strategy." http://icta.go.ke/pdf/NATIONAL%20CYBERSECURITY%20STRATEGY.pdf

Goldstein, J. & Rotich, J. (2008). "*Digitally Networked Technology in Kenya's 2007–2008 Post-Election Crisis* (Internet & Democracy Case Study Series No. 2008-09)," Berkman Center for Internet & Society, Harvard University, United States.

Hjort, J. & Poulsen, J. (2017). "The Arrival of Fast Internet and Employment in Africa," *WP 23582*. National Bureau of Economic Research, Cambridge, United States. www.nber.org/papers/w23582

Human Rights Watch. (2018a). "Kenya: Events of 2017." www.hrw.org/world-report/2018/country-chapters/kenya

Human Rights Watch. (2018b). "World Report 2018: Rights Trends in Kenya." www.hrw.org/world-report/2018/country-chapters/kenya

ICT Authority. (2018). http://icta.go.ke/open-data/

International Telecommunication Union. (2017). "Global Cybersecurity Index (GCI) 2017." www.itu.int/dms_pub/itu-d/opb/str/D-STR-GCI.01-2017-PDF-E.pdf

Internet World Stats. (2018). www.internetworldstats.com/africa.htm#ke

Kagwanja, P. & Southall, R. (2009). "Introduction: Kenya – A Democracy in Retreat?" *Journal of Contemporary African Studies*, 27(3): 259–277.

Kaimba, B. (2017a). "Africa Cyber Security Report 2017," Serianu Cyber-Threat Command Centre, Nairobi, Kenya. www.serianu.com/downloads/AfricaCyberSecurityReport2017.pdf

Kakah, M. (2018). "Court Suspends Portions of Cybercrime Law," *Daily Nation*. www.nation.co.ke/news/Court-suspends-portions-of-cybercrime-law/1056-4585936-thh4s5/index.html

Kamau, M. (2018). "Banks, Mobile Money Firms to File Cyber Security Reports," *Standard Digital*. www.standardmedia.co.ke/article/2001292863/banks-mobile-money-firms-to-file-cyber-security-reports

Kassujja, M. (2017). "Fury as Safaricom Suspends 'Public Likes' Paybill," *Nairobi News*. https://nairobi news.nation.co.ke/news/safaricom-suspends-public-likes-paybill/

Kazeem, Y. (2018). "E-commerce Is Thriving in Africa despite Hurdles to the 'Last Mile,'" *Quartz Africa*. https://qz.com/africa/1492628/africa-e-commerce-libya-tops-online-shopping/

Kenya News Agency. (2018). "Digital Sector Lifts Economic Growth," *Business Today*. https://busines stoday.co.ke/digital-growth-contributes-economic-growth/

Kenya Vision 2030. (2018). http://vision2030.go.ke/

Kritzinger, E. & von Solms, S. H. (2012). "A Framework for Cyber Security in Africa," *Journal of Information Assurance & Cybersecurity*. http://ibimapublishing.com/articles/JIACS/2012/322399/

Mäkinen, M. & Kuira, M. W. (2008). "Social Media and Postelection Crisis in Kenya," *The International Journal of Press/Politics, 13*(3): 328–335.

Matinde, V. (2017). "Is Kenya's Cyber Security Bill Good Enough?" *ITWeb Africa*. www.itwebafrica. com/security/515-kenya/238025-is-kenyas-cyber-security-bill-good-enough

Matinde, V. (2018). "Kenya Makes a Dent on Cybercrime but Threats Continue," *ITWeb Africa*. www. itwebafrica.com/security/515-kenya/244562-kenya-makes-a-dent-on-cybercrime-but-threats-continue

Macharia, K. (2017). "Aon Kenya Launches Cyber Security Insurance Product," *Capital FM*. www.capi talfm.co.ke/business/2017/09/aon-kenya-launches-cyber-security-insurance-product/

Mutisya, J. (2018). "Cybercrime Losses Surge above Sh20bn," *Daily Nation*. www.nation.co.ke/news plex/cybercrimei/2718262-4739020-fdefb7/index.html

Mutua, M. (2001). "Justice under Siege: The Rule of Law and Judicial Subservience in Kenya," *Human Rights Quarterly, 23*(1): 96–118.

Mwangi, O. G. (2018). "How Kenya Is Managing Security 20 Years after the Nairobi Blast," *The Conversation*. http://theconversation.com/how-kenya-is-managing-security-20-years-after-the-nai robi-blast-101143

Okuku, A., Renaud, K. & Valeriano, B. (2015). "Cybersecurity Strategy's Role in Raising Kenyan Awareness of Mobile Security Threats," *Information & Security: An International Journal, 32*(2): 2–20.

Olingo, A. (2018). "Kenya Banks, Telcos to File Cyber Security Rules," *The East African*. www.theeasta frican.co.ke/business/Kenya-banks-telcos-to-file-cyber-security-rules/2560-4730524-8329uv/index. html

Omondi, D. (2017, July 30). "How Kenyans Were Lured into Sh2 Trillion Public Likes Scam," *Standard Digital*. www.standardmedia.co.ke/article/2001249724/how-kenyans-were-lured-into-sh2-trillion-public-likes-scam

Rogito, P. K. (2017). "Multi-Tiered Security Architecture for Information Infrastructure Protection in Selected Commercial Banks in Kenya," United States International University, Nairobi, Kenya.

Souter, D. & Kerretts-Makau, M. (2012). "Internet Governance in Kenya-An Assessment."

Sunday, F. & Makau, M. (2017). "Poor Policy Slowing Kenya's ICT Sector as Neighbours Take Lead," *Standard Digital*. www.standardmedia.co.ke/article/2001259537/investment-poor-policy-slowing-kenya-s-ict-sector-as-neighbours-take-lead

Sutherland, E. (2018). "Digital Privacy in Africa: Cybersecurity, Data Protection & Surveillance," *SSRN Electronic Journal*. doi: 10.2139/ssrn.3201310

The Economist. (2015). "Why Does Kenya Lead the World in Mobile Money?" www.economist.com/ the-economist-explains/2015/03/02/why-does-kenya-lead-the-world-in-mobile-money

The National KE-CIRT/CC. (2012). www.ke-cirt.go.ke/index.php/about-us/

Turianskyi, Y. (2018). "Balancing Cyber Security and Internet Freedom in Africa," Occasional Paper No. 275, South African Institute of International Affairs, Johannesburg, South Africa.

Wabuke, E. (2017). "Improving Electoral Cybersecurity in Kenya," *Lawfare*. www.lawfareblog.com/ improving-electoral-cybersecurity-kenya

Wesangula, D. (2017). "Kenya's Supreme Court Has Stood Tall Instead of Ducking. It Gives US Hope," *The Guardian*. www.theguardian.com/commentisfree/2017/sep/04/kenya-supreme-court-stood-tall-hope-win-for-democracy

West, S. (2017, June 16). "The Threat al-Shabaab Poses to Kenya's Election," *The Jamestown Foundation*. https://jamestown.org/program/threat-al-shabaab-poses-kenyas-election/

47

CYBERSECURITY POLICY IN NIGERIA

A tool for national security and economic prosperity

Adewunmi J. Falode

Introduction

Nigeria has an active and expanding presence in cyberspace. Critical sectors of its economy, such as banking and telecommunications, are heavily dependent on access to cyberspace technology. Thus, Nigeria has taken proactive measures creating specialized agencies and units for cybersecurity protection, as well as enacting legislation and policies to fight cybercrime and protect the country's critical infrastructure.

Statement of National Cybersecurity Strategy

Nigeria has come to rely on cyberspace to carry out most of its socio-economic and political functions in the twenty-first century. The shift into cyberspace has exposed Nigeria and its citizens to digital threats that could compromise its overall security, compromise its critical infrastructure and restrict interactions with other states via the Internet. Threats include cybercrime (in all its varieties), cyberterrorism, and on-line child abuse and exploitation. Therefore, the Federal Government of Nigeria (FGN) has developed a National Cybersecurity Strategy (NCSS) as a cohesive response to these challenges. The NCSS derives from the 2014 Nigerian Cybersecurity Policy (NCSP). The NSCP presents four important doctrines: the Doctrine on Cyberspace, Doctrine on Cyberspace Critical Assets and Infrastructure, Doctrine on Cyber-Risk Exposure, and Doctrine on Cybersecurity. The Cyberspace Doctrine recognizes cyberspace as an arena for critical and non-critical national functions that support economic prosperity and security. Such critical and non-critical functions include trade and commerce, national security and defense, communication, medical and health, government operations, and economic development.

According to the Doctrine, Nigeria's cyberspace encompasses all forms of digital engagements, interactions, socializations, transactional activities, contents, resources, and assets deployed through interconnected networks. The Doctrine on Cyberspace Critical Assets and Infrastructure is anchored on safe and secure national critical information infrastructure policies and processes with skilled manpower to manage such national structure. Nigeria's conception of its cyberspace is somewhat broader and holistic compared to what is obtained in other climes. The concept of the cyberspace is woven into the country's economic, political, social, and security fabric. Nigeria has a ready pool of skilled manpower that it has deployed to man aspects of this national critical infrastructure. What comes to mind here is the financial and telecommunication services sectors that are crucial to the socio-economic and political well-being of the state. The Doctrine on Cyber-Risk Exposure recognizes and acknowledges the threats and vulnerabilities that the country constantly faces in cyberspace. Particular risks are those related to cybercrime, specifically, those of hacking, illegal theft, illegal interception, and phishing in the financial services sector. These are not uniquely Nigerian phenomena but they are the most prevalent in the country. Nigeria is further aware that interdependent networks of critical information infrastructures do not exist in isolation from global networks. Therefore, national functions are recurrently vulnerable to predictable and unpredictable risks in cyberspace. The Doctrine emphasizes the consequences and the damage a disruption to the critical national functions would have on the confidentiality, resilience, integrity, availability, and accessibility of the Internet in Nigeria. For example, a DDoS attack in the banking sector will not only affect financial institutions but will also have a serious negative effect on the millions of Nigerian customers that rely on electronic monetary transactions. The Doctrine of Cybersecurity is anchored on the provision of sustainable, proactive, and holistic measures to mitigate, protect, and safeguard the nation from cyberspace's risks, threats, and vulnerabilities.

Nigeria's NCSP identifies three approaches needed to establish a cybersecurity program: public–private sector partnership, multi-stakeholder engagement, and international cooperation. The strategic areas of focus are, among other things:

1   The establishment of a legal framework to tackle the different facets of cybersecurity threats in cyberspace;
2   The creation of a national cybersecurity coordinating center in the Office of the National Security Adviser (ONSA);
3   The creation of a Critical Infrastructure Protection and Resilience (CIIPR) program.

The National Security Strategy that is derived from the National Security Policy contains strategic initiatives and programs congruent with the national doctrines, principles, vision, goals, and objectives in the NCSP. It emphasizes the development of an all-inclusive framework that looks at cybersecurity from both national security and economic interest perspectives. The NCSS spells out short-, medium- and long-term strategies, including articulating proactive and holistic measures for the protection, security, and defense of the nation's cyberspace. NCSS's (2014) core areas include:

1   The provision of a national mechanism for developing and implementing legal and policy measures;
2   National incident management;
3   Critical information infrastructure protection;
4   Cybersecurity assurance framework;
5   Global cooperation on cybersecurity.

The vision of the NCSS is to create a safe, secured, resilient, vibrant, and trusted internet space that gives opportunities to the citizenry, protects national assets and interests, and promotes peaceful interactions in cyberspace for national prosperity.

Definitions

Nigeria uses standard definitions of most cyberspace terms drawn from the US and European Union (EU) understandings:

Cyberspace simply means the interdependent network of critical and non-critical national information infrastructure, convergence of interconnected information and communication resources using information and communication technologies (National Cybersecurity Policy, 2014: Part 2, Section 2.1.1.).

Cybersecurity means the series of sustainable proactive measures that mitigates, protects and safeguards the nation from cyberspace risks, exposures, and threats (National Cybersecurity Strategy, 2014, Chapter 1, Section 1:2). Echoing what is found in the cybersecurity policies of the European Union and the United States, Nigeria's conception of cybersecurity has within it: confidentiality, integrity, availability, information, and resilience. Integrity means that the system and the data in it have not been altered or changed without authorization. Information is currency in cyberspace and protecting that information is of paramount importance. Technical tools such as access control, encryption, and legal protections guarantee confidentiality. Availability implies that the system will behave as expected when used. Resilience is what enables a system to endure security threats instead of critically failing. The key to resilience is accepting the inevitability of threats and limited failures in security defenses (Singer & Friedman, 2014: 36).

Cyberthreat refers to those challenges that are inimical to national growth, security, and prosperity in cyberspace. The core threats are cybercrime (wire fraud and phishing), cyberterrorism, cyberespionage, and child online abuse and exploitation.

These threats directly affect the level of risk exposure, resilience, and protection of associated national critical and non-critical infrastructure. It is important to emphasize here that although Nigeria listed five areas, cybercrime, cyberespionage, cyberterrorism, cyberconflict, and online child exploitation as critical cyberthreats issues, the most important one here is cybercrime. Cybercrime, unlike the remaining four, has come to define the country's identity in the international community. This is why Nigeria has devoted considerable resources and efforts to tackling the menace in its NCSS. In Nigeria, CIIP is known as Critical Information Infrastructure Protection and Resilience (CIIPR) (National Cybersecurity Strategy, 2014: Section 6.1.2.). CIIPR is defined as the detection, prevention, and deterrence of cyberthreats on CII and, crucially, the continued operation of CII in the face of all hazards. Nigeria's CIIPR includes the following: communications sector, government facilities sector, manufacturing sector, dams sector, defense sector, chemical sector (oil and gas), power and energy sector, commercial facilities sector, financial services sector, food and agriculture sector, emergency services sector, transportation systems sector, public health and healthcare sector, water and waste water systems, and Information Technology sector (National Cybersecurity Policy, 2014: Part 7, Section 7:1).

International law

The Convention on cybercrime of the Council of Europe, otherwise known as the Budapest Convention is the only binding international instrument on cybersecurity (Council of Europe, 2001). Some of the cyber offenses covered by the Convention include: data interference, system interference, computer-related forgery, computer-related fraud, offenses related to child pornography, and illegal access. In 2017, Nigeria was invited to sign the Budapest Convention based on the years of cooperation between it and the Council of

Europe (Council of Europe, 2017). Although, Nigeria is yet to sign the treaty, the invitation shows that the country agrees in principle with its aims. This Convention is of particular significance to Nigeria. Fraudsters have become extremely adept at using the Internet to perpetuate digital crimes that transcend borders. The banking and finance sectors have been particularly exposed to this kind of cybercrime in Nigeria. "Advanced Fee Fraud," known as "419" or "yahoo-yahoo" in local parlance, is a dangerous form of cybercrime that has wreaked havoc on the banking and financial sectors in the country (Salu, 2005). This sort of crime is very difficult to prevent, detect, and prosecute because the perpetrators hide behind the anonymity of cyberspace to commit trans-continental crimes. The Convention of Budapest makes it easier for this type of cybercrime to be tackled. Interestingly, Nigeria ranks third in global internet crimes behind the United Kingdom and the United States (Vanguard, 2017). While the advanced countries experience the five variants of cyberthreats, Nigeria has a preponderant share when it comes to cybercrime, especially wire fraud. Nigerian cyber criminals are also very adept in using simple malwares like Predator Pain, ISR Stealer, Keybase, and Pony to remotely access or steal data from infected machines. The frequency of malware attacks has spiked from a few hundred attacks in 2014 to over 8,000–9,000 per month by 2017 (Technology Times, 2016). However, with the passage of the comprehensive Cybercrime Act and the country's membership of G8 24/7 Network, Nigeria has shown its readiness to tackle cyber-related threats.

International governance

Nigeria plays a vital role in both regional and international governance of cyberspace. Through its compliance with the directives of the European Union General Data Protection Regulation (GDPR) and the country's technology regulatory agency National Information Technology Agency (NITDA), Nigeria has ensured that the privacy of its citizens and foreigners in the country is guaranteed in cyberspace (Zakariyya, 2018). The GDPR prevents the abuse and exploitation of personal data of foreigners (Europeans) and Nigerians in cyberspace. It gives users the ability to restrict the amount of their personal data that can be posted and used online. At present, Nigeria's data is stored within the country in the databases of different federal agencies. It is hoped that in the near future, the country will adopt the EU GDPR model to harmonize the data, protect, and secure the privacy of its citizens.

In May 2007, the Internet Society organized an international conference with the theme, "Internet Governance in Africa," in Nigeria (Internet Society, 2015). The conference had in attendance participants from over one hundred countries. Internet governance issues such as the state of play in Africa and international level access issues and Internet-related priorities for Africa were extensively discussed. In July 2016, US IT experts trained Nigerian public officials on global best practices on the implementation of cybercrime law. This training was conducted under the auspices of the West Africa Cyber-Security Initiative Bilateral Workshop that took place in Nigeria (PM NEWS, 2016). The workshop trained the public officials on things such as: cybersecurity strategies and civil liberty issues; countering violent extremism; and digital evidence skills. Nigeria, being a key player in IT development and penetration in Africa, has been able to use such knowledge to strengthen Internet regimes on the continent. In 2017, the Nigerian Telecommunications Commission (NCC) partnered with the International Telecommunications Union (ITU) to set up the Africa Regional Cybersecurity Center (RCC) in Abuja (iTedge News, 2017). The center will play a critical role in the continent's drive to shield Africans from exposure, risks, dangers, and challenges from cyberthreats. The center will also be used as a hub to share information on cyberattacks, threats, malwares, worms, and viruses and train countries in the regions on cyber-related issues.

Sovereignty

Nigeria sees cyberspace as the fourth pillar in its security architecture. In addition to threats from land, sea, and air, Nigeria realized that threats from cyberspace, if left unchecked pose serious dangers to the country's CIIPR, economic prosperity, and sovereignty. Internet penetration and access in the country is above average. As in most developing societies, Nigeria grapples with nation-building challenges such as ethno-religious conflicts and terrorism. This situation has forced Nigeria to not only police its cyberspace but also make legislation that would deter and punish those that would want to use the Internet to undermine the country's security and prosperity. As of January 2018, a Bill in Nigeria's parliament targets those that would want to use hate speeches, via cyberspace, to destabilize the country (Busari, 2018). The aim of this Bill is not to police or censure the Internet, à la the Chinese, but to stop cyberspace from being used to promote ethno-religious intolerance. Additionally, because of the existential threats that cybercrime, especially that in the banking and financial services sectors, constitutes to the overall security and prosperity of the country, Nigeria passed into law the Cybercrimes Act on May 15, 2015. The Act protects Nigeria's CIIPR from cyberattacks and provides a holistic, effective, and unified legal and institutional framework to tackle cyberthreats.

Cultural understanding

The Nigerian understanding of Cybersecurity Culture (CSC) in cyberspace is influenced by its early exposure to cybercrime. Cybercrime has a tripartite structure: socio-economic, psychosocial, and geopolitical cybercrime. Socio-economic cybercrime includes cyber fraud, cyber embezzlement, cyber piracy, romance scams, cyber extortion, illegal on-line gambling, and cyber terrorism. Examples of psychosocial cybercrime are child pornography, cyber bullying, cyber stalking, revenge porn, cyber hate speech, and obscenity. Geopolitical cybercrime includes hacktivism, cyber vandalism, cyber espionage, cyber sabotage, cyber rebellion, cyber assault, and cyber riot. Nigeria tends to experience cybercrime in its socio-economic and psychosocial variations. The motivations behind cyber frauds include self-satisfaction, the need for peer respect and commercial advantage. The most important cybercrime that has gone a long way in influencing Nigeria's CSC in cyberspace is the "Advance Fee Fraud." This fraud is also known as "419," a code which refers originally to the section of the Nigerian Penal Law that deals with specific fraud schemes (Adogame, 2007). This cultural understanding, that is the erroneous belief that the cyberspace is a safe and fast means for the fraudulent acquisition of wealth, spawned a new generation of young Nigerians who are known as "Yahoo-Yahoo Boys." This is a catchall phrase that describes any young Nigerian with an Internet connection and a laptop or desktop computer that is used to dispossess people of their money in any part of the world.

The 419-scam combines the threat of impersonation fraud with a type of an advance fee scheme in which a letter, email or fax is received by the potential victim. The communication from individuals representing themselves as Nigerian or foreign government officials offers the recipient the opportunity to share in a percentage of millions of dollars, soliciting for help in placing large sums of money in overseas bank accounts. The scheme relies on convincing a willing victim to send money in several instalments of increasing amounts for a variety of reasons. At present, issues such as privacy and surveillance do not influence Nigeria's understanding of cybersecurity issues. Rather, it is the notion of cybercrime in cyberspace, especially that related to the banking and financial services sectors in the Nigerian economy, and how to proactively and holistically tackle this crime, that has been the driving force.

Cybersecurity institutions in Nigeria

In tackling cyberthreats, the FGN has been proactive and effective in its response. Beginning in the early 2000s, Nigeria established several governmental institutions related to cybersecurity. In April 2004, Nigeria created the Presidential Committee on Illegal On-line Activities (PCIAO) (National Cybersecurity Policy, 2014: Part 1, Section 1:3). PCIAO is an inter-agency body that comprised all relevant law enforcement, security, intelligence, and IT agencies of government and private organs in the IT sector. The PCIAO laid the groundwork for the prosecution of computer crimes, provided technical assistance to the National Assembly on cybercrime, and developed technical guidelines for the establishment of an industry on cybersecurity. During the same period, Nigeria established the Nigerian Cybercrime Working Group (NCWG) (Udotai, 2015). The NCWG members comprised all the security, financial, and IT agencies in Nigeria such as the Economic and Financial Crimes Commission (EFCC), Nigeria Computer Society (NCS), Office of the National Security Adviser (ONSA), the Nigerian Communications Commission (NCC), and Internet Services Providers' Association of Nigeria (ISPAN). Before its term expired in 2006, the NCWG sponsored the Cybercrime Bill in 2005. In 2006, the FGN created the Directorate of Cybersecurity (DfC) as a permanent autonomous body within the ONSA to take over all the assets and liabilities of the NCWG (Udotai, 2007). Its mandates include the development and implementation of a national cybersecurity policy for Nigeria, establishment of a national computer emergency readiness, development of an effective framework and interface for inter-agency collaboration on cybersecurity and cybercrime, and the establishment a national computer forensics laboratory.

In May 2015, the ONSA commissioned the Nigeria National Computer Emergency Response Team (ngCERT) operations center (Policy Competition and Economic Analysis of Department, n.d.). The ngCERT was specifically created to combat cyberthreats and attacks on Nigeria's Internet. In 2007, Nigeria passed the National Information Technology Development Agency Act (NITDA) (Gamatie, 2015: 61). The Agency, which started its operations six years prior, has the major responsibility for administering ICT-related activities in Nigeria. It is mandated to, among other things, cover the implementation of policy guidelines for driving ICT in Nigeria, and play an advisory role in copyright law by verification and revision of applicable laws in the country (Gamatie, 2015). Nigeria places a high premium on its security architecture in cyberspace. The cyberspace is not just significant to the country as a medium of communication, it is also a key pillar in the country's economic and security structure. This relevance prompted Nigeria to place the twin issues of cyberspace and cybersecurity directly under the Presidency in the ONSA in 2014 (Osho & Onoja, 2015). The ONSA, with the help of other IT agencies has been responsible for the formulation, implementation and articulation of cyberspace-related policies in Nigeria. It was the ONSA that eventually released the two White Papers that have come to define Internet related issues in the country in 2014.

Role of the private sector

Recognizing the importance of the private sector in the achievement of cybersecurity and prosperity, Nigeria created the Public-Partnership Management Framework (PPMF) within the NCSS (National Cybersecurity Strategy, 2014: Chapter 10, Section 10:1). The key elements of the PPMF strategy include:

1   Facilitating cooperation and partnership among the stakeholders in the implementation of the NCSS in the country;
2   Setting up a Public–Private Partnership (PPP) for cybersecurity.

The PPMF defines roles and responsibilities, integrates capabilities, and facilitates joint ownership of the problems and challenges in cyberspace between public and private actors. As in many other nations, the private sector designs, invests, builds, owns, operates, and maintains most of the critical information infrastructure that supports government and public users alike. The partnership helps to build consensus on standards, rules, and best practices for cybersecurity (Udotai, 2015). The PPMF's brief also includes the development of an action plan to review, monitor and implement cybercrime and cybersecurity legislation, coordination of private sector groups from different critical infrastructure industries related to cybersecurity, and the establishment of a coordinated strategy for cybersecurity incidence and response management. For example, partnership with the Internet Service Providers (ISPs) is of crucial significance to Nigeria's cybersecurity. The partnership with the ISPs fosters easier access to network traffics and activity monitoring in cyberspace thereby ensuring safety of the citizens on the Internet (Osho & Onoja, 2015). The access to network traffics allows the government to respond proactively to the activity of cybercriminals in the Nigerian cyberspace.

The role of the legislature

Nigeria's legislature has played an integral part in the adoption of regional and international harmonized legislations against the misuse and abuse of cyberspace for criminal and other unlawful purposes (National Cybersecurity Policy, 2014: Part Nine, Section 9:4). Nigeria established the Cyber Security Legal Framework (CSLF) initiatives in the NCSS to combat cybercrime. The CSLF has four initiatives: to enact fit for purpose cybercrime legislation; prepare and revamp the judiciary for cybercrime legislations; promote institutional cooperation; and encourage public–private collaboration (National Cybersecurity Strategy, 2014: Chapter Four, Section 4.3). In 2005, the NCWG prepared a draft bill titled "Draft Nigerian Computer Security and Critical Information Infrastructure Protection Bill" (Martins Library, 2015). The Bill recommends, among other things, the creation of a legal and institutional framework in relation to the issue of cybercrime and the creation of a central agency to enforce. This Bill was eventually collapsed into the Cybercrime Act of 2015.

In 2006, the Nigerian legislature passed the first in a series of laws that targeted crimes committed via digital technology or electronic devices. The Advance Fee Fraud Act of 2006 criminalized the use of computers or electronic devices to carry out fraud practices (Saulawa, 2016). This Act is limited to offenses that border on fraudulent financial transactions. If convicted under the Act, offenders will be jailed for a maximum period of twenty years and a minimum of seven years without the option of a fine. The stiffer penalty is due to the severity and impact of the cybercrime threat in the country. Nigeria passed the Cybercrime

Act in 2013 to provide an effective and unified legal, regulatory, and institutional framework for the prohibition, prevention, detection, prosecution, and punishment of cybercrimes in the country. In 2015, the Nigerian legislature passed a more comprehensive bill, the Nigeria Cybercrime Act of 2015 that targets the various facets of crimes committed in cyberspace (Saulawa, 2016).

Cybercrime and cyberterrorism

Nigeria created both the Nigerian Computer Emergency Response Team (ngCERT) and the Computer Incident Response Team (CIRT) to tackle issues related to cybercrimes in the country. CIRT responds in real-time to curb, contain, curtail, and delete emerging threats like viruses, Trojans, and malwares, before they can cause or after causing critical damage. A CIRT team is meant to develop a written cyber incident response plan, and more importantly, to investigate and respond to cyberattacks in accordance with that plan (Policy Competition and Economic Analysis of Department, n.d.). Other functions include determining the scope for investigations and conducting investigations within the scope once attack occurs; promoting cybersecurity awareness; and determining the tools and technology that can be used to detect and prevent cyberattacks. ngCERT uses a Cyber Emergency Monitoring System (CEMS) to classify threats that constitute a national-level cyber incident that requires the group's involvement and the triggering of incidence response protocols (National Cybersecurity Strategy, 2014: Part 5, Section 5.).

CEMS operational procedure establishes the baseline security monitoring for broad detection of malicious or anomalous network activity within the cyberspace. CEMS also established specialized security monitoring for critical assets and critical processes within the context of the National Critical Information Infrastructure Protection Plan (NCIIPP). The core functions of ngCERT include, among other things: to direct and coordinate actions to immediately ensure that appropriate measures are put in place to stop an on-going incident at the right time once this has been validated by CEMS; to identify the scope and scale of the incident in order to activate the relevant countermeasures; to coordinate the activities of other sectoral CERT and facilitate cooperation and partnership of all cybersecurity stakeholders, including international and multilateral organizations; to sustain an optimal incident response readiness capacity, technical, and procedural capacity building for both law enforcement and judicial officers; to quickly and effectively coordinate communication among experts during security emergency; to build awareness of security issues across the Internet community; to identify and classify cyberattack scenarios; and to determine the tools and technology that can be used to detect and prevent attacks.

Nigeria also established a Directorate of Cybersecurity (DfC) as a permanent autonomous body within the ONSA with the mandate to develop and implement a national cybersecurity policy for Nigeria. The National Emergency Readiness and Response Mechanism with Early Warning System (EWS) and Alerts, and the National Computer Forensic Laboratory (NCFL) were created by Nigeria to combat cyberthreats that confront the country in cyberspace (Odunsi, 2014). The EWS tackles all cyber-related emergencies in the country while the NCFL coordinates the training and utilization of its facility by all law enforcement, security, and intelligence agencies and coordinates Nigeria's involvement in international cybersecurity operations. Besides, Nigeria established the Nigerian HoneyNet Project (NHP) to proactively and holistically tackle cyberthreats in cyberspace (Kovacs, 2014). The NIIP is a partnership between the government and the private sector comprising ISPs, telecommunication companies, and critical infrastructure organizations.

NHP makes it possible for these stakeholders in the Nigerian cyberspace to share information on malicious sources and cyberspace clean-up procedures.

Nigeria's response to cyberterrorism is coordinated through the ONSA. The following agencies are mandated to counter terrorism and terrorist finances in cyberspace: the Central Bank of Nigeria (CBN) with its anti-terrorism finance act known as the CBN Act or CBN (Anti-Money Laundering and Combatting the Financing of Terrorism in Banks and Other Financial Institutions in Nigeria) Regulations 2013 and AML/CFT (Saulawa & Marshall, 2015). This Act enables the CBN to diligently enforce AML/CFT measures and ensure effective compliance by financial institutions; provides guidance on Know-Your-Customer (KYC) measures to assist financial institutions in the implementation of these regulations; and encourages financial institutions in Nigeria to formulate and implement institutional controls and other procedures to deter criminals from using its facilities for money laundering and terrorism financing (Central Bank of Nigeria, 2013).[1] The Economic and Financial Crimes Commission (EFCC), established in 2004 by the FGN, plays a key role in the fight against cyberterrorism. EFCC created the Nigeria Financial Intelligence Unit (NFIU) in 2004 to combat terrorist finances in cyberspace (Economic and Financial Crimes Commission, 2020). The NFIU was created under the EFCC (Establishment) Act 2004 and Money Laundering (Prohibition) Act of 2004 to gather intelligence and analyze financial transactions in financial institutions in the country. In 2005, the Federal Executive Council created the Special Control Unit Against Money Laundering (SCUML) as an arm of the Federal Ministry of Commerce and Industry (Department for International Development, British Council, 2010). The SCUML monitors, supervises, and regulates activities of all Designated Non-Financial Institutions (DNFIs) in Nigeria in consonance with the country's AML/CFT regime.

Conclusion

Cyberspace has been very significant to the country's security and economic prosperity in the twenty-first century. The realization of the crucial role of the Internet in Nigeria's economic prosperity and security made the country proactive, systemic, holistic, and strategic in its response to threats from cyberspace. Cybercrime in its different variations constitutes the major threat that confronts the country in cyberspace. The seriousness with which Nigeria views these threats was responsible for the adoption of most of the steps listed in the NCSP and NCSS and the passage of the comprehensive Cybercrime Acts in 2015. Being fully aware of the danger that the threats from cybercrime portend for economic prosperity and national security in the country and the sub-region, Nigeria has been at the forefront of establishing a continent-wide taskforce to combat and check the menace.

Note

1 See Part II, Section 4 (2), Central Bank of Nigeria (Anti-Money Laundering and Combating the Financing of Terrorism in Banks and Other Financial Institutions in Nigeria) Regulations 2013, "Cyberterrorism."

Suggested reading

Adesina, O. S. (2017). "Cybercrime and Poverty in Nigeria," *Canada Social Science, 13*(4): 19–29.

Boniface, K. A., Michael, K. A. & Victor, K. O. (2015). "Cyber Security in Nigeria: A Collaboration between Communities and Professionals," *International Journal of Computer, Electrical, Automation, Control and Information Engineering, 9*(5): 1118–1122.

Ibikunle, F. & Eweniyi, O. (2013). "Approach to Cybersecurity Issues in Nigeria: Challenges and Solutions," *International Journal of Cognitive Research in Science, Engineering and Education*, 1(1): 1–11.

Olayemi, O. J. (2014). "A Socio-Technological Analysis of Cybercrime and Cyber Security in Nigeria," *International Journal of Sociology and Anthropology*, 6(3): 116–125.

Osho, O., Falaye, A. A. & Shafi'I, A. M. (2013). "Combating Terrorism with Cybersecurity: The Nigerian Perspective," *World Journal of Computer Application and Technology*, 1(4): 103–109.

References

Adogame, A. (2007, July). "The 419 Code as Business Unusual: Youth and the Unfolding of the Advance Fee Fraud Online Discourse," *International Sociological Association E-Bulletin*, 7: 4–25. www.isa-sociology.org/uploads/imgen/330-e-bulletin-7.pdf

Busari, K. (2018, March 2). "New Senate Bill Proposes Death Sentence for Hate Speech," *Premium Times*. www.premiumtimesng.com/news/top-news/260466-new-senate-bill-proposes-death-sen tence-hate-speech.html

Central Bank of Nigeria. (2013, September 3). "Federal Republic of Nigerian Official Gazette." www.cbn.gov.ng/out/2014/fprd/aml%20act%202013.pdf

Council of Europe. (2001, November 23). "Convention on Cybercrime," European Treaty Series No. 185, Budapest, Hungary. www.europarl.europa.en/meetdocs/2014_2019/documents/libe/dv/7_Conv_budapest_/7_Conv_budapest_en.pdf

Council of Europe. (2017, July 11). "Nigeria Invited to Join the Budapest Convention on Cyber Crime." www.coe.int/en/web/cybercrime/-/nigeria-invited-to-join-the-budapest-convention-on-cybercrime

Department for International Development, British Council. (2010). "Special Control Unit Against Money Laundering," *Security, Justice and Growth*. www.britishcouncil.org.ng/sites/default/files/spe cial_control_unit_against_money_laundering.pdf

Economic and Financial Crimes Commission. (2020). "Nigeria Financial Intelligence Unit." https://efcc nigeria.org/efcc/about-efcc/98-nfiu

Gamatie, A. (ed.). (2015). *Computing in Research and Development in Africa: Benefits, Trends, Challenges and Solutions*. London: Springer.

Internet Society. (2015, May 29). "Internet Development and Internet Governance in Africa," *Internet Society*, Abuja, Nigeria. www.internetsociety.org/resources/doc/2015/internet-development-and-internet-governance-in-africa/

iTedge News. (2017, November 29). "NCC, ITU Partner to Set up Africa Regional Cybersecurity Center." https://itedgenews.ng/2017/11/29ncc-itu-partner-africa-regional-cybersecurity-center

Kovacs, E. (2014 April 14). "Nigeria Launches Computer Emergency Readiness and Response Team," *Softpedia News*. www.news.softpedia.com/news/Nigeria-Launches-Computer-Emergency-Readi ness-and-Response-Team-437433.shtml

Martins Library. (2015, March). "A Critical Review of the Computer Security and Critical Information Infrastructure Protection Bill 2005 as Nigerian Specific Cybercrime Legislation." https://martinsli brary.blogspot.com/2015/03/a-critical-review-of-computer-security.html

National Cybersecurity Policy. (2014). https://cert.gov.ng/images/uploads/NATIONAL_CYBERSE CURITY_POLICY.pdf

National Cybersecurity Strategy. (2014). https://cert.gov.ng/ngcert/resources/NATIONAL_CYBESE CURITY_STRATEGY.pdf

Odunsi, W. (2014, June 19). "NSA Raises Alarm over Cyber Threat, Seeks Collaboration with Stakeholders," *Daily Post*. www.dailypost.ng/2014/06/19/nsa-raises-alarm-cyber-threat-seeks-collab oration-stakeholders/

Osho, O. & Onoja, A. D. (2015). "National Cyber Security Policy and Strategy of Nigeria: A Qualitative Analysis," *International Journal of Cyber Criminology*, 9(1): 120–143. www.cybercrimejour nal.comOsho&Onoja2015vol9issue1.pdf

PM NEWS. (2016, July 25). "US Trains 100 Nigerians on Cybercrime Law." www.pmnewsnigeria. com/2016/07/25/us-trains-100-nigerians-on-cybercrime-law/

Policy Competition and Economic Analysis of Department. (n.d.). "Understanding the Concept of Cyber Security." www.ncc.gov.ng/docman-main/industry-statistics/research-reports/682-under standing-the-concept-of-cyber-security/file

Salu, A. O. (2005). "Online Crime and Advance Fee Fraud in Nigeria – Are Available Legal Remedies Adequate?" *Journal of Money Laundering Control,* 8(2): 159–167.

Saulawa, M. A. (2016). "An Overview of the Legal Framework of Advanced Fee Fraud and Cybercrime in Nigeria," *Hasanuddin Law Review,* 2(2): 201–202.

Saulawa, M. A. & Marshall, J. B. (2015). "Cyberterrorism: A Comparative Legal Perspective," *Journal of Law, Policy and Globalization, 33.* www.iiste.org/journals/index.php/JLPG/viewfile/19332/19640

Singer, P. W. & Friedman, A. (2014). *Cybersecurity and Cyberwar: What Everyone Needs to Know.* Oxford: Oxford University Press.

Technology Times. (2016, October 11). "Cyber Crime in Nigeria 'Increasing at Alarming Rate'." https://technologytimes.ng/cyber-crime-in-nigeria-increasing-at-alarming-rate/

Udotai, B. (2007, May 4). "Framework for Cybersecurity in Nigeria," Directorate of Cybersecurity, Office of the National Security Adviser, Abuja, Nigeria. www.itu.int/ITU-D/cyb/events/2007/praia/docs/udotai-nigeria-cybersecurity-framework-praia-nov-07-pdf

Udotai, B. (2015, September 3). "Dealing with the Challenge of Cybercrime in Nigeria under the New Cybercrime Act 2015," The Lagos Chamber of Commerce and Industry 2015 Seminar of the Financial Services Group. http://lagoschamber.com/download/SPEAKER%201-%20cybercrime%20-%20%20UDOTAI.ppt

Vanguard. (2017, August 22). "Nigeria 3rd in Global Internet Crimes behind UK, U.S., Says NCC." www.vanguardngr.com/2017/08/nigeria-3rd-global-internet-crimes-behind-uk-u-s-says-ncc/amp/

Zakariyya, A. (2018, February 25). "Nigeria: Europe's Data Regulation – What Nigerians Should Know," *Daily Trust.* https://allafrica.com/stories/201802250001.html.

48

CYBERSECURITY IN GHANA

Past, present, and future

Anwar Ouassini and Mostafa Amini

Introduction

Ghana's information and communications technology industry has been at the forefront in Africa in trying to tackle the domestic, regional, and global questions surrounding cybersecurity in Africa. As Ghana gradually becomes interconnected with the global system, cybersecurity threats are increasingly impacting economic development, political stability, and international relations. In response to the domestic and global challenges, Ghana has acknowledged the central role that cybersecurity plays in maintaining its stability in West Africa. It has been comprehensively reforming legal and criminal justice institutions while collaborating with international partners to share expertise to build the necessary critical infrastructure. This chapter explores these issues in more detail by presenting an analysis on the information and communications technology infrastructure in contemporary Ghana. It provides an overview of Ghana's cybersecurity strategy with a focus on legal reforms, beginning in 2008 with the establishment of the National Information Technology Agency and up to the most recent development of the National Cyber Security Center in 2018. The chapter evaluates how these institutions have played a central role in developing the Ghanaian cybersecurity infrastructure to respond to domestic and international challenges. The chapter then discusses cybercrimes in the Ghanaian context with an emphasis on the enduring problem of the *Sakawa* culture and cyber-criminality. Finally, the chapter ends with new developments in the Ghanaian cybersecurity apparatus with a focus on the banking sector.

Statement of National Cybersecurity Strategy

The dominant paradigm capturing Ghana's perspective on cyber security can be characterized as a transition from disengagement, to an attempt at rapid modernization and centralization. The implementation of the Ghanaian internet strategy has been historically driven and controlled by the private sector which has since the 1990s registered over 100 internet and data service providers (Foster, Goodman, Osiakwan, & Bernstein, 2004). While the government has only recently placed emphasis on investing in a technological framework, the private sector has had full control over all the internet usage in the country, including the government's own access to the internet (Republic of Ghana, 2015). The void created by this lack of government authority has facilitated an environment where cybercriminals can flourish. Consequently, in 2008 the Ghanaian government began to acknowledge these threats and rolled out a network that would be the first of many national investments in internet and data technologies (Republic of Ghana, 2015).

The purpose behind this drastic move was to centralize already existing regulatory bodies that oversee internet activities, cybercrimes, and the emerging e-services that were increasingly becoming crucial to Ghana's economic development (Republic of Ghana, 2015). The formalization of this network was introduced in two phases. The first phase was in 2008, where the e-government services center moved officially under the control of the newly formed National Information Technology Agency (NITA). The second phase was instituted in 2011, as NITA became the sole provider of the internet and data services to almost all government agencies. This permitted regulatory agencies to work under government domains and led to, among other things, the creation of "digital certificates" to label and secure communication between government bodies and non-governmental bodies (Republic of Ghana, 2015).

The development of NITA authorized the government to begin a strategy to tackle cybercrime locally, regionally, and internationally. The rise of cybercrimes originating from Ghana produced negative attention on the government and society, questioning its reputation of stability in Africa. Moreover, the mobilization to establish a dynamic cybersecurity framework arose out of fears that criminal networks are also potentially undermining European and American economic investment and tourism. The recognition that cybersecurity is impacting domestic and foreign policy – especially concerning national security – led the Ghanaian government to act. National progress, national strength, image, economic well-being, defense and security, public health, and safety, were all key factors driving the rapid change (Republic of Ghana, 2015).

Consequently, for Ghanaian authorities, cybersecurity was framed as being fundamental to the social, political, and economic well-being of the nation. In recognition of these threats and opportunities, the government endeavored to maintain its independence from international actors to allow for self-reliance and promote stability and development in its territorial boundaries. The Ghanaian government maintains that this can only be accomplished through effective governance, a strong legislative and regulatory framework, a developed technology framework that reinforces cultural awareness, localized research, emergency readiness and international cooperation (Republic of Ghana, 2015: 26–28).

What does the drastic shift in perspective look like at the policy level? Several policies, national documents, and cybersecurity centers have been developed to address the issues facing the nation, including online threats and criminal activities. The necessity of these policies has been best explained by President Akkufo-Addo when he stated, "Ghana cannot fully reap the digital dividends, associated with her adoption of ICT as a means of our socio-economic transformation if it fails to mitigate both existing and emerging cybersecurity threats" (The Republic of Ghana, Ministry of Communications, 2019). The establishment of these policies institutionalized and embedded the emerging cybersecurity apparatus within Ghanaian political, economic, and social institutions. To better understand this sudden shift in policy, it is crucial to analyze the history of legislation driving Ghana's attitudes towards cybersecurity.

Legal reforms and the Ghanaian cybersecurity apparatus

The structure of the cybersecurity apparatus in Ghana is a symbiosis between private and public entities, not unlike that in the United States (Adu & Adjei, 2018). The role of each of these respective institutions constitutes the proactive implementation of safeguards and measures against cybercrimes, as well as proliferating awareness across the country on their dangers and potential solutions (Warner, 2011). In an effort to supplement national expertise, Ghana has made strides in forming communicative pipelines and initiatives with international institutions – including the Council of Europe, Oxford University, and the World Bank – to develop Ghana's infrastructure in the face of increased cyber threats ("Legislation on Cybersecurity Will Addresses Weakness in Our Cybercrime Laws," 2019). As a result of these key collaborations, other significant steps have also been implemented since the founding of National Information Technology Agency Act (NITA) in 2008, including the establishment of the Ghana National Cyber Security Policy & Strategy document and the construction of the National Cyber Security Centre (NCSC), under the Ministry of Communications. This pivotal institution heads and centralizes cybersecurity efforts in Ghana to "liaise with relevant state agencies and the private sector to oversee cybersecurity operations in the country" (GhanaWeb, 2017: n.p.). This new center will also centralize all other bodies under its umbrella with a strategy to tackle the micro, meso, and macro-level impacts that the cyber threat produces. To provide a look into the structure and policy driving cybersecurity in Ghana, we take a look at legislative efforts to institutionalize cybersecurity standards within the Republic. We will also take a look at the configuration of Ghana's formal policy and vision for combating cybercrime.

The backbone of Ghana's cybersecurity policies relies on three pieces of legislation: The Electronic Transactions Act of 2008 (ETA), the National Information Technology Agency Act of 2008 (NITA), and the Data Protection Act of 2012 (DPA) (Ennin, 2015). The National Information Technology Agency Act (NITA) was Ghana's effort at creating a formalized structure to "regulate the provision of information communications technology, ensure the provision of quality information communications technology, promote standards of efficiency and ensure high quality of service" (The National Information Technology Agency Act of 2008: 4). By establishing the National Information Technology Agency (or Technology Agency, "TA"), the Ministry of Communication provides a vision to its citizens and the international community on how seriously Ghana takes the growth of cybersecurity, the rise of cybercrime, and their goal of integrating economic, technological, and administrative aspects of government with this vision (The National Information Technology Agency Act of 2008: 4).

The Electronic Transactions Act of 2008 (ETA) provides legal validation and legitimacy of the usage of electronic forms of communication and transactions, from both a national and transnational perspective (Electronic Transactions Act of 2008). The ETA provides a framework for the usage of electronic transactions in court proceedings and the admissibility of evidence. While the ETA tries providing leverage to law enforcement bodies when dealing with crimes committed in the realm of cybercrime, the scope of the exact powers is limited and, at times, unclear (Ennin, 2015). Another critical power instituted by the Act is the creation of a "Certifying Agency," who has the power, among other functions, to issue "licenses for encryption and authentication service" (Electronic Transactions Act of 2008).

The Data Protection Act was initially established to protect consumer data from violations and breaches by organizations, who are required to abide by a set of established principles and instructions (Data Protection Act of 2012). The Act also facilitates the creation of the Data Protection Commission (DPC), which serves a regulatory body over the processing of personal information and oversees other privacy-related matters (Dagbanja, 2016). The DPC is instructed with the regulatory oversight of what the legislation terms as

"Data Controllers" and "Data Processors." The former is defined as a body who provides guidelines on how personal data will be utilized in their respective contexts, whereas the latter is simply a recognized representative of the former (Data Protection Act of 2012). The DPC is also served with the responsibility of maintaining another regulatory measure enabled by the DPA: The Data Protection Register. The Register is simply a repository of these "Data Controllers," who are required under the Act to apply to the DPC outlining their goals and objectives for processing private data, for their respective organization purpose (Bright, 2019). While it is unclear to what extent the DPA and its associated measures are being implemented and tracked, the mere establishment of the DPA as a critical piece of legislation is a symbolic transition in Ghana highlighting the seriousness with which the government is taking cybersecurity.

The aforementioned legislative initiatives by Ghana provide a structural framework of independent agencies, regulatory bodies, oversight tools, and empirical measures, all to accentuate cybersecurity, and thereafter moving to decrease cybercrime. Ghana has taken key steps in avoiding isolationism to combat the rise in cybercrime and, instead, collaborates with international organizations to achieve its outlined objectives. The foresight in implementing such legislation also shows its understanding of how cybersecurity has serious implications for a breadth of industries including finance, health, national security, and education. However, there still exist key barriers in the process of combating cybercrimes, including the lack of expertise from law enforcement and the lack of strong substantive measures in the implementation of these legislative provisions (Boateng, Longe, Mbarika, Avevor, & Isabalija, 2010).

In the process of developing a robust cybersecurity policy and structure, Ghana has identified various components of its Critical National Information Infrastructure (CNII), which provides goals and objectives in the enhancement of the cybersecurity structure. These include the protection of economic strength, international reputation, national security, public health, and the extent to which the government can fully operate unhindered (Republic of Ghana, 2015). Ghana's policy also highlights various sectors that are especially relevant to combating cybercrime, including the industries of finance, communications, health, and agriculture. With these areas in mind, some areas that are covered by Ghana's cybersecurity initiative include regulatory and technology frameworks, facilitating a culture of security, and international cooperation (Republic of Ghana, 2015: 19–21).

From a regulatory and technology perspective, the main strategy from Ghana includes setting up regulatory agencies that both provide guidance and incorporate recommendations from external entities (Republic of Ghana, 2015: 29). Ghana also seeks to establish universal standards and guidelines to be used by academia and law enforcement alike. Ghana's intent for developing cultural competence in cybersecurity seeks to use both grassroots training and legal enforcement. NGOs, professional certifications, and training are pivotal tools that will improve "awareness creations and online skill development for all stakeholders including children by developing a National Cyber Security Awareness program and portal targeted at all stakeholders by content providers using different packaging for different demographics" (Republic of Ghana, 2015: 31).

Finally, Ghana's intent to develop international cooperation in its cybersecurity apparatus is driven by strategic interests and necessity. The comprehensive manner in which Ghana seeks to address cybersecurity concerns via its institutions and active policy frameworks, speaks volumes to not only the historic dynamics that are unique to Ghana but also the general international sentiments towards cybercrime. Ghana holds a unique place in global cybersecurity concerns because of the nature of the crimes that originate within its borders.

Cybercrime and Sakawa

The legislative and government structures driving Ghana's policies are key in understanding where Ghana *was* in cybersecurity, and certainly where it is heading. However, a deeper look at what the characteristics of cybercrime look like is also imperative for a comprehensive picture. According to Warner (2011), the Ghanaian cybercriminal infrastructure has been dominated by three major forms of cybercrimes: identity fraud, fake gold dealers, and estate fraud. Identity fraud in Ghana is also known as "romance fraud" whereby a person "hooks" a prospective lover/partner from the United States or Europe and convinces them to send funds to support their relationship (Warner, 2011). This type of fraud has received the most attention in the United States and Europe contributing to "Ghana being blacklisted for money-laundering by the international watchdog the global Financial Action Task Force in 2012" (Darko, 2015).

Fraudulent gold dealers initiate their relationships online via email, online chat rooms, social media, and marriage sites and dupe the victims who are mostly from developed nations to pursue an investment in an upstart company to take advantage of the "flourishing gold market." Once the prospective "investor" sends the money, the company ceases to exist and all contact between the fraudster and victim is terminated (Levine, 2018).

Unlike identity and gold fraud, estate fraud primarily targets Ghanaians who live abroad and are seeking to invest in Ghana (Warner, 2011). Fraudsters employ fake websites propping up non-existent construction firms, sell blueprints of the land and homes to be built, and request large deposits to build the property. Once the deposit is received through a wire transfer, the shell company dissolves leaving the "customer" out of their funds (Warner, 2011). These criminal activities all utilize online tools to defraud both Westerners and Ghanaians living abroad of their wealth. While the underlying motivations towards cyber-criminality may be driven by poverty, unemployment, and minimal regulatory frameworks, there are also cultural processes that facilitate the practice (Baylon & Antwi-Boasiako, 2016).

One of the unique developments in the problem of cybercrime in Ghana is the cultural belief in Sakawa. Sakawa cybercriminal attacks utilize the internet to fraud and scam individuals and businesses of their money through bank, identity, and credit card fraud (Baylon & Antwi-Boasiako, 2016). This fraud often engages Juju spirits through black magic rituals to fortify the success of the witchcraft imposed on the process of defrauding the individual or business. It is believed that these Juju priests, for a price, negotiate with the spirits to protect the scammers from the authorities to ensure success in the scam (Baylon & Antwi-Boasiako, 2016). If the Sakawa boy conducts the supervised rituals and follows the precepts laid out by the Juju priest, then success will be forthcoming. If they fail to follow the rules and prescriptions laid out by the Juju priest, then they will be cursed and possessed by the spirits (Baylon & Antwi-Boasiako, 2016). This ritual is often paid for by the criminal gang's boss to ensure that the recruited scammer maintains their loyalty to the gang and the scam (Warner, 2011; Baylon & Antwi-Boasiako, 2016). As a result, the Sakawa boys act brazenly in their attempts at defrauding their victims because they believe the spirits are watching over them (Warner, 2011; Baylon & Antwi-Boasiako, 2016).

While many argue that this religio-ideological practice has its sources in Nigeria, (Warner, 2011) it has become popular and mainstream in Ghanaian cybercriminal culture. Warner cites Ghanaian blogger Linnet Taylor, stating that

> the Sakawa kid will go to the priest and [the priest] will say, "you must sleep for
> a night in a coffin [with a corpse], then sacrifice three chickens, then give me five

cedis [approximately $3.33].".' If the person does all this, their [sic] fraud will be successful. If not, they [sic] are disregarding the prescription of a juju priest, which, as everyone knows, is an unwise thing to do. [The process] usually involves you getting turned into an animal of some kind, or running naked through the market square ... There are also rumors [sic] about human sacrifices being made.

(Warner, 2011: 744)

This belief reveals that any strategy to combat and address cybercrimes in Ghana necessitates a holistic view that takes into account the technological, political, economic, and cultural frameworks that facilitate the growth and expansion of cybercriminality in Ghana. This is why President Akufo-Addo emphasized at the opening of the National Cyber Security Week that:

we have to promote a cyber-security culture among our people. In our everyday lives, we would not leave the doors to our homes or cars open, nor would we advertise to the public where we leave our prized possessions, we would never dream of exposing our children to known criminals but in the virtual world, we take these chances daily.

(Republic of Ghana, Ministry of the Interior, 2017: para 13)

The evolution of cybercrime and the Bank of Ghana's Cyber Security Directive for Financial Institutions

Within the first seven months of 2018, Ghana reported a loss of $97 million due to cybercriminal attacks, compared to a loss of $69 million in all of 2017, marking a forty per cent increase from 2017 to 2018 ("Awareness Creation on Cyber Crime Key for Digital Migration," 2018). Such a sharp rise is indicative, among other factors, of the evolution in cybercrime that is currently transpiring within Ghana. These nuanced cyberattacks are not only technically complex but are also administered domestically by citizens and internationally by foreign actors and adversaries alike. Among the more complex offenses are included direct cyberattacks on financial institutions and their infrastructure, as well as phishing attempts on individuals and government institutions. While the traditional cybercriminal activities of credit card fraud, email scams, and deceptive wires are still foundational tools for cybercriminals in Ghana, there are long-standing attempts to develop new methods to commit these outlined crimes. The context that is facilitating this development is the paradox of "simultaneous innovation," where advancement in technological infrastructure and capability in Ghana also inevitably facilitates more opportunities to participate in criminal activities, due to the expansion of the cyber "field." Along the line of this development, what further exacerbates this issue is precisely what makes the internet infrastructure such a useful tool for the banking industry: the "boundary-less" attributes of cyberspace constrain policing directives to regulate cybercrimes making it that much more difficult (Ndubueze, 2007; Baylon & Antwi-Boasiako, 2016).

At the crux of Ghana's effort to combat the ever-evolving range and sophistication of cyberattacks and cybercriminality, the Ghanaian government has worked with international partners to assist in bolstering its cybersecurity platforms. Aside from establishing the National Cyber Security Center to regulate all governing institutions, Ghana has formed key partnerships and sought consultations from the World Bank, the EU's Global Action on

Cybercrime Project, the United States' Security Governance Initiative, the FBI, and the Federal Reserve (Oxford Business Group, 2019). One expansion of Ghana's collaborative efforts to address the growing threat of cyberattacks on its critical infrastructure was to safeguard its vulnerable banking system ("Bank of Ghana's Cyber & Information Security Directive," 2018). The Ghanaian government established the Bank of Ghana's Cyber & Information Security Directive for Financial Institutions to streamline operations in order to secure and develop

> protocols and procedures for; routine and emergency scenarios, delegation of responsibilities, inter- and intra-company communication and cooperation, coordination with government authorities, establishment of reporting mechanisms, physical security measures for IT Data centers [sic.] and Control Rooms, and assurance of data and network security.
> *("Bank of Ghana's Cyber & Information Security Directive," 2018: 2)*

The Directive is Ghana's response to the evolving field of cybercrime, which has taken a keen interest in Ghana's banking infrastructure. Some of the fundamental provisions of the Directive instruct senior executives within the private banking sector to pay special attention to internal cybersecurity processes to manage risk, create robust security standards, and uphold privacy for individual customers and prospective investors. Furthermore, banks are urged to appoint Cyber and Information Security Officers (CISO) to act as the formal driving force in providing and implementing recommendations from the Directive (Kshetri, 2019). This will reinforce the sharing of information across banking institutions while focusing the efforts locally to address vulnerabilities and shore up defenses. The 130-page document comprehensively addresses several components of the banking sector including risk management, strategic responses to cyberattacks, user access to sensitive systems, provisions for securing mobile banking systems, training of employees, and even physical security ("Bank of Ghana's Cyber & Information Security Directive," 2018: 3–6 and 128). It even goes as far as to provide an implementation schedule that projects a one- to two-year duration, depending on the specific component implemented.

Conclusion

Even with the most advanced internet infrastructures in Africa, Ghana has a long way to go in developing the cybersecurity infrastructure to tackle the problems of cybercrimes. The Ghanaian government's effort to create a centralized body under the National Cyber Security Center has been successful, nevertheless increased investment in the internet infrastructure is necessary to continue to address the nation's cybersecurity challenges. The establishment of the National Cyber Security Center will have to ensure that information is shared amongst the local and national agencies while simultaneously working with regional and international actors to confront the ever-evolving varieties of cybercrime. Moreover, it is imperative to understand cybersecurity from within the Ghanaian experience which will ultimately produce different challenges from neighboring nations and the rest of the international community. This is important because many West African nations adopt cybersecurity institutional structures and strategies from Europe without taking into account the local context (Republic of Ghana, 2015). Finally, the strength of these institutions will be their ability to adapt to the exponential growth of technology that cybercriminals employ and the potential pool of victims who are increasing every day as the world shifts online.

Suggested reading

Baylon, C. & Antwi-Boasiako, A. (2016). "Increasing Internet Connectivity while Combatting Cybercrime: Ghana as a Case Study," *Global Commission on Internet Governance*, Paper Series 44. www.cigionline.org/publications/increasing-internet-connectivity-while-combatting-cybercrime-ghana-case-study

Ghana Talks Business. (2018, February 26). "Ghana's National Cybersecurity Policy and Strategy (NCSPS): Critique and Comparison with Best Practice." https://ghanatalksbusiness.com/ghanas-national-cybersecurity-policy-strategy-ncsps-critique-comparison-best-practice/

Republic of Ghana. (2015, June 23). "Ghana National Cyber Security Policy & Strategy." www.itu.int/en/ITU-D/Cybersecurity/Documents/Country_Profiles/National-Cyber-Security-Policy-Strategy-Revised_23_07_15.pdf

Warner, J. (2011). "Understanding Cyber-Crime in Ghana: A View from Below," *International Journal of Cyber Criminology*, 5(1): 736–749.

References

Adu, K. K. & Adjei, E. (2018). "The Phenomenon of Data Loss and Cybersecurity Issues in Ghana," *Foresight*, 20(2): 150–161.

"Awareness Creation on Cyber Crime Key for Digital Migration." (2018). www.crime-research.org/news/31.10.2018/4033/

"Bank of Ghana's Cyber & Information Security Directive." (2018). www.bog.gov.gh/wp-content/uploads/2019/09/CYBER-AND-INFORMATION-SECURITY-DIRECTIVE.pdf

Baylon, C. & Antwi-Boasiako, A. (2016). "Increasing Internet Connectivity while Combatting Cybercrime: Ghana as a Case Study," *Global Commission on Internet Governance*, Paper Series 44. www.cigionline.org/publications/increasing-internet-connectivity-while-combatting-cybercrime-ghana-case-study

Boateng, R., Longe, O. B., Mbarika, V., Avevor, I. & Isabalija, S. R. (2010). "Cyber Crime and Criminality in Ghana: Its Forms and Implications," Americas Conference on Information Systems. https://pdfs.semanticscholar.org/561f/cc5baef2a153903fb67a08b9e7917b0ddb0a.pdf

Bright, V. (2019). "Ghana: Data Protection 2019," in *The ICLG to Data Protection Laws and Regulations* (pp. 146–153). London: Global Leader Group Ltd.

Dagbanja, D. N. (2016). "The Right to Privacy and Data Protection in Ghana," in A. Makulilo (ed.), *African Data Privacy Laws* (pp. 229–248). Cham: Springer.

Darko, S. (2015). "Inside the World of Ghana's Internet Fraudsters," *BBC*. www.bbc.com/news/world-africa-32583161

Ennin, D. (2015). *Cybercrime in Ghana: A Study if Offenders, Victims and the Law* (PhD dissertation), University of Ghana, Accra, Ghana.

Foster, W., Goodman, S., Osiakwan, E. & Bernstein, A. (2004). "Global Diffusion of the Internet IV: The Internet in Ghana," *Communications of the Association for Information Systems*, 13(38): 1–47.

GhanaWeb. (2017, October 23). "Ghana to Establish National Cyber Security Centre." www.ghanaweb.com/GhanaHomePage/business/Ghana-to-establish-National-Cyber-Security-Centre-593389

Kshetri, N. (2019). "Cybercrime and Cybersecurity in Africa," *The Journal of Global Information Technology Development*, 22(2): 77–81.

"Legislation on Cybersecurity Will Address Weakness in Our Cybercrime Laws." (2019). https://cybersecurity.gov.gh/

Levine, M. (2018). "How One African Man's Gold Scheme Cost His American Victims Millions of Dollars." https://abcnews.go.com/International/african-mans-gold-scheme-cost-american-victims-millions/story?id=52610439

Ndubueze, P. (2007). "High-Tech Crimes, Boundaryless Policing and Cyber Security Policy in Nigeria: A Periscope," *Dutse Journal of Criminology and Security Studies*, 1(1): 89–102.

Oxford Business Group. (2019). "Cybersecurity of Top Priority for Ghanaian Banks." https://oxfordbusinessgroup.com/analysis/safe-and-secure-use-online-services-continues-grow-strengthening-cybersecurity-remains-top-area

Republic of Ghana. (2015). "Ghana National Cyber Security Policy & Strategy." www.sbs.ox.ac.uk/cybersecurity-capacity/system/files/Ghana_Cyber-Security-Policy-Strategy_Final_0.pdf

Republic of Ghana, Ministry of Communications. (2019). "MOC Celebrates National Cyber Security Week." www.moc.gov.gh/moc-celebrates-national-cyber-security-week

Republic of Ghana, Ministry of the Interior. (2017). "Ghana to Establish a National Cyber Security Centre, Says President Akufo-Addo." www.mint.gov.gh/ghana-to-establish-a-national-cyber-secur ity-centre-says-president-akufo-addo/

"The Data Protection Act." (2012). https://nita.gov.gh/wp-content/uploads/2017/12/Data-Protection-Act-2012-Act-843.pdf

"The Electronic Transactions Act." (2008). www.researchictafrica.net/countries/ghana/Electronic_Tran sactions_Act_no_772:2008.pdf

"The National Information Technology Agency Act." (2008). www.moc.gov.gh/sites/default/files/ downloads/National%20Information%20Technology%20Agency%20Act%20771.pdf

Warner, J. (2011). "Understanding Cyber-Crime in Ghana: A View from Below," *International Journal of Cyber Criminology*, 5(1): 736–749.

49

BUILDING A CYBER FORTRESS IN AFRICA

Uganda's cyber security capacities and challenges

Scott N. Romaniuk and David Andrew Omona

Introduction: Uganda's expanding role in cyberspace

Cyber security, "a body of technologies, processes, and practices designed to protect networks, devices, programs, and data from attack, damage, or unauthorized access" (Lord, July 15 2015), is very important for any country embracing digitization. For a nation to be regarded as a true digital nation, it needs to build up its cyber capacity to manage an array of current threats and to be ready to deal with them. This means developing cyber capacities in the form of "national abilities, processes, resources, institutions and knowledge that would allow" a country "to build a safe, secure, peaceful and prosperous cyber environment" (NRD Companies, 2017) is mandatory. Like any other country, Uganda is working to position itself in the digitalized world by expanding its overall presence in the cyberspace. The recently announced Global National Cyber Security Index by Estonia's E-Governance Academy Foundation Company, ranked Uganda first in Africa and 40th in the world in cyber security, with an index of 49.35 (Osekeny, September 24, 2018).

The September 21, 2018 ranking of the National Cyber Security Index measures preparedness of countries to prevent cyber threats and manage cyber incidents. Coming first in Africa and 40th in the world puts Uganda well ahead of many developing and developed countries in cyber security. In Africa, the position puts Uganda ahead of Mauritius, which came second in Africa and 43rd globally, Nigeria, which comes in third in Africa and 45th globally, and South Africa at 75th place globally. It also puts Uganda ahead of a number of other developed countries including Israel at 42nd place, Iceland at 44th, and China at a position of 62nd globally (Osekeny, September 24, 2018). If the level of technological advancement in some of these countries is looked at critically, one cannot compare it with that of Uganda. This means Uganda has, at least on a superficial level, learned from the mistakes of other countries and set itself on a path for any eventuality.

Overview of national cyber security strategy

Whereas Ugandans generally see Internet crime as an advanced type of crime that has not yet infiltrated the country (Paul, n.d.), there are many instances where Ugandans have suffered as a result of cyber related crimes. The carefree nature of Internet use, whereby anyone has the ability to publish anything and at any time, presents the country with a serious security threat by way of the vulnerability of its approximately 42 million citizens.

Since cybercrimes directly affect people when they lose vital data, and have their money stolen or their privacy violated, in an attempt to protect Ugandans, the government of Uganda has armed itself with a number of laws that ensure the security of the cyberspace. To this end, in an effort to provide an appropriate legal framework to deal with cybercrime and provide for secure electronic transactions, the government of Uganda developed and enacted a number of cyber laws – underpinned by previous laws, such as The Official Secrets Act, 1964 (Section 4(1)(d)) and The Security Organisations Act, 2005, to provide a foundation for the state to develop protection in a technological age – including The Computer Misuse Act, 2011, The Electronic Signatures Act, 2011, and The Electronic Transactions Act, 2011. The government of Uganda has also set in place the National Information Security Strategy (NISS), 2011, the National Information Security Framework (NISF), and the Communications Sector Computer Emergency Response Team (CERT) to oversee a robust preparedness in cyberspace security (ict.go.ug). Accordingly, Mwesigwa (2003) opined that the Electronic Transaction Bill (now an Act):

- Creates a light-handed regulatory regime for electronic transactions.
- It facilitates the development of e-commerce in Uganda by broadly removing existing legal impediments that may prevent a person from transacting electronically because of a lacuna in the traditional laws.
- It makes provision for functional equivalence; thus, paper transactions and electronic transactions are treated equally before the law.
- Establishes rules that validate and recognize contracts formed through electronic means.
- Sets default rules for contract formation and governance of electronic contract performance.
- Defines the characteristics of a valid electronic writing and an original document writing.
- Supports the admission of computer evidence in courts and arbitration proceedings.

The effects of the envisioned merits of the Electronic Transaction Bill (now an Act) can be observed in numerous ways in Uganda. While it is meant to curb crimes, it has reduced the overall costs of transactions between businesses of various size and scope.

The Electronic Signatures Act:

- Makes provision for the use of electronic signatures in order to ensure that electronic signatures are carried out in a secure environment.
- [E]stablishes a public key infrastructure for authenticity and security of documents.
- Recognizes the different signature creating technologies.
- Provides effective administrative structures e.g., establishment of Certification Author- ities (Mwesigwa, 2003).

While there are some complaints from unofficial sources concerning the Electronic Signature Act, equally some people think it has come to relieve business transactions and offers a significant degree of protection from scammers, fraudsters, other varieties of criminals and criminal activity.

The Computer Misuse Act:

- Takes cognizance of the fact that all computer operations are susceptible to computer crimes and our current legal system does not recognize computer crimes thus the importance of a legislation to provide for computer crimes.
- Creates several computer misuse offences e.g., unauthorized modification of computer material.
- Lays down mechanisms for investigation and prosecution of the offences.

As will be discussed at a later point in this chapter, the application of the Computer Misuse Act on other people helped to send warning signals to those who wrongly use ICT instruments.

Then the National Information Security Strategy (NISS) 2011 was established to:

- Enable Uganda to achieve her economic and societal goals through a secure online environment.
- Enable Uganda to evolve her means of protecting information and information processing infrastructure against today's threats.
- Enable Uganda to define and work towards achieving her Cyber Security vision and key objectives.
- Define an approach through which Uganda's knowledge, skills and capacity can be grown to improve her cyber security capabilities (NITA, 2011).

Indeed, following the above strategic programmatic areas ensures maintenance of the security of people's information and the envisioned development of a cyber-secure environment. The NISS works in tandem with the provision of The Computer Misuse Act, 2011, The Electronic Signatures Act, 2011, The Electronic Transactions Act, 2011, The Electronic Misuse Act, The Access to Information Act, 2005, and The Regulation of Interception of Communications Act, 2010 (GCSCC, OMS, UO, & CTO, 2016: 14), to ensure cyber security in and across the country. Although there is limited capacity by the law enforcement agencies to investigate all crimes, through use of these legal instruments, the government of Uganda's cyber security enforcers were able to identify and track some cybercrime offenders. In most cases, the Cyber Crime Unit, and Electronic and Counter Measures Department of the Uganda Police Force retain the technical capacity and training to undertake tracking and compile charges against offenders.

However, in spite of the available legal and institutional framework, "crimes such as cyber terrorism, intellectual property infringement, internet usage policy abuses, internet fraud, industrial espionage and altering of data, on-line child exploitation and pornography, illegal goods purchasing, piracy, impersonation and hacking" still exist in Uganda (Mulalira, n.d.). For example, in 2005, a Ugandan and two Congolese masterminded the internet bank transfer of a massive sum of money from Standard Charted Bank, Nairobi to Barclays Bank, Kampala (Tushabe, 2004). Similar crimes have been committed against other banks such as the Centenary Bank. Collectively, banks in Uganda have lost billions of Ugandan Shillings due to cybercrime. The amplification of cybercriminal activity can be credited to many companies operating with inadequate funding and financial capabilities in fighting cybercrime.

Dimensions of cybercrime and cyber terrorism

Since the dawn of Information and Communication Technology (ICT), numerous crimes related to internet space have been registered in Uganda. For the most part, cybercrime in Uganda has involved the hacking of people's email accounts and various website scams that target Ugandans and citizens of other countries. Common cybercrimes include hacking of other people's information, sending malware to others, cyber harassment, emails scams (that target individuals in relation to government services), cyber bullying, and social media fraud. Furthermore, crimes including the hacking of bank accounts and illegal online transfers of funds are reported in Uganda on a large scale. In most cases, cybercrime affects people directly in instances where data is lost, money is stolen, or a person's privacy is infringed upon. According to Paul (2017):

> The cybercrime landscape evolves year over year as criminals alter their operating strategies, develop new tools and techniques, and take advantage of changes in consumer and business behavior. Mobile [*money points*] continues to remain vulnerable to cybercriminals as its popularity as a banking and e-commerce channel grows and more services become available via mobile apps. Cybercriminals are also jumping on the internet of things (IoT) bandwagon by exploiting poor password practices to take over IoT devices for their own purposes.
>
> Way back in 2013, the Annual Police Report 2013 stated that cybercrime cost Uganda about UGX.18 billion. Another figure released by the Kaspersky Labs put the figure at UGX. 25 billion. Both figures were within the range that was released by the auditing firm, Deloitte.
>
> The reports in 2016 indicated that the country's monetary loss to cybercrime was UGX. 122 billion. Fast forward to 2017, cybersecurity researchers revealed that Uganda lost close to UGX. 15 billion ($42m) to cybercriminals in 2017 alone. In the period under review, 95.6% of cyber security incidents went unreported or unresolved and only 4.4% of the reported cases were followed through to a successful prosecution.

Given the aforesaid, people in Uganda are not any safer from cybercrimes than in any other countries. It is clear that the criminals, in their striving for survival, have become wiser than what many may have expected, including specialized agencies and organizations that focus exclusively on the electronic defense of people and the public at large. As in dialectics, once people try to set a strict regime to curb cybercrime in general, criminals devise an anti-thesis to counter the laws set in place to address their activity. This sort of maneuvering has established an act-and-response "choreography" between criminals and cyber defenders.

Cybercrime has also increasingly taken place beyond the individual level in Uganda, with various companies having been targeted over previous years. MTN Uganda, the country's largest telecommunications company, was the victim of one such scam that resulted in the company as well as the government losing millions of Ugandan Shillings (Ndagire, 2020).

Concomitantly, technological innovation and development facilitate cybercriminals to a greater extent than those targeted, with individuals and groups utilizing technology to their advantage in progressively more sophisticated and intricate attacks. Moreover, as cyber threats continue to come in diverse form, businesses and companies come under increasing pressure to develop enhanced cyber defense capacities, which many tend to lack. Skilled cyber personnel and professionals, who are able to devise and implement the necessary defenses are also too few in numbers. Data compiled by Uganda Serianu Cyber Intelligence in 2018 showed that only 400 cyber professionals with the necessary critical skills were in existence (Lyatuu, 2020; Ndagire, 2020).

Two cases of cyber harassment, among many, are prominent in the Ugandan media and courts. The first included Doctor Stellan Nyanzi, a Makerere University Lecturer accused of attacking the president of Uganda and members of his family in a Facebook posting. Whereas one of the posts was a birthday poem on September 16, 2016 for President Yoweri Museveni's 74th birthday, "prosecution sued Nyanzi claiming the poem was too vulgar and ridiculed the person of the president" (UBN, 2020). The second case was that of Brian Isiko, a 25-year-old student who was charged with cyber harassment and offensive communication when he sent love messages to the Kabarole district MP, Sylvia Rwabwogo (Kabahumuza & Odeng, 2018). These, and many other related cases, have pushed people to be more careful with what they are posting, and how they use their computers in order to avoid being targeted and punished through the Computer Misuse Act.

Since some people have used ICT to promote, support, facilitate, and/or engage in acts of terrorism, Uganda has experienced the same. On several occasions, terrorist organizations have used the Internet to instill fear by issuing threats of impending attacks on key locations in the country as well as to communicate and spread terrorist propaganda. Others have used ICT for recruitment, radicalization, and incitement of terrorism; terrorist financing; and terrorist training. Furthermore, terrorists use ICT for planning of terrorist attacks. They have severally carried out secret communication and open-source information; execution of terrorist attacks; and cyberattacks (see UNODC, 2012).

Terrorist organizations including Al-Shabaab, Allied Democratic Forces (ADF), and the Lord's Resistance Army (LRA), for example, have coordinated recruitment, attacks, and support through use of the information and communications technologies (ICT). While the LRA and ADF have been relatively silent, although foreign based, Al-Shabaab, which currently aims to punish the Ugandan Government for participating in African Union (AU) military operations, notably the African Mission in Somalia (AMISOM) launched in 2007, against the group, has been employing ICT for information gathering and attack-planning so as to compel Uganda to withdraw forces from Somalia (Williams, 2018). While they do not have a permanent presence in Uganda proper, they have propagated plans to renew attacks in Kampala (2020 CIA World Factbook and Other Sources).

Immediate challenges and threats

There are many immediate challenges and threats in countering cybercrime for and in Uganda. Enumerating Uganda's immediate challenges and threats of cyber security, Mwesigwa (June 2009), notes:

- Lack of awareness by users, law enforcement officials, and policy makers on the adverse impact of cybercrime and measures to safeguard against cybercrime;
- Lengthy process for putting in place necessary legislation;
- Rapid changes in technology hence requiring more sophisticated tools to combat cybercrime;

- Limited use of internet and low bandwidth availability, which discourage use due to spam, and other irrelevant messages and data.

Moreover, the Uganda Communications Commission (UCC) (2005), while highlighting the above views adds cost of protection, lack of coordination, and human resources to the challenges of cyber security in Uganda. The cost of protection becomes a challenge in that procuring the required gadgets required for protection is costly to many organizations. As such, it also affects coordination and information sharing between organizations. Furthermore, whereas the numbers of skilled labor in both computer networking and various Internet applications are increasing, though not yet to the required levels to address issues related to cyberattacks, the hiring of such technical personnel is still unaffordable for many organizations in Uganda. This therefore makes addressing cyber threats hard for many.

The fact that most of the software protection available requires regular renewal of licenses and subscriptions means that not many users of cyberspace in Uganda can afford the charges involved. Even some organizations as well as individuals, find it difficult to sustain the costs of maintaining the necessary standard of cyber security defense. Hence, many organizations and individuals in Uganda leave their fate to chance because of exorbitant costs involved in securing their personal data.

Many, if not most, organizations in Uganda do not have firsthand experience in cyber-related crimes and therefore, they have little knowledge about how to properly protect themselves from attackers (UCC, 2005: 4). Since only those who have experienced cyberattack first-hand know what it means to protect themselves against cyberattack, facilitating a broader public awareness and understand about the enormity of cybercrime is still a big hurdle to dismantle in Uganda.

The above laxity can be attributed to a general lack of awareness of the seriousness of cyberattacks and their implications. This is due to the fact that most individual users of cyberspace are only conversant with antivirus software. In most cases, many people do not renew their antivirus licenses when they expire but rather abandon them and install another given the abundance of free versions of antivirus at their disposal. To make the situation even more problematic, many people have developed the skills of hacking software for free. Hence, much work is required to create a more extensive public awareness in Uganda so that people can be brought up-to-date about the various dangers they are exposed to on a daily basis.

With its call for submissions on the Draft Data Protection and Privacy Bill, 2015, Uganda's Parliament created an opportunity for stakeholders to provide input to ensure the law, when enacted, measures up to internationally acceptable standards of data protection (Paul, 2017). There is, however, at this point no official National Cyber Security Strategy document in Uganda. As Paul (2017: n.p.) observes that:

> Instead, Uganda has a National Information Security Policy and a National Information Security Strategy. NITA-U brought together different stakeholders for consultation to develop both documents.
>
> To make matters worse, there is no centralized budget for cybersecurity. Every Ministry allocates its budget separately and depends on previous experience and future plans to allocate budget for cybersecurity. Law-enforcement cooperates with NITA-U and Uganda Communications Commission (UCC) the telecommunications regulator in Uganda.

The validity of Paul's statement is reflected on the NITA-U website, where a 2015 post reads "[t]he Government of Uganda through the Commonwealth Telecommunications Organization has obtained support from the United Kingdom to assist Uganda develop its National Cyber Security Strategy" (NITA-U, 2015). This indicates that the country has yet to formulate a National Cyber Security Strategy.

International law

Given cybercrime is a global phenomenon, state parties have formulated several legal frameworks to address it. In a publication by International Telecommunication Union entitled "Understanding cybercrime: phenomena, challenges and legal response," Gercke (2012) noted several such international legal frameworks for combating cybercrime. With reference to the United Nations Convention on the Rights of Children (UNCRC), he notes that member states are required to prevent the exploitative use of children in pornographic performance (Article 34). Then there is the Optional Protocol on the Rights of the Child on the Sale of Children, Child Prostitution, and Child Pornography, where Article 3 requires State parties to criminalize certain conducts including acts related to child pornography (Gercke, 2012: 116).

The Optional Protocol to the Convention on the Rights of the Child (2001), in Article 3(1)(c) prohibits the production, distribution, dissemination, sale, and possession of child pornography. The Preamble mentions the Internet as a means of distribution. The definition of child pornography, set forth in Article 2(3), is broad enough to encompass virtual images of children (2171 U.N.T.S. 227). Furthermore, the European Convention on the Protection of Children against Sexual Exploitation and Sexual Abuse (2007), expressly prohibits the use of "information and computer technology (ICT)" to access child pornography (Article 21(1)(f)), to distribute child pornography (Article 30(5)) or to solicit children for sexual purposes (Article 23) (C.E.T.S. 201).

The United Nations Convention Against Transnational Organized Crime (General Assembly resolution 55/25, November 15, 2000), also known as the Palermo Convention, obligates state parties to enact domestic criminal offenses that target organized criminal groups and to adopt new frameworks for extradition, mutual legal assistance, and law enforcement cooperation. Although the treaty does not explicitly address cybercrime, its provisions are highly relevant (2225 UNTS. 209).

The Council of Europe (CoE) established several conventions to combat cybercrimes. The Convention on Cybercrime (2001), also known as the Budapest Convention (July 1, 2004), represents the first international agreement aimed at reducing computer-related crime by harmonizing national laws, improving investigative techniques, and increasing international cooperation (ETS. 185). The Additional Protocol to the Convention on Cybercrime Concerning the Criminalization of Acts of a Racist or Xenophobic Nature Committed through Computer Systems (2003), requires state parties that have ratified the protocol to the Budapest Convention to enact laws to criminalize racist or xenophobic acts that are expressed or otherwise communicated online (ETS. 189).

Additionally, the UN General Assembly Resolutions 45/121 (1990), 55/63, and others are key documents in addressing cybercrime. Resolution 45/121, for instance, requires the prevention and control of computer related crimes. On the other hand, Resolution 55/63 identifies a number of measures to prevent the misuse of information technology:

- States should ensure that their laws and practices eliminate safe havens for those who criminally misuse information technologies;
- Law enforcement cooperation in the investigation and prosecution of international cases of criminal misuse of information technologies should be coordinated among all concerned States;
- Law enforcement personnel should be trained and equipped to address the criminal misuse of information technologies.

Since the aforesaid resolutions require state parties to devise necessary means to combat cybercrime on the national and international level, Uganda has been observing the aforementioned International legal frameworks in its effort to curtail cybercrime targeting the country and originating from within it.

International governance

Regarding the realm of international governance and management, the Ministry of ICT & National Guidance (2019), writes:

> The UK Government together with the Ugandan Government have held a cyber capacity building event in Uganda under the Commonwealth Cyber Declaration agreed at the 2018 Commonwealth Heads of Government Meeting which commits Commonwealth states to collective cyber security and building foundations. The Ministry of ICT & National Guidance is committed to building a safe and secure internet space as they move all Government services online. As part of a National Cyber Security Capacity Building initiative under the Ministry of ICT & National Guidance together with the National Information Technology Authority is conducting a 2019 National Cyber Security Risk Assessment (NCRA) workshop over the next few days.

Accordingly, Uganda has gone to great lengths to position itself at all flanks to ensure there is safety both at home and abroad. Besides the Computer Misuse Act 2011, the Electronic signatures Act 2011 and the Electronic Transactions Act 2011, the Government has also developed and implemented the National Information Security Strategy (NISS) 2011, the National Information Security Framework (NISF) and the Communications Sector Computer Emergency Response Team (CERT). As noted above, in spite of the presence of these bodies, the lack of policy framework that addresses cybercrimes directly still stands as a major undoing. In order to avert this, the country is required to have some specific policy framework that addresses cybercrime more directly. Since the government, in partnership with other organizations, has joined to address emergencies, they are able to boast a degree of achievement in this regard.

Partner institutions at home and abroad

Several partner institutions within and outside of Uganda are cooperating to address the challenges of cybercrime in Uganda. Since 2003, the government of Uganda undertook a process of establishing the Information Security Working Group under the Ministry of ICT with the following key terms of reference, among others:

- Developing guidelines for Computer Security Emergency Response Teams;
- Coordinating Computer security incident response;
- Collaboration with national, regional and international partners in information security;
- Conducting regular seminars, conferences, and workshops for local and central government (Mwesigwa, 2003).

This working group was composed of the Ministry of ICT; the Ministry of Finance, Planning and Economic Development; the Ministry of Internal Affairs; the Ministry of Foreign Affairs; the External Security Organization; and the Internal Security Organization. Furthermore, it includes the Uganda Police Force; the Directorate of Public Prosecution; the Judiciary; the Uganda Communications Commission; and Makerere University. The working group has been able to design guidelines that the National Information Technology Authority-Uganda (NITA-U) oversees.

The Internet Society, Uganda Chapter is another institution in Uganda augmenting the efforts of the government of Uganda to ensure limited occurrences of cybercrimes. The institution aims to:

- Raise awareness about cyber security management in Uganda;
- Promote online child safety in Uganda;
- Advocate for proper implementation of cyber security laws in Uganda;
- Cyber security awareness campaign;
- Participate in Safe Internet Day Celebrations;
- Research into the implementation of cyber laws in Uganda (Internet Society, Uganda Chapter, 2020).

Many of the aforementioned aims of the Internet Society, Uganda Chapter have made achievements in the cyber security realm.

Although a private organization, the Uganda Internet Governance Forum (UIGF), in partnership with the Collaboration on International ICT Policy in East and Southern Africa (CIPESA), is augmenting the work of the government in developing and protecting people from the effects of cybercrime. Since its inception, CIPESA, as a leading center for research and analysis of information, enabled policy makers in the region to understand ICT policy issues, and for various multi-stakeholders to use ICT to improve livelihoods (CIPESA, n.d.). As part of its work in the areas of research, advocacy, and awareness about how internet governance impacts on development and governance, Nanfuka (2014) lauded CIPESA's implementation of "the OpenNet Africa project, which monitors and promotes internet freedoms primarily in East Africa."

Standard Chartered Bank Uganda in partnership with Uganda Banker's Association has spearheaded industry discussions on Information and Cyber Security (ICS) as they have realized the principal risks arising from the digital and technological revolution. Consequently, Leah Kimata – the Country Information Security Risk Officer at Standard Chartered Bank East Africa – appealed "to all stakeholders including, Government, Financial and non-Financial institutions, and other organizations to strategically plan and implement structures and technologies to help in combating cyber threats" (EABW Editor, 2020: n.p.).

As a member of the East African Community, Uganda, with other members states, has robustly responded to the threat of cybercrimes. The Interpol of each member country is alerted about cross-border criminal gangs using the Internet to defraud unsuspecting institutions or institutions incapable of defending themselves due to a lack of cyber skill or for other reasons. This was why fraudulent financial transactions initiated in Kenya were easily detected in Uganda before they could be concluded.

Uganda is also a signatory to the AU's Convention on Cybersecurity and Personal Data Protection that was adopted by the 23rd ordinary session of the Assembly held in Malabo-Equatorial Guinea on June 27, 2014. The preamble and the content of the protocol is so exhaustive and it covers a range of areas so that application of it at national level would insulate citizens of member states against cybercrimes.

Alongside the above, since Uganda is also a signatory to the various conventions and protocols of the UN and other international organizations regarding cyber protection, such laws guide the country in collaborating with the international community to address issues of cybercrimes as cybercriminals and their activity evolve and expand.

Legislative developments and processes within the republic

Uganda has both criminal legislation, and Regulation and Compliance in place for protecting the people from cybercrime.

With respect to *criminal legislation*, Uganda has so far come up with some specific legislations so as to respond to the increasing cybercrime in the country. The key legal framework in this regard comprises the Electronic Signature Act, the Computer Misuse Act, the Electronic Transection Regulations, and the Penal Code Act.

The Electronic Signature Act-2011 was developed to "provide for the use, security, facilitation and regulation of electronic communications and transactions; to encourage the use of e-Government services and to provide for related matters" (ESA, No. 8, 2011, Preamble). This provision assists persons who are involved in online transactions and criminalizes those who become involved in dubious acts online.

The Computer Misuse Act, 2011 is an Act to:

> make provision for the safety and security of electronic transactions and informa-tion systems; to prevent unlawful access, abuse or misuse of information systems including computers and to make provision for securing the conduct of electronic transactions in a trustworthy electronic environment and to provide for other related matters.
>
> *(GOU, "The Computer Misuse Act," 2011, Preamble)*

This implies that any person found to contravene the requirement of the Act is regarded as a criminal and legal proceedings could be instituted against such a person.

The Electronic Transaction Regulation helps to authenticate and assess the integrity of data messages, and sets rules and procedures for tracking transmissions, hosting and caching. In the case of suspected criminal activity, it presents guidelines for the prosecution of the offender(s). Similarly, the Penal Code Act, 1950 guides in prosecuting a range of crimes committed by persons against others, even those that are computer related. All these legal instruments help in prosecuting cybercrimes in Uganda.

Concerning *regulation and compliance*, Uganda has enacted three specific cybersecurity regulation and compliance instruments. These are the National Information Technology Authority of Uganda (NITA-U) Act, 2009, Access to Information Act, 2005, and the

Electronic Signature Act, 2011. Each of these Acts gives specific regulation and compliance procedures in the use of and access to electronic information.

The potency of the National Information Technology Authority, Uganda Act, 2009, is contained in the set function:

1   to provide first level technical support and advice for critical Government information technology systems including managing the utilization of the resources and infrastructure for centralized data center facilities for large systems through the provision of specialized technical skills;

2   to identify and advise Government on all matters of information technology development, utilization, usability, accessibility and deployment including networking, systems development, information technology security, training and support;

3   to co-ordinate, supervise and monitor the utilization of information technology in the public and private sectors;

4   to regulate and enforce standards for information technology hardware and software equipment procurement in all Government Ministries, departments, agencies and parastatals;

5   to create and manage the national databank, its inputs and outputs;

6   to set, monitor and regulate standards for information technology planning, acquisition, implementation, delivery, support, organization, sustenance, disposal, risk management, data protection, security and contingency planning;

7   to regulate the electronic signature infrastructure and other related matters as used in electronic transactions in Uganda;

8   to promote and provide technical guidance for the establishment of e-Government, e-Commerce and other e-Transactions in Uganda;

9   in liaison with other relevant institutions, to regulate the information technology profession in Uganda in order to ensure its effective utilization promotion and development;

10 to act as an authentication center for information technology training in Uganda in conjunction with the Ministry responsible for Education;

11 to provide advice on information technology project management services to Government;

12 to provide for information management service through acting as a records management facility and an information depository;

13 to provide guidance on the establishment of an infrastructure for information sharing by Government and related stakeholders;

14 to provide guidance in information technology audit services to Government;

15 to undertake and commission research as may be necessary to promote the objects of the Authority;

16 to arbitrate disputes arising between suppliers of information technology solutions and consumers;

17 to protect and promote the interests of consumers or users of information technology services or solutions;

18 to undertake any other activity necessary for the implementation of the objects of the Authority.

Notwithstanding some uncertainties, by following the set functional processes, NITA-U is helping to monitor cybercrimes in the country. The Access to Information Act helps organizations to protect their information and also categorize whichever information ought to be for public consumption so that whoever is found in possession of confidential information is charged. In the same way, the Electronic Signature Act, 2011 provides for the use, security, facilitation and regulation of electronic communications and transactions, and encourages the use of e-Government services and related matters (GOU, "The Electronic Signature Act, 2011," Preamble).

Capacity building at home

Uganda is building capacity in terms of standardization, professional certification, education and development of capacity to curb cybercrimes.

As a way of *standardization*, the UCC, the NITA, and NISS work together to ensure a standardized-system exists in addressing cyber threats in the country. Since the UCC has joined both Kenya and Tanzania, as members of East Africa Regulatory Postal and Telecommunications Organization (EARPTO), it assists in raising awareness of the importance of the issues of security at regional levels (UCC, 2005).

With regards to *professional certification, education, and development*, a significant number of institutions in Uganda offer information security related courses both at certificate, undergraduate and postgraduate levels. Within the broader courses offered, there are modules that specifically focus on the subject of information security. There are also certified courses offered widely across Uganda mainly by private institutions. Some private institutions in the country also run courses and programs in information security assurance and awareness. Recently, some of the institutions have started to offer courses on basic cyber security awareness for targeted groups including judges, legal practitioners, and law enforcement officers. There is a noticeable increase in ISO certified experts and incident handlers in Uganda.

As part of its mandate to coordinate and collaborate with relevant national and international organizations and safeguard the interests of consumers and operators, in matters relating to communication, the UCC, in collaboration with the global Forum for Incident Response Teams (FIRST), has hosted technical cyber security training events in the country. During training, members learned about:

> Advanced Persistent Threat and targeted attacks, social networks used as an attack vector for targeted attacks; Advanced Persistent Threat incident handling; Digital Forensics and incident Response; Incident handling during an attack on Critical Information infrastructure; incident handling in Cloud; Large Scale incidents handling in live role-playing; conducting Exercise to improve incidences Response.
>
> *(Thembo, 2019)*

The topics handled during the training were carefully selected so as to equip those who attended it with requisite skills. Aside from the training, the UCC also signed an agreement with the International Telecommunication Union (ITU) in November 2011 to establish a Sector CERT. Consequently, on June 6, 2013, the Commission inaugurated the Computer Emergency Response Team (CERT) as an initiative to improve and secure communication services in Uganda (UCC Blog, 2019).

In working to expand the horizon of skilling Ugandans with cyber security skills so as to tackle the growing cyber threat, the UCC has launched a cyber security competition targeting university students. During its inaugural workshop on cyber security techniques, more than

500 university students aged 18–24 participated (Watchdog News, n.d.). This has been treated as an innovative way of preparing human capital with what has been deemed the requisite skills in identifying and addressing cyber threats. As a means of preparing Ugandan society for countering cybercrimes and threats, organizers will need to maintain a steady effort in this area and broaden efforts to reach a greater number of students. However, at the same time, authorities and experts in collaboration with the view to enhancing cyber security knowledge and preparedness will also have to turn their attention to other members of society not attending higher-level education though still relying on technology in their private homes and for running their businesses.

Child online protection

In Uganda, the production, viewing, and sharing online of naked pictures or videos showing children in sexual poses or engaged in sexual acts is regarded as dangerous and a crime. It is required that anyone who knows about producers, transmitters, and recipients should report them to the authorities, child helpline, or NITA. Although there is no specific law against online child sexual abuse, the criminal acts related to the abuse and exploitation can be criminalized under the following laws:

* Computer Misuse Act
* The Anti-Pornographic Act
* The Prevention of Trafficking in Persons Act

Since Uganda is a signatory to several International Conventions and protocols aimed at fighting child abuse and protecting the rights of children, such laws as applied at the international levels (UNICEF, n.d.) are addressing online child protection.

Whereas everyone is responsible for ensuring that children are protected from Online Child Sexual Exploitation, the government has put in place some institutions to oversee strict adherence to the laws. Those institutions include:

* The Ministry of Internal Affairs responsible for monitoring and overseeing crime management in the country.
* The Uganda Police Force with various key Departments related to management of the crime, including the Criminal Investigations Directorate, The department of Child & Family Protection, Community Policing Department, Cyber Crime Units under CID and Police Headquarters, Police ICT Unit and General Duties.
* Several Government Ministries responsible for carrying out respective activities related to protection of children, including: Ministry of Gender, Labour & Social Development, Internal Security Organization, Ministry of Education & Sports, Directorate of Public Prosecutions, Ministry of Justice & Constitutional Affairs, Law Reform Commission, Ministry of Foreign Affairs.
* The National Information Technology Authority (NITA) and Uganda Communications Commission (UCC), responsible for regulating Information Technology and Telecommunication services, including postal and broadcasting, respectively.
* Many International and Civil Society Organizations dealing in and supporting projects related to child protection issues, including UNICEF (UNICEF, n.d.: 6–7).

Notwithstanding the presence of the above institutions and the mechanisms to address the plight of children in the era of ICT, there are still gaps in implementing the law. Some of the key concerns are:

- The subject matter is new to all the duty bearers in the country and there is need for training and awareness right from the top managers and commanders.
- There is no specific law that constitutes the offence of on-line child sexual abuse and exploitation.
- There are no clear policy guidelines on how to handle the various aspects of the offences, especially in relation to management of victims, investigations and prosecutions.
- There are challenges of jurisdictions of the laws where part of the offence is committed outside Uganda.
- There is little literature about the subject matter.
- There is a challenge of making the general public appreciate the dangers of the crime.
- Daily technological advancement whereby several internet service providers keep coming up (UNICEF, n.d.: 7).

However, in following with international best practices, Uganda has adopted some strategic actions to counter on-line child sexual abuse and exploitation in the following ways:

- Creation of a Working Group on prevention of online child sexual abuse and exploitation to develop, coordinate and over-see implementation of national counter measures against the crime;
- Development of technical capacity to remove offensive pictures from the internet and to assist with investigations to rescue victims and track the perpetrators;
- Develop capacity to carry out effective investigations and prosecutions;
- Social and psychological rehabilitation of victims of the crime;
- Raising awareness on the existence, dangers and how to avoid becoming victims of Online child sexual abuse and exploitation (UNICEF, n.d.: 7).

Albeit with difficulties, some of the above strategies have greatly assisted in addressing rampant occurrences. Extensive questions orbit the issue of computer misuse in Uganda. Even as the government strives to enact legislation and measures to curtail online abuse and misuse, government and law enforcement authorities' interpretation of key concepts and acts as they relate to provisions have been a habitual problem and one that can disconcertingly favor or even serve the government. As noted, acts of harassment, disturbing the peace, and legitimate communication remain dense grey zones in Uganda's legal realm.

Sections of The Computer Misuse Act, though touted as falling in line with and being based on the provisions within the Budapest Convention and international standards or so-called best practices, deeply contravene standards of free speech and expression. As such, the implementation and employment of The Computer Misuse Act, alongside other legal provisions within the country can be an extension of anti-democratic practice on the part of the government in the digital realm. Cyberspace as a space to claim equality and equal rights and citizenship in the context of homosexuality and transgender identity is an example of tension between expression and government policing and management of the cyber realm as an extension of state society. While the cybersphere "provides a 'safe space' for the production of LGBT discourse by Ugandan bloggers" and non-LGBT supporters and allies, to "express resistance, contesting anti-gay discourse dominating the Ugandan public sphere" (Valois, 2013: 145), that same space can be targeted as a marshalling point for activity that threatens Uganda's state-driven heteronormativity. As society has evolved from a physical presence to an online one, the government has followed and in so doing extended its normative perspective of what Ugandan society should look like and what may constitute an overstep on the part of an individual or group and when.

Implications of cyber security policies and strategies

As touched upon in the previous section, there are both positive and negative implications of the cyber security policies and strategies. Positively, available cyber security policies and strategies in Uganda have provided a framework for following criminals who are abusing the Internet and computers to the disadvantage of others. Writing about "why cyber security strategy is important," Unni (2018) notes:

- You can gain a deeper understanding of your risk
- It is inherently proactive
- It enables early detection
- It allows for a shift response
- You can deter inside threats
- It provides optimal operation efficiency
- It enables you to stay ahead of the course

Indeed, the availability of cyber security policy and strategy, and their societal coverage facilitate those points Unni (2018) presents. Developing a cyber security strategy allows a country to understand their current environment and profile. By identifying inadequacies and vulnerabilities, they are able to make the necessary modifications to get to where they need to be. While eliminating threats entirely is a difficult, if not impossible, task, identifying them remains an integral element of risk reduction and by extension, security enhancement.

Since to a great extent, proactivity defines the potency of a cyber security strategy, having it in place can be immensely beneficial. Rather than waiting for cyber criminals to strike first, having a cyber security strategy positions a country and/or organizations in such a way that both response and preemptive action can be undertaken. Some countries and organizations have achieved this through:

- Penetration testing – Includes web application, mobile app, network and infrastructure testing;
- Security vulnerability scans – Looks for defects and misconfigurations that make a network susceptible to attack;
- Business continuity planning – Accelerates recovery and reduces downtime;
- Managed security – including active logging and monitoring of networks for security incidents (Unni, 2018).

Deploying resources in readiness of cyber threat by following the above procedures facilitates early detection of threats. With the rapid advancement in cyberattacks, having advanced defense mechanisms in place can help in safety because, the earlier you are able to identify an anomaly such as malicious code in your database, the better your odds are of resolving it.

Many smart organizations do acknowledge that no one is completely immune and able to thwart every single attack. The presence of cyber security policy and strategy in a country allows for a shift-response when threats occur, to deter within-state threats, to provide for optimal operation efficiency, and enable individuals and communities of people and business (as well as government agencies) to stay ahead of the threat wave.

Furthermore, given that cyberattacks and data breaches are potentially costly, as has been proven by Uganda's immense financial losses, the availability of cyber security policies is imperative. Even if employees become the weak links in an organization's security by sharing passwords, clicking on malicious URLs and attachments, using unapproved cloud applications, and neglecting to encrypt sensitive files, having a protective strategy can be of great assistance and serve as the frontline defense against cyberattacks and the threat of attack causing serious direct and indirect damage. The availability and accessibility of cyber security policies can help employees and consultants to understand how to maintain the security of organizational data and applications.

Conclusion: Uganda's cyber future

From the preceding discussion, it becomes clear that the cyber security landscape in Uganda appears as uneven terrain. While cyber security activities may require some degree of observation in order to be able to detect irregularities and protect cyber infrastructure and information, users of modern information infrastructures in Uganda ought to be conscious of existing and emerging threats. There is need for organizations to be attuned with the existing cyber security strategies and activities so as to build robust cyber surveillance regimes for monitoring and analyzing cyber threats. At the same time those regimes can only be strengthened and their potential realized when inherent gaps as a result of competency shortfalls are addressed. More so, the Internet Service Providers (ISPs) in the country ought to find a way to get direct link access (IP address) through which Internet crime unfolds. Uganda's current and palpable cyber security competencies gap is amplified by the state's lack of transparency and untapped collaborative efforts and partnering with institutions across the region. While Uganda has been successful in tracking and mitigating the damage as a result of cyberattacks, the country, including its private citizens and companies remains vulnerable to existing and emerging threats.

As well as the government, privacy regulators and advocates need to play active roles to ensure cyber security strategies, principles, action plans, and implementation of activities that promote privacy protection both as a guiding principle and an enduring standard. However, and again, we point to the skills-gap within the country and the state's current level of cyber talents that arguably fall short of the demands placed upon the state. To be able to achieve the desired end, all stakeholders working towards ensuring cyber security are required to increase global collaboration and adapt a stewardship approach that ensures accountability, and checks and balances on all stakeholders involved in cyber security activities.

Since modern cyber security practices require prompt notification of relevant authorities and individuals whose rights are likely to be jeopardized by any breach, all concerned parties need to play their part in doing so at the right time so that any unauthorized access to information which is likely to result in discrimination, damage to reputation, financial loss,

loss of confidentiality or any other economic or social disadvantage are disclosed once noticed and urgent measures are taken to address them. Invariably, the conveyor effect of cyber breach disclosure helps to ready corporations and government agencies to adopt tight timescales to report attempted and actual breaches on their systems. Striking the balance between maintaining an appropriate degree of cyber preparedness and security, and rights of private citizens and societal security has emerged as a challenge second to the immediacy of cyber threats themselves. The major challenge for Uganda will be in its forward strides in building a cyber fortress that foremost defends against looming threats and protecting the country without having a deleterious effect on those it seeks to protect.

Further resources

GOU, Statutory Instruments 2013 No. 42. The Electronic Transactions Regulations, 2013, available from www.nita.go.ug/sites/default/files/publications/Electronic%20Transactions%20Regulations%202013%20-%20SI%2042%20of%202013.pdf, accessed 27/3/2020.

GOU, The Computer Misuse Act, 2011, available from www.nita.go.ug/sites/default/files/publications/Computer%20Misuse%20Act%20%202011%20%28Act%20No.%202%20of%202011%29.pdf, accessed 27/3/2020.

GOU, The Electronic Signature Act- 2011, available from https://ulii.org/ug/legislation/act/2015/7-6, accessed 27/3/2020.

GOU, The Electronic Transaction Act, 2011, available from https://ulii.org/system/files/legislation/act/2011/8/electronic_transactions_act_rtf_16395.pdf, accessed 27/3/2020.

Kizza, J. M. (2014b). *Computer Network Security and Cyber Ethics* (4th ed.). Jefferson: McFarland & Company, Inc.

References

2020 CIA World Factbook and Other Sources. (2020). "Uganda Terrorism 2020." https://theodora.com/wfbcurrent/uganda/uganda_terrorism.html

EABW Editor. (2020, January 22). "Standard Chartered and Uganda Banker's Association in Fight Against Cybercrime." www.busiweek.com/standard-chartered-and-uganda-bankers-association-in-fight-against-cybercrime/

CIPESA. (n.d.). "History." https://cipesa.org/about-us/history/

GCSCC, OMS, UO, & CTO. (2016). "Cybersecurity Capacity Review of the Republic of Uganda."

Gercke, M. (2012), "Understanding cybercrime: phenomena, challenges and legal response." www.itu.int/ITU-D/cyb/cybersecurity/legislation.html

GOU. "Panel Code Act, 1950." https://ulii.org/ug/legislation/consolidated-act/120

GOU. (2013, September 30). "Statutory Instruments 2013 No. 42 – the Electronic Transactions Regulations, 2013." www.nita.go.ug/sites/default/files/publications/Electronic%20Transactions%20Regulations%202013%20-%20SI%2042%20of%202013.pdf

GOU. "The Computer Misuse Act, 2011." www.nita.go.ug/sites/default/files/publications/Computer%20Misuse%20Act%20%202011%20%28Act%20No.%202%20of%202011%29.pdf

GOU. "The Electronic Signature Act, 2011." https://ulii.org/ug/legislation/act/2015/7-6

GOU. "The Electronic Transaction Act, 2011." https://ulii.org/system/files/legislation/act/2011/8/electronic_transactions_act_rtf_16395.pdf

Internet Society, Uganda Chapter. (2020). "Internet Governance." https://isoc.ug/index.php/internet-governance/

Kizza, J. M. (2014a). *Computer Network Security and Cyber Ethics* (4th ed.). Jefferson: McFarland & Company, Inc.

Lord, N. (2015, July 15). "What is cyber security? Definition, best practices and more," *Digital Guardian's Blog*. www.digitalguardian.com

Ministry of ICT & National Guidance. (n.d.). "Information Security." http://ict.go.ug/initiatives/information-security/

Mularira, F. U. (n.d.). "Uganda's legal and institutional framework in combating cybercrime: A critical review of Uganda's ICT law new opportunities." www.academia.edu/3630851/INFORMATION_TECHNOLOGY_LAW_AND_CYBER_CRIME_IN_UGANDA?email_work_card=thumbnail

Mwesigwa, P. (June 2009). "Cyber Security Legislation and Policy Legislation and Policy Initiatives-Uganda Case," Paper presented at the 2009 ITU Regional Cybersecurity Forum for Africa and Arab States, Tunis, Tunisia, June 2–5 2009.

Lyatuu, J. (January 28, 2020). "Banks share ideas on fighting cyber attacks," *Daily Monitor.* www.monitor.co.ug/Business/Prosper/Banks-share-ideas-on-fighting-cyber-attacks—/688616-5435046-yw4g1qz/index.html

Nanfuka, J. (2014, December 6). "Internet Governance in Uganda." https://cipesa.org/2014/12/internet-governance-in-uganda/

Ndagire, B. (2020, January 30). "How fraudsters cheated govt, MTN in phone calls scam," *Daily Monitor.* www.monitor.co.ug/News/National/How-fraudsters-cheated-government-MTN-phone-calls-scam/688334-5437814-nfu2q6/index.html

NITA-U. (2015). "Development of the Uganda National Cybersecurity Strategy." www.nita.go.ug/media/development-uganda-national-cybersecurity-strategy, accessed 28/3/2020.

NRD Companies. (2017). "Cyber Defence East Africa 2017 financial sector security conference report," August 9–10, 2017, Kampala, Uganda. www.cybersecurity.ug

Osekeny, J. (2018, September 24). "Uganda Ranked 1st in Africa in the National Cyber Security Index." https://guru8.net/2018/09/uganda-ranked-1st-in-africa-in-the-national-cyber-security-index/

Paul, K. (n.d.). "Cybercrime in Uganda: computer Security." www.forensicsinstitute.org/cybercrime-in-uganda/

Thembo, J. (2019, May 13). "UCC invests in cyber-security capacity building in bid to safeguard consumer interest." https://theinsider.ug/index.php/2019/05/13/ucc-invests-in-cyber-security-capacity-building-in-bid-to-safeguard-consumer-interests/

Tushabe, F. (2004). "Computer Forensics for Cyberspace Crimes," (Master's thesis). Makerere University, Uganda.

UBN. (2020, February 20). "Harassing the president: court orders immediate release of Stella Nyanzi." https://observer.ug/news/headlines/63597-harassing-the-president-court-orders-immediate-release-of-stella-nyanzi

UCC Blog. (2019). "Cyber-security capacity building." https://uccinfo.blog/2019/05/13/ucc-cyber-security-capacity-building/

UCC. (2005). "The state of cybersecurity in Uganda," Paper presented at ITU/WISS thematic meeting on cybersecurity, Geneva, Switzerland, June 28–July 1, 2005.

UNICEF. (n.d.). "Child online protection safety handbook." www.nita.go.ug/sites/default/files/publications/Child%2520Online%2520Protection%2520Handbook%2520%283%29.pdf

UNODC. (2012). "The use of the internet for terrorist purposes," United Nations, New York, United States. www.unodc.org/documents/frontpage/Use_of_Internet_for_Terrorist_Purposes.pdf

Unni, A. (2018). "Why cyber security strategy is important." www.stickman.com.au/why-cyber-security-strategy-is-important/

Valois, C. (2013). "Virtual access: the Ugandan 'anti-gay' movement, lesbian, gay, bisexual and transgender blogging and the public sphere," *Journal of Eastern African Studies*, 9(1): 145–162.

Watchdog News. (n.d.), "UCC launches first ever cyber-security competition to tackle cyber threats." www.watchdoguganda.com/business/technology/20200222/87963/ucc-launches-first-ever-cyber-security-competition-to-tackle-cyber-threats.html

Williams, P. D. (2018). "Joining AMISOM: why six African states contributed troops to the African Union Mission in Somalia," *Journal of Eastern African Studies*, 12(1): 172–192.

50

CYBERSECURITY IN SOUTH AFRICA

Status, governance, and prospects

Raymond Steenkamp Fonseca and Jo-Ansie van Wyk

Introduction: cybersecurity in South Africa – awareness, breaches, and challenges

The South African State Security Agency published the National Cybersecurity Policy Framework (NCPF) in 2012 that calls for a coordinated national approach for establishing and maintaining cybersecurity. Since its adoption by Cabinet in 2012, South Africa has been working on the legislative and institutional mechanisms, for both defensive and offensive cybersecurity. This chapter presents a state-level overview of cybersecurity efforts in the South African civilian and military domains. There has been some progress in the passing of the Cybercrimes Bill in December 2018, and in building coherence of the administration of government departments (or "cluster") engaged with cybersecurity governance. However, only some of the elements of the legislative framework are in place, administration and service-delivery remain a wider challenge for the South African state, and a Cyber Warfare Strategy based on a national security policy has yet to be finalized. Although there has been some public input into the process, primarily through civil society organizations and the business community, for the most part individual citizens have not participated in a national debate on the extent of the problem of cybersecurity or on the desirability of the proposed solutions.

South Africa's approach to cybersecurity: norms, perception, and practice formulating and regulating cyberspace

South Africa's National Cybersecurity Policy Framework (NCPF) of 2012 applies the International Telecommunications Union (ITU) definition of cyber security (RSA, 2010). This is also aligned with the African Union (AU), which does not provide its own definition for cybersecurity, but also relies on the ITU. The ITU declares that cybersecurity is "the collection of tools, policies, security concepts, security safeguards, guidelines, risk management approaches, actions, training, best practices, assurance and technologies that can be used to protect the cyber environment and organization and user's assets" (ITU, 2008: 2). In the Memorandum on the Cybercrimes and Cybersecurity Bill, the South African government defined cybersecurity as: "technologies, measures and

591

practices designed to protect data, computer programs, computer data storage mediums or computer systems against cybercrime, damage or interference" (RSA, 2017a: 1).

Thus, aside from the range of actions of recognizing cyber threats and managing cyber risk, this approach to cybersecurity requires that the protection of cyberspace include the protection of IT equipment and of digital infrastructure. This could include, but is not limited to, telecommunications operators (landline and mobile), cable operators, datacentres, Internet eXchange Points (IXP), enterprise/institutional networks, and academic networks. Protecting the different elements of the Internet infrastructure would also entail protection of connected and end-user devices, "including the data and information stored or transmitted by them" (Orji, 2012).

Because of adopting this all-inclusive definition, South Africa's approach to cybersecurity needs to be multi-sectoral. This would include legal frameworks and regulatory mechanisms, as well as technological and non-technological solutions to improve the resilience of information systems. This also requires governmental coordination and, essentially, a horizontal, rather than vertical, agency with a wide authority to manage cooperation. It would also need to include private sector actors and experts, both technical and business, but also ideally informed by academic and civil society organizations. Moreover, rather than just being national, South Africa's approach does consider the international dimension of cyberspace and the need for harmonization at regional and continental levels.

Following Dunn Cavelty's (2016) views on cybersecurity, it can be considered in terms of three interrelated discourses. The first is a technical discourse dealing with the technical sub-structure where malware and viruses infiltrate information infrastructure and can compromise computer and network systems. The second discourse focuses on the interrelationship of cybercrime and cyberespionage, both economic and political. This has thus made cyberspace a strategic domain. The third discourse is one of cyberconflict, where the revolution in military affairs (RMA) has made the information domain an area of contestation through information warfare and cyber-confrontations. However, these discourses overlap in terms of emphasizing "information assurance," i.e. the basic security of information and information systems (Dunn Cavelty, 2016: 411). Applied to South Africa's multi-sectoral approach to cybersecurity, one can see these three discourses at play, even if they are essentially linked and overlapping.

Focusing on state actors, the main actors in the technical sphere would include computer technology experts in government departments, agencies such as the State Information Technology Agency (SITA) and in government-funded research centers such as the Council for Scientific and Industrial Research (CSIR). Their objects of reference are the computer networks that comprise the information infrastructure. The countermeasures proposed would include coordinated communication of computer experts through a Computer Emergency Response Team (CERT), which, in South Africa is called a Computer Security Incident Response Team (CSIRT) (Sutherland, 2017).

In the crime-espionage sphere, the main actors include law-enforcement agencies such as the South African Police Service (SAPS), the National Prosecuting Authority (NPA), and the intelligence community, primarily the State Security Agency (SSA). Their object of reference is government networks, including those of classified information and sensitive information in business networks and the cybercrime black market. As countermeasures, the development of cyberlaw and the definition of cybercrimes is, at the time of writing in 2019, in progress through the passage of legislation, the Cybercrimes Bill and the Cybersecurity Bill, in the National Parliament.

The third said discourse would include national security experts, primarily those in the South African National Defence Force (SANDF), and those linked within the defense industrial complex such as state-owned entities Armscor, Denel, and COMSEC, Ltd. Their object of reference is military networks and critical information infrastructure. Countermeasures for their protection would include cyber-deterrence, cyber-defense, and cyber-offence. The drafting of a Cyber Warfare Strategy and the creation of a Cyberwarfare Command Centre continues. This is regarded part of the SANDF's constitutional mandate of protecting South Africa against external threat. However, in the interim, the Office for Interception Centre (OIC), established 2002 and located in the SSA, provides centralized interception services to South Africa's law enforcement agencies mandated with national security (RSA, 2016).

Alongside these discourses on cybersecurity, however, there is a deeper debate in South Africa about the independence and integrity of state security services. Following allegations that the intelligence services have been used domestically as instruments of party political power struggles, there has been renewed concern that these agencies may willfully act outside the law (Duncan, 2015). Allegations that the prosecution services may also act selectively have also weakened the credibility of the criminal justice system (Schönteich, 2014). The South African government thus faces, in introducing cybersecurity legislation, the need to assure a commitment to security legislation consistent with the constitutional dispensation. Overall, what is largely absent from the discourse on cybersecurity in South Africa is an understanding of the moral, ethical, legal and security implications (Olivier, 2013).

South Africa's National Cybersecurity Policy Framework: policy, institutional design, and legislative context

In the absence of finalized cybersecurity legislation but the expectation for this to be finalized during the term of the sixth Parliament elected in 2019, it can be argued that South Africa's National Cybersecurity Policy Framework (NCPF) has been the legally authoritative document on cybersecurity.

Luiijf, Besseling, and de Graaf (2013) trace the origins of the agenda setting and policy formulation on cybersecurity that included initial workshops on cybersecurity in January 2009. In 2010, the Department of Science and Technology (DST) was replaced as the author of government's policy on cybercrime with the Department of Communications under the leadership of Retired General Siphiwe Nyanda as President Jacob Zuma's Communications Minister. A draft National Cybersecurity Policy was released in 2010, but, in May 2011, Minister Nyanda proposed another draft, marked confidential, that included new sections on Cryptography, Identity Management, National Critical Information Infrastructure (NCII), the creation of a National Cybersecurity Advisory Council (NSAC), and set out the roles and responsibilities of organs of state (RSA, 2010). These would become the main areas where civil society and others have raised concerns in the proposed legislation. The 2011 draft, however, also noted the need for state and private sector cooperation, a National Computer Security Incident Response Team (CSIRT), and a Computer Security Emergency Response Team (CSERT). The target dates set were for March 2012. However, in February of 2012, further changes to the author of the policy were made. Government decided to replace the Department of Communications with the Department of State Security (i.e., the national intelligence services). Cabinet approved the NCPF on 7 March 2012, but the Minister for State Security only published a final version for public information on 4 December 2015.

Newmeyer (2015), in a comparative study, commented that the draft NCPF was brief and, relative to the more comprehensive national strategies in other English-speaking countries, met only the essentials of recommended international guidelines. However, Sabillon, Cavaller, and Cano (2016) observe that South Africa's Cyber Security policy is based on similar strategies of Australia, Germany, Japan, Malaysia, and the United Kingdom. This is confirmed in the reference list of the draft dated May 2011 but, additionally, it also includes the USA's Rockefeller-Snowe Act. Luiijf, Besseling, and de Graaf's (2013) broader comparative study found that where others included as guiding principles the protection of civil liberties, democratic core values, and cooperation in public–private partnerships, South Africa's draft policy lacked reference to such guiding principles. South Africa was not included in the fourteen of the eighteen countries who expected in their policies for their "citizens to take an active role in cyber security" (Luiijf, Besseling, & de Graaf, 2013: 18) and instead placed greater emphasis on national security and critical infrastructure (CI) protection rather than protection of civil liberties.

While the South African policy framework undertakes to involve government, public and private sectors, society, and special interest groups, the work until now has been primarily in drafting the legislative framework and building the supporting institutional mechanisms. As noted, amongst the key aims of the NCPF are to:

- Centralize the coordination of cybersecurity activities by facilitating the establishment of relevant structures, policy frameworks and strategies in support of cybersecurity to combat cybercrime, address national security imperatives and to enhance the information society and knowledge-based economy;
- Promote compliance with appropriate technical and operational cybersecurity standards; and to
- Develop requisite skills, research and development capacity (RSA, 2015a).

The national security discourse, the cybercrime discourse, and the technical discourse as coherent and overlapping aims are evident in these stated aims. Further aims are to achieve concerted international action in regulating cyberspace, as well as the need for a democratic approach to:

- Promote international cooperation; and
- Foster cooperation and coordination between government, the private sector and civil society by stimulating and fostering a strong interplay between policy, legislation, societal acceptance and technology (RSA, 2015a).

The NCPF, therefore, seems to provide the measures and mechanisms for policy coordination across government departments, agencies, and regulators. Bramwell (2017) notes that the state is charged with implementing a government-led, coherent and integrated cybersecurity approach to:

1 Promote a cybersecurity culture and demand compliance with minimum security standards;
2 Strengthen intelligence collection, investigation, prosecution and judicial processes in respect of preventing and addressing cybercrime, cyberwarfare, cyber terrorism and other cyber ills;
3 Establish public–private partnerships for national and international action plans;

4   Ensure the protection of National Critical Information Infrastructure (NCII);
5   Promote and ensure a comprehensive legal framework governing cyberspace; and
6   Ensure adequate national capacity to develop and protect cyberspace.

From an institutional design perspective, South Africa has adopted an interagency approach to cybersecurity, recognizing that the cross-cutting nature of cybersecurity is such that it cannot be addressed by one department only. However, regardless of which government department is involved (and what it is called), these functions include governance and legal prescription and protection, law enforcement, intelligence, and military operations (Ducheine, Voetelink, Stnisen & Gill, 2012). However, there is a policy hierarchy here. The NCPF foresees "a dedicated policy, strategy and decision-making body to be known as the JCPS Cybersecurity Response Committee to identify and prioritise areas of intervention and focussed attention regarding Cybersecurity related threats" (Section 7) (RSA, 2015a). This Cybersecurity Response Committee (CRC) is chaired by State Security (South Africa's Intelligence Service) and is a "central point of contact on all Cybersecurity matters pertinent to national security (national defence, national intelligence and cybercrime)" (Section 5.3.2). The State Security Agency (SSA) is thus tasked with the overall responsibility of cybersecurity that includes the coordination, development and implementation of South Africa's cybersecurity measures as an integral part of its national security.

The SSA also hosts the South African Cybersecurity Response Team and Cybersecurity Centre (CSC) that is supposed to anticipate cyber-attacks in the country or on national critical information infrastructure (NCIIs) to mitigate these threats and attacks. The Centre also has "to promote cyber security knowledge and awareness" (Parliamentary Question NW3654, 2017). Hence, the CSC cooperate with other government agencies such as the Government CSIRT (Gov. CSIRT), the Cyber Security Hub (CSH), the National Cybercrime Centre (NCC), the Cyber Command (CC), and sector CSIRTs.

Technical cybergovernance and protection

The Department of Telecommunications and Postal Services (DTPS) renamed the Department of Communications and Digital Technologies (DCDT) in June 2019, is part of the Cyber Response Committee (CRC) established under the Cluster. Not only is it the key department in aligning with existing legislation, but it is also developing industry standards (with the assistance of ICASA and the South African Bureau Standards) and established the National Cybersecurity Advisory Council. Minister Carrim set up this National Cybersecurity Advisory Council to advise the Minister of Telecommunications and Postal Services on policy and technical issues, and other matters pertinent to cybersecurity. This seven-member council was expected to act independently of the other bodies set up under the NCPF. Barend Taute from the Council for Scientific and Industrial Research (CSIR) chaired. Other members were Ritasha Jethva (Accenture), Khomotso Kganyago (Microsoft's Chief Security Advisor), Tana Pistorius (Professor of Intellectual Property and IT at the UNISA), Sizwe Snail (Attorney), Mark Heyink (Attorney), and Collen Weapond (Advocate), most of whom served on government advisory boards in the past, including those advising on the Protection of Personal Information Bill (SAPA, 2013).

The CRC also manages the Cybersecurity Centre, the Cybersecurity Hub, the South African Government Electronic Communications Security Computer Security Incident Response Team (ECS-CSIRT), and any other CSIRT established in South Africa. Developing cybersecurity incident detection and response capabilities through the National

Cyber-Security Incident Response Team (CSIRT) has advanced (Burbidge, 2019). CSIRTs are responsible for receiving, reviewing, and responding to computer security incident reports and activity. The Hub acts as a national point of contact for the coordination of cybersecurity incidents, receives and analyses cybersecurity incidents, trends, vulnerabilities and threats, but also facilitates the establishment of sector, regional and continental CSIRTs. The Hub also initiates national cybersecurity awareness campaigns. The various presentations made by the Hub in Parliament indicate that it, by its own admission, is in a very early stage of establishing itself and functionality (Media Monitoring, 2018).

Globally, since the 1990s, governments have established Computer Emergency Response Teams (CERT) that have been included in the National Cybersecurity Strategies. Resolution 58 of the ITU, for example, encourages the creation of National Computer Security Incident Response Teams (CSIRTs) particularly for developing countries. These technical teams share threat information and provide cyber protection and resilience capabilities. The South African Cybersecurity Hub was launched in October 2015 and its initiatives include the formalization of Sector CSIRTs, with the finance sector being strongly advanced (Sutherland, 2017). South African financial markets and e-commerce institutions such as the Johannesburg Securities Exchange (JSE), the South African Reserve Bank (SARB), Bankserv, and STRATE, and industry associations such as the South African Insurance Association (SAIA), the Payments Association of South Africa (PASA), the Association of Savings and Investments South Africa (ASISA), and the South African Banking Risk Information Centre (SABRIC) participate in the Finance Sector CSIRT (RSA, 2017). Agreements for the establishment of the Logistics Sector CSIRT have been negotiated with the South African National Research Network (SANREN) and Transnet, a state-owned transport enterprise. Despite these elaborate governance structures, South Africa's coordinated threat monitoring and response to attacks remain a concern, even with the country's participation in the Forum for Incident Response and Security Teams (FIRST), an international global network of computer response teams (495Members). Besides government two South African private sector CSIRTs – the Standard Bank Group and First National Bank – also participate in FIRST (Sutherland, 2017: 90). Since May 2019, the University of Cape Town (UCT) has also been a full member of FIRST (UCT, 2019).

In the absence of public opinion surveys, it is difficult to determine the extent of South Africans' public understanding of and participation in cybersecurity issues, hence the establishment of the South African National ICT Forum in May 2015 to link government, labor, civil society, and business to discuss ICT sector issues. The Forum is structured around four chambers, namely Social, Economic, ICTs and disability, and Governance and security. The CEO of the Institute of Information Technology Professionals South Africa (IITPSA), formerly Computer Society of South Africa (CSSA), the professional body, for example, chaired the Governance and Security Chamber, for ICT practitioners. The NCPF is explicit that private business, non-governmental organizations, and the public should cooperate with government on cybersecurity, hence the participation in and collaboration of these sectors in the Cybersecurity Hub, which was established by the Minister of Telecommunications and Postal Services, Siyabonga Cwele in October 2015. However, at the launch of the Hub, the Minister was silent on the consultative and broad nature of the Hub, but rather emphasized the discourse of national security:

> We need to mobilise all our cybersoldiers to come on board to defend South Africa and her people. We can beat cyber attacks and disruptions. We need to mobilise our resources to train and equip our cybersoldiers with high-end skill and

technology to defend our nation. As Government, we will play our part in identifying young South Africans of talent to join this cyber army.

(RSA, 2015b)

Although speaking as the Minister of Telecommunications and Postal Services, Cwele was formerly the Intelligence Minister (Minister of State Security), and, since 1994, served on Parliament's Joint Standing Committee on Intelligence. Cwele, as Minister of Telecommunications and Postal Services, succeeded Yunus Carrim, widely seen as the best South Africa's Communications Minister. Cwele's appointment by President Jacob Zuma was part of the restructuring of the Ministry, placing under Zuma's control the state public broadcaster, the South African Broadcasting Corporation (SABC), the state communications agency, the Government Communication and Information System (GCIS), Brand SA, the regulatory body, the Independent Communications Authority of South Africa (ICASA), and the Media Development and Diversity Agency, a statutory body set up to ostensibly widen media ownership but seen by some as government interference curtailing media freedom (Wasserman & de Beer, 2005). A second appointment to Zuma's Cabinet in 2009 demonstrating and explaining the militarization of cybersecurity discourses was the appointment of Siphiwe Nyanda, Chief of the South African National Defence Force since 2005, as Minister of Communications. This has thus been the deployment of the country's top military general, with a twenty-year career as a military officer, to run the Communications Ministry, one of the key ministries dealing with cybersecurity.

Law Enforcement, Cybercrime, and Cyber Intelligence

Section 16 of the NCPF details the roles and responsibilities of the state regarding cybersecurity. Cabinet Ministers in the Justice, Crime Prevention and Security Cluster (JCPS Cluster) are assigned responsibility with the Department of Justice, and the National Prosecuting Authority (NPA), having overall responsibility for cybercrime prosecution and court processes. The aim has been the creation of an "integrated cybercrime legal framework and prosecution approach" (Section 16.1.b). A review and alignment of all cybersecurity law, led by the Minister of Justice, was to be submitted to the JCPS Cluster cybersecurity implementation team. A review of related legislation and South African laws with a focus on cybersecurity are dealt with below. However, legislation and executing authority often overlaps which results in inaction and thus poor cybersecurity. Viewed collectively, South African cybercrime legislation can best be described as "'silo-based' in that it only criminalizes cybercrime in relation to certain government departments or state bodies with the notable exception of the Electronic Communications and Transactions Act 25 of 2002 (Mangena, 2016: 33). Other cybercrime legislation includes the Prevention of Organised Crime Act 121 of 1998, and the Financial Intelligence Centre Act 38 of 2001.

The Electronic Communications and Transactions Act 25 of 2002 (ECTA)

South Africa's Electronic Communications and Transactions Act (ECTA) is the country's foundational cybersecurity legislation. The ECTA was promulgated in August 2002 and aims to "enable and facilitate electronic communications and transactions in the public interest." Section 2(1) of the ECTA defines electronic communications as "a communication by means of data messages."

The legislation was welcomed as it addresses important areas of digital commerce, including the legal validity of electronic data and the validity of electronically concluded agreements. This gave full legal status to commercial electronic transactions (Gereda, 2006). The Act also defines cybercrime, despite the fact that without the ECTA common and statutory law could be applied for the arrest and prosecution of online offenders (Snail, 2009). In the first statutory provisions, specifically on cybercrime, Section 85 of the ECTA defines cybercrime as the actions of a person who, after taking note of any data, becomes aware of the fact that he or she is not authorized to access that data and continues to access that data (Gereda, 2006: 282). This criminalizes unauthorized access to data (hacking), data interception, data interference (e.g. viruses and denial of service attacks) and computer related extortion, fraud and forgery. Section 87 introduces the cybercrimes of e-extortion, e-fraud, and e-forgery. Section 86(5) states that the person with intent to "interfere with access to an information system so as to constitute a denial, including a partial denial of services to legitimate users is guilty of an offence." From Section 80, the ECTA creates "cyber policing" in the form of cyber inspectors or cyber police with power to monitor any information system in the public domain, allowed under warrant, and according to Section 83(1) to "enter any premises or access an information system that has a bearing on an investigation."

The Regulation of Interception of Communications and Provision of Communication-Related Information Act 70 of 2002 (RICA)

For most South Africans, RICA refers to the mandatory requirement to register their SIM cards every time they buy a mobile phone. However, RICA is also the main domestic communications surveillance law, removing the ability to communicate anonymously. Promulgated in 2002, RICA is primarily concerned with the interception of fixed line and mobile communications, on both criminal justice and national security issues (Mare & Duncan, 2015). The RICA thus aims to regulate the interception of communications and related processes (metadata), to monitor signals and frequency spectrums, and to regulate and issue applications authorizing the interception of communications. Judicial authorization is required under RICA as the interception of domestic communications can only be done with the authorization of a designated judge when there are reasonable grounds to believe that a serious criminal offence has been, is being or probably will be committed. Internet service providers and telecommunications network operators are obliged to comply with any such warrant (Privacy International, 2019). RICA also obliges all communications providers to store all information about a person's communication for a minimum of three years, irrespective of whether or not they are suspected of criminal activity. Mass retention of a person's sensitive information violates their privacy (Right2Know Campaign, 2017).

Under the RICA regime, there have been numerous abuses of the state's surveillance powers and allegations that RICA has been abused to conduct extrajudicial surveillance (Media Monitoring Africa, 2018). Section 32 of RICA provides for a centralized interception service, the Office for Interception Centres (OIC) reporting to the Minister of State Security. However, there is already a National Communications Centre (NCC), which is the government's national facility for intercepting and collecting electronic signals, nominally foreign signals intelligence. This, however, has also been used domestically and abused for partisan reasons. Parliament's Joint Standing Committee on Intelligence (JSCI) reported in March 2010 that in the "three and half years that OIC has been established, three million interceptions were done" (RSA, 2010a). The Inspector-General of Intelligence investigated and reported on the surveillance of senior members of the African National congress (ANC), of opposition parties, businesspersons and public service officials in circumvention of the legal regime. A Ministerial Review Commission on Intelligence concluded that this surveillance (including mass interception of communications) is unlawful and unconstitutional (RSA, 2013a). The General Intelligence Laws Amendment Act 11 of 2013 specifically excludes surveillance of lawful political activity, advocacy, protest and dissent from the mandate of the intelligence agencies (Mare & Duncan, 2015).

RICA is not only deeply flawed, but is likely also unconstitutional. In April 2017, the amaBhungane Centre for Investigative Journalism launched a legal challenge to RICA based on constitutional flaws, including how the security services copy, share, or store data, and its failure to regulate bulk interception (Sole, 2019). The challenge also raises questions about the interception of the communications of journalists, in this case journalists investigating corruption in government. The South African National Editors' Forum (SANEF) has documented how various prominent journalists have been the target of state surveillance (SANEF, 2019). The applicant's affidavit also is concerned with cross-border privacy protection. As communication often travels to servers located internationally, thus outside of the borders of South Africa, this communication can be put under surveillance outside of the law and without a judge's warrant. Privacy International, an international NGO promoting the right to privacy, and the Right2Know campaign a South African NGO joined the case as a friend of the court. The judgement, handed down in September 2019, found that parts of RICA are indeed invalid and inconsistent with the constitution, and government is required to introduce new legislation within two years and allow Parliament to cure the defects (amaBhungane v Minister of Justice and Correctional Services, 2019).

The Protection of Personal Information Act 4 of 2013 (POPI)

POPI is the primary instrument regulating data protection in South Africa. The legislation aims to promote the protection of personal information processed by public and private bodies. The POPI Bill was released in 2009 and enacted in 2013, but according to some legal experts it has only partially come into full effect, as the substantive provisions have not yet been brought into force and face bureaucratic obstacles (Donnelly, 2018). On paper, POPI provides safeguards to protect all personal data and financial information, in line with international best practice, giving effect to the constitutional right to privacy and ensuring that companies and individuals who handle personal data do not misuse that information or violate their privacy. Section 5 of the Act includes the right of Data Subjects, the person to whom personal information relates, to object to the processing of their personal information. Individuals also have rights to request details of any personal information held about them and information about third parties who have or have had access to that information and rights to correct or delete certain personal information. However, the appropriate technical and organizational safeguards required by the Act are not yet in place (Media Monitoring Africa, 2018). Section 39 of POPI establishes the Information Regulator, a data protection agency, with responsibility for monitoring and enforcing compliance and handling complaints related to the enforcement of privacy laws. The appointment of a chairperson of the office of the Information Regulator was delayed as the person nominated, Pansy Tlakula, had been found by a court to have engaged in misconduct while chair of the Electoral Commission and had subsequently resigned (Pillay, 2014). Since her appointment in December 2016, the process of getting the office operational has been slow with a CEO and legal policy researcher only appointed in mid-2019 (Mzekandaba, 2019).

The Cybercrimes and Cybersecurity Bill

The Department of Justice and Constitutional Development published a draft Cybercrimes and Cybersecurity Bill in August 2015. According to Duncan (2015), the drafters of the Bill held that RICA and the Criminal Procedure Act 51 of 1977 are not adequate to investigate cybercrime. A period for public submissions on the Bill was given until 30 November 2015. It is crucial to emphasize that the period for public submissions closed before the government released the National Cybersecurity Policy Framework. Even though the NCPF had been approved by Cabinet on 7 March 2012, and could have been released immediately for public information, Minister of State Security, David Mahlobo, only published the NCPF in the Government Gazette of 4 December 2015. Nevertheless, the draft Bill drew significant opposition from civil society groups, and many parts of industry. A number of public submissions were made opposing the infringement on internet freedom and expansion of state surveillance power. As discussed below, these were instrumental in maintaining the legislative process and outcome to constitutional principles.

The Right2Know Campaign (R2K), launched in August 2010, describes itself as activist-driven raising public awareness through targeted advocacy. R2K focuses on freedom of expression and access to information as rights fundamental to democracy. The R2K rejected the draft Bill in that it grants wide-ranging powers, including invasive surveillance powers, to state security structures. Rather than the internet being considered as a common space for the public good, the bill frames "vast parts of the internet as assets of state-security" and "hands stewardship of the internet to the Ministry of State Security." (Right2Know Campaign, 2015: 2). The secretive operations of South African intelligence agencies and the lack of democratic controls had been identified as a problem by Parliament and by Minister Kasrils, Minister for Intelligence Services from 2004 to 2008, since at least 2005. Given this background of lack of effective democratic control, the potential in the Bill was that it was open to abuse by criminalizing "cyber-dissent by political actors critical of the ruling party" (Mare & Duncan, 2015: 16). According to R2K, the draft Cybercrimes Bill extended surveillance to investigation, search and seizure of electronic data communications.

Where RICA says that interception of communications should only be used for serious offences, the draft Bill's powers can be exercised to access information connected to any offence. The Internet Service Providers' Association (ISPA), a voluntary organization representing the interests of its members in the South African internet industry, was concerned that, in most cases, their industry should be dealt with no differently to offline suppliers of products and services. For the most part, much of the conduct criminalized by the provisions of the Bill is already unlawful under existing laws, and it is "not desirable to have two sets of legislation setting out separate offences in respect of broadly the same conduct" (ISPA, 2015: 24). Aside from the limitations on freedom of expression, other concerns included that the Bill gave the South African Police Service and the State Security Agency (and their members and investigators) extensive powers to investigate, search, access, and seize computers databases, or networks. The Centre for Constitutional Rights, in their submission, took issue with the power given in the Bill to the State Security Agency, for example to appoint an "investigator" as law enforcers – without being subject the Constitutional provisions on security services. (Centre for Constitutional Rights, 2017: 5). In their view, the State Security Agency are granted unconstitutional powers.

In response to these concerns, the Department of Justice and Constitutional Development formed an expert review panel and published a revised draft of the

Cybercrimes and Cybersecurity Bill in March 2017. In its passage through Parliament, there were extensive comments on the Bill during the public participation phase, particularly on onerous aspects of the Bill. The South African Human Rights Commission (SAHRC), a constitutionally created independent state institution that must review government policies in the light of human rights and may make recommendations, noted that "the Bill may impact the right to privacy on multiple grounds" (SAHRC, 2017: 3). There is also an effect on investigative journalism and whistleblowing where provisions affect freedom of speech and access to information. The Bill also "vests a disproportionate amount of discretion and power to the official" and affects the constitutional right to privacy (SAHRC, 2017: 4). R2K, in their 2017 submission, maintained that in order to ensure the right to freedom of expression, cybersecurity legislation should be "be transferred back to a 'civilian' department falling under the Ministry of Communications" rather than being the domain of the state intelligence structures (Right2Know Campaign, 2017: 3). Their recommendation was for the withdrawal of the Chapter on "Structures to deal with Cybersecurity" (Chapter 10). The Bill gives state security structures the power to declare any device, network, database or other infrastructure as "critical information infrastructure." This in turn places legal obligations on these entities (including private companies) to meet government security standards and submit themselves to security audits – a practice in which R2K see echoing China's 2016 Cybersecurity Law. This, it is argued, can give a legal and technical "backdoor" into networks and devices, and in turn potential for state interference and surveillance abuses. The R2K recommendation was for the Chapter on "Critical Information Infrastructure Protection" (Chapter 11) to be withdrawn or redrafted by civilian agencies. More to the point, their conclusion was to separate the Cybercrimes Bill, improving the fight against cybercrime, and the policy aims of a Cybersecurity Bill to upgrade the security of cyber infrastructure (Right2Know Campaign, 2017).

The Department of Justice and Constitutional Development presented an amended version of the Cybercrimes and Cybersecurity Bill that removed provisions relating to cybersecurity, specifically, Chapter 10 titled, "Structures to deal with Cybersecurity." This removal of provisions relating to cybersecurity, to be dealt with separately, required renaming the Bill from the "Cybercrimes and Cybersecurity Bill" to the "Cybercrimes Bill." Regarding policing, the Cybercrimes Bill states in Article 55(1) that the Cabinet member responsible for policing must: (a) establish and maintain sufficient human and operational capacity to detect, prevent and investigate cybercrimes; (b) ensure that members of the South African Police Service receive basic training in aspects relating to the detection, prevention and investigation of cybercrimes; and (c) in cooperation with any institution of higher learning, in the Republic or elsewhere, develop and implement accredited training programs for members of the South African Police Service primarily involved with the detection, prevention, and investigation of cybercrimes. This new Cybercrimes Bill was adopted by the National Assembly on 27 November 2018, but before it becomes law it still needs to pass consideration by the second legislative chamber, the National Council of Provinces (NCOP), a process that began in 2019. According to the Parliamentary Committee, cybersecurity-specific legislation is under development, and will be dealt with at a later stage in a separate Bill.

New proposed legislation

Proposed laws and amendments that implicate cybersecurity include the Critical Infrastructure Protection Bill, the Protection of State Information Bill (POSIB), and the Films and Publications Amendment Bill (FPAB), and the Defence Amendment (Media Monitoring Africa, 2018). Of these, the Critical Infrastructure Protection Bill [B22-2017] is likely to have a significant effect, as it will determine certain cybersecurity structures, mechanisms, and obligations. The Bill was passed by the National Assembly in August 2018, amended by the National Council of Provinces in December 2018, and passed by Parliament in March 2019. At the time of writing, it is with President Cyril Ramaphosa for signing into law (Ferreira, 2019).

Cyberwarfare

The Defence Review (2014), South Africa's national defense policy update, states that on "Information Warfare" "South Africa requires the protection of its cyber-domain, through (inter alia) a comprehensive information warfare capability, integrated into its intelligence-related information systems at the international, national and defence levels" (RSA, 2014: ix). However, the Review itself notes that, "[t]he Defence Force is in a critical state of decline" (RSA, 2014: 9). The Defence Review considers cyberwarfare, within the military concept of Information Warfare, to cover a broad range of operations within the Information Sphere (or InfoSphere). Information security is ensured by:

> dominating the electromagnetic spectrum (EMS), the network information systems spectrums (also known as the Cyberspace) as well as influencing human beliefs and behaviour in the physical, information and the cognitive (psychological) domains.
>
> *(RSA, 2014: 6–7)*

Joint Information Warfare will be integrated within all levels of war and throughout the spectrum of conflict. State activities in the InfoSphere need coordination at the national level and the Defence Review calls for the establishment of Information Operations. In this, defense has a supportive role to the other security agencies in the "protection of government information" against a cyber-threat, with the primary role being that of the State Security Agency. In 2002, the Electronic Communications Security (Pty), Ltd. (COMSEC Pty Ltd) was set up through an act of Parliament as a private company with the purpose of ensuring the security of critical electronic communications of the State (O'Brien, 2011) The General Intelligence Laws Amendment Act dissolved COMSEC into the newly created State Security Agency. This was part of a bigger restructuring of the security service in September 2009, in which President Zuma, by Presidential Proclamation, abolished the National Intelligence Agency and the South African Secret Service as national departments of state and created the State Security Agency as a state department. Some have noted that under Jacob Zuma there was an increased securitization of the South African state (Africa, 2012).

There has been a noticeable change in the discourse used by the South African Department of Defence (DOD) to describe their intentions for cyberspace. DOD documents such as annual budgets and annual reports (which often show little variation year to year) tend to identify a more hostile cyber environment, and a shift towards warfare capabilities rather than just security capabilities. This discourse shift is emphasized here in italics. For instance, the DOD Situational Analysis for 2017 notes that:

> While the nature of military conflict is not expected to change in the air, at sea, on land and the cyberspace in the coming decades, the means of warfare certainly will continue to evolve. Cyber and terror attacks remain a possibility to *contemplate*.
>
> *(RSA, 2017b: 8)*

This last sentence was changed in the 2018 DOD Situational Analysis to "Cyber and terror attacks remain a possibility *and thus require constant contemplation and response.*"(RSA, 2018: 8). The language of the 2018 DOD's Annual Performance Plan is more to the point

> There has been an increased [sic] cyber-attacks both globally and domestically in the past year against SA National Departments and companies. The DOD remains aware of the possibility of escalated cyber-attacks against South Africa should it become involved in a conflict perceived to be illegitimate. The DOD will implement robust network security architecture, including appropriate segregation and segmentation between the IT and control system (Including weapons systems) networks using firewalls and intrusion prevention/detection tools. The DOD will perform continuous network security monitoring thus enabling the identification of abnormalities on the network.
>
> *(RSA, 2018: 7)*

The wider picture regarding the defense budget however is that there has been a reduction in overall expenditure. Potentially there is a decline in capability although "Defence will continue with the implementation of the Cyber Warfare Plan and will contribute, pending resource allocation, towards capacitating a Cyber-security Institution through the establishment of a Cyber Command Centre Headquarters" (RSA, 2017: 20). Although the reference here is to a Cyber-security Institution, in 2018 the intention is made explicit that "… Defence will continue with the implementation of the Cyber Warfare Plan and pending resource allocation, towards capacitating a *Cyber-Warfare Institution* through the establishment of a Cyber Command Centre scheduled for FY2018/19" (authors' emphasis) (RSA, 2018: 22). What is meant by moving from a Cyber-Security Institution to a Cyber-Warfare Institution is not exactly clear at this stage, although the wording suggests a discourse of establishing offensive and not just defensive capabilities. Not much is known publicly as this is a classified project, but this Cyber Warfare Command Centre Headquarters was expected to be fully established during Financial Year 2018–2019, with R340 million been budgeted for this in the Defence Intelligence Programme. Ten departmental personnel are working on the establishment of the Cyber Command Centre, though implementation remains a challenge due to inadequate resource allocation (RSA, 2018: 7–8).

South Africa and the international legal rules that apply to cyberspace

South Africa's position in respect of cybersecurity at the regional and international level is unclear although the policy does refer to international cooperation. However, given that there are myriad concerns about the securitization policies and practices of some state actors, and that the international regulation of cyberspace is as yet unfolding with the slow emergence of international cyber norms (see Maurer, 2011) the prospects for an international treaty placing limitations on the militarization of cyberspace seem now more remote than in the past. South Africa's foreign and security policy does not seem to indicate support for initiating such an international treaty.

South Africa has supported a series of resolutions of the United Nations General Assembly in 2010 concerning technical aspects such as on Computer Security Incident Response Teams (CSIRTs), and protection of critical national infrastructure (CNIs). More generally, South Africa has supported the work of the UN Office on Drugs and Crime (UNODC, 2017), and is a signatory to the Budapest Convention on Cybercrime (Council of Europe, 2001). The Budapest Convention is the only international agreement that addresses cybercrime and aims to harmonize national laws and establishing international cooperation against cybercrime. South Africa signed the Convention in 2001, but never ratified it. According to the Department of Communication in 2013, the Cabinet decision to not ratify the convention, is based on considering instead a United Nations, African Union, or BRICS conventions on cybercrime (RSA, 2013).

South Africa has also signed, but not ratified, the African Union (AU) Convention on Cyber Security and Personal Data Protection (2014). The draft AU Convention on cybersecurity sets out options for an AU-wide cybersecurity policy, lays the foundation for cyber ethics and regulates issues related to the use of electronic transactions and electronic signatures as well as an institutional framework for the protection of personal data. South Africa is also a member of, Southern Africa Development Community (SADC), and a number of guidelines and model laws have been developed as a way to promote common approaches to common problems, including the SADC Model Law on Data Protection and the SADC Model Law on Cybercrime.

Suggested reading

De Lanerolle, I. (2016). "Internet Freedom: Why Access Is Becoming a Human Right." http://theme diaonline.co.za/2016/06/internet-freedom-why-access-is-becoming-ahuman-right/

Gcaza, N. & von Solms, R. (2017). "A Strategy for A Cybersecurity Culture: A South African Perspective," *The Electronic Journal of Information Systems in Developing Countries, 80*(6): 1–17.

Lewis, C. (2015). "SA Ranks High in Cybercrime." www.sabc.co.za/news/a/ebe2b3004a2f054d9f61d fa53d9712f0/SA-ranks-high-in-cybercrime-20151012

Lotz, B. (2015). "We Don't Have Enough People to Cope with Cybercrime," *Hawks. Cybersecurity News.* www.htxt.co.za/2015/09/10/we-dont-have-enoughpeople-to-cope-with-cybercrime-hawks/

SA Government Gazette. (2015). "National Cybersecurity Policy Framework for South Africa."

von Solms, R. & van Niekerk, J. (2013). "From Information Security to Cyber Security," *Computers & Security, 38*: 97–102.

References

Africa, S. (2012). "The Policy Evolution of the South African Civilian Intelligence Services: 1994 to 2009 and Beyond," *Strategic Review for Southern Africa, 34*(1): 97–134.

amaBhungane Centre for Investigative Journalism NPC and Stephen Patrick Sole v Minister of Justice and Correctional Services and 9 other respondents. (2019). Case no.: 25978/17, High Court of South Africa, Gauteng Division, Pretoria.

Bramwell, L. (2017, August 21). "Department of Telecommunications and Postal Services: Cybersecurity," Research Unit, Parliament Portfolio Committee of Telecommunications and Postal Services.

Burbidge, M. (2019, May 29). "Can SA Survive a Cyber Attack?" *IT Web.* www.itweb.co.za/content/ mQwkoM6Kayeq3r9A

Centre for Constitutional Rights. (2017, August 10). "Concise Submission on the Cybercrimes and Cybersecurity Bill [B 6-2017]."

Donnelly, L. (2018, June 22). "Another Day, Another Data Breach," *Mail and Guardian.*

Duncan, J. (2015). *The Rise of the Securocrats: The Case of South Africa.* Johannesburg: Jacana.

Dunn Cavelty, M. (2016). "Cyber-Security," in A. Collins (ed.), *Contemporary Security Studies* (4th ed. pp. 400–416). New York: Oxford University Press.

Ferreira, E. (2019). "National Assembly Approves Critical Infrastructure Protection Bill, IOL News." www.iol.co.za/news/politics/national-assembly-approves-critical-infrastructure-protection-bill-19647155

Gereda, S. L. (2006). "The Electronic Communication and Transactions Act," in L. Thornton, Y. Carrim, P. Mtshaulana & P. Reyburn (eds.), *Telecommunications Law in South Africa* (pp. 262 294). Johannesburg: STE Publishers.

Grobler, M., van Vuuren, J. J. & Leenen, L. (2011). "Implementation of a Cyber Security Policy in South Africa: Reflection on Progress and the Way Forward," in M. D. Hercheui, D. Whitehouse, W. McIver & J. Phahlamohlaka (eds.), *ICT Critical Infrastructures and Society* (pp. 215–225). HCC 2012. IFIP Advances in Information and Communication Technology, Vol. 386. Berlin and Heidelberk: Springer.

ISPA. (2015). "Submission on the Draft Cybercrime Cybersecurity Bill 2015." https://ispa.org.za/wp-content/uploads/2012/06/20151130-ISPA-Submission-on-the-Draft-Cybercrime-Cybersecurity-Bill-2015.pdf

ITU. (2008, April). "Overview of Cybersecurity: Recommendation ITU-T X.1205," Geneva, Switzerland. www.itu.int/rec/T-REC-X.1205-200804-I

Luiijf, E., Besseling, K. & de Graaf, P. (2013). "Nineteen National Cyber Security Strategies," *International Journal of Critical Infrastructures, 9*(1/2): 3–31.

Mangena, D. (2016). "Will Legislation Protect Your Virtual Space? Discussing the Draft Cybercrime and Cyber Security Bill," *De Rebus, 560*: 33–34.

Mare, A. & Duncan, J. (2015). "An Analysis of the Communications Surveillance Legislative Framework in South Africa," Media Policy and Democracy Project. www.mediaanddemocracy.com/uploads/1/6/5/7/16577624/comms-surveillance-framework_mare2.pdf

Maurer, T. (2011). "Cyber Norm Emergence at the United Nations – An Analysis of the UN's Activities Regarding Cyber-security," Discussion Paper 2011–11, Cambridge, MA: Belfer Center for Science and International Affairs, Harvard Kennedy School, September 2011.

Media Monitoring Africa, MMA. (2018). Inquiry into the role and responsibilities of the Independent Communications Authority of South Africa in cybersecurity: Submissions by Media Monitoring Africa on the discussion document. 30 November 2018. https://www.icasa.org.za/uploads/files/MMA-submission-discussion-document-on-cybersecurity.pdf

Mzekandaba, S. (2019, June 27). "Top-level UN Human Rights Role Gives Tlakula Extra Digital Power," *IT Web*. www.itweb.co.za/content/wbrpOMgPlrgqDLZn

Newmeyer, K. P. (2015). Elements of National Cybersecurity Strategy for Developing Nations," *National Cybersecurity Institute Journal, 1*(3): 9–19.

O'Brien, K. A. (2011). *The South African Intelligence Services: From Apartheid to Democracy, 1948–2005.* New York: Routledge.

Olivier, B. (2013, July 28). "Is There a Need for Cyber-ethics?" *Mail and Guardian.* https://thoughtleader.co.za/bertolivier/2013/07/28/is-there-a-need-for-cyber-ethics/

O'Reilly, K. (2013). "South African Law Coming to Grips with Cyber Crime," *De Rebus 530*: 14–15.

Orji, U. (2012). *Cybersecurity Law and Regulation.* Nijmegen: Wolf Legal Publishers.

Pillay, V. (2014, September 2). "IEC Chair Pansy Tlakula Resigns." *Mail and Guardian.*

Privacy International. (2019). "The State of Privacy in South Africa." https://privacyinternational.org/state-privacy/1010/state-privacy-south-africa

Right2Know Campaign. (2015, November 30). "Preliminary Position on the Draft Cybercrimes and Cybersecurity Bill."

Right2Know Campaign. (2017, August 10). "Cybercrimes, Cybersecurity, and Internet Freedom: Right2Know Campaign Submission on the Cybercrimes and Cybersecurity Bill."

RSA. (2010). "Draft Cyber Security Policy of South Africa," *Annex to Government Gazette, 536*(32963): 4–12.

RSA. (2010a). "Annual Report of the Joint Standing Committee on Intelligence for Financial Year Ending 31 March 2010." Parliament ATC110921.

RSA. (2013, November 26). "Department of Communication Review Report: E-commerce, Cybercrime and Cybersecurity – Status, Gaps and the Road Ahead."

RSA. (2013a). "Ministerial Review Commission on Intelligence (Matthews Commission)."

RSA. (2014). *South African Defence Review 2014.* Pretoria: Government Printer.

RSA. (2015a). "State Security Agency, Notice Number 609 of 2015," *Government Gazette, 609*(39475): 67–95.

RSA. (2015b). "Address by Dr. Siyabonga Cwele, Minister of Telecommunications and Postal Services at the Launch of the Cybersecurity Hub at CSIR," Pretoria, South Africa. www.gov.za/speeches/minister-siyabonga-cwele-launch-cybersecurity-hub-30-oct-2015-0000

RSA. (2017, February 28). "Department of Telecommunications and Postal Services (DTPS), Cybersecurity Briefing to the Portfolio Committee of Parliament."

RSA. (2017a). "Department of Justice and Constitutional Development Memorandum on the Objects of Cybercrimes and Cybersecurity Bill."

RSA. (2017b). *Department of Defence Annual Performance Plan for 2017*. Pretoria: Government Printer.

RSA. (2018). *Department of Defence Annual Performance Plan for 2018*. Pretoria: Government Printer.

Sabillon, R., Cavaller, V. & Cano, J. (2016). "National Cyber Security Strategies: Global Trends in Cyberspace," *International Journal of Computer Science and Software Engineering, 5*(5): 67–81.

SAHRC. (2017, August). "Submission on the Cybercrimes and Cybersecurity Bill [B 6-2017]."

SANEF. (2019, June 4). "SANEF Supports Landmark Constitutional Challenge to South Africa's Surveillance Law, RICA." https://sanef.org.za/sanef-supports-landmark-constitutional-challenge-to-south-africas-surveillance-law-rica/

SAPA. (2013, October 15). "Carrim Announces New Cyber Security Council." *Mail and Guardian.*

Schönteich, M. (2014). "A Story of Trials and Tribulations: The National Prosecuting Authority, 1998–2014." *SA Crime Quarterly* 50: 5–15. doi: 10.4314/sacq.v50i1.1

Snail, S. (2009). "Cyber Crime in South Africa – Hacking, Cracking, and Other Unlawful Online Activities," *Journal of Information, Law & Technology, 1*: 1–13.

Sole, S. (2019, September 18). "Analysis: Inside amaBhungane's Landmark Ruling on Surveillance," *Daily Maverick.* www.dailymaverick.co.za/article/2019-09-18-analysis-inside-amabhunganes-landmark-ruling-on-surveillance/

Sutherland, E. (2017). "Governance of Cybersecurity – The Case of South Africa," *The African Journal of Information and Communication, 20*: 83–112.

UCT. (2019, May 24). "Africa First for UCT Cybersecurity." www.news.uct.ac.za/article/-2019-05-24-africa-first-for-ucts-cybersecurity

Wasserman, H. & de Beer, A. (2005). "Which Public? Whose Interest? The South African Media and Its Role during the First Ten Years of Democracy," *Critical Arts, 19*(1–2): 36–51.

Appendix

In a Briefing to the Portfolio Committee of Parliament by Department of Telecommunications and Postal Services (DTPS) on 28 February 2017, information was provided on incidents, alerts, and warnings noted by the Cybersecurity Hub during 2016. These included:

- May 2016 – National Bank exploit
- June 2016 – National broadcaster website attack
- July 2016 – National military attack
- September 2016 – National IP addresses on DDos-for-Hire List
- October 2016 – International fraud in South Africa (Nigerian arrest)
- December 2016 – Online shopping scam & cybercrime on small businesses

Table 50.1 is derived from information presented at the briefing. The descriptors used for the types of incidents appear below the table.

Table 50.1 Incidents, Alerts, and Warnings per Month (January 16–December 16)

Month	January	February	March	April	May	June	July	August	September	October	November	December	TOTAL
Total Per Month	930	1920	673	1137	1664	2167	1425	1222	1774	2256	2878	1644	19,690
Abusive Content	33	56	38	157	235	320	155	215	249	220	242	154	2074
Malicious Code	188	147	165	238	154	446	291	142	247	672	634	549	3873
Information Gathering	55	156	42	273	253	260	225	258	270	350	469	323	2934
Intrusion Attempts	73	241	53	25	68	89	9	3	22	0	5	0	588
Intrusions	102	213	67	19	97	55	10	25	36	0	0	0	624
Availability	7	425	43	110	376	358	256	180	496	592	300	323	3466
Information Security	98	245	29	15	58	65	56	45	32	0	528	0	1171
Fraud	5	81	3	50	67	209	96	32	43	27	39	30	682
Vulnerability	369	356	233	250	356	365	327	322	379	395	661	265	4278

★ Abusive Content: (Spam, Cyberbullying, Cyber stalking, Child Pornography, Violence) 2. Malicious Code (Viruses, Worms, Trojans, Spyware, Dialer) 3. Information Gathering (Scanning, Sniffing, Phishing, Spoofing, Pharming) 4. Intrusion attempts (Exploitation of known vulnerabilities, Login attempts, New attack Signature) 5. Intrusions (Privileged account compromise, Unprivileged account compromise, Application compromise) 6. Availability (Denial of service, Distributed Denial of service, Sabotage) 7. Information security (Unauthorized access to information, Unauthorized modification of information, Ransomware) 8. Fraud (Unauthorized use of resources, Copyright infringement, Masquerade)

Source: Cybersecurity Briefing to the Portfolio Committee of Parliament by Department of Telecommunications and Postal Services (DTPS). 28 February 2017. Slide 20–22.

51

ALGORITHMS OF OPPRESSION?

AU's cybersecurity policy and its enforcement in Africa

Joshua Oreoluwa Akintayo

Introduction

Information and communication technologies, particularly the internet and mobile networks, are essential tools for governments, businesses, civil society, and individuals globally. These technologies have enabled tremendous economic growth and development and increased the unhindered flow of information. However, the growing importance of the internet has also brought about new challenges: As societies become more interconnected and highly dependent on the internet and ICTs, the tendency for authoritarian, hybrid, and even democratic governments to abuse or misuse the internet and technology to serve their interest increases. Moreover, the exponential growth of the internet has created new opportunities for perpetrating cybercrime on a global scale, and to exploit the inherent vulnerabilities.

As African countries increase their access to the internet, issues concerning cybersecurity and cybercrime are gaining traction. Cybersecurity concerns are broader than national security, and yet, few cybersecurity initiatives have been implemented at the continental level (Dlamini, Taute, & Radebe, 2011). Africa is facing several Internet-related challenges concerning security provisions to prevent and control technological and informational risks (Orji, 2014). Accordingly, the African Union (AU) has taken measures to address the existing gaps and to strengthen cyber defenses across the board in addition to striving for the development of a clear and logical strategy regarding cybersecurity in the context of states and their communities. In making cybersecurity strategies and policies a priority in and across Africa, including cross-national, regional, and international cooperation, African governments have deployed cybersecurity policy to serve their interest. This chapter aims to examine the African Union cybersecurity policy underscoring how it was domesticated and enforced in various African countries and its implications on democratic institutions in the country. Existing literature on cybercrime is dominantly focused on the global north with relatively little known about the issue in the global south, particularly sub-Saharan Africa. This chapter fills this gap and examines the AU cybersecurity policy, taking into account how the regional institutional protocol created the avenue for various African national governments to suppress opposition voices in the guise of enforcing this policy.

Moreover, the chapter contends that under the guise of enforcing AU cybersecurity policy, African governments are stifling civil liberties, thereby undermining democratic consolidation in the various nascent democracies in African countries. Thus, this chapter contributes to the ongoing discourse of the adverse effects of cybersecurity policy. The chapter begins by providing a background to the development of the AU Convention on cybersecurity. The next section examines the main features of the Convention. This is followed by a brief illumination of the interrelated concepts of cybercrime and cyberterrorism. The other parts of the work address how the African governments deploy the AU cybersecurity strategy to repress, oppress human rights and civil liberties, and the implications of the enforcement of cybersecurity policies on democratic consolidation in African states. The last section presents the conclusion of the chapter.

The African Union Convention on cybersecurity and personal data protection

Although Africa is a signatory to various international agreements, instruments, and protocols aimed at addressing the issue of cybersecurity and cybercrime (e.g., the Budapest Convention of cybercrime), until 2014, African states lacked a guiding protocol developed internally to curb cybercrime. Seeing the growth rate of the continent in terms of the technology, internet, and the growing interconnectivity of the world (Kshetri, 2019), African leaders were left with no choice than to commence plans to develop a regional protocol. Added to this reason is that all other continents and regions of the world have internally developed guiding mechanisms and measures to address cybercrime and cybersecurity issues, and it would only seem right not to be left out of the trend. This influenced the emergence of an African Union cybersecurity strategy.

Some initial moves and strategies preceded the eventual and final adoption of the AU Cybersecurity Convention in 2014. I categorize these stages into three, each with defining processes and activities. The first period, which can be referred to as the "Oliver Tambo Declaration," kickstarted the process and it was at this stage that the resolution for the development of the AU cybersecurity policy was adopted. The Ministers of Communications and Information Technologies in Africa in 2009 adopted a declaration [EXT/CITMC/MIN/Decl. (I)] (Olivier Tambo Declaration) where it was:

> requested [that] the African Union Commission develop jointly with the United Nations Economic Commission for Africa, a convention on cyber legislation based on the Continent's needs and which adheres to the legal and regulatory require-ments on electronic transactions, cybersecurity, and personal data protection.
>
> *(Amazouz, 2016)*

The second stage of activity can be termed the "Endorsement Phase." This endorsement was done by the 14th AU Summit of Head of State and government in 2010 [Assembly/AU/11(XIV)] (Amazouz, 2016). The third stage before the official signing into law of the Convention is the "Confirmation Phase." This was enabled in August 2010 by the third ordinary conference of Ministers of communication and ICT held in Abuja ([AU/CITMC/MIN/Decl. (III)] (Amazouz, 2016).

Following this was a draft convention on cybersecurity, which was developed in 2010–2011. Furthermore, various regional workshops were organized on Cyber Legislation and the AU Draft Convention on Cyber Security. These are ECCAS: Libreville, Gabon, November 2011, ECOWAS: Abidjan, Côte d'Ivoire, February 2012, and the tripartite [COMESA, SADC, CEAC] + UMA (Northern Africa): Addis-Ababa, Ethiopia, June 2012. In August 2012, the Final Expert Group meeting to finalize the Draft Convention was held before the CITMC-4 in Addis Ababa, Ethiopia. The Ministers of Information and Communication Technology gave the final endorsement of the AU last Draft Convention on cyber legislation at the 4th Ministerial Conference of the African Union Ministers of Communication and ICT. The Convention was then adopted by the Conference of Ministers of Justice and Legal Affairs. The AU and the Economic Commission for Africa (ECA) steered the development and implementation of the African Union Convention on Cybersecurity and personal data protection, a move that was approved by the African Union Heads of States and Governments at a Summit in June 2014 in Malabo (Amazouz, 2016).

The objective of the AU Malabo Convention is to get a unified and united approach on the issue of securing the cyberspace in Africa and set up minimum standards and procedures to set up a credible digital environment for developing the electronic communications and guarantee the respect of privacy online. The Malabo convention seeks the establishment of a legal framework for cybersecurity and personal data protection as well as setting guidelines for incrimination and repression of cybercrime and related issues. The Convention underlines the essential security rules for establishing and promoting a cybersecurity culture. The Convention is more comprehensive than most other regional approaches because of its inclusion of data protection and electronic transaction issues (Orji, 2014). The Convention has a broad scope covering three essential areas of cyberlaw/policy: electronic transactions, data protection, and cybersecurity/cybercrime. This chapter focuses solely on the cybersecurity and cybercrime aspects of the Convention.

Main features of the convention

The AU Malabo convention is divided into four main parts, with each part having different numbers of sections and articles. This part of the chapter will highlight the constituent parts of the convention and the sections contained. Part one is related to electronic commerce. It addresses various aspects such as contractual bond of an electronic provider of goods and services (see, Part 1, Section II, Chapter II), treaty requirements in electronic form (see, Part 1, Section IV), and security of electronic transactions (see, Part 1 Section V). The second part deals with issues of data protection (see, Part 2). The third part deals with the issue of promoting cybersecurity and combating cybercrime. The final part deals with the Common and final provisions. Section 1 contains five chapters: this includes a set of six definitions (electronic communication, computerized data, racism and xenophobia in ICTs, minors, child pornography, and computer systems) (see, Article III–I). The third part addresses the need of a national cybersecurity policy and a related strategy (see, Part 3, Chapter 1, Article I and II). The second chapter deals with general aspects related to legal measures. This includes standards related to statutory authorities, democratic principles, protection of essential information infrastructure, harmonization, double criminality, and international cooperation (see, Article III–I to Article III 1–7). The third chapter addresses issues related to a national cybersecurity system. These issues are culture of security, the role of the government, public–private partnership, education and training, and public awareness-raising (see, Article III 1–8 to Article III 1–12). The fourth chapter is committed to national cybersecurity monitoring structures. The fifth chapter deals with international cooperation. Section 1 includes a criminalization of illegal access to a computer system (see, Article III-2), illegal remaining in a computer system (see, Article III-3), illegal system interference (see, Article III-4), illegal data input (see, Article III-5), illegal data interception (see, Article III-6), and illegal data interference (see, Article III-7). Section 2 includes the criminalization of aspects of computer-related forgery (see, Article III-8), illegal use of data (see, Article III-9), illegal system interference with the intent to obtain advantage (see, Article III-10), data protection violations (see, Article III-11), illegal devices (see, Article III-12), and participation in a criminal organization (see, Article III-13). Section 3 deals with the criminalization of illegal content. The next section of this chapter unpacks the major concepts that will be used throughout this work.

Cybercrime and cyberterrorism: unpacking the concepts

An elaborate discourse of the concepts of cybercrime and cyberterrorism is beyond the scope of this chapter; however, attempts shall be made to give an overview of its definition as used by a few scholars and in policy documents, and how it would be used in this chapter. Despite it being on the top of agenda, discussions, and discourses globally, regionally, and nationally, it has remained a concept that is elusive of a universally accepted definition. In simple terms, cybercrime can be referred to as computer-enabled crime or computerized crime. One standard definition describes cybercrime as any activity in which computers or networks are the tools, targets, or abode of criminal activity. The Budapest Convention of the Council of Europe (2001) defines cybercrime thus: "Cybercrime is a deliberate, planned and intentional action of illegal access, interception, data interference, system interference, misuse of devices, computer-related forgery, computer-related fraud, offenses related to child pornography and offenses related to copyright and neighboring rights."

Colarik (2006) argues that defining the concept is not so straightforward and thus is considered computer crime by default. Acts of cybercrime include the selling or transport of contraband in cyberspace, the theft of property including people's identities, and a host of other offenses that are considered inappropriate by societies and by the government (Colarik, 2006). A recurring theme in all of these discussions concerns the centrality of the computer system in perpetuating/carrying out the cybercrime. Melzer (2011) describes cybercrime as a high-tech crime that is committed in cyberspace in a globally interconnected network of digital information and communication infrastructures. It includes the internet, telecommunications, and computer systems. For the sake of this chapter, cybercrime is described as crimes that make use of computers or other allied digital networks and technologies in either committing the crime or as the victim/target of the crime.

Cyberterrorism, just like cybercrime, is an esoteric concept devoid of a universal definition (McGuire, 2014). The esoteric nature of the concept and the absence of a universal definition has thrown it open to various definitions and discussions from both the academic and the policy arena, thus making it difficult to pinpoint what exactly constitutes cyberterrorism. However, these definitions cover areas such as the convergence of cyberspace and terrorism to "severe economic damage" (Denning, 2001). The Center for

Strategic and International Studies (1998) puts forward one of the first commonly accepted definitions of cyberterrorism thus, "cyberterrorism means premeditated, politically motivated attacks by subnational groups or clandestine agents, or individuals against information and computer systems, computer programs, and data that result in violence against noncombatants targets" (1998). In a related vein, the then deputy assistant director of the cyber division of the FBI Keith Lourdeau (2004), defined cyberterrorism as:

> a criminal act perpetrated by the use of computers and telecommunications capabilities, resulting in violence, destruction and/or disruption of services, where the intended purpose is to create fear by causing confusion and uncertainty within a given population, with the goal of influencing a government or population to conform to a particular political, social or ideological agenda.

Colarik (2006) also, gives a similar definition. He defined cyberterrorism as:

> premeditated, politically motivated criminal act by subnational groups or clandestine agents against information and computer systems, computer programs, and data that result in physical violence, where the intended purpose is to create fear in noncombatant targets.

This definition makes a clear connection between the traditional description of terrorism – which is to inflict fear in the minds of people – and the term cyber.

The definition explicitly spells out that there is a marked difference between cybercrime and cyberterrorism, although they may look similar (Denning, Keith, 2004). Hence, cyberterrorism can be referred to as cybercrime, but all cybercrimes do not fall into the remit of cyberterrorism. The motive and objective differentiate the two while the mode of operation and consequences unite them. The motive of cyberterrorists is to terrorize nations, by inflicting fear into the minds of noncombatant populace in order to achieve its political objectives of influencing government decisions. However, cybercrime is often committed out of a quest to explore the cyberspace for profit. Colarik (2006), posits that the differences between criminals and terrorists in cyberspace exist in the transfer of knowledge about these systems, and its destruction. This chapter, therefore, aligns with Colarik's (2006) definition of cyberterrorism, and it shall be used throughout the chapter.

Domestication of the cybersecurity protocol

Cybersecurity and cybercrime cannot be treated just like other regulatory topics or subject matter due to the grave danger they portend. Thus, cybersecurity has become a priority for all governments globally, and many have developed strategies to address the emerging security issues connected with the unlawful use of ICTs. These strategies developed by countries are referred to as national strategies and action plans. Pescatore (2009) argues that the national cybersecurity strategy of governments should capitalize on the strengths of the government to propel the advancement of security measures that the government and all other stakeholders use in their contact with cyberspace activities.

In Africa, efforts at addressing and improving cyberthreats and cybersecurity are underway (Kshetri, 2019). Also, ratifying, domesticating, as well as implementing national cybersecurity strategies have been and are still being put in place. A few African countries began making moves for the implementation of their cybersecurity strategies even before the development of the Malabo convention at national and sub-regional levels. Although a large number of African countries kickstarted their national policies after the declaration of the Malabo convention, this section of the chapter takes a look at the domestication of the AU cybersecurity policy by different African Countries. According to the November 2016 report of the African Union Commission (AUC) and the cybersecurity firm Symantec (cited in Kshetri, 2019), 11 countries in the continent had specific laws and strategies to deal with cybercrime and electronic evidence: Nigeria, Botswana, Cameroon, Côte d'Ivoire, Ghana, Mauritania, Mauritius, Senegal, Tanzania, Uganda, and Zambia. Also, 12 countries had taken remarkable legislative actions, although limited in nature.[1] Draft cybercrime laws were prepared in many other countries and bills presented to national parliaments. However, the ratification of the Malabo Convention has not been too impressive so far. Despite all the good deeds that the Convention promised to deliver to the issue of cybersecurity in Africa, it has experienced a meager rate of ratification (Kenyanito & Chima, 2016). To date, only three countries have ratified the Convention, while ten countries have signed it (Kshetri, 2019). However, while the cybersecurity protocol has been ratified and domesticated by African countries, these laws have been used to target and repress credible opposition, human rights activists, and journalists. In the next section, I examine the effects of the enforcement of cybersecurity policy in two African states.

The AU cybersecurity strategy: an algorithm of oppression?

In this section, the chapter examines how the AU Malabo Convention has been used by African governments as guise to repress various sections of the civil society in their respective countries. African governments have used their national cybersecurity laws/policies to target protest groups by shutting down the internet[2] and engage in other repressive mechanisms to stifle civil liberties. The vaguely worded[3] and overly broad nature of the AU cybersecurity strategy became a conveyor belt for various African governments to silence legitimate criticism of public officials and opposition groups. However some of these laws are with the touted goal of protecting online users, curbing cybercrimes, and ultimately protecting national security.

Although the AU Malabo Convention makes no provision for shutting down internet services, most African countries that have followed this path have justified their actions on the premise of protection of national security, curtailing the spread of disinformation and hate speech, in their respective countries. It is also worth remembering that the Malabo Convention supports this argument through Article 25, schedule No 4, which empowers states to ensure the protection of critical infrastructures of sectors regarded as sensitive for national security and well-being of the economy. Under this guise, some states have successfully ensured that internet services in their countries are either partially or fully shut during critical periods such as elections and as anti-government policy reactions. A 2018 report by Access Now group, states that there were 21 instances of internet shutdowns in 2018 alone, a notable and sharp increase from 2017. The next section of this chapter examines how cybersecurity policy was used to repress credible opposition through a case study analysis.

Country case analysis

This section undertakes an analysis of how cybersecurity/crime strategies have been used as algorithms of oppression by African governments by looking at two countries: Tanzania and Nigeria. Both were selected for the case study because they both implemented their cybercrime Act in 2015.

Tanzania

In Tanzania, there is no doubt that cybercrimes are a threat to the national security and other individuals' rights enjoyments because cybercrime is unlawful acts wherein the computer is either a tool or a target or both. To this end, on April 1, 2015, the Tanzanian government passed a cybercrime law that seeks to address pressing issues such as child pornography, cyberbullying, online impersonation, electronic production of racist and xenophobic content, unsolicited messages, illegal interception of communications, and publication of false information, bearing semblance with the AU Cybercrime Strategy of 2014. The Tanzanian Cybercrimes Act also sought to criminalize information deemed false, misleading, inaccurate, or deceptive (see, Section 16 of the Tanzanian Cybercrimes Act). The Cybercrimes Act guarantees freedom of expression through the internet but only within the scope and framework prescribed under the Act and the Tanzanian government. However, just like a recurring theme in African countries, the law has been used in draconian ways. It is argued that the law seeks more than addressing the above-highlighted issues; instead, it takes on a new phenomenon, which is the illegitimate use for punishing critics of the president or the government on social media. The law gives the security agents in Tanzania wide-ranging ability to search the houses of suspected violators of the law, seize electronic hardware, and also demand data from internet service providers (Macha, 2015). Some sections of the cybercrime law are structured in highly repressive terms and take on a repressive nature (see, Sections 16, 20, 31, and 32).

In addition, the enactment of the Cybercrimes Act has harmed the freedom of expression online with varying results such as self-censorship and the arrest/prosecution of journalists and activists. The Act empowers the state's security agencies to obtain computer data protected against unauthorized access without permission. It empowers police or law enforcement officers to storm the premises of a news agency and confiscate a computer system or device to prove an offense has been committed. The police are equally given the right to search devices like cell phones, laptops, or computers if they believe they contain information that can be used as evidence to prove a crime has been committed. Also, the Cybercrimes Act gives police powers to decide what they feel is a state-sanctioned truth. It restricts freedom of expression, cultivates online censorship, and can be used to suppress dissent. Importantly, section 16 of the Cybercrimes Act is coined in a mainly broad and vague nature, and it has been used to arrest and charge. Section 16 says,

> publication of false information: any person who publishes information or data pre-
> sented in a picture, text, symbol or any other form in a computer system knowing
> that such information or data is false, deceptive, misleading or inaccurate, and with
> intent to defame, threaten, abuse, insult, or otherwise deceive or mislead the public
> or concealing commission of an offence, commits an offence, and shall on convic-
> tion be liable to a fine of not less than five million shillings or to imprisonment for
> a term of not less than three years or to both.
>
> *(see, Section 16)*

According to a report by Amnesty International (2019a), the Cybercrimes Act increased censorship of online freedom of expression through its introduction and use of sweeping powers to police the internet. Section 31 of the Cybercrimes Act also gives the police unrestrained powers to assess published information with or without the help of the judiciary (see, Section 31). This puts enormous powers in the hands of the police to restrain contents that are considered to be anti-state in nature. Another section of the Cybercrimes Act that constitutes an impediment against human rights is section 20 of the Act. This section states that "A person shall not, with intent to commit an offense under this Act initiate the transmission of unsolicited messages; relay or retransmit unsolicited messages or falsify header information in unsolicited messages." "Unsolicited message" is defined in the Act as "any electronic message which is not solicited by the recipient" (see, Section 20). This section gives the police the power to request information from ISPs, mobile phone operators, and also to confiscate and search computers for information and data if the need arises.

Remarkably, the Cybercrimes Act has been enacted and implemented in a highly repressive nature. According to the Tanzanian Human Rights Defenders Coalition (2016), more than 20 cases or instances where the Cybercrimes Act was used to arrest and prosecute "culprits" have been documented. Similarly, the Tanganyika Law Society (TLS) in February 2019, cited in an Amnesty International report (2019a) states that about 56 people had been charged under section 16 of the 2015 Cybercrimes Act.

The Cybercrimes Act contains many questionable restrictions, which have raised concerns over their likely impact on limiting the Civil Society Organizations' (CSOs) space and interfering with freedoms of expression and independence of media. It contains sections that impose severe sanctions on several media-specific offenses, consequently restricting the space for both civil society and individuals' access to information. It is safe to say that the 2015 Cybercrimes Act not only violates the right to share and receive information online; it also gags and stifles every form of perceived opposition by the government. This is what Charlotte (2019) referred to as cyber policing in Tanzania.

Nigeria

In Nigeria, internet blackout is not typical to constrict freedom of expression, but there is a Cybercrime Act implemented in 2015 to curb the increasing problems of cybersecurity in the country. The Cybercrime (Prohibition & Prevention) Act 2015 gives a legal and regulatory framework "for the prohibition, prevention, detection, prosecution, and punishment of cybercrimes" in Nigeria (see, explanatory note of the Nigerian Cybercrime Act). However, the Act has been used by the government to oppress and harass journalists and activists, restrict the freedom of expression of citizens, thereby ultimately shrinking the civic space. It can be argued that Nigeria is acting out the AU Malabo Convention in her Cybercrime Act of 2015 on the premise that she has signed and ratified the policy. However, considering that the policy has not come into effect due to the inadequate number of ratifications, the argument does not hold water. Nevertheless, both Acts have some level of resemblance, and thus one cannot rule out the possibility of some level of imitation. One problematic aspect of the Cybercrime Act used by authorities is Section 24, which proscribed "cyberstalking." The section prescribes up to three years imprisonment or a fine of N7 million or both for anyone found guilty of "causing annoyance, inconvenience danger, obstruction, insult, injury, criminal intimidation, enmity, hatred, ill will or needless anxiety to another" (see, Section 24).

The section is part of the law's sweeping attempt to curtail freedom of expression of citizens online, making it difficult to criticize or organize mass action against government policies. Also, Section 38 is equally fearful because it empowers security agencies to gain access to citizens' private data with few checks for excesses (see, Section 38). Just as the Malabo Convention empowers states to use any possible means that they deem fit to ensure the protection of critical national infrastructure, the Nigerian Cybercrime Act was a response to this change. In the opening explanatory memorandum, it seeks to ensure protecting critical national information infrastructure. Thus, in a bid to do this, the Cybercrime Act specifically identifies cyberterrorism amongst others as one of the pressing issues it holds in high esteem and to which penalties are attributed. Although this is typical in other African countries, the Cybercrime Act gives the state so much power to "misbehave" and perpetuate what Davenport (2007) refers to as "Digital Repression."[4]

Incidences of journalist's harassment and arrest with the help of the Cybercrime Act are rife. According to Amnesty International (2019b):

> Between January and September 2019, at least 19 journalists and media practitioners have suffered attack …. While many of them faced indiscriminate charges such as "defamation," "terrorism" and "cyberstalking"… Worse still, many of the journalists were prosecuted under the Cybercrime Act.

The expansive powers of the Nigerian Cybercrime Act have become an instrument for curbing potentially critical speech of citizens on the internet. As such, very vocal activists are profiled, occasionally singled out, isolated, or neutralized in some way as a means of containing trouble and disheartening other activists, resulting in self-censorship. This practice and decision by the Nigerian government made way for various acts of abuse by the government through her security agents under the guise of protecting national security. This Act has enabled political leaders at the helm of affairs to label political opponents and activists as perpetrating acts of cyberterrorism and cyberstalking.

Just recently, a bill seeking to prohibit the transmission of false statements of facts scaled through the second stage of reading in the legislature (the senate section of the National Assembly) at the time of writing this chapter. The proposed bill, which is officially known as Protection from Internet Falsehood, Manipulations, and Other Related Matters Bill 2019, popularly known as the Social Media Bill, seeks to guide against the transmission of false statements or declaration of fact in Nigeria. According to the explanatory memorandum of the proposed bill, the goal of the Act reads as follows: "This Act is to provide protection from internet falsehoods and manipulations." Part of the aims and objectives of the Act includes: "to prevent the transmission of false statements/declaration of facts in Nigeria and to enable measures to be taken to counter the effects of such transmission" (retrived from https://techpoint.africa/wp-content/uploads/2019/11/Protection-from-Internet-Falsehood-and-Manipulation-Bill-2019.pdf).

It is claimed that the objective of the bill is to check the spread of fake news and falsehood in the country vis-a-vis its proliferation. However, just like the Cybercrime Act of 2015, the "social media" bill contains some elements that ultimately seek to gag the freedom of speech, rob Nigerians of every right that they still hold on to, and of course, restrict the civic space that demands accountability and questions the government. For instance, the proposed draft bill contains a section that grants an access blocking order to the communication regulatory commission (Nigerian Communication Commission) through the security agencies to order the various internet service providers to block and disrupt internet services for users. What this suggests is that social media platforms, where there is public discourse of socio-political issues by Nigerians can be shut down at the will of the security agencies if found to contravene the opinions of the government. Consequently, individuals are liable to face sanctions and fines. Additionally, the bill also states that:

A person must not do any act in or outside Nigeria in order to transmit a statement in Nigeria, knowing or having reason to believe that it is a false statement of facts, and it will diminish public confidence in the performance of any duty or function of, or the exercise of any power of the government.

(Hundeyin, 2019)

What this vague and ambiguously worded clause of the bill implies is that any news, post, or even tweet that projects the Nigerian government as immoral, incapable, or ineffective is tantamount to "false statement." This in turn gives unhindered powers to label any online information as false based on the judgement of the government alone. In clear terms, only the Nigerian government has the power to decide what is actually "fake news" or "false statement." Expressly, the bill does not define what it implies by false statements of facts, as this raises issues as to the extent a factually correct but incomplete statement could amount to a "misinforming" and consequently legally false statement, imperatively, empowering security agencies to arrest people in such situations under the guise of protecting national security. This further raises the issue and fears of the likelihood of censorship. The bill also makes it possible for the government to coerce an individual to admit their statement as false forcefully, and this can be done through the correction order. To this extent, the government solely determines what is right and false. The tendency for the Nigerian government to abuse this is very high going by the antecedents of the Nigerian state.

Other internet shutdowns in Africa

Notably, another significant concern in this chapter is the diverse ways, manifestations, and forms that oppression has been done apart from using and abusing cyberterrorism laws to incarcerate oppositions. Some of these major forms and ways include: internet shutdowns, stifling and restricting internet freedom, prosecution, and detentions related to online activities, blockages of access to social media. Various African governments have chosen the route of shutting down internet services in their countries. According to CIPESA (2019),

an internet disruption, often referred to as an internet shutdown, is the intentional blockage of access to the Internet or sections of the Internet such as social media platforms. Internet disruptions are mostly ordered by governments eager to disrupt communications and curtail citizens' access to information in order to limit what the citizens can see, do, or communicate.

Access Now 2018 report describes some common forms of internet shutdown to include: Bandwidth throttling, broadband internet shutdowns, mobile internet shutdowns, mobile phone call, and text message network shutdowns, service-specific (platform) shutdowns (Access Now, 2018). A 2018 report by Access Now group, states that there were 21 instances of internet shutdowns in 2018 alone, a notable and sharp increase from what was obtained in 2016 with 4 incidences and 2017 with 13 incidences.

Chad experienced a social media blackout for 300 days in 2018 and 2019 due to protests that emanated from the government's plan to amend the constitution to increase the term of the president in office (Chimbelu, 2019). During this period, various social media platforms were blocked, thereby ostracizing the citizens of the country from voicing their opinion. However, the official justification given by the government was that of national security concerns (Dahir, 2019). It is interesting to note that Chad does not have any national approved cybersecurity policy or strategy in place to date (ITU, 2015). Instead, it can be deduced that the decision of the government to enforce a social media blackout was initiated via the individual efforts of the Chadian government that felt the need to gag opposition voices that attempted to counter their constitutional amendments move. Also, in Sudan and Zimbabwe, Giles (2019) highlights how the governments of both countries blocked the internet in different situations under different circumstances, both using the guises of national security. In Sudan, there was a partial internet shutdown during the anti-government protests (Giles, 2019). The same experience occurred in Zimbabwe also, where the national government ordered a total internet shutdown in 2019 (CIPESA, 2019). Similarly, the national government is currently in the process of implementing new policies and regulations that seek to restrict access to the internet while at the same time giving them unlimited power and control (Giles, 2019). To this end, a ministry of cybersecurity, threat detection, and mitigation, which will focus exclusively on eliminating and curtailing "abuse and unlawful conduct" in cyberspace, has been proposed in Zimbabwe (Matfess & Smith, 2018).

Internet was shutdown totally in Gabon in the early part of 2019 due to an attempted coup, while in the Democratic Republic of the Congo (DRC), partial internet shutdown was experienced following the countdown to the presidential elections (Adepoju, 2019). In both cases, the government's official justification for the shutdown was hinged covertly on the protection of national security. Both countries have neither ratified or signed the Malabo Convention and consequently have not domesticated it in their respective countries, however, these actions can be seen to have indirectly taken refuge in Article 25, Schedule 4 of the AU Malabo Convention. In 2016, President Yoweri Museveni of Uganda issued a directive ordering that all social media sites be shut down during the elections so as to stop the spread of fake or misleading information (Ratcliffe & Okiror, 2019). Further to this, a social media tax was introduced in 2018. The main goal of this in the words of President Yoweri Museveni was to put an end "to gossip." This government decision was accompanied by a wide anti-government protest which also resulted in arrests. In Ethiopia, the government is known for being a regular internet censor, having shut down the internet countless times over the years. Interestingly, the government has also criminalized dissent through its 2009 Anti-Terrorism Proclamation (Matfess & Smith, 2018).

Implications of cybersecurity policies and strategies

The AU Malabo Convention on cybersecurity and the cybersecurity strategies of other African countries have had remarkable impacts and consequences. The top of this list is the issue of human rights implication. It is crucial to note that the right to privacy is fundamental for a free and self-governing society, and it constitutes a defining part of individual security and personal liberty. The advent of technologies increases the expedience of this respect for the right to privacy by democratic nations. According to the National Research Council (2007), there is increased tension and clash between the point of an individual's privacy (in all its forms) and a government's national security interests.

A common denominator present in most of the countries that have cybersecurity policies and strategies is the abuse of rights and disregard for the right to privacy. Cases of various forms of abuse and violations of rights are present in countries that have cybersecurity strategies. Abuse of rights, be it physical or digital, and violations of human and constitutional rights are the significant identifiable implications. Owing to the need to enforce their various cybersecurity policies, African countries have in the process trampled on the fundamental rights of their citizens. Considering that most of these policies contain elements that seek to restrain and control expression from the public against the government, the principle of freedom of expression by citizens has been curtailed to a large extent. Thus, citizens are not allowed to freely express their minds and participate in public discourse online again. This act of abusing citizens' digital rights is a prominent feature in almost all the cybersecurity policies of African countries. One blowback of this act is that such a government that allows this to happen is free to do whatever she likes without any form of opposition whatsoever and any input from the third sector. Policies and actions are implemented unchallenged without due consideration for the populace. The media, being a part of the third sector, is the principal victim of this abuse.

Considering that the internet and cyberspace are now used more frequently as a channel of communication by the media, African governments have taken to clamping down on "warring" media practitioners and journalists that seek to question and challenge governments' actions. This situation was mostly reported in Nigeria, where the Cybercrime Act of 2015 was believed to have targeted journalists. The cybercrime and terrorism laws in Nigeria have been abused by government authorities and charges have been trumped-up to intimidate journalists via harassment through verbal and physical assault, indiscriminate arrest, and detention and prosecution (Njoku, 2020 forthcoming). Abuse of physical rights is also a form of human rights implication of cybersecurity strategies. This form of rights abuse and violations is done via arbitrary arrests and incarcerations of those perceived to be troublemakers or "enemies of government" and a clampdown on protests. Considering that most digital activities may most likely be transferred to reality, the choking of digital rights has in most times, led to street protests by citizens.

However, African governments likewise moved their rights violations and abuse to the physical realm, for example, actively seeking to clampdown on street protests by citizens that challenge actions deemed to be unfavorable. These protests have been met by arrests, incarcerations and clampdown by security agents. In Zimbabwe the government clamped down on street protesters that took to the street to complain/protest about the internet blackout and the fuel hike. According to Burke (2019):

> six anti-government activists were abducted and tortured … the activists were taken from their homes at night by armed men in unmarked cars, accused of involvement in the protest, stripped, beaten and then abandoned.

The above discussion on the abuse of rights (digital and physical) can also be said to be violations of human and constitutional rights as enshrined in the constitutions of various countries. The ultimate consequence of all of these is the shrinking of the civic space in the state, a worsening situation of state–society relations that weakens the democratic consolidation of the already fragile state of democracy in Africa.

Another implication of the oppressive use of the cybersecurity policy and strategy is the erosion of democratic institutions in the affected countries. The most commonly affected democratic institution is the press. Following the analysis and evidence provided above, the press has been negatively affected by the various repressive actions of these African governments. The freedom of the press as an independent institution that is saddled with the responsibility of demanding accountability from the government on behalf of the citizens has been dramatically jeopardized on the altar of national security (Njoku, 2020). This has consequently affected the delivery and reportage of the press on the activities of the government, thus reducing the press to mere appendages of the ruling government. The various instances from Nigeria give credence to this claim; moreover, recent happenings in Nigeria indicate a situation where it is becoming quite dangerous to practice journalism freely in Nigeria without being victimized by the government. To date, over 19 journalists (including bloggers) have been arrested and incarcerated at different points in time since January 2019.

Conclusion

This chapter argued that the AU Malabo Convention on cybersecurity functioned as a livewire through which various African countries drew strength for their cybersecurity strategies, although most of them have not yet ratified the Malabo Convention. It highlights the resemblance between the Malabo Convention and the cybersecurity strategies of other countries. It further argued that the AU Malabo Convention reflected in other cybersecurity strategies has functioned as an algorithm of oppression in different forms such as internet shutdowns, social media blockage, and gagging of opposing voices – all done under cover of protecting national security. The Convention contains some elements and provisions that give enormous powers to the states and her security agents to wield their powers to control and repress perceived enemies of the state. The consequence(s) of this is the issue of human rights implication that it brings; abuse of digital and physical rights of citizens, and the violation of human and constitutional rights. This is reflected in the powers of the state to securitize some elements of the third sector that question government policies (Njoku, 2017). The media and civil society are denied rights to privacy and freedom of expression due to the construction of threats around their activities by the cybersecurity strategies, thereby setting not only a worrisome precedent in the polity but undercutting the already fragile nature of democracy in Africa.

In order to resolve the issues of human rights abuse inherent in the AU Malabo Convention and other African cybersecurity strategies, it is essential to review these laws. The expediency for review is also hinged on the idea that the practice of alienating and repressing civil liberties and shrinking the civic and private space while countering security challenges in the cyber realm is ultimately counterproductive, and would likely sustain existing security challenges. In turn, the lacunas in the 2014 AU Malabo Convention on cybersecurity around how it fosters human rights abuses should be reviewed in ways that significantly addresses these issues.

Notes

1 The 12 countries and the dates are as follows: Nigeria 2015, Botswana 2007, Cameroon 2010, Cote d'Ivoire 2013, Ghana 2008, Mauritania 2015, Mauritius 2003, Senegal 2017, Tanzania 2017, Uganda 2011, and Zambia 2018.
2 According to CIPESA (2019), "an internet disruption, often referred to as an internet shutdown, is the intentional blockage of access to the internet or sections of the internet such as social media platforms. Internet disruptions are mostly ordered by governments eager to disrupt communications and curtail citizens' access to information in order to limit what the citizens can see, do or communicate." Access Now 2018 report describes some common forms of internet shutdown to include: Bandwidth throttling, broadband internet shutdowns, mobile internet shutdowns, mobile phone call and text message network shutdowns, service-specific (platform) shutdowns.
3 This vagueness connotes the multiplicity of subjective meanings that some sections and articles in the cybersecurity policy is subjected to. For instance, article 25 of the policy is open/subject to various meanings, and can thus be interpreted in diverse ways with haphazard implications.

4 Digital Repression refers to the use of information and communications technologies (ICT) to surveil, intimidate, coerce and harass opponents in order to "impose a cost on the target" and deter specific activities or beliefs that challenge the state. It encompasses six techniques: surveillance, censorship, disinformation, cyberattacks and hacking, connectivity restrictions, and targeted arrests and violence.

References

Access Now. (2018). "Fighting Internet Shutdowns around the World." www.accessnow.org

Adepoju, P. (2019). "Internet Shutdown in Gabon, DR Congo Condemned," *IT Web Africa*. www.itwebafrica.com/security/513-africa/245309-internet-shutdown-in-gabon-dr-congo-condemned

Amazouz, S. (2016). "African Union Perspectives on Cybersecurity and Cybercrime," ITU-ATU workshop on cybersecurity strategy in African countries. www.itu.int/en/ITU-T/Workshops-and-Seminars/cybersecurity/Pages/Programme.aspx

Amnesty International. (2019a). "The Price We Pay: Targeted for Dissent by the Tanzanian State." www.amnesty.org/en/documents/afr56/0301/2019/en/

Amnesty International. (2019b). "Endangered Voices: Attack on Freedom of Expression in Nigeria." www.amnesty.org/en/documents/afr44/9504/2019/en/

Burke, J. (2019, January 1). "DRC electoral fraud fears rise as internet shutdown continues," *The Guardian*. Retrieved from: https://www.theguardian.com/world/2019/jan/01/drc-electoral-fears-rise-as-internet-shutdown-continues

Chimbelu, C. (2019). "The Government or the People. Telecoms Firms Trapped in Internet Shutdowns." www.dw.com/en/the-government-or-the-people-telecoms-firms-trapped-in-internet-shutdowns/a-49634343

CIPESA (Collaboration of International ICT policy for East and Southern Africa) (2019). "Despots and Disruptions: Five Dimensions of Internet Shutdowns in Africa." Retrieved from https://cipesa.org/?wpfb_dl=283

Colarik, A. M. (2006). *Cyber Terrorism: Political and Economic Implications*. USA and UK: Igi Global.

Cross, C. (2019). "Cybercrime and the Policing of Politics in Tanzania," in M. Dwyer & T. Molony (eds), *Social Media and Politics in Africa: Democracy, Censorship and Security* (pp. 195–213). London: Zed Books.

Dahir, A. L. (2018, January 24). "There's a decades-old law threatening digital freedom in DR Congo. Retrieved from Quartz Africa." Retrived from: https://qz.com/africa/1187727/the-dr-congo-is-using-a- decades-old-law-to-shut-down-the-internet/

Davenport, C. (2007). *State Repression and the Domestic Democratic Peace*. Cambridge: Cambridge University Press.

Denning, D. E. (2001). "Activism, Hacktivism, and Cyber Terrorism: The Internet as a Tool for Influencing Foreign Policy," in J. Arquilla & D. Ronfeldt (eds), *Networks and Netwar: The Future of Terror, Crime and Militancy* (pp. 239–288). Santa Monaca: RAND.

Dlamini, I. Z., Taute, B. & Radebe, J. (2011). "Framework for an African Policy Towards Creating Cyber Security Awareness." https://researchspace.csir.co.za/dspace/bitstream/handle/10204/5163/Dlamini_2011.pdf?sequence=1&isAllowed=y

Giles, C. (2019). "Africa Internet: How Do Governments Shut It Down." www.bbc.com/news/world-africa-47734843

Hundeyin, D (2019, November 26) "Nigerian Government Moves to Cage the Last Untamed Media Space." Retrieved from: https://newswirengr.com/2019/11/26/nigerian-government-moves-to-cage-the-last-untamed-media-space/

ITU. (2015). "Cyberwellness Profile: Republic of Chad." www.itu.int/en/ITU-D/Cybersecurity/Documents/Country_Profiles/Chad.pdf

Keith, L. (2004). "FBI Deputy Assistant Director, Testimony before the U.S. Senate Judiciary Subcommittee on Terrorism, Technology, and Homeland Security." www.fbi.gov/congress/congress04.htm

Kenyanito, E. P. & Chima, R. J. S. (2016). "Room for Improvement: Implementing the African Cyber Security and Data Protection Convention in sub-Saharan Africa." Access Now.

Kshetri, K. (2019). "Cybercrime and Cybersecurity in Africa," *Journal of Global Information Technology Management*, 22(2): 77–81.

Macha, N. (2015). "Two Tanzanians Accused of Posting 'False Information' Face Charges under New Cybercrime Law," *Global Voices advox*. https://advox.globalvoices.org/2015/10/19/two-tanzanians-accused-of-posting-false-information-face-charges-under-new-cybercrime-law/

McGuire, M. R. (2014). "Putting the 'cyber' into cyberterrorism: re-reading technological risk in a hyperconnected world," in *Cyberterrorism* (pp. 63–83). New York, NY: Springer.

Matfess, H. & Smith, J. (2018). "Africa's Attack on Internet Freedom," *Foreign Policy*. https://foreignpolicy.com/2018/07/13/africas-attack-on-internet-freedom-uganda-tanzania-ethiopia-museveni-protests/

Melzer, N. (2011). *Cyber Warfare and International Law*. Zürich: University of Zürich.

National Research Council. (2007). *Engaging Privacy and Information Technology in a Digital Age*. Washington, DC: National Academies Press.

"Nigerian Cybercrime Act 2015."

Njoku, T. E. (2017). "Politics of Conviviality? State-Civil Society Relations within the Context of Counter-Terrorism in Nigeria," *Voluntas: International of Voluntary and Nonprofit Organizations*, 1–23.

Njoku, T. E. (2020). "Counter-Terrorism Legislation and Press Freedom in Nigeria," in PTCIJ (ed), *Press Freedom in Nigeria Abuja: Premium Times Center for Investigative Journalism*.

Orji, U. J. (2014). "Deterring Cyberterrorism in the Global Information Society: A Case for the Collective Responsibility of State," *Defence against Terrorism Review*, 6(1): 31–46.

Pescatore, J. (2009). "Toward a national cybersecurity strategy, G00167598." Gartner Inc.

Ratcliffe, R. & Okiror, S. (2019). "Millions of Ugandans Quit Internet Services as Social Media Tax Takes Effect," *The Guardian*. www.theguardian.com/global-development/2019/feb/27/millions-of-ugandans-quit-internet-after-introduction-of-social-media-tax-free-speech

Tanzanian Human Rights Defenders Coalition (2016). "Report on the situation of Human rights Defenders in Tanzania 2016," Retrieved from: https://thrdc.or.tz/wp-content/uploads/2018/11/THRDC-SITUATION-REPORT-2016.pdf

The United Republic of Tanzania, *The Cybercrimes Act, 2015*. Retrieved from: https://rsf.org/sites/default/files/the_cyber_crime_act_2015.pdf

Webster, W. & Cilluffo, F. (1998). *Cybercrime, Cyberterrorism, Cyberwarfare, Averting an Electronic Waterloo*. Washington, DC: Center for Strategic and International Studies.

INDEX

Page numbers in **bold** refer to content in **tables**; page numbers in *italics* refer to content in *figures*.

hacker groups 134, 261, 269, 321, 334, 475, 486–487, 538; *see also* viruses/malware
hacktivism 398, 430, 484, 509–510
Halim, T. 351, 353
Hamas 420–422
Hammoudi, H. 535
hate speech 84, 357, 526, 545
Hathaway, M. 251
Havelsan 401
Helmbrecht, U. 73
Hezbollah 445
Hilmi, H. 528
Honasan, G. 315, 316, 319
HoneyNET 440
Honwana, A. 535
Huawei 373
human rights *see* freedoms; privacy
Hungary 4, 99; cultural understanding 104; cyber warfare, crime, and terrorism 107–108; definitional landscape 101–102; institutions 104–105; intellectual property (IP) 106–107; international law and governance 102–104; legislature's role 106; private sector's role 105–106; societal implications 108–109; strategy statement 99–101
Hurel, L. M. 1–2
hybrid war 187–189
Hyundai 321

IceShima Cyber Group (ISCG) 127
Ikenberry, G. J. 497
ILoveYou 202
India: Bangladesh cooperation 350–351; e-governance, surveillance, and data protection review 340–345; introduction of IT Act (2000) 337–338; and Singapore 385; weaknesses of IT Act (2000) 338–340
Individual Partnership Action Plans (IPAP) 43
Industrial Control Systems (ICS) 276
informational war 185, 187
Instagram 544
integrity principle 154, 165
intellectual property (IP) 106–107
Inter-American Development Bank (IDB) 479, 498, 499
International Atomic Energy Agency (IAEA) 42
International Conference on Cyber Conflict (CyCon) 233, 234–235, 236
international governance: Australia 370; Bangladesh 350–351; Colombia 497–498; Egypt 522–523, 527; Estonia 215–216; Japan 254; Mexico 489–490; Nigeria 556–557; Philippines 317; Russia 158; Singapore 383–384; Slovakia 170; Taiwan 278; Turkey 404–405; Uganda 580; United Kingdom (UK) 196–197

international law: Australia 369–370; Bangladesh 350–351; Colombia 496–497; Estonia 216; Japan 253–254; Nigeria 555–556; North Atlantic Treaty Organization (NATO) 233; Norway 147–148; Philippines 316–317; Singapore 382–383; Slovakia 169; South Africa 603–604; Taiwan 277–278; Turkey 404–405; Uganda 579–580; United Kingdom (UK) 195–196
International Multilateral Partnership Against Cyber Threats (IMPACT) 362, 404, 538
International Telecommunication Union (ITU) 6, 11, 26, 44, 390, 398, 404, 474–475, 556, 579, 591; Global Cybersecurity Index 11, 26, 43–44, **43–44**, 99, 312, 390, 500, 521, 538, 545
internet access/use: Bangladesh 352; China 285–286, *286*; Czech Republic 56; Estonia 211; Germany *79*; Iran 440; Italy 121; Kenya 543–544; Malaysia 326; Myanmar 357, 363; Poland 89; Saudi Arabia 428; Tunisia 536; Vietnam 297
Internet Assigned Numbers Authority (IANA) 159
Internet Corporation for Assigned Names and Numbers (ICANN) 159, 278, 463, 490
internet kill switches 255, 406, 466
Internet of Things (IoT) 255, 260, 276, 322, 414, 576
internet service providers (ISPs) 53, 58, 84, 121, 132, 371, 418, 419–420, 428, 525, 559, 588
internet shutdowns 255, 466, 613, 617–618
Internet Society 463, 556, 581
Interpol 389, 402, 500, 581–582
IP telephony 189
Iran 435–436; attacks on Saudi Arabia 432; comprehensive cybersecurity strategy 439–442; cyber crime 442–444; cyber operations for deterrence 444–446; foreign policy **438**, 439; national security strategy 436–439, *437*, **438**; viruses 204
Isiko, B. 577
ISIL (Islamic State) 538
Islam, S. 3
Islamic law 431–432
Israel: defense and security models 409–411; military-economy model 413–415; military's role 411–413; and Palestine 411–412, 419–423
Israel Electric Corporation 410
Italy 121–122; analysis of 2017 strategy 125–126; contribution to secure cyberspace 126–127; governance and policy 122–125, *123*; public-private cooperation 127–128

Jalali, G.-R. 445
Jamaica 473–474; cyber crime and security relationship 475–476; cybersecurity acts 477–479; definitional landscape 474–475; international